THE CAMBRIDGE HISTORY OF CHINA

General editors

DENIS TWITCHETT and JOHN K. FAIRBANK

Volume 15
The People's Republic, Part 2:
Revolutions within the Chinese Revolution
1966–1982

THE CAMBRIDGE HISTORY OF CHINA

Volume 15
The People's Republic, Part 2:
Revolutions within the Chinese Revolution
1966–1982

edited by
RODERICK MacFARQUHAR
and
JOHN K. FAIRBANK

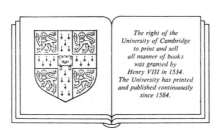

The right of the
University of Cambridge
to print and sell
all manner of books
was granted by
Henry VIII in 1534.
The University has printed
and published continuously
since 1584.

CAMBRIDGE UNIVERSITY PRESS
CAMBRIDGE
NEW YORK   PORT CHESTER
MELBOURNE   SYDNEY

Published by the Press Syndicate of the University of Cambridge
The Pitt Building, Trumpington Street, Cambridge CB2 IRP
40 West 20th Street, New York, NY 10011, USA
10 Stamford Road, Oakleigh, Melbourne 3166, Australia

First published 1991

Printed in the United States of America

Library of Congress Cataloging-in-Publication Data
(Revised for vol. 15)
The Cambridge history of China.
Vol. 1. edited by Denis Twitchett and Michael Loewe;
v. 7 edited by Frederick W. Mote and Denis Twitchett;
v. 11 edited by John K. Fairbank and Kwang-Ching Liu;
v. 13 edited by John K. Fairbank and Albert Feuerwerker;
v. 14–15 edited by Roderick MacFarquhar and
John K. Fairbank.
Includes bibliographies and indexes.
Contents: v. 1. The Ch'in and Han Empires,
221 B.C. – A.D. 220 – – v. 3. Sui and T'ang China,
589–906, pt. 1 – [etc.] – v. 14–15. The People's
Republic, pt. 1–2.
1. China – History. I. Twitchett, Denis Crispin.
II. Fairbank, John King, 1907– . III. Feuerwerker,
Albert.
DS735.C3145   951   76–29852
ISBN 0–521–21447–5

British Library Cataloguing in Publication Data
The Cambridge history of China.
Vol. 15, The People's Republic. Pt. 2, Revolutions within
the Chinese Revolution, 1966–1982.
1. China, history
I. Fairbank, John K. (John King), 1907–   II. MacFarquhar,
Roderick
951

ISBN 0–521–24337–8 hardback

GENERAL EDITORS' PREFACE

As the modern world grows more interconnected, historical understanding of it becomes ever more necessary and the historian's task ever more complex. Fact and theory affect each other even as sources proliferate and knowledge increases. Merely to summarize what is known becomes an awesome task, yet a factual basis of knowledge is increasingly essential for historical thinking.

Since the beginning of the century, the Cambridge histories have set a pattern in the English-reading world for multivolume series containing chapters written by specialists under the guidance of volume editors. *The Cambridge Modern History*, planned by Lord Acton, appeared in sixteen volumes between 1902 and 1912. It was followed by *The Cambridge Ancient History, The Cambridge Medieval History, The Cambridge History of English Literature*, and Cambridge histories of India, of Poland, and of the British Empire. The original *Modern History* has now been replaced by *The New Cambridge Modern History* in twelve volumes, and *The Cambridge Economic History of Europe* is now being completed. Other Cambridge histories include histories of Islam, Arabic literature, Iran, Judaism, Africa, Japan, and Latin America.

In the case of China, Western historians face a special problem. The history of Chinese civilization is more extensive and complex than that of any single Western nation, and only slightly less ramified than the history of European civilization as a whole. The Chinese historical record is immensely detailed and extensive, and Chinese historical scholarship has been highly developed and sophisticated for many centuries. Yet until the second quarter of the twentieth century the study of China in the West, despite the important pioneer work of European sinologists, had hardly progressed beyond the translation of some few classical historical texts, and the outline history of the major dynasties and their institutions.

Recently Western scholars have drawn more fully upon the rich traditions of historical scholarship in China and also in Japan, and greatly advanced both our detailed knowledge of past events and institutions and also our critical understanding of traditional historiography. In addition,

the present generation of Western historians of China can also draw upon
the new outlooks and techniques of modern Western historical scholarship, and upon recent developments in the social sciences, while continuing to build upon the solid foundations of rapidly progressing European,
Japanese, and Chinese sinological studies. Recent historical events, too,
have given prominence to new problems, while throwing into question
many older conceptions. Under these multiple impacts the Western revolution in Chinese studies is steadily gathering momentum.

When *The Cambridge History of China* was first planned in 1966, the aim
was to provide a substantial account of the history of China as a bench
mark for the Western history-reading public: an account of the current
state of knowledge in six volumes. Since then the outpouring of current
research, the application of new methods, and the extension of scholarship into new fields have further stimulated Chinese historical studies.
This growth is indicated by the fact that the *History* has now become
fifteen volumes, but will still leave out such topics as the history of art
and of literature, many aspects of economics and technology, and all the
riches of local history.

The striking advances in our knowledge of China's past over recent
decades will continue and accelerate. Western historians of this great and
complex subject are justified in their efforts by the need of their own
peoples for greater and deeper understanding of China. Chinese history
belongs to the world, not only as a right and necessity but also as a subject of compelling interest.

JOHN K. FAIRBANK
DENIS TWITCHETT

CONTENTS

PART II. THE CULTURAL REVOLUTION: THE STRUGGLE FOR
THE SUCCESSION, 1969–1982

MAPS

TABLES

CONVERSION TABLES

Pinyin to Wade-Giles

Pinyin	Wade-Giles	Pinyin	Wade-Giles	Pinyin	Wade-Giles	Pinyin	Wade-Giles
a	a	chu	ch'u	er	erh	hou	hou
ai	ai	chuai	ch'uai			hu	hu
an	an	chuan	ch'uan	fa	fa	hua	hua
ang	ang	chuang	ch'uang	fan	fan	huan	huan
ao	ao	chui	ch'ui	fang	fang	huang	huang
		chun	ch'un	fei	fei	hui	hui
ba	pa	chuo	ch'o	fen	fen	hun	hun
bai	pai	ci	tz'u	feng	feng	huo	huo
ban	pan	cong	ts'ung	fo	fo		
bang	pang	cou	ts'ou	fou	fou	ji	chi
bao	pao	cu	ts'u	fu	fu	jia	chia
bei	pei	cuan	ts'uan			jian	chien
ben	pen	cui	ts'ui	ga	ka	jiang	chiang
beng	peng	cun	ts'un	gai	kai	jiao	chiao
bi	pi	cuo	ts'o	gan	kan	jie	chieh
bian	pien			gang	kang	jin	chin
biao	piao	da	ta	gao	kao	jing	ching
bie	pieh	dai	tai	ge	ke, ko	jiong	chiung
bin	pin	dan	tan	gei	kei	jiu	chiu
bing	ping	dang	tang	gen	ken	ju	chü
bo	po	dao	tao	geng	keng	juan	chüan
bu	pu	de	te	gong	kung	jue	chüeh
		dei	tei	gou	kou	jun	chün
ca	ts'a	deng	teng	gu	ku		
cai	ts'ai	di	ti	gua	kua	ka	k'a
can	ts'an	dian	tien	guai	kuai	kai	k'ai
cang	ts'ang	diao	tiao	guan	kuan	kan	k'an
cao	ts'ao	die	tieh	guang	kuang	kang	k'ang
ce	ts'e	ding	ting	gui	kuei	kao	k'ao
cen	ts'en	diu	tiu	gun	kun	ke	k'o
ceng	ts'eng	dong	tung	guo	kuo	ken	k'en
cha	ch'a	dou	tou			keng	k'eng
chai	ch'ai	du	tu	ha	ha	kong	k'ung
chan	ch'an	duan	tuan	hai	hai	kou	k'ou
chang	ch'ang	dui	tui	han	han	ku	k'u
chao	ch'ao	dun	tun	hang	hang	kua	k'ua
che	ch'e	duo	to	hao	hao	kuai	k'uai
chen	ch'en			he	ho, he	kuan	k'uan
cheng	ch'eng	e	o	hei	hei	kuang	k'uang
chi	ch'ih	ei	ei	hen	hen	kui	k'uei
chong	ch'ung	en	en	heng	heng	kun	k'un
chou	ch'ou	eng	eng	hong	hung	kuo	k'uo

Pinyin	Wade-Giles	Pinyin	Wade-Giles	Pinyin	Wade-Giles	Pinyin	Wade-Giles
la	la	ni	ni	re	je	ti	t'i
lai	lai	nian	nien	ren	jen	tian	t'ien
lan	lan	niang	niang	reng	jeng	tiao	t'iao
lang	lang	niao	niao	ri	jih	tie	t'ieh
lao	lao	nie	nieh	rong	jung	ting	t'ing
le	le	nin	nin	rou	jou	tong	t'ung
lei	lei	ning	ning	ru	ju	tou	t'ou
leng	leng	niu	niu	ruan	juan	tu	t'u
li	li	nong	nung	rui	jui	tuan	t'uan
lia	lia	nou	nou	run	jun	tui	t'ui
lian	lien	nu	nu	ruo	jo	tun	t'un
liang	liang	nü	nü			tuo	t'o
liao	liao	nuan	nuan	sa	sa		
lie	lieh	nüe	nueh	sai	sai	wa	wa
lin	lin	nuo	no	san	san	wai	wai
ling	ling			sang	sang	wan	wan
liu	liu	o	o	sao	sao	wang	wang
lo	lo	ou	ou	se	se	wei	wei
long	lung			sen	sen	wen	wen
lou	lou	pa	p'a	seng	seng	weng	weng
lu	lu	pai	p'ai	sha	sha	wo	wo
luan	luan	pan	p'an	shai	shai	wu	wu
lun	lun	pang	p'ang	shan	shan		
luo	lo	pao	p'ao	shang	shang	xi	hsi
lü	lü	pei	p'ei	shao	shao	xia	hsia
lüe	lueh	pen	p'en	she	she	xian	hsien
		peng	p'eng	shei	shei	xiang	hsiang
ma	ma	pi	p'i	shen	shen	xiao	hsiao
mai	mai	pian	p'ien	sheng	sheng	xie	hsieh
man	man	piao	p'iao	shi	shih	xin	hsin
mang	mang	pie	p'ieh	shou	shou	xing	hsing
mao	mao	pin	p'in	shu	shu	xiong	hsiung
mei	mei	ping	p'ing	shua	shua	xiu	hsiu
men	men	po	p'o	shuai	shuai	xu	hsu
meng	meng	pou	p'ou	shuan	shuan	xuan	hsuan
mi	mi	pu	p'u	shuang	shuang	xue	hsueh
mian	mien			shui	shui	xun	hsun
miao	miao	qi	ch'i	shun	shun		
mie	mieh	qia	ch'ia	shuo	shuo	ya	ya
min	min	qian	ch'ien	si	szu, ssu	yan	yen
ming	ming	qiang	ch'iang	song	sung	yang	yang
miu	miu	qiao	ch'iao	sou	sou	yao	yao
mo	mo	qie	ch'ieh	su	su	ye	yeh
mou	mou	qin	ch'in	suan	suan	yi	i
mu	mu	qing	ch'ing	sui	sui	yin	yin
		qiong	ch'iung	sun	sun	ying	ying
na	na	qiu	ch'iu	suo	so	yong	yung
nai	nai	qu	ch'ü			you	yu
nan	nan	quan	ch'üan	ta	t'a	yu	yü
nang	nang	que	ch'üeh	tai	t'ai	yuan	yuan
nao	nao	qun	ch'ün	tan	t'an	yue	yueh
ne	ne			tang	t'ang	yun	yun
nei	nei	ran	jan	tao	t'ao		
nen	nen	rang	jang	te	t'e	za	tsa
neng	neng	rao	jao	teng	t'eng	zai	tsai

Pinyin	Wade-Giles	Pinyin	Wade-Giles	Pinyin	Wade-Giles	Pinyin	Wade-Giles
zan	tsan	zhan	chan	zhou	chou	zi	tzu
zang	tsang	zhang	chang	zhu	chu	zong	tsung
zao	tsao	zhao	chao	zhua	chua	zou	tsou
ze	tse	zhe	che	zhuai	chuai	zu	tsu
zei	tsei	zhei	chei	zhuan	chuan	zuan	tsuan
zen	tsen	zhen	chen	zhuang	chuang	zui	tsui
zeng	tseng	zheng	cheng	zhui	chui	zun	tsun
zha	cha	zhi	chih	zhun	chun	zuo	tso
zhai	chai	zhong	chung	zhuo	cho		

Wade-Giles to Pinyin

Wade-Giles	Pinyin	Wade-Giles	Pinyin	Wade-Giles	Pinyin	Wade-Giles	Pinyin
a	a	ch'ü	qu	hsiu	xiu	ku	gu
ai	ai	chua	zhua	hsiung	xiong	k'u	ku
an	an	chuai	zhuai	hsü	xu	kua	gua
ang	ang	ch'uai	chuai	hsüan	xuan	k'ua	kua
ao	ao	chuan	zhuan	hsüeh	xue	kuai	guai
		ch'uan	chuan	hsün	xun	k'uai	kuai
cha	zha	chüan	juan	hu	hu	kuan	guan
ch'a	cha	ch'üan	quan	hua	hua	k'uan	kuan
chai	zhai	chuang	zhuang	huai	huai	kuang	guang
ch'ai	chai	ch'uang	chuang	huan	huan	k'uang	kuang
chan	zhan	chüeh	jue	huang	huang	kuei	gui
ch'an	chan	ch'üeh	que	hui	hui	k'uei	kui
chang	zhang	chui	zhui	hun	hun	kun	gun
ch'ang	chang	ch'ui	chui	hung	hong	k'un	kun
chao	zhao	chun	zhun	huo	huo	kung	gong
ch'ao	chao	ch'un	chun			k'ung	kong
che	zhe	chün	jun	i	yi	kuo	guo
ch'e	che	ch'ün	qun			k'uo	kuo
chei	zhei	chung	zhong	jan	ran		
chen	zhen	ch'ung	chong	jang	rang	la	la
ch'en	chen			jao	rao	lai	lai
cheng	zheng	e	e, o	je	re	lan	lan
ch'eng	cheng	en	en	jên	ren	lang	lang
chi	ji	eng	eng	jeng	reng	lao	lao
ch'i	qi	erh	er	jih	ri	le	le
chia	jia			jo	ruo	lei	lei
ch'ia	qia	fa	fa	jou	rou	leng	leng
chiang	jiang	fan	fan	ju	ru	li	li
ch'iang	qiang	fang	fang	jua	rua	lia	lia
chiao	jiao	fei	fei	juan	ruan	liang	liang
ch'iao	qiao	fen	fen	jui	rui	liao	liao
chieh	jie	feng	feng	jun	run	lieh	lie
ch'ieh	qie	fo	fo	jung	rong	lien	lian
chien	jian	fou	fou			lin	lin
ch'ien	qian	fu	fu	ka	ga	ling	ling
chih	zhi			k'a	ka	liu	liu
ch'ih	chi	ha	ha	kai	gai	lo	luo, lo
chin	jin	hai	hai	k'ai	kai	lou	lou
ch'in	qin	han	han	kan	gan	lu	lu
ching	jing	hang	hang	k'an	kan	luan	luan
ch'ing	qing	hao	hao	kang	gang	lun	lun
chio	jue	hen	hen	k'ang	kang	lung	long
ch'io	que	heng	heng	kao	gao	lü	lü
chiu	jiu	ho	he	k'ao	kao	lüeh	lüe
ch'iu	qiu	hou	hou	kei	gei		
chiung	jiong	hsi	xi	k'ei	kei	ma	ma
ch'iung	qiong	hsia	xia	ken	gen	mai	mai
cho	zhuo	hsiang	xiang	k'en	ken	man	man
ch'o	chuo	hsiao	xiao	keng	geng	mang	mang
chou	zhou	hsieh	xie	k'eng	keng	mao	mao
ch'ou	chou	hsien	xian	ko	ge	mei	mei
chu	zhu	hsin	xin	k'o	ke	men	men
ch'u	chu	hsing	xing	kou	gou	meng	meng
chü	ju	hsio	xue	k'ou	kou	mi	mi

Wade-Giles	Pinyin	Wade-Giles	Pinyin	Wade-Giles	Pinyin	Wade-Giles	Pinyin
miao	miao	peng	beng	suan	suan	ts'eng	ceng
mieh	mie	p'eng	peng	sui	sui	tso	zuo
mien	mian	pi	bi	sun	sun	ts'o	cuo
min	min	p'i	pi	sung	song	tsou	zou
ming	ming	piao	biao			ts'ou	cou
miu	miu	p'iao	piao	ta	da	tsu	zu
mo	mo	pieh	bie	t'a	ta	ts'u	cu
mou	mou	p'ieh	pie	tai	dai	tsuan	zuan
mu	mu	pien	bian	t'ai	tai	ts'uan	cuan
		p'ien	pian	tan	dan	tsui	zui
na	na	pin	bin	t'an	tan	ts'ui	cui
nai	nai	p'in	pin	tang	dang	tsun	zun
nan	nan	ping	bing	t'ang	tang	ts'un	cun
nang	nang	p'ing	ping	tao	dao	tsung	zong
nao	nao	po	bo	t'ao	tao	ts'ung	cong
nei	nei	p'o	po	te	de	tu	du
nen	nen	p'ou	pou	t'e	te	t'u	tu
neng	neng	pu	bu	tei	dei	tuan	duan
ni	ni	p'u	pu	ten	den	t'uan	tuan
niang	niang			teng	deng	tui	dui
niao	niao	sa	sa	t'eng	teng	t'ui	tui
nieh	nie	sai	sai	ti	di	tun	dun
nien	nian	san	san	t'i	ti	t'un	tun
nin	nin	sang	sang	tiao	diao	tung	dong
ning	ning	sao	sao	t'iao	tiao	t'ung	tong
niu	niu	se	se	tieh	die	tzu	zi
no	nuo	sen	sen	t'ieh	tie	tz'u	ci
nou	nou	seng	seng,	tien	dian		
nu	nu		sheng	t'ien	tian	wa	wa
nü	nu	sha	sha	ting	ding	wai	wai
nuan	nuan	shai	shai	t'ing	ting	wan	wan
nüeh	nüe	shan	shan	tiu	diu	wang	wang
nung	nong	shang	shang	to	duo	wei	wei
		shao	shao	t'o	tuo	wen	wen
o	e, o	she	she	tou	dou	wo	wo
ong	weng	shei	shei	t'ou	tou	wu	wu
ou	ou	shen	shen	tsa	za		
		sheng	sheng	ts'a	ca		
pa	ba	shih	shi	tsai	zai	ya	ya
p'a	pa	shou	shou	ts'ai	cai	yang	yang
pai	bai	shu	shu	tsan	zan	yao	yao
p'ai	pai	shua	shua	ts'an	can	yeh	ye
pan	ban	shuai	shuai	tsang	zang	yen	yan
p'an	pan	shuan	shuan	ts'ang	cang	yin	yin
pang	bang	shuang	shuang	tsao	zao	ying	ying
p'ang	pang	shui	shui	ts'ao	cao	yo	yue, yo
pao	bao	shun	shun	tse	ze	yu	you
p'ao	pao	shuo	shuo	ts'e	ce	yü	yu
pei	bei	so	suo	tsei	zei	yüan	yuan
p'ei	pei	sou	sou	tsen	zen	yüeh	yue
pen	ben	ssu	si	ts'en	cen	yün	yun
p'en	pen	su	su	tseng	zeng	yung	yong

PREFACE TO VOLUME 15

Volume 14 of *The Cambridge History of China* took the story of the Chinese Communist experiment in social engineering up to the eve of the Cultural Revolution in 1965. At that point, the country appeared to have recovered from the disaster of the Great Leap Forward, and the regime was ready to launch its postponed 3rd Five-Year Plan. Despite the earlier break with the Soviet Union, China once again looked like simply a variation of the Stalinist-type state. Virtually all Chinese, including most top leaders, and all foreign observers were unaware that Mao Tse-tung was about to launch a new campaign to transform that image, a movement that in every respect except loss of life would be more shattering than any that had gone before.

The harbingers of the Cultural Revolution were analyzed in Volume 14. In Volume 15, we attempt to trace a course of events still only partially understood by most Chinese. We begin by analyzing the development of Mao's thought since the Communist seizure of power, in an effort to understand why he launched the movement. We grapple with the conflict of evidence between what was said favorably about the Cultural Revolution at the time and the often diametrically opposed retrospective accounts.

We go on to examine how Mao's last desperate effort to transform China spiritually was followed, after his death in 1976, by a new revolution, as his successor Teng Hsiao-p'ing set a fresh course, opening up China in an endeavor to transform the country economically. Far from making the Chinese more revolutionary, the effect of the Cultural Revolution seemed to have readied them to discard the principles of Karl Marx in favor of those of Adam Smith. Most of the contributors to this volume take their analyses of the new course through the early 1980s, when Teng's experiment was registering its first major achievements.

Our chapters on politics, economics, foreign relations, education, and intellectuals follow on from similar ones in Volume 14. But in addition, in two chapters we shift perspective from that of the policymakers in Peking to that of the people of China, to suggest what the revolution has meant for them. And we also look across the Taiwan Strait to the island province, which has used its insulation from the successive upheavals on the mainland to transform itself in a different way.

This is the sixth and final volume covering the nineteenth and twentieth centuries, at least for this edition of *The Cambridge History of China*. As before, our footnotes indicate how much we are in debt to others. It is a pleasure to point out that our citations of Chinese scholars have greatly increased as a result of the policy of *k'ai-fang* (openness) pursued in Peking during the past decade.

Joan Hill has been the anchor for Volumes 10 through 15 of this series. During a period of fifteen years she has cheerfully borne responsibility for manuscript production. In so doing, she has ably coped with authors' manuscripts, footnotes, and bibliographical essays, with the compiling of bibliographies (an arcane art), and with the accuracy of romanization in our six submissions to the Cambridge University Press. By this time, complexities, whether of authorial personality or of textual format, have no terrors for her. We take this inadequate means of expressing our great indebtedness and thanks.

We are also highly indebted to two young Harvard scholars who have taken time off from their own researches to help bring this enterprise to a conclusion. Gwendolyn Stewart has devoted long hours of painstaking toil to the heartbreaking and patience-straining task of preparing the Glossary-Index and ensuring the accuracy and consistency of the Bibliography. Yin Xiaohuang, a mainland scholar, has expended considerable effort to ensure the completeness and precision of the Chinese citations in the Bibliography. Nancy Hearst, the Fairbank Center librarian, and Timothy Connor and his colleagues at the Harvard-Yenching Institute, under the leadership of the doyen of East Asian librarians, Eugene Wu, have provided crucial backup, particularly in the later stages of editing. In the final stages, Nancy Hearst spent many careful hours copy-editing, proofreading, and checking corrections on the proofs and improved enormously a hitherto flawed text. The transformation of manuscript into book was carefully carried out by Nancy Landau and Martin Dinitz for the Cambridge University Press.

This volume, like its immediate predecessor, was assisted at an early stage by a working conference of contributors in January 1983, generously financed by the Rockefeller Foundation and run by Patrick Maddox under the aegis of Harvard's Fairbank Center. We are delighted also to reiterate our gratitude for the indispensable support of the Ford and Mellon foundations at various stages, as well as the help of the American Council of Learned Societies and the National Endowment for the Humanities.

Finally we express our thanks to Harvard University for housing this project throughout its existence and particularly to Nancy Deptula, administrative officer of the Council on East Asian Studies, for handling its finances over the years.

RLM
JKF

ACRONYMS

Some of these abbreviations represent publications; others stand for names and titles in the text. Characters for publications will be found in the Bibliography; those for names and titles, in the Glossary-Index.

APC	Agricultural Producers' Cooperative
BR	*Beijing Review*
CASS	Chinese Academy of Social Sciences
CB	*Current Background*
CC	Central Committee
CCP	Chinese Communist Party
CFJP	*Chieh-fang jih-pao*
CHOC	*The Cambridge History of China*
CKYC	*Chung-kung yen-chiu*
CI	Comintern
CIA	Central Intelligence Agency
CLG	*Chinese Law and Government*
CPPCC	Chinese People's Political Consultative Conference
CPSU	Communist Party of the Soviet Union
CQ	*China Quarterly*
CSYB	*Chinese statistical yearbook*
ECMM	*Extracts from China Mainland Magazines*
FBIS	Foreign Broadcast Information Service
FLP	Foreign Languages Press
FYP	Five-Year Plan
GLF	Great Leap Forward
GPCR	Great Proletarian Cultural Revolution
HC	*Hung-ch'i*
HHPYK	*Hsin-hua pan-yueh k'an*
HHYP	*Hsin-hua yueh-pao*
IASP	International Arts and Sciences Press
IMH	Institute of Modern History
JAS	*Journal of Asian Studies*

JMJP	*Jen-min jih-pao*
JPRS	Joint Publications Research Service
KMJP	*Kuang-ming jih-pao*
KMT	Kuomintang
KTTH	*Kung-tso t'ung-hsun*
LHCC	*Lu Hsun ch'üan-chi*
LSYC	*Li-shih yen-chiu*
MAC	Military Affairs Commission
Mao, *SW*	*Selected works of Mao Tse-tung* (English translation)
MC	*Modern China*
MTHC	*Mao Tse-tung hsuan-chi*
MTTC	*Mao Tse-tung chi*
NCNA	New China News Agency (Hsin-hua she)
NEFA	Northeast Frontier Agency
nei-pu	"Internal use only"
NFJP	*Nan-fang jih-pao*
NPC	National People's Congress
NSC	National Security Council
NYT	*New York Times*
OECD	Organization for Economic Cooperation and Development
PC	*People's China*
PKI	Communist Party of Indonesia
PLA	People's Liberation Army
PR	*Peking Review* (later *Beijing Review*)
PRC	People's Republic of China
SCMM	*Selections from China Mainland Magazines*
SCMP	*Survey of China Mainland Press*
SEATO	Southeast Asia Treaty Organization
SMR	South Manchurian Railway
SWB/FE	*Summary of World Broadcasts (Far East)*
TCNC	*T'ung-chi nien-chien*
URI	Union Research Institute
USC	Universities Service Centre
Wan-sui	*Mao Tse-tung ssu-hsiang wan-sui*

CHAPTER 1

MAO TSE-TUNG'S THOUGHT
FROM 1949 TO 1976

Like Lenin, Mao Tse-tung, on coming to power, continued to develop his ideas in a context different from that within which he had operated while in opposition. In so doing, he modified, adapted, and elaborated positions he had adopted earlier. In many respects there was substantial continuity, but there were also startling ruptures and reversals, and in addition, Mao struck out in new directions he had never previously had the occasion to explore.

One important constant in the development of Mao Tse-tung's thought was his concern to adapt Marxism, or Marxism-Leninism, to the economic and social reality of a backward agrarian country, and to the heritage of the Chinese past, which for Mao was no less real. Before the conquest of power, the first aspect of this project involved devising theoretical justifications for attributing to the peasantry a political role greater than that implied by the model of the October Revolution, and more specifically for the strategy of surrounding the cities from the countryside. In this respect, it might have been assumed, and probably was assumed by Mao himself in 1949, that Chinese practice, and Chinese theory, would move closer to that of the Soviet Union. Having taken power in the cities as well as in the countryside, the Chinese Communist Party was effectively in a position to develop modern industry, and thus to create its own supposed class basis as the "vanguard of the proletariat," and to open a road to convergence with more advanced countries under communist rule.

During the first few years of the People's Republic, such a trend appeared to be emerging, but it was rapidly reversed, and a decade after 1949 China and the Soviet Union were moving farther apart than they had ever been before. In *The Cambridge History of China*, Volume 14, these events are chronicled, and their causes analyzed. What interests us in this chapter is, of course, the role played by Mao Tse-tung and his ideas in these changes of direction. It will be argued here that the explanation lies partly in the continuing weight of the peasantry in Chinese society, as well as the influence on Mao himself of ideas current among the peasantry. But that is by no means the whole answer. The influence of the Yenan matrix, both in terms of an ethos of struggle and sacrifice and in terms of decentralized and self-reliant methods of economic work, must also be taken into account. Yet another factor manifestly important but difficult to assess, is Mao's goal, already mentioned, of adapting Marxism to China. Although the term he had put forward in 1938 to evoke this process, "the Sinification of Marxism," had gone out of use by the early 1950s, largely because Stalin resented the suggestion that there might be other theoretical authorities in the world communist movement apart from himself, the impulse it expressed remained very much part of Mao's thinking.

Mao's conviction that Chinese culture was a great, perhaps a unique, historical achievement strengthened his sentiments of national pride. On the other hand, his explicit aim was to enrich Marxism with ideas and values drawn from the national past, and thereby render it more potent as an agent of revolutionary transformation, and ultimately of Westerniza-tion, not to replace it with some kind of neotraditionalism in Marxist dress. Nonetheless, it became increasingly hard, especially in his later years, to determine whether the basic structure of "Mao Tse-tung Thought" was Chinese or Western.

This is particularly true of his theory of contradictions, although it can legitimately be asked whether Mao, during his last decade and a half, was as interested in such intellectual issues as he had been in the past, or whether he was above all preoccupied with achieving his own goals, which he regarded as by definition revolutionary. Another ambiguous element in Mao's thought is the stress on the role of subjective forces, "conscious activity," and the superstructure that runs through the whole of his career, from beginning to end. To the extent that this reflects a Promethean impulse, which was not prominent in premodern Chinese culture, or in other non-European civilizations, it cannot be seen as a traditionalistic element in Mao's thought. On the other hand, to the extent that the display of virtue by the ruler came to be seen as the chief guarantee of happiness, and the emulation of virtue became a key instru-ment of social control, the parallels with imperial China are obvious.

In Mao's final years, he was, of course, explicitly likened to the first Ch'in emperor, presented as a great revolutionary precursor and a master in the use of revolutionary violence. And yet, at the very same time, the idea of mass participation, and of relying on the masses, which was a real (though often misunderstood) element in the Yenan heritage, was also trumpeted more loudly than ever.

Proletarian party and peasant constituency, the logic of modernization and the ethos of revolutionary war, Marxism and the Chinese tradition, determinism and voluntarism, salvation through virtue and salvation through technology, autocracy and mass democracy – these are some of the contradictions with which Mao wrestled during the years from 1949 to 1976.

In discussing the complex record of his efforts to deal with these and other issues, an approach partly thematic and partly chronological has been adopted. In many important respects, the second half of 1957 constituted a geat climacteric in Mao's life, marked by changes in outlook and personality that were to cast their shadow over the whole of his last nineteen years. The account of many aspects of Mao Tse-tung's thought will therefore be divided into two halves, before and after 1957. This pattern will not, however, be applied rigidly, especially as some key ideas of Mao's later years did not even emerge untill well after 1957.

FROM PEOPLE'S DEMOCRACY TO
CONTRADICTIONS AMONG THE PEOPLE

Patterns of rule

This first theme is one for which, precisely, 1957 does not appear to have seen a decisive change in Mao's thinking, but there was very great continuity from the Ching-kang-shan and Yenan to the early 1960s. Throughout this period, his thought was strongly marked by an insistence on the need for firm leadership by a political elite.

This trait is, in fact, an integral part of the "mass line" itself, so often romanticized, or sentimentalized, during the Cultural Revolution to signify a project for allowing the people to liberate themselves and to run things in their own spontaneous way. In fact, while Mao Tse-tung saw the process of government as in part an educative process, he had no Spockian notions to the effect that the "students" should be entirely free to decide what they should learn. On the contrary, the "mass line," correctly understood, must be seen not as the negation or polar opposite of Lenin's conception of "democratic centralism," but as a complementary idea, emphasizing a particular dimension of the relation between leaders and led.[1]

At the same time, it must be recognized that the concept of the "mass

---

1 For a discussion of the complex and ambiguous relation between "traditional" and "modern" elements in Mao's thought and behavior, see Stuart R. Schram, "Party leader or true ruler?: Foundations and significance of Mao Zedong's personal power" in S. Schram, ed., *Foundations and limits of state power in China*.

reason for maintaining the slightest ambiguity about the Party's immediate political goals. Mao therefore spelled out, on 30 June 1949, in an
article written to commemorate the twenty-eighth anniversary of the
foundation of the Chinese Communist Party, the precise nature of the
"people's democratic dictatorship" that he proposed to establish three
months later.

The term "people's democracy" had, in fact been introduced by Mao as
early as May 1939, in his speech on the twentieth anniversary of the May
Fourth Movement. "The present stage," he said then, "is not socialism,
but destroying imperialism and the feudal forces, transforming this [pres-
ent] semi-colonial and semi-feudal position, and establishing a people's
democratic system (*jen-min min-chu chu-i ti chih-tu*)."[7] Now, in 1949,
characterizing the new people's democratic regime, Mao made use of a
distinction he had employed in "On New Democracy" between the "state
system" (*kuo-t'i*) and the "system of government" (*cheng-t'i*).[8] Not surprisingly, since they viewed the matter in a Marxist framework, Mao and
other writers in the early years of the Chinese People's Republic defined
the state system primarily in class terms. Thus, one reference work for
political study by basic-level cadres, first published in 1952, said in part:

The state system is the class essence of the state. The question of the state system
is the question of the place of the various social classes in the state, i.e., it is the
question of which class controls the political power of the state. For the most
part, the state system of the various countries of the world at the present time can
be divided into three types: (1) the capitalist state system, marked by the dictatorship of the reactionary bourgeoisie; (2) the socialist state system, marked by the
dictatorship of the working class; and (3) the new-democratic state system,
marked by the joint dictatorship of the various revolutionary classes, led by the
working class and with the worker-peasant alliance as the foundation.[9]

This had been the classification laid down by Mao in 1939-40. The
state established in 1949 was called a people's dictatorship rather than a
proletarian dictatorship, because it was seen as a hybrid form adapted to
the circumstances prevailing during the "period of transition" from postwar reconstruction to the building of socialism. Although it was an axiom
of Marxism that power in a society where capitalism had begun to
develop could be exercised only by the proletariat or by the bourgeoisie,
and not by any intermediate class or combination of classes, Lenin had

7 Takeuchi Minoru, ed., *Mao Tse-tung chi*, 6.238. (Hereafter *MTTC*.) Apart from variations resulting
   from changes in the Chinese text, the translation in Mao, *SW*, 2.243 is so imprecise that "people's
   democratic system" becomes simply "people's democracy."
8 Mao, *SW*, 2.351–52.
9 Ch'en Pei-ou, *Jen-min hsueh-hsi tz'u-tien* (People's study dictionary). (2nd. ed.), 288–89.

put forward, in 1905, the formula of the "revolutionary-democratic dictatorship of the workers and the peasants" to characterize the political system under which certain reforms could be carried out in Russia before the establishment of a full-blooded proletarian dictatorship. Mao's "people's democratic dictatorship" was a lineal descendant of this Leninist concept, which had been applied to China and other Asian countries by the Comintern in the 1920s and 1930s.[10]

In 1949, Mao defined the locus of sovereignty in such a state in terms of concentric circles, or of an atom or onion metaphor. The hard or heavy center was made up of the working class, which was to exercise hegemony through the Party presumed to represent it. Next to the center were the peasants, said to constitute the most reliable allies of the proletariat. Then came the petty bourgeoisie, who were to be largely followers. As for the national bourgeoisie, they had a dual nature; they were patriotic, but they were also exploiters. They therefore dwelt on the outer fringes of the "people," perpetually in danger of flying off into the camp of the "non-people" hostile to the revolution.

These four classes (corresponding, of course, to Stalin's "four-class bloc" of the 1920s) were to exercise the "people's democratic dictatorship." Since the "state system" was thus made to include not only the class nature of the state but also the mode of rule (dictatorship), what realm of meaning was left to be covered by "system of government"? Most definitions of the *cheng-t'i* of the Chinese People's Republic in its earliest years[11] refer back to Mao's formulation in "On New Democracy," where he wrote in part:

As for the question of the "system of government,"[12] this is a matter of how political power is organized, the form in which one social class or another chooses to arrange its apparatus of political power to oppose its enemies and protect itself.... China may now adopt a system of people's congresses, from the national people's congress down to the provincial, county, district and township people's congresses, with all levels electing their respective governmental bodies. But if there is to be a proper representation for each revolutionary class according to its status in the state, a proper expression of the people's will.... then a system of really universal and equal suffrage, irrespective of sex, creed, property or education, must be introduced. Such is the system of democratic centralism....

10 On Mao's evolving ideas regarding the role of various classes in the Chinese revolution and the hegemony of the proletariat, see *CHOC*, 13.851–58.
11 See, for example. *Jen-min ta hsien-chang hsueh-hsi shou-ts'e* (Handbook for the study of the people's constitution), 135, and *Jen-min ta hsien-chang hsueh-hsi tzu-liao* (Materials for the study of the people's constitution), 31.
12 In the original version, this reads "political power" (*cheng-ch'üan*), rather than "system of government" (*cheng-t'i*), but the latter term is used in the first sentence of the ensuing paragraph, so the overall sense of the passage is not substantially affected. (See *MTTC*, 7.165–66.)

The state system, a joint dictatorship of all the revolutionary classes and the system of government, democratic centralism – these constitute the politics of New Democracy.[13]

This passage was, of course, written in 1940, when Mao was still operating within the context of the United Front with the Kuomintang and the position of the Chinese Communist Party was relatively weak. By 1949, his idea of a "republic of New Democracy" stressed rather the need for dictatorship over the "reactionary" classes than direct elections based on universal suffrage as the key to genuine democracy. The affirmation of "democratic centralism" as the basic organizational principle of the new state remained, on the other hand, intact.

But while he showed his debt to the Soviet example by maintaining key Leninist slogans such as democratic centralism, Mao also used, in his article of 30 June 1949, terms and concepts pointing in a different direction. Thus he employed the old-fashioned word *tu-ts'ai*, or "autocracy," as a synonym for dictatorship (*chuan-cheng*). To be sure, this compound had sometimes been employed in years past, when Marxist expressions did not all have standard equivalents in Chinese, as a translation for "dictatorship." Mao cannot, however, have been unaware of the traditional overtones *tu-ts'ai* would have for his readers, any more than he was unaware of the connotations of the ancient term *ta-t'ung*, or "Great Harmony," which had been refurbished half a century earlier by K'ang Yu-wei, and which he employed as a synonym for "communism."

In 1953, when a committee headed by Mao was engaged in drafting a constitution for the People's Republic of China, an eight-line rhyme was coined to sum up the criteria for the proper functioning of the political system:

> Great power is monopolized,
> Small power is dispersed.
> The Party committee takes decisions,
> All quarters carry them out.
> Implementation also involves decisions,
> But they must not depart from principles.
> Checking on the work
> Is the responsibility of the Party committee.[14]

In other words, there should be participation, by the citizens and by lower-level cadres, but it must be kept firmly under centralized control.

Mao's speech of 25 April 1956 to the Politburo, entitled "On the ten

---

13 Mao, *SW*, 2.352
14 "Sixty articles on work methods," *Wan-sui* (supplement), 34. (S. Schram's translation; see also the version in Jerome Ch'en, ed., *Mao papers: anthology and bibliography*, 68–69.)

great relationships," is unquestionably one of his half-dozen most important utterances after 1949, and one of the two or three most authoritative statements of his administrative philosophy. This remains true, in my view, even though the economic ideas Mao expounded on this occasion were in large part derived, as will be noted, from reports by the planners.

Section V of the speech, on the relationship between the Center and the localities, must be interpreted in the context of the speech as a whole, which tended above all to argue that the one-sided and doctrinaire pursuit of any policy goal was self-defeating. Thus, if you really want to develop heavy industry, you must not neglect light industry and agriculture; and in order to build up new industrial centers in the hinterland, you should make proper use of the existing industry in the coastal areas. Reasoning in similarly dialectical fashion, Mao said, on the question that concerns us here:

The relationship between the Centre and the localities is also ... a contradiction. In order to resolve this contradiction, what we now need to consider is how to arouse the enthusiasm of the localities by allowing them to run more projects under the unified plan of the Centre.

As things look now, I think that we need a further extension of local power. At present it is too limited, and this is not favourable to building socialism.[15]

In the last analysis, Mao continued to attach supreme importance to the cohesion and efficiency of the state as a whole, and he valued decentralization and grass-roots initiative within the limits thus set. Summing up his discussion in Section V of "On the ten great relationships," he declared:

There must be proper enthusiasm and proper independence.... Naturally we must at the same time tell the comrades at the lower levels that they should not act wildly, that they must exercise caution. Where they can conform, they ought to conform.... Where they cannot conform ... then conformity should not be sought at all costs. Two enthusiasms are much better than just one.... In short, the localities should have an appropriate degree of power. This would be beneficial to the building of a strong socialist state.[16]

The emphasis on centralism is even stronger in the official version than in the unofficial text from which I have been quoting. The new text adds, at this point: "In order to build a powerful socialist state, we must have strong and united leadership by the Centre, we must have unified plan-

---

15 This quotation is taken from the version of Mao's speech reproduced by the Red Guards in 1967–69, as translated in S. Schram, *Mao Tse-tung unrehearsed: talks and letters, 1956–71*, 71–72.
16 Schram, *Mao unrehearsed*, 73.

ning and discipline throughout the whole country; disruption of this necessary unity is impermissible."[17]

Although these differences of emphasis were clearly evident at the time when the official version of "On the ten great relationships" was published three months after Mao's death, it was impossible at that time to assess their significance for lack of information about the sources, and the course of editorial work on this key text. Indeed, some observers regarded the new passages added at that time as forgeries. Information subsequently published enables us to clarify these issues.

This talk, while it dealt at length with the problems of patterns of rule that concern us here, was in the first instance an attempt to define an overall strategy for economic development. For a month and a half, in February and March 1956, Mao Tse-tung had listened, in the company of some leading members of the Party and of the government, to reports from a large number of economic departments. On 25 April 1956, he summed up his own understanding of the conclusions that flowed from these discussions at an enlarged session of the Politburo; on 2 May, he repeated substantial portions of this talk, in revised form, before the Supreme State Conference. The official version is a marriage of the two.[18]

Despite his abiding emphasis on a strong centralized state, Mao's immediate concern in 1956 was with widening the scope of local authority, since he regarded the existing degree of centralization as self-

17 Mao, *SW*, 5.294.
18 The 25 April version was disseminated only to upper-level Party cadres at the time; in December 1965, "On the ten great relationships" was circulated down to the *hsien* and equivalent levels, but this text, though dated 25 April, was in fact an edited version of the 2 May 1956 talk. The latter, because it was delivered before a non-Party audience, was understandably less explicit and forceful in dealing with various issues such as relations with the Soviets. (On one point, the proclamation of the "Hundred Flowers" slogan, Mao had in fact gone well beyond his April position on 2 May, but that passage, discussed later in the chapter, was not included in the December 1965 text.) It was such a truncated version of Mao's 2 May talk that the Red Guards reproduced under the title "On the ten great relationships" and that was translated in the West in the 1970s. Only in July 1975 were the two speeches combined, at the suggestion of Teng Hsiao-p'ing, into what was to become the official version. The editorial work was done by Hu Ch'iao-mu, under Teng's authority. Approved by Mao at the time for inner-Party distribution, it was published only in December 1976. In the light of these facts, the title of an article written immediately after its appearance (Stuart Schram, "Chairman Hua edits Mao's literary heritage: 'On the ten great relationships,' " *CQ*, 69 [March 1977]) now appears slightly ironic.

    All of the information in the above note is taken from *Kuan-yü chien-kuo-i-lai tang-ti jo-kan li-shih wen-t'i ti chueh-i chu-shih pen (hsiu-ting)* (Revised annotated edition of the Resolution on certain questions in the history of our party since the founding of the PRC, 243–45.) (Hereafter, "1981 resolution, annotated edition.") This volume, compiled by the "Research Center on Party Literature under the Central Committee (Chung-kung chung-yang wen-hsien yen-chiu-shih), the organ responsible for the publication of all writings by Mao Tse-tung (as well as other leaders including Liu Shao-ch'i, Chou En-lai, and Teng Hsiao-p'ing) is unquestionably authoritative. The openly published, revised edition of this work is slightly fuller than the original *nei-pu* version that appeared in 1983, and is therefore to be preferred. In the case of "On the ten great relationships," the relevant passage is virtually identical.

defeating. In another talk at the same April 1956 Politburo meeting, he said: "The relationship between the lower echelons and the higher echelons is like that of a mouse when it sees a cat. It is as if their souls have been eaten away, and there are many things they dare not say."[19]

But how was effective centralization to be combined with an "appropriate degree" of local power? This problem, in Mao's view, was inextricably linked to the issue of dual versus vertical control (see *CHOC*, 14, ch. 2), which is explicitly raised in Section V of "On the ten great relationships":

At present dozens of hands are meddling in local affairs, making them difficult to manage.... Since the ministries don't think it proper to issue orders to the Party committees and people's councils at the provincial level, they establish direct contact with the relevant departments and bureaux in the provinces and municipalities and give them orders every day. These orders are all supposed to come from the central authorities, even though neither the Central Committee of the Party nor the State Council knows anything about them, and they put a great strain on the local authorities.... This state of affairs must be changed....

We hope that the ministries and departments under the central authorities will ... first confer with the localities on all matters concerning them and issue no order without full consultation.

The central departments fall into two categories. Those in the first category exercise leadership right down to the enterprises, but their administrative offices and enterprises in the localities are also subject to supervision by the local authorities. Those in the second have the task of laying down guiding principles and mapping out work plans, while the local authorities assume the responsibility for putting them into operation.[20]

The last paragraph of the above quotation refers to the policy, adopted in 1956–57, of keeping only large-scale or important enterprises, especially in the field of heavy industry, under the direct control of the central ministries, and handing other industrial and commercial enterprises over to the lower levels (see *CHOC*, 14, ch. 3). The complex pattern that resulted has been the subject of many studies. Two decades ago, Franz Schurmann drew a distinction that remains useful between what he called "decentralization I," involving the transfer of decision-making power to the production units themselves, and "decentralization II," signifying the transfer of power to some lower level of regional administration. He viewed Ch'en Yun as an advocate of the first plan, which would have led China in the direction of a Yugoslav-type economy, and

---

19 *Wan-sui* (1969), 35; *Miscellany of Mao Tse-tung Thought (1949–1968)*, 30.
20 This version is based primarily on the official Chinese text, as translated in Mao, *SW*, 5.293, but the translation had been modified in places, sometimes making use of the phrasing employed in Schram, *Mao unrehearsed*, 72.

Mao Tse-tung and Liu Shao-ch'i as partisans of the second. He found, however, that Ch'en Yun's approach constituted a "contradictory" combination of centralization, decentralization I, and decentralization II.[21]

Harry Harding, who uses a sixfold set of criteria for approaching the problem, likewise concludes that the policy (in fact drafted by Ch'en Yun) adopted by the Third Plenum in the autumn of 1957 was an "eclectic" one, combining centralization and decentralization.[22] Such a contradictory or "eclectic" approach was, in reality, characteristic of everyone in the leadership at the time; the differences were matters of emphasis. During the Great Leap Forward, Schurmann added, this policy of combining centralism and democracy in a "unity of true opposites" consisted of "centralization of general policy impulses and decentralization of specific policy impulses."[23] Plainly, what he calls here "general policy impulses" are in essence what Mao's 1953 jingle referred to as ta-ch'üan, or "great power"; "specific policy impulses" (or the right to generate them) can be equated with hsiao-ch'üan, "small power."

On 31 January 1958, Mao revised the "Sixty articles on work methods," the directive constituting in effect the blueprint for the Great Leap Forward. In Article 28 of this directive, the 1953 jingle is first quoted and then explained in the following terms:

"Great power is monopolized" [ta-ch'üan tu-lan] is a cliché which is customarily used to refer to the arbitrary decisions of an individual [ko-jen tu-tuan]. We borrow this phrase to indicate that the main powers should be concentrated in collective bodies such as the Central Committee and local Party committees; we use it to oppose dispersionism. Can it possibly be argued that great power should be scattered? ... When we say, "All quarters carry them out," this does not mean that Party members do so directly. It is rather that there must first be a phase in which Party members enter into contact with those who are not Party members in government organs, enterprises, co-operatives, people's organizations, and cultural and educational organs, discuss and study things with them, and revise those parts [of higher-level directives] which are inappropriate [to the particular conditions]; only then, after they have been approved by everybody, are they applied.[24]

This text, it will be seen, deals both with relations between levels, and with the co-ordinating role of the Party. Mao's deliberate emphasis on the parallel between the current maxim ta-ch'üan tu-lan and the term tu-tuan,

---

21 Franz Schurmann, *Ideology and organization in Communist China*, 167–175, 196–98.
22 Harry Harding, *Organizing China: The problem of bureaucracy 1949–1976*, 107–15, 175–82. Both Schurmann and Harding rely to a great extent on secondary sources for Ch'en's views; Ch'en Yun's own words can now be read in Nicholas Lardy and Kenneth Lieberthal, eds. , *Chen Yun's strategy for China's development: a non-Maoist alternative*.
23 Schurmann, *Ideology and organization*, 86–87.
24 *Wan-sui* (supplement), 34–35 (translation by Stuart Schram).

which normally refers, as he says, to the arbitrary or dictatorial decisions of an individual, shows once again that he did not shrink from asserting the need for strong, centralized rule – or from implementing such ideas in practice.

How could such centralization be combined with the exercise of real and significant, though subordinate, "small power" at lower levels? Primarily through the coordinating role of the Party, to which the greater part of Mao's commentaries on the 1953 jingle are devoted. Although he did not here employ the term *i-yuan-hua*, meaning "to integrate," "to make monolithic," or "to make monistic," which had figured so largely in his administrative philosophy during the Yenan period,[25] it is clear that the impulse expressed in this concept was at the center of his thinking. In remarks of April 1956, he recalled that, in response to the emergence of excessive decentralization and local independence in the base areas of the Yenan period, the Central Committee had adopted a resolution on strengthening the "party spirit" (*tang-hsing*, a translation of the Russian *partiinost'*). "Integration [*i-yuan-hua*] was carried out," he continued, "but a great deal of autonomy was preserved."[26]

In comments of January 1958 on the 1953 jingle, Mao referred to the fact that the system of one-man management had been discredited. He included among the most basic organizational principles to be observed "the unity of collective leadership and individual role," which he equated with "the unity of the Party committee and the first secretary."[27] This can be taken as a reaffirmation of Mao's Yenan-style understanding of *i-yuan-hua* or integrated leadership, as opposed to Kao Kang's ideas on the subject. For Kao, *i-yuan-hua* had a sense very close to its literal meaning of "to make monolithic." A monolithic pattern of organization implied, in his view, that each entity such as a factory could be responsible to only one outside authority, which in practice meant the relevant ministry in Peking. The factory manager, as the agent or point of contact of this authority, must therefore have unchallenged authority within the factory. According to Mao's view, which was the prevailing view in the late

25 For a more detailed discussion of the emergence and significance of this concept, see Schram, "Decentralization in a unitary state: theory and practice 1940–1984," in Stuart Schram, ed., *The scope of state power in China*, 81–125, esp. 87–89. On *i-yuan-hua* as "integrate," see also Schram's chapter in *CHOC*, 13.864–66.

26 *Wan-sui* (1969), 36; *Miscellany*, 31. The "Resolution on strengthening the party spirit" adopted by the Politburo on 1 July 1941 (Boyd Compton, *Mao's China*, 156–60) did not in fact use the term *i-yuan-hua* but referred to the importance of centralization, and of "unified will, action and discipline." Manifestly, Mao regarded this decision as the first step in a process of establishing integrated Party control, which found further expression in 1942 and 1943.

27 Talk of 11 January 1958 at the Nan-ning Conference, *Wan-sui* (1969), 148; *Miscellany*, 79–80. *Wan-sui* (supplement), 34–35.

1950s, integration had to be carried out not merely at the national level, but in the localities. Otherwise, even "small power" could not be dispersed without leading to confusion. And the agent of integration could only be the Party committee at each level. Party control, whether at the Center or in the localities, involved, as Mao made clear, first taking decisions on matters of principle, and then subsequently checking on their implementation.

Further discussion of the leading role of the Party can best be deferred until we consider Mao's political and economic strategy at the time of the Great Leap Forward as a whole. Meanwhile, to round off this discussion of patterns of rule, it suffices to recall that in his speech of January 1962, after asserting that centralism and democracy must be combined "both within the Party and outside," and stressing once again, as he had in Yenan, that centralism was even more important than democracy, Mao went on to say that genuine centralization was possible only on a basis of democracy, for two main reasons. On the one hand, if people were not allowed to express themselves, they would be "angry" and frustrated, and therefore would not participate willingly and effectively in political and economic work. And on the other hand:

If there is no democracy, if ideas are not coming from the masses, it is impossible to establish a good line.... Our leading organs merely play the role of a processing plant in the establishment of a good line and good ... policies and methods. Everyone knows that if a factory has no raw material, it cannot do any processing.... Without democracy, you have no understanding of what is happening down below; the general situation will be unclear; ... and thus you will find it difficult to avoid being subjectivist; it will be impossible to achieve unity of understanding and unity of action, and impossible to achieve true centralism.[28]

Here the term "democratic centralism" is made to cover both the fundamental dilemma of combining effective "centralized unification" with active support and initiative from below, and the problem of the upward and downward flow of ideas evoked by the slogan of the "mass line." Mao's overall view of this cluster of issues is clearly reflected in the metaphor of the processing plant. To be sure, this plant is incapable of producing anything meaningful if it is not constantly fed with information and suggestions, but in the last analysis the correct line can only be elaborated by the brain at the center. The deprecatory adverb "merely" before "processing plant" does not change the fact that this is where the decisive action takes place.

<hr />

28 Schram, *Mao unrehearsed*, 163–64.

Such was, broadly speaking, Mao's view of democracy and centralism, from Yenan days to the early 1960s. At the same time, although an overarching consistency marked, as noted at the beginning of this section, his line on these matters, there was undeniably a certain change of emphasis in 1957–58. This shift was closely linked to Mao's increasing radicalism, both in economic matters and in the domain of class struggle, which will be discussed in the following sections. It had, however, a direct impact on the questions of the structure of power we are considering here.

We have already seen that although Mao did seek, within the limitations imposed by his ultimate attachment to the ideal of a "strong socialist state," to foster the participation of the people in the country's affairs, the scope for political choice involved in such practices was slight. Above all, Mao gave little thought to the establishment of a political system democratic in its structure and mechanisms, and not merely in the sense that it was held to represent the "people."

That is, of course, one of the criticisms that has been made of him in China since 1978, and we shall return to it in the conclusion to the chapter. It is important to note, however, that from the time of the Great Leap, Mao Tse-tung attached even less importance to institutions than he had previously done. In a word, down to 1956 or 1957, while defining democracy in terms of the class character of the state, rather than in terms of political mechanisms, he nonetheless treated the state structure as something that had to be taken into account.

For example, in Mao's April 1956 discussion of centralization and decentralization, he declared:

According to our Constitution, the legislative powers are all vested in the central authorities. But, provided that the policies of the central authorities are not violated, the local authorities may work out rules, regulations and measures in the light of their specific conditions and the needs of their work, and this is in no way prohibited by the Constitution.[29]

In his speech of 27 February 1957 "On the correct handling of contradictions among the people," Mao emphasized that democracy was a means and not an end, and he poured scorn on Western ideas and practices such as parliamentary democracy and the two-party system.[30] China's own political system he treated whimsically and cavalierly, but he did at least take note of its existence. Discussing the problem of whether

29 Mao, *SW*, 5.294. This version is substantially identical in substance with the unofficial text (Schram, ed., *Mao unrehearsed*, 72), except that the latter contains an explicit reference to the National People's Congress as the sole legislative body.
30 Mao, *SW*, 5.398.

the not very numerous counterrevolutionaries still present in the country should be liberated in a big way (*ta fang*), even though under the constitution they were supposed to be objects of the dictatorship, Mao quoted an imaginary critic as saying: "This is laid down in the Constitution. You are the Chairman; aren't you supposed to observe the Constitution?" His very characteristic response to this dilemma was to suggest that most, though not all, of these people should be released, but that one should certainly not announce such a policy publicly.[31]

By the time of the Great Leap Forward, Mao had come to set very little store indeed by such institutional niceties. But because this evolution in Mao Tse-tung's thought was a direct consequence of the radical climate engendered by the ongoing revolution in the economy and in society, let us turn to those dimensions of the matter, before examining Mao's approach to political power in his later years.

Patterns of development

In approaching Mao's ideas regarding patterns of socialist development, it is perhaps worth emphasizing by way of introduction that his attitude toward modernization and industrialization was consistently positive. There has been a tendency in recent years to treat Mao as a believer in some kind of pastoral utopia, a partisan of a "steady-state" economy as an alternative to our so-called advanced industrial society. In reality, throughout the twenty-seven years during which he presided over the destinies of the People's Republic of China, Mao never ceased to call for rapid economic progress, and for progress defined in quantitative terms: tons of steel, tons of grain, and all the rest.

The very use of the term "modernization" was often taken, in the recent past, as a manifestation of Western cultural arrogance because it seemed to imply that in joining the "modern" world, the peoples of Asia and Africa would necessarily become like the Americans or the Europeans. In fact, Mao himself had no such scruples, and consistently defined China's economic aims in these terms, from the 1940s to the 1960s. Thus, for example, in his report of April 1945 to the Seventh Party Congress, he said China's agriculture must be made to progress from its "old-style, backward level" to a "modernized [*chin-tai-hua ti*] level," in order to pro-

---

31 This passage had been removed from the June 1957 edited text of Mao's speech (Mao, *SW*, 5.398–99). See the text as delivered in *Hsueh-hsi wen-hsuan* (Selected documents for study), 201–2. The content of Mao's February 1957 speech is discussed in detail later in this section.

vide markets for industry, and "make posssible the transformation of an agricultural country into an industrial country."[32]

Industry was, in Mao's view, of primary importance because of the role it played, or could play, in assuring the wealth and power of the Chinese state. Noting, in his article "On the people's democratic dictatorship," that "imperialism, a most ferocious enemy, is still standing alongside us," Mao added (in a comment removed from the *Selected works* text): "A very long time must elapse before China can achieve genuine economic independence. Only when China's industry has been developed, so that economically China is no longer dependent on foreign countries, will she enjoy genuine independence."[33]

The introduction to this chapter spoke of the continuing weight of the peasantry in Chinese society, and of the influence of this fact, and of peasant ideology, on Mao Tse-tung himself. This factor undeniably existed, and was of crucial importance, but it manifested itself very much more strongly from 1955, and especially from 1958, onward. On the eve of the conquest of power, in contrast, Mao repudiated, or in any case played down, the significance of the Party's rural experience. "From 1927 to the present," he declared in March 1949,

the centre of gravity of our work has been in the villages – gathering strength in the villages, using the villages in order to surround the cities, and then taking the cities. The period for this method of work has now ended. The period of "from the city to the village" and of the city leading the village has now begun. The centre of gravity of the Party's work has shifted from the village to the city.[34]

In other words, hitherto we have been doing it the unorthodox way, because that is the only way in which we could win victory, but henceforth we will do it in the orthodox Marxist, or Leninist, way, with guidance and enlightenment radiating outward from the urban industrial environment to the backward peasants in the countryside. Such a perspective was clearly in evidence in Mao's article of June 1949 "On the people's democratic dictatorship," in which, after declaring that state power could not be abolished yet because imperialism and domestic reaction still existed, and that the present task, on the contrary, was to strengthen the people's state apparatus, he went on to say, "Given this condition, China can develop steadily, under the leadership of the working class and the Communist Party, from an agricultural into an industrial country, and from a

---

32 *MTTC* 9.244. (The clause referring to agricultural modernization had been excised from the current official version of this speech in Mao, *SW*, 3.297.)

33 *MTTC* 10.304; see also Mao, *SW*, 4.421, where the last two sentences quoted are missing.

34 Mao, *SW*, 4.363.

new-democratic into a socialist and communist society, abolish classes and realize the Great Harmony [*ta-t'ung*]." In this task of guiding the development of China "from an agricultural into an industrial country," it would be relatively easy, in Mao's view, to reeducate and remold the national bourgeoisie. "The serious problem," he declared, "is the education of the peasantry." For, he added, "The peasant economy is scattered, and the socialization of agriculture, judging by the Soviet Union's experience, will require a long time and painstaking work."[35]

Mao's stress on educating the peasants, and on working-class leadership of the "people's dictatorship" that was to do the educating, appears to offer clear confirmation of the reversal of priorities between cities and countryside he had announced in March 1949.

Another intriguing indication to this effect may be found in Mao's decision of December 1951 to abandon a formulation, put forward the previous spring by Liu Shao-ch'i and used thereafter by the Central Committee, according to which the "semi-working class" (*pan kung-jen chieh-chi*) in the countryside was, like the urban working class, one of the classes leading the revolution. Although Mao himself had earlier characterized the "semi-proletariat (the poor peasants)" as a leading class in the new-democratic revolution, he now found it "erroneous" to attribute leadership to any class save the urban workers. This plainly marked a shift toward greater orthodoxy.[36]

Moreover, in the early 1950s, these ideological trends were translated into action by an energetic attempt to draw large numbers of real flesh-and-blood workers into the Chinese Communist Party, in order to "improve" its class composition (see Chapter 2).

And yet, despite Mao's statement, in 1962, that during these early years there had been no alternative to "copying from the Soviets,"[37] he did not, like the Soviets, confuse the industrial revolution with the socialist revolution. And although scientific and technical modernization was a central and crucial strand in Mao's conception of socialist development, one may legitimately ask whether his broader vision of the Chinese revolution, even as he entertained it in 1949, would ultimately prove compatible with such technical modernization.

At the outset, the economic policies explicitly formulated by Mao were prudent and gradualist ones. Thus, in June 1950, he called for "maintaining the rich peasant economy in order to facilitate the early rehabilitation of rural production," and summed up the overall goals as follows:

35 Ibid., 418–19.
36 "Chih Liu Shao-ch'i" (To Liu Shao-ch'i), 15 December 1951, *Mao Tse-tung shu-hsin hsuan-chi*, 427–28.
37 Schram, *Mao unrehearsed*, 178.

... existing industry and commerce should be properly readjusted, and relations between the state sector and the private sector and between labour and capital should be effectively and suitably improved; thus under the leadership of the socialist state sector all sectors of the economy will function satisfactorily with a due division of labour to promote the rehabilitation and development of the whole economy. The view held by certain people that it is possible to eliminate capitalism and realize socialism at an early date is wrong, it does not tally with our national conditions.[38]

Even after the beginning of the 1st Five-Year Plan (FYP), Mao's perspective on these matters remained essentially similar. In August 1953, he defined the "general line" for the period of transition as "basically to accomplish the country's industrialization and the socialist transformation of agriculture, handicrafts and capitalist industry and commerce over a fairly long period of time."[39]

In September 1954, he declared:

The people of our country should work hard, do their best to draw on advanced experience in the Soviet Union and other fraternal countries, be honest and industrious, encourage and help each other, guard against boastfulness and arrogance, and gird themselves to build our country, which is at present economically and culturally backward, into a great industrialized country with a high standard of modern culture in the course of several five-year plans.[40]

In November 1954, Mao Tse-tung called the attention of Liu Shaoch'i and Chou En-lai to what he described as an "erroneous formulation" in the extracts from the Soviet textbook of political economy just published in *People's Daily*: "Until socialism has been built completely or to a very large extent, it is impossible that there should be socialist economic laws."[41] In repudiating this view, Mao was quite plainly concerned with the theoretical foundations for China's claim to be already in some degree socialist in nature.

Nevertheless, as late as March 1955, Mao recognized that the road to socialism would be a long one:

It is no easy job to build a socialist society in a large country such as ours with its complicated conditions and its formerly very backward economy. We may be able to build a socialist society over three five-year plans, but to build a strong, highly industrialized socialist country will require several decades of hard work, say fifty years, or the entire second half of the present century.[42]

---

38 Mao, *SW*, 5.29–30.   39 Ibid., 102.   40 Ibid., 148–49.
41 "Chih Liu Shao-ch'i, Chou En-lai teng" (To Liu Shao-ch'i, Chou En-lai and others), 18 November 1954, *Mao Tse-tung shu-hsin hsuan-chi*, 484–85.
42 Mao, *SW*, 5.155.

Then, suddenly, in the middle of 1955 Mao's attitude changed, and (as described in *CHOC*, 14, ch. 2) he launched a movement for more rapid cooperativization in the countryside that, almost overnight, transformed the whole atmosphere of Chinese society. Mao's new mood, as well as his new framework of analysis, is vividly evoked by his annotations in the volume *Socialist upsurge in China's countryside*, written at the end of 1955, when the acceleration of cooperativization for which he had called on 31 July was proceeding even faster than he himself had predicted.[43]

In these texts, we can see clearly foreshadowed certain basic themes of the Great Leap Forward, and even of the Cultural Revolution, such as Mao's belief in the omnipotence of the subjective efforts of the mobilized masses to transform themselves and their environment. For example, in a passage praising the Wang Kuo-fan cooperative, nicknamed "The Paupers' Co-op," which had accumulated "a large quantity of the means of production" in three years by their own efforts, Mao commented: "In a few decades, why can't 600 million paupers, by their own efforts, create a socialist country, rich and strong?" Noting, in another passage, that tens of millions of peasant households had swung into action during the second half of 1955, thus completely transforming the atmosphere in China, Mao commented: "It is as if a raging tidal wave has swept away all the demons and ghosts."[44]

In this context of enthusiasm for the zeal and fighting spirit of the peasants, Mao wrote in December 1955:

If you compare our country with the Soviet Union: (1) we had twenty years' experience in the base areas, and were trained in three revolutionary wars; our experience [on coming to power] was exceedingly rich.... Therefore, we were able to set up a state very quickly, and complete the tasks of the revolution. (The Soviet Union was a newly established state; at the time of the October Revolution, they had neither army nor government apparatus, and there were very few Party members.) (2) We enjoy the assistance of the Soviet Union and other democratic countries. (3) Our population is very numerous, and our position is excellent. [Our people] work industriously and bear much hardship, and there is no way out for the peasants without co-operativization. Chinese peasants are even better than English and American workers. Consequently, we can reach socialism more, better, and faster.[45]

Thus, Mao suggested as early as 1955 that because they came to power after twenty years' struggle in the countryside, instead of by suddenly seizing the reins of government in the capital city, the Chinese Com-

---

43 *Socialist upsurge in China's countryside*, passim: Mao's commentaries are also reproduced in Mao, *SW*, 5.235–76.
44 *Socialist upsurge*, 5–6.159–60.   45 *Wan-sui* (1969), 27; *Miscellany*, 29.

munists knew more in 1949 than Lenin and his comrades had known in 1917 about exercising authority over the population at the grass roots, and securing their support. Moreover, the Chinese peasantry, in his view, provided splendid human material for building a socialist society.

And yet, it was by no means a one-sided "rustic" revolution that Mao sought to promote at this time. Though a distinctive feature of his 31 July 1955 speech on cooperativization had been the demand that in China, collectivization should come before mechanization, it was not to come very *far* before it, and the provision of the necessary tractors, pumps, and other industrial products was therefore urgent. More broadly, Mao continued to subscribe to the view he had put forward in 1949, according to which "the serious problem" was "the education of the peasantry." The implication plainly was that these rural dwellers would have to be brought into the modern world by causing them to assimilate knowledge, and especially technical knowledge, originating in the cities. And in this process, scientists, technicians, and other intellectuals would have a key role to play. Indeed, Mao recognized this in January 1956 when he declared, in the context of his twelve-year program for agricultural development, that the Chinese people "must have a far-reaching comprehensive plan of work in accordance with which they could strive to wipe out China's economic, scientific and cultural backwardness within a few decades and rapidly get abreast of the most advanced nations in the world." And he added that "to achieve this great goal, the decisive factor was to have cadres, to have an adequate number of excellent scientists and technicians."[46]

Mao therefore called, in January 1956, for a conciliatory and understanding approach to the intellectuals inherited from the old society. At a conference on the problem of the intellectuals called by the Central Committee, Mao underscored the various respects in which China was industrially and technologically backward, and in a dependent position because it could not make key products for itself, and commented:

There are some comrades who say not very intelligent things, such as "We can get along without them [i.e., the intellectuals]!" "I'm a revolutionary" [*lao-tzu shih ko-ming ti*]! Such statements are wrong. Now we are calling for a technical revolution, a cultural revolution, a revolution to do away with stupidity and ignorance [*ko yü-chun wu-chih ti ming*], and we can't get along without them. We can't do it by relying only on uneducated people [*lao-ts'u*] like ourselves.[47]

46 Speech of 25 January 1956, *JMJP*, 26 January 1956; extracts translated in Hélène Carrère d'Encausse and Stuart R. Schram, comps., *Marxism and Asia: an introduction with readings*, 293.
47 *Wan-sui* (1969), 34.

Mao's overall approach to building socialism in the mid-1950s is most cogently summed up in his speech of 25 April 1956 to the Politburo, "On the ten great relationships." In every domain, the lesson of this well-known utterance was the same: Understand the interconnectedness of things, and do not seek to maximize one while neglecting the effects on others. Thus, as we have already seen, he called in the political domain for an increase in the power and initiative of the localities, in order to contribute to the building of a strong socialist state. In the economic field, he called for reducing (but not reversing, as is sometimes suggested) the overwhelming priority to heavy industry, at the expense of agriculture and light industry, which he held to be self-defeating. But at the same time (thus illustrating his balance and evenhandedness at the time), he urged that proper attention should be given to developing further the existing industrial base in Shanghai and other coastal cities, rather than putting all the available resources into spreading industry throughout the hinterland.[48]

In drafting this speech Mao Tse-tung had, as noted earlier, taken careful account of the views of Ch'en Yun and other experts in economic work, and "On the ten great relationships" as a whole undoubtedly represented an attempt on his part to lay down a compromise position that would command wide agreement within the Party. The fact that Mao thus adopted a moderate and conciliatory attitude on specific issues by no means implied, however, that he was prepared in all respects to bow to the will of the majority of his leading comrades.

Already, in his manner of launching an accelerated collectivization drive in 1955, Mao Tse-tung had shown his disposition to ride roughshod over all opposition on a matter close to his own heart.[49] In mid-1956, he revealed a similar intolerance once again, in a more veiled, but ominous, manner. In early 1956, Mao had been persuaded that, as a result of the success of the "high tide" of socialism in the countryside, all economic work could be accelerated. When, in the face of the resulting contradictions and disequilibrium, the important editorial of 20 June 1956 on "Opposing adventurism" was drafted under the supervision of Chou En-lai, Mao saw the text in advance but did not express himself one way or the other. His colleagues were left with the impression that he had endorsed this statement, but in fact he had reservations about it. While acknowledging that it was undesirable to go *too* fast in economic development, he was persuaded that China could go very fast. For a year and a

48 Schram, *Mao unrehearsed*, 61−83; official text in Mao, *SW*, 5.284−307.
49 See the discussion in *CHOC*, 14. 110−17, 167−69, and also the analysis by Schram in "Party leader or true ruler?," 214−16.

half, he harbored his resentment at this editorial in general and at Chou En-lai in particular, before giving vent to his feelings on the eve of the Great Leap Forward.[50]

Meanwhile, in the spring and summer of 1956, Mao not only launched the slogan of a "Hundred Flowers" but also adopted a very soft approach toward problems of classes and class struggle, the relation between the Communist Party and other forces in society, and the relation between right and wrong. These issues were dealt with in more detail in his speech of 27 February 1957, "On the correct handling of contradictions among the people," but Mao had frequently referred to them in earlier texts. Because of the importance that "class struggle" was to assume from 1957 to 1976, this theme merits detailed discussion in a separate section.

People, classes, and contradictions

The theoretical framework in which Mao considered these matters before February 1957 was essentially that laid down in 1937 in "On contradiction." In this article, Mao had argued that although contradiction "permeates each and every process from beginning to end," and although all contradictions involved struggle, they were not necessarily antagonistic, and contradictions different in nature should be resolved by different methods. In the text of this essay as Mao originally wrote it, the realm of "non-antagonistic contradictions" was defined very broadly, and the scope of class struggle thereby restricted:

For instance, the contradictions between correct and incorrect ideas in the Communist Party, between the advanced and the backward in culture, between town and country in economics, between the forces and relations of production, between production and consumption, between exchange value and use value, between the various technical divisons of labour, between workers and peasants in class relations, between life and death in nature, between heredity and mutation, between cold and hot, between day and night – none of these exist in antagonistic form [*tou mei-yu tui-k'ang hsing-t'ai ti ts'un-tsai*].[51]

---

50 For Mao's continuing optimism and impatience, see his speech at the Second Plenum of 15 November 1956, Mao, *SW*, 5.332–35. The importance of Mao's psychological reaction to the criticism of "adventurism" is widely stressed in recent Chinese accounts of this period. In a conversation of 24 April 1986, Kung Yü-chih characterized it as perhaps the first step on the road to the Cultural Revolution. For a summary of evidence regarding Mao's anger at this editorial published during the Cultural Revolution, see Roderick MacFarquhar, *The origins of the Cultural Revolution*, 1: *contradictions among the people 1956–1957*, 86–91. Regarding Chou En-Lai's contribution to the writing of the article of 20 June 1956, see Hu Hua, *Chung-kuo she-hui-chu-i ko-ming ho chien-she shih chiang-i* (Teaching materials on the history of China's socialist revolution and construction), 146.

51 Nick Knight, *Mao Zedong's "On contradiction": an annotated translation of the preliberation text*, 38. (Translation slightly modified on the basis of the Chinese text.)

In the revised version of 1951, which constituted, of course, the standard of ideological orthodoxy during the period we are considering here, Mao drew the lines much more carefully, explaining that "as long as classes exist, contradictions between correct and incorrect ideas in the Communist Party are reflections within the Party of class contradictions," and that such contradictions *could* become antagonistic "if the comrades who had committed mistakes did not correct them." He also noted that, while the contradiction between town and country was nonantagonistic in the base areas, or in a socialist country, it was "extremely antagonistic" in capitalist society, and under the rule of the Kuomintang.[52]

These are important differences as far as the tone of the work is concerned, and reflected an emphasis on the need to wage class struggle that Mao Tse-tung was to exhibit to a greater or lesser degree throughout the 1950s, but as regarded the attitude adopted toward the only two classes that (as we have seen from our earlier consideration of "On the people's democratic dictatorship") constituted a serious problem for the new regime, the line laid down was not significantly altered in 1951. The contradiction between the proletariat and the bourgeoisie was still to be resolved "by the method of socialist revolution"; and that between the workers and peasants in socialist society, which in 1937 was supposed to be resolved by the "socialization of agriculture," now called for the method of "collectivization and mechanization in agriculture," which was really a more concrete way of saying the same thing.[53]

In June 1950, Mao Tse-tung confirmed the basic moderation of his approach at that time in a speech to the Third Plenum entitled, in the *Selected works*, "Don't hit out in all directions" – in other words, don't struggle with too many classes at the same time. Summing up the Party's current attitude toward that ambiguous class, the national bourgeoisie, he declared:

The whole Party should try earnestly and painstakingly to make a success of its united front work. We should rally the petty bourgeoisie under the leadership of the working class and on the basis of the worker–peasant alliance. The national bourgeoisie will eventually cease to exist, but at this stage we should rally them around us and not push them away. We should struggle against them on the one hand, and unite with them on the other.[54]

By June 1952, things had progressed to the point where, in Mao's view, the contradiction between the working class and the national bourgeoisie had become the "principal contradiction" in China; hence it was

52 Mao, *SW*, 1.344–45.   53 Knight, *Mao Zedong's "On contradiction."* Mao, *SW*, 1.321–22.
54 Mao, *SW*, 5.35.

no longer appropriate to define the national bourgeoisie as an "intermediate class."[55]

And yet, in September 1952 he wrote to Huang Yen-p'ei that it would be unreasonable, throughout the whole period of the 1st FYP (i.e., until 1957), to expect more than a small fraction of the bourgeoisie to accept socialist ideas. They must accept working-class leadership, but to ask them to accept working-class thought, and not to be concerned with making money, was "impossible, and should not be done."[56]

In the summer of 1955, Mao Tse-tung gave renewed impetus to class struggle in the countryside, in particular by adopting the distinction between "upper" and "lower" middle peasants, and treating the line between these two categories as the fundamental cleavage in Chinese rural society. Summing up the situation in his concluding speech at the Sixth Plenum of October 1955, which formally endorsed his rural policies, Mao repeated that the Communists had two alliances, one with the peasants and the other with the national bourgeoisie. Both of them were "indispensable," but of the two, the alliance with the peasants was "principal, basic and primary," whereas that with the bourgeoisie was "temporary and secondary." Stressing the interrelationship between these two alliances, he said:

At the Third Plenary Session in 1950, I spoke against hitting out in all directions. The agrarian reform had not yet been carried out in vast areas of the country, nor had the peasants come over entirely to our side. If we had opened fire on the bourgeoisie then, it would have been out of order. After the agrarian reform, when the peasants had entirely come over to our side, it was possible and necessary for us to start the movements against the "three evils" and the "five evils" [i.e., the Three Antis and the Five Antis]. Agricultural co-operation will enable us to consolidate our alliance with the peasants on the basis of proletarian socialism and not of bourgeois democracy. That will isolate the bourgeoisie once and for all and facilitate the final elimination of capitalism. On this matter we are quite heartless! On this matter Marxism is indeed cruel and has little mercy, for it is determined to exterminate imperialism, feudalism, capitalism, and small production to boot.

During the fifteen-year period of the first three five-year plans (of which three years had already elapsed), "the class struggle at home and abroad will be very tense," he noted.[57] In fact, the socialist transformation of agriculture and of capitalist industry and commerce, which Mao said in the speech just quoted would take about three five-year plans, was carried through on all fronts by the end of 1956 (see *CHOC*, 14, ch. 2). Already,

55 Ibid., 77.
56 "Chih Huang Yen-p'ei" (To Huang Yen-p'ei), 5 September 1952, *Mao Tse-tung shu-hsin hsuan-chi*, 441–43.
57 Mao, *SW*, 5.213–15.

by early 1956, sensing the favorable prospects and feeling himself in a position of strength, Mao Tse-tung took, as we have seen, a far softer and more conciliatory line on class struggle, and especially on the role of bourgeois intellectuals, and stressed the importance of scientists and technicians.

Another reflection of the same trend was the ending of the discrimination previously exercised against nonproletarian elements in recruiting new Party members. As already noted, strenuous efforts had been made in the early years of the Chinese People's Republic to recruit more workers into the Party, in order to improve its class composition. Then, in 1956, the more rigorous selection procedures formerly applied to nonworkers were abolished in the new Party constitution, on the grounds that, as Teng Hsiao-p'ing put it in his Report to the Eighth Congress, "the former classification of social status has lost or is losing its meaning." It is perhaps worth recalling the details of Teng's argument, for they provide the background against which Mao's views on class developed during the last two decades of his life:

The difference between workers and office employees is now only a matter of division of labour within the same class.... Poor and middle peasants have all become members of agricultural producers' co-operatives, and before long the distinction between them will become merely a thing of historical interest.... The vast majority of our intellectuals have now come over politically to the side of the working class, and a rapid change is taking place in their family background.... Every year large numbers of peasants and students become workers, large numbers of workers, peasants, and their sons and daughters join the ranks of the intellectuals and office workers, large numbers of peasants, students, workers and office workers join the army and become revolutionary soldiers.... What is the point, then, of classifying these social strata into two different categories?[58]

To the extent that Teng here attached more importance to subjective attitudes, and willingness to work for the revolution, than to family origins, his views are consonant with a continuing (though not a consistent) trend in Mao's thinking. But to the extent that he indicated that class struggle within Chinese society was rapidly dying away, his ideas obviously go completely against the tide that was later to rise, and to swamp the Party. That does not, of course, mean that Mao Tse-tung disagreed with him at the time. Even during the first upsurge of the Cultural Revolution, in 1966, when K'ang Sheng complained that the political report at the Eighth Congress had contained the theory of the disappearance of classes, Mao recognized that he had shared these views in 1956: "I read

58 *Eighth National Congress of the Communist Party of China*, 2.213-14.

the report, and it was passed by the congress; we cannot make these two – Liu and Teng – solely responsible."[59]

How and why did Mao come to change his attitude toward classes and class struggle so dramatically that Liu became a decade later the "number one capitalist-roader"? The general context is well known. An aspect that merits emphasis is the crucial generational change in China's educated elite, which was inevitable in any case but was accelerated by the events of 1957. During the early years after 1949, both technical and managerial cadres were, of necessity, largely people inherited from the old society, "bourgeois" in their social origins or in that they had been trained in the West or in universities staffed by graduates of European, American, or Japanese schools. Mao believed that the loyalty of these people could be gained, and that being already expert, they could be made red as well. The "Hundred Flowers" policies Mao launched in the spring of 1956 were primarily designed to serve this aim of drawing the pre-1949 intellectuals into active participation in political and social life, improving their morale, and remolding them in the process.

In his speech "On the ten great relationships" as originally delivered to the Party on 25 April 1956, Mao Tse-tung, while reiterating that "inner-Party controversies over principle" were "a reflection inside the Party of the class struggle in society," stressed the importance of exchanging ideas, especially in the scientific domain, with people in and outside China.[60] The Hundred Flowers formula emerged in the course of the discussion of his report by the Politburo. In an intervention of 28 April, Mao declared that if one's views were true, more and more people could be expected to believe in them, adding that the Party's orientation (*fang-chen*) in literature should be "Let a Hundred Flowers bloom," and in scholarly matters, "Let a Hundred Schools contend."[61]

It was in the version of "On the ten great relationships" presented on 2 May 1956 to the Supreme State Conference that Mao gave, for the first time, a systematic account of his ideas on this topic. According to the fullest available summary, he declared that spring had now come, and that a hundred flowers, and not just a few kinds, should be allowed to bloom. The formula of a hundred schools of thought contending dated, he recalled, from the Spring and Autumn and Warring States periods, when there were a hundred schools of leading philosophers, with many different doctrines, all freely engaging in controversy. The same thing, he said, was necessary at present. Within the limits set by the constitution, the

59 Schram, *Mao unrehearsed*, 269.   60 Mao, *SW*, 5.301–6.
61 *1981 resolution, annotated edition*, 253–54.

partisans of every sort of scholarly theory should be able to argue about the truth or falsity of their ideas, without interference. We still haven't sorted out, he remarked, whether Lysenko's ideas are right or wrong, so let each school put forward its ideas in the newspapers and journals.[62]

Not only were Lysenko's ideas discussed in the newspapers, but in August 1956 at Tsingtao, a large-scale scholarly conference debated for a fortnight the opposing views of genetics, under the slogan "Let a hundred schools of thought contend!"[63] When one of the participants in this gathering subsequently expressed his enthusiasm in an article published in *Kuang-ming jih-pao*, Mao Tse-tung personally decided that it should be reprinted in the *People's Daily*, with a new subtitle supplied by Mao: "The way which the development of science must follow" (*fa-chan k'o-hsueh pi-yu chih lu*).[64]

The related but distinctive idea of contradictions among the people first emerged in the autumn of 1956, in the aftermath of de-Stalinization in the Soviet Union, and of the Polish and Hungarian events. In his speech of 15 November 1956 to the Second Plenum, Mao indicated that class contradictions within Chinese society had already basically been resolved, although he spoke out firmly in support of class struggle and the dictatorship of the proletariat in dealing with counterrevolutionaries, and against Khrushchev's ideas of peaceful transition by the parliamentary road.[65]

So far as is known, Mao first used the actual term "contradictions among the people" on 4 December 1956 in a letter to Huang Yen-p'ei, a leading representative of one of the minor parties. On this occasion, he stated that although class struggle within China (as opposed to conflicts with imperialism and its agents) had "already been *basically* resolved" (*i-ching chi-pen-shang chieh-chueh le*), problems among the people would, in future, "ceaselessly arise."[66] Plainly, the suggestion is that they would be more numerous.

The *People's Daily* editorial of 29 December 1956, entitled "More on

62 Ibid., 254.
63 The full record of the formal discussions at this conference was published nearly thirty years later. See *Pai-chia cheng-ming – fa-chan k'o-hsueh ti pi-yu chih lu. 1956 nien 8 yueh Ch'ing-tao i-ch'uan hsueh tso-t'an hui chi-shu* (Let a hundred schools of thought contend – the way which the development of science must follow. The record of the August 1956 Tsingtao Conference on Genetics).
64 Ibid., 10 (Introduction). For a fuller account, see Kung Yü-chih, "Fa-chan k'o-hsueh pi-yu chih lu – chieh-shao Mao Tse-tung t'ung-chih wei chuan-tai 'Ts'ung i-ch'uan-hsueh t'an pai-chia cheng-ming' i wen hsieh ti hsin ho an-yü" (The way which the development of science must follow – presenting Comrade Mao Tse-tung's letter and annotation relating to the republication of "Let a hundred schools of thought contend viewed from the perspective of genetics"), *KMJP*, 28 December 1983.
65 Mao, *SW*, 5.341–48 passim; *1981 resolution, annotated edition*, 51.3
66 "Chih Huang Yen-p'ei" (To Huang Yen-p'ei) 4 December 1956, *Mao Tse-tung shu-hsin hsuan-chi*, 514–15. (Mao himself underscored the adverb "basically.")

the historical experience of the dictatorship of the proletariat,"[67] constituted the first public exposition of Mao's ideas on this topic.[68] This text,
which aimed to combat excessive discrediting of Stalin and of Soviet
experience in the wake of the Polish events and the Hungarian revolt,
took a slightly harder position, stating that no one adopting the standpoint of the people should "place the contradictions among the people
above the contradictions between the enemy and ourselves," adding:
"Those who deny the class struggle and do not distinguish between the
enemy and ourselves are definitely not Communists or Marxist-Leninists."[69]

At a conference of provincial and municipal Party secretaries on 27
January 1957, Mao declared, "During the period of building [socialism],
our experience of class struggle (which is partial), and contradictions
among the people (which are primary) has been inadequate. This is a science, and we must study it very well."[70]

A month later, Mao devoted the greater part of his celebrated speech
"On the correct handling of contradictions among the people" precisely
to this science. In the original version of this talk, Mao expressed some
reservations about the December editorial (even though he had personally revised it),[71] saying that it had not dealt explicitly with the problem of
the national bourgeoisie, and had not made plain that the contradictions
with this class were definitely contradictions among the people. To be
sure, under certain circumstances, they could become antagonistic, but
one should not mistake well-intentioned criticisms for hostile attacks.
Lenin had not had time to analyze this problem properly, and Stalin did
not even try to make the distinction:

You could only speak favourably, and not unfavourably; you could only sing
praises to his successes and virtues, but were not allowed to criticize; if you
expressed any criticisms he suspected you of being an enemy, and you were in
danger of being sent to a camp or executed.

Leftists are left opportunists. The so-called "leftists" raise the banner of the
"left," but they are not really left, for they exaggerate the contradictions between
ourselves and the enemy. Stalin, for example, was such a person.

---

67 For a translation, see *The historical experience of the dictatorship of the proletariat*, 21–64.
68 The novelty of this formulation was widely noted at the time, and these ideas were commonly
   attributed to Mao. (This passage was included in Stuart R. Schram, *The political thought of Mao
   Tse-tung* in 1963.) The fact that Mao had not previously expressed the same ideas in any unpublished text is confirmed by Liao Kai-lung, "She-hui-chu-i she-hui chung ti chieh-chi tou-cheng ho
   jen-min nei-pu mao-tun wen-t'i" (The problem of class struggle and of contradictions among the
   people in socialist society), in Liao Kai-lung, *Ch'üan-mien chien-she she-hui chu-i ti tao-lu* (The road to
   building socialism in an all-round way), 245.
69 *The historical experience*, 25.   70 *1981 resolution, annotated edition*, 532.
71 *Wan-sui* (1969), 89; *Miscellany*, 61. This source indicates simply that the meeting took place in
   January 1957; the date of 27 January is given in the version published in Mao, *SW*, 5.359–83,
   which does not, however, include this passage.

China, too, said Mao, had suffered from such errors, especially during the campaign against counterrevolutionaries.[72]

The original text of Mao's 27 February speech contained extremely long and important passages both on the differences between China and the Soviet Union and on the related problem of war and peace, which will be discussed in a later section, on the Sino-Soviet split. It also dealt in passing with a variety of issues that cannot be taken up in this chapter, such as the "anarchism" prevailing in the realm of birth control,[73] or the inability of China at the present stage to provide secondary education for all.[74] Regarding the problem concerning us here, Mao declared that the "basic" (*chi-pen-ti*) contradiction in Chinese society was that between the relations of production and the productive forces, or between the basis and the superstructure.[75] At the same time, he made plain that, in his view, class struggles had basically come to an end in China.[76]

One can find a similar emphasis on the crucial role of contradictions among the people in the official text of Mao's February 1957 speech. For example, he declared: "It is precisely these contradictions [among the people] that are pushing our society forward"; since contradictions were, in Mao's view, the motor of change, the particular contradiction, or type of contradiction, that moves society forward ought logically to be the principal contradiction. Moreover, in the same passage, Mao went on to say:

Contradictions in socialist society are fundamentally different from those in the old societies, such as capitalist society. In capitalist society contradictions find expression in acute antagonisms and conflicts, in sharp class struggle; they cannot be resolved by the capitalist system itself and can only be resolved by socialist revolution. The case is quite different with contradictions in socialist society; on the contrary, they are not antagonistic and can be ceaselessly resolved by the socialist system itself.[77]

Such statements apper to support the view, put forward by some leading Chinese theoretical workers in recent years, to the effect that Mao's ideas of late 1956 and early 1957 implied the replacement of class struggle by contradictions among the people (which cannot, generally speaking,

---

72 *Hsueh-hsi wen-hsuan*, 193–95. For another version of this passage in the original February 1957 text, see *Mao Chu-hsi wen-hsien san-shih p'ien* (Thirty documents by Chairman Mao) (Peking: Special Steel Plant, 1967), 94–95.

73 *Hsueh-hsi wen-hsuan*, 209.   74 Ibid., 211.   75 Ibid., 212–13.

76 Ibid., passim, esp. 201. See also Su Shao-chih's assessment in *Tentative views on the class situation and class struggle in China at the present stage* ("Selected writings on studies of Marxism," No. 6), 35. (Chinese text, "Shih lun wo-kuo hsien chieh-tuan ti chieh-chi chuang-k'uang ho chieh-chi tou-cheng," in *Hsueh-shu yen-chiu-k'an*, 1 [October 1979].)

77 Mao, *SW*, 5.393.

be regarded as a form of class struggle) as the "principal contradiction" in Chinese society after the socialist transformation of 1955–56.[78]

An issue closely related to that of contradictions among the classes making up Chinese society is the problem of the role of the intellectuals. Mao's relatively tolerant and gradualist attitude toward the elimination of class differences in this domain was expressed in a statement of January 1957 noting that 80 percent of university students in China were still children of landlords, rich peasants, upper middle peasants, and the bourgeoisie. "This situation," he commented, "should change, but it will take time."[79] Nonetheless, he stressed forcefully, in the original version of his speech on "contradictions among the people," the importance of making the intellectuals reform themselves, so as to do away with their self-indulgent attitudes. All they wanted, he said, was two things: a high salary and "an old lady" or an "old man" (*t'ao lao p'o, t'ao lao kung*) – in other words, "to eat and to produce children."[80]

Mao's disdain for goals such as these (in both of which, it is hardly necessary to observe, he had himself freely indulged) was expressed in another passage of the 27 February 1957 speech on the corrupting effects of material well-being. The Chinese, he said, had two characteristics: Their standard of living was low, and their cultural level was low. Both of these traits, he said, were ambiguous:

If China becomes rich, with a standard of living like that in the Western world, it will no longer want revolution. The wealth of the Western World has its defects, and these defects are that they don't want revolution.... Their high standard of living is not so good as our illiteracy [*laughter*].[81]

This strain in Mao's thought was to come to the fore and find further expression during the Great Leap Forward, as we shall see. Meanwhile, however, Mao remained on the whole, in early 1957, relatively well disposed toward both the bourgeoisie and the intellectuals.

As late as 2 May 1957, an editorial in the *People's Daily*, which according to a well-informed Chinese specialist "reflected completely Comrade Mao Tse-tung's views at the time," argued: "Following the decisive victory in socialist transformation, the contradiction between the proletariat and the bourgeoisie in our country has already been basically resolved, and the previous several thousand years of history in a system of class exploitation has been basically concluded." As a result, the editorial

78 Liao Kai-lung, "She-hui-chu-i she-hui chung ti chieh-chi ...," 246–53; Su Shao-chih, *Tentative views on the class situation*, 22–26.
79 Mao, *SW*, 5.353.   80 *Hsueh-hsi wen-hsuan*, 207.   81 Ibid., 225–26.

stated, the principal contradiction in China was no longer that between hostile classes, but the contradiction between "the demand to build an advanced industrial country and the reality of a backward agrarian country," and others of a similar nature.[82]

But in mid-May, Mao's attitude changed radically as a result of continuing harsh criticism, and he perceived among the members of the Party "a number of" revisionists and right deviationists, whose thinking was a "reflection of bourgeois ideology inside the Party," and who were "tied in a hundred and one ways to bourgeois intellectuals outside the Party."[83]

Rewriting his February speech in June 1957, Mao qualified his original conclusion that class struggles were over by adding: "The large-scale, turbulent class struggles of the masses characteristic of times of revolution have basically come to an end, but class struggle is by no means entirely over."[84] This was still a relatively soft position, but Mao progressively hardened it. Thus, in July 1957, as the Hundred Flowers Campaign was being transformed into an Anti-Rightist Campaign, he asserted, "To build socialism, the working class must have its own army of technical cadres and of professors, teachers, scientists, journalists, writers, artists and Marxist theorists.... This is a task that should be basically accomplished in the next ten to fifteen years." To be sure, he added that his new army would include intellectuals from the old society "who would take a firm working-class stand after having been genuinely remoulded," but it was plain that most members of this army were to be young people of good class background. "The revolutionary cause of the working class," he added, "will not be fully consolidated until this vast new army of working-class intellectuals comes into being."[85]

As for the existing intellectuals, Mao warned them disdainfully:

Intellectuals are teachers employed by the working class and the labouring people to teach their children. If they go against the wishes of their masters and insist on teaching their own set of subjects, teaching stereotyped writing, Confucian classics or capitalist rubbish, and turn out a number of counter-revolutionaries, the working class will not tolerate it and will sack them and not renew their contract for the coming year.[86]

82 "Wei shih-mo yao cheng-feng?" ("Why do we want to carry out rectification?"), *JMJP*, 2 May 1957. For the judgment quoted above regarding Mao's approval for the article, see Liao Kai-lung, "Kuan-yü hsueh-hsi 'chueh-i' chung t'i-ch'u ti i-hsieh wen-t'i ti chieh-ta" (Answers and explanations regarding some questions which have been posed in connection with study of the "Resolution"), *Yun-nan she-hui k'o-hsueh*, 2 (March 1982), 104–5. (At a meeting of Party and state cadres in Yunnan on 8 October 1981.)
83 "Things are beginning to change," 15 May 1957. Mao, *SW*, 5.440.   84 Ibid., 395.
85 "The situation in the summer of 1957," July 1957, Mao, *SW*, 5.479–80.
86 "Beat back the attacks of the bourgeois rightists," 9 July 1957, Mao, *SW*, 5.469–70.

From this time forward, Mao increasingly saw "ghosts and monsters opposed to the Communist Party and the people" everywhere.[87]

MAO'S SEARCH FOR A "CHINESE ROAD"

As argued in the introduction to this chapter, the Anti-Rightist Campaign of autumn 1957 constituted a major turning point not only in Chinese politics generally, but in the development of Mao Tse-tung's thought. The changes that took place at this time made themselves felt across the whole range of Mao's intellectual interests and political concerns, from economics to philosophy, and from China's own internal problems to relations with the Soviet Union. In substantial measure, however, the central core of these new trends in Mao Tse-tung's thinking, and the impulse that led to their emergence, can be found in his ideas about "building socialism."

Determinism and utopian visions:
the theory of the "Great Leap Forward"

One aspect of the sea change in Mao's mind and thought that took place at this time was, as just noted, a sharp reversal of his attitude toward the intellectuals. By their harsh and, to his mind, negative and destructive criticisms, the scholars and writers participating in the "great blooming and contending" of early 1957 had cast doubt on Mao's own judgment in pressing ahead with these policies in the face of opposition from many of his senior comrades, and thereby, in Mao's view, undermined his prestige and authority. He therefore turned savagely against them. Henceforth, apart from training new, red intellectuals of good class origin, Mao Tse-tung would rely rather on the enthusiasm and creativity of the masses.

As for those wretched bookworms who had so betrayed his confidence during the Hundred Flowers period, who needed them? Mao therefore made repeated statements, and actively promoted policies, entirely at variance with his view of 1956 that scientists were the decisive factor, stressing that "all wisdom comes from the masses," and that "the intellectuals are most ignorant." In March 1958, he declared:

Ever since ancient times the people who founded new schools of thought were all young people without much learning. They had the ability to recognize new things at a glance and, having grasped them, opened fire on the old fogeys.... Franklin of America, who discovered electricity, began as a newspaper boy....

87 Ibid., 444.

Gorki only had two years of elementary schooling. Of course, some things can be learned at school; I don't propose to close all the schools. What I mean is that it is not absolutely necessary to attend school.[88]

However pithy and forceful we may find this, and Mao's many other anti-intellectual statements of the Great Leap period, it would be wrong to take any of them as a full and balanced expression of his view on these matters. At this time, he was still striving to hold together in creative tension, and to manipulate, polarities such as mass creativity and the scientific inputs necessary to economic development, or the rural and urban sectors in Chinese society.

In December 1958, Mao wrote to Lu Ting-i endorsing a report from the Tsing-hua University Party Committee about correcting the leftist errors committed in dealing with teachers in the Physics Department, and requesting that it be reproduced for general distribution. There was a widespread feeling, said this document, that "intellectuals are objects of the revolution during the period of the socialist revolution, and even more so during the transition to communism, because the overwhelming majority of them are bourgeois intellectuals and belong to the exploiting class. Even assistant professors who are members of the [Communist] Youth League are regarded as objects of the revolution." The only reason for having them around at all, in this prevalent view, was to set up an object of struggle; if the professors refused to reform, and to cut their salaries voluntarily, they should be sent to an old people's home.

This view Mao (like the Tsing-hua University Party Committee) entirely rejected, on the grounds that it was necessary to rally as many teachers and research workers as possible of all ranks to serve proletarian education, culture, and science.[89] But nevertheless, the weight of Mao's interest, and of his hopes, had unquestionably shifted toward the masses and the countryside.

Apart from Mao's exasperation with urban intellectuals, an important factor contributing to the turn of his thoughts, and also of the main thrust of Party policy, toward the countryside was the growing trend in the direction of creating larger rural organizations to cope with tasks such as mechanization and irrigation. Already in late 1955, in one of his editorial annotations to *Socialist upsurge in China's countryside*, Mao had proclaimed the superiority of big co-ops, adding: "Some places can have one co-op for every township. In a few places, one co-op can embrace

88 Schram, *Mao unrehearsed*, 119-20.
89 "Chih Lu Ting-i" (To Lu Ting-i), 22 December 1958, *Mao Tse-tung shu-hsin hsuan-chi*, 554-55. (For some reason, the name of the university is omitted here.) Both Mao's letter and the text of the relevant document are included in *Wan-sui* (1969), 267-69.

several townships. In many places, of course, one township will contain several co-ops."[90]

During the period from the spring of 1956 to the autumn of 1957, when the campaign against "adventurism" and other factors had led to the eclipse of some of Mao's more radical policy initiatives, this advice had, on the whole, not been put into effect. (See *CHOC*, 14, chs. 2 and 3, the discussion of political and economic developments in the run-up to the Great Leap.) During the winter of 1957–58, however, a movement for the amalgamation of the existing higher-stage cooperatives emerged. At the Chengtu Conference of March 1958, Mao threw his weight behind this development, and on 8 April 1958, the Central Committee issued a directive in the same sense, reading in part:

... if the agricultural producers' co-operatives are on too small a scale, there will be many disadvantages in future concerning both organization and development. In order to adapt to the needs of agricultural production and cultural revolution, small co-operatives must, in those localities where the conditions exist, be combined into large-scale co-operatives.[91]

By a coincidence far too striking to be accidental, this directive was issued the very day after Mao's visit to the "big co-op" at Hung-kuang in Szechwan had been announced in the press. (The visit had taken place in mid-March, while the Chengtu Conference was in session.)[92]

As already noted, the impulse toward larger-scale organization had emerged from the concern with creating a more effective infrastructure in the countryside, and above all with promoting the development of water-works. It is thus not surprising that during the very same Chengtu Conference of March 1958 at which he advocated larger cooperatives, and at the Nanning Conference that had led up to it, Mao Tse-tung should have devoted a considerable amount of time to listening to conflicting views regarding the "Three Gorges" plan for a giant dam to control the waters of the Yangtze, and chairing meetings to decide policy on this issue.[93]

At the early stage of the Chengtu Conference, the *ta-she*, or "big co-ops," were not yet formally invested with the administrative and military functions that were one of the distinctive aspects of the "people's communes" as endorsed in August 1958 at Peitaiho, and one cannot say,

90 *Socialist upsurge*, 460; Mao, *SW*, 5.273–74.
91 *1981 resolution, annotated edition*, 323–24. Mao's intervention at Chengtu in favor of *ta-she*, referred to here, does not appear in the texts of any of his three speeches at this meeting available outside China. (See Schram, *Mao unrehearsed*, 96–124.)
92 David S. G. Goodman, *Centre and province in the People's Republic of China: Sichuan and Guizhou, 1955–1965*, 144–45.
93 See Li Jui, *Lun San-hsia kung-ch'eng* (On the Three Gorges project), 8–10, 94–99, 171, 245, and passim.

therefore, that they were communes in all but name. They were, however, already beginning to take on some of these characteristics, and thus constituted a stage in a process of development that soon culminated in the communes.

The history of the emergence of the communes is not, of course, in itself our concern here, but the facts just presented are relevant to the theme of this chapter because they demonstrate that Mao's own thought and action contributed directly to the institutional revolution that burst on the scene in the summer of 1958 and was to shape Chinese rural society for a quarter of a century.

The inspiration for this trend can be found not simply in Mao's identification with the rural world, but in the millenarian visions that had gripped him during the collectivization drive of 1955. These ideas found expression in the thesis, repeatedly expounded by Mao between 1956 and 1958, according to which the Chinese people could draw positive advantages from the fact that they were "poor and blank." "Poor people," he wrote in April 1958, "want change, want to do things, want revolution. A clean sheet of paper has no blotches, and so the newest and most beautiful words can be written on it, the newest and most beautiful pictures can be painted on it."[94]

Mao was here making the same two linked points he had conveyed in different language in his speech of 27 February 1957 when he referred to the superiority of China's "illiteracy" over the wealth of the West. To the extent that the peasants were even blanker than the Chinese people as a whole, that is, even less corrupted by material well-being, and even more innocent of the wiles of the modern world, they were evidently superior in virtue, and in revolutionary capacities.

The roots of this strain in Mao's thinking go back deep into the past, to the twenty-two years of bitter struggle in the countryside that preceded his triumphal entry into Peking. I argued in the conclusion to my chapter on Mao's thought down to 1949 in Volume 13 of *The Cambridge History of China* that the economic policies of the late 1950s could not be characterized in terms of a "Yenan model," because the concrete circumstances were too different.[95] There was, however, an existential continuity with the *spirit* of Yenan, and of the Ching-kang-shan.

This continuity is revealed with extraordinary vividness in Mao Tsetung's speeches at the Peitaiho meeting of August 1958, which officially endorsed the formation of the people's communes. Calling repeatedly for the abolition of the wage system, and the reintroduction of the free

94 HC, 1 June 1958, 3–4; PR, 15 (10 June 1958), 6.   95 CHOC, 13.868–69.

supply system followed during the war years, Mao declared that just feeding men was no different from feeding dogs. "If you don't aid others, and engage in a bit of communism, what's the point?" The wage system, he asserted, was "a concession to the bourgeoisie," and its result had been "the development of individualism." Some people, he remarked, argue that egalitarianism makes for laziness, but in fact that is the case of the grade system.[96]

This whole ethos of struggle and sacrifice Mao linked explicitly to the past of armed struggle. "Our communism," he declared, "was first implemented by the army. The Chinese Party is a very special Party, it fought for several decades, all the while applying communism." Now, in the twin struggle against imperialism and the forces of nature, the goals were equally clear, and the introduction of the free supply system would in no way reduce people's motivation or commitment.[97]

Arguing that the communes contained "sprouts of communism," Mao contrasted them with the cities, where people wanted "regularization" (cheng-kuei-hua), and which were full of big yamens divorced from the masses. Calling for desperate efforts (p'in-ming kan) to make steel, Mao noted that some criticized backyard steel production as "a rural work style" or "a guerrilla habit." In fact, he declared, such views were the expression of "bourgeois ideology," which had already eliminated many good things in the Party's heritage.[98]

Speaking to a reporter on 29 September 1958, Mao repeated publicly this denunciation of those who regarded mobilizing the masses for industrial production as "irregular" or a "rural work style."[99] Less than a year later, in July 1959, he was obliged to recognize that this had been a misguided undertaking that led to "chaos on a grand scale" and a substantial waste of resources.[100]

Mao Tse-tung was only dissuaded from going ahead with his plan for the introduction of a military-communist style of free supply system because Chou En-lai produced detailed estimates, based on materials from various ministries, to show that it would be ruinously expensive as compared to the wage system.[101] It constitutes, incidentally, remarkable

96 Speeches of 21 August 1958 (morning) and 30 August 1958 (morning), Hsueh-hsi wen-hsuan, 304, 306–7, 318. (This is a different collection from that cited in note 31.)
97 Speech of 30 August 1958, ibid., 318. (See also speech of 21 August, 306.)
98 Speeches of 17 August, 21 August (morning), and 30 August (morning) 1958, ibid., 302, 305–7 passim, 318.
99 Schram, Political thought, 353.   100 Schram, Mao unrehearsed, 144–46.
101 Liao Kai-lung, "Li-shih ti ching-yen ho wo-men ti fa-chan tao-lu" (The experience of history and the path of our development), CKYC, September 1981, 123. This report, delivered on 25

testimony both to Chou's steadiness of purpose and to his prestige that he was able to persuade Mao on this point even though he had been a primary butt of the fierce attack on those who had "opposed adventurism" in 1956, which Mao had launched at the Nanning Conference of January 1958 and pressed home at Chengtu in March.[102] But though Mao accepted that this idea was impracticable for the moment, he continued to dream such rural utopian dreams.

And yet, Mao recognized as early as the First Chengchow Conference of November 1958 that the peasants displayed a certain attachment to their own material interests, declaring: "The peasants after all remain peasants, throughout the period when the system of ownership by the whole people has not yet been implemented in the countryside, they after all retain a certain dual nature on the road to socialism." At the Second Chengchow Conference of February–March 1959, he reiterated this statement several times, adding that at the present stage the workers, not the peasants, still played the role of "elder brother" in the relationship between the two.[103]

Perhaps Mao never truly resolved, either in practice or in his own mind, the dilemma of a peasantry that was simultaneously the salt of the earth and the "younger brother" of the working class in building socialism.

A particularly suggestive symbol of the overall pattern of socialist development that Mao Tse-tung sought to promote at the time of the Great Leap Forward was the theory of the "permanent" or "uninterrupted" revolution, which he defined as follows in the "Sixty articles on work methods" of January 1958:

Our revolutions follow each other, one after another. Beginning with the seizure of power on a nation-wide scale in 1949, there followed first the anti-feudal land reform; as soon as land reform was completed, agricultural co-operativization was begun…. The three great socialist transformations, that is to say the socialist revolution in the ownership of the means of production, were basically completed in 1956. Following this, we carried out last year the socialist revolution on the political and ideological fronts [i.e., the Anti-Rightist Campaign]…. But the problem is still not resolved, and for a fairly long period to come, the

October 1980 at a meeting for the academic discussion of the history of the Chinese Communist Party called by the Central Party School, has been officially published in China only in a revised version, but there is every reason to believe that the original text as reproduced in Taipei is authentic. It is translated in *Issues & Studies*, October, November, and December 1981; the passage cited here appears in the October issue, p. 84. For the new version, see Liao Kai-lung, *Tang-shih t'an-so* (Explorations in Party history), 308–65. The historical overview of the 1950s and 1960s has been significantly condensed in the official version, and does not contain details about Chou's role in persuading Mao to abandon the "free supply system."

102 See, in particular, the passage in his talk of 22 March 1958, Schram, *Mao unrehearsed*, 122.
103 *Wan-sui* (1969), 247; *Wan-sui* (1967), 12, 17, 49, etc.

method of airing of views and rectification must be used every year to solve the problems in this field. We must now have a technical revolution, in order to catch up with and overtake England in fifteen years or a bit longer.[104]

As this passage makes plain, it was characteristic of the Great Leap Forward, as of Mao's approach to revolution generally, that economic, social, political, and cultural transformation were to be carried out simultaneously. At the same time, a dramatic raising both of technical levels and of levels of material production was very much part of the Maoist vision in 1958. This concern found clear expression in Mao's call for a "technical revolution," as well as in the slogan "Overtake England in 15 years," which had been proclaimed in December 1957.

Twice, indeed, in the course of the radical phase of the Great Leap, Mao dated the beginnings of the process of modernization and change in China from the moment when, at the end of the nineteenth century, Chang Chih-tung embarked on his program of industrialization. In September 1958, Mao measured progress in terms of numbers of machine tools; in February 1959, his criterion was the growth of the Chinese working class. In both cases, he compared China's achievements before and after 1949 in catching up with the more advanced countries of the world.[105]

This does not mean, of course, that Mao regarded industrialization, or even economic development in general, as the whole essence of revolution. In a speech at the Second Session of the Eighth Party Congress in May 1958, at which the Great Leap Forward was officially proclaimed, he asserted his resolve to press ahead with rapid economic growth, but indicated that revolution would not result from development alone:

We do not put forward the slogans "Cadres decide everything" and "Technology decides everything," nor do we put forward the slogan, "Communism equals the Soviets plus electrification." Since we do not put forward this slogan, does this mean that we won't electrify? We will electrify just the same, and even a bit more fiercely. The first two slogans were formulated by Stalin, they are one-sided. [If you say] "Technology decides everything" – what about politics? [If you say] "Cadres decide everything" – what about the masses? This is not sufficiently dialectical.[106]

Thus, although China intended to "electrify," that is, to develop its economy (in Lenin's metaphor) just as fast as the Soviets, Mao saw this process as intimately linked to human change.

The Great Leap Forward thus involved the juxtaposition of many

104 *Wan-sui* (supplement), 32–33; translation from Schram, "Mao Tse-tung and the theory of the permanent revolution 1958–1969," *CQ*, 46 (April–June 1971), 226–27.
105 *Wan-sui* (1969), 245, and *Wan-sui* (1967), 15.   106 *Wan-sui* (1969), 204.

diverse inspirations and imperatives, the simultaneous insistence on technical revolution and political mobilization being only one instance of this.
One of the most flagrant of such contradictions was that between the
stress on unified Party leadership, expressed in the slogan "Politics in
command," and the fragmentation of economic initiative and control to
such an extent that, as Mao later recognized, effective planning largely
ceased to exist. This problem arose in large part because the system of
"dual rule," which had been reintroduced in 1956 (see CHOC, 14, ch. 3),
was tilted so far in favor of the Party in 1958 that effective control at every
level was vested in Party cadres who had no machinery at their disposal
for checking, even if they had wanted to, on the wider consequences of
economic decisions.

At the time, Mao suggested that this was nothing to worry about, since
disequilibrium was a "universal objective law" that acted as a spur to
progress.[107] Back of this ideological formulation lay the conviction that it
was imperative to mobilize the population as a whole to play a dynamic
role in economic development. This, in turn, implied not only stressing
the creativity of the masses, as opposed to the experts, but attributing to
the "revolutionary people" as a whole (experts, or at least "red" experts
among them) virtually unlimited capacities to modify their own environment. Thus we find, in ideological writings of the Great Leap period
manifestly reflecting Mao's viewpoint, quite extraordinary statements
such as "There is no such thing as poor land, but only poor methods for
cultivating the land," or even "The subjective creates the objective."[108]

It might be said that at the time of the Great Leap, a decade before the
events of May 1968, Mao grasped and illustrated the slogan that the students of Paris were later to make famous: "L'imagination au pouvoir!"
The difference was, of course, that he really *was* in power. In the summer
of 1958, fantasy rather than sober observation came all too often to be the
criterion for defining truth and reality generally.

Summing up the situation in September 1958, Mao declared that the
national grain output had more or less doubled, and might be expected to
double again in 1959, so that soon there would be too much even to feed
to the animals, and there would be a problem in disposing of it.[109]

In his speech of 9 December 1958 at the Sixth Plenum of the Central
Committee in Wuchang, Mao Tse-tung noted that, at the informal discussions which had taken place just before the plenum, the slogan "Seek

107 See Schram, "Mao Tse-tung and the theory of the permanent revolution," esp. 232–36.
108 Wu Chiang, article in *Che-hsueh yen-chiu* 8 (1958), 25–28; extracts in Schram, *Political thought*, 99,
        135–36.
109 *Wan-sui* (1969), 228.

truth from facts" had been put forward once again. He interpreted this to mean that in planning work, it was necessary to be both hot and cold; to have lofty aspirations and yet at the same time to carry out considerable scientific analysis. Concretely, Mao said that, when he had forecast a production of 120 million tons of steel in 1962, he had been concerned only with the demand for steel in China, and "had not considered the problem of whether or not it was possible." In fact, he said, such a target was neither possible nor realistic. Nor should the Chinese confuse the transition to socialism with the transition to communism, or seek to enter communism ahead of the Soviet Union.[110]

In the early months of 1959, as the "wind of communism" blew across the land, Mao himself once again entertained unrealistic hopes. In March 1959, he told Anna Louise Strong that if steel production met the targets set for 1959, as it had done in 1958, 6 million tons a year could be allocated to the production of agricultural equipment, and mechanization would soon be completed.[111] By July, he had come to regard the backyard furnaces as an ill-advised adventure for which he was to blame.[112] Nevertheless, though the time scale for achieving a decisive economic breakthrough was soon revised in the direction of greater realism, the ultimate aim of rapid and decisive economic progress remained unchanged.

In order to achieve this goal, effective coordination of efforts on a national scale would be required. Mao, who in July 1959 took responsibility also for the dismantling of the planning system during the high tide of the Great Leap,[113] therefore endorsed the slogan, adopted in early 1959: "The whole country a single chessboard."

At the same time, while accepting the need for more effective centralized control of the industrial sector, Mao took the lead in decentralizing ownership and control in the communes. In March 1959, intervening to settle a sharp argument as to whether the basic level of accounting and distribution should be pushed down one level or two, Mao opted for the second and bolder solution.[114] (The unit in question was the *sheng-ch'an tui*; normally translated "production team," this meant, in the context of 1959, what is now called the brigade, that is, roughly the equivalent of the old higher-stage APC.) The intermediate solution, which Mao rejected, would have consisted in taking as the basic unit an entity equivalent to the administrative area, which was subsequently abolished. For further details, and an account of later developments, see *CHOC*, 14, ch. 8.

110 *Wan-sui* (1969), 262–62, 264–65; *Miscellany*, 141–42, 144–45.
111 Anna Louise Strong, "Three interviews with Chairman Mao Zedong," *CQ*, 103 (September 1985).
112 Schram, *Mao unrehearsed*, 143.   113 Ibid., 142.
114 *Wan-sui* (1967), 106–7. (Letter of 15 March 1959.)

Mao was persuaded that the system of people's communes was basically sound, and could easily be consolidated by the adjustments carried out in the spring and early summer of 1959.[115] Probably he thought that, by himself taking action to correct defects in the system he had devised, or in any case promoted, he would disarm potential critics in the Party. If this was indeed his expectation, he was bitterly disappointed. At the Lushan Plenum of July–August 1959, P'eng Te-huai, Chang Wen-t'ien and others openly attacked the whole range of Great Leap policies.[116]

It would be hard to overestimate the impact of the confrontation on Lushan, not only on Mao's attitudes toward his comrades, but on the substance of his thought. As in 1957, he had committed errors of judgment, and the experience had not chastened him, but rather rendered him more sensitive regarding his own dignity. Psychologically, the consequence was that, from Lushan onward, Mao Tse-tung not only sought to punish everyone who disagreed with him, but came increasingly to regard any and every idea he put forward as the standard of orthodoxy. In other words, dissent from orthodoxy as defined by Mao became "revisionism," if not outright counterrevolution.[117]

Synthesis or eclecticism: Chinese and Marxist elements in Mao's thought

This evocation of Mao's image of himself as ruler necessarily raises the problem of another duality that became prominent in his thought from the late 1950s on: the relation between Marxism and the Chinese tradition. In May 1958, at the Second Session of the Eighth Party Congress, Mao declared that the new policies of the Great Leap Forward represented an attempt to vie with China's "teacher" in revolution, the Soviet Union. And he added, "We have two parents: Kuomintang society and the October Revolution."[118] This statement, he made plain, was intended to apply to politics as well as to economics.

Of the two "parents" acknowledged by Mao, the significance of the

---

115 Strong, "Three interviews," 496–97.
116 Chang Wen-t'ien's three-hour intervention was, in fact, more systematic, and couched in more rigorous theoretical terms, than P'eng Te-huai's "Letter of opinion." See the analysis of Li Jui, who was present at the time, in his article "Ch'ung tu Chang Wen-t'ien's ti 'Lushan ti fa-yen'" (On rereading Chang Wen-t'ien's intervention at Lushan), *Tu-shu*, 8 (1985), 28–38. The text of Chang's speech has now been published in *Chang Wen-t'ien hsuan-chi* (Selected works of Chang Wen-t'ien), 480–506.
117 The fullest and most accurate account in English of the events at Lu-shan and their significance is that of Roderick MacFarquhar, *The origins of the Cultural Revolution. 2. the Great Leap Forward 1958–1960*, 187–251.
118 *Wan-sui* (1969), 222; *Miscellany*, 121.

October Revolution requires little comment or explanation. China, he is saying, has learned about the theory and practice of making revolution, and in particular of establishing a socialist state, from Lenin, Stalin, and Soviet experience since 1917. The reference to "Kuomintang society," on the other hand, means far more than might at first be apparent. The Chinese People's Republic, he is saying, is the creation of the Chinese people as they existed in 1949, and therefore reflects the ideas, attitudes, and institutions that they have developed not only during the two decades of Kuomintang rule but throughout the whole of their long history.

To be sure, China needed a revolutionary transformation guided by Marxist theory, but this did not mean turning the country into a carbon copy of the Soviet Union. "There are some things," said Mao in March 1959, "which need not have any national style, such as trains, airplanes and big guns. Politics and art should have a national style."[119] Back of this statement, we can sense once again the conviction, expressed by Mao in 1938, that the assimilation of the past provides not only raw material but also a "method" for elaborating a correct line today.

By the time of the Great Leap, Mao was thus placing side by side, on the same level, the Marxist-Leninist and Soviet tradition, on the one hand, and the lessons of Chinese history, on the other, and even mentioning Kuomintang society first among the two "parents" of the current stage in the revolution. Six or seven years later, he had shifted the emphasis still further, remarking several times to comrades in the Party: "I am a native philosopher, you are foreign philosophers."[120]

Mao's claim, in 1964 and 1965, to be a "native" or "indigenous" thinker by no means signified that he had abandoned Marx for Confucius. It does, however, confirm beyond any question that the traditional roots of his thinking remained important to the end of his life. But how, precisely, were the Chinese and Western elements in Mao's thought combined in the late 1950s and early 1960s? Were they fused together or integrated into a new synthesis? If so, which of the two components defined the structure of his system as a whole? Did "Mao Tse-tung Thought" remain essentially a variant of Marxism, and hence in the last analysis a vehicle of Westernization? Or was, rather, the logic and pattern of his thought increasingly Chinese? Or was there no system, and no clear structure, but two skeletons working sometimes to reinforce each other, sometimes at cross purposes, in an unwieldy body composed of disparate elements?

119 *Wan-sui* (1967), 48.   120 Schram, *Mao unrehearsed*, 225, 239.

There can be little doubt that, as has already been suggested, both the nature of Mao's thought and his own perception of it changed as the years passed. In the early years of the People's Republic, he still saw a theory of Western origin – Marxism – as the warp, and Chinese culture as the woof, of the new social and political fabric he was bent on weaving. But by the late 1950s, his interpretation of Marxist theory was beginning to evolve in directions that reflected simultaneously the influence of the political climate of the Great Leap and a growing stress on modes of thought derived from the Chinese past.

In "On contradiction," Mao Tse-tung had accepted implicitly the "three basic laws" of Marxist and Hegelian dialectics (the unity and struggle of opposites, the transformation of quantity into quality, and the negation of the negation), but at the same time he had given a hint of a new approach to these problems by characterizing the "law of the unity of opposites" as the "fundamental law of thought," thus seemingly placing it in a higher category than the other two.[121] To be sure, Lenin had said, in a passage quoted by Mao in January 1957, "In brief, dialectics can be defined as the doctrine of the unity of opposites." But he had immediately added, "This grasps the kernel of dialectics, but it requires explanations and development."[122] Mao, on the other hand, was ultimately to move toward the view that the law of the unity of opposites in itself summed up the whole essence of dialectics.

In the section "On dialectical and historical materialism" that he contributed to the *History of the CPSU* in 1938, Stalin had enumerated four "principal features" of the Marxist dialectical method: that phenomena are all interconnected; that nature is in a state of continuous movement and change; that development takes the form of gradual quantitative change leading to qualitative changes or "leaps"; and that contradictions are inherent in all things, and the struggle between opposites "constitutes the internal content of the process of development."[123]

In his talk of January 1957 with Party secretaries, Mao explicitly took issue with Stalin's views on this topic, criticizing both the philosophical inadequacy of his fourfold classification and its political implications:

Stalin says Marxist dialectics has four principal features. As the first feature he talks of the interconnection of things, as if all things happened to be interconnected for no reason at all.... It is the two contradictory aspects of a thing that

---

121 Mao, *SW*, 1.345. See also Schram's chapter on Mao's thought to 1949 in *CHOC*, 13, and note 87
       thereto. In "On dialectical materialism," Mao had explicitly confirmed that Marxist dialectics as
       developed by Lenin comprised the three laws. (See *MTTC*, 6.300.)
122 Mao, *SW*, 5.366. (Talk of 27 January 1957.)
123 *History of the Communist Party of the Soviet Union (Bolshevik). Short Course*, 106–10.

are interconnected.... As the fourth feature he talks of the internal contradiction in all things, but then he deals only with the struggle of opposites, without mentioning their unity.

Clearly the reference here is to Stalin's stress, from 1938 onward, on class struggle, which Mao, at this stage, did not wish to exacerbate to the same degree. But he then went on to discuss other differences between his conception of dialectics and that of Stalin:

Stalin's viewpoint is reflected in the entry on "identity" in the *Shorter Dictionary of Philosophy*, fourth edition, compiled in the Soviet Union. It is said there: "There can be no identity between war and peace, between the bourgeoisie and the proletariat, between life and death and other such phenomena, because they are fundamentally opposed to each other and mutually exclusive." ... This interpretation is utterly wrong.

In their view, war is war and peace is peace, the two are mutually exclusive and entirely unconnected.... War and peace are both mutually exclusive and interconnected, and can be transformed into each other under given conditions. If war is not brewing in peace-time, how can it possibly break out all of a sudden? ...

If life and death cannot be transformed into each other, then please tell me where living things come from. Originally there was only non-living matter on earth.... Life and death are engaged in constant struggle and are being transformed into each other all the time. If the bourgeoisie and the proletariat cannot transform themselves into each other, how come that through revolution the proletariat becomes the ruler and the bourgeoisie the ruled? ...

Stalin failed to see the connection between the struggle of opposites and the unity of opposites. Some people in the Soviet Union are so metaphysical and rigid in their thinking that they think a thing has to be either one or the other, refusing to recognize the unity of opposites. Hence, political mistakes are made. We adhere to the concept of the unity of opposites and adopt the policy of letting a hundred flowers blossom and a hundred schools of thought contend.[124]

The following month, in the original version of "On the correct handling of contradictions among the people," Mao repeated many of these criticisms of Stalin as a philosopher, in very similar terms. Stalin, he said, was relatively deficient (*hsiang-tang ch'üeh-fa*) in dialectics, though not completely without it. His dialectics was a "dialectics of hemming and hawing" (*t'un t'un t'u t'u pien-cheng-fa*). Mao's overall verdict was that Stalin had been 70 percent a Marxist, and 30 percent not a Marxist.[125]

The political lesson is clear enough, though as we have seen, Mao's view on class struggle shifted dramatically six months later. The philosophical implications are, however, somewhat more obscure, or at least ambiguous. The discussion of the interrelation between life and death evokes unmistakably the old Taoist dialectics of the ebb and flow of na-

124 Mao, *SW*, 5.367–96.   125 *Hsüeh-hsi wen-hsüan*, 212–13, 220.

ture. And yet, in April 1957, Mao remarked: "Dialectics is not a cyclical theory."[126]

How was it possible to preserve the basic feeling for the essence of the dialectical process reflected in the passages of 1957 quoted above, and in many other statements by Mao, while remaining within a modern and Marxist system of categories? Mao's solution to this dilemma was of startling simplicity – so much so that, when confronted with it, I (and to my knowledge, all other foreign students of these problems) totally failed to grasp its significance.

In the "Sixty articles on work methods," to which he put his name in January 1958, when this directive was distributed in draft form, Mao included a sentence that, a decade ago, I translated as follows: "The law of the unity of opposites, the law of quantitative and qualitative change, the law of affirmation and negation, exist forever and universally."[127] What is rendered here as "law of affirmation and negation" (*k'en-ting fou-ting ti kuei-lü*) I took to be the kind of elliptical formula commonly used in Chinese political and philosophical language, "affirmation and negation" being intended to evoke the Hegelian and Marxist progression "affirmation, negation, and negation of the negation." On the basis of this assumption, I subsequently wrote that, in contrast to the views he was to put forward in the mid-1960s, Mao in 1958 had "reaffirmed" the classic formulation of the three laws by Engels.[128]

It turns out that the Chinese expression just cited should in fact be translated "the law of the affirmation of the negation," and that it was so understood, and treated as a major theoretical innovation by Chairman Mao, in China at the time.[129]

This may seem a very abstruse point, of little interest to anyone save hairsplitting expositors of Marxist doctrine. In fact, the implications, both political and intellectual, are of considerable moment. There is, first of all,

126 *Wan-sui* (1969), 104; *Miscellany*, 66.
127 Schram, "Mao Tse-tung and the theory of the permanent revolution," 228.
128 "The Schram, Marxist," in Dick Wilson, ed., *Mao Tse-tung in the scales of history: a preliminary assessment*, 63. As early as 1976, Steve Chin had grasped that this formulation involved a significant new departure, but unfortunately he got things backward, taking it to mean "the negation of the affirmation." See Chin, *The thought of Mao Tse-tung: form and content*, 60, 66–67, etc.
129 See two important compilations from Mao's writings produced in 1960 for internal use: *Mao Tse-tung che-hsueh ssu-hsiang (chai-lu)* (Mao Tse-tung's philosophical thought – [extracts]), 195–220; and *Mao tse-tung t'ung-chih lun Ma-k'o-ssu-chu-i che-hsueh (chai-lu)* (Comrade Mao Tse-tung on Marxist philosophy – [extracts]) (preface dated May 1960), 150 et seq. Both volumes contain extended sections bearing the title "The law of the affirmation of the negation," although the materials for these are drawn largely from writings of the Yenan period, and of the mid-1950s, about combining the old and the new, Chinese and foreign ideas, and so on. (It is perhaps worth noting that the first of these volumes contains, broken up into sections by theme, the whole of the lecture notes on dialectical materialism of which Mao denied authorship in his 1965 interview with Edgar Snow.)

the issue of Mao's personal authority in the philosophical domain. A recent work by a scholar who was, in Yenan days, a member of Mao's small philosophical study group, declares: "In the 'Sixty articles on work methods' Comrade Mao Tse-tung changed the name of what had used to be called the law of the negation of the negation to the law of the affirmation of the negation. This is an important question which he left to us, *without providing any sort of further demonstration* [*ping wei chin-hsing keng to ti lun-cheng*], and which our philosophical circles must inquire into [*t'an-t'ao*] further."[130]

It is hardly necessary to elaborate on the significance of the words italicized in the preceding sentence. Thus, a phrase inserted by Mao Tse-tung into a directive, and never subsequently elaborated, became for two decades a new law, accepted without question by China's philosophers. The parallel with Stalin's "contributions of genius" in biology, linguistics, and other domains is unmistakable.

The trends of thought on Mao's part underlying this theoretical innovation are, however, also worthy of attention. In March 1983, Chou Yang went so far as to state explicitly that by failing to correct Stalin's "one-sided" view casting doubt on the "negation of the negation" because it smacked of Hegelianism, Mao ultimately opened the door to the destructive excesses of the Cultural Revolution. The core of Chou Yang's argument is that Mao's misgivings about the old concept reflected a tendency to exaggerate the absolutely antithetical and mutually exclusive nature of successive moments in the dialectical process, and to lose sight of the fact that "negation" meant the supersession of some elements of the thing negated, while retaining others and incorporating them into a new synthesis.[131] If that is what Mao meant, then the new theory did indeed point

---

130 Yang Ch'ao, *Wei-wu pien-cheng-fa ti jo-kan li-lun wen-t'i* (Some theoretical problems of materialist dialectics) (hereafter *Problems of dialectics*), 211. This was a revised version of a book originally devoted explicitly to Mao's thought: Yang Ch'ao, *Lun Mao Chu-hsi che-hsueh t'i-hsi* (On Chairman Mao's philosophical system), 2 vols. (hereafter *Mao's philosophical system*) (Nei-pu t'ao-lun kao [Draft for internal discussion]). Regarding Yang Ch'ao's participation in Mao's philosophical study group in 1939, see Wen Chi-tse, "Mao Tse-tung t'ung-chih tsai Yenan shih-ch'i shih tsen-yang chiao-tao wo-men hsueh che-hsueh ti?" (How did Comrade Mao Tse-tung teach us to study philosophy during the Yenan period?), in *Ch'üan-kuo Mao Tse-tung che-hsueh ssu-hsiang t'ao-lun hui lun-wen hsuan* (Selected essays from the national conference to discuss Mao tse-tung's philosophical thought), 69. The other members of the group, apart from Mao himself, were Ai Ssu-ch'i, Ho Ssu-ching, Ho P'ei-yuan, and Ch'en Po-ta.

131 Chou Yang, "Kuan-yü Ma-k'o-ssu-chu-i ti chi-ko li-lun wen-t'i ti t'an-t'ao" (An exploration of some theoretical questions of Marxism), *JMJP*, 16 March 1983, 4. This article, based on Chou Yang's speech on the occasion of the centenary of Marx's death, was criticized during the campaign of the winter of 1983–84 against "spiritual pollution" because of references to alienation under socialism, but there has never been any suggestion that Chou Yang's analysis of Mao's dialectics was erroneous. For the circumstances surrounding the publication and criticism of this speech, see Stuart Schram, *Ideology and policy in China since the Third Plenum, 1978–84*, 41–56.

straight toward Cultural Revolution notions of overthrowing everything and negating everything.

Yang Ch'ao, for his part, declares that in Mao's view most of the previous phase was eliminated at each negation. He also suggests that Mao had doubts about the old formulation, and replaced it by a new concept that "enriched its content," because he thought it implied that the end result of the whole process was a return to the *initial* affirmation, rather than a progression to a new and higher level. And he adds that Mao believed in the dialectical unity of the opposites "affirmation" and "negation," just as he believed in the unity of peace and war, life and death, proletariat and bourgeoisie, and so forth. All things, in Mao's view, were "contradictory entities made up of affirmation and negation."[132]

It is, perhaps, possible to combine these two perspectives, and thereby to arrive at a reasonably good understanding of what Mao was seeking to achieve by introducing this new concept. Plainly, the formulation "affirmation of the negation" stresses the fact that, in the historical process, new things are constantly emerging. It also suggests, however, that such new things do not arise simply as a reaction against what has come before ("negation of the negation"), but that they are affirmed or asserted by historical actors: classes, or those leaders and parties that claim to speak for classes. In other words, "affirmation of the negation" evokes both the ceaseless change that is the essence of "permanent revolution" (not surprisingly, since the two terms were used side by side in the "Sixty Articles" of January 1958), and the role of the will. Or to put it another way, it corresponded to a further shift in emphasis from the basis to the superstructure.

In terms of the concrete political significance of Mao's ideas, the concept of the affirmation of the negation can perhaps best be seen as the symbolic expression of the "poor and blank" hypothesis discussed above. In other words, it is a way of saying that the negative can be transformed into the positive, or that a situation comprising many negative factors can, in the course of a process of transformation baptized "affirmation" instead of "negation" (of the negation), be turned into a new situation, rich with promise for the future. To the extent that we accept Chou Yang's analysis, this "affirmation" would consist in the chiliastic hope of a rapid and total change, rather than a gradual and incrementalist strategy building on what has already been achieved.

Then, in the 1960s, Mao went beyond simply renaming and in some degree redefining the negation of the negation to repudiating this basic

132 *Problems of dialectics*, 199–217, esp. 212–13; *Mao's philosophical system*, 247–63.

Marxist concept altogether. On 18 August 1964, in the course of a conversation on philosophy with K'ang Sheng, Ch'en Po-ta, and others, K'ang asked the Chairman to "say something about the problem of the three categories." Obviously he knew that Mao had new ideas to put forward, as indeed the Chairman proceeded to do:

Engels talks about the three categories, but as for me I don't believe in two of those categories. (The unity of opposites is the most basic law, the transformation of quality and quantity into one another is the unity of the opposites quality and quantity, and the negation of the negation does not exist at all.) The juxtaposition, on the same level, of the transformation of quality and quantity into one another, the negation of the negation, and the law of the unity of opposites is "triplism," not monism.... Affirmation, negation, affirmation, negation ... in the development of things, every link in the chain of events is both affirmation and negation. Slave-holding society negated primitive society, but with reference to feudal society it constituted, in turn, the affirmation. Feudal society constituted the negation in relation to slave-holding society but it was in turn the affirmation with reference to capitalist society. Capitalist society was the negation in relation to feudal society, but it is, in turn, the affirmation in relation to socialist society.[133]

The following year, at the Hangchow Conference of December 1965, Mao summed up his view very succinctly once again, on the eve of the Cultural Revolution:

It used to be said that there were three great laws of dialectics, then Stalin said there were four. In my view there is only one basic law and that is the law of contradiction. Quality and quantity, positive and negative ... content and form, necessity and freedom, possibility and reality, etc., are all cases of the unity of opposites.[134]

In the past, some Western scholars, including Frederic Wakeman and Stuart Schram, have seen in this development a turn, or reversion, on Mao's part toward a more traditional approach to dialectics.[135] Whether or not one accepts such a view of this point, there can be no doubt that in the 1960s the influence of traditional Chinese thought across the board came increasingly into prominence in Mao's thought as a whole.

One important index of Mao's evolving attitude toward traditional Chinese culture was manifestly his evaluation of Confucius. Mao, who denounced teachers of Chinese literature during the May Fourth period as "obstinate pedants" who "forcibly impregnate our minds with a lot of stinking corpse-like dead writings full of classical allusions,"[136] had come

---

133 Schram, *Mao unrehearsed*, 226.   134 Ibid., 240.
135 Frederic Wakeman, *History and will*, 323–26; Schram, "The Marxist," 63–64.
136 "The great union of the popular masses"; Schram translation from *CQ*, 49 (January–March 1972), 80–81.

to take the view, as early as 1938, that the classical heritage had a positive as well as a negative aspect, and that it was therefore necessary to deal selectively with it. On the one hand, he had no more doubts than he had ever had since the May Fourth period about the reactionary and harmful character of Confucianism as an answer to the problems of the twentieth century. But at the same time, from the 1930s to the 1950s, he alluded with approval to various attitudes defined by tags from the Confucian classics, such as Confucius's practice of going about and "enquiring into everything,"[137] his attitude of "not feeling ashamed to ask and learn from people below,"[138] and the recommendation from the *Mencius*: "When speaking to the mighty, look on them with contempt."[139]

It was in 1964, however, that Mao's turn back to the Chinese classics for inspiration led him to a surprisingly favorable view of Confucius. While criticizing the Sage for his contempt for manual labor, and for his lack of interest in agriculture, Mao declared in February 1964, at the Spring Festival Forum on Education:

Confucius was from a poor peasant family; he herded sheep, and never attended middle school or university either.... In his youth, he came from the masses, and understood something of the suffering of the masses. Later, he became an official in the state of Lu, though not a terribly high official.[140]

The following August, in his philosophical conversations with K'ang Sheng and Ch'en Po-ta, Mao quoted with approval a passage from the *Shih-ching*, commenting: "This is a poem which accuses heaven and opposes the rulers. Confucius, too, was rather democratic."[141]

Perhaps the most distinctive expression of a "Chinese national style" in Mao's approach to politics is to be found in his emphasis on the political relevance of moral values and, more generally, on the educational function of the state. In January 1958, Mao included in the directive that constituted the blueprint for the Great Leap Forward a call to train new, communist intellectuals, in the following terms:

The various departments of the Centre, and the three levels of the province, the special area and the *hsien*, must all compete in training "*hsiu-ts'ai.*" We can't do without intellectuals. The proletariat must definitely have its own *hsiu-ts'ai*. These people must understand relatively more of Marxism-Leninism, and they must also have a certain cultural level, a certain amount of scientific knowledge and of literary training.[142]

137 "Oppose book worship," in Mao, *Selected readings*, 34. (*Analects* VII.2; Legge, *The Chinese classics*, 1.195.)
138 Mao, *SW*, 4.378. (*Analects* V. 14; Legge, *The Chinese classics*, 1.178.)
139 Schram, *Mao unrehearsed*, 82. (*Mencius* 6.ii, 34; D. C. Lau, *Mencius*, 201.)
140 Schram, *Mao unrehearsed*, 208.   141 Ibid., 215.
142 *Wan-sui* (supplement), 37. (Article 47 of the "Sixty Articles.")

The deliberate use of the term *hsiu-ts'ai* or "cultivated talent," the popular name for the lowest-level graduates of the imperial examination system (*sheng-yuan*), with all of its traditional connotations, cannot be dismissed as a mere pleasantry. No doubt Mao intended the parallel to be taken with a pinch of salt, but there is also implicit in it the deep-seated conviction, which lay at the heart of the Confucian orthodoxy, that people are educated in order to assume political responsibilities, and that having been educated, it is their duty to take up the burdens of power.

Another echo of the past can be found in Mao's statement, in May 1958, at the Second Session of the Eighth Party Congress, that "for the layman to lead the expert" (*wai-hang ling-tao nei-hang*) is a universal law. To be sure, he noted that this question had been raised in the previous year by the rightists, who had created a tremendous disturbance, claiming that laymen could not lead experts.[143] In other words, his formula was a refutation of the view, which Mao had already dismissed in the "Sixty articles," that "we are petty intellectuals, incapable of leading the big intellectuals."[144] But apart from the resentment of the normal-school graduate against the "bourgeois academic authorities" who had criticized him in the spring of 1957, it is hard not to see, in the argument advanced by Mao in this same speech of May 1958 to the effect that "politicians handle the mutual relations among men," a reaffirmation of the moral basis of politics and society.

A few months later, at the Peitaiho meeting of August 1958, Mao declared, in discussing the question of rule by law (as advocated by Han Fei-tzu) and rule by men (as advocated by the Confucians):

You can't rely on law to rule the majority of the people; for the majority of the people you have to rely on cultivating [the right] habits ... I took part in establishing the Constitution, but I don't remember it.... Every one of our [Party] resolutions is a law; when we hold a meeting, that's law too. Public security regulations will only be respected if they rely on cultivating habits.... Our various systems of constitutional instruments [*hsien-chang chih-tu*] are concocted for the most part, to the extent of 90 per cent, by the bureaux. Basically, we do not rely on all that, we rely mainly on our resolutions ..., we do not rely on civil or criminal law to maintain order. The National People's Congress and the State Council have their stuff [*t'a-men na-i-t'ao*], while we have this stuff of ours.[145]

Apart from the implications of this passage regarding the relation between the Chinese Communist Party and the administrative machine,

143 *Wan-sui* (1969), 210–11; *Miscellany*, 110–11.
144 Schram translation, from "Mao Tse-tung and the theory of the permanent revolution," 227.
145 Speech of 21 August, *Hsueh-hsi wen-hsuan*, 310.

Mao here conveys very forcefully his feeling for the traditional role of the state as supreme educator.

In April 1964, Mao discussed problems of reform through labor with the minister of public security, Hsieh Fu-chih. "In the last analysis," said Mao, "what is most important – transforming people, the production output of those engaged in reform through labor, or both of them equally? Should we attach importance to men, to things, or to both? Some comrades think only things, not men, are important. In reality, if we do our work with men well, we will have things too." To this, Hsieh replied, "I read out the 'Double Ten Articles' [also called the First or Former and the Later Ten Points, guidelines for the Socialist Education Campaign then under way, which has been discussed in *CHOC*, 14, ch. 7] to the prisoners of the Shou-shih production team of the First Prison of Chekiang Province.... Afterward, the overwhelming majority of the prisoners who had not confessed before now admitted their guilt, and many obstinate prisoners also underwent a conversion."[146]

I would not go so far as to suggest that reading a directive on the Socialist Education Campaign in the countryside to political prisoners was strictly equivalent to convoking the population in the old days to listen to the reading of the imperial edicts (*hsiang-yueh*), but surely there is a certain underlying continuity in the conviction that moral exhortation is an important dimension of political leadership. Perhaps it was implicit in Mao's view that intellectuals in the new society should be Marxist or "proletarian" in their political outlook, "bourgeois" in the sense that they must be the bearers of the modern knowledge developed under capitalism, and "feudal" to some extent in their conception of their own role.

As for the problems of the structure of power discussed in the first section of this chapter, the relation between Marxism-Leninism and the Chinese tradition was perhaps, in this domain, an even more ambiguous one. The blend of Confucianism and Legalism that defined, on the whole, the orthodox view of the state in late imperial times, was hierarchical and authoritarian, and so too was Leninism, to a very high degree. To this extent, there was convergence. Moreover, if Mao saw in politics the "leading thread" that always had priority over economics, and ultimately shaped the pattern of social change, he was following in this not only Lenin but also the monistic and state-centered vision of the social order that had prevailed in China for two thousand years.[147] At the same time,

---

146 *Wan-sui* (1969), 493; *Miscellany*, 347.
147 On this theme, see Schram, prefaces to *The scope of state power* and *The foundations of state power*, and the latter volume, passim, especially the contributions of Jacques Gernet and Benjamin Schwartz.

there were profound differences between Mao's ideas and those of the Chinese past, regarding both the persons and the institutions that were seen as the wielders of the transformative power of correct thought, and the goals of political action.

In view of the overriding emphasis on centralism in Mao's thinking about the state, which was, as we saw in a previous section, starkly consistent in all of his writings from the 1940s to the 1960s, it is not surprising that he should have spoken out repeatedly in praise not only of the first Ch'in emperor, but of other strong rulers in the Chinese past as well. "King Chou of the Yin dynasty [commonly known as the "Tyrant Chou"], who was well versed in both literature and military affairs, Ch'in Shih-huang and Ts'ao Ts'ao have all come to be regarded as evil men," he wrote in 1959. "This is incorrect."[148] And in a famous passage from one of his speeches to the Second Session of the Eighth Party Congress in May 1958, Mao had hailed Ch'in Shih-huang-ti as a "specialist in stressing the present and slighting the past," quoting with approval Li Ssu's proposal, endorsed by the emperor, that "those who make use of the past to disparage the present should be exterminated together with their whole families" (*i ku fei chin che tsu*). He had also boasted that the Chinese Communist Party had executed a hundred times as many counterrevolutionary intellectuals as Ch'in Shih-huang-ti, who had buried only "460 Confucian scholars."[149]

And what, if anything, did Mao Tse-tung take from that other tradition, often seen as the ideology of the failures and misfits of the imperial system, Taoism? As already noted, events in the Chinese People's Republic, under Mao's leadership, were marked by a succession of campaigns, interspersed with periods of repose, to make a pattern of what G. William Skinner and Edwin Winckler have called "compliance cycles," and which Mao himself characterized as alternating "hard fighting" and "rest and consolidation" in a "wavelike form of progress."[150]

Angus Graham has remarked that the *Lao-tzu* "advises Doing Nothing as a means of ruling, not as an abdication of ruling."[151] Some curious parallels can be observed between aspects of Mao's role as Chairman during the last two decades of his life, when he first retired to the "second line," and then, although reasserting his authority, remained in seclusion except for the first Red Guard rallies, and the principles asserted in the chapter of the *Chuang-tzu* entitled "The Way of Heaven":

148 Schram, *Mao unrehearsed*, 101.   149 *Wan-sui* (1969), 195.   150 Schram, *Mao unrehearsed*, 106–7.
151 Angus Graham, *The book of Lieh-tzu*, 10.

... those who of old reigned over the empire, though wise enough to encompass heaven and earth would not do their own thinking, though discriminating enough to comprehend the myriad things would not do their own explaining, though able enough for all the work within the four seas would not do their own enacting.... Emperors and kings do nothing, but the world's work is done.... This is the Way by which to have heaven and earth as your chariot, set the myriad things galloping, and employ the human flock.[152]

Looking at the pattern of Mao's thought and action throughout his career, and especially in the period after 1949, it seems evident that he was, in the last analysis, more strongly influenced by the "great" than by the "little" tradition.[153]

These paratraditional ideas regarding the role of the ruler were to grow still more in importance during Mao's last decade, and constitute, with the leftist attitudes he increasingly displayed in economic and political matters, one of the roots of the Cultural Revolution. A third, and in many respects crucial, dimension of the situation was, however, the unfolding of Sino-Soviet relations, and Mao's response to these developments.

CAUSES AND CONSEQUENCES OF THE SINO-SOVIET SPLIT

From the very inception of the Chinese Communist Party, Soviet influence on its development was, of course, many-sided and profound. Moscow was at once the locus of authority and the source of inspiration for the world communist movement from the 1920s to the 1940s and beyond. Mao's response to these two dimensions of the Soviet role was markedly different. The validity of the Soviet model he called into question only progressively, and relatively late. The notion that China was not merely a junior partner in the cause of communism but should subordinate itself entirely to a worldwide revolutionary organization, and lose its own identity in the process, he was, on the contrary, never at any time willing to accept.

In a sense, the whole of this dimension of the problem is summed up in Mao's reply to Edgar Snow when, in 1936, Snow asked him whether, in the event of a Communist victory, there would be "some kind of actual merger of governments" between Soviet China and Soviet Russia. "We are not fighting for an emancipated China in order to turn the country over to Moscow!" Mao shot back at him, adding: "The Chinese Commu-

---

152 Angus Graham, *Chuang-tzu: The seven inner chapters and other writings from the book "Chuang-tzu,"* 261.
153 For further discussion of this point, and a refutation of Wolfgang Bauer's ideas to the contrary, see Schram, "Party leader or true ruler?"

nist Party cannot speak for the Russian people, or rule for the Third International, but only in the interests of the Chinese masses."[154]

The evolution of relations between the Soviet and Chinese Communist Parties, and between Mao and Stalin, during the Yenan period falls outside the scope of this chapter. It does seem appropriate, however, to note, by way of introduction to what happened after 1949, Mao's own assessment of Stalin's behavior during the crucial years of civil war, beginning in 1945. Recalling, at a meeting of the Central Committee of the Chinese Communist Party in September 1962, that since 1960 the Chinese had been distracted from their internal tasks by the need to "oppose Khrushchev," he commented: "You see that among socialist countries and within Marxism-Leninism, a question like this could emerge." Then, turning back to earlier events, he continued:

In fact its roots lie deep in the past, in things which happened very long ago. They did not permit China to make revolution: that was in 1945. Stalin wanted to prevent China from making a revolution, saying that we should not have a civil war and should co-operate with Chiang Kai-shek, otherwise the Chinese nation would perish. But we did not do what he said. After the victory of the revolution he next suspected China of being a Yugoslavia, and that I would become a second Tito. Later when I went to Moscow to sign the Sino-Soviet Treaty of Alliance and Mutual Assistance, we had to go through another struggle. He was not willing to sign a treaty. After two months of negotiations he at last signed. When did Stalin begin to have confidence in us? It was the time of the Resist America, Aid Korea campaign, from the winter of 1950. He then came to believe that we were not Tito, not Yugoslavia.[155]

In June 1949, on the eve of victory in the civil war, Mao nonetheless proclaimed that solidarity with the Soviet Union would be the cornerstone of the new China's foreign policy, which he summed up as follows: "Unite in a common struggle with those nations of the world which treat us as equals and unite with the peoples of all countries. That is, ally ourselves with the Soviet Union, with the People's Democracies and with the broad masses of the people in all countries, and form an international united front."

Replying to an imaginary interlocutor to whom he attributed the comment "You are leaning to one side," he elaborated on the reasons for this policy:

Exactly. The forty years' experience of Sun Yat-sen and the twenty-eight years' experience of the Communist Party have taught us to lean to one side, and we are firmly convinced that in order to win victory and consolidate it we must lean to

154 Schram, *Political thought*, 419. 155 Schram, *Mao unrehearsed*, 191.

one side. In the light of the experiences accumulated in these forty years and these twenty-eight years, all Chinese without exception must lean either to the side of imperialism, or to the side of socialism. Sitting on the fence will not do, nor is there a third road.[156]

Although this was the clearly enunciated foreign policy line in 1949, Stalin's attitude did not always make it easy, or agreeable, for Mao to carry it out. When Mao went to Moscow in December 1949, it took him, as he himself later recalled, two months of negotiations, "amounting to a struggle," to get Stalin to offer China even that minimum of assistance and support which Mao regarded as essential. One dimension of the problem was, of course, the clash between the national interests of China and the Soviet Union, and the place of these two states in the larger unity known in the 1950s as the "Socialist camp." Mao explained his own approach to these matters during the Moscow negotiations of 1950 in a speech of March 1958:

In 1950 I argued with Stalin in Moscow for two months. On the questions of the Treaty of Mutual Assistance, the Chinese Eastern Railway, the joint-stock companies and the border we adopted two attitudes: one was to argue when the other side made proposals we did not agree with, and the other was to accept their proposal if they absolutely insisted. This was out of consideration for the interests of socialism.[157]

Back of these discords lay, of course, not merely Stalin's lack of enthusiasm for the emergence of another communist great power that might ultimately be a rival to the Soviet Union, or at least demand the right to have its say as to how the "interests of socialism" should be pursued on the world scene, but twenty years of conflict between Mao and Stalin as to the way in which the Chinese revolution should be carried out. Referring to the events of the 1920s and 1930s, Mao said, in his important speech of 30 January 1962:

Speaking generally, it is we Chinese who have achieved understanding of the objective world of China, not the comrades concerned with Chinese questions in the Communist International. These comrades in the Communist International simply did not understand, or we could say they utterly failed to understand, Chinese society, the Chinese nation, or the Chinese revolution. For a long time even we did not have a clear understanding of the objective world of China, let alone the foreign comrades![158]

---

156 Mao, *SW*, 4.415.   157 Schram, *Mao unrehearsed*, 101.
158 Ibid., 172. The officially published text does not underscore quite so strongly the point that the foreign comrades were even more incapable of understanding the Chinese revolution. (See *PR*, 27 [1978], 14.)

"Understanding the objective world of China" meant, of course, grasping the special circumstances of a revolution under communist leadership in a vast and overwhelmingly peasant country, and devising a pattern of struggle based on agrarian reform and guerrilla warfare from rural bases. But it also meant working out new methods for transforming society and developing the economy once the struggle for power had been carried to a victorious conclusion. The crucial years during which Chinese and Soviet perceptions of these realities gradually diverged to the point of sharp, if as yet undeclared, conflict extended from the beginning of the 1st Five-Year Plan in 1953 until the Great Leap Forward of 1958–60.

The problem of the relation between foreign and domestic developments during this period is a complex one, and there was undoubtedly action and reaction in both directions. The Chinese probably soon became aware, after the upheavals in Poland and Hungary in the autumn of 1956, that Moscow would henceforth be in a position to offer less economic assistance, because it was necessary to spend more on Eastern Europe in order to stabilize the situation there. To this extent, the emphasis on "self-help" in Chinese policy beginning especially in 1958 did not reflect a purely arbitrary decision on Mao's part, but also constituted a response to the realities of the international situation. There was also the behavior of the "ugly Russian," who was plainly no more appealing than the "ugly American" who served in certain other countries during the same period as adviser and technical specialist. But apart from these diplomatic and psychological aspects of Sino-Soviet economic and technical cooperation, reliance on foreign experts for leadership in China's program of economic development also raised more basic problems of the role of the Chinese people themselves in shaping their own future.

Mao's overall approach to the various interrelated aspects of the problem of a Chinese road to socialism is clearly and forcefully projected in a passage from his speech of 30 January 1962. In the first few years after 1949, he said,

the situation was such that, since we had no experience in economic construction, we had no alternative but to copy the Soviet Union. In the field of heavy industry especially, we copied almost everything from the Soviet Union, and we had very little creativity of our own. At that time it was absolutely necessary to act thus, but at the same time it was also a weakness – a lack of creativity and lack of ability to stand on our own feet. Naturally this could not be our long-term strategy. From 1958 we decided to make self-reliance our major policy, and striving for foreign aid a secondary aim.[159]

159 Schram, *Mao unrehearsed*, 140–41.

Mao's formulation here strongly emphasizes considerations of national dignity; wholesale imitation of foreign experience, he says, however necessary for a time, simply "could not be" the long-term strategy of the Chinese people. In 1958, when the economic and social experiments of the communes and the Great Leap Forward were first implemented, Mao stated bluntly that he was aware of the resentment that the Soviets might feel at China's refusal to follow them blindly − and could not care less. In a discussion of the need to smash "blind faith" in the Soviet example, specifically in the military field, he said: "Some people mentioned that when the Soviet comrade advisers saw that we were not copying their [combat regulations], they made adverse comments and were displeased. We might ask these Soviet comrades: do you copy Chinese regulations? If they say they don't, then we will say: if you don't copy ours, we won't copy yours."[160]

Mao's insistence on breaking with the Soviet model was not, however, motivated simply by considerations of pride; for several years before 1958, he had been having increasing doubts about the value of Russian methods in the Soviet Union itself, as well as about their applicability to China. In the speech of April 1956 "On the ten great relationships," which marked the beginning of his attempt to sketch out in systematic form the ideas underlying the Chinese road to socialism, Mao declared:

We have done better than the Soviet Union and a number of Eastern European countries. The prolonged failure of the Soviet Union to reach the highest pre-October Revolution level in grain output, the grave problems arising from the glaring disequilibrium between the development of heavy industry and that of light industry in some Eastern European countries − such problems do not exist in our country.... The Soviet Union has taken measures which squeeze the peasants very hard.... The method of capital accumulation has seriously damp-ened the peasants' enthusiasm for production. You want the hen to lay more eggs and yet you do not feed it, you want the horse to run fast and yet you don't let it graze. What kind of logic is this?[161]

Despite these misgivings about the Soviet experience of economic development, and despite his own criticism both of Stalin's obsession with class struggle, and of Stalin's weaknesses as a dialectician, Mao Tse-tung had serious reservations regarding both the manner and the sub-stance of the enterprise of de-Stalinization launched by Khrushchev in 1956. It is time to consider more systematically his response to these events.

160 Ibid., 126−27.
161 Mao, *SW*, 5.185 and 291. For the reasons explained in the first section of this chapter, this official text of Mao's "On the ten great relationships" is more explicit in its criticism of the Soviets
than that reproduced by the Red Guards and translated in Schram, *Mao unrehearsed.*

De-Stalinization and "modern revisionism"

The problem of the Chinese reaction to the Twentieth Soviet Party Congress, which was for so long the object of speculation and controversy on the basis of fragmentary texts released by one side or the other, can now be examined in the light of an abundant, though not altogether complete documentation, and it is dealt with in Volume 14, chapter 6, of *The Cambridge History of China*. As early as April 1956, the Central Committee of the Chinese Communist Party had decided on the assessment of 30 percent for mistakes and 70 percent for achievements in looking at Stalin's career as a whole. Mao declared in "On the ten great relationships" that the editorial of 5 April 1956 had been written "on the basis of this evaluation," although the figures do not actually appear there.[162] Despite Stalin's wrong guidance of the Chinese revolution, Mao thought the thirty–seventy assessment was "only fair."[163]

Half a year later, in the aftermath of the Hungarian and Polish events, Mao made his famous remarks, at the Second Plenum on 15 November 1956, regarding the "sword of Stalin" and the "sword of Lenin." In Mao's view, even the first of these should not simply be discarded, in the name of opposition to "so-called Stalinism." Although he criticized Stalin's mistakes, he felt the Soviet leader's reputation should be protected. As for the "sword of Lenin," that is, the insistence on the model of the October Revolution, as opposed to the "parliamentary road," Mao argued that it should under no circumstances be abandoned.[164]

This trend of thought was continued in the *People's Daily* editorial of 29 December 1956, "More on the historical experience of the dictatorship of the proletariat," which placed greater emphasis both on Stalin's merits and on the continuance of class struggle under socialism than that of the previous April. In his speech of 27 February 1957, on contradictions among the people, on the other hand, Mao Tse-tung spelled out his views about Stalin, and about related issues, both theoretical and concrete, in a somewhat different spirit.

The first section of this chapter quoted a passage about Stalin's propensity to exterminate his critics. Following on from this, Mao developed, under the heading of eliminating counterrevolutionaries, a comparison between China and the Soviet Union as regarded the use and abuse of revolutionary violence:

How has the work of eliminating counter-revolutionaries been carried out after all in our country? Very badly, or very well? In my opinion, there have been

162 *The historical experience*, 18–19.   163 Mao, *SW*, 5.304.   164 Ibid., 341–42.

shortcomings, but if we compare ourselves with other countries, we have done relatively well. We have done better than the Soviet Union, and better than Hungary. The Soviet Union has been too leftist, and Hungary too rightist.

China, too, he acknowledged, had at times committed leftist errors, but mostly in the base areas in the South, under Soviet influence; these had been rectified by the directive of 1942 against killings and excessive arrests. Even after that, there had been some shortcomings, but nothing like the Soviet Union when Stalin was in power: "He didn't deal with this matter well at all [*t'a na-ko tung-hsi kao-ti pu-hao*]. He had two aspects. On the one hand, he eliminated genuine counterrevolutionaries; this aspect was correct. On the other hand, he wrongly killed a large number of people [*hsu to jen*], important people, such as delegates to the Party Congress."

Here Mao alluded to the figures for percentages killed given by Khrushchev in his secret speech, before confirming that in 1950–52, 700,000 had been executed in China, a measure he characterized as "basically correct."[165]

Apart from criticizing Stalin's policy of sending to a camp or killing anyone who dared to say anything negative about the Party or the government, Mao also commented once again, as he had done in his talk of January 1957 to Party secretaries, on Stalin's deficiencies as a Marxist theoretician. This time, however, he went further, and claimed philosophical originality for himself as compared to Marx and Lenin, as well as to Stalin:

Contradictions among the people, and how to resolve this problem, is a new problem. Historically, Marx and Engels said very little about this problem, and though Lenin referred to it, he only just referred to it [*chien-tan t'an-tao*]. He said that in a socialist society, antagonisms died away, but contradictions continued to exist; in other words, ... the bourgeoisie had been overthrown, but there continued to be contradictions among the people. [Thus] Lenin said there were still contradictions among the people, [but] he didn't have time to analyze this problem systematically. As for antagonism, can contradictions among the people be transformed from non-antagonistic to antagonistic contradictions? It must be said that they can, but in Lenin's day there was as yet no possibility of investigating this problem in detail. There was so little time allotted to him. Of course, after the October Revolution, during the period when Stalin was in charge, for a long time he mixed up these two types of contradictions.[166]

165 *Hsueh-hsi wen-hsuan*, 197–98. The Soviet Union is not even mentioned in the corresponding section of the official revised text (Mao, *SW*, 5.396–99) – not surprisingly, since this was first published in June 1957, when any such negative comments would have been quite out of the question.
166 *Hsueh-hsi wen-hsuan*, 194. For a comparison of Mao's ideas regarding nonantagonistic contradictions with those of Lenin and Stalin, see Stuart Schram, *Documents sur la théorie de la "rév-*

Lenin's failure to develop the concept of contradictions among the people Mao excused by the lack of experience in those early days of the revolution.[167] Stalin's mistakes, on the other hand, Mao attributed to his inherently inadequate understanding of dialectics.[168]

Summing up regarding the criticism of Stalin at the Twentieth Congress, Mao declared that this business had a dual nature. On the one hand, to smash blind faith in Stalin, and to take the lid off, was a "liberation movement" (*i-ko chieh-fang yun-tung*). But on the other, Khrushchev's manner of doing it, without analysis, and without taking account of the consequences in the rest of the world, was wrong. We have, said Mao, complained of this in face-to-face discussions with the Soviets, saying that they were great-nation chauvinists.[169]

When he visited Moscow for the second time, in November 1957, to attend the conference of Communist and workers' parties, Mao remarked that he still had a "belly full of pent-up anger, mainly directed against Stalin," although he would not elaborate on the reasons, because it was all in the past. He then proceeded, in characteristic fashion, to do precisely that: "During the Stalin era, nobody dared to speak up. I have come to Moscow twice and the first time was depressing. Despite all the talk about 'Fraternal Parties' there was really no equality."

Now, he said, we "must admit that our Soviet comrades' style of work has changed a lot." Consequently, he expressed the opinion that "first of all, we must now acknowledge the Soviet Union as our head and the CPSU as the convenor of meetings, and that, secondly, there is now no harm in doing so."[170] Although the available record of the Moscow meetings suggests a reasonably cordial atmosphere between Mao and Khrushchev, a formulation such as this clearly does not indicate a degree of veneration for Soviet ideological or political authority that would make it in any way surprising that, within a year, signs of conflict were to emerge. A major factor in this deterioration of relations was, of course, Moscow's reaction to the new economic policies of the Great Leap Forward.

olution permanente" en Chine, xxxii–xxxviii. In the official text of the 27 February 1957 speech, Mao's judgment on his predecessors is turned into its opposite; Lenin, it reads, "gave a very clear exposition of this law." (Mao, *SW,* 5.392–93.)

167 *Hsueh-hsi wen-hsuan,* 211–21.   168 Ibid., 212–13.

169 Ibid., 223–24. (The text as printed in this collection actually says "our great nation-chauvinism," but I take *wo-men* to be a misprint for *t'a-men.* Alternatively, Mao might have indicated that when he criticized Khrushchev's handling of the problem of Stalin, the Soviets denounced *China's* great-nation chauvinism, that is, her insistence on having a voice in such matters.

170 Speech of 14 November 1957, translated by Michael Schoenhals in *The Journal of Communist Studies,* 2.2 (June 1986).

The Soviets, not surprisingly, saw only the heterodoxy of some of Mao's new methods, and not the basic consistency of many of his policies and aims with the logic of Leninism. They took a particularly dim view of the people's communes, set up in the summer of 1958, which Khrushchev ridiculed first privately, and soon afterward in public as well. (See *CHOC*, 14, ch. 11.)

Undoubtedly, the Soviets were also shocked and irritated by what they saw as the extravagant and boastful claims of the Chinese in the domain of industrial production. They must have been particularly taken aback when one of the most extreme of these, the call to overtake England in fifteen years in the output of steel and other major industrial products, was first put forward by Mao under their very noses, at the November 1957 meeting of Communist and workers' parties.[171]

Mao's new approach to internal problems, accompanied as it was by a greater reluctance to rely on Soviet assistance, implied in itself a loosening of the ties between China and the Soviet Union. As late as December 1956, Mao had reaffirmed unequivocally the policy of "leaning to one side" that he had first put forward in 1949:

The principal components of the socialist camp are the Soviet Union and China. China and the Soviet Union stand together. This policy line is correct. At present, there are still people who have doubts about this policy. They say, "Don't stand together." They think that China should take a middle course and be a bridge between the Soviet Union and the United States. This is the Yugoslav way, a way for getting money from both sides. Is this way of doing things good or not? I don't think it is good at all, it is not advantageous to our people. Because on one side is powerful imperialism, and this China of ours has suffered from imperialist oppression for a long time. If China stands between the Soviet Union and the United States, she appears to be in a favorable position, and to be independent, but actually she cannot be independent. The United States is not reliable, she would give you a little something, but not much. How could imperialism give you a full meal? It won't.[172]

In 1958, however, there took place a sharp deterioration in the relations between Mao and Khrushchev going far beyond what was implied by the logic of the Great Leap policies. This growing estrangement was not simply, or even primarily, the result of disagreement about de-Stalinization, although, as we have seen, Mao had strong reservations about the way in which Khrushchev had carried out that operation, with-

---

171 See Mao's speech of 18 November 1957, as translated by Schoenhals in ibid. These events are also discussed in Hu Hui-ch'iang, "Ta lien kang-t'ieh yun-tung chieh-k'uang" (A brief account of the campaign to make steel in a big way), *Tang-shih yen-chiu tzu-liao* (Materials for research on Party history), 4.726.
172 *Wan-sui* (1969), 62-63.

out consulting him. For at the same time, Mao nourished strong resentment against Stalin for his high-handed treatment of the Chinese, and he therefore approved – up to a point – Khrushchev's effort to cut him down to size. "Buddhas," he said in March 1958, "are made several times lifesize in order to frighten people.... Stalin was that kind of person. The Chinese people had got so used to being slaves that they seemed to want to go on. When Chinese artists painted pictures of me together with Stalin, they always made me a little bit shorter, thus blindly knuckling under to the moral pressure exerted by the Soviet Union." And in April 1958, he declared: "This Comrade Stalin of ours had something of the flavour of the mandarins of old.... In the past, the relations between us and the Soviet Union were those between father and son, cat and mouse."[173]

But nevertheless, he objected, he said in March 1958 at Chengtu, to Khrushchev's action in "demolishing Stalin at one blow." Stalin's errors should be criticized, but it was necessary to recognize that he also had a correct side, and that correct side "we ought to revere and continue to revere for ever."

Despite his reservations on this point, Mao still held up Khrushchev, at the same conference in Chengtu in March 1958, as an example of those excellent and vigorous revolutionaries who emerge from the local Party organizations: "Comrades working in the provinces will sooner or later come to the Centre. Comrades at the Centre will sooner or later either die or leave the scene. Khrushchev came from a local area. At the local level the class struggle is more acute, closer to natural struggle, closer to the masses. This gives the local comrades an advantage over those at the Centre."[174]

It is fair to say, I think, that never again, after the middle of 1958, would Mao have spoken of Khrushchev in such basically positive terms as these. A decisive episode in the deterioration of relations between the two men was, of course, the foreign policy crisis (or crises) of the summer of 1958. Khrushchev's attempt to solve the Middle Eastern conflict of July 1958 without the participation of Peking was clearly a major source of annoyance. Even more important, perhaps, was Mao's conviction that the Soviet leader was trying to dictate China's foreign policy.

On 29 July 1959, as the confrontation with P'eng Te-huai at the Lushan meeting of the Central Committee was approaching its climax, Mao wrote a brief annotation to three documents regarding foreign criticism of the communes, including press reports of Khrushchev's remarks on the subject in the United States. Three days later, he sent a copy of

173 Schram, *Mao unrehearsed*, 99; also *Wan-sui* (1969), 183.   174 Schram, *Mao unrehearsed*, 114–55.

these materials and of his accompanying comment to an old comrade, with a note saying in part:

The Khrushchevs oppose or are dubious about these three things: letting a hundred flowers bloom, the people's communes, and the Great Leap Forward. I think they are in a passive position, whereas we are in an extremely active position. What do you think? We must use these three things to fight the whole world, including a large number of opponents and skeptics within the Party.[175]

Obviously Mao was both angry and contemptuous at the suggestion that his methods for building socialism were not compatible with Marxist orthodoxy. At the same time, his resentment at slurs against the communes, and more broadly at Khrushchev's meddling in the internal affairs of the Chinese Communist Party (through his criticisms of the communes, his relations with P'eng Te-huai, etc.) was greatly exacerbated by the anxiety he felt because the Soviet reservations were shared in some degree within China.

There followed, in the autumn of 1959, the incident of the TASS communiqué, and then a series of other clashes with the Soviets, which Mao summarized briefly as follows in his speech at the Tenth Plenum:

... in September 1959 during the Sino-Indian border dispute, Khrushchev supported Nehru in attacking us and Tass issued a communiqué [in this sense]. Then Khrushchev came to China and at our Tenth Anniversary Celebration banquet in October, he attacked us on our own rostrum. At the Bucharest Conference in 1960 they tried to encircle and annihilate us. Then came the conference of the Two Communist Parties [of China and of the Soviet Union], the Twenty-Six-Country Drafting Committee, the Eighty-One-Country Moscow Conference, and there was also a Warsaw Conference, all of which were concerned with the dispute between Marxism-Leninism and revisionism.[176]

Mao's use in this context of the term "encircle and annihilate" (*wei chiao*), which was that employed by Chiang Kai-shek in the 1930s to characterize the campaigns of extermination launched by him against the Communists, vividly reflects the degree of hostility that Mao perceived in his erstwhile comrades. But although he reacted to this hostility with anger, he remained wholly imperturbable in the face of it. In a speech of March 1960, he expounded the reasons for his confidence:

After all, who are the people of the so-called great anti-China [movement or chorus]? How many are there? There are merely imperialist elements from certain Western countries, reactionaries and semi-reactionaries from other countries, and

---

175 Letter to Wang Chia-hsiang, in *Mao Chu-hsi tui P'eng, Huang, Chang, Chou fan-tang chi-t'uan ti p'i-p'an*, 14.
176 Schram, *Mao unrehearsed*, 190–91.

revisionists and semi-revisionists from the international communist movement. The above three categories of people can be estimated to constitute a small percentage, say 5 per cent of mankind. At the most, it cannot be more than 10 per cent.... So far as we are concerned, their anti-China activities are a good thing, and not a bad thing. They prove that we are true Marxist-Leninists, and that we are doing our work pretty well.... The hatred which has grown up between the United States and us is somewhat greater, but they do not engage in anti-China activities daily either. Not only is there now a brief pause between two waves of anti-China activities, but also there may be a pause of longer duration in the future.... [I]f the entire party, and the entire people really unite as one, and we can catch up with or overtake them in gross output and per capita output of our main items of production, then such pauses will be prolonged. This is to say that this will compel the Americans to establish diplomatic relations with us, and do business with us on an equal basis, or else they will be isolated.[177]

The improvement in Sino-American relations that Mao predicted in 1960 was not to materialize for another decade. Meanwhile, China's relations with the Soviet Union rapidly moved toward a climax. A month after Mao made the speech just quoted at length, the Chinese opened a massive ideological offensive with the publication of an editorial entitled "Long Live Leninsim!" and a series of other texts, ostensibly directed against the "revisionists" mentioned by Mao as members of the "great anti-China chorus," that is, against the Yugoslavs, but in fact aimed at the Soviet "semi-revisionists," who were soon to become openly the principal villains in Mao's book. A decisive turning point was reached in January 1962, when Mao Tse-tung, at the Seven Thousand Cadres Conference, called, in effect, for the overthrow of the existing Soviet regime.

In a passage from his remarks on this occasion (published as a "directive" in 1967) Mao said:

The Soviet Union was the first socialist country, and the Soviet Communist Party was the party created by Lenin. Although the Party and state leadership of the Soviet Union have now been usurped by the revisionists, I advise our comrades to believe firmly that the broad masses, the numerous Party members and cadres of the Soviet Union are good; that they want revolution, and that the rule of the revisionists won't last long.[178]

Although this speech was not publicly divulged at the time it was delivered, the Soviet leaders assuredly soon grasped the fact that Mao considered them beyond the pale. In any case, the rupture between Moscow and Peking was made abundantly manifest in the public polemics of 1963–64. The history of the Sino-Soviet dispute is dealt with in CHOC 14, ch. 11, and even though authorship of the nine Chinese replies to the

177 Wan-sui (1969), 316–18.   178 Schram, Mao unrehearsed, 181.

Soviets, from 6 September 1963 to 14 July 1964, has been attributed to Mao, I shall not review their contents here. What is relevant in this context is how rapidly Mao himself gave ideological and policy substance to the anti-Soviet rhetoric generated beginning in early September.

In late September 1963, the Politburo held an enlarged meeting. On 27 September, Mao put forward in this context a "Directive on opposing revisionism in Sinkiang." The first point, he said, was to do economic work well, so that the standard of living of the population was improved until it surpassed not only the level that had existed under the Kuomintang, but that "in the Soviet Union under revisionist domination" (*hsiu-cheng-chu-i t'ung-chih hsia ti Su-lien*). Less grain should be requisitioned, and in order to heighten the favorable contrast with the situation across the border, the supply of cotton cloth, tea, sugar, and so forth, should be "a bit more ample than in other areas."

Against this background, Mao then enunciated the second point:

2) We must put politics in command, and strengthen ideological and political education. We must carry out very well anti-revisionist education directed at the cadres and people of every nationality.... Cadres of the Han nationality should study the languages and literatures of the minority nationalities, they must pay attention to dealing well with relations among nationalities, and to strengthening solidarity among them. We must educate cadres and people of the Han nationality strictly to observe the Party's policy toward nationalities, to uphold a class viewpoint, and to implement a class line.... In the anti-revisionist struggle, we must have participation by units of the army and of the militia made up of national minorities, in order to guarantee the success of the anti-revisionist struggle.

The third point for attention was the education of the local Han population to respect the customs and habits of the local minorities. Some idea of what this signified is conveyed by the fact that under this heading Mao called for assistance to the Han workers sent to Sinkiang in resolving their "marriage and other difficulties." The fourth point was constant attention to the situation on the border, and intensifying the "anti-revisionist struggle on the border." The fifth point was vigilance against subversion and sabotage, as well as military incursions, by the "Soviet modern revisionists." The last point, finally, was "integrated leadership" (*i-yuan-hua ling-tao*) of the antirevisionist struggle.[179]

Mao Tse-tung was, in fact, convinced that China was rapidly catching

---

179 *Mao Chu-hsi kuan-yü kuo-nei min-tsu wen-t'i ti lun-shu hsuan-pien* (Selections from Chairman Mao's expositions regarding problems of nationalities within the country, October 1978), 40–41.

up with the Soviet Union in terms of standard of living, not only in Central Asia, but in the country as a whole. "Khrushchev," he told Anna Louise Strong in January 1964,

has said that we have one pair of trousers for every five people in China, and sit around eating out of the same bowl of watery cabbage soup. Actually, when he said that, his own economic situation was getting worse, and he said it for the Soviet people to show how well off they were. Now they are getting shorter on trousers and their soup is getting more watery. Actually, the livelihood of the people in the Soviet Union now is not much better than that of our own people.[180]

Whether or not Mao actually believed this, he was assuredly persuaded that the Soviet Union sought to use its primacy in the socialist camp to promote its own selfish economic interests. In his reading notes of 1960 on the Soviet textbook of political economy, Mao had attacked Moscow's policy of economic specialization within Comecon, the Soviet-dominated Eastern European economic organization – a policy designed to keep certain countries in the position of suppliers of agricultural raw materials to their more advanced neighbors, in particular to the Soviet Union.[181] This point continued to rankle, and in his January 1964 interview with Anna Louise Strong, Mao declared, "The problem with the socialist countries is that Khrushchev wants them to stick to a one-sided economy producing to meet the needs of the Soviet Union. It's hard to be the son of a patriarchal father."[182]

Thus, in the late 1950s and early 1960s, Mao Tse-tung voiced an increasingly assertive nationalism as a response not only to the boycott of China by the imperialists, but to Soviet great-power chauvinism. Linked to this trend, and to the evolution of Sino-Soviet relations generally, was a growing radicalism, manifesting itself above all in an emphasis on class struggle. This turn toward the left was, as noted in this chapter's first section a natural outgrowth of the Great Leap policies, but further impetus was given to it by Mao's revulsion at Khrushchev's "goulash communism." Moreover, having been struck by the emergence of revisionism within the Soviet Union, Mao Tse-tung began to discern the existence of similar phenomena within China itself. Thus yet another factor was injected into the complex process that ultimately culminated in the Cultural Revolution.

180 Strong, "Three interviews," 504.
181 *Wan-sui* (1967), 226–27; *Miscellany*, 296.   182 Strong, "Three interviews," 504.

The enemy within: Mao Tse-tung's growing obsession with class struggle

As noted at the end of the first section of this chapter, Mao drastically changed his position regarding the nature of the contradictions in Chinese society during the summer of 1957. The consequences of this shift for economic policy have already been explored, and some of its implications in the philosophic domain have also been evoked. Now, having reviewed the interaction between trends in Mao's thought after 1957 and the Sino-Soviet conflict, it is time to consider how Sino-centrism, a radical interpretation of Marxism, and leftist sentiments engendered by nostalgia for the heroic virtues of the past, came together to lead Mao toward unprecedented experiments.

A central element in the growing radicalization of Mao Tse-tung's thought and political stance in the early 1960s was, of course, his increasingly strident and persistent emphasis on the existence and importance of class struggle within Chinese society. Let us therefore begin by reviewing briefly the evolution of Mao's ideas regarding classes and class struggle from the Greap Leap to the eve of the Cultural Revolution.

The first systematic formulation of his new approach was contained in Mao's speech of 9 October 1957 at the Third Plenum. Abandoning the position that had been adopted a year earlier at the Eighth Congress, and that, as we have seen, he had himself reiterated in February 1957, to the effect that the basic contradiction in China at the present stage was between the productive forces and the relations of production, Mao asserted that

the contradiction between the proletariat and the bourgeoisie, between the socialist road and the capitalist road, is undoubtedly the principal contradiction in contemporary Chinese society.... Previously the principal task for the proletariat was to lead the masses in struggles against imperialism and feudalism, a task that has already been accomplished. What then is the principal contradiction now? We are now carrying on the socialist revolution, the spearhead of which is directed against the bourgeoisie, and at the same time this revolution aims at transforming the system of individual production, that is, bringing about co-operation; consequently the principal contradiction is between socialism and capitalism, between collectivism and individualism, or in a nutshell between the socialist road and the capitalist road. The resolution of the Eighth Congress makes no mention of this question. It contains a passage which speaks of the principal contradiction as being that between the advanced socialist system and the backward social productive forces. This formulation is incorrect.[183]

183 Mao, *SW*, 5.492–93.

It is, of course, Mao's revised formulation just quoted that is now seen in China as incorrect. Right or wrong, however, it was the emphasis on class struggle, against the bourgeoisie and between the "two roads," that was to characterize Mao's thought for the rest of his life. Within this broad orientation, there were, however, to be significant twists, turns and fluctuations during the ensuing nineteen years, both in the vigor and harshness with which Mao Tse-tung promoted class struggle and in his analysis of the existing class relations.

On the eve of the Great Leap, Mao spelled out his view regarding the class structure of Chinese society in rather curious terms, stating that "the reciprocal relations between people" were "determined by the relationship between three big classes": (1) "imperialism, feudalism, bureaucratic capitalism, the rightists, and their agents"; (2) "the national bourgeoisie," by which he said he meant all the members of this class except the rightists; and (3) "the left, that is to say the labouring people, the workers, the peasants." To this last category Mao added, more or less as an afterthought, the parenthetical remark: "In reality there are four classes – the peasants are a separate class."[184]

In his speech of 6 April 1958 to the Hankow Conference, Mao corrected one anomaly – the failure to single out the particular role of the peasantry – but continued to include the "imperialists" among the classes existing in China. On this occasion, he put the matter as follows:

... there are four classes within the country, two exploiting classes and two labouring classes. The first exploiting class consists of imperialism, feudalism, bureaucratic capitalism and the remnants of the Kuomintang, as well as 300,000 rightists. The landlords have now split up, some of them have been reformed, and others have not been reformed. The unreformed landlords, rich peasants, counter-revolutionaries, bad elements and rightists resolutely oppose communism. They are the Chiang Kai-shek and the Kuomintang of the present day, they are the class enemy, like Chang Po-chün. The rightists in the Party are just the same.... If you add up all these people, they come to roughly 5 per cent of the population, or about 30 million.... This is a hostile class, and still awaits reform. We must struggle against them, and at the same time take hold of them.... If we succeed in transforming 10 per cent of them, this can be accounted a success.... After a few years, when they demonstrate a sincere change of heart and are genuinely reformed, their exploiting class hats can be removed.[185]

The second exploiting class, made up of the national bourgeoisie, including the well-to-do middle peasants in the countryside, Mao described as a vacillating and opportunistic class. As for the "two labouring

184 Schram, *Mao unrehearsed*, 112–13.   185 *Wan-sui* (1969), 180–81; *Miscellany*, 85–86.

classes, the workers and the peasants," Mao remarked: "In the past, their minds were not as one, and they were not clear about ideology or about their mutual relations." And he added; "The workers and peasants work and till the land under the leadership of our Party, but in the past we did not properly handle the problem of their mutual relations."

In the aftermath of the Great Leap Forward, Mao's previous approach to the problem of class, which combined objective and subjective criteria, was modified by the addition of a new dimension: the notion that privileged elements among the cadres and intellectuals constituted an embryonic class. This trend was linked to the generational change referred to above, for it had long been understood that, because they were accustomed to a certain standard of living, intellectuals of bourgeois origin must be paid high salaries. This was extensively discussed in the Chinese press in 1956–57, and in January 1957, Mao himself defended what he called "buying over" at a "small cost" the capitalists plus the democrats and intellectuals associated with them.[186] Obviously the same considerations did not apply to the newly trained young people, who did not have such expensive tastes, and who might be assumed to have a higher level of political consciousness.

I have already noted Mao's advocacy, at the Peitaiho meeting of August 1958, of the "free supply system." His speech on this occasion was not, of course, openly published at the time, but much of the substance of his thinking was conveyed in an article by Chang Ch'un-ch'iao reproduced in the *People's Daily* in October 1958. Chang's article, which had originally appeared in Shanghai in September, did not, in fact, represent simply an accidental convergence between his views and Mao's, but was the result of a clever political maneuver. K'o Ch'ing-shih, the leftist mayor of Shanghai, who was present at the Peitaiho meeting, had read out to Chang Ch'un-ch'iao over the telephone his notes of Mao's speech, and this had provided the inspiration for Chang's piece. Mao's decision, on reading the article, to have it reprinted in Peking was therefore evidence both of his own susceptibility to flattery, and of the functioning, already at this time, of a Shanghai link, if not a Shanghai network.[187]

In the editorial note he wrote to accompany Chang's article when it appeared in the *People's Daily*, Mao said the views expressed were "basically correct," but he judged the article "one-sided," and "incomplete" in

186 Mao, *SW*, 5.357.
187 Information regarding the role played by K'o Ch'ing-shih from a conversation of 23 April 1986 with Hu Hua, confirmed by Kung Yü-chih in a conversation of 24 April 1986.

its explanation of the historical process.[188] But even though Mao thought Chang was in too much of a hurry to eliminate the "ideology of bourgeois right" or bourgeois legal norms defined by Marx, the issue evoked by this term remained posed in his speeches and writings from this time forward. In brief, Mao regarded the inequalities resulting from compensation according to work, even under a socialist system, as qualitatively similar to the "bourgeois right" defined by Marx with reference to capitalist society, and it was this that provided the theoretical basis for his view that the Party, because it contained the greatest number of high cadres attached to their privileges, was a nest of bourgeois or bourgeois-minded elements.[189]

I have already stressed the importance of the Lushan Plenum of 1959 as a turning point toward an ever greater emphasis on class struggle. Condemning P'eng and his allies as anti-Marxist "bourgeois elements" who had infiltrated the Chinese Communist Party,[190] Mao declared that the struggle at Lushan had been a class struggle, "the continuation of the life-and-death struggle between the two great antagonists of the bourgeoisie and the proletariat in the process of the socialist revolution during the past decade," and predicted that such struggle would last "for at least another twenty years.'[191] (In the event, Mao very nearly saw to it that it did.)

188 Chang Ch'un-ch'iao, "P'o-ch'u tzu-ch'an-chieh-chi ti fa-ch'üan ssu-hsiang" (Eliminate the ideology of bourgeois right), *JMJP*, 13 October 1958.
189 For the most authoritative recent Chinese analysis of this trend in Mao's thought, see Shih Chung-ch'üan, "Ma-k'o-ssu so-shuo-ti' tzu-ch'an-chieh-chi ch'üan-li' ho Mao Tse-tung t'ung-chih tui t'a ti wu-chieh" (The "bourgeois right" referred to by Marx, and Comrade Mao Tse-tung's misunderstanding of it), *Wen-hsien ho yen-chiu*, 1983, 405–17, and the revised openly published version of this in *HC*, 11 (1985), 12–22. This article, like many other recently published accounts, asserts unequivocally that Mao played the central role in introducing the concept of "bourgeois right" into Chinese political discourse from the Great Leap onward. The term commonly rendered into English as "bourgeois right" has as its *locus classicus* Marx's "Critique of the Gotha Programme," where he makes use of it in criticizing the notion of a "fair distribution of the proceeds of labour." (Karl Marx and Frederick Engels, *Selected works*, 317–21.) *Recht* means, in German, both right, in the sense of entitlement to the rewards of one's labor (or of human rights), and legal order. Marx is in effect referring, in the passage in question, to both these dimensions, as he makes plain when, after stating that "equal right is still in principle bourgeois right," he goes on to note: "Right by its very nature can consist only in the application of an equal standard." In other words, right (or rights) in the sense of entitlement is defined by a system of legal or quasi-legal norms. The Chinese have further compounded this confusion by rejecting the translation of the term used by Mao, *tzu-ch'an chieh-chi fa-ch'üan* (meaning literally "bourgeois legal rights"), since 1979, in favor of *tzu-ch'an chieh-chi ch'üan-li*, which points rather toward the rights of the individual subject. In any case, Mao's concern was primarily with the fact that, as he saw it, the strict application of the socialist principle of "to each according to his work" failed to take into account the social needs of the individual, and was therefore in some degree heartless, just as the capitalist system of wage labor was heartless.
190 Speech of 11 September 1959 to the Military Affairs Committee, Schram, *Mao unrehearsed*, 147–48.
191 "The origin of machine guns and mortars," 15 August 1959, *CLG*, 1.4 (1968–69), 73.

Discussing Mao Tse-tung's "errors regarding the problem of class struggle" in the period just before the Cultural Revolution, Teng Li-ch'ün has pointed to another source for Mao's increasing radicalism: "In reality, after 1958, he basically paid no attention to economic work. This affected his estimate of the situation regarding classes and class struggle."[192] The above statement should not be taken literally to mean that Mao henceforth took no interest in anything related to the economy. After all, it was in 1960 that he produced his "Reading notes on the [Soviet] textbook of political economy," and Mao is now said to have taken personal charge of the drafting of the "Sixty Articles" on the communes in March 1961.[193] Teng Li-ch'ün's point, therefore, was that although Mao continued to talk about the political and ideological dimensions of the economic system, he took little serious interest in economics or in economic reality. In this sense, Teng's conclusion is undoubtedly justified.

Mao's growing conviction, form 1959 on, that the bureaucratic tendencies which not only he, but also Liu Shao-ch'i and others, had long denounced in the Chinese Communist Party were not simply the result of a defect in "work style," but reflected an incipient change in the class character of the Party and its cadres, was inspired to a significant extent by his observations regarding the Soviet Union. But the comments he made in 1960 regarding the emergence of "vested interests groups" in a socialist society after the abolition of classes, although they occur in his reading notes on the Soviet textbook of political economy, were obviously intended to apply to China as well.

Indeed, there are scholars in China today who take the view that Mao's analysis of Soviet "revisionism" had as its primary purpose the forging of a weapon against those in the Chinese Communist Party who did not share his ideas. That is probably putting it too strongly; Mao undoubtedly did have an acute distaste for Khrushchev's Russia and all it had come to stand for in his eyes. In fact, he even traced the defects in the Soviet system back to its very origins. After the October Revolution, he asserted, the Soviets had failed to deal properly with the problem of "bourgeois right." As a result, a pattern of stratification reminiscent of the tsarist era had emerged; most Party members were the children of cadres, and ordinary workers and peasants had no chance of advance-

---

192　Teng Li-ch'ün, answering questions about the resolution of 27 June 1981 at an academic discussion held on 11 and 12 August 1981, in the context of a national meeting on collecting materials for Party history, in *Tang-shih hui-i pao-kao-chi*, 145.

193　T'ao K'ai, "K'ai-shih ch'üan-mien chien-she she-hui-chu-i ti shih-nien" (The ten years which saw the beginning of the all-round construction of socialism), in *Hsüeh-hsi li-shih chüeh-i chuan-chi* (Special collection on the study of the Resolution on [Party] history), 121.

ment.[194] He also noted that the Soviets had failed to smash bourgeois freedom, and thereby to promote proletarian freedom; China's political and ideological revolution had been more thorough.[195] Nonetheless, Mao's most acute concern was with the threat that such unwholesome tendencies might take root in China. Already at this time, he attributed to the Chinese bearers of such contagion two traits that were to remain central to his ideas on this theme in later years. On the one hand, they were attached to their privileges, founded in the principle of distribution "to each according to his work" — in other words, to the "ideology of bourgeois right." And at the same time, they behaved like overlords. "This animal, man, is funny," said Mao, "as soon as he enjoys slightly superior conditions he puts on airs."[196]

In January 1962, in a speech mainly stressing the need to continue the struggle against the old reactionary classes (landlords and bourgeoisie), which he said were "still planning a comeback," Mao stated explicitly that in a socialist society, "new bourgeois elements may still be produced."[197] And in August 1962, at a preliminary meeting of the Central Committee in Peitaiho before the Tenth Plenum, Mao declared; "In the book *Socialist upsurge in China's countryside* [which he had himself edited] there is an annotation saying that the bourgeoisie has been eliminated, and only the influence of bourgeois ideology remains. This is wrong, and should be corrected.... The bourgeoisie can be born anew; such a situation exists in the Soviet Union."[198]

As it stands, this statement that the bourgeoisie can be "born anew" leaves open the question, central for our purposes, of whether Mao means the old bourgeoisie can be reborn, or whether he is referring to the reincarnation of the soul or essence of the bourgeoisie in a new form, adapted to the conditions of a socialist society. He probably was talking about the second of these things, in other words about what Djilas and others have called the "new class" — although Mao himself may never have used that term. He seemed unable to make up his mind, however, in the mid-1960s, as to whether these "new bourgeois elements" were merely isolated individuals, corrupted by the advantages drawn from the misuse of their status, or whether *all* cadres, because of the privileges and power they enjoyed, were prone to take on this character.

194 *Hsueh-hsi wen-hsuan*, 305. (Speech of 21 August 1958, in the morning.)
195 Ibid., 311. (Speech of 21 August 1958, in the afternoon.)
196 *Wan-sui* (1967), 192. For an earlier reference to "putting on airs like overlords," see Mao's speech of November 1958 on Stalin's *Economic problems of socialism in the USSR* in *Wan-sui* (1967), 117–18.
197 Schram, *Mao unrehearsed*, 168. 198 *Wan-sui* (1969), 424.

In the early 1960s, he appeared to lean in the first direction, by stressing the corrupting effects of money, and advantages bought with money. Thus, while continuing to acknowledge that material incentives were necessary in Chinese society at the present stage, he argued that they should be subordinated to "spiritual incentives" in the political and ideological domains, and that individual interests should be subordinated to collective interests.[199]

In his speech of 30 January 1962 to a central work conference, Mao related the "five bad categories" to the social origins of the individuals in question: "Those whom the people's democratic dictatorship should repress," he declared, "are landlords, rich peasants, counter-revolutionary elements, bad elements and anti-communist rightists. The classes which the counter-revolutionary elements, bad elements and anti-communist rightists represent are the landlord class and the reactionary bourgeoisie. These classes and bad people comprise about four or five per cent of the population. These are the people we must compel to reform."[200]

At the Tenth Plenum of September–October 1962, Mao put forward the slogan "Never forget the class struggle!" and personally revised the communiqué of the plenum that summed up his thinking.[201] Like his speech five years earlier, at the Third Plenum, and the confrontation at Lushan, this occasion marked yet a further turn toward a policy of promoting "class struggle." The nature and locus of the classes being struggled against remained, however, fundamentally ambiguous. In his speech of January 1962, Mao had referred to "classes and bad people." In other words, although the counterrevolutionaries and other "bad elements" were said by Mao to "represent" the landlords and the reactionary bourgeoisie, they did not necessarily come from these classes. Two passages from speeches by Mao during the period from the summer of 1962 to the spring of 1963, when the Socialist Education Campaign was in the process of taking shape, stress more heavily the class origins of deviations within the Party, but at the same time underscore the continuing importance, in Mao's view, of transformation through education.

In his talk of 9 August at Peitaiho, Mao said:

The composition of Party membership [*tang-yuan ti ch'eng-fen*] includes a large number of petty bourgeois, a contingent of well-to-do peasants and their sons and younger brothers, a certain number of intellectuals, and also some bad people who have not yet been properly transformed; in reality, [these last] are not

199 *Wan-sui* (1967), 206, 210. (From Mao's reading notes of 1960 on the Soviet textbook of political economy, now known to be edited versions of his remarks at sessions discussing the Soviet text.)
200 Schram, *Mao unrehearsed*, 169–70.   201 *1981 resolution, annotated edition*, 359.

Communist Party members. They are called Communist Party members, but they are really [members of the] Kuomintang.... As for the intellectuals and sons and brothers of landlords and rich peasants, there are those who have been transformed by Marxism [*Ma-k'o-ssu-hua le ti*], there are those who have not been transformed at all, and there are those who have not been transformed to a satisfactory level. These people are not spiritually prepared for the socialist revolution. we have not educated them in good time.[202]

In May 1963, on the eve of the promulgation of the first directive regarding the Socialist Education Campaign (the "Former Ten Points"), Mao defined the class composition of the Party quite differently, but discussed the problem of "transformation" in very similar terms:

With respect to Party composition, the most important class components are workers, poor peasants and farm labourers. Consequently, the main class composition is good. However, within the Party there is a large number of petty bourgeois elements, some of whom belong to the upper stratum of the urban and rural petty bourgeoisie. In addition, there are intellectuals, as well as a certain number of sons and daughters of landlords and rich peasants. Of these people, some have been transformed by Marxism; some have been partly, but not totally transformed by Marxism-Leninism; and some have not been transformed at all. Organizationally they may have joined the Party, but not in terms of their thought. They are not ideologically prepared for the socialist revolution. In addition, during the last few years some bad people have wormed their way in. They are corrupt and degenerate and have seriously violated the law and discipline.... This problem requires attention, but it is relatively easy to deal with. The most important problem is the petty-bourgeois elements who have not been properly reformed. With respect to intellectuals and the sons and daughters of landlords and rich peasants we must do more work. Consequently, we must carry out education, and yet more education, for Party members and cadres. This is an important task.[203]

It is evident from these two quotations that although objective social origins remained important for Mao, personal transformation through political education was likewise a crucial aspect of the problem of class taken as a whole. If anything, the stress on "transformation," that is, on subjective criteria, is greater in 1963 than in 1962.

In May 1964, as the Socialist Education Campaign unfolded, Mao declared, at a meeting with four vice-premiers:

We must definitely pay very close attention to class struggle. The "four cleanups" in the countryside is a class struggle, and the "five antis" in the cities is also

---

202 *Wan-sui (1969)*, 426.

203 *Tzu-liao hsuan-pien* ([Peking], January 1967), 277. For a conveniently available translation of this whole directive, see Richard Baum and Frederick C. Teiwes, *Ssu-ch'ing: the Socialist Education Movement of 1962–1966*, 58–71. (The passage by Mao is on pp. 70–71.) This text was first openly published in the ninth Chinese reply to the Soviet open letter; see Schram, *Political thought*, 367.

a class struggle.... Class status [ch'eng-fen] must also be determined in the cities. As for how such class lines should be drawn criteria must be formulated when we come to do this work. We cannot take account only of [inherited] class status [wei ch'eng-fen lun]. Neither Marx, Engels, Lenin nor Stalin had working-class family origins [ch'u-shen].[204]

A directive on drawing class distinctions, undated but almost certainly from late 1964, discusses explicitly the relation between subjective and objective criteria:

It is necessary to draw class distinctions.... Of the two, [objective] class status [chieh-chi ch'eng-fen] and the behaviour of the person in question [pen-jen piao-hsien], it is the behaviour of the person in question which is most important. The main thing in drawing class distinctions is to ferret out the bad elements.

We must moreover clearly distinguish between family origins [ch'u-shen] and the behaviour of the person in question. The emphasis must be placed on behaviour; the theory that everything depends on class status alone [wei ch'eng-fen lun] is wrong, the problem is whether you take the stand of your class of origin, or whether you adopt a different class stand, that is, on the side of the workers and the poor and lower-middle peasants. Moreover, we must not be sectarian, but must unite with the majority, even including a portion of the landlords and rich peasants, and their children. There are even some counter-revolutionaries and saboteurs who should be transformed; it suffices that they be willing to be transformed, and we should be willing to have them, one and all.[205]

It can be argued that, in Mao's later years, certain pairs of opposites that had hitherto coexisted in dynamic and creative tension became dissociated, thus unleashing forces that ultimately propelled his thought and action into destructive channels. In several crucial and interrelated respects, this unraveling of the previous synthesis began with the Tenth Plenum in the fall of 1962. Increasingly, Mao came to perceive the relation between the leaders, with their privileges, and the rest of society, as an antagonistic contradiction rather than a contradiction among the people. The consequence that inevitably flowed from this insight was that the Party, considered as an entity that included virtually all of these privileged power holders, must not be simply tempered and purified in contact with the masses, but smashed, at least in large part.

Apart from the relation between the Party, or privileged elements in the Party, and the masses, the very complex process of dissociation or disaggregation of the structure of Mao Tse-tung's thought that took place

204 Miscellany, 351; Wan-sui (1969), 494—95.
205 Miscellany, 351; Wan-sui (1969), 602—3. (For the dating of this text, see the discussion in volume 2 of the index to Mao's post-1949 writings published in 1981 by Kyoto Daigaku Jimbun Kagaku Kenkyūsho [Research Institute of Humanistic Studies, Kyoto University], p. 47.)

beginning in the 1960s involved a number of other polarities. I have already dealt at some length with the interaction between Marxism and the Chinese tradition, and also with the issue of the relation between the Soviet model and Chinese experience.

The Sino-Soviet conflict also played an important role in shaping Mao Tse-tung's philosophical thought by contributing to the context in which the key idea of "One divides into two" emerged. On 26 October 1963, Chou Yang delivered to the Chinese Academy of Sciences a speech entitled "The fighting task confronting workers in philosophy and the social sciences." This speech, which was published, by an altogether too striking coincidence, on Mao's seventieth birthday (26 December 1963), plainly represented Mao Tse-tung's own thinking. In it Chou Yang surveyed the history of the workers' movement from Marx's own day to the present in terms of the axiom "One divides into two."[206]

Mao himself had, in fact, used this expression in a speech of 18 November 1957 at the Moscow meeting, although on that occasion his emphasis was not on divisions within the socialist movement, but on the fact that all societies, including socialist society, "teem" with contradictions, and on the fact that there is good and bad in everyone. "One divides into two," he concluded. "This is a universal phenomenon, and this is dialectics."[207]

Very soon after Chou Yang's speech of 1963, the slogan "one divides into two" came to evoke above all, in Mao's own usage, the need to struggle against "capitalist roaders" in the Chinese Communist Party. In other words, it was, by implication, a call for class struggle. (It was also, as discussed in *CHOC*, 14. 466–69, the rallying cry for the purge and persecution of Yang Hsien-chen and other partisans of the opposing formulation, "Two combine into one.")

This principle, Mao declared, constituted "the heart of dialectical materialism." He drew from it the conclusion that the electron, like the atom, would ultimately be split.[208] But above all, he was persuaded that social categories and political forces would continue to split, now and forever.

In the last analysis, Mao's conflict with others in the leadership revolved, of course, around the fundamental political and economic strategy that should be adopted for building socialism. The domain of culture

---

206 *PR*, 1964.1, 10–27, esp. p. 14; Chinese in *HC*, 1963.24, 1–30. (The expression *i fen wei erh* appears on pp. 4–5.) On Mao's involvement with this report, see also Schram, *Ideology and policy*, 44–45.

207 Mao, *SW*, 5.516.   208 Strong, "Three interviews," 499–500.

was, however, a crucial battleground as well, In the early 1960s, Mao perceived certain developments in literature and philosophy not only as the expression of unwholesome tendencies, but as weapons for attacking the very foundations of socialism through the agency of the superstructure. It is thus no accident that Mao should have first expressed his anxieties in cogent form precisely at the Tenth Plenum, simultaneously with his call for class struggle:

Writing novels is popular these days, isn't it? The use of novels for anti-party activity is a great invention. Anyone wanting to overthrow a political regime must create public opinion and do some preparatory ideological work. This applies to counter-revolutionary as well as to revolutionary classes.[209]

The clear implication of this statement was that "counter-revolutionary classes" were still at work in China, thirteen years after the conquest of power, seeking to overthrow the dictatorship of the proletariat, and that constant struggle in the realm of the superstructure was necessary in order to keep them in check. There is here present in embryonic form the idea of "continuing the revolution under the dictatorship of the proletariat" that was to loom so large during the Cultural Revolution decade. In view of the ambiguity of Mao's notion of class at this time, this development clearly represents a further manifestation of the accent on the superstructure, and on subjective forces, which had characterized Mao's thought from the beginning.

Just as Mao's call for class struggle at the Tenth Plenum had led to the Socialist Education Campaign, so this statement gave the impetus to a movement for literary rectification, and encouraged Chiang Ch'ing to launch the reform of the Peking Opera. These policies and their consequences have been described and analyzed in *CHOC*, 14, chapter 10. Here it will suffice to mention briefly two directives by which Mao continued to pour fuel on the fire. In December 1963, he complained that the "dead" still ruled in many departments of art, literature, and drama. "The social and economic base has already changed," he declared, "but the arts as part of the superstructure, which serve this base, still remain a great problem today.... Isn't it absurd that many communists are enthusiastic about promoting feudal and capitalist arts, but not socialist art?" In June 1964, his judgment was even harsher. The Chinese Writers Union, he said, "for the past fifteen years had *basically* [Mao's italics] ... not implemented the Party's policy." Instead of uniting with the workers and peasants,

---

209 Schram, *Mao unrehearsed*, 195. A similar concern with the influence of the media, and with the superstructure as a crucial realm of political struggle, had already been expressed by Mao in his then unpublished "Reading notes" of 1960 on the Soviet textbook of political economy. See *Wan-sui* (1969), 342–43; *Miscellany*, 266.

they had acted as bureaucrats and overlords, going to the brink of revisionism. Unless they mended their ways, they would become another Petröfi Club.[210] In other words, they would be outright counterrevolutionaries, and would be treated as such.

At the same time, in 1963–64, Mao showed greatly increased skepticism regarding the role of intellectuals in revolution and development. Without carrying his distrust of intellectuals to the point of characterizing them, as would the Gang of Four, as the "stinking ninth category," Mao therefore moved toward education policies infinitely more extreme than those of the Great Leap Forward. "We shouldn't read too many books," he said in February 1964. "We should read Marxist books, but not too many of them either. It will be enough to read a dozen or so. If we read too many we can move toward our opposite, become bookworms, dogmatists, revisionists."[211]

In all of these various domains – art and literature, philosophy, education – Mao attacked leading intellectuals not so much because they were privileged elements exploiting the masses (although he could make a good case to show that they were), but because they failed to share his utopia of struggle, and to obey wholeheartedly his directives.

In the summer of 1964, Mao referred scathingly to material corruption throughout the Party. "At present," he said, "you can buy a branch secretary for a few packs of cigarettes, not to mention marrying a daughter to him."[212]

The reference here to lower-level cadres would suggest that at that moment, shortly before Liu Shao-ch'i produced his "revised later ten points," Mao did not wholly disagree with the view that the Socialist Education Campaign should be directed at the grass roots, as well as at the higher echelons. He was, however, particularly exercised about the attitudes and behavior of the privileged urban elite. In a talk of June 1964 on the 3rd Five-Year Plan, he remarked:

Don't strive for money all the time, and don't spend it recklessly once you've got it.... In accordance with our policy, bourgeois intellectuals may be bought when necessary, but why should we buy proletarian intellectuals? He who has plenty of money is bound to corrupt himself, his family, and those around him.... In the Soviet Union, the high-salaried stratum appeared first in literary and artistic circles.[213]

As discussed in *CHOC*, 14, ch. 7, the final confrontation between Mao Tse-tung and Liu Shao-ch'i took place in December 1964, when

210 These are two of the "five militant documents" on art and literature published in May 1967. For a translation (somewhat modified here) of the directives of 12 December 1963 and 27 June 1964, see *PR*, 1967.23, 8.
211 Schram, *Mao unrehearsed*, 210.   212 Ibid., 217.   213 *Wan-sui* (1969), 498–99.

Mao, dissatisfied with what he perceived as the distortion and watering-down of his original strategy for the Socialist Education Campaign, put forward a new twenty-three–article directive that Liu, Mao later claimed, refused to accept. On this occasion, he made a number of observations regarding the "new bourgeoisie" in which power, rather than money, began to appear as the decisive factor.

It is perhaps worth noting in passing that although the problem of status and wage differentials was obviously of very acute concern to Mao, he displayed toward it even at this time a relaxed and humorous attitude scarcely to be found in the writings of the glum and fanatical ideologists of the Gang of Four. "This business of eating more and possessing more is rather complex!" he declared. "It is mainly people like us who have cars, and houses with central heating, and chauffeurs. I earn only 430 yuan, and I can't afford to hire secretaries, but I must."[214]

It is hard to resist reading this passage in the light of Mao's remark, earlier in the same year of 1964, "Hsuan-t'ung's salary of a little over a hundred yuan is too small – this man is an emperor."[215] One has the impression that for Mao, there existed, in addition to "worker," "poor peasant," "son of revolutionary martyr," and so on, yet another *ch'eng fen*: that of ruler. As for those who did not share this status with him, and with the former emperor, they could not be allowed to grow attached to their privileges.

In a discussion of 20 December 1964, he thus castigated once again those "power holders" among the cadres who were primarily concerned about getting more wage points for themselves, and agreed that the "hat" of "new bourgeois elements" should be stuck on "particularly vicious offenders" among them. He warned, however, against overestimating their number, and said they should be referred to as elements or cliques, not as "strata" – still less, obviously, as a fully formed class.[216] A week later, on 27 December 1964, Mao declared that there were "at least two factions" in the Chinese Communist Party, a socialist faction and a capitalist faction; these two factions thus incarnated the principal contradiction in Chinese society.[217]

Such formulations, and Mao's determination to direct the spearhead of the Socialist Education Campaign against "those in authority taking the

214 Ibid., 587.
215 Schram, *Mao unrehearsed*, 198. (Remarks at the Spring Festival Forum on Education.) Hsuan-t'ung was the reign title of the last Manchu emperor, a boy at the time of his abdication in 1912, and also known as Pu-yi (P'u-i) when he was emperor of the Japanese puppet state of Manchukuo from 1932 to 1945. He was still living in Beijing in 1964.
216 *Wan-sui* (1969), 582–88.   217 Ibid., 597–98.

capitalist road," led, of course, directly to the confrontation with Liu and others in the Party, and to the Cultural Revolution.

THE IDEOLOGY OF THE CULTURAL REVOLUTION

Before addressing the substance of Mao's thinking during the Cultural Revolution, it may be useful to ask ourselves precisely why he launched this movement, and what was the relationship between this decision and the "unraveling" of the Great Leap and post–Great Leap synthesis evoked above. Did he adopt extreme lines of conduct because his thinking had become skewed or distorted, or did he think as he did because he was obsessed with certain existential problems – above all, with the desire to punish and ultimately to destroy his critics?

As I have already suggested, especially in discussing his changing ideas on dialectics, and on class struggle, there were, in my view, elements of both these processes at work, but the predominant factor was the second one. In other words, the political and psychological roots of his ideas were notably more important than the intellectual ones. As a Chinese author has put it, Mao was so thoroughly persuaded that his own views were the only correct exposition of Marxism-Leninism that anyone who failed to agree with him automatically became a revisionist in his eyes. As a result, "The more it proved impossible to put his ideas into practice, the more he saw this as the reflection of class struggle, ... and of the emergence of 'counter-revolutionary revisionist elements' within the Party."[218]

Dictatorship, rebellion, and spiritual transformation

Among the multifarious ideological and policy innovations of the Cultural Revolution, it was the radical calling into question of the Party, and of authority in all its forms (except that of the Chairman), that attracted the most attention at the outset of this upheaval. In retrospect, it is clear that Mao's repudiation of leadership from above was not so sweeping as it appeared at the time. Nevertheless, he did go very far.

In his comments of 1960 on the Soviet manual, Mao had declared: "No

218 Wang Nien-i, "Mao Tse-tung t'ung-chih fa-tung 'wen-hua ta-ko-ming' shih tui hsing-shih ti ku-chi" (Comrade Mao Tse-tung's estimate of the situation at the time when he launched the "Great Cultural Revolution"), *Tang-shih yen-chiu tzu-liao*, 4.772. For a more extended discussion of the psychological roots of the Cultural Revolution, see Schram, "Party leader or true ruler?" 221–24, 233–37. Also, Stuart Schram, "The limits of cataclysmic change: reflections on the place of the 'Great Proletarian Cultural Revolution' in the political development of the People's Republic of China," *CQ*, 108 (December 1986), 613–24.

matter what, we cannot regard history as the creation of the planners, it is the creation of the masses."[219] And yet, he had always held, down to the eve of the Cultural Revolution, the view that the masses could exercise this role of making history only if they benefited from correct leadership. As the great confrontation with the Party approached, in December 1965, he went a step farther, proclaiming that democracy meant "dealing with the affairs of the masses through the masses themselves." There were, he added, two lines: to rely entirely on a few individuals, and to mobilize the masses. "Democratic politics," he said, "must rely on everyone running things, not on a minority of people running things." At the same time, however, he called once more for reliance on "the leadership of the Party at the higher level and on the broad masses at the lower level."[220] It was only with the actual onset of the Cultural Revolution in March 1966, that Mao sounded a much more radical note, suggesting that the masses could dispense with centralized Party leadership:

The Propaganda Department of the Central Committee is the palace of the King of Hell. We must overthrow the palace of the King of Hell and set the little devils free. I have always advocated that whenever the central organs do bad things, it is necessary to call upon the localities to rebel, and to attack the centre. The localities must produce many Sun Wu-k'ungs to create a great disturbance in the palace of the King of Heaven.[221]

Two months later, these "Monkey Kings" burst upon the scene, using Mao's own rhethoric, including the slogan "To rebel is justified!" which he had coined in 1939, attributing it — irony of ironies — to Stalin.[222] "Daring to ... rebel is ... the fundamental principle of the proletarian Party spirit," proclaimed the Red Guards of Tsing-hua University Middle School. "Revolutionaries are Monkey Kings.... We wield our golden rods, display our supernatural powers, and use our magic to turn the old world upside down, smash it to pieces, pulverize it and create chaos – the greater the confusion the better! We are bent on creating a tremendous proletarian uproar, and hewing out a proletarian new world!"[223] The "old world" these Red Guards wanted to smash was, of course, that controlled by the Party; they did not propose to rectify it, but to dissolve it in the chaos of the Cultural Revolution, and replace it by a completely new order.

Mao himself never proclaimed such a goal. At a central work confer-

219 *Wan-sui* (1967), 206.
220 *Wan-sui* (1969), 630. (Talk of 21 December 1964 with Ch'en Po-ta and Ai Ssu-ch'i.)
221 *Wan-sui* (1969), 640.
222 *MTTC*, 7.142; translated in Schram, *Political thought*, 427–28.
223 *JMJP*, 24 August 1966; translated in *PR*, 1966.37, 2–21.

ence on 23 August, he remarked, "The principal question is what policy we should adopt regarding the so-called disturbances [*so-wei luan*] in various areas. My view is that we should let disorder reign for a few months [*luan t'a chi-ko yueh*].... Even if there are no provincial Party committees, it doesn't matter; aren't there still district and *hsien* committees?"[224]

The phrase "for a few months" should probably be taken literally, to mean three or four months, or six at the outside. That in itself would have made the Cultural Revolution more like a conventional rectification campaign. Nevertheless, by accepting the prospect that for a time the Party might survive only in the form of local-level committees, the central organs having been effectively smashed and put out of action, Mao was at the very least taking the risk of destroying the political instrument to which he had devoted more than four decades of his life, in order to purge it of his enemies.

When events moved in such a direction, in late 1966 and early 1967, that the threat to the very existence of the Party became acute, Mao was forced to choose between Leninism and anarchy. He had no hesitation in preferring the former. Speaking in February 1967 to Chang Ch'un-ch'iao and Yao Wen-yuan, Mao noted that some people in Shanghai had demanded the abolition of "heads," and commented: "This is extreme anarchism, it is most reactionary. If instead of calling someone the 'head' of something, we call him 'orderly' or 'assistant,' this would really be only a formal change. In reality, there will still always be heads."[225] Discussing the objections to setting up communes as organs of government, as Chang and Yao had just done in Shanghai, Mao queried: "Where will we put the Party? ... In a commune there has to be a party; can the commune replace the party?"[226] The history of the ensuing nine years made it abundantly clear that in the Chairman's view it could not.

Another contradiction that became acute at this time was the one between Mao's consistently held view that the Party should command the gun and the gun should never be allowed to command the Party, and the increasingly dominant role of the People's Liberation Army in Chinese politics from 1960 on. This trend had begun, of course, as an essentially tactical maneuver on Mao's part to develop a power base in Lin Piao's PLA because he felt the Party to be slipping from his grasp, and not because of any innovation or brusque mutation in his thought. The pursuit of these tactics, however, soon led Mao in directions that, whatever his own original intentions, had major theoretical implications.

---

224 *Wan-sui* (1969), 653. 225 Schram, *Mao unrehearsed*, 277.
226 *Wan-sui* (1969), 670–71; *Miscellany*, 453–54.

The most important of these developments was the establishment in the course of the "Learn from the PLA" campaign launched in February 1964 (see *CHOC*, 14, ch. 7) of political departments, modeled on that of the army, in industrial enterprises, schools, and other units throughout the country. Not only did the army provide the model for these departments; it also provided the personnel, as Mao himself had decided in advance. On 16 December 1963, he wrote to Marshals Lin Piao, Ho Lung, and Nieh Jung-chen and to General Hsiao Hua, saying in part:

In every branch of state industry people are now proposing to emulate the People's Liberation Army from top to bottom (i.e., from the ministry down to the factory or to the mine), to set up everywhere political departments, political offices and political instructors, and to put into effect the Four Firsts and the Three-Eight work style. I too propose that several groups of good cadres be transferred from the Liberation Army to do political work in the industry ministries.... It looks as though we just can't get by without doing this, for otherwise we will be unable to rouse the revolutionary spirit of the millions and millions of cadres and workers in the whole industrial sector (and commerce and agriculture too).... I have been considering this question for several years.[227]

Such colonization of other organizations by the army rather than the Party was without precedent in the history of the world communist movement. Of equally great symbolic importance was the fact that by 1964 the People's Liberation Army was becoming increasingly the ideological and cultural mentor of the Chinese people. It was the army that compiled and published, in May 1964, the first edition of the "little red book," *Quotations from Chairman Mao*. Moreover, Mao himself, although he is not known to have participated in the work of compiling this breviary, had a share in the authorship of it, for the preface was drawn in large part from a resolution of the Military Affairs Commission of October 1960 that he had personally rewritten and approved at the time.[228] Thus the stage was set for the dialectic between anarchy and military control during the period 1966–72, and for the further and final unraveling of the polarities of Mao Tse-tung's thought.

By no means the least of the paradoxes of the Cultural Revolution period lay in the role of youth. On the one hand, Mao called on the Red Guards, at the outset of the movement, to serve as the vanguard, as he and his own generation of students had burst upon the stage of his-

---

227 *Tzu-liao hsuan-pien*, 287; translated in Stuart Schram, "New texts by Mao Zedong, 1921–1966," *Communist Affairs*, 2.2 (1983), 161.

228 The resolution of 20 October 1960 is translated in J. Chester Cheng, ed., *The politics of the Chinese Red Army; a translation of the Bulletin of activities of the People's Liberation Army*, 66–94. The passage corresponding to the preface to the *Quotations* appears on p. 70; on p.33 of the same volume, it is noted that the resolution has been revised "by Chairman Mao himself."

tory in 1919; and yet, on the other hand, the policies of 1966 and after involved downgrading sharply the role of this very educated elite. Part of the explanation is to be found in the undisciplined and self-indulgent behavior of the Red Guards, for which Mao castigated them in the summer of 1968, before sending them to the countryside, beginning in December 1968, to learn "proletarian class consciousness" from the peasants. But this paradox also reflects a deeper ambiguity, in Mao's thinking and policies, regarding the role in building socialism of expertise, and of the highly trained people who are the bearers of expertise.

Theoretically, all these contradictions should have been subsumed in a larger unity under the slogan "Red *and* expert." In fact, the emphasis was shifted so far, in the aftermath of the Cultural Revolution, in the direction of politics as a substitute for, rather than as a complement to, knowledge and skills, that the whole foundation for the enterprise of modernization to which, as we have seen, Mao was committed, was substantially undermined.

The fountainhead for many of these excesses was Mao's directive of 21 July 1968, which reads as follows:

It is still necessary to have universities; here I refer mainly to the need for colleges of science and engineering. However, it is essential to shorten the length of schooling, revolutionize education, put proletarian politics in command and take the road of the Shanghai Machine Tools Plant in training technicians from among the workers. Students should be selected from among workers and peasants with practical experience and they should return to practical work in production after a few years' study.[229]

Mao commented on this text, or perhaps on the talk from which it is drawn, in his conversation of 28 July 1968 with Red Guard leaders. On this occasion, he showed himself less exclusively concerned with technical knowledge for practical purposes, but in some respects even more skeptical about the value of formal education. "Should we continue to run universities?" he asked. "Should universities continue to enrol new students? To stop enrolling new students won't do either. You should make some allowances for [the context of] that talk of mine. I spoke of colleges of science and engineering, but I by no means said that all liberal arts colleges should be closed." Mao then went on, however, to say that if liberal arts colleges were unable to show any accomplishments, they should be overturned. In any case, he argued, courses in senior middle schools merely repeated those in junior middle schools, and those in

229 Schram, *Political thought*, 371. For the example of the Shanghai Machine Tools Plant, see *PR*, 1968.37, 13–17.

universities repeated those in senior middle schools. The best method, he held, was independent study in a library, as practiced by Engels, and by Mao himself in his youth, or setting up a "self-study university" (as Mao had done in 1921). "The real universities are the factories and the rural areas," he concluded.[230]

Some account must be taken, in interpreting these remarks, of the fact that Mao had at the same time a very stern and indeed harsh message to convey to his Red Guard interlocutors, namely that the party was over and the activities in which they had been indulging for the past two years would no longer be tolerated. In these circumstances, it was understandable that he should sweeten the pill by expressing agreement with them on some things. Thus he also went on to say that examinations were a waste of time. "All examinations should be abolished, absolutely abolished. Who examined Marx, Engels, Lenin and Stalin? Who examined Comrade Lin Piao? Who examined me? Comrade Hsieh Fu-chih, call all the students back to school."[231]

The students were indeed to be called back to school, and though the academic discipline of examinations was (for the moment at least) to be abolished, social discipline was to be forcefully restored. Explaining to the Red Guard leaders why he was obliged to put a stop to the bloody internecine conflicts that had already claimed thousands of victims, Mao declared:

The masses just don't like civil wars.... For two years, you have been engaged in the Great Cultural Revolution, that is, in struggle-criticism-transformation, but at present you are neither struggling nor criticizing nor transforming. It's true that you are struggling, but it is armed struggle. The people are unhappy, the workers are unhappy, the peasants are unhappy, Peking residents are unhappy, the students in most schools are unhappy.... Can you unite the realm in this way?

"If you are unable [to handle the problem]," he warned, "we may resort to military control, and ask Lin Piao to take command."[232] That was, of course, exactly what Mao did do, but whatever the Soviets or leftists of various persuasions may think, military dictatorship was not his ideal. He "resorted to military control" because there was no other instrument, apart from the People's Liberation Army, capable of putting down factional fighting conducted not merely with bricks and slingshots, but with rifles and even with mortars and other heavy weapons. As soon as circumstances appeared to permit it once again, he undertook to reestablish the primacy of the Party over the "gun." Justifying this step in

230 *Wan-sui* (1969), 693, 706, 695; *Miscellany*, 475, 488, 471.
231 *Wan-sui* (1969), 714; *Miscellany*, 496.   232 *Wan-sui* (1969), 698, 688; *Miscellany*, 481, 470.

his talks of August–September 1971 with military commanders, he suggested that the PLA was not the best instrument for exercising leadership in complex political and economic matters. "I approve of the army's traditional style of quick and decisive action," he said. "But this style cannot be applied to questions of ideology, for which it is necessary to make the facts known and reason with people." The main thrust of these talks was, in fact, the reestablishment of unified Party leadership, and the subordination of the army to the Party. "Now that the regional Party committees have been established," said Mao, "they should exercise unified leadership. It would be putting the cart before the horse if matters already decided by regional Party committees were later turned over to Army Party committees for discussion."[233]

The Ninth Congress of the Chinese Communist Party in April 1969 was presented at the time, and was widely seen outside China as marking the conclusion of the Cultural Revolution. In retrospect, and despite the symbolic significance of the formal disgrace of Liu Shao-ch'i on this occasion, the overarching continuity of events from 1966 to 1976 was such that it is probably more accurate to speak, as the Chinese have done since the Third Plenum of 1978, of the "Cultural Revolution decade." Nonetheless, the phase inaugurated by the Ninth Congress did see the emergence of significant new themes and formulations in the thought of Mao Tse-tung.

Marx and Ch'in Shih-huang-ti: the ambiguous legacy

Thus far, the term "Cultural Revolution" has served as a convenient label for the period beginning in 1966, without further inquiry into its meaning. Before proceeding in the analysis of the ideological content of the so-called Great Proletarian Cultural Revolution, as it continued to unfold after 1969, let us consider the appropriateness of the expression.

Leaving aside the adjective "great," the force of which is purely rhetorical or emphatic, was it "proletarian"? Was it "cultural"? Was it a revolution? Plainly Mao believed it to be all three of these things. To my mind, it was in truth none of them. The question of why Mao thought it *was* is, however, central to any understanding of his thought during his last decade.

In reality Mao's reasons for attributing to the movement he launched in 1966 each of these three qualities overlap to such a significant extent that they stand or fall together. In other words, either it was proletarian,

233 Schram, *Mao unrehearsed*, 296.

cultural, and revolutionary, or it cannot appropriately be characterized by any of these terms.

If we consider the three attributes in the order in which they are commonly placed, "proletarian" might signify, to begin with, "related to the urban working class." In that sense, the upheaval of 1966 was assuredly not proletarian. As indicated in the next chapter, the shock troops of the movement, during its first and formative stage, were students rather than workers. And though so-called revolutionary rebels among the workers subsequently played a significant role in political events, their intervention scarcely reflected the qualities of discipline, and of orientation toward technological modernization that Marx attributed to the urban proletariat.

The Cultural Revolution might, in a slightly looser sense, be legitimately called "proletarian" if it contributed to industrial development, and thereby to expanding the working class, and laying the material foundations for a society dominated by the proletariat. That was assuredly not the case, either. In December 1968, when Mao issued his directive ordering educated young people to go to the countryside to be reeducated by the poor and lower-middle peasants, this was interpreted to signify that the sons and daughters of urban workers would receive "a profound class education" from the poor peasants in the countryside.[234] And although, as has already been stressed repeatedly, Mao never ceased to call for rapid economic development, arguing even that the policies of the Cultural Revolution would produce economic and technical miracles, he showed increasing anxiety about the consequences of economic development.

In August 1958 at Peitaiho, he had called for the revival of the spiritual heritage of Yenan, but nevertheless, at that time the emphasis was overwhelmingly on economic goals. In April 1969, on the other hand, at the First Plenum of the new Ninth Central Committee, he spoke with nostalgia of the very high proportion of comrades killed during the struggle for power, and went on to say:

For years we did not have any such thing as salaries. We had no eight-tier wage system. We had only a fixed amount of food, three mace of oil and five of salt. If we got 1½ catties of millet, that was great.... Now we have entered the cities. This is a good thing. If we hadn't entered the cities Chiang Kai-shek would be occupying them. But it is also a bad thing because it caused our Party to deteriorate.[235]

234 PR, 1968.52, 6–7.   235 Schram, *Mao unrehearsed*, 288.

Although Mao concludes that it was, after all, right to enter the cities, his sentiments toward the consequences of modernization and economic development were, thus, profoundly ambiguous.

If the Cultural Revolution did not reflect either the role or the ideals of the urban working class, there remains only one sense in which it might qualify as proletarian: by its conformity to "proletarian" ideology as defined by Mao. We have already noted the threefold framework in which Mao Tse-tung had begun to view classes in the late 1950s and early 1960s. During the Cultural Revolution, while objective class origins were never regarded as *irrelevant*, high and generally decisive importance was attributed to subjective factors as the main criterion of class nature.

Lenin, for his part, had written in an orthodox Marxist vein, "The fundamental criterion by which classes are distinguished is the place they occupy in social production." In November 1966, Mao's evil genius, K'ang Sheng, said that Lenin's definition had proved inadequate, for class differentiation also fell under political and ideological categories, and in 1970 K'ang stated more precisely: "The existence of the capitalist class is particularly manifest in relations of economic exploitation. In socialist society, although there are economic contradictions among the various classes, the existence of classes shows itself ideologically and politically."[236]

Leaving aside for the moment the question of just where and how the existence of classes in this sense "showed itself" in China at this period, it is evident that to define class in ideological terms brings, in effect, the matter of the "proletarian" character of the movement launched by Mao in 1966 into the cultural domain. In other words, this "revolution" was proletarian only to the extent that it was also cultural.

The notion, propagated at the time by some naive observers, that the events of 1966 constituted a "cultural revolution" in the same sense as the May Fourth Movement, and indeed as the legitimate continuation of the May Fourth Movement, was altogether absurd. A bitter joke current in China in the years after Mao's death, *Wen-hua ko-ming shih ko wen-hua ti ming* ("The Cultural Revolution was about doing away with culture"), is nearer the mark. This upheaval did grow, nonetheless, as we have seen, out of Mao's reaction to certain cultural phenomena, and from beginning to end it was marked by an overwhelming stress on cultural and psychological transformation.

To mention only a few manifestations of this tendency, which clearly

---

236 Mao, *SW*, 18–19.

reflects Mao's long-standing conviction that by changing people's attitudes through indoctrination or thought reform, one can change their objective nature, there was the emphasis on a "great revolution which touches people to their very souls." That is to say, the Cultural Revolution was to constitute a process of subjective transformation leading to a new political identity. There was also the whole range of ideas and policies summed up by the slogan "Fight self, oppose revisionism," with the implication that "bourgeois" tendencies were to be found even in the hearts of veteran revolutionaries and proletarian fighters, if not in that of the Chairman himself.

Finally, however violent the resulting struggles, and however frenzied the enthusiasm they unleashed, can these events be called a revolution? Broadly speaking, there are two commonly accepted meanings for the word "revolution"; it may refer either to the conquest of power by a different class, social category, or political faction, or to the use that is made of power, once attained, to transform society. Theoretically, China had, in Mao's view, been carrying out socialist revolution in this second sense since 1949, and especially since 1955. As I have already noted, however, the concrete economic dimension of "building socialism" did not figure very extensively in Mao's scheme of things during his last decade. The transformation of attitudes is, of course, a form of social transformation, but even this came, in the end, to play a relatively limited role. The dominant concern was rather with the "seizure of power" from the "bourgeoisie."

Such an enterprise was possible in a country that had been ruled for seventeen years by a "dictatorship of the proletariat" only thanks to the redefinition of the class enemy from whom power was to be seized as the "bourgeois elements" and "capitalist roaders" in the Party – that is, all those who had ventured to disagree with Mao Tse-tung about anything from material incentives to literature and philosophy. So in the last analysis, the Cultural Revolution was a "revolution" only by virtue of an ideological and cultural definition of its target and goal.

Ironically, the Cultural Revolution, which had opened with manifestos in favor of the Paris Commune model of mass democracy, closed with paeans of praise to that most implacable of centralizing despots, the first Ch'in emperor. This decade saw the rise and fall of Lin Piao and of the influence of the PLA; the fall, rise, and renewed partial eclipse of the Party, in favor of the "Legalist leading group around the emperor (or around the empress)."[237]

237 Liang Hsiao, "Yen-chiu Ju-Fa tou-cheng ti li-shih ching-yen" (Study the historical experience of the struggle between the Confucian and Legalist schools), HC, 1974.10, 60; PR, 1975.2, 11.

Apart from Lin Piao's probable reluctance to accept the renewed subordination of the army to the Party, the reasons for his fall are of little interest here. This affair, though it throws light on the functioning of the Chinese political system, is scarcely relevant to the analysis of Mao Tse-tung's thought. The "Campaign to criticize Lin Piao and Confucius," on the other hand, is not merely a fascinating puzzle for Pekingologists; it also had significant theoretical implications.

One crucial aspect of the campaign in this respect was the veritable cult of Ch'in Shih-huang-ti that developed in 1973–74. It is only an apparent paradox that the "Shanghai radicals" should have propagated such an ideal of centralized rule by an autocratic leader, for anarchy and despotism are two maladies of the body politic which engender one another.

In the Great Leap period, as we have seen, Mao had not hesitated to praise Ch'in Shih-huang-ti and to evoke him as a precursor. But this does not necessarily mean that he took, then or later, the same view of the historical significance of the Ch'in unification of the empire as did the ideologists of 1973–75. At that time, Chairman Mao was said to have expounded, in his speech of 1958, quoted earlier, "the progressive role of revolutionary violence, and exposed the reactionary essence of attacks on Ch'in Shih-huang as attacks on revolutionary violence and the dictatorship of the proletariat."[238] The conclusion, which is never stated outright, but is clearly implicit in materials of the mid-1970s, is that the Ch'in Shih-huang-ti analogy should, as it were, be turned inside out. Lin Piao had criticized Mao as a despot; right-minded people should, on the contrary, see Ch'in Shih-huang-ti as a revolutionary leader and the Ch'in autocracy as a kind of protoproletarian dictatorship.

The analogy obviously requires that there should have been a change in the "mode of production," that is, in the ruling class, and not merely a change in the organization of the state, with the founding of the dynasty. The transition from slaveholding society to feudalism, which Mao himself had earlier placed (in the original version of "The Chinese revolution and the Chinese Communist Party") in the eleventh century B.C., was therefore brought forward to the fifth, or even the third, century B.C. Conceivably, Mao might have changed his mind on this point since 1939, and in any case the views put forward in 1972–74 had long been held by some Chinese historians. It is quite another matter to suggest, however, even if there *was* a change in the ruling class at the end of the third century B.C., that the "new rising landlord class" was consciously reshaping Chinese society, taking Legalist ideology as its guide, in the same sense that the

238 Chin Chih-pai, "P'i-K'ung yü lu-hsien tou-cheng" (Criticism of Confucius and two-line struggle), *HC*, 1974.7, 32; *PR*, 1974.33, 11 (and note 2).

Communists, armed with Marxism-Leninism–Mao Tse-tung Thought, are doing so today. Such a view was totally un-Marxist, and historically absurd, and there is no evidence that Mao ever espoused it.

The only justification for this line of argument would appear to reside in a desire to demonstrate that China had revolutionary power, and revolutionary ideology, before anyone else. In other words, in putting forward the Ch'in Shih-huang-ti analogy, Yao Wen-yuan and the other theoreticians of the Gang of Four were, in reality, disciples of Lin Piao, baptizing "class struggle" an exceedingly old-fashioned Chinese view of politics as a succession of palace coups. Mao's position was subtler, and despite his pride in China's cultural heritage, less narrowly nationalistic.

Nevertheless, the mid-1960s had seen, as already stressed, a further unraveling of the polarity between Marxism and the Chinese tradition in Mao Tse-tung's thought, in the context of a general trend toward the dissociation of opposite insights held in creative tension.

As has already been suggested, it can be argued that the changes in Mao's philosophical outlook at this time resulted from the resurgence of Chinese influences in his thinking, and in particular from a drift toward a quasi-Taoist understanding of the relation between opposites in terms of ebb and flow, such that the direction of historical change was no longer built into the structure of the dialectical process. But Mao's pessimism about the prospects for revolution also grew out of his fear of "restoration" in China and the Soviet Union. It was because the pursuit of the more moderate course that he had himself worked out with Chou En-lai only a year or two earlier conjured up once more in his mind the specter of "revisionism" that Mao had endorsed, in 1973, the *P'i-Lin p'i-K'ung* campaign of which Chou was the real target. It was the same bugbear that led him to support wholeheartedly the "campaign to study the theory of the proletarian dictatorship" launched by Chang and Yao in the spring of 1975.[239]

Joseph Esherick draws a distinction between Lenin, who "always identified the primary threat of capitalist restoration with the spontaneous capitalist tendencies of the 'small-producer economy,'" and Mao, who saw the main danger of restoration in the emergence of a new class in the Party and state bureaucracy.[240] This approach leads him to put forward the idea of the new bourgeoisie as a potential hereditary ruling class in a socialist society that has taken the road of revisionism and "restoration." He calls attention to a striking passage in Mao's notes of 1960 on the Soviet textbook regarding the defects of the children of cadres:

239 Liao, "Li-shih ti ching-yen," 147; English in *Issues & Studies* (November 1981), 98.
240 Joseph W. Esherick, "On the 'restoration of capitalism': Mao and Marxist theory," *Modern China*, 5 (January 1979), 57–58, 71–72.

The children of our cadres are a source of great concern. They have no experience of life and no experience of society, but they put on very great airs, and have very great feelings of superiority. We must teach them not to rely on their parents, nor on revolutionary martyrs, but to rely entirely on themselves.[241]

Recalling Mao's disparaging comments in the 1960s, to Snow and others, about the defects of China's youth, Esherick argues that, in Mao's view, these sons and daughters of cadres might inherit the status and privileges of their parents, thus constituting a "vested interest group" that, by perpetuating itself over several generations, would transform itself into a class.[242]

The difficulty with this argument is that it fails to provide any serious analysis of the relation between such a bureaucratic stratum and the rest of society, or any real justification for calling it a class. I do not mean to suggest that an argument cannot be made for focusing on control rather than ownership of the means of production, and treating existing socialist systems as forms of "state capitalism," ruled by a "new class" or "new bourgeoisie" defined in this context. From Djilas to Bahro, a great many people have done just that during the past three decades. Moreover, on the basis of all the available evidence, it appears that Mao himself leaned in this direction in his later years. Not only did he accept K'ang Sheng's view that in a socialist society, classes manifested themselves "ideologically and politically" rather than in terms of relation to the means of production, but he actually did subscribe to the view, put forward in 1975–76, that in China the bourgeoisie was to be found primarily, or decisively, in the Party. Moreover, he accepted the logical conclusion from such a premise, namely, that these "new bourgeois elements" exploited the workers and peasants through the mechanism of the socialist system, that is, of the state apparatus.[243]

Even if we conclude, however, that Mao held such a view in the early 1970s, he did not produce a systematic argument to justify it – indeed, by that time he was probably incapable of doing so. Nor, in my opinion, have those Western scholars who have written on these issues done so on his behalf.[244]

On the problem of the relation between the old and the new bourgeoisie, Chang and Yao, while discussing at considerable length the sel-

241 Wan-sui (1969), 351.
242 Esherick, "On the 'restoration of capitalism,'" 66–68.
243 This statement regarding Mao's position during his last years corresponds to the view commonly expressed by responsible theoretical workers, at the Chinese Academy of Social Sciences and elsewhere, in conversations conducted in April and May 1982. See also Liao, "Li-shih ti ching-yen," 135–36; English in Issues & Studies (November 1981), 84–85.
244 The study by Richard Kraus, Class conflict in Chinese socialism, is a far more important contribution to the subject in general than Esherick's article. On many aspects of the problem of the relation

fish and corrupt behavior of privileged strata among the leading cadres, in terms derived from Mao, treat these "extremely isolated persons" rather as the tools of those remnants of the "overthrown reactionary classes" who desire the restoration of capitalism in the literal sense. If the role of "bourgeois right" and material incentives is not restricted, writes Yao Wen-yuan:

... capitalist ideas of making a fortune and craving for personal fame and gain will spread unchecked; phenomena like the turning of public property into private property, speculation, graft and corruption, theft and bribery will increase; the capitalist principle of the exchange of commodities will make its way into political and even into Party life, undermining the socialist planned economy; acts of capitalist exploitation such as the conversion of commodities and money into capital, and labour power into a commodity, will occur.... When the economic strength of the bourgeoisie has grown to a certain extent, its agents will demand political rule, demand the overthrow of the dictatorship of the proletariat and the socialist system, demand a complete changeover from socialist ownership, and openly restore and develop the capitalist system.[245]

This analysis is likewise ill worked out, and even more difficult to reconcile with reality than that in terms of a new bureaucratic elite controlling the means of production. Was the pre-1949 bourgeoisie really so powerful in China a quarter of a century after the revolution? Above all, how could the "new class elements" within the Party, who reveled in their power and perquisites under the existing order, willingly participate in the restoration of actual capitalism, involving the private ownership of the means of production? Surely they must have realized that, in such a system, they would be very poorly equipped to compete with the "real" capitalists of yore, and would soon lose their privileged position? And yet, both of the perspectives just evoked regarding the role of the "new class" in Chinese society build explicitly on tendencies apparent in Mao's own writings from the late 1950s onward.

To a large extent, Mao's primary concern was with the resurgence in China, after the revolution, of "bourgeois" attitudes such as attachment to money, pleasure, and privilege. Such deviations would, in his view, be encouraged by inequality of material rewards – hence his support, qualified or not, for the campaign of 1975 against "bourgeois right." But in the last analysis he was more concerned with the struggle to transform

between stratification based on class origins, and "class as political behavior," Kraus offers extremely subtle and illuminating analyses. I believe that he errs, however, as does Esherick, in arguing that in his later years, Mao defined class primarily in terms of the privileges, and the control of the means of production, derived by cadres from their relationship to the state.

245 Yao Wen-yuan, On the social basis of the Lin Piao anti-Party clique, 7–8.

"hearts" or "souls." If he focused his attention on "bourgeois elements" in the Party, this was partly because such people enjoyed more of the privileges likely to corrupt them, and more of the power and influence that would enable them to corrupt others.

At the same time, it should be stressed that in Mao's view, the source of corruption was not merely the rewards of power, but power itself. In one of the very last directives published in his lifetime, Mao was quoted in May 1976 as saying that revolutions would continue to break out in future because "junior officials, students, workers, peasants and soldiers do not like big shots oppressing them."[246] There is no way of verifying the authenticity of this text, but it sounds very much like the irrepressible Mao. Although he remained committed to the need for leadership, and for a strong state, he was plainly skeptical that anyone – except the emperor himself – could be trusted with power.

I have stressed repeatedly that the remarkable and extreme tendencies in Mao's thought and behavior during his last years were based, to a substantial extent, on his conclusions regarding the measures necessary to ensure the thoroughgoing and systematic realization of Marxist ideals or principles such as struggle against the class enemy, the reduction of the differences between town and countryside, and the creation of a more egalitarian society. But although such ideas of Western origin, however oddly interpreted, remained a significant component of his thought, there is no denying the increasingly large place occupied in Mao's mind, and in the Chinese political system, by Chinese and traditional influences.

Apart from the cult of Ch'in Shih-huang-ti discussed above, a notable manifestation of this trend was the stress on devotion to the Leader and his Thought, symbolized by the value of "loyalty" (*chung*). Not only were "proletarian revolutionaries" such as the Red Guards to learn by heart the "little red book," so they could repeat a suitable saying on every occasion and thereby demonstrate their mastery of Mao Tse-tung Thought. They were also to be "boundlessly loyal to Chairman Mao," and this quality above all others was the touchstone for distinguishing genuine from sham revolutionaries in the China of the late 1960s and the early 1970s.

In the *Tso-chuan*, under the ninth year of Duke Ch'eng, it is written: *Wu ssu, chung yeh.* Loosely translated, this can be taken to mean "He who is selfless is truly loyal [to the ruler]." The Chinese, in Mao's last years, read this equation both backward and forward. On the one hand, he who was genuinely selfless, who was willing to serve the people like Lei Feng as a "rustless screw," was a true and loyal disciple of Chairman Mao and a genuine proletarian revolutionary. But conversely, he who was loyal to Mao Tse-tung and Mao Tse-tung Thought became, by that very fact, selfless and proletarian, and endowed with all the other revolutionary virtues.[247] In this respect, as in the use of the parallel with Ch'in Shih-huang-ti, Mao truly moved, at the end of his life, from expressing Marxist ideas in a language accessible to the Chinese people to a somewhat eclectic position in which traditional values and ideas played an increasingly large part.

CONCLUSION: IN SEARCH OF MAO'S IDEOLOGICAL LEGACY

The term "Mao Tse-tung Thought," or "Mao Tse-tung's Thought," has at least three different meanings. First of all, it can be used to signify what Mao himself actually thought, in the course of his long life, as evidenced by contemporary sources for the writings of each period. Second, it may have the sense given to it in China from the 1950s until Mao's death (or, indeed, until the Third Plenum, in December 1978); that is, it may refer to the orthodox doctrine at any given time, as laid down in the post-1951 edition of the *Selected works* and in other speeches and writings openly published, including the extracts issued during the Cultural Revolution period as "supreme directives." Third, it can be used as the Chinese use it today, to designate that portion of the total corpus of Mao Tse-tung's writings still regarded as correct, complemented by works in which Chou En-lai, Liu Shao-ch'i, Chu Te, and others further developed some of Mao's ideas, but without those writings by Mao reflecting the "errors of his later years."

This chapter has continued the attempt begun in the closing chapter of Volume 13 of *The Cambridge History of China* to trace the development of Mao Tse-tung's thought, in the first sense, from 1917 to 1976. The present chapter has also dealt with the problem of changing patterns of orthodoxy grounded in Mao's writings, which did not exist for the period before 1949 because there was no official canon and no such ortho-dox interpretation of "Mao Tse-tung Thought." Now, the task remains of summing up the essence of Mao's theoretical contribution, but of doing so on a basis rather different from that currently adopted in China.

It is often suggested that the approach of the present leaders of China

247 For a discussion of the significance of *chung*, and more broadly of the nature of Mao's rule in his last days, see Schram, "Party leader or true ruler?" 223–25, 233–43.

to Mao Tse-tung Thought is altogether arbitrary, manipulative, and cynical – in other words, that they characterize as "correct" those ideas of Mao's which will serve to justify the policies they have laid down on a quite different basis. That seems to be far too simple a view. Apart from the need to adopt enough of Mao's ideological heritage to demonstrate that they are his legitimate successors, those engaged in defining and elaborating Mao Tse-tung Thought today are for the most part veterans of decades of revolutionary struggle under Mao's leadership, who cannot but have internalized and built into their own thinking many ideas and practices from the era of Mao Tse-tung. It is therefore not implausible to accept that the current attempt at a redefinition of Mao's Thought has the aim that is attributed to it, namely, to determine what portions of his heritage are correct, in the dual sense of being good Marxism, and of being adapted to China's needs.

Even if this is so, however, the goals, and therefore the logic and the criteria, of the ongoing Chinese reassessment are different from those of this chapter. Here, our concern is rather with what constitutes the essence of Mao's thinking about problems of socialist development, from 1949 to 1976.

In the past, this chapter's author referred to the substance of Mao Tse-tung's positive contribution to the theory of building socialism as "mainstream Maoism," and suggested that it could be found in the period 1955–65, and more precisely in the early 1960s.[248] In other words, "mainstream Maoism" was defined as the rational kernel of the "Chinese road to socialism" devised by Mao, minus the excesses of the Great Leap and the Cultural Revolution. On further reflection, this usage seems less than satisfactory. As argued, the progression from 1958 to 1966 was in many respects inexorable, and the leftist tide that carried everything before it in the course of both these radical experiments might well be regarded as more characteristic of Mao's last quarter century (if not of his life as a whole) than the relatively prudent and realistic position he adopted in the early 1960s, and again in the early 1970s.

"In all things, one divides into two," said Mao in March 1964. "I, too, am a case of one divides into two."[249] That is, perhaps, the first and most fundamental thing that must be said by way of conclusion. On the one hand, Mao's thought from beginning to end, and especially his thought of the 1950s and 1960s, was an uneasy juxtaposition of disparate ideas and imperatives. And second, the provisional and unstable synthesis he had

248 See in particular Stuart Schram, *Mao Zedong: a preliminary reassessment*, 71.
249 *Wan-sui* (1969), 477; *Miscellany*, 343. (Remarks at a briefing.)

managed to forge between these elements began to unravel and fly apart with the onset of the Cultural Revolution.

If we look at Mao's economic ideas during and after the Great Leap Forward as formulated at the time, we must recognize, in my opinion, that they are far less one-sided and simplistic than they have commonly been made out to be in recent years, in interpretations based on the Cultural Revolution reconstruction of the "struggle between two lines." We find him placing stress equally on moral *and* material incentives, on redness *and* expertise, and on large- and small-scale industry. The policy of "walking on two legs," which was in some respects the heart of his whole economic strategy, was a policy of walking as fast as possible on both legs, and not of hopping along on the leg of small-scale indigenous methods alone.

And yet, there are aspects of Mao Tse-tung's approach to development, even after he had retreated from the extravagant illusions of the summer of 1958, that reflect a fundamental ambiguity toward the implications of industrialization and technical progress. One of these, to which I devoted considerable attention earlier, was his attitude toward the intellectuals. Another was his conception of the political process, and of the relation between the leaders and the masses.

In 1960, discussing the Soviet Constitution, Mao Tse-tung said that this constitution gave the workers the right to work, to rest, and to education, but that it gave the people no right to supervise (*cheng-li*) the state, the economy, culture or education, whereas these were the most basic rights of the people under socialism.[250] A parallel passage in the "Reading notes" uses the term *kuan-li*, instead of *cheng-li*.[251] Although there is a significant nuance between these two expressions, both are relatively ambiguous, and their ambiguity reflects, once again, the contradictions we have already noted in Mao's theory and practice of the "mass line." *Kuan-li*, the term that appears in Mao's own words as reproduced by the Red Guards, may mean "manage," "run," "administer," or "supervise"; *cheng-li*, employed by Liao Kai-lung in his paraphrase, signifies "put in order," "straighten out," or "arrange." The first is obviously more concrete, evoking an organizational context rather than simply a process. Both are equally vague as to whether the workers, or toilers (*lao-tung che*) are intended by Mao essentially to keep track of what is going on, and to make sure that political authority is exercised in accordance with their wishes, or whether he means they should actually *run* things themselves.

250 Liao, "Ch'üan-mien chien-she she-hui-chu-i ti tao-lu," 2.
251 *Wan-sui* (1969), 342–43.

One of the English translations of Mao's "Reading notes" has "run" and "manage" for *kuan-li*; the other has "administer" and "take charge."[252] I have preferred "supervise," which does not imply that the workers, collectively, are all actually taking charge to the same degree, because such a reading corresponds better to Mao's thought in 1960 as I understand it. This choice is, admittedly, arbitrary, but no more so than that of the other translators. The ambiguity is in fact there, in Mao's own language, and in his thought.

Another case in point is the passage of 1965 asserting that democracy means "dealing with the affairs of the masses through the masses themselves" (*ch'ün-chung ti shih-ch'ing yu ch'ün-chung lai kuan-li*).[253] For the character *yu* can mean either *by* the masses, in the sense that they are the effective agents, or *through* the masses, in other words, to mean that the matter is laid before them and they are consulted. Here, it is translated as "through" because the clear statement, in the same text of December 1965, about the need for Party leadership from above confirms that, at the time, Mao still held to the view, which he had clearly and repeatedly stated, that centralism was even more important than democracy. And yet by 1965 his approach to these matters was clearly beginning to shift.

During the period before and after the Great Leap, the emphasis on centralism took the form of an insistence on the crucial and decisive role of Party leadership. As noted in the first section of this chapter, Mao revived the concept of *i-yuan-hua*, or integrated Party control, which had been so much stressed in Yenan.

Generally speaking, Mao's view during the Great Leap period was that integration or *i-yuan-hua* had to be carried out not merely at the national level, but in the localities. Otherwise, even the "small power" referred to in the 1953 jingle could not be dispersed without leading to confusion. And the agent of integration could only be the Party committee at each level. Party control, whether at the center or in the localities, involved, as Mao made clear in 1958, first taking decisions on matters of principle, and then subsequently checking on their implementation.

With the approach of the Cultural Revolution, this whole philosophy was undermined because Mao Tse-tung called into question in theory, and then denied in practice, the legitimacy and political rectitude of the Party that was supposed to exercise the function of "integration." One of the first and most dramatic hints of what was to come is to be found in the famous passage from the Ninth Reply to the Soviets, dated 14 July

---

252 Mao Tse-tung, *A critique of Soviet economics*, tr. Moss Roberts, 61; *Miscellany*, 266.
253 *Wan-sui* (1969), 630.

1964, stating that if cadres were to be "corrupted, divided, and demoralized" by the class enemy (made up of "the landlords, rich peasants, counter-revolutionaries, bad elements and monsters of all kinds"), then "it
would not take long ... before a counter-revolutionary restoration on
a national scale inevitably occurred, the Marxist-Leninist party would
undoubtedly become a revisionist party or a fascist party, and the whole
of China would change its colour."[254]

Although Mao reasserted, in his conversations of February 1967 with
Chang and Yao, that there had to be a Party as a leading nucleus, and
although he continued to strive to combine in some fashion the need for
leadership with the anti-elitism and the encouragement of initiative from
below that had constituted the justification (if not the principal motive)
for the Cultural Revolution, this whole enterprise was distorted and
vitiated by the fact that the right of the masses to "rebel" against the
Party hierarchy and state bureaucracy was guaranteed only by a figure
exercising personal authority of a kind that soon came to be officially
likened to that of the first Ch'in emperor.

It is in this light that one must interpret the calls by Wang Hung-wen
at the Tenth Party Congress[255] and by Chang Ch'un-ch'iao at the National People's Congress in January 1975[256] for the "integrated [i-yuan-hua]
leadership" of the Party over the state structure, and over everything
else. For by this time, neither Chang, nor indeed Mao himself, were so
much interested in the relation between organizations as in imposing Mao
Tse-tung's personal authority. Henceforth, truth and authority resided
not in the Party, but in Chairman Mao, the leader invested by history
with the mission of educating the Chinese people and guiding them
toward communism.

Throughout his career, from the Ching-kang-shan and Yenan to the
1960s, Mao Tse-tung treated democracy and centralism as two indisso-
lubly linked aspects of the political process, one of which could not be
promoted without reference to the other. The Cultural Revolution saw
the emergence of two quite different concepts. Democracy was replaced
by "rebellion"; centralism was replaced by chung, or personal loyalty to
the great leader and helmsman. No doubt Mao Tse-tung saw these
tendencies as bound together in a dialectical unity, like democracy and
centralism, which he had not in principle repudiated. Nevertheless, he
allowed a situation to develop in which the "heads," of which he himself
acknowledged the necessity, at all levels of society and the economy,

254 HC, 1964.13, 31-32; PR, 1964. 29, 26. (Originally from a note by Mao on a document of 9 May
      1963 regarding cadre participation in productive labor in Chekiang.)
255 HC, 1973.9, 22, 27; PR, 1973.35-36, 25, 28.   256 HC, 1975.2, 17; PR, 1975.4, 19.

could not in fact function as heads, because although they were held accountable, they had no power to make decisions. The alliance between the leader and the masses took the form, on the national level, of an unstructured plebiscitary democracy, sadly reminiscent of earlier examples. At lower levels, it produced a mixture of arbitrary rule by ad hoc committees, military control, apathy, and confusion.

The roots of these last developments go back to the 1960s, and in particular to Mao's repeated statements, beginning in 1963, asserting the axiom "One divides into two." For it is only if the Party is in reality symbolized by and incarnated in one man that the two principles of *i-yuan-hua* or "making monolithic," and *i fen wei erh*, or the divisibility of all things (and the propensity of their components to struggle with one another) can coexist. In other words, the Communist Party could split, and yet remain one, capable of carrying out its mission of integration, only if its oneness and integrity were the emanation of Chairman Mao, who (despite his remark quoted earlier) did not split, but remained permanently in charge, even though his thoughts teemed with contradictions.

Another duality central to the interpretation of Mao's thought was, as I have stressed throughout this account, that between Marxism and the Chinese heritage. The fact that, in Mao's later years, the leader had come to be the focus of loyalty and the fount of truth is not in harmony with Marxist theory, or indeed with Mao's own reminder, in 1971, of the words of the "Internationale" denying the existence of "supreme saviours."[257] This does not, in itself, make of his rule a species of oriental despotism, nor does it even signify that the ideology to which he lent his name was primarily Chinese rather than Western. There were, after all, sufficient Western or Westernizing sources for the cult of the leader – including Stalin's red fascism, as well as the original doctrines of Hitler and Mussolini. Moreover, in the complex process of acculturation, if new Western ideas can be made to serve old Chinese goals and values, Chinese forms can also be turned to purposes defined by foreign doctrines.[258] The final balance is therefore not easy to draw up, but the problem merits a few final reflections.

Between the mid-1950s and the mid-1960s, Mao Tse-tung moved from the rejection to the acceptance of Chang Chih-tung's principle "Chinese learning as the substance, Western learning for practical application." In his "Talk to music workers" of August 1956, he adopted the relatively balanced view he had expounded since 1938, namely that China must

257 Schram, *Mao unrehearsed*, 297.
258 On this theme, see Schram, "Party leader or true ruler?"

learn many things from the West, while remaining herself. Marxism, he declared, was a "general truth which has universal application." This "fundamental theory produced in the West" constituted the foundation, or *t'i*, of China's new regime, although it must be combined with the concrete practice of each nation's revolution.[259] In December 1965, at Hangchow, on the other hand, he said in effect that Chang Chih-tung was right: "We cannot adopt Western learning as the substance.... We can only use Western technology."[260]

Even though Mao declared in the same speech, as noted earlier, that he was a "native philosopher," such remarks should not be understood to mean that Mao no longer proposed to take anything from Marxism, or from the West. They were rather an emphatic way of saying that China's revolutionary doctrine today must be rooted in her culture, and in her past, if borrowings from the West were to be put to good use. The problem is not, however, one that can fruitfully be approached in purely intellectual terms, through the dissection of Mao's theoretical formulations. Deep-rooted feelings also come into it, and color even his political or ideological statements.

In March 1958 at Chengtu, Mao declared: "First classes wither away, and then afterward the state withers away, and then after that nations [*min-tsu*] wither away, it is like this in the whole world."[261] Talking to Edgar Snow on 18 December 1970, Mao put the matter as follows:

What is a nation [*min-tsu*]? It includes two groups of people [*liang pu-fen jen*], one group consists of the upper strata, the exploiting classes, a minority. These people know how to speak [effectively], and to organize a government, but they don't know how to fight, or to till the land, or to work in a factory. More than 90 per cent of the people are workers, peasants, and petty bourgeoisie; without these people, it is impossible to constitute a nation [*tsu-ch'eng min-tsu*].[262]

Mao's remarks of 1970 illustrate once again his tendency, in his later years, to see class struggle as a conflict between a small group of "big shots" and the people as a whole. But they also underscore, as does his comment of 1958, the fundamental importance he attached to the nation as a primary form of social organization.

Although Mao quite unquestionably always regarded China as the "central place," and Chinese culture as the "central flower" (*chung-hua*), we should by no means draw from this trait the conclusion, commonly put forward by the Soviets and their supporters, as well as by Trotskyites

259 Schram, *Mao unrehearsed*, 85-86.   260 Ibid., 234-35.
261 *Mao Chu-hsi kuan-yü kuo-nei min-tsu wen-t'i* ..., 8.
262 Ibid., 6-7. (This quote is from the official Chinese record of the talks; to my knowledge, Snow never made use of this passage in his own writings.)

and other leftists of various persuasions, that Mao was, after all, nothing but an old-fashioned Chinese nationalist with very little of the Marxist about him.

The fact remains that, during the Cultural Revolution decade especially, the synthesis toward which Mao had been bending his efforts for many decades largely fell apart, at least as regarded his own ideas and attitudes. Moral and political criteria drawn from the *Tso-chuan* and similar sources thus loomed very large in 1976, when Mao, as he put it to Edgar Snow, "saw God," or "saw Marx" (or perhaps both of them), and a new era opened under his successors.

If we look, however, not at these last sad, anticlimactic years but at the soberer elements in Mao's Thought, from 1935 to 1965, it seems to constitute, in the last analysis, rather a revolutionary ideology of Western origin, and a vehicle of Westernization.

No doubt, the crucial link between this Westernizing thrust and Mao Tse-tung's indisputable Sino-centrism is provided by his view regarding what has been called the "dialectics of backwardness." In his "Reading notes" of 1960, one of the quintessential expositions of "mainstream Maoism," Mao devoted a section to the topic "Is revolution in backward countries more difficult?" Needless to say, he concluded that it was not. The poisons of the bourgeoisie were, he said, extremely virulent in the advanced countries of the West, after two or three centuries of capitalism, and affected every stratum of society, including the working class. Lenin's dictum " The more backward the country, the more difficult its transition from capitalism to socialism" was therefore incorrect:

In reality, the more backward the economy, the easier, and not the more difficult, the transition from capitalism to socialism. The poorer people are, the more they want revolution.... In the East, countries such as Russia and China were originally backward and poor. Now not only are their social systems far more advanced than those of the West, but the rate of development of the productive forces is far more rapid. If you look at the history of the development of the various capitalist countries, it is again the backward which have overtaken the advanced. For example, the United States surpassed Britain at the end of the 19th century, and Germany also surpassed Britain in the early 20th century.[263]

This extravagantly optimistic vision has, of course, today been repudiated in China, and emphasis has been placed, rather, on the need to develop the productive forces as a precondition to the transformation of the social system. Mao's view, expressed in the passage just quoted, that in the West (and, by implication, in China, once the economy has been

263 *Wan-sui* (1969), 333–34; *Miscellany*, 258–59.

developed) "the important question is the transformation of the people" (*jen-min ti kai-tsao*) has not, however, been similarly abandoned.

Perhaps, in the end, this vision of China's place in the world and this emphasis on the human and moral dimension of politics will remain among Mao Tse-tung's main contributions to the theory and practice of revolution, because these insights are grounded in a long historical perspective.

PART I

THE CULTURAL REVOLUTION: CHINA IN TURMOIL, 1966–1969

CHAPTER 2

THE CHINESE STATE IN CRISIS

The Great Proletarian Cultural Revolution, which by official Chinese reckoning lasted from the beginning of 1966 to the death of Mao Tse-tung some ten years later, was one of the most extraordinary events of this century. The images of the Cultural Revolution remain vivid: the young Red Guards, in military uniform, filling the vast T'ien An Men Square in Peking, many weeping in rapture at the sight of their Great Helmsman standing atop the Gate of Heavenly Peace; veteran Communist officials, wearing dunce caps and placards defiling them as "monsters" and "freaks," herded in the backs of open-bed trucks, and driven through the streets of major cities by youth only one-third their age; the wall posters, often many sheets of newsprint in size, filled with vitriolic condemnations of the "revisionist" or "counterrevolutionary" acts of senior leaders. The little red book carried by the Red Guards – a plastic-bound volume containing selected quotations from Chairman Mao – remains a symbol of the revolt of the young against adult authority.

From a purely narrative perspective, the Cultural Revolution can best be understood as a tragedy, for both the individual who launched it and the society that endured it. The movement was largely the result of the decisions of a single man, Mao Tse-tung. Mao's restless quest for revolutionary purity in a postrevolutionary age provided the motivation for the Cultural Revolution, his unique charismatic standing in the Chinese Communist movement gave him the resources to get it under way, and his populist faith in the value of mass mobilization lent the movement its form. Mao's breadth of vision and his ability to shape the destiny of 800 million Chinese are the elements of myth, producing a man who appears larger than life.

But, as in classical tragedy, these seemingly heroic elements were, in the end, fatally flawed. Mao's quest for revolutionary purity led him to exaggerate and misappraise the political and social problems confronting China in the mid-1960s. His personal authority gave him enough power to unleash potent social forces, but not enough power to control them. And his confidence that the masses, once mobilized, would be the sal-

MAP 1. China's physical features

0 ⊢———⊢———⊢———⊢———⊢ 500 km
0 ⊢———⊢———⊢———⊢ 300 miles

┉┉┉ Grand Canal

〰〰〰 Great Wall

)(Pass

vation of the country proved woefully misplaced as the mass movement degenerated into violence, factionalism, and chaos. The Cultural Revolution, which Mao hoped would be his most significant and most enduring contribution to China and to Marxism-Leninism, instead became the monumental error of his latter years.

Because of Mao's ability to move China, what was a tragedy for the man became simultaneously a tragedy for the nation. China's leaders now describe the Cultural Revolution as nothing less than a calamity for their country. Although the economic damage done by the Cultural Revolution was not as severe as that produced by the Great Leap Forward, and although the human costs were not as devastating as those of the Taiping Rebellion, the Japanese invasion, or the Communist revolution itself, the effects of the Cultural Revolution in terms of careers disrupted, spirits broken, and lives lost were ruinous indeed. The impact of the movement on Chinese politics and society may take decades finally to erase. What is more, these costs of the Cultural Revolution were largely the predictable consequences of Mao's perception that China was on the brink of the restoration of capitalism, and of his prescription that the mobilization of urban youth was the best way to prevent it.

From a different point of view, that of political analysis, the Cultural Revolution is equally intriguing. Political scientists have become accustomed to speaking of "crises" of political development, during which established political institutions are challenged and shaken by the pressures of economic transformation, intellectual ferment, political mobilization, and social change.[1] Unless effective reforms can be undertaken, political crises can produce violence and disorder, and even revolt and revolution. In this sense, the Cultural Revolution appears at first glance to have been similar to crises of political modernization experienced by many other developing countries in the twentieth century. The Chinese Communist Party faced high levels of urban protest, rooted in widespread dissatisfaction with a variety of social, economic, and organizational policies. It proved unable either to suppress the dissent or to accommodate it effectively. The result of these circumstances, in China as elsewhere, was chaos and anarchy, until the military intervened to restore order and begin the reconstruction of political institutions.

What is unique about the Cultural Revolution, however, is that this political crisis was deliberately induced by the leader of the regime itself. It was Mao who called into question the legitimacy of the Chinese Communist Party. It was Mao who mobilized the social forces that would

---

1 Leonard Binder, et al., *Crises and sequences in political development.*

undermine his own government. And it was Mao who provided the political and ideological vocabulary for protest and dissent. The man who had undertaken a revolution against China's old regime now sought to launch a revolt against the new political establishment that he himself had created.

But Mao's victory in his first revolution was not matched by comparable success in the second. Successful revolutions are, as Mao himself recognized, acts of construction as well as destruction: They build a new order, even as they destroy an old one. Mao's first revolution was guided not only by a critique of the existing system but also by a relatively coherent image of a new economic and political order. Similarly, the first revolution not only mobilized mass discontent but also produced a disciplined revolutionary organization, the Chinese Communist Party, that could govern effectively after the seizure of power. Mao's second revolution, in contrast, had no clear guiding vision, and produced no unified organization to implement a new set of programs and policies. It toppled the old regime, but left only chaos and disorder in its place.

This chapter is a history and analysis of the first three and a half years of the Cultural Revolution, from its initial stirrings in late 1965 to the convocation of the Ninth National Congress of the Chinese Communist Party in April 1969. This is the period that some have described as the "Red Guard" phase of the Cultural Revolution, and others as its manic stage. It is the period in which the political crisis induced by Mao was the deepest, the chaos the greatest, and the human costs the highest.

These three and a half years encompass several shorter periods, each of which is dealt with in turn in this chapter. First, there was the growing confrontation between Mao and the Party establishment from the fall of 1965 to the summer of the following year. During that period, Mao began to develop a power base with which to confront those leaders in the Party whom he regarded as revisionists. Using his political resources, Mao secured the dismissal or demotion of selected officials within the armed forces, the cultural establishment, the Peking municipal government, and the Politburo itself. Then, at the Eleventh Plenum in August 1966, Mao obtained the formal endorsement of the Party's Central Committee for a criticism of revisionism on an even broader scale.

The second period, from the Eleventh Plenum through the end of 1966, was one in which Mao's assault on the Party establishment spread across the country, with the Red Guards now its major instrument. The outcome of this period was not, however, what Mao had intended. He had apparently hoped that the Red Guards would form a unified mass movement, that officials would accept criticism from these ad hoc organizations in a sincere and open manner, and that the Party would therefore emerge from the Cultural Revolution with its orientation corrected and its authority intact. In fact, none of these developments occurred. The Red Guards split into competing organizations, with some attacking the Party establishment and others defending it. Party leaders at the provincial and municipal levels sought first to suppress the mass movement, then to co-opt it, and finally to evade it. The escalation of conflict, both between competing Red Guard organizations and between the mass movement and the Party establishment, served not to strengthen the authority of the Party but to weaken it. By the end of 1966, the political institutions in many of China's most important cities were in total collapse.

During the third period, from January 1967 until mid-1968, Mao ordered that political power be seized from the discredited Party establishment. After a few weeks of uncertainty as to the procedures by which this would be done, Mao decided that political power be shared, at the provincial and municipal levels, by coalitions of three forces: the mass organizations that had emerged during the Cultural Revolution, those cadres who were able to survive the movement, and the People's Liberation Army (PLA). The problem was that none of these groups was completely reliable. The mass organizations were prone to violence and anarchy, and the cadres and the PLA, particularly at the provincial and municipal levels, tended to work together to suppress the most obstreperous of the Red Guard activists. Unable completely to control the forces he had unleashed, Mao's only recourse was to play one against another. Once again, the result was near chaos, and Mao ultimately concluded that the only way to prevent collapse was to demobilize the Red Guards and allow the PLA to restore order.

This decision marked the beginning of the final stage under consideration in this chapter: the reconstruction of the Chinese political system. This process culminated with the Ninth Party Congress in April 1969, which elected a new Central Committee, approved a new Politburo, and adopted a new Party constitution. Given the preeminent role of the Chinese military during this period, it should not be surprising that army officers occupied the plurality of the leadership positions filled at the Ninth Congress, or that Minister of Defense Lin Piao secured anointment as Mao's successor. But even the growing power of the military in civilian affairs was not sufficient to restore political stability. Power remained divided among the radical intellectuals who had mobilized the Red Guards, the veteran officials who had survived their assault, and the military who had finally suppressed them. As later chapters in this volume will reveal, the legacy of the Red Guard stage of the Cultural Revolution was chronic instability that was ultimately to be removed only by the death of Mao Tse-tung, the purge of the radicals, and the emergence of Teng Hsiao-p'ing as China's preeminent leader.

TOWARD A CONFRONTATION

Sources of political conflict

Mao Tse-tung surveyed the political scene in China in the early 1960s with increasing dissatisfaction. On issue after issue, the Party had adopted policies that Mao regarded as unnecessary or unacceptable: a return to private farming in agriculture, the resurrection of material incentives in industry, a concentration on urban medicine in public health, the development of a two-track system in education, and the reappearance of traditional themes and styles in literature and the arts. Most of these policies had been advanced by their proponents as ways of restoring social cohesion and economic productivity after the Anti-Rightist Campaign and the Great Leap Forward. In Mao's view, however, these measures were creating a degree of inequality, specialization, hierarchy, and dissent that was incompatible with his vision of a socialist society.[2]

Mao's dissatisfaction with Party policies was exacerbated by growing personal tensions between the Chairman and some of his chief lieutenants. There were, to begin with, an increasing number of incidents that Mao chose to regard as acts of *lèse-majesté*. Although Mao had supposedly withdrawn voluntarily from day-to-day leadership in late 1958, he increasingly resented the way in which some leaders, particularly the Party's secretary-general, Teng Hsiao-p'ing, failed to consult with him before making decisions on major issues. In October 1966, for example, Mao would complain that "Whenever we are at a meeting together, [Teng] sits far away from me. For six years, since 1959, he has not made a general report of work to me."[3] In March 1961, when he discovered that Teng had made some major decisions on agricultural reorganization without consulting him, Mao asked sarcastically, "Which Emperor decided these?"[4] Mao was irritated by the allegorical criticisms of his leadership that began to appear in Chinese literature and journalism in the

---

2 On the emerging conflict between Mao and his colleagues in the early 1960s, see Byung-joon Ahn, *Chinese politics and the Cultural Revolution: dynamics of policy processes*; Harry Harding, *Organizing China: the problem of bureaucracy, 1949–1976*, ch. 7; Roderick MacFarquhar, *The origins of the Cultural Revolution. 2: the Great Leap Forward 1958–60*; and Kenneth Lieberthal's chapter in Volume 14 of *CHOC*.

3 Jerome Ch'en, ed., *Mao papers: anthology and bibliography*, 40.

4 Parris H. Chang, *Power and policy in China*, (rev. ed.), 131.

early 1960s, and must have been even more angered that officials responsible for intellectual matters, including P'eng Chen and Lu Ting-i, were
doing nothing to bring the offending writers to task.

In addition, Mao became increasingly frustrated by his inability to
bend the bureaucracy to his will. Between 1962 and 1965 he tried, in five
areas of long-standing personal interest, to alter the policies that the Party
had adopted in the immediate post-Leap period. Mao attempted to halt
trends toward private farming in agriculture, proposed reform of the
curriculum and examination system in higher education, criticized the
concentration of public health facilities in urban areas, proposed the creation of peasant organizations to uncover corruption and inefficiency
among rural Party and commune cadres, and denounced the reappearance
of traditional themes and revisionist theories in intellectual affairs.

Although the Party establishment ultimately responded to each of these
initiatives, it did so in a way that Mao justifiably believed to be half-
hearted and unenthusiastic. In part, this was because many senior leaders
continued to support the policies that had been adopted in the post-Leap
period and were reluctant to alter them at Mao's behest. In part, too, the
sluggishness in responding to Mao's wishes reflected the normal attempt
of bureaucracies to act gradually and incrementally, preserving as much
of existing routines as possible even while undertaking some of the
new initiatives that Mao proposed. Moreover, Mao's intentions were
often expressed in vague and ambiguous language, with the Chairman
better able to criticize emphatically tendencies he disliked than to suggest
concrete alternatives.

In any event, Mao's conclusion was that the sluggishness of the
bureaucracy, the emergence of traditional and "bourgeois" ideas in intellectual life, and the emphasis on efficiency in national economic strategy
together created the danger that revisionism – a fundamental departure
from a genuinely socialist path of development – was emerging in China.
At first, Mao voiced these concerns in a rather low-keyed manner. In
1962, for instance, he called on the Party to overcome revisionism, but
said that this task should not "interfere with our [routine] work ...
or be placed in a very prominent position."[5] Equally important, Mao
initially attempted to overcome revisionist tendencies in the Party
through rather modest and traditional means: the launching of campaigns
within the bureaucracy to study Marxist-Leninist doctrine and to emulate
model leaders.

But as the ineffectiveness of these measures became apparent, Mao's

5   Stuart R. Schram, ed., *Chairman Mao talks to the people: talks and letters, 1956–1971*, 193–95.

warnings became more pointed. He ultimately concluded that revisionism was more widespread than he had anticipated, and that the highest leaders of the Party, because of their reluctance to cope with the problem effectively, were possibly guilty of revisionist thinking themselves. At a work conference in September 1965, Mao asked his colleagues, "If revisionism appears in the Central Committee, what are you going to do? It is probable that it will appear, and this is a great danger."[6]

It was only gradually that these warnings about revisionism were transformed into a systematic theory justifying a Cultural Revolution. Significantly, in fact, the movement itself was launched before a full theoretical justification was provided for it. But two editorials published in 1967 have been identified by the Chinese as laying out in fullest form Mao's emerging theory of "continuing the revolution under the dictatorship of the proletariat."[7] Although these essays were not written by Mao himself, there is little reason to doubt that the ideas expressed in them reflected the Chairman's views.

Taken together, the editorials conclude that, in Mao's eyes, the greatest danger to a successful socialist revolution is not the threat of attack from abroad, but rather the restoration of capitalism at home. Mao believed that the experience of the Soviet Union after the death of Stalin proved that the restoration of capitalism could occur if "revisionists" usurped power within the ruling Communist Party. To prevent this, it would be necessary to wage continuing class struggle against those "Party persons in authority" who might attempt to follow the capitalist road. Indeed, this would be the major form of class struggle in socialist society after the nationalization of industry and the collectivization of agriculture. The method for waging this class struggle would be to "boldly arouse the masses from below" in a Cultural Revolution, in order to criticize not only revisionist power holders within the Party but also the selfish and liberal tendencies within their own minds. Because the problem of revisionism was thus rooted in human selfishness, it would be necessary to have a succession of Cultural Revolutions over many decades to preserve the purity of purpose of a socialist society.

---

6 Ch'en, *Mao papers*, 102.
7 Editorial department of *Jen-min jih-pao* and *Hung-ch'i*, "A great historic document," 18 May 1967, in *PR*, 19 May 1967, 10–12; and editorial departments of *Jen-min jih-pao, Hung-ch'i,* and *Chieh-fang-chün pao,* "Advance along the road opened up by the October socialist revolution," 6 November 1967, in *PR*, 10 November 1967, 9–11, 14–16. Recent accounts have revealed that the latter essay was drafted under the supervision of Ch'en Po-ta and Yao Wen-yuan. See Sun Tun-fan et al., eds., *Chung-kuo kung-ch'an-tang li-shih chiang-i* (Teaching materials on the history of the Chinese Communist Party), 2.268. (Hereafter *Li-shih chiang-i.*)

Forging Mao's power base

By 1964, the basis began to be created for such an assault on the Party
establishment. The elements of this power base were created, initially,
in a piecemeal and seemingly uncoordinated manner. One element was
produced by the impersonal operation of social and economic policy,
which created disadvantaged and disenchanted groups in society, particularly among the urban young. A second, under the guidance of Mao's
wife, Chiang Ch'ing, began to emerge in the intellectual and cultural
spheres. A third was produced, within the army, by Minister of Defense
Lin Piao. Between 1964 and 1966, these three elements were more systematically assembled into a political coalition that, under Mao's leadership,
was powerful enough to conduct the Great Proletarian Cultural Revolution against even an entrenched Party apparatus.

The People's Liberation Army. The most crucial element in Mao's power
base, given its control of organized armed force in China, was the
People's Liberation Army under the leadership of Lin Piao.[8] After succeeding P'eng Te-huai as minister of defense at the Lushan Plenum in
1959, Lin had devoted particular attention to reviving political work in
the military apparatus – a policy intended both to ensure the loyalty of the
armed forces to Maoist leadership and to bolster his own reputation in
Mao's eyes. Lin rebuilt the Party branches at the basic levels of the PLA,
resurrected the network of political departments that had deteriorated
under P'eng's stewardship, and tightened the control of the Party's Military Affairs Commission over military matters. Lin intensified the army's
program of political education, basing it in large part on a new compilation of quotations from Mao Tse-tung, a collection that would serve as
the model for the little red book later used by the Red Guards.

At the same time, Lin also sought to restore some of the military
traditions of the revolutionary period. In the 1950s, the organizational
and tactical principles of guerrilla warfare as practiced in the 1930s and
1940s had been set aside in favor of those characteristic of more regu-
larized armed forces. A formal system of ranks and insignia had been
instituted. The militia had been deemphasized, with P'eng Te-huai proposing that it be supplanted by a more formal system of military reserves.

8 On the People's Liberation Army in the early 1960s, see John Gittings, "The Chinese army's role
   in the Cultural Revolution," *Pacific Affairs*, 39.3–4 (Fall–Winter 1966–67), 269–89; John Gittings,
   The role of the Chinese army, ch. 12; Ellis Joffe, "The Chinese army under Lin Piao: prelude to political intervention," in John M. H. Lindbeck, ed., *China: management of a revolutionary society*, 343–74;
   and Ellis Joffe, *Party and army: professionalism and political control in the Chinese officer corps, 1949–
   1964*.

Greater priority had been placed on hierarchy and discipline, as against the "military democracy" of earlier years. Soviet military doctrine, with its stress on positional warfare and modern ordnance, replaced the Maoist doctrine of mobile warfare using primitive weapons.

A reaction against the abandonment of the PLA's revolutionary heritage in favor of these "foreign doctrines" was apparent as early as the mid-1950s. Accordingly, some attempts to redress the balance were undertaken in the latter part of the decade, while P'eng Te-huai still served as minister of defense. But the process of "re-revolutionization" accelerated under Lin Piao's leadership. New military manuals stressed such traditional concepts as joint command by political commissars and line officers, the importance of political work in maintaining the loyalty and morale of the troops, close ties between the army and civilian society, and egalitarian relations between officers and men. Military strategy once again emphasized the infantry (as opposed to specialized services), the militia (as opposed to the regular forces), and small-unit tactics (as opposed to maneuvers by larger, multiservice forces). Finally, in a step with enormous symbolic significance, military ranks were abolished in 1965, and officers removed the Soviet-style uniforms and insignia they had worn since the mid-1950s and returned to the unadorned olive-drab uniforms of the Yenan years.

And yet, Lin Piao never allowed this policy framework to weaken the military prowess of the PLA. Even as he proclaimed that men were more important than weapons in ensuring military victory, Lin simultaneously sponsored the modernization of the air force and the development of China's nuclear capability. He said that political education should have the highest priority in military training, but he saw to it that the troops actually devoted more time to military exercises than to ideological study. Lin reasserted the PLA's adherence to the principle of people's war, but the level of militia activity declined from the heights reached during the Great Leap Forward, and rural militia units devoted more attention to agricultural production and internal security than to military affairs.

Thus, during the early 1960s, Lin presided not only over the revitalization of the political structure in the armed forces and the restoration of some traditional military concepts, but also over the successful border campaign against India in 1962 and the detonation of China's first atomic bomb two years later. These achievements indicated that the "redness" of the PLA did not come at the expense of its military expertise.

The successful performance of the PLA in the early 1960s contrasted with the widely perceived decay of the Party and state agencies during the same period. It is little wonder, therefore, that Mao came to see Lin Piao as a more effective organizational manager and a more loyal lieutenant than either Liu Shao-ch'i or Teng Hsiao-p'ing, and began to identify the PLA as a model for civilian bureaucracies to emulate. To that end, a nationwide campaign to "Learn from the People's Liberation Army" was launched in February 1964. As part of that movement, the government bureaucracy was ordered to form political departments, modeled on those in the PLA, which would be responsible for the regular political education of civilian officials. Between 30 and 40 percent of the positions created in those new political departments were held by demobilized PLA cadres or by officers seconded from the armed forces.[9]

Lin Piao was hardly reluctant to see the army assume this new role. It is quite likely, in fact, that Lin suggested the formation of political departments in state agencies in the first place; and it is even possible that he proposed they be placed under the supervision of the General Political Department of the armed forces. If adopted, such a recommendation simultaneously would have dramatically increased the influence of the PLA in civilian affairs and would have made significant inroads into the traditional responsibilities of the Party organization. Although Liu Shao-ch'i accepted Mao's decision to establish political departments within government bureaus, he allegedly insisted that they be placed under the jurisdiction of the Party agencies responsible for economic work, rather than under the PLA's political apparatus.[10]

Even so, the initiation of the "Learn from the People's Liberation Army" Campaign and the creation of the political departments in the government bureaucracy gave the PLA and Lin Piao more influence over civilian affairs than at any time since the early 1950s. In February 1966, the PLA held a conference on cultural matters which, while nominally dealing only with literature and art in the armed forces, had great impact on civilian cultural circles as well.[11] And in March 1966, Lin wrote a letter to a work conference on industrial and commercial affairs advocating that economic administrators be more active in the study of Maoism – a relatively innocuous message, but one that symbolized Lin's growing ability to speak out on matters concerning national economic policy.[12]

9 On the campaign to learn from the People's Liberation Army, see Ahn, *Chinese politics*, ch. 6; John Gittings, "The 'Learn from the army' campaign," *CQ*, 18 (April–June 1964), 153–59; Harding, *Organizing China*, 217–23; and Ralph L. Powell, "Commissars in the economy: The 'Learn from the PLA' movement in China," *Asian Survey*, 5.3 (March 1965), 125–38.

10 Radio Peking, 16 December 1967, cited in John Gittings, "Army-Party relations in the light of the Cultural Revolution," in John Wilson Lewis, ed., *Party leadership and revolutionary power in China*, 395.

11 Kenneth Lieberthal, *A research guide to central Party and government meetings in China 1949–1975*, 238–39.

12 Michael Y. M. Kau, ed., *The Lin Piao affair: power politics and military coup*, 321–22.

The radical intellectuals. The second element in the nascent Maoist coalition was a group of radical intellectuals who, by mid-1966, would come to serve as the doctrinal arbiters and mass mobilizers of the Cultural Revolution. The key person in assembling these leftist propagandists and writers was Mao's wife, Chiang Ch'ing, who quickly realized that the emerging tensions between Mao and the Party establishment gave her an unusual opportunity to realize her own political ambitions.

Before traveling to Yenan to join the Communist movement in 1937, Chiang Ch'ing had been a second-string actress and an active participant in Shanghai's artistic and political demimonde. Her liaison with Mao in 1938 seemed at first to offer this ambitious woman the chance to switch from the theater to politics. But, given Chiang Ch'ing's rather checkered background, her marriage to the Chairman was bitterly opposed by many other senior Party leaders, and may have been accepted only after she agreed to refrain from political activity for thirty years.[13] Ill health forced her to keep the bargain throughout the 1950s; but in the early 1960s, with her health if not her temperament somewhat improved, she undertook a new project: the reform of Chinese culture. This was a task for which her earlier theatrical career had given her some minimal credentials, and for which Mao's growing impatience with "revisionism" in culture provided substantial encouragement and support.

Chiang's initial efforts to reform traditional Peking Opera encountered the disdain of established performers, the opposition of officials responsible for cultural affairs, and thus the neglect of the press.[14] Faced with these obstacles, Chiang turned to a group of young, relatively radical, intellectuals in Peking and Shanghai. Compared with more prestigious members of China's urban intelligentsia, these were younger men, lower in rank, less cosmopolitan in outlook, and more exclusively steeped in Marxist intellectual traditions. Many had taken, out of a combination of conviction and careerism, relatively radical positions on academic and cultural matters ever since the Anti-Rightist Campaign of 1957, and had been engaged in an ongoing debate with their more liberal seniors throughout the cultural relaxation of the early 1960s.[15]

Chiang Ch'ing developed contacts with two main groups of these radical intellectuals: one was centered in the Institute of Philosophy and Social Science of the Chinese Academy of Sciences in Peking (including

13 Ross Terrill, *The white-boned demon: a biography of Madame Mao Zedong*, 154.
14 On Chiang Ch'ing's role in this period, and her relationship with young, radical intellectuals, see Merle Goldman, *China's intellectuals: advise and dissent*, ch. 3; and Roxane Witke, *Comrade Chiang Ch'ing*, 321–22.
15 The distinction between the Shanghai and the Peking groups is drawn from Goldman, *China's intellectuals*, ch. 3.

Kuan Feng, Ch'i Pen-yü, and Lin Chieh), and another was centered in the Municipal Propaganda Department in Shanghai (including Chang Ch'un-ch'iao, the director of the bureau, and Yao Wen-yuan). The former group, more academic in character, specialized in history and philosophy. The Shanghai group, in contrast, was more experienced in journalistic criticism and more knowledgeable about the creative arts. Chiang's entrée to these groups was facilitated, in the case of Peking, by Ch'en Po-ta, who for years had served as Mao Tse-tung's personal secretary and theoretician; and, in the case of Shanghai, by K'o Ch'ing-shih, the Party chief for the East China region, who, unlike many Party leaders, remained close to Mao even after the debacle of the Great Leap Forward.

Between 1963 and 1966, Chiang Ch'ing and her coterie of intellectuals focused principally on cultural and artistic matters, particularly on her interest in the reform of Peking Opera and other performing arts. (In this undertaking another regional Party secretary, T'ao Chu of the Central-South region, also proved supportive of Chiang Ch'ing.) Gradually, however, as the confrontation between Mao and the Party establishment grew more intense, the radical intellectuals began to turn to more overtly political themes, providing, as we shall see, both the criticism of Mao's rivals and the ideological rationale for the Cultural Revolution.

This second element in the Maoist coalition, to use Lowell Dittmer's apposite expression, played the role of "imperial favorites."[16] The radical intellectuals had narrow careers, rather dogmatic and idealistic political positions, and little political standing independent of their association, through Chiang Ch'ing, with Mao. They had little stake in the established political order in China, and perceived clearly that their own careers would be advanced more rapidly through opposition to the system than through patient accommodation. But their power would increase as Mao found that their loyalty to him, their skills at propaganda, and their mastery of radical doctrine made them useful tools in his assault on the Party establishment.

A mass base. The final element in the Maoist coalition, latent until the middle and latter parts of 1966, was a mass base, composed of those elements of urban Chinese society that regarded themselves as disadvantaged. Paradoxically, social tensions in Chinese cities had been substantially increased by two policies, adopted under Mao's prodding, that were supposed to create a more egalitarian society: the reemphasis on class background in educational recruitment and job assignment, and a program of part-time industrial employment for suburban peasants.

16 Lowell Dittmer, "Bases of power in Chinese politics: a theory and an analysis of the fall of the 'Gang of Four,'" *World Politics*, 31.1 (October 1978), 42.

The most active in Mao's mass base were China's high school and college students. Their participation in the Red Guard movement of the Cultural Revolution can be explained in large part by the normal idealism of the young, which made them ready to share Mao's indignation at the elitism, inequality, and bureaucratic stagnation that seemed to be plaguing China in the mid-1960s. China's student population doubtless also welcomed the sense of importance and power provided by their involvement in Mao's campaign against revisionism.

In addition, the educational policies of the early 1960s had produced serious cleavages and grievances among China's students. While opportunities for primary and junior middle school education were expanding, enrollment at both senior middle schools and universities declined sharply from the levels attained during the Great Leap Forward, as the state sought to retrench overextended budgets during a period of serious economic recession. There was a sharper differentiation between elite middle schools, whose graduates had a good chance to go to college, and lesser institutions, whose graduates had little prospect for higher education. By 1964–65, furthermore, in a program foreshadowing the mass rustification policies of later years, middle school students who had not been placed in universities or industrial enterprises were being sent, in large numbers, to frontier and rural areas.[17]

These declining opportunities for upward mobility – and the real danger of a permanent transfer to the countryside – focused student concern on the standards for advancement. Formally, three criteria were important in assigning students to elite middle schools, universities, and the most desirable jobs: class background, academic achievement, and political behavior. But the relative weight of the criteria was changing in the mid-1960s, with class background and political behavior becoming more important, and academic achievement becoming less so. By the eve of the Cultural Revolution, the most fortunate students were thus those from cadre or military families. These students' academic records were not always superior, but they were increasingly benefiting from the new emphasis on class background as a criterion for enrollment in senior middle schools, universities, and the Communist Youth League. Next came students from worker and peasant families, whose good class background now offered some compensation for what was often mediocre classroom performance. At the bottom were students from bourgeois or intellectual families, who often enjoyed superior academic records, but

17 On educational policy in the early 1960s, see John Gardner, "Educated youth and urban-rural inequalities, 1958–66," in John Wilson Lewis, ed., *The city in communist China*, 235–86; and Donald J. Munro, "Egalitarian ideal and educational fact in communist China," in Lindbeck, *China*, 256–301.

whose "bad" or "middling" class background was becoming an ever greater obstacle to advancement.[18]

Just as students were divided by the policies of the early 1960s, so too were urban workers. The economic policies of the 1950s had already produced cleavages between permanent workers and apprentices, between skilled and unskilled laborers, and between workers at large state factories and employees of smaller collective enterprises. In each case, the former received substantially higher salaries and job benefits than did the latter.

These divisions, the result of the application of the Soviet model to China, were widened by the implementation of the "worker-peasant system" of industrial employment in 1964. Under this policy, industrial workers were hired from suburban communes on a temporary or part-time basis, as required by specific factories and enterprises. The system was officially justified as an effort to reduce the social and economic disparities between city and countryside by producing a class of people who were simultaneously workers and peasants. In practice, however, the principal appeal of the worker-peasant system was much less noble: Factories welcomed the opportunity to hire temporary contract workers who were paid lower wages, who were ineligible for the pensions or medical benefits that state enterprises were required to provide to permanent employees, and who could be fired for poor performance.[19]

The consequence of the worker-peasant system, therefore, was to exacerbate social tensions rather than to ameliorate them. This employment policy not only produced an underclass of dissatisfied workers, who received less remuneration and less job security for the same work than did permanent employees, but also raised the specter of downward mobility for many more. The tendency in many state enterprises was to reassign positions from the permanent payroll to the more flexible worker-peasant system. Thus, apprentices saw the opportunities for advancement drying up, and even permanent workers faced the danger that they would find themselves transferred to the countryside to become contract employees.

When the Cultural Revolution broke out in mid-1966, and when mass protest was officially encouraged, many of these collective resentments, as well as individual grievances, formed the emotional fuel for the Red Guard movement. As in any complex social movement, there was only a

18 This categorization of Chinese students is based on Hong Yung Lee, *The politics of the Chinese Cultural Revolution: a case study*; and Stanley Rosen, *Red Guard factionalism and the Cultural Revolution in Guangzhou (Canton)*.
19 Lee, *Politics of the Cultural Revolution*, 129–39.

loose correlation between one's socioeconomic standing in the mid-1960s and one's political orientation during the Cultural Revolution. But a common pattern in the Red Guard movement was the anger against the Party establishment by students from "bad" or "middling" classes, who felt that their chances for upward mobility were steadily declining, and by those workers who occupied lower positions on the ladder of economic specialization.[20]

The emerging crisis

The issues and tensions just discussed came to a head between the fall of 1965 and the summer of 1966, as Chinese leaders engaged in heated controversies over Chinese military policy, strategy toward Vietnam, policy toward the literary community, and the rectification of the Party. These debates enabled Lin Piao and Chiang Ch'ing, with Mao's backing, to push potential rivals aside, extend their control over China's military and cultural establishments, and thus strengthen Mao's political base. In the case of the PLA, a dispute over China's response to the escalating conflict in Vietnam provided the occasion for the purge of the chief of staff, Lo Jui-ch'ing, who was potentially able to challenge Lin's control over the armed forces. In the cultural realm, an early skirmish over a historical drama that was allegedly critical of Mao led ultimately to the dismissal of the first Party secretary in Peking, the reorganization of the Party's Propaganda Department, and the appointment of Ch'en Po-ta, Chiang Ch'ing, and K'ang Sheng – a longtime public security specialist with close ties to Mao – as leaders of the unfolding campaign against revisionism. Within a few months, Mao had broken decisively with Liu Shao-ch'i over the way to extend that campaign from the cultural community into the universities and the bureaucracy.

The spring of 1966 also witnessed the gradual melding of the three elements of Mao's political base – the army, the radical intellectuals, and the disenchanted youth – into a relatively coherent coalition that could spearhead the Cultural Revolution. A linkage between Chiang Ch'ing and Lin Piao was forged at a forum on literature and art in the armed forces in February 1966, at which Chiang Ch'ing, who had had little connection with the PLA in the past, came to assume a leading role in the military's cultural activities. Within the next few months, the radical civilian and military leaders surrounding Mao Tse-tung began to mobilize support

20 Marc J. Blecher and Gordon White, *Micropolitics in contemporary China: a technical unit during and after the Cultural Revolution.*

among disenchanted sectors in urban China. During June and July, the Cultural Revolution Group under Ch'en Po-ta, Chiang Ch'ing, and K'ang Sheng started to build connections with radical students and faculty in key universities in Peking, and encouraged them to launch intense criticism of university, Party, and government leaders. By the end of July, the PLA had begun to provide supplies and logistical support to the leftist organizations that were springing up on major campuses.

Finally, in August 1966, the Central Committee of the Chinese Communist Party held a rump session in Peking. Attended by little more than half the members of the Central Committee, and packed with Red Guards, the plenum adopted a resolution authorizing the mobilization of China's urban population to criticize "those persons in authority who are taking the capitalist road." It was this decision that authorized what, by year's end, had become an all-out assault by Mao and his lieutenants against the Party establishment. With it, the Cultural Revolution entered its most chaotic and destructive period.

Lo Jui-ch'ing. The military policies of Lin Piao had not gone unchallenged in the high command of the PLA. Lin's principal rival was the chief of staff, Lo Jui-ch'ing, who came to question the appropriateness of Lin's military policies in 1964–65, as the escalation of American involvement in the war in Vietnam presented China with an unexpected threat on its southern borders.[21]

In retrospect, Lo Jui-ch'ing's challenge to Lin Piao still appears somewhat surprising. Lo had been a political commissar through much of his pre-1949 career, and had served as minister of public security (rather than a troop commander) during the 1950s. There was little reason, therefore, to suspect that Lo would have opposed the emphasis on ideological indoctrination and political loyalty that characterized Lin's service as minister of defense. What is more, Lin and Lo had had a close personal relationship during the Communist revolution. Lo had served under Lin in the 1st Corps of the Red Army in the early 1930s, and had been Lin's deputy at both the Red Army College and K'ang-ta (the Resist-Japan Military and Political University in Yenan). When Lin Piao became minister of defense in 1959, Lo was promoted to the position of chief of staff. If Lo's appointment was not at Lin's initiative, it was at least with his approval.

Lin Piao had, since the early 1950s, been a victim of chronic illness –

21 On the Lo Jui-ch'ing affair, see Harry Harding and Melvin Gurtov, *The purge of Lo Jui-ch'ing: the politics of Chinese strategic planning*; and Michael Yahuda, "Kremlinology and the Chinese strategic debate, 1965–66," *CQ*, 49 (January–March 1972), 32–75.

variously described as a war wound, stomach difficulties, tuberculosis, or a combination – that periodically forced him to curtail his physical and political activities. The recurrence of these physical ailments in the early 1960s apparently created serious tensions between Lin and Lo Jui-ch'ing. At a minimum, Lo may have wished, in light of Lin's illness, to be granted greater operational authority over the armed forces; or, alternatively, Lo may have hoped that Lin would resign as minister of defense in his favor. According to one dramatic account, Lo actually told Lin to his face that "a sick man should give his place to the worthy! Don't meddle! Don't block the way!"[22]

The growing participation of American forces in the Vietnam war – a step Chinese leaders had apparently not anticipated – also strained the relationship between the two men. Lo began to propose more intensive military preparations, in case the United States should decide to carry the war to China. As Lo put it in May 1965:

> It makes a world of difference whether or not one is prepared once a war breaks out.... Moreover, these preparations must be made for the most difficult and worst situations that may possibly arise. Preparations must be made not only against any small-scale warfare but also against any medium- or large-scale warfare that imperialism may launch. These preparations must envisage the use by the imperialists of nuclear weapons as well as of conventional weapons.

Moreover, Lo also argued that if war did come to China, the PLA should be prepared to defend the country from prepared positions, and then counterattack across China's borders to destroy the enemy "in its own lair."[23]

Lo's recommendations, which may have reflected the views of China's professional military planners, proved unacceptable to Lin Piao. For one thing, the strategy of linear defense that Lo proposed contradicted the principles of people's war, according to which the Chinese Army would attempt to lure an invader deep inside China so as to overextend his supply lines and destroy him piecemeal. What is more, Lo's insistence that, as he put it in September 1965, there were "a thousand and one things to do" before China was ready for war,[24] implied that the PLA should reorder its priorities, at least temporarily, so as to place greater stress on military preparation. Of these two considerations, it was the second that was probably the more controversial. The PLA was playing an

22 Harding and Gurtov, *Lo Jui-ch'ing*, 10.
23 Lo Jui-ch'ing, "Commemorate the victory over German fascism! Carry the struggle against U.S. imperialism through to the end!" *PR*, 20 (14 May 1965), 7–15.
24 Lo Jui-ch'ing, "The people defeated Japanese fascism and they can certainly defeat U.S. imperialism too," *CB*, 770 (14 September 1965), 1–12.

ever larger role in civilian society, and was becoming a critically important part of Mao's power base in his emerging confrontation with the
Party establishment. If adopted, Lo's proposals would have reversed this
process: They would have drawn the army from political affairs, and thus
largely removed it from the Maoist coalition.

The controversy between Lin Piao and Lo Jui-ch'ing reached its climax in early September, when the two men published articles on the
twentieth anniversary of the surrender of Japan at the end of World War
II that contained very different implications for Chinese defense policy.[25]
Lo argued that China "certainly must have sufficient plans and certainly
must complete preparations" in case the United States should attack
China. Lin, in contrast, implied that the Americans were unlikely to be so
rash, and that even if they were, there would be ample time to mobilize
"the vast ocean of several hundred million Chinese people in arms." This
was to be Lo's last major public utterance, and by the end of November, he
dropped from public view altogether. Lin Piao began assembling a bill of
particulars against his colleague, which he presented to a Central Committee conference in Shanghai on 8 December . The conference appointed
a seven-man team, headed by Marshal Yeh Chien-ying, to examine Lin's
case against Lo.

The investigation soon took an inquisitorial turn. The team, accompanied by representatives from various branches of the military, engaged in what was later described as "face-to-face" struggle against Lo in
March 1966. After Lo's self-criticism was rejected as inadequate, he tried
unsuccessfully to commit suicide by leaping from the building in which
he was confined. On 8 April, the investigation team concluded its work
by recommending to the Central Committee that Lo be dismissed from all
his posts in the PLA, as well as from his duties as a vice-premier and a
member of the Party Secretariat. That report, in turn, was approved by an
enlarged meeting of the Politburo in early May. There is some reason to
believe that P'eng Chen, a Politburo member serving concurrently as first
Party secretary in Peking, defended Lo during the course of the investi-
gatory process, but his views were rejected.[26]

The Lo Jui-ch'ing affair was important for two reasons. It provided
persuasive evidence that Mao and Lin had the will and the ability to
secure the dismissal of officials who disagreed with their policies and who
challenged their personal standing. It also enabled the two to increase
their control over two key elements in the coercive apparatus of China.
The dismissal of Lo as chief of staff, and his replacement somewhat later

25 Lo, "The people defeated fascism"; Lin Piao, *Long live the victory of People's War*.
26 On the fate of Lo, see Ahn, *Chinese politics*, 203–4; and Lieberthal, *Research guide*, 248–49.

by Yang Ch'eng-wu, gave Lin further influence over the main forces of the PLA. In addition, the purge of Lo was followed by the dismissal of some of his former lieutenants in the Ministry of Public Security, thus enabling K'ang Sheng to strengthen his control over the state security apparatus.

Wu Han and P'eng Chen. At the same time as Lo Jui-ch'ing was coming under serious attack, Mao also turned his attention to the problem of dissent among the intellectuals.[27] He focused his fire on *Hai Jui dismissed from office* (*Hai Jui pa kuan*), a play by Wu Han, an author and scholar who served concurrently as a deputy mayor of Peking. The Chairman charged that this historical drama, which nominally depicted an upright Ming dynasty official unjustly dismissed by the emperor, Chia-ch'ing, was actually an allegorical criticism of Mao's purge of P'eng Te-huai at the Lushan Plenum in 1959. That Mao may well have encouraged Wu to write the play in the first place did not affect the Chairman's judgment of the final product.

In dealing with Wu Han and *Hai Jui*, Mao took a two-pronged approach. Initially, he assigned the responsibility of criticizing Wu Han's play to a Five-Man Group on revolution in culture (*wen-hua ko-ming wu-jen hsiao-tsu*), headed by P'eng Chen, which had been established in 1964. This put P'eng in a difficult position, for, as first Party secretary of Peking municipality, he was responsible for the actions of one of his own deputy mayors. Perhaps because of his personal connections with Wu Han, as well as his more general beliefs about the best way to handle policy toward intellectuals, P'eng soon made clear what his approach would be: to focus on the historical issues raised by Wu Han's play rather than on its possible allegorical content, and to discuss those issues in an open way in which "everyone is equal before the truth."[28]

Aware of Peng's predilections on the case, Mao decided simultaneously to take a second tack. He asked Yao Wen-yuan, one of the Shanghai intellectuals associated with Chiang Ch'ing, to prepare his own criticism of Wu Han's play. Mao emphasized that Yao's article should address what he considered to be the crucial issue: that Wu Han had intended Hai Jui to be a historical analogue for P'eng Te-huai. The extent of Mao's

---

27 On the Wu Han affair, see Ahn, *Chinese politics*, 195–213; Goldman, *China's intellectuals*, ch. 5; Jack Gray and Patrick Cavendish, *Chinese communism in crisis: Maoism and the Cultural Revolution*, ch. 4; Lee, *Politics of the Cultural Revolution*, ch. 1; and James R. Pusey, *Wu Han: attacking the present through the past.*

28 "The Great Proletarian Cultural Revolution – a record of major events: September 1965 to December 1966," *JPRS*, 42, 349. *Translations on Communist China: political and sociological information* (25 August 1967), 3.

personal interest and involvement in this matter is suggested by his reviewing Yao's essay three times before agreeing that it was ready for publication.[29]

Yao's article — a harsh direct attack on Wu Han — was published in Shanghai in early November, before the Five-Man Group in Peking had taken any formal action on the Wu Han case. P'eng Chen's reaction was one of outrage, not merely because his subordinate was being criticized so strongly, but also because he believed that publication of such an article, without the formal approval of the responsible Party organs, was a violation of the principles of inner-Party struggle. Together with Lu Ting-i, director of the Party Propaganda Department and a member of the Five-Man Group, P'eng succeeded in blocking republication of Yao's essay in any central or Peking municipal newspapers. It was only after the personal intervention of Chou En-lai, apparently acting at Mao's behest, that the article appeared in newspapers with wider circulation — first in the *Chieh-fang-chün pao* with a laudatory editorial note, and then in the *Jen-min jih-pao* (People's Daily) with a skeptical introduction.

Even though he had lost the battle to suppress the publication of the Yao Wen-yuan essay, P'eng still vigorously attempted to keep criticism of intellectuals on what he considered to be the proper course. With a working majority on the Five-Man Group (of whose members only K'ang Sheng was a firm supporter of Mao's position), P'eng continued to obstruct the publication of further articles by radical writers such as Ch'i Pen-yü that he considered to be excessively critical of Wu Han. He stuck to this position despite direct criticism from Mao toward the end of December, when the Chairman accused P'eng of ignoring the possible analogy between Hai Jui and P'eng Te-huai. P'eng defended himself on the somewhat narrow grounds that there had been no personal contact between P'eng and Wu, and that Wu Han was therefore innocent of any factionalist behavior. But P'eng promised Mao that the Five-Man Group would reach a final decision on the issue within two months.

The Five-Man Group held at least two crucial meetings on the subject: the first on 2 January 1966, and the second on 4 February. Despite all the evidence that Mao would be dissatisfied with their report — evidence provided not only by Mao's conversations with P'eng in December but also by warnings from K'ang Sheng — the group decided to stick with the approach P'eng Chen had originally adopted. On 3 February, two deputy directors of the Propaganda Department, Yao Chen and Hsu Li-ch'ün,

29 Yao Wen-yuan, "On the new historical play *Hai Jui dismissed from office*," *Wen-hui pao*, 10 November 1965, trans. in *CB*, 783 (21 March 1966), 1–18.

drafted a statement summarizing the views of the majority of the Five-Man Group.

This document, known as the "February Outline" (*erh-yueh t'i-kang*), acknowledged the problem of bourgeois tendencies in culture but emphasized the desirability of focusing on the academic issues involved.[30] Implicitly, the outline distinguished two different approaches to the problem of "people like Wu Han." The first approach would treat such problems as a political issue, would characterize dissenting views or unorthodox approaches as antisocialist or counterrevolutionary, and would use administrative means to suppress them. The second approach, in contrast, would treat such matters as serious academic issues that should be "reasoned out," under the principle of "seeking truth from facts."

The outline opted decisively for the second approach, declaring that the Party's policy toward intellectuals should continue to be guided by the principle of "letting one hundred schools of thought contend." The goal should be to overcome dissidence and unorthodoxy through superior academic work, not by "beating them [dissident intellectuals] politically." The process should be a lenient one, and critics should not "behave like scholar-tyrants who are always acting arbitrarily and trying to overwhelm people with their power." Above all, the outline proposed that the struggle against bourgeois ideology be conducted "under leadership," "prudently," and over a "prolonged period of time."

The February Outline departed decisively in two significant ways from the views of Mao Tse-tung and the radicals around Chiang Ch'ing. It pointedly avoided any conclusion as to whether Wu Han had intended *Hai Jui* as an indirect criticism of Mao's dismissal of P'eng Te-huai, and thus evaded the responsibility that Mao had explicitly assigned it. What is more, the outline criticized the radical intellectuals exemplified by Yao Wen-yuan as much as the allegedly revisionist scholars such as Wu Han. The Five-Man Group refrained from criticizing any radical writers by name. But it warned that some "revolutionary Leftists" were acting like "scholar-tyrants," and even called for the "rectification" of the incorrect ideas among the left.

The February Outline was discussed and approved by the Standing Committee of the Politburo, chaired by Liu Shao-ch'i, on 5 February. P'eng Chen and others then traveled to Wuhan to discuss the matter with Mao. As expected, Mao apparently objected to the harsh treatment of the radicals in the outline report and its failure to issue a decisive criticism of

---

30 "Outline report concerning the current academic discussion of the Group of Five in charge of the Cultural Revolution," in *CCP documents of the Great Proletarian Cultural Revolution, 1966–1967*, 7–12.

Wu Han. Nonetheless, P'eng returned to Peking claiming that Mao had approved the February Outline, and the document was circulated under the imprimatur of the Central Committee on 12 February.

In the fall of 1965, Yao Wen-yuan's direct criticism of Wu Han had stood in sharp counterpoint to the milder approach favored by P'eng Chen and the Party Propaganda Department. Now, in February 1966, the outline issued by the Five-Man Group would stand in contrast to another document prepared under the joint auspices of Lin Piao and Chiang Ch'ing. The document was the summary of the meeting on literary and art work in the armed forces, held in Shanghai 2–20 February 1966, that forged the political alliance between Chiang Ch'ing and Lin Piao.[31] Like Yao Wen-yuan's earlier article, the Forum Summary (known in Chinese as the February Summary, or *erh-yueh chi-yao*) was drawn up under Mao's personal supervision, and was reportedly revised by Mao three times before it was circulated through inner-Party channels.

The Forum Summary took a position on intellectual problems that was diametrically opposed to that of the February Outline. It not only described China's cultural life as having been characterized by "sixteen years of sharp class struggle" between the revolutionary and revisionist perspectives, but also claimed that cultural affairs were now under the "dictatorship of a black anti-Party and anti-socialist line" – a sharp attack on the leadership provided by the Propaganda Department and the Five-Man Group. The Forum Summary called for active mass criticism of these tendencies, rather than the more lenient and scholarly kind of criticism envisioned by the February Outline.

The Forum Summary ignored the case of Wu Han and *Hai Jui* altogether. This was because the issue at this point was no longer Wu Han but, rather, the behavior of P'eng Chen, the Party Propaganda Department under Lu Ting-i, and the Five-Man Group they controlled. At a Central Work Conference at the end of March, Mao Tse-tung harshly attacked P'eng Chen, Wu Han, and the February Outline; and threatened to disband the Five-Man Group, the Peking Municipal Party Committee, and the Central Committee's Propaganda Department. As he said to K'ang Sheng, using vivid imagery drawn from ancient Chinese mythology:

The central Party Propaganda Department is the palace of the Prince of Hell. It is necessary to overthrow the palace of the Prince of Hell and liberate the Little Devil.... The local areas must produce several more [Monkey Kings] to

31 "Summary of the forum on the work in literature and art in the armed forces with which Comrade Lin Piao entrusted Comrade Chiang Ch'ing," *PR*, 10.23 (2 June 1967), 10–16.

vigorously create a disturbance at the palace of the King of Heaven. If P'eng Chen, the Peking Municipal Party Committee, and the central Propaganda Department again protect the bad people, then it will be necessary to dissolve the Peking Municipal Committee, and it will be necessary to dissolve the Five-Man Group. Last September, I asked some of the comrades what should be done if revisionism emerged in the central government. This is very possible.[32]

After the work conference, P'eng Chen apparently realized that further defiance of Mao would be useless. In a desperate attempt to preserve his own position, he encouraged the Peking Party Committee to intensify its criticism of Wu Han, began an attack against Teng T'o, another Peking Party official who had written veiled criticisms of Mao's leadership, and even began to prepare his own self-criticism. In early April, according to one Red Guard account, P'eng called a joint meeting of the Five-Man Group, the leadership of the Propaganda Department, and members of the Peking Municipal Party Committee at his residence. With deep emotion, he acknowledged that he had made serious mistakes in his handling of the revolution in culture, but insisted that the rest of his political record was exemplary. He pleaded for the support of his colleagues: "As the old saying goes, we depend on [our] parents' protection at home but depend on [our] friends' kind help outside. I am now looking forward to your help."[33]

But it was too late. At a meeting of the Party Secretariat between 9 and 12 April, P'eng found himself the target of criticism not only by K'ang Sheng and Ch'en Po-ta, but also by Teng Hsiao-p'ing and Chou En-lai. The Secretariat decided to disband P'eng Chen's Five-Man Group, and to propose to the Politburo the establishment of a new leading group for cultural reform that would be more sympathetic to Mao's concerns.[34] During many of these dramatic developments, Liu Shao-ch'i was away from Peking on an ill-timed visit to Pakistan, Afghanistan, and Burma, and was thus unable to lead a defense of P'eng Chen and Lu Ting-i.

The May Politburo meeting. The final fates of the two principal targets thus far – Lo Jui-ch'ing and P'eng Chen – were decided together at an enlarged meeting of the Politburo between 4 and 18 May. The highlight of the meeting was an impromptu speech by Lin Piao, much of the data for which, it was later charged, had been provided by Chang Ch'un-ch'iao.[35] In it, Lin linked the question of Lo Jui-ch'ing with that of P'eng Chen and Lu Ting-i by accusing the three men of planning, in conspiracy

32 *Miscellany of Mao Tse-tung Thought*, 2.382.   33 Ahn, *Chinese politics*, 207.
34 Lieberthal, *Research guide*, 246–47; "Record of major events," 10–11.
35 Lieberthal, *Research guide*, 248–49; Kau, *Lin Piao*, 326–45; *JMJP*, 18 May 1978, in FBIS *Daily Report: China*, 24 May 1978, E2–11.

with Yang Shang-k'un, the director of the Secretariat of the Central Committee, a military coup against Mao and the radicals. "You may have smelled it – gunpowder," Lin told the Politburo melodramatically.

Lin supported these fantastic charges with a detailed discussion of the role of military force in acquiring political power. He emphasized the prevalence of military coups in both Chinese and contemporary world history, chronicling assassinations and usurpations in nearly every major dynasty, and noting that there had been an "average of eleven coups per year" in the Third World since 1960. Although these facts were intended to make his case against Lo, P'eng, Lu, and Yang more plausible, they also reflected Lin's fascination with the use of military force to pursue political goals. And he revealed that he had already put this historical lesson into practice: Acting under Mao's orders, Lin said, loyal troops had been sent into radio broadcasting stations, military installations, and public security offices in Peking to prevent further attempts at "internal subversion and counterrevolutionary coups d'état."

Equally interesting was Lin's sycophantic portrait of Mao. Accusing Lo, P'eng, Lu, and Yang of being "opposed to Chairman Mao and opposed to Mao Tse-tung Thought," Lin went on to extol Mao's genius, and to identify loyalty to Mao as a key criterion for holding Party or government office. "Chairman Mao has experienced much more than Marx, Engels, and Lenin.... He is unparalleled in the present world. ... Chairman Mao's sayings, works, and revolutionary practice have shown that he is a great proletarian genius.... Every sentence of Chairman Mao's works is a truth; one single sentence of his surpasses ten thousand of ours.... Whoever is against him shall be punished by the entire Party and the whole country."

The enlarged meeting of the Politburo received, and approved, the report of the work group that had investigated Lo Jui-ch'ing, and instructed that it be circulated within the Party and the armed forces. It also issued a circular on 16 May, which Chiang Ch'ing later claimed to have drafted, on problems in cultural affairs.[36] The 16 May Circular (*wu i-liu t'ung-chih*) revoked the February Outline, charging that it tried to "turn the movement to the Right" by obscuring the contemporary political issues that were being discussed within the intellectual community, and that it attempted to "direct the spearhead against the Left" by criticizing the emergence of "scholar-tyrants." The circular blamed P'eng Chen for the February Outline, dissolved the Group of Five, and estab-

---

36 "Circular of the Central Committee of Communist Party of China," in "Collection of documents concerning the Great Proletarian Cultural Revolution," *CB*, 852 (6 May 1968), 2–6. On Chiang Ch'ing's role, see Witke, *Chiang Ch'ing*, 320.

lished a new Cultural Revolution Group (*wen-hua ko-ming hsiao-tsu*) that would report directly to the Standing Committee of the Politburo (i.e., to Mao) rather than to the Party Secretariat (i.e., to Teng Hsiao-p'ing and Liu Shao-ch'i) as had its predecessor. Whereas a majority of the Five-Man Group had opposed Mao's views on the handling of the Cultural Revolution, the new Cultural Revolution Group was dominated by Mao's personal supporters and the radical intellectuals surrounding Chiang Ch'ing. The group was headed by Ch'en Po-ta, with K'ang Sheng as an adviser, and with Chiang Ch'ing, Chang Ch'un-ch'iao, Yao Wen-yuan, Ch'i Pen-yü, Wang Li, and Kuan Feng as members.

While the principal purpose of the new Cultural Revolution Group was to continue the criticism of "bourgeois" ideas in the cultural sphere, the 16 May Circular also warned that ranking Party and state officials might well suffer the same fate as P'eng Chen and Lo Jui-ch'ing. It was necessary, the circular said, to eliminate the

representatives of the bourgeoisie who have sneaked into the Party, the government, and the army. When conditions are ripe, they would seize power and turn the dictatorship of the proletariat into a dictatorship of the bourgeoisie. Some of them we have already seen through, others we have not. Some we still trust and are training as our successors. There are, for example, people of the Khrushchev brand still nestling in our midst.

In this way, the circular represented a major escalation of Mao's drive against revisionism: from a movement directed principally at intellectuals, to one aimed at the Party as a whole.

The May Politburo meeting set the stage for the reorganization of the Peking Municipal Party Committee, the Party Propaganda Department, and the Party Secretariat, which was announced in early June. P'eng Chen was replaced as Peking's first secretary by Li Hsueh-feng, then the first secretary of the North China Bureau; Lu Ting-i was replaced as head of the Propaganda Department by T'ao Chu, previously first secretary of the Party's Central-South Bureau; and Yang Shang-k'un was replaced as staff director of the Party Secretariat by Wang Tung-hsing, a vice-minister of public security who concurrently commanded the elite guards unit in the capital.

The dismissals of men of such rank in late May and early June showed that Mao was determined to have his way on issues that were of importance to him, and that he was able to secure the replacement of officials who did not comply with his wishes. Moreover, each reorganization – of the General Staff Department of the PLA, of the group responsible for cultural reform, of the Peking Municipal Party Committee, of the Party

Propaganda Department, of the Party Secretariat – strengthened Mao's coalition and weakened those who would resist or oppose him. Rather than appeasing Mao, in other words, each purge simply made it easier for him to escalate his assault on revisionism in the Party.

The Fifty Days. By warning of "representatives of the bourgeoisie" who had "sneaked into the Party, the government, and the army," the 16 May Circular indicated that Mao wanted a thoroughgoing purge of "revisionism" throughout China, not just in the cultural sphere but throughout the bureaucracy. Still away from Peking, in relative seclusion in Central China, Mao left the conduct of this effort in the hands of Liu Shao-ch'i, a man whom he would later say he already suspected of revisionism, and who other radicals would claim was one of the officials referred to indirectly in the 16 May Circular as "people of the Khrushchev brand" being trained as Mao's successors.

Whether or not Liu was fully aware of Mao's suspicions, he did face a serious dilemma in June 1966. On the one hand, if he were to have any hope of survival, he would have to show enthusiasm and efficiency in combating revisionism. On the other, he had to do so in a way that preserved central control over a rapid process of political mobilization, particularly on college campuses, and that protected what was left of his eroding political base. Liu's attempts to resolve this dilemma were reflected in his actions during a fifty-day period in June and early July 1966, during which, in Mao's absence from Peking, he was principally responsible for the day-to-day affairs of the Party.

By this time, radical students and teachers, particularly in Peking, were well aware of the debate over cultural reform and of Mao's views about the February Outline. In part, this was simply because younger professors who were members of the Party had access to the documents on the subject, such as the 16 May Circular, that were being circulated within the Party organization. But it was also because the leaders of the newly established Cultural Revolution Group were sending representatives to major college and university campuses in Peking to mobilize mass support.[37]

On 25 May, a group of radical professors and teaching assistants at Peking University (Peita) led by Nieh Yuan-tzu, a teaching assistant in the philosophy department, wrote a large-character wall poster (*ta-tzu-pao*) criticizing the university's leadership for having supported the liberal policies of the February Outline, and for having prevented mass discussion of the political issues raised by the *Hai Jui* affair. According to

37 Sun Tun-fan, *Li-shih chiang-i*, 2.247.

accounts published well after the Cultural Revolution, Nieh received direct encouragement from a "theoretical investigation group from the central authorities," led by K'ang Sheng's wife, Ts'ao I-ou, which had arrived at Peita under orders to "kindle the flames and spread the fire to upper levels."[38]

The university administration, not surprisingly, took prompt action to suppress this kind of dissent. In this they were supported by Chou En-lai, who sent a second central work group to criticize Nieh's wall poster the night it was displayed at Peita. But, having learned of the contents of the ta-tzu-pao, Mao Tse-tung ordered that it be broadcast and published nationally, with favorable commentary, on 1 June. This decision, followed presently by the announcement that the entire Peking University leadership was being reorganized, served to legitimate spontaneous mass protest as part of the campaign against revisionist officials. So, too, did increasingly inflammatory editorials that began to appear in *Jen-min jih-pao* after the newly reorganized central Propaganda Department had undertaken a restaffing of the central news media.

With this encouragement, wall posters written by students and faculty began to appear at university campuses and in middle schools throughout China. Most probably focused on educational issues – the admissions process, course examinations, and curricula were the questions of greatest concern – but some accused university leaders and higher-level officials of supporting revisionist policies. As at Peita, it is very likely that much of this explosion of dissent was encouraged and coordinated by the new Cultural Revolution Group under Ch'en Po-ta, Chiang Ch'ing, and K'ang Sheng. In short order, the authority of university leaders on other campuses collapsed, and discipline among students and faculty quickly eroded.

It was this rapid process of political decay – the rise of dissent and the collapse of authority – that must have been of particular concern to Liu Shao-ch'i.[39] Operating without clear instructions from Mao, he decided on several measures he hoped would simultaneously demonstrate his willingness to combat revisionism and bring the student movement under Party leadership. To begin with, he ordered the suspension of university enrollment for half a year, to permit a thorough reconsideration and reform of the examination system and the university curriculum. At the same time, he organized a large number of work teams – perhaps four

---

38 The events at Peita are drawn from *HC*, 19 (October 1980), 32–36.

39 On the Fifty Days, see Ahn, *Chinese politics*, ch. 9; Jean Daubier, *A history of the Chinese Cultural Revolution*, ch. 1; Lowell Dittmer, *Liu Shao-ch'i and the Chinese Cultural Revolution: the politics of mass criticism*, 78–94; and Harding, *Organizing China*, 225–29.

hundred teams with more than ten thousand members in all – and dispatched them to universities and high schools and to bureaucratic agencies responsible for finance, trade, industry, and communications. Given the frequent use of work teams in past Party rectification campaigns, Liu doubtless considered his decision to be routine, appropriate, and noncontroversial.

What was ultimately Liu's undoing was less the principle of dispatching work teams than the instructions under which they operated. They apparently were told that large numbers of ordinary bureaucratic officials and university faculty were to be subject to criticism, and possibly dismissal. In the Ministry of Finance, for example, 90 percent of the cadres reportedly were criticized; in the Ministry of Culture, work teams were authorized to dismiss two-thirds of the ministry's officials. In universities, large numbers of administrators and faculty came under attack, beginning a reign of terror that would last for a decade.

The work teams were also told to reestablish Party leadership over the student movement in the nation's major universities and high schools. A Politburo conference on 13 July, after reviewing the Cultural Revolution in Peking's middle schools, concluded that the most important task on each campus was to "restore the leading role of the Party branch" and to "strengthen the work teams."[40] Putting the same point in somewhat blunter language, the first Party secretary of Anhwei province announced that, "for units where the leadership is not in our hands, work teams must be sent immediately to win it back."[41]

The reassertion of Party leadership over the student movement implied the demobilization of the radical students and their faculty supporters. National policy was still to permit student demonstrations, rallies, and wall posters as long as they were confined to campus. But many local Party committees and work teams, in their zeal to impose control over the student movement, took a stricter approach. In some places, *ta-tzu-pao* and rallies were banned altogether, while in others they were allowed only if permission had been obtained from the work team. Some radical students were expelled from the Communist Youth League, others were subjected to struggle meetings, and still others were sent to the countryside for a stint of labor reform. As a result of such stringent measures, the work teams were able to restore a modicum of normality to many universities.

But while some students were persuaded to cease political activity, the

40 Sun Tun-fan, *Li-shih chiang-i*, 2.250.   41 Radio Hofei, 16 July 1966.

restrictions imposed by the work teams drove others into deeper opposition. Secret student organizations, some of which took on the name "Red Guards" (*hung-wei-ping*), formed to resist the activities of the work teams, despite Liu Shao-ch'i's ruling that such organizations were "secret and [therefore] illegal."[42] Other student groups were organized at the behest of the work teams to provide them with support. The result, in other words, was not only the partial demobilization of the student movement, but also the polarization of the remaining activists.

The work teams' suppression of the radicals soon became a matter of considerable controversy at the highest levels of the Party. In early July, the case of K'uai Ta-fu, one of the leading radical students at Tsing-hua University, who had been criticized by the work teams sent there, was the subject of a high-level Party meeting in Peking. In that meeting, Liu Shao-ch'i attacked K'uai as a troublemaker, while K'ang Sheng defended his right to criticize revisionism in the Party. It was by this time common knowledge that activists such as K'uai Ta-fu had direct connections with the central Cultural Revolution Group advised by K'ang Sheng, whereas the work teams with which K'uai had come into conflict had been dispatched on the order of Liu Shao-ch'i. What gave this particular case special poignancy was the fact that the leader of the work team sent to Tsing-hua was none other than Liu Shao-ch'i's wife, Wang Kuang-mei.[43] In this way, Liu's political future had become inextricably intertwined with the performance of the work teams.

As Mao Tse-tung saw it, the work teams repeated the same mistakes that Liu Shao-ch'i had committed during the rural Socialist Education Campaign earlier in the 1960s.[44] In that campaign, directed against corruption and "capitalist tendencies" among rural cadres, Liu's approach had been to dispatch large numbers of work teams to grass-roots Party organizations, restrict peasant participation in cadre rectification, criticize large numbers of commune officials, and downplay the responsibility of higher-level Party leaders. In Mao's eyes, Liu's conduct of the rectification of the universities and the urban bureaucracy in mid-1966 was guilty of similar errors. Once again, large numbers of lower-level officials were being attacked and mass involvement was being restricted, without any recognition that the ultimate cause of revisionism lay in the sympathetic attitudes of higher officials.

---

42 "Record of Major Events," 25. 43 Ahn, *Chinese politics*, 218.
44 On the Socialist Education Movement, see Ahn, *Chinese politics*, ch. 5; Richard Baum, *Prelude to revolution: Mao, the Party, and the peasant question, 1962–66*; and Harding, *Organizing China*, ch. 7.

The Eleventh Plenum

Thus, in mid-July, angered at Liu Shao-ch'i's conduct of the campaign against revisionism in the bureaucracy and his management of the radical student movement, Mao abruptly ended his stay in Hangchow and headed for Peking. On the way back to the capital, Mao stopped for a swim in the Yangtze River – an act intended to demonstrate that he had the physical vigor needed for the political battles ahead. Although Mao had been active behind the scenes in Hangchow, this was his first public appearance in many months, and it received unprecedentedly sycophantic coverage in the Chinese media. The official report of the event carried by the New China News Agency began with the sentence "The water of the river seemed to be smiling that day," and went on to tell of a militiaman from the Hankow Thermal Power Plant who "became so excited when he saw Chairman Mao that he forgot he was in the water. Raising both hands, he shouted: 'Long live Chairman Mao! Long live Chairman Mao!' He leapt into the air, but soon sank into the river again. He gulped several mouthfuls, but the water tasted especially sweet." Thereafter, the president of the World Professional Marathon Swimming Federation invited Mao to take part in two forthcoming races, for the Chairman's speed, as reported by the New China News Agency dispatch, was nearly four times the world record.[45]

Upon his arrival at the capital, Mao called a meeting of regional Party secretaries and members of the Cultural Revolution Group where he demanded the withdrawal of the work teams dispatched by Liu Shao-ch'i. "The work teams know nothing. Some work teams have even created trouble.... Work teams only hinder the movement. [Affairs in the schools] have to be dealt with by the forces in the schools themselves, not by the work teams, you, me, or the provincial committees."[46] The Peking Municipal Party Committee immediately announced that work teams would be withdrawn from all universities and high schools in the city, and would be replaced by "Cultural Revolution small groups" to be elected by the teachers, students, and staff at each school.[47]

But Mao was not mollified by the Peking Party Committee's quick capitulation. He began preparations for a Central Committee plenum, the first since 1962, that would endorse the measures already undertaken and legitimate his vision of a revolution against revisionism in China. The session, which convened in early August, was probably attended only by

45 "Quarterly chronicle and documentation," *CQ*, 28 (October–December 1966), 149–52.
46 Ch'en, *Mao papers*, 26–30.   47 Sun Tun-fan, *Li-shih chiang-i*, 2.250.

about half of the full and alternate members of the Central Committee – a reflection of both the depth of division within the Party and the haste with which the meeting had been called. The plenum was packed, not only by Party officials who were not members of the Central Committee but also by "representatives of revolutionary teachers and students from the institutions of higher learning in Peking."[48] In addition, Lin Piao apparently reinforced military control over key installations in the capital area – thus tightening the grip over the city which he had first announced at the enlarged Politburo meeting in May. Even so, Mao himself later admitted that he received the support of a bare majority of those attending the meeting.[49]

This rump session of the Central Committee made decisions in three principal areas. On personnel matters, it agreed to the promotion of several of Mao's principal supporters, and the demotion of those who had resisted him or who had misread his intentions over the past several months. The plenum endorsed the May Politburo decisions concerning the dismissals of P'eng Chen, Lo Jui-ch'ing, Lu Ting-i, and Yang Shang-k'un; and dropped P'eng and Lu from the Politburo. For his mishandling of the "Fifty Days" Campaign, Liu Shao-ch'i was stripped from his Party vice-chairmanship and demoted from the second to the eighth position in the Party hierarchy. Lin Piao succeeded Liu as second-in-command, and was made sole Party vice-chairman, thus replacing Liu as Mao's heir apparent. Ch'en Po-ta and K'ang Sheng, leaders of the new Cultural Revolution Group, were promoted from alternate membership on the Politburo to full membership. And Minister of Public Security Hsieh Fu-chih, who came to form a rather close association with the Cultural Revolution Group, was appointed an alternate member of the Politburo and named the member of the Party Secretariat responsible for all political and legal matters, the position formerly held by P'eng Chen.

Not all the new appointments to the Politburo were close associates of Lin Piao or Chiang Ch'ing. Other personnel decisions made at the Eleventh Plenum seemed to reflect compromises that Mao, Lin Piao, and the Cultural Revolution Group made with the Party and military establishments. A number of veteran civilian and military officials, not closely associated with Chiang Ch'ing, Chen Po-ta, or Lin Piao, were added to the Cultural Revolution Group. Four senior provincial leaders – T'ao Chu, the new director of the Propaganda Department; Li Hsueh-feng, the new first Party secretary in Peking; and regional Party secretaries Sung Jen-ch'iung and Liu Lan-t'ao – received appointments as Polit-

---

48 Lieberthal, *Research guide*, 255–57.   49 *Miscellany of Mao Tse-tung Thought*, 2.457–58.

buro members. And three more PLA marshals – Yeh Chien-ying, Hsu Hsiang-ch'ien, and Nieh Jung-chen – were also added to the Politburo, perhaps as a way of counterbalancing Lin Piao's growing political influence.

On policy matters, the formal political report given by Liu Shao-ch'i was overshadowed by the text of Lin's May talk on coups d'état and by a friendly letter sent by Mao to a group of Tsing-hua Middle School Red Guards in late July, both of which were circulated among the delegates to the plenum.[50] In reviewing the crucial issues of the early 1960s, the plenum's communiqué endorsed all the positions associated with Mao Tse-tung, and indirectly criticized some of those taken by Liu Shao-ch'i. Mao's approach to the Socialist Education Campaign, as embodied in the Former Ten Points of May 1963 and the Twenty-three Articles of January 1965, was said to be the correct way of dealing with organizational problems in the countryside. The plenum cited with approval Mao's concern with promoting revolutionary successors and his theory that class struggle continues in socialist society. It also noted favorably his calls to learn from such model units and organizations as the Ta-chai production brigade, the Ta-ch'ing oil field, and the People's Liberation Army.

Finally, the plenum adopted a Sixteen Point Decision on the Cultural Revolution (*wen-ko shih-liu t'iao*), laying out Mao's vision for the movement.[51] The principal goal was nothing less than to "change the mental outlook of the whole of society." It was to

struggle against and overthrow those persons in authority who are taking the capitalist road, to criticize and repudiate the reactionary bourgeois academic "authorities" and the ideology of the bourgeoisie and all other exploiting classes, and to transform education, literature and art, and all other parts of the superstructure not in correspondence with the socialist economic base.

The principal mechanism was to be the mobilization of "the masses of the workers, peasants, soldiers, revolutionary intellectuals, and revolutionary cadres." Even though they could be expected to make mistakes, the Decision proclaimed, the key to success in the Cultural Revolution was "whether or not the Party leadership dares boldly to arouse the masses." It was improper either to resist the movement, or even to attempt to control it.

The Sixteen Points, reflecting serious differences within the Central

50 Sun Tun-fan, *Li-shih chiang-i*, 2.251.
51 *Decision of the Central Committee of the Chinese Communist Party concerning the Great Proletarian Cultural Revolution.*

Committee, were highly ambiguous on the question of the degree of disorder that would be tolerated during the Cultural Revolution. On the one hand, the Decision acknowledged approvingly that there were likely to be "disturbances" in the course of the Cultural Revolution. It cited Mao's remarks in his 1927 report on the Hunan peasant movement that revolutions cannot be "so very refined, so gentle, so temperate, kind, courteous, restrained and magnanimous." It also set a sweeping goal for the movement: the "dismiss[al] from their leading posts [of] all those in authority who are taking the capitalist road [so as to] make possible the recapture of the leadership for the proletarian revolutionaries." And it prohibited any kind of reprisals against students in high schools or universities who participated in the movement.

On the other hand, reportedly at the instigation of Chou En-lai and T'ao Chu, the Decision also contained several specific provisions that were clearly intended to moderate the conduct of the Cultural Revolution.[52] It emphasized the possibility of uniting "ninety-five per cent of the cadres," and prohibited the use of coercion or force. It largely exempted ordinary scientists, technicians, and cadres, and Party and government agencies in the countryside, from the full force of the movement. It insisted that the Cultural Revolution not be allowed to hamper economic production. And it stipulated that although "bourgeois academic 'authorities'" and revisionists in the Party should be criticized, they should not be attacked by name in the press without the approval of the cognizant Party committee.

Even so, the general tone of the Eleventh Plenum was significantly different from what these formal caveats might suggest. Even as the plenum was in session, Mao wrote his own ta-tzu-pao, which he posted outside the Central Committee's meeting room, in which he accused "some leading comrades" – the reference was clearly to Liu Shao-ch'i and Teng Hsiao-p'ing – of "adopting the reactionary stand of the bourgeoisie" by sending out work teams to college campuses and government offices during the Fifty Days.[53] And the plenum itself endorsed the decision to dismiss or demote three of the twenty-one members of its Politburo. Together, these two developments symbolized the broad significance of the Eleventh Plenum: to legitimate a broad attack on the Party establishment and the intellectual community, at the personal initiative of Mao Tse-tung, that would entail a high degree of mass mobilization and an intense degree of political struggle.

52 JMJP, 5 January 1986, in FBIS Daily Report: China, 24 January 1986, K12–22.
53 Ch'en, Mao papers, 117.

THE COLLAPSE OF AUTHORITY

The emergence of the Red Guards

The Eleventh Plenum endorsed Mao's vision of the Cultural Revolution as the "arousal of the masses" to criticize revisionist tendencies in "all ... parts of the superstructure not in correspondence with the socialist economic base." In so doing, it brought together two themes that had been present in Mao's thinking since the early 1960s: first, that the Party establishment itself had been responsible for the emergence of revisionism in China since the Great Leap Forward and, second, that the best way to combat revisionism was to mobilize the ordinary citizenry of China – and especially China's young people – against it.

The Sixteen Point Decision of the Eleventh Plenum on the Cultural Revolution envisioned a mechanism for popular participation that survived for only a few weeks. The plan was to establish popularly elected Cultural Revolution committees (*wen-hua ko-ming wei-yuan-hui*) in grassroots units from factories and communes to universities and government organs. These organizations were to be modeled after the Paris Commune of 1871, in that their members were to be selected through a system of general election and were to be subject to criticism and recall by their constituents at any time. They were, in short, to be broadly representative of the organization in which they were formed.

Significantly, however, the Cultural Revolution committees were not expected to replace the Party committees or the administrative structure. Instead, the Decision of the Eleventh Plenum described them somewhat ambivalently as a "bridge to keep our Party in close contact with the masses." On the one hand, the committees were supposed to be permanent organizations for criticizing revisionism and struggling against "old ideas, culture, customs, and habits." But on the other, the Decision also specified that they were to remain "under the leadership of the Communist Party."

The problem, from a Maoist perspective, is that this conception of the Cultural Revolution committees had inherent flaws that stripped them of their effectiveness. To begin with, the stipulation that the committees accept Party leadership made it possible for the local Party committees to co-opt or control them by ensuring that the masses "elected" committee members who were relatively conservative in outlook. And the provision that the committees be elected virtually ensured, in the universities at least, that they be divided in reflection of the increasingly polarized student body. In many cases, the Cultural Revolution committees were dominated by the children of high-level cadres, not only because children from cadre families had come to constitute the largest single group among university students, but also because higher level Party committees were likely to favor their colleagues' children as leaders of the mass movement. What is more, the Cultural Revolution committees were preoccupied with the problems of their particular units rather than with the broader questions of national policy that the Maoists intended should be the more important focus of the Cultural Revolution.

But another model of popular participation was immediately available: that of the Red Guards. Just before the Eleventh Plenum approved the concept of Cultural Revolution committees, Mao Tse-tung wrote a letter to a group of Red Guards at the Tsing-hua Middle School in Peking that tacitly endorsed that alternative form of organization. Although the Eleventh Plenum's Decision on the Cultural Revolution did not even mention the Red Guards by name, Red Guard representatives were present in the meeting room. Compared to the Cultural Revolution committees, the Red Guards must have appeared to be a way of lifting the Cultural Revolution out of an exclusive concern with the affairs of grassroots units and toward the consideration of broader issues and criticism of higher-level leaders. Whereas the Cultural Revolution committees seemed likely to fall under the control of the Party apparatus, the Red Guards could more readily be manipulated by the Cultural Revolution Group.[54]

Thus, within a week after the close of the Eleventh Plenum, a series of massive Red Guard rallies began in Peking. Although the Cultural Revolution committees were never repudiated, and even received sporadic attention in the press for the rest of the year, it was clear nevertheless that they had been eclipsed by the Red Guards. The eight rallies, organized with the logistical support of the PLA, brought together 13 million Red Guards from all over China in the three months between 18 August and 26 November 1966.[55] Films of the events present vivid images of these enraptured young middle school students: some chanting revolutionary slogans, tears streaming down their faces; others waving their copies of Mao's quotations at the distant deity reviewing them on the Gate of Heavenly Peace. The Red Guard organizations bore such martial names as the "Red Flag Battalion," the "Three Red Banners Group," and the "Thorough Revolution Corps." Many Red Guards wore military uniforms, and Mao himself put on a Red Guard armband, thus conveying

---

54 On the interplay of these two models of organization, see Harding, *Organizing China*, ch. 8.
55 Sun Tun-fan, *Li-shih chiang-i*, 2.254.

the clear message that the Red Guards had the support of both Mao and the PLA. Directives issued by the Cultural Revolution Group in the name of the Central Committee gave the Red Guards the right to organize parades and demonstrations, use printing presses and publish newspapers, and post *ta-tzu-pao* criticizing Party committees at all levels.

The Red Guard movement drew on many of the socioeconomic cleavages and grievances discussed earlier in this chapter, particularly the tension between class background and academic performance as criteria for success in China's educational system. Beyond this, the mobilization of Red Guards was also facilitated by several other factors: a sense of excitement at being called upon by the leader of their country to become involved in national affairs; a sense of opportunity that one's future would be fundamentally affected by involvement in the Cultural Revolution; the suspension of classes and admissions examinations, which relieved millions of middle school and university students of academic responsibility; and, above all, the provision of free railway transportation to Red Guards seeking to travel around the country to "exchange revolutionary experiences." The Red Guard organizations drew not only on urban youth but also on large numbers of young people who had been sent down to the countryside in the early 1960s, and who now took advantage of the disorder of the time to return to the cities.

But the Red Guard movement did not, in the fall of 1966, achieve the goals that Mao had foreseen for it. To begin with, the Red Guards remained fascinated with what the Chairman must have regarded as secondary, even trivial, issues. Taking seriously the injunction of the Eleventh Plenum to combat the "four olds" – old ideas, old culture, old customs, and old habits – the Red Guards took to the streets looking for evidence of "bourgeois" culture. Young men and women wearing long hair were stopped on the streets and shorn on the spot. Women wearing tight slacks were subjected to the "ink bottle test": If a bottle of ink placed inside the waistband could not slip freely to the ground, the pants would be slashed to shreds. Shopkeepers were forced to take down signboards bearing traditional store names and to replace them with more revolutionary labels. Red Guards themselves often changed the names of streets, occasionally arguing among themselves over which new name would be the more progressive. One group of Red Guards proposed that the meaning of traffic signals be changed so that red, the color of revolution, would signify "go" rather than "stop."

Another Red Guard organization from a middle school in Peking drew up a list of one hundred examples for "smashing the old and establishing the new," which give some flavor of this aspect of the Cultural Revolution. They told "rascals and teddy boys" to "shave away your long hair" and "remove your rocket-shaped shoes." They insisted that people should stop drinking, desist from smoking, and give up the "bourgeois habits of keeping crickets, fish, cats, and dogs." Laundries, they said, should refuse to launder the clothing of "bourgeois families," and "bath houses must as a rule discontinue serving those bourgeois sons of bitches, and stop doing massage for them." This group of Red Guards also demanded that their own school change its name from the "No. 26 Middle School" to the "School of Mao Tse-tung's Doctrine."[56]

Some Red Guard activities were much less amusing. Teachers and school administrators were often regarded as principal representatives of the "bourgeois" class in China, and untold numbers were harassed, beaten, or tortured at the hands of their own students – often to death. Homes of former industrialists or landlords were invaded and ransacked, in a search for "contraband materials" or hidden wealth. Art objects were confiscated, ornate furniture smashed or painted red, and walls covered with quotations from Mao Tse-tung. Members of the pariah classes, such as landlords, were rounded up and forcibly deported from major cities. At Peking University alone, one hundred homes of faculty and staff were searched, books and other personal effects seized, and 260 persons forced to work under "supervision" with placards around their necks listing their "crimes."[57] The descent into often mindless violence and brutality simply continued and intensified, albeit under less official auspices, the reign of terror against China's "bourgeois" classes, particularly intellectuals, that had begun under Party leadership during the Fifty Days earlier the same year.

From the outset, the Red Guard movement was plagued with serious factionalism, with the main issue under dispute being the identity of the principal targets of the Cultural Revolution. To a very large degree, the divisions among the students occurred along the fault lines created by the educational policies of the early 1960s.[58] Students from cadre or military families usually insisted that the Red Guard movement remain under Party leadership, and tried to moderate the criticism leveled at the Party establishment. Instead, they sought to direct the spearhead of the movement against a different set of targets: intellectuals, scholars, former

56 SCMM, 566 (6 March 1967), 12–20.
57 For descriptions of Red Guard violence, see Gordon A. Bennett and Ronald N. Montaperto, Red Guard: the political biography of Dai Hsiao-ai; Ken Ling, The revenge of heaven: journal of a young Chinese; and HC, 19 (October 1980), 32–36.
58 On cleavages within the Red Guard movement, see Lee, Politics of the Cultural Revolution; Rosen, Red Guard factionalism; and Anita Chan, "Images of China's social structure: the changing perspectives of Canton students," World Politics, 34.3 (April 1982), 295–323.

industrialists and landlords, and signs of "bourgeois culture" in China's urban society.

Students from bourgeois backgrounds, in contrast, saw the Cultural Revolution as an opportunity to overcome the discrimination they had experienced in the early 1960s, when the growing emphasis on class background had put them at a disadvantage in university admissions, Youth League and Party recruitment, and job assignments. From their perspective, the Red Guard movement offered an unparalleled chance to demonstrate a degree of revolutionary conduct that would outweigh their undesirable family origins, and a legitimate opportunity to vent their grievances against the Party establishment. Maoist sympathizers who had been suppressed and persecuted during the Fifty Days now saw the possibility of reversing the verdicts that had been imposed on them by the work teams. They argued that their resistance to the teams had been an act of rebellion against "incorrect" Party leadership – a right now guaranteed them by the Sixteen Points adopted at the Eleventh Plenum.

The divisions within the student movement have been captured in a number of detailed case studies of Red Guard organizations in Peking and Canton. One reveals that, in a sample of nearly 2,200 middle school students in Canton, the overwhelming majority of students from cadre families (73 percent) joined organizations that defended the Party establishment, while a slightly smaller majority of students from intellectual backgrounds (61 percent) and a plurality of students from other "bourgeois" families (40 percent) joined rebel organizations. Analyzed somewhat differently, the same data show that the "loyalist" organizations drew the bulk of their membership (82 percent) from children from cadre and worker backgrounds, while the "rebel" organizations recruited their members principally from families of intellectuals (45 percent).[59]

From a Maoist perspective, this was an irony of the highest order, in that the most radical students in a revolutionary campaign against revisionism were representatives not of the proletariat, as the rhetoric of the day insisted, but rather of the bourgeoisie itself. From a less ideological point of view, however, the divisions within the student movement are much more understandable. Those who criticized the Party most vehemently were those who had gained the least from the Party's educational policies and whose families had been the principal victims of the Party's "class line," whereas those who supported the Party against attack were the children of Party officials and were those who had benefited the most from the prevailing system of Party recruitment, university admissions, and job assignments.

59 Chan, "Images of China's social structure," 314, Table 2.

The reaction of the Party establishment

The failure of the Red Guard movement to follow the course that Mao had intended, and its descent into disorder, factionalism, and violence, can be attributed to a number of causes. In part, it was because the restraints on the mass movement contained in the Sixteen Points were not strong enough to counterbalance the inflammatory rhetoric of that same document, of the official Party press, and of the leaders of the Cultural Revolution Group. In part, it was because the Cultural Revolution was conducted in a way that significantly departed from the original vision embodied in the Eleventh Plenum, in that the movement was implemented not by Cultural Revolution committees under Party leadership, but rather by Red Guard organizations that took as their right and obligation the rejection of Party authority. Perhaps most important, it was the result of a decision to mobilize millions of immature young people in a highly charged political atmosphere, to encourage them to engage in "revolutionary struggle" against vaguely defined targets, and to denounce as "suppression of the masses" any attempt to bring them under leadership or control.

Another reason for the difficulties of the Red Guard movement can be found in the opposition of the Party establishment itself. Officials could only have been bewildered by the notion that their records were to be evaluated by loosely organized groups of high school and university students, wearing military uniforms and waving small red books of Mao's quotations. But it was clear that their jobs were at stake. The Eleventh Plenum Decision had spoken of dismissing Party people in authority taking the capitalist road. And, in a speech to the plenum, Lin Piao had discussed the same matter in even blunter terms. The Cultural Revolution, he said, would involve "an overall examination and overall readjustment of cadres" according to three political criteria: whether they "hold high the red banner of Mao Tse-tung Thought," whether they "engage in political and ideological work," and whether they are "enthusiastic about the revolution." Those who met the criteria were to be promoted or retained in office; those who did not were to be dismissed, so as to "break the stalemate" between those who supported Mao's programs and those who opposed them.[60]

Even more alarming, it was rapidly becoming apparent that more than careers were involved. As already mentioned, an untold number of teachers and principals had by this time been beaten, tortured, and even murdered by their own students. And Party cadres were by no means

60 Kau, Lin Piao, 346–50.

exempt from similar forms of violence. In the first few months of the Red Guard movement alone, at least one Party official – the first secretary of Tientsin municipality – died as a result of a struggle meeting with radical students, and another – P'an Fu-sheng of Heilungkiang – was hospitalized after being denied food for four days.[61]

In some places, officials may have heeded the Party's injunctions to submit themselves freely to interrogation and criticism by the Red Guards. But the overall pattern was one in which officials tried to delay, divert, or disrupt the movement.[62] Initially, some attempted to ban the Red Guard organizations outright, on the grounds that they had not been officially sanctioned by the Eleventh Plenum. Another tactic was to permit the formation of Red Guard organizations, but then to place their activities under tight restrictions, similar to those imposed by the work teams during the Fifty Days, that prohibited them from holding parades or demonstrations, posting wall posters, or printing their own newspapers.

The convocation of the huge Red Guard rallies in Peking, and the publication of laudatory editorials in the central press, however, soon made it impossible to deny the legitimacy of the Red Guard organizations. Consequently, local officials began to employ a more subtle approach. Some tried to sacrifice a few subordinates (in an analogy with chess, the Chinese used the phrase "sacrificing the knights to save the king" to describe this tactic) as a way of demonstrating sincerity without placing themselves in jeopardy. Some staged "great debates" to discuss whether or not their Party committee had exercised truly "revolutionary" leadership, but manipulated the meetings so as to ensure the correct outcome. Some sought to prevent Red Guards from posting wall posters by covering blank walls with quotations from Mao Tse-tung, in the confident belief that covering such sayings with ta-tzu-pao would be tantamount to sacrilege. Still others tried to evade the Red Guards by moving their offices to local military compounds, which the radical students could not enter.

The principal tactic, however, was for provincial and local cadres to encourage the formation of conservative mass organizations to defend them against criticism by the radicals. Working through the Party organization and the Youth League within each university and middle school, it was possible to organize students who had a stake in maintaining the

---

61 Dittmer, *Liu Shao-ch'i*, 132.
62 On the response of Party officials to the Red Guard movement, see Parris H. Chang, "Provincial Party leaders' strategies for survival during the Cultural Revolution," in Robert A. Scalapino, ed., *Elites in the People's Republic of China*, 501–39; and Richard Baum, "Elite behavior under conditions of stress: the lesson of the 'Tang-ch'üan p'ai' in the Cultural Revolution," in Scalapino, *Elites*, 540–74.

status quo, and to portray more radical Red Guard groups as being members of bourgeois families seeking revenge on the Party. Working through the trade unions, the local leaders also organized more conservative workers into "Scarlet Guards" (*ch'ih-wei-tui*) to defend Party and government buildings against assaults by radical Red Guards. As a result of such maneuvers, the Red Guard movement, which had originally been based on college and middle school campuses, began to move outward into the ranks of the industrial work force.

This tactic was facilitated by a set of central regulations that, ironically, favored the Party establishment over the Cultural Revolution Group. Central policy at first restricted membership in Red Guard organizations to students from what were called "five red" family backgrounds – workers, peasants, soldiers, cadres, or revolutionary martyrs – and prohibited students from "bourgeois" backgrounds from participating in the Red Guard movement. This not only limited the size of the student movement – only 15 percent to 35 percent of middle school and university students belonged to the original Red Guard organizations in the late summer and early fall of 1966[63] – but it also paradoxically restricted membership in the Red Guards to precisely those students who were more likely to defend the Party establishment.

Why did officials resist the Red Guard movement in all these ways? Part of the answer lies in their desire for self-preservation in the face of a movement they must have regarded as anarchic and uncontrolled. But local and provincial officials must have also believed that they had support in Peking, and that their best strategy would be to try to ride out the worst of the campaign and hope that it would soon be brought to an end. After all, neither Liu Shao-ch'i, Teng Hsiao-p'ing, nor Chou En-lai had been dismissed from the Politburo by the Eleventh Plenum. Liu, to be sure, had been demoted in rank, but he remained president of the People's Republic. Teng and Chou retained their positions as secretary-general of the Party and prime minister of the State Council. And T'ao Chu, the former head of the Party's Central-South regional bureau, who had been named director of the Party Propaganda Department in early June, was also attempting to prevent the Red Guard movement from claiming too many victims. All these central leaders, in their speeches, actively supported efforts to restrict membership in the Red Guards to students from "five red" backgrounds, to maintain unity and discipline of Red Guard organizations, and to use the principle of majority rule to subordinate the radical minority to the more conservative majority.

63 Lee, *Politics of the Cultural Revolution*, 85.

The response of the Maoists

By the end of September, therefore, it was becoming clear to Mao, Lin, and the Cultural Revolution Group that the Cultural Revolution was not proceeding as originally intended. There had been much criticism of the "four olds," but little criticism of leading officials. Only a few lower-level cadres had been forced to resign. The main trend was for the Party establishment to evade, subvert, and co-opt the movement.

Accordingly, early October saw a substantial radicalization of the Cultural Revolution, and the strengthening the Cultural Revolution Group at the expense of the Party establishment. This development was first reflected in a series of speeches and editorials, most of which were written by members of the Cultural Revolution Group, on the occasion of China's National Day on 1 October. These statements criticized Party cadres for their resistance to the Cultural Revolution, reiterated that the Red Guards had the right to rebel against the Party organization, and emphasized that the main target of the Cultural Revolution was revisionists in the Party and not, as conservative organizations had argued, the "four olds." Perhaps most important, they also announced that the restrictions on membership in Red Guard organizations would be overturned so that radical students from "bad" class backgrounds could legally join the mass movement.

Moreover, between 9 and 28 October a central work conference was held in Peking to assess the Cultural Revolution's progress thus far, and to find ways of overcoming the obstacles it had encountered.[64] At first, Mao and Lin sought to gain the delegates' support for the Cultural Revolution by reassuring them about the movement's purposes. They promised that most cadres would be able to "pass the test" of the Cultural Revolution, if only they would welcome, instead of trying to evade, mass criticism. "If [cadres] have made mistakes," Mao said, "they can probably correct them! When they have corrected them, it will be all right, and they should be allowed to come back and go to work with a fresh spirit." Mao even submitted his own self-criticism, in which he acknowledged that the emergence of revisionist policies in the early 1960s was partly the result of his own choice to retire to a "second line" of leadership and relinquish responsibility for day-to-day decisions. What is more, Mao admitted, he had not anticipated the "big trouble" that was created by the mobilization of the Red Guards.[65]

64 Lieberthal, *Research guide*, 259–62. The dates, which differ somewhat from those given by Lieberthal, are from Sun Tun-fan, *Li-shih chiang-i*, 2.255.
65 Ch'en, *Mao papers*, 40–45; and Jerome Ch'en, ed., *Mao*, 91–97.

But the delegates to the work conference were still not mollified. What was originally expected to be a three-day meeting stretched on to more than two weeks, and what was supposed to have been a conciliatory atmosphere gradually became more and more acrimonious.[66] Ch'en Po-ta gave a report charging that the struggle between the "proletarian" and the "bourgeois" lines that had been evident in the early 1960s was now being reflected in the conduct of the Cultural Revolution. Mao Tse-tung and Lin Piao stopped giving reassurances to worried cadres, and now vehemently attacked officials who tried to check or elude the movement. Mao complained that "only a very few people firmly place the word 'revolt' in front of other words. Most people put the word 'fear' in first place." Lin attributed the resistance of the Party to the obstruction of some central officials, and he named Liu Shao-ch'i and Teng Hsiao-p'ing as the probable culprits. Both men were compelled to submit self-criticisms to the conference.

The effect of these developments in October 1966 was greatly to reduce the influence of conservative mass organizations.[67] Late in the year, some loyalist organizations in Peking did engage in a last stand, attacking radical Red Guard groups, criticizing Lin Piao, defending Liu Shao-ch'i, and insisting that the proper course was to "kick away the Cultural Revolution Group to make revolution on our own." But their power was clearly on the wane. Some conservative organizations submitted self-criticisms, some were taken over by radical students, and others collapsed as their leaders were arrested by public security forces.

The Cultural Revolution Group was also able in late 1966 to intensify the mass assault on the Party establishment. Easing restrictions on membership in mass organizations quickly increased the size of the radical factions. At the same time, the Cultural Revolution Group strengthened its liaison with those organizations which it considered to be most sympathetic, and urged them to amalgamate into larger, more effective bodies. In November and December, Red Guards were allowed to enter factories and communes, and workers were authorized to form their own "revolutionary rebel" organizations, thus breaking the effective monopoly previously enjoyed by the Party establishment in organizing workers and peasants. Free transportation to Peking was ended, so as to encourage Red Guards to end their "revolutionary tourism" and return to their

---

66 Sun Tun-fan, *Li-shih chiang-i*, 2.255.
67 On events following the October work conference, see Daubier, *History of the Cultural Revolution*, ch. 3; Dittmer, *Liu Shao-ch'i*, ch. 5; Lee, *Politics of the Cultural Revolution*, 118–29. The escalation is also reflected in the central directives issued during the period, in "Collection of documents."

home cities and provinces to "make revolution" against local Party committees.

Most important of all, the Cultural Revolution Group began to identify high-ranking officials for the mass organizations to attack, and provided friendly Red Guards with information that could be used as the basis for their criticisms. Red Guard delegations were sent from Peking to major provincial capitals with quite specific instructions as to which local officials should be put to the "test." Radical Red Guard organizations were informed that Liu Shao-ch'i and Teng Hsiao-p'ing had opposed Mao Tse-tung, and could be subjected to criticism. The Cultural Revolution Group provided the Red Guards with copies of Liu's and Teng's self-criticisms at the October work conference, and wall posters attacking the two men began to appear in greater numbers in November and December. According to evidence presented at the trial of the "Gang of Four" in 1980–81, Chang Ch'un-ch'iao met with the Tsing-hua student radical K'uai Ta-fu at Chung-nan-hai on 18 December and told him to discredit Liu and Teng publicly. "Make their very names stink," Chang is alleged to have said. "Don't stop halfway."[68] And, toward the end of the year, T'ao Chu was dismissed from the directorship of the Propaganda Department, for attempting to shield provincial officials and central propaganda and cultural affairs cadres from criticism, and for allegedly seeking to strip control over the movement from the Cultural Revolution Group. Five other important central officials – Yang Shang-k'un, Lo Jui-ch'ing, Lu Ting-i, P'eng Chen, and Ho Lung – were forced to attend mass rallies in Peking where they were denounced and abused for hours on end.

The message of these developments was clear: No one in China, save Mao Tse-tung himself, was to be exempt from criticism; and the methods of criticism could be harsh indeed.

The collapse of provincial authority

The result of the escalation of the Cultural Revolution in the last three months of 1966 differed from one part of China to another. In more remote provinces, where the mobilization of radical students was difficult, provincial leaders remained well entrenched. But where mobilization did occur, the consequence was not the rectification of local officials, as Mao had hoped, but rather the nearly complete collapse of provincial authority.

68 *A great trial in Chinese history: the trial of the Lin Biao and Jiang Qing counter-revolutionary cliques, Nov. 1980–Jan. 1981*, 35.

Shanghai provides the best example of this latter process.[69] The inflammation of central rhetoric in October encouraged the formation of the first radical, citywide workers' organization, the "Workers' Headquarters," early the following month. This organization, composed primarily of such underprivileged workers as apprentices and temporary contract laborers, was apparently formed by some lower-level cadres (such as Wang Hung-wen of the No. 17 State Cotton Mill, who would rise to national prominence later in the Cultural Revolution) with the assistance of radical students. The mayor of Shanghai, Ts'ao Ti-ch'iu, had by some accounts been willing to comply, albeit reluctantly, with the central directives on the Cultural Revolution. But he resisted the formation of the Workers' Headquarters, on the grounds that the creation of independent workers' organizations had not yet been sanctioned by central directives, and that the formation of such groups would almost certainly interfere with production.

When the Workers' Headquarters approached Ts'ao, seeking official recognition and material support, he therefore denied their request. Angered, the leaders of the Headquarters commandeered a train and left for Peking to present their case to the central leadership. Ts'ao ordered the train sidetracked at a suburban station outside Shanghai, where his representatives again tried to explain his position.

At first the central Cultural Revolution Group supported Ts'ao's stand. But when the workers still refused to return to their factories, the radical leaders in Peking sent Chang Ch'un-ch'iao to negotiate with them. Chang undercut Ts'ao Ti-ch'iu by agreeing to recognize the Workers' Headquarters, on the condition that their Cultural Revolutionary activities not be permitted to interfere with their normal production assignments – a decision that Ts'ao had no alternative but to endorse.

The city government's position was further weakened by the arrival, in Shanghai, of Nieh Yuan-tzu, apparently with instructions to expose the head of the city's education department as a revisionist, and to accuse Ts'ao Ti-ch'iu of shielding him. In the aftermath of her arrival, a group of radicals took over the local newspaper, the *Chieh-fang jih-pao*, demanding that it distribute copies of Nieh's address. Several days later, the city government capitulated.

The collapse of Ts'ao's authority, however, was not primarily the result of these actions by radical workers and intellectuals. It was, instead, the result of a countermobilization, at least partly spontaneous, by more

<hr />

69 Accounts of events in Shanghai in this period can be found in Neale Hunter, *Shanghai journal: an eyewitness account of the Cultural Revolution*; and Andrew G. Walder, *Chang Ch'un-ch'iao and Shanghai's January Revolution*.

MAP 2. PRC: political (Wade-Giles romanization)

MAP 3. PRC: political (*pinyin* romanization)

conservative Shanghai citizens. During the occupation of the *Chieh-fang jih-pao*, groups of Scarlet Guards and other supporters attempted to storm the building to retake it from the radicals. Postal workers refused to distribute copies of the tabloid containing Nieh's speech. The Scarlet Guards issued demands that Ts'ao repudiate his "capitulation" to the radicals, and that he not concede anything further to them.

Ts'ao's response to this process of polarization was, according to the careful study by Andrew Walder, to "sign any and all demands that were made to his office" by either faction.[70] The result was a torrent of requests by disadvantaged sectors of society for economic benefits. Workers who had been transformed into temporary laborers, and contract workers who had been laid off, demanded reinstatement and back pay. Permanent workers lobbied for higher wages and for increases in benefits, and charged that the disruption of production by the radicals would cause a reduction in their own bonuses.

Fights and riots broke out between the conservative and radical factions, and after one in which eight conservatives were reportedly killed, the Scarlet Guards called a general strike. This, coupled with the strategy of the besieged municipal government – to meet the demands of all factions – led to the collapse of the Shanghai economy: runs on banks, hoarding of supplies, disruption of electricity and transportation. By the end of December, China's largest city was in chaos.

THE SEIZURE OF POWER

The "January Revolution"

The situation in Shanghai was, in extreme form, representative of what had happened in much of urban China by the end of 1966. Essentially, three processes were at work, which taken together caused the collapse of Party authority. First of all, there was the mobilization of large sectors of Chinese society, who were making ever greater demands on the Party bureaucracy. The process had begun as a deliberate attempt by the Maoists in Peking to organize a force to criticize the Party. But once it began, the process fed on itself, with mobilization by the Maoists engendering a form of countermobilization – some spontaneous, some highly organized – in support of the Party establishment.

Accordingly, the process of mass mobilization produced a high degree of polarization in Chinese society, mirroring the intense factionalism that

70 Walder, *Chang Ch'un-ch'iao*, 36.

already existed at the highest levels of the Party leadership. In calling on the students (and later the workers) of China to criticize revisionism in the Party, Mao seems to have naively believed that they would act as a relatively unified force – that the "great union of the popular masses," of which he had spoken and written since the mid-1920s, would form in the course of the Cultural Revolution.[71] What happened was precisely the opposite. Mass mobilization aggravated deep cleavages within Chinese society, particularly those separating students of cadre families from those with bourgeois backgrounds, and those separating skilled permanent workers from less skilled and temporary employees.

Third, mobilization and polarization were accompanied by the delegitimation of Party authority. By authorizing the Red Guards to "rebel" against revisionists in the Party, and by asserting that people should obey only those Party directives that corresponded with Mao Tse-tung Thought, the Maoists in effect stripped the Party of unconditional legitimacy, without providing any alternative structure of authority in its place. At the same time, the delegitimation from above was reinforced by a withdrawal of legitimacy from below. As beleaguered Party organizations sought to cope with the explosion of popular demands by trying to please everyone, they ultimately pleased no one. The Shanghai experience vividly illustrates the authority crisis that occurs when a regime loses control over an escalating process of mobilization and countermobilization.

Mao's response to the collapse of authority was, in effect, to authorize radical groups to push aside the discredited (or recalcitrant) Party committees and constitute new organs of political power in their place. Once again, Shanghai was the frontrunner in this stage of the Cultural Revolution.[72] On 6 January 1967, a mass rally in Shanghai confirmed officially what had already occurred in fact: It dismissed Ts'ao Ti-ch'iu and other municipal officials from their posts. On that same day, Chang Ch'un-ch'iao, as a representative of the Cultural Revolution Group, returned to Shanghai from Peking to establish a new municipal government to replace the overthrown Party committee. With his encouragement, and with the support of the Cultural Revolution Group, constituent organizations of the radical Workers' Headquarters issued demands for the restoration of social order and economic production: demands that the economic grievances of workers be shelved until a "later stage" of the Cultural Revolution, that workers remain at their posts, and that enter-

71 On this tendency in Mao's thinking, see Stuart R. Schram, "From the 'Great Union of the Popular Masses' to the 'Great Alliance,' " *CQ*, 49 (January–March 1972), 88–105.
72 On events in Shanghai, see Walder, *Chang Ch'un-ch'iao*, ch. 7. A similar seizure of power took place in Shansi.

prise and bank funds be frozen. At the same time, rebel organizations, backed by units of the People's Liberation Army, began taking over factories, docks, newspapers, and other economic enterprises. From these beginnings, it was only a short time before the ultimate step was taken: The radical organizations announced the formation of a new organ of political power in Shanghai that would assume the political and administrative functions of the old Party committee and municipal government.

In the latter part of the month, this sort of power seizure was authorized for all of China. On 22 January, a vitriolic editorial in *Jen-min jih-pao* encouraged radical organizations throughout the country to rise up and take power away from the Party committees:

Of all the important things, the possession of power is the most important. Such being the case, the revolutionary masses, with a deep hatred for the class enemy, make up their mind to unite, form a great alliance, [and] seize power! Seize power!! Seize power!!! All the Party power, political power, and financial power usurped by the counterrevolutionary revisionists and those diehards who persistently cling to the bourgeois reactionary line must be recaptured![73]

The following day, a formal Central Committee directive repeated *Jen-min jih-pao*'s call for a mass seizure of power from "those in authority who are taking the capitalist road." It described the Cultural Revolution not simply as a criticism of bourgeois and revisionist tendencies in China, as had the Decision of the Eleventh Plenum, but rather as "a great revolution in which one class overthrows another."[74]

The radicalization of the goals of the Cultural Revolution was accompanied by a radicalization of the composition of the Cultural Revolution Group. In January and February 1967, all the representatives of the PLA and the regional and provincial Party organizations that had been appointed to the group the previous year were removed – along, of course, with T'ao Chu, who lost membership in the group when he was purged as director of the Propaganda Department in December. This meant that, once again, the Cultural Revolution Group reflected solely the interests of the radical intellectuals associated with Chiang Ch'ing, K'ang Sheng, and Ch'en Po-ta. No longer was their viewpoint moderated by the more conservative outlooks of senior Party and army officials.

The Central Committee's 23 January directive also initiated an escalation of the Cultural Revolution along a second dimension. Through the

---

73 *JMJP*, 22 January 1967, in *PR*, 10.5 (27 January 1967), 7–9.
74 "Decision of the CCP Central Committee, the State Council, the Military Commission of the Central Committee, and the Cultural Revolution Group under the Central Committee on resolute support for the revolutionary masses of the left," 23 January 1967, in "Collection of documents," 49–50.

latter half of 1966, the People's Liberation Army had played a somewhat aloof and ambivalent role in the Cultural Revolution. In some ways, to be sure, it had been actively involved on the side of the Maoists: by providing a forum for Chiang Ch'ing's assault on the prevailing line in literature and art; by providing, through the *Chieh-fang-chün pao*, a mouthpiece for radical viewpoints in the spring of 1966; by securing Peking during such crucial meetings as the May 1966 central work conference and the Eleventh Plenum, in August; and by providing logistical support for the Red Guards. In other ways, however, it had stood on the sidelines, or even taken a hostile position. The Decision of the Eleventh Plenum had specifically exempted the army from the jurisdiction of the Cultural Revolution Group, and other directives had apparently ordered military units to take a posture of "noninvolvement" in the confrontation among mass organizations and between radical groups and the Party establishment. And in many areas, the PLA had served as an "air raid shelter," providing sanctuary for local and provincial Party officials and a force for suppressing radical organizations.

Until 23 January, then, the most active elements in the Maoist coalition had been the radical brain trust, as symbolized by the Cultural Revolution Group, and the mass base, as typified by the radical Red Guard and revolutionary rebel organizations. Now, in light of the general stalemate that had occurred throughout the fall, and the collapse of authority that had begun to appear around the turn of the year, Mao decided to throw the army – the third element of his power base – more fully into the fray. The 23 January directive, citing a recent directive from the Chairman that "the PLA should support the broad masses of the Left," ordered that the armed forces drop any pretense of noninvolvement, stop serving as an "air raid shelter for the handful of Party power holders taking the capitalist road," give "active support … to the broad masses of revolutionary Leftists in their struggle to seize power," and "resolutely suppress" any "counterrevolutionaries or counterrevolutionary organizations" that offered resistance.

Once the decision had been taken to authorize the seizure of power, however, other equally important decisions remained. Who should seize power? Who should exercise it? Through what organizational forms? Perhaps the most pressing issue in this regard was whether or not "the masses" could really assume the role that had been assigned to them. The language of the 22 January *Jen-min jih-pao* editorial and the Central Committee directive of the following day suggested a kind of Marxist jacquerie: a mass uprising to depose those who had usurped power and departed from correct policies. But the "masses" of China were deeply divided into competing interests and largely ignorant of the details of political administration, rather than a unified political force that could provide an effective alternate government.

Both these problems were reflected in the wave of "power seizures" across the country in late January. In some places, competing mass organizations each claimed to have seized power, and appealed to Peking for support. In other places, Party officials used friendly mass organizations to stage what were later described as "sham" seizures of power. In still other localities, mass representatives entered Party or government offices, demanded the seals with which official documents were "chopped," and then walked out, in the belief that the capture of the symbols of power meant that power itself had somehow been seized. As Chou En-lai himself put it, power was "surrendered" by the Party but was not effectively "retained" by the Red Guards.[75]

The extent of these difficulties was indicated by the fact that China's central news media acknowledged and endorsed only four of the thirteen power seizures that occurred across the country at the end of January. An important editorial published on 1 February in *Hung-ch'i* (Red Flag), the Party's theoretical journal, tacitly admitted that the concept of a Marxist jacquerie was unworkable. Instead, the editorial stipulated that power should be seized not simply by a "great alliance" of mass organizations, but rather by a "three-in-one combination" (*san-chieh-ho*) of representatives of the "revolutionary masses," local military officers, and Party and government officials whose attitude was judged to be sufficiently "revolutionary." The presence of mass representatives would reflect the original populist ethos of the Cultural Revolution. But, as the editorial admitted, "it will not do to rely solely on the representatives of these revolutionary mass organizations." Without the other two components of the "three-in-one combination," "the proletarian revolutionaries will not be able to solve the problem of seizing and wielding power in their struggle ..., nor can they consolidate power even if they seize it." Cadres were necessary because of their administrative experience and their knowledge of the details of policy and programs; military representatives, who became, as we will see, the most important part of the "three-in-one combination," would be able to ensure discipline and suppress any opposition to the seizure of power.[76]

With this issue resolved, the second problem taken up by the Maoist center was the form that the new organs of power would assume. For a brief period, the Maoists flirted with the idea of re-organizing China

75 Philip Bridgham, "Mao's Cultural Revolution: the struggle to seize power," *CQ*, 34 (April–June 1968), 7.
76 *HC*, 3 (1 February 1967), in JPRS, 40,086, *Translations from Red Flag* (1 March 1967), 12–21.

around the principles of the Paris Commune: All officials would be drawn from the ranks of ordinary citizens, be chosen by general election, be paid the same salaries as ordinary workers, report regularly to their constituents, and be subject to recall at any time. These principles, which imply a form of government completely different from that of classic bureaucracy, had been endorsed by Marx, Engels, and the pre-1917 Lenin as the form of political institutions that the dictatorship of the proletariat would introduce, replacing the bureaucracies that, in Lenin's words, were "peculiar to bourgeois society."[77]

The model of the Paris Commune had been fashionable among Chinese radicals in 1966, the ninety-fifth anniversary of the Commune's short existence. A long article in the February issue of *Hung-ch'i*, well before the Eleventh Plenum, had recounted the history of the Commune and advocated that its principles be applied to China. The plenum itself, in authorizing the formation of Cultural Revolution committees, had provided that these new organizations embody the principles of the Commune, even though it simultaneously stipulated that the committees would supplement, and not supplant, the more bureaucratic Party and state organizations.[78]

With this as background, it was not surprising that radical Chinese would again turn to the model of the Paris Commune once the decision had been taken to seize power from the Party and state bureaucracies in January 1967. Implicitly echoing comments by Marx a century earlier that the proletariat could not simply take over the state machinery of the bourgeoisie but would have to create new forms of organization, the *Hung-ch'i* editorial of 1 February argued that the revolutionary rebels of China could not merely seize power in the existing Party and government agencies, but would have to create completely new organizational forms. Although it provided no clear guidelines as to what these new forms should be, the editorial strongly implied that they should be patterned after the Paris Commune. In keeping with this suggestion, many of the new provincial and municipal governments formed in late January announced that, in line with the principles of the Commune, their officials would be selected through mass elections and would be subject to supervision and recall. Some, such as Shanghai and Harbin, actually proclaimed themselves to be "people's communes."

77 Vladimir I. Lenin, "The state and revolution," in Henry M. Christman, ed., *Essential works of Lenin*, 290.
78 *HC*, 4 (15 February 1966), in JPRS, 35,137, *Translations from Red Flag* (21 April 1966), 5–22; *Decision*, sec. 9. On the use of the Paris Commune as a model in this period, see John Bryan Starr, "Revolution in retrospect: the Paris Commune through Chinese eyes," *CQ*, 49 (January–March 1972), 106–25.

In the situation prevailing in early 1967, however, such a step was as unrealistic as had been the earlier call for a mass uprising to seize power. The situation in Shanghai, for example, in no way reflected the exercise of immediate democracy, Paris Commune style. In organizing the Commune, Chang Ch'un-ch'iao had ignored the principle of direct election, promising only that such elections might be held at some future point "when conditions become ripe." In fact, the formation of the Shanghai Commune immediately produced grumblings that Chang had favored representatives of the Workers' Headquarters at the expense of other groups and that he was using the PLA to suppress opposition. Some people complained that he was ignoring the economic demands raised by workers in late December, and that he himself, as a former director of the municipal Propaganda Department and a current member of the central Cultural Revolution Group, was hardly an "ordinary citizen." As Andrew Walder has pointed out, "Despite the utopian images conjured up by the commune..., the Shanghai Commune was probably supported by less than one-fourth of Shanghai's politically active working population and relied heavily upon the PLA for its very survival."[79]

Realizing that talk of "people's communes" raised expectations of immediate democracy that could not possibly be realized in a highly mobilized and polarized setting, Mao Tse-tung called Chang Ch'un-ch'iao and Yao Wen-yuan back to Peking to persuade them to change the name of the Shanghai Commune. Mao's concern was that a faithful implementation of the Paris Commune model would produce a further collapse of political authority, the exclusion of cadres and military representatives from the "three-in-one combination," an inability to restore order and suppress "counterrevolutionaries," and problems in finding a role for a reconstituted Chinese Communist Party later on. All these tendencies the Chairman labeled "most reactionary."[80]

Thus on 19 February, the day after Mao's meetings with Chang and Yao, the Central Committee banned the use of the term "people's commune" at the national, provincial, or municipal levels.[81] (It retained its original meaning, of course, as the name of the largest level of joint economic and political administration in the countryside.) Instead, the Central Committee resurrected a term from revolutionary days – the "revolutionary committee" (*ko-ming wei-yuan-hui*) – to describe the "revo-

79 Walder, *Chang Ch'un-ch'iao*, 61.
80 For the texts of Mao's remarks, see *Miscellany of Mao Tse-tung Thought*, 2.451–55; and JPRS, 49,826, *Translations on Communist China* (12 February 1970), 44–45.
81 "CCP Central Committee's notification on the question of propagandizing and reporting on the struggle to seize power," 19 February 1967, in "Collection of documents," 89; Ch'en, *Mao papers*, 136–37.

lutionary, responsible, and proletarian provisional power structures"
formed as a result of the seizure of power. The historical reference was
particularly apt, for the revolutionary committees of the 1940s had also
been three-in-one combinations of mass representatives, Party cadres, and
military personnel, formed as provisional governments in areas recently
"liberated" by the Red Army. But the use of the term in 1967 also underlined a key point: like their predecessors of the Yenan years, the revolutionary committees of the Cultural Revolution were now regarded only
as provisional governments, pending the organization of something more
permanent. Already, it seemed, Mao was envisioning ways of reducing
the high level of mass mobilization that the Cultural Revolution had
produced.

The third issue at stake in early 1967 was the process by which these
revolutionary committees would be formed. With the notion of general
elections discarded, and the Party apparatus in shambles, the only element
of the three-in-one combination that was in a position to organize the
revolutionary committees on a nationwide basis was the People's Liberation Army. Thus, the procedure authorized by Peking was that, after the
overthrow of the local Party committees, the local military garrison (for
cities) or military district command (for provinces) would form a "military control committee" (*chün-shih kuan-chih wei-yuan-hui*), responsible for
restoring order, maintaining production, and beginning the selection of
the mass representatives, cadres, and military officers to serve on the revolutionary committee. In essence, the army became a national work team,
with responsibility for deciding not only which cadres would survive the
Cultural Revolution, but also which mass organizations deserved representation on the revolutionary committees.[82]

The overthrow of the Party committees in early 1967 has been described by the Chinese themselves as the "January Revolution" (*i-yueh
ko-ming*), and has been described outside the country as tantamount to a
military seizure of power. But neither the analogy of a mass revolution
nor that of a military coup is an adequate way of understanding this
period. It is true that the January Revolution involved a level of popular
dissent, mass organization, and political protest unknown since 1949. But
official rhetoric notwithstanding, the main purpose of the seizure of
power in January was less to overthrow authority than to restore order.
Granted, too, that the main beneficiary of the seizure of power was the
People's Liberation Army, as the country fell under military rule. But
military intervention in Chinese politics in early 1967 occurred at the

82 Harding, *Organizing China*, 253.

behest of civilian authorities in Peking, not in defiance of them. If the events of January 1967 in China amounted to a revolution, in other words, it was a revolution from above; and if they resulted in military rule, then that outcome reflected the decision by one civilian faction to use military force to overthrow another, rather than a military coup against civilian authority.

The main participants in the "three-in-one combination"

The establishment of the three-in-one combination as the official framework for the creation of revolutionary committees defined the principal issue for the next ten months. In how many administrative units and at what levels of government should power be seized? What balance should be struck among the three components of the three-in-one combination as each revolutionary committee was formed?

The principle of the three-in-one combination also illustrated quite clearly the main lines of cleavage in Chinese politics produced by the Cultural Revolution. At the provincial and municipal levels, cadres, mass organizations, and military units all competed for representation on the revolutionary committees. In Peking, in turn, each component of the three-in-one combination had its sponsors at the highest levels of Party leadership: Chou En-lai and other senior civilian leaders represented the interests of cadres; the Cultural Revolution Group, under Chiang Ch'ing, Chen Po-ta, and K'ang Sheng, represented the interests of the radical mass organizations; and Lin Piao and his associates in the Military Affairs Commission of the Party sponsored the interests of the armed forces.

But it would be incorrect to imply that these three vertical networks were internally unified. Just as there was conflict within the mass movement among radical and conservative Red Guard organizations, so too were there cleavages inside the armed forces between those sympathetic with Lin Piao and those who opposed him, and divisions between those cadres who were willing to accommodate to the Cultural Revolution and those who chose to resist it. And, significantly, none of the three organizational networks, nor their elite sponsors in Peking, was able to secure or maintain the unqualified support of Mao Tse-tung.

An understanding of the events of the remainder of 1967 and the first half of 1968 can therefore be facilitated by a brief analysis of the interests and behavior of each of these three vertical networks in Cultural Revolutionary China, beginning with what remained of the Party and state bureaucracy. By the end of January 1967, it was clear that every government and Party official in China was subject to criticism, dismissal, and even physical assault by radical organizations. Some cadres had already fallen from power, including the early targets of the Cultural Revolution, such as P'eng Chen, Lu Ting-i, and Lo Jui-ch'ing; and the victims of the radicalization of the Red Guard movement in late 1966 and the first power seizures in January 1967, such as T'ao Chu and Ts'ao Ti-ch'iu. Still others, such as Liu Shao-ch'i and Teng Hsiao-p'ing, and Chou En-lai and his vice-premiers, had come under heavy criticism but had not actually been dismissed. Elsewhere, the fate of the vast majority of cadres was still uncertain. Leaders at each level waited to see whether they could se-cure appointment to the revolutionary committees that were now being formed under military sponsorship, while their subordinates remained in office with their authority weakened but not completely eliminated.

The interest of the cadres, as symbolized by Chou En-lai, was primarily to moderate the impact of the Cultural Revolution on the state and Party bureaucracy. Chou's goals throughout the movement were, to the great-est degree possible: (1) to exempt the most important agencies of the Party and government from the most disruptive Cultural Revolutionary activities, (2) to prevent mass organizations from seizing power without authorization from a higher level, (3) to limit the geographic scope of operation of any particular mass organization, and (4) to ensure the main-tenance of normal production and administrative work.[83] In addition, Chou sought to protect a number of high-level officials from Red Guard attack. In January, he reportedly invited between twenty and thirty cabi-net ministers to take turns living in the guarded leadership compound in Chung-nan-hai, and enabled the first Party secretaries from a number of regions, provinces, and major cities to move to Peking, where they would be free from harassment or criticism by local Red Guards.[84]

Despite the common interests of cadres in limiting the scope of the Cultural Revolution, there were differences of outlook within the ranks of Chinese officialdom. Some cadres, particularly those of lower ranks, saw the Cultural Revolution as an opportunity for more rapid advancement, or for revenge against colleagues with whom they had poor personal relations. In some provinces and municipalities, therefore, a pattern emerged by which lower-echelon officials joined with radical mass organi-zations in seizing power from their superiors. Important examples include Hua Kuo-feng, a secretary of the provincial Party committee in Hunan; Chi Teng-k'uei, an alternate secretary in Honan; and, of course, Chang

83 On Chou En-lai's role in the Cultural Revolution, see Thomas W. Robinson, "Chou En-lai and the Cultural Revolution," in Thomas W. Robinson, ed., The Cultural Revolution in China, 165–312.
84 Sun Tun-fan, Li-shih chiang-i, 2.260–61.

Ch'un-ch'iao of Shanghai – all of whom rose to positions of even greater prominence in their provinces as a direct result of the Cultural Revolution. This would be the basis for later controversy, as those cadres who benefited from the Cultural Revolution in this way came into confrontation in the latter half of the 1970s with those who had been its principal victims.

The second main vertical network was that of the Cultural Revolution Group and the radical mass organizations it mobilized, protected, and to some degree directed. The main interests of the Cultural Revolution Group appear to have been to discredit as many cadres as possible, to give mass organizations the greatest scope and autonomy in their activities, and to maximize the participation of mass representatives on revolutionary committees. To this end, the Cultural Revolution Group began, as early as August 1966, but on a wider scale late in 1967 and in 1968, to draw up lists of Central Committee members, provincial Party and state leaders, and members of the National People's Congress and Chinese People's Political Consultative Conference whom they considered to have been "capitulationists" during the revolutionary period or "revisionists" after 1949. By August 1968, for example, K'ang Sheng had allegedly compiled a list of more than a hundred members of the Central Committee, and thirty-seven members of the Party's central disciplinary apparatus, whom he wanted to see expelled from the Party.[85] In addition, the Cultural Revolution Group used friendly Red Guard organizations to organize mass demonstrations and criticism against Party and government officials, to seize compromising materials from their homes, and to obtain useful information through detention and torture of suspected "revisionists" and, in some cases, members of their families, their servants, or their office staff.[86]

These activities brought the Cultural Revolution Group into conflict with both of the other two vertical networks active in the Cultural Revolution. The Cultural Revolution Group tried to expand the scope of political struggle to include virtually all officials at all levels of the bureaucracy, whereas the cadres obviously sought to narrow the targets of the Cultural Revolution to a smaller number. The Cultural Revolution Group wished to grant radical mass organizations greater autonomy to seize power from Party committees and government agencies, whereas civilian officials such as Chou En-lai attempted to place power seizures under the control of higher authorities, and to restrict mass organizations to supervisory rather than administrative functions.

85 Ibid., 2.271.   86 *Great trial*, passim.

In addition, the Cultural Revolution Group came into increasing conflict with the PLA over the military's role in the Cultural Revolution. In
January 1967, when the seizure of power first got under way, Ch'en Po-ta
contrasted the Cultural Revolution with the final stages of the revolution
in China in the 1940s. Then, he said, the Red Army seized power, "exercised military control, and issued orders from top to bottom." During
the Cultural Revolution, he said, it would be the "masses," and not the
military, "who take over."[87] The role that Mao granted to the PLA in
overthrowing the Party establishment and organizing revolutionary
committees was thus far greater than the Cultural Revolution Group
would have preferred. Even worse, the local military forces did not always appoint mass representatives to revolutionary committees in the
numbers that the Cultural Revolution Group wanted, or from the mass
organizations that it supported. The formation of revolutionary committees inevitably led, therefore, to attacks on local military headquarters
by some dissatisfied Red Guard organizations, and thus to tensions
between the PLA and the Cultural Revolution Group in Peking.

This leads to the third vertical network active in the Cultural Revolution: the People's Liberation Army itself. The role of the army, as we
have seen, escalated steadily through 1966 and early 1967. Now, once the
Cultural Revolution entered the stage of the seizure of power, the military
played an even greater part in Chinese politics. Its job was not only to
help seize power from the Party establishment, as it was ordered to do on
23 January, but also to ensure thereafter that order was maintained. This
second purpose was served by military occupation of key warehouses,
banks, broadcasting stations, and factories; military supervision of spring
planting; military management of civil aviation; and establishment of
military control commissions in major administrative jurisdictions where
power had been seized.[88] Altogether, 2 million officers and troops of the
PLA participated in civilian affairs during the Cultural Revolution.[89]

In general, the military appears to have had a single major interest during the Cultural Revolution: to maintain order and stability, prevent
the collapse of the Chinese social and political fabric, and thus avoid a
situation in which China would be vulnerable to foreign invasion.
In addition, some military officers had a related interest in maximizing
their own influence on the new revolutionary committees, increasing the

87 *Huo-ch'e-t'ou*, 7 (February 1967), in *SCMP*, 3898 (14 March 1967), 4–7.
88 The escalation of military involvement can be traced through the central directives in "Collection
   of documents."
89 Edgar Snow, *The long revolution*, 103.

numbers of military representatives, and protecting the military against attacks by Red Guards.

Beyond these common interests, however, the divisions within the military during the Cultural Revolution appear to have been every bit as great as those within ranks of the cadres or among the country's mass organizations.[90] Some of the cleavages were structural, resulting largely from the division of the PLA into local and main forces. The main forces – including the navy, air force, and the elite elements of the ground forces – were better equipped and directly subordinated to central command. The local forces, in contrast, were composed of lightly equipped infantry forces, commanded by military districts (corresponding in virtually all cases to provinces) and military regions (comprising several neighboring provinces), and responsible for a wide range of civilian activities.

During the Cultural Revolution, it was the main forces that remained more faithful to central directives from Lin Piao, not only because they came directly under the command of a General Staff and a Military Affairs Commission that he had packed with his own supporters, but also because they were the main beneficiaries of the program of military modernization that Lin had undertaken in the early 1960s. In contrast, the local forces, whose commanders often had close ties with local Party officials, often acted in conservative fashion as defenders of the provincial and municipal Party establishments. A study by Jürgen Domes, for example, has suggested that, of the twenty-nine military district commanders at the outset of the Cultural Revolution, only five gave the movement their backing, eight gave it nominal support only after they had brought local mass organizations under their control, and sixteen were unsupportive.[91]

A second set of cleavages within the military formed around personal factions. During the latter part of the Communist revolution, the Red Army had been divided into five great "field armies," each responsible for liberating a different part of the country. The personal associations established during this period formed the basis for factional networks of officers far after 1949. It was widely believed that Lin Piao, in seeking to consolidate his control over the PLA after his appointment as minister of

---

90 See Jürgen Domes, "The Cultural Revolution and the army," *Asian Survey*, 8.5 (May 1968), 349–63; Jürgen Domes, "The role of the military in the formation of revolutionary committees, 1967–68," *CQ*, 44 (October–December 1970), 112–45; Harvey W. Nelsen, "Military forces in the Cultural Revolution," *CQ*, 51 (July–September 1972), 444–74; and Harvey W. Nelsen, "Military bureaucracy in the Cultural Revolution," *Asian Survey*, 14. 4 (April 1974), 372–95.
91 Domes, "Role of the military."

national defense in 1959, had favored officers from the field army he had commanded (the Fourth) over officers from other factions.[92] After his purge, Lin was accused of having assembled derogatory materials about ranking officers from other field armies, particularly Nieh Jung-chen, Hsu Hsiang-ch'ien, Ho Lung, and Yeh Chien-ying, who might have thwarted his attempt to establish exclusive personal control over the armed forces.[93]

As a final element in this assessment of the major participants in the three-in-one combination, it is important to underscore the tensions and conflicts that emerged from time to time between Mao and each of these three vertical networks. Mao's main differences were obviously with the Party and state cadres, for it was they whom he suspected of revisionism, and against whom he directed the Cultural Revolution. On the other hand, Mao seems to have acknowledged the need for trained administrators to serve on the revolutionary committees. He claimed to hope that the cadres would be able to "pass the test" of the Cultural Revolution ("Who wants to knock you down? I don't," he told the central work conference in October 1966),[94] and he protected a few ranking civilian officials, particularly Chou En-lai, from Red Guard criticism.

But Mao also had his differences with both Lin Piao and the Cultural Revolution Group. Although Mao had selected Lin to head the Ministry of Defense in 1959, and chose him as his heir apparent at the Eleventh Plenum in 1966, the Chairman apparently questioned many of Lin's views on questions of history and ideology. In a letter to Chiang Ch'ing in early July 1966, he criticized Lin for overstating the importance of military coups and military power in the history of China and the history of developing countries, and for exaggerating Mao's own personality cult. "I have never believed that those several booklets of mine possessed so much magic," Mao wrote to his wife. "This is the first time in my life that I have involuntarily agreed with others on an issue of major significance."[95]

Much of Mao's criticism of Lin could simultaneously be read as a criticism of the Cultural Revolution Group, for the encomiums to Mao Tse-

---

92 The *locus classicus* for an analysis of the importance of field armies in Chinese military politics is William W. Whitson with Chen-hsia Huang, *The Chinese high command: a history of communist military politics, 1927–71*. See also Chien Yu-shen, *China's fading revolution: army dissent and military divisions, 1967–68*; and William L. Parish, "Factions in Chinese military politics," *CQ*, 56 (October–December 1973), 667–99.

93 *A great trial*, 82–89.   94 Ch'en, *Mao papers*, 45.

95 *CLG*, 6.2 (Summer 1973), 96–99.

tung Thought in mid-1966 and the sycophantic treatment of Mao in the Chinese press were as much its responsibility as that of the PLA. Some of Mao's statements in January about the Shanghai Commune suggest that Mao was concerned about anarchistic tendencies among the Cultural Revolution Group, and about their desire to overthrow all of the country's cadres.[96] There is no evidence to suggest that Mao was ever willing to authorize the use of armed force by mass organizations, as Chiang Ch'ing and her colleagues on the Cultural Revolution Group were sometimes prepared to do.

Mao had a variety of resources and strategies to employ against any of these three networks should they prove insubordinate or recalcitrant. The cadres were the most easily controlled, as they had the weakest power base at the time. As a general instrument, Mao could allow the central Cultural Revolution Group to intensify its criticism of Party and government officials, confident that this would be promptly reflected in the actions of radical mass organizations. More specifically, Mao could identify particular cadres for exclusion from revolutionary committees, for punishment, or for protection.

The PLA, in contrast, had much more power than civilian officials, for army officers controlled the organized armed force that now was essential to the stability of the regime. But the army could be controlled – in part by increasing the leeway given to radical mass organizations to criticize army officials, and in part by disciplining errant officers through the military chain of command. Thus, commanders unsympathetic to the Cultural Revolution were removed or transferred in five military regions and six military districts in the spring of 1967, and about eight more district commanders met similar fates later that year. In extreme situations, as we shall see, Mao and Lin could dispatch main force units into provinces where local commanders had been particularly obdurate.

Mao also had a variety of mechanisms for controlling the mass organizations. He could tighten restrictions on radical mass activities, giving Red Guard and revolutionary rebels less leeway to criticize civilian and military officials when their tendencies toward fragmentation and violence seemed to get out of hand. In addition, Mao and his representatives could label particular organizations as either "revolutionary" or "counterrevolutionary," depending on their subservience to central directives, and could give local military units the authority to suppress and disband mass organizations that had been deemed counterrevolutionary.

96 *Miscellany of Mao Tse-tung Thought*, 2.451–55; and JPRS, 49,826, *Translations on Communist China* (12 February 1970), 44–45.

The shifting balance

Given these cleavages – within each vertical system, among the three organizational networks, and between each vertical system and Mao Tse-tung – the formation of revolutionary committees in 1967–68 was thus an exceedingly complicated task. In only a few places – Heilungkiang, Shanghai, Kweichow, and Shantung – were revolutionary committees formed smoothly in the first two months of 1967. Here, the key was the existence of alternative leadership, usually from the pre–Cultural Revolution provincial or municipal Party establishment, which was able quickly to fill the collapse of authority that occurred in January. In other provinces, where the existing military and civilian leadership was divided, and where the mass organizations were deeply fragmented, the formation of revolutionary committees was a much more protracted process, involving continued conflict and competition.

The twenty months during which the revolutionary committees were selected, March 1967 to October 1968, were essentially a period of shifting balances among the three competing organizational networks, in which each would periodically gain or lose power relative to the others. Throughout the period, Mao retained the ability to determine the balance of power among the three vertical networks, although his decisions were clearly made in response to the actions of the cadres, the military, and the mass organizations, and although he never controlled the situation completely. The dynamics of the period can best be understood by examining four key turning points: the "February Adverse Current" of February–March 1967, the Wuhan Incident of late July 1967, the purge of a so-called "516" Group of radicals in early September, and the dismissal of Chief of Staff Yang Ch'eng-wu and the disbanding of the Red Guards in the summer of 1968.

Each of these turning points is important both for its origins and for its consequences. Each episode emerged from the tensions within and among the three key vertical networks already discussed. Each reflected, from Mao Tse-tung's perspective, the unreliability of one or more of the three organizational systems: the February Adverse Current showed that senior Party leaders still resisted the Cultural Revolution and the Red Guard movement; the Wuhan Incident demonstrated that high-ranking military commanders, particularly at the regional level, tended to side with conservative mass organizations against their radical opponents; and the "516" affair and the disbanding of the Red Guards in mid-1968 reflected the proclivities of the mass movement, and, indeed, the leaders of the Cultural Revolution Group itself, toward violence and disorder.

Together, the three episodes also produced a shift in the balance of power among the three organizational systems that dominated Chinese politics during this period. Although the three networks had begun, at least in theory, as equal participants in the three-in-one combination, by the end of 1967 it was evident that the PLA was well on its way to establishing predominance over both the civilian cadres and the mass organizations. The disbanding of the Red Guards in mid-1968, and the transfer of millions of young people to the countryside, removed these participants from the Chinese political stage altogether.

The February Adverse Current. The Decision on the Cultural Revolution adopted by the Eleventh Plenum in August 1966 had envisioned a mass movement that would be sweeping yet controlled. The emphasis on mass mobilization and mass criticism – particularly on the part of young people – promised to make life much more complex for the nation's Party and government officials. But significant limits were imposed in three areas. First, the cadre policy outlined in the Sixteen Points involved strict criticism but lenient treatment. The Eleventh Plenum had stipulated that most cadres were "good" or "relatively good," and had implied that they could remain at or return to their posts once they had made "serious self-criticism" and "accepted the criticism of the masses." Second, the movement was undertaken in the name of the Party, and was to be conducted under the leadership of the Central Committee, if not the Party apparatus at lower levels. And third, Cultural Revolutionary activities within the PLA were to be insulated from those in the rest of society and placed under the leadership of the Party's Military Affairs Commission rather than that of the Cultural Revolution Group.

By the end of January 1967, however, it was abundantly clear that the Cultural Revolution was overstepping each of these boundaries. A number of ranking cadres, including P'eng Chen and Lo Jui-ch'ing, had been "detained," without any warrant or other legal sanction, by radical mass organizations. Others were paraded through the streets of China's cities, with dunce caps on their heads and placards around their necks listing their "counterrevolutionary offenses." At least one member of the State Council, Minister of Coal Industry Chang Lin-chih, had been beaten to death, and other high-ranking officials had been physically abused. Liu Shao-ch'i and Teng Hsiao-p'ing had come under virulent verbal attack.

The authorization to mass organizations to "seize power," and the creation of Shanghai Commune, suggested that even the principle of Party leadership was being abandoned, for, as Mao himself pointed out, there was no room for a vanguard Party within the structure of a Paris

Commune. What is more, the turmoil of the Cultural Revolution now threatened to spread into the ranks of the armed forces, as the PLA was ordered to intervene in civilian politics in support of the "left." And Lin Piao himself seemed eager to incite his followers within the armed forces to criticize, in Red Guard style, those senior marshals, such as Chu Te, Ho Lung, and Yeh Chien-ying, who might challenge Lin's control over the armed forces.[97]

To cope with these problems, the central authorities issued a series of directives and statements throughout the month of February that were intended to limit the chaos being produced by the Cultural Revolution. The attempts at political stabilization proceeded along four tracks. First, as we have already seen, the model of the Paris Commune, which promised direct democracy without Party leadership but would have delivered little but factionalism and disorder, was repudiated by Mao personally. It was replaced by the model of the revolutionary committee and the directives to the PLA to intervene in the Cultural Revolution to "support the left" – both of which measures were intended to provide an organizational framework for restoring order and discipline to the country. As part of the implementation of the three-in-one combination, the central media began a campaign to publicize Mao's policy of relative leniency toward cadres who had "committed errors" either before the onset, or during the early months, of the Cultural Revolution.

Second, Mao also intervened to limit the use of force and violence by Red Guard organizations. Writing to Chou En-lai on 1 February, Mao criticized the tendency to force cadres under criticism to "wear dunce caps, to paint their faces, and to parade them in the streets." Describing such actions as "a form of armed struggle," Mao declared that "we definitely must hold to struggle by reason, bring out the facts, emphasize rationality, and use persuasion.... Anyone involved in beating others should be dealt with in accordance with the law."[98] Similar injunctions against the use of force were contained in a directive issued by the Military Affairs Commission on 28 January, a document said to have been drafted under the sponsorship of such senior military officials as Yeh Chien-ying, Hsu Hsiang-ch'ien, and Nieh Jung-chen, and then approved by Mao. The directive declared: "Arresting people at will without orders is not permitted; ransacking of homes and sealing of doors at will is not permitted. It is not permitted to carry out corporal punishment or disguised corporal punishment, such as making people wear tall caps

97 "Collection of documents," 19–20, 21; Great trial, 160, 164.
98 JPRS, 49,826, Translations on Communist China (12 February 1970), 22.

and black placards, parading them in streets, forcing them to kneel, etc. Earnestly promote civil struggle, resolutely oppose struggle by brute force."[99]

Third, attempts were also made to limit the impact of the Cultural Revolution on those state and military organizations that were crucial to the maintenance of economic production and political order. In February, outside mass organizations were ordered to leave all central Party departments and those central state ministries and bureaus responsible for national defense, economic planning, foreign affairs, public security, finance and banking, and propaganda; power seizures in the armed forces were limited to such peripheral organizations as academies, schools, cultural organs, and hospitals; and all Cultural Revolution activities of any kind were "postponed" in seven crucial military regions.[100] In addition, the Central Committee and the State Council issued a further directive attempting to preserve the confidentiality of all secret documents and files, including the personnel dossiers of Party and state cadres, which had been the source of much of the evidence used by mass organizations in their criticism of leading officials.[101]

Finally, central directives also tried to narrow the scope of activity allowed to mass organizations, to the point that, if these directives had been implemented, the Red Guard movement would have been brought to an end. Mass organizations were told to stop traveling about the country to "exchange revolutionary experiences," and were ordered to return to their native cities and towns. Middle school students were told to return to school, resume classes, and "attend their lessons on the one hand and make revolution on the other." National alliances of Red Guard organizations, which had begun to form spontaneously (or with encouragement from the Cultural Revolution Group) during the January Revolution, and which potentially threatened to become so powerful that they could not be controlled, were described as "counterrevolutionary organizations" and were ordered to disband immediately. Disgruntled elements of the work force, notably contract workers, temporary laborers, and workers who had been transferred to jobs in border regions, were told that they should stay at their posts and that their demands would be dealt with at a later stage of the Cultural Revolution.[102]

Encouraged by these developments, a group of senior Party leaders, from both the civilian and military spheres, began to launch an attack on

---

99 "Collection of documents," 54–55. See also Dittmer, *Liu Shao-ch'i*, 152–53.
100 "Collection of documents," 56, 61, 66, 71–72, 78–79, and 89.
101 Ibid., 84.   102 Ibid., 72, 82, 83, 85, and 87–88.

the whole concept of the Cultural Revolution.[103] These officials included Marshals Yeh Chien-ying, Nieh Jung-chen, and Hsu Hsiang-ch'ien; and Vice-Premiers Ch'en I, Li Fu-ch'un, Li Hsien-nien, and T'an Ch'en-lin. They used the occasion of a series of meetings on "grasping revolution and promoting production" that were convened by Premier Chou En-lai in mid-February to express their criticism of the Cultural Revolution. These veteran cadres apparently raised four principal issues: whether it was proper to separate the mass movement from the leadership of the Party; whether it was correct to attack so many senior officials; whether it was justified to produce disorder in the armed forces; and, on that basis, whether the Cultural Revolution should be continued or, as these officials clearly believed, be brought to a rapid end.

The most dramatic of these meetings occurred in Huai-jen Hall, inside the Chung-nan-hai complex in Peking, on an afternoon in mid-February. At this meeting, the contending groups were literally arrayed along two sides of a long table, with Chou En-lai sitting at one end. To Chou's left were Ch'en Po-ta, K'ang Sheng, Hsieh Fu-chih, and other members of the Cultural Revolution Group; to the prime minister's right were the three marshals, the five vice-premiers, and State Council officials Yü Ch'iu-li and Ku Mu. The meeting soon turned into a shouting match between the two sides, with T'an Chen-lin, the vice-premier responsible for agricultural work, at one point rising from the table and declaring his intention to resign, only to be restrained by Ch'en I and Chou En-lai.

An account of the proceedings — distorted, it was later charged — was soon relayed to Mao Tse-tung by members of the Cultural Revolution Group. Mao was furious at some of the opinions expressed at the meeting, which he considered to be a repudiation of his leadership. Aware of Mao's anger, the radicals soon described these meetings as a "February Adverse Current" (erh-yueh ni-liu), and used them as evidence in their mounting campaign to purge all surviving senior cadres from office.

In some ways, therefore, the result of the meetings in Chung-nan-hai was similar to that of the Lushan Conference of the summer of 1959, during the Great Leap Forward. On both occasions, China was in the midst of a tumultuous mass movement launched by Mao Tse-tung. In both cases, the disruptive consequences of the campaign had already become apparent, and efforts were under way to limit them. But on both occasions, some senior officials not only criticized the excesses of the

103 This account of the "February Adverse Current" is based on *JMJP*, 26 February 1979, in FBIS *Daily Report: China*, 28 February 1979, E7–20; and the recollections of Nieh Jung-chen, in *Hsin-hua jih-pao*, 21 and 22 October 1984, in FBIS *Daily Report: China*, 6 November 1984, K21–24. See also Lee, *Politics of the Cultural Revolution*, ch. 6; Daubier, *History of the Cultural Revolution*, ch. 5.

campaigns but also expressed some opposition to the movement as a whole. In both cases, Mao took the criticisms as a challenge to his personal leadership. As a result, not only did the two movements continue long after their adverse consequences had become clear, but some of the measures originally intended to remedy those consequences were canceled or postponed.

Thus, the February Adverse Current had the effect of re-radicalizing the Cultural Revolution, by discrediting the attempts that had been made earlier that month to restore order. One manifestation of this development was the decision to move criticism of Liu Shao-ch'i and Teng Hsiao-p'ing from Red Guard wall posters and tabloids into the official Party press, albeit through the use of such epithets as "China's Khrushchev" and "The Number Two Party Person in Authority Taking the Capitalist Road." Given the fact that Liu and Teng served respectively as president of the Republic and the general secretary of the Party, this step removed any remaining doubts that all cadres throughout the country were legitimate targets of attack. In a related measure, the 16 May Circular of 1966, with its harsh attack on "representatives of the bourgeoisie" in the Party, government, and army, appeared in the public media on the first anniversary of its adoption.

Emboldened by these developments, radical mass organizations issued stronger and more frequent criticisms of a number of surviving civilian officials throughout the spring of 1967. A prominent target was T'an Chen-lin, who had been one of the most active participants in the February Adverse Current, and whose outspokenness made him a favorite quarry of the radicals. At the climactic meeting at Huai-jen Hall, T'an had described K'uai Ta-fu, the Tsing-hua University radical who was then one of the darlings of the Cultural Revolution Group, as a "counterrevolutionary clown." T'an allegedly sent several written reports to Mao and the Central Committee urging an end to the Cultural Revolution, in one of which he called Chiang Ch'ing a "latter-day Empress Wu Tse-t'ien." According to accounts sympathetic to the radicals, T'an had also attempted to reinstate Ministry of Agriculture officials who had been overthrown during the January Revolution.

Another goal of the radicals was the dismissal of Foreign Minister Ch'en I, who, like T'an Chen-lin, made no attempt to hide his acerbic attitude toward the Cultural Revolution and the Red Guard movement. In one widely circulated, although possibly apocryphal, account, Ch'en I responded to an unpleasant encounter with one group of Red Guards by waving his own copy of the little red book, the *Quotations from Chairman Mao Tse-tung*, and saying: "Now it's my turn. Allow me to quote for you from Chairman Mao, page 320. Chairman Mao has said: 'Ch'en I is a good and faithful comrade.'" It was up to the Red Guards to discover that the Chinese edition of the *Quotations* had no such page.[104]

But the ultimate target of many of the radical mass organizations, and possibly the Cultural Revolution Group, was Chou En-lai, who was regarded by the radicals as the "backstage supporter" of the February Adverse Current and the protector of officials such as T'an and Ch'en. In Peking, a number of wall posters were displayed that began as attacks on T'an and Ch'en but ended with criticisms of Chou En-lai.

In this way, the February Adverse Current placed senior cadres in an increasingly vulnerable and passive position. To be sure, there were still periodic interventions by Mao, reasserting his conviction that 95 percent of China's cadres could be redeemed. Mao and Chou also attempted to save some cadres from public criticism and physical assault, at least for a time. Chou himself was protected by Mao, and Chou worked to protect such officials as Liao Ch'eng-chih, Ch'en I, Li Fu-ch'un, and Li Hsien-nien. It was at this point that a number of provincial and municipal officials were brought to Peking, so that their physical safety could be ensured.

But such measures did not protect everyone, nor prevent the progressive weakening of the political positions of veteran civilian officials. Liu Shao-ch'i and Teng Hsiao-p'ing were placed under house arrest sometime in the summer of 1967. The central Cultural Revolution Group came to assume many of the powers of the Politburo and the State Council. And the radicals continued to use the February Adverse Current as evidence that senior cadres opposed the Cultural Revolution, the Cultural Revolution Group, and Mao's leadership. Of the three vertical networks in the Cultural Revolution, the veteran officials were now in by far the weakest position.

The Wuhan Incident. Three of the most significant developments in China in mid-1967 were the serious divisions that emerged between radical and conservative mass organizations, between conservative and radical forces within the PLA itself, and between the Cultural Revolution Group and the armed forces. The Wuhan Incident of 20 July (referred to in Chinese as the "7/20 Incident," the *ch'i-erh-ling shih-chien,* after the date on which it occurred) provides the best example of the development and implications of these cleavages.[105]

---

104 Daubier, *History of the Cultural Revolution,* 220.
105 This discussion of the Wuhan Incident is drawn from Ch'en Tsai-tao, "Wu-han 'ch'i-erh-ling shih-chien' shih-mo" (The beginning and end of the "July 20th Incident" in Wuhan), *Ko-ming-shih tzu-liao,* 2 (September 1981), 7–45; and Thomas W. Robinson, "The Wuhan Incident: local strife and provincial rebellion during the Cultural Revolution," *CQ,* 47 (July–September 1971), 413–38.

When the PLA was ordered to supervise the formation of revolutionary committees at the provincial and municipal level across the country, that task was assigned principally to the military regions, and the local and garrison forces under their command. Many regional commanders had close personal associations with the Party officials in the provinces, which disposed them to side with the more conservative mass organizations to protect the Party establishment. Similarly, the PLA's proclivity for maintaining order and discipline placed it in conflict with more radical mass organizations that sought to overthrow all officials and disregarded economic production for the sake of "making revolution."

During the month of February, therefore, many regional commanders, using as justification the restrictions on the Cultural Revolution that had recently been issued by the central authorities, began to clamp down on the most obstreperous radical organizations. In the Wuhan Military Region, this involved decisions by the commander, Ch'en Tsai-tao, first to dissociate himself from, and then to order the disbanding of, a coalition of radical organizations known as the Workers' General Headquarters on the grounds that they were persistently engaging in disruptive activities that endangered both social order and economic stability.

The criticism of the February Adverse Current gave radicals in both Peking and the provinces the opportunity to protest the "suppression" of leftist mass organizations by the PLA. On 2 April, *Jen-min jih-pao* published an editorial calling for "proper treatment of the Young Generals" (i.e., the Red Guards) that was based on information supplied by disgruntled radicals in the Wuhan and Chengtu Military Regions. The same week, the Central Committee and the Military Affairs Commission published separate directives that greatly reduced the PLA's ability to suppress radical mass organizations.[106] The directives stripped the armed forces of the authority to declare any mass organization to be "counterrevolutionary," to suppress those who criticized military leadership, or to make mass arrests. Henceforth, the power to classify mass organizations was to be made by Peking alone, and those who had been labeled as counterrevolutionaries by regional military commanders were to be pardoned. The directives were reportedly the result of joint efforts by Lin Piao and members of the Cultural Revolution Group, which suggests that, at this point at least, there was still a high degree of cooperation between these two elements of the Maoist coalition.

Because these directives greatly reduced the PLA's ability to restore order, they also significantly increased the degree of conflict between con-

---

106 "Collection of documents," 111–12, 115–16.

servative and radical mass organizations. Radicals began to seize weapons from military armories and, in southern China, from shipments of munitions intended for North Vietnam. In some places, the PLA responded by supplying weapons to more conservative organizations. The incidence of armed struggle vastly increased, exacting a toll not only in human lives but also in economic production. In Wuhan, the principal consequence was that the radicals launched a series of protests and demonstrations calling for a reversal of the "adverse currents" in the city. These activities apparently received Chiang Ch'ing's personal endorsement.

Because the directives of early April had provided that only the central authorities would have the right to decide on the political orientation of competing mass organizations, Ch'en Tsai-tao requested a meeting with Chou En-lai and the Cultural Revolution Group to discuss the situation in Wuhan. According to Ch'en's own account, the meeting concluded that the behavior of the Wuhan Military Region had been basically correct, and that the radicals in the city should be told to stop attacking it. Unfortunately for Ch'en, word of this agreement leaked out in Wuhan before it had been officially announced in Peking, thus leading Chiang Ch'ing to charge that Ch'en was taking undue advantage of his success, and emboldening her to try to undo the agreement.

Meantime, the struggle among mass organizations in Wuhan intensified. In mid-May there came into existence a conservative umbrella organization known as the "Million Heroes," which took as its program the defense of the military region and the majority of veteran cadres. According to Ch'en Tsai-tao, the Million Heroes counted among their membership about 85 percent of the Party members in Wuhan, and enjoyed at least the tacit support of most of the local armed forces. Ch'en claimed that the military region command officially took a neutral position between the competing mass organizations, and called for unity between them. But it is likely that the true preferences of Ch'en and his subordinates were clear to all those involved.

Thus a second series of meetings was held, this time in Wuhan in mid-July, to try again to resolve the problems in the city. Participating in the meetings from Peking were Chou En-lai, two representatives of the central military command (Li Tso-p'eng and Yang Ch'eng-wu), two members of the Cultural Revolution Group (Wang Li and Hsieh Fu-chih), and, for some of the meetings, Mao himself. Both Mao and Chou now criticized Ch'en for his disbanding of the Workers' General Headquarters in February, and ordered that that organization be reinstated. But Mao apparently urged unity of the competing mass organizations, and disclaimed any intention of "knocking down" Ch'en Tsai-tao.

Chou then returned to Peking, leaving Hsieh and Wang to convey the results of the meetings to all parties in Wuhan. Fairly or not, the two men presented Mao's and Chou's instructions as a repudiation of the military region command, a criticism of the Million Heroes, and an endorsement of the city's radical mass organizations. Angered by this development, representatives of the Million Heroes stormed the hotel where Hsieh and Wang were staying, and then a group of soldiers from the local garrison seized Wang Li, detained him, and possibly beat him. Hsieh was spared only by his formal position as a vice-premier and minister of public security.

This insurgency was suppressed by dispatching Chou back to Wuhan to secure Wang Li's release, and by mobilizing substantial numbers of naval and airborne forces to seize control of Wuhan. Wang, Hsieh, and Ch'en Tsai-tao all flew off to Peking, the first two to receive a hero's welcome, the latter to undergo criticism and interrogation.

As in the case of the February Adverse Current, the immediate results of the Wuhan Incident were remarkably limited. Like T'an Chen-lin, Ch'en Tsai-tao received much less punishment than one might have expected for his act of disloyalty – for what in Ch'en's case was portrayed by the radicals as an act of mutiny. He was dismissed as military region commander but was otherwise treated relatively leniently, and was rehabilitated less than two years after the fall of Lin Piao. Ch'en himself has attributed this to the goodwill of Mao and Chou En-lai, but one also wonders about the degree to which Lin Piao would have welcomed the complete humiliation of a regional commander, even a recalcitrant one, at the hands of the Cultural Revolution Group.

The purge of the "516" Group. Although the Wuhan Incident had relatively slight effects on its principal participants, its broader consequences were devastating. Radicals, including members of the Cultural Revolution Group, took the occasion to call for a further assault against conservatives and "revisionists" in both Peking and the provinces. On 22 July, only two days after the Wuhan Incident, Chiang Ch'ing introduced the slogan "attack with words, defend with force" (*wen-kung wu-wei*).[107] This was the first time a leader of her rank had endorsed the armed struggles that were sweeping the country, and her statement only complicated any efforts to restore order.

The targets of this upsurge of radicalism included foreign diplomats in China, the Ministry of Foreign Affairs, and Chou En-lai. Diplomats from a number of countries were harassed, and the British legation was burned

107 *SCMP, Supplement*, 198 (August 1967), 8.

to the ground. A young diplomat named Yao Teng-shan, who had formerly been stationed in Indonesia, engineered a power seizure in the Foreign Ministry, directed not only against Ch'en I but also, by implication, against Chou En-lai, who had attempted to protect Ch'en.[108] Radical wall posters written during this period called for the downfall of the "old government," for the criticism of the "backstage boss of Ch'en Tsai-tao," and for dragging out "another Liu Shao-ch'i, one who has stood guarantee for the greatest number of people."[109] Chou was apparently detained in his office for two and a half days by radical Red Guards, who wanted to drag him out for "struggle."

The most important target this time was not Chou En-lai, however, but the People's Liberation Army itself. An editorial in *Hung-ch'i* in early August called on radicals to strike down the "handful of military leaders taking the capitalist road."[110] That there might be revisionists in the PLA was hardly an unprecedented notion: It had been contained in the 16 May Circular of 1966, as well as numerous editorials in the first half of 1967. But in the aftermath of the Wuhan Incident, such a slogan was explosive and had immediate consequences. Regional commanders, including some closely associated with Lin Piao, came under attack: Huang Yung-sheng, commander of the Canton Military Region and an ally of the defense minister, was described as the "T'an Ch'en-lin of Canton" by radical Red Guards.[111] If not checked, such a formula threatened the ability of the armed forces to maintain any kind of order in China.

Mao, Chou, and Lin all had common cause for opposing this escalation by the Cultural Revolution Group: Lin, because it threatened the unity and legitimacy of the armed forces; Chou, because it threatened his control over foreign affairs and the State Council and brought his own political position under attack; and Mao, because it moved China ever farther away from the elusive goal of unity that he appeared to seek.

In late August, therefore, the Cultural Revolution Group was reorganized. Four of its most radical members – Wang Li, Mu Hsin, Lin Chieh, and Kuan Feng – were dismissed, and a fifth, Ch'i Pen-yü, fell from power four months later. The Party's theoretical journal *Hung-ch'i*, which, under the editorship of Ch'en Po-ta, had been the mouthpiece of the Cultural Revolution Group, was forced to suspend publication. This "516" Group (*wu-i-liu ping-t'uan*) – named after the 16 May Circular of

108 On the struggles in the Ministry of Foreign Affairs during this period, see Melvin Gurtov, "The Foreign Ministry and foreign affairs in the Chinese Cultural Revolution," in Robinson, *Cultural Revolution*, 313–66.
109 On the renewed surge of radicalism in this period, see Lee, *Politics of the Cultural Revolution*, ch. 8, and Daubier, *History of the Cultural Revolution*, ch. 8.
110 *HC*, 12 (August 1967), 43–47.   111 Daubier, *History of the Cultural Revolution*, 207.

1966 – was accused of using the February Adverse Current as a pretext for criticizing first Yü Ch'iu-li, then Li Hsien-nien, Li Fu-ch'un, and Ch'en I, all with the ultimate goal of overthrowing Chou En-lai himself. The radicals were assigned responsibility for the wall posters attacking Chou En-lai in August.[112]

On 5 September, all four of the central authorities in China – the Central Committee, the Military Affairs Commission, the State Council, and the Cultural Revolution Group – issued a joint directive attempting to end armed struggle in the country and to revive the tattered authority of the PLA. Red Guard organizations were forbidden to seize arms from the armed forces, and the army was forbidden to transfer arms to mass organizations without central authorization. The PLA was now allowed to use armed force, as a last resort, against mass organizations that resisted its attempts to restore order.[113]

That same day, in a rambling extemporaneous speech to a Red Guard rally in Peking, Chiang Ch'ing sought to distance herself and the survivors of the Cultural Revolution Group from the four who had been dismissed. Without referring to them by name, she described the "516" Group as a small number of "extreme leftists" who had attempted to seize control of the mass movement. She repudiated the call to "drag out a handful from the PLA" as a "trap" set by these ultra-leftists to bring China into chaos. While still defending her own formulation "attack with words, defend with force," she now argued that the situation in China did not warrant the use of force in any circumstance. Despite doing her utmost to deny any personal responsibility for the "516" Group, Chiang Ch'ing had in fact been forced into making a statement that amounted to self-criticism.[114]

The chaos of August and the "516" affair had important implications for the course of the Cultural Revolution. First, as we will see below, it shifted the focus of the Cultural Revolution from the destruction of the old political order to the creation of a new one. In September, Mao Tse-tung revealed his "great strategic plan" for the rest of the Cultural Revolution, based on his travels across the country throughout the summer. In essence, this called for an end to disorder, and the most rapid possible progress toward the formation of revolutionary committees in the twenty-two provincial-level units in which they had not yet been organized.

112 On the fall of the "516" Group, see CB, 844 (10 January 1968); and Barry Burton, "The Cultural Revolution's ultraleft conspiracy: the 'May 16 Group,'" Asian Survey, 11.11 (November 1971), 1029–53.
113 SCMP, 4026 (22 September 1967), 1–2.   114 Ibid., 4069 (29 November 1967), 1–9.

As that process got under way toward the end of 1967, it appeared that the events of the summer had also readjusted the balance between the radical mass organizations and the regional military commanders in favor of the latter. In the spring of 1968, as we shall see shortly, there was a final resurgence of radicalism, but it never reached the high-water mark set in August 1967. When forced to choose between the mass movement and the PLA – between continued disorder and the only hope for political stability – Mao selected the latter. As a result, the military was now able to move relatively steadily toward institutionalizing its dominant position in the new provincial revolutionary committees.

The "516" affair also changed the pattern of alignment among the central leadership in Peking. Of all the leading members of the Central Cultural Revolution Group, the one most closely associated with the victims of the "516" purge, and thus the one most seriously weakened by it, was Ch'en Po-ta. All five victims of the "516" affair had apparently served as deputy chief editors of *Hung-ch'i* directly under Ch'en; all had been closely associated with Ch'en in the radical intellectual and journalistic establishment in Peking in the early 1960s; and the closing of *Hung-ch'i* could only be interpreted as a repudiation of Ch'en's editorial policies. Realizing that his position was weakening, Ch'en Po-ta now sought new sources of political support. He appears to have chosen Lin Piao. This was a marriage of political convenience that offered advantages to both parties. Ch'en could offer Lin the ideological and theoretical trappings that had been noticeably lacking in Lin's own public pronouncements. In turn, Lin could grant to Ch'en the backing of the vertical network – the PLA – that now seemed certain to emerge from the Cultural Revolution in the strongest position. It is highly plausible that Ch'en Po-ta began to work more closely with Lin Piao in late 1967, offering the ghostwriting services he had earlier provided to Mao and the Cultural Revolution Group.

The purge of Yang Ch'eng-wu and the suppression of the Red Guards. The "516" affair notwithstanding, there was one final resurgence of radical mass activity in the spring and early summer of 1968. This brief radical revival was made possible by a still mysterious leadership shuffle within the PLA: the dismissal, in March 1968, of Acting Chief of Staff Yang Ch'eng-wu, along with the political commissar of the air force and the commander of the Peking Military Region.[115]

115 Accounts of the dismissal of Yang Ch'eng-wu by participants in the event include those by Lin Piao, in Kau, *Lin Piao*, 488–50; by Nieh Jung-chen, in *Hsin-hua jih-pao* (9 and 10 October 1984), in FBIS *Daily Report: China*, 5 November 1984, K18–21; and by Fu Ch'ung-pi, in *Pei-ching wan-pao*, 12 April 1985, in ibid., 1 May 1985, K9–10. See also Harvey W. Nelsen, *The Chinese military system: an organizational study of the Chinese People's Liberation Army*, 97–101.

The purge of Yang Ch'eng-wu appears to have been a prototypical example of the cleavages produced by the Cultural Revolution: the divisions between radicals and conservatives in the provinces, the conflict between Chou En-lai and the Cultural Revolution Group, and the tensions within the PLA among representatives of different field-army factions. All of these conflicts seem to have played their part in Yang's sudden fall from grace.

Toward the end of 1967, Yang had been responsible for resolving a number of provincial disputes, just as he had accompanied Mao to Wuhan on a similar assignment in July. In both Shansi and Hopei, Yang supported the conservative factions against their more radical opponents. In Shansi, Yang refused to back the radical chairman of the provincial revolutionary committee against a challenge from more conservative military officers in the province; and in Hopei, Yang supported a coalition of conservative military units and mass organizations against a similar coalition of radicals that had been endorsed by Hsieh Fu-chih.

What is more, Yang Ch'eng-wu and Fu Ch'ung-pi, the commander of the Peking Military Region, took Chou En-lai's side in the premier's dispute with the Cultural Revolution Group and radical mass organizations. It was apparently Yang and Fu who provided military protection for a number of civilian and military leaders close to Chou. And after the dismissal of Ch'i Pen-yü, Yang encouraged Fu Ch'ung-pi to send a small force of soldiers to the offices of the Cultural Revolution Group, nominally to arrest Ch'i's followers and to search through the files looking for evidence of wrongdoing. Whatever Yang's ultimate intentions, it was not unreasonable for the remaining members of the Cultural Revolution Group, including Chiang Ch'ing and Hsieh Fu-chih, to believe that Yang was looking for materials that might incriminate them.

Finally, Yang was also involved in internecine struggles within the armed forces. Although Yang had some historical ties to Lin Piao, he had served in the final years of the revolution in the Fifth Field Army, not the Fourth. Yang's relations with Lin's closest lieutenants, including air force commander Wu Fa-hsien, were quite strained, and Lin apparently came to doubt Yang's loyalty. At the same time, Lin could also use the purge of Yang Ch'eng-wu as a way of attacking his own rivals Nieh Jung-chen and Hsu Hsiang-ch'ien, who had served as Yang's superiors in the Fifth Field Army.

Yang Ch'eng-wu was therefore accused of having supported a second February Adverse Current, which, like the first, had as its intention the protection of conservative forces, particularly senior cadres, against attack by the radicals. The immediate effect of his dismissal was twofold.

First, it enabled Lin Piao to strengthen his control over the Administrative Office of the Party's Military Affairs Commission, which exercised day-to-day control over the armed forces. Lin was now in a position to staff this crucial body with five people personally loyal to him: Wu Fa-hsien; Huang Yung-sheng, the commander of the Canton Military Region who now replaced Yang Ch'eng-wu as chief of staff; Li Tso-p'eng, the political commissar of the navy; Ch'iu Hui-tso, the head of military logistics; and Yeh Ch'ün, Lin's own wife.[116]

The second consequence of the Yang Ch'eng-wu affair was to legitimate a resurgence of activity by radical mass organizations, in protest against their alleged underrepresentation on the new revolutionary committees. Violence was particularly widespread in Shansi, Hopei, Shantung, and Kwangtung. At Peking's Tsing-hua University, rival factions barricaded themselves in campus buildings behind cement barricades and wire fences, and used catapults to launch chunks of brick and concrete against their adversaries.

In provinces such as Kwangsi, where the revolutionary committee had not yet been formed, factional violence flared to even greater proportions. Competing organizations stole weapons from trains carrying military supplies to Vietnam, and fought each other with machine guns, bazookas, and even antiaircraft weapons. The victims of the violence, often bound and trussed, floated down the Pearl River to be discovered in the waters off Hong Kong.

It was the violence at Tsing-hua University that caused the final suppression of the mass movement and the demobilization of the Red Guards. Mao ordered troops from Unit 8341, the elite security force protecting central Party leaders, together with workers from a knitwear mill and a printing plant in Peking, to enter Tsing-hua in late July. A few days later, on the night of 28 July, Mao met with student leaders from both Tsing-hua and Peking universities. Noting that K'uai Ta-fu had complained that a "black hand" had sent workers to the universities to suppress the Red Guards, Mao declared: "The black hand is still not captured. The black hand is nobody else but me." Mao complained that the Red Guards were engaged in factional armed struggle, instead of carrying out the Cultural Revolution in a principled way:

In the first place, you are not struggling; in the second place, you are not criticizing; in the third place, you are not transforming. Yes, you are struggling, but it is armed struggle. The people are not happy. The workers are not happy. The peasants are not happy. Peking residents are not happy. The students in most of

116 Sun Tun-fan, *Li-shih chiang-i*, 2.270–71.

the schools are not happy. Most students in your school are also not happy. Even within the faction that supports you there are people who are unhappy. Can you unite the whole country this way?[117]

Unless the Red Guards could shape up, Mao warned, "we may resort to military control [of the schools], and ask Lin Piao to take command."

Shortly thereafter, just as Mao had threatened, "worker-peasant Mao Tse-tung Thought propaganda teams," supervised by military officers, began to enter China's major universities. On 5 August, Mao sent some mangoes, which he had received from a group of Pakistani visitors, to the propaganda team at Tsing-hua as a personal endorsement of their activities. Mao justified the suppression of the Red Guards by arguing that the leadership of the Cultural Revolution should be in the hands of the "working class" rather than students. In the middle of the month, Mao issued a directive declaring that "it is essential to bring into full play the leading role of the working class in the Great Cultural Revolution." A few weeks later he ordered that the "masses of the workers," in cooperation with "Liberation Army fighters," should take the lead in the "proletarian revolution in education."[118]

Toward the end of August, Yao Wen-yuan, whose article on Hai Jui had launched the Cultural Revolution, now wrote another essay, which, in essence, brought the Red Guard stage of the movement to an abrupt end. Entitled "The working class must exercise leadership in everything," Yao's article was a scathing critique of the excesses of the mass movement, written by a man who had ridden to power on its back. The anarchism and factionalism of the Red Guard movement were ascribed to the "petty-bourgeois" outlook of its participants. "The facts show," Yao stated, "that under [the] circumstances it is impossible for the students and intellectuals by themselves alone to fulfill the task of struggle-criticism-transformation and a whole number of other tasks on the intellectual front; workers and People's Liberation Army fighters must take part, and it is essential to have strong leadership by the working class."[119] Under such leadership, the remaining mass organizations were disbanded, and Red Guard newspapers and periodicals ceased publication.

By the end of the year, the demobilization of the Red Guard organizations had been accompanied by the physical removal of millions of youths from the cities to the countryside. In December, Mao issued yet another directive that deemed it "very necessary for educated young people to go to the countryside to be reeducated by the poor and lower-middle

117 Miscellany of Mao Tse-tung Thought, 2.470.
118 Ch'en, Mao papers, 105.   119 PR, 11.35 (30 August 1968), 3–6.

peasants. Cadres and other city people should be persuaded to send their sons and daughters who have finished junior or senior middle school, college, or university to the countryside." By the end of 1970, about 5.4 million youths had been transferred to rural areas, mostly in their home provinces, but often to remote border and frontier regions. Few had any hope that they would ever be able to return to their homes.[120]

THE RECONSTRUCTION OF THE POLITICAL SYSTEM

With the purge of the "516" Group in late August 1967 and the demobilization of the Red Guards the following spring, the emphasis of the Cultural Revolution shifted from the destruction of the old order to the creation of a new one – from what the Chinese called a period of "struggle and criticism" (*tou-p'i*) to one of "criticism and transformation" (*p'i-kai*). Reconstructing the political system involved two principal elements: the completion of the organization of revolutionary committees, and the rehabilitation of the Party itself.

What is particularly noteworthy about this period is that the formal structure of China's "new" political order differed very little from that which existed on the eve of the Cultural Revolution.[121] The movement began with utopian rhetoric about "overthrowing" bureaucracy and establishing direct democracy, along the lines of the Paris Commune. But when the work of political reconstruction actually got under way, the blueprint that was followed was much less visionary. Officials were "reeducated" in "May 7 cadre schools" (*wu-ch'i kan-hsiao*) where, through physical labor and political study, they were supposed to cultivate a more selfless and efficient style of work. The revolutionary committees, and the bureaucracies they supervised, were supposed to be smaller, more capable, and more committed to Maoist values than their predecessors. And because they contained a small number of mass representatives, they were presumed to be more responsive to popular concerns. Still, the organizational policies of the period of reconstruction made it clear that government institutions would still be structured along bureaucratic lines, and that the Chinese Communist Party would remain a Leninist organization that would guide the work of the revolutionary committees.

What distinguished the new political system from its predecessor was less its structure than its staffing. Military officers played a much more

---

120 Thomas P. Bernstein, *Up to the mountains and down to the villages: the transfer of youth from urban to rural China*, 57–58.
121 For a description and evaluation of organizational changes wrought by the Cultural Revolution, see Harding, *Organizing China*, chs. 8–9, passim.

important role, particularly at higher levels, than at any time since the early 1950s. Veteran civilian officials were pushed aside in favor of men and women who were less experienced, less educated, less cosmopolitan, and less qualified – although not necessarily any younger. Party recruitment was resumed, and emphasized the absorption of large numbers of mass activists from the Red Guard movement. Moreover, Party and state organizations were plagued by serious factionalism, as a result of the unresolved conflicts among the victims, activists, and bystanders of the Cultural Revolution.

Mao's "strategic plan"

In September 1967, Mao Tse-tung devised what was described as his "great strategic plan" for concluding the Cultural Revolution. While defending the disorder of the previous twenty months ("Don't be afraid of making trouble. The bigger the trouble we make, the better"), Mao acknowledged that this troublemaking had served its purpose and should now be brought expeditiously to an end. "The car will overturn if it is driven too fast," Mao warned. "It is therefore necessary to be cautious."[122]

The immediate task as Mao saw it was to complete the formation of China's twenty-nine provincial revolutionary committees. Up until then, the process had been agonizingly slow: Only six revolutionary committees had been established at the provincial level between January 1967 and the end of July. "What we must principally accomplish now," Mao instructed, "is the great alliance and the three-in-one combination." This Mao hoped could be done by January 1968.

Mao appears to have believed that two guidelines would facilitate the formation of the remaining revolutionary committees. To begin with, Mao was now prepared to see the People's Liberation Army dominate the process, in fact if not in name, and was therefore willing to testify to the army's authority and loyalty and to forgive its occasional failures. As he put it in late summer, "The army's prestige must be resolutely safeguarded. There can be no doubt whatsoever about that." In a rather magnanimous reference to the Wuhan Incident, Mao continued: "It was unavoidable that the army should have made mistakes in tackling for the first time the large scale fighting tasks of supporting the left, supporting industry and agriculture, and carrying out military control and military training. The chief danger at the moment is that some people want to beat down the PLA."[123] The importance Mao assigned to the army was reflected in his reluctance to see the PLA become a target of general criticism after the dismissal of Yang Ch'eng-wu the following spring.[124]

As a second guideline, Mao recognized that the formation of revolutionary committees could be accelerated if their mass representatives were drawn from a broad spectrum of mass organizations, rather than solely from those that had been endorsed by local military commanders. This concept of inclusiveness was embodied in an instruction that the PLA should "support the left, but no particular faction," and in Mao's directive that "the working class has absolutely no reason to split into two hostile factional organizations."[125] The promulgation of Mao's ideal of national unity was accompanied in late 1967 by increasingly virulent press attacks against factionalism and anarchism, both of which were now described as manifestations of "petty bourgeois" ideology.

The completion of the formation of revolutionary committees occurred in two stages after Mao's tour of China in the summer of 1967. Between August 1967 and July 1968, committees were formed in eighteen provincial-level units. The last five, in such deeply divided provinces as Fukien and Kwangsi, and in such sensitive border areas as Sinkiang and Tibet, were created after the final suppression of the Red Guard movement in July. In general, the committees were produced in a series of negotiated settlements, in which local military commanders and Peking leaders sought to impose unity on competing mass organizations.

Because of Mao's stipulation that they should be broadly representative of a wide range of viewpoints, the revolutionary committees were generally large and unwieldy organs, composed of between one hundred and two hundred fifty members each.[126] The standing committees of the revolutionary committees, however, were more manageable bodies, often smaller than the comparable Party and state leadership groups that had existed before the Cultural Revolution. The composition of the standing committees varied with the trends of the times, with more mass representatives appointed in more radical periods, and fewer named in more moderate phases. Although mass representatives secured a reasonable number of places on the revolutionary committees formed during this period (61 of the 182 chairmen and vice-chairmen), effective power was concentrated in military hands. Of the twenty-three chairmen, thirteen were troop

123 Nelsen, *Chinese military system*, 83.
124 Philip Bridgham, "Mao's Cultural Revolution: the struggle to consolidate power," *CQ*, 41 (January–March 1970), 5.
125 *Chieh-fang-chün pao*, 28 January 1968, in *PR*, 11.5 (2 February 1968), 8–9; and Ch'en, *Mao papers*, 146.
126 Frederick C. Teiwes, *Provincial leadership in China: the Cultural Revolution and its aftermath*, 27, 29.

commanders, and five were professional commissars. Of the first vice-chairmen, fourteen were commanders, and five were commissars. All the rest were Party officials; not one was a mass representative.[127]

Over the longer term, Mao also foresaw the reconstruction of the Party once the revolutionary committees had been established as provisional governments in all China's provinces. From the beginning, the Chairman had seen the Cultural Revolution as a movement to purify the Party, not to destroy it. The purpose of the Cultural Revolution committees, as described in the Sixteen Points of the Eleventh Plenum, had been to serve as a bridge linking the Party to the masses, and not to act as a replacement for the Party. Similarly, the purpose of the Red Guards had been to overthrow "capitalist roaders" in the Party, but not the Party as an organization. Mao's principal objection to applying the model of the Paris Commune to China in early 1967, it will be recalled, was that there was no clear role for the Party in such a structure. "If everything were changed into a commune, then what about the Party? Where would we place the Party? ... There must be a party somehow! There must be a nucleus, no matter what we call it. Be it called the Communist Party, or Social Democratic Party, or Kuomintang, or I-kuan-tao, there must be a party."[128] If the Party had been set aside by the Red Guards and the revolutionary committees, that was a temporary phenomenon, not an ultimate goal of the Cultural Revolution.

Now, in September 1967, Mao believed that the time had come to think about the reestablishment of the Party. "The party organization must be restored," Mao said, and "party congresses at all levels should be convened." Mao was optimistic that this could be accomplished relatively quickly: "I see that it will be about this time next year [i.e., September 1968] that the Ninth Party Congress is convened."[129] Mao assigned the task of rebuilding the Party to Chang Ch'un-ch'iao and Yao Wen-yuan, with Hsieh Fu-chih, who was responsible for political and legal affairs during the Cultural Revolution, also playing an active role. On 10 October, Yao presented a preliminary report that laid out some basic principles for Party reconstruction.[130] Yao's report envisioned a top-down process, which would begin with the convocation of a national Party Congress to select a new Central Committee and to adopt a new

---

127 These data are based upon those in Richard Baum, "China: year of the mangoes," *Asian Survey*, 9.1 (January 1969), 1–17.
128 *Miscellany of Mao Tse-tung Thought*, 2.453–54. The I-kuan-tao, in Communist historiography, was a reactionary secret society during the Nationalist period.
129 *CLG*, 2.1 (Spring 1969), 3–12.
130 On Yao's report and the two subsequent Party documents, see Lee, *Politics of the Cultural Revolution*, 296–301.

Party constitution. The delegates to the Congress would be appointed by the central authorities after "negotiation" with the provinces. After the conclusion of the Party Congress the rebuilding of the Party at lower levels could begin. New Party committees at each level would embody, according to Yao's report, no fewer than three "three-in-one combinations": Each would be a combination of the old, the middle-aged, and the young; of workers, peasants, and soldiers; and of masses, army officers, and cadres.

On the basis of Yao's report, the Central Committee issued, on 27 November, a "Notice on the opinions about convening the Ninth Party Congress," and then, on 2 December, a further document "On the opinions regarding the rectification, restoration, and reconstruction of the Party structure." These documents followed the outlines of Yao's report, with two important amendments. First, the "Notice" added a decision that had been implicit from the beginning of the Cultural Revolution: that Lin Piao was now to become Mao's successor. "A great many comrades suggest," the "Notice" declared, "that the Ninth Party Congress vigorously propagandize the fact that Vice-Chairman Lin is Chairman Mao's close comrade-in-arms and successor, and that this be written down into the Ninth Party Congress's reports and resolutions so as to further enhance Vice-Chairman Lin's high prestige."

Second, the Central Committee documents announced the resumption of "Party life" at the basic levels. Provisional Party branches, often called Party core groups, were formed within revolutionary committees to guide the rectification of the Party at the basic levels. Their task was to begin a "purification of the ranks" of Party members, expelling those who had been shown to be revisionist, and absorbing "fresh blood" from the activists of the Cultural Revolution.

The Twelfth Plenum

Although the reconstruction of the Party was thus anticipated in the fall of 1967, the process did not really get under way until the formation of the last provincial-level revolutionary committees in September 1968. Once that crucial task had been accomplished, however, the surviving central leadership quickly convened the Twelfth Plenum of the Central Committee, which was held in Peking between 13 and 31 October.

Like the Eleventh Plenum, in August 1966, the Twelfth Plenum was a rump session of the Party's Central Committee. Only fifty-four full members of the Central Committee attended the meeting, representing a bare quorum of the surviving members of the body.[131] Furthermore, like its predecessor, the Twelfth Plenum was packed with people who were not Central Committee members. But where the additional observers in 1966 had been the "revolutionary students and teachers" from the Red Guard movement, in 1968 the extra participants were members of the Cultural Revolution Group, representatives of the provincial revolutionary committees, and "principal responsible comrades of the Chinese People's Liberation Army" – the officials, in other words, who were now the survivors and beneficiaries of the Cultural Revolution.[132]

The radicals entered the meeting with ambitious goals: to win endorsement of the events of the preceding two years and to complete the purge of the highest levels of the Party establishment. They were more successful in the first objective than the second. The plenum's final communiqué praised the accomplishments of the Cultural Revolution, lauded Mao's theory of "continuing the revolution under the dictatorship of the proletariat," held that Mao's "important instructions" and Lin's "many speeches" given during the movement were "all correct," and described the Cultural Revolution Group as having "played an important role in the struggle to carry out Chairman Mao's proletarian revolutionary line." It endorsed Mao's assessment that the Cultural Revolution was "absolutely necessary and most timely for consolidating the dictatorship of the proletariat, preventing capitalist restoration, and building socialism." It declared that "this momentous Cultural Revolution has won [a] great and decisive victory." And, with an eye to the future, the plenum adopted a new draft Party constitution and announced that the Ninth Party Congress would be held "at an appropriate time."[133]

In perhaps its most important decision, the plenum announced that Liu Shao-ch'i was being dismissed from all his government and Party positions, and was being expelled from the party "once and for all." The plenum's resolution on the subject – the first time Liu had been criticized by name in an official public document during the Cultural Revolution – disparaged Liu in inflammatory language. He was described as a "ren-

---

131 On the participants in the Twelfth Plenum, see Hu Yao-pang, "Li-lun kung-tso wu-hsu-hui yin-yen" (Introduction to theoretical work conference), in *Chung-kung shih-i-chieh san-chung ch'üan-hui i-lai chung-yang shou-yao chiang-hua chi wen-chien hsuan-pien* (Compilation of major central speeches and documents since the Third Plenum of the Eleventh Central Committee), 2.55; and Teng Hsiao-p'ing, "Remarks on successive drafts of the 'Resolution on certain questions in the history of our Party since the founding of the People's Republic of China,' " in *Selected works of Deng Xiaoping (1975–1982)*, 290.

132 For the communiqué of the Twelfth Pienum, see *PR*, 11.44 (1 November 1968), supplement, v-viii.

133 The text of the draft Party constitution is in Union Research Institute, *Documents of the Chinese Communist Party Central Committee, September 1956–April 1969*, 235–42.

egade, traitor, and scab hiding in the Party," as "a lackey of imperialism, modern revisionism, and the Kuomintang reactionaries," and as having "committed innumerable counter-revolutionary crimes." And yet, the supporting documents circulated after the plenum (at least those available in the West) dealt principally with Liu's activities in 1925, 1927, and 1939, during the early stages of the revolution, and said little about his behavior after the establishment of the People's Republic.[134] This would suggest that the plenum was unable to agree on how to characterize Liu's post-1949 activities.

During the small group sessions surrounding the meeting of the Central Committee, the Cultural Revolution Group and Lin Piao launched a vigorous attack upon the February Adverse Current of 1967. Curiously, Mao's closing speech to the plenum took a more conciliatory view of that episode than he had in the past. The Chairman now described the infamous meeting in Huai-jen Hall as an occasion for members of the Politburo to exercise their right to express their opinions on critical political issues. Nonetheless, Mao did nothing to prevent the plenum's communiqué from denouncing the February Adverse Current as an attack on the "proletarian headquarters with Chairman Mao as its leader and Vice Chairman Lin as its deputy leader."

But despite their best efforts, the radicals were unable to secure the removal from the Central Committee of any of the most active participants in the February Adverse Current, save for T'an Chen-lin, who had already been purged the previous year. Li Fu-ch'un, Li Hsien-nien, Ch'en Yi, Ye Chien-ying, Hsu Hsiang-ch'ien, and Nieh Jung-chen all remained on the Central Committee. Above all, the Cultural Revolution Group's proposal that Teng Hsiao-p'ing not only be removed from the Central Committee but also be expelled from the Party altogether, along with Liu Shao-ch'i, was rejected after a personal intervention by Mao Tse-tung.[135]

Beyond these points, the Twelfth Plenum made few important policy decisions. It spoke vaguely of a "revolution in education" that would be undertaken under the leadership of the workers' propaganda teams, but did not indicate what specific new programs would be adopted. Similarly, it described the Cultural Revolution as "promoting the emergence of a new leap in our socialist construction," but announced no new economic plans. The Cultural Revolution may have been intended to repudiate some of the economic and social policies of the early 1960s that Mao

134 The indictment of Liu Shao-ch'i, entitled "Report on the examination of the crimes of the renegade, traitor, and scab Liu Shao-ch'i," is in URI, *Documents of the Central Committee*, 243–50.
135 For these aspects of the Twelfth Plenum, see Sun Tun-fan, *Li-shih chiang-i*, 2.274; and the recollections of Nieh Jung-chen, in *Hsin-hua jih-pao*, 23 October 1984, in FBIS *Daily Report: China*, 7 November 1984, K20–21.

regarded as "revisionist," but the plenum indicated that no new "rev-olutionary" policies had yet been established to replace them.

The Ninth Party Congress

The Ninth Party Congress, convened in April 1969, reflected many of these same trends. Much of the political report, delivered to the Congress by Lin Piao, was an attempt to justify the Cultural Revolution as a "new and great contribution to the theory and practice of Marxism-Leninism."[136] Lin praised both the army and the Cultural Revolution Group for their achievements since 1966, and, in a veiled reference to the surviving senior civilian cadres, again criticized the February Adverse Current (here described as an "adverse current lasting from the winter of 1966 through the spring of 1967") as a "frenzied counterattack" on the Cultural Revolution that was intended to "reverse the verdict on the bourgeois reactionary line."

On matters of domestic policy, Lin's political report – like the com-muniqué of the Twelfth Plenum – said virtually nothing. It simply noted that the economic situation was good – that there had been "good harvests," "a thriving situation in industrial production," a "flourishing market," and "stable prices" in the preceding years – and concluded that it was "certain that the great victory of the Great Proletarian Cultural Revolution will continue to bring about new leaps forward on the eco-nomic front." It also claimed that the seizure of power in "departments of culture, art, education, the press, health, etc." would end the domina-tion of these sectors by "intellectuals" and "persons of power taking the capitalist road," but did not indicate what new policies would result. The report also referred at some length to the expulsion of old members from the Party and the recruitment of new ones, but did not provide any fresh clues as to the process by which this would occur.

The contribution of the Ninth Party Congress to China's political reconstruction, then, lay in the decisions it took about the new Party constitution and central Party leaders. Compared to the previous Party constitution, adopted by the Eighth Party Congress in 1956, the new document stressed the guiding role of Mao Tse-tung Thought and the importance of continued class struggle – neither of which concepts had

---

136 Lin Piao's report is in *PR*, 12.18 (30 April 1969), 16–35. The drafting of this report is subject to various interpretations. Chou En-lai reported at the Tenth National Congress in 1973 that the first draft had been written by Lin Piao and Ch'en Po-ta but was "rejected by the Central Committee." See *The Tenth National Congress of the Communist Party of China (Documents)*, 5. More recently, Hu Yao-pang has claimed that the report was written by K'ang Sheng and Chang Ch'un-ch'iao. See Hu, "Li-lun kung-tso wu-hsu-hui yin-yen," 57.

appeared in the earlier version.[137] In addition, opportunities for membership in the Party were now offered only to those who had the proper class background. The 1956 constitution had opened the doors of the Party to anyone who "works and does not exploit the labor of others" and who accepted the responsibilities of Party membership. The 1969 constitution, in contrast, restricted Party membership principally to those from worker, poor and lower-middle peasant, and military backgrounds.

The most important feature of the new constitution, however, was its brevity and lack of precision. Containing merely twelve articles, the new document was only about one-fifth as long as the 1956 constitution. The new constitution contained no reference to the rights of Party members. No attempt was made to specify in any detail the structure and powers of Party committees and various levels, the procedures for disciplining Party members, the frequency of national Party congresses, or the relation between the Party and the state – all of which had been important features of the earlier constitution. Eliminated from the Party structure were the Secretariat, which had supervised the central Party apparatus; the office of the general secretary, who had overseen day-to-day Party functions; and the entire network of control commissions, which had been responsible for inner-party discipline. Thus, the organizational structure for the Party that emerged from the Ninth Party Congress was significantly more flexible, less institutionalized, and therefore more open to manipulation by elements of the top leadership, than had been the case before the Cultural Revolution.

The Ninth Party Congress also selected a new central leadership not only for post-Cultural Revolution China but, it appeared, for the post-Mao era as well. Lin Piao's position as sole vice-chairman and as "Comrade Mao Tse-tung's close comrade-in-arms and successor" was established as a formal provision of the new Party constitution. Only 54 of the 167 members of the previous Central Committee were reelected at the Ninth Party Congress. Those who were removed from the Party elite at this point included a large number of provincial and regional Party leaders who had not been appointed to revolutionary committees, as well as important economic specialists, such as Po I-po and Yao I-lin, who had previously served in the State Council. After a protracted campaign by the radicals, most of the veteran civilian and military officials connected with the February Adverse Current lost their positions on the Politburo, although they retained their memberships in the Central Committee. The most prominent victim of the Ninth Party Congress was

---

137 The 1969 Party constitution is in *PR*, 12.18 (30 April 1969), 36–39. The 1956 constitution is in URI, *Documents of the Central Committee*, 1–30.

Teng Hsiao-p'ing, who was dropped from the Central Committee, but who still was not criticized by name in the official Congress documents.

The delegates to the Congress, and the Central Committee it elected, gave plain evidence of the effects of the Cultural Revolution on the Chinese political system. First, they illustrated the preeminence of the military. An analysis of the films of the Congress revealed that approximately two-thirds of the fifteen hundred delegates appeared in military uniforms. Of the Central Committee, 45 percent were military representatives, as compared with 19 percent of the Central Committee elected at the Eighth Party Congress in 1956.[138] The rise of the military came at the expense of both civilian officials, who were the main targets of the Cultural Revolution, and mass representatives, who might have been expected to be its principal beneficiaries. Mass representation on the new central Party organs was minimal. To be sure, 19 percent of the Central Committee members were "of the masses," but they tended to be older workers and peasants rather than the younger mass activists who had emerged during the Cultural Revolution. Greater representation of military officers also meant a decline in representation of civilian officials, particularly from the State Council, who fell to about a third of Central Committee membership. Given the differences in education and career path between the PLA and those government leaders, this change in the composition of the Central Committee was correlated with a decline in the level of education and amount of experience in foreign countries.

Second, and equally important, the Congress demonstrated the decentralization of power that had been produced during the Cultural Revolution. In 1956, about 38 percent of the Central Committee held provincial offices, and the rest occupied positions in the central military, Party, and government agencies. In 1969, in contrast, fully two-thirds of the Central Committee members were provincial representatives. This trend was not, however, so clearly reflected on the Politburo. Only three of the members of the Politburo on the eve of the Cultural Revolution could be classified as provincial or regional representatives. By comparison, two civilian officials with exclusively provincial responsibilities (Chi Teng-k'uei and Li Hsueh-feng) and three local military commanders (Ch'en Hsi-lien, Hsu Shih-yu, and Li Te-sheng) were elected to the Politburo at the Ninth Party Congress.

138 For analyses of the composition of the Ninth Central Committee, and comparisons with its predecessor, see Gordon A. Bennett, *China's Eighth, Ninth, and Tenth Congresses, Constitutions, and Central Committees: an institutional overview and comparison*; and Robert A. Scalapino, "The transition in Chinese Party leadership: a comparison of the Eighth and Ninth Central Committees," in Scalapino, *Elites*, 67–148.

Third, the Ninth Central Committee saw a shift of power to a more junior generation of leaders, although not to a younger one. Indeed, "inexperience without youth" is one way of characterizing the Central Committee produced by the Ninth Party Congress. Of the 170 full members of the Committee, 136 (and 225 of the 279 full members and alternates) had not served on the Central Committee before the Cultural Revolution. But, with an average age of about 60, the Ninth Central Committee was only slightly younger than the one it replaced, and was substantially older than the Eighth Central Committee had been at its election in 1956. Furthermore, the Ninth Central Committee was of distinctly lower rank than its predecessor, because of the influx of regional military leaders, second-echelon provincial officials, and mass representatives into Central Committee membership.

In a final development, the Politburo approved by the Central Committee illustrated the continued fragmentation of power at the highest levels in Peking. The twenty-five full and alternate members of the Politburo included, in addition to Mao and Lin, five central military officials closely linked to Lin, six people associated with the Cultural Revolution Group, three regional and provincial military commanders not closely tied to Lin, two senior civilian officials attacked during the Cultural Revolution, one other PLA marshal to counterbalance Lin Piao, three midlevel Party officials who had risen to power as a result of the Cultural Revolution, and three veteran Party leaders well past their prime. The composition on the Politburo thereby reflected the divisions among the victims, survivors, and beneficiaries of the Cultural Revolution; between the military and the civilian radicals who had come to power during the movement; between Lin Piao and his rivals in the central military leadership; and between the central military establishment and the regional commanders.

In short, despite the successful attempts to end the violence of the Red Guard movement, and the preliminary efforts to begin the reconstruction of the Chinese political system, the Ninth Party Congress left the country with a volatile political situation. The outlines of post-Cultural Revolution policy were undecided; power was divided among groups with noticeably different interests; and the structure of the Party and state was vague and uninstitutionalized. Although he was the nominal successor to Mao Tse-tung, Lin Piao's power base was highly fragile. Over the next two years, Lin would attempt to strengthen it by perpetuating military dominance of civilian affairs and by putting forward a policy platform that he believed would have wide appeal. These efforts, however, ultimately led to Lin's physical demise, as well as his political downfall.

CONCLUSIONS

How can we fairly judge the origins and development, consequences and significance, of this first stage of the Great Proletarian Cultural Revolution in China? The task is an unusually difficult one, bedeviled by the complexity of the events, the uncertain reliability of the information contained in the Red Guard press, and the lack of clear historical perspective on events that, as of this writing, took place less than twenty years ago.

The job of analysis is also entangled in the extreme and changing evaluations of the Cultural Revolution that have appeared in both China and the West since the Ninth Party Congress. During the late 1960s and early 1970s, the Chinese described the Red Guard movement as a creative and effective way, in Mao Tse-tung's words, "to arouse the broad masses to expose our dark aspect openly, in an all-round way, and from below." In the official interpretation of the day, the Cultural Revolution enabled the Chinese working classes to "smash revisionism, seize back that portion of power usurped by the bourgeoisie," and thereby "ensure that our country continues to advance in giant strides along the road of socialism."[139] As late as 1977, even after the purge of the "Gang of Four," Chinese leaders continued to portray the Cultural Revolution in glowing terms. "Beyond any doubt," Hua Kuo-feng declared at the Eleventh Party Congress, "it will go down in the history of the proletariat as a momentous innovation which will shine with increasing splendor with the passage of time." Indeed, Hua promised that further Cultural Revolutions "will take place many times in the future," as a way of continuing the struggle against bourgeois and capitalist influences within the Party.[140]

Within two years, however, the official Chinese line had completely changed. In mid-1979, Yeh Chien-ying described the Cultural Revolution as "an appalling catastrophe suffered by all our people." The interpretation that has prevailed more recently is that China was never in danger of a capitalist restoration, that Mao's diagnosis of China's political situation in 1966 "ran counter to reality," that the programs produced in the latter stages of the Cultural Revolution were impractical and utopian, and that the Red Guards were naive and impressionable youth led by "careerists, adventurists, opportunists, political degenerates, and the hooligan dregs of society."[141] An official resolution on Party history, adopted in 1981,

139 These quotations are drawn from Lin Piao's report to the Ninth Party Congress, in PR, 12.18 (30 April 1969), 21.
140 The Eleventh National Congress of the Communist Party of China (Documents), 51–52.
141 Beijing Review, 5 October 1979, 15, 18, 19.

condemned the Cultural Revolution as causing "the most severe setback and the heaviest losses suffered by the party, the state, and the people since the founding of the People's Republic."[142]

The reassessment of the Cultural Revolution in China has been fully replicated in the West. During the 1970s, the Cultural Revolution was described by many Americans as a worthy example of Mao's desire to preserve communitarian, egalitarian, and populist values in the course of economic development, and his conviction that "bureaucracy and modernization do not necessarily lead to an improved quality of life." The origins of the movement were said to lie in Mao's "noble vision" of a society in which "the division involving domination and subjection will be blurred, the leaders will be less distinguishable from the led..., and the led will take part more directly in the policy-making process." It was believed that the Cultural Revolution would devise socioeconomic programs that would prevent China from "ossifying in the morass of bureaucratism and statism."[143]

As the Chinese have become more critical of the Cultural Revolution, so too have Western observers. Mao's "fanaticism" has been compared to that of Hitler and Stalin, and the Cultural Revolution has been likened to the Inquisition and the Holocaust. The origins of the movement are traced not to a noble vision, but to a perverted perception of China's social and political problems in the mid-1960s. The decade from 1966 to 1976 is portrayed as a period of "chaos and destruction" that produced "one of the worst totalitarian regimes the ancient land had ever seen." By "destroy[ing] the intellectuals, wip[ing] out the universities, and ... wreck[ing] what there was of China's economy, the Cultural Revolution set back China's modernization for at least a decade."[144]

These rapidly changing interpretations of the Cultural Revolution should raise doubts about our abilities to portray accurately and fairly the tumultuous events of the late 1960s. Nonetheless, what is now known about the Cultural Revolution suggests the following assessment of the origins and consequences of the movement.

Origins

The ultimate responsibility for the Cultural Revolution rests squarely with Mao's diagnosis of the problems confronting Chinese society in the

142 "Resolution on certain questions in the history of our party since the founding of the People's Republic of China," FBIS *Daily Report: China*, 1 July 1981, K14.
143 These quotations are drawn from Harry Harding, "Reappraising the Cultural Revolution," *The Wilson Quarterly*, 4.4 (Autumn 1980), 132–41.
144 These quotations are taken from Harry Harding, "From China, with disdain: new trends in the study of China," *Asian Survey*, 22.10 (October 1982), 934–58.

early and mid-1960s. It cannot be denied that many of the shortcomings Mao identified were indeed rooted in observable reality. Local Party organizations, particularly in the countryside, had become seriously corrupt and ineffective. Higher-level administrative agencies, both state and Party, were overstaffed, underskilled, and enmeshed in bureaucratic routine. The social and economic policies introduced in the aftermath of the Great Leap Forward were reviving industrial and agricultural performance, but at the cost of growing inequality between skilled and unskilled workers, between communes blessed with fertile land and those to whom nature had been less kind, between bright students and their more mediocre classmates, and between urban dwellers and rural folk.

But Mao characterized these problems in extreme form. He chose to interpret the emergence of bureaucratism and inequality as signs that China was proceeding along a revisionist course, and to trace their origins to the presence of disguised "capitalists" and "bourgeois elements" at the highest levels of Party leadership. In so doing, Mao brought his lifelong concern with class struggle in China to its logical conclusion. For most of the first two-thirds of his life, Mao had waged revolution against those whom he considered to be the enemies of the Chinese people. For a short period in the mid-1950s, after the unexpectedly successful collectivization of agriculture and nationalization of industry, Mao briefly considered the notion that class struggle in his country might now basically be over. But it was difficult for him to hold to such a conclusion for long. By the Anti-Rightist Campaign in late 1957, he had developed the view that the struggle between antagonistic classes continued to be the principal political contradiction in the socialist period, just as it had been in China's presocialist years. And if not by the Lushan Plenum of 1959, then certainly by the Tenth Plenum in January 1962, Mao had come to the conclusion that the focal point of this class struggle was inside the leadership of the Party itself.

Thus, contemporary Chinese leaders and intellectuals are correct in saying that Mao was accustomed to seek the "class origins" (*chieh-chi ken-yuan*) of problems in Chinese society, and to interpret differences of opinion inside the Party as evidence of class struggle. As one Chinese historian has concisely put it, "Mao thought that inequalities and shortcomings in society were a sign that class struggle had not been handled well."[145]

145 Shao Hua-tse, "Kuan-yü 'wen-hua ta ko-ming' ti chi-ko wen-t'i" (On several questions concerning the "Great Cultural Revolution"), in Ch'üan-kuo tang-shih tzu-liao cheng-chi kung-tso hui-i ho chi-nien Chung-kuo kung-ch'an-tang liu-shih chou-nien hsueh-shu t'ao-lun-hui mi-shu-ch'u (Secretariat of the National Work Conference on Party Historical Materials and the

Mao was also strongly influenced by developments in the Soviet Union in the late 1950s and early 1960s. Confronted with evidence of Moscow's attempts to manipulate China's foreign policy and to control its economy, and concerned by signs of growing inequality and stagnation inside the Soviet Union, Mao reasoned that the "great power chauvinism" and "revisionism" apparent in Soviet foreign and domestic policy could only reflect the degeneration of the leadership of the Communist Party of the Soviet Union. Once having reached this conclusion, Mao logically inferred that the risk of a similar retrogression existed in China as well.

In his analysis of the Soviet Union, Mao stressed the consequences of the political succession from Stalin to Khrushchev. Although Mao had been quick to criticize Stalin's shortcomings, he was still persuaded that Stalin remained, on balance, a great Marxist revolutionary. Concerning Khrushchev, the Chairman reached the opposite conclusion. From the Twentieth Congress of the CPSU onward, Mao appears to have become ever more persuaded that Stalin's successor was himself a revisionist, whose rise to power had made possible nothing less than the restoration of capitalism in the birthplace of the October Revolution. Given Mao's own advanced years in the mid-1960s, the lesson was poignant. As he said to Ho Chi Minh in June 1966, "We are both more than seventy, and will be called by Marx someday. Who our successors will be — Bernstein, Kautsky, or Khrushchev — we can't know. But there's still time to prepare."[146]

Mao's strategy for dealing with the emergence of revisionism in the course of succession is also of crucial importance in understanding the origins and outcomes of the Cultural Revolution. Mao's approach was to call on the country's university and middle school students to criticize capitalist tendencies in China, first on their own campuses and then at higher levels of the Party bureaucracy. Paradoxically, however, Mao's view of Chinese youth in the mid-1960s was tinged with large doses of skepticism. In 1965, he told Edgar Snow that since the young people of China had not yet personally experienced their own revolution, they might "make peace with imperialism, bring the remnants of the Chiang Kai-shek clique back to the mainland, and take a stand beside the small percentage of counter-revolutionaries still in the country."[147] But Mao

Academic Conference in Commemoration of the Sixtieth Anniversary of the Chinese Communist Party), ed., *Tang-shih hui-i pao-kao-chi* (Collected reports from the Conference on Party History), 353.

146 Shao, "Kuan-yü…chi-ko wen-t'i," 356.
147 Mao is quoted in Snow, *Long revolution*, 221–22.

seemed confident – unwarrantedly so, as later developments would prove – that relying on the youth would serve to temper them as well as to purify the Party. In this sense, the Cultural Revolution was to provide a revolutionary experience for an entire new generation of Chinese, even as it offered a means of testing the revolutionary commitment of an older generation of Party officials.

The strategy was characteristically Maoist in at least two regards. First, it embodied long-standing populist elements in his thinking: his conviction that even the vanguard Party needed to be rectified and reformed through criticism from the people it led, and his belief that the masses of China should be encouraged to become involved in even the highest affairs of state. In the fall of 1967, in evaluating the results of the Cultural Revolution, Mao would stress the degree to which this populist ideal had been realized: "The important feature of this excellent situation is the full mobilization of the masses. Never before in any mass movement have the masses been mobilized so broadly and deeply as in this one."[148]

Second, Mao's strategy for the Cultural Revolution also reflected his tendency to rely on the unreliable in uncovering the darker side of Party leadership. For Mao deliberately to seek criticism of the Party from those very groups that lacked firm commitment to socialism was not unprecedented. In the mid-1950s, he had done so from intellectuals, during the Hundred Flowers Campaign. During the Socialist Education Campaign of the early 1960s he had mobilized the peasantry to purify the rural Party organization, although he simultaneously acknowledged the existence of spontaneous capitalist tendencies even among the poorer peasants. And now, in the mid-1960s, he would mobilize millions of students – at best naive and immature; at worst, in Mao's own words, ready to "negate the revolution" – to attack revisionism in the Party.[149]

Although this strategy was characteristic of Mao, it was still highly unorthodox for the Party. As Frederick Teiwes has demonstrated, the mobilization of students to criticize "Party persons in authority taking the capitalist road" ran counter to at least three major Party traditions: that Party leaders should not be penalized for their views on matters of policy, and should be allowed to retain their opinions even if they were in the minority; that Party rectification campaigns should result in mild sanctions rather than "merciless blows"; and that mass participation in Party rectification, if allowed at all, should be under the firm leadership either of the regular Party apparatus or *ad hoc* Party work teams.[150] What

---

148 Stuart R. Schram, *The political thought of Mao Tse-tung*, rev. ed., 370.
149 Snow, *Long revolution*, 223.
150 Frederick C. Teiwes, *Leadership, legitimacy, and conflict in China: from a charismatic Mao to the politics of succession*, ch. 3.

is more, by launching the Cultural Revolution through irregular procedures, in the face of reluctance or opposition from the greater part of the central Party leadership, Mao simultaneously violated a fourth norm as well: that of collective leadership and majority rule.

Only a leader with Mao's unique authority within the Chinese Communist movement could have successfully abandoned all these simultaneously. It is no exaggeration, therefore, to conclude that the principal responsibility for the Cultural Revolution – a movement that affected tens of millions of Chinese – rests with one man. Without a Mao, there could not have been a Cultural Revolution.

But if Mao was a necessary condition for the Cultural Revolution, he was not a sufficient one. To begin with, Mao had, as we have seen, crucial political resources in addition to his own personal legitimacy. These included, first, a quite sizable popular base. This mass support included both the sincere and the opportunistic, both the enthusiastic and the acquiescent. Some participated out of personal devotion to Mao, the man who had liberated their country from imperialism and warlordism. Others joined the Cultural Revolution for the same reason that so many supported reform in the 1980s: their concern that a Soviet model of development would take China down the road of ossification, inequality, and authoritarianism. Still others became Red Guards and revolutionary rebels because of specific grievances against particular cadres. As a former Red Guard has put it, Chinese used the Cultural Revolution to "get back at their superiors for everything from tiny insults to major abuse of policy."[151]

Over time, this mass base began to dissipate, as many of those who participated in the Cultural Revolution became disillusioned with the violence and chaos it engendered. Nonetheless, Mao was able to mobilize enough mass support in late 1966 and early 1967 to shake the Chinese Communist Party to its very foundations. And for this, the Chinese people themselves must bear some accountability.

Mao also relied on political support within China's national leadership. As we have repeatedly emphasized in this chapter, Mao's resources included a group of ambitious political ideologues and organizers in both Peking and Shanghai who could develop more systematically his rather inchoate observations about the dangers of revisionism in China, enhance Mao's personal charisma through the manipulation of the mass media, mobilize the disenchanted sectors of urban society, and, to a degree, direct the activities of the mass movement. At the same time, Mao also enjoyed the support of important elements of the People's Liberation

151 Liang Heng and Judith Shapiro, *Son of the revolution*, 47.

Army, particularly Lin Piao and major figures in the high command, who provided political support to the Chairman in early 1966, gave logistical assistance to the Red Guard movement later that year, overthrew the Party establishment in early 1967, and then undertook the restoration of order between mid-1967 and mid-1969.

But responsibility must also be assigned to the rest of the Party establishment for not resisting Mao more vigorously. The official Chinese version of the Cultural Revolution now places great stress on the opposition to Mao, at both central and local levels, that emerged after January 1967. The February Adverse Current of 1967 is singled out for particular credit as an example of "unceasing struggle" carried out by the Party against the Cultural Revolution. But by this time the Cultural Revolution had already received the formal endorsement of the Eleventh Plenum of the Central Committee. The forces of mobilization, conflict, and chaos were already irreversible.

The Party establishment might have been able to stop the Cultural Revolution if, earlier, it had acted in a more unified way to oppose Mao rather than acceded to his decisions. Of particular importance was Chou En-lai's assistance in securing the wider publication of Yao Wen-yuan's article on Hai Jui in November 1965, his involvement in the criticism of P'eng Chen in April 1966, his defense of radical students such as K'uai Ta-fu in September and of the Cultural Revolution Group as late as December 1966, and his failure to associate himself unambiguously with the February Adverse Current of February 1967. Of special interest is the revelation that Chou was the author of one of the most vitriolic denunciations of bureaucracy to come out of the Cultural Revolution, a document previously attributed to Mao Tse-tung.[152] This suggests that Chou may have genuinely believed that the danger of bureaucratic rigidification required drastic measures. Alternatively, Chou may have supported Mao for reasons of personal loyalty or self-preservation. In either event, Teng Hsiao-p'ing later acknowledged that Chou had done things during the Cultural Revolution for which he later had been "forgiven" by the Chinese people.[153]

But Chou should not be singled out for blame. Yeh Chien-ying and Yang Ch'eng-wu were involved in drafting the report justifying the purge of Lo Jui-ch'ing.[154] Teng Hsiao-p'ing appears to have joined Chou in the criticism of P'eng Chen in April 1966. And, more generally, the

152   *JMJP*, 29 August 1984, in FBIS *Daily Report: China*, 31 August 1984, K1–4.
153   Teng Hsiao-p'ing, "Answers to the Italian journalist Oriana Fallaci," in *Selected works of Deng Xiaoping*, 329–30.
154   Lieberthal, *Research guide*, 243, 249.

entire Politburo consented to the dismissal of Lo Jui-ch'ing, the reshuf-
fling of the Peking municipal Party committee, and the purge of the Party
Secretariat and Propaganda Department in May 1966, and to the adoption
of the Sixteen Points on the Cultural Revolution at the Eleventh Plenum
in August.

On the complicity of the Party leadership in the early stages of Mao's
assault against it, the official resolution on Party history is silent. But
Chinese historians have been more forthcoming. As one has put it, the
Politburo may have adopted such measures as the 16 May Circular without believing in them, or even because it felt compelled to do so; but it
endorsed Mao's decisions nonetheless, and must therefore "bear some
responsibility" for the Cultural Revolution.[155]

In explaining the acquiescence of the Party establishment in the spring
and summer of 1966, the Chinese have emphasized the importance of
Mao's personal authority over the rest of his colleagues on the Politburo
and the Central Committee. This implies that Mao enjoyed charismatic
standing among the Party leadership, as well as among the Chinese
masses. It further suggests that his ability to lead the Chinese Communist
Party to victory against enormous odds in the late 1930s and 1940s had
given him an air of infallibility that had been only slightly tarnished by
the disaster of the Great Leap Forward.

Recent Chinese accounts have also revealed that Mao was, in effect,
presenting the Party with a choice between Lin Piao and Liu Shao-ch'i
as his successor, and that many Party leaders initially agreed that Lin was
the better man. In the words of Teng Li-ch'ün, a man who was Liu Shao-
ch'i's secretary before the Cultural Revolution and who was responsible
for propaganda work in the early 1980s, Mao's preference for Lin "could
not be said to have been without support within the Party." This was
because, compared to Liu Shao-ch'i, Lin was more loyal to Mao, appeared to have a deeper commitment to ideology, and certainly had a better understanding of military matters. At a time when China was faced
with the escalation of American involvement in the Vietnam conflict and
a deepening military confrontation with the Soviet Union, many senior
Party leaders apparently were persuaded by the argument that "to run a
country and a Party like ours well, it won't do only to know politics and
not military matters."[156]

155 Chin Ch'un-ming, "'Wen-hua ta ko-ming' ti shih-nien" (The decade of the "Great Cultural
Revolution"), in Chung-kung tang-shih yen-chiu-hui (Research Society on the History of the
Chinese Communist Party), ed., Hsueh-hsi li-shih chueh-i chuan-chi (Special publication on studying
the resolution on history), 159–60, and Shao, "Kuan-yu...chi-ko wen-t'i," 378.
156 Teng Li-ch'ün, "Hsueh-hsi 'Kuan-yü chien-kuo-i-lai tang-ti jo-kan li-shih wen-t'i ti chueh-i' ti
wen-t'i ho hui-ta" (Questions and answers in studying the "Resolution on certain historical
questions since the founding of the state").

Just as Mao can be held accountable for the origins of the Cultural Revolution, so too must he bear much of the blame for its outcomes. Many of the most devastating consequences of the movement – particularly the violence, disorder, and loss of life – can be considered the predictable, if not inevitable, results of the strategy that Mao employed. In mobilizing the masses, Mao sanctioned the use of highly inflammatory rhetoric, casting the movement as nothing less than a Manichaean struggle between the forces of revolution and counterrevolution in China. He brought to the surface deep cleavages and grievances within Chinese society, without creating any mechanisms for organizing or directing the social forces he unleashed. He seems to have envisioned a self-disciplined revolutionary movement, but produced a divided and factionalized force over which he, the Cultural Revolution Group, and even the army could exercise only limited control. He expected Party cadres to welcome and support mass criticism of their own leadership, and reacted in disappointment and outrage when, not surprisingly, they attempted to suppress or manipulate the mass movement in order to preserve their own positions.

The flaw in Mao's strategy, in other words, was that he waged only half a revolution between 1966 and 1969. He failed to design a viable and enduring alternative political order to replace the one he sought to overthrow, or to transform the political resources he had mobilized from a destructive force into a constructive one. In this sense, the Cultural Revolution was the second unsuccessful Chinese revolution of the twentieth century. In 1911, Sun Yat-sen had succeeded in overthrowing the Manchu dynasty; but he was unable to create effective republican institutions to replace the fallen monarchy, and China fell under military rule. In the late 1960s, Mao succeeded in seizing power from the Party establishment, but was unable to design effective populist institutions to replace the Leninist Party-state. Once again, political power fell into the hands of the Chinese military.

In Mao's defense, perhaps the most that can be said is that at the height of the Cultural Revolution, he did try to moderate its destructive impact on the Party apparatus and on society as a whole. Mao attempted to prevent armed struggle and physical persecution, as is apparent in a number of central directives that he authorized forbidding beating, house raiding, looting, incarceration, and destruction of personal property.[157] He criticized the factionalism that had plagued the mass movement, and

157 See, in particular, the 6 June 1967 directive prohibiting "armed struggle, illegal arrest, looting, and sabotage," in CCP documents of the Great Proletarian Cultural Revolution, 463–64. Recent Chinese accounts attribute this directive to Mao personally. See Chin, " 'Wen-hua ta ko-ming' ti shih-nien," 164.

called on revolutionary committees to include representatives of all competing mass organizations. Mao not only repeatedly emphasized that the majority of cadres were good but was also personally responsible for protecting a number of high-ranking officials, the most important of whom was Chou En-lai, against attack.[158]

The problem was that these interventions were not completely successful in controlling the factionalism and violence of the Cultural Revolution. In the final analysis, the only way in which Mao could have regained control over the movement would have been to repudiate it completely. And this he refused to do. He never abandoned the concept of the Cultural Revolution, the theory behind it, or the strategy it reflected. Nor did Mao repudiate his own lieutenants who were responsible for much of the violence. To the end of his life, he continued to believe that the Cultural Revolution was a timely, necessary, and appropriate device for ensuring that China would follow a truly revolutionary course after his death.

Consequences

There is a certain all-or-nothing quality to the Cultural Revolution between 1966 and 1969. Important sectors of Chinese society were affected in a thorough manner, while other equally important parts of the country were hardly touched at all. Similarly, some of the consequences of the Cultural Revolution have already proved ephemeral, while others will continue to affect China for decades to come.

The Cultural Revolution largely spared rural China, and the 620 million people who lived there in the late 1960s. The exceptions were a relatively small number of communes close to large and medium-sized cities, especially those in suburban counties located within municipal boundaries. These suburban areas did experience some Cultural Revolutionary activities, as peasants engaged in struggles for power at the commune and brigade level, and participated in mass protest in the neighboring cities. In his careful study of the Cultural Revolution in the Chinese countryside, Richard Baum has identified 231 places in which rural disorder was reported by the Chinese press between July 1966 and December 1968. Of these, 42 percent were in suburban counties, especially around Peking, Shanghai, and Canton; and another 22 percent were within fifty kilometers of large or medium-sized cities. Less than 15 percent, in contrast, were more than a hundred kilometers away from an urban place. Baum's findings do not imply, of course, that only 231

158 Witke, *Comrade Chiang Ch'ing*, 363.

communes were directly involved in the Cultural Revolution. But his data do suggest that the Red Guard stage of the Cultural Revolution did not have a deep impact far beyond the major cities of China. It was, instead, principally an urban movement.[159]

If the countryside was touched lightly, relatively few urban residents remained unaffected by the Cultural Revolution, since the movement was conducted in virtually every high school, factory, university, office, and shop in China. In an interview with Yugoslav journalists in 1980, Hu Yao-pang estimated that 100 million people – roughly half the urban population, and virtually all those of working age – were treated "unjustly" during the Anti-Rightist Campaign, the Cultural Revolution, and other Maoist movements. Allowing for a bit of exaggeration, we can regard Hu's figure as a reasonably accurate indication of the comprehensive impact of the Cultural Revolution on urban China.[160]

Economically, China suffered surprisingly little from the Red Guard phase of the Cultural Revolution. Grain production rose in both 1966 and 1967, fell substantially in 1968, but then regained 1966 levels in 1969. The poor performance registered in 1968 may have been partly related to the political turmoil of that year, but it also reflected the fact that the weather in 1968 was significantly worse than in 1967. Moreover, the rapid recovery of grain production the following year suggests that the Cultural Revolution had only limited and temporary effects on agricultural output.

A similar pattern was evident in industry. Industrial output fell some 13 percent in 1967, as a result of the disruption of the normal work of both factories and transportation lines. As a result, state revenues, state expenditures, and investment in state-owned enterprises also fell precipitously in 1967 and 1968. But the industrial economy quickly revived. Industrial ouput in 1969 once again exceeded the level of 1966, and state revenues, expenditure, and investment followed suit the following year.[161] By the beginning of 1971, according to Western estimates, industrial production had achieved full recovery, regaining the levels that would have been projected from the growth rates of the early 1960s.[162]

159 Richard Baum, "The Cultural Revolution in the countryside: anatomy of a limited rebellion," in Robinson, *Cultural Revolution*, 367–476.
160 Tanjug, 21 June 1980, in FBIS *Daily Report: China*, 23 June 1980, L1. Some Western accounts mistakenly assign responsibility for these 100 million victims to the Cultural Revolution alone; see, for example, *Washington Post*, 8 June 1980.
161 Data on industrial and agricultural output are drawn from Arthur G. Ashbrook, Jr., "China: economic modernization and long-term performance," in U.S. Congress, [97th], Joint Economic Committee, *China under the Four Modernizations*, 1.104. Data on state revenues, expenditures, and investment are from *Beijing Review*, 19 March 1984, 27–28.
162 Robert Michael Field, Kathleen M. McGlynn, and William B. Abnett, "Political conflict and industrial growth in China: 1965–1977," in U.S. Congress, [95th], Joint Economic Committee, *Chinese economy post-Mao*, 1.239–83.

Thus the effects of this phase of the Cultural Revolution on the Chinese economy were limited in extent and duration; they were certainly far less severe than those of the Great Leap Forward one decade earlier. But the consequences of the Cultural Revolution for cultural and educational affairs were much greater.[163] The Chinese stage and screen stopped presenting any work of art other than a handful of "revolutionary" films, operas, and ballets written under the sponsorship of Chiang Ch'ing. The sale of traditional and foreign literature was halted, and libraries and museums were closed. Universities were shut down in the summer of 1966, and middle schools suspended instruction in the fall, so that their students could participate in the Cultural Revolution. Although middle school education was resumed the following spring, college classrooms remained dark for the next four years. It was only in the summer of 1970 that the first new class of university students was recruited, and even that process was limited to a fraction of China's institutions of higher learning.

From a strictly curricular perspective, the damage of the early phase of the Cultural Revolution to the Chinese educational system was only moderate. More detrimental were policies implemented after 1969 that politicized the curriculum, reduced the length of training, required lengthy doses of physical labor, and selected students on the basis of class background rather than academic promise. On the other hand, many cultural and educational institutions sustained serious physical damage. The collections of many libraries and museums were damaged, disrupted, or dispersed. Red Guards defaced or destroyed numerous historical sites, religious structures, and cultural artifacts. And the military, once it had been sent into the universities to restore order, requisitioned many campus buildings for its own use. Many of these effects were not fully remedied until well after the death of Mao Tse-tung in 1976.

The most serious impact of the Cultural Revolution in the cultural and educational spheres was on scholars, writers, and intellectuals. No precise figures are yet available on the persecution and harassment suffered by cultural circles between 1966 and 1969, but the trial of the Gang of Four in 1980–81 has provided some illustrative data. The indictment in that trial claimed that 2,600 people in literary and art circles, 142,000 cadres and teachers in units under the Ministry of Education, 53,000 scientists and technicians in research institutes, and 500 professors and associate professors in the medical colleges and institutes under the Ministry of

163 This discussion of the effects of the Cultural Revolution on the educational system draws upon Marianne Bastid, "Economic necessity and political ideals in educational reform during the Cultural Revolution," *CQ*, 42 (April–June 1970), 16–45.

Public Health were all "falsely charged and persecuted," and that an unspecified number of them died as a result.[164] Most suffered at the hands of relatively autonomous Red Guard organizations in their own units, but a minority were victimized by Chiang Ch'ing personally. Concerned that damaging information about her career in Shanghai in the 1930s might be released by her opponents, Chiang Ch'ing organized groups to search the homes of writers and artists in Shanghai to confiscate letters and photos relating to her past.

The persecution of intellectuals was fully matched by the maltreatment of Party and government leaders. The rate of political purge was extremely high. It reached 70–80 percent at the regional and provincial levels, where four of six regional Party first secretaries, and twenty-three of twenty-nine provincial Party first secretaries, fell victim to the Cultural Revolution. In the central organs of the Party, the purge rate was about 60–70 percent. Only nine Politburo members out of twenty-three, four secretariat members out of thirteen, and fifty-four Central Committee members out of one hundred sixty-seven survived the Cultural Revolution with their political positions intact. Only about half of the fifteen vice-premiers and forty-eight cabinet ministers remained on the State Council at the end of the movement.[165]

The rates of purge were not, of course, uniform throughout the bureaucracy.[166] Studies of the organizational impact of the Cultural Revolution have suggested that the turnover was higher in some functional areas (especially agriculture, industry, planning, and culture and education) than in others (such as national defense, and finance and trade); that, predictably, the higher one's rank, the more likely one was to fall victim to the Cultural Revolution; and that, somewhat ironically, non-Party cadres suffered somewhat less from the Cultural Revolution than did officials who were Party members. All told, the level of purge can be estimated in a rough manner by reference to a Chinese claim that some 3 million cadres who had been labeled as revisionists, counterrevolutionaries, or "Party persons in authority taking the capitalist road" were rehabilitated in the late 1970s. This may have represented as much as 20 percent of a bureaucracy of 15 million to 20 million officials.

The Cultural Revolution was not characterized by the great purge trials

164 *A great trial*, 182–83.
165 On the rates of purge, see Bennett, *China's Eighth, Ninth, and Tenth Congresses, Constitutions, and Central Committees*; Donald W. Klein and Lois B. Hager, "The Ninth Central Committee," *CQ*, 45 (January–March 1971), 37–56; Scalapino, "The transition in Chinese Party leadership"; and Teiwes, *Provincial leadership in China*.
166 Richard K. Diao, "The impact of the Cultural Revolution on China's economic elite," *CQ*, 42 (April–June 1970), 65–87.

and mass executions of the Stalin period. Most victims of the Cultural Revolution survived the movement, and secured their political rehabilitation after the death of Mao and the purge of the Gang of Four. But the experience for China's bureaucracy was still not pleasant. A large number – again perhaps as many as 3 million – were sent to May 7 cadre schools, usually in rural areas, to engage in physical labor, conduct intense ideological study, and forge "close ties" with neighboring peasants. Although some officials, especially those younger in years, found the experience to be rewarding in ways, the May 7 schools represented a true physical hardship for older cadres, especially those who remained in the schools, separated from their families, for a long period of time.

Other officials experienced fates worse than a stint in the May 7 cadre schools. Some were placed in isolation in their own work units, where they underwent severe psychological harassment aimed at inducing "confessions" of political malfeasance. An unknown number were beaten and tortured. Some were killed, some died in confinement, and others committed suicide. Liu Shao-ch'i was placed under house arrest in 1967, beaten by Red Guards later that year, and died in prison in 1969. Ho Lung, a marshal in the Chinese armed forces, was hospitalized for the malnutrition he suffered while under house arrest, and then died after glucose injections complicated his diabetic condition.[167] Other ranking officials known to have died during the Cultural Revolution include P'eng Te-huai and T'ao Chu, both members of the Politburo; two Peking municipal Party secretaries, Liu Jen and Teng T'o; Wu Han, the author of *Hai Jui* who was concurrently a deputy mayor of Peking; Shanghai's Mayor Ts'ao Ti-ch'iu and Deputy Mayor Chin Cheng-huan; and Vice-Minister of Public Security Hsu Tzu-jung. Lo Jui-ch'ing, the former chief of staff, attempted suicide.

The children of leading officials also suffered political persecution and physical torture. Some, like Teng Hsiao-p'ing's daughter, joined their parents in internal exile. Others, like Teng's son, were crippled for life at the hands of Red Guards. An adopted daughter of Chou En-lai's was allegedly tortured by Red Guards. And others were subject to intense criticism and abuse because they were the sons and daughters of their parents.

The total number of deaths attributable to the Cultural Revolution is not known with certainty. Of the 729,511 people named in the indictment of the Gang of Four as having been deliberately "framed and persecuted" by them and their associates, 34,800 are said to have been persecuted

167 David Bonavia, *Verdict in Peking: the trial of the Gang of Four*, passim.

to death. These include nearly three thousand people in Hopei, fourteen thousand in Yunnan, sixteen thousand in Inner Mongolia, and more than one thousand in the PLA. [168] Fox Butterfield attributes to a well-informed Chinese the estimate that four hundred thousand people died during the Cultural Revolution.[169] Extrapolations based on deaths in particular provinces, such as Fukien and Kwangtung, are somewhat higher, ranging between seven hundred thousand and eight hundred fifty thousand, but these figures are based on provinces that experienced higher than the average level of violence and disorder. It might not be unreasonable to estimate that approximately half a million Chinese, of an urban population of around 135 million in 1967, died as a direct result of the Cultural Revolution.

Beyond the immediate effects just considered, the events of 1966–69 also had longer-term consequences. To begin with, the Red Guard years produced an explosive combination of a deeply fragmented leadership and weak political institutions. Leadership at the central and provincial levels was divided among veteran Party officials, regional and main force military commanders, mass representatives, and lower-level cadres who had risen to power as a result of the Cultural Revolution. The authority of the Party itself had been brought into serious question, but the institutions that had taken the place of the Party, the revolutionary committees, were described as only temporary organs of government. The Cultural Revolution had discredited the socioeconomic policies and organizational norms of the early 1960s, but the new leadership had not yet come to any consensus on what should replace them.

This fragmentation of power established the patterns that dominated Chinese politics for the next seven and a half years, until the death of Mao Tse-tung in September 1976. There was, first, a struggle between civilian and military leaders over the role of the armed forces in post–Cultural Revolution China. Lin Piao's unsuccessful effort to institutionalize military dominance of civilian politics was followed, after his death in the fall of 1971, by more effective attempts to disengage the People's Liberation Army from civilian affairs. The events of the late 1960s also produced a struggle over the definition of post-Cultural Revolution programs, pitting more conservative officials, who sought to resurrect the policies of the early 1960s, against radical leaders, who wished to formulate a set of more egalitarian and populist programs in industry, agriculture, and intellectual life. And the fragmentation of power so evident in the

---

168 *A great trial*, 21.   169 Fox Butterfield, *China: alive in the bitter sea*, 348.

Politburo selected at the Ninth Party Congress also led ineluctably to a serious struggle to succeed Mao Tse-tung among the officials (like Teng Hsiao-p'ing) who had been victims of the Cultural Revolution, the ideologues and organizers (like Chiang Ch'ing) who had led it, the military officers (like Lin Piao) who had ended it, and the middle-level cadres (like Hua Kuo-feng) who had survived it. In short, the "manic phase" of the Cultural Revolution from 1966 to 1969 produced seven or eight years of lesser turmoil, resolved only by the purge of the Gang of Four in October 1976 and the emergence of Teng Hsiao-p'ing's reform program in December 1978.

The restoration of order in 1976, and the initiation of economic and political reform in 1978, did not, however, mark the final elimination of the effects of the Cultural Revolution. Two enduring consequences remained very much in evidence as China entered the mid-1980s. One was a deep-seated factionalism, infecting almost every government agency, industrial and commercial enterprise, and Party committee. Factional conflict was created by the struggle for power at the height of the Cultural Revolution, was preserved by the insistence on broad consensus and representation in the formation of revolutionary committees, and was strengthened by the rehabilitation of large numbers of victims of the Cultural Revolution during the mid-1970s. Such conflict seriously reduced the effectiveness of political institutions by making both policy decisions and personnel appointments captives of factional considerations.

Second, the events of the late 1960s created a serious crisis of confidence among the young people of China. For the more than 4 million high school and university students – many of them former Red Guards – who were relocated to the countryside in 1968 and 1969, the suspension of normal patterns of schooling meant a dramatic and often devastating change in their future prospects. Although almost all were able to return to their homes by the end of the 1970s, the fact that most were unable to complete their education meant that their career paths and life chances had changed for the worse. The fact that so calamitous an event was launched in the name of Marxism served to undermine their faith in ideology; and the inability of the Party to prevent the Cultural Revolution served to weaken their confidence in the existing political system.

The process of disillusionment occurred for different youth at different times. For some, the turning point was the restriction and eventual demobilization of the Red Guards after the January Revolution, a clear sign that those who had once been told that they were the leaders of the movement were now to be made its scapegoats. For others, the critical event was the discovery of the poverty of the Chinese countryside, whether during the "exchange of revolutionary experiences" in 1966–67 or during the rustification programs of later months. One former Red Guard, who experienced both these awakenings, spoke for an entire generation when he vented his rage and frustration in an interview with American scholars after his escape to Hong Kong in 1967:

Nothing can describe my anger at the way the situation had developed in March [1967]. Those sons of bitches [the PLA and the military training platoon in his middle school] had thrown us all out the window.... We had virtually succeeded in seizing power, in making a true revolution. Now the bastards had thrown it all away.

[My time in the countryside] was another eye-opening experience. [The peasants] ceaselessly complained about their hard life. They said they had little food to eat, even in good crop years.... Times had been better, they felt, even under the Kuomintang, when a man could work, save some money, invest it, and improve himself.... They also preferred Liu Shao-ch'i to Mao because they identified Liu with the private plots which gave them the chance to put some savings [away] and move up the ladder.... I had thought that only capitalist roaders and counterrevolutionaries had such thoughts. But I had just heard them from the mouth of a revolutionary poor peasant who had worked for the Party for more than twenty years.... In ten short days, my world outlook had been challenged by the reality of peasant life and attitudes.[170]

The effects of that disillusionment also varied from individual to individual. For some young people, China's so-called Lost Generation, the consequences were political cynicism, a passivity and lack of initiative in work, and a growing materialism and acquisitiveness. This crisis of confidence among youth, coupled with the decline in the rule of law during the Cultural Revolution, is widely believed to have contributed to a rise in crime and antisocial activities in the late 1970s. For others, especially those who had received some college education before 1966, time in the countryside provided an opportunity for reading, reflection, and debate about the future of their country. Many of these former Red Guards later constituted a group of younger intellectuals who, in the late 1970s and early 1980s, helped to formulate the general principles and specific policies for the economic reforms of the post-Mao era.

As of the late 1980s, in fact, it appeared that, paradoxically, the chaos of the Cultural Revolution had been an important condition for the reforms of the post-Mao era. The fact that so many senior cadres had suffered so greatly during the Cultural Revolution, and yet had survived it, helped create the leadership for economic and political liberalization once the movement had come to an end. The disillusionment of thousands of

170 Bennett and Montaperto, *Red Guard*, 214–17 and 222–24, passim.

educated youth and intellectuals during the Red Guard movement stimulated many of the radical ideas that would later be translated into concrete reforms. And the devastating impact of the Cultural Revolution on the Chinese Communist Party, all in the name of preventing revisionism, weakened the Party's ability to resist a restructuring of the political and economic order that went far beyond that which Mao had found so objectionable in the Soviet Union. In short, had there been no Cultural Revolution, it is unlikely that reform in the post-Mao period would have gone as far or as fast.

But the long-term consequences of the Cultural Revolution remain uncertain. It is not yet clear whether the Cultural Revolution served as a precedent for, or immunization against, the recurrence of similar undertakings in the future. From the vantage point of the 1980s, of course, the innoculatory effects of the Cultural Revolution appeared to be the greater. The damage done by the Red Guards, without any countervailing accomplishments, warns strongly against launching a similar "open door" rectification soon. Over time, however, it remains possible that memories will dim, and that the Cultural Revolution will appear more noble and salutary in retrospect than it does today. If so, the Cultural Revolution could still serve as a prototype for another struggle for political power in China, or another attempt to purify the country of inequality, corruption, and elitism through mass mobilization. The issue is whether the post-Mao reforms will create sufficient political institutionalization, economic prosperity, social stability, and cultural modernization such that the Cultural Revolution will have little appeal even after the inoculatory effects have worn off.

CHAPTER 3

CHINA CONFRONTS THE SOVIET UNION: WARFARE AND DIPLOMACY ON CHINA'S INNER ASIAN FRONTIERS

During the "active phase" of the Cultural Revolution, up to 1969, China deliberately adopted a low profile in foreign policy, as the country was consumed by internal disorder. The conscious foreign policy of the Cultural Revolution was to have as little of it as possible. China purposely went into diplomatic isolation, kept foreigners out of the country, lowered the level of commercial intercourse with other countries, steered clear of international institutions, and substituted Maoist rhetoric for more tangible means of policy. For a while, China was not a factor of consequence in global politics or even in Asian international relations.

Nevertheless, a chapter on this brief period can illustrate several verities of Chinese foreign policy. Among these are the interdependence and interpenetration of Chinese domestic developments and the international environment.[1] Even though the Cultural Revolution was a period of almost exclusive Chinese attention to internal events, its causes were partly international, its initiation was delayed by occurrences outside China's borders, its effects were felt directly by China's neighbors and strongly even by nations and foreign offices at great distances from Peking, and its direction was abruptly altered by the threat of war in 1969 and after.

Another verity is the dependence of Chinese internal policy and international actions on the policies and actions of the United States and the Soviet Union. American intervention in Vietnam precipitated the strategic debate of 1965 that, in turn, helped divide the leadership along pro— and anti—Cultural Revolution lines; and Soviet intervention in Czechoslovakia in 1968 caused the Chinese leadership to take fright over the Soviet military buildup along the Chinese border and to catch the Soviets

---

1 This follows Thomas W. Robinson, "Political and strategic aspects of Chinese foreign policy," in Donald C. Hellmann, ed., *China and Japan: a new balance of power*, 197–268, and Thomas W. Robinson, "Restructuring Chinese foreign policy, 1959–1976: three episodes," in K[al] J. Holsti et al., *Why nations realign: foreign policy restructuring in the postwar world*, 134–171.

off guard with the Chen-pao Island raids early the next year. The un-expectedly strong Russian reaction led to the end of the "active phase" of the Cultural Revolution.

A third verity is that the Cultural Revolution affected the fate of lead-ing Chinese officials. Many of them chose to – or had to – comment on foreign policy issues merely in order to participate effectively in the highly charged, factionalized infighting that characterized Chinese poli-tics throughout the 1960s. Thereby they left themselves open to Maoist/Red Guard attack once the purge stage was reached.

Of scarcely less importance is that the foreign policy of the Cultural Revolution, and the dilemma in which the Chinese leadership found itself as a result, served as the foil against which Chinese foreign policy for the next decade and more reacted so severely. Not only was Peking's general opening to the world – economic and institutional as well as diplomatic – based on retreat from Cultural Revolution extremes, but the rapproche-ment with the United States (the foundation of Chinese policy during the 1970s) also had its roots in decisions taken during the Cultural Revolu-tion. So although the period stood as an exception to the flow of past and future foreign policies, it nonetheless served as the point of departure for subsequent events.[2]

Finally, it is possible to take a revisionist approach to Chinese foreign policy during the Cultural Revolution. It turns out that Peking's policy was more dynamic and participatory than was generally thought at the time. Not only was there much activity along the border with the Soviet Union (actions reflecting deliberate decisions in the Chinese capital) and continuing contact with the United States (over Vietnam and regarding the politics of the strategic triangle), but trade, foreign aid, and reception of high-level visitors continued, albeit at reduced levels. The period of self-imposed isolation was thus short. Added to that are the spillover effects of Cultural Revolution violence and ideological enthusiasm. Hong Kong suffered major disturbances and came close to anarchy, and Burma and Cambodia altered their policies toward China after Red Guard–induced violence in their capitals. The siege of the Soviet embassy in Peking, the mob violence directed against Russian diplomatic dependents during their evacuation, and anti-Soviet antics by Chinese Red Guards in Moscow and elsewhere – all induced a highly emotional reaction in the Kremlin. Though temporarily kept in restraint, from 1969 on these

2 See the companion chapter in the present volume by Jonathan Pollack; G[olam] W. Choudhury, *China in world affairs: the foreign policy of the PRC since 1970*; Thomas Fingar et al., eds., *China's quest for independence: policy evolution in the 1970s*; and Robert Sutter, *Chinese foreign policy after the Cultural Revolution*.

events created a "never again" syndrome of military and diplomatic overreaction.

On balance, then, the foreign policy of the active phase of the Cultural Revolution seems to have been less exceptional than it at first appeared. In fact, it was generally in line with Peking's policies before 1965 and after 1969, and came out of the same complex of determinants. The framework and the "driving variables" were the same. This chapter suggests that even with a near absence of foreign relations, in reality China was responding to the combined influence of well-understood domestic and international pressures.

At the domestic level, those pressures took three forms:[3] the influence of politics, personalities, and the political culture back of them; the weight of the Chinese past, recent and ancient, particularly of "lessons learned" during the Chinese Communist Party's formative pre-1949 era; and the influence of ideology, including both Marxism-Leninism-Maoism and the Chinese weltanschauung.

International pressures also took three forms: the policies of the United States and Soviet Union, the only two states that mattered critically to Peking; the overall configuration of the global international system – political, economic, and security – the shape of the Asian regional system, and their respective operational "rules"; and the complex of Chinese national/state interests relative to those of other relevant states and to the growth in Chinese national power. Chinese foreign policy during the Cultural Revolution showed what the costs were when the Party elected to run the risk of violating several of the cardinal principles of its own policy and of international systemic behavior.

FOREIGN POLICY ORIGINS OF THE CULTURAL REVOLUTION

Our approach combines a rough chronological sequence with an analytic bias. First, we specify the foreign policy origins of the Cultural Revolution under three aspects: the broadening, particularly in the mind of Mao Tse-tung, of the issue of ideological revisionism from Sino-Soviet relations to the Chinese domestic political and socioeconomic arena; the alleged delay of the Cultural Revolution necessitated by the American military intervention in Vietnam and the debate over the appropriate Chinese response; and the influence of these and other foreign policy issues on interpersonal relations among top Party leaders. Each are text-

3 This draws on the author's unpublished manuscipt "Explaining Chinese foreign policy: contributing elements and levels of analysis."

book examples of the complex intermingling of foreign and domestic factors.

The long and tortuous path from the original Chinese criticism in the mid-1950s of the Kremlin's handling of the Stalin question to Mao Tse-tung's conclusion that China as well as the Soviet Union was following the path of ideological revisionism and capitalist restoration is reasonably clear.[4] Mao concluded that the reason Soviet foreign policy had gone so far astray – as evidenced by its combination of peaceful coexistence, adventurism, and capitulationism toward the United States and its policy of chauvinism, splittism, and all-around opposition toward China – was that the Soviet leadership under Khrushchev and, after him, Brezhnev had deliberately departed from the true Leninist path of revolution and socialist construction to restore capitalism within the Soviet Union. The Chinese series of nine polemics in the early 1960s catalogued these most clearly as the Kremlin's sins.[5]

The Sino-Soviet dispute would have remained purely a foreign policy matter if Mao had not drawn logical and empirical conclusions about the development of socialism after the Communist Party takes power. Logically, there must be solid Marxist reasons if the Soviet Union had erred so greatly and consistently. Truly socialist countries are incapable of such departures, so the Soviet Union was no longer a socialist country and had, progressively, restored capitalism. The Soviet Communist Party was therefore a bourgeois capitalist institution, complete with all the attitudinal and political-organizational manifestations of the property-holding and imperialist class. Because the Soviet Union under Lenin and Stalin was socialist, and because mere individuals could not lead Moscow back to capitalism, the causes of regression were the forces and relations of production as industrial modernization proceeded and the still weighty influence on the economic base of the political-ideological-social superstructure, that is, the influence of the Russian past. Since the Soviet Union was the first and thus the oldest (formerly) socialist country, revisionism had had a chance to progress the farthest there. But if that were so, the process of regression was probably similar in all socialist states, and its manifestations could also be detected in younger socialist countries, albeit at a less advanced stage. In particular, signs of revisionism ought to be

4 The literature on the Sino-Soviet dispute from 1956 to 1964 is extensive. Among other entries, see Donald S. Zagoria, *The Sino-Soviet conflict, 1956–1961*; William E. Griffith, *The Sino-Soviet rift* and his *Sino-Soviet relations, 1964–1965*; Alexander Dallin, ed., *Diversity in international communism: a documentary record, 1961–1963*; and Richard Lowenthal, *World communism: the disintegration of a secular faith*.

5 Most are reprinted in Harold C. Hinton, ed., *The People's Republic of China, 1949–1979: a documentary survey*, 2.1051–1193.

appearing in China itself, since by the 1960s the Chinese Party had been in power for nearly a decade and a half.

Having gone through this logical process (the evidence for which is to be found throughout his writings and Central Committee documents produced under his guidance),[6] Mao, ever the experimental social scientific Marxist, turned to the empirical world for confirmation. He, of course, found what he was seeking, convincing himself that the normal administrative-bureaucratic-ideological behavior of his colleagues, charged with developing a large and diverse nation and using a highly imperfect method of socialist organization, was indeed a species of revisionism and therefore that they were "capitalist roaders." The progression of Mao's thinking on revisionism inside China can be traced through his increasing dissatisfaction with the Socialist Education Campaign, and with the activities of almost every Party leader, save only his wife, Chiang Ch'ing, Lin Piao, and a few others.[7]

By early 1965, Mao concluded that only a major purge would save China and the Party and that it was best to begin as soon as possible, lest the forces of capitalist restoration within the Party become too strong. Indeed, Mao was prepared to broaden the Socialist Education Campaign into the Cultural Revolution.[8] It was only necessary to find the correct combination of personal and class allies, and to make sure that the international environment would remain reasonably benign. To accomplish the former, Mao placed his suspected Party opponents Liu Shao-ch'i, Teng Hsiao-p'ing, and P'eng Chen in charge of implementing the Socialist Education Campaign, thus testing their loyalty; put the defense minister, Lin Piao, in charge of the Socialist Education Campaign in the army, of producing the "little red book" of Maoist aphorisms, and helping to organize the student Red Guards; and began organizing poor peasants in class struggle detachments.[9] All that would take time, essentially most of 1965.

6 These are translated in *Miscellany of Mao Tse-tung Thought (1949–1968)*, and in John Bryan Starr and Nancy Anne Dyer, comps., *Post-Liberation works of Mao Zedong: a bibliography and index*.

7 The standard works on this era are Richard Baum, *Prelude to revolution: Mao, the Party, and the peasant question, 1962–66*; Parris H. Chang, *Power and policy in China*; Byung-joon Ahn, *Chinese politics and the Cultural Revolution: dynamics of policy processes*; Frederick C. Teiwes, *Politics and purges in China: rectification and the decline of Party norms, 1950–1965*; and William F. Dorrell, "Power, policy, and ideology in the making of the Chinese Cultural Revolution," in Thomas W. Robinson, ed., *The Cultural Revolution in China*, 21–112.

8 See Chang, *Power and policy in China*, 147–56; Baum, *Prelude to revolution*, 11–42; and Ahn, *Chinese politics and the Cultural Revolution*, 89–122.

9 Teiwes, *Politics and purges in China*, 493–601; Andrew C. Walder, *Chang Ch'un-ch'iao and Shanghai's January Revolution*; Richard Baum and Frederick C. Teiwes, *Ssu-ch'ing: the Socialist Education Movement of 1962–1966*; Thomas Robinson, "A politico-military biography of Lin Piao, Part II, 1950–1971."

The international atmosphere, however, turned threatening almost coincidentally with Mao's decision deliberately to radicalize China. The Vietnam conflict had been heating up since the United States during the Kennedy administration began to intervene militarily in support of the southern government. It escalated several rungs with the Tonkin Gulf incident in the late summer of 1964 and the American retaliatory bombardment of North Vietnamese oil depots and naval bases. Lyndon Johnson had nonetheless been elected president in November 1964 on a platform of no further escalation and a negotiated settlement. Despite that, when Viet Cong forces successfully attacked American advisers' barracks and destroyed many American aircraft at Pleiku, the American president took advantage of the situation to carry out renewed, regular, and increasingly severe air bombardment of the North and to increase the number of American ground forces in the South. The United States seemed now to be in the conflict for its duration and the urgent question for China became: Would Washington invade the North and force Peking to confront American ground troops, as in Korea, with contingents of its own, as the Chinese Politburo made clear it would?[10]

If so, all thought of inducing internal revolution, however necessary Mao thought it would be for the survival of socialism in China, would have to be put aside. A subsidiary question was how much cooperation, if any, was necessary with the Soviet Union to coordinate defense of North Vietnam. For some time, but particularly after the American air attacks in February 1965, the Russians had been pressing for "united action" with China and other socialist countries in defense of the North.[11] If Mao were to assent to Soviet requests (minimal under the circumstances but still broad enough to require toning down anti-Soviet polemics), his own dual campaign to denigrate the Kremlin's foreign policy and to root out incipient revisionism in China would suffer a major setback.

Mao was, therefore, extremely reluctant to meliorate opposition to the Russians, the more so since Chinese foreign policy energies after 1960 had gone into the uphill struggle against Moscow for leadership of the international communist movement. Indeed, in early 1965 it appeared to the Chinese leader that success was just around the corner, given the failure of the Soviet-called March meeting of nineteen Communist parties (boycotted by China and many others) and given Chinese-led progress toward the convening of a "second Bandung" Afro-Asian Conference in Algiers that would, presumably, exclude and therefore isolate the

10 Stanley Karnow, *Vietnam, a history*; Leslie H. Gelb, with Richard K. Betts, *The irony of Vietnam: the system worked.*
11 Donald S. Zagoria, *Vietnam triangle: Moscow/Peking/Hanoi.*

Russians.[12] The trick was therefore to keep up momentum in the anti-Soviet offensive while at the same time assisting the Vietnamese against the Americans. The answer was to gain assurances, tacit or explicit, from the Americans that, despite air bombardment, there would be no ground invasion of the North, and to arm the Vietnamese sufficiently to withstand American military pressures on their own.

Both aims were successfully accomplished. The assurance came slowly, via a tacit Sino-American agreement produced by differential diplomatic and military responses to the American air escalation.[13] Although it was not clear until 1967 that the Americans would not invade the North, it was reasonably apparent by mid-1965 that the United States would likely confine its ground activities to the South and that Washington had understood and heeded Chinese warning signals.[14] Arming the Vietnamese also took time, given the necessity to construct new airfields in southern China, step up military production and transfers to the North Vietnamese, conduct military training and joint exercises with Hanoi, and send to Vietnam a 50,000-man PLA road-and-rail construction force complete with antiaircraft divisions.[15] But these commitments were made good eventually.

Once the decision was made to proceed on both fronts, Mao could with confidence continue his struggle against the Kremlin and move ahead with preparations for the Cultural Revolution. There seems little doubt, however, that his timetable was upset by the American intervention and that what could have occurred (i.e., the opening of the Cultural Revolution) in mid-1965 did not take place until November. Two internal and two external processes were at work simultaneously, making rigorous logical-chronological conclusions impossible.

Internally, Mao wished to see how his suspected Party opponents would handle the assignments in carrying out the Twenty-three Articles,[16] while the Chinese leadership as a whole debated how best to respond to the American challenge and to Soviet offers to sign an ideological peace treaty. Given that the same personnel were involved in both

---

12 Charles Neuhauser, *Third World politics: China and the Afro-Asian People's Solidarity Organization, 1957–1967.*

13 Allen S. Whiting, "The use of force in foreign policy by the People's Republic of China," *The Annals of the American Academy of Political and Social Science*, 402 (July 1972), 55–66; Allen S. Whiting, *The Chinese calculus of deterrence*, ch. 6.

14 Allen S. Whiting, "How we almost went to war with China," *Look*, 33 (29 April 1969), 6; Edgar Snow, "Interview with Mao," *New Republic*, 152 (27 February 1965), 17–23.

15 *Strategic Survey 1966; New York Times*, 17 January 1965, 1; *New York Times* (hereafter *NYT*) 12 August 1966, 4.

16 Teiwes, *Politics and purges in China*, 546ff. The Twenty-three Articles are translated in Appendix F of Baum and Teiwes, *Ssu-ch'ing*, n. 9.

processes, they naturally tended to fuse, leading Mao to convince himself even further that his Party opponents were also serving the cause of Soviet revisionism.

Externally, the anti-Soviet campaign and, concomitantly, Chinese efforts to lead the newly decolonized states against both superpowers were both set back by the Vietnam conflict and by the Kremlin's success in moving Hanoi back to a neutral position in the Sino-Soviet dispute.[17] Finally, in the fall of 1965 Chinese policy disasters in Algiers, Jakarta, and various sub-Saharan African capitals called into question Mao's presumption of a parallel between the Chinese revolution and postcolonial radicalization in the Third World. These processes also took time to unfold and thus further delayed the Cultural Revolution.

The Chinese leadership's so-called strategic debate over the Vietnam War of mid-1965 has been much analyzed, and certain conclusions seem reasonable despite differences among observers.[18] Most important, although the debate was genuine, by the time it was manifest in June 1965, Mao had probably already made up his mind that China need not worry about American intervention in North Vietnam, that the traditional people's war mode of conflict was proper and would eventually prove successful in Vietnam (albeit with such modern add-ons as air defense weaponry), and that, therefore, Peking need not compromise severely with Moscow.[19]

Chief of Staff Lo Jui-ch'ing's call[20] to gird more seriously for war (including smoothing over domestic political conflicts, increasing military production and service budgets at the expense of the civilian economy, and going along with the Soviet proposal for "united action") was thus already anachronistic. It was also politically diversionary and hence dangerous, since it gave only secondary emphasis to the domestic struggle against revisionism and since it would have taken the People's Liberation Army out of the center of domestic politics (as organizational headquarters for the Cultural Revolution buildup, role model for China's

17 William E. Griffith, "Sino-Soviet relations, 1964–65," *CQ*, 25 (January–March 1966), 66–67.
18 Harry Harding and Melvin Gurtov, *The purge of Lo Jui-ch'ing: the politics of Chinese strategic planning*; Tang Tsou, ed., *China in crisis*, vol. 2: *China's policies in Asia and America's alternatives*, chapters by Ra'anan and Zagoria; Michael Yahuda, "Kremlinology and the Chinese strategic debate, 1965–66," *CQ*, 49 (January–March 1972), 32–75; and Donald S. Zagoria and Uri Ra'anan, "On Kremlinology: a reply to Michael Yahuda," *CQ*, 50 (April–June 1972), 343–50.
19 During this period, Mao was vitriolic in his attacks on both the United States and the Soviet Union. See, for instance, his remarks to the visiting Japanese Communist Party delegation on 29 March 1966, as reported in Michael B. Yahuda, *China's role in world affairs*, 185, and the "Communiqué," 12 August 1966, *PR*, 34 (19 August 1966), 4–8.
20 Lo Jui-ch'ing, "Commemorate the victory over German fascism! Carry the struggle against U.S. imperialism through to the end!" *HC*, 5 (1965), in *PR*, 8.20 (14 May 1965), 7–15.

youth, etc.) and confine it to being a mere instrument of foreign policy. Moreover, it was essential to retain the primacy of the people's war thesis, for China's enemies – both capitalist and revisionist – could thereby be kept at bay with the least expenditure of Chinese military resources.

Finally, the debate brought into the open the opinions of Mao's opponents. On the one hand were the relatively hard-line professional soldiers, exemplified by Lo, who advocated taking up cudgels against the United States in Vietnam and making necessary, temporary compromises, in practical policy if not ideology, with the Soviet Union. On the other hand were the domestically oriented rationalist-revisionists, led by Liu Shao-ch'i and Teng Hsiao-p'ing, who were afraid that Vietnam intervention and bigger military budgets would severely constrict rapid economic growth and inhibit needed socioeconomic reforms. To make sure that intervention in Vietnam would be unnecessary and to arrange for resumption of Soviet economic assistance and high trade levels, this group apparently was also prepared to compromise many of China's policy differences with the Soviet Union. Both groups thus agreed on the Soviet component of China's foreign policy but differed on how to deal with the Vietnam issue and so disagreed over domestic policy priorities. Mao and his associates, particularly Lin Piao and possibly even Chou En-lai, stood apart from both. They favored continued stringent anti-Sovietism, and continued support of Vietnamese resistance against the Americans. They were more relaxed about American activities in Indochina (witness Mao's January remarks to Edgar Snow),[21] and certainly were vehemently opposed to the domestic changes proposed by the rationalists – which were revisionist in Mao's eyes and in reality as well.

Mao's tactic in dealing with both groups was similar: give them enough rope and they would eventually hang themselves.[22] Thus, he put the revisionists in charge of carrying out the later stages of the Socialist Education Campaign and he allowed the professional military to have their say, both in print and in Party councils. Thanks to American caution in Vietnam, Soviet lack of success in the ideological debate, and – paradoxically – reversals in Indonesia and Africa in early fall 1965,[23] the foreign policy issue was comparatively easy to deal with. The Lin Piao article on people's war, issued in early September,[24] was therefore the signal that the issue had been resolved – that there would be no direct

21 Snow, "Interview with Mao," n. 14.
22 For details, see the chapter in *CHOC*, 14, by Kenneth Lieberthal.
23 Arthur J. Dommen, "The attempted coup in Indonesia," *CQ*, 25 (January–March 1966), 144–70; "Quarterly chronicle and documentation," *CQ*, 26 (April–June 1966), 222–23.
24 Lin Piao, "Long live the victory of People's War!" *PR*, 8.36 (3 September 1965), 9–30.

Chinese intervention in Vietnam, that there would be no compromise with the Soviet Union, and that foreign policy henceforth would be a secondary concern.

The Lin Piao article (which even Lin himself admitted he did not personally write and which was in no manner original, even to the Chinese themselves) thus was important more for timing and symbolization than for content. To be sure, it was a classic restatement of Chinese belief in the revolutionary war process and an expansion of the original formula, by analogy, from the Chinese rural scene to the "world countryside."[25] But it was certainly no declaration of war against the developed world. In the context of the Third World defeats that China had already incurred or that would shortly take place, it was more a declaration of faith in eventual victory and restoration of revolutionary progress. In that sense, it was a conservative statement.[26] In the context of the Cultural Revolution, however, it indicated that China would put increasing proportions of its energy not into exporting people's war but in assuring revolutionary continuity inside the country. There were thus two "opening guns" of the Cultural Revolution: the Lin Piao editorial on people's war on 3 September, and the Yao Wen-yuan article on Wu Han on 10 November 1965.[27] The one would not have been possible without the other.

The origins of the Cultural Revolution were also linked, causally and chronologically, with the failure of China's Third World policy in 1964 and 1965. Following the shock in 1960 of the Soviet removal of advisers, the cutting off of Russian economic assistance, and the "three bitter years" of Great Leap Forward–incluced depression, Chinese foreign policy had been largely quiescent while Mao's more practical-minded associates strove to put the country back together. Only with the Sino-Indian conflict of October 1962 did Peking return to foreign policy activism.[28] This time, however, policy was based not merely on anti-Americanism and anti-Sovietism but, in addition, on expanding state ties and promoting revolution in the Third World. Peking conceived its mission to become the leader of the newly independent or underdeveloped countries of Asia, Africa, and Latin America, not only to beat the Russians at their own game but also as a policy for its own sake. The

25 Benjamin I. Schwartz, in his "Essential features of the Maoist strategy," *Chinese communism and the rise of Mao*, 189–204.
26 Thomas W. Robinson and David P. Mozingo, "Lin Piao on People's War: China takes a second look at Vietnam."
27 Yao Wen-yuan, "On the new historical play *Hai Jui dismissed from office*," Shanghai *Wen-hui pao*, 10 November 1965, reprinted in *Chieh-fang-chün pao*, 10 November 1965.
28 Whiting, *The Chinese calculus of deterrence*, 22–28, chs. 3 and 4; J. Chester Cheng, ed., *The politics of the Chinese Red Army*.

ideological altruism of supporting socialist and antiimperialist revolutions everywhere now combined with the national interest of expanding China's own power for the first time in its history, to reach the four corners of the globe. Such a policy accorded well with Mao's own personal revolutionary élan, since its success could be regarded as proof that the Chinese revolution was indeed the vanguard of history.

Thus, from 1963 to late 1965 China had devoted much policy attention to, and expended considerable resources in, the Third World.[29] Superficially, much progress was seen. Chou En-lai, the premier, toured Africa from late 1963 to early 1964 and again in mid-1965.[30] China began a foreign aid program, also centered on Africa, and sent out military supplies and trained insurgent leaders. Peking attempted, with some success, to counter Soviet influence in Third World organizations and to transform them into instruments of its own policy. Particular attention was devoted to the Afro-Asian People's Solidarity Organization and to preparations for a "second Bandung" meeting in Algeria in mid-1965, from which the Russians would be excluded.

But the Chinese approach encountered obstacles. First, Peking was clearly manipulative, being often more interested in beating the Russians than in assisting the economic development of the former colonies. Second, China lacked the policy "reach" to make its programs effective: Peking's ambitions stepped too far ahead of its ability to project sufficient power far from its border. Third, and most important, was the glaring contradiction between China's pretensions of leading a united Third World and the reality of its armed support of domestic Communist Parties trying to overthrow their governments. So it was not surprising that Chinese Third World policy was not wholly successful. The Soviets were not about to leave the battlefield without a fight. The Third World was not so completely anti-Western nor so totally taken with socialism as the Chinese had let themselves believe. Many Afro-Asian statesmen grew suspicious of Chinese intentions, went looking for proof of Chinese duplicity, and usually found it in the form of arms caches or Chinese-supported antiregime guerrilla training bases.[31]

The surprising thing was how rapidly China's Third World policy came apart. Chou En-lai's African tours were only indifferently success-

29 For details, see Neuhauser, *Third World politics*, n. 12; and Peter Van Ness, *Revolution and Chinese foreign policy: Peking's support for wars of national liberation.*
30 Robert A. Scalapino, *On the trail of Chou En-lai in Africa.*
31 Robert A. Scalapino, "Africa and Peking's united front," *Current Scene*, 3.26 (1 September 1965), 1–11.

ful.[32] Indeed, he was chastised by local heads of state for his dual policy and was forced to beat a verbal retreat. The Chinese effort to create revolutionary bases in the Congo in 1964 failed because of superior American and Belgian military-cum-covert prowess. A Chinese-assisted plot to murder the president of Burundi was discovered in early 1965 and that state broke diplomatic relations with Peking. The Algiers Conference, toward which the Chinese had been working so assiduously, was postponed "indefinitely" because of general African dissatisfaction with Chou En-lai's manipulative and excessively anti-Soviet tactics and because China had too quickly switched its affections from Ben Bella, the Algerian head of state, who was inconveniently overthrown shortly before the meeting was scheduled in late June, to his successor, Boumedienne. The conference never did meet. The entire Chinese effort thus went for naught, and Chou had to go home empty-handed.[33]

China also moved to assist "people's war" in Thailand by setting up a Thai Patriotic Front and supplying it with Chinese arms and training, thus guaranteeing Bangkok's enmity and a major increase in American influence there.[34] In South Asia, the Chinese were shown to be paper tigers by first egging on the Pakistanis to attack India in the Rann of Cutch in mid-1965, by then jumping in diplomatically with a near ultimatum to India, and by finally doing nothing when New Delhi stood firm. They found, to their chagrin, Soviet Premier Kosygin successfully stepping in to mediate the Indian-Pakistani conflict in Tashkent.[35]

All these were blows to Peking's Third World ardor but could have been rationalized as the normal high start-up costs. A much more serious setback occurred in Indonesia in September 1965, when the Chinese-supported (and, some say, materially assisted) Indonesian Communist Party (PKI) attempted to lop the head off the Indonesian military by assassinating the country's top generals and thus to seize power in a Jakarta coup. The attempt succeeded only partly and the surviving military leaders turned around and led a popular suppression of the PKI throughout the country that left several hundred thousand dead within days.[36] Because the Chinese were apparently heavily implicated in the

32 W. A. C. Adie, "Chou En-lai on safari," *CQ*, 18 (April–June 1964), 174–94; Donald W. Klein, "Peking's diplomats in Africa," *Current Scene*, 2.36 (1 July 1964), 1–9; George T. Yu, "Sino-African relations: a survey," *Asian Survey*, 5.7 (July 1965), 321–32; Bruce D. Larkin, *China and Africa, 1949–1970: the foreign policy of the People's Republic of China*, 38–88.
33 Neuhauser, *Third World politics*, n. 12, has details.
34 Daniel D. Lovelace, *China and "People's War" in Thailand, 1964–1969*.
35 Bhabani Sen Gupta, *The fulcrum of Asia*, 141–241.
36 Antonie C. A. Dake, *In the spirit of the Red Banteng: Indonesian communists between Moscow and Peking 1959–1965*, 479; John Hughes, "China and Indonesia: the romance that failed," *Current Scene*, 19

affair, and because the loss of life was so terrible (to say nothing of the viability of the PKI, which was promptly outlawed and disappeared as a factor in Indonesian politics), Peking suffered an enormous and immediate loss of prestige, which in turn took the wind completely out of the sails of China's revolutionary policy.

All these events took place in foreign countries, and several were the culmination of trends over which China had little control. In every instance, however, Chinese policy induced negative local reaction. If the Cultural Revolution had not broken out just after the Indonesia fiasco, Chinese Third World policy would have been adjudged an even more blatant failure. As it was, the timing of these events, especially those in Jakarta and Algiers, was fortuitous, providing Mao with one more excuse to pull back from untenable foreign policy positions into which he had led the country since the split with the Russians and the recovery from the Great Leap. Not that Mao and Lin Piao admitted failure. They merely brought out the old Stalin argument that history proceeds in waves and thus that temporary setbacks are to be expected.[37] In any case, the Cultural Revolution gave the Chinese leadership a chance to divert attention from these problems, to claim victory (through Maoist propaganda) from defeat, and to assert that the only instrument of policy left to Peking – rhetoric – was the only one necessary.

It was therefore almost a footnote when the coup de grace to Chinese revolutionary playacting occurred in early 1966. First, Chinese diplomats in two African states, Dahomey and the Central African Republic, were caught engaging in plainly subversive activity and those countries broke diplomatic relations with China.[38] Second, Peking's Latin American policy collapsed when the Cuban leader, Fidel Castro, supposedly a textbook example of how a revolutionary communist Third World country achieves success, broke with China on grounds of Chinese interference in Cuban affairs (the Chinese were found to be distributing anti-Soviet leaflets to Cuban army officers) and of China's using Cuba's need for rice to bribe Havana into changing its stance toward the Soviet Union.[39] Thenceforth, Castro was firmly in the Soviet camp (where the Soviets made sure he would stay by bankrolling the Cuban economy and fi-

---

(4 November 1969), 1–15; David P. Mozingo, *Chinese policy toward Indonesia, 1949–1967*, 303; Sheldon W. Simon, *The broken triangle: Peking, Djakarta and the PKI*, 674; Justus M. Van der Kroef, "The Sino-Indonesian partnership," *Orbis*, 8.2 (Summer 1964), 332–56.

37 "Circular of [the] Central Committee [of the] CCP [on the Cultural Revolution]," 16 May 1966, in *PR*, 21 (19 May 1967), 6–9; Lin Piao, "Address at the enlarged meeting of the CCP Central Politburo," 18 May 1966, in *CLG*, 5.4 (Winter 1969/1970), 42–62.

38 Larkin, *China and Africa*, n. 32, pp. 167–93.

39 Cecil Johnson, *Communist China and Latin America, 1959–1967*.

nancing Havana's arms requests, neither of which China was capable of countering). Third and perhaps most symbolically, Kwame Nkrumah, the Ghanian leftist head of state, was overthrown just as he arrived in Peking.[40] His successors soon broke state ties with China after the Chinese continued to treat him as the titular leader he no longer was.

From that point all the way to the late 1970s, China had to put aside its revolutionary policy in the face of the military challenge from Moscow, the consequent necessity to make peace with Washington, and the requisites of societal reconstruction and economic development. During the "active phase" of the Cultural Revolution, however, Mao could get away with claiming to have an unadulterated, purist foreign policy based solely on principle, since neither Moscow nor Washington was overly concerned with China and since a country at war with itself regarded economic progress and relations with the external world as secondary matters. Chinese revolutionary rhetoric rose to historic peaks during the 1966–69 period, and there were occasional Chinese activities that could be called "revolutionary" in foreign states and cities – Hong Kong, Rangoon, Moscow, and so forth. But these are more properly catalogued as external manifestations of disorders inside the country. For the most part, revolutionary activity was mothballed along with most of the other components of Peking's foreign policy.

FOREIGN POLICY AT THE START OF THE CULTURAL REVOLUTION, 1965–1967

The two major assumptions of Chinese foreign policy, such as it was, during the Cultural Revolution were that the country could deal with the external world on China's own terms and that the international environment would continue to be benign; that is, no external events would occur requiring inordinate policy attention or resources and no foreign power would unduly threaten China internally. The general ideas were to break the hitherto strong linkage between events at home and developments abroad, to insulate the country from the outer world, and to approach other states, peoples, and issues only in terms and at times set by Peking itself. Those were quite a set of presumptions and reflected both the unreality of the entire Cultural Revolution ethos and Mao's arrogant belief that only he had found the truth, and that others (even foreigners) would, if sufficiently and correctly educated, willingly assent to its veracity. So long as these assumptions were borne out in the Cul-

40 Larkin, *China and Africa*, n. 32, 167–93.

tural Revolution, little trouble arose. But when China violated its own precepts, the international environment in the form of a fearsome military threat took its revenge and forced both the Cultural Revolution and Chinese foreign policy to change course drastically. Even during the height of China's putative separation of internal from external developments, however, linkage continued. In general, the phases, decisions, and turning points of the Cultural Revolution reflected Peking's international attitudes, policies, and actions, even though they were severely attenuated.

The foreign policy of the "active phase" of the Cultural Revolution can be divided into three periods. From its unofficial beginning in November 1965 to shortly after the official inauguration in August 1966 at the Eleventh Plenum of the Party's Eighth Central Committee, Peking did very little internationally. Decisions had already been taken regarding the Soviet Union, the United States, and the Vietnam conflict; not much was left of its Third World policy except words; and the leadership's attention was riveted on the question of its own internal unity, and so no new policy initiatives could or need be taken. The second period after the emergence onto the streets of the Red Guards in August 1966 lasted through the height of disorders in the summer of 1967 and was symbolized by the Wuhan Incident and the burning of the British embassy. Now China cast its attitudinal approach to the outer world strictly in Cultural Revolutionary terms, while Chinese actions and contact with other peoples and governments accorded almost entirely with the level of disorder inside the country. The two important occurrences in Chinese foreign policy were thus internal: the Red Guard takeover of the Foreign Ministry accompanied by the temporary ouster of Ch'en I from his post as foreign minister, and the treatment of foreign diplomats in China, particularly the officially sponsored violence against the Russians and the British. China's international relations, in the sense of events outside the periphery influenced by Peking's policies, were mere spillovers from the disorders at home, even though in the cases of Hong Kong, Cambodia, and Burma they were severe.

The third period began in the summer of 1967 with the decision to dispense with violence, bring the army in as martial law administrators, and attend to the important question of the Maoist succession. These initiatives – along with Soviet military activities – led directly to the Sino-Soviet border incidents in March 1969, and subsequently to the decision at the First Plenum of the Ninth Central Committee in April to put the pieces of China's shattered foreign policy back together, to the Soviet campaign of political-military coercion ending in the Chou-Kosygin meeting at Peking airport in October 1969, and eventually to Sino-American rapprochement. Chinese foreign policy at the end of the Cultural Revolution's "active phase" was thus similar to that when it had begun: Peking was again heavily engaged with the superpowers on their terms, and the traditional close linkage between domestic developments and foreign policy had been restored.

Phase one, 1965–1966

In the first period, Peking had only three foreign policy worries: whether even further American escalation in Vietnam would require more direct Chinese response; how to structure, that is, keep bad but not too bad, relations with Moscow; and what to do about Indonesian suppression of Overseas Chinese in that country and mob attacks on Chinese diplomatic posts in Jakarta and elsewhere in Indonesia. In late 1965 and throughout 1966, the United States severely increased its air attacks on North Vietnam and, inevitably, brought under bombardment Chinese military aid personnel and civilian technicians stationed in Hanoi and elsewhere, as well as Chinese ships in Haiphong harbor.[41] This naturally raised concern once again in Peking that more direct action would have to be taken, especially if the Americans carried the air war to southern China itself. But the United States took great pains not to allow the war to spill over to Chinese airspace, and a tacit agreement arose separating the two air forces.[42] It was also understood that so long as China continued to send military supplies to the North, station troops there, and establish repair facilities, they would remain under threat of American attack. The period was therefore characterized by much shrill rhetoric from Peking, an escalation of warning statements concomitant with the increasing severity and frequency of attacks, and mass rallies in Chinese cities, but no actual intervention save defensive reactions when American warplanes trespassed into Chinese airspace. In these circumstances, China was bound to turn aside the first overtures of the Johnson administration[43] to improve Sino-American relations by tying any melioration not merely to the Taiwan issue, as it always had, but also to cessation of American escalation in Vietnam. China had no interest in reciprocating these definitive American hints of rapprochement, even though they were later repeated, and, together with Soviet military pressure, eventually caused Peking to take notice.

41 NYT, 1 July 1966, 4, 11.   42 Whiting, The Chinese calculus of deterrence, 170–83.
43 NYT, 1 November 1968, 1, 10.

Chinese relations with the Soviet Union were largely conditioned by the Soviet role in the Vietnam conflict and by the possibility, however faint at the time, of a Soviet-mediated negotiated peace between North Vietnam and the United States.[44] The Chinese worried about détente-related Soviet-American "collusion" concerning the several American attempts to use the Kremlin's good offices (although they were hardly that) to bring the Vietnamese to the negotiating table. None bore fruit, since Hanoi had no intention of settling once again for partial gains.[45] But that did not diminish Chinese suspicions that Soviet-American agreement might reach beyond Vietnam and the strategic arms control realm to include a worldwide understanding, shearing away Soviet nuclear protection of China against American attack. Peking thus continued to attack the Russians whenever and wherever it could: in the increasingly small number of intracommunist forums open to both, in the increasingly large anti-Soviet rallies inside China, and in the Chinese media.[46] When possible (and so long as there was no real danger of Soviet overreaction), the Chinese struck at the Russians directly. Thus, Peking refused to attend the Twenty-third CPSU Congress in Moscow in early 1966 and other Soviet meetings later, and rebuked the Russians for sending out a secret letter to other ruling Communist parties. Peking denied all the long list of Soviet allegations against China contained therein, campaigned in particular to counter the repeated rumors (and Russian accusation) that China had held up Soviet shipments across Chinese territory of military equipment bound for Hanoi (there appears to have been truth in this charge), and deliberately began a program of baiting the Kremlin – in this instance by issuing regulations allegedly controlling Soviet shipping on the Amur and Ussuri border rivers.[47]

Although Peking's relations with Hanoi were almost totally conditioned by the Vietnamese conflict with the Americans, there were indications that below the surface not all was well between the two Communist parties. Hanoi rightly suspected that Peking was using interruptions of Soviet supplies as a political instrument, and not merely for anti-Soviet purposes. The Vietnamese hardly appreciated the Chinese telling them (in Lin Piao's article on people's war) how to conduct their struggle when Giap had already decided to move from guerrilla to con-

---

44 Henry Kissinger, *White House years*, 266–69.   45 Karnow, *Vietnam, a history*, n. 10, ch. 12.
46 Neuhauser, *Third World politics*, n. 12, ch. 4; FBIS *Daily Report: Far East*, for August–December 1966.
47 "Quarterly chronicle and documentation," *CQ*, 26 (April–June 1966), 216–17, for the secret letter and attendant events; *JMJP*, 20 April 1966, for the river regulations; if the Soviets had acceded to these Chinese rules, which they did not, they would have admitted Chinese sovereignty over all the disputed riverine islands and over the two waterways as a whole.

ventional operations with large units. And the Lao Dong Party disliked being pressured by the Chinese Party to take its side in the Sino-Soviet dispute no matter how much it might injure Vietnamese-Soviet relations.

Finally, even at that early date Ho Chi Minh and his associates knew that China did not favor the North's conquest of the South and the reestablishment of a single Vietnamese state, much less a Vietnam-dominated Communist Indochina.[48] Long-term Chinese policy for Southeast Asia seemed to be: communist yes, united no. Such differences were, for the while, put aside in the face of the American military threat, but it was clear to Peking that the Vietnamese Communists were much too independent for China's good. After all, the Chinese understood the advantages of self-reliance and themselves used that status to its utmost in their campaign against the Russians. They could hardly have wished to have seen the same weapon used against themselves. The roots of the Sino-Vietnamese conflict of the 1970s are thus to be found in the manner in which they dealt with each other in the 1960s, particularly during the Cultural Revolution.[49]

The enforced passivity of Chinese foreign policy during this phase is graphically illustrated by Peking's inability to deal effectively with the challenge to Chinese state interests made by Indonesia. As a consequence of the failed PKI coup attempt in September 1965, the Suharto regime conducted a witch-hunt of all Communists and suspected Communists, allowing the army and the populace to kill as many as could be found, often including their families as well.[50] China was, of course, embarrassed and greatly distressed but could do nothing. When, however, attacks spread to the Overseas Chinese in Indonesia and then to Chinese diplomatic and other official personnel and installations in Jakarta and other cities, the way was open for legitimate intervention. Anti-Chinese Indonesian violence peaked in early and mid-1966 with attacks, raids, forced searches, sacking of the Chinese embassy and several consulates, and expulsion of Chinese diplomatic personnel. But China could still do little except protest, withdraw official persons and students, and cut off eco-

48 W. A. C. Adie, "China and the war in Vietnam," *Mizan*, 8.6 (November–December 1966), 233–41; Tai-sung An, "The Sino-Soviet dispute and Vietnam," *Orbis*, 9.2 (Summer 1965), 426–36; Harold C. Hinton, "China and Vietnam," in Tsou, *China in crisis*, 2.201–36; John W. Lewis, "China and Vietnam," in University of Chicago Center for Policy Studies, *China briefing*, 53–56; Lawrence Pratt, *North Vietnam and Sino-Soviet tension*, 197; Robert A. Rupen and Robert Farrell, eds., *Vietnam and the Sino-Soviet dispute*, 120; Donald S. Zagoria, "Moscow, Peking, Washington, and the war in Vietnam," in Allan A. Spitz, ed., *Contemporary China*, 14–20.

49 Eugene K. Lawson, *The Sino-Vietnamese conflict*; Liao Kuang-sheng, *Antiforeignism and modernization in China, 1860–1980: linkage between domestic politics and foreign policy*; David W. P. Elliott, ed., *The third Indochina conflict*, chapters by Sutter, Porter, and Garrett.

50 Donald Hindley, "Political power and the October 1965 coup in Indonesia," *JAS*, 1969. 27. 237–49; Dommen, "The attempted coup in Indonesia," 144–70.

nomic assistance. When persecution of the Overseas Chinese reached widespread proportions, the Chinese Ministry of Foreign Affairs did demand that it be allowed to send ships to pick up all those who wished to return to the motherland.[51] In late 1966, Indonesia allowed a Chinese passenger ship to fetch those who wished to go home. Eventually, it transported more than four thousand such people.

Given Indonesian provocations, China should have broken diplomatic relations immediately. That it did not demonstrated how paltry were the instruments of policy then available. It was Indonesia, not China, that took decisive action at every stage. Only later, at the height of Cultural Revolution disorders in 1967, was the table turned on the Indonesians, when their embassy in Peking was invaded and burned by a Red Guard mob. The emerging demands of the Cultural Revolution, together with Peking's inability to project its power much beyond its boundaries, caused China's foreign policy to remain largely reactive and passive. As in China's relations with the Soviet Union, the United States, and Vietnam, the only option available was to react verbally to initiatives taken by others and to international events and decisions over which Peking had no say.

Phase two, 1966–1967

In the Red Guard phase of the Cultural Revolution, September 1966–August 1967, what foreign policy China had was strictly the product of the riots, rebellions, and revenge seeking that constituted the country's internal affairs for a full year and more. China no longer had to react to developments abroad, since the rest of the world accurately judged that China wished for nothing more than to be left alone. Now its foreign policy had to respond to events within China's own borders. At one point, when Red Guards seized the Ministry of Foreign Affairs itself and put Ch'en I up for mass criticism and ridicule, Peking's external policy was reduced to negotiating with the riotous mass of "revolutionary" youth at the front door of the building. China had finally achieved that total independence from the demands and controls of other states toward which it had striven so long, but only at the cost of having no foreign policy at all.

There was almost total correspondence between the scale of disorders inside the country and the degree of verbal pugilism directed against the external world. Until the Foreign Ministry went under in June 1967,

---

51 "Quarterly chronicle and documentation," *CQ*, 28 (October–December 1966), 193, and 29 (January–March 1967), 196–97.

China practiced foreign policy by mass rally, reminiscent supposedly of the Paris Commune. Thus, whenever China wished to give vent to its displeasure at some Soviet action, huge demonstrations were staged in front of the Soviet embassy. The first of these took place in January 1967 and lasted night and day for three weeks.[52] Moreover, Peking attempted to teach the Kremlin the art of revolution right in the Soviet capital; Chinese students passing through Moscow stopped off in Red Square to provoke the Russians, drew a few drops of Russian blood, and then spent the rest of their Siberian train ride showing passengers their bandages covering alleged wounds inflicted by tsarist Russian–like cavalry charges and showering Russian train stations with anti-Kremlin propaganda.[53] Demonstrations in Peking against other states' embassies also took place periodically throughout this period, particularly against those of Great Britain, Burma, and Indonesia, in retaliation for some presumed sinful action on the part of their government or merely for possessing, in Chinese eyes, the sociopolitical characteristics for which they were well known.

Sino-Soviet relations, of course, plunged even further as the Russians became the negative object of practically every Chinese verbal initiative. Diplomatic relations were nearly severed a number of times as tit-for-tat rounds of expulsions of official persons and others, especially correspondents, regularly occurred.[54] Chinese students in other countries – for instance, France and Iraq – also carried out demonstrations before the local Soviet embassy and then claimed hero status when the police knocked their heads together.

The Chinese international information apparatus turned its entire attention (that is, as much as was left after extolling the Cultural Revolution through quotations from Mao) to broadcasting to the Soviet Union, increasing its schedule to twenty-four-hour coverage. The most costly Chinese mistake was to attack Soviet citizens in China directly. Not only were parts of the Soviet embassy invaded and sacked, but officers of a Russian ship anchored in Dairen harbor paraded through the city streets for refusing to wear Mao badges.[55] In addition, Russian dependents being evacuated via Peking airport were forced to run a gauntlet of thousands of jeering, threatening, and spitting Red Guards assembled for the occasion.[56] These activities would, in 1969 and later, cost the Chinese

---

52 FBIS Daily Report: Far East, 30 January, 1967.
53 "Quarterly chronicle and documentation," CQ, 29 (January–March 1967), 193–95, and 30 (April–June 1967), 242.
54 Ibid., CQ, 30 (April–June 1967), 244.
55 O. B. Borisov and B. T. Koloskov, Soviet-Chinese relations, 1945–1970, 294–95.
56 Ibid., 304.

heavily in delayed Soviet emotional retaliation. There was also continued Chinese criticism of the Kremlin on all the litmus paper issues: "collusion" with the United States, revisionism at home and abroad, deliberate use of the (remnants of the) international communist movement against China, sham support but real sellout of the Vietnamese, and so forth.[57] But since relations with Moscow were frozen and since China wanted no improvement at all, the diplomatic component was of reduced importance. More important, but still behind the scenes, was the military situation at the border, where incidents and force buildups were already taking place,[58] and where the stage was being set for the explosion that would soon occur and require a halt to the Cultural Revolution itself.

China's foreign policy goal during this period – to insulate the country as thoroughly as possible from the outer world – was accomplished for the most part. For instance, all foreigners, with the exception of officially credited persons, were told to leave the country, while visits of foreign dignitaries were halted or kept to the bare minimum. But China could not be hermetically sealed, especially in the atmosphere of social breakdown, power seizure, demonstrations, and scapegoating. Spillovers inevitably took place. The most important was in Hong Kong.

Riots in Hong Kong

This British colonial remnant was an inviting and logical target for extremists. When the Foreign Ministry ceased to function and when what was left of Chinese foreign policy fell into the hands of local officials wishing to show how revolutionary-minded they had become, it was only a matter of time before the crown colony directly felt the effects of revolutionary street action. Besides, Hong Kong satisfied the Maoist criteria of readily ignitable socioeconomic timber, being the world's last outpost of rampant, no-holds-barred capitalism and the most vicious latter-day exemplar of Karl Marx's own description of how bourgeois society supposedly really operated.

The matter began with a local labor dispute in early May 1967, and would undoubtedly have stopped there had not China intervened by egging on the strikers and then officially supporting them and their demonstrating relatives. From the outset, such backing included radio broadcast instructions beamed to Hong Kong, loudspeaker relays attached to the Bank of China in downtown Victoria, payment to strikers

---

57 Any issue of PR, from September 1966 through mid-1967, will have at least one such article.
58 Thomas W. Robinson, "The Sino-Soviet border dispute: background, development, and the March 1969 clashes," *American Political Science Review*, 66.4 (December 1972), 1177–83.

and demonstrators, and resolutions of support passed by the Chinese trade unions. Thus the situation quickly mushroomed into full-scale riots and soon threatened the very existence of British rule. Arrests quickly mounted into the hundreds, sometimes on a daily basis, and strikes spread first to other private enterprises, then to such public services as transportation and gas supply, and finally into the government bureaucracy itself.

But the British government held firm against these challenges, sending in an aircraft carrier laden with helicopters and marines, while the Hong Kong police, 99 percent of whom were Chinese, neither broke in the face of the onslaughts nor joined the rioters. With the further breakdown of order in China, however, the crisis exacerbated in July. The border between China and Hong Kong was partially opened by the local Kwangtung authorities, apparently on their own initiative, and serious incidents occurred in border villages, including the killing by machine-gun fire of several Hong Kong police. With a permeable border, China-based terrorists penetrated into the heart of Kowloon, and by summer's end around 160 bomb explosions had been recorded in connection with intimidation of Chinese workers.[59]

From the very beginning, the Chinese raised the matter to the diplomatic level – first, by officially serving five demands on the Hong Kong government (which, if acceded to, would have transferred effective political power to the rioters); second, by surrounding the British embassy in Peking with howling mobs abusing British diplomats to a degree not seen in China in the twentieth century, and in July and August destroying embassy buildings there as well as the consulate in Shanghai; and, third, by provoking disturbances around the Chinese embassy in London (which then were used as excuses for further violations of British diplomatic immunity in China and stringent restrictions on British official personnel).[60] This staged escalation was probably not the consequence of a carefully timed series of Foreign Ministry moves designed to drive the British out of the colony or even decisions by Mao, Chou En-lai, and others occupying the "Party Center" (by the summer of 1967 all that was left of central political power in China except for direct military rule). Rather, it seemed to reflect the step-by-step disintegration of the Foreign Ministry, even to the point where foreign policy was effectively in the hands of a junior official, Yao Teng-shan, and his Red Guard associates,[61]

59 William Heaton, "Maoist revolutionary strategy and modern colonization: the Cultural Revolution in Hong Kong," *Asian Survey*, 10.9 (September 1970), 840–57; Edward Earl Rice, *Mao's way*, 364–75; "Quarterly chronicle and documentation," *CQ*, 31 (July–September 1967), 212–17.
60 *CQ*, 32 (October–December 1967), 221–23.
61 On whom more discussion will appear later in this chapter.

where Ch'en I was powerless, and where even Chou En-lai, presumably against his better judgment, had to associate himself with the revolutionary actions in Hong Kong.

The maltreatment of the British chargé in Peking, Donald Hopson, and his consul in Shanghai, Peter Hewitt,[62] would normally have been reason enough for any foreign power to break diplomatic ties with China. The burning of the embassy alone should have provided sufficient cause. But London did not take that logical step, for several reasons. Most obviously, with no diplomatic relations, Hong Kong would have been placed in ultimate jeopardy (as things were, although the riots were serious enough, trade, tourism, and manufacturing held up remarkably well and there was little capital flight). Moreover, London realized that the Chinese antics were the consequence of reducing Chinese foreign policy to an offshoot of internal mob action, and that probably the storm would pass, as it did, soon enough. Britain determined to show China that intimidation as a policy would not work and that if China pretended to be a civilized state, it would have to behave like one. This view had a nineteenth-century ring to it.

In the end, this policy paid off. By the fall of 1967, with the Foreign Ministry's being put back in order and military rule's finally taking effect across China, order was restored in the colony, the border was again subject to normal cooperative passage, and (most important) British diplomats in Peking were allowed to move about within the metropolitan area. China, of course, claimed victory when there was none and then lifted pressure on British diplomats in China. That, however, took time, and not until mid-1968 was London able even to begin to get its diplomats out of the country. Even then, however, the Reuters correspondent Anthony Grey was still under house arrest (where he had been since July 1967) late in the year, while British ship captains and other seamen were still being regularly detained, tried, and deported, and at least one British subject, an engineer named George Watt, was sentenced to three years' imprisonment, allegedly for spying. (The rest of the staff of the Vickers-Zimmer Company, which had been building a synthetic fiber plant, was deported in July 1968.)[63]

The British experience in China during the Cultural Revolution was the most extreme instance of its kind. It was paralleled, nonetheless, by those of most of the Western European states that elected to keep open their China missions, had Chinese embassies to contend with in their own

62 *NYT*, 25 May 1967, and *Far Eastern Economic Review*, 1 August 1967, 229.
63 "Quarterly chronicle and documentation," *CQ*, 36 (October–December 1968), 172.

capitals, or at least maintained economic relations with China. The experience of states on China's borders or within reach of Chinese influence was somewhat different. There, Cultural Revolution spillover problems were felt more directly, if in a shorter time span and in a more manageable manner. Cambodia and Burma met crises, while India, Nepal, Ceylon, Kenya, and Algeria also felt leftist-induced pressures.[64]

Spillover in Southeast Asia

In Phnom Penh, the situation was complicated by the Vietnam War. Prince Sihanouk wanted to use China's alleged friendship to prevent the conflict from spreading westward, while his armed opposition, the Khmer Rouge, had a history of support by Peking. China's aims were not to upset the Cambodian leader too much about Viet Cong use of his territory, to maintain Phnom Penh's ultimate independence from the Vietnamese, to keep alive the Khmer Rouge movement but not to make it an overt Chinese tool, and to support Sihanouk's neutrality in the Sino-Soviet dispute.[65] The problem for Peking was that it could not control events. Not only were the Russians, the Americans, the Vietnamese, and the domestic Cambodians all independent actors, but during this phase of the Cultural Revolution the export of revolutionary Chinese voluntarism became an additional disturbing element.

In May 1967, the Chinese embassy in Phnom Penh took it upon itself to distribute Maoist propaganda, encourage local Chinese youth in Red Guard-like activities, pass out money to the Khmer-China Friendship Association, and publicly involve itself in details of Cambodian politics.[66] Sihanouk could not allow these affronts to pass unchallenged, even though he was dependent on Chinese diplomatic support and economic largesse. He therefore felt constrained to adopt countermeasures that effectively stopped such activities. He also severely criticized the Cultural Revolution itself.[67]

The matter could have ended there but for the events in China that summer. With the Foreign Ministry in a shambles by August, Chou En-lai was forced to tell the visiting Cambodian foreign minister, Prince

64 Ibid., *CQ*, 31 (July–September 1967), 219–21; 32 (October–December 1967), 225–26; 34 (April–June 1968), 192; and 35 (July–September 1968), 194–97; Larkin, *China and Africa*, 125–47.

65 Roger M. Smith, *Cambodia's foreign policy*; Michael Leifer, "Cambodia and China: neutralism, 'neutrality,' and national security," in A. M. Halpern, ed., *Policies toward China: views from six continents*; and Michael Leifer, *Cambodia: the search for security*; Melvin Gurtov, *China and Southeast Asia, the politics of survival: a study of foreign policy interaction*, ch. 3.

66 Gurtov, *China and Southeast Asia*, 77–78.   67 Ibid., 79–81.

Phurissara, in effect that China had lost control of its Cambodian embassy's activities.[68] Moreover, Chinese support for the Friendship Association, which Sihanouk had by then banned, did not cease, and Chinese media began to attack the Cambodian head directly. These actions led Sihanouk to accuse China, accurately, of interfering in Cambodia's internal affairs.[69] Together with the burning of the British embassy in Peking in August and China's conduct in the parallel situation in Burma, they also caused him in September to announce the withdrawal of Cambodian embassy personnel from Peking. Even though Chou En-lai subsequently talked him out of this incipient break in diplomatic ties, the damage was done and relations between the two countries remained distant for the remainder of the Cultural Revolution.

In Burma events went to a much greater extreme, showing how quickly an otherwise reasonable bilateral relationship could get out of hand once the Cultural Revolution influenced the Foreign Ministry directly. Historically, China's ties with Burma were reasonably good, based on Rangoon's sensible policy of not offending China overtly and on Peking's goals of promoting good state relations while laying the groundwork for eventual support of violent communist revolution. Thus, Peking was patient with the Burmese policy of neutrality and noninvolvement, of relatively close control of the domestic leftist movement, and of departure from China in a number of policy matters, including its attitude toward the Vietnam conflict, arms control, and what the best Third World stance should be toward the West and the Soviet Union. So long as Burma was reasonably cooperative and the domestic communist movement relatively weak (it had split between Red Flag and White Flag branches, with a further division in the mid-1960s within the pro-Peking White flags), there was little that China could, or needed to, do in Burma. Therefore, China signed a boundary treaty with Burma in 1960, followed that with a treaty of friendship and nonaggression in 1961, looked the other way when the Ne Win government suppressed Communist fronts after his talks with leftist factions collapsed in 1963, and did not object openly when, in 1964, government nationalization of banks and major industries adversely affected Chinese citizens in Burma.[70]

It was a different matter once the Cultural Revolution began. For one thing, the White Flag Communists converted themselves, after a violent internal struggle and blood purge, into a Maoist-style, purist politico-military organization under the direction of China-trained Red Guard—

like leaders.[71] For another, Burma did not follow China's policy line sufficiently closely on the Vietnam conflict, the anti-Soviet struggle, or in the Third World, despite multiple top-level visits to Rangoon by Liu Shao-ch'i, Ch'en I, and Chou En-lai in 1965 and 1966.[72] Moreover, the Chinese embassy and the NCNA in Rangoon not only financed local Chinese schools but introduced a strong Maoist content into their curriculum, which was heavily reinforced at the outset of the Cultural Revolution. This effectively converted these Chinese students into foreign-based Red Guards. Finally, with the progressive collapse of the Chinese Foreign Ministry in the spring and summer of 1967, Chinese diplomats returning to Rangoon after Cultural Revolution indoctrination earlier that year began openly to distribute the "little red book" of Mao quotations, Mao buttons, and other inflammatory propaganda. When challenged by local authorities, they insisted that they had every right to do so.[73]

These acts, particularly the last, were too much for the Rangoon population and the Ne Win government. Anti-Chinese riots therefore broke out when embassy-encouraged students refused to remove their Mao buttons as required by government regulation. The riots quickly escalated into attacks on the Chinese embassy, the NCNA office, the Chinese-run schools, and finally on many Burmese Overseas Chinese. These disturbances were not quashed by the Rangoon police, and the rioting spread to the point where a Chinese embassy aide was killed. Peking responded much as it had in the Hong Kong instance (which, like the events in Phnom Penh, was developing concurrently). First, Peking sent warning memoranda in late June, then served a list of demands on Rangoon (which, because of their severity, Burma could not but reject), followed that with massive demonstrations around the Burmese embassy in Peking, and finally escalated diplomatically with yet another series of demands.[74]

The problem would still have been contained, even at that point, had not Peking radicalized the situation completely by coming out openly (for the first time) in support of the White Flag Communists' campaign to

71 John H. Badgley, "Burma and China: policy of a small neighbor," in Halpern, ed., *Policies toward China*, 303–28; Robert A. Holmes, "Burma's foreign policy toward China since 1962," *Pacific Affairs*, 45.2 (Summer 1972), 240–54; Lynn B. Pascoe, "China's relations with Burma, 1949–1964," in Andrew Cordier, ed., *Columbia essays in international affairs: the dean's papers, 1965*; Frank N. Trager, "Sino-Burmese relations: the end of the Pauk Phaw era," *Orbis*, 11.4 (Winter 1968), 1034–54; Justus M. Van der Kroef, "Chinese subversion in Burma," *Indian Communist*, 3.1–2 (March–June 1970), 6–13.
72 Gurtov, *China and Southeast Asia*, 107–8.   73 Ibid., 114.   74 Ibid., 115–16.

overthrow the Burmese government by violence. Peking verbally attacked the Burmese government and Ne Win personally, called on the Burmese people to take up arms against their government and establish a Communist one in its place, and placed Chinese media at the disposal of the White Flags.[75] This major escalation, which occurred in the space of three days at the end of June, was clearly the work of the radicals inside the Chinese Foreign Ministry. It reversed (indeed, destroyed) the entire Chinese position in and with regard to Burma that had been constructed with such care ever since 1949. Burma, both government and citizenry, reacted accordingly. Demonstrations spread throughout the country during July and August, Chinese-backed propaganda organs were banned, a massive crackdown on leftist groups occurred, a government-backed media campaign against China and its local fellow travelers was conducted, and several Chinese correspondents were expelled.[76] The inevitable diplomatic break followed. China and Burma withdrew their ambassadors in midsummer, and Sino-Burmese relations did not even begin to recover until a year later.

Radicalization of the Foreign Ministry

These events – in Hong Kong, Phnom Penh, Rangoon, and to a lesser extent elsewhere – had multiple causes. But they would probably not have occurred at all had the Chinese Foreign Ministry not suffered radicalization during this mid-1967 period, had Foreign Minister Ch'en I not been subject to personal attack, and had physical destruction of some ministry records not taken place. Any understanding of Chinese foreign policy during this phase of the Cultural Revolution, as well as for a lengthy period after, must take these developments into account, for the Foreign Ministry was the nexus between internal Chinese events and the country's dealings with the rest of the world.

The bureaucratic expression of the Cultural Revolution was the interference of work teams, Red Guards, revolutionary rebels, revolutionary committees, and other disruptive elements in the workings of the ministries and committees of the State Council. The timing of these activities, however, varied, depending on the ministry and the general direction and staging of Cultural Revolution violence. The Foreign Ministry was one of the last to be invested; it suffered for a comparatively short time (although during that period, the summer of 1967, it was very hard hit); and in contrast to many other government organs, it continued in operation throughout the entire period with which we are concerned. But Foreign Ministry operations were compromised, and the content and direction of Chinese foreign policy were changed in close accordance with the disordering and reordering of the Cultural Revolution.

Thus, in the summer of 1966, Foreign Minister Ch'en I accepted work teams the Party sent into his organization, but like other ministers he used them to defend the organizational integrity of his institution and to keep the radical students away.[77] In the fall of 1966, after the Eleventh Plenum formally opened the Cultural Revolution, Mao recalled the work teams and permitted Red Guards to form revolutionary committees in the Foreign Ministry as in other State Council institutions. But Ch'en I did not allow them to interfere in the making or execution of Chinese foreign policy, and he himself continued unimpaired in his duties. His effort was parallel to those of other ministry heads. Each fought a delaying action in the hope that the overall situation would improve.[78]

Radicalism, once loosed, however, could not be put back into the bottle. By late 1966 and early 1967 student-worker mobs began to conduct "power seizures" everywhere. The January Revolution thus brought intentionally perpetrated chaos across the land and within most governmental organizations, including the Foreign Ministry. In the ministry, a Revolutionary Rebel Liaison Station was established on 18 January. Attacks against Ch'en I, which had begun in the fall, now reached a crescendo. Ch'en was forced to deliver a self-criticism before a mass rally of ten thousand, during which he admitted to seven major "crimes."[79] Ch'en's idea, of course, like that of Chou En-lai (who presided over this rally), was to use his own "confession" to deflect the radicals from interfering in ministry operations and to save his own position by hiding behind the authority of Chou and, by implication, of Mao Tse-tung. This tactic worked reasonably well: Some leftists within the ministry liaison office were removed. For the next two months the content of foreign policy remained reasonably rational.

But structural changes then occurred, causing this modus operandi to disintegrate by early summer. First, China called back all its ambassadors (save one, Huang Hua, in Cairo)[80] for the duration of the Cultural Revolution, as well as most of the top embassy staff members, the latter for

77 Melvin Gurtov, "The Foreign Ministry and foreign affairs in the Chinese Cultural Revolution," in Robinson, *The Cultural Revolution in China*, 317–18.
78 Ibid., 318–22.   79 Ibid., 322–25.
80 It is still not clear why Huang Hua alone was kept at his post. Perhaps it was thought necessary to have at least one seasoned observer in that part of the world, especially after China's problems in Africa had led to the forced withdrawal of so many Chinese embassy personnel stationed on that continent.

indoctrination. This action, obviously, severely impaired Peking's ability to perceive and analyze events abroad. But an equally important consequence was that it radicalized both the embassies, once the staff returned to them, and the Foreign Ministry departments at home. Second, in January 1967 the PLA was called in by Mao to provide support to the leftists in their power seizures. The military acted temporarily as a stabilizing and comparatively conservative force by giving primacy within the "three-way alliance" (among the PLA, senior cadres, and Red Guards) to the older, experienced, and presumably less radical bureaucrats. But by April the military was criticized for this ploy (called "false power seizures") and had to give added power to the radicals. Thus, within the Foreign Ministry, Ch'en I found himself once again under pressure, this time from the so-called Criticize Ch'en I Liaison Station. Soon open demonstrations were being held in Peking against him. With the assent of Chou En-lai, in May 1967, Ch'en was once again subjected to criticize-and-struggle rallies.[81]

Third, the radicals found leaders of putatively heroic quality to stand against the foreign minister on an equal basis. The final break between China and Indonesia had occurred in April 1967 when Jakarta expelled the Chinese chargé, Yao Teng-shan. Yao returned to China on 30 April to a tumultuous welcome at Peking airport attended by the entire Chinese leadership. Thereafter he was lionized throughout the city and was the main attraction at a denounce-Indonesia rally in mid-May. Once back in the Foreign Ministry building, Yao set about the task of providing authoritative leadership to the radical forces directed against Ch'en, who was once again attempting to shield the conduct of China's foreign relations (as well as his senior staff) from the rising tide of internal violence.[82]

The consequence was the ripping apart of the Foreign Ministry by the combined onslaught of internal strains and external attacks. A series of violently destructive incidents occurred on 13 May, wherein hundreds of Liaison Station-controlled radicals invaded the ministry, shut down operations, beat up officials, and took away classified information after scattering files. This act was repeated on 29 May. Thereafter the Foreign Ministry was only quasi functional. One major cause of the rapid downward spiral in China's relations with Hong Kong, Cambodia, and Burma already outlined, and less severely with more than thirty other states, was the combination of physical inoperability of the ministry in the summer

81 Gurtov, "The Foreign Ministry," 326–31.
82 Ibid., 332–36.

of 1967 and the competition for power within its walls between Ch'en I's associates and Yao's cohorts. That there was any foreign policy at all was perhaps due to Chou En-lai, who not only intervened with the radicals to save Ch'en (typically, by telling them to prepare their case against Ch'en more thoroughly and thus buying time) but also stepped back into the foreign ministership temporarily and directed its affairs from his own office.[83]

But the violence mounted to a peak in midsummer 1967, as Mao sought to give the Chinese people that renewed revolutionary experience he thought they needed. Armed clashes occurred in the provinces. This affected the Foreign Ministry, and therefore policy, in two ways. First, it focused the attention of the central leadership almost entirely on real military struggle. Mao and his followers tended to forget about the problems caused by Peking's policies toward other states and to leave the Foreign Ministry to work out its internal differences without any assistance from them.

Second, the most important of these midsummer battles, the so-called Wuhan Incident,[84] produced in July a new (if temporary) hero, in Wang Li. He returned, like Yao Teng-shan, to Peking in triumph, and power quickly went to his head. He chose the Foreign Ministry as one of the places in which to try to exercise it. On 7 August, Wang gave a speech that signaled his and Yao's final assault on the ministry and Ch'en I. For the next two weeks, the Foreign Ministry was entirely under the control of the rebels, and Ch'en I was subjected once more to mass struggle sessions (on 11 and 27 August, at which he confessed to a new list of "crimes").[85] Chinese foreign policy was in chaos.

It was during this period that the crises with Burma and Cambodia came to a head and the British embassy was burned. They were the direct consequences of Yao's and Wang's excesses. Yao also sent out telegrams to Chinese missions abroad of his own volition, "went everywhere making reports and creating trouble,"[86] and acted to all intents and purposes as foreign minister. The Party Center, that is, Mao and his Cultural Revolution Group, was either unwilling or unable to put a stop to these excesses until the end of August.

The British embassy incident, together with the realization of where deliberately encouraged civil war had led the country, finally shocked the

83 Ibid., 347; Thomas W. Robinson, "Chou En-lai and the Cultural Revolution," in Robinson, ed., *The Cultural Revolution in China*, 259–65.
84 Thomas W. Robinson, "The Wuhan Incident: local strife and provincial rebellion during the Cultural Revolution," *CQ*, 47 (July–September 1971), 413–38.
85 Gurtov, "The Foreign Ministry," 347–51.
86 *Hung-wei pao*, 15 September 1967.

Maoist leadership into drawing back. A fundamental turn in the direction of the Cultural Revolution was decided on 1 September: There would be no more "struggles by force" or "power seizures"; Red Guards would no longer be allowed to travel but would have to stick to their own units; political struggle would replace armed struggle as the principal means of ridding the country of the "capitalist roaders"; and the revolutionaries were told to stop "beating, smashing, burning, invading, and obstructing."[87] The effect on the Foreign Ministry of this volte-face was immediate: Yao, Wang, and their henchmen were removed and tried; Ch'en I was able to reoccupy his office (literally as well as figuratively); embassies abroad were instructed to cease making revolution; and power seizures in and against the ministry were specifically forbidden.[88] It is true that relations between China and many countries had been damaged so badly that the wounds could not be sewn up nor the scars healed overnight. Ties with such countries remained either broken or severely strained for a long time. But a change for the better had occurred.

THE NADIR OF CHINESE FOREIGN POLICY, 1967–1968

China did essentially nothing in the international sphere for practically a year and a half after the summer wars of 1967. But the real tragedy of Chinese foreign policy thereafter was that the enormous difficulty with the Russians, which the Chinese brought on themselves in early 1969, was avoidable and unnecessary. The early March 1969 border incident between Chinese and Soviet armed units caused military overreaction by the Russians and mortgaged Chinese foreign policy as a whole for a decade thereafter. It was caused almost entirely by Cultural Revolution–induced internal political problems and by Mao's own unwise decisions. Before proceeding, let us outline what there was of Chinese policy during 1968 and mention a few other matters connected with foreign relations that were not tied in with chronological developments.

The year 1968 was one of maximum Chinese isolation from the rest of the world. Violence continued throughout the year despite official injunctions to end it. It took a long time even to begin the political reconstruction of the Party and the government ministries.[89] China literally had reduced its policy instruments to zero. Peking could only look on outside events, comment on them from time to time, and begin the extended process of resuscitating its ties with the countries with whom things had

87 Jürgen Domes, *The internal politics of China, 1949–1972*, 188–99.
88 Gurtov, "The Foreign Ministry," 364–66.
89 Rice, *Mao's way*, chs. 24 and 25.

gone sour during the previous three years. Toward the United States, China could think only of bad things to say, principally in connection with the American military role in Vietnam.[90] There was no movement, therefore, or even hint, of any warming up of Sino-American relations. That came only after the Soviet overthrow of the Czech government in the summer of 1968.

Toward Vietnam, Peking continued to express its fear that Hanoi would negotiate in earnest with the United States instead of using the American bombing halts and the various peace talk proposals and sessions as time to be gained to regroup for the next battle.[91] Despite these misgivings and despite its disagreement with Giap's military strategy, as evidenced by the Tet offensive, China did continue its own supply of military and economic goods to North Vietnam. But public evidence of discord in Sino-Vietnamese relations also continued to be displayed. In June 1968 demonstrations took place before the Vietnamese consulates in Canton, Kunming, and Nanning protesting Hanoi's acceptance of the American (and Soviet-mediated) Paris peace talks proposal. The consulate in Kunming was severely damaged.[92]

The Chinese once again found nothing good to say about the Russians, and spent an increasing amount of media space denouncing the Kremlin on all the standard issues.[93] At least there was no repetition of the violent untoward acts that had characterized Chinese policy toward Moscow in the previous two years. The major event in Sino-Soviet relations (aside from border-related matters, discussed in the next section) took place in East Europe, when in August 1968 the Red Army invaded Czechoslovakia. Up to that point, Peking had kept its distance from the Czech Communist Party led by Alexander Dubček because of its obvious reformist-revisionist character. Once Russian tanks were in Prague, However, China turned around and verbally supported the (now ousted)

90 Hinton, ed., *The People's Republic of China, 1949–1979*, vol. 4, documents 425 and 439; and "Quarterly chronicle and documentation," CQ, relevant sections nos. 34–37.

91 Henry S. Albinski, "Chinese and Soviet policies in the Vietnam crisis," *Australian Quarterly*, 40.1 (March 1968), 65–74; King C. Chen, "Hanoi vs. Peking: policies and relations – a survey," *Asian Survey*, 12.9 (September 1972), 807–17; G. P. Deshpande, "China and Vietnam," *International Studies*, 12.4 (October–December 1973), 568–81; Ishwer C. Ojha, *The changing pattern of China's attitude toward a negotiated settlement in Vietnam, 1964–1971*, 23; D. R. Sardesar, "China and peace in Vietnam," *China Report*, 5.3 (May–June 1969), 13–18; Brian Shaw, "China and North Vietnam: two revolutionary paths," *Current Scene*, 9.11 (November 1971), 1–12; Hsiang Nai-kuang, "The relations between Hanoi and Peiping," *Chinese Communist Affairs*, 1.4 (December 1964), 9–21; Alexander Woodside, "Peking and Hanoi: anatomy of a revolutionary partnership," *International Journal*, 24.1 (Winter 1968–69), 65–85; Yao Meng-hsien, "Chinese communists and the Vietnam War," *Issues & Studies*, 1.9 (June 1965), 1–13.

92 "Quarterly chronicle and documentation," *CQ*, 35 (July–September 1968), 199.

93 Author's perusal of FBIS *Daily Report: China* for 1967 and 1968.

Czech leader, if not his program.[94] The Soviet military action badly frightened the Chinese, especially after Brezhnev justified the Kremlin's acts with the doctrine that the Soviet Union had the unilateral duty to make sure that a country once communist would stay that way. The obvious extension was to China itself. The Russians now began to say, in print, that China was no longer a Marxist-Leninist state, and they greatly raised the level and the shrillness of their denunciations.[95] The fear, however unfounded, that China could be next on the Soviet military hit list played a substantial role in the decision to spill Russian blood onto the Ussuri ice in early 1969. To Mao's way of thinking, cold-blooded murder would throw the Russians off balance and perhaps bring them to their senses before they attacked China.

China's dispute with Britain over Hong Kong and maltreatment of British diplomats in China continued. There was an intermittent flow of new incidents throughout the year, although none were as serious as those of 1967.[96] The same was true of Peking's relations (or lack of them, in the diplomatic sense) with Indonesia and Burma, particularly the former. In late 1967, in retaliation for the earlier sacking of the Indonesian embassy in Peking, the Chinese embassy in Jakarta was stormed, with the injury of twenty Chinese inside and the loss of several Indonesian lives, some from Chinese gunfire.[97] Both countries thereupon withdrew all their diplomats from each other's capitals. Peking's ties with Cambodia warmed slightly, despite Sihanouk's continued suspicions, voiced publicly, of China's dualistic motives. The rapprochement, such as it was, stemmed directly from the American decision to bomb Viet Cong positions and North Vietnamese supply routes in Cambodia. China promised Sihanouk "all-out support" to help repel the Americans, and a flow of Chinese military assistance did begin early in 1968.[98] (Peking also stepped up its arms provision and training of the anti-Sihanouk Khmer Rouge at the same time, however, and the Prince's inability to persuade Peking to stop the material backing of these domestic rebels was one factor, a few years later, in Sihanouk's removal from office.)

In 1968, Chinese policy toward the three other Asian states of conse-

---

94 See, for instance, the speech by Chou En-lai on 23 August 1968, "Chinese government and people strongly condemn Soviet revisionist clique's armed occupation of Czechoslovakia," *PR* supplement to no. 34, III–VIII.

95 See, for instance, the series of three articles in *Kommunist*, 6 (April), 102–13; 7 (May), 103–14; 8 (May), 95–108; 9 (June), 93–108; and 10 (July), 90–99.

96 "Quarterly chronicle and documentation," *CQ*, 32 (April–June 1968), 189–90; 35 (July–September 1968), 193–94; 36 (October–December 1969), 172–73; 37 (January–March 1969), 165–66.

97 Ibid., *CQ*, 33 (January–March 1969), 178.

98 *JMJP*, 28 December 1967, 1, and Gurtov, *China and Southeast Asia*, 129–37.

quence to itself – Japan, India, and North Korea – came into some prominence. Toward Tokyo, Peking's attitude hardened. China continued periodically to arrest and deport Japanese correspondents, as it had since the beginning of the Cultural Revolution, on the grounds of too close an inquiry into Chinese domestic goings-on, but in 1967 and again in late 1968 this treatment was extended to Japanese businessmen.[99] The consequence was a drastic decline in the number of such people traveling to China, even to the Canton trade fair, which in turn negatively affected Sino-Japanese trade. Peking also showed how badly it could stray from the facts when in April it conjured up the accusation that Tokyo was bent on nuclear rearmament (later it was even to charge that Japan and South Korea were secretly cooperating militarily against China).[100] This is a good example of the elementary errors into which Chinese foreign policy fell as a result of the destruction of Foreign Ministry records of its own past policies toward important foreign states.

Toward India, Peking pulled out the propaganda stops, calling for the overthrow of the Indian government by force, surreptitiously supplying arms and training to Naga guerrillas, praising the Naxalbari peasant rebels, hailing the unrest in Bihar, and verbally encouraging the pro-Peking branch of the Indian Communist Party (which by then had split into three parts) to forsake the parliamentary path and take to the rebel road.[101] As a *People's Daily* editorial in February had it: "A single spark can start a prairie fire.' Let the peasants' revolutionary storm in India strike harder!" The predictable result was a strong Indian government reaction, both on the scene and internationally. New Delhi moved even closer to Moscow, resolved to build up its military forces more strongly against China, and limited still further the foreign policy autonomy of the Himalayan border states. The degree to which the Sino-Indian military equation had already changed from the time of the 1962 Chinese invasion had already been made manifest in September 1967. A week-long fight between regular Indian and Chinese troops occurred on the Sikkim–Tibet border, with loss of life on both sides. This time, there was a standoff (the product of better Indian training and equipment) and Peking therefore tacitly cooperated with New Delhi to hush up the incident.[102]

In 1968, China realized that North Korea had become too independent for Peking's own good and that Pyongyang could well drag China against

99 "Quarterly chronicle and documentation," *CQ*, 35 (July–September 1968), 196.
100 *JMJP*, 5 April 1968, 1; 28 February 1968, 1; Chae-jin Lee, *Japan faces China: political and economic relations in the postwar era*, 49, 163, 188.
101 "Quarterly chronicle and documentation," *CQ*, 34 (April–June 1968), 192; 35 (July–September 1968), 195.
102 Ibid., *CQ*, 32 (October–December 1967), 225.

its will into another war with the United States. In January, the North seized an American electronic spy ship, the *Pueblo*, outside of Pyong-yang's territorial waters, causing a crisis on the peninsula. More import-ant, throughout the 1965-69 period, North Korea markedly stepped up its attempts to infiltrate the South, escalated the number of military incidents along the demilitarized zone (DMZ) and inside South Korea, and vastly increased its military budget to more than 30 percent of an already growing gross national product. To make matters worse for Peking, Pyongyang swung over to the Soviet side of the fence, both ideo-logically and by accepting a large volume of Soviet military supplies. Moreover, Chinese Red Guards strongly criticized North Korean "revi-sionism" and Kim Il Sung by name as a "millionaire and an aristocrat." Finally, in 1969 armed clashes took place between regular units from both states, probably the result of Ladakh-like Chinese roadbuilding activity in-side territory that hitherto had been regarded by both sides as Korean.[103] In 1968 and even more pronouncedly in 1969, therefore, the Chinese leaders decided they had better reverse this trend, which was against Chinese interests. The only way to do so was to work hard to befriend Kim, through protestations of comradeship, verbal support of his policies toward the South, military and economic assistance, and ideological relaxation. That would take time, of course, and the next several years were spent repairing ties with North Korea. But at least a start was made during this stage of the Cultural Revolution.

Two final indications of the nadir to which Chinese foreign relations had sunk were the annual votes on China's admission to the United Nations and the effect on China's foreign trade of these years of socio-political breakdown. An argument can be made that had the Cultural Revolution not occurred, Peking would have regained China's seat in the United Nations several years earlier than 1971. In the years immediately before 1965, the voting trend was modestly favorable, thanks mostly to China's relatively moderate policy toward former colonies and their wholesale admission to the principal international organization. But the Cultural Revolution changed that, and the voting margins went heavily against Peking from 1966 through 1968.

During the heyday of the Cultural Revolution, Peking had no chance

---

103 Carol Bell, "Korea and the balance of power," *Political Quarterly*, 25.1 (January–March 1954), 17–29; Donald S. Zagoria, "North Korea and the major powers," in William J. Barnds and Young Kun Kim, eds., *The two Koreas in East Asian affairs*, 19–59; Ilpyong J. Kim, "Chinese Communist relations with North Korea: continuity and change," *JAS*, 13.4 (December 1970), 59–78; Roy U. T. Kim, "Sino-North Korean relations," *Asian Survey*, 8 (August 1968), 17–25; Joseph C. Kun, "North Korea: between Moscow and Peking," *CQ*, 31 (July–September 1967), 48–58; Chin Chung, *P'yongyang between Peking and Moscow: North Korea's involvement in the Sino-Soviet dispute, 1958–1975*.

of admission. It thus regularly denounced the world organization (although it drew back from the Indonesian-sponsored idea of 1965 to found a new "revolutionary" international organization pointed against the West).[104]

The *Sturm und Drang* of the Cultural Revolution could not but affect China's foreign trade. But total trade did not decline more than marginally, from $3.8 billion in 1965 to $3.7 billion in 1968, and rebounded with reasonable rapidity, standing in 1971 at $4.5 billion.[105] The absolute figures are not high, of course, because during the Cultural Revolution, as before, China had not become the great trading nation of the latter 1970s and beyond. The effects on trade were indeed minimized for several reasons. First, the portion of the country's gross national product devoted to trade was quite small. Second, many of the export industries were comparatively unaffected, or only lightly so, by the destructiveness of the Cultural Revolution. Third, agriculture, the principal source of Peking's exports, also suffered relatively little. Such dislocations as did occur were due more to disruptions in transportation and in selected industries than to generalized disorder, indicating that the Cultural Revolution tended to be highly specific in locale and by industry. Moreover, total trade declined because of the Chinese propensity to keep imports and exports in close balance on an annual basis; thus, as exports dropped off, imports were also restricted. As grain imports declined the most, one would have expected repercussions in the Chinese diet and its caloric content. In fact, these did not occur, because Chinese agriculture was largely immune from the urban-based disorders.

One change of note was the continuation of the shift, begun in the early 1960s for political reasons, of trade away from the Soviet Union and Eastern Europe and toward the industrial countries of the capitalist West (except, of course, the United States). Developed countries took 53 percent of China's trade in 1970, as opposed to 39 percent in 1965, while communist countries fell from 30 to 20 percent during the same six years. Most of China's manufactures and technology imports now came from Japan and Western Europe, as well as a surprisingly high percentage of its imports of primary produce. The result was a consistent trade deficit with such countries, which was made up by a trade surplus with Hong Kong and the less developed noncommunist countries. Even with the communist countries, however, trade rose in absolute terms beginning in

104 Samuel S. Kim, *China, the United Nations, and world order*, 99–105.
105 A. H. Usack and R. E. Batsavage, "The international trade of the People's Republic of China," in United States Congress [92nd], Joint Economic Committee, *People's Republic of China: an economic assessment*, 335–37.

late 1970. After falling to a nearly infinitesimal $47 million in 1970, Sino-Soviet trade rebounded to $145 million the next year, and Chinese trade with Eastern Europe did not suffer the temporary nosedive experienced by the Russians.

It is somewhat surprising that Sino-Soviet trade registered at all in 1971, given the Soviet force buildup described in the next section and the political aftermath of the 1969 border incidents. The reason seems to be that China's need for the items that Moscow and its Eastern European satraps were willing to provide – mostly civil aircraft and manufactured spare parts – outdistanced its capacity to punish the Russians for their politico-military transgressions. Chinese trade throughout the period did follow the general direction – in fact, the vagaries – of Peking's foreign policy. But it was so small in absolute terms that whatever China did in this area was more symbolic than consequential. Only later could China develop trade as a principal instrument of policy.

THE 1969 SINO-SOVIET BORDER CONFLICT

The Cultural Revolution would have been an unfortunate, but relatively harmless, aberration in the general development of China's foreign relations had it not been for one overriding event: Peking's decision in early 1969 to militarize the long-standing border dispute with the Soviet Union. Why China elected to do so at a moment of comparative weakness, or to do so at all, remains a mystery. No convincing single explanation has yet been put forward for the 2 March 1969 violent outburst at Chen-pao Island in the Ussuri River.[106] Here a composite, if tentative, answer is offered although the essential facts will probably never be known. Yet the event did occur, Chinese foreign policy and the Cultural Revolution both veered dramatically off course, and the entire structure of relations within the Sino-Soviet-American strategic triangle changed accordingly.[107]

Sino-Soviet border differences have a long history, stretching back to the first treaties between Russia and China in the seventeenth century.[108]

---

106 Robinson, "The Sino-Soviet border dispute," n. 58.
107 Vernon Aspaturian, "The USSR, the USA and China in the seventies," *Survey*, 19.2 (Spring 1973), 103–22; William E. Griffith, ed., *The world and the great power triangles*; Michael Tatu, *The great power triangle: Washington, Moscow, Peking*; Ronald J. Yalem, "Tripolarity and world politics," *The Yearbook of world affairs*, 28.23–42; Thomas W. Robinson, "Detente and the Sino-Soviet-U.S. triangle," in Della W. Sheldon, ed., *Dimensions of detente*, 50–83; Thomas W. Robinson, "American policy in the strategic triangle," in Richard A. Melanson, ed., *Neither cold war nor detente?* 112–33.
108 Tai-sung An, *The Sino-Soviet territorial dispute*.

In the post-1949 period, however, the border was not a problem until after the Soviet and Chinese Communist Parties had their initial falling-out in the late 1950s. The issue thus not a cause of the Moscow–Peking split. Nevertheless, the border was always a place where differences could be expressed. There were also specific border-related problems that fed the buildup of Sino-Soviet tensions: differences over the exact location and ownership of certain pieces of real estate; questions about the historical process of arriving at the border treaties; differences over treaty implementation; and problems of administering the border area, including river navigation and the special issue of island ownership and riparian rights.[109]

These matters were purposely overlooked or easily managed until the ideological spilt cracked the broader Moscow-Peking military alliance irreparably. Then all such residual problems gradually reemerged and soon became active components of serious Sino-Soviet differences. Starting about 1966, adding the military dimension led to an increasing concentration on the border problems, which begat further Sino-Soviet tensions. Then it was only a matter of time until things took a violent turn and brought out hitherto dormant racial, historical, and irrationally emotional fears.

Border incidents increased in frequency from around 1960. The Russians allege that the number of Chinese "systematic provocations" began to increase in mid-1962. By 1967 border relations had become quite bad. Not only were there reports of a clash on the Ussuri in January 1967, but the Russians accused the Chinese of wildly provocative behavior during the Cultural Revolution. Other incidents occurred on 7–9 and 23 December 1967, and in late January 1968 on the Amur and the Ussuri, apparently continuing until the 2 March 1969 clash. The Russians gradually evolved a procedure for dealing with these incidents without violence, a procedure that was in effect at Chen-pao in March.[110]

As if to verify this Soviet version, Chinese complaints about Soviet border violations began only with an "intrusion" on 23 January 1967 at Chen-pao. The Chinese accused the Russians of "ramming Chinese fishing boats, robbing Chinese fishing nets, turning high-pressure hoses on Chinese fishermen, kidnapping Chinese," assaulting and wounding Chinese frontier guards, seizing arms and ammunition, and violating Chinese airspace. Further, the Chinese charged, the Russians sent tanks, armored cars, and boats into Chinese territory, "drove out many Chinese

109 Ibid., 58–90.   110 Robinson, "The Sino-Soviet border dispute," 1181–83.

inhabitants by force, demolished their houses, and destroyed their means of production and household goods."[111] Taken together, however, these Soviet and Chinese charges indicate little more than run-of-the-mill incidents between two unfriendly powers who disagreed about some specific border demarcations and who found the border a convenient place to express general tensions. Still, each took the other's activities more seriously as time went by, and tit-for-tat reprisals did begin after the January 1967 seizure-of-power phase of the Cultural Revolution. The question is, Why?

The long-term disposition of forces along the border had roughly balanced numbers of men – the Chinese having an edge in the Northeast and the Russians having superiority in the Sinkiang area. There was a Soviet advantage in weapons and logistics. Until 1959, the Chinese did not worry about this nor could they challenge it, while the Russians never made much of it. In the early 1960s, when Sino-Soviet ideological separation came about, force dispositions on both sides remained defensively oriented. Because the border incidents began in 1959 and increased annually until 1969, both powers might have been expected to augment their border forces proportionally. But no large buildup occurred before 1967 on either side, nor were traditional force-dispositions altered. Beginning in late 1965, however, Soviet forces were brought to a higher state of readiness and equipped with better and more weaponry, and their numbers were marginally augmented. The Soviets also signed a new defense agreement with Mongolia giving them the right to station troops and maintain bases in that country.[112]

On the Chinese side, nothing of a similar scale was done. The Chinese were in the midst of the 1965 military strategy debate, the power struggle preceding the Cultural Revolution had led to the purge of the army chief of staff, Lo Jui-ch'ing, and the army had lost capability due to Lin Piao's efforts to use Mao Tse-tung Thought to enhance military prowess. The Vietnam War, moreover, directed Chinese military attention primarily to its southern flank. Thus, the Chinese were not able to counter the Soviet buildup, however small it was.[113]

In 1967, border incidents associated with the Cultural Revolution not

---

111 NCNA, 3 March 1969; *JMJP*, 4 March 1969; NCNA, report on border film, 18 April 1969; "Statement of the government of the People's Republic of China," 24 May 1969, NCNA, 24 May 1969, in FBIS *Daily Report: China*, 26 May 1969, A1–10; and "Down with the new tsars!" *JMJP*, 3 March 1969, in *SCMP*, 4373 11 March 1969, 17–19.
112 Robinson, "The Sino-Soviet border dispute," 1183–85.
113 Harry Gelman, *The Soviet Far East buildup and Soviet risk-taking against China*, 12–15. Apparently, the Chinese knew of the Soviet buildup and complained accordingly to Moscow. See Robinson, "The Sino-Soviet border dispute," 1185–87.

only reached a new high but took on, in Soviet eyes, increasingly ominous overtones. They responded by increasing the size of their border-guard force, making it large enough to elicit a public complaint from Ch'en I.[114] The most important step in the Soviet military buildup was the stationing of strong military units on Mongolian soil. By November 1967, several divisions were occupying permanent bases in Mongolia. The magnitude of this buildup upset the military balance. The Chinese did their best to redeploy forces in response, and several divisions went to the Soviet-Mongolian border from the Fukien region. Peking also began again to stress the importance of the Production and Construction Corps in the borderland provinces.[115] But apparently Chinese leaders considered direct action more appropriate.

On the night of 1–2 March 1969, about three hundred Chinese frontier guards and regular soldiers dressed in white camouflage crossed the Ussuri River ice from the Chinese bank to Chen-pao Island, dug foxholes in a wooded area, laid telephone wire to the command post on the Chinese bank, and lay down for the night on straw mats.[116] Early in the morning, the duty man at the Soviet outpost south of the island reported activity on the Chinese bank. Around 11:00 A.M. twenty or thirty Chinese were seen moving toward the island, shouting Maoist slogans as they went. The Soviet commander, Strelnikov, and his subordinates set off for the island in two armored personnel carriers, a truck, and a command car. Arriving, Strelnikov and several others dismounted and moved out to warn the oncoming Chinese, as they had done several times previously. Following a procedure developed for such occasions, the Russians strapped their automatic rifles to their chests and linked arms to prevent the Chinese from passing. A verbal altercation took place at this point. The Chinese arrayed themselves in rows and appeared to be unarmed. But when the Chinese had advanced to about twenty feet from the Russian group, the first row suddenly scattered to the side, exposing the second line of Chinese, who quickly pulled submachine guns from under their coats and opened fire on the Russians. Strelnikov and six others were killed outright. Simultaneously, from an ambush to the Russians' right, the three hundred Chinese in foxholes also opened fire, catching the entire Russian unit by surprise. Mortar, machine-gun, and antitank fire also commenced from the Chinese bank. The Chinese then charged the Russians and hand-to-hand fighting ensued. The Soviet unit was overrun, and the Chinese (according to the Russians) took away nineteen prisoners

114 JPRS, 36.136, *Translations on international communist developments*, 852 (June 23 1966), esp. 13–14.
115 Chiang I-shan, "Military affairs of communist China, 1968," *Tsu-kuo*, 59 (February 1969), 20–36.
116 Robinson, "The Sino-Soviet border dispute," 1187–89.

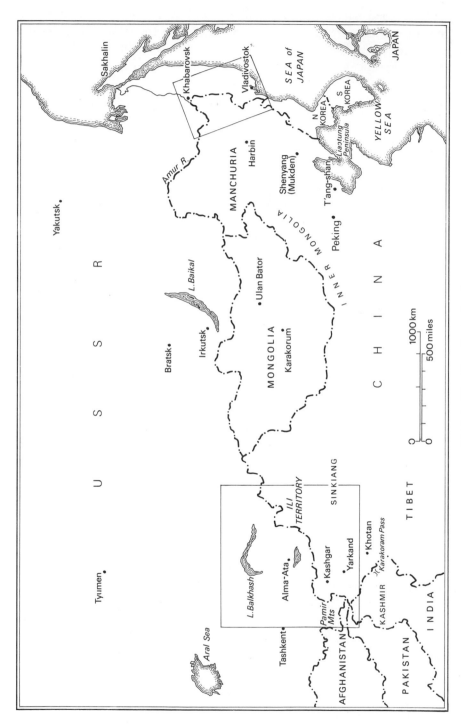

MAP 4. The Sino-Soviet border

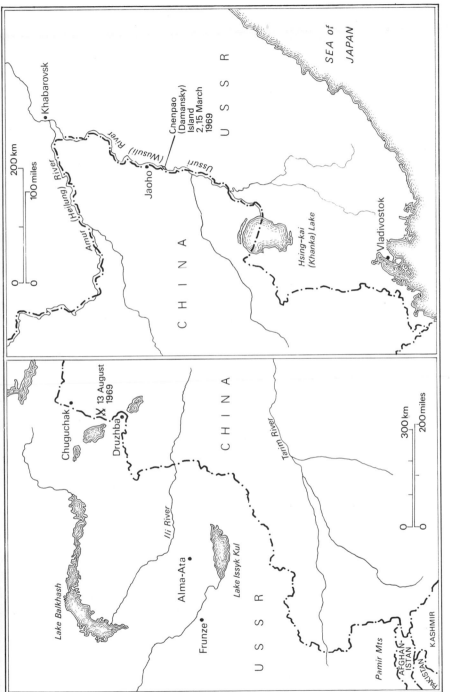

MAP 5. Sino-Soviet clashes, March and August 1969

and killed them on the spot. They also took away Soviet equipment, which they later put on display.

Seeing the battle, the head of the Soviet northern outpost, Bubenin, and his entire command set out for the scene. Racing up in an armored car, he succeeded in gaining the right flank of the Chinese, forcing them to divide their fire. But he also found himself in the middle of the ambush the Chinese had prepared for Strelnikov. Bubenin's vehicle was hit and he was wounded and shellshocked. He managed to get into another armored car and direct the battle from it. A series of melees ensued, with charges by both sides. Finally the Russians pinned down, for a time surrounded, and then forced the retreat of the remaining fifty or sixty Chinese to their own side of the bank.

The battle on 15 March was somewhat different.[117] Preparations on both sides were much more extensive, forces were larger, losses were higher, and the engagement lasted much longer. There was also no element of surprise. In contrast to the encounter on 2 March, it is not clear who began the conflict on 15 March. A small Russian scouting party did spend the night of 14–15 March on the island, and this group was used to lure the Chinese into a frontal attack. The Chinese say that the other side sent "many" tanks to the island and the river-arm about 4:00 A.M., attacking Chinese guards on patrol. It is not clear why such a large force would be needed to attack a patrol. The Russians state that their own early-morning patrol, consisting of two armored cars, discovered a group of Chinese, who had allegedly sneaked over the previous night, lodged on the island. Whatever the cause, the battle began around mid-morning, with mortar and artillery fire from the Chinese bank.

The Chinese now threw more than a regiment (about two thousand men) into the fray, charging across the ice and gaining possession of at least part of the island. When they saw this wave of Chinese, the Russians sought to block their advance with machine-gun fire from armored personnel carriers, but moved back when they saw the Chinese had more men. (Russian accounts speak of ten Chinese for every Russian.) The Chinese directed intense artillery fire not only at the Soviet troops but also at the eastern channel of the river, hoping to stop the movement of heavy vehicles over the ice. The Russians, adopting American Korean War tactics, allowed the Chinese to advance and then counterattacked with large numbers of tanks, armored cars, and infantry in armored personnel carriers. Soviet artillery launched a fierce barrage at 1:00 P.M., raking Chinese positions as far as four miles inland. Three such attacks were mounted, each breaking through Chinese positions. The first two

117 Ibid., 1189–90.

faltered when ammunition was gone, but the third broke up the Chinese, who retreated to their own bank, taking their dead and wounded. The battle was over at 7:00 P.M., having lasted more than nine hours. The Russians lost about sixty men (including the border-post commander); and the Chinese, eight hundred – both figures probably including both dead and wounded.

Explaining the March 1969 border incidents

Because we are dealing with a single event and there is an almost total absence of high-quality primary data, no final explanation is possible as to why the Chinese pulled the trigger on 2 March 1969. Explanatory possibilities fall into three clusters: rationales flowing from the local and regional situation in China, rationales concerning politics in the Chinese capital, and foreign policy–related motivations.[118]

At the local-regional level, three possibilities stand out. First, the local Chinese border commander may have possessed enough latitude to initiate military action if growing border tensions seemed to warrant it. Delegating authority in a large military organization is a reasonable administrative device to police a very long national boundary. And given the uncertainty of the local political situation, especially in early 1969 when the military had taken effective power throughout the country, it is possible that an impatient commander might have taken things into his own hands. But the facts, if we are to believe them, speak of a degree of deliberateness and a level of preparation that reflect control from a higher level.

Second, there is a chance that what happened on 2 March may in reality have been a local firefight between ordinary patrols that happened to meet at Chen-pao. That is what seems to have happened with India the year before. If so, the Soviets would claim it was a Chinese ambush to cover the fact that they lost the battle, and the Chinese would say nothing in hopes that the Russians would not retaliate. Essentially this is a statistical argument and as such cannot be refuted. Some such incident would have happened eventually; it took place on 2 March and at Chen-pao. However, the degree of detail and the level of moral outrage pouring forth from the Russians gives rise to the suspicion that a deliberately staged incident did in fact take place.

Third, differences of opinion, of failures of communication, may have existed between the Heilungkiang Revolutionary Committee, the Shenyang Military Region, the local Chinese commander at the scene, and

118 This follows ibid., 1190–94, and the sources cited therein.

their superiors in Peking. Ch'en Hsi-lien, the Military Region commander, may have wanted to demonstrate his importance to Lin Piao or, conversely, local commanders their value to Ch'en. But military forces usually do not work this way. They are top-down command organizations, and if such attempts to draw attention to the efficient carrying out of one's duties really did occur, we would expect, given the horrendous consequences to China of the incident, the individuals in question to have been summarily removed. Nothing of the sort took place, so far as we know.

The more likely locus of explanation is at the national political level. The most important possibility is that factional strife in Peking was so fierce that some groups, realizing they were literally fighting for their lives, took extreme measures. In early 1969, many factions were competing for power in China: the ideologues of the Cultural Revolution Group, the bureaucrats under Chou En-lai, the military led by Lin Piao, the remaining mass revolutionary organs, and – presiding over the continuing chaos and thereby maximizing his own power – Mao Tse-tung. However, only Lin Piao and Mao Tse-tung had the possible motives, the power, and the command structure to order the ambush of a Soviet unit. Chiang Ch'ing and her followers lacked the command structure, and Chou En-lai would not have been so foolish as to think that China could get away with such a blatant act without retribution.

Lin Piao certainly had plenty of reasons to enhance his own authority. He was Mao's anointed successor but had hardly generated the kind of support that would have seen him through the dangers of the immediate succession period. Throughout the Cultural Revolution, moreover, he not only had made enemies but also had not convinced anyone (other than Mao) that he was fit for the job. Further, there was clearly tension between Lin and Chou over which institution, army or government, should govern the country in the new stage of the Cultural Revolution that began on 1 September 1968. Lin may have felt that a foreign threat would provide additional argumentation for continued military administration and thus enhance his own chances of long-term survival. There is sufficient Pekinological evidence to give credence to this possibility, especially given the subsequent struggle for power leading to Lin's demise in late 1971.[119]

---

119 The literature on Lin's demise, although large, is as yet unconvincing. It is also contradictory and must be used only with great care. See, for instance, Yao Ming-le, *The conspiracy and death of Lin Biao*. This book is almost certainly bogus. More reliable is Michael Y. M. Kau, ed., *The Lin Piao affair: power politics and military coup*. See also, Robinson, *A political-military biography of Lin Piao, Part 2, 1950–1971*.

A second national-level explanation is that the leadership as a whole (i.e., Mao, Lin, Chou, and Chiang Ch'ing) decided that a foreign incident was necessary to divert popular attention from domestic tensions. The ensuing war scare and its concomitant outpouring of nationalism would enable the leadership to carry through an ideologically based permanent restructuring of Chinese society previously planned but sabotaged by the bureaucrats. It is clear that by late 1968 or early 1969, an impasse had come about between those who wished to reverse course and put society back together and those who wanted to press forward with what were later called the Cultural Revolution's "Socialist newborn things" – institutions and processes that presumably would guarantee China would never again run the risk of "capitalist restoration." If Mao and Lin were, with Chiang Ch'ing, in favor of the latter course, as we must presume (Chou would then have had to go along), they may have considered that the best way to break the impasse would be a sudden and spectacular move. Drawing Soviet blood would provide the necessary popular enthusiasm and also overcome bureaucratic foot-dragging. Of course, it would have to be assumed that the Soviet Union was indeed a paper tiger, in other words, that Moscow's reaction would be manageable or that if the Russians did react frontally, their deeds could be used as the most recent example of the frightful nature of social imperialism – what happens when countries go the full distance of capitalist restoration.

The final set of rationales addresses Peking's foreign policy motives. First, and most important, China was already taken aback at the Soviet invasion of Czechoslovakia in August 1968, with the Kremlin's promulgation of the Brezhnev doctrine, with the strengthening of the Red Army east of Lake Baikal, and with aggressive Soviet border patrol tactics. Mao and his associates may have decided that they had no choice but to move before it was too late, to confront the Russians head-on and thus to warn them off from further military adventures. The risk of Soviet military retaliation would have to be taken, since Russian tanks would soon be massing on China's borders anyway.

Second, and consistent with the first, is the idea that whenever the Chinese Communists perceived a superior force about to attack, the proper strategy (learned through bitter experience during the Shanghai-Kiangsi-Yenan days) was to preempt the situation at a place and time of one's own choosing, thus throwing the enemy off balance and perhaps even preventing his coming ahead at all. Hence Chen-pao.[120]

---

120 William W. Whitson, *The Chinese high command: a history of communist military politics, 1927–71*, ch. 11, "Strategy and tactics."

Third, Mao may have feared that despite all his success in teaching the Chinese people the evils of revisionist-based social imperialism, additional measures were needed, since the revisionist bacterium was still alive and circulating in the Chinese body politic. A vaccine was needed against its spread. Thus inoculated, the Chinese people would never again be tempted by the "bourgeois revisionist line." The Chen-pao incident was staged to sow dragon's teeth between China and the Soviet Union.

The most likely explanation is a combination of the three foreign policy rationales, which are mutually supportive, and the two national political motivations. These are also mutually consistent and buttress the former. There is, further, additional evidence from both spheres. Domestically, there is no indication that the Soviet threat engendered any debate over how to respond. On all prior occasions (the last of which was the "strategic debate" of 1965, already reported), such a debate did take place, showing the existence of factional differences on that issue and other more general problems. The absence of a debate after Prague indicates a reasonably united political leadership, meaning either that factional differences had not developed sufficiently or that (more likely) all realized the magnitude of the foreign threat and the likelihood that if the Russians were to attack, the Cultural Revolution, and perhaps rule of China by the CCP, would be over.

Internationally, the evidence is clear that Peking considered the Soviet threat strong enough to begin to seek assistance from foreign powers. There was only one place, however implausible it might have seemed to some in the leadership, to go: the United States. Beginning in the late fall of 1968, therefore, Peking gingerly and tentatively began to respond to the signals that the Johnson administration had been sending out periodically since 1965. Specifically, polemics against Washington ceased and Peking proposed resumption of the Warsaw talks.[121] The fact that Sino-American conversations did not proceed far before March 1969 does not obviate the point that China had already concluded that insurance against the Russians should be sought by bringing to bear the interests and policy means of the other nuclear superpower.

This phase of Chinese foreign policy thus ended in a manner similar to how it had begun. Chinese domestic politics and foreign policy were once again closely intertwined, and China was deeply enmeshed with, and heavily dependent on the relative power of, the United States and the Soviet Union. It took a few more years, to be sure, for that to become fully evident. In the meantime, China had to pay heavily for its trans-

121   Thomas M. Gottlieb, *Chinese foreign policy factionalism and the origins of the strategic triangle.*

gression against the Soviet Union and its own interest. It lost once again the foreign policy freedom, however dubious it had been, that it had temporarily gained during the Cultural Revolution. And the revolutionary forward movement of the Cultural Revolution, which was Mao's principal goal in the first place, was dissipated in useless anti-Soviet demonstrations and civil defense tunnel digging.

Defusing the border crisis, 1969

Beginning with the second Chen-pao incident, the Soviet Union put into practice a new strategy of coercive diplomacy toward the Chinese. This combined diplomatic and military pressure to make China see the desirability not only of negotiating the border problem itself but also of using the border settlement as the basis for all-around improvement in relations. Coercion at the border thus had two purposes: to solve important problems in Soviet-Chinese relations and to "talk" to Peking about resolving other ideological and national differences. The Kremlin determined that "success" on the border issue (border talks leading to a negotiated settlement) was worth pursuing in its own right, even if the cost in the short term was lack of progress on other issues.

The Soviets took a risk in employing coercive diplomacy. Diplomatic moves were of necessity accompanied by punishing military actions and by threat of more severe losses. They also felt it necessary to strengthen their forces along the entire length of the Soviet-Mongolian-Chinese border, to support the new politico-military campaign, and to deter and defend against repetition of the first Chen-pao incident. The Kremlin sought to control the local situation by absolute superiority in conventional forces and the strategic situation by absolute superiority in combined forces, including nuclear arms. This meant a huge buildup against China, which would dislocate the Soviet economy and push Peking toward the West. To preserve Soviet security in the narrow sense, then, Moscow took a chance that it could handle any long-term Chinese response and any short-term anti-Soviet realignment of political forces. In retrospect, that was not a worthwhile gamble: Border security was ensured but at the cost of (1) China's fear and hostility, (2) its resolve to modernize its economy and military to counter the Soviets directly, (3) lack of the border treaty that was the secondary object, and (4) threat of an anti-Soviet entente composed of all the other powerful states in the world headed by the United States and China.

Without a much better factual basis, no firm conclusions can be drawn regarding the seriousness of these military occurrences and their connection as means of pressure on, or indicators of, the state of the border talks and of Soviet-Chinese relations in general. Nonetheless, it is clear that from the March 1969 incidents to the Chou–Kosygin meeting in Peking on 11 September, the Soviet Union used border clashes as a means of applying pressure on China to reopen the border talks, recessed since late 1964. After the September meeting and the reconvening of the talks on 20 October, public reportage of additional incidents serves as a rough indicator of the stage of the negotiations, while their frequency, location, and intensity provide some indication of the degree of progress of the negotiations. Even when their occurrence was not publicly admitted, military clashes served to test the defenses of the other side and reinforce the negotiators' positions.

After March 1969, border incidents may be divided into those occurring before the Chou–Kosygin meeting and those thereafter. A Soviet-initiated campaign began shortly after the Chen-pao incidents in March 1969 and, supported by well-orchestrated hints of nuclear attack and other untoward consequences, rose to a crescendo by late August. Publicly admitted clashes took place on 10–11 June, 8 and 20 July, and 13 August,[122] and the two governments charged each other with having perpetrated dozens of other incidents from April through July.[123]

Publicized affairs took place in widely scattered locations along the border: some along the Ussuri River, scene of the March events; others on islands in the Amur River; still others along the Sino-Mongolian border, while more occurred in the Sinkiang-Kazakhstan region not far from the Lop Nor Chinese nuclear test site and the historic Dzungarian Gate invasion route between the two countries. Given the preoccupation of the Chinese military with internal Cultural Revolution political and administrative matters, given Soviet strategic superiority, and given the concomitant Soviet campaign of hints and innuendos of more drastic measures if China did not reconvene the border talks, it is difficult to imagine that the Chinese took the military initiative. In some instances, the Chinese forces on the spot may have taken the offensive to forestall a perceived attack,[124] but this was not Chinese strategy in general, given their relative weakness. Rather, the period before 11 September 1969

122 *10–11, June*: NCNA, 11 June 1969; *NYT*, 12 June 1969; *Pravda*, 12 June 1969; *8 July*: *NCNA*, 6 July; *NYT*, 8 July; *Pravda*, 8 July; Radio Moscow, 10 July; FBIS *Daily Report: USSR*, 14 July, A30–A32; *20 July*; *Pravda*, 11 September, *13 August*: *Pravda*, 13 August; *NYT*, 14, 15, 16 August; *Christian Science Monitor* (hereafter *CSM*), 14 August 1969; FBIS *Daily Report: USSR*, 15 August, A1–A4; *Izvestia* and other Soviet sources, 16 August; FBIS *Daily Report: USSR*, 28 February 1974, C2–3.

123 *SCMP*, 4435; 24 (12 June 1969), NCNA, 19 August 1969; *NYT*, 9 September 1969.

124 Preemptive attack as a local tactic – but not usually as a general strategy – has been used by the Chinese Communist military throughout its history. See Whitson, *The Chinese high command.*

must be seen as a textbook case of the combined use by Moscow of political, military, and propaganda means to force its opponent to take an action – renew the talks – it otherwise resisted, and to teach the Chinese the desired lesson not to attempt more surprises like Chen-pao.

These Soviet military actions were thus accompanied by a series of diplomatic notes setting forth the Soviet position on the border problem and suggesting that all differences would be settled by agreeing on a new border treaty. Moscow parried each Chinese counterargument with historical or ideological points of its own, all the while coordinating diplomatic notes with military action. The Soviets had in their major policy statement of 29 March offered to reopen the talks,[125] a proposal repeated on 11 April.[126] Earlier, on 21 March, Premier Alexei Kosygin had attempted to telephone the Chinese but had been rebuffed by Lin Piao, who refused to speak with him via that medium.[127] They evidently feared that the Soviets would threaten further military action if negotiations were not reopened and thus chose to sever direct verbal communications. The Soviets continued further border incidents as a means of bringing the Chinese to the negotiating table, and now sought to test the Chinese response. The Chinese Ninth Party Congress was held 1–24 April, at which time Lin Piao, Mao's then successor-designate, stated that the Chinese side was still "considering its reply" to the Soviet proposal; that is, China was stalling.[128]

The Russians resolved to probe the Chinese readiness to reestablish full-scale border talks by using the forum of the border river navigation talks, which had been conducted annually since 1951, as a testing ground. Thus, on 26 April Moscow proposed that these lower-level discussions resume in May in Khabarovsk.[129] The Chinese delayed until 11 May, replied in the affirmative, but proposed mid-June as the meeting time,[130] which the Russians accepted on 23 May.[131] The talks opened on schedule but the Chinese and the Soviets could not agree on the agenda, for on 12 July the Soviets stated that the Chinese had "flatly refused" to continue,

---

125 TASS, *Pravda*, and *Izvestia*, 30 March 1969 (translation in *Current Digest of the Soviet Press* [*CDSP*], 16 April 1969, 3–5, and FBIS *Daily Report: USSR*, 1 April 1969, A1–7).

126 FBIS *Daily Report: USSR*, 14 April 1969, A1.

127 Lin Piao, "Report to the Ninth National Congress of the Communist Party of China," *PR*, 18 (30 April 1969), 33.

128 Ibid., 33.

129 *Pravda*, 3 May 1969, and *Izvestia*, 5 May 1969 (translation in *CDSP*, 21 May 1969, 22).

130 FBIS *Daily Report: China*, 12 May 1969, A1–2, and *SCMP*, 4417 (16 May 1969), 21–22. The Chinese note attempted to blame the Soviets for the lack of a meeting the previous year and therefore treated their agreement to attend the new session as a magnanimous concession.

131 FBIS *Daily Report: USSR*, 23 May 1969, A4. The Chinese replied on 6 June. See FBIS *Daily Report: China*, 9 June, A3–4, and *SCMP*, 4436 (13 June 1969), 22–23.

apparently because they attempted to bring up the unequal treaties question. As in the abortive discussions in 1968, Peking hoped this would cause the Soviets to walk out of the meeting altogether, but this time the Russians stayed and apparently threatened the Chinese with further military action (there had just been, on 8 July, an incident on the Amur and the Soviet Pacific Fleet concurrently was holding "training exercises" on the river), for within several hours of their first declaration the Chinese "decided to remain in Khabarovsk and agreed to the continuation of the commission's work."[132] Negotiations then proceeded more to the point of the meeting's original intent of river navigation maintenance work and new navigation rules, for on 8 August a new annual agreement was announced (separately; the Russians underscored its significance for further talks on the border question as a whole, whereas the Chinese downplayed the occasion).[133]

This test case convinced Moscow that Peking could be brought to the negotiating table and made to sign an agreement if the proper kinds and amounts of pressure were brought to bear. The principal means continued to be the use and threat of force. In addition, the Soviets persevered in the long-term task of isolating the Chinese, diplomatically and ideologically. There were built-in contradictions in Moscow's policy toward Washington of continuing détente while at the same time competing for influence in the Third World and increasing its strategic force levels to rival those of the United States. Moreover, the weakness in the Soviet position would soon be revealed by the Sino-American détente itself.

Moscow did possess an important instrument in the communist world, however, in its ability to marshal support for its declared positions. For some time, it had been attempting to convene a conference of all supportive parties, ruling and nonruling, to consider issues of current ideological and diplomatic importance and to issue a collective statement that, like similar documents issued in years past, could serve as a standard position agreed upon by all. China, of course, refused to participate in any such efforts and did not attend the International Meeting of Communist and Workers' Parties, which met in Moscow 5–17 June 1969.[134] Before the conference, the Soviets had given assurances to the Rumanians and others that they would not turn the meeting into a forum for attacking China nor attempt to read Peking out of the movement as a whole.

132   FBIS *Daily Report: USSR*, 14 July 1969, A1–2, and *NYT*, 14 July 1969.
133   *NYT*, 9 August (for the Soviet announcement) and 12 August 1969 (for the Chinese statement).
134   The speeches and documents of the conference are translated in *CDSP*, 2, 9, 16, 23, and 30 July 1969, and FBIS *Daily Report: USSR*, 18 June 1969. Brezhnev's major speech is in *CDSP*, 2 July 1969, 3–17, and is summarized in *NYT*, 8 June 1969.

Nonetheless, the major Soviet address, delivered by the CPSU general secretary, Leonid Brezhnev, was as hostile to the Chinese leadership as could be imagined. On the boundary question, he accused the Chinese of purposely fomenting border clashes and of regarding war as a "positive historical phenomenon." Still, he renewed the Soviet offer to negotiate a settlement. Inveighing against China's "groundless claims of a territorial nature," Brezhnev said that "the future will show whether or not the Chinese leaders are actually seeking talks and want an agreement."[135] The Basic Document adopted by the conference did not mention the border situation, or China, at all, in keeping with the Soviet promise not to take up the matter.[136] Nonetheless, Brezhnev's post-Congress report in *Kommunist* brought the matter back in by asserting that Mao's policy had "received an impressive condemnation at the conference."[137]

The Chinese, after having put off as long as possible a reply to the Soviet proposal to reconvene the talks, issued on 24 May a long statement on the border issue.[138] The statement set forth five conditions under which China would negotiate a new treaty and delimit the boundary. These conditions indicate the overall Chinese negotiating stance at the talks, once they had later convened, and as such merit summary:

The Soviets must admit to the unequal nature of the existing treaties; once having done so, the Chinese would be willing to use them "as the basis for determining the entire alignment of the boundary line between the countries and for settling all existing questions relating to the boundary."

The Russians must return "in principle" to China all territory allegedly taken in violation of the unequal treaties. Once this was done, "necessary adjustments at individual places could be made in accordance with the principles of consultation on an equal footing and of mutual understanding and mutual accommodation."

The Soviets must cease all "provocation and armed threats," from exchange of border gunfire to nuclear attack.

Neither side should advance beyond the line of control, and in the case of riverine islands, the thalweg (i.e., the deepest part of the channel) should determine the line of control.

Where "habitual practice" has established "normal productive activities" of one side's citizens on the territory of the other (as in the case of some riverine islands such as Chen-pao or of sheepherders in the Pamirs), these practices should be maintained until a definitive boundary line is set out.

135 *CDSP*, 2 July 1969, 12.
136 *Pravda* and *Izvestia*, 18 June 1969, 1–4 (translation in *CDSP*, 6 August 1969, 14–24, and FBIS *Daily Report: USSR*, 18, June 1969, A21–47.
137 *Kommunist*, 11 (July 1969), 3–16 (translation in *CDSP*, 3 September 1969, 3–8), quotation from p. 4.
138 "Statement of the Government of the People's Republic of China," 24 May 1969, in FBIS *Daily Report: China*, 26 May 1969, A1–10, and *SCMP*, 4426 (29 May 1969), 24–36.

If the Soviets would agree to these conditions, the statement concluded, the Chinese would open negotiations with a view to arrive at an
equitable agreement. The first two conditions were the very reasons why
the 1964 negotiations had broken down. If Moscow had agreed to the
first, the way would have been opened to possible return of vast stretches
of territory acquired from the seventeenth to nineteenth centuries, or
more likely, the Kremlin would have given away an important point at
the outset without any compensating gain. Perhaps of equal importance
(since there was no likelihood of the Russians returning such amounts of
land) was the second condition. Since the boundary was never delimited
to the satisfaction of both parties, and since Russia before 1917 had
indeed taken possession of marginal numbers of square miles that China
declared to be its own land, Soviet assent to this condition not only would
place all power of decision on the matter in the hands of Peking but also
would return to the Chinese such vital areas as Hei-hsia-tzu Island, which
stands at the confluence of the Amur and Ussuri rivers and protects
Khabarovsk from encroachment. Given that the Soviet Union had long
since rejected Chinese proposals along these lines, the Chinese statement
offering negotiations upon acceptance of the five conditions was not
serious. Moreover, the last three conditions, which sprang from China's
desire to protect its territory from impending Soviet attack, would have
left the Russians with no means of protecting their own territory from
Chinese forays as at Chen-pao; would have caused Moscow to admit
Chinese ownership of all Soviet-held riverine islands on the Chinese side
of the thalweg; and would have left the Chinese still able to move about
on Soviet soil as they had, apparently, for many years, thereby (in the
new, tense circumstances) maximizing the probability of further military
or propaganda incidents.

Nonetheless, the Chinese had opened the door, if only a bit, to resuming negotiations, and the Soviets chose to emphasize this rather than
totally reject the Chinese offer. Thus, in their note to China of 13 June
1969[139] the Soviet government, after rejecting the five Chinese conditions
for resuming negotiations, took a narrow interpretation of the border
differences and proposed that the two sides meet within two or three
months to work out definitive agreements. The restrictive limit of the
Soviet stance is clearly seen in the operative section of the note:

The Soviet side is in favor of the following: stating the uniform opinion of the
two sides on those sections of the border on which there is no disagreement,

139 *Pravda*, 14 June 1969 (translation in *CDSP*, 9 July 1969, 9–13). This followed a Chinese protest
note of June 6 (FBIS *Daily Report: China*, 9 June 1969, A9–13), and was in response to that note
as well as the 2 May statement.

reaching an understanding on the location of the border line by means of mutual consultations on the basis of treaty documents; with respect to sections that have undergone natural changes, determining the border line on the basis of the treaties now in force, observing the principle of mutual concessions and the economic interest of the local population in these sections; and registering the agreement by the signing of appropriate documents by the two sides.

The Soviets thus adopted a *pacta sunt servanda* position regarding the treaties and focused on marginal changes and delimiting more accurately existing frontiers regarding the locations of the borderline. The Chinese adopted a *rebus sic standibus* position regarding the treaties, attached conditions to the very opening of negotiations, but also focused on marginal border changes – to be sure those in their favor – regarding the whereabouts of the actual boundary.[140]

Given these differences (which flowed basically from the differing ideological positions of the two Communist parties and more immediately from the military balance in favor of the Russians), it is not surprising that negotiations did not resume forthwith. Given Chinese delaying tactics and reluctance to meet the Soviets face-to-face, Moscow had to decide whether it would allow the issue to stand unresolved or whether it should force the matter to a head. Because border incidents continued throughout the late spring and early summer of 1969 (thus demonstrating the danger of a laissez-faire policy), and because the river-navigation talks had shown the Chinese could be pushed into negotiations, Moscow elected to use a combination of force buildup, calculated escalation of border incidents, threats of more serious applications of violence, and offers of negotiations without prior conditions to bring Peking around. This process occupied the summer of 1969, but by early September the Chinese still had not knuckled under. At this point, Ho Chih Minh conveniently died, leaving behind a legacy that included an express request that the Russians and the Chinese settle their differences. His funeral in Hanoi provided neutral meeting grounds. Moscow hastily advanced such a proposal, but Peking, not wishing to meet the adversary after a summer of military reversals and nuclear threats and still weak domestically, implicitly rejected it by withdrawing the Chinese funeral delegation, led by Chou En-lai, from Hanoi before the Soviet group could confront it.[141]

However, the Russians evidently sent Peking an unequivocal message, for on his way home from Hanoi (his plane had already landed in Soviet

140 *Pacta sunt servanda* is the "international law doctrine that treaties are binding" and are to be carried out in good faith by the contracting parties. The opposite doctrine in international law is that treaties shall be binding only so long as "things stand as they are" (*rebus sic standibus*), e.g., only so long as no vital change of circumstance has occurred.
141 *NYT*, 12 and 13 September 1969.

Tadzhikistan) Alexei Kosygin, the head of the Soviet delegation, received a message from Moscow to proceed to Peking instead of Moscow and meet with Chou there. The historic meeting between the two statesmen occurred on 11 September.[142] The Chinese, having done their best to avoid the Russians, made their displeasure clear: The meeting lasted no more than three and a half hours and was held, over Soviet objections, at the Peking airport, that is, not in the city, a calculated insult of the sort inflicted on foreigners for centuries past. Nonetheless, the content of the agreement reached gave Moscow what it was seeking: resumption of the negotiations and cessation of border incidents. Although neither side officially revealed details of the airport agreement, semi-authoritative leaks[143] have pointed to the following, proposed by Kosygin:

1. Maintenance of the *status quo* along the frontier
2. Avoidance of new military confrontations
3. Creation of demilitarized zones at select points in the frontier area
4. Reconvention of border negotiations looking to adjustments in the boundary line, taking as the negotiating basis the existing treaties and the actual situation at the spot
5. Restoration of movement of frontier inhabitants, particularly Soviet workers in regions near the Amur River where China claims territorial rights

This was obviously a victory for the Soviet side's narrow interpretation of the issues to be discussed and of the basis for negotiations, but the first three points were of advantage to China, too, because the Soviet military threat was partially neutralized. The questions of which demili-

---

142 Ibid. Apparently the Rumanian Communist leader, Nicolae Ceausescu, acted as go-between. He sent his premier, Ion Georghe Maurer, to the Ho funeral and then on to Peking, where he met with Chou a few hours before Kosygin arrived.

143 *Le Monde*, 10–11 November 1974. Later, Chou En-lai revealed his understanding of the sense of the meeting (there was no signed agreement). Both parties, in his view, had agreed (1) to maintain the status quo along the frontier until negotiations had produced a permanent settlement; (2) both sides would strive to avoid further armed clashes *and* both parties would withdraw military forces from the immediate border region; (3) both parties would negotiate a "new realignment of the boundary," which, Chou thought, "would not be a difficult matter to settle." See *NYT*, 24 November 1973 (Chou's interview with C. L. Sulzberger), and Kyodo, 28 January 1973 (Chou's interview with Japanese Diet members). Chou's interpretation differed from Kosygin's in connection with the process of carrying out the agreement. First, Chou considered that negotiations would begin – or continue, or come to fruition – only after the other aspects had been taken care of. Second, the term "status quo" was interpreted differently. To Kosygin, it meant no further border incursions from either side. To Chou, it meant as well no major change in the military balance in the border regions. Third, the two differed on the question of demilitarization. Kosygin evidently thought this meant *unilateral* troop withdrawal in *certain* sectors that had produced incidents in the past or that had that potentiality. Chou – whether or not he knew of Kosygin's interpretation – presumed it meant *Soviet* troop withdrawal only in those sectors that were *in dispute*, i.e., Soviet territory that China claimed. These differences formed much of the basis for the disagreements that followed.

tarized zones to create and of their exact dimensions would be bones of contention between the two sides and issues that the Chinese would use to prevent or delay discussion on substantive boundary matters. Nonetheless, the Chinese had agreed to reactivate the talks as a means of shunting aside the Soviet military threat, and this was what the Russians desired.

Some short-term salutary effects were noticeable immediately after 11 September. The Soviets ceased polemics against the Chinese;[144] border incidents stopped;[145] trade talks resumed;[146] and steps were taken to send back the two countries' ambassadors, who had been withdrawn earlier during the Cultural Revolution. Still, the Chinese continued to drag their feet. No date had been set for the actual resumption of talks, and it is not even clear that the Chinese agreed in Peking to the Kosygin proposals. Moreover, even if there was an agreement, it was subject to varying interpretations. There were indications, aside from the fact that only a short, noninformative communiqué[147] was issued on 11 September, that no agreement had been reached – even that no agreement to try to reach an agreement had been concluded.

One sign was the publication in the London *Evening News* of 17 September of an article by the Soviet intelligence agent and journalist Victor Louis conveying further veiled Soviet threats of military action against China. Extension of the Brezhnev doctrine asserting Soviet "right" to interfere unilaterally in the affairs of other socialist countries was specifically mentioned, as was the possible use of nuclear weapons against the Lop Nor nuclear center. The second was an interview in Tokyo with the then Soviet trade union head, Alexander Shelepin.[148] Shelepin stated that "the Chinese seemed to be positive toward solving the border question" and that "we expect negotiations ... to be held," which is to say the Chinese had not yet accepted the Soviet proposal nor even, on 30 September, formally replied to Moscow. Even after the

144 *NYT*, 17 September 1969.
145 Ibid., 19 September 1969.
146 Ibid., 25 September 1969, reporting an interview with Gus Hall, the American Communist leader, who met Brezhnev on his way home from Hanoi. Brezhnev told him Kosygin had made three sets of proposals to Chou: one dealing with the border, the second concerning restriction of diplomatic representation at the ambassadorial level, the last proposing higher levels of trade. Trade talks were reported in progress in early October. See FBIS *Daily Report: USSR*, 3 October 1969, A4, reporting a Yugoslav source in Moscow. They may already have begun in August, however. See FBIS *Daily Report: China*, 7 October 1969, A2.
147 The Chinese version of these communiqués said that Kosygin was "passing through Peking on his way home from Hanoi." This was hardly true and indicates that China accepted Kosygin under duress. See *SCMP*, 4498 (18 September 1969), 25, and *Far Eastern Economic Review* (hereafter *FEER*), 25 September 1969, 759.
148 Reuters, 30 September 1969, and *NYT*, 1 October 1969.

Chinese National Day, 1 October, Peking had not replied, according to diplomatic reports in Moscow.[149]

The burden was now on the Chinese to come up with necessary face-saving compromises to make negotiations possible. They sent official letters to the Russians on 18 September and 6 October (evidently there was a Soviet reply in the interim, but the contents of this exchange have not been revealed),[150] and finally on 7 and 8 October issued major public statements. In the 7 October statement, China revealed that the two governments had agreed to restore the 1964 talks, which would reconvene at the vice-ministerial level (e.g., at a higher level than originally proposed by Moscow) and that sessions would be held in Peking. The statement also indicated clearly that the only territorial points of difference were those that stemmed from alleged Russian or Soviet occupation of areas in violation of the "unequal" treaties, as detailed on the (as yet unpublicized) Chinese map exchanged during the 1964 negotiations. The statement of 8 October[151] was a refutation of the Soviet note of 13 June. At its conclusion, however, the Chinese advanced five principles for settling the border question, which constituted Peking's negotiating position at the upcoming talks. The first three were essentially equivalent to those just outlined as part of the Chinese statement of 24 May. The last two repeated much of the Kosygin proposal in September and showed for the first time that the Chinese were willing to talk about the matter if an equitable basis could be found. But they also revealed two important differences.

First, the Chinese wanted a new treaty defining the overall boundary line to replace all the old "unequal" treaties. This was no different from the Chinese position in 1964, and did differ substantially from the Soviet proposal to redefine the existing boundary more exactly but neither to replace the old treaties at all nor to agree to their "unequal" nature before signing a new document. Second, China reiterated its demand that, for an overall settlement, both sides withdraw from all disputed areas, for instance, those areas the Chinese claimed the Russians had occupied in contravention to the "unequal" treaties. The Soviets obviously could not comply with this condition without jeopardizing the security of Khabarovsk and possibly other vital areas.

Nonetheless, the Soviets took the Chinese statement positively, and negotiation did begin, on 20 October 1969. Thus, six months after the

149 NYT, 4 October 1969.
150 "Statement of the government of the People's Republic of China," 7 October 1969, in PR, 41 (10 October 1969), 3–4, and NYT, 8 October 1969.
151 "Document of the Ministry of Foreign Affairs of the People's Republic of China," 9 October 1969, in PR, 41 (10 October 1969), 8–15, and SCMP, 4517 (10 October 1969), 30–39.

Chen-pao incidents, the two states had agreed – mostly because of Soviet pressure – to attempt once again to solve the problem peaceably. For China, resumption of the talks was a lightning rod to conduct away at least part of the Soviet military potential, and it seems reasonably clear, in retrospect, that in 1969 Peking had no intention of arriving at any compromise agreement, that is, one that would depart measurably from its previously enunciated "principles." The Soviet negotiating team, which arrived in Peking 19 October, was led by Vice–Foreign Minister Vasily V. Kuznetsov, and included seven others. The Chinese side was headed by Vice–Foreign Minister Ch'iao Kuan-hua, and also comprised seven others.[152]

SINO-SOVIET NEGOTIATIONS, 1969–1975

After the talks began, publicly reported incidents declined to a frequency of one to three per year and with a much reduced level of severity.[153] In general, the impression after September 1969 is of a border closely guarded by both sides but with each taking extreme precautions not to allow local clashes to occur accidentally and to forestall escalation to the use of more destructive weapons systems or to the employment of large numbers of men. In most cases, the forces engaged were KGB-controlled border troops on the Soviet side and probably Production and Construction Corps formations on the Chinese side.[154] Given the vast increase in

152 *NYT*, 8, 19, and 21 October 1969; *Pravda* and *Izvestia*, 19 October (in *CDSP*, 12 November 1969, 15); *SCMP*, 4523 and 4524 (24 and 27 October 1969), 30 and 27, respectively; *JMJP*, 21 October 1969; and *PR*, 43 (25 October 1969), 4–5.

153 See *NYT*, 19 September 1969; 19 November 1970; 11 December 1972; *Ming pao*, 19 January 1970; *New Times*, 36 (1973), 19 (accusing the Chinese of 151 "military exercises" at the Mongolian border, deliberate penetration into Mongolia of fifteen to twenty kilometers' depth, shooting at herds, verbal abuse of bodyguards, and spreading propaganda leaflets); *Komsomolskaya Pravda*, 12 January 1972 (in FBIS *Daily Report: USSR, D7*); *Los Angeles Times*, 11 December 1972; FBIS *Daily Report: USSR*, 12 December 1972; *CSM*, 19 September 1972; *Turkmenskaya Iskra*, 5 February 1974 (in FBIS *Daily Report: USSR*, 15 February 1974, R6–8), *Soviet Analyst*, 28 November 1974, 2 (reporting a former Soviet citizen's account of a major battle on the Chinese-Mongolian border that produced high casualties but was not publicly achnowledged to have occurred); *Daily Telegraph*, 17 December 1974 (in FBIS *Daily Report: USSR*, 17 December 1974, W1–2); David Floyd's report of five clashes in November at the Mongolian border, denied by both Chinese and Soviet authorities as reported in FBIS *Daily Report: China*, 19 December 1974, E2; FBIS *Daily Report: USSR*, 19 December 1974, C1; and Yumjagin Tsedenbal (the Mongolian Party leader), "K Sotsialisticheskomu Obshchestvennomu Stroiu Minuya Kapitalizm" (Toward a socialist social order, by-passing capitalism), *Problemy Dal'nego Vostoka* (Problems of the Far East), 4 (1974), 6–29, in which he alleged that "groups of Chinese soldiers violate the border, fell forests, start forest fires, and herd into Mongolia tainted cattle infected with highly contagious diseases," *FEER*, 28 January 1974, 18–19, reported details of alleged Chinese violations of the Sino-Mongolian border on 2 June 1970, 26 May 1971, and 20 April 1973.

154 After the March 1969 incidents, new Production and Construction Corps divisions were formed, especially in Inner Mongolia and the Northeast, composed of former Red Guard youths sent out from the cities.

troop dispositions by both sides along the frontier after March 1969, this drastic decline in publicly reported incidents indicates that both sides agreed, tacitly or explicitly, to carry out the relevant clause of the Chinese proposal of 8 October 1969, to maintain the status quo along the frontier until the exact location of the boundary was agreed on, to avert armed conflicts, and to desist from sending forces into disputed areas.[155]

Before pursuing the successive phases of negotiation, let us note briefly the general trend of events that accompanied it. Quiet along the frontier resulted from the Peking agreement, the military buildup on both sides, and the border negotiations. Neither side appeared to wish to engage the other frequently, although occasional deliberate forays were made to test the opposition. Each side charged the other with this sort of activity – the Soviets accusing the Chinese of conducting training operations only meters from the Mongolian boundary, and the Chinese charging that the Russians often flew aircraft several kilometers into Chinese territory – but neither reacted violently. Both sides agreed to suppress news of further incidents. In 1974, for instance, there were rumors and allegations of a large-scale clash on the Sinkiang–Kazakhstan border, and in November of that year both Moscow and Peking denied a Western report of five battles along the Sino-Mongolian frontier.[156]

There were a few other specific occurrences related to border tensions: the seizure and expulsion of two Soviet diplomats in Peking in 1974 on spy charges,[157] the detention of a Soviet helicopter and its crew in China after the Russians alleged it had lost its bearings and run out of fuel while on a medical evacuation mission,[158] Soviet prohibition of Chinese ships'

---

155 This "proposal" merely reiterated the Chinese position stated in several notes of the previous five months and in fact was little different from the Soviet proposal. The Chinese later attempted to use an additional condition – prior withdrawal of both sides' troops to a set distance from the boundary – as a precondition to further agreement on the issue.

156 *Daily Telegraph*, 17 December 1974; *Pravda*, 20 December 1974; Reuters and Agence France Presse, 17 December 1974 (in FBIS *Daily Report: China*, 18 December 1974, E2); TASS, 19 December 1974 (in FBIS *Daily Report: USSR*, 19 December 1974, C1).

157 NCNA, 19 January 1974, in FBIS *Daily Report: USSR*, 23 January 1974, A3–4; *NYT*, 20, 21 and 24 January 1974; NCNA, in FBIS *Daily Report: China*, 23 January 1974, A1–5; *CSM*, 25 January 1974; NCNA, in FBIS *Daily Report: China*, 25 January 1974, A1–2; *Economist*, 26 January 1974, 43. The Chinese allegedly "caught" two Soviet diplomats handing over a spy kit to a Chinese citizen under a bridge outside Peking. The Chinese confessed and the Soviets were expelled. The Soviets in turn expelled a Chinese diplomat in Moscow. The Chinese charged the Soviets with wholesale spying in the Far East. See *Atlas World Press Review*, February 1975, 15–20, reprinting a previous *FEER* article.

158 The helicopter landed in Chinese territory near Beleski in the Altai region of Melkosopochnik County on 14 March. See *Pravda*, 21 March 1974 (in *CDSP*, 17 April 1974, 3). The Chinese placed the craft in Habake County in Sinkiang (*PR*, 29 March 1974, 5), accusing the Russian crew of being on a military espionage mission. A long series of verbal exchanges then ensued, in which the Soviets attempted to secure the release of the machine and its three-man crew and the Chinese used the issue for propaganda purposes and as means of forcing the Soviets to suspend

navigating the Kazakevichevo channel near Khabarovsk without permission during the summer low-water season,[159] a maritime accident off Hainan,[160] and slowness or inability to settle the annual navigation agreements.

More broadly, each side took precautions within its own boundary to build up the economy and population, invest in infrastructure, cement the loyalties of local native peoples to the national government, and (especially in the Chinese case) send out from their respective core areas large numbers of members of the dominant ethnic group. On the Soviet side, the government provided additional monetary incentives to settlers willing to relocate near the boundary. It began construction of the Baikal-Amur railway, placed farming communities on previously uninhabited (or fitfully inhabited) riverine islands, sought to prove that disputed areas had long been occupied by peoples now part of the Soviet Union, and changed names of border towns to more Slavic-sounding titles.[161]

Apparently the Soviets also harbored renewed ambitions of making Sinkiang a Mongolia-like buffer state. There were persistent reports of the authorities' organizing a Free Turkestan Movement, complete with its own military force, composed of those who had fled Sinkiang in the 1962 Ili disturbances. Based in Alma Ata and led by, among others, General Zunun Taipov, a former Sinkiang Uigur leader of long standing, this move reached its peak in the early 1970s. Thereafter, it seems to have received less Soviet support, as the Chinese sent in large numbers of former Red Guards, boosting the population of Han Chinese to more than half of the nearly 10 million inhabitants.[162] The Russians charged the Chinese with forcibly assimilating border minority peoples, especially in

further activities of the sort. At one point, the Soviets appealed to the International Red Cross to intercede, while the Chinese threatened to bring the crew to trial and allegedly took them around the country in cages for exhibition purposes. See, inter alia, *NYT*, 20, 23, 28, and 29, March; 3, 6, and 9 May; FBIS *Daily Report: USSR* (reporting a wide variety of Soviet sources), 29 March, C1; 5 April, C1–2; 29 April, C1–2, 30 April, C1–2; 3 May, C1–2; 6 May, C1; 7 May, C6–7; 13 May, C1–10; 16 May, C5–6; 23 May, C1–2; 10 June, C1–2; 24 June, C1; 28 June, C1 and C2; 8 August, C1–4; and 4 November, C3–4; FBIS *Daily Report: China*, 24 June, A4; *SCMP*, 1–4 April 1974, 65–66; *Economist*, 22 June 1974, 27–28; and *Daily Telegraph*, 26 June 1974.

159 *CDSP*, 12 June 1974, 4, reporting *Pravda* of 24 May.

160 NCNA, 18 April 1971 (in FBIS *Daily Report: China*, 19 April, A1), reporting an incident on 31 March 1971 in which the Soviet motor ship *Ernst Thaelman* collided with a Chinese fishing junk, sinking it and causing the death of eleven and injury to another eleven. The Chinese claimed the Soviet ship made no strenuous efforts to rescue the thirty survivors, while the Russians claimed (TASS, 31 March) that the Chinese ship was sailing without lights.

161 *NYT*, 28 January, 2 February, and 3 August 1970; 8 and 25 March and 5 August 1973; 4 April 1975, NCNA, 6 March 1973.

162 Harrison E. Salisbury, "Marco Polo would recognize Mao's Sinkiang," *New York Times Magazine*, 23 November 1969; *NYT*, 3 March, 5 July, and 16 August 1970; *FEER*, 16 January 1971, 46–47; *NYT*, 5 August 1973 and 3 January 1974; Tania Jacques, "'Shärqiy Türkstan' or 'Sinkiang'?" *Radio Liberty Research*, 7 March 1975.

Inner Mongolia, where an uprising was allegedly quelled. The Chinese also sent more than 150,000 former Red Guards into Heilungkiang to augment the Production and Construction Corps and began a major archaeological effort to prove that border regions historically had been part of China.[163]

Phase one, 1969–1970

One part of the agreement to resume negotiations was that the talks should remain secret. There are thus no official data on how they transpired aside from the obvious fact that because no agreement was reached, little or no progress took place. Nonetheless, a reasonably clear outline of developments can be deduced from the unofficial revelations, mostly by Chinese, plus the author's conversations with participants and others close to events, press reports, and evidence from the general trends in Soviet and Chinese domestic politics and foreign policies. Almost immediately after September 1969, for instance, it was apparent that the Chinese decision to return to the negotiating table had been taken against internal opposition.[164] Later, with the exposure of the Lin Piao–Mao Tse-tung controversy, the source of that opposition became clear. Aside from this, before a month had passed, Peking let it be known that the negotiations had become deadlocked. On 6 November, the CCP-controlled *Ta-kung pao* in Hong Kong stated that "negotiations on the boundary question have not been proceeding smoothly" and that the Soviets had not acceded to the Chinese "principles" (in particular, they had not withdrawn from the "disputed areas"). The Soviet side had allegedly tried to broaden the content of the talks to include general rapprochement and "other objectives," and stated its contentions "from a position of strength." If the Russians were to cease these obstructionist meneuvers, the article stated, an agreement would be possible.[165] The last of these amounted to an admission that China could not sign a border agreement with the Soviet Union until there was rough equality of military forces deployed in the border regions and also in the strategic sense. Because the military balance continued to favor the Soviet Union, it is not surprising that no agreement was reached in the decade and a half thereafter.

163 *NYT*, 8 November 1973; FBIS *Daily Report: USSR*, 18 June 1974, C1–2; *FEER*, 16 January 1971, 47; 8 April 1974, 5; FBIS *Daily Report: China*, 19 March 1975, E5–6.
164 *NYT*, 12 October 1960.
165 A translation of the article is in *Daily Report: China*, 6 November 1969, A1. Other analyses are in *NYT*, 6 and 20 November; *Los Angeles Times*, 7 November; *FEER*, 13 November 1969, 344; and *Washington Post*, 21 November 1969.

The trick for the Chinese was to keep the Soviets interested enough in the talks to justify their continuation or, conversely, to prevent Moscow from finding in their lack of meaningful progress an excuse for breaking them off and possibly launching a military attack. At the same time, the Chinese were not about to go to the opposite length, with talks still in progress, of meliorating their general line of propaganda and ideological attack against the Soviet leadership and its policies. Hence, the Chinese walked a tightrope. Moscow could at any time cut off the talks, while Peking, for the sake of internal political consistency and momentum if not for other reasons, had to continue its verbal forays against the Russians. Because the Chinese delegation was evidently under instructions from Mao neither to agree with Moscow nor even to give way on its enumerated questions of "principle," the best they could do was work at changing some of the external parameters. One was obviously the military balance, but it took time to change that, especially in the face of PLA involvement in political administration and the emerging Mao–Lin battle. Another was to try to dampen, however temporarily, the conflict with the United States, particularly as concerned Taiwan, the Vietnam War, and diplomatic recognition plus United Nations seating. A third was to begin building a global coalition of Third World forces against the Soviet Union, or at least to prevent Moscow from fashioning such a coalition against China. Peking attempted to move simultaneously on all these fronts, holding the negotiations constant in the meanwhile. Much of what occurred in the negotiations after late 1969 is understandable only when developments in these other arenas are kept in mind.

The Chinese did not cease, or even decrease the level of, polemics against the Soviet Union. On a number of occasions in the month following 20 October 1969, moreover, they cast aspersions directly on the Soviet position concerning the border.[166] Since public attitudes are reasonably accurate indications of progress in private talks, it is not surprising that Kuznetsov and his deputy head left Peking on 14 December, using the excuse of attending the upcoming Supreme Soviet session (of which he was a member) and "temporarily adjourning" the talks.[167] Concurrently, the Soviets made known their disappointment at the lack of progress, blamed the Chinese, and resumed direct verbal attacks against the Chinese leadership.[168] In Moscow, Kuznetsov reported that the two sides had not even been able to agree on an agenda. The Chinese wished to limit negotiations to the border question, the Soviets desired to

166 *Washington Post*, 21 November 1969; *Los Angeles Times*, 24 November 1969; *FEER*, 4 December 1969, 484; and *PR*, 49 (5 December 1969).
167 *NYT*, 21 December 1969. 168 Ibid.

broaden the discussion to include the whole range of Sino-Soviet differences and to work cautiously up to a border agreement by means of successes in such other areas as trade, culture, and level of diplomatic representation.[169] Kuznetsov also said the two sides had met twelve times (i.e., slightly more than once a week), that he had been the subject of wall poster vilification in Peking, and had been socially ostracized by his Chinese hosts.[170]

The Chinese, in January 1970, publicly agreed that negotiations had quickly reached a stalemate:[171] Their demand that the Soviets withdraw from disputed areas before negotiations could proceed had met with a peremptory Russian refusal, as did their call upon Moscow to admit the "unequal" nature of the existing treaties before working out a new agreement. Meanwhile, the Chinese reinstated contacts with the United States in Warsaw – thus beginning the long and delicate process that resulted in the Shanghai Communiqué of February 1972 – and began to swing around to a pro-Japan policy; they thereby attempted to extricate themselves from diplomatic isolation from the most important noncommunist powers on their periphery.

Kuznetsov returned to Peking on 2 January 1970 (this time without his deputy head, Major General Vadim A. Matrosov, the border commander),[172] and the talks resumed on 14 January.[173] They bogged down almost immediately, however, over the two sides' conflicting interpretations of the Chou–Kosygin agreement (if indeed there was any), the scope of the talks, and the agenda.[174] Kuznetsov reportedly offered to transfer to Chinese sovereignty many of the Ussuri River islands, including Chen-pao itself, and to open discussion on the Pamir sector of the Chinese claims, as a means of clearing the way for a general border agreement.[175] In exchange, the Chinese would be expected to drop their unequal treaties argument. But the Chinese refused to accede and continued to insist that the Russians carry out Peking's understanding of the September agreement. By mid-March, Moscow publicly admitted the talks were stalled and warned that Kuznetsov would be brought home (i.e., replaced by another negotiator at a lower rank) unless a breakthrough was reached.[176] About this time, rumors again circulated on border clashes[177] and the

169 Ibid., 31 December 1969.   170 Ibid.
171 See *FEER*, 25 December 1969, 664; 9 January 1970 (translation in FBIS *Daily Report: China*, 9
     January 1970, A1); *Los Angeles Times*, 9 January 1970, and *Financial Times*, 15 January 1970.
172 *NYT*, 30 December 1969, 2 and 3 January 1970; FBIS *Daily Report: China*, 2 January 1970, A1;
     SCMP, 4574 (12 January 1970), 43; *Pravda*, 3 January 1970; *PR*, 2 (9 January 1970), 31.
173 *NYT*, 14 January 1970, and *Washington Post*, 2 January 1970.
174 *NYT*, 8 March 1970.
175 Ibid., 1 March 1970; FBIS *Daily Report: China*, 13 January 1970, A31, and 17 January 1970.
176 *NYT*, 20 March 1970.   177 Ibid., 1 March 1970.

Soviet Union had to issue an official denial that it was about to launch a general attack on China.[178]

Propaganda exchanges now rose to a peak, for China hoped to forestall any Soviet attack by claiming loudly that one was imminent, and the Soviet Union chose to denigrate Mao's own personal past. Moscow warned China not to resort to verbal abuse in an attempt to extract concessions at the talks, and Peking, in a major editorial on the occasion of the hundredth anniversary of Lenin's birth, accused Brezhnev of following a Hitlerlike policy toward China.[179] The Soviets also nominated Vladimir I. Stepakov, the party propaganda chief and the person in charge of diatribes against China and Mao personally, as ambassador-designate to China – a gross insult[180] (later his name was withdrawn when Peking declared him unacceptable) – and Brezhnev spoke out publicly on the issue.[181]

In this heated atmosphere, Kuznetsov returned to Moscow for a seventeen-day period on 22 April 1970.[182] Just before his return, he had apparently made a further try at breaking the deadlock by accepting the Chinese proposal for withdrawal of forces (i.e., Soviet) from "disputed areas."[183] Unconfirmed reports said that the Soviet Union coupled this with a refusal to accede to the Chinese demand for establishing a military status quo along the frontier and continued to insist that the two sides concentrate on specific territorial differences and not on the general question of the "unequal" treaties. When the Chinese did not agree to this Soviet proposal, Kuznetsov left for home. Despite his failure to achieve a breakthrough and in the face of the Chinese verbal broadside on Lenin's birthday, Kuznetsov went back to Peking again on 7 May. Nothing happened at the negotiating table, however, and Kuznetsov himself was sent back to Moscow on 20 June 1970,[184] reportedly ill and, in any case, not again to return to Peking. Propaganda attacks on both sides tapered off. Nonetheless, Moscow did level a blast at Peking on 18 May in express reply to the Chinese attack of 26 April against Brezhnev, but while no kind words were wasted on the Chinese, significantly the border issue was

178 Ibid., 14 March 1970 reporting *Pravda* of that day (translation in *CDSP*, 14 April 1970, 19).
179 *Pravda*, 17 March 1969; *NYT*, 20 March, 1 and 15 April, and 3 May 1969; *JMJP*, 25 April 1970.
180 *NYT*, 3 May 1970.   181 *Pravda*, 15 April 1970 (translation in *CDSP*, 12 May 1970, 1–4).
182 *Times* (London), 22 April 1970; *NYT*, 7 May 1970.
183 *Los Angeles Times*, 16 April 1970. The Soviet military appears to have gone along with this proposed unilateral withdrawal on grounds that they could easily reenter the areas and could in any case control them militarily – through air and artillery power – without occupying the territory.
184 FBIS *Daily Report: USSR*, 1 July 1970, A20, quoting Budapest MTI Radio of 20 June.

described as only one aspect of the entire range of Soviet-Chinese differences.[185] Thereafter, for a period, Chinese polemics of a major sort also ceased.

It remained for Kosygin himself to sum up this first nine-month phase of the negotiating period. In his Supreme Soviet "election speech" on 10 June, he accused the Chinese of following a policy "which does not permit the realization of any progress in the normalization of our relations in general, or in the border talks in Peking." Still, he continued, "despite the complexity of the talks in Peking, which are hampered by the Chinese side, the Soviet Union intends to continue them in order to find an agreement that meets the interests of the Soviet Union, China, and the entire world."[186] These sentiments were echoed by Soviet President Podgorny and CPSU General Secretary Brezhnev in similar talks.

It would not have been to Peking's interest to let the talks founder completely, as that would have exposed the Chinese to possible Soviet attack at a time when their military defenses were still weak and their diplomatic campaign hardly under way. Moscow, too, did not wish to see the negotiations come to naught, since it had invested so much of its energy and diplomatic prestige in forcing the Chinese back to the negotiating table. Moreover, for Moscow as well as Peking, there was no alternative to negotiations except the measurably enhanced probability of war, which neither side wished nor could wage without suffering severe casualties. Both, therefore, sought to keep the talks going. For this they used the previous year's device, the annual river-navigation talks. The two sides agreed in June to reconvene on 10 July.[187] These talks quickly became enmeshed in procedural and substantive disagreements and concluded only six months later. Even then, the Chinese refused to acknowledge having signed a new annual agreement, instead (as on the previous occasion) signing their name to a "summary" of the proceedings.[188]

Phase two, 1970–1973

The Russians' next move was to switch chief negotiators. The dispatch of Vice–Foreign Minister Leonid Ilichev on 15 August 1970 to replace Kuznetsov signified a Soviet decision to gird for the long run; negotia-

---

185 *Pravda*, 18 May 1970 (translation in *CDSP*, 16 June 1970), 1–7; *NYT*, 10 May 1970.
186 *NYT*, 11 June 1970, and *FEER*, 18 June 1970, 4.
187 FBIS *Daily Report: China*, 1 July 1970, A1; *FEER*, 9 July 1970, 4, 16–17; *NYT*, 11 July 1970; *Pravda*, 11 July 1970 (translation in *CDSP*, 11 August 1970, 15).
188 *CSM*, 22 and 24 December 1970; *NYT*, 21 and 25 December 1970; FBIS *Daily Report: China*, 24 December 1970, A1; *PR*, 1 (1 January 1970), 7; and *Pravda*, 20 December 1970 (in *CDSP*, 19 January 1971, 26).

tions were placed at a lower diplomatic rung, and Ilichev, a former party propaganda expert, could be counted on to reply in kind to Chinese charges of ideological infidelity.[189] The Soviets also replaced Stepakov's name as ambassador-designate to China with that of Vasily S. Tolstikov, the Leningrad Party chief, while the Chinese indicated that Vice–Foreign Minister Liu Hsin-ch'ü would be their nominee for the Moscow post.[190] These men took up their posts in late November.[191] Finally, border provincial officials of the two states managed to sign a local accord for trade across the Amur River.[192] These moves signified that the two states did not want to see the overall character of their relations sink to such depths that no alternative but military conflict remained. Later (on 23 November) it was announced that the two states had, after eighteen months of negotiation, signed a one-year trade agreement.[193]

During the fall of 1970 Ilichev evidently forwarded to the Chinese side an offer for a nonaggression pact, apparently along the lines of the accord Moscow had signed in August with West Germany. We know very little about this initiative except that it was summarily rejected by the Chinese.[194] Ilichev then flew home, on 3 December, the same day that Chinese ambassador Liu called on Kuznetsov in Moscow.[195] Ilichev did not return until 14 January 1971, after the Supreme Soviet session to which he was a delegate, was over.[196] Again nothing transpired except a still unexplained meeting of Ilichev, Tolstikov, Chou, and Chi Peng-fei (who was acting as foreign minister) in Peking, which the Soviets thought important enough to report in *Pravda*. Ilichev and Tolstikov returned to Moscow in April for the meeting of the Twenty-fourth CPSU Congress, arriving back in Peking only on 19 April.[197] As if to demonstrate the stalled nature of the talks, the Soviet delegation was taken on the annual diplomatic corps tour of China, from which the Chinese had previously excluded Soviet delegations. It was only after public Soviet protest that Peking allowed them to join in.[198]

Later, it became clear that two additional factors were driving the

189 *FEER*, 23 July 1970, 4; *Los Angeles Times*, 16 August 1970; FBIS *Daily Report: China*, 17 August 1970, A1; *PR*, 32 (7 August 1970), 8–9; *Pravda*, 16 August 1970 (in *CDSP*, 15 September 1970, 8); *NYT*, 16 August 1970.
190 *NYT*, 3 July and 16 August 1970.
191 *Pravda*, 3 December 1970 in *CDSP*, 22.48 (29 December 1970), 32; *NYT*, 19 and 24 November 1970.
192 *NYT*, 24 September 1970.   193 Ibid., November 24, 1970.
194 *FEER*, 10 October 1970, 4; *Free China Weekly*, 25 October 1970.
195 Tanjug (Belgrade), in FBIS *Daily Report: China*, 15 January 1971, A3; *Pravda*, 3 December 1970.
196 *Pravda*, 15 January 1971 (in *CDSP*, 23.2 [9 February 1971]).
197 *Pravda*, 24 March 1971; FBIS *Daily Report: China*, 19 April 1971, A1.
198 *Pravda*, 20 February 1971 (in *CDSP*, 23 March 1971, 20); *CSM*, 29 May 1971; FBIS *Daily Report: China*, 24 May 1971, A11–12; *Pravda*, 22 May 1971 (in *CDSP*, 22 June 1971, 16); *NYT*, 22 May 1970.

Chinese even farther from a border pact. Perhaps the more important was the approaching denouement of the Mao–Lin struggle for power. According to charges posthumously placed against Lin, he was opposed to Mao's policy of negotiations as a means to ward off Soviet attack, differed with Mao on what military strategy to employ against the Russians, and was even accused of wishing to compromise the border issue as a whole with Moscow. These developments effectively precluded the Chinese from facing the Soviets, militarily or politically, with the necessary unity. Therefore, it was their best policy to procrastinate until domestic political order had been restored. Effectively, that point was not reached until after the turn of the year 1971–72. At this point, the Chinese found it to their advantage to delay serious negotiations even further, as a result of the second factor, the sea change in Chinese relations with the United States. The summer of 1971 saw the de facto American diplomatic chief, Henry Kissinger, take his historic secret trip to Peking to set up the visit of President Richard Nixon in February 1972.

These events deterred China's serious negotiations: If the Chinese could put Sino-American differences over Taiwan on ice and begin to restore full diplomatic relations, it would pay Peking to delay talks with Moscow until the full weight of the emerging Sino-American relationship could be brought to bear. The Chinese would not be interested in making headway on the border issue until after the American president's visit and the Shanghai Communiqué, which outlined the new Peking–Washington relationship. The border negotiations were stalled for the rest of 1971.[199]

In 1972 Moscow reiterated its proposal for a nonaggression pact, this time disclosing that it had made such a proposal in 1970 and that China had rejected it.[200] The proposal was evidently placed again before the Chinese negotiating team by Ilichev after he returned to Peking, 20 March 1972.[201] The river navigation talks were renewed 6 December 1971 and adjourned again without agreement, 21 March 1972.[202] The Chinese replaced their chief negotiator, Ch'iao Kuan-hua, with a new man of lower rank, Vice–Foreign Minister Yü Chan.[203] The Soviet delegation, having nothing to do, took another tour of Chinese cities.[204] Ilichev went

199 Propaganda attacks continued. See *Pravda*, 1 July 1971, "Alexandrov" article (in *CDSP*, 5 October 1971, 1–5); *CSM*, 18 March 1971; *CSM*, 30 September 1971; *International Affairs* (Moscow), November 1971, 17–24.
200 *Pravda*, 23 September 1972, and *NYT*, 24 September 1972.
201 He had gone back to Moscow so as not to be in Peking at the same time as Nixon.
202 *NYT*, 27 March and May 1972, passim; *Pravda*, 21 March 1972 (in *CDSP*, 19 April 1972, 18); and *CSM*, 27 March 1972. The Chinese did not report Ilichev's return to Peking. FBIS *Daily Report: China*, 22 March 1972, A1; *FEER*, 1 April 1972, 4 and 8 April 1972, 9.
203 *CSM*, 26 August 1970.
204 FBIS *Daily Report: USSR*, 1 May 1972, D1; *NYT*, 1 May 1972; FBIS *Daily Report: China*, 2 May 1972, A5.

home for a "vacation" in September, returning only on 17 October.[205] Propaganda attacks on both sides petered out, although the standard range of Chinese attacks could still be found at some time during the year, as could the normal range of Soviet denials and denunciations of the Chinese. Thus, 1972 was a year of waiting for both China and the Soviet Union.

The hiatus continued throughout 1973. Peking found it could continually postpone resolution of the border question by dragging out the negotiations, just as before. Moreover, events outside the conference room were more important in determining the course of negotiations. The complex maneuvers – factional, bureaucratic, and military – leading up to the CCP's Tenth Congress in August 1973 once again rendered China less than completely united against the Soviets. Although no struggle for political primacy was equally critical in Moscow, the Kremlin's diplomatic attention was diverted to dealings with the United States – the Brezhnev–Nixon Washington summit, the Watergate affair, the various maneuverings concerning the European Security Conference, and, late in the year, the crisis over the two superpowers' handling of the Arab-Israeli War. The Vietnam War was perhaps the most important of the influences on the triangular relations among the United States, China, and Russia: With the slow ending of the American involvement in 1972 and 1973, and the consequent stop-and-go nature of Sino-American and Soviet-American détente, both Moscow and Peking concentrated their attention on the American leg of the strategic triangle. Finally, it was only after Nixon's visit to Peking that Chinese military reinforcements to the border regions began in earnest, along with politico-military transfers of command. The scale of the Soviet buildup – and the consequent need to spend several years in bringing the balance more nearly into equilibrium – gave the Chinese additional incentive to delay an agreement.

Russia and China thus took opposite bets on the influence of their changing relations with the United States on the Sino-Soviet conflict. Moscow favored détente with Washington, among other reasons, in order to isolate Peking or at least to prevent the rise of a new Sino-American combination that, including Western Europe and Japan, would be the centerpiece of a grand anti-Soviet coalition. Peking sought to lessen tensions with the United States so as to confront the Soviets with the prospect – however unreal – of such a combination.

205 *PR*, 31 (4 August 1972), 7–9; *Pravda*, 30 September 1972 (in *CDSP*, 25 October 1973, 16); FBIS *Daily Report: USSR*, 17 October 1972, D1; *NYT*, 18 October 1972; FBIS *Daily Report: China*, 15 December 1972, A1.

Thus, 1973 also saw no progress in the talks. Soviet criticism of China varied with the international climate and the intensity of Chinese verbal forays.[206] Moscow ceased anti-Chinese diatribes at the beginning of the Paris Conference on Vietnam in an attempt to promote a united Soviet-Chinese front against the United States.[207] Kosygin denied Chinese charges that Moscow was militarily threatening China,[208] an "Alexandrov"-authored article appeared in *Pravda* rebutting Chinese charges, and Brezhnev, on 14 June, tried out the nonaggression proposal and the Chinese rejected it. (The Chinese "did not even take the trouble of answering," lamented the Soviet leader.)[209]

The river navigation commission met again, from 5 January to 5 March, with the same lack of results as previously.[210] The Soviet delegation took another tour of China,[211] and Ilichev went home 19 July for vacation and instructions, but this time he did not return for a full year.[212] Thus, the negotiations were effectively broken off in mid-1973.

The Chinese did not seem particularly perturbed by this possible danger signal: They were preoccupied with the Tenth Congress. Chou En-lai, in his report to the Congress, reiterated Chinese willingness to settle the border dispute so long as military force was not applied or threatened. Chou's remarks on Sino-Soviet relations were of significance in showing that China no longer feared immediate Soviet attack; rather, China took to warning the West that the Russians were now "making a feint in the east while attacking in the west." Of perhaps equal importance, Chou asserted Peking's willingness to improve state relations on the basis of peaceful coexistence. Presumably this included settlement of the boundary disputes.[213] These sentiments were echoed in Chou's interview with C. L. Sulzberger in late October,[214] and in the Chinese greetings to the Supreme Soviet (i.e., not to the CPSU Presidium) on the October Revolution anniversary.[215]

206 *NYT*, 8 August, 6 September, 19 November, and 22 December 1972; *CSM*, 26 August 1972.
207 *NYT*, 25 February 1973.
208 *Los Angeles Times*, 6 June 1973; *Pravda*, 2 June 1973 (in *CDSP*, 27 June 1973, 4 and 12); FBIS *Daily Report: USSR*, 1 June 1973, D1.
209 *Los Angeles Times* and *NYT*, 25 September 1973; *Economist*, 29 September 1973, 42; *CSM*, 2 October 1973; *International Affairs* (Moscow), 5 (May 1975), 37.
210 FBIS *Daily Report: China*, 9 March 1973, A3; *NYT*, 9 March 1970.
211 *Pravda*, 1 May 1973.
212 *NYT*, 20 July 1973. He had returned to Peking 13 January. See ibid., 25 February 1973.
213 *PR*, 35 and 36 (7 September 1973), 23. For a review of the Congress, see Thomas W. Robinson, "China in 1973: renewed leftism threatens the 'New Course,'" *Asian Survey*, 14.1 (January 1974), 1–21.
214 *NYT*, 29 October 1973.
215 Ibid., 11 November 1973; *Pravda*, 10 November 1973 (in *CDSP*, 5 December 1973, 6).

Phase three, 1974–1975

Ilichev's return to Moscow in mid-1973 had ended the second phase of the negotiations. The third phase did not begin until his return to Peking on 20 June 1974.[216] By then, Sino-Soviet relations had hit a new low as a result of the Chinese expulsion of alleged Soviet spies from Peking in January, the helicopter incident in March, China's military action in the Paracel Islands off South Vietnam, and the Kazakevichevo Channel controversy. The first two evidently kept Ilichev from returning to Peking early in the year, as he was involved in Moscow with Russian efforts to secure the release of the helicopter crew.[217] The third incident caused concern in Moscow because of its implications for China's border policy as a whole.[218] The last seems to have precipitated Ilichev's return to the Chinese capital.

On 22 May 1974, the Soviet foreign ministry sent a note to Peking about the Kazakevichevo Channel, which forms the southwest leg of the triangle separating Hei-hsia-tzu Island from the mainland. The Amur and the Ussuri form the other two legs, and Khabarovsk is on the mainland bank opposite the northeast corner of the island, where the Amur meets the Ussuri. The Soviet note recognized the channel as the maritime border between the two states and not the major rivers themselves.[219] The Soviet note went on to "view favorably China's request for passage of its vessels" through the Amur-Ussuri route during the dry (summer) season when the channel itself is unnavigable, but said for the first time that advance notice would be required in every case. It asserted its right to do this on the basis of "Russian-Chinese treaty documents," presumably correspondence following the Treaty of Peking in 1860.[220] The Chinese immediately rejected the Soviet argument;[221] but there was little they

216 *Los Angeles Times*, 26 June 1974; *NYT*, 26 and 30 June 1974; FBIS *Daily Report: USSR*, 25 June 1974, C1; *Financial Times*, 26 June 1974; Reuters, 26 June 1974; FBIS *Daily Report: China*, 21 June 1974, A1; *Le Monde*, 27 June 1974.

217 *Pravda*, 3 May 1974 (in *CDSP*, 29 May 1974, 15); *NYT*, 21, 24, and 29 March 1974; *Economist*, 26 January 1974, 43; FBIS *Daily Report: USSR*, 24 June 1974, C1.

218 *NYT*, 9 and 10 February 1974; *CSM*, 15 February 1974; Jean Riollot, "Soviet reaction to the Paracel Island dispute," *Radio Liberty Dispatch*, 11 February 1974. This was the first time since the Sino-Indian border wars of 1959 and 1962 that China used force in a territorial matter. To Moscow it demonstrated that Peking would use force to have its way once the military situation was favorable.

219 *Pravda*, 24 May 1974 (in *CDSP*, 12 June 1974, 4); *NYT*, 24, 25, and 28 May 1974; FBIS *Daily Report: USSR*, 23 May 1972, C1.

220 See Neville Maxwell, "A note on the Amur/Ussuri sector of the Sino-Soviet boundaries," *Modern China*, 1.1 (January 1975), 116–26.

221 *NYT*, 28 May and 1 June 1974; FBIS *Daily Report: China*, 31 May 1974, A1; *PR*, 23 (7 June 1974), 7.

could do to secure dry-season passage past Khabarovsk, because the Soviet Union had stationed gunboats since 1967 at the point where the channel splits off to the south from the Amur.[222] The Soviet motives were obvious: By raising the issue at that time, they hoped to secure leverage for the release of the helicopter crewmen, give the Chinese some motivation to reopen the border talks as a whole, counter the Chinese contention for ownership of most of the Amur–Ussuri Islands on the thalweg principle,[223] and provide a means of pressuring the Chinese to sign a new annual river-navigation agreement (the negotiations for which again ended in failure on 21 March).[224]

This Soviet tactic seemed to achieve at least part of its purpose, for the border talks reconvened in late June 1974. A month later, Ilichev again left Peking after no apparent progress was made, returned, and left once again for Moscow on 18 August.[225] Given the sterile past, it might be presumed that negotiations would not henceforth have resumed and that, having served their short-term purpose for Peking as a lightning rod, they could successfully be dispensed with. Rumania tried to act as a mediator when Kosygin, Li Hsien-nien – one of Chou En-lai's close associates – and Yü Chan were all in Bucharest at the same time in August for the thirtieth anniversary of the World War II liberation of Rumania, but the most that could be produced was a single pro forma handshake.[226]

Nonetheless, on 6 November the Chinese opened the door a tantalizing crack (or perhaps the Soviets kept their foot in it by some as yet unknown inducement) when they included in an otherwise unnoteworthy October Revolution greeting to Moscow the following:

The Chinese Government has repeatedly proposed that talks between the two sides be held in good faith.... [I]t is necessary first of all to conclude *an agreement of mutual non-aggression and non-use of force* against one another, on maintaining the status quo on the border and on averting armed conflicts and departure of the armed forces of both sides from disputed areas, and then to proceed toward the solution of the border questions as [a] whole by way of talks. [Emphasis added.][227]

222 Maxwell, "A note on the Amur/Ussuri sector," 122.
223 *NYT*, 24 May 1974. Maxwell, "A note on the Amur/Ussuri sector," 121, argues, plausibly but without supportive evidence, that Moscow "has developed and hardened its claim to a boundary along the Chinese bank so as to create a bargaining counter to be exchanged for a Chinese concession on a related but separate issue – the question of where exactly the boundary runs at the point where the Amur and the Ussuri meet."
224 *SCMP*, 5582 (2 April 1974), 33; FBIS *Daily Report: China*, 25 March 1974, A13; *FEER* 3 June 1974, 14.
225 *NYT*, 26 July, 19 August, and 2 October 1974; *Pravda*, 19 August 1974 (in *CDSP*, 11 September 1974, 16); FBIS *Daily Report: USSR*, 19 August 1974, C1; FBIS *Daily Report: China*, D18; and *Pravda*, 1 October 1974 (in *CDSP*, 23 October 1974, 7).
226 *NYT*, 3 September 1974; *CSM*, 26 August 1974; FBIS *Daily Report: China*, 23 August 1974, A1–2.
227 *Manchester Guardian*, 8 November 1974; FBIS *Daily Report: China*, 7 November 1974, A1–3; *NYT*, 8 November 1974; Reuters, 8 November 1974.

Why did the Chinese now apparently assent to what the Soviets had proposed to them for the past three years? There are several possible answers.

First, it is not clear that the Chinese were entirely serious about a nonaggression treaty, for the relevant phrase was wrapped in a package of other proposals, none of which were new; some of which (e.g., Soviet withdrawal from territory claimed by the Chinese) had previously been rejected by Moscow and stood no chance of acceptance now; and all of which – including the nonaggression clause itself – were proffered as preconditions to further negotiation. Second, China needed to reassert itself diplomatically with regard to the border question, given its rejection of all Soviet proposals; the nonaggression agreement suggestion was therefore a means of recovering the diplomatic initiative, which had been in Moscow's hands from the beginning. Third, there was every indication that the proposal was designed in part to arouse more notice in Washington than in Moscow. The Chinese had found the United States reluctant to move beyond the liaison-offices stage in improving their relations, and Washington was felt to lack any motive to change Sino-American relations further, since it now had ambassadorial-level representation in both Peking and Taipei. Inclining ever so slightly toward the Soviet Union was Mao's way, therefore, of informing Washington that it could not indefinitely count on the Sino-Soviet conflict as a means of forcing Peking to lessen its opposition to continued American recognition of, and protectorate over, Taiwan. Peking seemed to be telling Washington that China, as well as the United States, could use the new triangularization of international politics to its own advantage.

These reasons for the Chinese diplomatic departure are not entirely consistent with one another, but the initiative (if it can be called that) had its intended effect, at least on Moscow. Immediate Soviet reaction was cautiously noncommittal.[228] The short-term response was a firm and definite rejection. On 26 November, in Ulan Bator, Brezhnev stated his reasons for considering the Chinese November telegram not worthy of a positive reply:

Actually, Peking advances as preliminary condition no more no less than a demand for the withdrawal of Soviet border guards from a number of areas of our territory to which Chinese leaders have now decided to lay claim and so have begun to call "disputed areas." And Peking declares outright that it will agree to talks on border questions only after its demands concerning the so-called "disputed areas" have been satisfied.... Such a position is absolutely unacceptable.[229]

228 *NYT*, 9 November 1974.
229 *Pravda*, 27 November 1974 (in *CDSP*, 25 December 1974, 1–6); *NYT* and *CSM*, 27 November 1974. Earlier, Moscow had used the Hugarian media to indicate it would reject the Peking initiative. See FBIS *Daily Report: USSR*, 15 November 1974.

And in the official Soviet note sent the same day, the Kremlin opined that

What was said in your telegram of November 6th, this year, on ways of settling some questions of Soviet-Chinese relations, the presentation of all kinds of preliminary conditions, is a repetition of the former position of the Chinese leadership and, of course, does not furnish foundations for an understanding.[230]

The longer-term Soviet response was different. In early February 1975, Moscow sent Ilichev back to Peking and the talks were reopened.[231] The Soviet purpose was to see if there was in fact any change in the Chinese position; their private response to the Chinese telegram was therefore different from their public one.[232] Moreover, at the Fourth National People's Congress (NPC), convened in Peking after a long preparatory period, Chou En-lai's speech contained several phrases on the border question that seemed conciliatory. Chou distinguished between the non-aggression pact proposed several times by Moscow and the agreement in principle on mutual nonaggression, the claimed product of his September 1969 airport meeting with Kosygin. Although this was linked, as usual, with the demand that Soviet troops leave the "disputed areas," Chou did call upon the Russians to "sit down and negotiate honestly, do something to solve a bit of the problem and stop playing such deceitful tricks."[233] Moscow took Chou at his word and dispatched Ilichev to test the atmosphere for possible changes.

The atmosphere in reality was none too good. The Chinese had indicated their intention of putting the Soviet helicopter crew on trial, which would have been a serious move inviting material Soviet retaliation.[234] In December, the Chinese had published, in the first number of the reissued journal *Li-shih yen-chiu* (Historical research), a harsh attack on Soviet border policy, calling on the Russians to withdraw their troops from Mongolia, end military maneuvers in frontier areas, and reduce border-region troop levels to the level of 1964.[235] The new Chinese state constitution, adopted at the Fourth NPC, officially inscribed anti-Sovietism as a primary aspect of Chinese foreign policy.[236] For its part, Moscow continued its own propaganda campaign against Peking, generally accusing the Chinese of not responding to its own series of proposals, charging

230 *Pravda*, 25 November 1974 (in *CDSP*, 18 December 1974, 1).
231 *NYT*, 13 and 18 February 1974; FBIS *Daily Report: USSR*, 12 February 1974, C1; FBIS *Daily Report: China*, 12 February 1974, A1; *Daily Telegraph*, 13 February 1974.
232 Negotiations were not renewed before February because the Chinese were caught up in the preparations for and the holding of the Fourth NPC, which met in January.
233 *PR*, 4 (24 January 1975), 25; *Washington Post*, 24 January 1975; *FEER*, 31 January 1974, 14–15.
234 FBIS *Daily Report: USSR*, 15 October 1974, A13.
235 *LSYC*, 1975 1.
236 "The Constitution of the People's Republic of China," "Preamble," in *PR*, 4 (24 January 1975), 12.

the leadership with substituting Maoism for Marxism as the principal state and Party ideology,[237] and challenging the Chinese to come forth with "really constructive steps" toward settling the border problem.[238]

Still, Ilichev and his new Chinese counterpart, Han Nien-lung (who now replaced Yü Chan, reportedly ill), managed to meet, on 16 February 1975.[239] It is possible that aside from procedural and diplomatic courtesy matters, the Soviets attempted to include the helicopter crew matter and the question of Amur-Ussuri shipping on the agenda, for these topics were tending to interfere more and more in the broader context of the talks. As in previous years, however, there appears to have been no easy progress, and the Soviet delegation soon (in April) found itself on the now standard tour of South China cities.[240] By mid-1975, it was not even clear that the talks were continuing, even on an intermittent basis.

Thus, in the twelve years since the two sides first began negotiations in 1964, there had been no visible progress. Prospects for settlement depended essentially on the course of events outside the negotiating room, particularly on the longevity of Mao Tse-tung and the pattern of succession politics in China. Nonetheless, the period since 1969 had not been wasted. Were the political situation to change, the Soviets and the Chinese knew each other's positions well enough that a definitive settlement could have been reached in a very short time. That was not to come for at least another decade and a half.

APPENDIX: CHINESE AND SOVIET FORCE BUILDUPS, 1969–1975

The Russian and Chinese diplomatic efforts already detailed, however important, were nonetheless secondary to the military buildups. It was the Soviet force augmentation – startlingly swift, broad, and deep – that engendered Chinese fears of Russian aggression, that wreaked havoc with the domestic economy in the early 1970s, and that drove Peking into the waiting hands of the Americans. Later, however, the Chinese sent reinforcements sufficient to make a major Russian ground offensive very costly. It remained impossible for the PLA to prevent the Red Army from seizing large amounts of territory, but by the mid-1970s China had built up its ground strength enough to begin deploying army units closer to the border. Together with Chinese deployment of more than minimal

237 *Pravda*, 22 February 1974, "Alexandrov" article in *CDSP*, 19 March 1975, 1–5.
238 *CDSP*, 19 March 1975, 5; *NYT*, 23 February 1975.
239 Reuters, 17 February 1974; *Financial Times*, 19 February 1975; FBIS *Daily Report: China*, 18 February 1975, A1.
240 FBIS *Daily Report: USSR*, 30 April 1975, C1.

nuclear delivery capability, tactical and strategic, these changes partially redressed the imbalance of the early 1970s.

From the beginning, the Soviet Union had no intention of launching a major land offensive against China, either to overthrow its government or to seize territory. It shared with China the wish to secure the inviolability of its borders from what it perceived to be the predatory behavior of the other side. Both countries pursued a buildup program that was rational. And both capitals modified their stance toward the United States in a manner that helped allow Washington to pursue détente toward the Soviet Union, conclude the Vietnam War, and restore diplomatic contacts with China.

Moscow was generally alarmed, it is true, at Chinese behavior at Chen-pao Island, which it attributed to Cultural Revolution excesses and Mao Tse-tung's own perfidy. The Kremlin therefore resolved to garrison its (and the Mongolians') border with China heavily enough to make a repetition of the March 1969 events very costly to Peking, and to use the threat of more widespread military action to force the Chinese leadership into resuming the border talks. Hence the Soviets increased the number of divisions in the border regions from fifteen understrength formations to forty, and later to more than fifty, at higher levels of readiness.[241] They also provided the most advanced equipment, including nuclear missiles and tactical warheads; filled out border troop divisions; engaged in constant patrolling of land and water; augmented civil defense measures in cities within Chinese nuclear range (which included more and more of the Soviet Union with each passing year);[242] and began a massive construction program to lay in the necessary logistical base on a permanent basis.[243]

Although the Russians meant the program to be defensive, the Chinese evaluated it as threatening. Because Peking was innately sus-

241 FEER, 24 October 1970, 4; Chung-kung yen-chiu (Studies in Chinese communism) (hereafter CKYC), 3.7 (July 1969), 9; NYT, 7 August 1969; Economist, 21–22 September 1969, and 12 April 1970; FEER, 30 April 1970, 112–14; NYT, 22 July 1970; FEER, 4 September 1970, 359; CSM, 4 January 1970; Henry Bradsher, "The Sovietization of Mongolia," Foreign Affairs, 5.3 (July 1972), 545–53; Economist, 6 May 1972, 49; NYT, 10 September 1972; CSM, 10 and 14 September 1973; F. O. Miksche, "USSR: Rot-China – An der Ostgrenze Russlands Wacht die Dritte Weltmacht," Wehr und Wirtschaft (October 1974), 424–28; Die Welt, 10 July 1969; Los Angeles Times, 13 September 1969; NYT, 30 November and 30 December 1969, 7 October 1971, 6 May and 10 September 1972, 24 February 1974; Le Monde, 5 September 1970; Aviation Week and Space Technology, 20 May 1974, 64.
242 NYT, 16 August, 28 October, and 7 December 1969, 22 July 1970; FEER, 26 February 1972, 18–19; Krasnaya Zvezda (Red Star), 5 March 1970, 4; Tanjug, 17 February 1971 (in FBIS Daily Report: USSR, 9 May 1974, R6–7); FBIS Daily Report: USSR, 17 June 1974, R19–22; Daily Telegraph, 15 June 1974; Baltimore Sun, 5 August 1974; Ming Pao, 103, 104, 105 (July, August, and September 1974), article by Huang Chen-shih, et al.; CSM, 23 April 1975.
243 NYT, 3 February and 19 May 1970, 1 November 1971; FBIS Daily Report: USSR, 20 March, 1974. VI.

picious of the Soviets for ideological reasons and because they had to judge the Soviet military machine by its capabilities and perceived tactics (which often were offensive), the Chinese were forced to increase the size, change the disposition, and upgrade the equipment of their own forces. This cost them dearly in the short run: the Cultural Revolution had to be cut short, the PLA had to divide itself between politico-industrial administration and training and defense duties, support of such allies as Pakistan and North Vietnam had to take second place to opposition to the Soviet threat, and compromises had to be made with the United States over Taiwan to obviate the possibility of a two-front conflict. The Chinese did match the Soviet increase in numbers[244] if not in modernity of equipment (though they did not send significant additional divisions to the border regions until 1972, four years after the Russian buildup commenced). They increased their defense budget,[245] sent out large numbers of urban youth to man newly formed Production and Construction Corps in the northern and western provinces,[246] strengthened the militia program,[247] began a crash civil defense effort including the well-known tunnel networks in major cities,[248] and made a number of administrative changes in provincial boundaries — including the division of much of Inner Mongolia among its neighbors allegedly for defense purposes.[249] By 1974 these changes had gone part of the distance to redressing the felt imbalance of forces as of 1969–70.

Equally important, the Chinese nuclear and missile program not only continued but also changed its direction to reflect the combination of increased Soviet, and decreased American, threats. In particular, an effort was made to counter the Soviet menace by concentrating on short- and medium-range missiles; deploying them in diverse, semihardened

244 *CKYC*, 3.7 (July 1969), 9; *NYT*, 6 July, 17 and 30 August, 12 September, and 30 November 1969; *Economist*, 21–26 September 1969; *NYT*, 12 April 1970; *FEER*, 4 September 1970, 359; Miksche, "USSR: Rot-China – An der Ostgrenze Russlands," n. 16; *Die Welt*, 10 July 1969; *NYT*, 25 July 1972; *Daily Telegraph*, 15 July 1974; *CSM*, 7 November 1974.

245 *Krasnaya Zvezda*, 25 February 1972, 3 (in *CDSP*, 24.9 [29 March 1970], 1–4 and *NYT*, 26 February 1972); *New Times* (Moscow), 30 November 1972, 16; *FEER*, 5 August 1972, 23–24; *CSM*, 23 March 1973; FBIS *Daily Report: China*, 13 December 1973, A4–6; *FEER*, 11 March 1974, 33; FBIS *Daily Report: China*, 8 April 1974, A12–13; FBIS *Daily Report: USSR*, 16 July 1974, C1.

246 *FEER*, 17 October 1970, 35–36, which reported 600,000 men in the Sinkiang Corps, 200,000 in Inner Mongolia, 200,000 in Heilungkiang, and 100,000 in Tsinghai; *NYT*, 6 July and 7 November 1969, 28 January, 1 March, and 22 July 1970; FBIS *Daily Report: China*, 30 September 1969, G1; *PR*, 23 June 1972, 22–23, 2 June 1973, 14–15; *FEER*, 26, March 1975, 5.

247 *NYT*, 6 July and 30 November 1969; *FEER*, 16 January 1971, 46–47; FBIS *Daily Report: China*, 23 May 1974, K1–7; *Daily Telegraph*, 15 July 1974; FBIS *Daily Report: China*, 5 August 1974, K1, L1; *FEER*, 29 November 1974, 30–32, FBIS *Daily Report: China*, 2 February 1975, 61–62.

248 *CSM*, 16 November 1972; *NYT*, 21 November and 28 December 1969; *FEER*, 4 December 1969, 485–86, and 22 January 1970, 4; *NYT*, 4 January and 5 June 1971; and *FEER*, 9 April 1973.

249 *NYT*, 21 June, 5 and 20 July 1970; Bradsher, "The Sovietization of Mongolia"; *FEER*, 22 January 1972, which gives many details; *NYT*, 5 July 1973, 2 January 1974.

locations; and forgoing the expected (by the Americans) deployment of intercontinental missiles. Nuclear-weapons production and testing also continued and, based on older jet bombers and increased production capacity, a significant air-delivery capability emerged.[250] With such aircraft and weaponry dispersed around the full complement (around two hundred) of Chinese air bases reasonably near the Soviet border, a Soviet preemptive strike could no longer ensure destruction of the Chinese retaliatory capacity so that no Soviet cities, or only a small number of them, would be destroyed in return. Thus, by the mid-1970s there was a partial but significant redress of the nuclear imbalance along the border.

It is difficult to describe and evaluate the details of Soviet and Chinese dispositions: particulars are closely held secrets and force composition varies with circumstances. It is usually stated, for instance, that the Soviet Union had by 1975 built its ground forces up to 45 divisions, including 2 to 4 in Mongolia and others in the Trans-Baikal Military District available for quick reinforcement. Only about one-third of these were in the highest category of readiness. But many more divisions could have been brought in, given the vast investment in logistics, construction, and repositioning of equipment that took place after 1969. Much the same could be said of the Chinese. By 1975 they had about 50 divisions in the Shenyang and Peking Military Regions, 15 in the Lanchow Military Region, and perhaps 8 divisions in Sinkiang. As in the Soviet case, not all were engaged in border duties while, on the other hand, additional numbers could in an emergency quickly be sent from other areas of the country. Each state in addition maintained a certain percentage of its total forces for possible duty in other regions: the Soviet Union in Eastern and Western Europe, and in the Middle East; and China in South Asia, the Fukien Straits, and Korea. Both, particularly China, also maintained large formations for internal duties. Thus, even without sketching out scenarios, evaluation of the force levels available to both sides varies widely.

Geographic circumstances determined much of the specific location of Russian and Chinese forces and constrained Moscow and Peking to adopt different strategies. Because so much of the Russian population in Siberia and the Soviet Far East is necessarily concentrated along the Trans-Siberian railway, and because this vital transportation artery runs quite

250 *NYT*, 13 September, 2 November 1969; *Krasnaya Zvezda*, 21 January 1970, 4; *FEER*, 26 February 1972; *Economist*, 6 May 1972, 49; *NYT*, 10 September 1972; *CSM*, 14 September 1973; *Le Monde*, 5 September 1970; *Los Angeles Times*, 21 June 1974; *Economist*, 4 August 1973, 36; *Literaturnaya Gazeta*, 15 May 1974, 9 (FBIS *Daily Report*: USSR, 21 May 1974, C1); FBIS *Daily Report*: USSR, 7 August 1974, C1–2; *NYT*, 29 September 1974; *FEER*, 6 May 1974, 30–34; Harry Gelber, "Nuclear weapons and Chinese policy," 13–17; and Ralph Clough et al., *The United States, China, and arms control*, 140–43.

close to the Chinese border, Moscow had to deploy its forces and station its equipment close to the boundary, indeed, mostly south of the railway track. This location was naturally taken by Peking as a threat to Chinese territory to the immediate south – Sinkiang, Kansu, Inner Mongolia, and Heilungkiang. Since the Russians had nowhere to retreat north except tundra and ice (or, in the case of the Primorskaya, ocean water), Moscow had to adopt a strategy of preventing incursion by any Chinese force and turn down out of hand any Chinese suggestion for mutual withdrawal from the border. This was especially the case with Vladivostok and Khabarovsk, the latter being directly across the river from land claimed by China.

Chinese forces dared not approach the border too closely, because they would risk being destroyed or being surrounded in the Sinkiang, Kansu, and Inner Mongolian deserts. Moreover, the Chinese population lives quite a bit to the south in almost all cases. Those who do live near the Soviet border are minority peoples whose cousins are Soviet citizens and who, in the case of the Sinkiang Kazakhs, have attempted to reunite with their kinfolk. Chinese strategy and force locations were as follows: The main force had to remain back from the border to defend important cities (such as Peking itself) and facilities (such as the Lop Nor/Shuang Ch'eng-tze nuclear and missile sites); the minority peoples had to be watched and overcome by an influx of Han settlers who would at the same time act as a paramilitary barrier to advancing Soviet forces and spread themselves out, through agricultural colonization, to form a wall against the invader; and in case of invasion, the army and the people, mostly peasants in communes, would coalesce to present the Russians with a combination of conventional defense and guerrilla war tactics – "people's war." As the colonization effort proceeded and as the military felt stronger, the army would advance ever closer to the Soviet border. Meanwhile, aggressive patrolling and surveillance by border divisions would presumably prevent, forestall, or give warning of Soviet attack.

Central to both Soviet and Chinese strategies was their possession of sizable numbers of nuclear weapons. Moscow possessed enough nuclear weapons to punish China severely for any territorial transgression. This constituted only a background factor until the 1969 clashes, however, and even then their use was hardly a viable strategy except in the most severe circumstances. It was scarcely imaginable, despite talk of preemptive strikes at Chinese nuclear production and test facilities and at rocket, nuclear storage, and airbase sites.[251] But once sizable Soviet ground forces

---

251 Kissinger, *White House years*, 183 and passim.

began to be deployed, the entire Chinese position, strategic and tactical, was threatened, because tactical nuclear weapons are integral to Soviet divisions and because Soviet troops are trained to fight on nuclearized battlefields. It was now possible for a Soviet preemptive attack to destroy nearly all Chinese nuclear and missile facilities, airbases, seabases, and ground formations and then to occupy significant portions of the Chinese land mass, including the capital region itself. Hundreds of millions would be killed, including millions in neighboring countries, and this, together with the resultant weakened Soviet strategic position vis-à-vis the United States and the certainty of an alliance against the Soviet Union of all other states, made such a scenario quite unlikely. Nonetheless, it was plausible enough to the Chinese for them to take its likelihood seriously and to adjust their military and diplomatic posture accordingly.

Other scenarios also had to be faced by Peking. The most serious was the prospect of Soviet interference in the post-Mao succession struggle, supporting militarily one or another faction in order to help emplace a pro-Soviet government. Failing this, there was the possibility that, in a period of Chinese weakness during a succession struggle, Soviet forces might move into such critical border regions as Sinkiang or Heilungkiang. While the Soviet side undoubtedly viewed these possibilities with incredulity and was quick to disclaim any offensive intentions, the Chinese, combining an evaluation of actual Soviet military capabilities with the legacy of their own heavy criticism of Soviet ideological policies, could only plan for the worst. It was therefore the nuclear potential of a strong Soviet military force adjacent to the Chinese border that drove the Chinese to reinforce their own border defenses, to devote, in the early 1970s, increasing portions of their domestic product to conventional hardware production and non-ICBM ballistic missiles, to take PLA units out of politicoeconomic administration and relocate them closer to the Soviet border, and to interrupt Red Guard revolutionary activities and assign many of them to Production and Construction Corps units next to the boundary.

By 1975, the Chinese effort had gone some small distance toward redressing the imbalance. An infantry division had been converted to an armored unit, demonstrating at least that Peking now had the productive capability for such changes. By possessing a second-strike nuclear retaliatory potential of sufficient size to deter Soviet preemptive attack and to threaten major cities in European Russia, including Moscow itself, China advanced from minimal deterrence to a strategy based on increasingly hardened and dispersed missiles targeted against the Soviet homeland.

Changes in Soviet and Chinese force structures and dispositions are

TABLE I

Soviet and Chinese force levels, 1969–1976[a]

Year	Total Force	Total Army[b]	Total Divisions	Infantry	Mechanized	Airborne	Border Troops
			Soviet Union				
1969–70	3.30	2.00	147	90	50	7	250
1970–71	3.30	2.00	157	100	50	7	230
1971–72	3.38	2.00	160	102	51	7	300
1972–73	3.38	2.00	164	106	51	7	300
1973–74	3.42	2.05	164	107	50	7	300
1974–75	3.52	2.30	167	110	50	7	300
1975–76	3.58	2.32	166	110	49	7	300
Change	+0.28	+0.32	+19	+20	−1	+0	+0
			China				
1969–70	2.82	2.50	118[c]	108	8	2	300
1970–71	2.78	2.45	118	108	8	2	300
1971–72	2.88	2.55	120	110	8	2	300
1972–73	2.88	2.50	130	120	8	2	300
1973–74	2.90	2.50	130	120	8	2	300
1974–75	3.00	2.50	136	119	11	6	300
1975–76	3.25	2.80	142	125	11	6	300
Change	+0.43	+0.30	+24	+17	+3	+4	+0

[a] Total forces and total army in millions. Border troops in thousands.
[b] Includes air defense forces.
[c] Includes main forces divisions only, not local forces divisions.
Source: The Military Balance (London: International Institute for Strategic Studies [IISS], yearly), and author's conversations with American, Chinese, and Soviet officials, 1974–84.

detailed in Tables 1 and 2.[252] In Table 1, changes in the total amounts and composition of the ground forces of the two countries are shown. For China, there was a larger increase in the number of troops over the period 1969–75, about 300,000. The number of ground divisions grew from 118 to 142, an increase of 24, most of the gain before 1975 coming almost solely from transferring soldiers from Cultural Revolution–related administrative duties to line military units. Such a transfer, of approximately 200,000 troops, is a measure of the degree to which the PLA had become involved in nonmilitary affairs in China during the Cultural Revolution, and the timing of the transfer corresponds closely with the disappearance of soldiers from factories, offices, and political bodies observed by travelers to China during the period.

Changes in force structures and dispositions for the Soviet Union are also revealing. There are striking similarities between changes in Soviet

252 These are derived from *The Military Balance*, 1968–69 through 1974–75 (annual) and *Strategic Survey*, 1969 through 1975 (annual), both published by the International Institute for Strategic Studies, London.

and Chinese force levels, 1969–75. As with China, the total size of the military increased only marginally, from about 3.3 million to a reported 3,575 million men, an increase of about 275,000. The Red Army reportedly added about 320,000 troops, however, and the number of motorized rifle divisions increased by 20, from 90 to 110. All of these units went to deter the Chinese threats. The number of armored and airborne units changed hardly at all, again a pattern quite similar to that of China (the relevant difference being, of course, the much larger number of such Soviet units, reflecting the greater Soviet industrial base). Soviet border troops increased by approximately 60,000, and probably all of these were set to patrolling the border with China. But their total number was approximately that of China, around 300,000 men. In general, then, the Soviet Union and China increased their total manpower levels by nearly equivalent amounts. Given the magnitude of the threat that each perceived in the other, it is somewhat surprising that each raised its force levels by comparatively modest amounts. Perhaps this indicates the defensive nature of both sides' strategies. The approximate equality in the increase in force levels is evidence that both Moscow and Peking were aware that a very large increase by one side would engender a proportional increase by the other, thus precipitating an arms race costly to both.

With some exceptions, these conclusions are supported by the location of both sides' units near the border. Table 2 shows the time-differentiated changes in postings of division-size units in the relevant districts in the Soviet Union and China. Historically, China had more units in her border regions – Peking, Manchuria, Inner Mongolia, Lanchow, and Sinkiang – than the Soviet Union maintained in the Soviet Far East and the relevant areas of southern USSR, for example, Turkestan. Up to 1968, there were 47 ground divisions in these regions of China as opposed to perhaps 22 such units in the Soviet Union (15 in the Soviet Far East and possibly 7 of the 22 units in southern USSR). Table 2 shows clearly the rapidity of the Soviet buildup in the early 1970s, during which period the Chinese made only marginal additions to their own formations. By the end of 1973, the initial Soviet buildup of numbers of units was largely complete. Additions thereafter consisted mostly of logistical support units, equipment arrivals, and existing combat units being brought to higher degrees of readiness. Chinese additions began only at that point, going from 47 to 70 divisions within an eighteen-month period and to 78 divisions by mid-1975. The reason for this tardiness was to be found in Chinese domestic politics and Peking's relations with Washington: Only in late 1971 was the Lin Piao affair resolved, allowing Mao and his group

TABLE 2

Soviet and Chinese force dispositions, 1969–1976 (divisions)

Soviet Union

Year	Eastern Europe	European USSR	Central USSR	South USSR	Soviet Far East (including Trans-Baikal)
1968–69					22
1969–70	32	60	8	19	28 (2 in Mongolia)
1970–71	31	60	8	21	37 (3 in Mongolia)
1971–72	31	60	8	21	40 (2 in Mongolia)
1972–73	31	60	8	21	44 (2 in Mongolia)
1973–74	31	60	5	23	45 (2 in Mongolia)
1974–75	31	63	5	23	45 (2 in Mongolia)
1975–76	31	63	6	23	43 (2 in Mongolia)
Change	−1	+3	−2	+4	21

China

						Sino-Soviet border			
Year	Fukien	Canton/ Wuhan	Hainan	Southwest	Tibet	Peking, Northeast, Inner Mongolia	Lanchow	Sinkiang	Total Sino-Soviet border
1969–70	28	25	3	12	3	32	11	4	47
1970–71	28	25	3	12	3	32	11	4	47
1971–72	28	25	3	12	3	33	11	5[a]	49
1972–73	25	17	3	12	8[a]	40	15	10[a]	65
1973–74	20	17	3	12	8[a]	45	15	10[a]	70
1974–75	25	17	3	12	6[a]	50	15	8[a]	73
1975–76	25	18	3	12	6	55	15	8	78
Change	−3	−7	0	0	+5	+23	+4	+4	+31

[a] The IISS *Military Balance* for these years combines the divisional location listings for the Tibet and Sinkiang Military Regions. We assume the ratio is the same during previous years, i.e., 3 Tibet and 4 Sinkiang.

TABLE 3

Soviet and Chinese nuclear delivery vehicles, 1969–1976

Year	ICBM	MRBM/IRBM	SLBM	Soviet Union Tu-20, Tu-95, Mya-4	Tu-16	Tu-22	SSM[a]	Total[b]
1969–70	1050	700	159	150	600	150	900	3709
1970–71	1300	700	280	140	550	150	900	4020
1971–72	1510	700	440	140	500	200	900	4390
1972–73	1530	600	560	140	500	200	900	4430
1973–74	1527	600	628	140	500	200	900	4495
1974–75	1575	600	720	140	500	200	900	4635
1975–76	1618	600	784	135	475	170	1000	4782
Change	+ 568	− 100	+ 625	− 15	− 125	+ 20	+ 100	+ 1073

Year	ICBM	MRBM	IRBM	China SLBM	Il-28	Tu-16	SSM	Total
1969–70	—	—	—	—	150	—	—	150
1970–71	—	—	—	—	150	10–20	—	120–60
1971–72	—	c.20	—	—	150	c.30	—	200
1972–73	—	20–30	15–20	—	200	c.100	—	335–50
1973–74	—	c.50	15–20	—	200	c.100	—	365–70
1974–75	—	c.50	20–30	—	200	c.100	—	370–80
1975–76	2	c.50	20–30	—	300	c.60	—	432–42
Change	+ 2	+ 50	+ 30	—	+ 150	+ 60	—	+ 282–92

Note: Calculating China's totals at 20% of Soviet totals for 1975 would give the following figures: ICBM, 329; MRBM/IRBM, 125; SLBM, 175; Mya-4, 27; Tu-16, 95; Tu-22, 34; SSM, 200; total, 985.
[a] SSM = surface-to-surface missiles: the IISS figure. These are integral to ground units. Tactical nuclear warheads, other than SSMs, are not listed as there is no accurate estimate, aside from the IISS figure of 3,500 for 1970–71, which would include the 900 SSMs.
[b] Totals do not include any Soviet fighter-bomber aircraft, such as MiG-17s, -19s, -21s, -23s, etc., most of which are nuclear-capable. It is assumed that all these aircraft, like comparable Chinese planes, are devoted to interceptor duty or non-nuclear tactical air support.

to move units and change commanders,[253] and only after the Nixon visit in early 1972 did China feel secure enough to withdraw significant forces from the Fukien front opposite Taiwan. After this period of intensive activity, the Chinese moved only 8 additional ground units into the border area during the next two years. In the interim, the Chinese attempted to fill the gap by building up the Production and Construction Corps, training more militia, and stressing civil defense.

If these numerical totals and force locations reveal a rough equality, by 1975, of Soviet and Chinese forces ranged along or near the border, the same was not true of force structures and firepower. Table 3 displays data

253 For details, see Thomas W. Robinson, "China in 1972: socio-economic progress amidst political uncertainty," and Robinson, "China in 1973," *Asian Survey*, January 1973 and January 1974, respectively, and the sources cited therein.

as to strategic and tactical nuclear weapons available to Soviet and Chinese units. A tremendous disparity favored the Soviet Union in numbers of nuclear-capable delivery vehicles and, therefore, of nuclear warheads. Although the Soviet Union had to retain a large proportion of these for the deterrent relationship with the United States and waging war against America and her allies in Europe and elsewhere, the residue available for potential use against China was still enormous and represented (presuming that on average each such vehicle was capable of delivering more than one nuclear warhead) a destructive potential of horrendous proportions. China by 1975 possessed about 430 nuclear delivery vehicles (not counting MiG-19s, MiG-21s, and F-9s, which presumably were configured for interceptor, reconnaissance, and tactical support functions), while the Soviet Union disposed of some 4,735 vehicles (again, not counting its vast supply of jet fighter aircraft, many of which, however, were nuclear-capable). Were only 20 percent of the Soviet force to have been earmarked for the Chinese theater, about 950 craft would have been available. The Soviet Union also possessed a strong and dispersed air defense system that could have intercepted and destroyed a large percentage, if not all, of Chinese Il-28s and Tu-16s. Finally, each Soviet ground unit had nuclear capacity, in the form of ground-to-ground missiles or small unit-carried tactical nuclear weapons. Using the 1970 IISS figure of 3,500 such warheads, and presuming they were available for use against China roughly in proportion to the percentage of the Red Army deployed against China (in 1975, 43/166 or about 26%), this would mean another 880 warheads. This is to say nothing of the absolute superiority Moscow enjoyed in conventional firepower, artillery, armor, and battlefield mobility. Thus, as of 1975, the overall military balance weighed heavily in favour of the Soviet Union.

PART II

THE CULTURAL REVOLUTION: THE STRUGGLE FOR THE SUCCESSION, 1969–1982

CHAPTER 4

THE SUCCESSION TO MAO AND THE END OF MAOISM

INTRODUCTION

The Great Proletarian Cultural Revolution was an attempt to shape the future of China. Its method was to change the nature of the Chinese people. It was to be a "great revolution that touches people to their very souls."[1] The masses were to liberate themselves by class struggle against the main target, "those within the Party who are in authority and are taking the capitalist road."[2] These so-called Soviet-style revisionists were alleged to be seeking to corrupt the masses by using old ideas to restore capitalism. By transforming the ideological realm – education, literature, the arts – and embracing Mao Tse-tung Thought, the Chinese people were to inoculate themselves against poisonous contagion.

Mao's objective was a China that was pure though poor, more egalitarian and less privileged, more collectivist but less bureaucratic, a society in which all worked as one, not so much because they were led by the Communist Party as because an inner compass – Mao Tse-tung Thought – pointed them toward the magnetic pole of true communism.

The goal of the Cultural Revolution was to provide the right answer to the question, After Mao, what? But success would depend on the answer to an earlier question, After Mao, who? If alleged capitalist-roaders like head of state Liu Shao-ch'i survived the Chairman in positions of power, then China would "change its color." China must not only be guided by the correct line and policies, but had to "train and bring up millions of successors who will carry on the cause of proletarian revolution."[3] In the storm of the Cultural Revolution, new leaders were to emerge, steeled in

The author is grateful to Thomas Bernstein, John Fairbank, Merle Goldman, Kenneth Lieberthal, and Michael Schoenhals for comments and suggestions on drafts of this chapter.

1 "Decision of the Central Committee of the Chinese Communist Party concerning the Great Proletarian Cultural Revolution," URI, *CCP documents of the Great Proletarian Cultural Revolution, 1966–1967*, 42.
2 Ibid., 45, 46.
3 "On Khrushchev's phoney communism and its historical lessons for the world," *The polemic on the general line of the international communist movement*, 477. This is the last and most important of the nine polemics issued by the CCP against the "revisionism" of the CPSU in 1963–64. These documents are crucial for understanding Mao's concerns on the eve of the Cultural Revolution.

struggle, "proletarian" in outlook, in whose hands the Maoist brand of socialism would one day burn fiercely.

In the interim, Mao had to cleanse the top ranks of the CCP and install a new successor whom he could trust implicitly to preserve his vision and hand it down. Hence the internecine struggle and purges described in Chapter 2, "The Chinese state in crisis." Mao's victory in that battle was heralded at the CCP's Ninth Congress in the spring of 1969, which rubber-stamped his personal choice as heir, Defense Minister Lin Piao. But this produced a new conundrum, After Mao, which? Was it the demoralized and decimated Party that would run China, or the army, a body with equally revolutionary credentials, which had emerged after three years of Cultural Revolution as the master of the country? This was an institutional issue of supreme importance, with momentous implications for hundreds of millions of Chinese. But for the most part it was fought out between small coteries of leaders, plotting in their residences, clashing at central meetings, with the liquidation of one clique or the other finally emerging as the only viable solution.

THE MILITARIZATION OF CHINESE POLITICS

The CCP's Ninth Congress in April 1969 was a triumph for Lin Piao individually and for the PLA institutionally. Defense Minister Lin's position as second only to Mao, first achieved at the Eleventh Plenum of the Central Committee (CC) in August 1966, was confirmed. The new Party constitution formally designated him Mao's successor, the first time a comrade-in-arms of the Chairman had achieved that distinction.[4] Lin's military colleagues, as Chapter 2 pointed out, were very prominent at the congress; PLA representation on the Central Committee rose from

---

4 Indeed, the only time any Communist Party has ever taken such a step. Lin Piao's new status was attested to by the extravagant praise lavished on him by Chou En-lai in his speech to the CCP's Ninth Congress; Chou's address is included in a sixteen-page unpublished collection of speeches to the Congress, and has been translated and annotated for publication by Michael Schoenhals.

A Party historian has stated that when the presidium for the Ninth Congress was being appointed, Mao suggested that Lin should chair it and that he, Mao, should be vice-chairman, only to be interrupted by a loud shout of "Long live Chairman Mao" from Lin Piao.

The same historian has suggested that Mao indicated his preference for Lin Piao as his successor as early as 1956. It seems that when votes were cast for Party Chairman at the first plenum after the CCP's Eighth Congress in September that year, Mao was one vote short of unanimous approval. It was established that Mao had not voted for himself, nor for his number two, Liu Shao-ch'i, but for Lin Piao! See T'an Tsung-chi, "Lin Piao fan-ko-ming chi-t'uan ti chueh-ch'i chi-ch'i fu-mieh" (The sudden rise of the Lin Piao counterrevolutionary clique and its destruction), in *Chiao-hsueh ts'an-k'ao: ch'üan-kuo tang-hsiao hsi-t'ung Chung-kung tang-shih hsueh-shu t'ao-lun-hui, hsia* (Reference for teaching and study: national Party school system's academic conference on CCP history, vol. 2) (hereafter *Chiao-hsueh ts'an-k'ao, hsia*), 40, 42. The author is grateful to Michael Schoenhals for sharing both these items with him.

19 percent to 45 percent.[5] At the First Plenum of the new Central Committee after the Congress, the number of active-service soldiers appointed to the Politburo rose dramatically.[6]

The rise of Lin Piao and the military was in some ways a logical culmination of the Chinese revolution, and indeed conformed to a pattern familiar from Chinese history. Whenever political control broke down, often under the impact of economic disaster, uprisings took place. Force was met with force, and a process of militarization of the upper levels of the polity took place. Eventually some more able and ambitious rebel leader, sometimes a peasant, more often an aristocrat, would seize the chance to overthrow the dynasty by force, eliminating other aspirant rebel chiefs in the process. The generals who had backed the founding emperor in his struggle for power would assume powerful positions under the new dynasty.[7]

This process of replacement of one dynasty by another normally took many decades, a period of warfare disguised by the neat traditional assignment of a single year as the moment of passage of the mandate of heaven. This is particularly evident in the long-drawn-out decline and fall of the Ch'ing dynasty and the subsequent struggle for power between aspirant successor regimes, culminating in the CCP victory in 1949.

During the decades that followed the defeat of the Ch'ing by the British in the first Opium War (1839–42), the Manchus were beset by both foreign invaders and domestic rebels. The dynasty's initial response was to rearm on traditional lines, but this proved quite ineffective. Regional loyalists had to set up their own forces to supplement hapless imperial armies.[8] Finally, the dynasty embarked upon defense modernization, with sufficient success to ensure that the creator of the new army, Yuan Shih-k'ai, emerged as both the power broker who arranged the abdication of the last emperor in 1912, and the power holder who dominated early republican politics.[9] The era of the general as political leader had begun.

5 See Chapter 2. In view of the participation of virtually every older member of the CCP leadership in armed struggle at some point in his career, the calculation of military representation on the CC is often a question of definition. The "Quarterly Chronicle" of the CQ (39, [July–Sept. 1969], 145) estimated it at about 40 percent, Ying-mao Kau (CLG [Fall–Winter 1972–73], 8) at 38 percent. Domes, on the other hand, has estimated PLA representation as 40.3 percent at the Eighth Congress and 50 percent at the Ninth; see Jürgen Domes, The internal politics of China, 1949–1972, 210.

6 See Table 4.

7 For the Ch'in–Han transition, see CHOC, 1.110–27; for the Sui–T'ang one, see CHOC, 3. 143–68; for the Yuan-Ming, see CHOC, 7.44–106.

8 See CHOC, 11, ch. 4, and Philip A. Kuhn, Rebellion and its enemies in late imperial China: militarization and social structure, 1796–1864.

9 See CHOC, 11.383–88, 529–34, and CHOC, 12, ch. 4.

TABLE 4

Politburo named after CCP's Ninth Congress, April 1969

(Leaders named to the Politburo after the two sessions of the Eighth Congress in 1956 and 1958 appear in ordinary type; those added at the CC's Eleventh Plenum in 1966 appear in caps; those added after the Ninth Congress are in boldface.)

Standing committee: ranked

Mao Tse-tung	Chairman
Lin Piao	Vice-chairman

Standing committee: unranked

Ch'en Po-ta	Chair, CRG[a]
Chou En-lai	Premier
K'ang Sheng	Adviser, CRG

Full members: unranked

Yeh Ch'ün	PLA CRG
YEH CHIEN-YING	Marshal
Liu Po-ch'eng	Marshal
Chiang Ch'ing	Vice-chair, CRG
Chu Te	Marshal
Hsu Shih-yu	Gen.; CO Nanking MR[a]; Chair, Kiangsu RevCom[a]
Ch'en Hsi-lien	Gen.; CO Shenyang MR; Chair, Liaoning RevCom
Li Hsien-nien	Vice-premier
Li Tso-p'eng	Gen.; Navy Political Commissar
Wu Fa-hsien	Gen.; Air Force CO
Chang Ch'un-ch'iao	Vice-chair, CRG; Chair, Shanghai RevCom
Ch'iu Hui-tso	Gen.; Head, PLA Logistics
Yao Wen-yuan	Member, CRG; Vice-chair, Shanghai RevCom
Huang Yung-sheng	Gen.; PLA chief of staff
Tung Pi-wu	Vice–head of state
HSIEH FU-CHIH	Min. Public Security; Chair, Peking RevCom

Alternates: unranked

Chi Teng-k'uei	Vice-chair, Honan RevCom
LI HSUEH-FENG	Chair, Hopei RevCom
Li Te-sheng	Gen.; Chair, Anhwei RevCom
Wang Tung-hsing	CO Central Bodyguard

Actual ranking[b]

Mao Tse-tung
Lin Piao
Chou En-lai
Ch'en Po-ta
K'ang Sheng
Chiang Ch'ing
Chang Ch'un-ch'iao
Yao Wen-yuan

Note: (1) Of 23 members of pre-GPCR Politburo, 14 dropped. (2) Of 16 new members since GPCR started, 10 = military. (3) Of 25 members of new Politburo, 12 = military; of these, 10 were on active service. This compares with 7 out of 26 in 1956–58 Politburo, of whom only 2 were on active service. 8th CC: civil = 76.3%, PLA = 23.7%; 9th CC: civil = 52.5%, PLA =47.5%. (4) 3 men with provincial jobs in pre-GPCR Politburo, 8 in this one. Provincials in 8th CC = 37%; 9th CC = 58.6%.

[a] CRG = Cultural Revolution Group; MR = Military Region; RevCom = Revolutionary Committee.
[b] Derived from picture in *Chung-kuo kung-ch'an-tang ti-chiu-tz'u ch'üan-kuo tai-piao ta-hui (hua-ts'e)* (Ninth Congress of the Chinese Communist Party [picture volume]).

After the collapse of Yuan Shih-k'ai's ill-judged attempt to set up a new dynasty and the death of the would-be emperor himself shortly thereafter, China entered upon the warlord era (1916–28), during which none of Yuan's erstwhile subordinates and rivals proved sufficiently powerful to take over his role.[10] But as control of China's nominal government in Peking passed from one warlord to another, it became clear to the revolutionaries who had conspired to overthrow the Ch'ing dynasty and then been thrust aside by Yuan, that without military power of their own they would remain helpless or beholden to the unreliable favors of a warlord. It was then that Sun Yat-sen turned to Moscow, and in 1924 his military aide Chiang Kai-shek set up the Whampoa Military Academy with Soviet advisers, in order to train officers for a revolutionary army loyal to the Kuomintang.[11]

Had Sun lived longer, perhaps the reshaped KMT would have emerged as a powerful political organization able to subordinate its army to its purposes. But his death in 1925 unleashed a struggle for the succession, which was soon won by Chiang Kai-shek because of his military power base. Although the KMT played an important role when Chiang set up the Nationalist government in 1928, the army remained the ultimate source of power within his regime.[12]

On Moscow's orders, the newborn Chinese Communist Party (CCP) had collaborated with the KMT, and Communist officers and cadres served in the Northern Expedition that enabled Chiang to triumph over the warlords. But when Chiang turned on the CCP in 1927, it became clear to Mao Tse-tung, as it had become clear to Sun before him, that without its own military force, there was no future for a political movement in China. Political power grew out of the barrel of a gun.[13] On Ching-kang-shan and in the Kiangsi Soviet, he and his colleagues created the forces and developed the strategy which brought victory in the civil war with the KMT two decades later.[14]

There was a fundamental difference between what the CCP later called the People's Liberation Army (PLA) and Chiang Kai-shek's forces. Mao insisted that the Party should command the gun and that the gun must never be allowed to command the Party.[15] The PLA was not to be just another warlord army, or even a military-dominated party-army amalgam on the KMT model, but a revolutionary force led by the CCP in the service of a cause delineated by it.

But it was never quite that simple. Theoretical principles of Party con-

10 See *CHOC*, 12, ch. 6.   11 See *CHOC*, 12.540.
12 See Lloyd E. Eastman, *The abortive revolution: China under Nationalist rule, 1927–1937*.
13 Mao, *SW*, 2.224.   14 See *CHOC*, 13, ch. 4.   15 Mao, *SW*, 2.224.

trol may be hard to enforce in the heat of battle when life or death rests on the decision of the military commander.[16] Military subordination may be impolitic to insist on if, like Mao, you rely on the support of the generals for your rise to power.[17] Mao's personal political power did indeed grow out of the barrel of the gun; his way of ensuring political control of the army was to retain his chairmanship of the CC's Military Affairs Commission (MAC) from 1935 until his death more than four decades later.

Moreover, when political triumph has been engineered by generals can they be denied the fruits of power? Not with impunity. When Kao Kang made his bid to be recognized as Mao's successor in the mid-1950s, he sought and found support from generals who, he argued, had been short-changed in the post-Liberation distribution of posts.[18] Although Kao Kang lost out, the Party leadership got the message. Lin Piao, one of the military men who seems to have been attracted by Kao's arguments, was quickly raised to the Politburo, and after the CCP's Eighth Congress in 1956, seven of the PLA's ten marshals emerged as members of that body.[19]

The importance of the military within the polity was further demonstrated at the Lushan Conference in 1959, when then defense minister P'eng Te-huai implicitly challenged Mao's handling of the Great Leap Forward. P'eng's willingness to stick his neck out can be attributed to a number of factors; but its significance is that only the current head of the military establishment had the institutional base from which to initiate an attack that impugned the Chairman's competence and thus his authority. The extent to which Mao felt threatened and outraged by an assault from within what he had always considered his stronghold can be gauged from the bitterness of his rebuttal; only by portraying the issue as

16 During the Anti-Japanese War, P'eng Te-huai launched the Hundred Regiments campaign in clear defiance of the principles laid down by Mao on avoiding major offensives that carried no certainty of victory. In his memoirs, P'eng admitted mistakes with respect to this campaign, including launching the offensive early without consulting the CC's Military Affairs Commission, but cited a telegram from Mao as indicative of the Chairman's approval. In view of the shrill attacks made on P'eng over this issue during the Cultural Revolution after the passage of a quarter of a century, it seems possible that this campaign may have been launched against Mao's wishes or at least against his better judgment, and that his approval had been forthcoming only to preserve a facade of unity. For Mao's views on strategy in the Anti-Japanese War, see Mao, *SW*, 2.180–83, 227–32; for P'eng Te-huai's version, see his *Memoirs of a Chinese Marshal*, 434–47.

17 See Raymond F. Wylie, *The emergence of Maoism: Mao Tse-tung, Ch'en Po-ta and the search for Chinese theory, 1935–1945*, 68–71.

18 See *CHOC*, 14.97–103.

19 The founder of the Ming dynasty, Chu Yuan-chang, who came to power after long military campaigns, was careful to award noble titles to all his principal generals shortly after his proclamation as emperor; see *CHOC*, 7.105.

a choice between himself and the turbulent defense minister did he force the other marshals to accept P'eng's dismissal.[20]

Ironically, P'eng Te-huai's disgrace led to an increase in the PLA's status within the polity. P'eng's replacement as defense minister by Lin Piao, Mao's disciple from the early 1930s, gave the Chairman greater confidence in the military's loyalty to himself and his ideas. As Lin promoted the study of Mao Tse-tung Thought, and issued the first edition of the "little red book" of Mao quotations to the armed forces, the PLA was designated the exemplar, even to the CCP.[21]

Thus when Mao launched his assault on the Party leadership at the outset of the Cultural Revolution, he could be confident that the other major revolutionary institution would support him. Later, when the Red Guards found the overthrow of provincial leaders harder than expected, Mao was able to call on the PLA to support the left. When the triumphant Red Guards fell to internecine warfare, and many cities of China were the scenes of armed clashes, it was a general – Ch'en Tsai-tao in Wuhan in the summer of 1967 – who blew the whistle. Although Ch'en himself was disciplined, ultra-leftist cadres were also purged, and a year later Mao authorized the rustication of the Red Guards. The mass base of the Central Cultural Revolution Group was dissolved. The way was clear for the triumph of Lin Piao and his generals at the Ninth Congress.[22]

For Mao the issue must have seemed stark, even though among his colleagues he dismissed Soviet attacks on China's "military bureaucratic dictatorship" as not worth refuting.[23] All his life he had insisted on the primacy of the Party over the army; after his death, the prospect was that the army would dominate the Party. The CCP might go the way of the KMT. Could he accept this?

THE FALL OF LIN PIAO

The CCP's Ninth Congress should have signaled a return to some semblance of normalcy: Mao's "proletarian revolutionary line" reigned unchallenged, his enemies had been defeated, a new leadership was in place, civil strife had been suppressed. Mao had heralded a "great victory" as early as October 1968, and in his political report to the Con-

---

20 See *CHOC*, 14.311–22. The K'ang-hsi emperor was not so fortunate; he had to fight an eight-year-long civil war to subdue the dynasty's three most powerful generals before consolidating the Ch'ing regime in the late seventeenth century; Lawrence D. Kessler, *K'ang-hsi and the consolidation of Ch'ing rule, 1661–1684*, 74–90.
21 See *CHOC*, 14.335–42.   22 See Chapter 2.
23 At the First Plenum of the Ninth CC; see Wang Nien-i, *1948–1989 nien-ti Chung-kuo: Ta-tung-luan-ti nien-tai* (China from 1949 to 1989: decade of great upheaval), 395.

gress, Lin Piao proclaimed: "The victory of the Great Proletarian Cultural Revolution is very great indeed."[24] When discussing the future, Lin Piao talked of "continuing the revolution in the realm of the superstructure,"[25] that is, building the new society for which the Cultural Revolution had been launched. For the victors, if not for the victims when they were finally able to rewrite the histories, the Cultural Revolution was over. The year 1969 was meant to mark a new beginning after revolution, like the Liberation twenty years earlier.

But if this had been a "Congress of Victors," the calm it should have presaged was as short-lived as that after the CPSU's Seventeenth Congress in 1934 for which that appellation was coined. Insofar as the Cultural Revolution meant a struggle for power among the elite to determine who had the right to shape the future, it was far from over, and indeed was soon to take an even more dangerous turn. There were three arenas: the reconstruction of the Party; the rebuilding of the state structure; and foreign affairs. Underlying all three was the specter of Bonapartism conjured up by Lin Piao's rise to power.

The reconstruction of the Party

In the absence of any properly constituted lower-level Party committees, delegates to the Ninth Congress had supposedly been chosen either by "consultation" between revolutionary committees and local "rebel" groups,[26] or simply by directive from the higher levels.[27] Because the PLA dominated the revolutionary committees,[28] it was hardly surprising that the military were so much in evidence at the Congress. With the Congress resulting in many promotions for PLA officers, it was even less surprising that the process of provincial party construction reflected the prevailing power realities.

Mao had begun to call for the reconstruction of the Party as early as October 1967 with his "fifty character policy" statement, directing that party organs should be formed from advanced elements of the proletariat. At the new CC's First Plenum after the Ninth Congress, he repeated his call to revive the Party. But although the declared hope of the leadership was to rebuild from the bottom up, and in 1970 the CC publicized the

---

24 *CB*, 880 (9 May 1969), 37.   25 Ibid., 34.
26 These were organizations of blue-collar workers, the Red Guard groups having been disbanded.
27 Teaching and Research Office for CCP History of the [PLA] Political Academy, ed., *Chung-kuo kung-ch'an-tang liu-shih-nien ta-shih chien-chieh* (A summary of the principal events in the 60 years of the Chinese Communist Party), 559.
28 Of twenty-nine provincial revolutionary committees, twenty-one were headed by PLA officers; Domes, *The internal politics of China*, 205.

party construction experience of Peking University, Peking No. 27 Rolling Stock Plant, and the No. 17 State Cotton Mill in Shanghai as models,[29] Party branches proved difficult to set up.

By late 1969, the major effort had been transferred upward to the counties and municipalities, but even at this level progress was slow. In the year between November 1969 and November 1970, only 45 of the nation's 2,185 counties had set up Party committees. Presumably recognizing the futility of proceeding on these lines, the central leadership authorized the prior formation of provincial-level committees. The first was formed in Mao's home province, Hunan, in December 1970, with one Hua Kuo-feng as its first secretary, and by mid-August 1971 all twenty-nine provincial-level units were similarly endowed, with the PLA well in evidence. The military had supplied twenty-two of the twenty-nine first secretaries and 62 percent of the cadres running the provincial secretariats.[30]

According to post–Cultural Revolution accounts, Party rebuilding resulted in the induction of many disruptive "rebel" elements and the exclusion of old officials. Although a prime focus of the continuing "purify the class ranks" campaign launched in May 1968 had been to exclude ultra-leftist elements, allegedly the net was cast far wider, and the campaign used against blameless cadres.[31] This in itself probably displeased Mao, who appears to have wanted to reeducate, rehabilitate, and reemploy experienced cadres as part of an effort to restore stability and unity. But the more pressing issue was the clear failure of Lin Piao and the PLA to accept his injunctions to help rebuild a civilian Party that would reestablish its control over army and nation.[32] Well before the formation of the last provincial Party committees, it must have been obvious that the PLA would dominate them as it dominated the provincial revolutionary committees. Moreover, Lin Piao was giving evidence of wanting to dominate the state structure at the center as well as in the provinces.

Rebuilding the state structure

On 8 March 1970, Mao gave his opinions on rebuilding the state structure. He advocated convening the Fourth National People's Congress, at which a revised state constitution would be agreed upon. The consti-

29 Hao Meng-pi and Tuan Hao-jan, eds., *Chung-kuo kung-ch'an-tang liu-shih-nien, hsia* (Sixty years of the Chinese Communist Party, part 2), 610.
30 See Domes, *The internal politics of China*, 215.
31 Hao and Tuan, *Chung-kuo kung-ch'an-tang liu-shih-nien*, 608–11.
32 Philip Bridgham, "The fall of Lin Piao," *CQ*, 55 (July–September 1973), 429–30.

tution would abolish the position of head of state. The following day the Politburo endorsed Mao's opinion, and on 16 March formulated some principles regarding the NPC session and the constitution, which were submitted to the Chairman and endorsed by him. On 17 March, a central work conference met to flesh out what had been agreed on. But Lin Piao soon joined issue on the question of the office of head of state. On 11 April, he proposed in writing that Mao should resume the office of head of state, which he had ceded to the late Liu Shao-ch'i in 1959, otherwise "it would not be in accord with the psychology [*hsin-li chuang-t'ai*] of the people." The Chairman summarily rejected this suggestion, telling the Politburo on 12 April: "I cannot do this job again; this suggestion is inappropriate." At a Politburo conference toward the end of the month, Mao used a historical analogy from the period of the Three Kingdoms in the third century A.D. when stating for the third time that he would not take on the state chairmanship and that the post should be abolished.

Yet Lin Piao persisted. Two of his military allies in the Politburo were on the constitution-drafting group: Wu Fa-hsien, the air force head, and Li Tso-p'eng, the navy's chief commissar. In mid-May, Lin asked them to include a clause on the post of head of state, and despite a fourth disclaimer by Mao in mid-July that one should not create a post for the sake of a person, behind the scenes Lin Piao's wife Yeh Ch'ün kept promoting the idea with Lin's supporters. Yeh asked Wu Fa-hsien plaintively what Lin Piao would do if the state chairmanship were not reestablished, an indication of Lin's own interest in the post if Mao continued to decline it.[33]

Why would the Chairman's formally anointed successor in the Party press this issue in the teeth of Mao's opposition? Why would he want a ceremonial post with no more prestige than its occupant's status within the Party? Philip Bridgham has argued that Lin was dismayed that the new constitution would leave him junior in governmental status to Premier Chou En-lai, in whose cabinet he was a vice-premier and minister of defense, and at the implication that the Chairman was now contemplating a joint leadership of Lin and Chou to succeed him.[34] It can also be argued that Mao's tenure in the state chairmanship had conferred a certain aura on it, certainly a status senior to the premier's, and that Liu Shao-ch'i's tenure in the post before the Cultural Revolution had shown that it guaranteed considerable publicity, as well as exposure in the international arena.

33 Wang, *Ta-tung-luan-ti nien-tai*, 392–94; Hao and Tuan, *Chung-kuo kung-ch'an-tang liu-shih-nien*, 613.
34 Bridgham, "The fall of Lin Piao," 432–33.

The key to Lin Piao's behavior in this matter, however, is almost certainly a deep sense of insecurity, probably exacerbated by the relative isolation to which illness and temperament confined him.[35] He had emerged
as Mao's principal colleague as early as 1966, but he still required the
reassurance never granted to Liu Shao-ch'i of being named successor in
the Party constitution. Now he sought the further reassurance of being
named head of state. Personal psychology aside, this insecurity probably
stemmed in part from an uneasy consciousness that the manner in which
he had risen to power was illegitimate, and bitterly resented by survivors
of the Cultural Revolution among his generation of leaders. Even this
would have mattered little, had he had total confidence in Mao's backing.
He was surely unnerved by Mao's suggestion to him that since he (Lin)
was also old, he, too, should have a successor, and that Chang Ch'un-
ch'iao would be a good candidate;[36] and as the documents circulated after
Lin's fall indicate, he seems to have viewed Mao as someone always ready
to knife his closest associates in the back:

Today he uses sweet words and honeyed talk to those whom he entices, and
tomorrow puts them to death for fabricated crimes.... Looking back at the history of the past few decades, [do you see] anyone whom he had supported
initially who has not finally been handed a political death sentence? ... His former
secretaries have either committed suicide or been arrested. His few close
comrades-in-arms or trusted aides have also been sent to prison by him.[37]

Why, then, did Lin Piao defy Mao so blatantly? Possibly he felt that the
Chairman might relent; possibly he wanted to use the issue as a litmus test
of Mao's attitude toward himself. Or possibly, with his military colleagues grouped around him, he now felt strong enough to force Mao to
concede; after all, Mao had been dependent upon the PLA for the success
of the Red Guards, and later the generals' anxieties had helped compel
Mao to suppress them. Could not the dominant role of generals within
the Politburo be used to promote the defense minister's interests?

35 See Chang Yun-sheng, *Mao-chia-wan chi-shih* (An on-the-spot report on Mao-chia-wan), passim.
    Chang was one of Lin Piao's secretaries from 19 August 1966 until 17 November 1970. Lin appar-
    ently feared light, wind, water, and cold, and hated to sweat. He did not take baths and did not eat
    fruit. He insisted that his accommodation should be kept at a constant 21 degrees C. (about 70
    degrees F.), with no greater variation than half a degree. (Yeh Ch'ün liked her room temperature
    to be 18 degrees C.!) But probably the most debilitating aspect of Lin's condition, as far as carrying
    out his duties was concerned, was his inability or refusal to read documents, with the result that
    his secretaries had to select and summarize from the mass of paper that reached his office as much
    as they could read to him in thirty minutes. Ibid., 8–12; Wang Nien-i, *Ta-tung-luan-ti nien-tai*,
    373–75, 377.
36 Ibid., 387–88.
37 Michael Y. M. Kau, *The Lin Piao affair: power politics and military coup*, 87. These words were
    probably written by Lin Piao's son, but they clearly reflect the knowledge and experience of the
    older man.

Moreover, Lin Piao had another important ally in his quest for status: Ch'en Po-ta, Mao's longtime ideological adviser and onetime political secretary.[38] Ch'en had headed the Central Cultural Revolution Group from its creation in the spring of 1966, a confirmation of his closeness to the Chairman, and he soon rose to the fourth position in the leadership under Mao, Lin, and Chou En-lai, a ranking confirmed by pictures taken at the Ninth Congress. Yet, a year later, Ch'en, after years of loyal service to Mao, had chosen to support Lin Piao in defiance of the Chairman's repeatedly stated views.

One explanation is that the dissolution of the Cultural Revolution Group in late 1969 had deprived Ch'en of a starring role in the post–Ninth Congress constellation, and that he may have felt threatened by the campaign against ultra-leftism.[39] Equally, the crumbling of the original coalition that backed Mao at the outset of the Cultural Revolution under the impact of events from 1966–69 may have left Ch'en feeling isolated. The Shanghai leftists Chang Ch'un-ch'iao and Yao Wen-yuan were linked through Chiang Ch'ing (Madame Mao) to the Chairman; indeed, the youthful Yao seemed to have replaced Ch'en Po-ta as the favored bearer of Mao's message. Yet, at the outset of the Cultural Revolution, Chang, Yao, and even Chiang Ch'ing had been Ch'en's subordinates in the Cultural Revolution Group. In preparation for the Ninth Congress, Ch'en had originally been chosen as the principal drafter of Lin Piao's political report, with Chang and Yao as his aides; but when Ch'en proved unable to produce a satisfactory draft in time, Chang and Yao took over the task, under the supervision of K'ang Sheng. K'ang, Mao's longtime aide in the internal security field, also had close ties to his fellow provincial Chiang Ch'ing, and Ch'en appears to have been jealous of K'ang's connections.[40]

Lin Piao, on the other hand, had consolidated his position on a PLA base and no longer seemed to need the support of the leftists. Indeed, Lin and his followers and Chiang Ch'ing and hers were increasingly divided into rival camps; and whereas Lin may have had long-term worries about the security of his role, he seems to have had excessive confidence that in the short run he could dominate Chiang's clique. Perhaps Ch'en Po-ta agreed and, looking to the future, thought his best prospect was to offer

38 For Mao's indebtedness to Ch'en Po-ta, see Wylie, *The emergence of Maoism*, passim.
39 Bridgham, "The fall of Lin Piao," 432.
40 See Chung K'an, *K'ang Sheng p'ing-chuan* (A critical biography of K'ang Sheng), 15–16,146–47. For Ch'en Po-ta's jealousy of K'ang Sheng, see Chang, *Mao-chia-wan chi-shih*, 190–92; for Ch'en's problems with the report for the Ninth Congress, see ibid., 210–11, and Wang, *Ta-tung-luan-ti nien-tai*, 387. According to the latter source, Ch'en Po-ta, miffed, continued working on his own draft, but it was the Chang–Yao one that Mao, after several revisions, eventually approved. Lin Piao was apparently only interested in Mao's input and the final version of the report.

to perform for Lin Piao the same role he had previously performed for Mao.[41] The decision was to prove disastrous for Ch'en's career.

The struggle over the state chairmanship came to a head at the Ninth CC's Second Plenum, held at the ill-starred Lushan mountain resort from 23 August to 6 September 1970. Once again, Mao was locked in struggle with a defense minister, although this time he was not sure enough of his own strength or the minister's discipline to risk a direct confrontation at this stage.

On the eve of the plenum, 22 August, the Politburo Standing Committee, consisting of Mao, Lin Piao, Chou En-lai, Ch'en Po-ta, and K'ang Sheng, met to agree on the main themes of the plenum. Mao pointedly stressed the need for unity and the avoidance of factionalism, his habitual device when seeking to undercut opposition.[42] But Lin Piao and Ch'en Po-ta again proposed the retention of the state chairmanship and urged to Mao to assume it. Mao refused once more, but pointedly added that whoever wanted to take on the job should do so.[43]

The plenum was opened the next day by Chou En-lai, who listed the agenda as the revision of the state constitution, the national economic plan, and war preparedness. Unexpectedly, and without clearing his remarks with Mao in advance,[44] Lin Piao intervened to express his conviction that it was extremely important for the new constitution to express Mao's role as the great leader, head of state (*kuo-chia yuan-shou*), and supreme commander, as well as the guiding role of Mao Tse-tung Thought as the national ideology. Implicitly, he was threatening the opponents of retaining the state chairmanship with accusations of being anti-Mao.[45]

As in the past, Lin was stressing Mao's transcendent genius and role in order to display his own devotion and thus achieve his own ends, a strategy which Mao appears to have been aware of and uncomfortable with even from the beginning of the Cultural Revolution.[46] But for most of the

41 At his trial in the winter of 1980–81, Ch'en Po-ta said only that "after he learned of the power struggle between Lin Biao and Jiang Qing, he sympathized with Lin Biao"; see *A great trial in Chinese history*, 116. For the development of rival camps and the confidence of Lin's side, see Chang, *Mao-chia-wan chi-shih*, 382–89, and Wang, *Ta-tung-luan-ti nien-tai*, 382–88.
42 Cf. Mao's behavior at the 1959 Lushan Conference; see Roderick MacFarquhar, *The origins of the Cultural Revolution*, 2.220.
43 Hao and Tuan, *Chung-kuo kung-ch'an-tang liu-shih-nien*, 613–14.
44 Kao Kao and Yen Chia-ch'i, *"Wen-hua ta-ko-ming" shih-nien shih, 1966–1976* (A history of the ten years of the "Great Cultural Revolution," 1966–1976), 348.
45 Ibid., 614.
46 See Mao's letter of 8 July 1966 to Chiang Ch'ing in *CLG*, 6.2 (Summer 1973), 96–99. Later that year, in a speech to the Military Academy devoted to the theme of raising the study of Mao's writings to a new stage, Lin Piao praised the Chairman as the "greatest talent of the present era" and urged everyone studying Marxism-Leninism to devote 99 percent of their effort to his works; see *Issues & Studies*, 8.6 (March 1972), 75–79.

255 CC members present who were not in the know, Lin Piao was giving the opening, keynote address on behalf of the central leadership, and they were hardly likely to express opposition. His wife, Yeh Ch'ün, sought to press home this advantage, urging Lin's PLA allies Wu Fa-hsien, Li Tso-p'eng, and Ch'iu Hui-tso, the chief of logistics, to speak up in support, and to lobby CC members from their own arm of the services. Another PLA supporter, Chief of Staff Huang Yung-sheng, was telephoned in Peking and informed of Lin's demarche.[47] At a Politburo meeting held that evening to discuss the economic plan, Wu Fa-hsien proposed revising the following day's arrangements so that the plenary session could listen to a tape recording of Lin's speech and discuss it. That night, without formal authorization, Ch'en Po-ta was busy drafting a clause on the state chairmanship for the constitution, and collecting quotations on the theory of genius.[48]

It is not clear whether Mao attended the Politburo session on the evening of 23 August – presumably not – or if Wu Fa-hsien's proposal was accepted and the plenum listened to the Lin Piao tape the following morning. But on the afternoon of 24 August, after agreeing on their plan of action, Ch'en Po-ta, Yeh Ch'ün, Wu Fa-hsien, Li Tso-p'eng, and Ch'iu Hui-tso divided up and spoke in favor of the Lin line at the sessions of the North China, Central-South, Southwest, and Northwest regional groups. They distributed a selection of quotations from Engels, Lenin, and Mao on the theory of genius to bolster Lin's position, and Ch'en Po-ta told the North China group that anyone opposing Mao's assumption of the state chairmanship was opposing the concept of Mao as a genius. Reports of their remarks were printed in the group bulletins and distributed. No one at the group meetings suggested Lin Piao for head of state.[49]

Mao, it was later claimed, was well aware that Lin's tactic was for the CC to agree that the new constitution should retain the state chairmanship and then to take the position himself if Mao persisted in refusing it.[50] If so, then Mao's remark at the Politburo Standing Committee meeting on the eve of the plenum was perhaps a provocation, designed to suggest to Lin that Mao's real objection was not to the post but to occupying it himself. Thus Lin and his supporters would be encouraged to

47 Hao and Tuan, *Chung-kuo kung-ch'an-tang liu-shih-nien*, 614.
48 *Chung-kuo kung-ch'an-tang liu-shih-nien ta-shih chien-chieh*, 561–62.
49 Hu Hua, ed., *Chung-kuo she-hui-chu-i ko-ming ho chien-she shih chiang-i* (Teaching materials on the history of China's socialist revolution and construction), 300; Teaching and Research Office on CCP History, *Chung-kuo kung-ch'an-tang liu-shih-nien ta-shih chien-chieh*, 562; Kao and Yen, "*Wen-hua ta-ko-ming*" *shih-nien shih*, 348; Hao and Tuan, *Chung-kuo kung-ch'an-tang liu-shih-nien*, 614. For quotations from these speeches, see ibid., 614–15, n. 1; Wang, *Ta-tung-luan-ti nien-tai*, 398–99.
50 Hao and Tuan, *Chung-kuo kung-ch'an-tang liu-shih-nien*, 615–16.

promote the state chairmanship proposal and, given enough rope, would hang themselves.

Certainly Mao acted speedily when the speeches of Lin's supporters in the regional groups were brought to his attention by Chiang Ch'ing and Chang Ch'un-ch'iao on 25 August, an action Mao later described as his wife's meritorious service against Lin. Chiang and Chang, whose political base outside Shanghai had crumbled with the rustication of the Red Guards and the suppression of civil strife, presumably had no wish to see Lin Piao's already formidable power and status increased further. Indeed, by now, their own hopes of inheriting any portions of Mao's mantle clearly depended on the erosion of Lin Piao's position, and Chang Ch'un-ch'iao had earlier clashed with Wu Fa-hsien on the Lin program in a group discussion.[51]

Mao must have realized that Lin's supporters were moving so fast that the plenum might be jockeyed into supporting the state chairmanship proposal if he did not declare himself. Even Wang Hung-wen, a close follower of Chang Ch'un-ch'iao and the latter's deputy in Shanghai, was sufficiently enthused or naive to trumpet the praises of Lin Piao's keynote speech in the Shanghai caucus, and was preparing to repeat the perform-ance before the East China group.[52] So, later on 25 August, Mao called the Politburo Standing Committee into session, an expanded meeting, presumably in order to allow the Chairman to pack it with additional supporters such as his wife and Chang Ch'un-ch'iao. It was decided that discussion of Lin Piao's speech in the group sessions should cease forth-with, and the bulletin of the North China group with Ch'en Po-ta's offending remarks was recalled. Ch'en was ordered to make a self-criticism.[53]

Mao set the tone for a counterattack by circulating, on 31 August, "A few of my opinions," a document in which he exposed his erstwhile ide-ological adviser's "bourgeois idealism" and accused him of rumor-mongering and sophistry. Mao's broadside provided ammunition for the criticism of Ch'en, Wu Fa-hsien, and Lin's other supporters in group sessions.[54] Only Ch'en Po-ta, however, was hounded out of office, per-haps because he could be credibly accused of being the fount of Lin's theoretical position. Probably more important, his disgrace did not

51 Ibid., 616; Wang, *Ta-tung-luan-ti nien-tai*, 402.
52 Kao and Yen, "*Wen-hua ta-ko-ming*" *shih-nien shih*, 349. After Mao's intervention, Wang hastily changed his speech of approval into a criticism of Ch'en Po-ta.
53 Teaching and Research Office on CCP History, *Chung-kuo kung-ch'an-tang liu-shih-nien ta-shih chien-chieh*, 562.
54 Hao and Tuan, *Chung-kuo kung-ch'an-tang liu-shih-nien*, 616; a full text of Mao's remarks is in Wang, *Ta-tung-luan-ti nien-tai*, 403–4.

threaten Lin directly, as the dismissal of one of his PLA allies would have done. Mao knew Lin Piao's power and, as he later admitted, he was not yet ready to confront him. He spoke privately to Lin, but told other leaders that his deputy had to be protected.[55]

Even so, Lin Piao had got the real message. In a brief two and a half days,[56] Lin's attempt to obtain the state chairmanship had been defeated, an awesome reminder of Mao's power to manipulate the Party elite. Before leaving Lushan after the close of the plenum on 6 September, Lin summed up the lesson he had learned to Wu Fa-hsien: "Doing things in the civilian manner didn't work; using armed force will work."[57]

Disagreement over foreign policy

The issues of party building and the reconstruction of state institutions basically were about power. There also seems to have been one issue of policy dividing Mao and Lin, although it is given less attention in Chinese sources: the opening to America. Since this is dealt with elsewhere in this volume,[58] it will only be sketched here.

The origins of the startling turnabout in Sino-American relations that brought President Nixon to China in February 1972 are well known. The bloody reverse sustained by the Chinese in a frontier clash with Soviet troops on Chen-pao (Damansky) Island in the Ussuri River in March 1969 clearly aroused concern in Peking that Moscow was going to escalate what had hitherto been a series of minor confrontations. There was subsequently a series of clashes on the northwestern frontier, a particularly serious one occurring in Sinkiang in August, and rumors began to emanate from Eastern European sources that the Russians were sounding out their allies about a "surgical strike" against Chinese nuclear weapons installations.

The immediate tension was somewhat defused by the brief meeting between Premier Kosygin and Premier Chou En-lai at Peking airport on 11 September, but the Chinese clearly continued to take the danger very seriously. In the aftermath of the Ussuri River clash, the Peking press had already drawn an analogy with the Soviet invasion of Czechoslovakia in the summer of 1968, a move the Russians had subsequently justified with the "Brezhnev doctrine," which effectively allowed the Soviet Union to

---

55 Kao and Yen, "*Wen-hua ta-ko-ming*" *shih-nien shih*, 349–50.
56 I.e., from 23 August through noon on 23 August; ibid., 349.
57 "*Kao wen-ti pu-hsing, kao wu-ti hsing*"; see Hu, *Chung-kuo she-hui-chu-i ko-ming ho chien-she shih chiang-i*, 302.
58 See Chapter 5.

overthrow any communist government of which it did not approve. The question for the Chinese leadership was how to achieve national security in these new circumstances.

It is conceivable that the clash on Chen-pao Island began with an ambush by the Chinese, and that this was intended by Lin Piao to provoke a frontier flare-up, in order to impress upon delegates to the CCP's Ninth Congress the importance of the heroic PLA, and so justify the role it was assuming within the Party.[59] Whether or not this is correct, the lesson learned by Mao and Chou En-lai from the clashes of 1969 was almost certainly the opposite: the Soviet Union was embarked on a far tougher line on the border,[60] and, however determined in border clashes, the PLA probably would be incapable of defending China effectively if the Soviet Union were to launch a major attack. Hence the receptivity of Peking to the overtures of the Nixon administration. An opening to Washington could undermine the calculations of the Russians as to the impunity with which they could attack China. Indeed, even before the forging of the Sino-American link, the Nixon administration had indicated that Moscow could not assume its benevolent neutrality in the event of Soviet aggression.[61] The original Sino-Soviet rift derived in large measure from Chinese anger at Soviet-American détente; Chinese denunciations of the revisionism of the CPSU leadership began after the Russians and the Americans had signed the partial test-ban treaty; the Cultural Revolution had been launched in order to prevent the emergence of similar revisionism in China. It is hardly surprising, therefore, that the breakthrough in Sino-American relations would require a great deal of explanation for Chinese nurtured on a diet of ideological principle rather than realpolitik.[62]

Lin Piao may well have felt revulsion at what looked like an Asian equivalent of the Nazi-Soviet pact. He may have reasoned that if China really could not stand alone threatened by both superpowers simultaneously, would it not be better to come to terms with a revisionist Soviet Union rather than an imperialist United States? Lin's position on this issue has never been fully clarified. He was later accused of "isolationism"

59 A 29-year-old commander involved in the Chen-pao clash, Sun Yü-kuo, was introduced to the Ninth Congress by PLA chief of staff Huang Yung-sheng, and was given an emotional welcome by Mao; see Mao's brief remarks in a collection of major speeches to the Ninth Congress available in the library of Harvard's Fairbank Center.
60 See, for instance, the estimate of a Chinese officer involved in the clashes as reported in Neville Maxwell, "The Chinese account of the 1969 fighting at Chenpao," *CQ*, 56 (October–December 1973), 734. See also Chapter 3.
61 Henry Kissinger, *White House years*, 184.
62 See, for instance, the documents circulated within the Kun-ming Military Region in *Chinese Communist internal politics and foreign policy*, 115–45.

and "great nation chauvinism,"[63] which suggests that he opposed any link-up with the United States or the Soviet Union[64] and argued that China was strong enough to protect itself. Mao told Nixon and other foreign visitors that Lin Piao had opposed contacts with America.[65]

If Mao were reporting accurately, it is easy to understand his motives. The PLA would loom larger than ever in a China isolated and menaced. And under conditions of national peril, the right of one of the great revolutionary marshals to inherit the mantle of Mao could not be disputed. The arts of peace and diplomacy, the province of Chou En-lai, would seem less important.

Unfortunately for Lin, Mao felt he had to buy time with diplomacy, and on 7 October the NCNA announced that Sino-Soviet border negotiations were about to begin. Yet Mao remained suspicious of the Russians, and in mid-October the Politburo decided to heighten vigilance immediately. On 17 October 1969, apparently acting on Mao's somber analysis of the world situation, Lin issued his "Order No. 1," putting the PLA on emergency alert and ordering the evacuation of cities.

Lin was resting in Soochow at the time, in a house once owned by Madame Chiang Kai-shek. According to the secretary who transmitted Lin's order to Chief of Staff Huang Yung-sheng in Peking, the defense minister's concern was that the Russians might be preparing a surprise attack when the PRC's guard was down because of the arrival of the Soviet negotiating mission. Mao was apparently sent a copy of the order for approval two hours before Huang was sent his copy, and evidently did not countermand it. Later condemnation of Lin's order was probably at least partly due to contemporary concern about the sharp reactions to it by the Russians, the Americans, and the Taiwan regime; so obvious a preparation for war might have been used by the Russians as an excuse for further military action on the border. After Lin was disgraced, Mao was able to blame him for an action that was clearly sparked by himself.[66]

---

63 Ibid., 132.   64 See Chapter 3.

65 Kissinger, *White House years*, 1061; *NYT*, 28 July 1972, quoted in Bridgham, "The fall of Lin Piao," 441–42. See also Chapter 5. Yet Lin Piao's secretary testifies that his late chief took virtually no interest in foreign affairs; Chang, *Mao chia-wan chi-shih*, 329–33.

66 Chang, *Mao-chia-wan chi-shih*, 316–23; CCP CC Party History Research Office, *Chung-kung-tang-shih ta-shih nien-piao* (A chronological table of major events in the history of the Chinese Communist Party), 372. Chang's account affords a sobering look at how casually members of the Chinese leadership took steps that might have resulted in war.

The evacuation order probably had an additional motivation: to get senior cadres, potential threats to Lin Piao's power, out of Peking. A number of marshals were dispersed along the Peking–Canton railway line: Ch'en I at Shih-chia-chuang, Nieh Jung-chen at Han-tan, Hsu Hsiang-ch'ien at K'ai-feng, Yeh Chien-ying at Ch'ang-sha, Liu Po-ch'eng at Hankow, Chu Te and former chief planner Li Fu-ch'un in Ts'ung-hua county in greater Canton. Some had probably lined up against Lin Piao at the recent Lushan Plenum; all but Li were potential obstacles if he

The border negotiations began on 20 October without mishap. Simultaneously, the Chinese and the Americans were initiating what Henry Kissinger later called an "intricate minuet"[67] as they cautiously probed through twenty years of hostility and suspicion. By the end of 1969, it was clear to the Americans that their signals, messages, and hints had borne fruit. Throughout 1970, as Lin Piao was campaigning to become head of state, Sino-American contacts grew. By 21 April 1971, when Chou En-lai invited Kissinger to visit Peking,[68] Lin's civilian route to more power had proved a dead end, and he was launched upon a more perilous course.

"Throwing stones, mixing in sand, and digging up the cornerstone"

Lin Piao's decision to seize power by force was almost certainly triggered by his political rebuff at the Lushan Plenum, but its timing was probably determined by the relentless campaign that Mao waged against his associates after that meeting. During the autumn and winter of 1970–71, it must have become clear to the defense minister that if he did not act soon, he would be finished. Mao's actions seem almost provocative, as if he wanted to force Lin Piao to make a false move. If he did, he would court death.

The postplenum campaign against Ch'en Po-ta took a number of forms. First, there was the denigration of Ch'en himself, the gradual buildup of a campaign from November 1970 through April 1971 and beyond, which started from the premise that he was anti-Party and a sham Marxist. Simultaneously, senior cadres were told to study Marxism-Leninism and prescribed six books by Marx, Engels, and Lenin and five articles by Mao, the proclaimed objective being to enable them to distinguish materialism and idealism. In fact, Mao was hitting at Lin Piao, who had advocated shelving the study of the Marxist-Leninist classics and reducing the study of Mao's Thought to the recitation of quotations. Ch'en's crimes were investigated by Yeh Chien-ying, who visited Fukien, Kwangtung, and Kwangsi to look into his activities, and were made the

---

wanted to use military means to achieve power. For the dispersal process, see Nieh Jung-chen, *Nieh Jung-chen hui-i-lu, hsia* (The memoirs of Nieh Jung-chen, part 3), 861–64. Yeh Chien-ying was soon back in harness investigating Ch'en Po-ta. The NCNA report on the Sino-Soviet negotiations is quoted in Kissinger, *White House years*, 186. See also Chapter 3.

67 Kissinger, *White House years*, 187.

68 Ibid., 193, 684–703, 714. Kissinger speculates that an attempt by PRC fighter planes to intercept an American intelligence-gathering aircraft a hundred miles off the Chinese coast on 2 July, at a time when diplomatic relations were improving, may have been a reflection of an internal power struggle in Peking; ibid., 697. In view of Lin Piao's close relationship with PLA air force chief Wu Fa-hsien, this seems a reasonable speculation.

excuse for a rectification campaign clearly designed to wean cadres from loyalty to Lin.[69]

Mao later described his tactics against Lin Piao and his followers as "throwing stones, mixing in sand, and digging up the cornerstone."[70] "Throwing stones" meant sniping at Lin's allies. At Lushan, Chou En-lai had privately told Wu Fa-hsien, Li Tso-p'eng, and Ch'iu Hui-tso that they should make self-criticism to the Central Committee. The day after the plenum ended, at Chiu-chiang airport at the foot of Lushan, Lin Piao posed for a souvenir snapshot with them and Huang Yung-sheng, and discussed tactics with them and his wife. It was agreed that Wu's position had to be restored, Lin and Huang had to be protected, and that in response to Chou's order, false self-criticisms would be made.[71]

But when the written self-criticisms appeared on Mao's desk the following month, he scribbled dissatisfied comments all over them. When the Military Affairs Commission (MAC) called a conference of 143 officers on 9 January 1971, and Lin's allies neither criticized Ch'en Po-ta nor self-criticized despite Mao's repeated strictures, the Chairman expressed his displeasure by ordering the proceedings of the conference to be ignored. Finally, on 29 April, at a central meeting called to discuss progress in the anti-Ch'en Po-ta rectification campaign, Chou En-lai accused Huang Yung-sheng, Wu Fa-hsien, Yeh Ch'ün, Li Tso-p'eng, and Ch'iu Hui-tso of mistakes in political line and factionalism.[72]

"Mixing in sand" meant adding Mao loyalists to bodies otherwise dominated by Lin's people. Chi Teng-k'uei, elected to alternate membership of the Politburo at the Ninth Congress, and a general, Chang Ts'ai-ch'ien, were appointed to the MAC's administrative group on 7 April 1971, to offset the power there of Huang Yung-sheng and Wu Fa-hsien. Mao had already taken other organizational measures to ensure his control of personnel and propaganda. On 6 November 1970, a new Central

---

69 The CC's first anti-Ch'en document, issued on 16 November 1970, already set out the main accusations against him: anti-Party, sham Marxist, careerist, and plotter. On 26 January 1971, the CC issued a collection of materials to document Ch'en's "crimes" throughout his career. Two CC notifications, on 21 February and 29 April, detailed how the movement to criticize Ch'en should be carried out. See Hao and Tuan, *Chung-kuo kung-ch'an-tang liu-shih-nien*, *617–18*; Wang, *Ta-tung-luan-ti nien-tai*, 406–9. For Yeh's investigation, see *Ying-ssu lu: huai-nien Yeh Chien-ying* (A record of contemplation: remembering Yeh Chien-ying), 265, 294, 301–4.

70 "*Shuai shih-t'ou, shan sha-tzu, wa ch'iang-jiao;*" *CLG*, 5.3–4 (Fall–Winter, 1972–73), 38; Hu Hua, *Chung-kuo she-hui-chu-i ko-ming ho chien-she shih chiang-i*, 302.

71 Kao and Yen, "*Wen-hua ta-ko-ming*" *shih-nien shih*, 349–50. The photograph at Chiu-chiang is reproduced in Yao Ming-le, *The conspiracy and murder of Mao's heir*, 57.

72 Hao and Tuan, *Chung-kuo kung-ch'an-tang liu-shih-nien*, 619–20; Hu, *Chung-kuo she-hui-chu-i ko-ming ho chien-she shih chiang-i*, 302; *CLG*, 5.3–4 (Fall-Winter 1972–73), 38.

Organization and Propaganda Group, reporting directly to the Politburo, was set up to oversee the CC's Organization Department, the Central Party School, the *People's Daily*, the theoretical journal *Hung-ch'i* (Red flag), the New China News Agency, the Central Broadcasting Bureau, the *Kuang-ming Daily*, and a number of other organs. The group head was K'ang Sheng, and its members were Chiang Ch'ing, Chang Ch'un-ch'iao, Yao Wen-yuan, Chi Teng-k'uei, and a general, Li Te-sheng. K'ang Sheng soon cried off because of illness and Li Te-sheng became first secretary of the new Anhwei provincial Party committee in January 1971. Mao's wife and her Shanghai colleagues were left in charge, taking over what had once been Ch'en Po-ta's media empire,[73] thereby achieving a major national power base for the first time since the end of the Red Guard movement.[74]

"Digging up the cornerstone" meant reorganizing the Peking Military Region (MR). In an increasingly tense confrontation with his minister of defense, Mao had to be sure that the troops in charge of the capital were loyal to himself and not Lin Piao. On 16 December 1970, he called for a conference to explain why the Party committees of the North China region and the North China Military Region had allowed Ch'en Po-ta to become their backstage boss (*t'ai-shang-huang*) when he had not been given the appropriate powers by the CC. Insofar as there may have been any justice in the accusation – and it is easier to picture the bookish Ch'en Po-ta as a surrogate for Lin Piao than as the *éminence grise* of a military unit – it probably only reflected the normal deference any sensible party official would pay to a member of the Politburo Standing Committee; it is hard to imagine so lofty an individual being quizzed about his credentials. No matter: For Mao, who himself disdained going through channels, any credible infraction of organizational discipline was grist to his mill.

Chou En-lai called a North China conference on 22 December 1970, ostensibly to criticize Ch'en Po-ta's crimes and those of his imitators in the region. During the course of the month-long conference, the leadership of the Peking Military Region was reorganized: Lin Piao's followers, the commander and the second political commissar, were reassigned, and the Thirty-eighth Army, thought to be loyal to the defense minister, transferred out.[75]

73 *A great trial in Chinese history*, 226.
74 Hao and Tuan, *Chung-kuo kung-ch'an-tang liu-shih-nien*, 618.
75 Ibid., 618; Hu, *Chung-kuo she-hui-chu-i ko-ming ho chien-she shih chiang-i*, 302; Ying-mao Kau, "Introduction," *CLG*, 5.3–4 (Fall-Winter, 1972–73), 12.

"571": Lin Piao's abortive coup

According to subsequent testimonies, Lin Piao authorized the preparation of plans for a possible coup during a visit to Soochow with his wife and son in February 1971. The planning for the coup was to be conducted by a small band of relatively junior officers led by his son, Lin Li-kuo, from his base in the air force. The precipitating events were presumably Mao's rebuff to Lin Piao's allies' stand at the recent MAC meeting and the reorganization of the PLA in the capital. How was Lin to respond? He evidently opted for attack as the only method of defense.

Perhaps the most extraordinary aspect of Lin's bid for power, apart from its ineptitude, was his demonstrated weakness in his own bailiwick. Despite his position as minister of defense, he did not rely on his Politburo allies at the head of various arms of the PLA. According to the evidence brought out at the trial of Lin Piao's surviving supporters in 1980-81, whatever else they did, Huang Yung-sheng, Wu Fa-hsien, Li Tso-p'eng, and Ch'iu Hui-tso were not involved in any plot to assassinate Mao.[76]

Lin Li-kuo's formal position in the air force, which he owed to his father's influence, was deputy director of the General Office – a key bureau through which all paper flowed – and concurrently deputy chief of operations. According to the evidence of his chief, Wu Fa-hsien, at his trial in 1980, from 6 July 1970, "everything concerning the Air Force was to be reported to Lin Liguo and everything of the Air Force should be put at his disposal and command."[77]

Lin Li-kuo formed his group of conspirators (see Table 5), known as the "joint fleet," from an investigation team Wu Fa-hsien had authorized him to set up. Most members were thus officers of the PLA Air Force (AF). Lin Li-kuo's "command unit" was drawn, apart from himself, entirely from the Nanking Military Region, which controlled East China.

In February 1971, Lin Li-kuo picked up Yü Hsin-yeh, a deputy director of the PLA AF Political Department, in Hangchow, summoned another deputy director, Chou Yü-ch'ih from Peking to Shanghai, where

---

76 See *A great trial in Chinese history*, 117–25. The following account of Lin Piao's plot has been put together from a number of sources, but virtually all are official or semiofficial versions, written by the victors or based on their evidence. In events so momentous as the demise of an heir apparent, there are many reasons why evidence should be doctored, and there can be no guarantee that if the CC's innermost archives are one day opened, another version will not emerge. It still seems worthwhile to spell out in detail the currently most believable version of the Lin Piao affair in order to depict the nature of Chinese politics of the time. Any revised version is likely only to underline the way in which the fate of China was settled by the ambitions and intrigues of a very small group of desperate leaders and their families.

77 Ibid., 93.

TABLE 5

Lin Piao's team: allies and conspirators

Lin Piao[a]
Yeh Ch'ün[a]

Allies

Politburo members
Huang Yung-sheng, PLA chief of staff[b]
Wu Fa-hsien, PLA AF CO[b]
Li Tso-p'eng, PLA Navy, 1st political commissar[b]
Ch'iu Hui-tso, director, PLA logistics dept.[b]

Others
(Cheng Wei-shan, acting CO, Peking MR?)

Conspirators

"Joint Fleet"
Lin Li-kuo, deputy director, PLA AF General Office[a]
Wang Wei-kuo, political commissar, PLA AF 4th Group, Nanking
Ch'en Li-yun, political commissar, PLA AF 5th Group, Chekiang
Chou Chien-p'ing, deputy CO, PLA Nanking units
Chiang T'eng-chiao, former political commissar, PLA AF, Nanking[b]
Chou Yü-ch'ih, deputy director, PLA AF Political Dept., Peking[c]
Hu P'ing, deputy chief of staff, PLA AF, Peking
Kuan Kuang-lieh, political commissar, PLA unit 0190
Li Wei-hsin, deputy director, PLA AF 4th Group political Dept.
Liu Pei-feng, PLA AF HQ CCP office[a]
Lu Min, director, PLA AF Operations Dept., Peking
Wang Fei, deputy chief of staff, PLA AF, Peking
Yü Hsin-yeh, deputy director, PLA AF political dept, Peking[c]

[a] Killed in air crash in Mongolia.
[b] Tried in 1980–81.
[c] Committed suicide after failure of 571.

between 20 and 24 March he plotted with them and Li Wei-hsin, a deputy director of the Political Department of the PLA 4th Group in Nanking, on the basis of his father's orders.

The discussions of the conspirators indicate an assessment of the political situation by the Lin family that the moment to strike was almost nigh, and that delay in a time of stability could allow civilian leaders to strengthen their positions; Mao was engaged in his habitual playing off of factions, building up Chang Ch'un-ch'iao to offset the defense minister.[78] Yet a "peaceful transition" to power seems not to have been ruled out even at this stage. A second possibility was that Lin would be thrown

78 Kau, *The Lin Piao affair*, 90–91.

out. Again, surprisingly, in view of events at the Second Plenum and since, some conspirators felt this was unlikely in the next three years. But Lin Li-kuo at least knew the perils of such forecasts: "Nothing is predictable. The Chairman commands such high prestige that he need only utter one sentence to remove anybody he chooses." When Yü Hsin-yeh objected that Lin Piao had been Mao's personal choice, Lin Li-kuo reminded him dryly that Liu Shao-ch'i had been accorded the same honor.[79]

The third option for Lin Piao was to assume power "ahead of time." Two alternative scenarios were discussed: to get rid of his rivals, principally Chang Ch'un-ch'iao, and to get rid of Mao himself. The conspirators expressed no qualms about the latter act but were concerned as to how it could be presented to the nation without negative repercussions. Chou Yü-ch'ih suggested that the blame for Mao's murder could be put on others, even Chiang Ch'ing, but added that politically, Lin "would pay a very high price for resorting to this alternative." So the decision was taken to strive for Lin's peaceful transition to power, but to make preparations for a coup.[80]

Lin Li-kuo decided to code-name the plot "571," because the Chinese words for these numbers (*wu ch'i i*) are a homonym for armed uprising (*wu[-chuang] ch'i-i*). Mao was referred to as "B-52." As initially discussed, the plot involved only arresting Chang Ch'un-ch'iao and Yao Wen-yuan. The idea of assassinating Mao seems to have been devised by Yü Hsin-yeh late in the day,[81] and perhaps in response to the Chairman's activities in southern China.

No actions of the Chairman could have been better calculated to have alarmed Lin Piao than the comments Mao made during his whistle-stop tour from mid-August to mid-September 1971. His principal visits were to Wuhan, Changsha, and Nanchang, and he met Party and PLA officials from Hupei, Honan, Hunan, Kwangtung, Kwangsi, Kiangsu, and Fukien.[82] Talking to them, he described the activities of Lin Piao's allies at the Second Plenum as a "two-line struggle," thus equating it with the cases of Liu Shao-ch'i, P'eng Te-huai, Kao Kang, and other anathematized former leaders.

At first, refraining from blaming Lin Piao by name, Mao accused his henchmen of "planned, organized, and programmed" "surprise attacks and underground activities" at the Second Plenum. However, no one could have failed to realize his real target when he remarked: "A certain

79 Ibid., 92.   80 Ibid., 92–93.   81 Ibid., 93–95.
82 Hao and Tuan, *Chung-kuo kung-ch'an-tang liu-shih-nien,* 621.

person was very anxious to become state chairman, to split the Party, and to seize power." When he finally mentioned Lin's name it was more in sorrow than in anger, but the defense minister could not have been deceived: "This time, to protect Vice-Chairman Lin, no conclusions concerning individuals were reached. But, of course, he must take some of the responsibility. What should we do with these people?"[83]

Mao's likely answer to his own question could not have been in doubt in the Lin household. Equally interesting, however, was the clear indication in the Chairman's remarks of why he was pursuing his struggle against his anointed successor. At one point he criticized the practice of local Party committees taking their decisions to PLA Party committees for approval. At another, he modified his own earlier slogan that "the whole country should learn from the PLA" by adding on "the PLA should learn from the people of the whole nation."[84] It was the threat of military domination of the polity that moved Mao.

The Chairman must have known and intended that his remarks would soon reach Lin Piao. They were, in fact, reported to navy commissar Li Tso-p'eng, who informed Chief of Staff Huang Yung-sheng and Logistics Director Ch'iu Hui-tso on 6 September. Huang immediately telephoned Yeh Ch'ün, who was with her husband and son at the seaside resort Peitaiho. Two days later, Lin Piao issued Lin Li-kuo with what was allegedly his authorization to activate the plan for a coup: "Expect you to act according to the order transmitted by Comrades Liguo [Lin Li-kuo] and Yuchi [Chou Yü-ch'ih]." The same day, Lin Li-kuo left for Peking to make the final arrangements for Mao's assassination.[85]

From 8 to 11 September, Lin Li-kuo and members of his "joint fleet" discussed a number of methods for killing Mao as his special train journeyed north back to the capital: attacking the train with flame throwers, 40-mm rocket guns, or 100-mm antiaircraft guns; dynamiting a bridge the train had to cross; bombing the train from the air; or, less dramatic but perhaps surer, face-to-face assassination by pistol.[86]

All these plans were to prove fruitless. While the conspirators were learning about Mao's activities, the Chairman had got wind in Nanchang

83 Kau, *The Lin Piao affair*, 57–61. 84 Ibid., 64.
85 *A great trial in Chinese history*, 96–97. According to a much later account based on an interview with Lin Piao's daughter, Lin Tou-tou, Huang telephoned on 5 September, but since she was not in Peitaiho when the call came through and the trial version tells of telephone logs, 6 September seems the more likely date for Huang's call; see "Lin Tou-tou who lives in the shadow of history," *Hua-ch'iao jih-pao* (Overseas Chinese news), 15 June 1988, 3. However, one recent mainland history states that Lin Li-kuo was informed directly by one of the participants in Mao's meetings late on the night of 5 September; see Hao and Tuan, *Chung-kuo kung-ch'an-tang liu-shih-nien*, 621.
86 *A great trial in Chinese history*, 97.

at the end of August that Lin Piao might be up to no good.[87] On his return journey, therefore, Mao made sudden departures and curtailed stopovers, leaving Shanghai far sooner than expected, heading back to Peking on 11 September, passing through the places where his special train might have been intercepted before the plotters were ready.[88] On the afternoon of 12 September, he stopped the train at Feng-t'ai station just outside Peking and held a two-hour conference with senior military and civilian officials based in the capital, before pulling into the main station later that evening.[89] There is no indication that Mao's precipitate action was triggered by any knowledge of a specific plot, let alone its details. Possibly he had acted on an instinct for survival honed by long years of guerrilla warfare. Whatever the motives, his run for cover precipitated the crisis the Chinese now refer to as the "13 September Incident" (*chiu i-san shih-chien*).

The 13 September Incident

When Lin Li-kuo learned the Chairman had escaped death, he immediately put into high gear a plan to set up a rival regime in Canton, which Lin Piao and Yeh Ch'ün had been considering for some time; it had been prepared simultaneously with the assassination plot. It was agreed that Lin and Yeh would fly south on 13 September, leaving Peitaiho at 8:00 A.M., and expect to rendezvous in Canton with Lin's top military allies – Huang Yung-sheng, Wu Fa-hsien, Li Tso-p'eng, and Ch'iu Hui-tso – and Lin Li-kuo's co-conspirators. After completing arrangements in Peking, Lin Li-kuo flew to Shanhaikuan, the airport for Peitaiho, in one of China's few British-built Tridents, secretly commandeered through his network of air force supporters, to supervise the evacuation of his parents.[90] He would perhaps have succeeded, but for the intervention of his sister, Lin Li-heng.

Lin Li-heng was better known by her nickname Tou-tou (Bean Curd) which her father had given her because of his fondness for that food. Tou-tou was very close to Lin Piao, but was treated brutally by her mother Yeh Ch'ün, whom both she and her brother called "Director Yeh!"[91] Driven to distraction, Tou-tou began to believe that Yeh Ch'ün

---

87 Hao and Tuan, *Chung-kuo kung-ch'an-tang liu-shih-nien*, 622; "Lin Tou-tou who lives in the shadow of history."
88 Kao and Yen, "*Wen-hua ta-ko-ming*" *shih-nien shih*, 379–80.
89 Hu Hua, *Chung-kuo she-hui-chu-i ko-ming ho chien-she shih chiang-i*, 309.
90 Kao and Yen, "*Wen-hua ta-ko-ming*" *shih-nien shih*, 381–83.
91 "Lin Tou-tou who lives in the shadow of history," *Hua-ch'iao jih-pao*, 14 June 1988. According to one admittedly suspect source, Lin Tou-tou was born in 1941 in the Soviet Union. This would have been toward the end of Lin Piao's three-year period of hospitalization there; see Yao, *The conspiracy and murder of Mao's heir*, 130.

could not possibly be her real mother, and the doctor who had delivered her in Yenan had to be summoned to testify that Yeh was.[92] On one occasion, Tou-tou had tried to commit suicide. Director Yeh's reaction was "Let her die"; Tou-tou's father was not told.[93]

On 6 September, Lin Tou-tou had been summoned to Peitaiho from Peking by her brother on the pretext that her father was ill. When she arrived, Lin Li-kuo had informed her of Mao's activities in southern China, indicated that Lin Piao's back was against the wall, and candidly revealed the three options being considered: to kill Mao; to set up a rival government in Canton; or to flee to the Soviet Union. Tou-tou argued with her brother for two days, rejecting all three courses, suggesting that Lin Piao should simply retire from the political limelight like China's senior soldier, Chu Te.[94]

According to her account, Tou-tou's sole concern was her father's safety. She encouraged the servants to eavesdrop on Lin Piao, Yeh Ch'ün, and Lin Li-kuo to find out what they were up to; on 8 September, after her brother had left for Peking, she got word to the detachment of PLA Unit 8341 – the guards regiment assigned to CCP leaders – stationed by her parents' house, to be sure to protect Lin Piao whatever happened.[95] Despite Tou-tou's agitated behavior, no one had the courage to intervene, especially because Yeh Ch'ün had been putting it about that her daughter was distraught because she was in love; indeed, she was on the verge of becoming formally engaged.[96]

The engagement celebrations took place on the afternoon of 12 September, beginning before Lin Li-kuo's return from Peking. On his arrival, he told his sister he had come especially for the occasion, but aroused her suspicions by immediately hurrying off to confer with his parents. At about 10:20 P.M. Tou-tou went personally to alert the CO of Unit 8341. This time the commander telephoned Peking.[97]

When the report reached Premier Chou En-lai at about 10:30 P.M., he

---

92 "Lin Tou-tou who lives in the shadow of history," *Hua-ch'iao jih-pao*, 14 June 1988. It may have been this story that was the ultimate source for the assertions by Jaap van Ginneken that Tou-tou was the child of Lin Piao's first wife, Liu Hsi-ming, and that Yeh and Lin Piao were not married until 1960; *The rise and fall of Lin Piao*, 263, 272. The date of Yeh's marriage to Lin Piao is uncertain; see Klein and Clark, *A biographic dictionary of Chinese communism, 1921–1965*, 1.567; but one resident of Yenan in the mid-1940s has confirmed that they were married then (private communication). For a longer account of Tou-tou's unhappy position in the Lin–Yeh household, see Chang, *Mao-chia-wan chi-shih*, 256–92, 429. Despite Chang's critical account of Yeh's activities, he asserts that working for her was slightly better than working for Chiang Ch'ing; ibid., 429.
93 *Hua-ch'iao jih-pao*, 15 June 1988.   94 Ibid.   95 Ibid., 15 and 16 June.
96 Kao and Yen, "*Wen-hua ta-ko-ming*" *shih-nien shih*, 384.
97 Ibid., 384–85. Another account says Tou-tou approached the guard commander at about 8:30 P.M.; see "Lin Tou-tou who lives in the shadow of history," *Hua-ch'iao jih-pao*, 16 June 1988. Wang, *Ta-tung-luan-ti nien-tai*, 427–30, has an account of the events of 11 and 12 September as seen by Lin Li-kuo's fiancée, Chang Ning.

was chairing a meeting at the Great Hall of the People to discuss his government report to the Fourth NPC session. He immediately telephoned Wu Fa-hsien and Li Tso-p'eng to check whether or not there was a Trident at Shanhaikuan airfield.

While all this was going on, Yeh Ch'ün had spent a quiet hour gossiping on the telephone with Madame Ch'iu Hui-tso. Alerted via Lin Li-kuo's network to Chou's inquiries, Yeh decided to try to disarm suspicion. At 11:30 P.M. she telephoned the premier to tell him of the Lin family's interest in leaving Peitaiho to go to a hot-springs resort. In response to the premier's queries, she said they wanted to go by air rather than rail, but had not arranged a plane. Chou warned that the weather was currently bad and that he would discuss the Lins' proposed air journey with Wu Fa-hsien.[98]

Once Yeh was off the line, Chou again called Wu Fa-hsien and Li Tso-p'eng, who, as senior naval officer, was in charge of the Shanhaikuan naval air base, and ordered that the Trident was not to be allowed to take off unless permission was jointly given by Chou, Li, Huang Yung-sheng, and Wu Fa-hsien. In Peitaiho, Yeh sprang into action. With Lin Li-kuo, she aroused Lin Piao, who had taken a sleeping pill, telling him that people were coming to arrest him. Papers were burned, and the family got into their car and left for the airport. The Unit 8341 guards were too timid to stop them. Fortunately for the fugitives, Li Tso-p'eng had distorted Chou En-lai's instructions and had told the Shanhaikuan base authorities that the Trident could take off if just one of the four men named gave permission, which Li did. At 12:32 A.M., Lin Piao, with his wife and son, took off.[99]

Chou had been informed at about midnight that the Lins had fled their compound. On hearing the news, Chou ordered Wu Fa-hsien to ground all aircraft in China, and then sent an aide to Wu's headquarters to keep an eye on him.[100] Chou then drove to Mao's residence in the Chung-nan-hai to brief him personally. When radar indicated the Trident would be crossing into Mongolian territory, Wu Fa-hsien telephoned to ask

98 Yü Nan, "Chou tsung-li ch'u-chih '9.13' Lin Piao p'an-t'ao shih-chien ti i-hsieh ch'ing-k'uang" (Some of the circumstances regarding Premier Chou's management of the 13 September incident when Lin Piao committed treachery and fled), *Tang-shih yen-chiu* (Research on Party history), 3 (1981), 59; Wang, *Ta-tung-luan-ti nien-tai*, 431; Hao and Tuan, *Chung-kuo kung-ch'an-tang liu-shih-nien*, 622; Kao and Yen, "*Wen-hua ta-ko-ming*" *shih-nien shih*, 386; *Hua-ch'iao jih-pao*, 16 June 1988. The latter account says it was Chou who telephoned Yeh.

99 *Hua-ch'iao jih-pao*, 16, 17 June 1988; Hao and Tuan, *Chung-kuo kung-ch'an-tang liu-shih-nien*, 622; *A great trial in Chinese history*, 99; Kao and Yen, "*Wen-hua ta-ko-ming*" *shih-nien shih*, 387–91. According to Wang, *Ta-tung-luan-ti nien-tai*, 432, Mao's imprimatur had also to be obtained.

100 *Tang-shih yen-chiu*, 3 (1981), 59. The air force CO failed to prevent some of Lin Li-kuo's collaborators from trying to escape by helicopter; *A great trial in Chinese history*, 99–100.

whether the plane should be shot down. Chou asked Mao for his orders. Mao is quoted as replying philosophically: "Rain has to fall, women have to marry, these things are immutable; let them go."[101] Chou, not knowing the details of Lin's activities and wanting to prevent any threat to Mao's safety, got the Chairman to leave his residence and move to the Great Hall.

Only now did Mao order Chou to summon senior officials there for a Politburo conference, the clearest indication of how China was ruled. The meeting convened after 3:00 A.M., but Mao did not attend, whether for security reasons or out of embarrassment at the defection of his personally chosen heir is uncertain. Chou informed his Politburo colleagues of Mao's return to the capital the previous afternoon and of Lin Piao's flight. He warned them to be prepared for anything.[102] It was not until the afternoon of 14 September that Chou learned from the PRC embassy in Ulan Bator that Lin Piao's Trident had crashed at approximately 2:30 A.M. on 13 September near Undur Khan in Mongolia, killing the eight men and one woman on board.[103]

A more recent, unofficial account throws doubt on this description of events by focusing on the main question it prompts: Why did the Lins not fly south as arranged? The new account suggests that the Lin family did not immediately abandon their original plan to set up a rival regime in Kwangtung, a plan that, after all, they would have had to advance by only about eight hours. This version argues that the Trident was in the air for almost two hours, whereas the flying time to Undur Khan for such a plane should have been less than an hour. It claims that the Trident in fact first flew south for about ten minutes, and then returned to Shanhaikuan, but found the airbase closed as Chou En-lai had instructed. Why the Lins should have abandoned their southern strategy is not explained, but the implication of the story is that Chou refused to let Lin land to force the latter to flee to the Soviet Union, thus putting himself beyond the pale as a national traitor.[104] Whatever the truth, the most

101 "*T'ien yao hsia-yü, niang yao chia-jen, tou-shih mei-yu fa-tzu-ti shih; yao ta-men ch'ü pa.*" See Hao and Tuan, *Chung-kuo kung-ch'an-tang liu-shih-nien*, 623.
102 *Tang-shih yen-chiu*, 3 (1981), 59. This account was written partly to dispel rumors that Chou had withheld the news of the flight from Mao until just before the plane was about to cross the frontier. A more hard-nosed view preferred by some scholars to explain Mao's apparent relaxed attitude toward Lin Piao's escape is that the PLA Air Force's night-fighter capability was too limited to permit it to bring down the fleeing plane.
103 Ibid.
104 See *Hua-ch'iao jih-pao*, 17 June 1988. An alternative explanation could be that the Trident did not fly a straight course toward Mongolia, but zigzagged to avoid interception. Another version retailed by a former public security official to a China scholar was that Premier Chou managed to talk the pilot into flying back into Chinese airspace, but that the latter was then shot by Lin Li-

dangerous threat to Mao's power and person since the Liberation was over. The specter of Bonapartism had been exorcised for the time being.

The impact of the fall of Lin Piao

The death of Lin Piao enabled Mao and Chou En-lai to purge the Politburo of the central military leaders who had been his allies, if not his co-conspirators. On the morning of 24 September, Chou En-lai summoned PLA chief of staff Huang Yung-sheng, PLA AF head Wu Fa-hsien, PLA navy political commissar Li Tso-p'eng, and PLA Logistics Director Ch'iu Hui-tso to the Great Hall to tell them that they were dismissed and had to make thorough self-examinations. Each left under arrest, and each would eventually stand trial. The survivors among Lin Li-kuo's group of young turks in the PLA AF were also swept away.

But although the PLA had lost its most powerful figures in the civilian leadership and its high-profile role had been diminished, it was far from the end of PLA institutional dominance within the civilian polity. A major military presence in Party and government remained. Yeh Chien-ying, one of China's ten marshals and a longtime ally of Chou En-lai, took charge of a revamped Military Affairs Commission, directed the investigation into Lin Piao's activities within the major military units,[105] and played an increasingly important political role. His loyalty to Mao and the premier could be assumed, but he was nevertheless a representative of the military establishment.[106] Wang Tung-hsing, the CO of the central bodyguard, PLA Unit 8341, was even more committed to the Chairman and was a public security official rather than part of the military mainstream,[107] but he was certainly not a civilian cadre. These men, in

kuo, who took over the controls. Lin proved unable to handle the plane and it crashed. An even more sensational, supposedly "insider" account of the demise of Lin Piao, discounted by many scholars as fabricated, alleges that he was killed on Mao's orders in a rocket attack when driving home after a banquet at the Chairman's villa outside Peking on 12 September. See Yao, *The conspiracy and murder of Mao's heir*, ch. 16.

105 Hao and Tuan, *Chung-kuo kung-ch'an-tang liu-shih-nien*, 624; *Ying-ssu lu*, 305–8, 346. For the dismissal of Lin's senior military allies, see *Tang-shih yen-chiu*, 3 (1981), 59.

106 Among Mao's remarks during his southern tour in the summer of 1971 is an admonition on 28 August to respect Yeh Chien-ying because of his firmness in crisis, as demonstrated by his loyalty to the future Chairman during the latter's struggle with Chang Kuo-t'ao in 1935. This comment, which occurs in what appears to be an unexpurgated manuscript version of Mao's remarks available in Harvard's Fairbank Center Library, illustrates both the importance of Yeh to Mao in his dealings with the military at this time as well as how the Chairman never forgot a favor or a slight. I am grateful to Michael Schoenhals for bringing this remark to my attention.

107 Wang Tung-hsing is not listed among the senior officers named "Wang" whose biographies are given in volumes 1 and 2 of the official, *Chung-kuo jen-min chieh-fang-chün chiang-shuai ming-lu* (The names and records of marshals and generals of the Chinese People's Liberation Army).

contrast to Lin Piao, would faithfully support Mao in his continuing efforts to recivilianize the polity.

The continuing power of PLA cadres in the provinces was symbolized by the continuing presence within the Politburo of three generals with top provincial responsibilities: Hsu Shih-yu, chairman of the Kiangsu Revolutionary Committee and CO of the Nanking Military Region; Ch'en Hsi-lien, chairman of the Liaoning Revolutionary Committee and CO of the Shenyang Military Region; and alternate member Li Te-sheng, chairman of the Anhwei Revolutionary Committee and CO of the Anhwei Military District. All of them had kept on the right side of Mao during the Cultural Revolution.

What is less easy to assess is the impact of Lin's fall on Mao. Liu Shao-ch'i had been axed in the heat of the Cultural Revolution, at a time when Mao had generated enough momentum to gain widespread support for the need to change leaders. Even Liu's former secretary, Teng Li-ch'ün, later admitted that in 1966 he had felt it was probably right that Mao's successor should be someone able to handle military as well as Party affairs; and he testified that this was a common opinion within the CCP.[108] Lin Piao was an authentic revolutionary hero, and unquestionably a longtime Mao loyalist. The Chairman's assessment that Lin was a better bet than Liu may have been resented by the latter's followers in the Party machine, but probably accepted unquestioningly within the broader political world.

Now the "best pupil" had not merely been found wanting but, as Chou En-lai would reveal at the CCP's Tenth Congress in 1973,[109] had even attempted to assassinate the Chairman himself. How could Mao have been so wrong for so long? His letter to Chiang Ch'ing in 1966 expressing concern about Lin Piao's activities was quickly circulated within the Party,[110] but it underlined rather than explained away Mao's failure to

---

108 See Teng Li-ch'ün, "Hsüeh-hsi, 'Kuan-yü chien-kuo-i-lai tang-ti jo-kan wen-t'i ti chüeh-i ti wen-t'i no hui-ta" (Questions and answers in studying the "Resolution on certain historical questions since the founding of the state"), in *Tang-shih hui-i pao-kao-chi* (Collected reports from the Conference on Party History), 153. Confirmation that Teng Li-ch'ün was not exceptional in this regard is in T'an Tsung-chi, "Lin Piao fan-ko-ming chi-t'uan-ti chüeh-ch'i chi-ch'i fu-mieh," *Chiao-hsüeh ts'an-k'ao, hsia*, 42, 43. According to this latter source, when Liu Shao-ch'i was criticized at the Eleventh Plenum and a new number two had to be found from the Politburo Standing Committee, Teng Hsiao-p'ing was ruled out because he, too, was under fire; Ch'en Yun, because he was rightist; Chu Te, because he was too old; and Chou En-lai, because Mao was not satisfied with him and Chou himself had often said that he was not able to assume command (*wo che-ko jen shih pu-neng kua-shuai-ti*). That left only Lin Piao; T'an, ibid., 42.
109 *The Tenth National Congress of the Communist Party of China (Documents)*, 5–6.
110 Hao and Tuan, *Chung-kuo kung-ch'an-tang liu-shih-nien*, 625–26; also see above, note 43. This letter was so convenient for Mao to be able to circulate after the death of Lin Piao that post–Cultural Revolution Party historians seem to have questioned its authenticity. In response, one senior his-

prevent this dangerous man from emerging as his officially anointed successor. Was the Chairman unable to detect traitors and sham Marxists among men who had been close to him for decades?

Perhaps equally damaging was the revelation of how the top ranks of the CCP were riddled with treachery and intrigue worthy of the palace politics of the old imperial Chinese court, with plenty of obvious equivalents for the traditional panoply of empresses and eunuchs, officials and generals. Was this the purified politics the Cultural Revolution should have produced? While the turbulence and purges of the early years of the Cultural Revolution probably disillusioned most of Mao's closest colleagues, the fall of Lin Piao almost certainly spread that disillusionment among a far wider group,[111] and would be a source of political malaise when Mao's successors tried to rebuild after his death.

THE RISE AND FALL OF THE GANG OF FOUR

The succession problem

For the moment, Mao's main problem was to reconstruct the top leadership and in particular to select a credible successor. He had destroyed the very procedures by which he had hoped to spare China the succession struggles experienced by other totalitarian states, notably the Soviet Union after the death of Stalin. His "two fronts" system had been devised in the 1950s to give his colleagues experience and exposure in the front line while he monitored them from the second line. Liu's takeover from Mao of the post of head of state had been part of that process, but it did not outlast Liu himself. Similarly, the "best pupil" model could not outlast Lin Piao.[112] How was the Chairman to solve the problem of "After Mao, who?" and the even more crucial question "After Mao, what?"

Three groups began to emerge in the Politburo in the wake of Lin: radicals, survivors, and beneficiaries of the Cultural Revolution. The

torian recounted the following episode: Lin Piao had been most agitated when he had learned about Mao's letter in 1966, so much so that Mao decided not to have it circulated and indeed ordered it burned. When the burning ceremony took place, the leftist propagandist Ch'i Pen-yü protested to Chou En-lai that Mao's words were too precious to be destroyed in this way; the premier reassured him that he had ordered T'ao Chu, then director of propaganda, to make a copy. It was copies of this copy that had to be circulated after Lin's death, presumably giving rise to doubts about authenticity. See T'an Tsung-chi's account in *Chiao-hsueh ts'an-k'ao, hsia*, 41. This fascinating anecdote, which tells as much about Chou En-lai as Lin Piao, was first noticed by Michael Schoenhals.

111 Hao and Tuan, *Chung-kuo kung-ch'an-tang liu-shih-nien*, 624. This argument has also been made to the author by Chinese friends who experienced this disillusionment at that time.

112 For a longer discussion of the problem of succession under Mao and Teng Hsiao-p'ing, see Roderick MacFarquhar, "Passing the baton in Beijing," *New York Review of Books*, 35.2 (18 February 1988), 21–22.

radicals were the rump of the original ultraleftist coalition that had formed around Mao to launch the Cultural Revolution. By 1967, the interests of Lin Piao and the Cultural Revolution Group had already begun to diverge sharply, but they remained on the same side in important ways. With the disappearance of Lin Piao and his allies, the former coalition was reduced to K'ang Sheng, Chiang Ch'ing, Chang Ch'un-ch'iao, Yao Wen-yuan, and Hsieh Fu-chih, who had not originally been a member of the core group but had made himself extremely useful to it as the Cultural Revolution got under way from his vantage point as minister of public security. K'ang Sheng, however, appears to have played an increasingly nominal role, owing to failing health; and Hsieh died in 1972, leaving a rump of Chiang, Chang, and Yao.

The survivors were those senior officials who had collaborated with Mao, even though they almost certainly opposed the main thrust of the Cultural Revolution: Premier Chou En-lai, Vice-Premier Li Hsien-nien, acting head of state Tung Pi-wu, and three old marshals, Chu Te, Liu Po-ch'eng, and Yeh Chien-ying. Of these, only Chou, Li, and Yeh were active politically, while the other three had survived in the Politburo because their loyalty to Mao could be relied upon under almost any circumstances; indeed, Liu Po-ch'eng's continued membership was essentially a courtesy to a great revolutionary warrior, who was apparently mentally competent but physically blind and politically inert.

After the shock of the Lin Piao affair, Mao seems to have felt it expedient to reinforce his ties to this group by agreeing to rehabilitate a number of senior officials whose fall could credibly be blamed on Lin Piao. Those early critics of the Cultural Revolution known as the "February adverse current" were restored to grace if not to their old offices. When one of them, former Foreign Minister Ch'en I, died in January 1972, Mao unexpectedly attended the memorial ceremony and gave a high appraisal of the old marshal.[113]

One rehabilitation would profoundly affect China's history: that of "the number two Party person in authority taking the capitalist road," former CCP general secretary Teng Hsiao-p'ing. Teng and some of his family were in Kiangsi province, where they had been moved from Peking as a result of Lin Piao's evacuation order in October 1969. Teng

---

113 Hao and Tuan, *Chung-kuo kung-ch'an-tang liu-shih-nien*, 624. For a description of Mao's last-minute decision to attend the Ch'en I memorial ceremony on 10 January 1972, at which he told Prince Sihanouk of Cambodia that Ch'en had supported him, whereas Lin Piao had opposed him, see the series of eleven articles by Chang Yü-feng, "Anecdotes of Mao Zedong and Zhou Enlai in their later years," in *KMJP*, 26 December 1988–6 January 1989, translated in FBIS *Daily Report: China*, 27 January 1989, 16–19, and 31 January 1989, 30–37. This was the last such ceremony that Mao was able to attend.

worked a half day as a fitter in a county tractor plant. When Lin Piao fell, he wrote twice to Mao, in November 1971 and August 1972, asking to be allowed to work once more for the Party and nation. After receiving the second letter, Mao made approving comments on Teng's revolutionary record, although it was not until March 1973 that the formalities for his return to Peking were completed.[114] The reasons for Teng's second coming and its results will be explored later in the chapter.

The beneficiaries of the Cultural Revolution were those officials who had risen as a result of the purge of their seniors, as well as through their own ability to manipulate the turbulent politics of the late 1960s and early 1970s. In the immediate aftermath of the fall of Lin Piao, these were principally military figures: Hsu Shih-yu, Ch'en Hsi-lien, Li Te-sheng, and Wang Tung-hsing; but they also included a civilian cadre, Chi Teng-k'uei, who was involved in the post-Lin cleanup and would achieve increasing prominence.[115]

The problem for Mao now was that there was no obvious successor among the three groups likely to preserve the gains of the Cultural Revolution. Chou En-lai was, without question, the highest-ranking official under Mao. If the Chairman had considered him an appropriate successor, he could have appointed him long since, to widespread approval. But Mao was not prepared to entrust his ultra-leftist program to any of the survivors. Chou anyway could not be assumed to outlive Mao, for in May 1972, in the course of a regular checkup, he was found to have cancer, at an early stage.[116]

The rump of the old Cultural Revolution Group was the obvious place for Mao to look for a like-minded successor. The Chairman must have been aware, however, that the PLA was unlikely to accept as supreme leader anyone who had done so much to stir up violence, bloodshed, and disorder as Chiang Ch'ing or Chang Ch'un-ch'iao. Nor, apparently, did

---

114 See Kao and Yen, *"Wen-hua ta-ko-ming" shih-nien shih*, 528–30; Hao and Tuan, *Chung-kuo kung-ch'an-tang liu-shih-nien*, 624. For a more detailed account of Teng's sojourn in Kiangsi, see Ch'iu Chih-cho, "Teng Hsiao-p'ing tsai 1969–1972" (Teng Hsiao-p'ing in 1969–1972), *Hsin-hua wen-chai* (New China digest), 112 (April 1988), 133–55. A copy of Teng's letter of 3 August 1972 is available in the library of Harvard's Fairbank Center. In it, he expresses his support for the Cultural Revolution, without whose "incomparably immense monster-revealing mirror" (*wu-pi chü-ta-ti chao-yao-ching*) men like Lin Piao and Ch'en Po-ta would not have been exposed. The letter, which Michael Schoenhals drew to my attention, is a combination of flattery, self-abasement, and an account of Teng's own opinions and experience of Lin and Ch'en.

115 For Chi's role in the post-Lin cleanup, see *Hua-ch'iao jih-pao*, 18 June 1988. For an explanation of Chi's promotion under Mao's aegis, see Wang Ling-shu, "Ji Dengkui on Mao Zedong," *Liao-wang* (Outlook), overseas edition, 6-13 February 1989, translated in FBIS *Daily Report: China*, 14 February 1989, 22–26.

116 For the claim that the cancer was discovered in May, see Kao and Yen, *"Wen-hua ta-ko-ming," shih-nien shih*, 474. *Pu-chin-ti ssu-nien* (Inexhaustible memories), 583, provides the information that the cancer was in its early stages, and tells how Mao ordered a special group to be set up to supervise Chou's treatment. Curiously, *Chou tsung-li sheng-p'ing ta-shih-chi* (Major events in the life of Premier Chou), 494, gives only the year, though it provides a month-by-month chronology.

any beneficiary of the Cultural Revolution yet have the stature to attract broad-based support and the Chairman's endorsement.

In these difficult circumstances, Mao took an extraordinary step. He helicoptered a junior radical into the very apex of the leadership. Wang Hung-wen, aged only 36 at the time of Lin Piao's demise, had risen during Shanghai's "January Revolution" from a humble position as a Shanghai factory security chief to a workers' leader in support of Chang Ch'un-ch'iao and Yao Wen-yuan. By this time he was the effective boss of China's most populous city and leftist stronghold, and political commissar of its PLA garrison.[117] In the autumn of 1972, Wang was transferred to Peking, appearing in public there for the first time in October at the celebration of the fiftieth birthday of Prince Sihanouk in the Great Hall of the People, to the bewilderment of junior Chinese officials.[118] At Mao's direction, Wang was effectively inducted into the Politburo in May 1973, along with two beneficiaries of the Cultural Revolution: Hua Kuo-feng, the Hunan first secretary who seems to have distinguished himself in the post–Lin Piao investigations,[119] and Wu Te, the Peking first secretary.[120]

The rise of Wang Hung-wen was clearly designed to provide a more acceptable image for the radical faction. Wang, at 37, was good-looking and personable, and symbolized two constituencies critically important in the Cultural Revolution: youth and the workers. Through Wang, the radicals may have hoped to rekindle the youthful enthusiasm that had been dampened by the disbanding of the Red Guards. Wang's proletarian credentials could be expected also to attract the support of the urban workers. And whatever Wang's role in Shanghai, no general could blame him for the nationwide urban anarchy in 1967 and 1968.

After the CCP's Tenth Party Congress in August 1973, Wang was thrust into the Party's number-three position and was named a vice-chairman and member of the Politburo Standing Committee.[121] The

---

117 For Wang Hung-wen's life, see Ting Wang, *Wang Hung-wen, Chang Ch'un-ch'iao p'ing-chuan* (Biographies of Wang Hung-wen and Chang Ch'un-ch'iao), 49–134. See also Kao and Yen, *"Wen-hua ta-ko-ming" shih-nien shih*, 442–48. Neale Hunter, *Shanghai journal: an eyewitness account of the Cultural Revolution*, and Andrew G. Walder, *Chang Ch'un-ch'iao and Shanghai's January Revolution*, cover the period of Wang Hung-wen's emergence, but with little mention of Wang himself.

118 The present author witnessed officials' inability to explain what Wang Hung-wen was doing in Peking, shaking hands with the assembled VIPs along with elders and betters like Chou En-lai, Li Hsien-nien, and Foreign Minister Chi P'eng-fei. Curiously, a banquet given for Prince Sihanouk was made the occasion for another equally amazing first appearance in Peking, the return of Teng Hsiao-p'ing to public life on 12 April 1973; see John Gardner, *Chinese politics and the succession to Mao*, 62.

119 See Ting Wang, *Chairman Hua: leader of the Chinese Communists*, 77–80

120 Hao and Tuan, *Chung-kuo kung-ch'an-tang liu-shih-nien*, 628.

121 The consternation in China at Wang's meteoric rise can be guessed at when one remembers the disbelief with which American politicians and press reacted during the 1988 presidential campaign to then Vice-President Bush's choice of an unknown 41-year-old senator, Dan Quayle, as his running mate, a position that, unlike Wang's, conferred only potential power.

fourth member of what would later be known as the Gang of Four was now in place, outranked only by Mao and Chou En-lai. With only six years' experience of revolutionary struggle and politics, he was expected to keep up with, and contend against, men like the premier, who had survived six decades of revolutions, civil wars, foreign invasion, and Party infighting. It was a grossly unequal contest, another Maoist gamble that would fail.

Chou En-lai's anti-leftist offensive

When Wang Hung-wen arrived in Peking, his radical colleagues, Chiang Ch'ing, Chang Ch'un-ch'iao, and Yao Wen-yuan, were on the defensive. They had benefited from the fall of Lin Piao and his military clique, which removed a major obstacle to their inheriting Mao's mantle; but Lin Piao's actions had tarnished the leftist cause. Some of the dishonor he had incurred inevitably rubbed off on his erstwhile allies from the Cultural Revolution Group.

Chou En-lai took advantage of the radicals' disarray in the wake of the 13 September Incident to renew his year-old campaign to stabilize administration and encourage production. In December 1971, he lectured officials of the State Planning Commission (SPC) on the need to restore order and responsibility to an anarchic industrial management system. Intimidated by leftist threats, plant directors were afraid to maintain discipline. The guidelines produced by the SPC as a result of Chou's prodding were vetoed by Chang Ch'un-ch'iao and thus could not be distributed as formal documents. It was claimed that they nonetheless had a salutary effect on industrial production, although the figures do not bear this out.[122]

In agriculture, Chou ordered that the egalitarianism of the Ta-chai brigade should be imitated only when local circumstances permitted.[123] One such manifestation of egalitarianism had been a tendency to shift the accounting unit from production team to production brigade. During the

122 Hao and Tuan, *Chung-kuo kung-ch'an-tang liu-shih-nien*, 626; *Kuan-yü chien-kuo-i-lai tang-ti jo-kan li-shih wen-t'i ti chueh-i chu-shih-pen (hsiu-ting)* (hereafter *Chu-shih-pen*) (Revised annotated edition of the resolution on certain questions in the history of our party since the founding of the People's Repulic), 414–16. According to the PRC State Statistical Bureau, *Chung-kuo t'ung-chi nien-chien, 1981* (Chinese statistical yearbook, 1981), 233, steel production figures for these years were as follows (m. = million): 1969–13.3 m. tons; 1970–17.7 m. tons; 1971–21.3 m. tons; 1972–23.3 m. tons; 1973–25.2 m. tons; i.e., bigger increases in the years up to and including Lin Piao's fall than thereafter. See also Yen Fang-ming and Wang Ya-p'ing, "Chi-shih nien-tai ch'u-ch'i wo-kuo ching-chi chien-she ti mao-chin chi ch'i t'iao-cheng" (The blind advance in our national economic construction in the early 1970s and its correction), *Tang-shih yen-chiu*, 5 (1985), 55–60. For an analysis of the relative lightness of the effect of the Cultural Revolution on industry after the anarchy of 1967–68, see Chapter 6.

123 *Chu-shih-pen*, 416.

grim famine years after the Great Leap Forward when incentives for the peasants were vital to stimulate production, the Party had made the production team into the unit for accounting. The team was the smallest, lowest-level organization in the three-tier setup of the rural communes, and accounting at the team level meant that income was distributed within the most cohesive and homogeneous rural collective entity. When the right to act as the accounting unit was ceded by a group of teams to the production brigade, of which they were part, it entailed redistributing income from richer to poorer teams. This aroused great resentment. The radicals had encouraged a movement toward brigade accounting starting in 1968, but this had already been checked in 1970, before Chou En-lai's counterattack.[124] Another indicator of rural radicalism was the tolerance accorded peasants' private plots. Here, too, leftism seemed to be on the retreat as early as 1970, well before the fall of Lin Piao.[125] Nor do grain output figures suggest a general boost in agricultural production after 13 September 1971.[126]

Nevertheless, 1972 could be called Chou En-lai's year. There was relaxation in the cultural sphere. With the premier's encouragement, a call for a restoration of educational standards and scientific research was published by a leading academic, albeit not in the *People's Daily*, which was controlled by the radicals, and not without a counterattack by Chang Ch'un-ch'iao and Yao Wen-yuan.[127] At a major conference of more than three hundred senior central and provincial officials held in Peking from 20 May till late in June 1972, Chou deepened the attack on Lin Piao and won a ringing personal endorsement from the Chairman.[128] Yet the pre-

---

124 See David Zweig, *Agrarian radicalism in China, 1968–1981*, 57–60, and ch. 5; also Zweig, "Strategies of policy implementation: policy 'winds' and brigade accounting in rural China, 1966–1978," *World Politics*, 37.2 (January 1985), 267–93.

125 Zweig, *Agrarian radicalism in China*, 57–60, and ch. 6.

126 The grain output figures are as follows: 1969–210.9 m. tons; 1970–239.9 m. tons; 1971–250.1 m. tons; 1972–240.4 m. tons; 1973–264.9 m. tons; see State Statistical Bureau, *Chung-kuo t'ung-chi nien-chien, 1983*, 158.

127 That 1972 was the year of Chou En-lai is the assessment in Laszlo Ladany, *The Communist Party of China and Marxism, 1921–1985: a self-portrait*, 355–56, which deals with issues that will be covered in this chapter. Chou took the opportunity to try to rebut decisively an allegation that he had betrayed the CCP in 1932, which had apparently been discreetly encouraged by K'ang Sheng and Chiang Ch'ing in 1967. But although he circulated a brief statement from Mao that exonerated him, the Gang of Four continued to use the charge against him almost until his death; see "Kuan-yü kuo-min-tang tsao-yao wu-mieh ti teng-tsai so-wei 'Wu Hao ch'i-shih' wen-t'i ti wen-chien" (Document on the problem of the Kuomintang maliciously concocting and publishing the so-called "Wu Hao notice"), *Tang-shih yen-chiu*, 1 (1980), 8; "Wu Hao" was one of Chou En-lai's aliases at that time. See Hao and Tuan, *Chung-kuo kung-ch'an-tang liu-shih-nien*, 626–27, for a discussion of the article on educational reform by Chou P'ei-yuan; and Merle Goldman, *China's intellectuals: advise and dissent*, 162–66, for a general discussion of the attempt to revive science. For Chou's inability to control the *People's Daily*, see Chin Ch'un-ming, " 'Wen-hua ta-ko-ming' ti shih nien" (The decade of the Great Cultural Revolution), 203–4.

128 Hao and Tuan, *Chung-kuo kung-ch'an-tang liu-shih-nien*, 625–26.

mier was unable to liquidate the leftist positions because, in the last analysis, the radicals were still backed by Mao. By December 1972, the Chairman had decided that the antileftist tide had gone too far. In response to the urgings of Chang and Yao, he decreed that Lin Piao had not been an ultra-leftist after all, but an ultra-rightist![129] The radicals resumed their offensive.

The Tenth Party Congress

Wang Hung-wen, Chang Ch'un-ch'iao, and Yao Wen-yuan were put in charge of preparing the three main documents for the Tenth Party Congress, held in Peking from 24 to 28 August 1973, striking proof that they had recaptured the ideological high ground. The documents were the political report, which was delivered by Chou En-lai; the report on the revision of the Party constitution, delivered by Wang; and the draft new constitution.[130]

Not surprisingly, the reports and the constitution reflected the line of the Ninth Congress, despite the dramatic developments within the Chinese leadership since then. In Wang Hung-wen's words, "Practice over the past four years and more has fully proved that both the political line and organizational line of the Ninth Congress are correct."[131] Naturally, Lin Piao's name was excised from the new constitution, but the radicals would not have wanted to discard a document that reflected the ideals and achievements of the first three years of the Cultural Revolution. Instead they reaffirmed the concept of the Cultural Revolution, inserting into the general program of the new constitution the words: "Revolutions like this will have to be carried out many times in the future."[132] There is no way of knowing if they attempted to make Chou En-lai say something similar, but no such assertion appears in his report.[133]

Other additions to the constitution reflected other major concerns of the radicals: criticizing revisionism; going against the tide; the need to train revolutionary successors; the inviolability of Party leadership over

129 For a discussion of this politically necessary but ideologically bizarre redefinition, see a series of ten articles by Wang-Jo-shui entitled "Ts'ung p'i 'tso' tao-hsiang fan-yu ti i-tz'u ko-jen ching-li" (The experience of one individual of the reversal from criticizing 'leftism' to opposing rightism), in *Hua-ch'iao jih-pao*, 12–21 March 1989.

130 Hao and Tuan, *Chung-kuo kung-ch'an-tang liu-shih-nien*, 628.

131 *The Tenth National Congress of the Communist Party of China (Documents)*, 42. Chou En-lai used virtually the same words; ibid., 9–10.

132 Ibid., 45.

133 William A. Joseph has argued that Chou's report contains subtle hints that Lin Piao really was a leftist not a rightist; see his *The critique of ultra-leftism in China, 1958–1981*, 138–39. If so, then Chou presumably modified the draft after Wang and Chang submitted it to him.

other institutions, most importantly the PLA; the impermissibility of suppressing criticism.[134]

The new central leadership of the CCP, chosen at the postcongress CC plenum, reflected the resurgence of the radicals. The Politburo Standing Committee was greatly enlarged, nine members as compared with five in 1969. Of those nine, Mao, Wang Hung-wen, K'ang Sheng, and Chang Ch'un-ch'iao could be regarded as strong supporters of the goals of the Cultural Revolution; Chu Te (age 86) and Tung Pi-wu (age 87) were grand old men with little remaining political clout, whose presence might have comforted a few nostalgic senior officials, but who (if consulted) would almost certainly back Mao; Li Te-sheng, a dark-horse entrant soon to become CO of the Shenyang Military Region, had shown himself sensitive to radical demands during the early years of the Cultural Revolution, and could be counted as an opportunistic supporter of the radicals. This left only Chou En-lai and Yeh Chien-ying as effective voices of moderation.

New entrants to the Politburo like Hua Kuo-feng, Wu Te, and Ch'en Yung-kuei (the peasant Stakhanovite who headed the Ta-chai brigade) were nearly all beneficiaries of the Cultural Revolution who could presumably be expected to support its goals. Senior cadres like Li Ching-ch'üan and T'an Chen-lin, whom Chou had managed to get rehabilitated during the antileftist interlude, made it onto the Central Committee but failed to return to the Politburo.

In the aftermath of their success, the radicals dipped their brushes in vitriol as they prepared to denounce their most formidable opponent, Premier Chou En-lai himself.

"P'i Lin, p'i K'ung"

On 18 January 1974, with Mao's approval, the Party center circulated a document prepared under the direction of Chiang Ch'ing entitled "The doctrines of Lin Piao, Confucius and Mencius."[135] According to one account, the original authorization for this bizarre-seeming linkage was a comment by Mao to a Tsing-hua University study group in August 1973 that Lin and Confucius could be criticized together.[136] But the Tsing-hua inquiry itself must have been sparked by Mao's remark in March 1973 at

---

134 *The Tenth National Congress (Documents)*, 47, 48, 50, 52, 55.
135 "Lin Piao yü K'ung-Meng chih tao"; see Hu, *Chung-kuo she-hui-chu-i ko-ming ho chien-she shih chiang-i*, 316.
136 Yue Daiyun and Carolyn Wakeman, *To the storm: the odyssey of a revolutionary Chinese woman*, 323.

TABLE 6

Leadership changes, April 1969 – August 1973

(Names in boldface are of new entrants into the Politburo; names in capitals represent promotions within the Politburo as of the Ninth Congress. At both congresses, only the chairman and vice-chairmen were ranked; the rest were given in order of the number of strokes in the characters of their surnames. The order of the post-Ninth Congress Politburo has been juggled to make it easier to note the changes between 1969 and 1973.)

9th Congress		10th Congress	
Mao Tse-tung	PSC	Mao Tse-tung	PSC
Lin Piao	PSC		
Chou En-lai	PSC	Chou En-lai	PSC VC
Ch'en Po-ta	PSC		
		Wang Hung-wen	PSC VC
K'ang Sheng	PSC	K'ang Sheng	PSC VC
Yeh Chien-ying		YEH CHIEN-YING	PSC VC
Li Te-sheng	(alt)	LI TE-SHENG	PSC VC
Chu Te		CHU TE	PSC VC
Chang Ch'un-ch'iao		CHANG CH'UN-CH'IAO	PSC
Tung Pi-wu		TUNG PI-WU	PSC
Chiang Ch'ing (f)		Chiang Ch'ing (f)	
Yeh Ch'ün (f)			
Liu Po-ch'eng		Liu Po-ch'eng	
Hsu Shih-yu		Hsu Shih-yu	
Ch'en Hsi-lien		Ch'en Hsi-lien	
Li Hsien-nien		Li Hsien-nien	
Li Tso-p'eng			
Wu Fa-hsien			
Ch'iu Hui-tso			
Yao Wen-yuan		Yao Wen-yuan	
Huang Yung-sheng			
Hsieh Fu-chih			
Chi Teng-k'uei	(alt)	CHI TENG-K'UEI	
Li Hsueh-feng	(alt)		
Wang Tung-hsing	(alt)	WANG TUNG-HSING	
		Wei Kuo-ch'ing	
		Hua Kuo-feng	
		Wu Te	
		Ch'en Yung-kuei	
		Wu Kuei-hsien (f)	(alt)
		Su Chen-hua	(alt)
		Ni Chih-fu	(alt)
		Saifudin	(alt)

Notes: PSC = Politburo Standing Committee; VC = vice-chairman; alt = alternate member; (f) = female.

a central work conference called to criticize Lin Piao that it was also necessary to critize Confucius. Mao reinforced his message in a couple of poems written in May and August criticizing China's senior intellectual, Kuo Mo-jo, for praising the Confucians and reviling their principal tormentor, China's First Emperor, Ch'in Shih-huang-ti.[137] It was not inapposite that Mao himself was often seen by his countrymen as a founding emperor similar to Ch'in Shih-huang-ti,[138] a ruler excoriated as a tyrant by generations of Chinese historians.

By August, Mao's words must have been widely known among the political cognoscenti. That month, the *People's Daily*, controlled by the radicals, carried an article by a Canton professor that laid out some of the major themes of the subsequent campaign, including the one most relevant to current politics. The Confucian *Analects* were quoted as saying: "Revive states that have been extinguished, restore families whose line of succession has been broken and call to office those who have retired to obscurity." This was an oblique but unmistakable critique of Chou's rehabilitation of senior cadres, particularly clear to those who knew that this passage referred to the actions of Chou's namesake, the great statesman of the twelfth century B.C. the Duke of Chou.[139]

While this article was being debated up and down China, Chiang Ch'ing got Tsing-hua to form a group to provide the intellectual ammunition for a full-scale and credible official campaign.[140] The group was led by Ch'ih Ch'ün, formerly the political commissar of the central guards, PLA Unit 8341, but by this time the chairman of the Tsing-hua University Revolutionary Committee, with responsibility also for educational reform at the capital's other major institution of higher education, Peking University. His second-in-command was Hsieh Ching-i, also originally from PLA Unit 8341, a woman who had served as Chiang Ch'ing's secretary, then moved to Tsing-hua to become Ch'ih Ch'ün's deputy chairman.[141]

In autumn 1973, these two recruited twelve scholars (a number later increased to thirty-two) from Tsing-hua and Peking universities to do the research and writing needed to link Lin Piao and Confucius and, presum-

---

137 Teaching and Research Offce on CCP History, *Chung-kuo kung-ch'an-tang liu-shih-nien ta-shih chien-chieh*, 568. Mao pursued his comparison of Confucius and Ch'in Shih-huang-ti in conversation with a doubtless mystified visiting Egyptian leader; ibid. I have been unable to trace the poems referred to in this source. Mao was accustomed to using Kuo Mo-jo's poems as a foil for his own; see, for instance, *Chinese Literature*, 4 (1976), 43–44, 48–50. But there is no indication in *Mo-jo shi-tz'u hsuan* (Selected poems of Mo-jo) of any recent poems of Kuo's to which Mao might have been replying.
138 *The case of Peng Teh-huai*, 36.
139 "Quarterly chronicle and documentation," *CQ*, 57 (January–March 1974), 207–10. The fact that remarks by Chou En-lai on foreign affairs, a field he had made very much his own, were criticized by the Politburo in November 1973 at Mao's suggestion, of course encouraged the Gang of Four to believe their moment was coming; Wang, *Ta-tung-luan-ti nien-tai*, 417.
140 Yue and Wakeman, *To the storm*, 323. The key role of Tsing-hua in the launching of the *p'i Lin*, *p'i K'ung* campaign, and Chiang Ch'ing's links with that institution, suggests that she may have prompted its original submission to Mao.
141 Ibid., 303. For a transcript of discussions between Chiang Ch'ing and these two, see Wang, *Ta-tung-luan-ti nien-tai*, 479–89.

ably, to pinpoint the historical analogies that could be used for more urgent current purposes. This ideological hit team was designated the Peita–Tsing-hua Two Schools Big Criticism Group, and known as *Liang Hsiao* (Two Schools) for short. Its members were moved into special accommodation, given special food, and taken on fact-finding missions, often in the company of Chiang Ch'ing.[142] They became the core of a network of followers that the Gang established up and down the country.[143] The document circulated on 18 January 1974 was *Liang Hsiao's* first major product.

This marked the formal start of the official campaign to "Criticize Lin Piao, criticize Confucius" (*P'i Lin, p'i K'ung*), masterminded by Chiang Ch'ing and Wang Hung-wen, and foreshadowed by the 1974 New Year's Day joint editorial in the *People's Daily, Hung-ch'i,* and the *Liberation Army News.*[144] This might have seemed like an amplification of the ongoing drive to weed out supporters of Lin Piao in the Party and the PLA. Indeed, it was later alleged that a "Book-reading Group" (*tu-shu pan*) headed by Wang Hung-wen attempted to gain control in military units. But its real purpose, formulated by K'ang Sheng, was to undermine Chou En-lai, as had been clear from the first salvo the previous August.[145]

On 24 January, allegedly without permission but probably with Mao's consent, Chiang Ch'ing held a *P'i Lin, p'i K'ung* rally for the Peking garrison; the following day she held a similar one for central Party and government cadres, at which she, Yao Wen-yuan, Ch'ih Ch'ün, and Hsieh Ching-i made speeches.[146] Thereafter, she and her team traveled far and wide, penetrating even high-security military establishments, making speeches, or "lighting fires," as their activities were later described.[147] The campaign flooded the media and dominated the political activities of units in town and country.[148]

142 Yue and Wakeman, *To the storm*, 323–26. Yue Daiyun's knowledge of this group is extensive because her husband, T'ang I-chieh, was one of the twelve scholars.
143 Chin, "*Wen-hua ta-ko-ming*," 194.
144 Kao and Yen, "*Wen-hua ta-ko-ming*" *shih-nien shih*, 495.
145 Hu, *Chung-kuo she-hui-chu-i ko-ming ho chien-she shih chiang-i*, 316. See *Ying-ssu-lu*, 295–96 for the allegation about the reason for the *tu-shu pan*; Michael Schoenhals has brought to my attention a reference to these study groups in *Chung-kung chung-yang tang-hsiao nien-chien, 1984*, 4, which suggests they had less ambitious aims. For K'ang Sheng's role, see Chung, *K'ang Sheng p'ing chuan*, 310–11. Merle Goldman argues that Chou En-lai was able partly to diffuse the campaign, in *China's intellectuals*, 166–76. A leading member of the *Liang Hsiao* group has since claimed that he at no time wrote or supervised articles that were aimed consciously at Chou.
146 Goldman, *China's intellectuals*; Hao and Tuan, *Chung-kuo kung-ch'an-tang liu-shih-nien*, 634; Wang, *Ta-tung-luan-ti nien-tai*, 489–94.
147 Yue and Wakeman, *To the storm*, 325–27; Kao and Yen, "*Wen-hua ta-ko-ming*" *shih-nien shih*, 496–97; Hao and Tuan, *Chung-kuo kung-ch'an-tang liu-shih-nien*, 634.
148 "Quarterly chronicle," *CQ*, 58 (April–May 1974), 407; ibid., 59 (July–September 1974), 627–30.

The unjustified restoration of old familes was one theme. It was emphasized that there was an ongoing battle between those who wanted to go forward and those whose desire was to turn back the wheel of history.[149] Another was the contrast between the Confucians and the Legalist scholar-statesmen who worked for Ch'in Shih-huang-ti.[150] It was the Legalists who had convinced the Ch'in dynasty of a ruler's need to impose stern discipline and harsh punishments, an analogy perhaps intended to elevate class struggle over rehabilitation. The misdeeds of the Duke of Chou figured largely in speeches and articles.[151]

Whatever the psychological impact of this historical onslaught on the living Chou, the premier was increasingly incapacitated by his cancer, having to cut engagements, and finally to agree to surgery.[152] He left his office in the Chung-nan-hai complex on 1 June 1974 and moved into the Capital Hospital, which became his base for the remaining eighteen months of his life.[153] He left the hospital only occasionally, mainly to make sorties for important political purposes.[154] But if the radicals had cause to rejoice that a foe whom they had so far failed to topple was weakening, their satisfaction was short-lived. The terminal illness of Chou En-lai posed Mao a major political problem, and he solved it in a manner repugnant to his radical followers.

The return of Teng Hsiao-p'ing

Mao had to find someone to take Chou En-lai's place, to oversee the day-to-day running of the country. Although the Chairman evidently considered it nationally therapeutic and probably also personally exhilarating to encourage upheaval, he was well aware of the need for a stabilizing force to prevent total chaos. During the early years of the Cultural Revolution, and on earlier occasions like the Great Leap Forward, too, Chou had played that role. Although he could still rise to (or rather, for) the occasion – most notably, leaving the hospital to deliver the report on the

---

149 Ibid., 58 (April–May 1974), 407–8.   150 Ibid., 408.
151 Teaching and Research Office on CCP History, *Chung-kuo kung-ch'an-tang liu-shih-nien ta-shih chien-chieh*, 569.
152 Chou always insisted on getting Mao's permission before submitting to surgery; see *Pu-chin-ti ssu-nien*, 583. For his letter to Mao reporting in detail on his condition and asking permission for his third operation in March 1975, see *Chou En-lai shu-hsin hsuan-chi* (Chou En-lai's selected letters), 633–35.
153 *Chou tsung-li sheng-p'ing ta-shih-chi*, 504; *Huai-nien Chou En-lai*, 585–86.
154 Chou also made at least one sortie for sentimental reasons, when in September 1975 he paid his last visit to his barber of twenty years in the Peking Hotel; see Percy Jucheng Fang and Lucy Guinong J. Fang, *Zhou Enlai: a profile*, 184.

work of the government at the first session of the Fourth NPC on 13 January 1975 – it was no longer possible for him to work the long hours needed to supervise every major national concern.

Unfortunately for Mao, Wang Hung-wen turned out not to have the political skills that the Chairman presumably thought he had detected in the young man when he was operating in Shanghai.[155] More important: Despite his senior ranking, Wang had proved to be little more than a cat's-paw in the hands of Chiang Ch'ing and Chang Ch'un-ch'iao,[156] thus destroying his credibility as an independent new force. Although post–Cultural Revolution historians have axes to grind, there seems little reason to doubt their evidence that during the *P'i Lin, p'i K'ung* campaign, Wang Hung-wen had collaborated so closely with Chiang and Chang as to force Mao to realize he was not a viable replacement for Chou. By the time Mao started warning Wang against allying with Chiang, it was already too late.[157]

Quite apart from her activities on Mao's behalf earlier in the Cultural Revolution, Chiang Ch'ing was barred from power by the prejudices built into the political culture by two millennia of Chinese male historiography. Mao recognized that, as a woman, Chiang Ch'ing was a political liability. Female rulers were traditionally denounced by male historians for their disruption of the Confucian patrilinear succession system and for their alleged misdeeds. From 1974, Chiang Ch'ing tried belatedly to revise the negative historical images of the Empress Lü of Han and Empress Wu of T'ang,[158] who were, along with the Empress Dowager of the late Ch'ing, the historians' main bêtes noires.

What is less easy to understand about this period is Mao's periodic dissociation from Chiang Ch'ing and her Shanghai followers, while they remained so important to the promotion and preservation of his Cultural Revolution goals. Marital conflict is a possible explanation. According to Terrill's account, in 1975 Chiang Ch'ing moved out of the Chung-nanhai compound, where China's leaders lived, and took up residence in the Tiao-yü-t'ai guest house complex. This source implies that political dif-

155 Wang Hung-wen's most spectacular failure, his inability to restore order to strife-torn Hangchow in 1975, was still to come; see Gardner, *Chinese politics and the succession to Mao*, 74.
156 Chin, "*Wen-hua ta-ko-ming,*" 187.
157 Hao and Tuan, *Chung-kuo kung-ch'an-tang liu-shih-nien*, 638.
158 Kao and Yen, "*Wen-hua ta-ko-ming" shih-nien shih*, 513–17. For K'ang Sheng's role in this campaign, see Chung, *K'ang Sheng p'ing-chuan*, 315. See also Roxane Witke, *Comrade Chiang Ch'ing*, 464–66, 473; Ross Terrill, *The white-boned demon: a biography of Madame Mao Zedong*, 308–11; History Writing Group of the CCP Kwangtung Provincial Committee, "The ghost of Empress Lü and Chiang Ch'ing's empress dream," *Chinese Studies in history*, 12.1 (Fall 1978), 37–54; Yuan Ssu, "Bankruptcy of Empress Lü's dream," *Chinese Studies in History*, 12.2 (Winter 1978–79), 66–73.

ficulties may have been the cause rather than the result of the rift.[159] Mao certainly chose to give that impression, telling her on 21 March 1974: "It's better not to see each other. You have not carried out what I've been telling you for many years; what's the good of seeing each other anymore. You have books by Marx and Lenin and you have my books; you stubbornly refused to study them." It was at a Politburo meeting in July 1974 that the Chairman first criticized his wife's political actions in front of their colleagues, and referred to her and her allies as a "Gang of Four." Chiang Ch'ing, he told people, represented "only herself," had "wild ambitions," wanting "to become chairman of the Communist Party."[160] But a story widespread in Chinese political circles is that Chiang Ch'ing moved because she was outraged by Mao's liaison with a young railway-car attendant whom he had introduced into his household.[161] Yet another version is that Chiang Ch'ing, whatever her views of Mao's amours, had in fact moved out of his house long before the Cultural Revolution. What does seem certain is that politically Mao and Chiang Ch'ing still needed each other, and it is significant that whatever his strictures, he usually maintained that her errors were corrigible,[162] lending some credence to one Chinese view that Mao's attacks on the Gang of Four were part of an elaborate smoke screen designed to disarm their foes by implying he had deserted their cause. If so, then his principal dupe was Teng Hsiao-p'ing.

On 4 October 1974, no longer able to ignore the implications of Chou En-lai's illness, Mao proposed that Teng Hsiao-p'ing should take the premier's place in charge of the government with the title of first vice-premier. One of Mao's two principal victims at the onset of the Cultural Revolution was to return to run China. The meteoric rise of Wang Hung-wen had been extraordinary enough, but this was an even more astonishing appointment. Yet it had been clear since the end of the previous year that Teng's star was again in the ascendant and why. The issue was the PLA's role in the polity.

Mao had told a Politburo conference on 12 December 1973 that he wanted the COs of the military regions reshuffled, clearly to deprive them of their long-standing PLA commands and connections and their recently acquired Party and government posts. He complained that the Politburo did not deal with politics and that the MAC did not deal with military

159 Terrill, *The white-boned demon*.
160 Ibid., 324–25; Witke, *Comrade Chiang Ch'ing*, 476; Hao and Tuan, *Chung-kuo kung-ch'an-tang liu-shih-nien*, 637–38.
161 Terrill recounts this story in *The white-boned demon*, 317.   162 Chin, "*Wen-hua ta-ko-ming*," 210.

affairs, a not very suble hint to the military to get out of politics. To lessen
the anxiety of the generals at the implications of these proposals, Mao did
two things: He suggested that Teng Hsiao-p'ing should enter the MAC
and take on the job of chief of staff, and he criticized himself for being
taken in by Lin Piao's denunciation and harsh treatment of the PLA's
revolutionary heroes. Whether this explanation deceived the generals as
to the ultimate responsibility for the mistreatment of their colleagues is
doubtful, but it was at least an apology, coupled with a plea to let bygones be bygones.

Mao got his way: The MAC promulgated the reshuffle of eight COs of
military regions, and on the same day the CC authorized Teng's return to
a major political role in the MAC and a place on the Politburo. The
elements of the bargain were clear. In return for giving up political
power, the generals were promised that it would be put into the responsible hands of a trusted old comrade. Teng later commented approvingly,
perhaps even wonderingly, that all eight COs reported for duty at their
new posts within ten days.[163] To the disgust of the Gang, Teng was
chosen to lead the Chinese delegation to a special session of the United
Nations in April 1974 and deliver a speech introducing Mao's theory of
the three worlds to a global audience.

The Gang of Four could at least console themselves that by rehabili-
tating Teng, Mao had weakened their strongest potential opponents, the
military. But when in October Mao revealed his intention of putting
Teng in charge of the country, the Gang of Four were spurred into furious activity to try to deflect the Chairman from his purpose. Wang
Hung-wen flew secretly to see him in Changsha on 18 October.[164]
Through Wang and other emissaries, the Gang alleged that Chou was
shamming illness and secretly plotting in the hospital with Teng, and the
atmosphere in the capital had the flavor of the 1970 Lushan Conference.
Mao rejected their protests, praising Teng's ability. When Chou En-
lai, disregarding his illness, flew with Wang Hung-wen to Changsha on
23 December, the Chairman reaffirmed his commitment to Teng, and
proposed to implement his earlier suggestion that Teng be made a vice-
chairman of the MAC and PLA chief of staff. Political balance was preserved by the appointment of Chang Ch'un-ch'iao as director of the
PLA's General Political Department and second-ranking vice-premier.

163 *Chung-kung tang-shih ta-shih nien-piao*, 386; "Quarterly chronicle and documentation," *CQ*, 58
      (April–May 1974), 410; for an analysis of the regional reshuffle, see ibid., 57 (January–March
      1974), 206–7; for Teng's comment, see *Selected works of Deng Xiaoping (1975–1982)*, 97.
164 For a description of Wang Hung-wen's visit to Mao, see Chou Ming, *Li-shih tsai che-li ch'en-ssu*
      (History is reflected here), 2.196–203.

At a CC plenum in Peking from 8 to 10 January 1975, presided over by the ever vigilant Chou En-lai, these appointments were formally agreed upon, along with the even more striking decision that Teng should return to the Politburo Standing Committee as a vice-chairman of the Party.[165] The stage was set for the last great campaign of Mao's career.

Teng Hsiao-p'ing's year in charge

Teng Hsiao-p'ing has not revealed his thoughts on assuming day-to-day control of both Party and government in January 1975.[166] Did he believe that the Chairman had turned his back on the Cultural Revolution, and licensed him to revive the more rational policies that had been pursued on its eve?

There were some encouraging signs: the rehabilitation if not reinstatement of men like himself; Chou En-lai's speech to the Fourth NPC promoting, with Mao's support, long-term economic planning and what later became known as the "four modernizations" – of agriculture, industry, defense, and science and technology;[167] most important, there was Mao's call for stability and unity, and his criticism of the factional activities of the Gang of Four. Mao also seemed to wish to turn back the clock to more permissive policies in the cultural sphere, advocating the restoration to office of former officials like Chou Yang, and telling Teng Hsiao-p'ing that a hundred flowers should bloom again in all branches of the arts. Encouraged, perhaps led on, by the Chairman, Teng Hsiao-p'ing and his principal supporters, Yeh Chien-ying and Li Hsien-nien, criticized the Gang at Politburo meetings in May and June for their allegations that an eleventh "line struggle" was in progress and that the new leadership was guilty of pragmatism. Ever a weather vane, Wang Hung-wen made a

---

165 Hao and Tuan, *Chung-kuo kung-ch'an-tang liu-shih-nien*, 637–39; Kao and Yen, *"Wen-hua ta-ko-ming" shih-nien shih*, 530–37. Recent mainland historians are coy about how Chang Ch'un-ch'iao's appointment was brought about, presumably because they wish to avoid clouding their image of Mao playing a strongly positive role in the restoration of Teng at this time. An alternative or an additional explanation for Mao's recall of Teng, still current in China, is that he wanted to use him to displace Chou En-lai. According to this scenario, Mao worried that Chou might outlast him; the premier had cancer, but the Chairman allegedly had a serious stroke in late 1972, which could have convinced him that he might still die first. Mao's preference for Teng may have been partly because he considered him a less formidable opponent for the Gang of Four; it might also have had to do with his close earlier relation with him – Teng had remained loyal to Mao when the latter's back was up against the wall; for the Mao–Teng relationship, see MacFarquhar, *Origins*, 1.140–45.

166 Hao and Tuan, *Chung-kuo kung-ch'an-tang liu-shih-nien*, 639–40.

167 When Chou had first called for the four modernizations in 1964, he had not cited Mao in his support; see Gardner, *Chinese politics and the succession to Mao*, 67.

self-criticism, thereafter retiring to Shanghai for a few months, but his three comrades remained stubbornly silent.[168]

Teng energetically tackled pressing problems:[169] first, the military issue, which was a prime motive for Mao to recall him to office. Of Teng's eight speeches made in 1975 republished in his *Selected works*, three dealt with military affairs. Less than three weeks after he had formally assumed his military offices, Teng was attacking the bloated size and budget of the PLA, its inefficiency and lack of discipline, and the factionalism endemic among its officer corps. He stressed the need for PLA obedience to Party policies. In a later speech, he added conceit and inertia to his list of PLA faults.[170]

A more urgent problem was labor unrest, most notably the strikes and sabotage by railway workers at Hsu-chou, Nanking, Nanchang, and elsewhere, apparently resulting from leftist rabble-rousing during the *P'i Lin, p'i K'ung* campaign. Communications had been disrupted on four major trunk lines, causing massive economic dislocation. Teng restored order by a mixture of threats and conciliation, and the reinstatement of central control.[171] Wang Hung-wen had been unable to settle leftist-fomented strife in Hangchow. Teng simply sent in the PLA and arrested the trouble-makers.[172]

In search of solutions to deep-seated, longer-term problems relating to the economy, Teng called conferences and launched a number of initiatives. Three major policy documents were produced: "Some problems in accelerating industrial development" on 18 August, prepared by the State Planning Commission: "Outline report on the work of the Academy of Sciences" on 26 September, prepared by Hu Yao-pang, Hu Ch'iao-mu, and others;[173] and "On the general program of work for the whole Party and nation" in mid-October, written by Teng Li-ch'ün.[174]

168 Hao and Tuan, *Chung-kuo kung-ch'an-tang liu-shih-nien*, 645–47; Fang Wei-chung, ed., *Chung-hua jen-min kung-ho-kuo ching-chi ta-shih-chi (1949–1980)* (A record of the major economic events of the PRC [1949–1980]), 544–45; Chin, "*Wen-hua ta-ko-ming*," 212. A struggle over the political line was, of course, the most serious type of intra-Party dispute: The Lin Piao affair had been numbered the tenth such struggle, the Liu Shao-ch'i purge the ninth.

169 For a summary of Teng Hsiao-p'ing's activities from January through October 1975, at which point he was no longer able to exercise effective power, see Hao and Tuan, *Chung-kuo kung-ch'an-tang liu-shih-nien*, 640–41.

170 *Selected works of Deng Xiaoping (1975–1982)*, 11–13, 27–42.

171 Jürgen Domes, *The government and the politics of the PRC: a time of transition*, 127; Fang, ed., *Chung-hua jen-min kung-ho-kuo ching-chi ta-shih-chi (1949–1980)*, 541–43. The trunk lines were: Tientsin–P'u-k'ou; Peking–Canton; the Lung-hai (Lien-yun-kang–T'ien-shui) line, a major east-west artery linking coastal Kiangsu with Kansu in the northwest; and the Che-kan line joining Hangchow and Nan-chang.

172 John Gardner, *Chinese politics and the succession to Mao*, 74.

173 For an analysis of the drafting of these two documents, see Kenneth Lieberthal, *Central documents and Politburo politics in China*, 33–49.

174 Fang, *Chung-hua jen-min kung-ho-kuo ching-chi ta-shih-chi (1949–1980)*, 550–55; translations exist in Chi Hsin, *The case of the Gang of Four*, 203–86.

The industry document dealt with the roots of a wave of strikes that broke out in the middle of the year in Central and South China in response to leftist agitation for a more egalitarian wage system.[175] The document talked of "a handful of bad people sabotaging the work under the banner of 'rebellion' and 'going against the tide'"; of management being "in chaos"; of low productivity, low quality, expensive maintenance, high costs, and frequent breakdowns; and of the particularly serious problems in the raw materials, fuel, and power industries.[176] In his comments when the document was presented to the State Council, Teng stressed the need to support agriculture, introduce foreign technology, strengthen industrial research, bring order to management, to put "quality first," enforce rules and regulations, and restore material incentives.[177] A month later, in the discussions of the report on the Academy of Sciences, Teng pressed for better training, higher educational standards, more expert leadership, and more time to be spent on science (and by implication, less on politics).[178]

But it was the document formulating a general program for Party and nation that struck at the leftists most broadly, copiously quoting from early Mao writings to drive home the point that revolution could not be stressed to the detriment of production: "It is purely nonsense to say that a certain place or work unit is carrying out revolution very well when production is fouled up. The view that once revolution is grasped, production will increase naturally and without spending any effort is believed only by those who indulge in fairy tales."[179] No wonder Chiang Ch'ing denounced these documents as "three great weeds" and characterized this one as a "political manifesto for the restoration of capitalism."[180]

Chiang Ch'ing joined battle with Teng also on the issue of agriculture. At the First National Conference on Learning from Ta-chai [brigade] in Agriculture, which brought together 3,700 delegates from 15 September to 19 October, she called for a return to the commune ideal of the height of the Great Leap Forward in 1958, with an emphasis on egalitarianism and class struggle. Teng, on the other hand, looked back to the early 1960s, and the various incentives used then to encourage peasant initiative.[181]

175 Domes, *The government and politics of the PRC*, 128.
176 Chi, *The case of the Gang of Four*, 246, 247, 257.
177 *Selected works of Deng Xiaoping*, 43–46; Fang, *Chung-hua jen-min kung-ho-kuo ching-chi ta-shih-chi (1949–1980)*, 550–52.
178 Chi, *The case of the Gang of Four*, 287–95.   179 Ibid., 227.
180 Teaching and Research Office on CCP History of the [PLA] Political Academy, *Chung-kuo kung-ch'an-tang liu-shih-nien ta-shih chien-chieh*, 576.
181 Domes, *The government and politics of the PRC*, 129–30; Fang, *Chung-hua jen-min kung-ho-kuo ching-chi ta-shih-chi (1949–1980)*, 552–53.

In another bizarre example of invoking historical or literary texts for contemporary political purposes, Chiang Ch'ing used her Ta-chai speech to get at Teng Hsiao-p'ing by excoriating the hero of a famous old novel, the *Shui-hu chuan* (Water margin). She asserted that "this book must be read carefully to see the features of this renegade.... That man Sung Chiang had many double-dealing tricks![182] ... Sung Chiang made a figurehead of Ch'ao Kai; aren't there people just now who are trying to make a figurehead of the Chairman? I think there are some."[183] Typically, the *Shui-hu chuan* analogy was not her idea but stemmed from criticism by Mao of Sung Chiang's capitulationism or revisionism, a theme immediately pounced on by the Gang's sophisticated polemicist, Yao Wen-yuan.[184]

Mao's behavior throughout Teng Hsiao-p'ing's year in power was contradictory.[185] He backed Teng's measures, and defended them from attacks by the Gang of Four, but he simultaneously propounded his own leftist views and allowed Chang Ch'un-ch'iao and Yao Wen-yuan to publicize theirs. He bemoaned wage differentials, payment according to work, and commodity exchange; in those respects, he said, the PRC did not differ much from pre-1949 China, only the system of ownership had changed. Encouraged by Mao's statements, Chang Ch'un-ch'iao and Yao Wen-yuan published in the *People's Daily* a set of thirty-three quotations from Marx, Engels, and Lenin on the theory of proletarian dictatorship, carefully choosing comments that lent credence to their own position.[186] With the Chairman's permission, Chang and Yao both wrote major theoretical exegeses to justify their own views and his: on the overriding importance of class struggle and the proletarian dictatorship; on the danger of commodity exchange undermining the socialist planned economy; on the worrying emergence of new bourgeois elements encouraged by material incentives; on the urgency of pressing forward to higher stages of collective ownership, and then to state ownership; and on the continuing danger of China turning revisionist.[187]

Mao's ambivalence may have reflected indecision, a genuine conflict

---

182 *Chinese studies in history*, 12.1 (Fall 1978), 55.

183 Teaching and Research Office on CCP History of the [PLA] Political Academy, *Chung-kuo kung-ch'an-tang liu-shih-nien ta-shih chien-chieh*, 574.

184 Ibid., 573–74. For a detailed discussion of the *Shui-hu chuan* affair, see Goldman, *China's intellectuals*, 201–13.

185 Hao and Tuan, *Chung-kuo kung-ch'an-tang liu-shih-nien*, 648.   186 Ibid., 644–45.

187 Yao Wen-yuan, "On the social basis of the Lin Piao anti-Party clique," and Chang Ch'un-ch'iao, "On exercising all-round dictatorship over the bourgeoisie," are translated in Raymond Lotta, *And Mao makes 5: Mao Tse-tung's last great battle*, 196–220.

between head and heart. It may also have been a manifestation of his increasing infirmity. From early 1974 until August 1975, when he had an operation to remove one of two cataracts in his eyes, he was unable to read; with his confidential secretary terminally ill in hospital, Mao was forced to depend on his young female companion, Chang Yü-feng, to read official documents and newspapers to him. By the end of 1975, Parkinson's disease was rendering him literally speechless, even in some of his meetings with foreign VIPs, able to communicate only by writing or by grunts comprehensible only to his attendants. According to Chang:

Having trouble speaking, he could only utter some mumbled words and phrases. Having worked around him for a long time, I could manage to understand what he said. Whenever the Chairman talked with other leading comrades, I had to be present to repeat his words. But when his speech and pronunciation became extremely unclear, all I could do was to lipread or guess from his expression. When his speech was at its worst, he could only write down his thoughts with a pen. Later, the Chairman had a great difficulty getting about. He could not walk on his own; he could not even move a step without help.[188]

Mao's leftist nephew, Mao Yuan-hsin, seems to have been transferred from the Northeast in late September 1975 to act as the Chairman's liaison officer with the Politburo. He, too, weighed in against Teng. Iago-like, Mao Yuan-hsin slanted his reports and poured his doubts about Teng's loyalty to the Cultural Revolution into the Chairman's ear. He found a sympathetic listener.[189]

All these factors may have helped shape Mao's attitude. But in the light of Mao's long acquaintance with Teng, it seems unlikely that, in 1973, the Chairman was so naive as to think that the onetime number two capitalist-roader had changed his spots. The more likely hypothesis is that Mao's elevation of Teng Hsiao-p'ing was a tactic designed partly to hoodwink the military in order to deal more effectively with the problem "After Mao, which?" and partly to buy time while he sought a solution to the problem "After Mao, who?" The views he expressed during 1975 give no indication that he had changed his long-cherished ideas on the correct answer to "After Mao, what?"

---

188 Chang, "Anecdotes of Mao Zedong and Zhou Enlai in their later years." Ross Terrill in *Mao*, 395–97, 400–401, 411–13, 417–18, traces the Chairman's deteriorating health as manifested at his meetings with successive foreign visitors through the summer of 1976.
189 Hu, *Chung-kuo she-hui-chu-i ko-ming ho chien-she shih chiang-i*, 326; Hao and Tuan, *Chung-kuo kung-ch'an-tang liu-shih-nien*, 648–49. One report suggests that Mao Yuan-hsin was only with his uncle until November 1975, but other indications are that he remained in Peking at the Chairman's side until his death.

The death of Chou and the fall of Teng

Even before the death of Chou En-lai on 8 January 1976, there was a
rising tide of criticism of Teng Hsiao-p'ing's policies. Probably the Gang
of Four realized that the Chairman's tolerance of Teng was wearing thin,
and decided to move in for the kill. As at the start of the Cultural Revolution, the initial battleground was the intellectual sphere.

A Tsing-hua University Party official, perhaps instigated by Teng's
supporters, had written twice to Mao, complaining of the ideas and life-
style of the Gang's loyal followers there, Ch'ih Ch'ün and Hsieh Ching-i.
Mao took this as an attack on the Cultural Revolution, and his reply
in support of Ch'ih and Hsieh was publicized by them on 3 November as
the opening salvo of a campaign to "repulse the right deviationist wind
to reverse the verdicts."[190] They also seized their chance to attack the
minister of education, Chou Jung-hsin, who at Teng's request had been
pressing for a restoration of educational standards.[191] At stake for Mao
and the Gang of Four was one of the surviving legacies of the Cultural
Revolution, or "new socialist things," an egalitarian education system
emphasizing simpler and more practical courses that would be more easily accessible to worker-peasant-soldier entrants to universities.[192]

Toward the end of November, at Mao's orders, the Politburo called a
notification conference, at which Hua Kuo-feng read out a summary of a
speech by the Chairman, thereafter circulated to senior Party officials in
the provinces. The burden of the Mao text and subsequent supportive
central documents was that from July through September, political
rumors had been rife, attempts had been made to split the top leadership,
and attacks had been made on the Cultural Revolution in an effort to
reverse its verdicts.[193] Effectively Mao had withdrawn his mandate from
Teng, and reshaped the current campaign into a drive to "criticize Teng
and repulse the right-deviationist wind to reverse the verdicts."

It was at this point that Chou En-lai died, precipitating a political crisis
that would reverberate through China during the rest of the year. Chou
had been relatively inactive for months, but while he still lived, he

190 "*Fan-chi yu-ch'ing fan-an feng*"; see Hao and Tuan, *Chung-kuo kung-ch'an-tang liu-shih-nien*, 649.
191 Gardner, *Chinese politics and the succession to Mao*, 75–76. For a detailed analysis of educational
     developments during the Cultural Revolution, see Chapter 7.
192 Other new socialist things included Chiang Ch'ing's revolutionary operas; the rural "barefoot
     doctor" or paramedic system; the May 7 cadre schools where officials spent months, sometimes
     years, performing manual labor; emulation of the collectivism of Ta-chai brigade. See "Nothing
     is hard in this world if you dare to scale the heights," *JMJP, HC, Chieh-fang chün pao* (Liberation
     Army news) Joint editorial, 1 January 1976, translated in "Quarterly chronicle and documenta-
     tion," *CQ*, 66 (June 1976), 412.
193 Hao and Tuan, *Chung-kuo kung-ch'an-tang liu-shih-nien*, 649.

symbolized rationality and restraint, a guarantee that however chaotic the country became, somewhere, someone was attempting to restore order and to protect people from the worst effects of the Cultural Revolution. Teng Hsiao-p'ing, who had been a worker-student with him in Paris in the early 1920s, probably summed up the general attitude to Chou in an interview four years later:

> Premier Zhou was a man who worked hard and uncomplainingly all his life. He worked 12 hours a day, and sometimes 16 hours or more, throughout his life. ... Fortunately he survived during the "Cultural Revolution" when we were knocked down. He was in an extremely difficult position then, and he said and did many things that he would have wished not to. But the people forgave him because, had he not done and said those things, he himself would not have been able to survive and play the neutralising role he did, which reduced losses. He succeeded in protecting quite a number of people.[194]

Chou held the office of premier until the day he died. Now the choice of his successor could no longer be put off. Teng was the obvious candidate. His selection would have signaled a continuing willingness to retain a moderating figure at the helm. Despite the mounting tide of leftist criticism of his restorationist policies, Teng had not yet suffered any public humiliation, and was allowed to give the memorial address at Chou En-lai's funeral.[195]

But Mao must have calculated that to allow Teng to inherit Chou's mantle would make him virtually immovable, certainly after his own death. Teng had to be struck down now or he would eventually remove those who sincerely sought to preserve the Maoist vision and the achievements of the Cultural Revolution. The same argument militated against the succession of other leading survivors like Yeh Chien-ying and Li Hsien-nien.

The likeliest radical candidate for the premiership was the most capable member of the Gang of Four, the second-ranking vice-premier under Teng Hsiao-p'ing, Chang Ch'un-ch'iao. But Mao had almost certainly decided long since that a radical would not be a viable successor to Chou. Far from being able to preserve Maoism, a radical premier would precipitate a backlash that would remove both person and program.

So Mao had to choose a beneficiary of the Cultural Revolution, presumably on the shrewd assumption that such a person would be sufficiently indebted to Mao and committed to the Cultural Revolution to try to tread

---

194 "Answers to the Italian journalist Oriana Fallaci," in *Selected works of Deng Xiaoping (1975–1982)*, 329–30. For a suggestion that at the outset of the Cultural Revolution, Chou En-lai took a positive view of it, see Chou, *Li-shih tsai che-li ch'en-ssu*, vol. 1, 57–58.
195 Teng's speech is in "Quarterly chronicle and documentation," *CQ*, 66 (June 1976), 420–24.

the same path. A beneficiary might also want to preserve a radical element in the leadership to balance any threat to his own position from the old guard. Thus the pure Maoist torch would be kept alight within the Politburo, even if not at its very apex.

Mao chose Hua Kuo-feng, for reasons that are still not known; perhaps the Chairman simply made another mistake in selecting an appropriate heir. Hua's work as an official in Mao's home province had brought him early to the Chairman's favorable attention.[196] It has also been suggested that Hua played a key role in the post–Lin Piao cleanup, but so did Chi Teng-k'uei, another potential candidate as successor. Hua's position as minister of public security, assumed at the Fourth NPC a year earlier, gave him a power base that Mao may have thought an untested successor would need. On 21 and 28 January, he conveyed to the Politburo that Hua should be made acting premier and take over from Teng the control of the Party's daily work.[197] Mao also ordered that Teng's ally Yeh Chien-ying be replaced as head of the MAC by a military beneficiary of the Cultural Revolution, Ch'en Hsi-lien, presumably to prevent Hua being outflanked.[198] The covert campaign against Teng was stepped up.

The Gang of Four's strategy

The Gang of Four were furious at the elevation of Hua Kuo-feng, especially Chang Ch'un-ch'iao, who had apparently long coveted the premiership.[199] This led them to commit a major strategic error which probably cost them whatever slim hope they might have had of retaining power after Mao's death. Instead of collaborating with potential allies, they went all-out for power.

196 See Michel Oksenberg and Sai-cheung Yeung, "Hua Kuo-feng's pre–Cultural Revolution Hunan years, 1949–1966: the making of a political generalist," *CQ*, 69 (March 1977), 29–34.
197 Why "acting"? Conceivably for protocol reasons: Hua could not formally be named premier until so appointed by the NPC; but when he did obtain the full title in April, it was not as a result of some constitutional process. Possibly Mao, conscious of the error he had made in elevating an untried Wang Hung-wen into a top slot, put Hua on probation to minimize the damage if he proved equally incompetent. Or possibly he wished to diminish opposition from among his old comrades by implying that Teng had not been permanently displaced but only temporarily set aside. The latter hypothesis might also serve to explain why Mao, in his attacks on Teng, was careful to say that the latter's sins were contradictions among the people and could be resolved; see Hao and Tuan, *Chung-kuo kung-ch'an-tang liu-shih-nien*, 650.
198 Fang, *Chung-hua jen-min kung-ho-kuo ching-chi ta-shih-chi (1949–1980)*, 559. According to this account, Ch'en Hsi-lien was to replace Yeh Chien-ying while the latter was sick, but since no other account I have seen (e.g., Hao and Tuan, *Chung-kuo kung-ch'an-tang liu-shih-nien*, 649; Kao and Yen, *"Wen-hua ta-ko-ming" shih-nien shih*, 575) mentions this as a motive, one must assume it was a political illness brought on by anger at Mao's decision about Hua. Certainly Yeh had been well enough to attend Chou's memorial service on 15 January.
199 For Chang Ch'un-ch'iao's reactions to his personal setback, see Kao and Yen, *"Wen-hua ta-ko-ming" shih-nien shih*, 575–76.

TABLE 7

The political complexion of the Politburo after the death of Chou En-lai

(Names in boldface are of members of the Standing Committee; those in capitals are of full members, others are of alternate members. A name in parentheses means the person probably was politically dormant owing to age or illness.[a])

Radicals	Beneficiaries	Survivors
Mao Tse-tung	**Hua Kuo-feng**	**Teng Hsiao-p'ing**
Wang Hung-wen		**Yeh Chien-ying**
Chang Ch'un-ch'iao		(Chu Te)
CHIANG CH'ING	LI TE-SHENG[b]	LI HSIEN-NIEN
YAO WEN-YUAN	CH'EN HSI-LIEN	(LIU PO-CH'ENG)
	CHI TENG-K'UEI	HSU SHIH-YU
	WANG TUNG-HSING	WEI KUO-CH'ING
	WU TE	
	CH'EN YUNG-KUEI	
	Wu Kuei-hsien	Su Chen-hua
	Ni Chih-fu	Saifudin

[a] K'ang Sheng and Tung Pi-wu died in 1975.

[b] For reasons that are not clear, Li Te-sheng "asked to be relieved of" his vice-chairmanship of the CCP and membership of the PSC when Teng Hsiao-p'ing took over the running of the country in January 1975; see *Chung-kung tang-shih ta-shih nien-piao*, 391. Li had been a commander in the Second Field Army led by Liu Po-ch'eng and Teng Hsiao-p'ing during the Civil War. In 1982, he wrote the preface to one of the many accounts of their military exploits: see Yang Kuo-yü, et al., eds., *Liu Teng ta-chün cheng-chan chi* (A record of the great military campaigns of Liu [Po-ch'eng] and Teng [Hsiao-p'ing]), 1.1–4.

The political complexion of the Politburo at this time was not unfavorable to the Gang. (See Table 7.) The survivors from among the pre–Cultural Revolution old guard were on the defensive and weak in active members. With Teng and Yeh Chien-ying neutralized on the sidelines, Wang Hung-wen and Chang Ch'un-ch'iao could have worked with Hua Kuo-feng to dominate the Party from their vantage point within the Politburo Standing Committee. Hua would presumably have welcomed such support at this critical time, especially since it would have come with Mao's blessing. The Gang's natural allies were beneficiaries like Hua. They were relatively young and active; and, as Mao probably sensed, because of the manner in which they had risen to power, they would be suspected by and suspicious of the survivors. Moreover, the beneficiaries included key military and political figures who could be important allies in any showdown: Ch'en Hsi-lien, the commander of the Peking Military Region; Wang Tung-hsing, the commander of the leaders' guards, PLA Unit 8341; Wu Te, the party boss of the capital.[200]

200 The suitability of these men as allies of the radicals is underlined by the fact that Teng Hsiao-p'ing insisted on their removal when he returned to power after the death of Mao. These three together with Chi Teng-k'uei were nicknamed the "little gang of four."

But without Mao in firm daily control, the Gang brooked no compromise, instead allowing their naturally combative attitudes free rein. Accustomed until recently to acting as the Chairman's gatekeeper and representative,[201] Chiang Ch'ing was not about to play second fiddle to a political upstart. As early as the Ta-chai conference the previous autumn, she had begun sniping at the timidity with which the rising Hua Kuo-feng, whom she described as a "nice gentleman of Malenkov's ilk," sought to pursue their shared goals.[202] Now, instead of reassessing their position in the wake of Hua's appointment, the Gang stepped up their campaign against him,[203] thus ensuring he would eventually have to turn to the survivors for support. Yet the reality of interdependence was about to be dramatically demonstrated.

Not content with pursuing Teng and undermining Hua, the Gang recklessly flouted what they must have known was popular sentiment about Chou En-lai. When the premier died, no announcement was made that he would be cremated, or where and when the ceremony would take place. But the news got out, and an estimated 1 million people lined the route from T'ien An Men Square to the Pa-pao-shan Cemetery, many clutching white paper chrysanthemums to symbolize their mourning. At one point, the crowd surged forward and stopped the cortege to demand that Chou be buried, which would be in accordance with the Chinese custom; only after Chou's widow, Teng Ying-ch'ao, got out of her car and assured the crowd that cremation had been the premier's wish was the cortege allowed to continue.[204] In the weeks that followed there was evidence from all around the country of the popularity of Chou and the unpopularity of his enemies.[205]

The Gang's reaction was not to lie low for a time, but rather to confront Chou's memory. Their control of the media enabled them to restrict the public airing of grief and to sanction blatant attacks on his policies, although he was not denounced by name.[206] They finally overstepped the mark on 25 March, when the *Wen-hui pao*, a major Shanghai newspaper controlled by them, printed a front-page article in which Chou En-lai was unmistakably referred to as a "capitalist-roader." In Nanking, there were strong student-led protests against the Gang, which were not covered by the media. But the news reached Peking and other cities because students,

201 Chin, "*Wen-hua ta-ko-ming*," 191–92.
202 Domes, *The government and politics of the PRC*, 130.
203 Kao and Yen, "*Wen-hua ta-ko-ming*" *shih-nien shih*, 576–77.
204 Roger Garside, *Coming alive!: China after Mao*, 8–9.
205 Kao and Yen, "*Wen-hua ta-ko-ming*" *shih-nien shih*, 582–86.   206 Ibid., 581–82.

using tar, wrote slogans on the outside of railway carriages.[207] This "Nanking incident" was the prelude to a far more dramatic demonstration of support for Chou and Teng and hatred for the Gang of Four in the heart of the capital, right in front of the large portrait of Mao on the Gate of Heavenly Peace, the T'ien An Men.

The T'ien An Men incident, 1976

It was the time of the traditional Ch'ing Ming Festival when ancestors were remembered and their graves swept. In an effort to stamp out "superstition" years earlier, the CCP had attempted to transform this festival into a time for remembering revolutionary heroes. Now the people of Peking seized this opportunity to commemorate one of the greatest of all the CCP's heroes and to express their views on the current political situation.

Pupils of Peking's Cow Lane Primary School placed the first wreath by the Heroes' Monument in the center of T'ien An Men Square on 19 March. Four days later, a man from Anhwei province laid another one, with a dedication to Chou En-lai's memory. Both were swiftly removed by the police. The head of the capital's public security bureau muttered darkly about a "serious class struggle at the back of the wreaths." At dawn on 25 March, a middle school left its wreath, and shortly thereafter some workers left their memorial board beside it. On 30 March, the first group of soldiers left theirs. These tributes were not removed and they had a galvanizing effect on the city's population.[208]

From 30 March on, the laying of wreaths at the monument escalated rapidly, in defiance of the orders of the city authorities. Column after column, dozens of units, thousands of people, marched to the square to place their wreaths, declaim their tributes, and read those of others. On the festival day, 4 April, a Sunday holiday, an estimated 2 million people visited the square.

The bottom part of the Heroes' Monument was buried in wreaths. Surrounding it, an army of wreaths mounted on stands marched outward toward the sides of the square. A typical wreath was homemade of paper flowers, usually in mourning white, with a picture of Chou En-lai in its center, and two ribbons of white silk hanging from it, inscribed with a memorial tribute. Many had eulogies or poems pinned to them; other

207 Ibid., 586–97; Hao and Tuan, *Chung-kuo kung-ch'an-tang liu-shih-nien*, 652; Garside, *Coming alive!* 110–14.
208 Kao and Yen, *"Wen-hua ta-ko-ming" shih-nien shih*, 598–99.

poems were pasted on the monument. It was these tributes that became the focus of attention of the crowds, packed tight but eager to find out to what degree others shared their feelings.[209]

Some eulogies simply commemorated the premier:

He left no inheritance, he had no children, he has no grave, he left no remains. His ashes were scattered over the mountains and rivers of our land. It seems he left us nothing, but he will live forever in our hearts. The whole land is his, he has hundreds of millions of children and grandchildren and all China's soil is his tomb. So he left us everything. He will live in our hearts for all time. Who is he? Who is he? He is our Premier![210]

Such sentiments were widely shared, but it was the attacks on the Gang of Four that were most keenly read. Some were hidden behind veils of allusion. Others were totally transparent:

> You must be mad
> To want to be an empress!
> Here's a mirror to look at yourself
> And see what you really are.
> You've got together a little gang
> To stir up trouble all the time,
> Hoodwinking the people, capering about.
> But your days are numbered....
> Whoever dares oppose our Premier
> Is like a mad dog barking at the sun –
> Wake up to reality![211]

In the face of this verbal onslaught, the Gang of Four temporarily woke up to reality. They collaborated with the beneficiaries in the Politburo to take strong action. The Politburo had already met on 1 April to agree that the Nanking incident had been splittist and supportive of Teng Hsiao-p'ing. On the basis of that negative assessment, the Peking police had begun to take action in T'ien An Men Square on 2 and 3 April, trying to inhibit the mourners, removing some wreaths.[212]

On the evening of 4 April, as the Ch'ing Ming Festival drew to a close,

---

209 Garside, *Coming alive!* 115–36. Garside, a Chinese-speaking British foreign service officer who had been posted back to the British embassy in Peking in January 1976, gives an elegiac eyewitness account of these events. The fullest and most vivid Chinese account is probably that in Kao and Yen, *"Wen-hua ta-ko-ming" shih-nien shih*, 598–637; the estimate of the numbers in the square on 4 April is in this source, 611. The present author was in Peking from 1 to 4 April, but this account relies heavily on these two sources.

210 Quoted in Garside, *Coming alive!* 117.

211 Xiao Lan, *The Tiananmen poems*, 29–30. This set of English translations comprises only a small fraction of the poems and eulogies pasted up in the square at this time. See, for instance, *Ko-ming shih ch'ao* (A transcript of revolutionary poems), in two volumes, republished later as T'ung Huai-chou, ed., *T'ien-an-men shih-wen chi* (Poems from the Gate of Heavenly Peace).

212 Hao and Tuan, *Chung-kuo kung-ch'an-tang liu-shih-nien*, 652.

the Politburo met again to assess the situation in T'ien An Men Square. Prominent members of the old guard – Chu Te, Yeh Chien-ying, Li Hsien-nien, and the general Hsu Shih-yu who had supported them – were not present;[213] Teng Hsiao-p'ing could not have been there either. The beneficiaries and the Gang of Four appeared to be in total command. Hua Kuo-feng blamed provocateurs for what was happening in T'ien An Men Square, and opined that some poems were vicious direct attacks on the Chairman and many others in the central leadership. Another beneficiary, the Peking Party first secretary, Wu Te, detected coordinated activity, and attributed it directly to preparations made by Teng during 1974–75. He said, "The nature of [the activity] is clear. It's a counterrevolutionary incident."[214] Chiang Ch'ing asked if the safety of the central leadership was guaranteed and why their opponents had not been arrested.[215]

The basis for continued collaboration between the Gang of Four and the beneficiaries became clear during the meeting. Both groups felt threatened. What they stood for was being rejected. If Hua were correct in asserting that Mao personally was a target of some of the mourning verses, then even the ultimate basis of their shared power was being questioned.[216] If that could happen while the Chairman was still alive, what about when his backing was only posthumous? At the very least, this massive and unprecedented upsurge of support for Chou meant that the Chinese people now rejected Mao as the unique and godlike guide to their future. There was an alternate path and they preferred it. They rejected, too, Mao's choice of successor. The implication of their homage to Chou was that they wanted Teng Hsiao-p'ing back as his rightful heir. Everyone at the Politburo meeting that night knew that his return would spell disaster for them.

It was thus necessary to act swiftly and firmly. Mao Yuan-hsin relayed the conclusions of the meeting to his uncle, and when the Chairman sent back his agreement, the police were ordered into action. By 4:00 A.M. on 5 April, the square had been totally cleared of wreaths and writings; people who stayed late to read the verses or stand guard over the memorials were arrested.[217] By about 5:00 A.M., Wang Hung-wen was instructing the police on how to behave when day came.[218]

213 Ibid.   214 Hu, *Chung-kuo she-hui-chu-i ko-ming ho chien-she shih chiang-i*, 331.
215 Kao and Yen, "*Wen-hua ta-ko-ming*" *shih-nien shih*, 619.
216 One clear dig at Mao and his "feudal-style" cult came in a reference to the emperor Ch'in Shih-huang-ti, to whom the Chairman was often implicitly compared: "China is no longer the China of the past, And the people are no longer wrapped in utter ignorance, Gone for good is Qin Shi Huang's feudal society ..." Quoted in Garside, *Coming alive!* 127.
217 Hu, *Chung-kuo she-hui-chu-i ko-ming ho chien-she shih chiang-i*, 331.
218 Kao and Yen, "*Wen-hua ta-ko-ming*" *shih-nien shih*, 621.

News of the authorities' action spread rapidly, and people began converging on the square from all over the city, this time as individuals rather than in groups. But one group, ten middle school students, did turn up just after 6:00 A.M. to lay their tribute only to find their way barred by soldiers and workers' militia who surrounded the monument, explaining that it had to be cleaned.[219] A foreign eyewitness who arrived at 8:00 A.M. reported that already there were ten thousand people in the square. Facing the Great Hall of the People on the west side of the square, they shouted, "Give back our wreaths! Give back our comrades-in-arms!"[220] Ordered to disperse, but given no explanation for the removal of the wreaths, the crowd lost its temper. A police van was overturned and its occupants forced to apologize for alleging that the crowd was being led astray by "class enemies." A radical and presumably rehearsed Tsing-hua student who had the temerity to criticize wreath laying on behalf of the "biggest capitalist-roader in the Party" was roughed up and forced to retreat. By the early afternoon, several police vehicles had been burned, and a police command post had been stormed and set on fire.[221]

At 6:30 P.M., Wu Te broadcast an appeal through the square's loudspeaker system, calling on people to disperse.[222] Most did, all but a few hundred, according to Chinese accounts.[223] Then, at 9:35 P.M., the square was suddenly flooded with light. Martial music was played over the loudspeakers. Members of the militia, the public security forces, and the Peking garrison troops, who had been assembled in the Forbidden City behind the T'ien An Men, appeared on the square, armed with sticks, and began beating people. By 9:45 P.M., the carnage was over and the wounded members of the "masses" were taken away for interrogation.[224]

Meeting that evening, the Politburo concluded that this "incident" had been a "counterrevolutionary riot." On 7 April, informed of the events by Mao Yuan-hsin, the Chairman ordered the publication of the *People's Daily*'s version of what had happened together with the text of Wu Te's appeal. Teng was to be relieved of all his posts, but allowed to retain his Party membership in case he reformed; what else might have befallen him is unclear, for on the same day he was spirited away to safety in the south

219 Ibid., 622.
220 "*Huan wo hua-ch'üan, huan wo chan-yu*;" *Chung-kung tang-shih ta-shih nien-piao*, 401; Garside, *Coming alive!* 129.
221 Garside, *Coming alive!* 129–31.
222 The text is in Kao and Yen, "*Wen-hua ta-ko-ming*" *shih-nien shih*, 629–30.
223 Ibid., 633; Hao and Tuan, *Chung-kuo kung-ch'an-tang liu-shih-nien*, 653, specifies 388 arrests. Garside, *Coming alive!* 132, says four thousand remained in the square after Wu Te's speech, but this was on the basis of estimates rather than police records.
224 Hao and Tuan, *Chung-kuo kung-ch'an-tang liu-shih-nien*, 653; Kao and Yen, "*Wen-hua ta-ko-ming*" *shih-nien shih*, 634–35. Garside cites contemporary noncommunist reports of a hundred killed; *Coming alive!* 132.

by the PLA, where his allies on the Politburo, Hsu Shih-yu and Wei Kuo-ch'ing, controlled the local armed forces.[225]

In perhaps his most important decision on 7 April, Mao ordered that Hua Kuo-feng should be immediately elevated to the premiership and first deputy chairmanship of the CCP.[226] Either the situation was too dangerous to delay longer or Hua had met whatever test Mao had set him; at any rate, the Chairman had made his final choice of successor. Three weeks later, on the evening of 30 April, after the new first deputy chairman reported to him on the state of the country, Mao used the legitimating words that Hua would later brandish as a talisman: "With you in charge, I'm at ease."[227] In fact, Hua was to prove no more viable than any of his three predecessors. But Mao would never know.

The death of Mao

For superstitious or tradition-minded Chinese, which probably meant the majority of the nation, the year 1976 was replete with omens of disaster. The death of Chou in January was followed in July by the death at 89 of the grand old soldier of the revolution, Chu Te, the general whose loyalty to Mao during the early years in the wilderness had ensured military subservience to the Party. Three weeks later, a massive earthquake hit the area of the North China coal-mining city of T'ang-shan, killing more than 242,000 people and leaving more than 164,000 seriously injured.[228]

Throughout the country there was unrest, sparked on the one hand by leftist agitation against Teng Hsiao-p'ing, and on the other by popular anger over the way he had been purged. There were stoppages again on the railways. Steel production was 1.23 million tons below target in the first five months of 1976. The production of chemical fertilizer, cotton yarn, and other key industrial goods fell precipitously, causing a drop of 2 billion yuan in national financial receipts. Targets for the annual plan had to be scaled back.[229]

At this time of natural disaster, political turmoil, and economic disruption, it became clear to the elite that Mao's life was drawing to a close.[230] With Teng down but not yet out, it would clearly have been sensible for

---

225 Domes, *The government and politics of the PRC*, 132. I am unaware of any Chinese source that has admitted this was how Teng's safety was preserved.

226 Hao and Tuan, *Chung-kuo kung-ch'an-tang liu-shih-nien*, 653.

227 "*Ni pan shih, wo fang-hsin*"; Kao and Yen, "*Wen-hua ta-ko-ming*" *shih-nien shih*, 699.

228 Fang, *Chung-hua jen-min kung-ho-kuo ching-chi ta-shih chi (1949–1980)*, 568.

229 Ibid., 567. For reports of pro-Teng popular unrest, see Kao and Yen, "*Wen-hua ta-ko-ming*" *shih-nien shih*, 641–59; for an analysis of leftist agitation, see ibid., 662–76.

230 For an account of Mao's parlous condition at the time of the annual Spring Festival, see Chang, "Anecdotes of Mao Zedong and Zhou Enlai in their later years."

the Gang of Four to solidify the alliance forged with the Politburo beneficiaries during the T'ien An Men riot in order to be sure of weathering
the critical weeks ahead. But they threw away their last opportunity by
attacking Hua Kuo-feng at a national planning conference in July. They
had evidently decided to confront the beneficiaries by military force if
necessary, and in August, as the Chairman's life was ebbing away, they
began to put the Shanghai militia, which they had been building up since
1967, into a state of readiness.[231]

The generals, too, were preparing. As the senior marshal by virtue of
his place on the Politburo, Yeh Chien-ying was lobbied by General Wang
Chen to move against the Gang of Four. Yeh's fellow marshal Nieh
Jung-chen and General Yang Ch'eng-wu also had frequent strategy
sessions with him. Yeh was having consultations with members of the
Politburo, presumably including Hua Kuo-feng and other beneficiaries
whom the Gang had spurned. He also traveled to his native Kwangtung,
where he reportedly found Teng Hsiao-p'ing in a combative mood:

Either we accept the fate of being slaughtered and let the Party and the country
degenerate, let the country which was founded with the heart and soul of our
proletarian revolutionaries of the old generation be destroyed by those four
people, and let history retrogress one hundred years, or we should struggle
against them as long as there is still any life in our body. If we win, everything
can be solved. If we lose, we can take to the mountains as long as we live or we
can find a shield in other countries, to wait for another opportunity. At present,
we can use at least the strength of the Canton Military Region, the Fuchou Military Region, and the Nanking Military Region to fight against them. Any pro-
crastination and we will risk losing this, our only capital.[232]

But Yeh wanted to wait. He indicated to Wang Chen that he did not
think it appropriate to move before Mao's death;[233] he justified procras-
tinating with the phrase "Spare the rat to save the dishes" (*t'ou shu chi
ch'i*),[234] implying that he did not want to humiliate Mao by arresting his
wife as a counterrevolutionary while he was still alive. When Mao died at

231 Hao and Tuan, *Chung-kuo kung-ch'an-tang liu-shih-nien*, 654–55; Kao and Yen, *"Wen-hua ta-ko-
    ming" shih-nien shih*, 678–79. In early September, Chiang Ch'ing was revisiting the Ta-chai bri-
    gade when an urgent message came from Peking saying the Chairman was sinking fast. She alleg-
    edly went on playing poker with her guards and medical attendants for some time before leaving
    for the capital; Kao and Yen, ibid., 691.
232 Quoted in Garside, *Coming alive!* 140–41; the source of the quotation is unclear. Garside does
    not explore the implications of Teng's remark about finding "a shield in other countries."
233 Hsueh Yeh-sheng, ed., *Yeh Chien-ying kuang-hui-ti i-sheng* (Yeh Chien-ying's glorious life), 342–
    43. Formally, Yeh and Nieh were ex-marshals, as military ranks had been abolished under Lin
    Piao before the Cultural Revolution.
234 Wang Nien-i, "'Wen-hua ta-ko-ming' ts'o-wu fa-chan mai-lo" ("Analysis of the development of
    the errors of the 'Great Cultural Revolution,'") *Tang-shih t'ung-hsun* (Party history newsletter),
    October 1986.

ten minutes past midnight on 9 September, Yeh Chien-ying was ready to act.[235]

The arrest of the Gang of Four

The strategic mistake of the Gang of Four had been to fail to make common cause with the beneficiaries. Their tactical error was for all of them to remain in Peking after Mao's death. Lin Piao's plan to set up a rival CC in Canton, Teng's retreat to his allies' bailiwick in the south, indeed, the whole history of the Chinese revolution, should have taught them the critical importance of relocating to a secure base area when faced with potentially superior force. They ignored those lessons.

Chiang Ch'ing and her colleagues were clearly affected by hubris. They had risen to power rapidly and easily by virtue of Mao's support, and they had exercised that power in an imperious manner with his acquiescence. All of them had luxuriated in a degree of privilege that the CCP had launched a revolution to eliminate, but which, as Milovan Djilas has pointed out, is an inevitable companion of bureaucratic dictatorship.[236] In an earlier century, they would have been a court cabal, presuming upon their closeness to the emperor, insufficiently acquainted with the realities of power outside his penumbra.

Unlike most such cabals, the Gang of Four had a considerable regional power base in Shanghai to which they could have temporarily retreated. Instead, they apparently assumed that the combination of their relationship to Mao, membership in the Politburo Standing Committee, and control of the media had equipped them to take power in the capital, and they bent all their efforts to that goal. At the predawn Politburo meeting just after Mao's death, Chiang Ch'ing appeared to be more interested in securing the immediate expulsion of Teng Hsiao-p'ing from the CCP than in settling the funeral arrangements.[237]

The Gang seem to have had a three-pronged plan of action: to assert their right to Mao's ideological mantle; to attempt to gain control of the Central Party apparatus; and to prepare for armed confrontation. Under Yao Wen-yuan's direction, the main media organs were soon trumpeting

---

235 At some point during Mao's last days (hours?) of life, all members of the Politburo were brought in one by one to pay their final farewell; see Fan Shuo, "The tempestuous October – a chronicle of the complete collapse of the 'Gang of Four,'" *Yang-ch'eng wan-pao*, 10 February 1989, translated in FBIS *Daily Report: China*, 14 February 1989, 17.

236 Milovan Djilas, *The new class: an analysis of the Communist system*, 42–47. Terrill devotes much space to a discussion of Chiang Ch'ing's privileged life-style, and to a comparison of her and outstanding Chinese empresses; see *The white-boned demon*, esp. 317–23.

237 Hsueh, ed., *Yeh Chien-ying kuang-hui-ti i-sheng*, 342.

the importance of Mao's alleged deathbed injunction (*lin-chung chu-fu*): "Act according to the principles laid down" (*An chi-ting fang-chen pan*). Not to do so would be to "betray Marxism, socialism, and the great theory of continuing the revolution under the dictatorship of the proletariat."[238] Clearly the objective was to head off any attempt either to reverse the current campaign against Teng Hsiao-p'ing or, even more threatening, to disavow the Cultural Revolution.

By creating an appropriate ideological climate through the press, the Gang could sway lower-ranking cadres' judgment of the balance of forces in the capital.[239] But this was not tantamount to taking over the reins of power. Shortly after Mao's death, the Gang attempted to assert a right of leadership over provincial organs. Wang Hung-wen set up his own "duty office" in the Chung-nan-hai, sending a message to provincial committees in the name of the CC's General Office ordering all major problems to be referred to himself.[240] From 12 September, the Gang promoted a write-in campaign to pressure the Politburo to appoint Chiang Ch'ing chairman in Mao's place.[241] Pictures published on the occasion of the obsequies for the late Chairman were designed to accustom the public to the idea of Chiang Ch'ing emerging as his successor.[242]

The Gang pressed for a swift decision. On 19 September, Chiang Ch'ing demanded that the Politburo Standing Committee – at this point consisting of Hua Kuo-feng, Wang Hung-wen, Yeh Chien-ying, and Chang Ch'un-ch'iao – hold an emergency conference and that she and Mao Yuan-hsin should attend, but Yeh should not. At the meeting, Chiang proposed that Mao Yuan-hsin should be entrusted with sorting through his uncle's papers, presumably with a view to his discovering, or

---

238 Hao and Tuan, *Chung-kuo kung-ch'an-tang liu-shih-nien*, 656. According to post–Cultural Revolution accounts, Mao actually said to Hua Kuo-feng on 30 April 1976, "Act according to past principles" (*Chao kuo-ch'ü fang-chen pan*); see Kao and Yen, *"Wen-hua ta-ko-ming" shih-nien shih*, 699. One analysis of the difference between the formulations argues that the Gang of Four's version suggests obedience to specific policies that they had been promoting on Mao's behalf or that they might claim to have documentary proof of in the Chairman's papers, whereas the Hua Kuo-feng version advocates no more than a vague continuity. See Gardner, *Chinese politics and the succession to Mao*, 111–13.

239 Provincial papers immediately began repeating Mao's alleged deathbed injunction; see Hu, *Chung-kuo she-hui-chu-i ko-ming ho chien-she shih chiang-i*, 335.

240 Whether in doing this Wang exceeded his authority as a member of the Politburo Standing Committee as afterward alleged must remain uncertain. Two years earlier, Wang had apparently attempted to insert Shanghai cadres in central CCP and government organs, though with what success is unclear; see Chung, *K'ang Sheng p'ing-chuan*, 316.

241 Ibid., 334–35; *Chung-kung tang-shih ta-shih nien-piao*, 403.

242 Ladany, *The Communist Party of China and Marxism, 1921–1985*, 385. For an eyewitness account of the memorial service on 18 September, see Garside, *Coming alive!* 147–49. In late September, a mimeographed copy of Mao's purported last wishes reached Hong Kong; according to it, Mao had asked a group of leaders in June to help Chiang Ch'ing in "hoisting the Red Flag" after he was dead. See Ting, *Chairman Hua*, 112.

at least "discovering," a last will favoring her takeover. The vote went in favor of keeping the Chairman's papers locked up in the CC's General Office.[243]

On 29 September, at another Politburo conference, Chiang Ch'ing and Chang Ch'un-ch'iao tried to force the issue of her future role. They rejected a proposal from Yeh Chien-ying and Li Hsien-nien that Mao Yuan-hsin should return to his job in Liaoning province, countering with a suggestion that he should be entrusted with preparing the political report for the next CC plenum.[244] The Gang were outvoted, however: Mao Yuan-hsin was ordered back to Liaoning, and the leadership question was shelved.[245]

The Gang's third measure was to prepare for confrontation. The militia in Shanghai, perhaps 100,000 strong, was issued with weapons and arms, and warned to be ready for a fight. Secret contacts were established with Ting Sheng, the CO of the Nanking Military Region. Wang Hung-wen and the others breathed fire in speeches before friendly audiences.[246]

Mao Yuan-hsin caused a momentary panic on 2 October when he ordered an armored division to move to Peking; but a telephone call to Yeh Chien-ying from the Military Region headquarters elicited an immediate countermanding order.[247] Despite, or perhaps because of, the vicissitudes of the Cultural Revolution, the military chain-of-command loyalty was firmly in place, and the Gang and their adherents were not part of it.

Post–Cultural Revolution historians may well have exaggerated the extent to which the Gang were bent on a military coup. Even in their wildest fantasies, they could not have believed that their Shanghai militia could prevail over the likely opposition of most of the PLA. Shanghai could perhaps be a last-ditch stronghold, but not a Yenan-style springboard for victory. Indeed, by remaining in Peking, Chiang Ch'ing and her colleagues gave every impression of having deluded themselves into thinking that even after Mao, it would be politics as usual. The struggle would go on, but under Cultural Revolution rules that had always brought the Gang out on top. But their patron was dead, and they were

---

243 Chin, "*Wen-hua ta-ko-ming*," 214–15. Another version has Chiang Ch'ing and Mao Yuan-hsin bullying Mao's secretary into handing over some documents, which were only returned after Hau Kuo-feng's intervention; see Ting, *Chairman Hua*, 111.
244 Chin, "*Wen-hua ta-ko-ming*," 214–15.
245 Hsueh, *Yeh Chien-ying kuang-hui-ti i-sheng*, 345.
246 Hao and Tuan, *Chung-kuo kung-ch'an-tang liu-shih-nien*, 655–66; Chin, "*Wen-hua ta-ko-ming*," 214–15.
247 Kao and Yen, "*Wen-hua ta-ko-ming*" *shih-nien shih*, 699.

up against men who had fought long years to win China, and had made a
revolution by disregarding the rules and taking swift and ruthless action
when need be.

Sooner or later, such action was inevitable, for the reasons Teng
Hsiao-p'ing had given in his southern hideout. Yeh Chien-ying apparently felt that Hua Kuo-feng had to play a key role because of his
positions as the CCP's first deputy chairman and premier. Yeh found Hua
indecisive. Hua had originally wanted to convene a CC plenum to settle
the leadership dispute with the Gang of Four, but after the Politburo confrontation on 29 September, and after Yeh had promised him the support
of the old comrades if he stood up and fought, Hua became convinced
that the time for formal procedures was long past.[248]

An ideologically uncompromising article in the *Kuang-ming jih-pao* on 4
October, following provocative speeches by Chiang Ch'ing and Wang
Hung-wen, finally triggered the coup against the Gang, according to one
account.[249] There were worrying indications that the Gang were planning
some sort of action, for their followers were told to expect good news by
9 October. Alarmed, Yeh Chien-ying went into hiding in the capital.
Then, on 5 October, Hua Kuo-feng, Yeh Chien-ying, and Li Hsien-nien
held a Politburo conference at the PLA General Staff HQ in the Western
Hills outside Peking, to which the Gang were not invited. It was
unanimously agreed that Chiang Ch'ing, Wang Hung-wen, Chang Ch'un-
ch'iao, Yao Wen-yuan, Mao Yuan-hsin, and their principal supporters
had to be seized. Wang Tung-hsing and PLA Unit 8341 were ordered to
carry out this decision. They did so on 6 October. When Chiang Ch'ing
was arrested at her residence, her servant spat on her. The Cultural
Revolution was over.[250]

248 Hsueh, *Yeh Chien-ying kuang-hui-ti i-sheng*, 344–45.

249 This article was prepared by two members of the *Liang Hsiao* group, apparently at the urging
     of the editors of the *KMJP*. According to one of the authors, the article was dashed off with
     no prior consultation with members of the Gang of Four. Nevertheless, it was sufficiently
     disquieting for Politburo member Ch'en Hsi-lien to return immediately to Peking from T'ang-
     shan to consult with Yeh Chien-ying.

250 There is some disagreement as to the precise manner and moment of the arrest of the Gang of
     Four. According to Fan, "The tempestuous October," 21, a meeting of the Politburo Stand-
     ing Committee was called (presumably by Hua Kuo-feng) to discuss the final proofs of the
     fifth volume of Mao's *Selected works* and to study the proposals for the Mao mausoleum to be
     built in T'ien An Men Square. In addition to Wang Hung-wen and Chang Ch'un-ch'iao, who
     would come to the 8:00 P.M. meeting in the Huai-jen-t'ang in the Chung-nan-hai complex as of
     right, Yao Wen-yuan was also invited under the pretext that as the nation's leading propagan-
     dist, he would be the obvious person to carry out any last-minute revisions or polishing for the
     Mao volume. When each arrived, Hua Kuo-feng read out an agreed statement: "The central
     authorities maintain that you have committed unforgivable crimes, and have made a decision on
     investigating your case. You are prohibited from having access to the outside world during the
     investigation." Thereupon, Wang Tung-hsing's personnel escorted the prisoners away. Simul-
     taneously, Chiang Ch'ing and Mao Yuan-hsin were being arrested in their residences elsewhere

INTERREGNUM

In the immediate aftermath of the death of Mao and the purge of the Gang of Four, the urgent national need was for calm and stability. The Party, the PLA, and the people had to be reassured that the era of upheaval was over, and that the country was under firm but moderate leadership. A somewhat contradictory image of change combined with continuity had to be conveyed.

A priority was to settle the question that had rent the leadership since the outset of the Cultural Revolution: "After Mao, who?" The leading survivors, Yeh Chien-ying and Li Hsien-nien, presumably decided that this was no time for renewed struggle within the rump of the Politburo, already reduced by death and defeat to sixteen of the twenty-five appointed at the Tenth Congress only three years earlier. Whatever his merits, Hua Kuo-feng wore the mantle of legitimacy and had the rights of occupancy. He had been the Chairman's choice, he was in place, and he had led the beneficiaries into the anti-Gang camp. On 7 September, his assumption of Mao's posts as chairman of both the Party and its Military Affairs Commission was announced. Because he retained the premiership, Hua was now formally the heir of both Mao and Chou En-lai. By combining the roles of both men, he seemed to have been placed in an impregnable position. He would discover that position conferred prestige and privilege, but power had deeper roots.

Simultaneously with agreeing on a new leader, the Politburo had to neutralize the country's one radical bastion. Fortunately Shanghai turned out to be a paper tiger. Deprived of their national leaders, the Gang's deputies there vacillated, allowed themselves to be lured to Peking by transparent stratagems, and finally collapsed without fulfilling any of their threats of a fight to the finish. In the event, there was a week of light armed resistance. The Politburo dispatched two of their alternate members, Su Chen-hua and Ni Chih-fu, to take control; Hsu Shih-yu temporarily reassumed his old command of the Nanking Military Region, displacing the unreliable Ting Sheng, to provide the politicians with any necessary military backup.[251] With Shanghai reclaimed, it was now up to Hua Kuo-feng to provide the country with leadership.

in the Chung-nan-hai. See also Wang Nien-i, *Ta-tung-luan-ti nien-tai*, 607–9; Hsueh, *Yeh Chien-ying kuang-hui-ti i-sheng*, 345–46; *Ying-ssu lu*, 74–75. According to Kao and Yen, "*Wen-hua ta-ko-ming" shih-nien shih*, 700–703, however, the Gang of Four were all arrested in residences in the Tiao-yü-t'ai in the early hours of 6 October.

251 Kao and Yen, "*Wen-hua ta-ko-ming" shih-nien shih*, 703–8; Hao and Tuan, *Chung-kuo kung-ch'an-tang liu-shih-nien*, 657; *Chung-kung tang-shih ta-shih nien-piao*, 405. Domes's account suggests greater bloodshed – *The government and politics of the PRC*, 138.

Hua Kuo-feng's dilemma

From the outset, Hua Kuo-feng's leadership was hamstrung by an insol-
uble dilemma, symbolized by the contradictory heritages of Mao and
Chou that he had been bequeathed. On the one hand, there was no doubt
that Mao wanted the goals and gains of the Cultural Revolution to be
maintained. To disavow the Cultural Revolution would be to undermine
the position of the man who had chosen him as his successor, and indeed
to negate the whole period whose upheavals had permitted Hua to rise
from relative obscurity to his current eminence. Hua's only claim to legitimacy was Mao's blessing, and he moved swiftly to ensure that only he
had control of Mao's legacy. On 8 October, it was announced that a fifth
volume of the late Chairman's selected works would be published under
the editorial control of Hua Kuo-feng. A simultaneous decision was to
erect a mausoleum for Mao in T'ien An Men Square, in defiance of a
twenty-seven-year-old rule agreed to by the Chairman and his colleagues
not to emulate the Soviet pattern of honoring leaders by erecting tombs
and renaming cities and streets.[252] Hua had no doubt of Mao's continuing
significance for himself; he, and presumably his fellow beneficiaries,
wanted to try to ensure that Mao's continuing significance for the country
would be set in marble.

Hua's personal amulet was Mao's now oft-echoed sentence "With you
in charge, I'm at ease." But it was necessary to coin a slogan that would
convey in the ideological realm the symbolism enshrined in the mausoleum: The Chairman is forever with us. Appropriately, Hua approved a
formula proposed by Wang Tung-hsing that seemed to set Mao Tse-tung
Thought in concrete: "Whatever policy Chairman Mao decided upon, we
shall resolutely defend; whatever directives Chairman Mao issued, we
shall steadfastly obey." Their aim was to head off questioning of the actions of the later Mao, which had helped to bring them and other members of what came to be known as the "whatever faction" to power.[253]
Moreover, the preservation of the Mao cult provided a basis and a justification for the burgeoning cult of Hua Kuo-feng himself, badly needed if
this unknown successor was to establish a position among Party and
people.[254]

But the attempt of Hua and the "whatever faction" to don Mao's

---

252 *Chung-kung tang-shih ta-shih nien-piao*, 405.

253 First divulged in a joint editorial of *JMJP*, *HC*, and the Chieh-fang chün pao on 7 February
     1977; *Chung-kung tang-shih ta-shih nien-piao*, 406–7; Hao and Tuan, *Chung-kuo kung-ch'an-tang
     liu-shih-nien*, 670.

254 Ibid., 670. Books and pamphlets about Hua were churned out by the presses. According to
     Stuart R. Schram, writing in 1984, the card index in the library of Peking University contained
     approximately three hundred entries of books and pamphlets contributing to the Hua cult, a

protective mantle had already been challenged by Teng Hsiao-p'ing's protectors in the south. In a letter to Hua, Hsu Shih-yu and Wei Kuo-ch'ing queried the advisability of hushing up Mao's shortcomings, which were known to all; indicated that Mao's blessing of Hua as successor was insufficient legitimation and that it had to be confirmed by a CC plenum; and hinted broadly of a challenge to Hua at such a plenum if Mao's incorrect verdict on Teng were not reversed.[255]

Hua fought back. At the central work conference held from 10 to 22 March to discuss progress on the anti-Gang campaign, he reaffirmed the "two whatevers," repeated formulas from the Cultural Revolution, maintained that the T'ien An Men incident was counterrevolutionary, and asserted that the campaign against Teng and the right-opportunist wind to reverse the verdicts had been correct. He even denounced the Gang of Four as extreme rightists (the tactic *they* had used in the aftermath of the Lin Piao affair) in an effort to defend the continuation of leftist policies.

Hua came under fire from Party veterans, notably Ch'en Yun, who had been a member of the Politburo Standing Committee and its predecessor for more than two decades up to the Cultural Revolution. Ch'en and another critic, Wang Chen, focused on the linked questions of the assessment of the T'ien An Men incident and the need for a second rehabilitation of Teng Hsiao-p'ing, which they claimed was universally demanded. Hua must have wondered if this was the support of veteran cadres that Yeh Chien-ying had promised him in return for taking a lead against the Gang of Four. At any rate, he rejected the demands of Ch'en and Wang and even refused to allow their speeches to be printed in the conference record.[256]

There is no suggestion in Chinese accounts of this work conference that Yeh Chien-ying or Li Hsien-nien joined in their old comrades' criticisms of Hua's position. Almost certainly their feelings must have been mixed. Formally, it would have been unusual for a member of the Politburo Standing Committee like Yeh to criticize another member of that select body in front of a large gathering of more junior Party officials. More importantly, Yeh and Li owed a certain loyalty to Hua, who was now in a sense their creation as well as Mao's. And while Yeh and Li

small fraction, in his judgment, of those published around the country; Stuart R. Schram, "'Economics in command?' Ideology and policy since the Third Plenum, 1978–84," *CQ*, 99 (September 1984), 417, n. 1. A favorite publicity photograph of Hua at this time was of him with Mao, supposedly at the moment when the late Chairman had uttered the magic words of benediction. Some observers claimed to detect that Hua changed his hairstyle to make him resemble Mao.

255 Domes, *The government and politics of the PRC*, 146–47.
256 Hao and Tuan, *Chung-kuo kung-ch'an-tang liu-shih-nien*, 670–71; *Chung-kung tang-shih ta-shih nien-piao*, 407–8. The gist of Ch'en Yun's speech is to be found in *Ch'en Yun wen-hsuan (1956–1985)* (Selected works of Ch'en Yun [1956–1985]), 207.

had doubtless supported everything Teng had tried to do during 1975, they must have been ambivalent about him returning in 1977. With Teng absent, they dominated the political picture as elder statesmen guiding Hua; with Teng back, they would at the very least have to cede part of that role to him. And what would be Teng's attitude toward them? Would he not feel that they, like Chou, had done and said things they regretted in order to survive the Cultural Revolution? And if so, would he forgive the living as well as the dead?

Yet Yeh and Li would have appreciated the strength of sentiment within the Party and PLA and realized that with Mao gone it would be difficult to hold the line against Teng's return. They must have known, too, that Teng was more likely than Hua to be able to engineer the post–Cultural Revolution turnaround that most desired. Political confusion, factional battles, and indiscipline encouraged by years of leftist agitation were once again damaging the economy. There were widespread reports of strikes, sabotage, and renewed disruption of rail traffic. The 1976 plan results, affected in part by the T'ang-shan earthquake, had been considerably below target, and the estimated losses over the last three years of the Cultural Revolution, 1974–76, were 28 million tons of steel, 100 billion yuan in value of industrial production, and 40 billion yuan in state revenues.[257] Hua Kuo-feng had called for a return to "great order," but Teng was more likely to bring it about.

After the work conference, Yeh and Li must have advised Hua that to resist the Teng tide could be politically disastrous for him. The most that could be done was to obtain a guarantee from Teng that he would let bygones be bygones. On 10 April, Teng wrote to the Central Committee condemning the "two whatevers," and proposed instead the use of "genuine Mao Tse-tung Thought taken as an integral whole." He was subsequently visited by two "leading comrades" of the CC's General Office, one presumably its director, Wang Tung-hsing, seeking to negotiate a deal before the beneficiaries, now the whatever faction, agreed to his return. Teng, to judge from his own account, was not in a mood for compromise, pointing out that if the two whatevers were correct, there could be no justification for his rehabilitation or reversing the verdict on the T'ien An Men incident. Even Mao himself had never claimed that whatever he said was correct, nor had Marx or Lenin.[258]

Teng's letter has never been released, so it is uncertain whether in it

---

257 Fang, *Chung-hua jen-min kung-ho-kuo ching-chi ta-shih-chi (1949–1980)*, 573–74; Domes, *The government and politics of the PRC*, 140–42.
258 *Selected works of Deng Xiaoping (1975–1982)*, 51–52; Hao and Tuan, *Chung-kuo kung-ch'an-tang liu-shih-nien*, 671.

or an earlier communication he indicated, as rumored, his willingness to support Hua Kuo-feng's continued leadership of the Party.[259] Some such undertaking seems likely, or there would have been no reason for the whatever faction to agree to his return. If it were given, that could be why the letter was not included in Teng's *Selected works*: It would have contrasted sharply with Hua Kuo-feng's eventual fate.

Whatever the understanding, it enabled Teng Hsiao-p'ing to attend the Tenth CC's Third Plenum from 16 to 21 July, and be reinstated in all his offices: Party vice-chairman and member of the Politburo Standing Committee; vice-chairman of the MAC; vice-premier; and PLA chief of staff. Hua Kuo-feng had his positions formally endorsed, and stubbornly maintained his support for the two whatevers and the Cultural Revolution. The available text of Teng's speech indicates that he repeated his advocacy of an integrated view of Mao Tse-tung Thought, but was discreet enough not to attack the two whatevers frontally at this time; he had to prepare the ground before his next attack. Instead, he promoted an old slogan of Mao's which was to become the essence of Teng Hsiao-p'ing's post-Mao policies: Seek truth from facts.[260]

On the basis of the compromise cemented at the plenum, the CCP was able to hold its Eleventh Congress in August. On this occasion, it was Hua's turn to be discreet, not reasserting the two whatevers or repeating his estimation of the T'ien An Men incident as counterrevolutionary. But he clearly felt unable to criticize Mao or disavow the Cultural Revolution without undermining his own position. Instead, he opened with a long and effusive eulogy of the late Chairman, went on to reaffirm the necessity for, and success of, the Cultural Revolution, the correctness of the line of the Tenth Congress (at which he entered the Politburo), and the need to persist with class struggle and continue the revolution under the proletarian dictatorship; and he observed chillingly that "Political revolutions in the nature of the Cultural Revolution will take place many times in the future."[261]

Teng Hsiao-p'ing emerged at the Congress as the CCP's third-ranking leader, after Hua and Yeh Chien-ying (who reported on the new Party constitution). Teng's brief closing speech was the only other address to be accorded publicity. He referred to Hua as "our wise leader" but did

259 Garside, *Coming alive!* 174. For Teng's expression of support in conversation with Hua Kuo-feng, see the manuscript minutes of Hua's visit to Teng and Liu Po-ch'eng in a hospital on 26 October 1976, available in Harvard's Fairbank Center Library. I am grateful to Michael Schoenhals for drawing my attention to this source.
260 The slogan *Shih-shih ch'iu-shih* dates back to the Han period; *Selected works of Deng Xiaoping*, 55–60; *Chung-kung tang-shih ta-shih nien-piao*, 409–10.
261 *The Eleventh National Congress of the Communist Party of China (Documents)*, 52.

not emulate his wisdom by praising the Cultural Revolution. He avoided controversy by calling for a return to honesty and hard work, modesty and prudence, plain living and hard struggle, and, of course, seeking truth from facts. But he, too, had to compromise and express support for the current line to "grasp the key link of class struggle" and "continue the revolution under the dictatorship of the proletariat," dogmas of the Eleventh Congress later condemned by Chinese Party historians.[262] No wonder Teng chose not to include this speech in his *Selected works*, despite the importance for him and the CCP of the occasion on which it was given.

Out of this Congress there emerged a leadership that was purged of the left but that did not particularly favor the left's victims. One third of the CC elected at the Tenth Congress disappeared, which included more than 75 percent of its representatives from mass organizations, presumably for leftist sympathies. Another category of probable leftists, the more recent entrants into the Party, also suffered heavily, being reduced by more than 70 percent.

The Politburo was also a compromise, but weighted in favor of survivors and beneficiaries of the Cultural Revolution, with only six of twenty-six members drawn from the ranks of the victims. One man who would later help spearhead Teng's reform program secured a toehold as an alternate member: Chao Tzu-yang. In the new five-man Politburo Standing Committee, Teng was the only one who would later emerge as a strong critic of Hua and the whatever faction. Hua was now buttressed by his key supporter in that grouping, Wang Tung-hsing, who was presumably being recognized both for his service against the Gang and for the power he wielded as head of PLA Unit 8341. Yeh Chien-ying was joined by his joint guarantor of Hua's position, Li Hsien-nien.[263]

Hua's "great leap"

Insofar as Hua Kuo-feng had a vision of "After Mao, what?" it seems to have been an unlikely combination of mid-1960s radicalism and mid-1950s economics. Certainly, the more generally acceptable part of Hua's dual heritage was Chou En-lai's commitment of China to the four

---

262 Ibid., 191–95; Hao and Tuan, *Chung-kuo kung-ch'an-tang liu-shih-nien*, 674. One report has it that Teng was originally scheduled to deliver a speech on seeking truth from facts, written by Hu Ch'iao-mu, but that when Teng was assigned the closing address, Nieh Jung-chen gave the Hu text, which was later published in *Red Flag*, though no longer described as a Congress speech; I am indebted to Michael Schoenhals for this information.

263 *The Eleventh National Congress of the Communist Party of China (Documents)*, 227–36. For a more detailed breakdown of the composition of the new CC and Politburo, see Domes, *The government and politics of the PRC*, 150–51.

modernizations. Here was a goal around which all except the most rabid leftists could unite. And surely Hua visualized a successful development program as providing the answer to the many who were asking themselves what right he had to be at the top. An unexceptionable but also unexceptional bureaucratic career in the provinces before the Cultural Revolution; junior enough not to have been in the first group of provincial officials to be targeted by the Red Guards; the luck still to be around when the tide turned and experienced cadres were once again in demand; senior enough to be transferred to the capital when the Lin Piao affair left large gaps in the leadership; competent enough and leftist enough to have been acceptable to Mao when Wang Hung-wen failed him – no one could blame Hua for being lucky, but was his record justification enough for him to try to lead China after Mao and Chou when his elders and betters were available? Probably not, in many people's eyes, and hence Hua's need to prove himself.

Unfortunately for Hua, his need to deliver the goods outstripped China's ability to produce them. At the first session of the new (Fifth) NPC in February–March 1978, Premier Hua unveiled his grandiose version of the original Ten-Year Plan (1976–85) foreshadowed by Chou in his last NPC speech in 1975. The plan target for steel output in 1985 was 60 million tons (1977: 23.7 m. tons), for oil, 350 million tons (1977: 93.6 m. tons). For the remaining eight years, Hua called for the construction of 120 major projects, 14 major heavy industrial bases, and capital investment equivalent to that expended in the previous twenty-eight years. The plan failed to take account of the lessons of the 1960s and the economic damage of the 1970s.[264] As is explained in Chapter 6 of this volume, the plan could not have reflected any careful thought or accurate data: The oil fields on which expanded production would supposedly be based were a pipe dream; the foreign exchange costs would have been enormous, because what came to be known as Hua's "great leap outward" placed heavy reliance on machinery imports. Instead of picking up Chou's torch, Hua had mimicked Mao's grandiose visions. Instead of covering himself with glory, he had pointed China toward another economic disaster. This, too, would be used against him.

The Third Plenum

The manner in which Teng Hsiao-p'ing turned the tables on Hua and the whatever faction is an illustration of the mysterious nature of power in the PRC. Hua was supreme leader in all branches of Party and state, Teng

264 Fang, *Chung-hua jen-min kung-ho-kuo ching-chi ta-shih-chi (1949–1980)*, 595–96.

was not. The whatever faction were in power, Teng's supporters were
not. Yet, in the relatively short period between the Third Plenum of the
Tenth Central Committee, in July 1977, and the Third Plenum of the
Eleventh CC, in December 1978, those power relations had been turned
around. The method appears to have been mobilization of elite opinion
through the press.

On 11 May 1978, the *Kuang-ming jih-pao* published a pseudonymous
article entitled "Practice is the sole criterion for testing truth," which
became a second rallying cry for the Teng forces. The author of the
article, Hu Fu-ming, was then vice-chairman of the Philosophy Department of Nanking University and a Party member. He later claimed he had
submitted the article for publication in the autumn of 1977 in opposition
to the "two whatevers" entirely on his own initiative, because he felt that
without rebutting that doctrine there was no hope of Teng returning to
power.[265] Self-generated it may have been, but the article that appeared
had undergone considerable revision and strengthening on the basis of
the ideas of two theoreticians working at the Central Party School under
Hu Yao-pang.[266] It struck at the roots of Cultural Revolution doctrine,
which, whether expressed by Lin Piao, Chiang Ch'ing, or Hua Kuo-feng,
held that Mao's writings and statements were eternal verities that should
not be tampered with, whatever the circumstances.

To the annoyance of Hua Kuo-feng and Wang Tung-hsing, the article
was quickly republished in the *People's Daily* and the *Liberation Army
News* and was the spark that lit a prairie fire of nationwide debate.[267] Teng
Hsiao-p'ing himself joined in the fray in a speech to a PLA political work
conference in June, when he reasserted the need to "seek truth from
facts."[268] Astutely, he used quotations from Mao's works to prove that

265 See Stuart R. Schram's report of his interview with Hu in his "'Economics in command?'"
      417–19.
266 For instance, Hu Fu-ming's original title had been "Practice is a criterion of truth," which was
      then revised to read "Practice is the criterion of all truths" before finally appearing as "Practice is
      the sole criterion of truth." The genesis of this article has been minutely investigated by Michael
      Schoenhals, who presented a seminar paper on the subject at Harvard's Fairbank Center on 3
      February 1989.
267 Hao and Tuan, *Chung-kuo kung-ch'an-tang liu-shih-nien*, 680–83; Domes, *The government and politics
      of China*, 187. On hearing of the negative reaction of leading politicians, Hu Fu-ming, according
      to Schoenhals, got so worried that he dissociated himself from the article (which was noted in
      internal bulletins) on the grounds that it had been changed beyond recognition. A follow-up
      article, by one of Hu Yao-pang's two acolytes, was published in the *Liberation Army News* as a
      result of the intervention of Lo Jui-ch'ing; this was Lo's last major political act before his death
      in August 1978.
268 *Selected works of Deng Xiaoping*, 127–32. Hu Chi-wei, the editor of *JMJP*, had been reprimanded
      by his former chief at the paper, Wu Leng-hsi, for republishing the article, and Hu Ch'iao-mu
      rebuked Hu Yao-pang for the activities of his subordinates. Teng's intervention was thus a cru-
      cial development and was given big play by Hu Chi-wei in *JMJP*; Schoenhals seminar.

this principle did not mean rejecting him but, on the contrary, represented a return to the best traditions and practice of the Chairman himself,[269] and concluded with a rhetorical flourish:

Comrades, let's think it over: Isn't it true that seeking truth from facts, proceeding from reality and integrating theory with practice form the fundamental principle of Mao Zedong Thought? Is this fundamental principle outdated? Will it
ever become outdated? How can we be true to Marxism-Leninism and Mao
Zedong Thought if we are against seeking truth from facts, proceeding from
reality and integrating theory with practice? Where would that lead us? Obviously, only to idealism and metaphysics, and thus to the failure of our work and
of our revolution.[270]

At this stage the battle was far from won. Earlier at this PLA conference, Hua Kuo-feng and Yeh Chien-ying had both spoken, but neither
had saluted Teng's banner of truth.[271] Yet on 24 June, the *Liberation
Army News* published an article supporting Teng, immediately republished in the *People's Daily*, which had been prepared under the direction
of Lo Jui-ch'ing.[272] Lo had been dismissed as chief of staff on the eve of
the Cultural Revolution but had rejoined the CC at the Eleventh Congress; if his authorship were widely known within the elite, it would
doubtless have influenced a lot of senior officers to throw their weight to
Teng's side. Certainly, from this point on the debate heated up, and by
mid-September, when Teng returned to the attack on the two whatevers
in a speech in the Northeast,[273] something he had eschewed in Hua and
Yeh's presence in June, conferences in ten provinces had supported his
position.[274] Perhaps as dispiriting for the whatever faction, that quintessential survivor, Li Hsien-nien, had hinted that he was prepared to abandon Hua and back the new line. By November, leading officials in all
provinces and military regions had thrown their weight on Teng's side. It
was at this point that a central work conference, originally proposed by
Teng two months earlier, convened in Peking on 10 November.[275]

The principal elements on the agenda were how to reinvigorate agriculture and settling the 1980 economic plan. But Ch'en Yun again took
a lead in quickly transforming the meeting into a full-scale debate on the

---

269 Schram, " 'Economics in command?' " 419.
270 *Selected works of Deng Xiaoping*, 132.
271 Domes, *The government and politics of the PRC*, 156.
272 Hao and Tuan, *Chung-kuo kung-ch'an-tang liu-shih-nien*, 682. Michael Schoenhals tells me that the
   Liberation Army News article was the first to criticize the two whatevers.
273 *Selected works of Deng Xiaoping*, 141.
274 Domes, *The government and politics of the PRC*, 157.
275 Hao and Tuan, *Chung-kuo kung-ch'an-tang liu-shih-nien*, 682–83, 686–87. Teng was touring in
   Southeast Asia and missed the opening of the conference.

errors of the Cultural Revolution. He wanted retrospective justice to be done to Po I-po, whose revolutionary record had been besmirched, and posthumous justice done to T'ao Chu, who had fallen at the end of 1966, and P'eng Te-huai, who had been dismissed in 1959 and then been publicly denounced during the late 1960s. K'ang Sheng's grave errors should be acknowledged. But Ch'en's most provocative proposal for the whatever faction was his insistence that the positive nature of the T'ien An Men incident be affirmed.[276]

Ch'en Yun's speech triggered a wave of supporting speeches, notably from T'an Chen-lin, demanding that a whole series of incidents during the Cultural Revolution should be reassessed.[277] Hua Kuo-feng had evidently anticipated this onslaught, or moved very quickly to accommodate himself to it. On 15 November, it was announced that the Peking Party committee had reassesed the T'ien An Men incident as "completely revolutionary," and the following day that Hua himself had written an inscription for the first officially approved anthology of T'ien An Men poems. Similar reassessments of similar incidents in Nanking, Hangchow, and Chengchow had been announced earlier.[278] With that position conceded, it was less surprising that the whatever faction were also prepared to accept the rehabilitation of a large number of victims of the Cultural Revolution, most of whose fates were not directly attributable to themselves.

A far more dangerous setback for Hua Kuo-feng and the whatever faction was the entry of a group of victims into the Politburo at the CC's Third Plenum, held 18–22 December to formalize the results of the work conference, large enough to tip the balance of the leadership in Teng's favor. Ch'en Yun was restored to his old position as a CCP vice-chairman and a member of the Politburo Standing Committee, and made first secretary of a new body, the Discipline Inspection Commission, which set out to purify the Party ranks of Cultural Revolution leftists.[279] Three other Teng supporters, Hu Yao-pang, Wang Chen, and Teng Ying-ch'ao, Chou En-lai's widow, joined the Politburo. In addition, nine senior victims were made full CC members. At a Politburo meeting summoned on

276 Ch'en Yun wen-hsuan (1956–1985), 208–10.
277 Hao and Tuan, Chung-kuo kung-ch'an-tang liu-shih-nien, 689.
278 Garside, Coming alive! 200–201; the text of the Peking Party announcement is in "Quarterly chronicle and documentation," CQ, 77 (March 1979), 659.
279 Teng Hsiao-p'ing made clear in his speech to the plenum that the kind of people whom he detested were those who had engaged in "beating, smashing and looting, who have been obsessed by factionalist ideas, who have sold their souls by framing innocent comrades, or who disregard the Party's vital interests. Nor can we lightly trust persons who sail with the wind, curry favour with those in power and ignore the Party's principles"; Selected works of Deng Xiaoping, 160.

25 December, an embryo central secretariat was re-created, with Hu Yao-pang at its head; Wang Tung-hsing was simultaneously sacked from his leadership of the CC General Office, which had functioned as a secretariat during the Cultural Revolution.[280] Wang and other members of the whatever faction maintained their positions on the Politburo, but the writing was now on the wall for them.

Their predicament was underlined by the decisive swing away from leftism, even of their variety, that the conference and plenum represented. The two whatevers were rejected. Class struggle was no longer to be the "key link"; the four modernizations were to take precedence. The theory of "continuing the revolution under the proletarian dictatorship" was abandoned. Teng indicated in his speech to the plenum that the time had not yet come for an overall appraisal of the Cultural Revolution and Mao himself.[281] But the policies adopted by the plenum represented a radical turn from the previous decade.

First and foremost, the Third Plenum took the first steps away from agricultural collectivization so strongly maintained by Hua Kuo-feng. As already indicated, where rural socialism was concerned, Hua differed only in pace and not in goal from the Gang of Four. Even after the latter had been purged, he pressed forward with policies for greater egalitarianism, such as promoting brigade accounting and curbing private plots and rural fairs. By mid-1978, reflecting Hua's weakening position, those policies were beginning to be attacked.[282] The Third Plenum rejected Hua's program and the Ta-chai model. To unleash the "socialist enthusiasm" of the peasantry, the plenum returned to the policies of the early 1960s and established a framework that proved to be only the beginning of a radical restructuring of rural China:

The right of ownership by the people's communes, production brigades and production teams and their power of decision must be protected effectively by the laws of the state; it is not permitted to commandeer the manpower, funds, products and material of any production team; the economic organizations at various levels of the people's commune must conscientiously implement the socialist principle of "to each according to his work," work out payment in accordance with the amount and quality of work done, and overcome equalitarianism; small plots of land for private use by commune members, their domestic side-occupations, and village fairs are necessary adjuncts of the socialist econ-

---

280 For a full summary of the results of the work conference and the Third Plenum, as well as some of the events leading up to them, see: Materials Group of the Party History Teaching and Research Office of the CCP Central Party School, *Chung-kuo kung-ch'an-tang li-tz'u chung-yao hui-i-chi, hsia* (Collection of various important conferences of the CCP), 274–80.

281 *Selected works of Deng Xiaoping (1975–1982)*, 160–61.

282 Domes, *The government and politics of the PRC*, 163–64.

omy, and must not be interfered with; the people's communes must resolutely implement the system of three levels of ownership with the production team as the basic accounting unit, and this should remain unchanged.[283]

Not even in the industrial sphere was Hua's program endorsed. His Ten-year Plan went conspicuously unmentioned. Instead, Ch'en Yun's influence was again clearly visible in the plenum's call for more balanced and steadier growth, rather than the massive investment in heavy industry preferred by Hua.[284] When he addressed the annual session of the NPC in June, he had to announce that rather than press ahead at the hectic speed he had espoused a year earlier, reassessment by the State Council since the Third Plenum had led to a decision to dedicate the years 1979–81 to "readjusting, restructuring, consolidating and improving" the economy.[285]

Democracy Wall

The defeat of Hua and the whatever faction at the Third Plenum was mainly the product of successful mobilization by Teng Hsiao-p'ing and his supporters of the "silent majority" of cadres and officers who had always opposed the Cultural Revolution. But the work conference and plenum took place against a backdrop of vigorous public support in the capital for Teng's line that could not but have influenced a leadership with vivid memories of the impact of the T'ien An Men incident.

That incident had demonstrated the degree to which national discipline, so strikingly instilled in the early 1950s, had been weakened by the Cultural Revolution. "To rebel is justified," Mao had proclaimed, and on 5 April 1976, thousands in the capital had rebelled against the political leadership and the economic and social program that the Chairman was attempting to set in place for after his demise. The strikes, slowdowns, and simple hooliganism taking place in various parts of China in the mid-1970s underlined that it was not simply the politically aware inhabitants of the capital who understood that the authority of the CCP had been gravely undermined.

The death of Mao, and the gradual reemergence of leaders who wished to disavow the whole Cultural Revolution, triggered a new outburst of public activity in the capital designed to help that process along. The T'ien An Men incident had been Act 1 in the popular struggle to rehabilitate Teng and what he stood for. The entr'acte had been the replacement of Mayor Wu Te, heavily responsible for the repression of the T'ien An

283   Quoted in "Quarterly chronicle and documentation," *CQ*, 77 (March 1979), 170.
284   Ibid., 169.   285   "Quarterly chronicle and documentation," *CQ*, 79 (September 1979), 647.

Men protesters, in October 1978 after eighteen months of veiled attacks in the press and open attacks in posters.[286] Democracy Wall was supposed to be Act 2. But this time the curtain was rung down early, and by Teng himself.

A week after the beginning of the central work conference, the first posters went up on a stretch of wall along the Ch'ang-an ta-chieh, the wide avenue that passes the T'ien An Men, not far from the square.[287] The very first, put up by a mechanic, criticized Mao by name for support-ing the Gang of Four and dismissing Teng Hsiao-p'ing. Another early one called Teng "the living Chou En-lai" and denounced the authorities' handling of the T'ien An Men incident. A third attacked a "small group of highly placed people," clearly the whatever faction, for preventing a reassessment of the alleged counterrevolutionary nature of the incident.

These themes of support for Teng, antagonism toward the whatever faction, and criticism of Mao characterized many of the posters. They must have given Teng and his supporters at the work conference a feeling of satisfaction that at this critical juncture they could claim popular back-ing. But the poster writers did not stop there. Soon they were putting out pamphlets, papers, and magazines and setting up discussion groups such as the Human Rights Alliance and the Enlightenment Society. Within a week of the first poster going up, people at Democracy Wall were no longer content simply to read each other's posters, but were actively de-bating issues, and even with foreigners. On 26 November, the American syndicated columnist Robert Novak was given questions to ask Teng Hsiao-p'ing when he interviewed him the following day. When, on the evening of the 27th, Novak's colleague John Fraser, the Toronto *Globe and Mail*'s Peking correspondent, relayed to a mass audience the fact that Teng had told Novak that Democracy Wall was a good thing, "pande-monium broke out"; but Fraser's excited auditors sobered up when they heard that Teng, in a foretaste of things to come, had said that not all the things written up at the wall were correct.[288]

Democracy Wall was a more profound phenomenon than the T'ien An Men incident. The latter was a brief burst of anger against Mao and the Gang of Four; most of the poems mourned Chou En-lai or excoriated Chiang Ch'ing. At Democracy Wall, on the other hand, young Chinese,

---

286 Garside, *Coming alive!* 194–96.

287 This following brief summary of Democracy Wall is based principally on the eyewitness reports of Garside, *Coming alive!* 212–98, and Canadian journalist John Fraser's *The Chinese: portrait of a people,* 203–71, and the analysis and poems contained in David S. G. Goodman, *Beijing street voices: the poetry and politics of China's democracy movement.* Both Garside and Fraser made many contacts with participants in "the democracy movement."

288 Fraser, *The Chinese,* 245.

mainly blue collar with a junior high or high school education,[289] explored a wide range of political and social problems, and though often displaying a considerable degree of naiveté, were clearly enthused with the possibility of China embracing the "fifth modernization," democracy:

> The 5th National People's Congress opens red flowers,
> Drawing up the people's new constitution.
> Eight hundred million people joyously sing together,
> Of one heart to establish a new nation.

> The fresh blood of the revolutionary martyrs is sprinkled,
> In exchange for today's new constitution.
> Protect democracy, protect people's rights,
> Advance the Four Modernizations.[290]

As his interview with Novak illustrated, Teng Hsiao-p'ing's first reactions to the democracy movement were broadly positive. The day before that interview, Teng had told a leading Japanese politician: "The writing of big-character posters is permitted by our constitution. We have no right to negate or criticize the masses for promoting democracy.... The masses should be allowed to vent their grievances!"[291] Unfortunately for the movement, Teng Hsiao-p'ing quickly perceived contradictions between democracy and the four modernizations, and, whatever his earliest reactions, soon found Democracy Wall more of an embarrassment than an advantage in his current political struggles.

The contradiction was that widespread political debate could get out of hand and undermine the stability and unity that he proclaimed as vital for China's economic advance. He surely remembered that it was when young people went on the rampage in the early Cultural Revolution that China's cities were thrown into chaos and the Chinese economy suffered its worst setbacks of that decade. The embarrassment was that the "silent majority" of old cadres and senior PLA officers upon whose support he relied in his struggle with the whatever faction were not happy at a new threat to their authority and position. They had not welcomed the overthrow of the Gang of Four just to allow some new form of Cultural Revolution to spring up.

Nothing could be done for fear of adverse publicity before Teng's visit to the United States from 28 January to 4 February. But despite that overseas triumph, Teng's position thereafter may have been weakened

---

289 This is the analysis of a Chinese participant quoted by Goodman, *Beijing street voices*, 141. This person, who was arrested in May 1979, blamed the "arrogance" of the intellectuals for their lack of participation.

290 From Li Hung-k'uan, "Ode to the constitution," quoted in Goodman, *Beijing street voices*, 70.

291 Quoted in Garside, *Coming alive!* 247–48.

temporarily as a result of the inability of the PLA to teach Vietnam a convincing military lesson during the border war from mid-February to mid-March, a cause that was close to Teng's heart. One report suggests that as late as mid-March, Teng was telling senior colleagues that suppressing the democracy movement would have unfavorable results: "Counter-revolution can be suppressed, sabotage can be restricted, but to walk back down the old road of suppressing differing opinion and not listening to criticism will make the trust and support of the masses disappear."[292] But he agreed to abide by majority opinion, and at the end of March he proclaimed that the four modernizations demanded that the country adhere to the "four cardinal principles": the socialist road; the dictatorship of the proletariat; the leadership of the CCP; and Marxism-Leninism and Mao Tse-tung Thought.[293] In justifying the introduction of criteria highly reminiscent of Mao's action at the outset of the Anti-Rightist Campaign in 1957, Teng said that

certain bad elements have raised sundry demands that cannot be met at present or are altogether unreasonable. They have provoked or tricked some of the masses into raiding Party and government organizations, occupying offices, holding sit-down and hunger strikes and obstructing traffic, thereby seriously disrupting production, other work and public order. Moreover, they have raised such sensational slogans as "Oppose hunger" and "Give us human rights," inciting people to hold demonstrations and deliberately trying to get foreigners to give worldwide publicity to their words and deeds. There is a so-called China Human Rights Group which has gone so far as to put up big-character posters requesting the President of the United States to "show concern" for human rights in China. Can we permit such an open call for intervention in China's internal affairs?[294]

Wei Ching-sheng, the editor of the journal *Exploration* and a prominent figure in the democracy movement, condemned Teng for laying aside "the mask of protector of democracy." Three days later the Peking authorities issued regulations to curb the democracy movement, and the following day Wei was arrested. At his trial in October 1979, he was given a fifteen-year jail term.[295] On the basis of a CC Plenum decision in February 1980, at the 1980 NPC session, the clause in the state constitution guaranteeing citizens free speech and the right of assembly was shorn of the commitment so dear to Mao: the right to engage in great debate and to put up big-character posters.[296] For the moment, the democracy movement had been shut down.

292 Quote in ibid., 256.   293 *Selected works of Deng Xiaoping*, 172.
294 Ibid., 181.   295 Garside, *Coming alive!* 256–57, 262.
296 *Chung-hua jen-min kung-ho-kuo ti-wu-chieh ch'üan-kuo jen-min tai-piao ta-hui ti-san-tz'u hui-i wen-chien* (Documents of the third session of the 5th NPC of the PRC), 169.

The fall of Hua Kuo-feng

The Third Plenum is rightly appraised by Chinese Party historians as a major turning point in post-1949 history. Had Hua Kuo-feng been adept or swift enough, he might have made common cause with the old cadres against Teng on the issue of the democracy movement. Perhaps it was concern that this could happen that led Teng to move so fast. But in fact Hua and the whatever faction were too mired in the Cultural Revolution for such an alliance to have had more than temporary success.

In the event, Hua watched helplessly as an anti-whatever coalition was inexorably built up within the top leadership. At the CC's Fourth Plenum from 25 to 28 September 1979, Chao Tzu-yang was promoted to full membership of the Politburo. The rehabilitated P'eng Chen, the former Peking first secretary who, after Teng and Liu Shao-ch'i, had been the most senior victim at the start of the Cultural Revolution, returned to the Politburo. Eleven other prominent old cadres were readmitted to the CC.

A bigger breakthrough for Teng occurred at the Fifth Plenum from 23 to 29 March 1980, when Hua's supporters in the whatever faction – Wang Tung-hsing, Chi Teng-k'uei, Wu Te, and Ch'en Hsi-lien (the "little gang of four") – were relieved of all their Party and state posts. Ch'en Yung-kuei, the model peasant leader from Ta-chai, who was regarded as incompetent rather than malevolent, was simply allowed to drop out of Politburo activities. Hu Yao-pang and Chao Tzu-yang were elevated to the Politburo Standing Committee. Hu, a Teng loyalist who had been leader of the Youth League in the 1950s, was made the CCP general secretary, a job that had been vacant since Teng was removed from it early in the Cultural Revolution. The newly reconstituted secretariat was staffed almost exclusively with Teng's supporters. Finally, it was agreed that all the charges against the Cultural Revolution's number one capitalist roader, Liu Shao-ch'i, were false and that he should be rehabilitated.[297]

Teng's next step was to eradicate the influence of the whatever faction from the State Council. Vice-premiers Ch'en Hsi-lien and Chi Teng-k'uei were removed in April 1980 as a consequence of the decisions at the Fifth Plenum, but ousting Hua Kuo-feng from the premiership proved more difficult. Teng advocated separating the functions of Party and government, and proposed that in addition to Hua, a number of other old cadres including himself would resign as vice-premiers, thus also permitting the rejuvenation of the State Council. Although Teng's desire to eliminate overlapping of the two institutions was genuine, this device could have

---

297 Materials Group, *Chung-kuo kung-ch'an-tang li-tz'u chung-yao hui-i-chi, hsia,* 281–89.

deceived nobody, least of all Hua. Hua may well have tried to use his chairmanship of the MAC to seek succor from the PLA; a brief report of his speech to a PLA political work conference in May 1980 suggested that he might have hoped to forge bonds of loyalty on the basis of shared Maoist values.[298] But even if PLA generals were beginning to get restive about some of Teng's policies, it was highly unlikely that they would select Hua as their champion.

After a Politburo conference in August (and a postponement of the annual NPC session until the very end of the month), the top leadership agreed that Hua should be replaced as premier by Chao Tzu-yang. Teng, Li Hsien-nien, Ch'en Yun, and three other senior cadres duly resigned as vice-premiers, and Ch'en Yung-kuei was also relieved of that duty.[299] Three new vice-premiers were appointed, including Foreign Minister Huang Hua, leaving the State Council purged of all beneficiaries of the Cultural Revolution and comprising only survivors and victims.[300]

The stage was now set for the shredding of Hua's reputation and his eviction from his remaining posts. At a Politburo meeting in November–December, at the request of a large number of high-ranking cadres, Hua's record was submitted to pitiless scrutiny. He was accorded merit for helping to get rid of the Gang of Four but was censured for serious errors and failure to correct himself on a number of issues of principle. Even the mistakes he had apparently corrected were brought up again.

He had persisted with the slogans of the Cultural Revolution; he had not taken the initiative in repairing the damage caused by it. Here he was again being attacked for pursuing the anti-Teng campaign after the Cultural Revolution and refusing to reverse verdicts on the T'ien An Men incident. He was held responsible for rushing a decision to create the Mao mausoleum and to publish the fifth volume of the Chairman's works, both of which had presumably been agreed to by Yeh Chien-ying and Li Hsien-nien. He was also blamed for hindering the rehabilitation of victims of the Cultural Revolution. He had been "pragmatic" [sic] in his attitude toward the Mao problem and hence his support for the "two whatevers." He was held largely responsible for the blind advance and

---

298 Hua stressed moral values alongside material incentives; see "Quarterly chronicle and documentation," CQ, 83 (September 1980), 615.

299 The announcement of the resignations of Teng and the five other senior cadres was made separately from that of Ch'en Yung-kuei, and in slightly different terminology, to indicate that Ch'en was going in disgrace rather than in honorable retirement; see Chung-hua jen-min kung-ho-kuo ti-wu-chieh ch'üan-kuo jen-min tai-piao ta-hui ti-san-tz'u hui-i wen-chien, 175–76.

300 Domes, The government and politics of the PRC, 173–75; Hao and Tuan, Chung-kuo kung-ch'an-tang liu-shih-nien, 705–9.

the resulting serious losses to the economy in the previous two years.[301] In sum, the meeting agreed that Hua "lacks the political and organizational ability to be the chairman of the Party. That he should never have been appointed chairman of the Military Commission, everybody knows."[302]

Totally humiliated, Hua asked to be relieved of all his posts, but in the interests of protocol and perhaps of saving Yeh Chien-ying's face,[303] he was not accorded the merciful release of a coup de grace. He would not be removed from the chairmanship of the Party or the MAC until a formal decision could be made by the CC's Sixth Plenum. But although he would thus retain his titles until the end of June 1981, at which point he would be demoted to a vice-chairmanship of the Party, his jobs were immediately taken over: the party chairmanship by Hu Yao-pang, and the MAC chairmanship by Teng himself – the person everyone knew should have been appointed chairman of the MAC!

In the end, because of delays in holding the CCP's Twelfth Congress,[304] Hua remained a titular member of the Chinese top leadership for perhaps eighteen months longer than had been intended. But in September 1982, Hua Kuo-feng was reduced to membership of the CC. His erstwhile collaborator Wang Tung-hsing scraped into the bottom place among the CC alternates. The Hua interregnum had formally ended.

TENG HSIAO-P'ING'S PROGRAM

After Mao, who?

At the time of the Third Plenum in December 1978, it became clear that Hua Kuo-feng, however imposing his titles, was only a stopgap heir and that Mao's real successor would be Teng Hsiao-p'ing. Ironically, Teng's

---

301 Hao and Tuan, *Chung-kuo kung-ch'an-tang liu-shih-nien*, 709–10; CCP CC Party History Research Office, *Chung-kung tang-shih ta-shih nien-piao*, 438–9; Materials Group, *Chung-kuo kung-ch'an-tang li-tz'u chung-yao hui-i-chi*, 290–91.

302 Quoted in Domes, *The government and politics of the PRC*, 176.

303 As was already argued, Yeh bore a certain responsibility for Hua's retention of the leadership after the purge of the Gang of Four in 1976, and for persuading him to readmit Teng to the leadership in 1977. When the Sixth Plenum did meet in June 1981, Yeh Chien-ying was absent, apparently ill, but sent a letter agreeing to the personnel changes and the criticisms of Hua Kuofeng. That an official Party account thought it necessary to publish extracts from this letter suggests concern lest his absence be misinterpreted. See Materials Group, *Chung-kuo kung-ch'antang li-tz'u chung-yao hui-i-chi* 293.

304 Domes points out that the Fifth Plenum in February 1980 had decided to call the CCP's Twelfth Congress ahead of time, i.e., before the Eleventh Congress's five-year term expired in 1982. He suggests that the hoped-for date was early in 1981, but that disagreement over the assessment of Mao and administrative reforms forced a delay, so that the Eleventh Congress ran its full term; see *The government and politics of the PRC*, 183.

eventual triumph was due in large part to Mao's own actions. If Mao had not recalled Teng to office as Chou sickened, Teng could not have emerged as the obvious man to run China in absence of the premier. If Mao had not purged him again after Chou's death, Teng would not have become the symbol of a new political order to replace that of the Cultural Revolution. Certainly, the triumvirate of Hua Kuo-feng, Yeh Chien-ying, and Li Hsien-nien would have been in a stronger position to keep the angry victims of the Cultural Revolution at bay.

What is striking about Teng's ascendancy was the way in which, from the very start, he shunned titular confirmation of his power. He insisted on ranking himself below Yeh Chien-ying in the list of CCP vice-chairmen long after Yeh's role as post-Mao power broker had ended.[305] At no time was there any suggestion that Teng contemplated taking over the Party chairmanship, general secretaryship, or the premiership. Instead, he quickly gathered around him the men he wished to succeed him, giving them posts and responsibilities so that they could gain experience and respect. This was the successor-training operation that Mao had talked about but never really implemented.

A principal reason for Teng's self-denial was his determination to avoid appearing to covet a Mao-like role. Indeed, the chairmanship was dropped from the Party constitution at the Twelfth Congress in order to prevent anyone attempting to assume Mao's mantle. Another preventive measure was the Party's long-expected reappraisal of Mao. The object was to demystify his godlike image by coolly assessing his achievements and his errors, especially during the Cultural Revolution. The CCP was better placed to be courageous than the CPSU had been with Stalin. When Mao's faults came to be listed, Teng, a victim, had no reason to fear the question reportedly shouted at Khrushchev, an accomplice, when he made his secret speech denouncing Stalin in 1956: "And where were you, comrade, when all this was going on?"

Nevertheless, Teng also had more reason to be cautious than Khrushchev had a quarter of a century earlier. However intemperate the Chinese may have considered the latter's secret speech, Khrushchev always knew that the CPSU had the untarnished image of Lenin on which to fall back. For the CCP, Mao was both Lenin and Stalin, and if an assessment were

---

305 In his letter to the Sixth Plenum (n. 304), Yeh suggested that the order of the top three members of the Politburo Standing Committee should be Hu Yao-pang, Teng Hsiao-p'ing, Yeh Chien-ying, thus reversing the standings of himself and Teng. This was perhaps politeness, perhaps realism in the wake of the fall of Yeh's protégé Hua, but Teng ensured that Yeh retained his senior ranking.

not carefully handled, both images might be damaged, with incalculable effect on the Party's legitimacy.

Moreover, even among those who deplored the Cultural Revolution, there were many who wanted Mao protected and some of his actions upheld as correct. PLA generals in particular did not want excessive condemnation either of the man who led them to victory or of their role in the Cultural Revolution. One device was to blame as much as possible Lin Piao and the Gang of Four, and from 20 November 1980 to 25 January 1981, the regime staged a Nuremberg-style trial of the surviving leaders of the Cultural Revolution.

The trial did publicize considerable evidence of their misdeeds. The claim was made that almost 730,000 people had been framed and persecuted and that nearly 35,000 of them had been "persecuted to death." Most of the accused meekly admitted their guilt and cooperated with the court. Chang Ch'un-ch'iao, on the other hand, chose to remain silent throughout the proceedings, while Chiang Ch'ing defended herself forcefully, repeatedly insisting that she had only done what Chairman Mao had told her.[306]

The trial was an effective means of allowing victims to see that their persecutors had been humiliated and punished, and of enabling some even to denounce them in public. But Chiang Ch'ing's testimony served to underline that the ultimate guilt was Mao's and that the Party would have to find some means of coming to terms with that fact, while steering clear of a root-and-branch condemnation that would be too damaging even for the survivors. Early indications that Mao would be accused of "crimes" during the Cultural Revolution did not materialize. Some PLA behavior in that period was assessed positively. Teng made sure that armchair historians would not undermine his important constituency in the PLA.[307]

Thus, in his earliest comments to the drafters of what eventually emerged as the "Resolution on certain questions in the history of our Party since the founding of the PRC," Teng insisted that the first and most essential point to be covered was

---

306 *A great trial in Chinese history*, 102–3; the figures for the numbers of victims are on 20–21. A good analysis of the trial, with extracts, is contained in David Bonavia, *Verdict in Peking: the trial of the Gang of Four*. The full official text of the proceedings is in Research Office of the Supreme People's Court, ed., *Chung-hua jen-min kung-ko-kuo tsui-kao jen-min fa-yuan t'e-pieh fa-t'ing shen-p'an Lin Piao, Chiang Ch'ing fan-ko-ming chi-t'uan an chu-fan chi-shih* (A record of the trial by the Special Tribunal of the PRC's Supreme People's Court of the principal criminals of the Lin Piao and Chiang Ch'ing counterrevolutionary cliques); Chiang Ch'ing's appearances are covered on 117–21, 194–99, 227–41, 296–302, 341–47, 399–414.
307 Domes, *The government and politics of the PRC*, 180–82.

... affirmation of the historical role of Comrade Mao Zedong and explanation of the necessity to uphold and develop Mao Zedong Thought.... We must hold high the banner of Mao Zedong Thought not only today but in the future.... The first [point] is the most important, the most fundamental, the most crucial.[308]

Three months later when he found the latest draft inadequate on this issue he called it "no good" and demanded rewriting. The tone of the draft was "too depressing"; criticizing Mao's personal mistakes alone would not solve problems.[309] In a later comment, he underlined how politically sensitive the issue was. Without an appropriate evaluation of Mao's merits and faults, "the old workers will not feel satisfied, nor will the poor and lower-middle peasants of the period of land reform, nor the many cadres who have close ties with them." He hinted at potential PLA dissatisfaction.[310]

After more than a year of discussions among thousands of officials and historians, the Resolution was adopted by the Sixth Plenum in time for the sixtieth anniversary of the founding of the CCP, on 1 July 1981. It placed the blame for the Cultural Revolution squarely on Mao: "The 'cultural revolution,' which lasted from May 1966 to October 1976, was responsible for the most severe setback and the heaviest losses suffered by the Party, the state and the people since the founding of the People's Republic. It was initiated and led by Comrade Mao Zedong."[311] After an analysis of all the crimes and errors of the period, the Resolution supplied the balance that Teng had insisted on. It described Mao's leftist error in the Cultural Revolution as, after all, "the error of a proletarian revolutionary." In his later years, Mao had confused right and wrong and mistakenly believed that his leftist theories were Marxist. "Herein lies his tragedy."[312] Even during the Cultural Revolution, he could be praised for protecting some cadres, fighting Lin Piao, exposing Chiang Ch'ing, and pursuing a successful foreign policy.[313] The Resolution concluded that although it was true that Mao had made "gross mistakes" during the Cul-

---

308 *Selected works of Deng Xiaoping*, 276, 278.   309 Ibid., 282, 283.

310 He did this by referring to PLA soldiers' approval when they read what he had said about Mao in an interview with a foreign journalist, i.e., PLA troops were keenly concerned with what was said publicly about Mao.

311 *Resolution on CPC History (1949–81)*, 32.

312 The description of Mao as a tragic hero was a repetition of the formula the CCP had suggested for Stalin in the aftermath of Khrushchev's secret speech in 1956. The concept was, in fact, a breakthrough. Hitherto, in both the Soviet Union and the PRC, there had been a Manichean insistence on the simple juxtaposition of good and evil, black and white, with no allowance made for shades of gray. If one committed an error, one either purged oneself of it totally or was condemned as a reactionary or a counterrevolutionary. The model of the flawed leader had implications for politics and literature.

313 *Resolution on CPC History (1949–81)*, 41–42.

tural Revolution, "if we judge his activities as a whole, his contributions to the Chinese revolution far outweigh his mistakes."[314]

The Resolution achieved the balance Teng had wanted while also explaining why Mao had gone wrong. As his prestige had increased, he had become arrogant and put himself above the CC. His colleagues failed to take preventive action, and collective leadership was undermined. Intra-Party democracy was not institutionalized; relevant laws lacked authority. The Stalinist model of leadership had had its impact, as had centuries of Chinese "feudal autocracy."[315] The assessment of Mao sounded right, but Teng's Resolution succeeded no better than Khrushchev's secret speech in explaining how democracy could be institutionalized or laws respected under a system of proletarian dictatorship and CCP rule.

If Teng would not reject the system he had helped create, he personally would attempt to learn the negative lessons of Mao's leadership. Yet his rejection of Mao's titles and cult failed to deal with tendencies deep in the "feudal" political culture. Teng had taught Hua that position did not confer power or authority. Now he himself had to come to terms with the corollary: Power and authority could not be wished away simply by refusing titles, the imperial tradition could not be exorcised by Party resolution. No matter how loudly he protested that he participated in only one or two key decisions a year, nobody believed him. Although he had abandoned routine administration, he was regarded by both supporters and opponents as the court of last resort.

Partly this was a matter of generations. In sharp contrast to post-Stalin Russia, in which only survivors and beneficiaries remained, in post-Mao China many of the leader's victims, who were also fellow Long Marchers, were still alive.[316] They could return to power untarnished by his errors and garlanded still with their revolutionary achievements. It was impossible for men like Hu Yao-pang and Chao Tzu-yang whom Teng picked out as his successors to match the legitimacy he could claim as of right.

Partly it was a question of relationships, *kuan-hsi*. Teng had a network of friends, colleagues, and contacts in both Party and army who could be vital to the successful promotion of a policy. Hu Yao-pang and, to a lesser extent, Chao Tzu-yang had their networks, too, but they were not comparable in power and prestige as allies for governing China.

Partly it was a question of emergent factionalism. In the initial post-Mao era, all the returning victims could agree on the urgent tasks of

314 Ibid., 56.   315 Ibid., 48–49.
316 Had Bukharin been allowed to survive, he would have been only sixty-four on Stalin's death. Teng was seventy-four at the time of the Third Plenum.

removing the beneficiaries of the Cultural Revolution and liquidating the policies of that era. As that task neared completion, the original coalition began to split over where to go next. Teng did not always see eye to eye with Ch'en Yun or P'eng Chen, to name the two most prestigious returned victims besides Teng himself. Had Teng been able to retire and take with him his whole revolutionary cohort, leaving Hu and Chao to cope with their own generation, the succession process would have been easier to manage. But since Teng's old comrades-in-arms evinced no desire to leave the stage, Teng had to stay on to prevent them from using *their* superior credentials to derail his protégés.

Partly it was a question of talent. Teng Hsiao-p'ing was clearly an exceptional leader even among an extraordinary array of revolutionary veterans. Neither Hu Yao-pang nor Chao Tzu-yang was able to prove himself an equally outstanding successor.

Partly it was a reflection of an only partially solved question: Which would dominate, Party or PLA?

After Mao, which?

When the Politburo summed up Hua's shortcomings in late 1980, it was far more contemptuous about his right to be chairman of the MAC than about his right to lead the CCP. Yet in a state where the Party commanded the gun, any leader whom the Party chose should automatically have received the respect of the generals. Clearly that was never accorded to Hua. He became MAC chairman in 1976 presumably because the obvious available candidate, Marshal Yeh Chien-ying, insisted on it and stood by Hua to lend him authority. When Teng returned as vice-chairman of the MAC and chief of staff of the PLA in mid-1977, the generals probably took little further account of Hua. When Teng effectively took over the chairmanship in late 1980, their world seemed correctly ordered again.

Teng may have felt he had no option but to assume this one of Mao's titles, but his action caused as many problems as it solved. It confirmed to the PLA generals that they had a right to be commanded only by the person with supreme authority in the country; that they had a direct line to the top without interruption by layers of bureaucracy; that although the minister of defense was responsible to the premier, who in turn was responsible to the Party, none of this mattered, because all important issues would be thrashed out in the MAC. It thus confirmed what everyone knew – that the PLA was an institution apart – just when the generals needed to be brought back into line.

Teng's objective was to restore PLA discipline and end its unwillingness to obey orders or to implement Party policies laid down by the CC.
As we have seen, he had brought up these problems in 1975, but he now
admitted that they had not been solved then.[317] He may well have thought
that only he could bring the PLA to heel. Given the difficulties even he
experienced, perhaps he was right. The problems were both political and
institutional.

The rehabilitation of Liu Shao-ch'i in May 1980 was one major political
issue. That action had undermined a major justification for the Cultural
Revolution and was thus a direct repudiation of Mao, whose reputation
the generals had consistently wanted to safeguard. Yeh Chien-ying, and
even Hsu Shih-yu, Teng's protector in 1976, evinced disapproval by failing to show up for the memorial meeting at which this symbolically
important act took place.[318] The generals were also angry at two successive rounds of severe military budget cuts in late 1980 and early 1981; it
may have been partly in retaliation for these that the PLA initiated a drive
for ideological discipline. But probably the more important reason was
the generals' desire to counter the more relaxed political atmosphere that
Teng and the reformers were trying to encourage but that had produced
many attacks on military privilege. An army writer, Pai Hua, was made
the exemplary target to stand for all critical intellectuals.

In the face of evident PLA anger, Teng must have decided to excise
from the Resolution on Party history any criticisms of the role of the PLA
in the Cultural Revolution. But even this failed to appease the generals,
for on the eve of the CCP's Twelfth Congress, in September 1982, an
article in the *Liberation Army News* attacked "some responsible comrades
in cultural fields" for supporting bourgeois liberal points of view. Teng's
reaction to this gross breach of military and political discipline was swift.
Immediately after the Congress, the director of the PLA's General Political Department, Wei Kuo-ch'ing (another Teng protector in 1976), and
the head of the navy were both dismissed.[319]

Teng evidently realized the institutional problem in the relationship
between the PLA and the CCP, but his efforts to remedy it failed. In the
new state constitution promulgated at the Fifth Session of the Fifth NPC
in late 1982, an important institutional innovation was included: the creation of a Central Military Commission, responsible to the NPC, to direct

317 *Selected works of Deng Xiaoping,* 29–30, 97–98.
318 Domes, *The government and politics of the PRC,* 171–72. Domes argues that in the case of Hsu, per-
      sonal pique at not being made defense minister or chief of staff may have been another motive
      for his action on this occasion.
319 Ibid., 178–82, 185.

the PLA. According to the explanation given by P'eng Chen in his speech to the NPC, "The leadership by the Chinese Communist Party over the armed forces will not change with the establishment of the state Central Military Commission. The Party's leading role in the life of the state, which is explicitly affirmed in the Preamble, naturally includes its leadership over the armed forces."[320] What P'eng Chen conspicuously failed to mention was that the preamble made no mention of the Party's MAC as the instrument of that leadership. What then was to be the relationship of the MAC to the new body?

An article in a Party journal gave a strong hint of what was in the wind. It detailed the history of the Central Military Commission, showing how at some times it had been a Party organ and at some times a state organ. Both types of military commission had been legitimate. Referring to the creation of the new state body, the writer affirmed that the MAC would continue to exist as a Party organ. Yet the implication was that the time had come to sever the direct CCP–PLA link and make the PLA simply a part of the state structure, as in most other countries. The history of the PLA showed that this had been normal practice from time to time and therefore nothing to be feared.[321] For double reassurance, Teng Hsiao-p'ing legitimated the new body at the NPC by taking on its chairmanship in addition to his chairmanship of the MAC.

If Teng's objective was to prepare the ground for the abolition of the MAC, he did not achieve it. The new commission raised the profile of the PLA in the state structure by subordinating it no longer to a mere State Council ministry but to an NPC commission, but no general seems to have been ready to accept it as a substitute for the MAC. Instead, just when Teng and his colleagues were urging a general retrenchment of the bureaucracy, the country was saddled with two identical military commissions, both led by Teng Hsiao-p'ing and Yang Shang-k'un (as executive vice-chairman).

Even when Teng would finally manage to resign from the Politburo at the CCP's Thirteenth Congress in 1987, taking all his old comrades with him, he still could not retire from his MAC chairmanship. The CCP constitution stipulated that the MAC chairman had to be a member of the Politburo Standing Committee, so Teng endorsed a constitutional revision that permitted him to stay on.[322] He installed the new CCP general

320 *Fifth session of the Fifth National People's Congress*, 94.
321 Yen Ching-t'ang, "Chung-yang chün-wei yen-ko kai-k'uang" (Survey of the evolution of the Central Military Commission), in Chu Ch'eng-chia, ed., *Chung-kung tang-shih yen-chiu lun-wen hsüan, hsia* (Selection of research papers on the history of the CCP), 3. 567–87.
322 *Documents of the Thirteenth National Congress of the Communist Party of China (1987)*, 85.

secretary, Chao Tzu-yang, as first vice-chairman of the MAC, which suggested that the MAC would be preserved and that the NPC equivalent had been set up in vain.

The recent history of the MAC has confirmed the tenacity with which the PLA has maintained its institutional position within the CCP over the years. Under Teng's leadership, civilian control of the PLA would be gradually reinstated, especially after he engineered the exodus of virtually all remaining generals from the Politburo and sharply reduced PLA representation in the CC during the major central meetings held in September 1985. But the MAC issue illustrated that civilian control was still on the PLA's terms: that it must be asserted through the MAC, and the MAC must be headed by Teng as long as possible. Perhaps when the PLA is further denuded of revolutionary generals and colonels by retirements and deaths, and the Long March is history not memory, the post-Teng generation of CCP leaders will be able to assert its primacy over the military and assign to it a more conventional role in the state system. Until then it can be assumed that the PLA, the agent of victory during the revolution and the repository of power during the Cultural Revolution,[323] will remain a major factor in the polity. As the above account has indicated, how its political influence will be utilized will depend on the CCP's program and policies.

After Mao, what?

The conservatism of the PLA generals was a factor that Teng Hsiao-p'ing had to take into account in his drive to revitalize China. For Teng's reform program challenged not merely the ultra-leftist Maoism of the Cultural Revolution, but also what might be called the "Sinified Stalinist" line pursued by Mao and his colleagues when copying the Soviet model in the 1950s. Moreover, the reforms relaxed central control and allowed more freedom of thought and action, a permissiveness unlikely to commend itself to the ultimate guardians of law and order in the wake of the upheavals of the Cultural Revolution.

The economic reforms and their impact are covered in detail in Chap-

---

323 During the discussions of the resolution on Party history, Teng got quite angry at the suggestion that the Ninth Congress should be declared illegitimate or that the Party should be considered to have ceased to exist during the Cultural Revolution. Perhaps it was partly because he realized that to say that would constitute a formal admission that the PLA had been the only functioning revolutionary organization during that turbulent decade, that it had survived whereas the CCP had not, and that it had run most of the country while the CCP had not; *Selected works of Deng Xiaoping*, 290–91.

ter 6.[324] Teng turned back the clock, dismantling the commune system set up during the Great Leap Forward in 1958, returning control over production to the farm family for the first time since land reform in the early 1950s. The regime might claim that no ideological change had taken place because the land was formally still owned by the collective; it was only contracted back to the peasantry. Peasants might worry that their newly granted freedom to plan their own cropping patterns, hire labor to assist them, and sell part of the harvest in rural free markets[325] would suddenly be snatched back in yet another 180-degree policy shift. But in fact, private farming had been reinstated, even in cases where the peasants were reluctant to forfeit the security of the collective.[326]

This second liberation of the peasantry, bolstered by higher procurement prices, had a massive impact on production and on rural incomes, as Chapter 6 shows. The political implications were also of enormous significance. A majority of the 800 million peasants had been given a major stake in the reform program, and they trembled when conservative ideological winds blew coldly from Peking. But even Chinese neoconservatives like Ch'en Yun had welcomed the short-lived experiments with agricultural responsibility systems in the early 1960s, and it eventually became clear that no Peking politician would challenge the rural new deal, unless either its economic justification declined drastically or its impact on rural and regional equity became so negative as to carry grave dangers of renewed class struggle.

Rural cadres were initially unhappy about their new tasks and diminished control.[327] But as they began to use their political skills and connections to preserve their status and increase their incomes by assuming brokering roles, the cadres realized that the new deal could benefit them too.[328] From a long-term perspective, the initial distrust of aging cadres was less important than the implications of the reforms for the Communist Party. Dynamic rich peasants (often former cadres) were held up as models, and their recruitment to the Party was mandated. In some cases

---

324 See below. For details about the various forms of rural reform in the early stages, see also Kathleen Hartford, "Socialist agriculture is dead; long live socialist agriculture!: organizational transformations in rural China," in Elizabeth J. Perry and Christine Wong, eds., *The political economy of reform in post-Mao China*, 31–61.

325 See Terry Sicular, "Rural marketing and exchange in the wake of recent reforms," in Perry and Wong, eds., *The political economy of reform in post-Mao China*, 83–109.

326 Hartford suggests that not all peasants welcomed the destruction of the commune system; ibid., 138–39.

327 See Richard J. Latham, "The implications of rural reforms for grass-roots cadres," in ibid., 57–73.

328 This comment is based on the author's own observations and conversations in China, along with those of others.

this aroused envy.[329] But provided that the recruitment policy was maintained, the prospect was the transformation of a poor peasant party into a rich peasant one, with considerable implications for class attitudes and ideological predilections. The "serve the people" ethos of the CCP was bound to be adulterated by the new slogan "To get rich is glorious." This in turn would almost certainly ensure that the CCP would continue to eschew class struggle and focus on economic development as its prime goal.

The complexities of industrial restructuring and market reform posed far greater problems for Teng Hsiao-p'ing and his colleagues, as Dwight Perkins shows. There was no single step, like decollectivization, capable of generating an economic breakthrough that could not be gainsaid. On the contrary, many people stood to lose by urban reform: bureaucrats who forfeited power as greater independence was ceded to managers of state enterprises; managers of state enterprises who envied the even greater freedom accorded "collective" and private companies; workers in state enterprises who feared harder work and job insecurity in the search for efficiency, and envied the rising incomes of workers in the non-state sector and peasants in the countryside; every urban dweller, including intellectuals and students, who was hurt by the higher prices accompanying the reforms.

The reform program also implied a fundamental if dimly perceived threat to the legitimacy of the CCP. Party cadres were told to "seek truth from facts" and told that "practice is the sole criterion of truth." They were instructed to acquire knowledge that would equip them for the new era. The long-standing tension within the CCP between the demand for "redness" (political fervor) and the demand for "expertise" (professional skills), which used to be resolved in favor of the *yang* of redness, now seemed to have been settled in favor of the *yin* of expertise.

This was a potential blow to the roughly 50 percent of Party cadres who had been recruited during the Cultural Revolution, for their strengths were presumably in the field of political agitation. But it also placed a question mark over the role of the Party itself. The claim of the CCP to its vanguard role, like that of the CPSU and other parties, was rooted in its ideology. The premise was that its mastery of the ever correct ideology of Marxism–Leninism–Mao Tse-tung Thought enabled it to understand the present and plan for the future with a sureness inaccessible to non-Marxists. But if correctness was now to be found in practice or facts, what was the function of ideology?

329 For a discussion, see Elizabeth J. Perry, "Social ferment: grumbling amidst growth," in John S. Major, ed., *China briefing, 1985*, 39–41, 45–46.

Ideology had already been greatly devalued by the hyperbole of the Cultural Revolution, and the attribution of almost supernatural powers to Mao Tse-tung Thought.[330] The new emphasis on practice was a very grave blow. Teng Hsiao-p'ing's declaration that Marxism–Leninism–Mao Tse-tung Thought was one of four cardinal principles that could not be questioned did little to soften it.[331] CCP rule, although itself one of the four cardinal principles, now appeared to be justifiable only by competence and success, shaky foundations in view of the problems facing post-Mao China. At risk was the deep-rooted attachment in the Chinese political culture to the concept of an elite bureaucracy sanctioned simply by its commitment to and mastery of a totalist ideology that claimed to explain the world and man's place in it.

The increasing irrelevance of the Party was underlined by reformers' attempts to separate its functions from those of the government.[332] The declared aim was to free Party cadres to concentrate on overall questions of principle and line. Local government functionaries and managers who were not all CCP members were to be granted greater leeway to get on with their jobs regardless of ideological considerations.

But in a state in which virtually all top government officials were senior Party members and participated in the discussions of the Politburo or the Central Committee, it was not clear what should be the role of the "pure" Party official. Of course, he had to run the Party machine, but its role, too, was unclear in an era when class struggle and movement politics had given way to economic development.[333] During his tenure as CCP general secretary, Hu Yao-pang ignored the separation of roles, seeming to want to assert a right as China's top leader to make pronouncements on all spheres of national life. He made a number of overseas trips as if he were head of state or government.[334]

---

330 See George Urban, ed., *The miracles of Chairman Mao: a compendium of devotional literature*, 1966–1970, 1–27.

331 See "Uphold the four cardinal principles," *Selected works of Deng Xiaoping*, 172–74, 179–81. The other three were the socialist road, the dictatorship of the proletariat, and the leadership of the Communist Party.

332 "On the reform of the system of Party and state leadership," ibid., 303.

333 The dilemma may be loosely compared to that of party officials in the Western European democracies. During periods of opposition, the life of the party qua party looms large, for it is the instrument of agitation with which "class war" is waged in the country at large in order to oust the government of the day. If the strategy is successful and party leaders become government ministers in their turn, the role of the party greatly diminishes as its leaders occupy themselves with running the country and ensuring its economic prosperity. Purely party officials from then on take a subordinate role and rarely interfere with government policy, but are expected, rather, to ensure the loyalty of the party rank and file to whatever the government does.

334 There was perhaps some justification for this during Hu's brief period as CCP chairman, after the sixth plenum of the Eleventh CC in June 1981, but none after the Twelfth Congress in September 1982 when the chairmanship was abolished and the newly supreme post of general secretary became his only job. I use the term "formal" because, of course, ultimate power rested with Teng Hsiao-p'ing whatever his nominal title.

The Party's powers were further restricted by the provision in its new constitution passed at the Twelfth Congress in 1982 that "the Party must conduct its activities within the limits permitted by the Constitution and the laws of the state." As Hu Yao-pang explained this "most important principle" in his report, it was now formally "impermissible for any Party organization or member, from the Central Committee down to the grass roots, to act in contravention of the Constitution and laws."[335] A constitutional provision by itself was hardly a guarantee. But the emphasis on legality after the Third Plenum, in reaction to the anarchy of the Cultural Revolution when the elite had suffered most, together with the passage of various legal codes for the first time, at least signified an understanding that the unbridled power of the Party ultimately threatened everyone.[336]

Such formal restrictions on the Party were accompanied by concrete attempts to diminish "bureaucratism," whose harmful manifestations included

standing high above the masses; abusing power; divorcing oneself from reality and the masses; spending a lot of time and effort to put up an impressive front; indulging in empty talk; sticking to a rigid way of thinking; being hidebound by convention; overstaffing administrative organs; being dilatory, inefficient, and irresponsible; failing to keep one's word; circulating documents endlessly without solving problems; shifting responsibility to others; and even assuming the airs of a mandarin, reprimanding other people at every turn, vindictively attacking others, suppressing democracy, deceiving superiors and subordinates, being arbitrary and despotic, practising favouritism, offering bribes, participating in corrupt practices in violation of the law.

According to Teng, such practices had reached "intolerable dimensions both in our domestic affairs and in our contacts with other countries."[337]

Attacks on bureaucratism were nothing new within the CCP, dating back at least to the Rectification Campaign in Yenan in the early 1940s. The Cultural Revolution itself could in part be explained as Mao's final and most devastating attempt to destroy bureaucratism in order to unleash the pure revolutionary fervor of the masses. Teng's methods were less devastating, but he, too, wished to unleash the masses, though to create wealth rather than make revolution. Here again, Party cadres were being pushed to one side.

Despite these limits on the authority of the Party, the average peasant, worker, manager, or intellectual continued to behave circumspectly in the

335 *The Twelfth National Congress of the CPC*, 49.
336 For a discussion of some of the issues involved in the new emphasis on legality in the PRC, see R. Randle Edwards, Louis Henkin, Andrew J. Nathan, *Human rights in contemporary China*.
337 "On the reform of the system of Party and state leadership," *Selected works of Deng Xiaoping*, 310.

presence of its officials. Habits of obedience and memories of suffering inhibited any attempt to test the new permissiveness too far. The bureaucracy might be on the defensive, but it was still enormously powerful.

That may be the historians' final verdict on the Cultural Revolution. By the CCP's Twelfth Congress, in 1982, the erosion of the Party's authority as a result of the Cultural Revolution, the subsequent moves to restrain arbitrary use of power, the decline in the force of ideology, the unleashing of the peasant and the attempt to free up the urban economy – all carried the potential for a role for society vis-à-vis the state possibly greater than at any previous time when China was united under a strong central government. Mao had always stressed that out of bad things came good things. Those burgeoning social forces would finally challenge the bonds of state authority in the T'ien An Men demonstrations of 1989.

CHAPTER 5

THE OPENING TO AMERICA

Among the legacies of the era of Mao Tse-tung, the opening to the United States ranks as one of the most important. More than any other foreign policy initiative in Mao's twenty-seven years in power, the Sino-American accommodation reflected the Chairman's determination to establish China's legitimacy among the world's major powers. In a near-term sense, the restoration of Sino-American relations reversed China's international isolation and estrangement of the Cultural Revolution period. In a more long-term perspective, it ended two decades of diplomatic abnormality between the United States and China, and without it Peking's international emergence in the 1970s and 1980s would have been incalculably more difficult, and probably much less successful.

From the earliest hints of Sino-American accommodation in 1968, Mao was vital to this process. Yet even as the Chairman understood that closer relations with the West were a strategic imperative, he remained to the last highly ambivalent about the longer-term implications of incorporating China within the existing international system. Strategic and political necessity dictated Peking's reconciliation with the capitalist world, in particular the accommodation with America and with Japan, China's main adversary of the first half of the twentieth century. For psychological as much as for political reasons, Mao rarely admitted that his actions were dictated by weakness and vulnerability, or even that China sought such accommodation at least as actively as its former enemies. As a result, Mao never fully accepted the larger consequences of linking China with the outside world. Mao's ambivalence persisted to the time of his death, as he continued to sanction the struggle of his Cultural Revolution allies against leaders far more prepared to recognize the political and ideological implications of an internationally engaged China.

The Sino-American normalization process was therefore highly uneven and incomplete, as those leaders who sought to implement Mao's foreign

The opinions in this essay are the author's and do not reflect the views of the RAND Corporation or any of its governmental sponsors.

policy directives negotiated the dangerous shoals of Chinese internal politics. Larger international uncertainties also bedeviled China's external course, as China jettisoned the accumulated baggage of its previous foreign policy (especially as related to Vietnam), but without fully resolving the longer-term character of relations with the United States and Japan. Perhaps most important, the imponderables of the Chinese succession process repeatedly stymied the accomplishment of broader foreign policy goals. Without clear, consistent direction from the top, Sino-American relations progressed erratically for much of the 1970s. It was only toward the end of the decade that external imperatives and Teng Hsiao-p'ing's domestic political resurgence permitted consummation of the Sino-American normalization process begun nearly a decade before.

The development of China's relations with the West therefore seemed less the product of a grand design and more the result of contending and often contradictory impulses at work in the Chinese and American political systems. The earliest years in particular seemed fragile and tentative, as Chairman Mao, Premier Chou En-lai, and subsequently Teng Hsiao-p'ing sought to resurrect ties largely moribund since the Chinese civil war. That a handful of senior leaders engineered these changes may have made the initial breakthroughs easier, but it also made the process highly vulnerable to stagnation or reversal. Mao's increasing decrepitude and Chou's deteriorating health combined with President Nixon's political vulnerabilities to complicate early completion of the Sino-American normalization process. Neither Mao nor Chou lived to witness the culmination of their efforts, and Richard Nixon – compelled by unrelated events to resign from office – saw Jimmy Carter usurp the glory of Nixon's boldest diplomatic triumph. Equally ironic, it remained for Teng Hsiao-p'ing – twice relegated by Mao to political oblivion – and Ronald Reagan, among the twentieth century's most ideological presidents and a long-standing advocate of close relations with Taiwan – to furnish a rationale for Chinese-American relations that did not depend as intimately on shared security goals.

What reasons explain the resumption of relations with the United States? How was this policy debated among leaders in Peking? What expectations dominated the thinking of the advocates of Sino-American rapprochement, and were these expectations met? How did the process of accommodation influence China's subsequent thinking about the outside world? What were the effects of these changes on Chinese internal politics? Finally, did the opening to the West mark a truly historic break with China's past, or was it simply necessitated by exigencies of national security that are unlikely to endure? Before addressing these issues, it is first necessary to sketch briefly the character of foreign policy decision making during this period, and how it influenced the opportunities for policy change.

THE POLITICAL PROCESS AND CHINESE FOREIGN POLICY

The opening to America reflected longer-term strategic developments that directly affected Peking's security calculations. Three changes were especially important: (1) the retrenchment in the American military presence in East Asia deriving from the gradual withdrawal of U.S. forces from Vietnam, (2) a simultaneous increase in Soviet conventional and nuclear forces deployed in Asia that posed a direct threat to the security of China, and (3) the Nixon administration's public dissociation from Soviet coercive designs on China that constituted a tacit but crucial American commitment to the security and territorial integrity of the People's Republic (PRC). Strategic developments of such magnitude could not be slighted by Peking; a shift away from the isolation and xenophobia of the Cultural Revolution was all but inevitable under such circumstances.

Geopolitical logic, however, cannot explain all of Peking's responses; the personalities and institutions responsible for Chinese foreign policy must also be considered. Among various internal considerations, three were especially important. The first was the role of individual leaders. Three Chinese officials of singular authority and prestige loomed disproportionately large in the process of accommodation with the West: Mao Tse-tung, Chou En-lai, and Teng Hsiao-p'ing. These three men dominated Chinese foreign policy strategy from the earliest hints of reappraisal in the late 1960s, to the first breakthroughs in relations in the early 1970s, to the consummation of full Sino-American diplomatic ties at the end of the decade, and through the estrangement and reconstitution of relations in the early 1980s. Other veteran officials, in particular a small circle of senior military strategists and a few of Chou's longtime colleagues from the Ministry of Foreign Affairs, also played a vital behind-the-scenes role in the process. But Mao, Chou, and subsequently Teng remained the final arbiters of Chinese policy.

The disproportionate responsibility of these leaders accords closely with the highly centralized character of foreign policy during most of the post-1949 period. Although others contributed to this process, very few had legitimate claim to influencing the "grand design" of Chinese foreign policy. Only in foreign and military affairs, for example, did Mao's reputation remain largely untarnished in the decade following his death. As the June 1981 resolution on Party history affirmed:

In [Mao's] later years, he still remained alert to safeguarding the security of our country, stood up to the pressure of the social imperialists, pursued a correct foreign policy, firmly supported the just struggles of all peoples, outlined the correct strategy of the three worlds and advanced the important principle that China would never seek hegemony.[1]

There seems little reason to question these assertions; Mao's ideas and actions dominated China's foreign relations for more than a quarter century, including the initiation of relations with the United States. Chou's reputation in the international sphere remains equally unsullied, and Teng's domination of the foreign policy process (even in a more permissive political context) was nearly as far-reaching.

At the same time, each Chinese leader developed a distinct style in his interactions with American officials. To Chinese officials, issues of personality and policy were merged rather than blurred. Thus, the earliest breakthroughs in relations derived substantially from the personal and political compatibility established among Henry Kissinger, Chou En-lai, and Mao Tse-tung, but this congeniality never developed between Kissinger and Teng Hsiao-p'ing, especially as American and Chinese foreign policy interests began to diverge. Similarly, Teng's clear preference for Zbigniew Brzezinski rather than Cyrus Vance was partly attributable to the differing policy orientations of the two senior U.S. foreign policy officials, but also to their contrasting personalities. From the first, senior Chinese officials placed great importance on their ability to achieve a close personal relationship with a single official in various American administrations; absent such a connection, Sino-American relations tended to founder or deteriorate. Richard Solomon has captured the essence of this interpersonal process:

The most fundamental characteristic of dealings with the Chinese is their attempt to identify foreign officials who are sympathetic to their cause, to cultivate a sense of friendship and obligation in their official counterparts, and then to pursue their objectives through a variety of stratagems designed to manipulate feelings of friendship, obligation, guilt, or dependence.[2]

Only with the fuller institutionalization of Sino-American ties in the 1980s did this phenomenon become less prevalent and less vital to sustaining the relationship.

A second factor concerns the issue-based character of foreign policy decisions. Even if a very small circle of officials formulated Chinese foreign policy strategy, their decisions were influenced by a broader process

---

1 *Resolution on certain questions in the history of our party since the founding of the People's Republic of China* [27 June 1981], 41–42.
2 Richard H. Solomon, *Chinese political negotiating behavior: a briefing analysis*, 2.

of strategic and political reassessment under way within the Chinese bureaucratic system.[3] Like-mindedness on crucial foreign policy questions was also linked to a compatible stance on domestic policy issues. Chou's advocacy of diplomatic activism correlated closely with his effort to rebuild China's party and state institutions in the late 1960s and early 1970s; similarly, those most comfortable with China simultaneously confronting both superpowers were also the least troubled by the disruption of the Cultural Revolution.[4] Even if an interrelated policy stance cannot always be proved, the relative political position of Chou or Teng at a particular moment clearly affected his capacity for foreign policy initiatives.

A variant of this approach emphasizes institutional differences and their embodiment in personal power rivalries. In the classic bureaucratic maxim, "Where you stand depends on where you sit." A policy breakthrough as dramatic as the opening to the United States had a substantial effect on bureaucratic alignments and the allocation of scarce resources. The most dramatic example concerns Minister of Defense Lin Piao, whose political power and claim on resources eroded virtually in direct proportion to China's breakthrough with the United States. Some of the connections between Lin's declining fortunes at home and the success of Mao and Chou in building a relationship with the United States will be explored in the next section.

The third approach posits intense interpersonal and political rivalries, but does not assume a clear or consistent connection to a given foreign policy. Policy debate is simply the medium for intense struggles over personal power inherent in the Chinese political process. Although policy differences have influenced such competition, they are generally secondary to factional tendencies within the political system.[5] The purest form of this phenomenon occurred during the intensifying struggle to succeed Mao in the early and mid-1970s. Although the attacks of the Gang of Four on Chou, Teng, and other officials were cloaked in ideological trappings, these were the veneer for the underlying battle for political predominance waged in Mao's twilight years.

The Chinese have repeatedly denied any link between factional differences or power rivalries and foreign policy strategy. These disclaimers reflect the inherent sensitivity and secretiveness attached to discussions of China's national security strategy; any acknowledgment of major leadership divisions over foreign policy would ipso facto weaken China in its

3 See Richard Wich, *Sino-Soviet crisis politics: a study of political change and communication.*
4 Thomas M. Gottlieb, *Chinese foreign policy factionalism and the origins of the strategic triangle.*
5 Lucian W. Pye, *The dynamics of Chinese politics.*

dealings with other states. Thus, the struggle between the Gang of Four and Teng Hsiao-p'ing was waged in highly personalized terms rather than on the loftier plane of global strategy; it seemed too unseemly and sharp a descent from the geopolitical logic favored by Mao and Chou. Unfortunately, Mao's capriciousness and ambivalence about the internal political consequences of relations with the West kept the pot boiling well after the meal was cooked.

At various times, therefore, all three internal considerations influenced the conduct of Chinese foreign policy. Mao was convinced of the need to open relations with the United States, thereby establishing a new design for Chinese global strategy. Notwithstanding Mao's increasing isolation and decrepitude, the Chairman's towering prestige and authority in foreign affairs left him unchallenged in this realm. Yet the Chairman's interest in relations with the outside world waxed and waned, as Mao brooded over the possible political repercussions that would follow his death. Chou En-lai's growing infirmity meant that Mao no longer had a trusted lieutenant to oversee the making of Chinese foreign policy. As a result, foreign policy inexorably became part of the broader struggle for power undertaken by rival coalitions led by Teng Hsiao-p'ing and Chiang Ch'ing. Even after the passing of the extreme isolation and xenophobia of the late 1960s, Chinese internal politics continued to inhibit the conduct of external relations. The imperatives of China's national security and the internecine warfare among rival domestic factions repeatedly intermingled in the early and mid-1970s. As a consequence, there was an unfinished, tentative character to Chinese foreign policy throughout much of the decade. To understand the interaction of these developments more fully, however, we must first review the events that prompted China's strategic reassessment in the aftermath of the Cultural Revolution.

THE ROAD TO PEKING, 1968–1972

As noted earlier, the opening to America resulted from a more differentiated assessment of the degree of threat posed to China by the two superpowers. A degree of subterranean debate over Chinese views of the United States and the Soviet Union appeared intermittently during the Cultural Revolution,[6] but leaders in Peking seemed far too preoccupied by the factionalism and chaos unleashed during these years to permit definitive reassessment of China's security needs. It was only following

---

6 For a provocative if overstated account of these debates, see Gottlieb, *Chinese foreign policy factionalism and the origins of the strategic triangle*, esp. 30–66.

the Soviet invasion of Czechoslovakia in August 1968 that three trends coincided: (1) a reconstitution of the authority of the Chinese Party and state bureaucracies, (2) a growing war-weariness in the United States that foretold an eventual U.S. withdrawal from Vietnam, and (3) the steady and increasingly ominous buildup of Soviet power along the contested border with China.

Beginning in 1965, the Soviet Union (alarmed by Mao's allusions to unresolved territorial disputes and by xenophobia directed against it) began to strengthen its deployments along the Sino-Soviet border. As early as 1966, Chinese spokesmen first made note of these increases along what had previously been a lightly guarded frontier. The augmentation of Soviet ground forces was coupled with Moscow's readiness to use them, initially through more aggressive border patrolling. The invasion of Czechoslovakia and the subsequent articulation of the concept of "limited sovereignty" for socialist states (known widely as the "Brezhnev doctrine") created the potential for Soviet intimidation or punitive military attack, possibly directed against China's infant nuclear weapons program. In the aftermath of the Czech invasion, Chou and other Chinese leaders for the first time described the USSR as a "social-imperialist state" – that is, socialist in name but imperialist in deeds – capable of initiating a surprise attack on the PRC.

Under such circumstances, Chou began to reassess the consequences of adhering rigidly to a "dual adversary" conception of relations with the two superpowers. Even as Chinese statements still gave predominant emphasis to the alleged "collusion" between the United States and the Soviet Union, the consequences of a direct Soviet military challenge were vastly different from the threat posed by the United States. Although Moscow would not lightly contemplate major military action against China, the long common border made China highly vulnerable to attack. The Manchurian campaign of 1945 meant that the Soviet general staff was intimately familiar with some of the terrain of potential military operations; they also possessed detailed information on the performance of virtually all Chinese weapons systems. Even though the eastern regions of the Soviet Union were far removed from sources of military supply, over time Soviet logistic capabilities could be expected to improve. Much more ominously, by the summer of 1969 the Soviets had redeployed bombers from Eastern Europe to central Asia, where U.S. intelligence detected preparations for possible attacks on China's nuclear facilities.[7] Unlike the United States, which relied principally on its air and naval

7 Allen S. Whiting, "Sino-American detente," *CQ*, 82 June 1980, 336.

power deployed thousands of miles from home to "contain" China, the Soviet Union had an inherent geographic advantage. Its military assets, including ground forces, air power, and nuclear missiles, were already on Soviet soil, posing an immediate, continuing threat to China's industrial heartland and to Peking's nascent strategic weapons capability.

These brewing tensions culminated in the bloody border clashes in the winter of 1969, focused initially on Chen-pao Island, along the Ussuri River. As discussed in Chapter 3, the March hostilities were most likely initiated by the Chinese, who seemed intent on warning the Soviet Union in deed as well as word about the risks posed by the buildup of Soviet forces. But the subsequent escalation of hostilities by the Soviet side and public warnings from the general staff in Moscow created the possibility of a far wider and more destructive conflict. Hostilities in Sinkiang in late August and ominous private hints from Soviet officials about the possibility of punitive war against China suggested the worst; officials in Peking seemed genuinely anxious lest a large-scale conflict be launched by Moscow.

China's response to the increase in Soviet military and political pressure entailed three principal elements: (1) in the near term, seeking to limit the risks of major military hostilities by direct negotiations with the Soviet Union; (2) over the longer run, deploying larger, better-equipped forces along the Sino-Soviet border without appearing overly provocative to Moscow; and (3) initiating a more active political and diplomatic profile, including direct overtures to Washington. All three approaches were pursued simultaneously, but the third and perhaps most crucial "leg" in this policy was the slowest to yield results.

China's maximum vulnerability to attack was in summer of 1969, but not until the late spring of 1971 did Peking unambiguously convey its readiness to entertain a high-level American emissary. Why did it take so long for these changes to materialize? First, the newly elected Nixon administration did not act expeditiously on the earliest indications of China's interest in renewed relations with the United States. On 26 November 1968, a spokesman from the Ministry of Foreign Affairs had declared China's readiness to resume the ambassadorial talks in Warsaw in late February. More important, the spokesman also voiced China's interest in reaching agreement with Washington on the Five Principles of Peaceful Coexistence, long the touchstone of Chinese interest in normal state-to-state relations, but absent from PRC policy toward the United States since the mid-1960s. Although the new administration agreed to the date proposed by Peking, in other respects President Nixon's earliest public comments on China sought to discourage the possibilities for any near-term improvement in relations. When on 24 January 1969 a low-ranking PRC diplomat sought asylum in the Netherlands, the Chinese protested, but still waited until 18 February (two days before the scheduled resumption of the ambassadorial talks) to cancel the meeting. It would not be until January 1970 that the discussions at Warsaw finally resumed.

Although the evidence is circumstantial, the lack of a more positive U.S. response to China's earliest overtures appears to have stymied foreign policy initiatives proposed after the Twelfth Plenum of the Chinese Communist Party (CCP), in October 1968.[8] A decidedly more constructive tone was evident at that time in Chinese internal affairs, and it extended to foreign policy, as well. On 19 October, the Chinese ended their five-month silence on the Paris peace talks between the United States and Vietnam, implicitly voicing support for the first time for a negotiated end to the war. In late November, Peking republished Mao's speech to the Seventh Central Committee Second Plenum in March 1949, with its intriguing assertion that "we should not refuse to enter into negotiations because we are afraid of troubles and want to avoid complications.... We should be firm in principle; we should also have all the flexibility permissible and necessary for carrying out our principles." In addition, Peking painted a picture of the United States in isolation and decline; this included the publication of a text of Nixon's inaugural address.

At the end of January, however, Mao appeared in public for the first time since the Twelfth Plenum. A major rally of the top leaders pointed to possible tensions at the top, perhaps prompted equally by domestic and external developments. By the time of Peking's cancellation of the impending Warsaw negotiations, the foreign policy mood had shifted sharply. The defection of the Chinese diplomat was described as a "grave anti-China incident deliberately engineered by the U.S. government"; Nixon and Lyndon Johnson were now depicted as "jackals of the same lair without the least difference." Other commentaries on the United States returned to the emphasis on Soviet-American "collusion" that had been somewhat downplayed in the aftermath of the invasion of Czechoslovakia. These commentaries bore all the hallmarks of the more confrontational foreign policy emphasized by Lin Piao during the Cultural Revolution. With Sino-Soviet tensions growing steadily in early 1969, the momentary thaw in Chinese foreign policy appeared to cease. China

8 For a more detailed analysis on which this discussion draws, see Wich, *Sino-Soviet crisis politics*, 75–95.

seemed increasingly on a war footing, with predominant emphasis on the buildup of military power along the Sino-Soviet border.

In the context of these potentially ominous developments, however, Chou En-lai initiated in earnest a major internal reassessment of Chinese strategic and foreign policy.[9] During the Cultural Revolution, Lin Piao and his close subordinates had achieved total predominance atop the military command structure, virtually supplanting the other surviving marshals in the design and execution of Chinese defense strategy. The principal victim had been Ch'en I, minister of foreign affairs and among Chou's closest political colleagues, but also still a major force in Chinese military matters. However, the restoration of a degree of political stability in late 1968 had occasioned initial steps to place Chinese diplomacy on a normal footing again. With the onset of the border clashes, Chou moved immediately to transform Ch'en I's subliminal political and strategic role into a far more active one.

On 5 March – the day of the first clashes on Chen-pao Island – Chou ordered Ch'en I to convene a special forum on the international situation, with Marshals Yeh Chien-ying, Hsu Hsiang-ch'ien, and Nieh Jung-chen as contributing members. (Mao had evidently authorized the creation of such a group before this date, but the Sino-Soviet clashes lent it special urgency.) Assisted by personnel from the Foreign Ministry in a supporting role, the forum convened twenty-three separate meetings between March and October 1969, and submitted many reports to the Party Center for consideration. The Soviet Union's capability and intention to launch a direct military attack on China was among the key issues discussed, as was the possibility of Soviet-American collusion against China. Ch'en argued that contention remained paramount between the superpowers, effectively negating the possibility of joint action against the People's Republic. Ch'en was allegedly the first participant to reach this judgment, but the others ultimately followed suit. As the marshal concluded in a report forwarded to Mao, the acute border tensions made imperative a much more active diplomatic posture, beginning with the immediate resumption of the Sino-American ambassadorial talks at Warsaw. It would still be more than a year before these discussions resumed.

Leaders in Peking were nevertheless heartened by public statements from the Nixon administration that dissociated the United States from

---

9 This section draws upon interviews in China and several published accounts of Chinese diplomatic strategy in the late 1960s and early 1970s. See Tieh Tzu-wei, "Ch'en I tsai wen-hua ta-ko-ming chung" (Ch'en I during the "Great Cultural Revolution"), *Kun-lun*, 5 (September 1985), esp. 140, 142; and Yeh Chien-ying Biographical Writing Group of the Military Science Academy, *Yeh Chien-ying chuan-lueh* (A brief biography of Yeh Chien-ying), esp. 271–72.

any Soviet coercive designs on China. In addition, American leaders began to signal their desire for opening relations with Peking. On 1 August 1969, President Nixon (while on a visit to Pakistan) informed President Yahya Khan of his desire to open relations with China, and asked the Pakistani leader to convey his message to Peking.[10] In the absence of an early political breakthrough with the United States, however, the Chinese had few options for utilizing this altered American policy stance to direct advantage. The immediate key to avoiding war was through discussions with Moscow, resulting in Peking's sudden invitation for Premier Alexei Kosygin to visit Peking following Ho Chi Minh's funeral in September. (Kosygin had already begun his return to Moscow when the Chinese offer was received and accepted, suggesting the urgency of the situation.) With the Chou–Kosygin agreement to resume border negotiations in October, the period of acute crisis in Sino-Soviet relations had passed. Although the border talks did not achieve any immediate breakthroughs, the resumption of regular political and diplomatic contact seemed likely to prevent the worst from occurring. The Nixon administration, although by now far more sensitized to the dangers of the Sino-Soviet confrontation and beginning to explore major shifts in China policy, had only begun to develop a channel for communicating with Peking.

Moreover, regardless of the Nixon administration's increasing hints about its desire to improve relations with Peking, U.S. policy in 1969 and 1970 retained numerous elements detrimental to Chinese political and security interests. The Nixon–Sato communiqué of November 1969, in which Japan acknowledged for the first time a responsibility for the security of Taiwan and South Korea, could hardly have been reassuring to the advocates of Sino-American accommodation in Peking, and in part explains China's virtually alarmist attacks on the threat of "Japanese militarism" that persisted until 1972. Similarly, the United States (notwithstanding Nixon's express desire to withdraw from Vietnam and encouragement to America's Asian allies to assume more responsibility for their own defense) remained deeply engaged in Vietnam. The U.S. thrust into Cambodia in May 1970 and the subsequent South Vietnamese incursions into Laos in early 1971 undoubtedly delayed the accommodation process. Amicable relations with Vietnam still mattered to Peking; the Chinese were not prepared to damage their relationship with Hanoi until the possibilities with the United States were far clearer.

In addition, China's foreign affairs bureaucracy was still largely in a

---

10 Henry Kissinger, *White House years*, 180–81.

shambles at the end of the 1960s and the beginning of the 1970s. It was only in May 1969 that Peking began to return its ambassadors to posts abroad, and then on a very limited basis. Chou had only a handful of trusted lieutenants to whom he might turn. Foreign Minister Ch'en I's health declined precipitously, and other senior officials who might have been recruited into the process were deeply engaged in the reconstitution of the Party and state system. Most of those knowledgeable about the United States and experienced in dealing with American officials in the 1940s (in particular, Ch'iao Kuan-hua and Huang Hua) were now pressed into service, to the degree that their political health allowed. Neither the numbers of people involved nor the extent of their political power furnished much ground for optimism; it was Chou and, by extension, Mao himself who alone could guarantee the policy.

Finally, the political arrangements operating between the conclusion of the Ninth Party Congress until the time of Lin Piao's death remained highly tenuous. The PLA, under the direct control of Lin and his top lieutenants, remained by far the most powerful institution in China, a fact underscored by the military's access to and control over a separate transportation and communications network. The preponderant position of Lin and his allies in the Politburo and the Central Committee made any major policy initiative antithetical to their interests extremely difficult to undertake. Indeed, at the time that the Sino-Soviet border negotiations resumed in October, Lin Piao and Chief of Staff Huang Yung-sheng promulgated General Order No. 1, allegedly for the purpose of "intensifying preparations against war and preventing sudden attacks from the enemy." These actions were supposedly taken on Lin's personal initiative, without Mao's approval and consent, so as to consolidate Lin's control over the military and strengthen his grip on political power, as well.[11] The general order not only placed the entire army on alert; it also enabled Lin to have most of the other marshals removed from Peking, allegedly to ensure their safety but thereby precluding their active role in policymaking. Indeed, it is far from clear that the Politburo was even functioning in regular fashion at the time. Mao's suspicions of Lin Piao and his military circle had supposedly grown so acute that the Chairman no longer resided in Chung-nan-hai, preferring instead to spend long periods of time in locations in Peking that he deemed safer.[12]

Viewed from this perspective, the extreme confidentiality that Peking deemed essential to the early Sino-American dealings becomes more com-

11 *Nieh Jung-chen hui-yi lu* (Memoirs of Nieh Jung-chen), 865–66.
12 Roxane Witke, *Comrade Chiang Ch'ing*, 372.

prehensible. The very limited number of officials involved in this process in both systems may have been vital to the success of the initiatives. Nixon and Kissinger believed that reliance on conventional bureaucratic channels would have doomed their efforts; Chou may have viewed it as a matter of political survival.

The Chinese have never furnished much detail about Lin Piao's seeming opposition to the Sino-American rapprochement, concentrating instead on the alleged plot to assassinate Mao and Lin's subsequent effort to defect to the Soviet Union.[13] Nor have the official accounts of Lin's treachery documented a direct link between Lin and the Soviet Union, only that he hoped to secure such support. But some elliptical comments from Chou and a more specific claim by Mao lend credence to allegations of such opposition. In Chou's letter of 21 April 1971 emphasizing Peking's readiness to welcome a special U.S. envoy, the premier explained the three-month lapse responding to President Nixon's letter of early January as "owing to the situation at the time."[14] Kissinger speculates that Chou was alluding to South Vietnamese operations in Laos in February or to the search for an appropriate secure channel to communicate with Washington, but the increasingly tense standoff between Mao and Lin Piao seems a more plausible explanation. The rapid acceleration of Sino-American negotiations in the spring of 1971 followed closely on Lin's growing political problems of the late winter, as power began to slip away from the minister of defense. During the Nixon visit, Mao further alleged that a "reactionary group [was] opposed to our contact with you.... The result was that they got on an airplane and fled abroad."[15]

Other evidence suggests military opposition to rapprochement with the United States during its early stages. According to Kissinger, in July 1970 two MiG-19s attempted "to intercept and possibly shoot down" a U.S. aircraft on a routine intelligence-gathering mission a hundred miles off the Chinese coast. It had been five years since the Chinese had undertaken such actions.[16] The air force, commanded by Lin's close ally Wu Fa-hsien, had been intimately associated with Cultural Revolution radicalism; downing of a U.S. aircraft could have been expected to derail or at least delay improved relations with Washington. Similarly, in a major Army Day speech in 1971 only weeks after Kissinger's secret visit, Huang Yung-sheng delivered a blistering attack on U.S. policy toward Vietnam, describing the United States and the Soviet Union as coequal

---

13 Hua Fang, "Lin Piao's abortive counter-revolutionary coup d'état," *Beijing Review*, 22 December 1980, 19–28.
14 Kissinger, *White House years*, 714.   15 Ibid., 1061.   16 Ibid., 697.

threats to Chinese security. The theme of superpower collusion was in stark contrast to the clear differentiation of the Soviet and American threats offered in an authoritative defense of the opening to the United States that had appeared in *Hung-ch'i* (Red Flag) simultaneous with Huang's remarks.[17] Chou En-lai (in an interview with James Reston at the time of Huang's speech) dismissed the chief of staff's statements as not reflecting China's foreign policy priorities, in particular the desire for closer Sino-American relations.[18] Indeed, Marshal Yeh Chien-ying was the only military figure associated publicly with the Sino-American accommodation, having been present at Pcking airport for Henry Kissinger's arrival in early July.

It seems quite doubtful, however, that Lin represented a "pro-Soviet" viewpoint that counterbalanced Chou's alignment with the United States. Following Lin's death, for example, an internal Party document quoted Lin as asserting (perhaps more out of pique than design), "if Chou can invite Nixon, I can invite Brezhnev."[19] Similarly, in his speech to the Tenth Party Congress of August 1973, Chou En-lai accused Lin and his co-conspirators of "want[ing] to capitulate to Soviet revisionist social imperialism and ally themselves with imperialism, revisionism, and reaction to oppose China, communism, and revolution."[20] But these charges do not allege an active pro-Soviet "tilt" on Lin's part. If anything, the aggressive border patrolling undertaken by the PLA and the subsequent national mobilization orders were both probably attributable to Lin and his close allies in the high command. In the atmosphere of acute tension and with rumors of war abounding during the summer and early fall of 1969, Lin was the immediate political beneficiary of the confrontation with Soviet military power. It was only after Chou En-lai's meeting with Soviet Premier Kosygin at Peking airport in September that tensions with Moscow began to ease, especially as the two sides agreed to resume border negotiations interrupted since 1964. Thus, Chou and Mao, but not Lin, seemed to recognize the potential dangers of remaining indefinitely on a war footing.

Lin's larger problems concerned his standing with Mao. He recognized the Chairman's growing disenchantment with him in late 1970 and early 1971, and the virtual certainty that Mao had decided to unseat him. If

---

17 "T'uan-chieh jen-min chan-sheng ti-jen ti chiang-ta wu-ch'i; hsueh-hsi 'Lun cheng-ts'e'" (A powerful weapon to unite the people and defeat the enemy: a study of "On policy"). Writing Group of the CCP Hupei Provincial Committee, ed., *HC*, 9 (2 August 1971), 10–17.
18 *NYT*, 4 August 1971.
19 Stanley Karnow, "Lin Piao believed to be dead," *Washington Post*, 27 November 1971.
20 Chou En-lai, Report to the Tenth CCP National Congress" (delivered 24 August 1973), *PR*, 35 and 36 (7 September 1973), 20.

more compelling evidence existed of Lin's working "hand in glove" with the Soviet Union, it would have been among the most damning pieces of evidence of Lin's political treachery, and would have very likely surfaced in the spate of accusations subsequently directed against him. But no such charges were ever leveled. Rather, Lin's alleged pro-Soviet inclinations assumed a successful defection or the creation of an independent power base in Canton. As one internal document asserted, Lin "planned to establish a rival Central Committee [in Canton; he] also intended to collude with the Soviet revisionists to attack us simultaneously from the north and the south."[21] Had Lin reached the Soviet Union in September 1971, his defection would have represented a propaganda and intelligence coup for Moscow of the highest order, but this event never came to pass.

Lin's stake in a "dual adversary" approach to China's relations with the superpowers was political as well as institutional. As minister of defense during the latter half of the 1960s, he had presided over extraordinary increases in Chinese military expenditure, reflecting China's acute vulnerability to military pressure along its southern and northern frontiers. Between 1965 and 1971, the annual increase in Chinese defense spending averaged 10 percent, an even more remarkable development in view of the chaos and economic dislocation of the Cultural Revolution. The preponderance of these increases was in the procurement of weapons and equipment and the construction of new military facilities in China's interior provinces, reflecting the increased combat responsibilities of the Chinese military establishment during this period.[22] It is somewhat problematic to assert that Lin welcomed such military pressure or that he relished the prospect of an isolated, vulnerable China confronting simultaneous military challenges from Moscow as well as Washington. But he was the clear beneficiary of these circumstances, as disintegration at home and threats from abroad made Lin and the military virtually indispensable to Chairman Mao. With his designation in the 1969 Party constitution as successor to Mao and the simultaneous enhancement of the PLA's power in the Ninth CCP Central Committee, as well as the Politburo, Lin's position seemed virtually unassailable.

But the vicissitudes of the Chinese political process – and, perhaps more important, the mounting suspicions of an aged Party Chairman wary of Lin's ambitions – sharply reversed these circumstances. In retro-

---

21 "Report on the investigation of the counterrevolutionary crimes of the Lin Piao anti-party clique," *Chung-fa*, 34 (1973), in Michael Yim Kau, ed., *The Lin Piao affair: power politics and military coup*, 113.
22 For relevant details, see United States Central Intelligence Agency, National Foreign Assessment Center, *Chinese defense spending, 1965–79*, 2–4.

spect, it appears that Mao sought to undermine Lin almost from the time that he was named Mao's constitutionally designated successor.[23] Regardless of the various lurid renderings of Lin's subsequent political downfall – the leitmotif being his alleged plot to assassinate Mao – the consistent element in all such accounts is unrelenting struggle for power.

Allegations of Lin's opposition to the rapprochement with the United States are best judged in this context. Under more normal circumstances, Lin, as a military commander, might have been wary of efforts to accommodate with a long-standing adversary. At the time when Chou and Mao were making their initial overtures to Nixon, the United States remained deeply engaged in combat in Vietnam, posing a serious threat to Chinese national security. But these were not normal times. Just as the prize of succession to Mao was within Lin's grasp, Mao decided to rebuild the structure of Party and state power severely damaged in the Cultural Revolution. These decisions redounded very much to the advantage of Chou and his political allies, and called into question Lin's authority and longer-term political position. Thus, the prospect of a major shift in Chinese foreign policy strategy would have been especially unsettling to Lin, for he undoubtedly viewed the overtures to Washington as part of a coordinated campaign to undermine his political power.

As Mao's attacks on Lin accelerated in the aftermath of the Second Plenum in August–September 1970, so, too, did the Chairman's gestures toward the United States. On 1 October, Edgar Snow and his wife were escorted by Chou En-lai to Mao's side atop T'ien An Men, and were photographed together reviewing the National Day celebrations. It was not only the first occasion that an American citizen had been afforded such an opportunity; Mao was now publicly identified for the first time with the still tentative moves toward the United States.[24] Although Chou's earliest communications with the Nixon administration (in December 1970 and January 1971) alluded to the concurrence of Lin Piao as well as Mao in proposing high-level contact with the United States,[25] these were the only instances where Lin allegedly played any role at all in the Sino-American accommodation. Chou's letter of late May 1971 extending the invitation to Kissinger for a secret visit and to Nixon for a subsequent public visit made mention only of Mao's approval, with Lin's name conspicuous by its absence.[26] If any further evidence was needed, Chou supplied it during

23 For a collection of the relevant Party documents, see Kau, *The Lin Piao affair*.
24 Kissinger, *White House years*, 698–99. The photograph of Mao and Snow did not appear in *JMJP* until Mao's birthday on 26 December 1970.
25 Ibid., 701, 703; Richard Nixon, *RN: the memoirs of Richard Nixon*, 547.
26 Nixon, *RN*, 551–52.

Kissinger's first visit, of 9–11 July 1971. When the national security adviser presented gifts for the senior Chinese leadership, Chou omitted Lin Piao's name from the Chinese officials thanking him for the gifts.[27] Virtually from the start, therefore, Lin was the odd man out in Peking's overtures to Washington. His isolation from the most important foreign policy shift since the initiation of the Sino-Soviet conflict testified to his rapidly disintegrating political position, climaxing in an ignominious effort to defect to the USSR in September 1971.

Although Lin's approach seemed entirely consonant with the isolationism and confrontational mentality of the Cultural Revolution, it was not suited to the altered circumstances of the early 1970s, when a clear differentiation was drawn between the Soviet Union as the primary enemy and the United States as only a secondary adversary. As a subsequent critique noted:

> Lin Piao declared: "We have no common language with the imperialists, revisionists, and reactionaries. We must draw a clear line of demarcation with them, wage a struggle against them and oppose them; we must not join with them in their evil deeds."…. One of the most important strategies … in the struggle against the enemy is: rally all forces that can be rallied, organize the broadest international united front, and concentrate the main strength to hit the most important enemy…. The theory of "hitting out in all directions" trampled down on many important Marxist-Leninist tactics…. The consequence … was enemies everywhere, bringing us to the brink of isolation.[28]

As an Albanian document observed, the rapprochement with the United States marked the end of the foreign policy strategy of the Cultural Revolution era:

> With Nixon's visit, China joined the dance of imperialist alliances and rivalries for the redivision of the world, where China, too, would have its own share. This visit paved the road to its rapprochement and collaboration with U.S. imperialism and its allies. At the same time … the alliance with the United States of America also marked the abandonment on the part of the Chinese leadership of the genuine socialist countries, the Marxist-Leninist movement, the revolution and the national liberation struggle of the peoples.[29]

More than any other event, the opening to America had unhinged a decade of ideological rigidity at home and abroad. The Nixon visit was the

---

27 Solomon, *Chinese political negotiating behavior*, 7.
28 Chang Ming-yang, "An analysis of Lin Piao and the 'Gang of Four's' ultraleft foreign policy line," *Fu-tan hsueh-pao* (Fudan journal), 2 (March 1980), in JPRS, 76141 *China report: political sociological and military affairs*, 103 (30 July 1980), 48–49.
29 Letter to the CCP Central Committee and the PRC State Council, 30 July 1978, in *Foreign Broadcast Informatin Service* [hereafter FBIS] *Daily Report East: Europe*, 1 August 1978, 17.

crucial opening move in this process; foreign policy had been released from its doctrinaire moorings, with Lin Piao the principal casualty.

Chinese accounts make only passing mention of Peking's unanswered overtures of late 1968 and of its seeming deferral of the Sino-American accommodation. They also downplay Peking's acute anxieties about the possibility of a Soviet attack during 1969. Rather, Nixon and Kissinger were consistently depicted as ardent suitors of the Chinese, earnestly hoping for an invitation to visit Peking. According to Edgar Snow, Chou En-lai in early November 1970 expressed considerable skepticism about American intentions:

[Chou] recalled that when President Nixon came to office in 1969 that he had announced that he favored relaxation of tension and wanted to negotiate with China. Further, Nixon had informed Peking that, if Warsaw was not an appropriate place, discussions could be held in China. Peking had replied, that's fine. Nixon could come there himself or send an emissary to discuss the Taiwan question. There was no response from Nixon, however. Then came the Cambodian invasion of March 1970. The Chinese concluded that Nixon was not to be taken seriously.[30]

Later in the month, however, an additional private message from President Nixon led to a more encouraging if still somewhat diffident response from Peking. As Mao observed to Edgar Snow in mid-December:

... the Foreign Ministry was studying the matter of admitting Americans from the left, middle, and right to visit China. Should rightists like Nixon, who represent the monopoly capitalists, be permitted to come? He should be welcomed because, Mao explained, at present the problems between China and the U.S. would have to be solved with Nixon. Mao would be happy to talk with him, either as a tourist or as President.[31]

At the same time, Mao was sensitive to the political implications in the United States should Nixon visit China: "Discussing Nixon's possible visit to China, the Chairman casually remarked that the presidential election would be in 1972, would it not? Therefore, he added, Mr. Nixon might send an envoy first, but was not himself likely to come to Peking before early 1972."[32] Thus, from the earliest tentative moves between the United States and China, a "who needs whom" debate surfaced. Peking, above all, did not wish to appear the needier party: It was the United States that desired such a meeting, and it was for the United States to cut the Gordian knot of Taiwan.

---

30 Edgar Snow, *The long revolution*, 11–12. All but the first sentence of this quotation was excised from the initial text approved by the Chinese.
31 Ibid., 171–72. 32 Ibid., 182–83.

This self-confidence was amply reflected in an internal report delivered by Chou En-lai on the eve of Nixon's visit:

The visit of the head of U.S. imperialism ... renders bankrupt the China policy of the U.S. ... When the U.S. got stuck in Vietnam, the Soviet revisionists used the opportunity to extend vigorously their sphere of influence in Europe and the Middle East. The U.S. imperialists have no choice but to improve their relations with China in order to counter the Soviet revisionists.... Because Nixon has encountered difficulties both domestically and internationally, he has requested eagerly to visit China. When he comes, he has to bring something along in his pocket; otherwise, he will find it hard to give explanations when he returns to the U.S.[33]

To a domestic audience, therefore, Chou depicted Nixon as urgently and earnestly soliciting ties with Peking; in the view of Mao and Chou, they were only consenting to American eagerness to secure such relations, asserting further that Nixon would not arrive empty-handed.

The reality was far more complicated. Although the Chinese may have felt vindicated that the Nixon administration (not to mention various Democratic Party aspirants for the presidency) eagerly sought approval for trips to Peking, China's own motivations were hardly detached. The frankest public justification of the opening to the United States, published in *Hung-ch'i* two weeks after Kissinger's secret trip, drew unambiguous distinctions between the degree of threat posed by the two superpowers to China and its effect on Peking's security calculations. Although nominally an assessment of CCP strategy in the war of resistance against Japan, the distinctions between "Japanese imperialism which is now committing aggression against China and the imperialist powers which are not doing so now" were of clear contemporary relevance. According to the article's authors, the proletariat needed to grasp the opportunities presented by the "many contradictions" among the imperialist powers, in particular the opportunity "to force our principal enemy into a narrow and isolated position." As the authors further concluded, "the tactical principles formulated by Chairman Mao for struggling against the enemy presented a dialectical unity of firm principles and great flexibility."[34]

The question of private understandings reached between the Chinese and the Nixon administration remains more conjectural. Several observers allege that Nixon and Kissinger had provided private assurances to China on crucial issues in exchange for Chinese support for U.S. policy

---

33 Chou En-lai, "Internal report to the Party on the international situation" (December 1971), in King C. Chen, ed., *China and the three worlds*, 137–38. Chou's report, acquired by Taiwan sources, seems a credible and authentic document.

34 "T'uan chieh jen-min," 14.

in other areas.[35] In all likelihood, Taiwan was high on this list; as Mao had indicated to Edgar Snow in late 1970, "[Nixon] can't come unless he wants to talk about Taiwan."[36] Indeed, crucial American concessions related to Taiwan had already been conveyed in January and February by Ambassador Walter Stoessel in Warsaw, with the United States pledging itself to reduce (and, by implication, ultimately withdraw) U.S. forces on Taiwan. Michel Oksenberg describes Stoessel's two 1970 meetings with Chinese chargé d'affaires Lei Yang as "extraordinary." According to Oksenberg, "the United States acknowledged for the first time that this was a matter to be settled peacefully by the Chinese themselves; the Chinese in turn abandoned their previous stance that until the issue was settled, no improvement in the relationship could take place."[37] In exchange for such assurances, the Chinese proffered invitations to Kissinger and Nixon.[38] But the larger U.S. concerns focused on Vietnam, and the Nixon administration sought to gain at least tacit Chinese consent to its strategy for withdrawing from the conflict.

In the aftermath of Kissinger's private visit, the Chinese began to urge Hanoi to reach an accommodation with Washington that would leave the Saigon regime intact in the South.[39] According to a white paper issued by the Vietnamese Foreign Ministry, Peking counseled Hanoi "to avail itself of every opportunity to first solve the question of U.S. troop withdrawal and pay attention to solving the U.S. POW issue. The overthrow of the Saigon puppet administration will take time." According to this document, however, the Chinese also made clear their ordering of preferences:

On 13 July 1971, a high-ranking Chinese delegation [led by Chou En-lai] said: Indochina is the most important problem in our meeting with Kissinger. Kissinger said that the United States links the settlement to the Taiwan issue. The United States let it be known that U.S. troops could be pulled out of Taiwan only after U.S. forces were withdrawn from Indochina. To China, the withdrawal of U.S. troops from South Vietnam is more important than the question of China being admitted to the U. N....

In early March 1972 ... a representative of the Chinese leaders explained [that] to normalize Sino-U.S. relations and to alleviate the situation in the Far East, it is necessary first of all to solve the Vietnam and Indochina problem. We have not demanded that the Taiwan issue be solved first. This issue is secondary.[40]

35 See, for example, Seymour Hersh, *The price of power: Kissinger in the Nixon White House.*
36 Cited in ibid., 367.
37 Michel Oksenberg, "A decade of Sino-American relations," *Foreign Affairs,* 61.1 (Fall 1982), 177. Oksenberg's observations are based on extensive access to the Sino-American negotiating record of the period.
38 Hersh, *The price of power,* 361.   39 Ibid., 375–76.
40 *The truth about Vietnam–China relations over the last 30 years* (4 October 1979), reprinted in FBIS *Daily Report: Asia and Pacific,* supplement, 19 October 1979, 22.

Yet Vietnam insisted that Chinese intentions were duplicitous. According to Vietnamese foreign minister Nguyen Co Thach:

After Nixon's visit to China, Mao Tse-tung told Prime Minister Pham Van Dong that his broom was not long enough to sweep Taiwan clean and ours was not long enough to get the Americans out of South Vietnam. He wanted to halt reunification and force us to recognize the puppet regime in the South. He had sacrificed Vietnam for the sake of the United States.[41]

At Washington's behest, Peking began to transmit U.S. warnings to Hanoi of the dangers of renewed escalation should Vietnam refuse American negotiating proposals.[42] Vietnam's relations with China were the first and perhaps the most important casualty of the Sino-American rapprochement, underscoring Hanoi's subsequent conviction that enhanced relations with Moscow would be crucial to deflecting growing political pressure from Peking.

By the time China and the United States were in regular if highly secret contact in the spring of 1971, the period of maximum danger along the Sino-Soviet border had passed. Although the outbreak of hostilities could still not be precluded, it seemed far less likely, especially as military predominance in internal Chinese politics receded and civilian authority was reestablished. With China under less severe compulsion and with Nixon increasingly eager for a breakthrough before the election year 1972, Mao and Chou concluded that their hand had grown much stronger.

Even as the Nixon visit approached, however, internal rivalries again intruded on Sino-American relations. Chiang Ch'ing and her allies, clearly sensing the political opportunity presented to Chou En-lai by the impending presidential visit, allegedly voiced objection to the premier's domination of the foreign policy process.[43] During Kissinger's second visit to Peking in November and in Alexander Haig's advance trip in January 1972, the radicals supposedly asserted their right to conduct negotiations with President Nixon. Their objection was not to Sino-American rapprochement per se (especially given Mao's central role in the accommodation process), but to the premier's exclusive control over the execution of Chinese foreign policy. At the time of the Haig visit, the radicals printed an article fiercely criticizing "American imperialism." Chou was supposedly incensed at its publication, asserting that it violated Chairman Mao's strategic instructions and did not reflect Chinese foreign

41 See Nguyen Co Thach's interview in Amsterdam, *De volkskrant*, 6 March 1982, as reported in FBIS *Daily Report: Asia and Pacific*, 17 March 1982, K2.
42 *The truth about Vietnam–China relations*, 22–23.
43 The information in the above paragraph was furnished to the author by a Chinese official familiar with Sino-American relations at the time.

policy. Although he was able to limit the damage caused by its appearance at an inopportune moment, the first warning signs of the radicals' obstructionist role had surfaced, within four months of Lin Piao's death. That Chiang Ch'ing subsequently hosted the Nixon entourage at a revolutionary ballet was notable in that it implied her assent to the opening to America; probably it was an effort by Chou to furnish the radicals with the appearance of involvement in the Sino-American relationship.

But the stakes were far too big during the Nixon visit to permit failure. From the moment that Chou greeted the president on the tarmac at Peking airport on 21 February 1972, the success of the visit was virtually assured. Although the United States had no guarantee of a Nixon–Mao meeting, the call to Chung-nan-hai on the president's first evening in Peking put American anxieties to rest. The extensive front-page coverage in the next day's *People's Daily* – Chou himself was observed by American reporters reviewing the page proofs following the opening banquet – sealed Mao's endorsement of the visit. Having by his own acknowledgment "voted for you [Nixon]" in 1968, Mao made the same choice in 1972. Moreover, by restricting himself largely to a behind-the-scenes role, Mao guaranteed that the Nixon visit would be Chou's triumph.

During Nixon's stay, the two sides devoted much of their attention to a document that would define the broad principles intended to govern future Sino-American relations. The Shanghai Communiqué of 28 February 1972 represented a particularly artful example of such a document; joint paragraphs were juxtaposed with unilateral statements of national policy.[44] For the Chinese, the most important aspects of the communiqué were fourfold: first, the joint pledge that "neither should seek hegemony in the Asia-Pacific region and each is opposed to efforts by any other country or group of countries to establish such hegemony"; second, the common statement that "neither is prepared to negotiate on behalf of any third party or to enter into agreements or understandings with the other directed at other states"; third, the shared opposition to "any major country ... collud[ing] with another against other countries, or for major countries to divide up the world into spheres of interest"; and fourth, a longer statement from the United States on policy toward Taiwan:

The United States acknowledges [*ren-shih tao*] that all Chinese on either side of the Taiwan Strait maintain there is but one China and that Taiwan is a part of China. The United States does not challenge that position. It reaffirms its interest in a peaceful settlement of the Taiwan question by the Chinese themselves. With

44 For a text from which all citations are drawn, see Richard H. Solomon, ed., *The China factor: Sino-American relations and the global scene*, 296–300.

this prospect in mind, it affirms the ultimate objective of the withdrawal of all U.S. forces and military installations from Taiwan. In the meantime, it will progressively reduce its forces and military installations on Taiwan as the tension in the area diminishes.

Although the United States was not unequivocally committed to the Chinese position on the inviolability of one China, the Nixon administration had decided not to contest claims to the unity of China and Taiwan. As proposed in an earlier book by two U.S. policy analysts, the American position was that of "one China but not now."[45] Chou and his lieutenants (in particular Vice-Minister of Foreign Affairs Ch'iao Kuan-hua) had been uncompromising on this most sensitive of issues; Nixon and Kissinger, seeking to avoid an impasse and maintaining the position first disclosed privately at Warsaw in early 1970, yielded without voicing objection to China's claims of sovereignty over Taiwan.

Thus, the Chinese felt they had won a singular victory in the negotiations. Their own concessions in the document had been minimal, whereas the United States faced the delicate task of carrying out its stated intent to draw down its forces in Taiwan as part of a longer-term policy of disengagement from the area. On an issue of utmost nationalistic sensitivity, the Chinese concluded that they had not bartered away principles for the sake of a Sino-American accord. But Mao and Chou had assented to an indeterminate prolongation of the division of China and Taiwan.

The Chinese had judged broader national security imperatives far more pressing than immediate resolution of the Taiwan question. As Kissinger observed in his memoirs, a credible relationship with the United States transformed the character of China's relations with the superpowers. It relieved the Chinese of the threat of a two-front war against equally imposing adversaries; it compelled Moscow to rethink its calculus of either coercing the People's Republic or of attacking China outright; and it provided assurance to Peking that there would be no collaborative anti-China strategy ("collusion") undertaken by Moscow and Washington.[46] In November 1971, the United States had made additional private pledges to assist China militarily should Sino-Soviet tensions related to the Indo-Pakistani war escalate to armed conflict initiated by the Soviet Union.[47] Although such a contingency was far more remote than Kissinger implied, it furnished additional evidence to Peking that Washington deemed China's territorial integrity and inviolability a vital underpinning of U.S. foreign policy.

The consequences of the rapprochement for regional security were also

45 Richard Moorsteen and Morton Abramowitz, *Remaking China policy: U.S.–China relations and governmental decisionmaking.*
46 Kissinger, *White House years,* 765.   47 Ibid., 906, 910–11.

important, both for what was precluded and for what was permitted. As President Nixon disclaimed any intention to threaten China, Mao responded that "neither do we threaten Japan or South Korea."[48] These understandings not only allowed reductions in U.S. forces deployed against China, they provided tacit Chinese acceptance of the U.S. military presence in the western Pacific, including the U.S.-Japan Mutual Security Treaty. Subsequent disclosures suggest that Sino-American exchanges over the role of Japan were far more heated. Peking's personal and political distaste for the government of Eisaku Sato had been unrelenting throughout the late 1960s and early 1970s, a point underscored not only by Sato's sympathies for Taiwan, but even more pointedly by the Nixon–Sato communiqué of November 1969, in which the prime minister had stated for the first time that "the security of the Republic of Korea was essential to Japan's own security" and that "the maintenance of peace and security in the Taiwan area was also a most important factor for the security of Japan."[49] The prospect that the United States might secure Tokyo's consent for a wider defense role in the region appeared a worrisome possibility to China, since Peking – already facing acute military pressure from the Soviet Union – might confront a renascent Japan before establishing a credible understanding with the United States.

Chou and Mao therefore sought clarification from Nixon and Kissinger on the scope of a Japanese security role within the region. To Peking, a Japan closely aligned with the United States was infinitely preferable to Tokyo assuming an autonomous defense role, even if sanctioned and encouraged by Washington. According to subsequent disclosures from President Nixon, however, the two sides had "tough negotiations" over the propriety of the Mutual Security Treaty, with Nixon asserting that "we told them that if you try to keep us from protecting the Japanese, we would let them go nuclear." And the Chinese said, "We don't want that."[50] It is not possible to determine the veracity of these reported remarks, but such blunt exchanges put Chinese warnings of the period about "the resurgence of Japanese militarism" in a more comprehensible context. It also helps explain the reference in the Shanghai Communiqué of China's opposition to the "revival and outward expansion of Japanese militarism" and support for an "independent, democratic, peaceful, and neutral Japan."[51]

48 The Mao–Nixon exchange is reported in ibid., 1061.
49 As cited in Chae-jin Lee, *Japan faces China: political and economic relations in the postwar era*, 85.
50 Nixon's remarks date from a 1975 deposition following his resignation from the presidency. They are cited in Hersh, *The price of power*, 380.
51 As cited in Solomon, *The China factor*, 297. Notably, the United States, while "[placing] the highest value on its friendly relations with Japan," made no reference in the Shanghai Communiqué to the U.S.-Japan Mutual Security Treaty.

Regardless of the differences and uncertainties, the breakthroughs of 1971 and 1972 constituted a very ample return on China's investment in relations with the United States. The Nixon visit also paved the way for the rapid acceleration of Sino-Japanese relations, with Peking pointedly waiting until Sato's departure from the scene before signaling its interest in full diplomatic relations.[52] The visit of an American president whose early career had been based on intense hostility to Chinese communism was highly vindicating to Peking, but the symbolism of the visit of Prime Minister Kakuei Tanaka, once a foot soldier in the Sino-Japanese War, seemed even more profound. In a remarkably short time, Mao and Chou had displaced Lin Piao; ousted Taiwan from the United Nations on 25 October 1971, at the very time when Kissinger was making a second visit to China; foiled Soviet hopes of isolating the PRC; and greatly enhanced Peking's political and diplomatic prestige. The largest political costs concerned Peking's relations with its longtime allies in the communist world, in particular Albania and Vietnam. But a deteriorating relationship with Tirana seemed a very small price, and closer links with America proved invaluable as Peking approached the impending denouement in Vietnam, and the likelihood that Hanoi would shift its principal loyalties toward Moscow. The opening to America had begun as a response to the profound changes of the late 1960s, but the onset of these ties redirected events in East Asia as a whole.

STAGNATION AND TURMOIL, 1973–1976

By early 1973, the outlook for Sino-American relations seemed highly promising. President Nixon's resounding election victory in November 1972 and the signing of the Paris peace accords between the United States and North Vietnam on 23 January 1973, portended not only the steady development of relations with Washington, but also decreased tensions in East Asia to which the American military withdrawal from Taiwan was explicitly linked. In all likelihood, China anticipated American derecognition of Taiwan and the establishment of a U.S. embassy in Peking well before the end of Nixon's second term, although it is not certain that any American official made this pledge explicit.[53] In addition, relations with the United States would no longer be distracted by hostilities in

---

52 Lee, *Japan faces China*, 106–11.
53 The evidence on the latter issue is obscure. According to one American participant in discussions with the Chinese, Teng told Kissinger that "the U.S. owes China a debt" because of Nixon's supposed commitment in 1972 to complete normalization by the end of his second term. Solomon, *Chinese political negotiating behavior*, 11.

Vietnam. Although leaders in Hanoi retained grave suspicions about Sino-American collusion at Vietnam's expense and the war in Cambodia continued to rage, the outlook for the region as a whole seemed much brighter than before.

Kissinger's February 1973 visit to Peking confirmed this optimism.[54] The warmth with which Mao and Chou greeted his arrival testified to the extraordinary progress made in only nineteen months. China's leaders engaged in far more wide-ranging strategic and foreign policy discussions, suggesting an increased confidence in prospects for relations with the United States. To Kissinger's surprise, Chou proposed that the two countries open liaison offices in each other's capital, which would provide ambassadorial-level representation before the establishment of full diplomatic relations. Although a diplomatic sleight of hand enabled Chou to assert that the initiative for this proposal came from the United States, the Chinese had decided to move quickly to solidify their American connection.

The optimism of early 1973 proved short-lived. Within a matter of months, the Watergate crisis had enveloped Nixon, leading to his political incapacitation and resignation in August 1974. Mao personally expressed befuddlement that what seemed a mere trifle could topple a sitting American president. In a later meeting with visiting Thai leader Kukrit Pramoj, he mused about the American fascination with technologies such as tape recorders, insisting that he could not comprehend why Nixon's use of a taping system in the White House should be judged a criminal offense.[55] Quite apart from Mao's limited grasp of American constitutional procedures, the Chairman probably suspected that the opponents of relations with China were responsible for Nixon's political troubles, hoping to derail Sino-American relations in the process.

But it was not only American internal politics that threatened to unravel Sino-American relations. Political storms were brewing in China, severely limiting Peking's room for maneuver in foreign policy. The proximate cause of this instability was Chou En-lai's deteriorating health. By the time of Nixon's visit in 1972, Chou already knew that he had cancer, having made elliptical references to his health to both Kissinger and Nixon.[56] Chou's recognition of his declining physical powers underscored the urgency of his three-part political agenda: a major expansion of

---

54 Henry Kissinger, *Years of upheaval*, 44–71.   55 *NYT*, 10 July 1975.
56 Solomon, *Chinese political negotiating behavior*, 7. An authorized Chinese biography of Chou asserts that his cancer was already quite advanced at the time of the Nixon visit. The authors further claim that Chou had suffered from a heart condition since 1966. Percy Jucheng Fang and Lucy Guinong J. Fang, *Zhou Enlai: a profile*, 115–16.

China's foreign policy activities (including solidification of relations with the United States), a shift toward economic modernization at home, and the full reestablishment of Party and state authority. This third goal was the most important and the most contentious, because it entailed the "reversal of verdicts" against dozens of senior officials toppled in the Cultural Revolution. Heading the list was Teng Hsiao-p'ing, who returned to Peking in Febuary 1973 and first appeared at a diplomatic function in April. No matter what the precise circumstances of his return, the politics of the succession to Mao and Chou had begun in earnest.

How was foreign policy (and relations with Washington in particular) linked to the succession struggle? Even in retrospect, it remains very difficult to disentangle the convulsive, highly personalized politics of this period. Much of the ambiguity is attributable to Mao, who seemed unwilling until after Chou's death in early 1976 to move decisively, effecting Teng's second fall from power. On the one hand, the Chairman in his February 1973 meeting with Kissinger described Sino-American trade as "pitiful" and endorsed the opening of liaison offices; according to Kissinger, Mao also acknowledged that "China ... would have to go to school abroad."[57] In an additional meeting with Kissinger in November, Mao rather than Chou hinted at a formula for resolving the Taiwan impasse that presupposed virtually open-ended restraint by the Chinese. As Mao said at the time, "I say that we can do without Taiwan for the time being.... Do not take matters on this world so rapidly. Why is there a need to be in such great haste?"[58] This extraordinarily detailed conversation with Mao served as what Kissinger termed "the bible of U.S.-Chinese relations" for the remainder of his tenure as secretary of state.[59] Finally, Mao warned that Chinese women "will create disasters" and that Kissinger should be wary of them.[60]

In a matter of weeks, Chiang Ch'ing and her allies launched virtual guerrilla warfare against Chou, Teng, and the opening to the West. By the end of 1973, Chou had withdrawn from involvement in Sino-American relations, having entrusted Chinese foreign policy to Teng, whose physical vigor was not in question. Kissinger, for example, notes that his Chinese interlocutors did not mention Chou's name even once in subsequent discussions, and instead made exclusive reference to the Chairman's instructions and statements. But the premier's withdrawal seems to have been as much political as physical. Chou's limited energies were concentrated on other issues, with the premier's involvement in foreign relations dwindling to near zero.

57 Kissinger, *Years of upheaval*, 67, 69.   58 Ibid., 692.   59 Ibid., 697.   60 Ibid., 68, 694.

Quite apart from China's political turmoil, the larger strategic design of U.S. foreign policy portended serious difficulties for the relationship. As direct American involvement in the Vietnam War ended and Washington reassessed its long-term policy goals, Chou and Mao began to suspect that the United States saw ties with the Soviet Union as a far more important priority, with China increasingly taken for granted. Despite Washington's repeated assurances that Peking would be fully informed on all important aspects of U.S. global strategy, as early as February 1973 Chou spoke of possible American readiness to "push the ill waters of the Soviet Union ... eastward."[61] These suspicions were compounded as an increasingly weakened Nixon proved unable to normalize relations with China, even as he sought to sustain and enhance collaboration with the USSR.

Gerald Ford's accession to the presidency did little to reassure the Chinese. The broad contours of American diplomacy remained intact, with Kissinger intent on sustaining Soviet-American détente. To leaders in Peking, Kissinger's efforts to reinvigorate accommodation with Moscow reflected persistent illusions about the malleability of Soviet power, and a seeming disregard for the implications of closer superpower relations for the security of China. Ford's November 1974 summit with Brezhnev underscored the perceived insensitivity to Chinese interests. Not only did Washington and Moscow announce preliminary agreement on a new strategic arms control accord, but the meeting was held at Haishenwai (Vladivostok), a tacit but telling American acknowledgment of Soviet political and strategic claims in an area contiguous to the still contested, heavily armed Sino-Soviet border. The East-West agreements signed at Helsinki the following summer further discomfited the Chinese, since they appeared to ratify Western acceptance of the postwar division of Europe, thereby potentially affording Moscow a far freer political hand in Asia.

Chou and Mao had admonished Kissinger gently, but Teng Hsiao-p'ing did not demonstrate comparable restraint. As Teng's political responsibilities grew steadily in 1974 and 1975, his blunt style exacerbated the differences with Washington. Kissinger is alleged to have described Teng as "that nasty little man," and Teng had an equal or greater contempt for his opposite number. This mutual antipathy was also reflected in the exchanges of Teng's lieutenants with their American negotiating partners. The personal bond between senior American and Chinese leaders dissipated as rapidly as it had developed. Unlike in 1972, when

61 Ibid., 52.

Mao understood how Nixon's China visit helped guarantee the president's reelection, Teng made no such gestures toward President Ford, pointedly inviting Secretary of Defense James Schlesinger (Kissinger's chief bureaucratic rival) and leading Democratic Party politicians to China. When Ford visited Peking at the end of 1975, his trip was notable for its minimal accomplishments and the evident testiness of the official exchanges.

The opening volleys in this campaign, however, were launched not by Teng but by Mao and Chou.[62] When Kissinger outlined his hopes of engaging Moscow in further negotiations on arms control and international security in early 1973, Chou made clear his skepticism. In the premier's view, the preferred goal of U.S. strategy was to lead a coalition that would restrain Soviet ambitions rather than provide opportunities for Moscow to lull the West into a false sense of security. Chou derided Kissinger's expectations that the Soviet Union would be willing to negotiate seriously; Mao seconded these views, emphasizing the risks of false détente when Soviet power was expanding, not diminishing. In Kissinger's view, however, the end of the Vietnam conflict had broadened American options, whereas China had no alternative but to depend on the United States to limit its vulnerability to Soviet power. As Kissinger wrote privately to Nixon, the United States could "have its mao tai and vodka too." Kissinger believed that the antipathies between Moscow and Peking were unbridgeable, providing the United States with leverage over both communist powers.

Kissinger's overconfidence reflected not only Chinese restraint on Taiwan but also Peking's readiness to assent far more openly to the American security presence in East Asia.[63] Chou's 1973 presentations to Kissinger were devoid of the alarmist specter of renascent Japanese militarism that had characterized earlier Sino-American discussions; in its place, the premier offered a virtual endorsement of the U.S.-Japan Mutual Security Treaty as well as the NATO alliance. In a similar vein, Mao proffered advice on the deployment of U.S. forces in Asia, arguing that they were "too scattered." The intent of Chou and Mao seemed clear enough: By endorsing America's regional role and warning of Soviet imperial designs, Peking hoped that the Nixon administration would see a much closer relationship with Peking as preferable to the uncertainties and risks of accommodation with Moscow.

In addition, Kissinger's grandiose declaration that 1973 would be "the year of Europe" implied that American policy toward various regions

---

62 This paragraph draws from ibid., 47–70.   63 Ibid., 56, 67.

and countries was a matter more of sequence than strategy. The seeming paternalism in Kissinger's pronouncements trivialized relations with China, and Peking did not want to leave such American pronouncements unchallenged. This argued for focusing attention on Chinese differences with Washington, even as Peking remained ready to test the opportunities for a more comprehensive relationship.

Chou took the lead in diverging from American strategic perceptions and prescriptions. The premier returned to a theme raised in Nixon's 1972 conversation with Mao: the focus of Soviet long-term strategy. Although the Chairman had acknowledged great concern about the growth of Soviet power directed against China, he insisted that Moscow's primary strategic objectives were still oriented toward Europe rather than Asia. Equally important, although Soviet forces opposite China continued to grow, the rate of increase began to slow in the early 1970s, suggesting that there were upper limits to Moscow's ability to deploy forces along the Sino-Soviet border. Under such circumstances, China's need for an American security guarantee (and hence its incentives for close relations with the United States) would be less pressing. In May 1973, Chou for the first time suggested that a Soviet surprise attack had been deterred.[64]

The slowdown of the Soviet buildup enabled Chou to echo Mao in asserting that the Soviet military threat was posed principally to the West rather than against China. Mao's larger anxiety had always been that Soviet-American détente would permit the USSR to increase its political and military pressure against the People's Republic. Three corollaries followed from this concern. First, Peking would deemphasize if not totally dismiss the immediate Soviet threat to China's national security. Second, the Chinese would emphasize the growing military dangers in Europe, hoping to keep Moscow as well as Washington preoccupied in locations far removed from China's borders. Third, Peking would emphasize its shared interests with the Third World as an independent political and economic force prepared to defy both superpowers.

Chou's artful presentation at the CCP Tenth National Congress in August 1973 captured the essence of Chinese views on all three issues.[65] The premier sought to deflect challenges from adversaries as well as presumptive allies. To Moscow, he asserted that China, although "an attractive piece of meat coveted by all," had proven "too tough even to bite," let alone "devour." Earlier in the 1970s, Chinese officials had spoken

---

64 Marquis Childs, "Talking with Chou En-lai," *Washington Post*, 26 May 1973.
65 Chou's remarks in this paragraph are drawn from his "Report to the Tenth National Congress" (24 August 1973), *PR*, 7 September 1973, 22.

ominously about the presence of "a million Soviet troops massed on China's borders and threatening China's security." (This declaration reflected arithmetic license by more than a factor of two.) Now these "mere million troops" were deemed insufficient to invade and subjugate China. A Soviet war against China was deterred, if only because no adversary would repeat Japan's fatal strategic blunder of the 1930s. Toward the two superpowers, Chou argued that their "contention is absolute and protracted, whereas collusion is relative and temporary." Thus, any moves against China were diversionary rather than a serious effort to subjugate the PRC, because "strategically the key point of their contention is Europe." At the same time, Chou emphasized the "awakening and growth" of the Third World as a "major event in contemporary international relations." China would therefore advocate a united front "against [the] hegemonism and power politics of the superpowers."

Chou sought to portray China as largely outside the sphere of great power competition, and hence effectively immune to external pressures and threats. China did not want to be exploited to America's advantage in its rivalry with the Soviet Union – what Mao had earlier described as "standing on China's shoulders to reach Moscow."[66] At the same time, however, Chou attacked the belief that superpower tensions were decreasing. Soviet-American competition was described as unrelenting and permanent – a reflection of both nations' "hegemonic ambitions," which existed "independent of man's will" and were "bound to lead to world war someday." China was conveniently omitted from this portrayal. Being neither imperialist in nature nor the "focus of superpower contention," China could stand on the side of various oppressed nations, but apart from the superpower fray. This formulation had utility in both a domestic and international context. By abstaining (at least in declaratory terms) from the power rivalries that marked the superpower competition, Chou sought to deflect criticism from the left that a more activist foreign policy would besmirch China's ideological principles.

The antipathies and suspicions of the Gang of Four toward Chou and Teng ran very deep, but the radicals could only surreptitiously attack the relationship with the United States. Mao's personal endorsement of Sino-American détente and the ignominious death of Lin Piao – not to mention the strategic benefits of China's relationship with the West – made a frontal attack on relations with the United States highly problematic. Chou and Teng nevertheless remained vulnerable to indirect criticism. Growing involvement with the West entangled China in the web of

66 Kissinger, *White House years*, 763.

"great power politics," thereby compromising Peking's stance toward the Third World; it undermined China's commitment to self-reliance in national development; and it assumed American sincerity and goodwill in implementing the commitment to one China embodied in the Shanghai Communiqué. On all these issues, Chiang Ch'ing and her allies appealed to the xenophobia that lurked near the surface of Chinese domestic politics.

The stagnation in U.S.-Chinese relations did not appear to inhibit Teng Hsiao-p'ing; if anything, his sharp criticisms of American policy toward the Soviet Union may have emboldened him. Having taken blunt issue with the United States both publicly and privately, Teng was not vulnerable to charges of being "soft on the United States." Teng's domestic agenda presupposed much broader Western involvement in the modernization of China, enabling his adversaries to accuse him of mortgaging China's independence and national sovereignty for rapid economic development. But it was Teng, not his radical opponents, who pointedly decried American weakness and appeasement. Indeed, Teng linked China's weakness and backwardness to mounting concerns about Soviet assertiveness: The imperatives of international security underscored China's need for rapid economic and technological advance.

Independent of the political difficulties with Washington, Sino-American trade had increased very rapidly in the early 1970s, spurred principally by China's disappointing agricultural performance. As Peking's need for imported grain diminished in the mid-1970s, U.S. exports to China plummeted, with sales of industrial items also remaining very low. Even as Washington undertook the first preliminary steps to expedite the flow of advanced Western technology to Peking, Japan remained China's principal supplier of industrial equipment and complete plants. Rapid increases in petroleum production enabled exponential growth in Chinese oil exports to Japan as a means to pay for these equipment purchases, but it also exposed Teng to attacks from the political left.

Despite these harsh criticisms, Teng continued to take the lead role in faulting the larger design of American diplomatic strategy. Mao had provided Teng with his political opening when the Chairman had spoken bluntly to Kissinger about "what he took to be American ineffectuality in resisting Soviet expansionism."[67] The Chairman's contradictory messages continued throughout his later years; he wanted resistance to the Soviet Union but without paying an ideological price. In January 1975, Mao

---

67 Ibid., 1060. Kissinger does not date Mao's concern, but by implication it dates from one of his late 1975 meetings with the Chairman.

pointedly abstained from attending the Fourth National People's Congress, where Chou in his last public appearance put forward a comprehensive agenda for national modernization. At the very same time, however, Mao had a private meeting with Franz Josef Strauss, the conservative Bavarian leader whose anti-Soviet positions were well known. Mao's actions in these two instances graphically conveyed the contradictions in his behavior; Soviet expansion and domestic revisionism were both of great concern, but Mao saw no need to choose.

Thus, neither Washington nor Peking had the wherewithal or leadership consensus to cement fuller ties. Teng berated Kissinger and other American officials for their seeming weakness in the face of a growing Soviet challenge and for the inability of the United States to normalize relations with Peking, but he avoided reference to his own vulnerabilities. It seems highly unlikely that Teng had the political latitude to achieve a negotiating breakthrough in the acutely factionalized atmosphere of the mid-1970s. Mao was too enfeebled and fickle; Chou, in self-imposed retirement, was virtually uninvolved; and Teng was preoccupied with holding his political enemies at bay.

As relations with the United States stagnated, the Chinese had fewer incentives to portray American power in a positive light. In the aftermath of the 1973 oil shock, President Nixon's political incapacitation, increased Soviet assertiveness in the Third World, and the collapse of the Saigon regime, the United States appeared a far less resolute and dependable partner. This tendency was especially pronounced after the fall of the South Vietnamese government in April 1975. Although Chinese leaders had long anticipated such an event, it tended to confirm a growing belief in American passivity and strategic weakness. By implication, the value of closer relations with Washington, although not unimportant to Peking, had appreciably diminished.

In the aftermath of Chou's death in January 1976 and Teng's second dismissal from power in April, the prospects for a breakthrough in Sino-American relations dwindled to near zero. President Ford, confronting a major struggle for his party's nomination, was unwilling to alienate further the conservative forces offended by the pursuit of closer relations with the Soviet Union and China. Any actions that further eroded America's relations with Taiwan could have caused irreparable harm to Ford's relations with the Republican right wing, so he opted to stand pat. But this inaction left U.S. policy vulnerable from the political left in China, who were again ascendant in Peking. In July, Vice-Premier Chang Ch'un-ch'iao – unconstrained by the foreign policy oversight previously exercised by Chou and Teng – issued an extraordinarily harsh denunciation of U.S. policy toward Taiwan to a visiting U.S. Senate delegation, and even warned of the possible use of force against Taipei. Chang's language vividly conveyed the slippage in Sino-American relations, but it also reflected political uncertainty, as both political systems approached the succession to new leadership.

Mao's death on 9 September 1976 and the arrest of the Gang of Four in October did not immediately alter these circumstances. Hua Kuo-feng, newly and unexpectedly elevated to the ranking positions in both Party and state as concurrently CCP chairman and premier, lacked the stature, experience, and political power to move decisively on foreign policy issues. The political drama in China during the year had been far too traumatic for bold policy initiatives to be possible. Indeed, to the extent that any group had leverage at the time of Hua's succession to power, it was probably the senior military leadership (including Yeh Chien-ying) who had been instrumental in displacing the Gang of Four. But the priorities of the moment were domestic, not external; China had only begun to come to terms with the havoc wreaked by the political and natural disasters of the preceding months. The political and security circumstances that had generated the Sino-American accommodation were still largely in place, but a newly refashioned leadership was not able to act in decisive fashion. The emphatic rejection of Soviet overtures for normalization in the aftermath of Mao's death also illustrated these circumstances: Immobilism was the order of the day.

The election in November 1976 of a Democratic president wholly unknown in Peking created additional uncertainties. Although relations with the Nixon and Ford administrations had grown increasingly testy during the mid-1970s, American officials (especially Kissinger) were well known in senior leadership circles. The Watergate affair had introduced the Chinese to the workings of American constitutional procedures; the election had sensitized them to the vicissitudes of the electoral process. As the architects of rapprochement in both systems passed from the scene, the Sino-American relationship had entered a period of uncertainty and reassessment.

THE ROAD TO NORMALIZATION, 1977–1979

The election of a new president brought forth both fears and hopes in Peking. On the one hand, President Jimmy Carter would not necessarily be burdened by the domestic political liabilities that ultimately plagued Nixon and Ford. The new president, however, was an unknown quantity to the Chinese; Peking would therefore have to begin the laborious process of cultivating personal relationships with senior officials with whom it was largely unfamiliar. At the same time, 1976 had been an extraordinary year in China: the deaths of Chou, Chu Te, and Mao; Teng Hsiao-p'ing's second dismissal from office; Hua Kuo-feng's unexpected accession to the premiership and Party chairmanship; the T'ang-shan earthquake; and the arrest and purge of the Gang of Four represented political and personal drama on a grand scale. China needed a breathing spell.

By the time of Secretary of State Cyrus Vance's visit to Peking in the late summer, however, the political situation in China had begun to stabilize. The August 1977 Party Congress, although nominally dominated by Hua Kuo-feng, was more notable for the reemergence of Teng Hsiao-p'ing, who had been restored to his previous positions by the plenum immediately preceding the meeting. Hua offered a lukewarm endorsement for relations with the United States, emphasizing how the absence of an active military threat from the United States had been turned to advantage. Quoting Lenin, Hua reminded his colleagues that "the more powerful enemy can be vanquished only by … making use without fail of every … 'rift' among the enemies … and also by taking advantage of every … opportunity of gaining a mass ally, even though this ally be temporary, vacillating, unstable, unreliable, and conditional."[68]

If leaders in Peking had hopes for rapid movement by the Carter administration, these expectations were quickly dashed. Although improved relations with China were deemed an important policy priority, other issues ranked much higher on the new president's early agenda. In the view of one of the principal participants in governmental decision making on China during this period, in 1977 the Carter administration "neglected China."[69] Indeed, for a time normalization of U.S.-Vietnamese relations was a higher policy priority. When Secretary of State Vance traveled to Peking – ostensibly to convey the administration's readiness to move toward full diplomatic relations – the Chinese objected forcefully to U.S. proposals to maintain an unofficial presence on Taiwan as well as Vance's insistence on the right to sell arms to Taiwan.[70] Despite the secretary of state's reaffirmation of the Shanghai Communiqué and a pledge to remove the residual U.S. military presence from the island, Foreign Minister Huang Hua saw these pledges as mere lip service to China's oft-stated three conditions for achieving full diplomatic relations.[71] The three

68 Hua Kuo-feng, "Political Report to the 11th National Congress of the Communist Party to China" (12 August 1977), PR, 26 August 1977, 60–61.
69 Oksenberg, "A decade of Sino-American relations," 184.
70 Ibid., 182.   71 Cyrus Vance, Hard choices, 82.

conditions were the cessation of Washington's recognition of Taipei as the government of China, the abrogation of the U.S.-ROC Mutual Defense Treaty, and the withdrawal of remaining U.S. military personnel from Taiwan. Similarly, Teng Hsiao-p'ing (who had been rehabilitated only weeks before Vance's arrival) decried the new U.S. position as a retreat from the pledges of the Ford administration to adhere to the "Japanese formula," the artifice that enabled Tokyo to maintain robust but unofficial ties with Taipei while formally recognizing Peking. As Vance concluded, "the Chinese did not seem ready to negotiate seriously."[72]

Chinese displeasure was conveyed both publicly and privately. When President Carter purportedly described the Vance visit as a success, senior officials in Peking (including Teng) quickly dissented. Contemptuous references to American concern for their "old friends in Taiwan" and assertions that the sale of arms to Taiwan following normalization would be "intolerable" and would "compel China to take Taiwan by force," and that the presence of "such a heap of counter-revolutionaries on Taiwan" meant national unification "cannot be managed without a fight," all appeared within weeks of the Vance visit.[73] The Chinese appeared particularly incensed at the implication they had shown flexibility on the Taiwan issue. In Michel Oksenberg's view, Teng "had too recently returned to office, his power still to be consolidated, to afford the label 'flexible.' He could not tolerate any misunderstanding over the Chinese principle that the United States had to sever official ties with Taiwan unambiguously."[74]

Equally telling, the Chinese quickly renewed their attacks on détente first launched during the Ford administration, implying that Secretary of State Vance was among the advocates of "appeasement" toward the Soviet Union. According to one authoritative Chinese assessment, improved Soviet-American relations would both strengthen the USSR and pose a direct challenge to China:

... a trend of appeasement similar to that of the 1930s has emerged in the West.... Like their precursors [in the 1930s], the advocates of appeasement try to divert the Soviet peril to the east, to China ... frighten[ing] the Soviet Union with the groundless prediction of "the arrival of third superpower, China, in 20 years or

72 Ibid., 82.
73 Harrison E. Salisbury, "China 'quite unhappy' with Carter over Taiwan, a top leader says," *NYT*, 30 August 1977; Louis Boccardi, "Teng says Vance trip set back normal ties," *NYT*, 7 September 1977; "Formulas for Taiwan accord with U.S. flatly rejected by high officials in China," *Wall Street Journal*, 3 October 1977; and "China's vice premier reaffirms rigidity on Taiwan, calls use of force inevitable," *Wall Street Journal*, 4 October 1977.
74 Oksenberg, "A decade of Sino-American relations," 182.

so...." The fact that Soviet social imperialism is doing its utmost to encourage illusions about "detente" and foment the trend of appeasement in the West makes things clear to all.[75]

As in its earlier dealings with the Ford administration, Peking had decided to choose sides in the bureaucratic rivalries that already dominated foreign policy decision making under President Carter. Twice in the winter of 1978, China tendered invitations to National Security Adviser Zbigniew Brzezinski to visit China. In Michel Oksenberg's view, "the Chinese turned to the official whose world view more closely corresponded to their own."[76]

Teng was well aware of the contrasting personalities and policy orientations of Brzezinski and Vance. The divisions among policymakers in Washington reflected both bureaucratic differences as well as major divergencies in U.S. strategy toward China and the Soviet Union. To the secretary of state, it was imperative that the United States "steer a balanced course" between Moscow and Peking. In Vance's view, good relations with the Soviet Union and completion of the long-delayed SALT II agreement were the cornerstones of U.S. foreign policy. He considered a major effort to engage in strategic cooperation with China provocative to Moscow, and likely to strain U.S.-Soviet relations even further.[77]

National Security Adviser Brzezinski and Defense Secretary Harold Brown (especially the former) did not share Vance's concerns. According to the secretary of state, prior to normalization both Brzezinski and Brown saw various "security enhancements" (the exchange of military attachés, technology transfer to the PRC, third-country sales of military equipment to China, and other forms of cooperation) as likely to caution rather than provoke Moscow. As Soviet advances in the Third World continued, Brzezinski argued to President Carter that "the China relationship is useful in showing the Soviets that their assertiveness is counterproductive and not cost-free."[78]

The coalescence of the Chinese leadership around an exceedingly ambitious modernization agenda also presumed much closer technological and economic ties with the capitalist world. At the First Session of Fifth National People's Congress in February 1978, Hua Kuo-feng pro-

75 Jen Ku-p'ing, "The Munich tragedy and contemporary appeasement," *JMJP*, 26 November 1977, in *PR*, 9 December 1977, 8–10.
76 Oksenberg, "A decade of Sino-American relations," 183.
77 See Vance, *Hard choices*, 120–39.
78 The citation is from Brzezinski's memo of 5 October 1979 to President Carter, as cited in Zbigniew Brzezinski, *Power and principle*, 566.

posed a ten-year development plan entailing the construction of 120 major industrial projects, with an estimated capital investment of $600 billion, of which approximately $60 billion to $70 billion was to be allocated for the purchase of imported technology and equipment.[79] Although subsequent events proved that China's reach vastly exceeded its grasp, the program's goals meant Peking would look abroad for an increasingly large portion of its development needs, beginning with a $20 billion trade agreement signed with Japan in February 1978.

Other developments were also pushing relations forward. Mounting American frustration over Soviet encroachment in the Third World enabled Brzezinski to move with increased vigor on China policy, simultaneous with Teng's steady consolidation of power. The rapid deterioration of Sino-Vietnamese relations provided an additional spur to action. By the time Brzezinski visited Peking in May 1978, relations with Hanoi were near the breaking point. The expulsion of several hundred thousand ethnic Chinese in the late spring and the expropriation of their property by the state prompted Peking to sever all remaining economic and technical links with Vietnam. By the end of July, the Chinese argued that "behind every anti-China step taken by the Vietnamese authorities is the large shadow of Soviet social imperialism.... Moscow needs ... a 'forward post' to dominate Southeast Asia [in its] global strategic plan ... to outflank and encircle Europe and isolate the United States."[80] Mounting U.S. concern with Soviet inroads in Angola and the Horn of Africa had fused with Chinese anxieties in Southeast Asia. The logic of "the broadest international united front against hegemony" – that is, one including the United States – had finally begun to jell.

Chinese policy calculations assumed that the United States had become a virtually benign force on the international scene:

Of the two imperialist superpowers, the Soviet Union is the more ferocious, the more reckless, the more treacherous, and the most dangerous source of world war.... All [the U.S.] can do at present is to strive to protect its vested interests and go over on the defensive in its global strategy.... The Soviet Union has decided to ... weaken and supplant U.S. influence in all parts of the world.[81]

At the same time, Brzezinski was insistent in his discussions with Teng that President Carter "had made up his mind" on the Taiwan issue, sig-

---

79 Richard Baum, "Introduction," in Richard Baum, ed., *China's four modernizations: the new technological revolution*, 4–6.
80 Commentator, "Ts'ung Yueh-nan tang-chü fan-hua k'an Su-lien ti chan-lueh i-t'u" (The Soviet strategic intention as viewed from the Vietnamese authorities' anti-China activities), *HC*, 8 (1 August 1978), 101–4.
81 *JMJP* Editorial Department, "Chairman Mao's theory of the differentiation of the three worlds is a major contribution to Marxism-Leninism," 1 November 1977, in *PR*, 4 November 1977, 22–23.

naling U.S. readiness to negotiate a formula on terms acceptable to China. Spurred by the success of his national security adviser's visit, Carter decided in June to push for full diplomatic relations by the end of the year. As an added consequence, by mid-October he deferred all plans to normalize U.S.-Vietnamese relations so as not to complicate the Sino-American normalization process. Although the Chinese were not informed of this decision, formal notification seemed superfluous, since discussions with Hanoi had foundered as the tempo of negotiations with Peking had increased.

China had achieved a major breakthrough: America's repeated declarations on the importance of close relations with Peking were now unambiguously evident in U.S. policy decisions. The United States was prepared to identify far more closely with China's security and development objectives, including lobbying on China's behalf with U.S. allies. As one component in American policy, the United States declared its intent to modify arrangements on the transfer of advanced technology to China, including the possible sale of arms and related equipment by America's European allies. As a further demonstration of a desire to work on China's behalf, Brzezinski also personally urged Tokyo to move toward early ratification of the long-stalled Sino-Japanese Treaty of Peace and Friendship.[82] The treaty's antihegemony clause implied a closer identification with China's anti-Soviet strategy than many in Japan preferred. However, the burgeoning economic opportunities with China, Washington's clear preference for the treaty, and extreme rigidity in Soviet diplomacy toward Japan had given momentum to the process. At the same time, Teng proved amenable to deferring indefinitely resolution of a festering Sino-Japanese territorial dispute over the Tiao-yü Tao (Senkaku Islands) that had threatened to abort negotiations over the treaty in the spring. China's declared intention to Tokyo that it would not renew the Sino-Soviet Treaty of Friendship, Alliance, and Mutual Assistance – thereby dissociating China from language describing Japan as an adversary – also proved highly reassuring to the Japanese. With China ultimately prepared to accept somewhat more tempered language in the final document, the peace and friendship treaty was signed in August.[83]

Without question, the Chinese had garnered a major return in their effort to secure closer relations with the United States and Japan. Although the evidence remains circumstantial, Teng had seemingly been

---

82 Brzezinski, *Power and principle*, 216–18.
83 For more extended discussion from which this paragraph draws, see Daniel Tretiak, "The Sino-Japanese Treaty of 1978: the Senkaku incident prelude," *Asian Survey*, 18.12 (December 1978), 1235–49.

able to persuade more skeptical leadership colleagues that U.S. policy toward China had crossed a major threshold. It remains very difficult to measure the extent of disaffection or doubt of other senior officials. For example, Hua Kuo-feng's dissent from the U.S. determination to continue arms sales to Taiwan was particularly forceful, although this was a question on which no Chinese leader could intimate much flexibility. Teng's latitude and room for maneuver was therefore somewhat limited, but this was also the impression that Chinese negotiators wished to convey regardless of the extent of internal debate.

China's ultimate willingness to accept a suitably ambiguous framework for future U.S. relations with Taiwan, including American assertions of the right to sell arms to the island, belied Peking's public protests. The United States did not expect nor did it receive explicit Chinese approval or sanction of these arrangements, but a certain tolerance was the order of the day. Moreover, in the months preceding the final negotiations over normalization, the Carter administration turned down several requests from Taiwan for major new aircraft purchases, limiting Taipei to additional sales of aircraft already in its inventory. President Carter further conveyed to Peking that it retained the right to continue "carefully selected arms sales to Taiwan that would not be threatening to China."[84]

Peking had ample reason to be gratified by these decisions. Although there was no prospect of an immediate end to U.S. arms sales to the island, the U.S. decision implied a qualitative ceiling on the systems it was prepared to sell. The fact that the United States reserved the right to sell arms did not mean that additional arms would be sold, only that they could be sold. Continued U.S. military sales precluded a Chinese declaration of peaceful intent toward Taiwan, but tacit restraints (the Chinese in their policy statements and reduced military deployments opposite Taiwan, the Americans in their pledges of intent and limited military sales) suggested an unspoken but pivotal linkage in Chinese and U.S. policy. The Chinese seemed persuaded that leaders in Taipei did not have an open-ended commitment from the Carter administration, and that U.S. support would diminish over time. With the reduction of Chinese military forces in Fukien province and continued political gestures toward the island, China anticipated an eventual cessation in U.S. weapons sales to Taipei. Washington's unilateral statement at the time of normalization in mid-December that it reserved the right to continue limited sales of defensive arms seemed a short-term, face-saving gesture, a conclusion underscored by the U.S. agreement to a one-year moratorium on arms sales.

84 Oksenberg, "A decade of Sino-American relations," 187.

Teng had concluded that time was on Peking's side; Chinese restraint and appeals to patriotism and national unity were ultimately expected to bring Taipei to the conference table. This optimism was underscored by the language of the joint communiqué on the establishment of diplomatic relations issued on 15 December 1978: "The United States recognizes the Government of the People's Republic of China as the sole legal government of China [and] acknowledges [*ch'eng-jen*] the Chinese position that there is but one China and Taiwan is part of China." Thus, the somewhat equivocal language of the Shanghai Communiqué had been supplanted by a much more vigorous endorsement of the Chinese position; all "commercial, cultural, trade and other relations with Taiwan" would be maintained exclusively "through nongovernmental means."[85]

Under such circumstances, Chinese incentives for a magnanimous and almost benevolent depiction of future policy toward Taiwan were self-evident. The appeals to Taiwan began 1 January 1979, the date of U.S.-PRC normalization and U.S. derecognition of the Taipei government. A message to "compatriots in Taiwan" from the National People's Congress marking the cessation of bombardments of the Nationalist-held offshore islands of Quemoy and Matsu pledged that "all state leaders ... will take present realities into account in accomplishing the great cause of reunifying the motherland and will respect the status quo on Taiwan ... and adopt reasonable policies and measures in settling the question of unification."[86] These and similar statements demonstrated sensitivity to the U.S. preference for a peaceful resolution of the island's future, but they underscored Peking's conviction that "the way of bringing Taiwan back to the embrace of the motherland and reunifying the country ... is entirely China's internal affair."[87]

In Teng's estimation, the uncertainties related to Taiwan were outweighed by the gains for Chinese security and his internal political position. According to Teng, both countries had approached the establishment of diplomatic relations "from a global viewpoint," paralleling the sentiments expressed by Mao in his 1972 discussions with Nixon and Kissinger.[88] As with the first Sino-American breakthrough, the rationale of national security had given the process direction and momentum, permitting concessions and risks that would otherwise have proven vastly more difficult. Brzezinski's ascendance over Vance in American decision

85 See the text in Solomon, *The China factor*, 300–302.   86 *Beijing Review*, 5 January 1979, 17.
87 The citation is from the unilateral Chinese statement issued at the time of the normalization agreement, in Solomon, *The China factor*, 304.
88 See Teng's interview with American correspondents on 5 January 1979, in *Beijing Review*, 12 January 1979, 17.

making was in Teng's eyes the best guarantee of the relationship; unlike Kissinger, Brzezinski showed virtually no disposition to reach comparable understandings with the Soviet leadership. The match between Chinese vulnerabilities and needs and the fervent desire of an American president to cement a distinctive and far fuller relationship had coalesced: The advocates of closer Sino-American relations carried the day in both national capitals.

Teng's international triumph was also fully reflected at the Third Plenum of the Eleventh Central Committee, convened within days of the announcement of forthcoming Sino-American diplomatic relations in mid-December 1978. The tide in Chinese politics had turned decisively in Teng's favor. His agenda for economic reform and readjustment and appointment of key political allies (including Hu Yao-pang) to positions in the Politburo was now ratified; Ch'en Yun, newly elevated to a Party vice-chairmanship, wasted no time in curtailing the grandiose development plans put forward by Hua Kuo-feng in the spring of 1978. The foreign policy breakthroughs, however, seemed more a symptom than the source of Teng's internal political strength. The Carter administration's overtures and concessions were crucial to accelerating the normalization process, but Teng's consolidation of power at home gave him the authority without which the agreements could not have been reached and his highly successful tour of the United States in January 1979 could not have taken place.

China's Vietnam War

Teng quickly sought to test the new relationship. Mounting tensions along the Sino-Vietnamese border were much on Teng's mind during his visits to Washington and Tokyo in January. The signing of the Soviet-Vietnamese Treaty of Peace and Friendship in early November 1978 was followed in late December by Hanoi's invasion of Cambodia, vindicating Chinese assertions about the aggressive designs of "the large and small hegemonists." With the conclusion of the agreement on Sino-American diplomatic relations and the ratification of the Peace and Friendship Treaty with Japan, Teng felt far less constrained in voicing China's determination to "teach Vietnam a lesson." Without approval or consent by Washington or Tokyo, the Chinese began preparations for an attack on Vietnam.

The brief, bloody war, from 17 February to 5 March 1979, culminated a prolonged deterioration of Chinese-Vietnamese relations latent since the first steps at Sino-American accommodation. From the time of Kissinger's secret trip but especially in the aftermath of the Nixon visit, leaders in Hanoi knew that Chinese and Vietnamese interests had begun to diverge. Although Peking in the early 1970s still sought to sustain the political and personal bonds with Hanoi forged in decades of struggle against the West, Vietnamese needs were increasingly subordinated to China's larger security requirements, beginning with the relationship with Washington. China's abrupt seizure in January 1974 of islands in the Hsisha chain in the South China Sea then held by South Vietnamese forces did little to reassure Hanoi about Peking's longer-term intentions. Thus did the maneuverings for power and predominance in Southeast Asia after the Vietnam War begin in earnest.

The nominal focal point of this struggle was Cambodia.[89] The Khmer Rouge forces that emerged victorious in the spring of 1975 had quickly and brutally imposed a nightmarish, primitive agrarian communism that wreaked untold havoc on Cambodian society, ultimately entailing the death of approximately a million Cambodians. The extreme xenophobia of the Khmer Rouge was directed principally against the Vietnamese, with the forces under Pol Pot determined to root out Vietnamese influence (both real and imagined) by all means possible. The Khmer Rouge's need for external support inexorably led to closer bonds with Peking, where the residual radicalism and latent antiforeignism of the mid-1970s comported well with the doctrinaire communism being imposed on Cambodia. The internal struggle in Peking thus had highly deleterious consequences in Indochina, with China increasingly supportive of an extremist government in Phnom Penh. Nor did the situation improve with the ouster of the Gang of Four, as an inexperienced Hua Kuo-feng quickly entered into major new military and economic aid agreements with the Khmer Rouge.

Quite apart from the presumed symmetry between Chinese and Cambodian ideologues, the two sides shared a complementary, reinforcing pattern of intense hostility toward Vietnam. As Teng reemerged politically following the Eleventh Party Congress in 1977, he demonstrated none of Chou En-lai's deftness or subtlety in seeking to balance (if not reconcile) Peking's political and security needs with those of its erstwhile ally in Hanoi. Vietnam, for its part, saw far less need to uphold its previous bonds with China once full victory had been achieved in 1975. Although Vietnam's tilt toward Moscow was not unambiguous or irrev-

---

89 For exhaustive treatment, see Nayan Chanda, *Brother enemy: the war after the war*, and Robert S. Ross, *The Indochina tangle: China's Vietnam policy, 1975–1979*.

ocable until late 1977 or early 1978, the trend was already clear: Hanoi would seek to reduce the challenge posed by its much larger neighbor to the north by aligning with a Soviet leadership intent on the encirclement of China. Moreover, Soviet political, economic, and military support would enable Vietnam to plan for the ouster of the Pol Pot forces from power and the establishment of a pro-Hanoi government in Phnom Penh.

By the spring of 1978, all efforts by Peking and Hanoi to avoid a major break in relations had ceased; both leaderships were intent on garnering the external support necessary to secure their long-term goals. Teng's antipathies toward Vietnam seemed intense and almost visceral, and other senior Chinese officials openly seethed at Hanoi's efforts to defy Peking and align with Moscow. Equally significant, China deemed Vietnam an ungrateful ally prepared to denigrate the vast amounts of moral and material support that Peking had provided Hanoi in its decades of struggle against the West. However, the persecution of the Hoa (Vietnamese citizens of Chinese descent) was perhaps the most serious affront to China: Hanoi was openly challenging the leadership in Peking on an issue of utmost sensitivity to all Chinese.

By the fall of 1978, Vietnam had begun to plan in earnest for its invasion of Cambodia. Hanoi may well have calculated that a forceful, abrupt action to displace the Khmer Rouge would elicit only indirect, political reprisals from Peking, especially in the aftermath of Vietnam's signing its treaty with the USSR. Thus, security guarantees from Moscow did not so much embolden as reassure Hanoi, since they would presumably caution China against initiating any major military actions against Vietnam.

Teng's efforts to achieve a breakthrough in relations with Washington therefore assumed special urgency in the context of mounting tensions with Hanoi. He may well have calculated that leaders in Washington would draw satisfaction from the highly punitive use of force against a state that had very recently humiliated the United States. Although explicit sanction from Washington was not necessary, a measurably closer relationship with America was expected to caution Soviet leaders from retaliating against China for any actions launched by Peking against its new treaty partner.

China's attack on Vietnam in mid-February 1979 was therefore the first major test of the new relationship with the United States. Teng had not obscured his intentions, having informed President Carter during his visit to Washington about the magnitude and duration of the operations that the PLA would undertake. What Brzezinski labeled the first "proxy war"

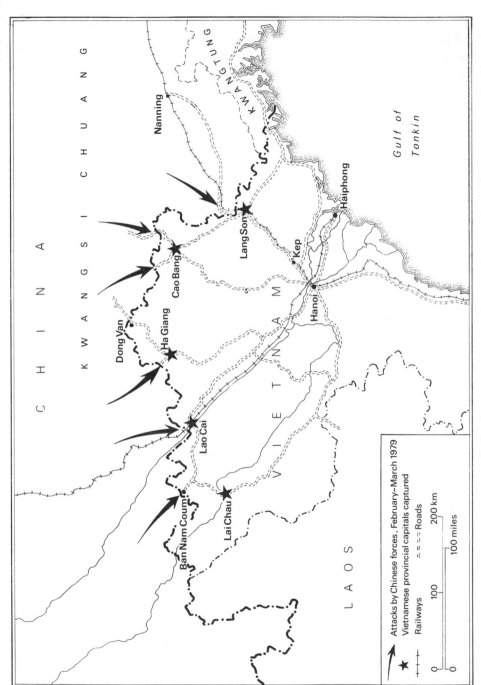

MAP 6. China's invasion of Vietnam, 17 February – 5 March 1979

between the Soviet Union and China would be brief, lasting no more than twenty days.[90] Teng did not expect a limited conflict to involve the Soviet Union, and he therefore did not envision or request American assistance. That America had recognized China and did not appear to dissuade Peking actively from such an undertaking seemed support enough. Indeed, according to Teng, Peking's attack on Hanoi fulfilled the PRC's part of the "anti-hegemony" bargain. Both states had to undertake parallel but complementary steps to punish "the large and small hegemonists" for their actions, thereby complicating their larger strategic design. In Teng's view, China's struggle against Vietnam was properly understood in a global rather then a regional context; Peking had assumed responsibility that would otherwise have fallen upon the United States to perform.

China's strategic reasoning was self-serving and self-fulfilling. By emphasizing the united front aspects of its military campaign against Vietnam and by highlighting Hanoi's collusion with Moscow, Peking heightened rather than diminished Soviet interest and involvement in Southeast Asia. Although China's immediate military objectives were limited, Hanoi's dependence on Moscow increased markedly in the aftermath of hostilities. Within several months, Soviet ships began regular use of Vietnamese naval facilities at Cam Ranh Bay, providing Moscow with a forward base in the Pacific for the first time since Khrushchev returned Port Arthur and Dairen to China in 1954. Chinese actions had ironically helped fulfill Peking's predictions that the USSR would seek an outpost in Southeast Asia to complement its earlier breakthroughs in Angola and the Horn of Africa.

Thus, the battle lines in Indochina had been drawn, effectively defining the character of Chinese policy toward Southeast Asia for the indefinite future. China would seek to bring together the disparate forces resisting Vietnam's occupation of Cambodia, including an unlikely coalition consisting of forces loyal to Prince Sihanouk, remnant anticommunist elements led by Son Sann, and the displaced Khmer Rouge regime. In Peking's estimation, only a broadly based coalition of "patriotic forces" would be able to disrupt Vietnam's long-term plan to subjugate Cambodia. Equally important, Peking sought to mobilize international opposition to the Vietnamese occupation by working closely with those states within the Association of Southeast Asian Nations (ASEAN) most determined to resist Hanoi.

The international opprobrium that greeted Vietnamese actions in Cam-

90 Brzezinski, *Power and principle*, 409–10.

bodia presented China with an unusual political and diplomatic opportunity.[91] Since the time of the American withdrawal from South Vietnam but especially following the collapse of the Saigon regime, Peking had sought to broaden its links with ASEAN, reassuring various Southeast Asian leaders that China's relations with remnant communist guerrilla movements were residual and inconsequential. Yet, lingering suspicions of Chinese long-term intentions toward the region led many to doubt Peking's assurances. Even though few within ASEAN had particular sympathy for Vietnam, Peking's readiness to use force against Hanoi left many uncomfortable with a more assertive China enlarging its political and security stake within the region.

The Sino-American accommodation and Vietnamese aggression, however, had legitimated a much higher Chinese profile in Southeast Asia. Although the United States steered clear of extensive policy coordination with the Chinese, Washington deemed Peking's political and diplomatic interventions generally supportive of U.S. interests. America's ignominious exit from Vietnam was too recent and too painful to permit any direct U.S. reentry into regional security. This abstinence enabled China to assume the role of indirect guarantor of the security of ASEAN, especially Thailand. In a transposition of roles that would have been unthinkable only a few years earlier, Teng and the other leaders were quickly pledging Chinese military support should Vietnam launch attacks across the Thai border.

The larger challenge for China was to convince regional leaders that its declarations reflected a genuine desire to support the security and territorial integrity of the ASEAN states, rather than create a Chinese sphere of influence at Vietnam's expense. Chinese leaders repeatedly emphasized that they harbored no long-term designs on the region, and sought only to compel Vietnam to yield the fruits of its aggression, thereby enabling the ultimate establishment of an independent, nonaligned Cambodian state.

Although many remained skeptical of Chinese pledges, Peking achieved significant headway in this regard, culminating in China's strong support for ASEAN at the UN conference on Cambodia in July 1981. In conjunction with Thailand and Singapore, a diplomatic "united front" blocked widespread recognition of the Vietnamese-installed government outside the socialist bloc. China was also able to realize Vietnam's isolation in Southeast Asia, at the same time that Peking's economic and political ties and diplomatic visibility in the region grew substantially. Thus,

91 For more extended discussion, see Pao-min Chang, *Kampuchea between China and Vietnam*, esp. 113–33.

the punitive war against Vietnam ironically helped create larger long-term political opportunities for Peking.

Viewed in a domestic context, however, China's war against Vietnam left a troubling legacy. Insisting that China had achieved a resounding victory against Hanoi, Teng's claims seemed hollow. The cost in men and matériel was far higher than had been expected, damaging the reputation of China's armed forces in the process. Vietnam had redeployed many of its frontline combat units to its northern provinces bordering China, but there was little appreciable effect on Vietnamese military operations in Cambodia, nor did Chinese military pressure compel Hanoi to reassess its policy to the west. Moreover, the largest consequence was a far more entangling and dependent Vietnamese security relationship with the Soviet Union.

Indeed, China rather than Vietnam had to adjust its policies. Replacement costs for the equipment losses in the Sino-Vietnamese War strained to the breaking point Chinese budgetary resources, already severely taxed by a late 1978 spending spree on foreign equipment and technology. The conjunction of spiraling budget deficits and a higher-profile foreign policy underscored the potential liabilities and risks of China's new political circumstances. The initial euphoria of the breakthroughs with the United States and Japan passed quickly, replaced by a much more sober estimate of the potential of both relationships, especially in the economic arena. As early as February 1979, Chinese officials were quietly informing Japanese firms that budget limitations made immediate fulfillment of contracts for industrial plants impossible. As the costs of the war against Vietnam became fully apparent, the need for drastic curtailment of capital construction and technology purchases rapidly moved to center stage of the policy agenda, leading to the adoption of a three-year "economic readjustment" policy announced in June.[92]

Twists and turns in Sino-Soviet relations

Although Hua Kuo-feng bore most of the immediate brunt of criticism for the grandiosely ambitious Ten-Year Development Plan of 1978, Teng's political credibility was also tarnished during this period. The Taiwan Relations Act, passed by the U.S. Congress and signed by President Carter in early April 1979, contained provisions and obligations (especially with respect to the security of Taiwan) that were far stronger than the Carter administration would have preferred and the Chinese had

92 Ryosei Kokubun, "The politics of foreign economic policy-making in China: the case of plant cancellations with Japan," *CQ*, 105 (March 1986), 23.

anticipated.[93] In private and public statements as early as mid-March, the Ministry of Foreign Affairs warned that the act "contravened the principles agreed upon by the two sides at the time of normalization" and threatened "great harm" to the embryonic relationship.[94] Teng followed these warnings in discussions with a U.S. Senate delegation in April, suggesting that the act was a virtual nullification of the normalization accords.[95] At the same time, the initiation of full Sino-American ties and China's coercive diplomacy toward Vietnam did not lead to a broader pro-Peking tilt in the U.S. foreign policy agenda. Officials in Washington remained wary of even tacitly endorsing future Chinese military actions in Southeast Asia, for fear that such approval would only further polarize the political and security situation in the region. In addition, the Carter administration's efforts to reach a SALT II agreement – against which Teng and other leaders had actively campaigned – remained a much higher U.S. policy priority than consolidating relations with Peking.

Thus, the new relationship with America seemed a mixed blessing, quite possibly at some cost to Teng's political reputation, if not his leadership position. More than any other high official, Teng had taken the lead in fostering relations with the United States, including pursuit of greater economic and technological collaboration with the West. These opportunities appeared more questionable in the aftermath of the cancellation or postponement of signed contracts with foreign firms. (Ironically, Japanese and Western European companies suffered disproportionately in these cancellations, having had an earlier foot in the China door.) Moreover, Teng's warlike posture toward the south clashed sharply with his hopes for a development program less inhibited by Soviet pressure.

It was in this context that the Chinese proposed the resumption of negotiations with the Soviet Union. On 3 April 1979, Foreign Minister Huang Hua notified the Soviet ambassador that China intended to let the thirty-year 1950 Treaty of Friendship, Alliance, and Mutual Assistance expire without seeking an extension. At the same time, however, Huang emphasized China's "consistent stand" for "the maintenance and development of ... normal state relations," and called for "negotiations ... of outstanding issues and the improvement of relations between the two countries."[96] Thus, the Chinese had initiated a call for unconditional negotiations on the full spectrum of Sino-Soviet relations, as distinct from the border talks of the 1969–78 period.

93 For a text, see Solomon, *The China factor*, 304–14.
94 *Los Angeles Times*, 25 March 1979.   95 *NYT*, 20 April 1979.
96 *Beijing Review*, 6 April 1979, 3–4.

Although there had been periodic efforts during the mid-1970s by both Peking and Moscow to reduce or at least contain military tensions along the border, neither state had chosen fully to reciprocate the other's gestures. Moscow had favored broader and somewhat more grandiose presentations on the principles for Sino-Soviet relations, which Chinese spokesmen repeatedly rejected. Even though the border negotiations continued on an irregular basis, they were endlessly mired in the conflicting claims and understandings put forward by the two sides. Chinese overtures were more measured and limited, most notably the December 1975 return of a Soviet helicopter crew that had strayed into Chinese airspace in early 1974. (Chinese diplomats acknowledged that earlier accusations of espionage activity had proven unwarranted, leading to a release of the crew.) However, such goodwill gestures were rare, and generally conducted at intermediate diplomatic levels, without expressions of support from higher political authorities.

Thus, the initiative from the Foreign Ministry had to reflect a decision at a higher level to explore improved relations with Moscow, or at least to open a channel for discussions on the broader spectrum of interstate relations. As such, it contrasted with China's sharp rejection of initiatives from Moscow immediately following Mao's death. For the first time since the deterioration of relations in the 1960s, the door was at least slightly ajar.

Hanoi's growing ties with Moscow may have convinced Teng of the need for a modest reduction of tensions with the Soviet Union. However, it is more likely that Teng, unexpectedly on the political defensive in the aftermath of economic setbacks, the Sino-Vietnamese border war, and mounting unease within the leadership about the "democracy movement" in China, agreed to foreign policy moves that undercut his plan to forge a security coalition with the West.[97] Indeed, efforts to stabilize China's security situation through negotiations with Moscow bore the clear imprint of Vice-Chairman Ch'en Yun, the principal architect of the economic readjustment policy. As early as the Third Plenum, Ch'en had emphasized that China "must walk gradually" in purchases of foreign equipment, making clear his dissociation from the frenetic buildup implied by the Ten-Year Development Plan.[98] Equally important, in mid-April 1979, China announced the posthumous rehabilitation of Foreign Ministry official Wang Chia-hsiang, who (along with Ch'en Yun)

97 In an interview in early 1981, Teng acknowledged that "we, including myself, have been too excited about economic construction." Cited in Kokubun, "The politics of foreign economic policy-making in China," 39.
98 Ch'en is cited in ibid., 23.

had advocated the reduction of tensions with China's external enemies in 1962 so as to permit increased attention to the internal economic crisis.

Given China's willingness to negotiate in the absence of any prior conditions, Moscow seemed obliged to respond positively to Peking's overtures. Even if the talks aroused Vietnamese suspicions, Chinese readiness to discuss major issues was a distinct plus for Moscow because it also suggested uncertainties and limits to the Sino-American rapprochement. When negotiations began in December 1979, however, Teng was again ascendant within China, and Peking quickly accused the Soviet Union of an absence of good faith in the discussions. Indeed, Teng may have initially acquiesced to such talks because he believed that Moscow would prove obdurate and unyielding on the crucial issues. At any rate, the onset of the Soviet invasion of Afghanistan later that month put such discussions on indefinite hold.

Even as Teng acceded to Sino-Soviet negotiations, he continued to test the waters of a far fuller relationship with the United States. In discussions with a U.S. Senate delegation in April, Teng for the first time raised the possibility of overt security cooperation with Washington, including naval port visits; purchases of U.S. weaponry (including advanced fighter aircraft); and (in an ironic gesture) the operation of U.S. monitoring equipment on Chinese territory to verify Soviet compliance with an arms control treaty.[99] Teng recognized that all three proposals entailed substantial problems and sensitivities, especially in the context of the passage of the Taiwan Relations Act. Teng also knew that U.S. policy continued to preclude any military sales to China, and that China was not in a position to make extensive purchases while undergoing a major budgetary retrenchment. But his audacious suggestions squared the circle of relations with America. Did the United States judge China reliable and important enough to supply highly sensitive technologies, even major weapons systems, or at least indicate its willingness to consider such a possibility? Was the United States sufficiently concerned about the erosion of its strategic position to view the augmentation of Chinese military power as an important gain for U.S. strategic interests, even if it seriously complicated the possibilities of an improved Soviet-American relationship?

Teng made clear his willingness to consider provision of American equipment to China, but he did not propose more binding forms of defense collaboration with the United States. No Chinese leader – least of all the one most intimately tied to relations with Washington – could

---

99 Jay Mathews, "China offers to monitor SALT data," *Washington Post*, 20 April 1979.

afford to appear beholden and yielding to a foreign power, especially one still accused of intervening in Chinese internal affairs. Should the United States grant China access to such sensitive technologies, however, it implied an American readiness to treat Peking as a quasi ally, and would also indicate that Washington no longer sought to follow an equidistant course between the two major communist powers.

Teng was fully aware that his initiatives would play directly into the internecine bureaucratic warfare then prevailing in the Carter administration. Over Secretary of State Vance's objections, National Security Adviser Brzezinski and Defense Secretary Brown repeatedly urged the president to alter U.S. technology transfer policy toward China, as well as opt for "benign neutrality" in possible Western European weapons sales to China. Mounting instability in Iran and growing Soviet involvement in Afghanistan and South Yemen shifted the weight of opinion in Washington; by early May 1979, President Carter made proposals to Peking that he elliptically described as an "embryonic U.S.-Chinese military relationship."[100] Although the Carter administration was still nowhere near a consensus on an appropriate long-term course for such dealings, Teng may well have concluded that U.S. policy was moving in the directions that he sought.

But Peking also seemed genuinely anxious about the possibility of Soviet expansion. As instability in Southwest Asia mounted in the aftermath of the Shah's overthrow, the Chinese voiced growing concern about a major Soviet breakthrough in both the Persian Gulf and Indochina. Chinese strategic analysts had long warned of the possibility of a two-pronged Soviet geopolitical advance in Southwest and Southeast Asia. Should Moscow gain control of vital strategic routes and lines of communication, it was asserted, it would achieve an economic stranglehold on the West and Japan. The omission of the implications for China's security seemed understandable; Peking saw no need to call attention to its own vulnerabilities. Teng was even blunter in his private comments. In Teng's view, the U.S. response to the Shah's ouster had been grossly inadequate, and called into question the U.S. ability to resist Moscow's steady geopolitical advance. Under such circumstances, it was far from certain to Peking that the United States could serve as a credible counterweight to the growth of Soviet power.

By early November, the *Hung-ch'i* Commentator painted a bleak picture of Western vulnerability, insisting that mounting instability in Southwest Asia "might even touch off a direct confrontation between the

100 President Carter's remarks are cited in Brzezinski, *Power and principle*, 421.

superpowers." While voicing gratification that "more and more people" understood the global character of China's antihegemonic strategy, Commentator warned that some Western politicians still sought to conciliate the Soviet Union, when the situation called for a more forceful response. "Realistic measures and practical actions," he concluded, were needed "constantly to upset the expansionist schemes of the planners of war, oppose the policy of appeasement and when necessary take retaliatory actions against aggressors."[101] Commentator's dire assessment seemed equally directed at any Chinese leader who still harbored thoughts of accommodation with Moscow.

The Soviet Union's invasion of Afghanistan in late December 1979 offered abundant confirmation of Peking's dire warnings. In an authoritative assessment of the Soviet invasion in mid-January, the *People's Daily* Observer attributed Soviet moves to a combination of internal instability within Afghanistan and American passivity.[102] Yet Observer hoped that Soviet actions would prompt the West into a more vigorous challenge to Soviet global strategy. By this reckoning, the United States may have been vacillating and unsteady in its past conduct, but unambiguous Soviet aggression was certain to shift thinking in the United States. As *Hung-ch'i* further observed, the "nature of Soviet social imperialism ... has been proved by new evidence. People no longer have doubts about it.... The concept of categorizing the present Soviet leaders as 'doves' and the hopes of securing world peace with these 'doves' is entirely wrong."[103]

Such admonitions seemed aimed equally at a domestic audience and at the West. The initial round of Sino-Soviet negotiations had concluded in Moscow in early December 1979, with both sides expressing their readiness to continue talks in Peking the following spring. Yet it was not until 19 January 1980 – that is, more than three weeks after the invasion of Afghanistan – that the Ministry of Foreign Affairs announced that Peking would not continue the talks, declaring further negotiations "inappropriate" under the new circumstances. Some Chinese officials still seemed reluctant to foreclose the negotiating option with Moscow, preferring to view the invasion as an act of weakness and desperation, rather than as part of a larger and more threatening strategic design. But this more

---

101 All citations are drawn from Commentator, "Tang-ch'ien chan-cheng wei-hsien yü pao-wei shih-chieh ho-p'ing" (The current danger of war and the defense of world peace), *HC*, 11 (November 1979), 53–58.

102 Observer, "Ching-chung ch'iao-hsiang liao" (An alarm has been sounded), *JMJP*, 15 January 1980.

103 Commentator, "Fan-mien chiao-yuan tsai kei ta-chia shang hsin-k'o: p'ing Su-lien ch'in-lueh ho chang-ling A-fu-k'an" (The teacher who teaches by negative example is giving everyone a lesson: commentary on the Soviet invasion and occupation of Afghanistan), *HC*, 2 (16 January 1980), 46–48.

benign view clearly represented a minority viewpoint. A protracted struggle had begun in both Southwest and Southeast Asia, and it presupposed that "all peace loving countries of the world" should step up their pressure on the Soviet Union as well as on Vietnam. Expanded cooperation with the United States seemed imperative under the circumstances; hints of accommodation and flexibility toward the Soviet Union would send the wrong signals to both Washington and Moscow.

China and South Asia

Moscow's invasion also reinforced the broader pattern of Chinese policy in South Asia. Since the mid-1960s, Peking had given priority emphasis in its South Asian policy to upholding the security and independence of Pakistan. In the aftermath of defeats at the hands of vastly superior Indian forces in the 1965 and 1971 border conflicts, Pakistan received vital political and security support from China, including extensive reequipping of its armed forces. At the same time, China did not rule out improved relations with India. However, the steady advance of Soviet-Indian ties during the late 1960s and early 1970s – especially in the military realm, and after the signing of the Indo-Soviet Treaty in August 1971 – made such a course far more problematic. Moreover, subsequent to the Sino-American accommodation, Chinese relations with both India and Pakistan were increasingly cast in terms of divergent Soviet and American interests on the subcontinent. This pattern was reinforced by Pakistan's quiet but very effective role in facilitating the Sino-American accommodation process, including the transmission of the Nixon administration's earliest messages to Peking and Kissinger's use of a Pakistani "cover" for his secret visit to China.

Despite such tendencies, Peking retained some hopes of inducing movement in relations between Pakistan and India, which could then serve as the basis for reinvigorating Chinese relations with New Delhi.[104] Over the course of the 1970s, Peking's evaluations of India became less strident, with the two states again exchanging ambassadors in 1976 after a fourteen-year hiatus. Indian policy was no longer automatically deemed an extension of its ties with the Soviet Union, leaving open the possibility of more differentiated relations between New Delhi and Peking. Although Chinese leaders did not invest undue energy in such a possibility, neither did they wish to preclude it, and in early 1979, Atal Behari Vaj-

104 For further discussion, see Yaacov Y. I. Vertzberger, *China's southwestern strategy: encirclement and counterencirclement*, 63–85.

payee, India's minister of external affairs, visited China, the highest-level Sino-Indian contact in nearly two decades.

However, Vajpayee's visit coincided with China's attack on Vietnam, which reminded New Delhi much too ominously of Peking's 1962 border war with India. Partly as an expression of support for Hanoi, but also reflecting anger at Peking's seeming disregard for Indian sensibilities, Vajpayee abruptly departed from China without completing his tour. Any improvement in Sino-Indian relations had again been left in abeyance, without serious exploration of the opportunity for understandings related to rival border claims.

Any near-term movement in Sino-Indian relations was made incalculably more problematic by the Soviet invasion of Afghanistan in December 1979, and New Delhi's unwillingness to take strong issue with Soviet actions. Moscow's behavior had greatly heightened the Soviet-American geopolitical rivalry in South Asia, with Peking and New Delhi on opposing sides of an increasingly polarized situation. In the aftermath of the Soviet invasion, Peking redoubled its support for Pakistan, both to buttress Islamabad's resolve in the face of potential Soviet intimidation and to open a conduit for military aid to resistance forces in Afghanistan. The essential requirements for possible movement in Sino-Indian relations were an absence of major political and military tensions and a measure of diplomatic fluidity; both commodities were in very short supply at the time.

In a longer-term sense, however, the prospect for accommodation remained open, especially as Prime Minister Indira Gandhi began to dissociate India from an overly encumbering relationship with Moscow in the early 1980s. In April 1981, China offered to begin discussions on the improvement of Sino-Indian relations. Peking's initiative led to Huang Hua's June visit to New Delhi, the first visit by a Chinese foreign minister in more than two decades, and the opening of border talks in Peking in December 1981. Although the two delegations largely restated their long-standing positions on this occasion and during a second round of discussions held in New Delhi in May 1982, the onset of the negotiations seemed more significant than the lack of an early breakthrough.[105] The possibility of a less overtly antagonistic relationship had emerged, but undiminished Soviet involvement in Afghanistan and continued Indian wariness about Sino-Pakistani relations imposed major constraints on political movement by either side.

105 Jerrold F. Elkin and Brian Fredericks, "Sino-Indian border talks – the view from New Delhi," *Asian Survey*, 23.10 (October 1983), 1132–34.

TOWARD AN INDEPENDENT POSTURE, 1980–1982

Thus, the invasion of Afghanistan set in train a whole series of political and strategic consequences. In particular, Moscow's actions shifted American opinion about the Soviet Union as had few events since the onset of the Cold War, resulting in major departures in Washington's ties with Peking. Defense Secretary Brown's scheduled arrival in Peking in early January 1980 – the first such visit by America's ranking defense official – had been preceded by heated debate over the directions of U.S. China policy, and the invasion proved the decisive factor. Soviet-American détente was placed on the back burner of American foreign policy, and Moscow would have to pay a price for its aggression. President Carter withdrew the SALT II treaty from further consideration in the U.S. Senate, imposed a grain embargo on the USSR, and withdrew the United States from the Moscow Olympics. He also explicitly defined the defense of the Persian Gulf as a vital U.S. security interest. Teng's years of intensive lobbying had paid off: The United States had shifted ground on all issues deemed crucial to Chinese security calculations. At the same time, the administration finally loosened its restraint on the export of various sensitive technologies to China. The United States would no longer maintain an equidistant posture in relation to China and the Soviet Union. Leaders in Peking now had much stronger evidence of China's political and strategic value to the United States.

Even in the context of the defense secretary's visit, however, the Chinese remained cautious and equivocal. Although the logic of an anti-Soviet united front drew China more fully into the deteriorating superpower relationship, Peking had no desire to become engulfed in growing tensions between Washington and Moscow. Teng understood that Sino-American relations were now a barometer of the status of Soviet-American relations, but he envisioned China as the beneficiary rather than the victim of this process. For all the foreboding talk emanating from Peking of a relentlessly expansionist Soviet Union, Chinese officials continued to assert that the threat of Soviet power was first and foremost to the West and Japan, and only secondarily to China.[106]

Teng conveyed the prevailing political mood in New Year's Day remarks to the Chinese People's Political Consultative Conference, which were amplified in a major policy address to a conference of high-level

---

106 See in particular, Special Commentator, "Su-lien cheng-pa shih-chieh ti chün-shih chan-lueh" (The military strategy of the Soviet Union for world domination), *JMJP*, 11 January 1980.

cadres convened by the Central Committee on 16 January.[107] In the latter address, Teng set forth three main goals for the 1980s: (1) "to oppose hegemonism still seemed very short on details. Finally, Teng's attention to motherland," and (3) "to step up economic construction." The third goal was considered the most important. Although acknowledging that the outlook for peace was uncertain ("the eighties will be a dangerous era and the beginning of the eighties was not good"), Teng was generally optimistic:

> We are confident that if the struggle to oppose hegemonism goes well, the outbreak of war can be postponed and a longer period of peace secured.... Not only the people of the world, but also we ourselves definitely need a peaceful environment. Therefore, in terms of our country, our foreign policy should seek a peaceful environment to carry out the four modernizations.

While asserting that "an attitude of doubt with regard to the domestic situation and the future of the four modernizations is completely erroneous," Teng was unspecific about how China could avoid war while opposing Soviet expansion. The concept of a united front to oppose hegemonism still seemed very short on details. Finally, Teng's attention to Taiwan, although perfunctory, implied that the political future of the island might yet again become a contentious issue between Washington and Peking.

U.S. policy toward Taiwan compounded these uncertainties. Only three days before Defense Secretary Brown's arrival in Peking, the Carter administration announced resumption of arms deliveries to Taipei. The United States had honored its commitment to a one-year moratorium on new arms sales to Taiwan following normalization, and Peking had likely assumed that this policy would continue in 1980. Instead, the administration even hinted that the United States might allow sales of a new air defense fighter to Taiwan. Although Peking refrained from a major public protest at the time, these developments were undoubtedly disconcerting, since it cast doubt on U.S. willingness to facilitate Peking's strategy of isolating Taiwan.

The presidential campaign also approached. The workings of the American electoral process had already proved quite befuddling and unpredictable to the Chinese. Having finally achieved the political breakthrough with the Carter administration sought but never fully consummated by Presidents Nixon and Ford, leaders in Peking may have hoped

---

107 Teng's 1 January remarks are not available. All citations are drawn from "The present situation and our tasks," 16 January 1980, in *Teng Hsiao-p'ing wen-hsuan* (Selected works of Teng Hsiao-p'ing), 169–95.

for a period of consolidation and stability in the Sino-American relationship. But Carter's mounting political liabilities did not augur well for his reelection prospects; like Ford before him, he faced a major challenge from within his own party.

Even more worrisome was the looming challenge from the Republican right wing, in the person of Ronald Reagan. Having been barely denied his party's nomination four years earlier, Reagan rapidly defeated his Republican rivals. Unlike Carter in 1976, however, Reagan was not an unknown quantity. On the one hand, his credentials as a harsh critic of U.S.-Soviet détente were unassailable, and he seemed equally intent on vigorously challenging Soviet advances in the Third World. But Reagan above all was an anticommunist, with well-established political sympathies for Taiwan. (Indeed, President Nixon had dispatched then governor Reagan to Taipei to reassure Chiang Kai-shek following Nixon's 1972 visit to the mainland.) Reagan had also taken heated issue with the Carter administration's derecognition of Taipei, and in the midst of the campaign for the nomination declared his intent to upgrade relations with Taiwan, possibly by dispensing with the fig leaf of "unofficial relations."

Alarmed by this prospect, even before Reagan's nomination Peking began issuing public warnings about the implications of such steps. When the Republican Party approved a platform with references to Taiwan that China deemed especially offensive, Reagan sent George Bush, his running mate and former head of the U.S. Liaison Office in Peking, to reassure the Chinese. Despite this unprecedented step, Teng and other senior officials approached the impending American election with disquiet. The long-sought relationship with America seemed at risk, compelling Peking yet again to assess the value of close ties with the United States and to define a foreign policy path that depended less intimately and immediately on close bonds with senior officials in Washington.

Thus, Ronald Reagan's resounding defeat of Jimmy Carter in November 1980 proved troubling to Peking. While castigating perceived American ineffectuality in coping with the Soviet challenge, the Chinese recognized that Carter had ultimately taken definitive steps toward Peking that Nixon and Ford had not. Reagan, however, was much less persuaded of the political and strategic value of aligning closely with China, and had spoken repeatedly of proving more attentive to Taiwan's needs. Less than a week after the inauguration of the new president, officials in Taipei renewed their long-standing request for more modern combat aircraft.[108] A positive decision would have constituted potent

108 Henry Scott Stokes, "Taiwan's premier hopes Reagan sends new arms," *NYT*, 25 January 1981.

evidence that the United States (notwithstanding its derecognition of Taiwan and its commitment to positive relations with Peking) had no intention of severing unofficial military ties with the island. In Peking's view, new U.S. weapons would only embolden Taipei and make Taiwan's reincorporation with the mainland an even more elusive goal. Thus, any American claims of continued responsibility toward Taiwan – and any backsliding in the unofficial status of U.S.-Taiwanese relations – severely diminished the credibility of U.S. policy in Peking. In all likelihood, therefore, Teng's room for maneuver within the leadership on the Taiwan question was very limited.

To justify the extraordinary departures in Chinese policy, Teng had portrayed China as backward, vulnerable, and in critical need of external assistance. At the same time, he had posed the Soviet challenge as global and unrelenting, which thereby called for heightened cooperation among all states threatened by Soviet power, including the United States and China. Under such circumstances, however, China would presumably not take excessive issue with Washington on other policy questions, potentially giving the United States a freer hand in areas where complementarity and consensus did not exist. Thus, American handling of the Taiwan question assumed significance as a larger indicator of the importance that the new administration placed on upholding and advancing relations with Peking.

Two major decisions on China policy – both holdover issues from the Carter administration – loomed on the horizon: one on new arms sales to Taiwan, and the other on possible Chinese purchases of U.S. weaponry and defense technology. For leaders in both capitals, the issues were interconnected. When former president Ford visited China in late March 1981, he proposed (at the behest of the Reagan administration) one possible solution: The United States would supply new arms to Taiwan but would also permit weapons sales to China.[109]

Mounting pressures to respond to Taiwan's repeated requests for new aircraft had thus converged with unresolved debates over the Reagan administration's larger China policy. Chinese leaders bluntly conveyed that a deal to sell arms to both Peking and Taipei was no deal at all, and that U.S. weapons sales to China would not be welcome under such circumstances. As a result, the prospective transfer of sensitive U.S. technologies to Peking was placed in limbo, pending clarification of U.S. policy toward Taiwan. Despite the potential risks for Peking, Chinese officials

---

109 Michael Parks, "Ford hopeful Taiwan arms sale issue can be solved," *Los Angeles Times*, 28 March 1981.

were openly hinting that further collaboration with Washington in opposing Soviet power was now hostage to a satisfactory resolution of the arms sale controversy.

The difficulties with the United States rekindled a long-standing quasi-academic debate during the winter and spring of 1981 about the consequences and risks of Westernization and the dangers of relying on foreign powers for China's security and development.[110] Although the debate nominally focused on the evaluation of various nineteenth-century reformers, it had undeniable relevance to China's urgent need for economic and technical assistance, counterbalanced by fears of foreign domination. But the debate lacked the visceral, biting quality associated with the allegorical criticisms of Chou En-lai and Teng Hsiao-p'ing during the anti-Confucian campaign of 1973–74 or the attacks on Teng in 1976 for his supposed "slavishness to things foreign."

Thus, the renewed allegorical debate did not presage another major campaign to unseat Teng Hsiao-p'ing. Teng's major challenge was to sustain the momentum of far-reaching political and administrative reforms that he had launched in 1980, including plans to abolish the existing leadership arrangements for the Central Committee and the Politburo.[111] When these plans stalled in early 1981, the slowdown was attributable principally to renewed difficulties in implementing the economic readjustment policies and to continued resistance among more conservative elements in the Chinese Communist Party wary of the consequences of Teng's reform agenda. But this opposition did not prevent Teng from displacing Hua Kuo-feng from his leadership posts, culminating with Hua's June 1981 resignation from the CCP chairmanship. Moreover, by late 1981, Teng had regained the political initiative, culminating in the Twelfth CCP National Congress in September 1982, where reform elements consolidated their hold on political power.

Thus, although Teng's political hand seemed momentarily weaker in 1981, it was not attributable in any significant measure to foreign policy setbacks. However, as the principal architect of the normalization accords, Teng was presumably subject to muted criticism that he had

---

110 For representative examples of these discussions, see Yang Tung-liang, "A brief analysis of the debate on coastal defense versus land border defense," *KMJP*, 10 February 1981, in FBIS *Daily Report: China*, 5 March 1981, L3–7; Ch'iao Huan-t'ien, "A discussion of Li Hung-chang's Westernization activities," *JMJP*, 30 March 1981, in FBIS *Daily Report: China*, 3 April 1981, K8–12, and Ch'iao Huan-t'ien, "The diplomatic activities of the Westernization proponents should not be cut off from the Westernization movement," *JMJP*, 7 May 1981, in FBIS *Daily Report: China*, 15 May 1981, K4–7.

111 For more extended discussion, see H. Lyman Miller, "China's administrative revolution," *Current History*, 82.485 (September 1983), 270–74.

oversold the Sino-American relationship. Teng's task was to avoid any accusation that he was excessively beholden to the West; the policy, but not Teng, was therefore subject to renewed scrutiny and challenge.

The debate over late Ch'ing reform suggested that China ran the risk of mortgaging its long-term independence to the caprices of a somewhat malign West. By implication, the task of long-term policy was to address the country's real economic and security needs, while avoiding the dangers of overreliance on foreign powers, whose interest in China was deemed selfish and potentially harmful. However, renewed isolation was not considered a solution. Enhancing Chinese policy independence and initiative in the context of growing ties with the outside would remain the preeminent challenge for national policy, and for Teng Hsiao-p'ing.

It was in the context of these heightened nationalistic sensitivities that Secretary of State Haig traveled to Peking in mid-June. Haig was well known to the Chinese, having participated actively in the early planning for President Nixon's visit to China. Along with Vice-President Bush, he was the senior official in the new administration toward whom the Chinese had the clearest personal affinity. Haig's tenure in office had already been marked by rancorous debates with the White House staff and the Department of Defense over control of the administration's security and foreign policies. He was also well known for his sympathies toward Peking, and deemed the further development of relations a "strategic imperative." But the Chinese did not seem as self-assured as in the past in injecting themselves into U.S. bureaucratic and policy struggles.

Although the Chinese were undoubtedly heartened by Haig's advocacy of closer relations, his voice had yet to carry the day. Even as Haig sought to reassure Peking of U.S. intentions – including the public disclosure that China would no longer be subject to previous restrictions on the munitions control list, and would be eligible for sales of lethal weaponry on a case-by-case basis – Chinese officials conveyed wariness and disgruntlement. A Foreign Ministry spokesman stated that "we have time and again made it clear that we would rather receive no U.S. arms than accept continued interference in our internal affairs by selling arms to Taiwan, to which we can never agree."[112] As a Hsin-hua correspondent also observed, "the crux to further strategic relations between the two countries remains that the United States stop developing all relations with Taiwan that go beyond non-governmental relations."[113]

Thus, the Chinese saw few incentives to cooperate when American

112 NCNA, 10 June 1981.   113 "A move doomed to failure," ibid., 11 June 1981.

intentions were deemed suspect. In banquet remarks following Haig's effusive declarations of China's importance to American interests, Foreign Minister Huang Hua's tone was guarded and noncommittal. Huang not only failed to allude to "Soviet hegemonism" (a standard reference in previous Chinese statements), but called attention to the Middle East, South Africa, and the need for "a new international economic order," where U.S. and Chinese policies differed sharply.[114]

Moreover, the Chinese appeared displeased that Haig publicly called attention to the supposed readiness of both countries to expand the framework of defense collaboration. Taking direct issue with Haig's claims of forward movement and President Reagan's renewed pledges of support for Taiwan, a Hsin-hua commentary declared that "U.S. relations with Taiwan, continued arms sales to Taiwan in particular, constitute the key link ... in the development of Sino-U.S. relations." As the commentary further observed:

There are Americans in the U.S. Government who are bent on giving Taiwan an international status as an independent political entity.... There are still Americans ... who contend that since China never fails to take the overall situation into consideration, it would ... swallow the bitter pill of U.S. arms sales to Taiwan. This is completely illogical.[115]

Further Sino-American political and security cooperation appeared endangered; Peking was beginning to explore its policy alternatives in the context of an increasingly unsettled relationship with Washington.

The strongest indications of change came from Teng Hsiao-p'ing. Speaking in mid-July to a leading Hong Kong journalist, Teng indelibly associated himself with the assertive, nationalistic mood evident in Chinese foreign policy. Others in the leadership may have questioned the logic of Sino-American accommodation, but Teng also had made very clear that he was not beholden to the United States:

The United States thinks that China is seeking its favor. In fact, China is not seeking any country's favor.... China hopes that Sino-American relations will further develop rather than retrogress. However, this should not be one-sided.... It is nothing serious even if the United States causes a retrogression in Sino-American relations. If worst comes to worst and the relations retrogress to those prior to 1972, China will not collapse.... The Chinese people ... will never bow and scrape for help.[116]

China, therefore, had embarked on the search for a political position that left future Sino-American relations indeterminate.

114 Ibid., 14 June 1981.
115 "A key link in development of Sino-U.S. relations," ibid., 19 June 1981.
116 Teng, interview in Hong Kong, *Ming pao*, 25 August 1981. The interview took place in mid-July but was not published until late August.

These steps necessitated doctrinal and policy adjustments. As Chinese incentives for collaboration with the United States increased over the course of the 1970s, Peking had dissociated itself from its earlier rhetoric extolling the unity of the Third World against the two superpowers. China's calls for a new international order had become far less visionary, with an increasing emphasis on the need for unity against Soviet expansion, and with far less emphasis on the need for a redistribution of global resources. By the late summer of 1981, however, the pendulum had again swung, with Peking renewing its past criticisms of U.S. policy in the Third World and again voicing support for the nonaligned movement. At the twenty-two–nation summit conference on international cooperation and development held in Cancun, Mexico, in October 1981, Premier Chao Tzu-yang (in his first major foray into international diplomacy) renewed earlier Chinese support for a new international economic order, declaring further that "the two superpowers in their worldwide rivalry are menacing and encroaching upon the independence and security of many countries."[117] At least for declaratory purposes, China had again linked the United States with the Soviet Union as a threat to international security.

The reality was more complicated. Peking was well aware that the Reagan administration continued to deliberate on future arms sales to Taiwan and enhanced technology transfer to China. But the Chinese were careful not to convey undue eagerness on the latter issue, for fear that it might be construed as evidence of Peking's acquiescence to renewed sales to Taipei. In Peking's estimation, a political position somewhat apart from the United States and an implied threat of political reprisal for actions deemed deleterious to Chinese interests afforded China a measure of latitude and protection.

Such a posture also left the door open to renewed negotiations with Washington. As the Reagan administration neared the climax of a year-long review of Taiwan's defense needs, Chinese officials intimated some flexibility in discussing the framework of future arms sales to Taiwan. Although Peking could not assent explicitly to U.S. sales, Chinese reactions to U.S. behavior would be governed by the scope and character of these transactions. China may have placed some political distance between itself and the United States, but there was an intrinsic importance to relations with Washington that Peking did not want to place at risk.

The proximate opportunity for moving relations in a more positive direction occurred in January 1982. The United States informed Peking

---

117 The citation is from Chao's address to the Mexican Congress following the Cancun summit, NCNA, 27 October 1981.

that it would approve continued coproduction on Taiwan of the F-5 E fighter, but had denied Taipei's request for the F-5 G, a new and much more advanced version of the aircraft. The worst had not occurred: By implication, the administration had placed a ceiling on the level of military technology it would sell to Taiwan, provided that Peking continue to exercise political restraint toward its neighbor. At the end of January, the Chinese indicated publicly for the first time that they might be willing to assent to continued sales over a period of time if the two sides could devise a formula for the eventual termination of U.S. arms transfers. Peking had concluded that informal assurances would no longer suffice: Without an official understanding, Sino-American relations were vulnerable to potential reversal or even rupture whenever the United States delivered additional weaponry to Taipei.

The ensuing six months were dominated by prolonged, frequently acrimonious negotiations between Washington and Peking on an appropriate formula for future arms sales. Throughout these discussions, Chinese statements warned repeatedly that Sino-American relations were "at a critical juncture" and in danger of "retrogression." Although Peking never defined explicitly the steps it might take in the absence of a satisfactory agreement, a broader spectrum of relations (including the enhancement of defense collaboration) was clearly on hold. At the same time, China issued a series of visceral attacks on U.S. China policy, in particular when U.S. statements suggested a continued American responsibility for the well-being of Taiwan. Taiwan remained an exceedingly sensitive issue for the Chinese leadership, frequently injecting an angry, intensely nationalistic tone in public as well as private settings. Teng and other senior officials remained wary and doubting about U.S. intentions, and this left them little room for maneuver.

Despite the strains and tensions permeating the negotiations, on 17 August 1982 China and the United States reached agreement on a joint communiqué governing future U.S. arms sales to the island. A third major document had thus been drafted and signed as a guide to long-term Sino-American relations, with Washington offering important concessions and assurances to Peking:

The United States states that it does not seek to carry out a long-term policy of arms sales to Taiwan, that its arms sales will not exceed, either in qualitative or quantitative terms, the level of those supplied in recent years ... and that it intends to reduce gradually its sales of arms to Taiwan, leading over a period of time to a final resolution.[118]

---

118 The citation is from the official U.S. text in *Department of State Bulletin*, October 1982, 20.

Although the agreement was immediately subject to radically different interpretations by Chinese and American officials, the communiqué explicitly addressed Chinese concerns and helped allay Peking's suspicions, thereby establishing a more predictable floor to support future ties. But there had been undeniable damage to Sino-American relations that would take some time to repair.

The prolonged uncertainties and diminished trust had led both countries (but especially China) to reassess the value attached to Sino-American ties. China had already sought to define a foreign policy strategy less dependent on intimate connections with the United States, especially in China's strategic positioning toward the Soviet-American competition. In terms of China's broader interests and needs, however, no change was discernible. In mid-April 1982, an authoritative commentary in *Hung-ch'i* again emphasized the importance that Peking attached to its economic relationship with the West. According to the essay, the attraction of foreign investment, the importation of advanced science and technology, and the further expansion of foreign trade would all remain integral to China's plans for long-term national development.[119] However, as Chao Tzu-yang conveyed almost simultaneously to a visiting Third World head of state, China's broad foreign policy principles would stress the country's identification with the Third World, antihegemonism, and pursuit of a long period of international peace.[120]

Thus, the Chinese sought to protect and enhance those dimensions of foreign relations that would strengthen China's power and position. This effort at doctrinal reformulation seemed especially germane to relations with Japan, which among the major capitalist powers had made the largest commitment to closer, long-term ties with China. Peking's economic reassessment of the early 1980s and the abrupt deterioration in U.S.-Chinese relations had been particularly unsettling to Tokyo, since both developments undermined the assumptions on which the Sino-Japanese alignment of the late 1970s had been based. Chinese leaders therefore repeatedly sought to reassure senior Japanese officials that relations with Tokyo would not be affected by the political uncertainties with Washington.

But Chinese views of the United States necessarily colored Peking's larger appraisal of regional politics and security, including its relations with Japan. As difficulties with the United States mounted, Chinese con-

---

119 Editorial Department, "Kuan-yü wo-kuo tui-wai ching-chi kuan-hsi wen-t'i" (On the questions of our country's external economic relations), *HC*, 8 (16 April 1982), 2–10.
120 See Chao's conversation with Joao Bernardo Viera, head of state of Guinea-Bissau, NCNA, 17 April 1982.

cerns about the military strength and political role of Japan had again grown. Efforts in the summer of 1982 by the Japanese Ministry of Education to dilute the language in textbooks describing Japan's aggression against China in the 1930s and 1940s provoked a firestorm of protest from Peking. For the first time since the normalization of relations with Tokyo in 1972, major Chinese policy statements again warned of the dangers of a potential "revival of Japanese militarism." Chinese support for the U.S.-Japan Mutual Security Treaty assumed a more equivocal tone as well. Although the Chinese leadership was mollified by subsequent retractions of the proposed textbook revisions, there had been undeniable damage to the political relationship with Tokyo.

In a larger sense, therefore, a duality had emerged in Chinese policies toward Washington and Tokyo. At a political level, China would strongly dissociate itself from explicit identification with U.S. and Japanese political and military strategies in the region. But this divergence would not affect Peking's larger incentives to collaborate with America and Japan, since these relations were crucial to China's hopes for economic, technical, and scientific advancement. The foundation of a nonconfrontational foreign policy had been laid: China would seek full cooperation when it served the interests of the modernization program, but it would avoid embroilment in the larger political and strategic rivalries that characterized great-power relations in East Asia.

Attributing international tension and turbulence to "the struggle for hegemony between the two superpowers" still left China free to define the degree of threat posed to Chinese security by either Moscow or Washington. In this respect, the distance that China sought to establish from the two superpowers was more hypothetical than real. In both public and private formulations, the Chinese continued to assert that the USSR remained on the offensive, posing a direct threat to the security of China. Over time, Chinese strategists asserted the United States could present a more effective challenge to the Soviet Union and the USSR might curtail the exercise of its power, but this day had yet to arrive.

The most important consideration was that China never again become a pawn in the U.S.-Soviet competition. As Foreign Minister Huang Hua told UN Secretary-General Pérez de Cuéllar in late August 1982, "China will never cling to any superpower. China will never play the 'U.S. card' against the Soviet Union, nor the 'Soviet card' against the United States. We will also not allow anyone to play the 'Chinese card.' "[121] This position was formally ratified and enshrined at the Twelfth CCP National

121 Ibid., 22 August 1982.

Congress. Speaking to the Congress on 1 September 1982, Party Chairman (soon to be general secretary under the new Party constitution) Hu Yao-pang declared that "China never attaches itself to any big power or group of powers, and never yields to pressure from any big power."[122] At least in doctrinal form, China had consummated the shift to an independent posture.

These circumstances still left largely undetermined the character of future Sino-Soviet relations. Teng, Hu, and other senior Chinese officials clearly recognized that their rivalry with Moscow represented a far more intractable, long-term problem than their disagreements with Washington. In his political report to the Twelfth CCP National Congress, Hu Yao-pang drew explicit attention to Soviet military activities throughout Asia that constituted "grave threats to the peace of Asia and to China's security." His urging that the Soviet leadership "take practical steps to lift their threat to the security of our country" was thus a direct challenge to Moscow to make good on its long-standing pledge to improve relations with Peking.[123]

During much of 1981 and 1982, Moscow had taken approving note of growing Sino-American differences, and clearly hoped to capitalize on the deteriorating political relationship between Washington and Peking. As Moscow's worst nightmares of Sino-American collusion began to recede, the Soviet leadership had obvious incentives to intimate flexibility toward Peking. But the Chinese remained exceptionally wary, especially in the context of undiminished Soviet military involvement in Afghanistan and Indochina. Although both states had begun to establish a more correct tone in interstate relations, their broader political and security differences remained undiminished. China in particular did not want difficulties with Washington to compel any abrupt moves toward Moscow.

By the fall of 1982, however, there were increased intimations of flexibility by both states. Peking's formal adoption of an independent foreign policy posture signaled to Moscow that China would no longer collaborate with the United States in policies generated explicitly by an anti-Soviet design. Perhaps even more important, the signing of the arms sale communiqué had halted the potential slide in Sino-American relations: Peking felt that it had increased latitude toward Moscow now that relations with the United States no longer seemed imperiled. The Chinese also wanted to position themselves to explore any political opportunities that might follow the impending succession to an increasingly infirm Leonid Brezhnev.

122 Ibid., 4 September 1982.   123 Ibid.

In October 1982, the Chinese decided to test Soviet intentions. Responding to overtures emanating from the Kremlin the previous spring, the Chinese proposed initiation of "consultations" at the level of vice–foreign minister to discuss the possible normalization of Sino-Soviet relations. Thus, the negotiations that had been canceled in the aftermath of the Soviet invasion of Afghanistan were now resumed, but in a more promising political context. A regular channel for Chinese and Soviet diplomatic contact had been reestablished, even if neither side anticipated an early or rapid improvement of relations. With Brezhnev's death the following month, the Chinese (in the person of Foreign Minister Huang Hua) were able to convey directly to a new Soviet leadership that Peking remained open to a fuller exploration of improved relations.

At the same time, China repeatedly made clear that shifts in Sino-Soviet relations would not come at the expense of relations with the West. China's stake in expanded economic and technical contact with the United States, Japan, and Western Europe was far too great to place it at risk for the tentative, still problematic political gains in relations with the Soviet Union. The uncertainty and instability of the early 1980s had been chastening to Peking, as well. But more differentiated relations with both adversaries and friendly states created at least the potential for the longer-term stability in foreign policy that had so long eluded the Chinese leadership. As 1982 drew to a close, Teng and other Chinese leaders had cause for quiet satisfaction, if not complacency: The outline of a credible long-term external course was finally discernible, if yet to be fully realized.

THE IMPLICATIONS OF SINO-AMERICAN RELATIONS

China's opening to America profoundly reshaped Asian international relations. By forgoing the adversarial relations that had dominated Sino-American ties since the Korean War, Peking began a process of realignment that altered the international system more markedly than any event since the onset of the Sino-Soviet conflict. Yet the results of this transformation were not foreordained. Both states had to grapple with the effects of improved relations on their respective political processes, at the same time that each interpreted the meaning and consequences of the rapprochement according to its own needs. Moreover, the architects of accommodation were not able to sustain their initial breakthroughs when attention in both systems quickly shifted from grand strategy to political survival.

By placing his imprimatur on the opening to America at an early date,

Mao provided the sanction without which accommodation with the United States could have been stymied or prevented. Yet Mao's identification with this policy guaranteed very little. It did not prevent attacks on Chou En-lai and Teng Hsiao-p'ing for their supposed "worshipping of things foreign," nor did it assure Mao's consistent support for relations with the United States. Mao was deeply troubled by the long-term threat posed to China by the Soviet Union, and felt that the lure of a relationship with Peking would lead the United States to proffer the security and political guarantees essential to China's well-being. His expectations were only partially met. More important, the political succession in Peking remained his larger preoccupation, setting limits on the authority of his political subordinates, especially Teng. The opening to America, therefore, remained incomplete. Mao was never fully reconciled to the implications of China's enhanced international involvement, viewing relations with America more as a means to escape China's acute security predicament rather than a path to economic and technological advancement.

The unevenness of China's accommodation with the West demonstrated the absence of a sustainable strategy in both national capitals in the earliest years of renewed relations; neither leadership proved able to make the concessions that the other deemed essential to its own political needs. Both countries sought to counter the growth of Soviet power; converting these concerns into a larger Sino-American understanding in both political systems proved far more difficult. It was only at the end of the decade, with Teng increasingly entrenched following his second return to power and with a different American administration in office far less equivocal about aligning with Peking, that full diplomatic relations were achieved. However, even this accomplishment proved ephemeral, as relations were severely tested and then redefined early in the Reagan administration.

Despite the fitful quality of Sino-American accommodation in the 1970s, it created the conditions for much more diversified relations in the 1980s. First, by reaching understandings at the highest levels of both systems, a floor had been created that withstood repeated challenges and pressures on both leaderships. Ties of greater weight and depth were ultimately built on this foundation. Second, the opening to America paved the way for China's fuller involvement within the existing framework of international institutions. China's admission to the United Nations was probably inevitable following Peking's emergence from the isolation of the Cultural Revolution, but Sino-American rapprochement unquestionably accelerated this process.

From the first, however, the Chinese policy agenda in international forums diverged sharply from U.S. policy preferences, in particular

Peking's advocacy of a "redistributionist" approach to major political and economic questions.[124] Only during the "high tide" of the Sino-American united front did Peking make a conscious effort to seek common ground with U.S. policy on a shared anti-Soviet platform. With China's foreign policy reassessment of the early 1980s, Peking resumed its effort to map a distinctive set of global policies that diverged sharply and repeatedly from U.S. policy, especially in relation to the Third World.

Third, the end of a twenty-year effort to isolate China opened the door to far fuller Chinese economic involvement both regionally and globally. Quite apart from the "globalist" orientation adopted by China in the United Nations and in other international organizations, Peking's actual behavior demonstrated an acute sensitivity to national needs. Over time, China's growing requirements for loans, investment, technology, and other forms of assistance from abroad demonstrated the gap between the normative thrust in Chinese policy pronouncements and Peking's determination to avail itself fully of the opportunities for economic advance, notably from the World Bank.[125] Without the explicit sanction provided by the American accommodation with Peking, however, it seems highly unlikely that China's incorporation within the international economic system would have been nearly as complete. These effects were especially pronounced with Japan, which in the context of the Sino-American rapprochement achieved unquestioned predominance as China's leading trading partner.

By the close of the 1970s, therefore, the abnormality of China's exclusion from the politics and economics of East Asia was drawing to an end. The prolonged turmoil of post–Cultural Revolution politics had delayed this process of integration, but the effects quickly receded in the early 1980s, as fuller ties were established with most of China's neighbors. At the same time, Peking had concluded that a durable framework for relations with the United States could not rest disproportionately on strategic cooperation, but instead required a much more diversified set of political, economic, and institutional relations between the two systems.

It was within the Chinese system, however, that the largest effects of the opening to the outside world were felt. The insularity and illusions bred by China's international isolation dissipated rapidly once Peking sought fuller participation in global and regional politics. A commitment to modernization and to China's emergence as an autonomous major power presupposed a continuing process of international engagement;

124 See Samuel S. Kim, *China, the United Nations, and world order.*
125 See Samuel S. Kim, "Chinese world policy in transition," *World Policy Journal*, Spring 1984, 603–33.

one could not be achieved without the other. Full relations with the United States did not resolve more than a century of internal debate about responding to the economic and technological superiority of the Western world, but it elevated this enduring question to central importance within the Chinese political process. The opening to America, therefore, marked a beginning as much as an end.

PART III

THE CULTURAL REVOLUTION
AND ITS AFTERMATH

CHAPTER 6

CHINA'S ECONOMIC POLICY AND PERFORMANCE

INTRODUCTION

Few really new economic ideas or policies were put forward during the Cultural Revolution decade (1966–76). There were economic debates leading up to and during the Cultural Revolution, but these debates had their roots in an earlier period, specifically in the Great Leap Forward and its immediate afftermath, when Chinese high and low attempted to understand what had gone wrong.

By 1956 the Chinese state had completed the takeover of private industry and commerce, and agriculture had been collectivized. The tools of planning and control over this socialized economy had been borrowed wholesale from the Soviet Union. China's economic strategy emphasizing machinery and steel was virtually a carbon copy of Stalin's development strategy for Russia in the 1930s.

This choice of planning tools and development strategy in part reflected a view among the leaders of many developing countries at the time that the Soviet Union represented the one real alternative to capitalist economic development, and a very successful alternative at that. China's leaders shared this view of Soviet accomplishments, but from the beginning they were uneasy with many features of the Soviet economic system. The sources of this uneasiness varied among the senior Chinese leaders. Some were concerned with the rigidities of the highly centralized system of planning and control, and others knew that China could not afford to follow the Soviet lead in neglecting agriculture. At some point, Mao Tsetung and those close to him became bothered by the implications the Soviet system held out for the increasing bureaucratization of society and its emphasis on values more consistent with capitalism than with the future communist ideal.

Virtually as soon as socialization was completed, therefore, Chinese leaders began tinkering with the system to make it better fit their perception of China's needs. In 1957, efforts were made to loosen the impact of overcentralization by reducing controls on certain private markets and by

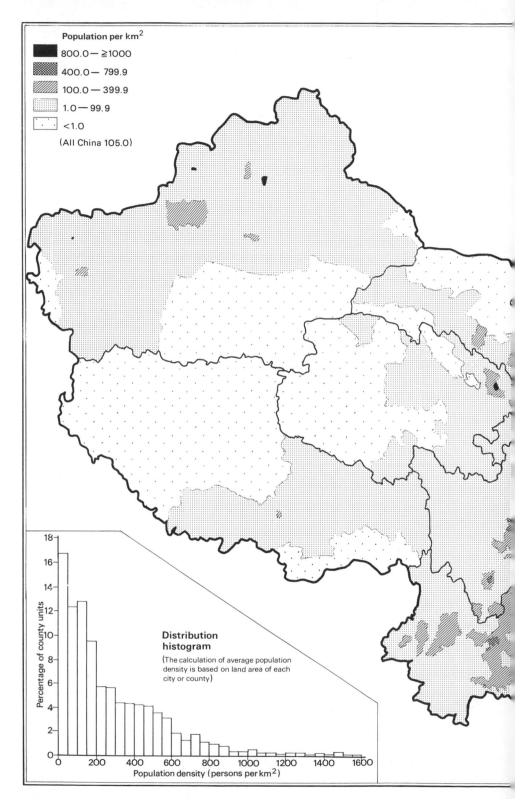

Population per km²

■ 800.0 — ≧1000
▨ 400.0 — 799.9
▨ 100.0 — 399.9
▦ 1.0 — 99.9
⬚ <1.0
(All China 105.0)

Distribution histogram

(The calculation of average population density is based on land area of each city or county)

Percentage of county units

Population density (persons per km²)

MAP 7. Population

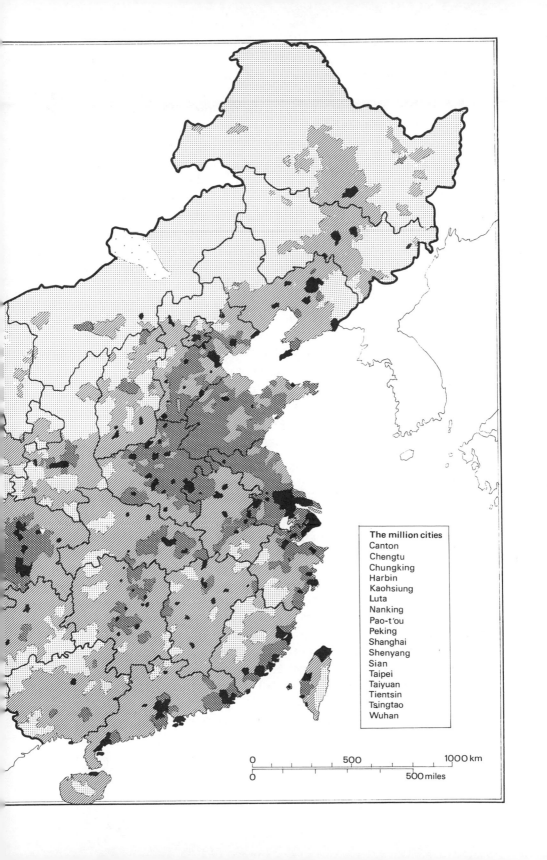

The million cities
Canton
Chengtu
Chungking
Harbin
Kaohsiung
Luta
Nanking
Pao-t'ou
Peking
Shanghai
Shenyang
Sian
Taipei
Taiyuan
Tientsin
Tsingtao
Wuhan

0		500		1000 km

0		500 miles

decentralizing some decisions to the province and below. In 1958 and 1959, there was the dramatic experiment of the Great Leap Forward and the people's communes. And with the collapse of the Great Leap in 1960, there was a return to centralized planning, combined with efforts to enhance the role of the market and to enhance private initiative, particularly in agriculture but also to a degree in industry.

Throughout much of the second half of the 1950s, the lines between what later came to be labeled "right" and "left," or "radicals" and "pragmatists," were not clearly drawn. On the one hand there were leaders, such as Ch'en Yun, who concerned themselves with economic matters. On the other were Mao Tse-tung and much of the senior Party leadership, whose concern was with political consolidation of the revolution. The concerns of the people with these portfolios did overlap because major issues, such as the pace of collectivization, involved both politics and economics. But Mao in particular did not concern himself with the central issues of economic development. His 1956 speech "On the ten great relationships" was probably more of a collective effort using his signature to give it authority than it was an attempt to articulate deeply held personal views.

Then, in 1958, Mao injected himself into economic decision making in a way that was to have a profound influence over the next two decades. In Mao's own words:

Before August of last year [1958], my main energies were concentrated on revolution. I am a complete outsider when it comes to economic construction, and I understand nothing about industrial planning.... But comrades, in 1958 and 1959 the main responsibility was mine, and you should take me to task. In the past the responsibility was other peoples'.... Who was responsible for the idea of the mass smelting of steel? K'o Ch'ing-Shih or me? I say it was me.[1]

As the above passage indicates, Mao not only intervened in economic decision-making in 1958 and 1959, but did so on the basis of a very modest understanding of economic development. The efforts of the Great Leap, in fact, owed more to political ideas than to anyone's concept of economics. The Great Leap was one long mass campaign designed to move China into the ranks of industrialized nations in a hurry. The key input was to be human effort – effort to make steel in backyard furnaces, effort to move millions of tons of dirt and rock so as to irrigate the parched fields of North China.

The quantitative dimensions of the disaster that followed this mass

---

1 Mao Tse-tung, "Speech at the Lushan Conference," 23 July 1959, in Stuart Schram, ed. *Chairman Mao talks to the people*, 142–43.

campaign are discussed elsewhere in this chapter. The key point of relevance here is that individual members of the leadership drew very different conclusions about the nature of the disaster. Analysis of what had happened was complicated by the fact that the weather was bad in the 1959–61 period and even more by the Soviet Union's decision to withdraw its technicians from China in 1960. Thus, those who shared Mao's vision could argue that the basic ideas of the Great Leap were sound, but poor implementation, bad luck (weather), and Soviet perfidy led to temporary failure. On the other side were those leaders who saw the very conception of the Great Leap as the main source of the disaster.

In the early 1960s these differences in viewpoint had only a modest impact on economic policy because all agreed that recovery was the number-one priority. But in 1962, evidence of disagreement was apparent from Mao's opposition to the agricultural responsibility system that he saw as undermining the rural collective economy. The more extreme forms of the responsibility system were, in fact, halted or reversed and did not appear again until the 1980s. Aside from efforts to contain the retreat from collectivism, however, Mao turned his attention to what he considered the root of the problem, the still unreformed values and attitudes of the great majority of the people, including much of the membership of the Chinese Communist Party (CCP). The result was, first, the effort to reform the army, followed by the launching of the Socialist Education Campaign.

If Mao also spent the early 1960s rethinking or refining his ideas about economic development, there is little evidence to that effect. There is little economic content of any but the most casual kind in Mao's speeches from that period. Nor were those close to Mao busy working out a development strategy that would retain the essence but eliminate the shortcomings of the Great Leap.

When the Cultural Revolution got under way in 1965–66, therefore, there were few guidelines for those who might want to promote a new, more radical path for the economy. The effort in the early 1960s to increase the role of financial targets and controls could be attacked as "putting profits in command," and Sun Yeh-fang, an advocate of financial controls, could be vilified. But there was little in the way of economic strategy that could be put in the place of the policies worked out under the leadership of Liu Shao-ch'i and Teng Hsiao-p'ing, except for the experiments of the Great Leap. But no one wanted an undiluted repeat of the Great Leap, either.

The strategy pursued from 1966 on, therefore, was an amalgam of policies from the 1950s as modified in the early 1960s plus pieces of the Great

Leap formulas of 1958–59. The nature of that strategy can best be understood not by reading the speeches of the leadership, left or right, but by dissecting the actual performance of the economy in the decade that followed. It may be that few leaders attempted to articulate a strategy because it was politically easier and safer to act from day to day in an ad hoc manner. But even policies designed to do little more than respond to short-run considerations can over time add up to a long-run strategy of a sort.

DISRUPTION IN THE ECONOMY, 1966 – 1969

Before turning to China's development strategy in the Cultural Revolution period, however, one must first deal with the argument that China had no coherent strategy in the period because the country was in continual chaos. Politics, of course, was frequently chaotic, but the question here is whether politics regularly spilled over into the economy, causing work stoppages and worse.

The principal data on which this analysis is based are presented in Tables 8, 9, and 10. The basic message in these tables is clear and consistent. First, the disruption was largely confined to three years, 1967, 1968, and 1969. Industry and transport were hit the hardest, but only in 1967 and 1968. By 1969, most industries had reached and surpassed the peak levels of 1966. Furthermore, even during the years of chaos, industrial output often did not fall farther than levels achieved in the "normal" year of 1965 and remained far above the depression figures of 1962. Although the degree of disruption varied between provinces, most provinces suffered severe disruptions in both 1967 and 1968. A notable exception to this pattern was Shanghai, where industrial production was disrupted in a major way in only one year, 1967. By 1968 Shanghai industry had recovered and passed the previous peak level of 1966.[2] Given that Shanghai was the base of the Cultural Revolution leadership, a more experimental and potentially disruptive set of economic policies could have been anticipated. What little we know about Shanghai's economic experience during the 1966–76 decade, however, suggests that it was much like that of the rest of the country. Overall industrial growth in Shanghai during this period was slower than the national average growth rate (8.3 percent versus 10.2 percent between 1965 and 1978), but this performance re-

2 Regional data for the 1966–70 period must be reconstructed from scattered sources. The statement here is based on data in R. Michael Field, Nicholas Lardy, and John Philip Emerson, *A reconstruction of the gross value of industrial output by provinces in the People's Republic of China: 1949–1973.*

TABLE 8

Indexes of industrial output during the Cultural Revolution (1966 = 100)

	1957	1962	1965	1966	1967	1968	1969	1970	1975
Electric power	23	56	82	100	94	87	114	140	237
Steel	35	44	80	100	67	59	87	116	156
Coal	52	87	92	100	82	87	106	140	191
Petroleum	10	40	78	100	95	110	149	211	530
Cement	34	30	81	100	73	63	91	128	230
Chemical fertilizer	6	19	72	100	68	46	73	101	218
Machine tools	51	41	74	100	74	85	156	253	319
Cloth	69	35	86	100	90	88	112	125	129
Bicycles	39	67	90	100	86	97	142	180	304

Source: State Statistical Bureau, *Statistical yearbook of China, 1981*, 225–31.

TABLE 9

Agricultural outputs and inputs during the Cultural Revolution (m. = million)

	1957	1962	1965	1966	1967	1968	1969	1970	1975
Grain									
(m. tons)	195	160	194.5	214	218	209	211	240	284.5
index	91	75	91	100	102	98	99	112	133
Cotton									
(m.tons)	1.64	.75	2.10	2.34	2.35	2.35	2.08	2.28	2.38
index	70	32	90	100	101	101	89	97	102
Hogs									
(m. head)	145.9	100.0	166.9	193.4	190.1	178.6	172.5	206.1	281.2
index	75	52	86	100	98	92	89	107	145
Chemical Fertilizer (m. tons)									
production	.15	.46	1.73	2.41	1.64	1.11	1.75	2.44	5.25
imports	1.22	1.24	2.73	3.15	4.88	5.21	5.55	6.42	4.94
supplied to farmers[a]	1.79	3.11	8.81	12.58	13.63	10.13	13.61	115.35	26.58
supply index	14	25	70	100	108	81	108	122	211

[a] These figures are given in terms of gross weight, whereas the production and import figures are in terms of nutrient.

Sources: State Statistical Bureau, *Statistical yearbook of China, 1981*, 229, 386; *Chung-kuo nung-yeh nien-chien, 1980*, 34, 40.

TABLE 10

Transport and commerce during the Cultural Revolution

	1957	1962	1965	1966	1967	1968	1969	1970	1975
Freight traffic (billion ton/km)	181.0	223.6	346.3	390.1	305.0	310.9	375.3	456.5	729.7
Railroad traffic (billion ton/km)	134.6	172.1	269.8	301.9	226.9	223.9	278.3	349.6	425.6
Retail sales (billion yuan)									
Urban	23.84	31.85	33.89	36.28	38.20	37.32	39.35	40.00	60.69
Rural	23.58	28.55	33.14	37.00	38.85	36.41	40.80	45.80	66.42
Farm products purchases (billion yuan)	21.75	21.11	30.71	34.59	34.48	33.82	32.40	34.78	47.86
Grain purchases (million tons)	45.97	32.42	39.22	41.42	41.38	40.41	38.45	46.49	52.62
Foreign trade (billion U.S. $)									
Exports	1.60	1.49	2.23	2.37	2.14	2.10	2.20	2.26	7.26
Imports	1.51	1.17	2.02	2.25	2.02	1.95	1.83	2.33	7.49

Source: State Statistical Bureau, *Statistical yearbook of China, 1981*, 283, 333, 345, 357.

flected policies started in the 1950s designed to relocate Chinese industry away from the coast.

Agriculture nationwide was less affected than industry. Grain output fell in 1968 and 1969 and cotton in 1969 and 1970. The number of hogs, usually a sensitive indicator of the status of private plots and the free market, was down significantly in 1968 and 1969. Some of this decline in agricultural output may have been because of bad weather, but in 1968 the principal problem was shortfalls in the availability of chemical fertilizer, supplies of which fell by more than 30 percent. The shortfall would have been worse if the sharp drop in domestic chemical fertilizer production had not been matched by a 65 percent rise in imports between 1966 and 1968. Somebody took responsibility to see that farmers did not suffer too severely from the disruption of industry.

By 1970, industry and agriculture had not only recovered to previous peak levels achieved in 1966 or 1967 but had surpassed those levels and regained the long-term trend line. In short, all of the worker strikes, the battles between workers and Red Guards, and the use of the railroads to transport Red Guards around the country had cost China two years of reduced output but little more, at least in the short run. Over the longer run, as the discussion in the next section makes clear, the ability of

China's planners to respond to new problems and opportunities was severely constrained by fears of political reprisals, although the difficulties these constraints created were not fully apparent until the late 1970s. Overall, the growth rate of national product in the 3rd Five-Year Plan (FYP) period (1966–70) may have averaged as much as 6 percent per year.[3]

The contrast between the disruption caused by the Cultural Revolution and that resulting from the Great Leap Forward of 1958–60 is striking. After the Great Leap, grain output fell 26 percent and cotton output by 38 percent from the 1958 peak.[4] The number of hogs in 1961 after private agricultural activity had been virtually eliminated was only 52 percent of the 1957 peak.

The industrial data for the Great Leap period and its aftermath are more difficult to interpret. In all cases output in the 1961–62 period was sharply below the peaks of 1958–59. But the 1958–59 peaks were inflated by price increases and by outright falsification of data. On the other hand, if there had been no Great Leap, industrial production would still have risen sharply in 1958 and 1959 because of all the new plant and equipment that was started earlier in the 1st FYP period (1953–57), but whose production was just coming on line at the beginning of the 2nd FYP (1958–62). In addition, many new complete plants were bought and delivered from the Soviet Union in 1958 and 1959, so that industrial production in the early 1960s should have continued to grow rapidly. In fact, industrial output declined sharply in 1961 and 1962 and had fully recovered by 1965 at the earliest.[5] The Soviet withdrawal of technical assistance in 1960 with only two weeks notice, of course, had more than a little to do with the slowness of this recovery.

In many respects the best comparisons of the degree of disruption in the Great Leap and the Cultural Revolution period are the figures for the productivity of investment (capital-output ratios) in Tables 14 and 15 in the following section. As these figures indicate, enormous amounts of investment produced only modest increases in production or none at all. The growth rate of national income for the entire 1958–65 period was less than half that of the 1966–78 period, and it took almost twice the level of

3 For example, grain output, which accounts for a substantial part of agricultural production, grew at an annual average rate of 4 percent in the 1966–70 period. Electric power output, a crude indicator of what was happening in the industrial sector, in 1970 was 71 percent above 1965, indicating an annual average rate of growth over the five-year period of 11 percent.

4 These figures on agriculture are all taken from *Chung-kuo nung-yeh nien-chien, 1980* (Chinese agricultural yearbook), 34–36, 38.

5 The industrial data on which this discussion is based are taken from State Statistical Bureau, *Statistical yearbook of China, 1981*, 255–31.

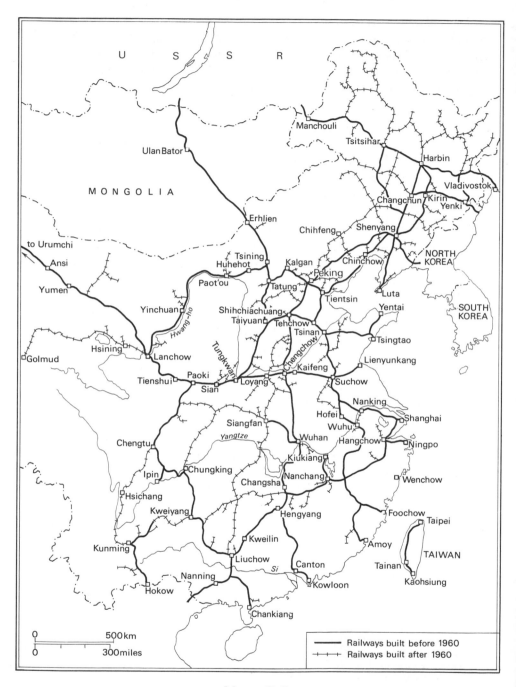

MAP 8. Railways

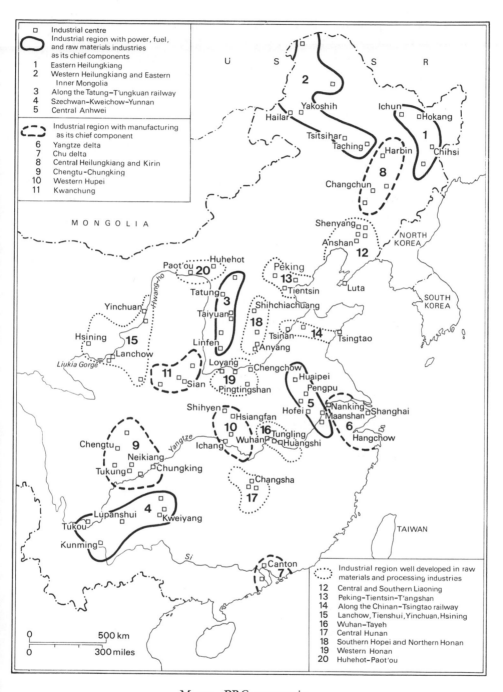

Legend:

□ Industrial centre

⬭ Industrial region with power, fuel,
and raw materials industries
as its chief components
1 Eastern Heilungkiang
2 Western Heilungkiang and Eastern
Inner Mongolia
3 Along the Tatung–T'ungkuan railway
4 Szechwan–Kweichow–Yunnan
5 Central Anhwei

⬭ (dashed) Industrial region with manufacturing
as its chief component
6 Yangtze delta
7 Chu delta
8 Central Heilungkiang and Kirin
9 Chengtu–Chungking
10 Western Hupei
11 Kwanchung

⸬ Industrial region well developed in raw
materials and processing industries
12 Central and Southern Liaoning
13 Peking–Tientsin–T'angshan
14 Along the Chinan–Tsingtao railway
15 Lanchow, Tienshui, Yinchuan, Hsining
16 Wuhan–Tayeh
17 Central Hunan
18 Southern Hopei and Northern Honan
19 Western Honan
20 Huhehot–Paot'ou

U S S R

MONGOLIA

NORTH KOREA

SOUTH KOREA

TAIWAN

Map labels: Yakoshih, Ichun, Hokang, Hailar, Tsitsihar, Taching, Harbin, Chihsi, Changchun, Shenyang, Anshan, Luta, Peking, Tientsin, Huhehot, Paot'ou, Tatung, Yinchuan, Taiyuan, Shihchiachuang, Hsining, Lanchow, Linfen, Tsinan, Tsingtao, Anyang, Loyang, Chengchow, Sian, Pingtingshan, Huaipei, Pengpu, Shihyen, Hsiangfan, Hofei, Nanking, Maanshan, Shanghai, Chengtu, Neikiang, Wuhan, Tungling, Huangshi, Hangchow, Tukung, Chungking, Ichang, Changsha, Lupanshui, Kweiyang, Tukou, Kunming, Canton

Hwang-ho, Yangtze, Si

Liukia Gorge

0   500 km
0   300 miles

MAP 9. PRC: economic

investment to produce a given increase in output in the former period as in the latter. In short, the Great Leap was a very expensive disaster. The Cultural Revolution at its peak (1967–68) was a severe but essentially temporary interruption of a magnitude experienced by most countries at one time or another.

The most damaging effects of the Cultural Revolution were not the result of the chaos of the Red Guard years. They were the result of the long-term impact of following a particular strategy of development and the quality of planning and management that accompanied that strategy. Thus, China's long-term economic problems could not be solved simply by bringing in the army to quell the Red Guards. More fundamental changes in strategy were required, but Chinese planners did not fully realize this until a decade later.

INDUSTRIAL DEVELOPMENT STRATEGY, 1966–1976

China's basic industrial development strategy was set in the 1st Five-Year Plan, of 1953–57. Inspired by the experience of the Soviet Union in build-ing a modern industrial sector on a crash basis, China hoped to accom-plish a similar transformation from an even more backward industrial foundation. The first phases of this process were described in *CHOC*, Volume 14. The question here is whether the Cultural Revolution altered this strategy in any significant way. Did the Cultural Revolution lead to a significant change in sectoral emphasis – a shift away from heavy indus-try, for example?

The short answer to these questions is no; the basic industrial strategy laid down in the 1950s continued unabated right through the late 1960s and early 1970s. Certain major changes in direction, in fact, did not come before 1979, others, not before 1977. It is interesting to speculate whether this consistency in policy was deliberate or the result of paralysis among economic planners during the Cultural Revolution. Some outside obser-vers have gone so far as to suggest that little planning of any kind took place in the late 1960s and early 1970s, but as the data in Table 11 indicate, plans were drawn up and, except for the years when disruption was severe, these plans had some relationship to economic results. Given the weakness of the bureaucracy and particularly the planners during the Cul-tural Revolution, the explanation that there was planning but that plan-ners' paralysis prevented serious consideration of changes in priorities is the more plausible one. If most new ideas are going to be attacked, the safest course is to continue doing whatever you were doing before.

This emphasis on caution was reinforced by the fact that much of the

TABLE 11

Realization of plan targets (actual output as percentage of plan target)

	1967	1969	1972	1977	1979	1980
Gross value of industrial output						
(% increase)	–	–	65.3	178.8	106.3	145.0
Light industry	–	–	–	–	115.7	–
Heavy industry	–	–	–	–	101.3	–
Steel	60.5	83.3	101.7	103.2	107.8	112.5
Coal	76.3	96.7	106.2	112.2	102.4	93.9
Petroleum	81.6	117.5	101.5	100.7	96.5	100.0
Electric power	81.5	95.9	101.6	107.1	–	103.7
Cement	67.1	–	–	–	–	–
Chemical fertilizer	99.5	–	–	–	–	–
Cotton yarn	76.9	75.9	103.9	106.9	–	110.5
Basic construction investment						
(within budget)	64.5	86.2	94.0	124.9	116.3	144.9

Sources: The actual output data were taken from State Statistical Bureau, *Statistical yearbook of China, 1981*, 225–31, and ibid., *1986*, 246–48. The plan data are from Fang Wei-chung, ed., *Chung-hua jen-min kung-ho-kuo ching-chi ta-shih-chi (1949–1980)* (A record of the major economic events of the Chinese People's Republic [1949–1980]), 430–31, 451–52, 488–89, 578, 606, 624.

top economic leadership was purged or at least disappeared from view during the late 1960s, often not to reappear until many years later. According to one estimate, of the 316 top economic officials, roughly one-third are known to have been purged and only one-quarter appeared in public or in some other way gave evidence of still being in office. Furthermore, the higher the position held, the more likely was the person to have been purged.

An in-depth history of how the economic ministries and commissions were run during the Cultural Revolution has yet to be written, and this chapter is not the place to attempt to do so. Clearly, however, the economic organs of government were deprived of experienced leadership. Few, if any, experienced replacements existed within the ranks of the political supporters of the Cultural Revolution. The decimated ranks of the economic ministries and commissions, therefore, were left to carry on as best they could. Lacking the strong leadership needed if major changes were to be made, the safest and only practical course was to continue on the preexisting course in determining what to produce and where to allocate investment.

If this view of how lower-level economic administrators kept the system running is correct, it may also help explain why Lin Piao's death in 1971 had little discernible impact on economic performance. The output of most industrial products grew through 1972 and 1973, and capital construction investment stayed at a high level, roughly double the level of 1966–69. Even farm income grew slightly despite a severe drought in 1972 that did reduce grain output. There were declines in certain key industrial products in 1974 and 1976, notably in steel and machine tools, but energy output and many other products grew even in those politically disruptive years. Thus, even the turmoil of a year such as 1976, which saw the deaths of Chou En-lai and Mao Tse-tung plus the T'ang-shan earthquake, did not have a lasting impact on economic performance comparable to that of 1967–68 and even less to that of the Great Leap Forward.

What was the industrial strategy that Chinese planners pursued so consistently? The core ideas are simple and can be described in a formal mathematical model without doing violence to reality. The model, usually called the Feldman–Mahalanobis model after the Soviet and Indian economists who independently developed it, makes several key assumptions.[6] The full model will not be presented here, but the assumptions will be described because Chinese planners, like their Soviet counterparts, at least implicitly operated under similar principles.

The key to the model is the belief that the most important choice facing planners is whether to invest in producer goods or in consumer goods – in items such as machinery and electric power, which can be used to manufacture other products, or in items such as clothing and food to be consumed. Two assumptions are necessary if one is to trace out the implications of this choice:

1. That the capital-output ratio is fixed: that is, that a given amount of investment will produce the same increase in output year after year.

2. That foreign trade is small relative to the size of the economy and to the size of total investment: If foreign trade is large relative to investment, planners can invest in consumer industries, then export these products in exchange for producer goods. If foreign trade is small, those producer goods must be manufactured at home or the country will run out of what is needed to construct new plant and equipment, and economic growth will come to a halt.

If these assumptions are valid, then it follows that economic growth

---

6 A good and reasonably simple discussion of this model can be found in Hywell G. Jones, *An introduction to modern theories of economic growth*, 110–19.

will be more rapid as a greater share of investment goes to producer goods. If the share of investment in producer goods is raised, consumption will suffer in the short run, but over time consumption as well will grow more rapidly and will eventually reach levels above what would have occurred if investment had been directed more to consumption in the first place. The only reason why planners would not channel most investment into producer goods is that in the short run consumption may be so low that people will starve (or revolt).

How valid were the key assumptions of this model in China in the 1960s and 1970s? The low foreign trade ratio or closed economy assumption, for one, was a reasonable approximation of reality. Chinese foreign trade and national income figures are presented in Table 12. Before the late 1970s, imports as a percentage of national income generally fluctuated between 5 and 7 percent. If all imports had been investment goods, China would still have provided less than 20 percent of its investment needs through such purchases abroad since investment in the late 1960s and 1970s was running at 30 percent of national income.[7] Four-fifths of all investment goods would have had to be manufactured in China. In fact, one-third or more of imports were either consumer goods or intermediate products, leaving the equivalent of only 3 percent of national income for imports of investment goods.[8]

This low foreign trade ratio was in part a reflection of China's large size and in part the result of deliberate policy choices. For reasons only partially understood, countries with large populations trade less (relative to their national product) than do small countries. India in the mid-1960s, for example, also imported an amount equivalent to 6 percent of its national product, and for Japan the figure was 9 percent. Smaller countries, such as Malaysia and Thailand, in contrast, had import ratios of 41 percent and 20 percent respectively.[9]

But as will become clear when policy changes in 1977 and 1979 and their impact are discussed, China's trade ratio could have been higher if planners had so desired. Chinese planners instead, like their Soviet counterparts, set out to minimize the nation's dependence on foreign trade, not just in the Cultural Revolution period, but beginning in the 1950s. As the figures in Table 12 indicate, the trade ratio fluctuated from one period

---

7 If imports are 5 percent of national income and investment is 30 percent, then, if all imports were made up of investment goods, 16.7 percent of investment would have been provided by imports (5/30) and the rest from domestic production.

8 Chinese figures indicate that 80 percent of all imports were "means of production," but the Chinese include many intermediate products such as textile fibers, rubber, etc.

9 These figures are from Hollis Chenery and Moises Syrquin, *Patterns of development, 1950–1970*, 192–95.

TABLE 12

Foreign trade ratios

	(1) National income	(2) Exports	(3) Imports	(4) (5) Foreign trade ratios	
				(2) ÷ (1)	(3) ÷ (1)
	(billions of current JMP)				
1952	58.9	2.71	3.75	.046	.064
1957	90.8	5.45	5.00	.060	.055
1962	92.4	4.71	3.38	.051	.037
1965	138.7	6.31	5.53	.045	.040
1970	192.6	5.68	5.61	.029	.029
1975	250.3	14.30	14.74	.057	.059
1978	301.0	16.77	18.74	.056	.062
1980	366.7	27.24	29.14	.074	.079
1982	426.1	41.43	35.77	.097	.084
1986	779.0	108.20	149.86	.139	.192

Sources: State Statistical Bureau, *Statistical yearbook of China, 1981*, 20, 357; ibid., *1986*, 40, 481; and State Statistical Bureau, *Chung-kuo t'ung-chi chai-yao, 1987* (Chinese statistical summary, 1987), 4, 89.

to the next, but there was no discernible trend. The lowest import ratios were in the early 1960s in the immediate aftermath of the severe disruption and bad harvests of 1959–61 and again in 1967–70 as a result of the disruptions of 1967–69.

What then was the impact of all the Cultural Revolution rhetoric against slavish dependence on foreign products and technology? Steel, copper, chemical fertilizer, and many other imports reached record highs in the late 1960s. Grain and other consumer goods declined, but mainly as a result of better domestic harvests. Imports of machinery and equipment did fall sharply in 1968 and 1969, probably in part as a result of the hostility of the "left" to foreign technology, but the general disruption of industry in 1967 and 1968 presumably was also a factor.[10] Overall the nominal value of total imports in 1966–70 was roughly the same as in 1953–57, and 1971–75 imports, again in nominal terms, were roughly double the level of 1953–57. When inflation and the rise in real national income are taken into account, the foreign trade ratio of 1966–70 was well below that of 1953–57, but had recovered to that earlier level by 1975. In short, even in the sphere of foreign trade the Cultural Revolution was more a continuation of than a departure from the closed economy strategy initiated during the 1st Five-Year Plan.

10 Imports of machinery, equipment, and scientific instruments fell from $348.7 million in 1966 to $136 million and $131.8 million in 1968 and 1969 before bouncing back to $276.6 million in 1970 (United States, Central Intelligence Agency, *People's Republic of China: international trade handbook* [December, 1972], 25).

TABLE 13

Investment in capital construction by sector (in %)

	1953–57	1958–62	1963–65	1966–70	1971–75	1976–80
Heavy industry	38.7	54.9	48.0	54.5	52.1	48.0
Construction	3.9	1.4	2.2	1.9	1.7	1.9
Geological prospecting	2.6	1.2	0.4	0.5	0.7	1.3
Transport	16.4	13.8	13.3	16.4	18.9	13.5
Subtotal	61.6	71.3	63.9	73.3	73.4	64.7
Light industry	6.8	6.5	4.1	4.7	6.1	6.9
Agriculture	7.6	11.4	18.4	11.4	10.3	11.0
Commerce	3.9	2.0	2.6	2.3	3.0	3.9
Education, health, etc.	8.1	3.9	6.0	3.0	3.3	5.7
Civil public utilities	2.6	2.3	3.0	1.9	2.0	4.2
Other	9.4	2.6	2.0	3.4	1.9	3.7
Subtotal	38.4	28.7	36.1	26.7	26.6	35.4
Total	100.0	100.0	100.0	100.0	100.0	100.0

Source: State Statistical Bureau, *Statistical yearbook of China, 1981*, 300–301.

Given a closed economy, China, like the Soviet Union before it, followed the main prescription for high growth laid out in the Feldman–Mahalanobis model. The lion's share of investment was directed toward the producer goods sector, not toward plants that would turn out more products for consumption. The classification of items in Table 13 is not precise, but the basic message is clear. Three-quarters of all investment went to make machines to make more machines or to provide the infrastructure required by that sector. The share of producer goods in 1963–65 was down, but more because of the immediate requirements of recovery from the 1959–61 crisis than from any long-term change in strategy. It made little sense to put most investment into new heavy industry plants when existing ones were underutilized and the population was barely meeting its minimum subsistence needs. Once the recovery was over, the share going to producer goods jumped back to Great Leap Forward levels.

This strategy, according to the model on which it was based, should have led to a high growth rate not only in national income and the producer goods industry but also in consumer goods and the standard of living of the people. In fact, the only prediction that the model forecast correctly was that the rate of investment would rise as a share of national income. The growth rate of national income did not rise – it fell; and the

TABLE 14

Investment-output ratios in selected industries

	1953–57	1958–65	1966–70	1971–75	1976–80
Electric power					
Investment	2.978	11.095	6.860	12.939	21.874
Increase in output					
(billion kwh)	32.24	34.1	75.3	75.2	77.25
Ratio	.092	.325	.091	.172	.283
Metallurgical industry					
Investment	4.661	20.317	9.879	17.308	18.969
Increase in rolled					
steel output					
(million tons)	6.88	–7.66	7.55	2.24	9.24
Ratio	.677	–	1.308	7.716	2.05
Machine building					
Investment	3.847	14.129	7.409	21.676	17.846
Increase in machine					
tool output					
(thousands)	99.6	–69.0	116.4	15.9	–61.5
Ratio	.039	–	.064	1.36	–
Coal					
Investment	2.968	11.213	4.665	9.074	13.625
Increase in output					
(million tons)	.011	0.0	.026	.063	.192
Transport					
Investment	9.015	21.708	15.001	31.759	30.245
Increase in freight					
volume (billion					
tons/km)	196.0	22.0	236.0	252.0	333.0
Ratio	.046	.987	.064	.126	.091
Petroleum					
Investment	1.198	4.154	3.884	8.900	13.142
Increase in petro-					
leum output					
(million tons)	2.94	11.08	31.42	46.72	10.64
Ratio	.407	.375	.124	.190	1.24

Notes: (1) All investment figures are in billions of yuan. (2) Output figures assume a lag of two years between investment and outputs. To eliminate some of the atypical year-to-year fluctuations, three-year averages have been used. Thus, the output increase for 1953–57 is actually the increase in the annual average of 1958–60 over 1953–5, etc. The 1976–80 increase is 1980–81 over 1976–78. (3) The ratio was obtained by dividing the investment row by the increase in output.
Source: State Statistical Bureau, *Statistical yearbook of China, 1981*, 227–31, 283, 300–302.

rate of increase in consumption fell as well. Data on consumption will be presented later, but the first task is to explain why events did not work out as Chinese planners hoped and the model forecast.

As is so often the case, the model itself was sound, but the assumptions

TABLE 15

The marginal capital-output ratio

	(1) Accumulation (as % of net material product)	(2) Growth rate of real net material product in 1980 prices	(3) Implied capital- output ratio (1) ÷ (2)
1953–57	24.2	6.62	3.66
1958–62	30.8	−4.30	–
1963–65	22.7	8.05	2.82
1966–70	26.3	6.50	4.05
1971–75	33.0	5.26	6.27
1976–80	33.2	5.57	5.96
1981–85	30.8	9.95	3.10

Note: The estimates of the growth rate of net material product (national income in Chinese termi-nology) were estimated by first deriving the sectoral deflation indexes and then using those deflation indexes to convert net material product in current prices into net material product in constant prices.
Source: State Statistical Bureau, *Statistical yearbook of China, 1986,* 40, 41, 49.

needed to make it work were invalid in the Chinese context. The key wrong assumption was that the capital-output ratio was fixed – that given levels of investment would produce the same level of output year after year. In fact, China's capital-output ratio began climbing in the late 1960s and early 1970s so that given levels of investment led to smaller and smaller increases in output.

The data needed to make this point are flawed, but certain relevant figures are presented in Tables 14 and 15. The statistics in Table 14 are not capital-output ratios in the strict sense, but the behavior of these ratios should be roughly similar to the behavior of the true capital-output ratios in these industries. Together the sectors represented in Table 14 accounted for 60 percent of all capital construction investment and most of the investment relevant to the producer goods sector.

What do the ratios show? In the 5th FYP (1976–80) period, it took three times as much investment to produce a kilowatt hour of electricity as it did in the 3rd FYP (1966–70), nearly twice as much investment to produce a ton of steel, and 40 percent more investment per ton kilometer of transport. Discounting for inflation, different assumptions about the underlying lags between the time investment funds are spent and the beginning of production would alter these results, but not the overall conclusion.[11] China was getting less and less for its money. The impact on a nationwide basis is reflected in the data in Table 15.

11 The inflation rate in Chinese prices was very modest in these periods.

TABLE 16

Real and nominal wages and rural collective incomes (in yuan per year)

	Average annual wage in state sector		Rural collective distributed income per capita	
	Nominal	Real (1952 prices)	Nominal	Real
1952	446	446	—	—
1953–57	559	522	41.75[a]	38.8
1958–62	546	461	42.9	35.8
1963–65	651	530	48.7	39.2
1966–70	623	525	59.5[a]	50.1
1971–75	614	513	63.8	54.4
1976–80	672	529	74.2	60.2

Note: Real wages were obtained by dividing nominal wages by the cost-of-living index for workers and staff. There is no appropriate price index for rural areas that would eliminate both changes in prices of purchased industrial goods and changes in accounting prices of goods distributed in kind. For lack of a better alternative, the general retail price index was used.

[a] Data are for 1956–57 and 1970 only.

Sources: *Chung-kuo nung-yeh nien-chien, 1980*, 41; State Statistical Bureau, *Statistical yearbook of China, 1981*, 411–12, 435–36.

We will speculate later in this chapter about the causes of this rapidly rising ratio. Declining worker incentives and bad planning are part of the story. Newer petroleum fields may have been in more difficult areas to develop, and new railroad lines may have been through particularly unfavorable terrain. Whatever the reasons, the national income growth rate was clearly falling, and because the investment rate was rising, the amount left over for consumption had little room for growth.

Consumption was further squeezed in the late 1960s by a rapid increase in defense spending, which according to Western estimates, rose from 24 billion yuan in 1965 to more than 40 billion yuan by 1971. This rise in defense spending may also have contributed to the increase in the capital-output ratio if much of this expenditure was for investment in the production of military equipment. Whatever the case, Lin Piao's fall brought this expansion to a halt. The military budget fell by several billion yuan in 1972 and then stabilized around 40 billion yuan until China's 1979 invasion of Vietnam.

Some indication of what was happening to consumption can be observed in the wage and rural income data in Table 16. Real wages did not rise at all between the 1st and 5th FYP periods. Rural collective income per capita per year did rise, but at a rate just under 2 percent per annum. Actually, urban income also increased because the ratio of employed workers to family members rose. Overall, between 1957 and 1978 national consumption rose at an annual rate of 4.5 percent a year or 2.5 percent per capita given a population growth rate of 2 percent.[12] At 2.5 percent per year, the material living standard of the Chinese people would double every twenty-eight years, a not insignificant accomplishment by the standards of the nineteenth-century experience of the United States or the United Kingdom. But 2.5 percent is a far cry from the promises of 5 percent a year and more that the Soviet model of growth seemed to hold out to China in the 1950s. At a 5 percent growth rate, consumption per capita would have risen fourfold between 1952 and 1980, and real wages would not have stagnated.

CHANGING INDUSTRIAL STRATEGIES, 1977–1980

Industrial strategy during the first two years after Mao's death in late 1976 represented only a limited departure from the industrial policies of the past. The key changes from the standpoint of industrial strategy were the increased emphasis on going abroad for foreign technology and the renewed reliance on material incentives to motivate greater and more efficient effort on the part of workers and farmers.

Planners in 1977 and 1978, however, do not seem to have recognized fully the significance for industrial investment policies of this shift in emphasis. Their thinking at the time was represented by the attempt to dust off and implement the Ten-Year Plan (1976–85) originally developed prior to Mao's death.[13] Steel output was to more than double by 1985 to 60 million tons and was still seen as the "key link" in industrial development. Of the 120 large-scale projects planned, 10 were iron and steel complexes; 9, nonferrous metal complexes; 8, coal mines; 10, oil and gas fields; 30, power stations; 6, new trunk railways; and 5, key harbors. Investment over the eight years remaining in the ten was to "far exceed" the total of the previous twenty-eight years combined. In short, the

---

12 These consumption estimates were obtained by taking the Chinese estimates of indexes of real national income and by removing the share in accumulation, leaving an index of consumption. China's method of linking its national income indexes may slightly overstate the growth rate and hence the consumption growth rate would also be overstated.

13 The Ten-Year Plan was discussed by the State Council in the summer of 1975, and this was followed by a draft plan that was approved by the Political Bureau but attacked by the Gang of Four. After Mao's death the plan was revised and presented to the National People's Congress in February 1978 for approval. See Hua Kuo-feng's "Report on the Work of the Government" at the First Session of the Fifth National People's Congress, 26 February 1978, *PR*, 10 (10 March 1978), 19.

Ten-Year Plan was a high investment–heavy industry plan of the Soviet type par excellence.

It is doubtful that much careful thought went into preparing this plan. Many important planners had yet to be rehabilitated and given positions of responsibility. Statistics were still being collected at the local level, but these figures were not being cross-checked, and in many cases were not even being compiled at the national level.[14]

One indication of the quality of the plan is the target of ten new oil fields, "ten new Ta-ch'ings," as the goal was referred to. Ten new Ta-ch'ings would have meant an increase in petroleum production from 100 million tons a year to around 400 million tons. In fact, these new oil fields were a pipe dream. Offshore exploration had not even been started. Onshore exploration was inadequate and had not come up with one new Ta-ch'ing, let alone ten, that was ripe for development. The reality in early 1978 was that Chinese petroleum output was peaking and it would take a major effort at least through 1982 to keep production from falling, but the plan was based on a severalfold rise. Instead of enjoying a large energy surplus available for export, China was about to enter a prolonged period of severe energy shortage. Planning for the steel sector was not much better than that for petroleum. One Western estimate indicated that the Chinese might have to spend as much as $40 billion in foreign exchange to accomplish the 60-million-ton target,[15] or $5 billion a year when total annual export earnings in 1978 were only $9.75 billion.

It was not just that planning was sloppy and based on poor data; planners, as already indicated, had not yet come to grips with the implications of the decisions to buy foreign technology in much greater amounts and to raise wages and the purchase prices of farm production in order to improve incentives. To increase imports significantly, China had either to increase exports significantly or to borrow abroad in large quantities. In practice, borrowing was never likely to provide more than a small fraction of China's foreign exchange needs, and so that left exports. But what kinds of exports could China hope to expand rapidly?

Agriculture, the traditional source of China's exports, directly or indirectly still provided more than half of China's foreign exchange in 1977 and 1978. But agricultural development was China's lagging sector, and the government was having trouble extracting enough food for its cities, let alone an increased surplus for sale abroad. Furthermore, with rising

14 This statement is based on, among other sources, a briefing given to an American Economic Delegation in Nanking in the fall of 1979 by Kiangsu statistical authorities.
15 United States, National Foreign Assessment Center, *China: the steel industry in the 1970s and 1980s.*

wages and farm incomes under the new incentive plan, the domestic demand for food would rise even more rapidly than in the past. Declining population growth would work the other way, but overall, China could not pay for its import requirements by exporting much larger amounts of food.

The drafters of the Ten-Year Plan may have hoped that petroleum would take up the slack, but that, as already indicated, was a vain hope. The only other possibility was to export manufactures, but what kind of manufactures? The plan called for more steel and machinery, but was China to become a major exporter of the products of heavy industry? To a degree, perhaps, but the efficient producers of these items are typically the more advanced industrial nations, not poor developing nations like China. That left consumer goods manufactures. Consumer manufactures were what fueled the export drives of China's neighbors: Japan in the 1920s and 1930s and South Korea, Taiwan, Hong Kong, and Singapore in the 1960s and 1970s.

China's emphasis on material incentives also drove the country in the direction of a greater emphasis on consumer goods, both industrial and agricultural. Increases in wages and farm prices would mean little if the new money could not buy anything. In fact, increased money incomes in the absence of expanded consumer goods production would be counter-productive. Not only would individual consumption not increase, but rationing of what goods were available would have to be tightened either formally (ration coupons) or informally (long queues).

There was, therefore, a basic contradiction between the goals of the Ten-Year Plan and the emerging outward-looking incentive-based strategy. As the year 1978 progressed, either existing planners became aware of this contradiction, or others who understood it all along regained influence, or both. Whatever the case, in December 1978 a decision was made to reorder industrial development priorities, at least temporarily.

The communiqué issued 22 December 1978 by the Eleventh CC's Third Plenum gave an indication of what was to come. More than half of the discussion of economic measures in the communiqué was devoted to the problems of raising agricultural output and the living standard of the people.[16] Of even greater significance was the election of Ch'en Yun as a CC vice-chairman and a member of the Politburo Standing Committee. Ch'en had been the behind-the-scenes architect of the recovery policies of the 1961–65 period; earlier, at the CCP's Eighth Congress in 1956, he had made a major speech advocating a greater use of the mar-

---

16 "Communiqué of the Third Plenary Session of the 11th Central Committee of the Communist Party of China" (adopted 22 December 1978), PR, 52 (29 December 1978), 11–13.

ket and limitations on excessive centralization.[17] Although he had been one of the central economic figures in the 1950s when the Soviet-type industrial strategy had been introduced, Ch'en was known as someone who had a keen appreciation of the dangers of overemphasis on heavy industry.

The public unveiling of the new priorities came at the meeting of the NPC in June 1979. Yü Ch'iu-li, head of the State Planning Commission, called for an emphasis on agriculture, light industry, and foreign trade development as top priorities. Planned heavy industry growth in 1979 at 7.6 percent was, for a change, to be below the planned light industry growth rate of 8.3 percent.[18] Investment in heavy industry was to be cut back from 54.7 percent of the total in 1978 to 46.8 percent in 1979, and the overall investment amount was to be held at the same level as 1978.

Plan targets are not always a good guide to what in fact to expect from actual performance. The Soviet Union's plans frequently call for greater emphasis on consumer goods, but when the year is over, heavy industry has retained its priority position in the actual allocation of funds and key inputs. In China, however, the shift in priorities was real.

Data for the first three years of what is called the "period of readjustment" are presented in Table 17. The indicated changes in priorities are dramatic. Not only did light industry grow faster in each of the three years; in 1981 the output of heavy industry actually fell. Perhaps the most significant change was the rapid growth of exports. Between 1952 and 1978, export growth averaged only 7 percent a year and the growth in real terms was even lower. In the 1979–81 period, the growth in nominal terms was at four times that rate (29 percent a year), and the difference in real terms was nearly threefold (18.6 percent a year).[19] Most of this increase in exports came from the sale abroad of manufactured products of which textiles was the largest but by no means the only item. The share of "industrial and mineral products" in exports, a figure that excludes textiles, rose from 37.4 percent to 51.8 percent of total exports between 1978 and 1980, owing in part to the rise in petroleum prices in 1979, but also because of the rapid expansion of exports such as bicycles, sewing machines, chinaware, and even machine tools.[20] By 1981, exports had

17 Chen Yun [Ch'en Yun], *Eighth National Congress of the Communist Party of China*, 2. 157–76.
18 These figures are from Yü Ch'iu-li, "Report on the 1979 draft national economic plan," *JMJP*, 29 June 1979, 1,3.
19 We do not have as yet an appropriate price index that can be used to deflate Chinese foreign trade data for this entire period. The 1979–81 figures in real terms are from *Chung-kuo tui-wai mao-inien-chien, 1984* China's foreign trade yearbook, 1984, 4.5.
20 In 1981, the Chinese changed the way they categorize foreign trade items, and available current data make comparisons of comparable categories between 1981 and earlier years impossible.

TABLE 17

Economic indicators during the first phase of the readjustment period, 1979–1981

Growth rates (%)	1979	1980	1981
Heavy industry	7.7	1.4	−4.7
Light industry	9.6	18.4	14.1
All industry	8.5	8.7	4.1
Agriculture	8.6	2.7	5.7
Investment in capital construction[a]	4.2	7.9	−20.7
Exports[a]			
Nominal	26.2	28.7	35.0
Real	25.6	20.3	10.6
Imports[a]			
Nominal	29.6	20.0	26.2
Real	15.7	6.5	−6.7

[a] Data for capital construction, exports, and imports are in current prices. All other percentages were derived from data in constant prices.
Source: State Statistical Bureau, *Statistical yearbook of China, 1981*, 136, 210, 299, 357, 390.

climbed to 9.5 percent of national income or nearly double the ratio of the previous quarter century.[21] In addition, the PRC had access to large subsidized credits from Japan and Western Europe and from its decision to take over China's seat in the International Monetary Fund and the World Bank. China no longer had a "closed" economy, and by opening up, China had greatly increased the options available to those setting future development strategy.

Military expenditures were also to be held down. The war with Vietnam did lead to a temporary burst of military spending in 1978 and 1979, but expenditures were cut back to mid-1970s levels by 1980. Military modernization was one of the "four modernizations," but there was little point in massive outlays to expand the number of obsolete tanks and aircraft. True modernization required first the upgrading of Chinese technology that could then form the base for the design and manufacture of advanced weapons systems.

This dramatic shift in priorities may in part have been a conscious move in the direction of the growth strategies of China's East Asian

21 "State Statistical Bureau report on the results of the 1981 National Economic Plan," *Chung-kuo ching-chi nien-chien, 1982*, 8.79, 82–83.

neighbors, but it was also in part making a virtue out of necessity. It was not just that investment was becoming less and less productive – that conceivably could have been tackled through managerial reforms without an accompanying change in industrial priorities. But managerial reforms could not overcome the fact that China did not have enough energy output to sustain a high-growth heavy industry strategy.

Total energy production between 1952 and 1978 grew at an average annual rate of 10.3 percent. The slower growth rate of coal production was more than offset in the 1960s and early 1970s by the rapid development of the Ta-ch'ing, Sheng-li, and other oil fields. Between 1978 and 1981, the increase in total energy output came virtually to a halt, rising at a minuscule 0.2 percent a year over the three-year period. Neglect in exploration efforts in earlier years, in the development of new coal mines, and in building the railroads to move the coal to where it could be used, had all taken their toll. If Chinese planners had continued the inefficient heavy industry strategy of the past, overall growth in national income would also have ground to a halt. Continued growth after 1978 was possible only if China shifted to industries in the consumer goods sector that required much less electric power per unit of output and began investing in energy-efficient equipment. Planners also began a major investment program to develop new sources of petroleum and coal and a supporting transport network, but these investments, even with the participation of the major international energy corporations, would not begin paying off in a major way until the mid-1980s. The readjustment period, therefore, was really the final outcome of the mistakes and inefficiencies of the Cultural Revolution industrial strategy and performance.

ACCELERATING INDUSTRIAL GROWTH, 1982–1987

The readjustment period in industry was expected to last through much of the 1980s. As it turned out, however, 1981 was the only year when overall growth slowed to the levels set by the readjustment targets in the 6th FYP of industrial growth of only 4 percent per year.[22] By 1982 China was in the early stages of an economic boom that was to continue throughout much of the 1980s.

Several events intervened to make the readjustment plan obsolete soon after it was introduced. To begin with, total energy production, which

---

22 *Sixth Five-Year Plan of the People's Republic of China for Economic and Social Development (1981–1985)*, 23.

TABLE 18

Growth of foreign trade

	1970	1975	1978	1980	1983	1986
			(in million U.S. dollars)			
Total exports	2,260	7,260	9,750	18,120	22,230	30,940
Total imports	2,330	7,490	10,890	20,020	21,390	42,920
Balance of trade	− 70	− 230	− 1,140	− 1,900	840	− 11,980
			1971–78		1979–83	1984–86
			(in % per year)			
Growth rate of exports:						
Value			20.0		17.9	11.7
Quantity			7.8		16.9	n.a.
Growth rate of imports:						
Value			21.3		11.2	26.1
Quantity			12.9		6.7	n.a.

Source: State Statistical Bureau, *Statistical yearbook of China, 1986,* 481; State Statistical Bureau, *Chung-kuo t'ung-chi chai-yao, 1987,* 89; *Chung-kuo tui-wai ching-chi mai-i nien-chien, 1984,* 4.5.

had fallen in 1980 and 1981, resumed growth in 1982, and by 1984 the growth rate of energy output had surpassed 9 percent a year, a figure comparable to the rates achieved in the early 1970s, before falling back in 1986 to growth of only 3 percent. No dramatic offshore oil discoveries or other breakthroughs accounted for renewed energy growth. These increases resulted instead from a broad effort to expand coal production, to use imported technology to extract more petroleum than had previously proved possible from existing fields, and a modest expansion in hydroelectric power, notably the completion of the first phase of the Ko-chou dam. Demands for energy by Chinese industry still exceeded supply by a wide margin, but excess demand is a characteristic of the Soviet-style bureaucratic-command economy.

Of equal or greater significance was the loosening of the foreign exchange constraint on Chinese industry. China's initial efforts to expand exports proved remarkably successful. Exports in the three years after 1978 more than doubled in nominal terms, wiping out the trade deficit by 1981 and generating a sizable surplus in 1982 despite a rapid increase in imports (Tables 18 and 20). The increase in exports was the result of an expansion in manufactured exports and the 1979 run-up in the price of oil. Petroleum exports briefly accounted for a quarter of all Chinese exports before falling off as the price of oil declined. (See Table 19.)

On top of this expansion of exports, China began to borrow significant

TABLE 19

Structure of Chinese exports

	Total exports (million U.S.$)	Manufactured exports (% of total)	Of which: heavy and chemical (% of total)	Primary exports (% of total)	Of which: petroleum and mining products (% of total)
1953	1,022	20.6	8.3	79.4	0.8
1957	1,597	36.4	10.1	63.6	1.1
1965	2,228	48.8	17.8	51.2	3.1
1970	2,260	46.5	12.8	53.5	2.8
1975	7,264	43.6	12.5	56.4	15.0
1978	9,745	46.5	10.4	53.5	13.8
1980	18,272	46.6	12.9	53.4	25.1
1983	22,197	53.8	22.0	46.2	21.2
1986	30,942	63.6	n.a.	36.4	11.9

Sources: Chung-kuo tui-wai ching-chi mao-yi nien-chien, 1984, 4.9; State Statistical Bureau, Chung-kuo t'ung-chi chai-yao, 1987, 89

TABLE 20

Financing China's trade deficit (all figures in million U.S. dollars)

	1978	1979–82	1983	1984	1985	1986
		(average per year)				
Balance of trade Deficit (−) or Surplus (+)	−1,140	−55	+840	−1,270	−14,890	−11,980
Foreign exchange from tourism	263	662	941	1,131	1,250	1,530
Foreign loans utilized	n.a.	2,718	1,065	1,286	2,688	5,015
Foreign direct investment utilized	n.a.	442	916	1,419	1,959	2,244
Foreign exchange Reserves – end of year (excluding gold)	2,154[a]	5,079	14,342	14,420	11,913	10,514

[a] This figure is for 1979.
Sources: State Statistical Bureau, Statistical yearbook of China, 1986, 499, 530; State Statistical Bureau, Chung-kuo t'ung-chi chai-yao, 1987, 80, 93.

amounts of money from abroad and to open the gates to large-scale tourism. Initially this borrowing took the form of subsidized credits from China's major trading partners. In 1980 China took its seat in the International Monetary Fund and the World Bank, and the first World Bank loan to China was approved in 1981.[23] Decisions were also made to allow direct foreign investment in the form of joint ventures and other arrangements. The decision to allow joint ventures meant that China had to codify this system formally with a joint venture law, new tax laws, and other laws that would introduce some predictability and stability into relations between foreign investors and the Chinese government. No amount of codification, however, could fully protect foreign investors from the uncertainties connected with an economic system where most inputs were allocated by the state rather than being freely available through a market. Nevertheless, companies in Japan and the United States began to invest sizable amounts in the hope of future profits. By far the largest amount of direct investment, however, came from Hong Kong and went into Kwangtung province next door to the colony. In the early 1980s personal connections based on cultural, linguistic, and family ties were probably a surer protection against the uncertainties of dealing with the Chinese government than was the country's fledgling legal system.

As the figures in Table 20 indicate, China was receiving $3 billion to $4 billion a year from tourism, loans, and direct investment at a time when the country had either a trade surplus or a small deficit. The result was a rapid run-up in China's foreign exchange reserves. These reserves passed $11 billion in 1982 and $14 billion in 1983. Despite increases in borrowing, China became a net lender on international financial markets. The combination of an investment slowdown caused by readjustment policies and this rapid increase in foreign exchange resources meant that China was accumulating more foreign exchange than it could effectively utilize. To continue the low-growth-rate targets of the readjustment period with this accumulating surplus made little economic sense.

Finally the Chinese leadership, somewhat to its surprise, found itself in the middle of an agricultural boom in the early 1980s. The year 1980 itself experienced a poor harvest after two very good years, but output bounced back in 1981 and then soared in 1982 and 1983. The reasons for this accelerated growth will be discussed later in this chapter. The point of mentioning it here is that slow agricultural growth in China places limits on the pace of development of industries. Agriculture is a major source of inputs to consumer goods industry. Agricultural exports are a source of foreign exchange, and agricultural imports were important users of foreign exchange. Chinese grain imports, for example, grew from

---

23 Harold K. Jacobson and Michel Oksenberg, "China and the keystone international economic organizations."

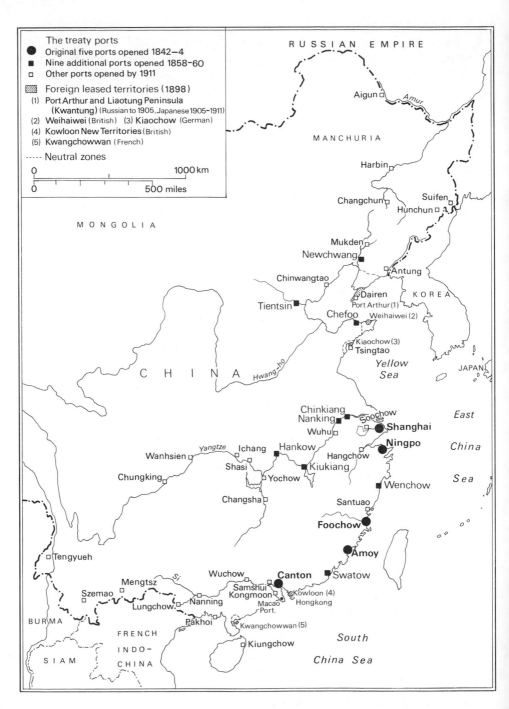

The treaty ports
- ● Original five ports opened 1842–4
- ■ Nine additional ports opened 1858–60
- □ Other ports opened by 1911
- ▨ Foreign leased territories (1898)
  - (1) Port Arthur and Liaotung Peninsula (Kwantung) (Russian to 1905, Japanese 1905–1911)
  - (2) Weihaiwei (British) (3) Kiaochow (German)
  - (4) Kowloon New Territories (British)
  - (5) Kwangchowwan (French)
- ----- Neutral zones

0   1000 km
0   500 miles

RUSSIAN EMPIRE

MANCHURIA

MONGOLIA

CHINA

KOREA

JAPAN

Aigun   Amur

Harbin

Changchun   Suifen
                   Hunchun

Mukden
Newchwang   Antung

Chinwangtao   Dairen
                     Port Arthur (1)
Tientsin   Chefoo   Weihaiwei (2)

                  Kiaochow (3)
                  Tsingtao

Hwang-ho   Yellow
                  Sea

Chinkiang   Soochow   East
Nanking   China
Wuhu   Shanghai
Yangtze   Hankow   Ningpo   Sea
Wanhsien   Ichang   Hangchow
          Shasi   Kiukiang
Chungking   Yochow   Wenchow
          Changsha
                  Santuao
                  Foochow

Tengyueh   Amoy

Mengtsz   Wuchow   Canton   Swatow
Szemao   Samshui   Kowloon (4)
          Kongmoon   Hongkong
Lungchow   Nanning   Macao Port.
          Pakhoi   Kwangchowwan (5)
BURMA
FRENCH   Kiungchow   South
INDO-
SIAM   CHINA   China Sea

MAP 10. Treaty ports under the unequal treaties to 1911

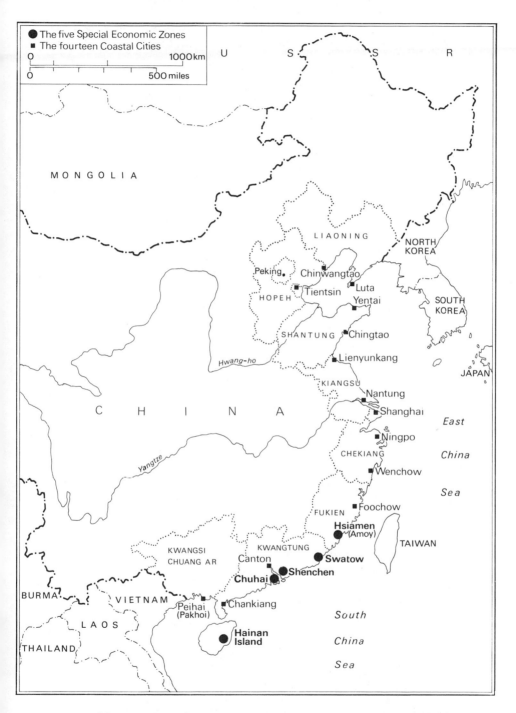

MAP 11. Coastal areas open to foreign investment, 1984

8.8 million tons in 1978 to 16.1 million tons in 1982, but fell back to only 6 million tons by 1985.[24] This fall in grain imports alone saved more than a billion dollars in foreign exchange.

The loosening of these three constraints on the economy coincided with policies introduced that had been designed to decentralize control over economic decision making further, including the allocation of investment.[25] In the 1971–79 period, for example, investment in state-owned enterprises that was carried out within the state budget was twice as large as investment in state-owned enterprises outside of the control of the budget. In the 1980–84 period, in contrast, investment in state enterprises outside the budget was 40 percent higher than that made through the budget.[26] Efforts to reassert central control over investment beginning as early as 1981, therefore, were not successful.

If the central government had been more successful in reasserting its control, it is far from clear that this would have led to measurable net benefits to the Chinese economy. What China achieved, partly as a result of earlier decentralization policies, was an industrial boom. Furthermore, the boom was concentrated to a large degree outside the state sector with its large-scale enterprises. More than half of the rise in the gross value of industrial output in the five years from 1982 through 1986 was accounted for by small- and medium-scale enterprises under collective rather than state ownership. A third of the total increase in industrial output was accounted for by enterprises in rural areas. (See Table 21.)

Rural industrialization in China began in the 1950s, but its development was aborted by the mistakes of the Great Leap Forward (1958–60). A renewed effort to develop rural industries to provide agriculture with key inputs such as fertilizer and cement was carried out in the late 1960s and early 1970s; and it is discussed at length in the section on rural development. Rural industrialization in the early 1980s, however, was different in character from these previous efforts. Much of this new rural industrial investment was concentrated in rural areas near some of China's major cities. The largest single concentration was in southern Kiangsu province around Shanghai, Wu-hsi, Nanking, and the other large cities of that region. Many of these new rural industries had subcontracting relationships with large state enterprises in the cities. Emphasis on small-scale

24 *Chung-kuo tui-wai ching-chi mao-i nien-chien, 1984*, 4. 118; and State Statistical Bureau, *Chung-kuo t'ung-chi chai-yao, 1987*, 91.
25 Barry Naughton, "Finance and planning reforms in industry," in U.S. Congress, Joint Economic Committee, *China's economy looks toward the year 2000*, 1.604–29.
26 Dwight H. Perkins, "Reforming China's economic system," *Journal of Economic Literature*, 26 (June 1988), table 2.

TABLE 21

Industrial growth, 1981–1986

	State industry	Rural collective industry	Urban collective industry and other	All industry
	(gross value of output) (billion yuan in 1980 prices)			
1981	405.44	60.10	80.04	545.58
1982	434.03	65.90	88.24	588.17
1983	474.78	78.91	100.29	653.68
1984	517.12	111.31	132.02	760.51
1985	584.02	170.28	171.28	925.58
1986	620.13	223.06	187.54	1,030.73
	annual growth rates (in %)			
1982	7.1	9.7	10.2	7.8
1983	9.4	19.7	13.7	11.2
1984	8.9	41.1	31.6	16.3
1985	12.9	53.0	29.7	21.7
1986	6.2	31.0	9.5	11.4
1982–86	8.9	30.0	18.6	13.6

Note: The figures for "Rural collective industry" and for "Total industry" include "village-run industrial enterprise output." Chinese data normally include village-run industrial output in gross agricultural output.
Sources: State Statistical Bureau, *Chung-kuo t'ung-chi chai-yao. 1987*, 24, 38; State Statistical Bureau, *Statistical yearbook of China. 1986*, 130, 227; ibid., *1984*, 194–95; ibid., *1983*, 215.

TABLE 22

Heavy and light industry: output and investment (%)

	1966–78	1979–81	1982–86
Gross value output of industry: total	10.2	7.1	11.8
Heavy industry GVO	11.8	1.3	12.5
Light industry	8.3	14.0	9.1
Share in capital construction:			
Heavy industry	50.0	40.8	38.3
Light industry	5.5	8.2	6.4
Housing	5.7	19.7	19.3

Sources: State Statistical Bureau, *Statistical yearbook of China, 1986*, 373, 375; and State Statistical Bureau, *Chung-kuo t'ung-chi chai-yao, 1987*, 65–66.

output did not mean a continuation of the readjustment period's emphasis on consumer goods. Investment in heavy industry remained below previous levels, but heavy industry output growth leapt ahead whereas the growth rate of light industry fell back to levels similar to those in the years 1966–78. (See Table 22.)

This boom nearly doubled Chinese industrial output between 1981 and

1986, but it was a development pace that could not be sustained. The major constraint on the especially rapid rate of industrial growth in 1984 and 1985, as it turned out, was foreign exchange. In 1985 China's foreign exchange reserves, especially that portion under the control of the central government, began to drop sharply. Only a major effort to expand borrowing abroad kept reserves from falling back to levels not seen since the 1970s. China's total external debt as a result grew, and may have reached $20 billion by 1987.

Accelerated industrial growth by stimulating a large annual increase in imports was the demand side of the problem. The supply-side part of the problem was caused by the slowdown in the growth of Chinese exports after 1981. The fall in petroleum prices did not have a major impact until 1986. The main difficulty was China's inability to maintain earlier growth rates of the export of manufactures. The barrier was not so much rising protectionism or the world recession abroad as it was a price system (including the exchange rate) that favored domestic over foreign sales. Enterprises could make larger profits selling on the domestic market. Devaluations of the Chinese currency beginning in 1985 together with other price adjustments helped correct this situation, and in 1986 manufactured exports rose by 45 percent making it possible for total exports to rise by 13 percent despite the sharp drop in petroleum prices. In 1987, Chinese manufactured exports leapt up again and imports were curtailed and China once again came close to a balance on its trade account despite an increase in the industrial growth rate.

It is not unusual during periods of rapid growth for the pace of industrial development to fluctuate widely. In Taiwan in the 1970s the annual growth rate of manufacturing was as low as minus 6.3 percent (in 1974) and as high as 25.6 percent (in 1976).[27] In the Republic of Korea in the same period the range was between 11.6 percent (in 1970) and 35.7 percent (in 1973).[28] Japan in the 1950s and 1960s before it acquired a chronic balance-of-payments surplus used to experience industrial booms followed by brief periods of slow growth caused by balance-of-payments constraints. The ups and downs of Chinese industrial growth rates, therefore, should be seen as a fairly typical accompaniment of rapid development. Analogies to China's own Great Leap Forward, when industrial output rose 110 percent over two years (1958–59) in a completely unplanned and uncoordinated way with disastrous consequences, are not relevant to the cycles in industrial performance in China in the late 1970s

27 Council for Economic Planning and Development, *Taiwan statistical data book, 1986*, 83.
28 Economic Planning Board, *Major statistics of Korean economy, 1986*, 83.

and 1980s. China's 7th FYP (1986–90) called for an annual average increase for industry of 7.5 percent per year,[29] more realistic than the 6th FYP (1981–85) target. Whether China would just make this target or surpass it would depend on the severity of the foreign exchange constraint and the overall progress of economic reform.

Reforming the industrial system

China's efforts to overcome energy and foreign exchange bottlenecks in order to achieve accelerated industrial growth are only part of the industrial-policy story of the 1980s. The changes with the most long-run significance are those involving efforts to change the system used to coordinate and manage industrial enterprises.

The urban industrial system China possessed in the 1970s was in many respects a carbon copy of the bureaucratic-command system in Soviet industry. Central planners decided what was to be produced and the inputs to be used in production. Enterprises received these inputs directly from state agencies responsible for such allocations. If more inputs were required, the enterprise either had to go back to the planners for an additional allocation or work out an informal (and often illegal) trade with some other enterprise that had a surplus of that particular item. The option of buying additional inputs on the market was not open because such markets did not exist.

Investment decisions were even more centralized. Special enterprises were set up to carry out major construction of new plant capacity that was then turned over to the producing enterprise when completed. The funding came directly from the government budget with no charge to the producing enterprise. The prime role of the banking system was not to be a major source of funds to finance investment, but was mainly to monitor compliance with the plan.

The rigidity of this Soviet-style system bothered Chinese economists from the beginning. Overcentralization of decision making was seen as one cause of the rising inefficiency of Chinese industry described earlier in this chapter. The main solution attempted before the 1980s was to decentralize decision making to the province and even to the county. The principal features of the bureaucratic-command system, however, remained intact. Allocations of key inputs were made by government agencies in

---

29 *Chung-hua jen-min kung-ho-kuo ching-chi he she-hui fa-chan ti-ch'i ko wu-nien chi-hua, 1986–1990* (The seventh five-year plan for the economic and social development of the People's Republic of China, 1986–1990), 23.

accordance with the plan. Markets played little or no role in these decisions.

In 1979 Chinese planners were already beginning experiments with reform of this bureaucratic-command system. These early efforts at reform involved such steps as allowing enterprises to compete with enterprises in other regions of the country where before each enterprise had a monopoly of its own region's market.[30] There were also attempts to improve the internal efficiency of the enterprise by reintroducing bonuses for workers and managers and by placing greater emphasis on the profits target in the government's plan rather than the gross value output target.

None of these early changes fundamentally altered the predominant role of central planning and the bureaucratic-command system. The role of market forces increased but was clearly subordinate to the plan. Efforts to increase the role of the market were resisted strongly by some members of the Politburo and they were reasonably successful in blocking radical reform in 1982 and 1983. Once again a central figure in the debate was Ch'en Yun, only now he was on the side of those resisting further change. Ch'en Yun saw a role for the market but firmly believed that planning and the bureaucratic-command system should predominate.[31]

It was not that Ch'en Yun's views had changed. What had happened instead was that a group of younger, much more radical reformers had acquired positions of power and influence. Foremost among this group was Chao Tzu-yang, who became premier in 1980. These more radical reformers were primarily responsible for the October 1984 document "On the reform of economic structure."[32] This document, written in language that somewhat obscured its full intent, was in practice a call for a major move away from the bureaucratic-command system and toward the use of market forces in all sectors of the economy.

The political battle over the appropriate role for market forces waxed and waned in the following three years (1985–87). Those favoring the market appeared to be gaining the upper hand in 1986, only to suffer a setback when Hu Yao-pang was demoted and reformers outside the economic sphere were purged in early 1987. By the Thirteenth CCP Congress in the fall of 1987, however, the market-oriented reforms were back on track, despite the presence of two members of the new Standing Committee of the Politburo who were seen as supporters of a continued role for the bureaucratic-command system.

---

30 William Byrd et al., *Recent Chinese economic reforms: studies of two industrial enterprises.*
31 See, for example, Ch'en Yun's statement of 8 March 1979, reprinted as "Planning and the market," *Beijing Review*, 29.29 (21 July 1986), 14–15.
32 "Decision of the Central Committee of the Communist Party of China on reform of the economic structure" 20 October 1984, *Beijing Review*, 27.44 (29 October 1984), I–XVI.

Whatever the political base of support for such reforms, the years after the October 1984 document witnessed a major expansion in the role of market forces, but an expansion that left elements of central planning and the command system intact.

There are five key elements in any attempt to make markets work in a way that will promote economic efficiency:

1. First, inputs and outputs of industry must be made available for purchase and sale on the market. As early as the first half of 1985 market sales by a sample of 429 enterprises had risen to 43.8 percent of total sales from 32.1 percent in 1984. Material inputs supplied by the market to these same firms had risen from 16.4 to 27.3 percent.[33] Those percentages have risen considerably since, but concrete statistics are not available.

2. Enterprise managers must behave in accordance with the rules of the market, or market forces will not lead enterprises toward efficient outcomes. There is little doubt that Chinese enterprise managers by the mid-1980s no longer attempted to maximize gross value output, as is typical in the Soviet command system but is completely inappropriate in a market system. Enterprises were concerned primarily with profits that could be used to pay bonuses, build housing, or otherwise provide for worker welfare.[34] But the key to an efficient market is to have enterprises raising profits by lowering their costs or raising sales, not by finding ways of extracting more subsidies from the government.

Chinese enterprises, however, still depend heavily on the bureaucracy for subsidies of various kinds. Tax rates, for example, are supposed to be calculated at a fixed rate according to one recent reform, but are still in practice negotiated rates set so that the enterprise can avoid making losses.[35] Bank loans are still too readily available at highly subsidized interest rates, despite efforts to harden up the terms on which bank loans are made. An effort has been made to pass a bankruptcy law, but in 1987 it was still being used on only a trial basis. Only one state firm in Shenyang had actually been allowed to go bankrupt, although small collective firms were often allowed to go out of business with or without a bankruptcy law.

In the mid-1980s, therefore, Chinese enterprise managers were responding to a mix of signals. Concern with profits led them to pay attention to market forces much more than was the case in the 1970s or earlier. But success for these managers still depended critically on their ability to cater to the desires of higher-level economic bureaucrats.

33 *Kai-ko: wo-men mien-lin ti t'iao-chan yü hsuan-tzu* (Reform: we face challenge and alternative), 45.
34 William Byrd and Gene Tidrick, "Factor allocation in Chinese industry."
35 See, for example, Andrew G. Walder, "The informal dimensions of enterprise financial reforms," in United States Congress, Joint Economic Committee, *China's economy looks toward the year 2000*, 1.630–45.

3. Getting prices to reflect the true relative scarcities in the economy is the third critical element in reform. If prices are distorted, inputs and outputs will not get to where they are most needed. But price reform is extremely difficult to implement in a system where the state sets most prices, as it did in China. Every time the state changes a price there is a winner (the producers who receive a higher price for their product) and a loser (those who must pay the higher price). The losers will do everything in their power to resist such changes. Because many of the losers in the Chinese case would be managers of large enterprises paying higher prices for energy and other inputs, their capacity to bring influence to bear on the price-setting bureaucracy was considerable. A few state prices were changed in the early 1980s, but most remained fixed at levels often set as many as twenty years earlier.

As more and more industrial inputs and outputs became available on the market, however, the Chinese discovered that there was much less resistance to fluctuating prices on these markets. What evolved, as a result, was a dual-price system. Goods allocated by the bureaucracy were paid for at the old prices fixed by the state. The same kind of product sold on the market was paid for at prices determined by supply and demand on the market. The key to price reform, therefore, was to expand the scope of goods available on this secondary market where prices were not fixed, and that was what in fact was happening in 1986 and 1987. Whether the market would eventually be allowed to set all prices or whether the state would retain a major price-setting role was still a subject for considerable debate.

4. A major reason for expanding the role of the market is to promote accelerated productivity growth. But markets enhance productivity in large part because of the forces of competition felt through the market. If each enterprise has a monopoly of its own market, there is little pressure to improve performance. In China in the early 1970s even county enterprises were given monopoly control over the local county market. Competition between enterprises was not over markets but took the form of contests to surpass norms set by the state, with the winner receiving a red flag or a trip to Peking.

State enforcement of enterprise monopolies began to disappear in the early 1980s. In the commercial sphere where collective and private traders competed directly with state retailers, the impact on improved performance (longer hours, more service-oriented sales personnel) was readily apparent. Industrial enterprises producing items that were in oversupply also had to cut their price, improve quality, or increase their sales effort. The problem was that many industrial enterprises faced markets where demand greatly exceeded supply. For those enterprises there was little competitive pressure to improve performance. Sales were automatic even where quality was low and service poor. Increasing competition involves more than simply abolishing state-enforced monopoly rights. Reform must also remove the sources of excess demand by getting managers to behave according to the rules of the market as described under (2) above.

5. Finally, an effectively operating market requires that the government maintain an acceptable level of price stability. Politics determines what is acceptable. In China consumers were used to long periods when prices did not rise at all or at most at 1 or 2 percent a year. Such stability was in part a reaction against the hyperinflation of the 1940s that had played an important role in undermining the Kuomintang government and bringing the CCP to power. Chinese politicians therefore had a low tolerance for price increases. When prices began to rise in the 1980s, their natural instinct was to reimpose price controls. But price controls in the face of excess demand lead to queuing and other forms of rationing, setting the economy on a path back toward the bureaucratic-command system. The problem in China was particularly acute in 1985 and 1986, when the official urban cost-of-living index rose by 12 percent and 7 percent respectively. Unofficially, it was widely believed that the rate of price increase was considerably higher. Urban residents in particular were disturbed by these increases, and their criticisms were an important force slowing the pace of market-oriented reform. The only solution for the reformers was to learn to do a better job of using macroeconomic controls to restrict excess demand and hence the rate of increase in prices. But the task was a difficult one, in part because the reformers had no prior experience with control of inflation through the indirect levers of macroeconomic policy.

By the end of 1987 China had made real progress on all five fronts in moving toward a more market-oriented system in the industrial sector. But bureaucratic controls over enterprise behavior, particularly the large-scale state enterprises, were still pervasive. Probably no one among the reformers envisaged moving all the way to a free market system such as the one prevailing in Hong Kong. But many saw the possibility of a mixed bureaucratic-command and market system with features in common with what existed in Japan in the 1950s or South Korea in the 1960s. The principal remaining difference between China and its East Asian neighbors would be in the area of public versus private ownership. In Japan, South Korea, and the province of Taiwan, private ownership predominated in industry, although there were many state-owned enterprises. In China virtually all large-scale firms other than joint ventures with foreign firms were owned by the state, and there were no plans to sell off any of them to the private sector.

The future of market-oriented reforms in China did not depend only on politics and the makeup of the Politburo. Of equal or perhaps even greater significance was what was happening with small- and medium-scale enterprises. In 1986 there were 400,000 such enterprises producing 40 percent of China's industrial output. There was no way that the center could hope to control these enterprises through the techniques of central planning. In practice in the mid-1980s most of these enterprises bought their inputs and sold their outputs on the market. The great majority of such firms were collectively owned, but private ownership of a sort was playing an increasing role.[36] As long as this small-scale sector continued to grow so rapidly, there was little prospect of the state's going back to a full Soviet-style command system as in 1956–57 or 1963–65. The efforts to promote rural and other collective industries in the mid-1980s, therefore, had the effect of reinforcing pressures to move toward more market-oriented reforms.

RURAL DEVELOPMENT STRATEGY

Chinese leaders could rationally decide to neglect investment in consumer goods before 1978–79 because of their belief in some version of the Stalinist or Feldman–Mahalanobis model of development. But Chinese planners had an additional reason for not being concerned in earlier years by the consequences of this neglect. Somewhere between two-thirds and three-quarters of all consumer goods were supplied by the agricultural sector.[37] And for agriculture China had a development strategy that did not require large-scale state investment in rural infrastructure.

The core idea of this rural development strategy was that farmers could accomplish most of what was needed without much outside help. The term "self-reliance" has meant different things over the past three decades in China, but in the 1960s and 1970s in rural areas it meant a strategy whereby farmers provided most of their own inputs, whether labor, capital, or current inputs, such as fertilizer.

Like so much else in the Cultural Revolution period, the ideas underlying this self-reliant strategy had their origins in earlier years – specifically, in the first phase of the nationwide collectivization campaign of 1955–56 and even more clearly in the Great Leap Forward years of 1958–59. What

36 The most systematic studies of rural industrialization that bring the story up to 1987 are in the papers prepared for the Chinese Academy of Social Science – World Bank Conference on Township Village and Private Enterprises held in Peking in November 1987.

37 In the late 1970s and early 1980s, food constituted about 65 percent of rural household budgets and 60 percent and more of urban household budgets. In addition, clothing, much of whose value comes from cotton, accounted for another 12–15 percent (*State Statistical Bureau, Statistical yearbook of China, 1981*, 439, 443).

were the characteristic features of this strategy? There were variations in emphasis over time, but the main components were there throughout until the change in policies in 1978–79 and some components even survived these changes. The main features were:

1. There was belief that China's large rural labor force was an asset that could be mobilized for development. If properly motivated and led, this labor force could provide its own infrastructure of irrigation systems, roads, and leveled fields. The key was how to provide the necessary motivation, and the "solutions" ranged from efforts through "socialist education" to encourage people to work altruistically for the good of society, to restructuring agricultural cooperatives (APCs) and communes to ensure that rural construction would serve peasants' material self-interest.

2. Particularly after the bad harvests of 1959–61 it became clear that agriculture had to have more modern inputs, such as chemical fertilizer and machinery, but the issue remained as to who was to provide those inputs. The solution during much of the 1966–76 period was to turn to small-scale enterprises in rural areas rather than to larger plants often imported from abroad and located in urban industrial centers.

These two main features had a clear relation to what actually happened in rural areas before the late 1970s. There were several other characteristic elements that often appeared in public rhetoric, but whose relation to what was actually happening was less clear. There was emphasis on reducing inequality both within the rural areas and between farm and city. There was the slogan "Take grain as the key link" that led to neglect of cash crops, but not as consistently as sometimes has been argued. The slogan "Take agriculture as the foundation" was interpreted by some analysts as indicating that agriculture had the number one priority in investment and in the allocation of key inputs, but, as the discussion above of investment priorities makes clear, this was far from the case. We shall return to issues of income distribution and overemphasis on grain, but first we need a clearer understanding of the central features of the self-reliant strategy and an appraisal of their actual impact on production and income.

Labor mobilization for infrastructure

The single most important economic justification for the nationwide formation of APCs in 1955–56 and rural people's communes in 1958 was the belief that their formation would make it possible to mobilize millions of "surplus" farm laborers to build the rural infrastructure of irrigation

systems and roads that China lacked. The idea was not a new one. Economists in the West (Nurkse, Myrdal, and many others) had long argued
that the rural areas of developing countries had a large, untapped resource
in the form of farmers who were less than fully occupied raising crops
on tiny plots of land. These farmers, the argument went, could make their
own capital equipment (shovels, baskets for carrying dirt) and use their
spare time to dig ditches, transform hilly wasteland into arable land, and
much else. If properly organized, this work could be done at no cost to
the central government budget and with no decline in agricultural output
even in the short run. Community development schemes in India and
rural public works programs around the world were founded on the
belief that surplus labor could be mobilized in this way. As it turned out,
many of these schemes were outright failures, and others existed only as
long as they received large subsidies from the central government or
international aid agencies.

China, however, was different because it had abolished private ownership on most agricultural land. Private ownership made it difficult to get
rural labor to volunteer for public works schemes because the people who
did the work were often not those who reaped the main rewards. With a
new irrigation canal, for example, the main beneficiaries were those who
owned land near the canal and had the most ready access to the water. But
those who did the work often had to be drawn from some distance away,
and many would be landless laborers or tenants. Either they saw no increase in productivity at all, or they lived near enough to the canal to
experience increased yields only to see those increases eaten up by higher
rents.

The formation of APCs and later communes made it possible to relate
effort to reward. An entire village could be mobilized to build a canal that
increased yields on only one-quarter of the village land. The villagers
(commune members) would be paid in "work points," the number varying according to the amount of work done. The increased output would
go not to those who farmed the more productive quarter, but to the
entire village. All output, including the increased portion, would be divided up among the villagers in proportion to the number of work points
earned.[38]

Following these principles, the Chinese mobilized tens of millions of

38 More precisely, the cooperative or production team, whichever was the basic accounting unit,
calculated its gross output and then deducted certain amounts for taxes, investment, current costs,
and the welfare fund. The amount remaining was divided by the total number of work points to
determine the value of a single point, and family collective incomes were set by multiplying this
amount times the total number of family work points.

TABLE 23

Growth rates of agricultural output (in % per year)

	1953–57	1958–65	1966–78	1979–82	1983–86
Grain	3.5	0	3.5	3.9	2.5
Cotton	4.7	3.1	0.2	13.5	−0.4
Oil-bearing crops	0	−1.8	2.8	22.7	5.7
Sugar cane	7.9	3.2	3.6	15.0	8.1
Meat	3.3	4.1	3.4	12.1	9.2
Gross value of agricultural output (minus sideline output)	5.2	0.9	3.1	6.4	5.8

Note: Sideline output, most of which is rural industry, was subtracted from total gross value of output and then all figures were converted into 1980 prices using price indexes derived from Chinese gross agricultural output figures in 1971 given in both 1957 and 1970 prices, and for 1980 given in both 1970 and 1980 prices.
Sources: State Statistical Bureau, *Statistical yearbook of China, 1986*, 130; and State Statistical Bureau, *Chung-kuo t'ung-chi chai-yao, 1987*, 28–31.

farmers in 1956–57 and even more in 1958–59. Enormous quantities of dirt and rock were moved, but there followed in 1959–61 the most serious crop failures of the post-1949 period. As with regard to so much else in the Great Leap Forward, it was difficult to sort out how much of the subsequent disaster could be attributed to bad weather, to bad management, and to the fact that the whole idea of labor mobilization may have been based on false assumptions in the first place. Lacking any clear basis for judgment, those who still felt labor mobilization was the key to rural development were in a position to reassert their position once recovery from the Great Leap crop failures had been achieved. Such models as the Ta-chai brigade and Lin county became famous throughout China for their achievements in turning uneven, parched land into large, level, well-irrigated fields. We have no good data on the amount of labor mobilized and construction completed in the late 1960s and early 1970s, but it was substantial. The question, however, is whether this construction had much of an impact on agricultural production.

Basic data on agricultural output in China are presented in Table 23. These indicate that production grew at a rate well above the population growth rate of 2 percent throughout the 1966–76 period. The issue is whether this rise in output was achieved through labor mobilization or as a result of increased amounts of such modern inputs as chemical fertilizer and improved plant varieties. Some relevant figures on agricultural inputs are presented in Table 24.

The main purpose of labor mobilization for rural construction is to

TABLE 24

Agricultural inputs

	1957	1962	1965	1970	1978	1982	1986
Rural labor force (millions)	205.7	213.7	235.3	281.2	303.4	332.8	379.9
labor force in agriculture[a]	n.a.	n.a.	233.0	n.a.	294.2	320.1	313.1
Arable land[b] (million ha)	112.0	102.3	103.9	101.2	99.4	99.6	96.85[d]
Irrigated area (million ha)	27.34	30.48	33.06	36.04	44.97	44.18	44.23
Power irrigated area (million ha)	1.20	6.07	8.09	14.99	24.90	25.15	25.03
Agriculture use machinery (million hp)	1.65	10.29	14.94	29.44	159.75	225.89	284.33[d]
Rural use of electric power (kwh per ha)	1.25	15.7	35.8	94.5	253.1	396.9	606.0
Consumption of chemical fertilizer (million tons of nutrient)	.373	.630	1.942	3.21[c]	8.84	15.13	19.35

[a] Figures are actually for the labor force in the primary sector and therefore include a small number of nonagricultural laborers.

[b] Land data were derived in part from data on mechanically plowed or irrigated acreage and the percentage of mechanically plowed or irrigated to total. Land data are widely believed to be underreported.

[c] Figures were derived from "standard weight" fertilizer assuming a nutrient content of .202 (the actual nutrient content in 1978).

[d] Figures are for the year 1985.

Sources: Chung-kuo nung-yeh nien-chien, 1980, 4.342–45; State Statistical Bureau, *Statistical yearbook of China, 1981,* 185; State Statistical Bureau, *Chung-kuo t'ung-chi chai-yao, 1987,* 17, 19, 36; State Statistical Bureau, *Statistical yearbook of China, 1986,* 4.111.

increase the amount or raise the quality of land used to grow crops. But the figures in Table 24 indicate that the amount of arable land actually declined slightly between 1965 and 1975, whereas the amount of irrigated acreage rose by 10 million hectares and accounted for 43 percent of all acreage, up from 32 percent in 1965. Because the arable land data are widely believed to be underreported,[39] it may be that there was a net increase in arable land during the Cultural Revolution period. On the other hand, most of the increase in irrigated acreage was due to the introduction of tube wells on the North China Plain, and tube wells have little if anything to do with labor mobilization.

39 *Chung-kuo ching-chi nien-chien, 1981,* 6.9, states that "cultivated acreage figures are biased downward, subject to future verification."

It may be that the main impact of rural construction was to protect farmers from drought and flood in bad years rather than to raise average yields in good years. But the area directly affected by flood and drought disasters in 1972, 1978, and 1980 was 17.2, 21.8, and 22.3 million hectares respectively. Only in the terrible years of 1960 and 1961, when the affected area was 25.0 and 28.8 million hectares, can one find higher figures in the post-1949 period.[40] No doubt the impact of these disasters on yields was less in the 1970s than in earlier periods, so some significant gains can be attributed to rural construction efforts, but the gains seem modest when put up against the enormous amounts of labor time involved over the two decades, 1956–76.

An alternative way of approaching the question of the contribution of labor mobilization to increases in agricultural output is to attempt first to estimate the contribution of modern inputs to that increase and then estimate the impact of labor mobilization by calculating the residual not explained by modern inputs. The method is known as "growth accounting" or "sources of growth" analysis and is usually used to estimate improvements in productivity.[41] The data needed to make these calculations are, in the Chinese case, crude and must be derived using assumptions that are arguable. Still, the results as presented in Table 25 are instructive. Taking the two decades of labor mobilization as a whole (1957–79), the biological package involving increases in chemical fertilizer, pesticides, and improved plant varieties accounts for nearly two-thirds of the total increase in crop output. Increased labor used directly on crops and augmented by labor-saving machinery[42] plus expansion of the irrigated acreage accounts for all the remaining increase in output and more. And most of this increase in irrigated acreage, as already indicated, was due to capital investment in modern power-driven tube wells, not to irrigation systems built by large labor corvées. The data for 1965–75 are less reliable but tell only a slightly different story. For that period the

---

40 These figures are from State Statistical Bureau, *Statistical yearbook of China, 1981*, 205–6.

41 Formally, growth accounting assumes a production function of the following form, $Q = F(L, Ld, K, C, t)$ where Q is output, L is labor, Ld is land, K is fixed capital, C is current inputs, and t is time. The specific form used here involves assuming constant returns to scale and differentiating a simplified version of this equation with respect to time, arriving at the following: $dQ/dt = F/t + F/C \times dC/dt + F/L \times dL/dt + F/Ld \times dLd/dt$, where chemical fertilizer is a proxy for current inputs and irrigated acreage increases represent the only significant changes in Ld.

42 The question of mechanization was a major issue during the Cultural Revolution period and before. Mechanization was in part done to break labor shortages, such as in a two- or three-crop-a year economy when one must harvest one crop and transplant another in a relatively short period. Mechanization, however, was also seen as serving sociopolitical ends, such as reducing the differences in work style between city and countryside and consolidating the collective economy. (Tractors, particularly when owned by the collective, helped reinforce the need to labor collectively.) See Benedict Stavis, *The politics of agricultural mechanization in China*.

TABLE 25

Accounting for China's agricultural growth (in billion 1970 yuan)

Contributing Inputs	1965–75	1957–79
Biological package (chemical fertilizer, improved plant varieties) [a]	8.35	22.7
Labor and labor augmenting machinery used in raising crops [b]	3.9	6.6
Expansion of irrigated acreage [c]	4.4	7.7
Change in gross value of crop output (1970) prices [d]	22.0	35.2
Residual-contribution of all other factors and increases in productivity $[4 - (1 + 2 + 3)]$ [e]	5.35	−1.8

[a] Although there are variations depending on local conditions, a ton of chemical fertilizer measured in terms of nutrient (NPK) usually produces about 10 tons of increases in grain output. The increases in fertilizer output were obtained from data in Table 24, were multiplied by 10 to obtain the increases in grain output, and further multiplied by 216.4 yuan, the average purchase price of grain in 1970 (*Chung-kuo nung-yeh nien-chien, 1980*, 381). If we had assumed that some of the fertilizer was used on cash crops, a slightly higher total would have been reached.

[b] This labor estimate involves the most assumptions based on the least reliable data. The rural labor force figures are from Table 24. We have assumed that each laborer devoted 130 days a year to raising crops. This figure is for 1957 and is from *T'ung-chi yen-chiu*, 8 (23 August 1958), 8. The most difficult problem is to estimate the marginal product of that labor without first estimating an agricultural production function. One Chinese survey indicated that the average value (income) of collective labor per day was 0.56 yuan in 1976, down from 0.70 yuan in 1956 and 0.68 yuan in 1957 (*KMJP* 7, December 1978). These are average product figures, and since they are falling, the marginal product was presumably below the average. Used here is an estimate of 0.5 yuan for the marginal product of a day spent laboring to raise crops.

[c] Data on the expansion of irrigated acreage are derived from Table 24. Irrigated land is assumed to produce two tons more grain per year than unirrigated land, and grain in 1970 prices is worth 216.4 yuan.

[d] The gross value of agricultural output (GVAO) figures for 1957 and 1965 in 1957 prices and 1970, 1975, and 1979 in 1970 prices are from *Chung-kuo nung-yeh nien-chien, 1980*, 41. Data on 1980 crop output in 1970 and 1957 prices indicates a deflater for crop output of 1.35, which is roughly the same as the farm purchase price index for 1970 over 1957 of 1.33. I converted the 1957 data into 1970 prices using 1.35. The 1975 crop output figure was obtained by assuming that 70 percent of GVAO was accounted for by crops.

[e] This figure is obtained by subtracting identified input contributions (1, 2, 3) from the change in gross value of crop output (4).

residual is at least positive, meaning that there is some part of the rise in crop output left over to be explained by factors other than the increase in modern inputs or the direct application of more labor and machinery to crops.

Slightly different assumptions would lead to somewhat different results, but only radical changes could alter the main conclusion. Either the massive effort to mobilize rural labor had a quite small impact on crop output directly or indirectly, or the impact was great but led to such inefficiency in the use of modern inputs that most of the gains were lost by this inefficiency. Put more concretely, chemical fertilizer and related inputs accounted for half or more of the rise in output if it was used efficiently and produced the expected yield response of ten kilograms of grain for one kilogram of nutrient. Or fertilizer was used inefficiently and produced a much lower yield response, in which case land improvements through labor mobilization may have accounted for a larger share of the rise in production. The technique of growth accounting as used here does not allow differentiation between these two alternative explanations.

Neither explanation leads one to conclude that labor mobilization for rural construction proved to be a successful way of achieving rapid increases in Chinese agricultural output. At best it was a supplementary contributor. The reason why the impact was not greater was partly because of management and incentive problems connected with the commune structure that was an essential part of the labor mobilization strategy. But it was also the case that rural construction projects of this type were not the appropriate technology to bring improved irrigation systems to those parts of China that lacked them. South China had begun building such systems a thousand years earlier, and, although these systems could be improved, the gains from such improvements were modest. North China desperately needed a more reliable source of water, but only in a few areas, such as on the edge of the T'ai-hang mountains where both Ta-chai and Lin counties are located, was it possible to achieve significant expansion of the irrigated acreage by labor mobilization alone. Elsewhere, one had to make more use of the water of the Yellow River, which meant first removing much of its silt, and that could be done only with a massive program of dam building and grassland development on the upper reaches of the river.[43] Or, as has been considered from time to time, one must find a way of diverting the waters flowing down the Yangtze northward, no mean trick under any circumstances and certainly not the job for a few million farmers working on their own with pickaxes and shovels.

Rural small-scale industry

Although modern inputs probably accounted for much of the rise in farm output, in the 1966–76 period at least many of these inputs were provided by quite small plants located in the countryside. As mentioned earlier, in the discussion of industrial strategy, like so much else during the Cultural Revolution period the basic idea for rural industrialization originated during the Great Leap Forward. But the design of the Great Leap small-scale–industry program was badly flawed. Backyard iron and steel

---

43 For discussions of North China's water problems, see James E. Nickum, *Hydraulic engineering and water resources in the People's Republic of China*; Alva Lewis Erisman, "Potential costs of and benefits from diverting river flow for irrigation in the North China plain"; and Dwight H. Perkins, *Agricultural development in China, 1368–1968*, 4.

furnaces that popped up all over were the prime example of the inappro-
priateness of the industries chosen for emphasis. These furnaces, like
most other commune-run enterprises, wasted materials and time and produced little of value. By 1963 their numbers had been reduced to 11,000
from a 1960 level of 117,000 commune enterprises, and by 1966 there
were still only 12,000.[44]

Between 1966 and 1970, however, commune industrial enterprises
were once again on the rise and were joined by many new county-level
state plants that fit within the small-scale category. But unlike the earlier
effort in the Great Leap, this program was based on something other than
the utopian wishes of the leadership. The key ideas in this period were
straightforward. Agriculture required modern inputs, but it would divert
a large share of the state investment and foreign exchange budget if these
inputs were to be supplied by large-scale and imported turnkey enterprises. Furthermore, high rural transport costs made it sensible to locate
enterprises near both their sources of raw material and the users of their
product. Cement, which uses limestone and coal as inputs, illustrates the
point. Because small outcroppings of limestone and coal can be found in
many of China's rural areas, it is possible to locate cement plants near
these outcroppings in order to produce cement for lining of canals, as
well as for other purposes. If the plant is small, local people can build the
plant themselves with only a limited amount of technical supervision
from outside. The alternative of building a large 1- or 2-million–ton
cement plant would have led to the production of higher-quality cement,
but most communes would have spent double and triple the original cost
of production to transport the cement to where they could use it.

Farm machinery illustrates another advantage of small plants located
near the users of their products. Tractors and other machines break down
frequently. In industrial countries a farmer can go to the repair shop of a
nearby distributor for a replacement part. But developing countries have
few distributors and inadequate or no inventories of spare parts. A farmer
could send his tractor off to Shanghai or Peking for repairs, but that
might take months or years. The solution is to have repair facilities located near users in the commune. But a major overhaul capacity involves
many kinds of skills and equipment needed to manufacture the item in the
first place, so it is not difficult to convert a major repair facility into a
manufacturing enterprise, and that is what the Chinese did.[45]

---

44 State Statistical Bureau, *Statistical yearbook of China, 1981*, 207.
45 There are a number of useful works on small-scale industry in the Great Leap and Cultural Revo-
    lution periods. See, for example, Jon Sigurdson, *Rural industrialization in China*; Carl Riskin,
    "Small industry and the Chinese model of development," *CQ*, 46 (April–June 1971); and Dwight
    H. Perkins, ed., *Rural Small-Scale Industry in the People's Republic of China*, report of the American
    Rural Small-Scale Industry Delegation.

TABLE 26

Small-scale cement plants

	No. of small-scale cement plants[a]	Annual growth rate of small-scale cement plants	Share of small-scale cement plants in total production (%)
1949	–	–	7.6
1953–57	–	–	2.6
1958–62	–	38.0	19.8
1963–65	–	77.1	26.8
1965	200	–	–
1966–70	–	14.9	39.0
1972	2,400	–	–
1971–75	–	20.8	53.0
1975	2,800	–	–
1976–80	–	14.8	65.9
1980	4,533	–	–

[a] Small-scale includes county as well as commune-run cement enterprises.
Sources: Kao Wen-hsi, "China's cement industry," *Chung-kuo ching-chi nien-chien, 1982,* 5.205; Jon Sigurdson, *Rural industrialization in China,* 153: and American Rural Small-Scale Industry Delegation, *Rural small-scale industry in the People's Republic of China,* 86.

Between 1965 and 1970 the number of small, commune-run enterprises had risen to 45,000, and by 1976 the number was 106,000, nearly back to Great Leap levels. Five industries received special emphasis – cement, farm machinery, chemical fertilizer, iron and steel, and electric power. By the early 1970s, half of China's total cement output and nearly all of the cement reaching the countryside were produced in small-scale plants. (See Table 26.) Roughly half of all chemical fertilizer also came from small-scale plants, mainly in the form of low-quality ammonium bicarbonate. In the late 1970s, China began closing down many small-scale enterprises on the grounds that they wasted materials and generally were run at prohibitively high cost. Not surprisingly, many of the decisions to build plants in the 1966–76 decade were made without adequate consideration of their economic efficiency. The surprising thing is that there were not many more plant closings for inefficiency given the highly politicized atmosphere in which decisions were made in the Cultural Revolution.[46]

One sector that was hard hit by the closing was the small-scale iron and steel industry, where three hundred of five hundred plants (mainly the smallest) were closed. Small chemical fertilizer plants also came in for much criticism, but output in such plants after many of the least efficient

46 A useful study of the post-1976 period is by Christine Wong, "Rural industrialization in the People's Republic of China: lessons from the Cultural Revolution decade," in U.S. Congress, Joint Economic Committee, *China under the four modernizations,* 394–418.

had been closed may have been three-quarters of its peak level.[47] Overall, however, small-scale industry kept growing at a rapid pace. By 1980, there were 187,000 commune-run enterprises, 80,000 more than in 1976.

Some of the original five small industries, notably cement, continued to grow in the late 1970s (Table 26). In 1979 machinery and construction materials (bricks as well as cement) still accounted for more than half of the rising gross value of output of commune-run enterprises, and chemicals and coal another 13 percent.[48] But at least in communes near urban industrial centers, there was an increasing effort to use commune industries as subcontractors to larger-scale, city-based enterprises. These and other changes led to the already described rapid expansion in small-scale collective industry that occurred in the 1980s. The developments in the 1980s, however, were a part of China's industrialization strategy and only secondarily related to issues of rural development. As such they were discussed earlier, in the section on industrial strategies, and that discussion will not be repeated here.

RURAL POLICY CHANGES AFTER 1979

In certain respects, notably in the continued development of small-scale industry, the post–Cultural Revolution period continued trends under way since 1966. In other respects, however, there were dramatic changes. The Ta-chai brigade was publicly pilloried for making false claims. Large labor corvées for rural construction may still exist, but their use has been sharply deemphasized.

In the minds of the Chinese leadership of the early 1980s, China's agricultural performance through 1977 had been inadequate to the country's needs, and the fault lay mainly with bad planning and management and with farmers who had little incentive to work hard or to take any initiative. Where Mao and his colleagues had relied on changes in organization to accomplish agricultural miracles through mass labor mobilization, Teng and his colleagues also relied on reorganization, albeit of a very different kind, to increase agricultural productivity.

The first step was to free up the market for rural subsidiary products and to encourage farmers to maximize both their collective and their private incomes. In principle, free markets and private household subsidiary production were restored in 1960 and 1961 and existed uninterrupted thereafter. Private household plots were also restored in 1960 and actually

---

47   This, at least, was the case in Shantung province (Wong, "Rural industrialization in the People's Republic of China," 413).

48   These figures are from *Chung-kuo nung-yeh nien-chien, 1980*, 368.

increased modestly in size in the early 1960s[49] and continued in existence throughout the Cultural Revolution period. In practice, private activities of all kinds were constantly under pressure from rural cadres responsible for collective production. These cadres were responsible both for seeing that grain and other collectively raised crop output and delivery targets were met and for ensuring that peasants acquired socialist values and styles of work. Private activities took time away from collective effort and encouraged values that were felt to be "capitalistic." Before 1979, therefore, private trading was on a small scale, and private household activity was probably mainly for one's own use, although no published data exist with which to verify this statement. By 1979, however, private activities, rather than being seen as an unfortunate necessity, were being actively encouraged, with results readily visible to the naked eye. Rural trade fairs blossomed, and farmers by the hundreds of thousands entered cities daily to sell the produce of their private plots. In 1964 private income accounted for about 19 percent of family income, in the 1966–76 period the figure was probably lower; but by 1982, private income, according to one survey, may have accounted for 38 percent of family income.[50]

By 1979 an even more profound change was under way in the organization of collective agricultural activity. In the poorest provinces of China, notably in Anhwei, China's leadership had begun to experiment with something called the "production responsibility system." From 1962 through the 1970s, the basic accounting unit of the collective system was based on the production team with an average of twenty-five families each.[51] The raising of collective crops was organized by the team and the collective income of team members was based mainly on the output of that team. In some cases, representing less than 10 percent of the rural population, the brigade, the next level up in the commune organizational structure with an average of two hundred families, was the basic accounting unit.[52] For the most part, however, the brigade and commune levels dealt with marketing and rural small-scale enterprises, not with the raising of crops. The main agricultural production unit, therefore, was small but its form still collective.

The production responsibility system retained collective or group

---

49 In 1964, in ten communes surveyed by a Pakistani delegation, for example, private plots accounted for 7.55 percent of the total arable land as contrasted to the 5 percent figure that was the declared government objective. Shahid Javed Burki, *A study of Chinese communes, 1965*, 35–36.

50 The 1960s figure is from ibid., 40. The 1982 figure is from State Statistical Bureau, *Statistical yearbook of China, 1984*, 471.

51 The figure fluctuates a bit from year to year. This figure is for 1965 (*Chung-kuo nung-yeh nien-chien, 1980*), 5.

52 Ibid.

farming in some cases, but in others responsibility devolved down to the household. In the poorest provinces, by 1981 or 1982, more than 90 percent of the households were responsible for farming formerly collective land on a household rather than a team basis, and the system was increasingly prevalent in the richer provinces as well. Income in some cases still depended on overall team results, but in other cases even income was determined by what the household itself produced.[53]

By the end of 1983 even these vestiges of collective agriculture had largely disappeared from the Chinese countryside. It no longer made sense to divide income between collective and private sources because almost all farm production was on a household basis. Even the names "commune" and "production brigade" were replaced with the older terms "township" (*hsiang*) and "village" (*ts'un*). Farming, after a quarter century of collective experiments, was once again based on the household as the main producing unit.[54]

The role of market forces in the rural areas was also expanded further. Conversion to a market-oriented system of coordination and distribution was inherently simpler in the rural areas than it was for the urban industrial sector. To begin with, a fledgling market for many agricultural products already existed and had been allowed to grow significantly, beginning in 1979, as already mentioned. Even for major crops under collective management before 1979, the market played some role. As a result, crop prices were occasionally changed even during the Cultural Revolution years, and these prices probably did not diverge from true relative scarcities as much as was the case in urban areas.[55] Perhaps most important, farm households as producing units naturally behaved in ways consistent with what the market required. Farm households were natural income or profit maximizers because higher profits meant a higher standard of living for household members. Furthermore, the only way to

53 For a discussion of the various kinds of responsibility systems as of 1981, see Liu Shu-mao, "An introduction to the several types of production responsibility systems currently in use in our rural areas," *Ching-chi guan-li*, 9 (15 September 1981), 9.12–14. These systems are discussed at greater length in Kathleen Hartford, "Socialist agriculture is dead; long live socialist agriculture!: organizational transformations in rural China," in Elizabeth J. Perry and Christine Wong, eds., *The political economy of reform in post-Mao China*, 31–62.

54 The process of transition to household farming has been described and analyzed by a number of authors. The early part of the process is ably described, in part based on firsthand village studies, in William L. Parish, ed., *Chinese rural development: the great transformation*. See also David Zweig, "Opposition to change in rural China: the system of responsibility and the people's communes," *Asian Survey*, 23.7 (July 1983); Frederick W. Crook, "The reform of the commune system and the rise of the township-collective-household system," in U.S. Congress, Joint Economic Committee, *China's economy looks toward the year 2000*, 1.354–75.

55 There were still substantial departures from true scarcity prices, however. See, for example, Nicholas Lardy, "Agricultural prices in China."

maximize profits was to increase output or cut production costs. There were no state subsidy schemes or friendly bankers standing by to bail out farm households that consistently ran losses, as there were in industry. The state stepped in only when starvation threatened. Finally, monopoly rights over particular markets were infeasible when one was dealing with several hundred million farm households. Competition was inevitable whether the bureaucracy approved of it or not.

The underlying conditions required by well-functioning markets, therefore, existed in the Chinese countryside. This fact, however, did not mean that all members of the state bureaucracy were comfortable with steps designed to let changes in relative prices govern what was produced and sold. Still, movement toward a market system made much greater progress in agriculture than in industry, and by the mid-1980s there was a decision in principle to have all farm output bought and sold through the market. Compulsory state purchase quotas for farmers were to be abolished and replaced with voluntary contracts. In practice, however, the state bureaucracy was reluctant to surrender that much control. Contracts, at least through 1987, were not completely voluntary.

The nature of the problem as seen through the eyes of the more reluctant reformers can be illustrated with the market for grain. By the mid-1980s the Chinese government was under great pressure to reduce its role in grain marketing because of the high cost of maintaining the subsidies involved. Urban sales prices for grain were well below the prices paid to farmers, particularly when transport and marketing costs were involved. The resulting losses were a major drain on the resources of the central government.

Simply freeing up grain prices was not a solution that could be taken easily. Urban food prices would have shot up immediately with consequences for political stability that could have been profound. This short-term danger was eased in part by the big grain harvests of 1982–84, about which more will be said later. With such large surpluses overhanging the market, grain price increases should have been moderated. Still, urban market prices for grain in 1985 were 88 percent higher than the state list prices so that abolition of all state grain sales would have led to a large price increase, although nothing so large as 88 percent.[56]

Even if the immediate political problem could have been managed,

56 Secondary market prices often will not reflect what would happen if dual markets (one controlled) were replaced by one single uncontrolled market. Prices would rise on this unified market above state control levels of the past, but higher prices would cut back consumption of grain so that demand and supply would normally reach equilibrium at prices below the full secondary market price. Determining the specific price reached, however, involves a variety of assumptions much too complex to deal with in this footnote.

from the point of view of Party conservatives there was another, more basic, long-term problem connected with reliance on the market for basic foodstuffs. The danger, from the conservatives' perspective, was what would happen if the market failed to stimulate adequate levels of grain output. A serious shortfall in supply could lead to sharp increases in prices or worse, even serious malnutrition, as occurred in parts of the country in 1960 and 1961. That 1960–61 crisis was a major element in causing the split within the CCP that culminated in the excesses of the Cultural Revolution. This danger did not seem very great in 1985 after three record harvests in a row, but by the end of 1987 the grain harvest for three years running had failed to match the 1984 peak and conservative fears seemed more plausible.

The reality was that in the mid-1980s China had ample supplies of grain and in 1985-86 was actually a net exporter despite increases in domestic consumption per capita. (See Table 27.) Furthermore, China was earning $30 billion a year from its exports as contrasted to less than $2 billion in 1960–61. In 1987 it was possible to import 10 million tons of grain for a price of around $1 billion. If China had experienced a major harvest failure in 1987 and had been forced to import, say, 50 million tons of grain at then existing world prices, the cost would have been under $6 billion, or less than 20 percent of China's foreign exchange earnings. Even if world prices of grain had risen sharply, as is possible if Chinese purchases had been so large, China had the foreign exchange to weather the shortfall without a fall in consumption. In any case, direct government intervention in what farmers were allowed to plant, the conservatives' answer to the danger, was a weak foundation on which to build an effective grain security policy. Government-set grain delivery quotas were no protection against bad weather. They did in the past limit farmers' ability to shift out of grain to cash crops, but almost certainly at the cost of a lower level of overall agricultural output than would have been the case in the absence of controls.

The real problem in Chinese agriculture was not the danger of a cyclical downturn caused by bad weather or a sudden decline in grain prices leading to an undesirably large shift of land out of grain. The central issue for Chinese agricultural and food policy was how to meet the nation's rapidly rising demand for food, given an arable-land endowment comparable to that found in Japan, Taiwan, or South Korea. China's East Asian neighbors dealt with this land problem by relying increasingly on food imports. South Korea in 1979, for example, was importing 145 kilograms of grain per year for each person in the country. An equivalent level of imports for China would have been 145 million tons of grain purchases

TABLE 27
Grain imports and exports (annual averages in million metric tons)

	Imports	Exports	Net imports
1950–60	.082	2.273	− 2.191[a]
1961–65	5.932	1.623	4.309
1966–76	5.015	2.772	2.243
1977–78	8.089	1.767	6.322
1979–81	13.203	1.419	11.784
1982–84	13.321	2.135	11.186
1985–86	6.867	9.372	− 2.505

[a] A minus sign indicates net exports.
Source: State Statistical Bureau, *Statistical yearbook of China, 1981*, 372, 388, 394, 398; ibid., *1984*, 397; State Statistical Bureau, *Chung-kuo t'ung-chi chai-yao, 1987*, 90–91.

from abroad. In the 1980s that level of imports would have been well beyond China's capacity to pay for in foreign exchange.

This longer-term problem was obscured in the early 1980s by the bumper harvests that followed the downturn in crop output in 1980. The reasons for these bumper harvests were varied. Good weather played some role. Freeing up farmers to decide themselves what to produce on their land led to a reallocation of inputs toward cash crops that raised overall agricultural productivity. But grain output also leapt ahead in 1982–84, suggesting that the relaxation of controls over farmer incentives had a positive impact that went beyond the shift out of grain to cash crops. Key inputs such as chemical fertilizer, farm machinery, and electric power also continued to increase in the 1980s. This chapter is not the place to attempt to measure the precise contribution to output growth of each of these components. The effect of one component no doubt reinforced the impact of the others. Without the introduction of household agricultural production under the responsibility system, however, there is little doubt that farm output growth would have been substantially lower than what in fact occurred in the early 1980.

China's spurt in agricultural growth in the 1980s, when farm output increases (excluding rural industry) averaged more than 9 percent annually, could not possibly have been sustained for long. The experience appears to have been a one-shot acceleration brought about by the removal of barriers to efficient production. Once higher levels of efficiency had been achieved, the Chinese agricultural growth rate fell back to a more sustainable level in 1985–87, although poorer weather may also have been a factor. Five percent annual increases in farm output are considered high by world standards, and anything higher is extraordinary. In

the East Asian context with its limited land endowment and rapid industrialization, much lower rates are the norm. In Japan, for example,
agricultural output in the early 1980s was essentially the same as in the
mid-1960s. Per capita grain production was only half as high as in the
mid-1960s.[57] In South Korea, a more relevant comparison, agriculture
averaged 4.3 percent per annum between 1965 and 1984, but grain grew
at only 1.2 percent a year.[58] The comparable figures for Taiwan over the
same period are 2.4 percent and minus 0.3 percent.[59] For China, therefore,
a growth rate of total agricultural output of 4 percent a year and of grain
of 2 to 3 percent a year would be an achievement.

China's long-term problem is that the demand for agricultural products, and for grain in particular, is growing faster than 3 to 4 percent. In
1980–84, Chinese demand for grain, for example, must have grown at
more than 5 percent a year,[60] but production grew at more than 6 percent
a year, generating a surplus that made it possible for China to become a
net exporter in 1985–86. If grain output were to grow on a sustained basis
at 3 percent a year, demand at current rates of industrialization and
national income growth will increase by at least 4 percent a year if not
higher, and China will revert to being a major grain importer like its East
Asian neighbors.

The responsibility system and the resulting spurt in agricultural development, therefore, gave China a brief respite from the country's long-
term agricultural problem. Industrialization could surge ahead and per
capita incomes in the rural areas could double without demand for food
outstripping the domestic supply. By 1987, however, China may have
gotten back on a more normal trend consistent with the country's having
only 0.1 hectare per capita of arable land. The agricultural choices for the
future, therefore, were more likely to resemble those faced in the late
1970s. Accelerated growth in real per capita income was possible provided that China invested enough in agriculture to ensure a growth rate
in that sector sufficient to keep agricultural imports from growing more
rapidly than China's ability to earn foreign exchange to pay for them. For
investment in agriculture to have this desired impact, it was also essential
for farmers to be given incentives to use this investment and other inputs
to maximum effect, as occurred in the early 1980s.

57 United Nations, *Statistical yearbook for Asia and the Pacific, 1984*, 277.
58 Economic Planning Board, *Major statistics of Korean economy, 1986*, 75.
59 Council for Economic Planning and Development, *Taiwan statistical data book, 1986*, 65, 67.
60 Chinese income was growing at about 9 percent per year. A conservative estimate of the income
    elasticity of demand for grain (including grain fed to animals) would be 0.6, which would mean
    that demand for grain would grow at 5.4 percent a year. Different assumptions give different
    results, but it is difficult to come up with plausible assumptions that result in a growth rate in
    demand of below 5 percent for this period.

A reversion to controls over farm output would have solved China's long-term excess demand for grain, mainly if it succeeded in lowering incentives by enough to slow markedly the growth in incomes and hence of demand. A turn inward away from an export promotion strategy would have had much the same result. By slowing national income growth overall because of slow import growth for all products, not just grain, demand for grain could be held down. Alternatively, the state could have reimposed a rigorous rationing system that would have held down grain consumption despite a rapid rise in income. Given those kinds of choices, it is hardly surprising that some reformers, at least, preferred a more market-oriented policy to encourage farmer incentives combined with vigorous export promotion to meet the foreign exchange requirements of anticipated increases in food imports.[61]

Income distribution

Whatever the virtues and drawbacks for production of the way agriculture was organized in the 1966–76 period, it was widely believed that the system at least reduced inequalities within the rural sector and between urban and rural residents. Policy changes after 1978, it was feared, would lead to increasing inequality. Data published in the early 1980s raise questions about both of these hypotheses. Land reform in the late 1940s and early 1950s, as Roll's estimates have shown, led to a major increase in income of the poorest 20 percent of the rural population, mostly at the expense of landlords, who lost most of their possessions without compensation.[62] Inequalities that remained in the 1953–55 period were those between rich and poor peasants in a given region and between rich and poor regions. The formation of APCs in 1955–56 eliminated differences in the amount of land owned. Inequality remaining within the cooperative (and later the production team) was due to variations between families in the ratio of healthy adult workers to nonworking dependents (children, aged parents, and the sick). Although these differences could be substantial, they were a far cry from inequalities caused by variations in the amount of land owned.

What impressed visitors to the Chinese countryside was this relatively egalitarian structure within any given collective unit. What visitors could not or did not see were the large disparities in income between regions. Collectivization could have no impact on these disparities at all.

---

61 Tu Jen-sheng, in a talk to a conference on township and village enterprises in Peking in November 1987, for example, made an explicit connection between export promotion policies and solutions to the grain problem.

62 C. R. Roll, "The distribution of rural income in China: comparison of the 1930s and the 1950s."

Farmers in poor mountainous regions banded together in a team with other poor farmers in the same region, as did rich suburban farmers. The better-off farmers in the mountainous region, whose income was still well below the national rural average, experienced a decline in income, whereas the less well-off suburban farmers, whose income was often double the national average, experienced a rise.

Data necessary for a definitive calculation are not available, but a manipulation of Roll's data suggests that inequality declined little if at all in 1956–57 as a result of collectivization.[63] Regional differences were great enough to dominate any decrease in inequality within collective units. The question of central relevance to this chapter is whether measures taken after 1965 in any way changed this outcome.

A decline in rural inequality could have been achieved in any of four ways: Progressive taxes on the rural communes could have reduced inequality, but there was little if any progressivity in the Chinese tax system. Welfare payments to the poorest regions would also have helped. Although there is much we do not know about the Chinese rural welfare system, transfers between regions appear to be quite small. Communes faced with serious malnutrition apparently got support, but most other communes were expected to fend for themselves. A third measure would have been to move peasants from the poorest regions into richer ones, but in a nation with little new land to open up this is a method guaranteed to produce severe rural conflict. Finally, the state could have directed investment and current inputs toward the poorest rural areas, and may on occasion have done so. But such a policy will frequently be at the cost of slower increases in productivity because the rate of return on investment in many poor areas is going to be low. It is often the richer areas that have the adequate supplies of water that make it possible to use more chemical fertilizer and improved plant varieties.

There is little reason, therefore, to expect that rural inequality, albeit low compared with that in most other developing countries, declined much in the 1960s and 1970s, and the few figures available appear to support this view. A standard measure of inequality is the gini coefficient whose value can range from "0" (perfect equality) to "1" (perfect inequality). Data on the distribution of brigade collective income in 1980, for example, suggest a gini coefficient of .232, which is virtually identical with the .227 coefficient obtained from Roll's data for the period after

63   Roll's data give the income of rich, middle, and poor peasants by region. If one assumes that all rich and poor peasants in a given region had the same income as middle peasants after collectivization, one can derive a gini coefficient for this simulated distribution of .211, only marginally less than the .277 figure for the precollectivization (and post–land reform) periods.

land reform and preceding collectivization.[64] This conclusion is reinforced by provincial data that suggest that 70 percent of the differences in per capita rural income between provinces can be accounted for by differences in the quantity and quality of land per capita.[65] Because the relative quality and quantity of land per capita between regions changed little over the 1960s and 1970s, relative incomes changed little as well.

Did changes after 1978 alter this picture? Generally, it is difficult to discern trends in income distribution over short periods, and available Chinese data are not suitable for such precise calculations in any case. It is possible, however, that already rich communes near cities and major transport lines benefited disproportionately from opportunities to expand cash crops and subsidiary activities. Poor mountainous regions, after all, cannot deliver vegetables to urban residents, nor are they usually in a position to do subcontracting work for urban enterprises. Liberalized economic controls, therefore, may have led to some rise in inequality in the early 1980s.

When we turn to the question of what happened to rural-urban differences in income, however, the connection between liberalized controls and greater inequality is much less clear. Liberalization, under certain conditions, in fact, could lead to a significant decline in inequality.

A central feature of the entire 1960s and 1970s period was the virtual prohibition on rural-to-urban migration. In addition, urban youth were shipped off to rural communes and state farms by the millions. At the same time, as described earlier in the chapter, the state continued to pour investment into urban-based industry. While this investment became increasingly capital intensive, there was still a steadily rising demand for labor in the urban areas, a demand that had to be met either by people who were already urban residents or by those who lived in nearby communes from which they could commute into the city and thus avoid the need for an urban residence permit. The result in the cities was a steady rise in the ratio of workers to dependents within the city population, and an increase in urban job opportunities for those communes that were already the richest in the nation. Wages did not rise, but urban per capita consumption, as a result, did rise much faster in the cities than in the countryside, as the data in Table 28 indicate. Comparable data on suburban communes are not available, but they would probably indicate a similar trend.

What happened after 1978? Part of the answer is that rural-to-urban

64 Roll, "The distribution of rural income in China," 72.
65 Dwight Perkins and Shahid Yusuf, *Rural development in China*, 115–19.

TABLE 28

Urban and rural consumption per capita (yuan in current prices)

	(1) Rural consumption	(2) Nonrural consumption	(3) Ratio (2)÷(1)
1952	62	148	2.39
1957	79	205	2.59
1965	100	237	2.37
1978	132	383	2.90
1980	173	468	2.71
1982	212	500	2.36
1986	352	865	2.46

Source: Chung-kuo ching-chi nien-chien, 1982, 7.28; and State Statistical Bureau, Chung-kuo t'ung-chi chai-yao, 1987, 98.

migration was not one of the liberalization measures introduced in that period. Many urban youth sent off to the countryside were allowed to return or returned on their own accord, and some rural people were allowed to move into the smaller towns by the mid-1980s, but rural residents still could not move to the cities easily. Large increases in purchase prices for farm produce did improve the rural residents' relative position, but because urban food sales prices were not raised, the cost of this measure to the central government budget was large and not likely to be repeated.[66] Large-scale investments in urban housing and general urban wage increases have helped urban residents keep their relative position vis-à-vis the rural areas. In any case, as long as farmers in the poorer regions of China are restrained from leaving those areas and moving to the cities or even to the county towns, rapid industrialization is likely to be accompanied by a large and possibly widening rural-urban income gap. The narrowing in 1980 and 1982 over 1978, therefore, should not be seen as the beginning of a long-term trend. The gap did in fact widen in 1986, although the quality of the data in Table 28 are such that strong conclusions cannot be drawn from small differences in the estimates.

CONCLUSIONS

Clearly, it is wrong to say that there was no economic strategy at all during the Cultural Revolution period. The investment plan was an unmodified version of a Stalinist emphasis on machinery and steel. Self-reliance

---

66 This issue is discussed at greater length in Lardy, "Agricultural prices in China."

or minimizing dependence on foreign imports and foreign technology had a Maoist ring when included in the rhetoric of the 1966–76 decade, but in practice self-reliance was not dramatically different from the Chinese autarkic policies of the 1950s or Russian policies toward foreign trade in the 1930s.

In rural China, policies owed much less to Soviet experience. To begin with, there was recognition that stagnation in agricultural output could be fatal. The question was how to achieve agricultural growth, not whether to do so, and China had a two-pronged strategy that combined the ideas of both "pragmatists" and "radicals" in an uneasy juxtaposition. The "pragmatists" pushed the rapid development of a chemical fertilizer industry plus increases in fertilizer imports. Those closer to Mao promoted the mass mobilization of labor and the Ta-chai model. They also insisted that a large portion of the modern inputs required by agriculture be provided by small-scale plants in rural areas.

In form, the system of planning and control over the economy remained true to the centralized Soviet model, modified only slightly by reforms instituted in the early 1960s. Five-year plans may have been problematic, but annual plans still governed what an enterprise was to produce. And key commodities and equipment were allocated by administrative means rather than through a market. Wages were paid in accordance with the Soviet eight-grade system, and rural collective incomes were based on the number of work points earned just as in the 1950s (except for the Great Leap) and the early 1960s.

If the form was the same, the actual implementation of policies within that form changed considerably in the late 1960s and early 1970s. The Soviet eight-grade wage system was designed to provide material incentives for more productive effort, but the Chinese removed these incentives by freezing promotions and eliminating bonuses. In the rural areas, political attitudes often counted for as much as effort in allocating work points. At the management level, enterprises continued to receive targets for cost and input reduction, but these targets did not have to be taken seriously if output targets were met. In addition, political considerations regularly interfered with judgments made in other countries on more technical grounds.

During the Cultural Revolution period itself, political interference and efforts to curtail the use of material incentives do not appear to have slowed growth. In fact, now that data are available with which to analyze growth in the late 1960s and early 1970s, development in the period, to the surprise of many analysts, was quite rapid except for the two years, 1967 and 1968, when political chaos was at a peak. But growth was built on ever higher levels of investment and inputs of energy that were being used more and more inefficiently with the passage of time. As long as the investment could continue to be raised and the Ta-ch'ing field poured out more and more petroleum, this was a viable means of maintaining growth, although a less effective means of raising the living standards of the population.

By the mid-1970s, however, labor discipline was breaking down after two decades of stagnant real wages, and production from the Ta-ch'ing and other oil fields peaked and threatened to decline. The rate of investment continued to rise, but the capital-output ratio may have been rising even faster. The years of steady growth based on the profligate use of human and material resources were coming to an end, whoever held the reins of political power.

Following Mao's death and the purge of the Gang of Four, in an attempt to accelerate development the interim leadership of China in 1977–78 made a dramatic turn outward, encouraging enterprises to import foreign technology in great quantity, and made an equally dramatic reversal of Cultural Revolution incentive policies by restoring bonuses, raising farm purchase prices, and implementing general wage increases and promotions. But the emphasis on machinery and steel continued, and this emphasis was not consistent with the new incentive and foreign trade policies.

In late 1978 and early 1979, Chinese planners finally abandoned Stalinist economics, at least temporarily. For the first time consumer goods received priority over producer goods both for home consumption and for export. China's development strategy had made a significant step toward the pattern pursued so successfully by its East Asian neighbors.

Some features of the first phases of the reform period did not last long. The effort to slow the overall growth rate so as to "readjust" the economic structure did not extend beyond 1981, when the growth rate in both industry and agriculture shot up. The deemphasis on heavy industry also proved to be temporary. In the 1982–86 period the ratio of heavy to light industry growth reverted back to levels similar to those prevailing during the Cultural Revolution. Stagnation in the supply of energy gave way to renewed growth in that crucial sector, making it possible once again to push the energy-using heavy industry sectors.

China's sectoral development strategy did not revert completely to earlier patterns, however. The turn outward, with an emphasis on expanded exports, borrowing abroad, and foreign direct investment in China, not only continued but grew and took on ever more diverse dimensions. The deemphasis on light industry and consumer goods was more apparent than real. The surge in agricultural production meant that consumer products to match the higher wages and other incentive payments were available.

In terms of sectoral growth strategies, China had made a significant move in the direction of the strategy that had proved so successful among its East Asian neighbors. Exports did not play as large a role in the development strategy of China as they did for, say, South Korea, but that was more a reflection of China's large size and the fact that trade is typically a smaller share of GNP in large countries than in small ones. China's trade ratios, though much smaller than those of South Korea or Taiwan, were similar to the ratios that prevailed in Japan in the 1960s. This Chinese trade ratio in comparison with the country's smaller neighbors was also an important reason why China had to pay more attention to the growth of heavy industry at this early stage of development as compared to South Korea, which in the 1960s could concentrate on light industry and meet its heavy industrial product needs through imports.

Changes in sectoral strategies were only one part of the reforms introduced after Mao's death in 1976 and the Third Plenum in December 1978. Of potentially greater significance were the moves fundamentally to change the system used to manage the economy.

Loosening of central management over foreign trade began as early as 1977, but centralized control had to be restored when enterprises took advantage of the situation to begin signing contracts for imports far in excess of China's ability to pay for them. The first reforms that lasted involved the removal of controls over the operation of rural markets. These were followed in the early 1980s by the introduction of the responsibility system that culminated in 1983 with the effective abandonment of collective agriculture. In five short years, 1979–83, China had gone from a collectivized agricultural system tightly controlled from above by a combination of state-set quotas and more informal slogans enforced by party cadres, to individual household agriculture controlled mainly through the indirect mechanisms of the market. A few marketing quotas remained, but steps were taken in the mid-1980s to begin removing these as well.

Removal of the Soviet-style system of planning and management in industry moved at a slower pace, in part because the changes required were much more complex than was the case with agriculture. Experiments with industrial systems reform began as early as 1979. These first efforts were in essence attempts to make the Soviet-style bureaucratic-command system work better. Changes were made in the way firms were managed internally, monopoly control over regional markets was relaxed in favor of competition, and the priority given to various plan targets was adjusted to give greater emphasis to efficiency-oriented targets and less emphasis to output targets.

By October 1984, in part because of the dramatic success of the rural reforms, the Party called for much more sweeping reforms in the industrial sector. Over the next three years important steps were taken toward changing China's industrial management and control system away from the centralized bureaucratic-command system of the past in the direction of a system combining market methods of control and coordination with continued bureaucratic control in key sectors. The goal, for some of the reformers at least, was a socialist version of the mix of market and state controls found in Japan or South Korea in the 1960s. The reality by the end of 1987, however, fell far short of this goal. Some members of the Politburo elected at the CCP's Thirteenth Congress in October 1987 probably still opposed changes of this magnitude in the economic system. Of equal or greater importance, bureaucratic systems of control were deeply entrenched and even the most determined reformers faced many obstacles in attempting to root them out.

In many ways China's changes in sectoral strategy and efforts to reform its economic system represented a long-delayed recognition of the country's underlying economic resources. The problem in agriculture was how to get the most food out of a very limited land endowment and an excess of labor power. Efforts to accomplish this goal through mass labor mobilization had failed. More chemical fertilizer and improved plant varieties were part of the answer, but equally important was the need to use these inputs more efficiently. Household-based agriculture had proved to be an efficient user of resources elsewhere in Asia and proved after 1981 that it could do equally well in China.

Similarly, a highly centralized system of planning and control was bound to be an inefficient method for controlling and coordinating several hundred thousand small-scale enterprises producing under widely varying conditions. Attempts to assert central control had led to local monopolies and other measures that seriously interfered with the growth and efficiency of the small-scale enterprise sector. When these controls were dismantled, the sector boomed.

With the boom in both agriculture and industry, China's gross national product rose at a rate nearly comparable to that experienced in the earlier booms of South Korea, Taiwan, and Japan. For eleven straight years from 1977 through 1987 China's net material product averaged a growth rate of over 8 percent a year. In per capita terms, gross national product doubled. Even with growth of this magnitude, however, China's economy in per capita terms was probably only comparable to that of Korea in the mid-1960s and to Taiwan's a few years earlier. The majority of China's labor force was still in agriculture, and an even larger percentage of the population still lived in rural areas. These percentages were falling rapidly in the 1980s, but it would take an additional decade or more of comparably rapid growth before most of China's population and work force would be urban and industrial.

The benefits of this first phase of accelerated growth were widely shared by the people of China. In fact, because the rural areas experienced the economic boom first, there even may have been some reduction in inequality nationwide in the early 1980s. The urban areas did less well, but their incomes did rise and most urban families began to purchase such consumer durables as refrigerators and television sets. Conceivably, continued rapid growth based on market principles could lead to increasing inequality. But in the late 1980s China still had a highly egalitarian distribution of the benefits of growth.

China by the end of 1987, therefore, was not a carbon copy of its East Asian neighbors on a mammoth scale. A socialist system evolving out of Soviet-style central planning was bound to end up somewhat differently from the mixed planning and market systems based on private ownership found elsewhere in East Asia no matter how hard Chinese reformers pushed for greater use of the market. China was also still some distance from the urban prosperity found in the rest of East Asia in the late 1980s. But China by the late 1980s had taken several giant steps away from the rural peasant economy steeped in poverty that had existed for millennia and that was still in evidence in modified form in the early 1970s.

CHAPTER 7

EDUCATION

THE ROLE OF THE SCHOOLS IN THE GPCR

Education emerged as both a means and an end during the Cultural Revolution decade. School-system reform was one of the movement's ultimate aims. But it was also launched from the schools with students and teachers mobilized as vanguards. Their influence extended well beyond education, setting the stage for changes in education and all other sectors as well. Because in retrospect the dual nature of education's role was often confused, this chapter distinguishes between the mobilization phase, which launched the movement, and the consolidation phase, aimed at institutionalizing the "revolution in education" thereafter.[1]

The events of 1966–68 can be interpreted as the mobilization phase of a mass movement like several others (beginning with the land revolution in the 1940s) that bear the Maoist imprint. This interpretation assumes that Mao, as initiator, had a larger aim in mind, namely, to ensure that the Chinese revolution would develop according to his own line for socialist construction and not that of others in the Party who disagreed with him. In this interpretation, the power struggle and mass participation in the assault against the bureaucracy are seen as the means rather than the end of the Cultural Revolution.

Mao's line had been introduced most systematically during the Great Leap Forward in 1958. Despite the economic disasters that had followed that venture, Mao was unwilling to abandon its goals even as the difficulties of achieving them divided the Party's leadership and crystallized the opposition against him. In accordance with his convictions, the socialist transformation of the economy was not sufficient; the realm of the superstructure had to be revolutionized as well. To accomplish that, ideas contradictory to his vision and the people who espoused them throughout the country had both to be changed. The Socialist Education Cam-

1 For sources for this interpretation, see note 14. Relevant later titles include Julia Kwong, *Cultural Revolution in China's schools, May 1966 – April 1969*; Liang Heng and Judith Shapiro, *Son of the revolution*; and Anita Chan, *Children of Mao*.

paign (as indicated in *CHOC* 14, Chapter 9) took up these goals but was inadequate to the task of achieving them. The Cultural Revolution, therefore, continued where that campaign left off, adding the necessary component of a power struggle within the ruling Party itself. Mao promoted the movement that would accomplish these ends as a successor in the continuous revolution that had begun with the democratic revolution, which took twenty-eight years to complete (1921–49), and the subsequent socialist revolution, which lasted seventeen years (1949–66).[2]

The 16 May 1966 Circular indicated the targets of the Cultural Revolution:

[to] thoroughly criticize and repudiate the reactionary bourgeois ideas in the sphere of academic work, education, journalism, literature and art and publishing, and seize the leadership in these cultural spheres. With this end in view, it is at the same time necessary to criticize and repudiate those representatives of the bourgeoisie who have sneaked into the Party, the government, the army and all spheres of culture, to clear them out or transfer some of them to other positions.

To launch so ambitious an enterprise, which entailed not just changing erroneous ideas but seizing power from those who espoused them, Mao turned to the mass movement. "Our experience since Liberation proves," asserted a key *People's Daily* editorial on 1 June 1966, "that the transformation of customs and habits can be accelerated if the masses are fully mobilized, the mass line is implemented and the transformation is made into a genuine mass movement." Mao then manipulated the mass movement to unleash the energies of the "masses" against the targets, much as he had used it to seize power in the villages of China during the land revolution. As land reform could not have succeeded as long as the old power structure dominated the countryside, so Mao's line and policies for socialist construction could not succeed until the power and authority of those opposed to them were broken. An important difference, however, was that those in authority who opposed him were the leaders of his own Party, which served as the vanguard of the entire revolutionary enterprise.

This was not the first time Mao had mobilized the masses to criticize the Party; but it was the most daring example thereof, given the nature and extent of the targets. The use of the masses in this way had a number of related functions. It was an effective method of attacking the targets; it permitted the masses to participate directly in the power struggle, thus giving them a personal stake in the process; and the natural leaders that

---

2 "Tsai chung-yang kung-tso hui-i shang ti chiang-hua" (Speech at a Central Committee work conference), 25 October 1966, in *Wan-sui* (1969), 658–59.

emerged among the masses during the movement provided a source of new recruits to succeed the overthrown power holders. In short, it would provide the successor generation to continue Mao's revolution after his demise.

Naturally, there would be "excesses." But Mao had discovered long before that excesses had a function. Hence, so long as these occurred during a "conscious struggle of the broad masses," they should be tolerated. They could be corrected afterward during the consolidation phase of the movement once the targets of mass anger had been overthrown. It would be wrong, therefore, to assume that all conditions obtaining at the height of the movement would be maintained during its later more moderate phases. These were the rules by which Mao had activated, promoted, and then curbed previous mass movements, and he followed the same pattern during the Cultural Revolution. Hence, he deliberately radicalized the movement from May 1966, allowing it on the one hand to take on a life of its own while on the other he manipulated the aroused masses until they had attacked all the points of resistance he had targeted including the leaders at the very top of the Party hierarchy. With the destructive phase having presumably achieved its purpose, the excesses could be corrected and a new superstructure could then be built by a new or at least a chastened set of leaders.

The changes introduced into the education system between 1968 and 1976 are to be seen as an integral part of the reconstruction phase of the movement because they could not have been instituted under the pre-1966 leadership. The abrupt and comprehensive return to the pre-1966 forms and structures that occurred after Mao's death in 1976 throughout the education system, and in many other sectors as well, provides added justification for this interpretation. With power lost, the policies were easily overthrown. The post-1976 reversals seem to offer final confirmation of the reality of the two-line struggle, except that it was settled then not on Mao's terms but on those of the enemies he had prophesied would require more than a hundred years and several more Cultural Revolutions to vanquish. He had also said, at the end of the first year of the Red Guard mobilization phase, that the consolidation of the movement would last for at least ten years.[3]

MASS MOBILIZATION

At the start, the big-character poster written by philosophy teacher Nieh Yuan-tzu, and others, at Peking University marked an intensification of

3 "Tui A-erh-pa-ni-a chün-shih tai-piao-t'uan ti chiang-hua" (Talk to the Albanian army representatives' group), 1 May 1967, in *Wan-sui* (1969), 677.

political activity in schools throughout the country. Nieh was secretary of the Philosophy Department's Party branch and among a group of Party members at Peita who had supported the 1964 Socialist Education Campaign at the university, crossing university president and Party Secretary Lu P'ing in the process. Her poster was put up on 25 May 1966; Mao had it broadcast nationwide and then published in the *People's Daily* on 2 June. It attacked two members of the Peking Party Committee and Lu P'ing for trying to restrain the development of the Cultural Revolution at the university, limit mass participation, and minimize the political significance of the movement by emphasizing its academic content.

In fact, political activity in the schools that spring had focused on academic matters. A critique of the education system had been gaining momentum following the same line of argument contained in Mao's 1964 Spring Festival commentaries already mentioned. The focus of the critique was similarly on curriculum, teaching materials, and political study. The debate over the play *Hai Jui dismissed from office* was also being treated as an academic controversy and a subject for student compositions rather than as a political attack against the critics of Mao's line for socialist construction.

Nieh Yuan-tzu's poster was significant for the sharper political focus it brought to the movement. Its publication on 2 June followed the equally provocative *People's Daily* editorial on 1 June entitled "Sweep away all monsters and demons." "In every revolution the basic question is that of state power," asserted this editorial. "In all branches of the superstructure – ideology, religion, art, law, state power – the central issue is state power. State power means everything. Without it, all will be lost."

Targets and participants

Students turned all of their attention to the movement after the 13 June announcement that the national college entrance examinations would not be held in July as usual that year. New enrollments would be delayed for a semester to allow the schools to carry out the Cultural Revolution and thoroughly reform the education system. In particular, a new form of enrollment would be devised to allow greater numbers of workers, peasants, and soldiers to attend college. But again, it was a question of power. The bourgeois authorities would never willingly give an inch. "If we don't hit them, they won't fall, and after they fall they try to stand up again," declared the *People's Daily* on 18 June. "Therefore the transformation of the educational system will certainly be a process of sharp and complex class struggle."

The Party organization continued to try to contain the movement. As noted in Chapter 2, work teams operating under the direction of Liu Shao-ch'i and Teng Hsiao-p'ing, in charge of the Party's day-to-day affairs, were sent into universities and middle schools throughout the country in early June. The teams had the most divisive effect in the universities. They tried to dampen the excitement, limit mass participation and violence, and isolate activity within individual campuses. In some places, the teams also apparently tried to deflect the target of the movement away from school Party leaders who, in Peking for example, had been attacked immediately after the publication of Nieh's poster. The work teams were later criticized for "pointing the spearhead downward" and attacking the many to protect the few. They also turned against the activists who had been most prominent during the preceding weeks and who resented the work teams' attempts to interfere with the new campaign.

During June and July, such violence as occurred was confined to campus. However, the movement developed differently in different parts of the country where the nature of the targets to be struggled against was not uniformly understood. Since the movement was being developed outside of and against the Party organization, the formal channels of direction from top to bottom were suspended. The movement therefore developed in the provinces on the basis of local initiatives in response to signals being given in the national news media, reinforced by such informal lines of communication as "letters from Peking" and report's of meetings by traveling Peking activists.

In Peking in June and July, leading university cadres were paraded around campus wearing dunce caps and criticized at school meetings for their bourgeois orientation toward education. In middle schools, mass criticism meetings were held against headmasters and Party secretaries. These were the first "monsters and demons" (*niu-kuei she-shen*, literally, cows' ghosts and snakes' spirits). During interrogation and criticism, they were held by the students under varying degrees of house arrest and confined in "cowsheds" (*niu-p'eng*). This was a figure of speech usually denoting not a barn but simply the room wherein the "cow's ghost" was being held. Eventually, the struggle against them ended and they were released to the surveillance of the masses, removed from office or "set aside," and made to do menial labor of some sort.

In Peking, where the movement was developing most rapidly, it was this sort of activity that the work teams tried to control and deflect, ultimately making targets of the rebel students such as K'uai Ta-fu at Tsing-hua University. There more than eight hundred students were labeled "counterrevolutionary" for such activities at this time.[4] They were themselves then placed under guard and restrictive surveillance and repudiated at mass meetings.

A few non-Party academic authorities were also struggled with and "set aside" at this stage. These were easy targets, people labeled in earlier campaigns if not for their bad class backgrounds, then for their pre-1949 associations with the Kuomintang (KMT) or their rightist inclinations and unregenerate behavior. Such persons were often referred to as the "five black categories" (*hei-wu-lei*), meaning landlords, rich peasants, counterrevolutionaries, bad elements, and rightists. Sometimes there were more black categories and sometimes fewer, depending on their presence in any given community. These targets, too, were held under varying degrees of surveillance for most of the next two years. In some parts of the country, they were the first "struggle objects"; the movement only turned against the administrative and Party leaders afterward, once it became known that bourgeois intellectuals were not intended to be the sole targets.

While trying to contain the movement, the work teams also mobilized a group of students to lead it in each school. These were mainly although not exclusively of good class background, that is, the children of workers, peasants, cadres (especially those who joined the Party before 1949), army men, and revolutionary martyrs. These were referred to as the "five red categories" (*hung-wu-lei*). Such students and those who otherwise supported the work teams were made leaders of the Cultural Revolution preparatory committees established in each school.

Mao ordered the work teams withdrawn from the schools at the end of July on the grounds that they were blocking the development of the Cultural Revolution. He subsequently referred to the work-team period, 10 June to 31 July, as the fifty days of "white terror." But when the work teams withdrew, they left the good class background students as leaders of the movement. These then imposed what they themselves advertised as a period of "red terror." In Peking it became known as "red August."

The diverse student groups began to take concrete shape after the work teams withdrew. Responding naturally to the impetus provided by the divergent signals coming from the center, students tended to split along similar lines. The "loyalists" (*pao-huang-p'ai* – literally: protect the emperor faction) or conservatives supported not so much the individual school leaders as the actions of the work teams and, by inference, Liu Shao-ch'i and the Party organization. The school preparatory committees

4 William Hinton, *Hundred day war; the Cultural Revolution at Tsinghua University*, 55.

served as the leadership for these students. The rebel students (*tsao-fan-p'ai*) stood in opposition. The resulting divisions grew into competing Red Guard groups.

Although the lines drawn between them were never absolute and tended to shift as the movement developed, with splinter groups and alliances forming and merging, nevertheless a pattern of participation developed that bore certain general similarities everywhere. Civilian and military cadres and their children tended to dominate the conservative side, and they were less inclined to attack the Party organization but more radical in acting against the other targets. People from middle-class and white-collar backgrounds – neither red nor white, as they often said of themselves – led the opposing rebel side. Bad class background individuals could also be found there when they participated at all. This side tended to be more radical in attacking the Party power structure, but less so with respect to the other targets with whom its members had many ties. Those of working-class origin were divided between the two sides and participated on both.

Most teachers and the lower-echelon cadres and staff – who did not qualify as targets of the movement, being neither bourgeois academics nor the handful of power holders taking the capitalist road – formed groups of their own. They, too, divided along similar lines and allied with corresponding student groups. Sometimes, as at Peking University, students and teachers participated together in the same groups from the start. Typically, the great majority of the middle school and college population thus participated at some time either actively or as sympathizers with one side or the other. For example, Chou P'ei-yuan, famous from 1972 on as a Peking University professor allied with Chou En-lai in the effort to raise the standards of university education, was actively associated in 1967–68 with the "rebel" faction at Peita. This group was opposed to Nieh Yuan-tzu's by then "conservative" Red Guard faction, which was more lenient in its orientation toward the Party authorities than were the rebels.[5]

Youth of good class background dominated the earliest Red Guard organizations, which were formed in August and September 1966. With the departure of the work teams, the struggle meetings against the targets grew more violent. The criticism of headmasters, Party secretaries, and bourgeois intellectuals continued, but in the process they were often beaten, ink bottles were thrown at them, and they were subjected to other indignities. The nature of the beatings and maltreatment varied from place to place only in degree, the most extreme cases being reported from middle schools in the provinces. The number of struggle objects also expanded somewhat under the "red terror." They now included bad class background students and others not initially targeted. These might be teachers never actually labeled "rightist" at any time but known to harbor rightist inclinations; or those with families and contacts abroad; or who had studied abroad and continued to enjoy a foreign bourgeois life-style although they had otherwise committed no political errors.

According to former teachers and students interviewed by the author in Hong Kong, about 10 percent or fewer of the teaching staff, concentrated among the older members, received the "monster and demon" treatment in each middle school and college. Intellectuals working in offices and research institutes were subjected to similar treatment. Hidden KMT agents and bad elements were ferreted out as well. During this period the homes of such struggle objects were ransacked as the Red Guards searched for bourgeois possessions and other incriminating evidence. Their immediate family members were also humiliated and mal-treated in different ways. Women were forced to kneel for hours on wash-boards, heads were shaved, confessions extracted, beatings administered. Individual deaths and suicides among the struggle objects did occur during this process and were reported from all localities.

Sometimes those who were not formally dubbed "monsters and de-mons" were similarly physically maltreated. Teachers were also partici-pants in the movement – students would put up wall posters denouncing teachers who held back from joining. All had to write self-criticisms analyzing how they had carried out the revisionist bourgeois line in edu-cation. All the students joined in this exercise, criticizing their teachers and evaluating their self-criticisms. For most teachers the matter ended there. Some with more serious "problems," even though not serious enough to merit a mass criticism meeting, were subjected to further investigation and interrogation. In the process, they were sometimes beaten and abused when answers were not readily forthcoming.

It was at this time that the Red Guards gained international attention as they marched out of their schools to attack the "four olds," that is, old ideas, old culture, old customs, and old habits, wherever they might be found. Old-fashioned street names were changed, and examples of "feudal" art and architecture defaced. Some schools were very strict in permitting only good class background Red Guards out onto the streets on their search-and-destroy missions. But in other schools, everyone went out, albeit divided into different formations, with good class background Red Guards together while middle-class youth moved in their own rebel groups.

Also in August, the Red Guards and others began traveling around the country free of charge to "exchange revolutionary experiences." Peking youth moved out into the provinces while provincial youth converged on Peking. There they participated in a series of huge rallies used by Mao and his followers to further mobilize and guide the movement. The first such rally was held on 18 August, attended by Mao himself, who accepted a Red Guard armband to demonstrate his support for their activities. Some 13 million young people journeyed to the capital that autumn before the offer of free travel was withdrawn. It was during such contact that Red Guards from the provinces learned, if they did not already know, about the true nature of the targets.

By autumn, Mao and his top followers now organized into the Central Cultural Revolution Group under the Central Committee were narrowing the focus of the movement directly onto the prime targets. These had become increasingly clear with the circulation of the 8 August "Sixteen Point Decision" of the Party Central Committee and Mao's own big-character poster, dated 5 August, entitled "Bombard the headquarters." Mao's poster praised that of Nieh Yuan-tzu and criticized those cadres who had tried to stifle the Cultural Revolution during the fifty days of the work-team period. This pointed directly toward Liu Shao-ch'i and Teng Hsiao-p'ing, who had sent out the teams. The Sixteen Point Decision stated that "the cultural and educational units and leading organs of the Party and government in the large and medium cities are the points of concentration of the present proletarian cultural revolution." It also cited rightists and reactionary bourgeois scholar despots as targets of the movement. But the Decision stated unequivocally that "the main target of the present movement is those within the Party who are in authority and are taking the capitalist road."[6]

Given the main target, Mao could not rely solely on the good class background Red Guards, because these were, if not led by children of the very cadres he aimed to overthrow, then at least predisposed to protect them. They could be mobilized easily to attack lower-ranking school headmasters and Party secretaries, but when the targets pointed clearly upward their usefulness became more problematic. Mao thus threw his support behind the rebels who had been on the defensive since June, unable to compete with the work teams and the early Red Guards. In Peking, finally exonerated for their earlier opposition, the rebels domi-nated the rally in T'ien An Men Square on 6 October. Everyone, not just those of good class background, was now encouraged to participate in the struggle to bring down the Party leaders who were taking the capital-

6 *JMJP*, 9 August 1966.

ist road. With the exclusivity of the good class background line officially criticized, loyalist strength waned while that of the rebels grew in late 1966. For a time they appeared to dominate the movement. For example, some ranking cadres' children and others who had led the movement at the start moved over to the rebel side; a few moved on to become antiestablishment "ultra-leftists"; others simply dropped out as the movement's targets moved closer to home.

Now the movement could develop a step further. The students were permitted to extend their range by entering other units to struggle with the power holders there. This expanded the action from the schools to factories and government offices, where the students joined in their struggles. It was officially forbidden to extort confessions by force (*pi-kung-hsin*), as it had not been during the early stage of the attack against school authorities. But the new targets were also beaten and maltreated. A popular practice at mass criticism meetings was "jet-planing" or forcing the accused to stand bowed during the proceedings with arms stretched out behind them.

Power seizure

By the end of 1966, the ultimate target was revealed: Liu Shao-ch'i was the chief capitalist-roader to be toppled. It had taken just half a year to escalate the movement from school headmasters to the Party Center. In January 1967, the Cultural Revolution leadership called upon the workers and peasants to join the intellectuals in seizing Party and state power. The January power seizure in the city of Shanghai was endorsed as official policy and swept the country, engulfing Party and government organs at all levels. The result was chaos as competing rebel groups and factions and the power holders themselves embarked on the struggle that was soon duplicated in one form or another in every province, city, and county throughout the country. The Party organization, carefully constructed to penetrate every work unit and administrative level, ceased to function. The popular movement spread until virtually the entire top echelon of the Party with the exception of Mao and Lin Piao were subject to mass criticism, together with all regional and provincial leaders.[7] Where protection was lacking, the power holders now found themselves subjected to the same kind of treatment that had earlier been directed at the lower-ranking and bad class background targets. This stage of the movement was symbolized by the criticism and humiliation of Liu Shao-

---

7 For a list of the ministers and deputy ministers responsible for education and culture who were criticized and removed from office at this time, see Julia Kwong, *Chinese education in transition: prelude to the Cultural Revolution*, 157.

ch'i's wife, Wang Kuang-mei, at a mass meeting orchestrated by K'uai Ta-fu and the Tsing-hua University rebels in April 1967. After the targets had been criticized and power seized, the lengthy and divisive process of setting up an alternative power structure began.

Mao clearly activated the nation's youth to serve as the spearhead of his revolutionary enterprise. But that he ever intended to hand over to the mobilized masses the control of Party and state power seems highly unlikely. Nevertheless, Mao's initial use of the masses not just to attack the powerholders but actually to overthrow them, was interpreted by some as the most significant feature of the Cultural Revolution, the end for which Mao initiated it. Certainly, it was unprecedented for a Communist leader to have allowed the non-Party masses to participate in a power struggle in this way. Hence the disillusionment that developed as the promise of mass participation in the subsequent exercise of political power gradually eroded after January 1967. It was essentially this issue that redivided the movement into "conservative" and "radical" wings.

What may never be known, however, is the extent to which Mao actually intended to allow the nation's mobilized rebel forces to share power after they had seized it from the incumbents, and the extent to which Mao's plans for the reconstruction of the power structure were ultimately determined by the factional warfare and bureaucratic resistance that developed in the wake of the January power seizures. Probably, Mao never meant to do more than chart a general course and unleash the mass movement in that direction, calculating that he could then work out the details of the route as he went along, in accordance with the "law of the mass movement," as he had done many times previously. Thus, the August 1966 Sixteen Point Decision did call for Cultural Revolution committees to be established as permanent mass organizations on the Paris Commune model to lead the movement (Article 9). But after the January power seizures, the task at hand was the creation not just of mass organizations but of a new form of state and administrative power. And Mao then opted for a more "conservative" variation, laying the groundwork thereby for the development of an "ultra-left" opposition as the dynamic of the movement played itself out.[8]

In February 1967, official policy shifted to curb the excesses created by January's unlimited power seizures. The center condemned anarchism, calling for revolutionary discipline and lenient treatment for cadres who corrected their mistakes. Mao himself endorsed the revolutionary committee, rather than the mass-dominated Paris Commune style of govern-

8 The best-known statement of the ultra-left position is "Whither China?" 6 January 1968, by the Hunan Provincial Proletarian Revolutionaries Great Alliance Committee, or Sheng-wu-lien, trans. in *SCMP*, 4190 (4 June 1968), 1–18.

ment, as the appropriate form for rebuilding the state power structure. The new revolutionary committees were to be based on three-in-one combinations initially made up at most levels of representatives of revolutionary cadres, army men, and mass leaders. Mao also gave the PLA a major role in the reconstruction process. The first call to the students to return to school to make revolution (*fu-k'o nao ko-ming*) was issued in early 1967, at the start of what would have been the spring semester. At that same time, in March 1967, Mao instructed that the "Army should give military training group by group and stage by stage in universities, middle schools and to senior classes in primary schools. It should also participate in the reopening of schools, the overhaul of organization, the establishment of leading organs based on 'three-way alliance,' and the carrying out of 'struggle-criticism-transformation work.' "[9]

These post–power seizure directives from the center gave the cadres and conservatives the opening they needed, and the rebels dubbed the ensuing swing against them the "February Adverse Current." The Cultural Revolution leadership accepted this verdict. To redress the balance created by the conservative current in favor of the power holders, the center issued a warning in March that the leaders of the mass organizations must not be relegated to a supporting role on the revolutionary committees or the Cultural Revolution would be negated. This led to an upsurge of criticism against the vice-premiers who together with Chou En-lai had tried to implement a moderate strategy for power seizure in the government ministries, thus giving strength to the Adverse Current.

Nevertheless, from this point forward, the center would never again allow the rebel masses to dominate the movement as they had been mobilized to do between October 1966 and January 1967. The March order to the PLA to enter the schools was symptomatic of Mao's restraint in this regard. Thereafter, the history of the movement was one of balancing and compromising with all of the forces in the power equation, namely, the Party–state bureaucracy led by Chou En-lai, the PLA led by Lin Piao, the Central Cultural Revolution Group, the membership of which itself was not united, and the feuding mass organizations. The three-way alliance that was established throughout the society in the revolutionary committees corresponded to the triumvirate of power at the top through which Mao manipulated the movement. Similarly, the divisions among the mass organizations after January 1967 also reflected differing orientations toward one or the other of the main forces in the power balance, even as all continued to declare their devotion to Chairman Mao.

<hr>

9 "Documents of the CCP Central Committee," trans. in *CB*, 852 (6 May 1968), 96.

The immediate task was daunting. The case of every cadre attacked had to be evaluated to determine the nature of his or her errors and standpoint in relation to Mao's thought. "Good" cadres could be reinstated and even allowed to sit on the new revolutionary committees. Considerable power was to have rested with the mass organizations because the revolutionary committees were to be formed on the basis of a democratic selection procedure. But here the problem was how to reach a consensus between and within the mass organizations, since they were split into a plethora of groups in every school and work unit. With the strife of recent months still fresh in everyone's memory, it was sometimes difficult to make members of different groups sit in the same classroom, much less agree on who the new leaders of the school should be. A cadre supported for reinstatement by one group would automatically be vetoed by its opponent and vice versa. Individual members would abandon one group and join another as disagreements grew.

By default if not design, the army representatives sent into each school following Mao's order of 7 March became the deciding force. In fact, they were supposed to reorganize the feuding groups into a single united all-school Red Guard unit that would then participate in the formation of the school's revolutionary committee. The aim from the start was to build the reorganized Red Guard organization into the successor of the Communist Youth League.

But the army representatives had the unenviable task of arranging a great alliance, establishing three-in-one revolutionary committees, and doing all of this in accordance with the center's class line policy. Conflicts did not arise over the regulations that excluded bad class background elements themselves (not their offspring) from participation in the mass organizations and even from returning to work as teachers or cadres if they remained unregenerate in thought and behavior. These were among the previously targeted "monsters and demons," and they were sent home to be reformed through labor under the surveillance of the masses. Tensions did occur, however, over the results of the ruling that those of good class background should be treated as the "mainstay" of the new Red Guard organizations in the schools. Moreover, "students who were not born of families of the laboring people may also join these organizations providing they have deep affection for Chairman Mao, have the revolutionary spirit of the proletariat and have consistently behaved themselves comparatively well politically and ideologically."[10]

10 "CCP Central Committee's regulations (draft) governing the Great Proletarian Cultural Revolution currently under way in universities, colleges, and schools," 7 March 1967, and "CCP Central Committee's opinion on the Great Proletarian Cultural Revolution in middle schools," 19 February 1967, both trans. in *CB*, 852 (6 May 1968), 87, 100.

The army was itself built upon good class background foundations and was, according to sophisticated city youth, dominated by simple "uneducated peasants." They were disciplined to obey orders and not inclined to tarry over the intellectually tedious exercise of assessing the revolutionary spirit among feuding middle-class rebels. The army therefore tilted in favor of the good class elements regardless of which groups they had belonged to or what actions they had engaged in previously. Naturally, it was good class individuals who became the leaders of the new Red Guard organizations and whose voices were weighted more heavily in the heated debates over the cadres and their reinstatement. As a rule, good class background people tended to accept the line coming from the center calling for a more lenient judgment on the cadres. They therefore became the natural allies of the PLA in the schools.

The middle-class students resented this reemergence of the class line that had initially excluded them from full participation in the movement. Now the new power structure was being rebuilt, and they were being relegated to second-class status once more. Some of them even refused to join the new Red Guard organizations. It was in this manner that the conservative–radical split reemerged in the spring of 1967. The line between the two sides was drawn as before primarily over power relationships, and the participants were usually although not always in the same place on either side of it. The line had shifted in late 1966 as the right to participate in the movement broadened and the targets were raised. In 1967, after the targets were overthrown, the mass organizations divided again over the question of who should participate in the new power structure.

The conservatives were generally distinguished from the radicals by a greater willingness to compromise with the former power holders. And these distinctions continued to be reinforced, although never absolutely in all cases, by the issue of class background. Those in the "five red categories" and especially those among them related by birth to the power holders inclined toward the conservative side. Although many different groups existed in any given school, these stood on one side or the other of the conservative-radical split, which was soon reinforced by city- and province-wide factional alliances. In Peking, the conservative groups associated themselves with the Heaven Faction, so named because of the dominant role played by a group at the Peking Aviation Institute. The opposing Earth Faction was led by a group at the Peking Geology Institute. In Kwangtung province, the conservative groups rallied under the banner of the East Wind Faction, while the radicals followed the Red Flag Faction.

But the radicals could not regain the initiative in the power balance unless official policy shifted back in their favor as it had in late 1966, and this did not happen apparently because Mao would not sanction it. Nevertheless, the center's posture was compromising and ambiguous as it officially tried to maintain the revolutionary momentum of January while searching for a workable balance within it. This allowed ample scope for individual leaders to manipulate the mass forces on all sides until armed conflict erupted among them. The divisions that emerged generally placed the Central Cultural Revolution Group on the side of the radicals and the PLA with the conservatives. Chou En-lai appeared to play the field in between while in fact leaning in the conservative direction.

When the army first entered the schools and began military training for everyone therein, the purpose was to promote alliance and instill discipline. To some extent it may have served that end. The Yenan Middle School in Tientsin was advertised as a model in this regard.[11] But what the military training also probably did was to add a new dimension to the conflict, because it was in the spring and summer of 1967 that factional strife escalated into serious armed clashes in many areas. The participants now turned their destructive impulses directly against each other.

It was after the Wuhan Incident in July 1967, when local conservatives kidnapped an investigator sent by the Central Cultural Revolution Group, that Chiang Ch'ing spurred the radicals on with her famous rallying cry, "Defend with weapons and attack with words." Thereafter, they raided military units for weapons and both sides soon had armed detachments. This period inspired a renewed radical upsurge. Some groups began attacking the entire power structure and all cadres within it whether or not they were "good" Maoists; some called for a complete and continuing redistribution of social and political power. They were now attacking simultaneously the government leaders, the conservative mass organizations, and the PLA.

At this point Mao again intervened on the side of moderation. The radical 16 May Group led by some members of the Central Cultural Revolution Group and aimed against Chou En-lai was exposed in early August; a planned radical campaign against power holders in the PLA was called off; and Chiang Ch'ing retracted her call to arms in early September. Measures were also announced that clearly signaled the onset of the consolidation phase of the movement. The tasks of rebuilding the Party and purifying class ranks were announced in the autumn. Workers rather than students were officially cited as the main force of the Cultural Revolution, and the students were criticized for having committed errors.

11 "*Chung-Fa* No. 85 (1967)," 8 March 1967, trans. in *CB*, 852 (6 May 1968), 96–98. For two collections of articles reflecting the situation in middle schools at this time, see also *CB*, 846 (8 February 1968) and 854 (24 May 1968).

They were told again, as they had been in the spring, that it was time to return to school. Mao issued a series of instructions in late 1967 all in the same vein, aimed at narrowing the targets, reaffirming a lenient policy toward the cadres, upholding the integrity of the PLA, and unifying the feuding mass factions.

It was on this basis that the provincial revolutionary committees were finally formed. Representative leaders of the provincial contenders for power including the PLA, the cadres, and the conservative and radical mass organizations were called to Peking. There they negotiated settlements among themselves, albeit under the active supervision of the Cultural Revolution Group, Chou En-lai, and the army. But instead of being submerged in the great alliance, the conservative-radical split was simply brought into the new governing revolutionary committees.

With the radicals now clearly on the defensive against the strengthening cadre-conservative coalition supported by the PLA, the center launched a final campaign against "rightist trends" in the spring of 1968. Violence again flared on both sides with factional fighters using weapons seized from the PLA and sometimes even drawing local army units into the conflicts. "The focal point of the contest for political power has all along been the struggle between the two lines on the question of cadres," declared one radical polemic at this time. Meanwhile, "bourgeois" cadres were being reinstated while revolutionary cadres were passed over and representatives of the radical mass organizations were being excluded from the middle school revolutionary committees. Even as fighting flared over these issues, some radicals were dropping out of the struggle anticipating that their side was sbout to become "part of the price paid for the revolution."[12]

The center issued orders banning armed conflict in July 1968. Mao summoned Peking Red Guards leaders to a meeting at which he castigated them for engaging in civil war.[13] When students refused to desist, Mao himself ordered the workers into the schools to stop the fighting. His gift of Pakistani mangoes to the Workers' Mao Thought Propaganda Team stationed at Tsing-hua University was advertised throughout the country as the symbol of Mao's support for the workers' presence in the schools. Once there, they together with the PLA ended the armed conflict and led the campaign to purify class ranks, while administering large doses of political study and Mao Thought propaganda to everyone. The

12 "Report on an investigation of right-deviation reversal of correct decisions in some middle schools in Canton" and "Though we've traveled all over these green hills we are not old yet," both in *Hung-se tsao-fan-che* (Red Rebels), new No. 2 (June 1968), trans. in *CB*, 861 (3 September 1968), 1–2, 20–21.
13 *Miscellany of Mao Tse-tung Thought (1949–1968)*, 469–97.

campaign to purify class ranks aimed to finalize once and for all the verdicts of the mass movement.

The officially designated targets to be formally removed from positions of authority and responsibility, and disciplined as necessary, were unregenerate bourgeois power holders and the five bad categories. But everyone came under scrutiny. All teachers were required to undergo one last round of mutual criticism and self-criticism to assess their behavior both during the movement and before against the Maoist standards now ascendant. Despite the evenhanded tenor of the directives from the center, the official bad class targets and the good class orientation of the new revolutionary committees, plus the presence of the workers and the PLA in all schools and colleges by the latter half of 1968, tipped the newly emerging power balance irrevocably toward the conservative-cadre side.[14]

The consolidation phase

The Ninth Party Congress, in April 1969, confirmed these developments. The Congress claimed victory with the establishment of the provincial revolutionary committees as organs of state power. But the revolution was not yet concluded since the struggle against the bourgeoisie would not die out with the seizure of political power. It remained to continue the struggle-criticism-transformation (*tou-p'i-kai*) stage and to "carry the socialist revolution in the realm of the superstructure through to the end." The Congress Report stressed that *tou-p'i-kai* must be carried out in every work unit in the country in the following stages: establishing a three-in-one revolutionary committee; carrying out mass criticism and repudiation; purifying the class ranks; consolidating the Party organization; simplifying administrative structures; and sending white-collar workers to participate in labor. To carry the revolution through to the end thereafter, it was imperative to carry out Mao's proletarian policies as stipulated at the start of the Cultural Revolution in the 16 May 1966 Circular and the Sixteen Point Decision.[15]

14 The definitive history of the mobilization phase of the Cultural Revolution remains to be written. The account here has relied on interviews conducted by the author in Hong Kong with former teacher and student participants in the events described, and also on the following: Byung-joon Ahn, *Chinese politics and the Cultural Revolution*; Lee, *The politics of the Chinese Cultural Revolution*; Stanley Rosen, *Red Guard factionalism and the Cultural Revolution in Guangzhou (Canton)* , part 2; David Milton and Nancy Dall Milton, *The wind will not subside: years in revolutionary China, 1964–1969*; Hinton, *Hundred day war*; Gordon A. Bennett and Ronald N. Montaperto, *Red Guard: the political biography of Dai Hsaio-ai*; Neale Hunter, *Shanghai journal*: an eyewitness account; Jean Daubier, *A history of the Chinese Cultural Revolution*; Ken Ling, *The revenge of heaven: journal of a young Chinese*; Ruth Earnshaw Lo and Katharine S. Kinderman, *In the eye of the typhoon* an *American woman in China during the Cultural Revolution*; Anita Chan, "Images of China's social structure," *World Politics* (April 1982), 295–323.

15 On the Ninth Party Congress documents, see *CB*, 880 (9 May 1969), also *CB*, 904 (20 April 1970).

Thus, the Cultural Revolution was proceeding more or less on the course Mao had initially charted: first seizing power and then using it to transform the superstructure in accordance with his line. The theme of *tou-p'i-kai* reiterating this logic of the mass movement ran throughout from the Sixteen Point Decision (Article 1) to Mao's March 1967 instruction sending the army into the schools, the Ninth Party Congress, and on into the early 1970s. The policy line for the revolution in education as part of this process was also similarly outlined from the start both in the June 1966 decision on changing the system of enrollment and in the August Sixteen Point Decision (Article 10).

According to these two policy statements, the education system would be thoroughly transformed. A new way of enrolling students into college and senior middle school would be devised because the existing method had failed to free itself from the set patterns of the bourgeois examination system. The new method of selection on the basis of recommendation and proletarian politics would aim to give greater access to working-class youth. In addition, all the arrangements for schooling, testing, and promotion would have to be transformed together with the content of education. The period of schooling would be shortened. Courses would be fewer and better. Although the main task of students was to study, they would also learn other things such as industrial and agricultural knowledge and military training. Studies would be conducted to determine how best to combine education with productive labor.

Teaching materials would be simplified and new ones compiled under the guidance of Mao's Thought. All students from the beginning of primary school through college would be required to study Mao's works. Such a thoroughgoing revolution would, within the context of the larger class struggle, eliminate one important power base of the bourgeois authorities in the ideological realm. It would destroy the breeding ground for intellectual aristocrats together with their imposing airs and hereditary treasures.[16]

EDUCATION IN THE GPCR

The Maoist–Red Guard critique of education

These principles constituted the foundation on which was built all three phases of the movement – struggle, criticism, and transformation – as it unfolded in the schools. Initially, as indicated, the Party organization had tried to concentrate the movement on intellectual matters and educational

16 *JMJP*, 18 June and 9 August 1966.

reform.[17] As the movement escalated out of the Party's control, Mao's educational principles provided the basis for the criticism of teachers and of the struggle objects. The language grew harsh and accusatory as it turned against the targets, imitating the polemical line of the official media to "drag out" the academic power holders and bourgeois intellectual authorities who had presided over the breeding ground for intellectual aristocrats.

The question of actually transforming the education system was then thrust into the background as the Red Guards moved out into society to bring down the power holders everywhere. Educational reform itself belonged to the consolidation phase of the movement and thus had to await the dampening of factional conflict. The first call to return to school to make revolution (*fu-k'o nao ko-ming*) was issued in early 1967. Primary schools were to resume classes following the Spring Festival holiday in February. Middle school teachers and students were told to stop going out to exchange experiences as of 1 March. Those at the college level were ordered back on campus before 20 March.[18] The obstacles thereafter encountered have already been described.

Nevertheless, some middle schools where factional strife was less intense did manage to restore some semblance of school life by the autumn semester of 1967, when the center again called on all schools throughout the country to resume classes immediately.[19] In between military training and Mao Thought study classes, the students were organized to criticize their textbooks and other features of the school system. By the end of 1967, the first groups of senior middle students were leaving school again, but this time to take up their first job assignments. By the spring semester of 1968, many middle schools were enrolling their first classes of new students since the start of the Cultural Revolution. Older students first served as class monitors for the new students and then were progressively sent out, the majority to work in the countryside and on state farms. For college students, demobilization did not begin until 1968. The 1965 and 1966 graduates were given work assignments in 1968, the target areas for them being the "mountains, villages, and border regions." The graduating classes of 1967 and 1968 were sent down under a uniform national policy for one year or more of manual labor on army-run

---

17 For criticisms dating from this period, of Chou Yang's effort to undermine the 1958 educational revolution after 1961, and of similar actions by the ex-head of the Education Department of the Peking CCP Committee, Chang Wen-sung, see *CFJP*, Shanghai, 11 August 1966 and *Pei-ching jih-pao*, 21 June 1966, trans. in *SCMP*, supplement, 155 (28 September 1966), 1–21.
18 According to the instructions issued in the name of the CCP Central Commitee for three school levels in February and March 1967, all trans. in *CB*, 852 (6 May 1968), 62, 87, 99.
19 *Chiao-yü ko-ming* (Education revolution), Peking, 17 November 1967, trans. in *SCMP*, supplement, 218 (20 February 1968), 1.

farms, after which they, too, were assigned work. Thus ended the turbulent school careers of the Red Guard generation of students.

But they left behind them a detailed if less than dispassionate critique of the pre-1966 education system. Since the critique was essentially a product of the 1967–68 demobilization phase, before reunification had been effectively imposed, it reflected the conflicting interests of the different groups that produced them. At Tsing-hua University where the combatants were still locked in struggle, the call to transform education was rejected by factional leaders on both sides. They argued that power was the crucial issue and that it was meaningless to discuss specific reforms until the question of which side would control the universities was settled.

In Kwangtung, it was the conservatives who more readily responded to the call from the center to focus on educational reform. The radicals initially resisted it as a conservative ploy to suppress the larger revolution. They remained preoccupied with the power struggle that they were then in the process of losing. Once it became clear that education reform was the next order of business, the two sides tended to interpret the issue from different perspectives. For example, the conservatives, dominated by good class background leaders, emphasized the responsibility of teachers and bourgeois intellectuals for the pre-1966 revisionist line, which discriminated against workers and peasants. The radicals, led by middle-class elements, blamed the power holders more than the teachers and focused on the unfair advantages enjoyed by their main competitors, the cadres' children. Whatever the variations, however, the critique was essentially inspired by guidelines coming from the center. Taken as a whole, therefore, it not only provided a detailed account of the pre-1966 system from a Maoist perspective but indicated the new directions for the future.

The Yenan experience and the system inherited from the KMT. The Yenan Anti-Japanese Military and Political College (K'ang-ta) was extolled as a model of proletarian education that had trained large numbers of revolutionary cadres. After 1949, a choice had to be made on the educational front whether to use the Yenan experience to transform the KMT system or vice versa. Mao was said to have advocated the former and Liu Shao-ch'i the latter. Liu and the revisionists maligned K'ang-ta–type education as "irregular" and "out-of-date," as character-building classes for cadres, and as inappropriate for national adaptation.

The Soviet experience. The capitalist-roaders therefore turned to the Soviet Union for inspiration. The education system, the curriculum, the substance of what was taught, teaching methods, examination methods –

everything was taken over from the Soviet Union. Some schools run along the lines of K'ang-ta were reorganized into "regular" universities. The style and forms of education developed in the old liberated areas before 1949 were thus obliterated.

The Great Leap Forward. In 1958, Mao launched a great education revolution. The monopoly of education by bourgeois intellectuals was broken; the system they led was repudiated as an unseemly mix of feudalism, capitalism, and revisionism. But Mao's opposition maligned the specific policies and measures advanced during the education revolution, calling it a "deviation," and in the early 1960s they set about restoring the education system to its pre-1958 form. Virtually every development that had occurred in education since 1960 that Mao had not personally sanctioned was reinterpreted as a perversion of his correct line for education, with Liu Shao-ch'i as the leader of the opposition.

Leadership. Mao's opposition advocated that the leading role of the Party branch in schools be abolished and the Party be demoted to the role of supervisor. Leadership would be handed back to the bourgeois intellectuals; those branded rightists would be exonerated; and all intellectuals would be honored for working in the service of socialism.

The two-track education system. From the early 1960s onward, Party leaders "taking the capitalist road" had concentrated on training bourgeois intellectuals. They had therefore emphasized the regular full-day schools at all levels. Most of the work-study schools set up during the Great Leap to expand education had been closed, particularly in the countryside. So had the school-run factories set up at the same time. But when Liu saw in 1964 that he could not override Mao's directives to reform the education system, he began to promote his "two-kinds of education systems" as a means of circumventing Mao's line. Lin's strategy was to divert Mao's demands for labor and practical training into the work-study stream while leaving the full-day schools unchanged. The result was the same as the "two-track" education systems of capitalist countries, with one kind of education for the talented and well-to-do and another kind for the working classes.

The keypoint schools. The imagery of the pagoda with its ranks and tiers was used to describe these schools. Liu was said to have advocated that the education system, with the key schools at its apex, take on the shape of the pagodas of old, which had accommodated fewer and fewer scholars for study and contemplation in each of their ascending tiers. Only the highest degree-holders were permitted to occupy the topmost level. Similarly, only a relative few of the "best" students were permitted to study in the precious pagoda keypoint schools, with their newly rebuilt and lavish surroundings. Meanwhile, ordinary students had to study in ordinary schools, while workers and peasants sometimes had no schools at all.

Social stratification. Red Guard groups from key schools publicized the class backgrounds of their student bodies. Different groups concentrated their criticism in different directions, depending on their own family background. But the net result was the same: Students from cadre and middle-class intellectual families predominated in the key schools; working-class youth were in a minority, and peasants few to nonexistent. This class composition was the combined result of the dual criteria of high academic achievement and good class background, which governed admissions to these schools in differing degrees during the pre-1966 period. At the college level, worker-peasant students admitted under the recommendation system in 1958 and 1959 were expelled or held back and ultimately weeded out. This was because they could not keep up with the course work under the more rigorous standards reinstituted in the early 1960s.

Teaching methods and content. Mao had personally set the tone for the critique in this area with his much-quoted comments beginning with those made at the 1964 Spring Festival Forum. Later he had also criticized the pedantic and impractical nature of college education. He recommended that everyone including administrators, faculty, and students should go to the countryside to see the land and the people. Red Guard critics elaborated on these themes. Teaching methods were based on cramming and memorizing texts. Students were locked into an examination life from the start of primary school onward. In such a system, they were of necessity studying "behind closed doors," cut off from production and practice.

The aims of study. In schools where politics and practice are neglected while the primary goal is book learning, the students must also be obsessed with grades, promotion rates, and the competition for a place in college. The system controls them in this manner and absorbs them into itself. Such students are ultimately motivated by selfish ambition to the exclusion of political or social objectives. The same was true for the schools themselves. All manner of stratagems were used to push up pass rates at the expense of the lower-scoring students so as to gain glory for the school. Special keypoint classes were set up within schools; students were channeled into different streams on the basis of their grades; those with lower marks were encouraged to drop out before graduation so as not to influence the school's promotion rates. Such were the conditions prevailing in the regular full-time schools. Hence their system of enrollment, examinations, and promotion with the threat of being held back in case of failure were "instruments for the bourgeoisie to exercise dictatorship in education" and exclude worker-peasant children from school. Such schools were havens for the best and most experienced teachers with high academic qualifications. These were passing on their bourgeois values to succeeding generations of students.

The youth-to-the-countryside program. Ideally, this program was a way of contributing to the socialist goal of reducing urban-rural differences. In reality, the program was being used as an appendage of the regular school system. The "best" urban youth were accommodated in that system; the "refuse" who were poor in conduct, study, and class background were sent to the countryside after junior middle school, and even the peasants looked down on them as a result.

Mao's response. Following the socialist transformation of the economy in China there appeared tendencies toward capitalist restoration within the CCP of which the revisionist line for education was a part. This coincided with a growing revisionist trend in the international communist movement. In order to prevent China from changing color, Mao developed his theory of class and class contradictions in socialist society and policies for continuing the revolution therein. Mao saw the struggle to win over the younger generation as "the most important question" in that endeavor and concluded that China's youth must be cultivated for the revolution in the storms of class struggle. He also personally issued many instructions on education work following his comments at the 1964 Spring Festival Forum. His aim was to create a system designed to reduce the three distinctions, that is, between mental and manual labor, between workers and peasants, and between town and countryside. But simple reforms in textbooks and teaching methods were not enough. Rather, it was necessary to "criticize and repudiate thoroughly the revisionist educational line, establish Chairman Mao's educational line, and cultivate successors to the revolutionary cause." The Cultural Revolution and the education revolution that was a part of it were the means Mao finally chose to realize his objectives.[20]

---

20 This critique is pieced together from many sources. Perhaps the single most comprehensive presentation of the official version is: "Shih-ch'i nien lai chiao-yü chan-hsien shang liang-t'iao lu-hsien tou-cheng ta-shih-chi" (Chronology of the two-line struggle on the educational front during the past seventeen years), *Chiao-yü ko-ming*, Peking, 6 May 1967, tran. in Peter J. Seybolt, ed., *Revolutionary education in China: documents and commentary*, 5–60. See also *JMJP*, 18 July, 28 October,

The Maoist transformation: national adaptation of the Yenan experience

In 1967–68, the official press was inundated with proposals aimed at revolutionizing education. Individual colleges, middle schools, and administrative districts were all urged to work out their own proposals. Inspired by the same Maoist principles which were also circulating in newly published compilations of Mao's quotations on education,[21] they soon transformed the above critique of the pre-1966 system into its opposite in the form of positive prescriptions for change. These were always tentative and experimental, advanced for "testing in revolutionary practice." A few individual proposals were singled out as models and pacesetters indicating that they in particular had official approval.

But the hallmark of the experiment was decentralization and flexibility, albeit always within the confines of Mao's educational principles. Hence, it is impossible to determine – as with the political objectives of the Cultural Revolution – the extent to which Mao intended the most radical proposals initially advanced to be retained, and the extent to which their gradual erosion during the early 1970s was the result of the clearly apparent resistance to them. Once again, the most plausible conclusion is that Mao meant only to chart the general course, pushing it to extremes initally in order to ensure that the changes he desired were made, and then allowing the dynamic of the movement to work itself out, assuming that with the necessary intervention from time to time he could keep the developing system on the line he had set.

In the process, it should be noted, the "conservative–radical" terminology that had been applied to the contending Red Guard factions took on a meaning almost diametrically opposite to that used by them. Thus the "conservative" leadership coalition of cadres, army , and workers was responsible for enforcing the "radical" education revolution in the schools. Meanwhile, among the former rebels and radicals there developed a conservative resistance to the reforms. On the new radical side at the center was what was left of the Central Cultural Revolution Group (after the purge of its left wing in 1968), led by Chiang Ch'ing in the name of Mao. This would become the radical Gang of Four and their followers. Arrayed against them would be former rebel intellectuals such as Chou

21 November, 22 November 1967, and Hinton, *Hundred day war*, 20–40, 139, 171–78. For the Red Guard variations and local elaborations, see Rosen, *Red Guard factionalism*, part 1; Stanley Rosen, *The role of sent-down youth in the Chinese Cultural Revolution: the case of Guangzhou*; Lee, *The politics of the Chinese Cultural Revolution*, 78–84, 306–8.

21 For example, *Mao Chu-hsi chiao-yü yü-lu* (Quotations from Chairman Mao on education), (Pei-ching tien-chi hsueh-hsiao, Tung-fang-hung kung-she, July 1967); and *Chairman Mao on revolution in education*, trans. in *CB*, 888 (22 August 1969).

P'ei-yuan, supported by Chou En-lai, and ultimately allied with the Cultural Revolution's main targets, both power holders and bourgeois academics.

The new education system that emerged after 1968 was never officially standardized on a nationwide basis. On many points, its "experimental" nature continued until the autumn of 1976. The result was a provisional system that changed almost from year to year and varied in detail from place to place. This also made it difficult for the observer to differentiate between variations that occurred within the spirit of the guidelines coming from the center and variations that went beyond. Nevertheless, these guidelines defined the basic parameters of the new education system.

Leadership and administration. The declared objective was to break the domination of the old power holders and the bourgeois academics. At the national level, the Ministries of Education and Higher Education ceased to function in 1966. Harking back to the 1944 Yenan reforms, the authority of the formal education bureaucracy was thus similarly circumscribed. Responsibility for making education policy was taken over by the Central Cultural Revolution Group and its special education committee. In 1972, the Science and Education Group was formed under the State Council. The Education Ministry was not revived until 1975, when its total working staff numbered only about three hundred.

Education administration was decentralized down to the level of the provincial education bureaus and beyond. What this meant, for example, was that at the college level the national unified curriculum, textbooks, and teaching materials fixed by the Education Ministry were all abandoned. Each institution devised its own curriculum and prepared its own teaching materials. At the secondary and primary levels, the nationally unified curriculum and textbooks were also abandoned. Responsibility for preparing these was sent down to the provincial education bureaus and beyond. Provinces, cities, and even communes made decisions on length of schooling, curriculum, and study plans that had previously all been centralized. The unified national college entrance examinations were also abolished, and responsibility for college enrollment was transferred to the candidates' work units. Middle school graduates were no longer permitted to go directly to college without working for a period of time first, hence the authority given to their work units in this matter.

At the county level, the authority of the state education bureaucracy vested in the county education bureaus was also set down. Rural primary schools were run by the production brigades within communes; existing state-run primary schools in the countryside were supposed to be transferred to production brigade management as well. Middle schools were also managed by the communes and brigades.

What this meant in practice was a system of dual administrative responsibility whereby leadership was exercised jointly by the county education bureaus and the localities. For example, state funds were shared out in different ways among all schools in the county, and then supplemented by local collective financing. Together with such local funding went personnel power or the right to hire, fire, and transfer teachers and staff. But this power was also shared in different ways since a typical rural primary school would have some teachers assigned and salaried by the state through the education bureau, and some hired locally and paid in work points from production brigade income. This was, in effect, the latter-day adaptation of the old *min-pan kung-chu* formula, or schools run by the people – now organized into a collective – with state help.

The circumvention of the formal education bureaucracy was institutionalized at the individual school level in the revolutionary committee. The first revolutionary committees, as noted, were formed on the basis of representative combinations of cadres, the mass organizations, and the army or militia. Once the Red Guard generation had been mustered out, the army generally withdrew from active participation in school leadership, at least at the lower levels. Its place on the middle school revolutionary committees and its role as guardian of discipline and order were inherited by the workers' propaganda teams. These remained in urban schools until after Mao's death, when they were officially withdrawn. The presence of the peasant propaganda teams in rural schools was much more of a formality and often only a temporary one at that. Local leadership was in any case exercised directly by the production brigade Party secretary and the commune Party organization.

Indeed, by the early 1970s after the Communist Party's organizational life had resumed, the school Party branch and its revolutionary committee were closely integrated. They constituted a form of unified leadership that was duplicated throughout the system from top to bottom. It was for the purpose of strengthening education work that first Party secretaries at all levels were made responsible for education work in the early 1970s. According to one source, Mao himself had "suggested" that the Party secretaries at the provincial, prefectural, and county levels take charge of education.[22]

---

22 Chang Hsueh-hsin, representative of the Higher Education Bureau, Ministry of Education, Peking, in an interview with the author, 19 July 1977; and Kwangtung radio broadcast, 21 August 1972, in *Union Research Service*, 69.5.

In individual schools, the unification of leadership was achieved through the familiar practice of concurrent positions. The leading members of the school's Party branch were always members of the school revolutionary committee. The head of the workers' propaganda team was always a Party member and would typically hold concurrent positions on the Party branch committee and revolutionary committee, being the worker representative thereon. The student mass representatives were soon dropped from the revolutionary committees. The Red Guard generation of student leaders were not replaced after they graduated and left school. Their places as mass representatives were taken by younger teachers who had distinguished themselves as activists in the movement or in some other way. But such mass leaders were quickly recruited into the Party so that they did not sit for long on the revolutionary committees as non-Party members. In fact, different kinds of three-in-one combinations were promoted, but the revolutionary committee was always closely integrated with the Party branch.

As for the cadre representatives, these were often transferred in from other schools in the same city or county. This was to avoid the difficulties that would arise if a leader tried to return to work at the same school where he or she had been repudiated by mass criticism. The hierarchical order by which the cadres lived and worked was itself never broken, however. The power holders had been submitted to great personal humiliation and required to perform menial labor at the height of the movement. But once the decision was made to reinstate them, as it was in most cases, the person was assigned work at a rank comparable to that held previously. This process, which occurred throughout the system, was exemplified at the national level by the return to power of Teng Hsiao-p'ing in 1973.

The authority of the "bourgeois academics" was more effectively circumscribed during the consolidation period than was that of the former power holders. Those among the older intellectuals who were deemed to be among the unregenerate five black elements were dismissed. In each school, there was at most only a handful of such people. More numerous, particularly in the good keypoint schools, were those who made up the "backbone" of the teaching staffs. These tended to be older experienced teachers, not landlords or capitalists themselves but often of bad class background or with some problem to cloud their political histories. Such teachers were typically among those reassigned to new schools or sent down to nearby rural schools to strengthen their teaching contingents. These teachers tended to regard themselves as being "sacrificed" to the new policy of equalizing the quantity and quality of schooling.[23]

At least three related changes were therefore occurring simultaneously in education administration under the impact of these reforms. One was decentralization within the education bureaucracy. A second was deprofessionalization with the authority of the intellectuals broken and that of the former power holders now diluted partly by leaders (the workers) brought in from outside the educational sphere and partly by younger activists brought up in the course of the movement. This development was summarized in the saying that nonprofessionals (*wai-hang*) should lead professionals (*nei-hang*). A third related change was the strengthening of local community and especially local Party control over education. Thus when deprofessionalization occurred, it was introduced primarily at the hands of the local Party authorities. Ironically, since the Cultural Revolution initially seemed designed to reduce the scope of Party in deference to popular control, the post-1968 changes actually strengthened local Party leadership over education.

Following the spirit of the Yenan reforms, however, the objective of these changes was to facilitate the development of an education system that would be appropriate to the life and work of each locality, but without fixing clear-cut hierarchies between different kinds of students. Flexibility was the hallmark of the new system. During previous phases of rapid expansion and reform, the regular academic system had continued to function more or less as before while the changes went on around it. With the reforms of the Cultural Revolution decade, the entire system was drawn into the movement.

Quantitative and structural changes at the primary and secondary levels. The two-track distinction between the full-time and work-study schools was abolished. So, too, were all forms of special and elitist education including the keypoint schools, special schools for cadres' children, schools that enrolled only girls or boys, Overseas Chinese schools, and those exclusively for national minorities. Most of these were converted into ordinary neighborhood schools. This facilitated a concurrent development, namely, The nationwide program of school expansion that was sustained throughout the period. The unified entrance examinations that had governed admission from the junior middle level upward were abolished. Students

---

23 On the political role of teachers and their tenacity in promoting their group interests in the face of overwhelming pressures to the contrary, see Gordon White, *Party and professionals: the political role of teachers in contemporary China.*

attended their nearest neighborhood school. At the primary level, the effort was to achieve universal schooling in areas that had not yet done so. Such areas were mainly rural. The expansion of secondary schooling occurred in both the cities and the countryside.

A 1944 statement by Mao was revived and frequently quoted to promote this expansion in the rural areas: "In our education we must have not only regular primary and secondary schools but also scattered, irregular village schools, newspaper-reading groups and literacy classes."[24] Thus, no effort was ever made to erase absolutely the regular-irregular distinction. Consequently the contemporary criticism of the "two-track" system should not be interpreted too literally. It was the division of the national educational system into a fixed hierarchy of learning that was challenged, not inequality and irregular schools as such.

As indicated, the chief means used to popularize rural schooling in the early 1970s was the adapted *min-pan kung-chu* formula. The pressure to promote schooling came from above and through the Party leadership. But the production brigades and the communes built the schools, hired sufficient local teachers to staff them often relying on sent-down city youth to supplement the rosters, and provided the administrative structure to maintain the rural school networks. Also, the specific content of the *min-pan kung-chu* formula now varied widely in practice depending on the wealth of the area and, in turn, on the size of its state education budget. This changing and varying nature of the formula was itself an indicator of development.

Thus, the prejudice against "irregular" schools, as exemplified by the local rejection of agricultural middle schools in the early 1960s, actually continued and applied to a certain extent to the *min-pan* primary schools as well. Just as virtually all the *min-pan* schools set up in the cities in the late 1950s were soon either closed or absorbed into the expanding state system, so there seemed an irresistible tendency for the rural *min-pan* primary schools also to push for increasing shares of state assistance whenever possible. When there are no schools at all the problem does not arise. But when development has progressed to the point where schools are not only widespread but where people generally accept the value of universal primary schooling – in itself an important change that has occurred in the Chinese countryside over the past thirty years – then the demands for equality appear. This popular demand is expressed at least in a lack of enthusiasm for clearly inferior alternatives. At the secondary level where

---

24 Originally from "The United Front in Cultural Work," 20 October 1944; quoted in *Chairman Mao on revolution in education*; also in *HC*, 6 (1971), 38, and *HC*, 6 (1973), 75.

the cost-benefit equation for local families is more complex, rural people prefer no school to the inferior agricultural middle school. At the primary level, they will support an inferior *min-pan* school, but not without demanding increasing amounts of state assistance if it is available.

In parts of Kwangtung, in Fukien, and in suburban Shanghai, therefore, the formula could just as appropriately have been "state-run with collective assistance." According to interviewees – mainly former teachers from these areas – many rural primary schools were by the mid-1970s already primarily state-financed. Student tuition was always collected even in such schools, however, and contributed something to education budgets. The production brigades were typically responsible only for paying the salaries of teachers hired within the brigade itself, and supplementing insufficient building and maintenance allocations.

In one suburban Peking commune, according to one of its ex-teachers, even the salaries of the locally hired teachers were paid from the education budget allocated by the state, and the primary schools were regarded by all as "state-run." This informant said that he always thought *min-pan* schools were "just some propaganda they made up for the newspapers." Neither he nor his wife, both of whom had worked for almost twenty years in several near and far suburban communes around Peking, had ever come across a *min-pan* school. For the more "classic" version, one had to look farther afield to more educationally underdeveloped provinces, such as Yunnan or Sinkiang. There it was easier to find communes and production brigades that themselves set up their schools, provided facilities, and financed them entirely from collective income. Nevertheless, the most common formula for the rural primary schools was some variant of local collective management and financing within the larger framework of state assistance. It was this formula, together with other measures designed to boost rural attendance rates, which made it possible to claim that primary school education was "almost universal" with 95 percent of all school-age children, or 150 million, in attendance at the end of the Cultural Revolution decade.[25]

The only area where interviewees report that expansion of primary schooling did *not* occur was in the Overseas Chinese districts of southern Fukien. Enrollments did not necessarily decline, but the number of schools did when Overseas Chinese funding largely ceased during the Cultural Revolution decade. In some communes of Ch'üan-chou prefecture, virtually every village had its own primary school and close to half of them were built and sustanied by contributions from Overseas Chinese

25 Education Ministry interview, 19 July 1977; see also Table 29.

in Southeast Asia. Instruction was often provided tuition-free in these schools because of generous endowments both from individuals and from clan organizations. The pattern of Overseas Chinese funding continued until 1966 and resumed in the late 1970s.

These schools, regarded as a latter-day version of the old private and clan schools, are not considered *min-pan* or collectively financed. Such externally funded schools also represent an exception to the general rule that, given a choice, local communities prefer to have a completely state-run school rather than one financed locally. So generous has been the support of Overseas compatriots that the schools they finance are said to be, particularly in their post-1976 reincarnations, sometimes even better outfitted than local keypoint institutions.

The *min-pan kung-chu* formula was also responsible for a substantial portion of the increase in rural secondary school enrollments during the Cultural Revolution decade. A common practice was to reduce primary schooling from six years to five, following official guidelines, and then to add junior middle classes of one or two years' duration to the existing primary schools to accommodate their graduates. The complete middle school established in the commune center was usually primarily state-funded, however. The rapid rise officially claimed for secondary school enrollments as shown in Table 29, is confirmed by all interviewees. The proclaimed standard of at least one four- or five-year complete middle school in every commune was the norm achieved, according to former teachers from Kwangtung, Fukien, Chekiang, and Shantung. Yunnan lagged well behind this standard. Suburban Shanghai and Peking, already well in excess of it before 1966, expanded on the existing base, building enough new schools to achieve universal junior middle schooling. Major cities, including Peking, Shanghai, Hangchow, and Canton, had achieved universal ten-year primary and secondary schooling by the end of the Cultural Revolution decade.[26]

Content and quality at the primary and secondary levels. That declining quality accompanies the development of mass education is axiomatic, and the Chinese case was no exception. The rapid expansion of schooling, made possible as it was by the combination of locally hired teachers, reduced number of years (from twelve years of combined primary and secondary to nine or ten years, according to local decision), and abbreviated curriculum, naturally had an adverse impact on qualitative output. But the mot-

26 The interviewees referred to in this section are more than sixty former residents of China interviewed by the author in Hong Kong. More than forty were former rural schoolteachers from all parts of the country, interviewed between mid-1980 and mid-1983.

toes of the period might well have been drawn from Yenan days: to "oppose uniformity" and not worry about "inequality of standards." Under the circumstances, some schools were naturally run better than others. The main changes that affected the content and quality of education were as follows:

Entrance examinations at the primary level, mainly to determine admission to key schools, were abolished. Unified city and county entrance exams for the secondary levels were also abolished; students attended their nearest neighborhood school. But wherever such schooling was not yet universal individual schools usually administered some kind of entrance exam and used it as a basis for enrollment.

Not only was the keypoint school system abolished, but all forms of what was called "elitist" education were forbidden, such as the practice of dividing students into ability groups or streams within schools. The practice of holding students back a grade was also forbidden, but former teachers indicate that the practice remained widespread, although it occurred only in individual cases rather than as prescribed procedure.

To accommodate the reduced length of schooling, courses and teaching materials were condensed, simplified, and revised. In the process, increased emphasis was placed on practical learning, politics, and manual labor. Subjects like physics, chemistry, and biology were all revised to emphasize their practical application in industry and agriculture. Geography and foreign languages were the most frequent casualties of the rapid expansion of schools; lack of teachers often made it impossible to offer these courses. Politics was sometimes combined with Chinese language and literature because they usually shared the same teaching materials, Mao's writings. By the mid-1970s, middle school students were doing about two months of manual labor per school year. Thus, everyone was in effect engaged in some form of work-study education. More time was spent on labor in the earlier years when students often contributed labor power to the building of new schools and other local work projects.

Teaching and testing methods were reformed to eliminate the "marks-in-command" approach inherited from the 1950s. Teachers were required to devise more flexible and informal teaching and testing methods. All interviewees report that midterms and final exams continued to be given throughout the period, but the rigorous examination life was effectively broken and students tended to be passed on from grade to grade regardless of performance. Individual students were required to repeat grades, but only if they and their parents agreed to the measure.[27]

27 See also Jonathan Unger, *Education under Mao: class and competition in Canton schools, 1960–1980*, part 2.

The tertiary level. The application of the Yenan spirit at the tertiary level had more serious consequences, and it is here that the post-1976 critique of the Cultural Revolution's impact on education has greatest validity. Most tertiary institutions did not enroll new students for at least four years. The teachers were sent to the countryside to be reeducated through labor, returning gradually as these institutions began to resume operations from 1970. Then the same principles were applied to them as elsewhere in the system.

Undergraduate course work was cut from four or five years to about three. Content was abbreviated and simplified, with heavy emphasis on practical application.[28] Even in institutions that did not participate in the ambitious open-door education experiments of the late Cultural Revolution period (1974–76), descriptions of undergraduate course work indicate that its content was reduced by about half. These curricular changes transformed the "appropriate technology" question as to whether an underdeveloped country can afford to spend scarce resources on the most advanced training at the elite level. The question in China became, instead, whether such a country could afford to do without that training altogether.

Equally important in terms of the goals of the education revolution, however, were the social changes intended to complete the transformation of the system as a whole. All young people were required to engage in manual labor after leaving secondary school, and especially before being eligible for college. This meant that most city youth had to accept work assignments in the countryside, given the lack of sufficient urban jobs. The national entrance exams were abolished and, as noted, candidates were selected on the basis of recommendations by their places of work.

These changes were an explicit attack against the tradition of intellectual elitism in China. The objective was a more egalitarian kind of higher education both in structure and content, capable of producing not only greater educational opportunities for workers and peasants but also a new type of worker-peasant intellectual. This objective clearly went beyond the pre–Cultural Revolution aim of expanding worker-peasant enrollments in college. The new emphasis on changing the nature of the education system itself was based on the assumption that workers, peasants,

28 Proposals for and articles about the education revolution at the tertiary level, as at the lower levels, abounded in the Chinese press in the late 1960s and early 1970s. The U.S. Consulate General, Hong Kong, collected many of these and translated them in a lengthy series of *Current Background* issues under the title "Socialist universities." See *CB*, 881, 890, 916, 923, 945, 955, 975, 996, 1007.

and even revolutionary cadres' children, educated in the conventional manner, could as easily be inducted into the intellectual elite as anyone else.

Moreover, the earlier suppositioin that the same kinds of students were probably being admitted to college despite the changed enrollment procedures, appears to be not entirely correct.[29] This conclusion was based on information that college enrollments in the early 1970s were concentrated among urban youth sent down to the countryside. Subsequent interviews with former rural teachers indicate that this pattern of enrollment was not uniformly followed. In addition, the plethora of new complete middle schools was beginning to contribute to the rural candidate's advantage by the mid-1970s. This became apparent in 1977 and 1978, after the national college entrance examinations were restored but before the new commune senior middle schools began to be closed. Rural students from these new schools did gain admission, albeit usually to low-prestige teacher training, agricultural, and junior college courses. Commune and production brigade cadres' children appear to have been disproportionately represented among these rural college students.

At the elite level, higher-ranking cadres – once their own political problems had been cleared – did typically manage to manipulate the enrollment procedures to their children's advantage. But the white-collar middle classes including the intellectuals – whose children had before 1966 shared primacy of place with cadres' children in the college preparatory stream – lacked the necessary advantages of position and good class background. Their children appear to have been the losers under the recommendation system of college enrollment.[30]

The reverse current. Mao mobilized the Red Guards at the start of the Cultural Revolution, to discredit and repudiate his opposition. The similarity with earlier mass movements has been noted. The difference in the Cultural Revolution was that the target was the ruling Party itself. For Mao, the need to compromise with the discredited landlord class never again arose, and capitalists and even intellectuals could be kept in their places if necessary. But the top Party leadership could not be completely obliterated, and presumably Mao never meant to do so. Hence the "liberation" of those criticized at the start of the Cultural Revolution, which progressed

---

29 Suzanne Pepper, "Education and revolution: the 'Chinese model' revised," *Asian Survey*, (September 1978), 871.

30 Further conclusions on college enrollments are drawn from Hong Kong interview data; also Suzanne Pepper, *China's universities: post-Mao enrollment policies and their impact on the structure of secondary education*, table 13. See also Robert Taylor, *China's intellectual dilemma: politics and university enrolment, 1949–1978*.

after 1970 at all levels and in all sectors. The assumption was, apparently, that such individuals, of whom Teng Hsiao-p'ing was the foremost, had been reeducated and reformed by their experience.

That this was not the case in education became apparent by about 1973. In 1972, Chou En-lai lent his prestige to a demand to improve standards at the tertiary level. Professor Chou P'ei-yuan's 6 October 1972 *Kuang-ming jih-pao* article brought the demand into public view and indicated that it had high-level backing. Under the circumstances, it was not an unwarranted demand. But in 1973, the movement for higher standards accelerated. The provinces gave unified college entrance examinations that summer. The new trend was thereupon treated by the radicals as an attempt at restoration, a "reverse current" being promoted by the academic professionals and their political supporters to restore the old order in education.

This sparked the going-against-the-tide campaign. It was launched with the publication of a letter written by candidate Chang T'ieh-sheng, a sent-down youth in Liaoning province, complaining about the unfairness of the 1973 examinations. The campaign then merged with the Criticize Lin Piao, criticize Confucius campaign. The following two years witnessed a resurgence of activism as students were mobilized again to fight the struggle between the two lines in education. The media gave national prominence to students who rebelled against their teachers, in the manner of Chang T'ieh-sheng.

At the secondary level, the activism often turned destructive. Breaking school windows was a widely reported pastime. Former teachers from some, but not all, areas recalled that regular classroom activity was again thoroughly disrupted at this time with students cutting classes at will to demonstrate their rebellion. Meanwhile, at Peking and Tsing-hua universities, among others, ambitious experiments in open-door and work-study education were launched that kept a large portion of the students off campus for months at a time during 1974–76.

Nevertheless, in early 1975, Chou Jung-hsin was appointed the first education minister since 1966. From what the wall posters at Peking University said about him at the end of the year, he spent most of his tenure criticizing the extremes to which the education revolution had been carried, particularly at the higher level. His views were identical to those of Teng Hsiao-p'ing, also circulating at this time and labeled by the radicals as "poisonous weeds." Yet the views of Teng and Chou did not appear to be extreme themselves. They were similar to those that had followed expansionist phases of development several times in the past. They were concerned that standards were too low; that education was now concerned only with the present and not with future needs; that universities were not engaged in theoretical and scientific research; and that intellectuals could not work properly so long as they continued to be derided as "damned intellectuals."[31]

THE NEGATION OF THE EDUCATIONAL REVOLUTION

In August 1977, just one year following Mao's death, the Eleventh National Congress of the CCP proclaimed the end of the Cultural Revolution. The restoration of the national college entrance examinations was announced two months later on 21 October. The dismantling of the education system created during the previous decade proceeded accordingly. Yet the total reversal came as something of a surprise to the uninitiated because it did not bear a direct relationship to the critique that had immediately preceded it. During the entire first year and more following the arrest of the Gang of Four in October 1976, the two main charges contained in the official polemic against them on the education front seemed to follow along the moderate lines of the 1975 critique. The Gang had pushed the Party's policies to excess, and had sought to use education as a tool in its struggle for power. Their opponents seemed loath to admit they might actually be playing out the reality of the two-line struggle in a manner anticipated by the Gang's own polemics before its downfall. Certainly, the early critique of the four contained no direct disavowal of the Cultural Revolution or the changes in education that accompanied it.

Within two years, however, it had become clear that, in the words of one Chinese university administrator interviewed in 1980, the Cultural Revolution was "completely negated." Formal questions on the entire decade were placed out of bounds for foreigners doing research on education in China. The two-line struggle had also ceased to exist. There was only one line, seriously disrupted during the 1966–76 "decade of disaster," which had now been restored to its rightful legitimacy. Mao was officially criticized for his role in precipitating the disaster. Liu Shao-ch'i was exonerated together with all of the Cultural Revolution's struggle objects. The class-line policy was dropped, at least for all spheres of activity not directly related to national security, on grounds that the question of class background was no longer applicable to the generations born and raised in post-1949 China. Enemies remained, but they were new po-

---

31 On the mid-1970s education debate, see Theodore Hsi-en Chen, *Chinese education since 1949: academic and revolutionary models*, 121–52; Unger, *Education under Mao*, 188–205. Chou Jung-hsin, despite serious illness, was forced to leave the hospital in January 1976 and undergo repeated interrogation. He died after one such session on 12 April 1976.

litical enemies, such as unregenerate radicals who were derided as "conservative" Maoist power holders from the Cultural Revolution era.

In education, power was restored to the academic authorities and recentralized in the state education bureaucracy led by the Ministry of Education. The ministry's staff rose immediately from about 300 to between 500 and 600 by 1980, approaching the 700 figure of the mid-1960s.[32] Primary, secondary, and college curricula, textbooks, and teaching materials were all reunified on a nationwide basis. Together with the recentralization of education and the return to power of the professionals went the proclaimed goal of reducing the Party's role to that of supervisor and guarantor. The degree of academic autonomy intended remained unclear, however, since this new goal was accompanied by a new demand to recruit more intellectuals into the Party.

With power thus restored to them, the professionals moved to restore the pre–Cultural Revolution system displaying a determination that pushed the "law of the mass movement" to its logical conclusion. The restoration of pre–Cultural Revolution policies, structures, names, and symbols – even on points where the educational value of the reversal was debatable at best – was systematic and complete. What occurred appeared to be not so much a pragmatic search for the most rational forms of educational development as a political repudiation of the Cultural Revolution experiment. Everything that was criticized during that decade was exonerated, and whatever was promoted then was subsequently discredited regardless of "objective" reasons and social consequences. It then became clearly apparent that however exaggerated the details of the polemics had been, there were indeed policy differences tied to the power struggle and the differences represented two diverse strategies of development.

In the process of the struggle between them, it also became clear that each in its own way had developed in reaction to the universal problems of educational development, and that each had its own ways of solving them. Each strategy did not cope with every problem equally well, however. In the best and most reasonable of worlds, a judicious mix would doubtless have been most effective. But the intensity of the political struggle was such that any substantive integration of the two appeared to be impossible. Hence the post-Mao Ministry of Education was willing to compromise only in unheralded areas and on marginal matters.

32 Suzanne Pepper, "China's universities: new experiments in social democracy and administrative reform," *Modern China* (April 1982), 190. This essay and the monograph on university enrollment policies already cited are based on data gathered during the author's three-and-a-half-month research trip to China in 1980. The material was collected primarily through interviews at a dozen universities and eight secondary schools. By prior agreement with the Ministry of Education, questions were officially confined to the post-1976 years, as it was still "too soon" to submit the Cultural Revolution decade to formal investigation.

Primary schooling

The post-Mao administration was openly critical of its predecessor's egalitarian ideals. As the new leaders saw it, the logic of materialism and the development process decreed that quantitative goals must to some degree be sacrificed to quality because to promote the two goals simultaneously was a luxury the Chinese economy could not afford.

At the primary school level the post-Mao administration was, without directly saying so, allowing the rural sector to absorb the loss. Educational authorities admitted privately to foreigners, although not for domestic publication, that peasant boys learned most of what they needed to know about tilling the land from their fathers. Local education bureaus were, therefore, no longer promoting the expansion of education in rural areas where the level of agricultural technology did not require it. This attitude of "benign neglect" replaced the active promotion of rural primary schooling that began in the early 1970s.

The new attitude was reinforced by a number of related developments. One was the officially advanced idea that the state should resume responsibility for all rural primary schools, following the national trend toward regularization. Also in deference to quality and the sudden disfavor into which labor and practical learning fell, many schools stopped running the various farms, workshops, and projects that had also contributed to school budgets. Finally, the new responsibility system and the decollectivization of agriculture weakened the structure that had sustained production brigade primary schools. In response to reports of the closing and merging of such schools in the late 1970s, there was an official clarification in 1979 that the state would not be able to take over responsibility for all rural schools immediately. The localities should therefore continue to run them in the interim.[33]

According to former teachers interviewed in Hong Kong, the localities were continuing to maintain their rural primary schools through different variations based on the "locally run with state assistance" formula. The main influence on primary schooling had come from the new individual responsibility system, which had led to increasing dropout rates, a phenomenon also widely reported in the Chinese press.[34] This was said to demonstrate that the peasants would rather augment the family income by

33 *JMJP*, 12 August 1979; also, *KMJP*, 24 July 1979; Changsha, Hunan radio, 29 May 1979, Foreign Broadcast Information Service *Daily Report: China* (hereafter FBIS), 31 May 1979, P4; Shenyang, Liaoning radio, 21 May 1979, *Summary of World Broadcasts* (hereafter *SWB*), FE/6126/BII/8, 26 May 1979.
34 See, for example, *Chung-kuo ch'ing-nien pao*, 9 May 1981; *KMJP*, 5 October 1981; *Kuang-chou jih-pao*, 4 August 1981; Premier Chao Tzu-yang also acknowledged this problem in his report to the Fourth Session of the Fifth National People's Congress in late 1981.

TABLE 29
Primary schools and enrollments

Year	Number of schools	Number of students	% of age group
1949	346,800	24,000,000	25
1965	1,681,900[a]	116,000,000	84.7[a]
1966		103,417,000	
1971		112,112,000	
1972		125,492,000	
1973		135,704,000	
1974		144,814,000	
1975		150,941,000	
1976	1,044,300	150,055,000	95+
1977		146,176,000	
1978		146,240,000	
1979	923,500	146,629,000	93
1980		146,270,000	
1981	894,074	143,328,000	
1982		139,720,000	

[a] Official statistics issued in the early 1980s for the Cultural Revolution decade are roughly similar to those given earlier in other sources. One source of confusion in the later official compilations is the failure to distinguish between the academic and calendar years. For a comparison between the later statistics as shown here and those issued earlier, see Suzanne Pepper, "Chinese education after Mao," CQ (March 1980), 6, table. One major unexplained discrepancy appears in the figures for 1965. The World Bank figures (China: socialist economic development, 3.134) show 682,000 primary schools instead of 1,681,900 as given in the source cited, and 70 percent of the age group enrolled instead of 84.7 percent. The number of students in school is, however, the same in all sources that cite this figure.

Sources: The number of schools from 1949–79 is from Chung-kuo pai-k'o nien-chien, 1980, 535. The number of schools in 1981 is from the same publication in 1982, 568. The number of students and percent of age group for 1949 and 1965 is from PR, 5 (3 February 1978), 16–17. The number of students from 1966–81 is from Chung-kuo t'ung-chi nien-chien, 1981, 441. The number of students in 1982 is from ibid., 1983, 511. The figure of 95 + percent of the age group was given at the end of the 1976–77 academic year together with a 150 million primary school enrollment figure, by a representative of the Education Ministry, in an interview with the author, 19 July 1977; see also, CQ, 72 (December 1977), 815–16. The 93 percent of the age group figure is from China: socialist economic development, 3.134.

putting their children to work than allow them to finish primary school. Rural schools were also lagging behind those in the cities in restoring the sixth year of primary school in accordance with the newly reunified national curriculum.

The net result of these changing policies and the official assumptions underlying them was a declining percentage of the age group claimed to be enrolled in primary school, that is, from "over 95 percent" in 1977 to 93 percent two years later. The declining number of primary schools and enrollments as recorded in official statistics is shown in Table 29. The number of students enrolled in primary school declined from a high of 150.94 million in 1975 to 139.72 million in 1982. The number of primary schools declined from just over a million in 1976, to 894,000 in 1981. Between 1979 and 1981, the number of students enrolled in the first year of primary school declined from 37.79 million to 27.49 million.[35] About 60 percent of those who entered primary school were said to graduate.[36] Estimates of dropout rates for earlier years are not available. It should be pointed out, howerer, that part of the declining numbers shown here will be due to declining birthrates. Birth control was enforced unevenly before 1979, but some areas, notably Shanghai, were already closing and merging primary schools at that time because of the reduced size of the school-age population.

Secondary schooling

At the secondary level, the Cultural Revolution policies were said not only to have tried to universalize (*p'u-chi*) schooling prematurely but also to have sought to unify (*tan-i-hua*) education in a manner inappropriate to China's needs and level of economic development. The new policies therefore sought to reverse the "equalization" of both quantity and quality that had occurred as a result of those policies. Since 1978, the declining numbers at the secondary level have been drastic and deliberate, accompanied by some social protest. In 1965, the total number of students in China's secondary schools was 14 million, as shown in Tables 30 and 31. The figure for the 1977–78 academic year was in the region of 68 million.[37] The new policy began to be implemented with the 1978–79 academic year. During 1980 alone, this resulted in the closure of more than 20,000 secondary schools. By 1982, total secondary enrollments had been cut by more than 20 million. The cutbacks have been most severe at the senior secondary level where, according to a claim made in the *Kuang-*

---

35 The 1979 figure for first grade enrollment is in *China: socialist economic development*, 3.205; the 1981 figure is from *Chung-kuo pai-k'o nien-chien, 1982*, 568. The sources for other figures are given in Table 29.

36 Chang Ch'eng-hsien, "K'o-fu tsou-ch'ing ssu-hsiang ying-hsiang, kao hao chiao-yü tiao-cheng" (Overcome the influence of leftist thinking, readjust education well), *HC*, 3 (1981), 28.

37 Earlier figures for the 1977–78 academic year claimed 68.9 million students in general secondary schools with an additional 800,000 in specialized technical schools (Clark Kerr et al., *Observations on the relations between education and work in the PRC* [Spring 1978], 93; the technical secondary enrollment figure was also given in *JMJP*, 28 June 1979). The new official figure is used in Table 30.

ming Daily on 12 October 1981, enrollments for 1981–82 were down by approximately two-thirds as compared with 1978. Of the 75,000 junior middle graduates in the entire Shanghai municipality in 1981, only a little over 20,000 or at most 30 percent were allowed to pass the entrance exams and continue on to the senior secondary level.[38] Similarly, only 54,000 or 39 percent of Peking's total of 139,000 junior secondary graduates were admitted to the senior middle level for the autumn 1981 semester.[39] The smaller size of Shanghai's secondary school-age population reflects the earlier and more rigorous attention paid to family planning in that city.

In the countryside, the plan that was implemented nationwide was to close the commune senior middle schools, leaving only one or a few remaining in each county. Also abolished were the junior middle classes attached to production brigade primary schools. The plan was to retain only one junior middle school in each commune, or the area equivalent to it as the commune organization was abolished.

When the senior middle sections of newly built schools began to be closed in 1979, local anger was contained in various ways. One interviewee described how it took three mass meetings to pacify local people in one Shantung county town. The message from the education bureau they were required to accept was that it was one-sided and selfish for them to demand costly senior middle schooling for their children when their chances of going on to college were so slight. They must therefore "sacrifice the current generation" for the long-term benefit of the nation as a whole.

Another interviewee left a particularly well-run commune middle school in Fukien before the final decision from the county education bureau had been issued. The commune members had demanded to be allowed to continue running the senior middle section as a *min-pan* school and hire their own teachers rather than close it down permanently. Yet a third former teacher, also from Fukien, dismissed such petitions as futile. He explained that the closure of schools was part of the current "line" and would have to be implemented everywhere so long as the education line itself and the central power equation at the top that determined it remained unchanged.

There was no suggestion of any attempt at an immediate proportional shift of student bodies from the general to the technical schools, as indicated in Tables 30 and 31. There was also no effort to coordinate the

38 *Wen-hui pao*, Shanghai, 21 October 1981, 4. On the small size of Shanghai's secondary-school-age population, see ibid., 25 February 1982.
39 *JMJP*, 12 November 1981.

TABLE 30

Secondary schools and students: general secondary

Year	Schools	Students		
1949	4,045	1,039,000		
1965	18,102	9,338,000		
1966		12,498,000		
1968		13,923,000		
1970		26,419,000		
1972		35,825,000		
1974		36,503,000		
1975		44,661,000		
1976	192,152	58,365,000		
			junior 43,529,000	
			senior 14,836,000	
1977		67,799,000		
1978		65,483,000		
1979	144,233	59,050,000		
			junior 46,130,000	
			senior 12,920,000	
1980		55,081,000		
1981	106,718	48,595,600		
			junior 41,445,800	
			senior 7,149,800	
1982		45,285,000		
			junior 38,880,000	
			senior 6,405,000	

Sources: (1) Schools: *Chung-kuo pai-k'o nien-chien, 1980*, 535; and *Chung-kuo pai-k'o nien-chien, 1982*, 568. The number of schools for 1976 and 1979 do not agree with those given in other sources, for example, Suzanne Pepper, "An interview on changes in Chinese education after the 'Gang of Four,'" *CQ, 72* (December 1977), 815−16; *Chung-kuo ching-chi nien-chien, 1981*, IV: 205−6; and *China: socialist economic development*, 3.134. (2) Students: *Chung-kuo pai-k'o nien-chien, 1980*, 536; *Chung-kuo pai-k'o nien-chien, 1982, 568; and Chung-kuo t'ung-chi nien-chien, , 1983*, 511−12.

closing of secondary schools with the declining school-age population. The curtailment of secondary schooling was immediate and proceeded independently of demographic trends as well as the expansion of technical and vocational schools.

China was, it should be noted, in the process of converting back to the pre-1966 twelve-year school system, that is, six years of primary and six years of secondary, with the latter divided into three years each at the junior and senior levels. This was necessary, it was said, because the newly unified national primary and secondary school curriculum created too much pressure on the students when taught within a ten-year syllabus.

Theoretically, therefore, the reduction in numbers of students at the senior secondary level need not mark a significant decline in the amount of education available. If universal primary and junior secondary edu-

TABLE 31

Secondary schools and students: specialized secondary

Year	Professional (*chuan-yeh*) technical and teacher training		Vocational/agricultural (*Chih-yeh*) (*nung-yeh*)		
	Schools	Students	Schools		Students
1949	1,171	229,000			
1957	1,320	778,000			
1965	1,265	547,000	61,626		4,433,000
1976	2,443	690,000			
1979	3,033	1,199,000			
1980	3,069	1,243,000	3,314		453,600
			390	vocational	133,600
			2,924	agricultural	320,000
1981	3,132	1,069,000	2,655		480,900
			561	vocational	213,100
			2,094	agricultural	267,800
1982		1,039,000			704,000

Sources: 1949–79: *Chung-kuo pai-k'o nien-chien, 1980*, 535–36; 1980: *Chung-kuo ching-chi nien-chien, 1981*, IV-205–6; 1981: *Chung-kuo pai-k'o nien-chien, 1982*, 568; 1982: *Chung-kuo t'ung-chi nien-chien, 1983*, 511–12.

cation were maintained, the total received by the majority would still be nine years of schooling. This was clearly not the case, however, given the increasing dropout rates in the rural areas and the growing proportion of youth not even gaining admission to the junior middle level. Enrollments for the first year of junior secondary school declined by 3 million from 17.7 million in 1979 to 14.1 million in 1981. Total junior secondary enrollments declined from 46.1 million in 1979 to 38.8 million in 1982.[40] Thus the net result of the new strategy of educational development was to narrow and sharpen the pyramid: A few would receive much more education in terms of both quantity and quality, while more young people were actually receiving less – although what they received was presumably of better quality than previously.

But although it was no longer fashionable in China to speak in terms of socialist ideals, the problems remained, and so did the critics. "It is unthinkable to rely on such a composition of the population to build a modern nation," declared an article in the theoretical publication *Journal of the Dialectics of Nature*. Focusing on the quality-over-quantity bias of current education policies, the author estimated what would happen to the 322 million young persons ranging in age from 6 to 18 years, given the existing level of education as of 1980. Some 20 million would grow up illiterate; at least 133 million would have no more than a primary

40 *China: socialist economic development*, 3.205; and *Chung-kuo pai-k'o nien-chien, 1982*, 568.

school education; while only 10 million would receive any kind of professional secondary or tertiary level schooling. Arguing that quantity and quality were two sides of the same coin, he criticized the current one-sided emphasis on the latter. "We should correct this right now," he concluded, "rather than wait until future generations sum up lessons when they write history."[41]

The qualitative equalization that occurred during the Cultural Revolution decade was reversed with similar determination. Much was initially made of the ratios between general and specialized secondary schooling. In fact, the former had always predominated, but it was claimed that a 1:1 ratio would be the most rational because graduates from the general secondary schools needed two to three years of training to prepare them for the jobs in which most would have to earn their living. Nevertheless, the expense of converting ordinary schools into technical ones was recognized at once as prohibitive. As shown in Table 31, the growth of these schools has been slow. The alternative has been to introduce vocational subjects into the curriculum of the ordinary non-keypoint schools at the senior secondary level. This is being done in accordance with guidelines approved by the State Council in October 1980.[42] The result is to make it essentially impossible for students in these schools to compete for college admission, while providing them with practical training that is not necessarily useful. The Chinese immediately encountered the same problem experienced by others who have tried to introduce vocational training at this level. The difficulty is to match teachers and specific training programs with the jobs available to the students upon graduation. For example, one of the first vocational courses introduced into one Fukien middle school was garment making. But there were no such factories in the area and the students had not been taught to make the whole garment which would have at least allowed them to go into business as private dressmakers or tailors. The course was therefore regarded as a failure.

The old work-study idea was revived briefly in the form of the agricultural middle schools that were officially promoted in the late 1970s. Some university intellectuals professed genuine surprise at the unanimity of the rural veto of these schools, which local officials nevertheless freely admitted. Rural people did not want to send their children to these schools for the same reasons that obtained twenty years previously. If a child could

41 Sung Chien, "Population and education," *Tzu-jan pien-cheng-fa t'ung-hsun* (Journal of the dialectics of nature), Peking, 3 (June 1980), 1–3, trans. in JPRS, 77745 *China report: political, sociological and military affairs*, 178, 3 April 1981, 43.
42 *Chung-hua jen-min kung-ho-kuo kuo-wu-yuan kung-pao* (Bulletin of the State Council of the People's Republic of China), Peking, no. 16 (1 December 1980), 493.

not attend a regular school in the county town, then a similar school in the commune seat was acceptable, and as primary schooling and junior secondary schooling had expanded, the demand for this kind of commune-level middle school had also grown. But to attend school to learn about agriculture from experienced peasants was a waste. Students could learn much the same from their elders and begin earning money at the same time. The few such schools established were already declining in number by 1981, as shown in Table 31.

If the countryside is the loser in this strategy, its pride is the urban keypoint system and the tertiary sector it supports. The former status of the keypoint schools as the college-preparatory stream has been fully restored, bolstered by generous budgets to replenish their aging facilities. These "pagodas" of learning, lauded as such, have been restored throughout the country at all levels from primary school through university. Some cities even announced the restoration of keypoint kindergartens. The newly reunified national curriculum and textbooks, strengthened and modernized particularly in science education, are geared to the level of the students in these schools.

Official policy now professes to be unconcerned with the social consequences of enrollment policies or the kind of education offered to different kinds of students. The attempt to promote worker-peasant intellectuals is officially derided as part of the premature attempt to reduce urban-rural and mental-manual differences. Both the earlier practice of giving preference to qualified working-class youths, and the later bias in favor of "good" class background candidates, has accordingly been dropped. Everyone is now more or less "equal before marks." Students are channeled into the hierarchy of schools on the basis of unified entrance examinations at all levels. Those most able to benefit from this system are said to be the children of cadres and intellectuals and their competition for scarce college seats now proceeds unobstructed. A majority of students entering keypoint middle schools originate in keypoint primary schools or the keypoint classes of ordinary primary schools. At the primary level, teachers indicate that the parents' background is considered because it is a commonplace that the children of educated and economically secure parents perform better in school.

Local officials freely acknowledge, however, the general criticism of the revived keypoint schools that exists "in society." This led to an outburst against them, aired briefly in the press in late 1981. The commentary echoed in substance if not intensity the Cultural Revolution critique and represented the first time that any such statements concerning these schools had appeared in the press since 1976. One writer listed three reasons for recommending the abolition once again of the key schools: (1) They could not contribute to raising the general quality of education because they depressed the enthusiasm for learning of the great majority of teachers and students to benefit only the few; (2) they were not beneficial to the all-around development of the nation's talent because they encouraged the one-sided emphasis on pass-rates to the detriment of learning; and (3) they were bad for the general development of education because they wasted financial and material resources.[43] But the public debate was soon terminated with little substantive result.

The sudden outburst against the keypoint schools was part of a developing controversy over the related practice of "streaming," or segregating students and teaching them separately according to ability; the inflexible rigors reimposed on the system by the need to pass entrance exams at each level; and the ensuing competitive drive to achieve high pass-rates. All sources agreed that the cramming and competition was if anything more intense than it had been before 1966. Teachers almost uniformly prefer the "regularity" of the unified national curriculum with its clear standards and demands: fixed progression of lessons, enforced by the full panoply of quizzes, tests, and examinations, all duplicating the pre-1966 system in every detail. Nevertheless, the logic of the pedagogical arguments against many of these details was also to a certain extent accepted. Teachers readily acknowledge, for example, that streaming students into ability groups makes teaching easier but benefits only the brightest students. Hence, when the defects of the system were permitted to develop unchecked, there was a basis for criticism even among the teachers. But any correctives had to come from the leading authorities responsible for fixing the centralized rules of the system. And predictably, given the additional logic of the two-line struggle, the correctives came not in the form of a rebuke for the new system but instead for that of its predecessor.

Responding to points of criticism raised by deputies to the National People's Congress meeting in December 1981, the then education minister, Chiang Nan-hsiang, conceded that the competition for college admission was being waged more intensely, with all the attendant evils, than at any time in the past; but he explained that the underlying reason was the disproportionate development of secondary and tertiary education. He

---

43 *Chung-kuo ch'ing-nien pao*, 21 November 1981. For other critical commentary at this time, see *Chung-kuo ch'ing-nien pao*, 31 October, 5 December, and 12 December 1981; *Wen-hui pao*, Shanghai, 21 October and 12 December 1981; *Pei-ching jih-pao*, 12 December 1981; *KMJP*, 7 November, 16 November and 5 December 1981; also *International Herald Tribune*, New York Times Service, Shanghai, 21 December 1981.

recalled that when the unified college entrance exams were first introduced in the early 1950s, they did not result in a preoccupation with pass
rates as there were not even enough middle school graduates in those
early years to meet the demand for college students. It was not until the
1960s, after senior secondary schooling had been significantly expanded,
that the various manifestations of the competitive drive for admission to
college developed. But even then, he maintained, the proportions of senior middle graduates going on to college varied between 30 percent and
40 percent. What had changed all this was the rash popularization of
senior secondary schooling during the 1966–76 decade. As a result, only
the top 4 percent to 5 percent of each year's senior secondary graduates
were gaining admission to college. The minister concluded that the
"extremely fierce competition" was the consequence not of the restored
entrance examinations but that the competition was due to the "unprecedentedly sharp contradiction between the vast numbers of senior middle school graduates and the low university enrollment quotas."[44]

Thus all arguments led to the same conclusion: the purpose of secondary schooling was to prepare for college and since only a small proportion
of those graduating from secondary school could continue their studies,
the solution was to cut back enrollments and reconcentrate resources
both human and material in the keypoint schools. In accordance with this
diagnosis, the number of senior middle school graduates was reduced
from an all-time high of 7.2 million in 1979, to 4.8 million by 1981.
Within three years, it would be reduced by an additional one million; the
intake of new students into the first year of senior middle school in 1981
was only 3.2 million.[45]

Higher-level education

At the tertiary level, however, the numbers were all moving in the
opposite direction in a declared effort to make up for the losses of the Cultural Revolution decade. The bias was weighted overwhelmingly in the
direction of science and technology regarded as most essential for the
nation's economic development. Total national enrollments rose from
565,000 in 1976 to 1.3 million in 1981, and the number of institutions
from 392 to 704 during that same time.[46] International development
experts maintain that a country China's size should have a college
enrollment of about two million, a target that was set for 1990. For the

---

44 *Wen-hui pao*, Hong Kong, 17 December 1981, or *Pei-ching jih-pao*, 3 January 1982.
45 *Chung-kuo pai-k'o nien-chien, 1980*, 538; and ibid., *1982*, 568.
46 *Chung-kuo pai-k'o nien-chien, 1980*, 535–36; and ibid., *1982*, 568.

first time since 1949, China turned directly to the capitalist West as a source of assistance and expertise. The first World Bank loans to China were extended for use in higher education to finance among other things the purchase of equipment and the further development of the national TV University network. Between 1978 and 1981, more than 10,000 Chinese students and scholars were sent abroad for study and research, the great majority to Western countries and Japan with the largest numbers going to the United States.[47]

The trend for uniformity and centralization enforced elsewhere in the system was evident at the tertiary level as well. National unified curricula were prepared by the Ministry of Education. Students and teachers throughout the country followed its inflexible routines much as they did when the centralized curriculum was first introduced in the 1950s. This was the environment under which the Kiangsi Communist Labor University (described in *CHOC*, 14, Chapter 9) was divested of its provincewide network of branches supported by their work-study schedules. The remaining main campus adopted the unified curriculum and full-time study schedule of "regular" agricultural colleges as decreed by the Education Ministry.

Meanwhile, university intellectuals were freed from what the older generation at least regards as three decades of Maoist oppression. Virtually all the old rightists and class enemies were rehabilitated and given work. All became intellectual laborers in the service of socialism, and improvements were quickly made in their living and working conditions. Nevertheless, many continued to look wistfully backward to what they once were and to colleagues abroad for what they might have become, and remained unreconciled. Their inclinations, however, coincided to a certain extent with the interest of the post-Mao leadership intent on adapting the secrets of Western technological success to their modernization program. Yet the initial result of their effort was to strengthen certain features of the education system originally taken from the Soviet model in the 1950s, while simultaneously attempting to dilute that model with features adapted from Western and especially American education. How this contentious mix will evolve in this new incarnation remains for the future to decide.

That the CCP and the intellectuals were not yet satisfied with or in agreement on the formula was demonstrated by the curious revival in the late 1970s of a turn-of-the-century controversy in modern guise. The question being debated was how much of Chinese society must be

---

47 *Chung-kuo pai-k'o nien-chien, 1982,* 573.

changed so that Western science and technology can fulfill their promise of economic prosperity. By 1983, Party leaders were sufficiently concerned to launch a campaign against "spiritual pollution" aimed among other things at discouraging the uncritical admiration for all things Western. But on one thing both the present Party leadership and the university intellectuals were in full agreement: Any lessons that may have been learned from the Yenan experience should be relegated firmly back to the rural sector that initially inspired them.

Employment and youth

In the countryside, young people are integrated into the work force from childhood. Indeed, they drop out of school to augment the family income by engaging in different kinds of sideline agricultural activities. In the cities, such opportunities are less abundant. The post-Mao administration has adopted a very different strategy from that of its predecessor for coping with the problem of employment for urban youth. The Cultural Revolution decade offered a two-pronged solution. First, it promoted the universalization of secondary schooling. Hence one reason cited by school administrators in China and interviewees in Hong Kong for the initial refusal in some localities to cut back secondary-school enrollments when the policy was first announced in 1978–79, was concern at the possible consequences of sending the young people out into the streets. The second measure followed during the Cultural Revolution decade was to assign urban youth to work in the rural areas.

The cost of the youth-to-the-countryside program during the Cultural Revolution decade was several million young people who never integrated with the peasants, even though they may have learned to live with them, and who fled the countryside by whatever means possible. It was also among this sector of the population, the educated sent-down youth of the Cultural Revolution decade, that dissident trends developed – almost as though they still lived by the old Maoist slogan "Rebellion is justified," which had mobilized them in the late 1960s. Some demanded liberalization of the socialist system; some rejected it altogether.

Virtually all of this generation returned to the cities, if they had not already found a way back, once the policy change permitted them to do so in 1978–79. They created a massive unemployment problem, which was gradually eased by their being allowed to engage in various kinds of private and collective endeavors previously forbidden as remnant capitalist activity. Urban school-leavers were thereafter allowed to stay in the cities. Nevertheless, ways still had to be found to deal with the large numbers of these young people who were now being factored out of the school system at an increasingly early age and for whom life held out few prospects. The solution ideally would be found in the convergence of falling birthrates and rising urban employment opportunities. In the meantime, the age for entering primary school was formally fixed at 6 in the late 1970s, but then immediately enforced at 7 in conjunction with the decision to cut back secondary enrollments. This delays by one year the emergence of the youth "into society." But their problems remained.

Such youth were said to have contributed to a rising tide of lawlessness, which was at least temporarily checked by a nationwide anticrime campaign during the latter half of 1983. But having stripped the youth-to-the-countryside program of any political significance, the government should not have expected any more enthusiasm than it received when it called upon urban youth to volunteer for settlement in the border regions, this time to help develop the remote province of Tsinghai. As it happened, this call coincided with the anticrime campaign, and a number of young urban offenders were sent out to Tsinghai for reform and education. Thus, the unfortunate connotation of the pre-1966 transfer programs, as the fate of urban failures and dropouts, was immediately restored. Even among the nation's elite, college administrators reported in 1980, it had never been more difficult to convince their graduates to accept unattractive work assignments far from hearth and home. The official post-Mao credo that one could serve the national interest by serving one's own was not without its drawbacks. But instead of acknowledging that some of these social problems were the result of contradictions in their own policies, Party leaders launched the "spiritual pollution" campaign to counteract the mechanical emulation of all things Western and disprove the proposition that alienation could exist under socialism.

THE "CHINESE MODEL" IN THIRD WORLD PERSPECTIVE

A congruence of concerns over problems of development in Third World countries and the unveiling of the new Cultural Revolution policies in China after 1970 produced an international movement of sorts to "learn from the Chinese model." It became fashionable to explore what could be learned from the Chinese experience and applied elsewhere.[48] The single-minded pursuit of economic development resulted in some impressive growth rates in a number of Third World countries. Yet the disparities both international and internal between the industrialized rich

48 See, for example, Ronald Dore, *The diploma disease: education, qualification and development.*

and the agrarian poor were not necessarily reduced and may actually have grown. The quantitative assumptions about economic growth rates took on new meaning once it was discovered how many of the world's population were not benefiting from them. Hence, most of the United Nations' Second Development Decade (1970–80) was spent in the search for more significant definitions and strategies of development. The priorities of the 1970s called for a concentration of development efforts in agriculture rather than in industry, on the countryside rather than the cities, and on ways to help those whose needs were greatest rather than on the growth of the gross national product alone.

In the field of educational development, a similar reordering of priorities occurred. The original academic bias of education shifted to an emphasis on vocational and technical training. But this effort, particularly at the vocational level, did not succeed, because it was difficult to match vocational curricula with the particular jobs available, and also because vocational curricula were regarded by too many as an inferior alternative for those who failed to gain admission to the academic stream. In the late 1960s and early 1970s, attention shifted to the failures of schooling in the countryside in particular, although it was realized that the basic problems of rural education did not rest primarily with education. But not content to await the solution of so fundamental a matter as the modernization of agriculture, educators began searching for ways to adapt schooling to a developing rural area. "Nonformal" education was one way; "ruralized" curricula was another. Again, the difficulty with these solutions was that they confined the students who might suffer them to ghettos of their own making, deliberately reinforcing and passing on from one generation to the next the inequalities inherent in the existing division of labor.

The next logical step for those planners and academics daring enough to advocate it was the restructuring of the entire education system. Even for those not so adventurous, decentralization, diversity, flexibility, and lifelong learning became the watchwords in the field of educational development. The goal was to design education systems built on these concepts that would at least minimize educational segregation by allowing both upward and lateral movement between courses and streams. Hence the excitement generated by the Cultural Revolution attempts to restructure Chinese education along just such lines. The international development community did not endorse socialism as a solution, but since the Chinese were addressing similar concerns and walking on common ground, it was felt that their experiments might be applied elsewhere. At least one country, Tanzania, made a serious effort to do so. In this sense, Chinese education did not just rejoin the rest of the world after Mao's death as was often popularly assumed. The Chinese experiment was at that time already very much a part of the international debates on educational development, except that then the rest of the world was asking what it could learn from China. Afterward, the post-Mao leaders refused to acknowledge that this had ever been so. Their only concern was to forget the past and learn what they could from the capitalist West.

Indeed, the effort to learn from the Chinese model did stop abruptly after Mao's death when the Chinese declared that the model the world had been studying so intently was all sham. Then it became clear that there were two Chinese models, not one; and the one that aroused so much international attention had been rejected before it had had a chance to develop fully. This makes the Chinese experience more difficult to assess and less conducive to cross-cultural emulation, leaving its lessons for academics to ponder. But the international development community can perhaps be forgiven for its fickleness. Once the post-Mao leadership set to work – dismantling the Maoist strategy, expunging its achievements from the public record, and forbidding anything but a negative verdict on every aspect of the entire Cultural Revolution decade – everyone, willingly or not, came under the spell of the new official line. When all other sources of information are cut off, even skeptics find themselves without alternative explanations.

Wisely, the World Bank did not allow itself to be drawn into the two-line struggle any more than was absolutely necessary when it prepared its first country-report for China. But in simply reproducing there the data it was given in 1979, it illustrated in statistical terms the strengths and weaknesses of the Chinese education system and also indicated which of the two strategies was responsible for what. The data were gathered in 1979, just as the new post-Mao policies were beginning to be implemented. The impact on the system of the cutbacks at the secondary level and the re-creation of the elite keypoint track at all levels had not yet been fully registered.

At the primary level, the net enrollment ratio of the age group, at 93 percent, placed China some 30 percentage points above the average enrollment ratio for 92 other developing countries. With girls constituting 45 percent of all primary school students (the average for other less developed countries was 43 percent), they probably represented the majority of the 7 percent of the age group not attending school. At the secondary level, the gross enrollment ratio (including underage and overage students) was 46 percent. By comparison, this ratio for other developing countries was only 26 percent. At both the primary and secondary levels, the greatest quantitative growth occurred during the

periods when the Maoist strategy predominated, that is, during the Great
Leap Forward of the late 1950s and again during the Cultural Revolution
decade.[49]

The percentage of the population over 25 years of age with no schooling was estimated at 38 percent in China. By comparison, other Asian
countries had the following "no schooling" rates: Pakistan, 81 percent;
India, 72 percent; Singapore, 48 percent; Thailand, 34 percent; Hong
Kong, 29 percent; Japan, 1 percent.[50]

Of total national expenditures for primary education in 1979 (4.4
billion yuan), an estimated 56.8 percent was allocated from the national
state budget; 27.2 percent was financed by the localities including rural
production brigades and urban enterprises; the private payment of tuition
and fees accounted for 15.9 percent.[51] The World Bank report noted that
localities and parents shared more of the financial burden than was common in most socialist countries. The *min-pan* school from China's past had
thus been adapted and promoted within a national framework of state
support and direction to achieve near-universal primary schooling in a
country that was still predominantly rural.

Balanced against the impressive quantitative performance at the primary and secondary levels, however, was the record at the tertiary level.
China had only 10.5 college students per 10,000 population. The comparable figure in India, noted for the disproportionate development of its tertiary level education by comparison with the primary and secondary
sectors, was 60. The United States had 500 college students per 10,000
population. Whereas China's enrollment ratios at the primary and secondary levels were well above the average for ninety-two other developing
countries throughout the 1970s, at the tertiary level the ratio began to fall
behind them in the early 1960s, fell drastically during the Cultural Revolution, and remained well behind in 1979.[52]

A further feature of the entire system, however, was that it was overstaffed, underutilized, and uneconomical. Teachers at the primary and
secondary levels thus taught fewer hours per week than their counterparts in other countries. The student-teacher ratio in China's primary
schools was 27:1, compared with the average ratios in other developing
countries of 38:1 to 34:1. The student-teacher ratio in academic secondary
schools was 19:1, compared to 22:1 or 23:1 in other developing countries.
At the secondary level, teaching loads of only twelve to thirteen hours per
week were common. At the tertiary level, the system was even less efficient, with a national student-teacher ratio of only 4.3:1.[53] Hence, expanding tertiary enrollments and improving quality at the lower levels could

49 *China: socialist economic development*, 3.147, 152–53, 211.
50 Ibid., 135.   51 Ibid., 181.   52 Ibid., 135, 164, 211.   53 Ibid., 150, 154, 168.

also have been achieved by a more efficient use of existing staff and facilities rather than the wasteful closing of schools and reduction of enrollments. Staff reductions were not made proportionlly to the cutback of student bodies so that by 1982, student-teacher ratios were even more uneconomical: 25.4:1 at the primary level; 16.4:1 at the secondary level. The new ratio for institutions of higher learning was 4:1.[54]

The strength of the Maoist strategy clearly lay in its determination and ability to promote universal mass education even in the rural areas, and to equalize the quantity and quality of education available to different kinds of students. The particular weakness of this strategy resided in its treatment of the tertiary sector reinforced by a rural socialist suspicion of the urban Westernized intelligentsia that presided over it. As a further characteristic, the Maoist strategy was implemented through the vehicle of the mass movement, achieving its greatest successes through the mobilization that accompanied it. But this method was itself costly in terms of the excesses deemed necessary to overcome resistance, as well as the waste and resentment inevitable during the consolidation phase of a movement. Thus, after Mao's death his strategy of development and the Yenan experience that inspired it were rejected as a model for the education system. Even the *min-pan* school formula was just tolerated, not heralded, as the only means for maintaining universal primary schooling in the rural areas.

The balance of forces that determined the nature of the education system after 1976 was similar to that during the 1950s, before the Anti-Rightist Campaign. Then Soviet structures and the Western-oriented intellectual community dominated the regular school system, which was itself the central focus of attention. Yet this balance of forces remained in an uncertain relationship with the mass base on which it rested. The protests "in society," both urban and rural, over closing schools and the elitism of the keypoint system was indicative of the tensions underlying the post-Mao strategy. Nor were Party leaders themselves, worried as they seemed to be about "spiritual pollution," completely at ease with the pro-Western orientation their policies had encouraged.

The outside observer cannot but speculate as to what might have been the result had Mao tried to harness the energies generated in the course of the mass movement, using them instead to devise a less disruptive but equally determined way to implement his objectives. Perhaps the achievement would not have been quite so impressive. But because the excesses would also have been muted and the costs therefore less, the inevitable backlash against them might not have been so extreme.

54 *Chung-kuo t'ung-chi nien-chien, 1983*, 514.

CHAPTER 8

CREATIVITY AND POLITICS

Ever since the establishment of the People's Republic, there has been a close relation between artistic creation and political life. The Cultural Revolution confirmed this, but also showed that variations in the relation were possible. In 1966 the relatively favorable political climate of earlier years, which had enabled literature to become a medium for veiled criticism of current politics, came to a sudden end. More fearful of artistic thought than any democratic government would be, the Chinese leaders supporting the Cultural Revolution turned against a number of literary works and operas and tried to replace them with new artistic productions. Almost all established writers were persecuted, and their role was taken over by lesser-known figures, who often preferred (or were forced) to work anonymously.

There are various ways to interpret and describe these events. One approach is to see literary production during the Cultural Revolution as a consequence of political interference in the arts. Severe ideological attacks on particular writers and the complete reorganization (or, rather, disorganization) of the cultural bureaucracy almost suffocated literary life. Another approach is to restrict oneself to a study of changes in the literary system – changes that, though political in origin, affected literature on the levels of the genre-system, the structure of the narrative, poetic form, and stage conventions. The political interference in literary life and the changes in the literary system, though interrelated, will be described separately. In fact, they can be distinguished also chronologically. When the first ideological criticisms were published, it was by no means clear whether literary production would be capable of meeting the newly formulated requirements. Only after a considerable lapse of time were specimens of the new art published, and even then their quality was dubious, even according to the new standards.

LAUNCHING THE CULTURAL REVOLUTION: IDEOLOGICAL
ATTACKS ON WRITERS, DISORGANIZATION OF
THE CULTURAL BUREAUCRACY

The Great Socialist Cultural Revolution, later rebaptized as the Great Proletarian Cultural Revolution, was announced in the *People's Daily* on 19 April 1966. The official announcement in the press, however, was preceded by careful preparations. Several intellectuals, such as the philosopher Yang Hsien-chen, the art historian Chou Ku-ch'eng, and the critic Shao Ch'üan-lin, had been criticized in 1964 and 1965, and the cultural apparatus was weakened by the criticism, notably by that of Shao Ch'üan-lin, whose ideas were close to those of Chou Yang, vice-director of the Propaganda Department of the Communist Party.

In November 1965, Yao Wen-yuan published his biting criticism of the historian and vice-mayor of Peking, Wu Han, whose historical drama *Hai Jui dismissed from office* (*Hai Jui pa kuan*), briefly performed as a Peking Opera in 1961, was singled out as a veiled attack on Maoist policies. Hai Jui had been an official under the Ming dynasty about whom Wu Han had written on other occasions. There can be no doubt that Wu Han "used the past to satirize the present" (*i ku feng chin*). In his earlier writings he had shown himself to be aware of this device. The incorruptible Hai Jui sides with the people who wish that the land be returned to them and their grievances be redressed. Yao Wen-yuan's interpretation that Wu Han was in fact suggesting the dissolution of the people's communes, is not too farfetched. Other radical critics equated Hai Jui with Marshal P'eng Te-huai, who in 1959 had expressed his opposition to the disastrous Great Leap Forward and the commune system, and had subsequently been dismissed. There are arguments in support of this reading as well.[1] Apart from these political interpretations, the play was heretical in its praise for an uncompromising moral attitude. This point, too, was repeatedly discussed in the hundreds of articles published in the Chinese press about Wu Han in late 1965 and the first half of 1966. The opinion that in feudal times there were occasionally incorrupt officials was considered to be incompatible with a Marxist interpretation of history. The radicals argued that the so-called good official was a contradiction in terms, as such persons had obscured the class conflict and therefore had impeded historical progress.

The criticism of Wu Han was not restricted to *Hai Jui dismissed from office* but pertained also to his historical work and critical essays. Between

---

1 James R. Pusey, *Wu Han: attacking the present through the past*, 35.

1961 and 1964, together with Liao Mo-sha and Teng T'o, respectively member and secretary of the Peking Party Committee, Wu Han wrote a series of articles for *Front Line* (*Ch'ien-hsien*) under the title *Notes from a three family village* (*San chia ts'un cha-chi*). In 1961–62 Teng T'o, who as a former editor in chief of the *People's Daily* was a figure of considerable political weight, published a similar series of essays under the title *Night talks at Yenshan* (*Yen-shan yeh hua*), which were reprinted in five slim volumes. Both series of articles were subjected to severe criticism. In early May 1966 the main thrust of the criticism was directed at Teng T'o, who, in a pamphlet by Yao Wen-yuan, was charged with having misused his position as editor in chief of *Front Line* and a secretary of the Peking Municipal Party committee for "anti-Party and anti-socialist" purposes and propagating a "right opportunist and revisionist line." It appeared that the criticism had less to do with literature than with ideological and political issues. The journalistic activities of Wu Han, Liao Mo-sha, and Teng T'o were taken to task because of their barely veiled criticism of Maoist policies. The form they had chosen for airing their views was the *tsa-wen*, the satirical essay, in which Lu Hsun had been a master, but which Mao Tse-tung in his Yenan "Talks on literature and art" had advised against using under the conditions of the dictatorship of the proletariat.

Although it provided an opportunity for implied and overt criticism, from a literary point of view the *tsa-wen* was not one of the main genres. Wu Han, Liao Mo-sha, and Teng T'o were also not well known as writers before they were attacked for political reasons. They were chosen as scapegoats primarily because the criticism of their writings provided an opening for an attack on the party leaders in Peking: P'eng Chen, mayor of Peking and first secretary of the Peking Municipal Party Committee, and as such the direct superior of both Wu Han and Teng T'o; Chou Yang, deputy director of the Propaganda Department of the Central Committee; Teng Hsiao-p'ing, general secretary of the CCP; and Liu Shao-ch'i, vice-chairman of the CCP and president of the People's Republic of China. From May 1966 on, the political purposes of the Cultural Revolution were evident. The consequences for creative literature, however, were less clear.

When on 1 July 1966 *Hung-ch'i* (Red Flag) published a criticism of Chou Yang, who had supervised literary production since 1949, the unmistakable charge was that the cultural policies under his responsibility had been totally wrong. Chou Yang was accused of being a right-opportunist of the Wang Ming sort, as had allegedly become apparent in 1936 when he endorsed the (opportunist) slogan "Literature for national

defense" (*kuo-fang wen-hsueh*) in order to counter Lu Hsun's (more proletarian) idea of a "Mass literature for the national revolutionary war"
(*min-tsu ko-ming chan-cheng-ti ta-chung wen-hsueh*). As so often in these
polemics, the critics delved deep into the past, but that it should have
taken thirty years to discover that Chou Yang was a revisionist, or worse,
was quite remarkable.

By presenting Chou Yang as an enemy of Lu Hsun the critics hoped to
curry favor with some of the writers and part of the reading public, who
for various reasons disliked Chou Yang and his bureaucracy. In an article
in the *People's Daily* of 3 January 1967, Yao Wen-yuan claimed that in the
past Chairman Mao had repeatedly tried to censure Chou Yang's revisionist ideas, but the effects had been nil. Yao held Chou Yang responsible for the publication in a literary journal in 1961 of an article on "The
problem of subject matter." It described the aim of literature as the representation of the world in all its complexity and suggested that not all
phenomena of life could be reduced to the simple scheme of the class
struggle. Yao interpreted this as a plea for "glorifying traitors, lackeys,
hooligans, landlords, rich peasants, counterrevolutionaries, bad elements
and rightists." He recalled that in 1959 Khrushchev had expressed a similar idea when he praised the short novel *Fate of a man* by Mikhail
Sholokhov as a story that "described the complex and rich spiritual world
of the ordinary citizen." According to Yao, Chou Yang believed that the
Chinese writers should publish similar "renegade literature."

Here the link between Chou Yang's and Khrushchev's conception of
the class struggle is important. Although Yao Wen-yuan's diatribe was
unreliable in its treatment of quotations and facts,[2] Chou Yang had
indeed used the term "literature and art of the whole people" in a speech
in 1962, which was reminiscent of the Khrushchevian concepts "state of
the whole people" and "Party of the whole people." Having patronized
Shao Ch'üan-lin's suggestion that "people in the middle," that is, people
wavering between the two classes or with an unclear class position,
should be described, Chou Yang had made himself vulnerable to the
accusation that he had supported the "theory of human nature" (*jen-hsing
lun*), which suggested that certain qualities of man transcended class
distinctions. This theory had been criticized on earlier occasions, not only
in the campaign to censure Feng Ting in 1964, but as early as in Mao's
Yenan "Talks."

It was not only his particular concept of the subject matter suitable for

---

2 Makiko Klenner, *Literaturkritik und politische Kritik in China: die Auseinandersetzungen um die
Literaturpolitik Zhou Yangs*, 193.

literature that differentiated Chou Yang from the radical Maoist position. Time and again he had emphasized the difference between art and science, literature and ideology. In his view of the creation and effects of literature, he relied heavily on the tradition of Russian literary theory, from the nineteenth-century critic V. G. Belinsky up to the theories of socialist realism. Inevitably he assimilated notions that originated in romanticism and idealism, such as Belinsky's view that "art is thinking in images." Of course, this was immediately pinpointed during the Cultural Revolution. As early as April 1966 Cheng Chi-ch'iao, later associated with the powerful Cultural Revolution Group, argued in *Hung-ch'i* that "thinking in images" could not be an alternative to abstract generalization and was incompatible with Marxist epistemology.[3] This argument played a considerable role in the repudiation of Chou Yang; in addition, it was essential for curbing the relative freedom that writers claimed for their imaginative writing. Cheng Chi-ch'iao and other radical critics denied the writers their private access to truth by artistic means. They proposed a plainly materialist conception of literature, which differed sharply from Soviet aesthetics. If carried to its logical conclusion, it was bound to collide with Friedrich Engels's famous evaluation of Balzac as a writer who, in spite of his conservative convictions, was progressive in his writings as a result of his artistic insight.

The new, strictly materialist theory of literary creation facilitated ideological censorship. Any work of art, any new image or typical representation, was believed to be based on abstract generalization. Writers could no longer escape from ideological control by recourse to ambiguous metaphors or reference to intuitive knowledge.

The radicals' view of artistic creation was largely based on a report of a forum on literature and art in the armed forces, organized by Lin Piao and Chiang Ch'ing in Shanghai in February 1966. It is probably correct to see the Shanghai Forum as being in opposition to the activities of the so-called Group of Five (headed by P'eng Chen), which in Peking in early February prepared a report on the Wu Han case, attempting to deflect the criticism into an academic debate without political consequences.[4] The results of the Shanghai Forum were not immediately published; it was more than a year before *Hung-ch'i* carried the summary report of it.[5]

In general the summary of the Shanghai Forum endorsed the tenets of

---

3 D. W. Fokkema and Elrud Ibsch, *Theories of literature in the twentieth century*, 107.
4 Merle Goldman, *China's intellectuals: advise and dissent*, 123–24.
5 *HC*, 9 (1967), 11–21. English translation: "Summary of the Forum on the Work in Literature and Art in the Armed Forces with which Comrade Lin Piao entrusted Comrade Chiang Ch'ing," in *Important documents on the Great Proletarian Cultural Revolution in China*, 201–38.

the Yenan "Talks," but also singled out certain points for specific and rather one-sided discussion. As in the Yenan "Talks," it was emphasized that literature had to serve the political struggle, now specified as a struggle against the "bourgeois and modern revisionist counter-current in literature and art" or simply "the sinister line." This struggle was depicted as arduous, complex, and "demanding decades or even centuries of effort," yet essential to the outcome of the Chinese revolution and the world revolution. The document explained that the literary and artistic production of the last twenty years had not met the Maoist standards as expressed in the Yenan "Talks." It repudiated various trends that at different times had been popular among writers, such as "the broad path of realism" (advocated as an alternative to socialist realism by Ch'in Chao-yang in 1956) and the representation of "characters in the middle" (defended by Shao Ch'üan-lin in 1962).

The overall effect of the argument, however, was a criticism of Chou Yang, although his name was not mentioned. For instance, the summary launched a fierce attack on "the literature and art of the 1930s": It had been Chou Yang's policy to keep the tradition of the great writers, such as Mao Tun, Pa Chin, and Lao She, as much alive as possible. The summary rejected the concept of literature propounded by Belinsky, N. A. Dobrolyubov, and other Russian critics: Chou Yang had patronized Chinese translations of their work and had assimilated their concept of literature and their ideas about artistic creation. The summary also disapproved of the way European, including Russian, classics had been acclaimed in China. Again, Chou Yang was responsible for the translation and distribution of foreign literature, in particular Russian literature, which he knew well and could read in the original. The summary betrayed its excessive detestation of foreign influence in judging that even Stalin had been too permissive with respect to the Russian and European classics. It stated, literally, that Stalin "uncritically took over what are known as the classics of Russia and Europe and the consequences were bad."

The Shanghai Forum prescribed quite clearly the topics socialist literature should deal with. It should represent heroic models of workers, peasants, and soldiers, the socialist revolution and socialist construction, as well as particular military campaigns during the liberation war. The restrictions on literary themes were quite specific: in the description of war, its cruel aspects should not be exaggerated in order to avoid the emergence of bourgeois pacifism; in the portrayal of heroic characters, one should avoid having them violate party discipline; in depicting the enemy, his class nature as an exploiter and oppressor should be clearly exposed. The reverse side of the medal, of course, was that any plot was made highly predictable.

Little was said about poetry, except that "the numerous poems by workers, peasants, and soldiers appearing on wall newspapers and blackboards" were believed to "herald an entirely new age." In fact, even less than narrative prose or drama, could poetry be considered a vehicle for political messages. With respect to the theater, the summary celebrated the rise of Peking operas on contemporary revolutionary themes and mentioned several of them, to be discussed later in the chapter. Again the question of subject matter is decisive here. In 1944, in a pronouncement that was published in May 1967 in the issue of *Hung-ch'i* that also carried the summary, Mao Tse-tung had criticized the traditional Chinese opera for staging "lords and ladies and their pampered sons and daughters" and presenting "the people as though they were dirt." In its emphasis on contemporary revolutionary themes, the summary followed this directive.

The issues dealt with at the Shanghai Forum were not new, but the emphasis was different from earlier statements about literature and art. In Marxist aesthetics there is always a tension between the ideological interpretation of reality as canonized by the Party on the one hand, and the artistic view of life as presented by literature and the arts on the other. Or, in Marxist terms, there is always a dialectical relation between the principle of Party spirit and that of typification. The Shanghai Forum overemphasized the Party spirit to such an extent that very little space was left for artistic creation. This will be exemplified in the next section.

CHANGES IN THE LITERARY SYSTEM

For political and ideological reasons, including those provided by the Shanghai Forum, the Cultural Revolution was hostile to literary creation. The ideological criticism of Wu Han and Teng T'o appeared to be a political instrument to eliminate the political enemies of Mao Tse-tung and Lin Piao. Similarly, the criticism of other writers, such as Pa Chin, Lao She, Ts'ao Yü, Lo Kuang-pin, Chou Li-po, Chao Shu-li, Liu Ch'ing, Yang Mo, Liang Pin, Wu Ch'iang, Chou Erh-fu, mainly served political purposes. They were subjected to political sanctions and often treated as criminals. Pa Chin was deprived of his civil rights and for many years kept under house arrest. Others were in prison for years. Lao She and Lo Kuang-pin committed suicide or were forced to do so. Chao Shu-li, Liu Ch'ing, and Wu Han died in captivity. Teng T'o was killed or committed suicide soon after his arrest in May 1966. Not only writers, but also painters, such as Ch'i Pai-shih and Lin Feng-mien, and musicians, such as

Ho Lu-ting, composer of "The East Is Red," as well as a great number of film producers and actors were criticized and persecuted. As long as there are no reliable figures about the number of intellectuals persecuted and killed during the Cultural Revolution, their suffering will remain unmeasurable. It is not extravagant, however, to compare the terror and bloodshed during these years to those of the Stalinist regime in Russia in the 1930s, or to the Holocaust of Nazi Germany, although in China the pace of the persecution was slower and the killing less systematic.

For the supporters of the Cultural Revolution, life was not comfortable either. They were divided by factional strife and often uncertain how to defend their voluntaristic Maoist ideals against the demands of practice. T'ao Chu, who, perhaps reluctantly, had succeeded Lu Ting-i as director of the CC's Propaganda Department in the summer of 1966, was arrested later that year and died in captivity as a victim of the Cultural Revolution. He was succeeded by Wang Li, an extreme leftist, who could keep his office no longer than eight months. In September 1967, Ch'en Po-ta, head of the Cultural Revolution Group, was made head of the Propaganda Department. The much-feared Cultural Revolution Group, active from mid-1966, was in complete disarray after little more than one year: Wang Li, Lin Chieh, Kuan Feng, and Mu Hsin, the most radical if junior members of the group, were arrested in September 1967. In February 1968, Ch'i Pen-yü, who had defended the Boxer uprising and extolled xenophobia as a means to combat imperialism and modern revisionism, was criticized and disappeared from the political stage. By then, the Cultural Revolution Group was, in effect, reduced to Ch'en Po-ta, Chiang Ch'ing, Chang Ch'un-ch'iao, and Yao Wen-yuan, with K'ang Sheng as an adviser. In 1970, Ch'en Po-ta, too, was purged, allegedly because he had plotted against Chairman Mao.

Because of internal dissent and external pressures, the Cultural Revolution Group never had the authority to give effective guidance to literary and artistic production and, except in the case of the promotion of modern Peking Opera on revolutionary themes, its interference in artistic life led nowhere. Like other branches of the administration, the cultural bureaucracy was highly disorganized. If the Cultural Revolution Group had wanted to return to Great Leap Forward policies in the field of literature, it would have been simply incapable of guiding and supervising another mass campaign for writing poetry. Moreover, it soon became clear that the Cultural Revolution Group wanted power, rather than ideological reform. In the struggle for power, literature and art were not the first priority.

It is not surprising that during the first years of the Cultural Revolution cultural life came almost to a standstill. In the criticism to which "revisionist" and other deviationist writers were subjected, fiction was usually interpreted as an expression of the author's political beliefs. No distinction was made between author and narrator, and even the political convictions of a particular character in a story could be directly attributed to the author. After the Shanghai Forum, the very distinction between political tract and fiction had been abolished. As a result reportage (*t'ung-hsun wen-hsueh*), mentioned by Mao Tse-tung in his Yenan "Talks," became a highly favored genre. Lin Piao, if we may believe his daughter Lin Tou-tou, admired reportage as "a style of writing that has the function of both a novel and an essay. It is more closely linked with political life. It bites, and plays a greater role in giving the people realistic education."[6] Lin Tou-tou herself wrote reportage, some of which appeared in English translation in *Chinese Literature* in 1967.

Reportage was, however, less suitable to meet the demand, stated in the Yenan "Talks," and repeated in the summary of the Shanghai Forum, that literature "ought to be on a higher plane, more intense, more concentrated, more typical, nearer the ideal, and therefore more universal than actual everyday life."[7] This almost Aristotelian view of literature was completely neglected during the first years of the Cultural Revolution, and writers did not dare to write anything that did not express positive support of the political goals of the day. During the years 1967–71 the *People's Daily* and *Hung-ch'i* never commented favorably on any modern or traditional novel, or on a volume of poetry by one single poet. The poems by Mao Tse-tung were an exception, but – though often quoted in a political context – they were never subjected to literary criticism.

Only after the death of Lin Piao in September 1971 did the conditions for literary creation begin to improve. The change was signaled by the publication of some poems by Kuo Mo-jo in the *People's Daily* on 19 September 1971. We should recall here that in April 1966, before the Cultural Revolution was officially launched, it was Kuo Mo-jo who was assigned the role of informing the nation (by means of an abject self-criticism) what was in store for intellectuals. The theme of his poems now published was political victory and the richness of the good life that resulted from it. A description of life and scenery in Sinkiang provided Kuo Mo-jo with an opportunity to invite writers to take up their brushes again:

6 Lin Tou-tou, "Vice-Chairman Lin Piao on writing." *Huo-chü t'ung-hsun* (Torch bulletin) (Canton), 1 (July 1968), quoted from *SCMM*, 630 (1968), 1–7.
7 "Summary of the Forum," 231.

Sheets of cloud serve as paper for poems,
The deep water in the lake our ink,
The pointed trees just so many brushes.[8]

Kuo Mo-jo also published a study about Li Po and Tu Fu (*Li Po yü Tu Fu*) in November 1971 to set the tone for more publications in the field of traditional literature. Although Kuo Mo-jo did not avoid historical-materialist explanations, the fact that he was allowed to publish his book meant a rehabilitation for historical research.

The change in the cultural climate was confirmed later in the year when, on 16 December 1971, the *People's Daily* printed Mao Tse-tung's saying "I hope that more and better works of literature and art will be produced." Mao's interference must be interpreted as an attempt to liberate literature from the impasse into which it had been maneuvered during the Cultural Revolution. After Lin Piao had fallen, the results of the Shanghai Forum, which he had organized with Chiang Ch'ing, could no longer be trusted and an updated statement on literary policy was badly needed. An editorial in the *People's Daily* on 16 December 1971 attempted to fill the gap. It emphasized continuity in Chinese literature. Literature should serve the workers, peasants, and soldiers. Heroes in literature should have a proletarian background. In this respect one should learn from the "revolutionary model plays" (*ko-ming yang-pan-hsi*), such as the Peking Operas on modern themes. Criticism of "the anti-Marxist views propagated by the political swindlers of the Liu Shao-ch'i type" should be continued and "the poisonous remains of the black policy of a revisionist literature and art" should be liquidated. Nevertheless, criticism alone was not enough. Also new creative work should be produced. All literature with a revolutionary content and a healthy form ought to be encouraged. It could be written both by amateurs and by professional writers. All literary and artistic genres might be developed, as long as writers were guided by the Marxist world view.

Although the last condition was potentially a severe restriction, the editorial was an encouragement to new literary production. Since the beginning of the Cultural Revolution several volumes of collectively written or anonymous poetry had been published, such as *Odes to Chairman Mao* and *A myriad of songs and poems devoted to the Party*.[9] These volumes continued the tradition of amateur-writing that was established during the Great Leap Forward. Now it became possible again for individual poets to collect their poetry. In 1972 Chang Yung-mei, Li Hsueh-ao, Li Ying, and Ho Ching-chih (one of the authors of the original version of

8 Quoted from the English translation in *Chinese Literature*, 1 (January 1972), 52.
9 *Sung ko hsien-kei Mao Chu-hsi; Ch'ien-ko wan-ch'ü hsien-kei tang.*

The white-haired girl) published volumes of poetry. They had all published before the Cultural Revolution and included some poems from earlier editions. Of course, their work was characterized by the optimistic view of life that is prescribed by Marxism, but the theme of struggle was less apparent than the myth of the good life under socialism, particularly in the poetry of Li Ying, who had made various attempts to present life in the countryside as an Arcadian idyll.[10]

The rehabilitation of the novel could not take place unless fiction were again differentiated from political documentation. Li Hsi-fan, who began his career as a critic in 1954 with a vehement criticism of Yü P'ing-po's interpretation of *Dream of the red chamber*, remained in the background during the first years of the Cultural Revolution, but in 1972 came forward with an important essay on Lu Hsun. He observed that the narrator in a story is *not* necessarily identical with the author of that story, and adds that Lu Hsun's stories are fiction, not something that happened to Lu Hsun.[11] His argument eliminated the basis of much criticism of so-called revisionist writers. It also encouraged the writing of new fiction. The point that fiction is different from reportage or history was also raised by Kao Yü-pao in a comment on how his novel *Kao Yü-pao*, originally published in 1955 and translated into English as *My childhood*, was written. When in 1972 the revised edition of his novel appeared, Kao Yü-pao declared: It "is not an autobiography. I wrote it as a novel." With a reference to the Yenan "Talks," he explained that life as reflected in a work of fiction ought to be on a higher plane and more typical than actual everyday life.[12]

The novels that appeared in 1972 were largely reprints. This was the case with novels by Li Yun-te, Li Ju-ch'ing, Kao Yü-pao, and Hao Jan. Although Hao Jan also began a new novel in several volumes, *The golden road (Chin-kuang ta-tao)*, he avoided referring to the political struggle during the Cultural Revolution. In fact, most novelists who published in the years 1966–76 were careful to keep away from political developments since 1960. In 1967, Hu Wan-ch'un was reported as working on a story about the Red Guards and on a short novel about the January Revolution in Shanghai.[13] In view of the continuous shifts in the official appreciation both of Red Guard groups and of the January Revolution, it is understandable that neither was published.

10 Cf. his poem "Hsiao" (Laughter) in Li Ying, *Tsao-lin ts'un chi* (Jujube village collection), 71–73. English translation in *Chinese Literature*, 8 (August 1972), 33–35.
11 Li Hsi-fan, "Intellectuals of a bygone age," *Chinese Literature*, 12 (December 1972), 24–32.
12 Kao Yü-pao, "How I became a writer," *Chinese Literature*, 6 (June 1972), 111–18.
13 Cf. the Red Guard newspapers *Ching-kang-shan*, 33 (7 April 1976), and *Pei-ching kung-jen* (The Peking worker), 27 May 1967.

Chin Ching-mai provided another negative example. His novel *The song of Ouyang Hai* (*Ou-yang Hai chih ko*) was published in *Harvest* (*Shou-huo*) in 1965, and appeared as a book in the same year. In April 1966, a second, revised edition appeared, to which further revisions were published in May 1967.[14] Chin Ching-mai's novel is the main source of information about the military hero Ouyang Hai, who died in an accident in 1963. In the first edition of his novel Chin described the positive influence of Liu Shao-ch'i's *How to be a good communist* on Ouyang Hai. Later he changed that passage and inserted a reference to the works of Chairman Mao. He also made a favorable comment on Lin Piao. When in 1971 Lin Piao fell into disgrace, the revised text was again out of date. Eventually, in 1979 a new edition was published, but it appeared too early to include again a posthumous tribute to Liu Shao-ch'i.

The fate of *The song of Ouyang Hai* exemplifies the dilemma of Chinese novelists. On the one hand, they have the obligation to represent the molding of heroic characters in the socialist revolution, but as soon as they go into detail and refer to recent political directives and documents, they run the risk that the Party line will have been changed by the time their novels are ready for printing. The dilemma between obedience to the Party line (Party spirit) and artistic generalization (typification) would be less awkward if the Party line did not shift with every change in the political and economic situation, or at least did not shift with the speed characteristic of the late 1960s and the 1970s.

Apart from a preference for describing the early history of the People's Republic, there were other constraints on the code of fiction. Since the main protagonists in a novel are expected to have some knowledge of Marxism and its potential to bring about a solution in any problematic situation, there is little space for indulging in psychological considerations. The narrator and main characters in a novel are extroverts and have access to an assumedly objective world. There is no time and no reason for much introspection and doubt, as Marxism is believed to be capable of providing the correct guidance to the correct goals. If the motivations of characters can have no basis in their psychological condition, the novelist must rely on motivation by social and economic determinants – in short, by class conflict. Indeed, all stories of the period 1966-76 were stories of conflict, and all conflict, according to Mao Tse-tung, boiled down to class conflict. (A conflict between class struggle and human nature was held to be impossible, as Mao Tse-tung did not recognize the existence of a human nature that transcended class differences. In

14 For detailed references, see D. W. Fokkema, "Chinese literature under the Cultural Revolution," *Literature East & West*, 13 (1969), 335–58.

addition, the struggle against natural catastrophes had to be interpreted in terms of class struggle, because different classes would react differently toward such disasters.)

Class conflict, however, can be dealt with in various ways: (1) as open class conflict, which has the disadvantage of being predictable from beginning to end; (2) as disguised class conflict, which may lure the writer into a too favorable presentation of the class enemy and a questionable description of the proletarian hero; or (3) as quasi-class conflict, which reduces the conflict to a misunderstanding, a test, or a joke. The latter solution has been rather popular with Chinese writers, such as Hao Jan, who in his stories has used the quasi-class conflict to depict what amounts to a literary idyll or a society without problems.[15]

Although the code of character description changed in the course of the Cultural Revolution, the following generalization seems to be warranted. In the early 1970s the class enemy (*chieh-chi ti-jen*) in fiction (also outside fiction) was a former landlord or rich peasant, a former member of the Kuomintang, a bookworm, a bureaucrat, or an egoist. He was usually rather old, but if young, he was deceived by an older person who had been spoiled by the old capitalist society. The class ally (*chieh-chi ch'in-jen*) was of poor, proletarian origin, member of a Party committee, maintained good relations with other progressives, and cared for other people.

There were also the following variations. During the first two years of the Cultural Revolution there was a tendency to invest the negative hero with Party membership, as in the 1967 fragments of *The song of Ouyang Hai*. Rather soon, however, this became impossible and Party membership was reserved for the positive hero, as before the Cultural Revolution. The attribute of studying books also shifted from the negative hero during the first years of the Cultural Revolution to the positive hero in later years. The author of the autobiographical novel *Kao Yü-pao* proudly named one of the chapters "I want to read books." This politically motivated shifting of the characteristics of enemy and hero made the task of the Chinese novelist all the harder. In fact, in writing a novel the novelist was a captive of the political configuration of the day. He had to adjust his codes of writing continuously to the political directives he was expected to obey. As soon as the political circumstances changed, the author was bound to alter his text, as did several of the novelists mentioned.

The necessity for such changes worked against the genre of the novel and favored shorter forms: the story and poetry. It also favored theatrical

15 E.g., "Bright clouds," trans. in *Chinese Literature*, 4 (April 1972), 13–28.

performances: Peking Opera, song-and-dance performances, and modern spoken drama (*hua-chü*), which relied on oral presentation that easily could be adjusted to unexpected changes in the political atmosphere.

THE MODEL PEKING OPERAS ON CONTEMPORARY REVOLUTIONARY THEMES

Ever since 1949, attempts had been made to modernize Peking Opera. One of the first modernized operas was *The white-haired girl* (1958), originally a play in the tradition of the rice-planting song (*yang-ko*). During the Cultural Revolution the plot was used for a ballet of the same name, which was added to the brief list of "revolutionary model plays," which Chiang Ch'ing baptized as such on 12 November 1967.[16] She could celebrate that moment as a victory (though with hindsight it turned out to be a Pyrrhic victory) in the long struggle with the cultural establishment over the performance of traditional plays. At the festival of Peking Opera on contemporary themes, held in June-July 1964, P'eng Chen and Lu Ting-i had maintained that historical plays could still be staged. Lu Ting-i advocated the performance of "good traditional plays such as those adapted from *Romance of the three kingdoms*, *Water margin*, *Generals of the Yang family*, and others. Nor do we oppose the staging of good mythological plays such as *Uproar in heaven*, or *Monkey Sun Wu-kung defeats the white-boned ghost*."[17] Chiang Ch'ing, who addressed a forum of theatrical workers participating in the same Festival of Peking Opera, offered a rather different emphasis:

We should take up historical operas only on the condition that the carrying out of the main task (that of portraying contemporary life and creating images of workers, peasants and soldiers) is not impeded. Except for those about ghosts and those extolling capitulation and betrayal, good traditional operas can all be staged.[18]

Lu Ting-i and Chiang Ch'ing both refer here to the issue of whether plays in which ghosts were impersonated should be staged; in 1961 Wu Han had defended the performance of plays with ghosts from a historical point of view.[19]

16 Cf. D. W. Fokkema, "The Maoist myth and its exemplification in the new Peking Opera," *Asia Quarterly*, 2 (1972), 341–61,
17 Lu Ting-i, "Speech at the opening ceremony of the Festival of Peking Opera on Contemporary Themes," in *A great revolution on the cultural front*, 82.
18 Chiang Ch'ing, "On the revolution in Peking Opera: speech made in July 1964 at a forum of theatrical workers participating in the Festival of Peking Operas on Contemporary Themes," *Chinese Literature*, 8 (August 1967), 120.
19 Wu Han, "Shen-hua-chü shih pu-shih hsüan-ch'uan mi-hsin?" (Do plays staging ghosts spread superstition?), *Chung-kuo ch'ing-nien* (Chinese youth), 15 (1961), 9–11.

It was not just the staging of ghosts that was at stake, however, but also the value of myths and traditional ethics. In "On contradiction" (1937), quoted by Wu Han, Mao Tse-tung had explained that "the best myths possess 'eternal charm,' as Marx put it."[20] Apparently supported by Chairman Mao, the resistance against banning traditional plays was strong. The *People's Daily* reported on 4 December 1966 that Chiang Ch'ing's attempts to modernize Peking Opera had long been frustrated by lack of cooperation on the part of the opera companies. This changed when in 1966 the First Peking Opera Company, the National Peking Opera Theater, and other companies were incorporated into the army and put under military discipline. Only then could Chiang Ch'ing, who held the official post of adviser on cultural work to the PLA, get her way and bring to fruition her plans for the modernization of Peking Opera. The operation was extremely important from an ideological point of view, but the quantitative aspect should be mentioned here as well. Modern spoken drama had never equaled Peking Opera in popularity. Of the 3,000 professional theatrical companies in China in 1964, according to Chiang Ch'ing, fewer than a hundred were staging modern drama and more than 2,800 were specializing in various kinds of traditional opera.[21]

The five Peking Operas on contemporary themes that were dubbed model theatrical works by Chiang Ch'ing in November 1967 were: *Raid on the White Tiger Regiment*, *Taking Tiger Mountain by strategy*, *Sha-chia-pang*, *The red lantern*, and *On the docks*. None of them was a new creation of the Cultural Revolution: The original versions of the first two operas were written in 1958, and the others dated from 1964.[22] In their rewritten versions, however, they represented the new Maoist ethics on stage and attempted to design a new Maoist myth.

Except for *On the docks*, they all dealt with themes of war and resistance. Precisely how the new Maoist hero should look was not immediately evident, and the librettos were repeatedly revised. The text of *Taking Tiger Mountain by strategy* (*Chih-ch'ü Wei-hu-shan*) of 1967 was followed by a revised text of October 1969, which, characteristically, did not refer to the earlier edition, as if in an attempt to erase history. Similarly, the novel from which the plot had been borrowed, Ch'ü Po's *Tracks in the snowy forest* (*Lin hai hsueh yuan*) of 1957, was almost completely ignored in the

20 Mao, *SW*, 1.341.
21 Chiang Ch'ing, "On the revolution in Peking Opera," 119.
22 Cf. Chao Ts'ung, *Chung-kuo ta-lu ti hsi-ch'ü kai-ko* (The reform of drama in mainland China). Model operas were filmed, and these apparently were virtually the only feature films made during the Cultural Revolution. Almost all films produced before 1966 were withdrawn during the Cultural Revolution. See Paul Clark, "The film industry in the 1970s," in Bonnie S. McDougall, ed., *Popular Chinese literature and performing arts in the People's Republic of China, 1949–1979*, 177–96.

rapturous discussions of the opera, which also must be interpreted as a deprecation of the history of the text. On one occasion, however, part of the pre-1967 history of the text was discussed in a disparaging way. It appeared that in the course of the many textual revisions, the representation of the main character had been embellished. In order to enhance his credibility, Yang Tzu-jung was initially represented as a semi-bandit, who sang obscene songs and flirted with the daughter of Vulture, his enemy. Soon after the beginning of the Cultural Revolution, however, someone had second thoughts about this and both the songs and the daughter were eliminated. The earlier portrayal of Yang Tzu-jung was castigated as "a living sample advertising Liu Shao-ch'i's reactionary military line of putschism, adventurism and warlordism."[23] The revision of Yang Tzu-jung as a character provides an example of the way in which the Maoist hero was further stylized and invested with puritanical features.

The ethical behavior of the heroic characters in the model Peking Opera was inspired by the propaganda for model-soldiers and model-workers from 1963 on, of which Lei Feng, Ouyang Hai, Wang Chieh, and Mai Hsien-te are the well-known examples. They, in turn, were inspired by the story of Chang Ssu-te. Whereas hero imitation was as old in China as Confucianism, the commemoration of Chang Ssu-te was the beginning of the Maoist hero emulation. Mao Tse-tung immortalized Chang Ssu-te in his short but important speech "Serve the people" (1944), which was one of the so-called much read articles (*lao-san-p'ien*) during the Cultural Revolution, and was printed in many millions of copies. Chang Ssu-te was a soldier in the Guards Regiment of the Central Committee. He joined the revolution in 1933, took part in the Long March, and was wounded in service. On 5 September 1944, when burning charcoal in the mountains of Ansai in northern Shensi, he was killed by the sudden collapse of a kiln. He died in the fire.

The reason why Chang Ssu-te could serve as a model for all Maoist heroes, both in and out of literature, lay in his complete commitment to the revolution, which led to his heroic death. It was typical that he excelled in both military affairs and at the production front. In Chang Ssu-te one recognizes the guerrilla who produces and the worker who is ready to fight. It is important that he dies before he has seen the inauguration of the Communist regime. He is no more than a link in the uninterrupted revolution that will never end. His story provided the plot for a

23 "Strive to create the brilliant images of proletarian heroes: appreciations in creating the heroic images of Yang Tzu-jung and others," by the Taking Tiger Mountain by Strategy Group of the Peking Opera Troupe of Shanghai, *Chinese Literature*, 1 (January 1970), 62.

play, entitled *Chang Ssu-te*, that aroused great interest in Peking in the autumn of 1967.

The heroes in the Peking operas on contemporary themes, including the puritanical version of Yang Tzu-jung, have many features in common with Chang Ssu-te. They share his unrelenting loyalty to Mao Tse-tung, his discipline and fighting spirit, his altruism, and his optimistic belief in the Communist victory. One of the most interesting heroes is Li Yü-ho in the model opera *The red lantern* (*Hung teng chi*). The text edition of May 1970, published in *Hung-ch'i*, was a revision adjusted to the personality cult of Mao Tse-tung, based on an older text by Weng Ou-hung and A Chia. The railway switchman Li Yü-ho cannot complete his assignment of passing a secret code to a unit of resistance forces. His daughter continues his work and so the chain of the revolution remains unbroken. The revolutionary tradition, symbolized by the switchman's red lantern, passes from the father to the daughter. He is not only unyielding in front of his Japanese interrogators, who resort to appalling tortures, but while sacrificing his own life provides for the continuation of the revolution. There is little action in this opera and the stubborn resistance of Li Yü-ho in Japanese captivity is the central theme. After having been tortured, he stumbles over the stage, controlling his movements in the traditional way as prescribed by the conventions of Peking Opera. His body is covered with blood, but his spirit remains indomitable.

Ostensibly, the medium of the opera provided welcome opportunities for the representation of heroes who were stylized according to the Maoist ethical code. It allowed for a severe reduction of psychological characterization yet still remained interesting as a spectacle, with traditional singing and music, highly stylized gestures and movements, acrobatics, and Grand Guignol. The return to a traditional style for representing a revolutionary ideal was, however, rather paradoxical. There are some, but not many, similarities between Maoist and Confucian ethics. Confucianism also employs hero emulation and is didactic. Both Maoism and Confucianism draw much of their strength from utopian schemes. On the other hand, the Confucian ideal of the incorruptible, good official, as represented in *Hai Jui dismissed from office*, derived its moral strength from a personal conception of duty and honesty. It is incompatible with the submissiveness implied in Lenin's metaphor of being a "cog-wheel" in the mechanism of the revolution. The difference may have to do with (but cannot be fully explained by) the far better system of communication in modern times: It is probably correct to assume that the Cultural Revolution would not have been possible without radio and telephone.

To some extent the Maoist hero was related to traditions other than

Confucianism, for instance, that of the knight-errant, whose cunning, foolhardiness, and protection of the weak have been described in traditional fiction. One difference is that the Maoist hero looked forward to a communist society, whereas the knight-errant was usually loyal to a dethroned dynasty. Another difference is that the knight-errant, as defined by James J. Y. Liu,[24] was often an outcast, a lonely individual who acted as he saw fit without bothering about other people's opinion or higher authorities; the Maoist hero, in conformity with Lenin's metaphor, had to respect Party discipline and had to be represented in accordance with the latest ideological prescriptions. Being a tool in the hands of the politicians, the Maoist hero did not succeed in creating a new myth. The audience for the model Peking Opera had too much knowledge of the discord, blackmailing, unlawful detention, suicides, and killing behind the scenes to believe in the operatic stylization of communist behavior.

1976 AND THE EMERGENCE OF "SCAR LITERATURE"

The Ch'ing Ming Festival in April 1976 was almost exclusively devoted to the commemoration of Premier Chou En-lai, who had passed away in January of the same year. In Peking, T'ien An Men Square was crowded by hundreds of thousands of people who wished to commemorate the premier by presenting funeral wreaths, delivering speeches, and reading poetry. In an evocation of the May Fourth Movement, this spontaneous demonstration received the name "April Fifth Movement" (*ssu-wu yun-tung*). Workers' militia and police, however, were used to suppress the demonstration, which in the *People's Daily* on 8 April was called a counterrevolutionary movement. It was more than two years before this judgment was exposed, on 21–22 November 1978, as having been contrived by the Gang of Four, and reversed. Subsequently, selections of the poetry in honor of Chou En-lai that had circulated only in *samizdat* editions were officially published.

It was only after the reversal of the verdict on the T'ien An Men incident that the cultural climate definitely began to change. The rehabilitation of writers criticized and arrested during the Cultural Revolution was taken as a further sign that the new political leadership was in favor of a different policy with respect to literature and the arts.

In 1978 the rehabilitation was made public of: Ai Ch'ing, poet, criticized 1957, sent to reform through labor in Sinkiang 1958–76; Chou Li-po, novelist, persecuted 1966; Chou Yang, theoretician and official,

---

24 James J. Y. Liu, *The Chinese knight-errant.*

in prison 1966–76; Liu Pai-yü, writer of short stories and official, criticized 1967; Hsia Yen, playwright and official, criticized 1965; Ouyang Shan, novelist, criticized 1965; Wang Jo-wang, critic and writer of short stories, criticized, in prison 1957, 1962.

In 1979 the rehabilitation followed of: Ch'en Huang-mei, critic, persecuted 1966; Chou Erh-fu, novelist, criticized 1969; Liao Mo-sha, essayist, criticized 1966; Liu Pin-yen, writer of short stories, criticized 1957; Ting Ling, novelist, criticized 1955, 1957, sent to reform through labor in the Northeast 1958–70, in prison 1970–75, in a people's commune 1975–78; Wang Meng, writer of short stories, criticized 1957; Wu Ch'iang, novelist, criticized 1968; Yang Han-sheng, playwright, criticized 1966; Yang Mo, novelist, criticized 1967.

For several writers rehabilitation came too late. In 1978 and 1979 posthumous rehabilitation was announced of: Chao Shu-li, novelist, criticized 1967, died in prison 1970; Feng Hsueh-feng, critic and poet, criticized 1957, died after long illness 1976; Lao She, novelist, criticized 1966, committed suicide or was killed 1966; Liu Ch'ing, novelist, arrested 1967, died in prison about 1977; Lo Kuang-pin, novelist, criticized 1966, committed suicide or was killed 1967; Shao Ch'üan-lin, theoretician and critic, criticized 1964, died in prison 1971; T'ao Chu, critic and official, arrested 1966, died in prison 1969; Teng T'o, essayist, criticized 1966, killed or committed suicide 1966; T'ien Han, playwright, criticized 1964, arrested 1966, died in prison 1968; Wu Han, playwright and essayist, criticized 1965, arrested 1966, committed suicide 1967.

The rehabilitation usually was without restrictions. Teng T'o's *Night talks at Yenshan* (1961–62), which had been subjected to the most devastating criticism in May 1966, was reprinted by Pei-ching ch'u-pan-she in 1979 in 150,000 or more copies. The work of the other writers who had been persecuted during the Cultural Revolution was made available again. Finally, in 1981 the rehabilitation of Hu Feng (arrested in 1955) took place. At the same time, the Chinese classics and the literature of the 1930s, as well as European literature, were rediscovered. In 1978 translations of Balzac, Galsworthy, Thackeray, Mark Twain, and Shakespeare were published, and this trend continued in subsequent years.

Among the new writers, Liu Hsin-wu was the first to deal critically with the adverse results of the Cultural Revolution and to draw national attention with his story "The class teacher" (1977).[25] He dealt with the effects of crime and the integration into normal life of young people who

25 Liu Hsin-wu, "Pan-chu-jen" (The class teacher), *Jen-min wen-hsueh* (People's literature), 11 (1977), 16–29. English translation in *Chinese Literature*, 1 (January 1979), 15–36.

had been victims of the Cultural Revolution. Another young writer who quickly became famous was Lu Hsin-hua, who in his story "The scar" (1978), also translated as "The wound," evaluated the relation between a so-called progressive daughter and her so-called revisionist mother in the light of the drastic change in the political atmosphere after the death of Mao Tse-tung and the arrest of the Gang of Four. The story received an award and was reprinted in a collection of short stories that attracted much publicity.[26] Lu Hsin-hua's story became a model for "scar literature" (*shang-hen wen-hsueh*), literature in which the sufferings of honest people under the Cultural Revolution were described. Again it appeared that, apart from a genuine impulse behind this literature of exposure, such writing served a political end: It strengthened the faction of Teng Hsiao-p'ing, who wanted to erase totally the effects of the Cultural Revolution. Other writers who joined the effort to settle accounts with the theory and practice of the Cultural Revolution were: Ch'en Kuo-k'ai, Ju Chih-chüan, Kao Hsiao-sheng, and Wang Ya-p'ing. Their work also often implies criticism of the Great Leap Forward. Of the generation that had been active during the Hundred Flowers period of 1956–57, Liu Pin-yen and Wang Meng reappeared and became amazingly vigorous.

Occasionally the question was raised as to whether it was wise to enlarge on the negative aspects of the Cultural Revolution. In the *People's Daily* of 31 July 1979, Li Chien advocated a more reserved treatment of the moral and economic chaos. In the same issue Wang Jo-wang, a victim of the Anti-Rightist Campaign, defended the stories exposing the scars of the Cultural Revolution. In his capacity as vice-president of the Chinese Federation of Writers and Artists, Chou Yang supported Wang's view.[27] Chou Yang, who had spent ten years in prison, had resumed many of his pre-1966 responsibilities. His authority, however, did not equal that in the days before the Cultural Revolution. Not only had he grown older, but he was also expected now to cooperate with writers whom he had opposed or even sent to jail during the Anti-Rightist Campaign – people like Liu Pin-yen, Ting Ling, and Wang Jo-wang. In his defense of Wang Jo-wang, Chou Yang explained that the Yenan "Talks" provided a valid rule of conduct but should not be interpreted in a dogmatic way. In contradistinction to the Shanghai Forum, he emphasized the particularity of literary creation: "If one wants to give guidance to the economy, one cannot ignore the laws of economy …, if one wants to guide literature

26 Lu Hsin-hua, "Shang-hen" (The scar), in *I-chiu-ch'i-pa nien ch'üan-kuo yu-hsiu tuan-p'ien hsiao-shuo p'ing-hsuan tso-p'in-chi* (Critical selection of the best short stories of the whole nation published in 1978), 244–58.
27 For Chou Yang's comment, see *Chinese Literature*, 1 (January 1980), 94–95.

and the arts, one needs to respect the laws of literature and the arts."[28] Although Chou Yang did not elaborate on the "laws of literature," it is evident that in the strained relationship between party spirit and typification he was prepared to put full emphasis on artistic creation or "typification." Like Chou Yang, other critics harked back to problems that had also been debated during the Hundred Flowers period. Old issues were taken up again, sometimes by the same protagonists – if they had survived the Cultural Revolution. Wang Jo-wang and Ch'in Chao-yang were two of these liberal critics who emphasized the difference between art and propaganda and advocated a broad concept of realism.

Both inside and outside China the polemics occasioned by the screenplay *Unrequited love* (*K'u-lien*) by Pai Hua in 1981 were interpreted as a test of the limits of freedom in writing. On 20 April, the *Liberation Army News* accused the author of negating patriotism and resenting Party policies. With Liu Pin-yen, Pai Hua had been among the most candid speakers at the Fourth Congress of Chinese Writers and Artists in 1979, deploring the growth of hypocrisy, the fear of trusting friends or keeping diaries. He also praised those young writers who had the courage and ability to think for themselves.[29] Two years later his script was criticized. In evaluating the widespread criticism, it should not be overlooked that Pai Hua was an officer in the cultural apparatus of the PLA, which made his case specially delicate. Furthermore, from the very beginning it was explained that the criticism was not the beginning of a new campaign against the writers. As late as July 1983, *Beijing Review* emphasized that Pai Hua had continued writing and that one of his recent plays had been staged in Peking. The criticism of Pai Hua showed not only the limits of creative freedom but also the dilemma of the CCP: how to allow a considerable degree of intellectual freedom throughout China, without having that freedom upsetting the familiar ideological patterns to the point of complete destruction. Perhaps the dilemma can be solved only if the Party relinquishes its supervision of cultural life and, consequently, is relieved of responsibility for the new tendencies in literature and the arts.

Such warning signals were symptomatic of an increasing concern on the part of such conservative Party leaders as Ch'en Yun and P'eng Chen, and their surrogates in the intellectual realm, Hu Ch'iao-mu and Teng Li-ch'ün, about the use being made by China's intellectuals of China's equivalent of *glasnost'*. They would be able to play upon Teng Hsiao-p'ing's own detestation of disorder to bring about the brief but threaten-

---

28 Chou Yang, "Yeh t'an-t'an tang ho wen-i ti kuan-hsi" (Speaking again of the relation between the Party and literature and the arts), *HC*, 11 (1979), 27.

29 W. J. F. Jenner, "1979: a new start for literature in China?" *CQ*, 86 (June 1981), 294.

ing campaign against "spiritual pollution" of late 1983 to early 1986, and the disciplining of such prominent intellectuals as the writer Liu Pin-yen, the physicist Fang Li-chih, the Marxist theoretician Su Shao-chih, and the editor Wang Jo-shui in early 1987. This was in the wake of the 1986 student demonstrations and consequent dismissal of Hu Yao-pang as CCP general secretary. Yet the freedom of writers is still probably greater than ever since 1949. At the very least, literary creation soon became remarkably different from the days of the Cultural Revolution. Social and political conditions still determined the themes of literature, but were radically different from the time of the Cultural Revolution. Current themes included the relation between bureaucratic power and individual responsibility, hope and disillusion, the relations between mother and daughter and between father and son, love, artistic creation, corruption, crime and nepotism.

The new opportunities for psychological description led Wang Meng (who later became minister of culture) and Ju Chih-chüan to experiments with the stream-of-consciousness technique and narration that did not respect the chronological order of events. The importance of the appearance of introspection in Chinese fiction as a cultural value can hardly be overestimated. Decisions dictated by individual conscience replaced unconditional obedience to Party directives. Whatever might be the political future of this trend, it at least led to a lively and diversified production of literature, which completely overshadowed the fewer than a dozen "model theatrical works" once chaperoned by Chiang Ch'ing.

PART IV

LIFE AND LETTERS
UNDER COMMUNISM

CHAPTER 9

THE COUNTRYSIDE
UNDER COMMUNISM

In his famous "Investigation of the peasant movement in Hunan," Mao Tse-tung described "four thick ropes binding the Chinese people, particularly the peasants." These ropes represented the bonds of four kinds of authority:

(1) the state system (political authority) ... ; (2) the clan system (clan authority), ranging from the central ancestral temple and its branch temples down to the head of the household; and (3) the supernatural system (religious authority), ranging from the King of Hell down to the town and village gods belonging to the nether world, and from the Emperor of Heaven down to all the various gods and spirits belonging to the celestial world. As for women, in addition to being dominated by these three systems of authority, they are also dominated by the men (the authority of the husband). These four authorities – political, clan, religious, and masculine – are the embodiment of the whole feudal-patriarchal system and ideology.[1]

In their drive for power, the Chinese Communists attempted to build a base of peasant support by severing and reweaving these bonds of authority; and they continued this process after they took control of the country in 1949. Although their efforts did indeed lead to important alterations in the fabric of Chinese rural life, the traditional patterns of peasant life seem to have had more resilience than the Communists had counted on, and the changes that actually occurred in those patterns were often different from what they had intended.

ESTABLISHING A NEW ECONOMIC AND POLITICAL
SYSTEM, 1949–1955

The fabric of rural Chinese society

Even today, when Chinese peasants discuss the size of their villages, they usually refer to numbers of households rather than numbers of indivi-

---

1 Mao Tse-tung, "Report on an investigation of the peasant movement in Hunan," in *Selected works of Mao Tse-tung*, 1.44.

duals – the product of a long tradition that sees the individual mainly in terms of his or her relation to a family unit. The household, the primary unit of life in the Chinese countryside, has for millennia ideally consisted of a husband and wife together with all of their married sons and daughters-in-law and all of their grandchildren. In practice, however, this ideal of an extended household has been only rarely realized, because the maintenance of such an ideal household requires above-average wealth and depends on exceptionally skillful management of interpersonal relations.[2] The more typical household has usually consisted only of a married couple and their children and perhaps the husband's elderly parents. The social structure of the fundamental Chinese family unit has traditionally been hierarchical and patriarchal, husbands having authority over wives, parents over sons, and the elder over the younger. Its moral ethos has been a vision of life that sees the family as transcending the existence of any of its individual living members, to the extent that the family includes deceased ancestors as well as the living, with the result that a particular moral responsibility is attached to the extended relations of kinship that link concentric circles of uncles and nephews and cousins by virtue of their common descent from ancestors in the male line. Before the Communist takeover of China, the economic base of this family unit was a parcel of land, ideally owned but often merely rented, the produce of which provided the family with its food and, through local trade, with some of the cash needed to buy the necessaries of life.

For all their centrality in social life, however, traditional Chinese peasant households were by no means self-sufficient. Clusters of households, often bound together by kinship ties, resided together in villages, within which they cooperated and competed with one another in an intricate variety of ways.[3] Residents of villages regularly reached beyond their home communities to buy and sell, to lend and borrow, to seek wives for their sons and marry off daughters, to acquire political protection and to secure the consolations of religious observance. Such relationships usually converged on a market town, the hub of economic and social life for perhaps a dozen and a half villages. Within such a town would be found the shops of grain sellers and carpenters, the offices of doctors and moneylenders, and an assortment of inns, teahouses, and temples. Periodically, perhaps every five days, or sometimes every three days or every other day, people

2 For analyses of these tensions, see Yueh-hwa Lin, *The golden wing: a sociological study of Chinese familism*; C. K. Yang, *The Chinese family in the communist revolution*; and Margery Wolf, *The house of Lim: a study of a Chinese farm family*.
3 See Morton Fried, *The fabric of Chinese society: a study of the social life of a Chinese county seat* and G. William Skinner, "Marketing and social structure in rural China," *JAS*, 24 (1964–65).

from surrounding villages would mingle with itinerant peddlers to hold a market, at which would be bought and sold everything from vegetables and livestock to clothing and handmade farm implements.

Such local market relationships, however, were never purely economic but were always constrained by custom and embedded in complex networks of interpersonal loyalties. As a woman in a village in Taiwan, discussing the plight of the rural shopkeeper with the anthropologist Margery Wolf, put it:

It really is hard to run a country store if you don't have a lot of money because all of your neighbors that you have known for generations and all of your relatives come and want things when they don't have any money, and so you just have to give them the things. Sometimes you know that if you give things to this person, he will never give you the money, and so you tell him this, and then he gets mad and says that you don't respect him and goes all around to people saying you have insulted his family. If you don't give things to people, they get mad at you, but if you do, you can't make any money. It really is hard to run a store in the country.[4]

Chinese peasants have often spoken of the extrafamilial bonds necessary for daily living in terms of the principles of *kan-ch'ing*, a word that literally means "feeling" but in common parlance refers to the particularistic ties that link superiors and inferiors in relations of patronage and clientage. In traditional rural life, each strand of such *kan-ch'ing* relations was somewhat different, its strength and resilience depending on the personal character of the parties to the relation, the exact quantity and quality of the material and spiritual goods exchanged by means of the relation, and the specific history of its development.[5]

As the Communists took power, this basic fabric of Chinese life underlay a wide variety of community settlement patterns in different parts of China. Villages varied in size and mode of solidarity from communities in parts of South China of perhaps five hundred households (around 2,500 persons), all of whom would claim descent on the male side from a single common ancestor and who would be organized as a single corporate lineage under the formal leadership of a small group of clan elders,[6] to communities in parts of North China with perhaps fifty households representing several different lineages. Marketing networks similarly varied in size and complexity.

4 Wolf, *The house of Lim*, 22.
5 One of the most systematic analyses of these loyalties is offered by Fried, *The fabric of Chinese society*, 99–134.
6 For the classic anthropological study of such organizations, see Maurice Freedman, *Lineage organization in southeastern China*.

Concrete patterns of economic and social inequality also differed widely from village to village and marketing area to marketing area. Almost all villages were divided into groups of households that were relatively land-rich and groups that were land-poor. The land-rich – those who owned more than they could farm themselves – rented out their surplus to households that did not own enough to support themselves. Some landowners were able to make enough income through rents so that they did not have to do any physical labor themselves. Others, not quite so well off, supplemented the income from their own labor with that from rents. Those who had to rent all the land that they tilled often had to pay about 40 percent of their crop as rent to their landlord. And in most villages there were some who could not even manage to rent any land for themselves and thus were forced to work as hired laborers. But the ratio of landlords to "poor and hired" peasants differed widely. In some highly fertile regions, where the richness of the land made landholding a profitable investment, villages might be polarized into a small group consisting of a few extremely wealthy landlords and a large mass of renters. In areas where the land was poor, villages often consisted mostly of "middle peasants," who subsisted on small plots of land that they owned themselves, with only a few landlords, living in something like genteel poverty, and a relatively small number of poor peasants and hired labor. Similarly, some marketing areas consisted of villages that were nearly equal in wealth and influence while others were characterized by more diversity.[7]

Relations between the land-rich and land-poor also varied widely in quality. Many of the wealthier landowners were absentee landlords, having left their villages for the cities. Having no personal relations with their tenants and sometimes relying on ruthless local agents to collect their rents, such landlords could be fiercely detested by the poor as greedy parasites. Other landlords, perhaps not so wealthy and still residing in their native villages, where they were connected to their tenants by ties of kinship or by strong strands of "good feeling," might be viewed by at least some of their tenants with genuine loyalty and respect.[8]

Actual patterns of affluence and misery also differed from community to community and were constantly in flux. Even though many poor peasant households might have access to barely enough land to feed them-

7 A sense of the range of such differences, as they existed on the eve of the Communist takeover, can be gained by reading C. K. Yang, *A Chinese village in early communist transition*; William Hinton, *Fanshen: a documentary of revolution in a Chinese village*; Isabel and David Crook, *Revolution in a Chinese village: Ten Mile Inn*; Isabel and David Crook, *Ten Mile Inn: mass movement in a Chinese village*; and Fried, *The fabric of Chinese society*.
8 See Fried, *The fabric of Chinese society*, 104–9.

selves in good harvest years, not to mention paying for the expenses of sickness or of a wedding or a funeral, such households could often supplement their farming income through handicraft production during the agricultural slack season or through seasonal labor by some of their members in the city. Also, the social and political unrest of the 1930s and 1940s often occasioned a great deal of social mobility, so that one reads many accounts of landlords going bankrupt through the calamities of war or failed business ventures or opium smoking or gambling, as well as some accounts of middle or even poor peasants getting rich (often enough through illegal activities such as narcotics smuggling).[9]

All of these complex factors often led to what the Chinese Communists called a "low level of class consciousness" in China's rural communities. The poor and hired did not necessarily see themselves as united by common interests against their community's rich landlords. Indeed, when most peasants first encountered the Communist rhetoric of class analysis, it must have seemed foreign and strange to them. The rhetoric involved, first of all, some new terminology: Village society was divided into "landlords," "rich peasants," "middle peasants" (a category further subdivided into "well-to-do middle peasants" and "middle peasants"), "poor peasants," and "hired workers." Although villagers were obviously aware of economic and political differences within their local communities, they did not ordinarily use such terms to make precise and systematic distinctions between gradations of wealth and power.[10] And even when they learned to use such terms, they did not necessarily feel that their primary loyalties were determined by such distinctions. Yet the Communists' land reform program was based on precisely the assumption that one's primary interests were, and one's primary commitments ought to be, so determined.

The land reform program aimed to untie all of the "feudal-patriarchal" bonds through which local society was woven into an intricate pattern of particularistic relations and to replace those bonds with rationalized frameworks of conflicting class solidarities. But the fabric of Chinese society resisted such easy unraveling. And as the process of land reform impinged on that fabric of life, it created enormously variegated patterns of human experience, which had in common mainly a lack of precise fit with official Communist prescriptions of how land reform should have taken place.

9 For an analysis of such mobility patterns, see Yang, *A Chinese village in early communist transition*, 122–27.
10 Richard Madsen, *Morality and power in a Chinese village*, 72–80.

Land reform

The experience of land reform varied, first of all, depending on exactly when it took place. In what the Communists called "old revolutionary base areas," like the area around Yenan in Shensi province, where the Communists had been established since the mid-1930s, land reform took place soon after 1946, in the politically and psychologically charged atmosphere of an impending civil war. The policy governing this land reform was a radical one, emphasizing the complete expropriation of the relatively wealthy and encouraging the use of violence. Under these circumstances, there frequently occurred, as Liu Shao-ch'i later wrote, "the phenomena of indiscriminate beating and killing."[11] Villagers sometimes used the guise of land reform to settle old grudges, branding as landlords local rivals who might objectively have been classified merely as middle peasants. Frustrated when the "fruits of struggle" – the redistributed property of the rich – were too meager to raise them out of poverty, poor peasants tried to reclassify as landlords or as rich peasants people who owned only modest amounts of land more than they did.[12] Such unrestrained peasant radicalism often led to economic crises by destroying all motivation on the part of skilled farmers to excel in economic endeavors. A speech by Mao Tse-tung in the spring of 1948 marked a turning away from the radical policy. The earlier land reform had been a "leftist deviation" based on notions of "absolute egalitarianism," he said. The immediate aim of land reform was the development of agricultural production, and this required that land reform proceed in a "step by step and discriminating way." Peasants were reclassified, and restitution was made to some who had been improperly expropriated.[13]

In "early liberated areas" like the Central-South provinces of Hupei and Hunan, on the other hand, land reform came around 1948 or early 1949, after this more moderate line had taken effect and in an atmosphere marked by the Communists' confidence in their ultimate victory over the Kuomintang. The "masses" were kept under tighter control; landlords were allowed to keep enough property to make a living from; and rich peasants were allowed to keep much of their land, farm tools, and draft animals.[14]

11 Liu Shao-ch'i, "Report on the question of land reform" delivered at the National Committee of the Chinese People's Political Consultative Conference, 14 June 1950; see *Liu Shao-ch'i hsuan-chi*, 29–47.
12 See Hinton, *Fanshen*, 280–475.
13 Ibid., 479–508. The speech by Mao was delivered on 1 April 1948 and is summarized in ibid., 486–87.
14 For a detailed account of land reform in this region, see Vivienne Shue, *Peasant China in transition: the dynamics of development toward socialism, 1949–1956.*

In "later liberated areas" like the southern provinces, land reform did not begin until well after 1949, in accordance with an even more moderate Agrarian Reform Law promulgated in June 1950, which emphasized the need to maintain the "rich peasant economy." By October 1950, however, the Korean War had begun, and with it came a much tougher line on land reform. Up to perhaps 800,000 landlords were eventually executed as "counterrevolutionaries."[15]

When it was carried out, land reform usually began at the village level with the arrival of a "work team" of about a dozen outside cadres, of whom half might be peasants familiar with the locality and half city people, often intellectuals, being sent down to prove their commitment to the Communist cause and to forge their revolutionary spirit in the fires of the land revolution. The tone of land reform in a region would be set by the initial experiences of work teams in a few carefully selected "keypoint villages."

A work team would spend an initial period of up to several months living in the village, helping with farm work, getting to know the local situation. Closely monitored by higher-level officials operating out of nearby towns, it would make a rough determination of the class status of village households. It would base its classification on the amount of land villagers owned (or had owned three years before land reform) and on the percentage of villagers' income that had been derived from "exploiting" others by renting land to them or by hiring them as wage laborers. Poor peasants and hired hands would be invited to form a Poor Peasants' Association, which (under the careful guidance of the work team, itself under the careful guidance of a Chinese Communist Party organization) would help to determine more precisely who belonged to what social class in the village. The initial classifications might be revised several times in the light of peasant comments and in accordance with higher-level instructions.

The classification of villagers into the new categories was the most fateful part of the land reform process. Where one's name was listed on the official announcements posted by work teams at a village's central meeting place would not only determine who would gain or lose what in the redistribution of land, but for decades to come it would decide who could officially be considered politically reliable and who could not. In some cases, a classification could literally make the difference between life and death. It must have caused many peasants considerable anxiety to realize that the process of determining who belonged to what class was inevitably extremely imprecise.

15 Benedict Stavis, *The politics of agricultural mechanization in China*, 29–30.

In the first periods of land reform, the official criteria for determining who was a landlord or a rich peasant, and so forth, were themselves imprecise. But even when rough guidelines were replaced by detailed regulations specifying a complex casuistry for discriminating between various classes, plenty of ambiguities remained. Exactly how much land did a family own? Even if one could measure the exact acreage to which it held title – often a difficult task in itself, given the lack of official records – one would have to take into account what percentage of this land was valuable, fertile land and what percentage only marginally cultivable, in order to determine the real value of those holdings. Since landholdings were often widely scattered in the form of small plots throughout a village, it could be extremely difficult to make such a determination. How much of one's income came from "exploitation"? In the absence of systematic written records, such figures were hard to come by. But they might spell the difference between being classified as a rich peasant or as a middle peasant. What was the exact value of the farm implements one's family owned? Was the family plow so broken down as to be almost unusable, or was it still a valuable farm tool? Was one's water buffalo or mule near the end of its working days, or did it still have a lot of life left in it? Answers to such questions could make the difference between being classified as a middle peasant or as a poor peasant. How much of a seemingly affluent person's income was from a legitimate commercial enterprise – say, a small medicine shop – and how much from the little plots of land that person rented out in the village? Such a discrimination could distinguish between a true landlord and merely a "small rentier" – and during some periods of land reform, perhaps the difference between life and death.[16]

In a supercharged political atmosphere, inexperienced work team cadres, themselves perhaps under conflicting political pressures from superiors, might try to explain such complex distinctions to illiterate peasants, tied to some of their fellow villagers and estranged from others by a maze of particularistic loyalties. Under such circumstances one could not expect the resultant decisions to be dispassionately objective or precisely accurate, and they were not. One legacy of the inevitable mistakes made by land reform work teams was an array of persistent grievances, which might underlie all sorts of personal and political conflicts in a village for decades to come. For instance, if many villagers thought that Old Wang really should have been classified as a rich peasant rather than as a middle

---

16 For eyewitness accounts of some of the mistakes made under these circumstances, see Hinton, *Fanshen*, 280–475, and Yang, *A Chinese village in early communist transition*, 131–52.

peasant, and if Old Wang had the kind of personality that irritated many of his fellow villagers, they might harbor against him resentment that could burst into a variety of minor or serious conflicts. Or if Little Li had been classified as a rich peasant, when many who knew him believed that he really should have been considered a middle peasant, his friends might harbor lasting grudges against those responsible for the classification.

The pressures of carrying out an accurate classification of the rural population also took their toll on the work team cadres responsible for directing this mission at the grass roots. Many such cadres were genuinely idealistic and honestly tried to do the right thing under the circumstances. Yet they had to contend not only with the intrigues and dissimulations of local peasants, traditionally suspicious of outsiders — for instance, with landlords "donating" some of their property to relatives and friends or otherwise hiding their wealth in order to appear poorer, with poor peasants trying to argue that some of their slightly more well-to-do neighbors were even better off than they appeared to be — but also with shifting government policies that might one month say that work teams should define the term "landlord" in a broad fashion and another month say that it should be defined in a more restrictive fashion. Or sometimes they had to reconcile their consciences with policies that at least implicitly assigned quotas demanding that they find a certain percentage of landlords in a village, no matter what the actual results of their investigations. Instead of becoming "steeled in revolutionary struggle" as a result of such experiences, some cadres were politically ruined or psychologically broken.[17]

After the classification had been completed, a "struggle phase" of the land reform would begin. The worst of the landlords — those called "local despots," who had been guilty of particularly exploitative and abusive behavior toward their tenants — and assorted other "local bullies" and "counterrevolutionaries" were brought before mass assemblies in the village. Under the guidance of the work team, villagers denounced and sometimes physically abused (and sometimes even beat to death) their former local elites. Often, villagers were initially reluctant to condemn their landlords in this way. Kinship ties or ties of "good feeling" sometimes connected them to the landlords. Sometimes they simply felt a basic respect for the former village leaders. Sometimes they were afraid of the consequences should the landlords someday regain their power. Basic-level work teams were sometimes reluctant to make the effort to overcome peasant hostility and had to be pressured by their superiors to persevere in pushing the peasants to get personally involved in the class

17 For a dramatic example of this, see Hinton, *Fanshen*, 364–68.

struggle. Once the ice was broken, however, and a few local "activists" (often brash, politically ambitious young men) took the lead in damning the landlords, a torrent of criticism often poured forth. In fomenting such active mass struggle against the old local elite, the Chinese Communist Party was attempting to destroy whatever legitimacy bolstered the traditional elite's power in the countryside. They appeared to have largely succeeded.[18]

From the point of view of the CCP, the political task of destroying the traditional power structure of rural China was indeed the main goal of land reform. From the point of view of the peasantry, however, the main goal was economic. Most poor peasants took part in land reform out of the hope of getting property. After the landlords (and, during radical phases of policy, the rich peasants) had been expropriated, a large proportion of their land, together with all land owned corporately by such traditional organizations as clans and temples, was redistributed to the poor, usually after heated discussions about who really was poor and who needed how much. The result of this redistribution usually was a village in which every household owned a small piece of land: Middle peasants kept the land they had already owned, landlords (those who survived beatings and were spared executions) were left enough property to make them the equivalent of middle peasants, rich peasants (at least under the policies that supported maintaining a "rich peasant economy") were allowed to keep much of their property and draft animals, poor peasants got to own for themselves about the amount of land (often, in fact, the same plots of land) that they had once rented, and hired laborers got about as much as the poor peasants.[19] Land, however, was not widely distributed among villages, so that a poor peasant in a rich village might thus end up with more land to farm and food to eat than a middle peasant in a poor village.

Mutual aid

The prevalent official slogan of the first few years after 1950 was "set up a household and become rich" (*fa chia chih fu*) — an encouragement to private enjoyment of the fruits of land reform. But most poor peasants had little realistic hope of becoming rich, at least not in the immediate future. True, they no longer had to pay rent on the land they farmed. But they

---

18 See Franz Schurmann, *Ideology and organization in Communst China*, 431–37.
19 For examples of the actual land distributions in different areas, see Hinton, *Fanshen*, 592; Yang, *A Chinese village in early communist transition*, 146–52; and Shue, *Peasant China in transition*, 61 and 90.

still had to pay taxes on what they produced; and although tax policies, like so much else, fluctuated considerably in the early 1950s, and although the manner of collection by local cadres differed in various regions, the overall tax burden on villages was stiffer than it had been under the old regime, even though it was distributed much more evenly than in the past.[20] And even though poor peasants might have somewhat more surplus after taxes than after rent payments under the old system, their poverty had been only partly the result of having to pay rent on the small parcels of land they farmed. It had also been the result of intractable economic, social, and personal limitations. They had lacked farm implements and draft animals to till their land efficiently, and all too often they had lacked credit to borrow money to improve their farming or to carry their families over emergencies. Often, too, the poor had been stuck in their unfortunate situation because they did not fit into whatever networks of extended kinship had dominated their villages or because, for whatever reasons, they had been estranged from the bonds of good feeling that traditionally tied cooperative neighbors together. Some of them had been poor because their families consisted of too few strong, healthy workers, or too few persons with the skills, motivation, and discipline for effective work.[21]

None of these problems was solved simply by redistribution of a village's land. Some were even made worse by the immediate consequences of land reform. Take, for example, the lack of farm tools and draft animals – one of the most crucial factors in effective farming. The supply of credit needed to buy such items almost dried up in the countryside after land reform. The main source of credit in the past had been local landlords and rich peasants, who loaned out money at usurious rates of interest (the ability to extend credit was, indeed, one of the major sources of their power), although interest rates might be lowered a little if a borrower's "human feeling" relationship with the lender was good and if the borrower was in severe straits. Private moneylending was still legally permitted after land reform, provided it was lent at reasonable rates of interest, but even those rich peasants who still had money to spare had no desire to lend it out, because moneylending would simply advertise one's wealth – a dangerous thing to do in the new society – and because the new government was giving no plausible guarantees that the money

---

20 Such, at least, is the conclusion of Yang, *A Chinese village in early communist transition*, 155–57. For a detailed account of the tax system during this period, see Shue, *Peasant China in transition*, 102–43.

21 Anita Chan, Richard Madsen, and Jonathan Unger, *Chen Village: the recent history of a peasant community in Mao's China*, 52.

would be repaid in the future.[22] Under such circumstances, agricultural production and disposable income among the poor remained stagnant. Inequalities between poor peasants and rich peasants remained in place. Some such inequalities even widened as poor peasants, unable to support themselves on their newly acquired land, began to hire themselves out as laborers to the rich peasants.

To solve such problems, the government could not expand the net amount of land available to villagers, and for the time being, at least, it would not expand the amount of capital. Its preferred solution was the establishment of mutual aid teams (MATs), a device presumably to make better use of what meager productive resources there were. This was, on the face of it, a modest innovation. Under the leadership of the Communist Party, villagers were supposed to build such MATs on the foundation of traditional patterns of cooperation. In the past, small groups of neighboring households, often related by kinship, had customarily worked out arrangements for cooperating during the busy harvest and planting seasons. At first, the new MATs were basically copies of these older arrangements, consisting of the perhaps three or four households that had helped one another out during the busy harvest and planting seasons in the past. The main difference was that labor exchange was now supposed to be based on more formal accounting procedures than in the past and was supposed to last throughout the years.[23]

The big barrier to extending labor exchanges had traditionally been the issue of assuring reciprocity: for instance, if one household had stronger workers and better tools than another, why should its members spend a day in their neighbor's fields if all they were going to get in return was an inferior day's labor with inferior tools? In the past, villagers had solved or at least avoided such problems, first, by restricting the scope of cooperation to small groups of roughly equal households bound together by close enough ties of kinship or friendship to encourage them to trust one another and, second, by limiting the exchanges of labor to specific tasks that could be easily monitored. But if better methods for objectively evaluating the contribution each household made to a common endeavor could be established, and if arrangements for assuring that each household contributed its fair share could be institutionalized, then the number of cooperating households might be broadened and the quantity and

---

22 Shue, *Peasant China in transition*, 247–50; and Yang, *A Chinese village in early communist transition*, 163–65.

23 See William Hinton, *Shenfan: the continuing revolution in a Chinese village*, 76–93; Shue, *Peasant China in transition*. 153–91; and Yang, *A Chinese village in early communist transition*, 203–14. For an account of pre-Communist mutual aid, see Fried, *The fabric of Chinese society*, 117–20.

quality of the labor exchanged might be increased. This could presumably enhance productivity and improve the livelihood of the peasants involved.

Thus, although the earliest MATs established under Communist sponsorship were very similar to traditional labor exchange groupings, they contained two important innovations: an official leader responsible for managing the team and a "work point" system for recording the amount of work each member contributed and for calculating the compensation for it. Once these two innovations were in place, local officials could push to expand the scope of the MATs' cooperation. Teams were to get bigger, and they now were to cooperate year-round instead of only at harvest and planting seasons.

Each step in expanding the size and function of the MATs, however, pulled at the traditional fabric of village life, causing tensions and conflicts. The more the MATs' membership expanded beyond small circles of neighbors and kin, the weaker were the bonds of trust and mutual understanding uniting the groups and the more difficult it became to establish consensus on an appropriate leader, an appropriate division of labor, and a reasonable production plan. A peasant interviewed by Jan Myrdal describes some of the conflicts that beset his fledgling MAT:

There were eight households in the group. We drew up a timetable and one day we worked for one household and the next day for another.... But it was not easy to make a timetable like that. There were many squabbles. Li Chung-ying was the worst; he always wanted to be first. Because it was often important to be the one who got ploughed first or his seed in first. In the end, we agreed to take it in turn. But he was never properly satisfied.[24]

The larger the MAT, the greater the variety in resources possessed by its different members and the greater the potential benefit from mutual aid. But the larger the MAT, the greater the chance that those with more resources – better tools and farming skills, greater willingness to work hard – would have reason to worry that they were subsidizing some of their less well-endowed or lazier teammates. Government officials had to maintain constant pressure on villagers (in some places with more success than in others) to resist the tendency of "generals to go with generals and soldiers to go with soldiers," that is, for those peasants who were better off to exclude those who were less well off. (Rich peasants, however, were excluded from MATs. The government was using formation of the teams as a way to isolate them.) Expansion in the size and diversity of MATs thus set the stage for chronic conflict within the work groups.

24 Jan Myrdal, *Report from a Chinese village*, 140.

Expansion of the varieties of work carried out by the teams could also occasion chronic conflict. The more different the kinds of tasks the MAT members performed, the greater the difficulty in determining the relative worth of each task – and the greater the potential for arguments about how much each member should be compensated for his or her labor. "Being leader of the labor group for mutual aid," says Myrdal's interviewee,

was a thankless task. Every day there was someone who said: "You are unfair." Sometimes, for example, a person would say: "Turn about, turn about! Can't you see that I have many more weeds in my field than he has? Weeds don't bother to grow in turn. If you don't weed my field today, I shall suffer for it." In the end we chose a small group that had to deal with all such questions.... But, as I said, it wasn't easy.... There was nothing but surliness and squabbling.[25]

Such tensions might have been minimized if the MATs had been expanded slowly and if MAT members could see that they were obviously getting benefits from the expanded production promised by the government. After a few years of fairly cautious experimentation with MATs, however, the government, by the end of 1953, began to speed up its efforts to establish and expand them. And the expansion brought only modest material benefits to the peasantry. The fact was that the establishment of MATs was being used not simply to provide peasants with a way to improve their livelihood but better to control them so as to extract greater surpluses from the countryside for the support of heavy industry in the cities.[26]

The mechanism for the extraction of such surpluses was the system of "unified purchase and supply" mandated in the fall of 1953 to eliminate the independent marketing of grain in the countryside. The prices of grain were now fixed by the state, and quotas were established for the amount of grain each locality had to deliver to the state. It would have been impossible for the government to establish quotas for each individual household. But it was possible to establish them for groups as large as MATs. Thus, it was imperative to get almost all peasants into MATs. And thus, from the point of view of the peasants, teams became mechanisms of social control, enforcing the government's demand for their hard-earned grain at an all too cheap price. They were efficient mechanisms. By the end of 1954 many regions were reporting grain shortages.[27]

When peasants found themselves not only working together in a new form of organization with people they would customarily not have want-

25 Ibid., 141.   26 Shue, *Peasant China in transition*, 185, 195–245.
27 Ezra Vogel, *Canton under communism: programs and politics in a provincial capital*, 1949–1968, 138–42.

ed to associate with, but getting less income for their hard work into the bargain, they naturally became contentious. At this period, however, the focus of their contention was not usually the Communist government. The new government had a great deal of legitimacy, at least among former poor peasants who had at last gained some land that they could call their own. Besides, it was too powerful to be openly challenged. So the pressures generated by tightened economic circumstances often burst forth in quarrels among MAT members. As suggested by the peasant quoted above (who had himself been a MAT leader), the focus of such quarrels was often the team's leadership and the methods it used for determining work points. "People were never satisfied and one was always being accused of being unfair and showing favoritism."[28] Such disputes over both leadership and work points constantly would accompany each new step toward higher levels of collective organization in the countryside.

And the countryside was indeed moving toward higher levels. Whether ordinary peasants realized it or not, mutual aid was only a preparation for complete collectivization.

REMAKING SOCIETY, 1955–1963

Collectivization

The way in which MATs were established throughout the countryside foreshadowed the way in which agriculture was collectivized. First there was heavy propaganda to convince peasants that the new form of agriculture would indeed be in their long-term self-interest. Then there was the establishment on a voluntary basis of some new forms of work organization that were only modestly different from what peasants were used to and were indeed apparently in the best interests of many peasants. Then there followed transformations in the state institutions that controlled rural economic life – transformations that made it economically unsound for peasants to resist joining the new organizations. Concomitantly, there was an expansion of the new organizations in ways that favored the state's ambition to transfer agricultural surpluses to urban industry. There was anger at this on the part of many peasants, but not much direct resistance, because most had found themselves pulled by indirect methods into the new situation before they had a chance fully to realize what was happen-

28 Myrdal, *Report from a Chinese village*, 141.

ing to them. For the few who did resist, there was swift and strong political coercion.[29]

Entrance into the first collective farming arrangements, called "Agricultural Producers' Cooperatives" (APCs), was voluntary. Even so, this
must have been a step taken with considerable trepidation by many of the
pioneer APC members. For the APCs were a radical departure – far more
than the MATs – from ordinary peasant visions of the basis of a good,
secure life. In the old society, the goal of every Chinese peasant was to
own land, as much as possible. As Vivienne Shue has pointed out, "this
was not the only way of getting rich in rural China, but it was probably
the safest and most honorable since, if it succeeded, the farmer's heirs
were granted a valuable inheritance."[30] In the new APCs, the peasants
exchanged the titles to their most important tangible possession, their
land, for a package of hopeful promises. "When three people unite, yellow dirt changes to gold!" peasants in Shansi province's Longbow village
were told.[31] Improved cooperation would lead to increased productivity,
and that would lead to more consumable income, fairly shared by all.

There was some plausibility to the promise that the APCs would
increase productivity. Each peasant had usually owned several scattered
plots of farmland, each plot separated from those of its neighbors by a
little path. If all the land could be pooled, the wasteful crazy quilt of
dividing paths could be plowed away and the consolidated land could be
worked in a more orderly, rational fashion. Nonetheless, the opportunity
for increased productivity was hedged by risks. The advantages of more
rationalized field management could easily be nullified if the members of
the collective failed to cooperate smoothly. In the first APCs, however,
the risks were lessened by the relatively small size of the collective
organizations, which only consisted of about thirty households, usually
from the same hamlet or the same neighborhood within a village – people
tied together by bonds of kinship or long-term familiarity. The obstacles
to achieving a reasonable degree of cooperation in such a group were not
overwhelming.

There were more uncertainties, though, associated with the promise
that APC members would receive a fair share of the increased production
from collective farming. Farmers with more land and better farming abilities had reason to worry that they would be subsidizing the poorer mem-

29 See the detailed, analytic accounts of collectivization in Shue, *Peasant China in transition*, 275–317;
    Yang, *A Chinese village in early communist transition*, 203–37; Vogel, *Canton under communism*, 146–77;
    and the lengthy descriptions in Hinton, *Shenfan*, 81–166.
30 Shue, *Peasant China in transition*, 276.   31 Hinton, *Shenfan*, 137.

bers of the collective. Although the government wished especially to encourage poor peasants to join the APCs, it also wanted middle peasants to participate in them, needed them, in fact, if the APCs were to have adequate supplies of capital and farming skills. It therefore minimized the risk of APC membership to middle peasants by tying remuneration from the APC to the amount of property one originally brought into it. When one joined an APC, one did not contribute one's property outright to the APC but one was considered to have rented one's property to it. Besides receiving a share of the net profits of the APC, dependent on the amount of work (measured in work points) one contributed to it, one also received a regular rent for one's property. Government regulations stipulated that the amount paid in rent had to be less than the amount paid for the APC member's labor. But they were vague about how much less. The proportions of income derived from labor and from land dividends varied widely: from perhaps 60 to 80 percent for labor and from 40 to 20 percent for dividends. The tendency was for the proportion of income derived from dividends to be set relatively high at first, to attract middle peasants, and then to be whittled away. Middle peasants had to wonder – and worry – about how long their property would pay any dividends at all. It would pay dividends only as long as the government said it would, and the main tendency of government policy was to press toward equality, wiping away any advantages inherited from the old society. As this happened, middle peasants often reacted bitterly, often directing their anger against their local officials.[32]

Another worrisome aspect of cooperativization for middle peasants had to do with the fate of their draft animals and farm implements. The key to modest economic security was not simply the amount of land one possessed but also the instruments one had available to farm it. Households that had been classified as middle peasants at the time of land reform had usually possessed a buffalo or a donkey or a mule or a horse, together with a workable plow. Rich peasants often had several such animals and tools. In the redistribution of property, middle peasants and rich peasants got to keep most of these important assets. Landlords lost most of theirs, but their expropriated animals and tools were usually not sufficient to meet the needs of the poor peasant population. Thus, most poor peasants and hired hands had not received draft animals and farm tools to go with their land. Those who did receive them (often those who

32 Shue, *Peasant China in transition*, 299–300, presents figures on the proportions of income that could be derived from rent and from labor; Hinton, *Shenfan*, 126–43, gives ancedotes about the tensions created by the new system.

had played "activist" roles in the land reform), or those who were able to purchase them in the years following land reform, tended to attain the economic status of middle peasants. They came, in fact, to be called "new middle peasants." Those who did not receive such assets remained mired in poverty. An important attraction of cooperativization to those peasants who remained poor was that they would have access to draft animals and farm tools. An important worry for middle peasants (and a fortiori for rich peasants, who, after having been excluded from MATs, were now being pressured into joining the APCs) was that they would lose their animals and tools. Regulations for the new APCs required that such assets be made available to the APC as a whole, but allowed them to be rented from middle and rich peasants. The owners of draft animals and farm tools had reason to worry, however, that when rented out, their property would be ruined. Often they reacted with bitter anger when they saw their oxen or donkeys overloaded and beaten by APC members eager to squeeze every bit of usefulness, as quickly as possible, out of the animals.[33]

After getting certain peasants to join "on a voluntary and mutually beneficial basis" (many of the first joiners were "activists" with local political aspirations) and showcasing the benefits achieved from the most successful APCs, the government steadily increased the pressure to expand membership. Its most effective way of doing this was to take away all incentives for peasants to go it alone. With the elimination of private money lending, government-run credit co-ops became the only source of loans, and they did not lend to private farmers. With the elimination of the free market in commodities, "supply and marketing co-ops" became the only buyers of grain and the only sellers of farm implements; and they gave favorable terms to APCs. Systems of grain quotas were manipulated in such a way as to discriminate against independent producers and give incentives to both poor peasants and rich peasants to join APCs.[34]

Thus, as the government's drive to expand membership in APCs

---

33 "In the case of draught animals ... the owner might continue to own and rear them, charging the co-op the going rate for their use; or else the owner might continue to own them but give the co-op the responsibility for rearing them and the right to use them at will, accepting a final payment; or else the owner might sell them outright to the co-op, accepting payment in installments over several years. Under the first two systems there was much room for recrimination if an ox should die or be injured. Therefore, outright purchases of animals were considered best, once co-ops were well established. The schemes actually adopted by co-ops to compensate peasants for draught animals, tools, and so on were extremely diverse" (Shue, *Peasant China in transition*, 290). See Hinton, *Shenfan*, 144–49, for descriptions of how prices of animals were manipulated to the benefit of the co-ops. See also *Shenfan*, 149–51, for some poignant stories about the anguish of peasants who saw their animals mistreated and overworked after they had been given over to the collective.

34 Shue, *Peasant China in transition*, 284–85, 299–300.

gained momentum in 1954 and 1955, peasants who did not think it in their interests to join them – this group perhaps consisted especially of middle and rich peasants but also included poor peasants who did not like or did not trust those neighbors with whom they would have to work if they joined a collective – were feeling immense pressure from the coercive power of the state. But it was in the main a vast, diffuse pressure, not simply the visible, personalized coercion of some identifiable, officious bureaucrats or some overbearing local officials. It was not the kind of pressure that could be directly railed against or argued with or resisted. As the peasantry was forced into APCs, its resistance was mainly passive, manifested in a lack of initiative and a lack of enthusiasm for hard work.

As production fell off, some worried officials in the central government advocated slowing down the pace of collectivization and decreasing the amount of grain being extracted from the peasantry through the APCs. But as recounted in Chapter 2 of *CHOC*, 14, Mao Tse-tung and his fellow advocates of a speedup in collectivization won the day. Not only was the pace of collectivization to be vastly accelerated but the size of the elementary APCs was to be expanded and their internal organization transformed so that they would no longer be "semisocialist" but, rather, fully socialist in nature.

Consisting on the average of between 200 to 300 families (about 1,000 to 1,500 persons), the new "higher-stage APCs" were up to ten times larger than the lower-stage or elementary APCs. All members participated in them on an equal footing, that is, no one received any rent for land or tools contributed to the collective. The property of rich peasants and middle peasants was in effect confiscated. In the process of doing this, the government raised once again the banner of class struggle.

If it was in the interest of anyone to join the new higher-stage APCs, it was in the interest of the poor peasants. Poor peasants were therefore cast as heroes in the struggle for collectivization and rich peasants as villains. Rich peasants who contested their expropriation (by destroying draft animals, for example) or who even complained publicly about the policies were often punished swiftly with "struggle sessions." From this time on, rich peasants joined landlords, counterrevolutionaries, and "bad elements" (hard-core criminals) to constitute the "four bad types" – a politically stigmatized pariah caste, members of which had virtually no civil rights, were constantly harassed, and had practically no way of erasing their stigma – in fact, they were considered to pass the stigma down to succeeding generations in the male line.

While not being consigned to this pariah caste, middle peasants were increasingly forced out of positions of authority – the policy was to "rely on poor peasants and to unite with middle peasants." But the practicalities of the new emphasis on class struggle necessitated a refinement in the casuistry of assigning class labels. After land reform had been completed, the majority of villagers had in the government's hopeful new class analysis fallen into the category of "middle peasants" because most (but not all) former poor peasant households had acquired enough land to make them the equivalent of middle peasants. In the years immediately following land reform, as we have seen, some of these new middle peasants prospered enough, through acquisition of draft animals and through good fortune in farming and entrepreneurship, to be at least as well off as the old middle peasants had been. Others, however, remained for all practical purposes poor, with about as much land as other middle peasants but without the animals, tools, and other assets to make them economically secure. Starting around 1955, these peasants were classified as "lower-middle peasants" and they were given an official status virtually equivalent to that of poor peasants. By the second half of the 1950s, the "good classes," those who could officially be relied on, were usually denominated, in a single breath, as the "poor and lower-middle peasants."[35] It was from the ranks of such people that activists were recruited to consolidate the higher-stage APCs.

These new APCs exceeded in size most of the natural networks of association that had facilitated cooperation in the countryside. In South China, where villages were as large as one or two thousand people, the APCs now encompassed the whole village. In other regions, where villages were smaller, the APCs encompassed several villages. Although peasants were used to being administered – kept under surveillance and controlled from the top down – through such units, they were not accustomed to cooperating voluntarily with all of the members of such units in common economic endeavors. Group animosities between various lineages or between hamlets or neighborhoods and personal animosities between various families within such a large unit all worked to undermine the basis of cooperation and to destroy the morale essential to increasing agricultural production.

In spite of such problems, the higher level APCs were welcomed by a number of actors on the rural scene. For many local officials – at least those peasants of poor and lower-middle-class background who had occupied leadership positions in the elementary APCs – the drive toward higher-level APCs must have seemed like a good thing. The obligation to pay special dividends according to a vague and frequently shifting for-

---

35 See Richard Baum, *Prelude to revolution*, 180n.

mula to middle and rich peasants had been a burden. It had forced them to deal with constant dissension while hampering their exercise of power. Now they were freed of that burden and had much more control over local economic affairs than ever before. Such local officials formed part of the popular base for what Mao called the "socialist upsurge in the countryside."[36]

Ambitious young men officially classified as poor and lower-middle peasants must have formed another part of that base. For many of them, the times were no doubt exciting. They had a chance now to grab the reins of village leadership. All they had to do was press the collectivization program forward with alacrity, loudly condemning rich peasants and all others who dragged their feet on the glorious road to socialism. But for middle and upper-middle peasants, the times were gloomy. And for those classified as rich peasants, the times were dark – they lost their property and their political rights.

For many middle-aged poor and lower-middle peasants, too, the times must have seemed full of uncertainty. Indirectly, at least, they gained the use of the rich peasants' and middle peasants' property. But they lost much control over their work. Now they would be ordered around, told what to do and how to do it by APC cadres, who often enough were strangers, belonging to other neighborhoods, other hamlets, other lineages, and to another generation – people who owed them nothing and possibly had no sympathy or loyalty toward them. Before the problems worried about by such people had a chance to come to pass, however, they were superseded by even bigger problems. In 1958, the Maoist government embarked on the Great Leap Forward (GLF).

From the point of view of ordinary peasants, the early beginnings of the GLF must have seemed innocent enough. Large numbers of city cadres started to arrive in villages, sent down by the government to help them increase production. Up to a point, many of these city people must have been welcomed. The extra labor power they provided would help more seeds to be planted, more grain to be harvested. The problem with this influx – and the problem with most policy innovations at this time – was that the government always sent too much of a good thing. More city people came down to the villages than could be absorbed.[37]

The sending down of urban cadres coincided with increasingly intense government demands for producing "more, faster, better, and more economically." One way to accomplish this was to build new and better water conservation projects, by mobilizing thousands of peasants to take

---

36 Shue, *Peasant China in transition*, 300.   37 Vogel, *Canton under communism*, 228–29.

part in constructing dikes and ditches during the agricultural slack seasons. The seasonal rhythm of work was being changed. Now there were no more "slack seasons," no more time between the hectic planting and harvesting periods when peasants could relax at home or engage in various private "sideline" enterprises. All seasons were now times for public work, labor for the collective good. When the regular planting seasons arrived, the peasants were told to make some innovations in plowing and planting techniques. If fields could be plowed deeper in rows placed closer together, grain production would expand greatly, peasants were told. In accordance with the policy of "walking on two legs," new rural industries, such as "backyard furnaces" for steel smelting, were to be established using simple technology and much hard work.[38]

Almost all of the new innovations being demanded at this time required massive investments of labor. Where were the laborers to come from? One source was the women of the countryside. In most parts of China, they had traditionally not been called upon to labor in the fields, being confined to domestic chores and handicraft production. Now, with the destruction of the rural free markets, there was little they could do to supplement the family income through cottage industry. But there was still the problem of housework and childcare. In Honan province, local officials set up community mess halls in order to release women from their cooking chores so that they could labor together with men in agriculture and in water conservancy. Arrangements were made for girls and older women to take care of the community's children, its sick, and its aged. Thus were disrupted the rhythms of domestic life.

How was all of this activity to be coordinated? Units the size of the higher-stage APCs were too small for the task. The solution was to consolidate the APCs into even larger organizational units. Honan province tried to do this in mid-1958, calling the new form of organization a "people's commune." Chairman Mao visited one of the first people's communes in Honan in August 1958, proclaimed that the commune was "good," and within a few months, communes had been established everywhere throughout China.

The new organizations were "one, big, and two, public," far surpassing in size any traditional units of social and economic cooperation. The new communes encompassed perhaps ten to twenty villages, with a total pop-

---

38 For some good accounts of the communization movement, see Vogel, *Canton under communism*, 243–52; Schurmann, *Ideology and organization*, 474–82; Chan, Madsen, and Unger, *Chen Village*, 24–26; Hinton, *Shenfan*, 169–247.

ulation on the average of about 25,000 people, generally the equivalent of several local marketing districts.[39] This massive unit publicly owned all of the means of production in its area – fields, farm animals, factories, and so forth. And it often appropriated for public use items that peasant common sense would have considered inalienably private – personal jewelry, cooking utensils, even the metal doorframes from their houses. All such goods were to be melted down to produce steel in the backyard furnaces or sold to finance new public economic endeavors. The unprecedented scale of formal organization represented by the people's communes posed mind-boggling management problems.[40] The commune headquarters was supposed to make decisions about how communewide projects, such as water conservancy or steel smelting, were to be carried out, and about what, where, and how various crops were to be grown. Then the headquarters would assign squads, teams, and brigades (the terminology was military, as was indeed the entire spirit of heroic endeavor that was supposed to dominate the commune) of workers chosen from the various villages throughout the commune to do the work. How would a few cadres at headquarters, working under immense time pressure, be able to determine which workers should be deployed for which tasks? Since it was impossible to make judgments about such matters with any degree of precision, much labor was wasted. How could the cadres at headquarters keep track of how much each worker was to be compensated for his or her work? They could not, so all workers received the same thing. In the fall of 1958, during the first rush of enthusiasm for the communes, there blew what villagers still call a "communist wind," an elusive idea with explosive practical consequences, that the communes were truly a communist rather than a mere socialist form of organization. Thus, the slogan governing remuneration was not "to each according to his work" but "to each according to his needs."

Not a few peasants appeared to welcome the communist wind at first. Indeed, it seemed in some places as if a millenarian spirit had arisen, an epidemic of enthusiasm that was similar perhaps to that which periodically arose throughout Chinese history when militant prophets called masses of peasants to rebellion with extravagant promises of an imminent new world order. Abundant food had often been a central dream in such visions, and during the GLF many peasants happily plunged themselves

39 There were, however, wide variations in the size of communes. See Byung-joon Ahn, "The political economy of the People's Commune in China: changes and continuities," *JAS*, 34.3 (May 1975).
40 Especially good analyses of these are found in Vogel, *Canton under communism*, 233–70; and Schurmann, *Ideology and organization*, 464–90.

into their work while being intoxicated by the dream of unlimited food. Since everyone could eat as much as he or she wanted from the community mess halls, without having to pay for it, it seemed as if the utopian dreams had come true. A peasant from Kwangtung still remembers fondly the seeming abundance of free food: "We ate wherever we happened to be; ah, in the beginning we were all so fat! We could eat anytime we liked at the canteens."[41] The early period of the commune movement was called by some peasants the "Eat It Up" period because one could eat at the mess halls as often as five or six times daily.[42]

But the dream of unlimited consumption soon turned into a nightmare. Higher-level officials passed down commands to try impractical new farming methods. Local leaders who said the methods would not work were accused of being "rightists." Faced with unreasonable demands, they reacted with untruthful replies, telling superiors whatever they wanted to hear about the glorious increases in production that were accompanying the new initiatives. As a consequence of some of the innovations, like extremely close planting, whole fields of grain were lost. Work was poorly allocated, so that laborers would be moved from one place or to another before a crucial job could be completed. Peasants would consume all of their local mess hall's grain, expecting other villages to pick up the burden of saving for seed grain. The whole process of communization had been, as some peasants put it, "too early, too fast, and too rude."[43] The social chaos produced by this "communist wind" combined with very bad weather conditions in 1959 to create economic disaster.

The famine that ensued was one of the greatest human tragedies of the twentieth century. According to recent demographic analyses, around 20 million people died directly or indirectly from starvation between 1959 to 1962. Death rates peaked in 1960, but in some rural areas starvation persisted into 1962. The statistics show that the rural population suffered more from the famine than did the urban.[44]

Yet, amazingly, there are very few written records to convey the personal, human dimensions of the tragedy expressed in these numbers. If

41 Chan, Madsen, and Unger, *Chen Village*, 25.
42 Ibid., 25.   43 Quoted in Ahn, "Political economy," 634.
44 For summaries of the statistical estimates about numbers of excess deaths during the famine, see Nicholas Lardy, "The Chinese economy under stress, 1958–1965," *CHOC*, 14, Ch. 8.370; and Penny Kane, *Famine in China, 1959–61: demographic and social implications*, 89–90. According to Lardy, the death toll was between 16 million and 27 million. Kane's estimates range from 14 million to 26 million. For the three paragraphs that follow, I am especially indebted to Kane's summary of sources of information on the famine.

a catastrophe of this magnitude happened almost anywhere else in the world, there would be volumes of eyewitness reports by journalists and social scientists vividly describing the scene. But Chinese writers were not allowed to report on the famine during this time, and foreign reporters were generally kept out of the country. (The few foreign reporters who did come at that time were "old friends" of China's, like Edgar Snow and Han Suyin, who believed the assurances of their hosts that although there were some difficulties, there was nothing terribly wrong, or who consciously covered up information about the famine.)[45] Peasants interviewed in the 1970s and 1989s have been reluctant to talk about their experiences of that time. When they do talk, their reports are spare in detail.

From the sketchy recollections of eyewitnesses that can be pieced together in the 1980s, there emerges the following portrait of typical grassroots responses to the famine. When grain ran out, peasants scavenged through the countryside for edible herbs, tree bark, and wild animals.[46] In some places especially hard hit, they left their homes and wandered in search of food – a measure that could work, of course, only if there were places with food surpluses sufficiently close and if those desperate for food could pay for it.[47] Production teams and brigades – those units of commune organization whose boundaries coincided closest with the natural villages where peasants lived – shared whatever surplus grain they had among their needy families. In some cases, brigades and teams that had managed not to follow orders during the GLF – those that had somehow resisted the most radical orders about collectivization or had hoarded grain they were supposed to share with the commune – were better able to take care of their own than were more compliant brigades and teams. Brigades and teams that did have surplus food were sometimes not scrupulous about charging outsiders exorbitant prices for it.[48]

Most who died because of the famine were infants or old people. Adult males usually got first priority on scarce food supplies, on the grounds

---

45 In her 1980 memoir, Han Suyin, the cosmopolitan author born of Chinese and Belgian parents, recalled how she hid the truth about the famine out of loyalty to her motherland. "Fiercely, wholeheartedly, I was defending China, even lying through my teeth (with a smile) to the diplomats and the newsmen who probed. Because only China was the heartbeat of my heart, the rise and fall of my blood, the substance of every cell of my body. I had not chosen this. It had chosen me. And all the more so when the wind howled like a wolf and winter fastened its iron will upon the land, and the whole world seemed to rise with glee to threaten China. Then, above all, I was China." Han Suyin, *My house has two doors*, 296.

46 See for example, Steven W. Mosher, *Broken earth: the rural Chinese*, 50.

47 Kane, *Famine in China*, 118.   48 There is an example of this in Hinton, *Shenfan*, 251–52.

that it was essential that they have enough energy to plant new crops.[49] In at least one place, many of the wives had to leave the village to go begging – and never returned to their husbands.[50] To conserve energy, children were kept out of school.[51] As one peasant quoted in Ch'en Village laconically summed up his memories of those times: "Some people became ill, and some of the elderly died. Our village became quiet, as if the people were dead."[52]

The deathly silence of that time perhaps bespoke a mood of exhausted resignation. Communist propaganda had claimed to provide a vision opposed to the fatalism of traditional peasant society. The Communist Party, it said, would forthrightly banish this aspect of peasant superstition by making peasants masters of their fate. At first it had seemed that the Party might actually be accomplishing this. The promise of land reform had been not only for land but also for control. Poor peasants would no longer have to submit to the will of landlords and moneylenders. Immediately after land reform started, it may well, in fact, have seemed to poor peasants that they had finally gotten power over their lives. Organized into Poor Peasants' Associations, they had struck down the landlords and redistributed their land. Later, the peasants had joined mutual aid teams on the basis of "voluntarism and mutual benefit." But the collectivization movement showed them how much they had lost control. As the movement progressed, the state's coercive power gradually tightened around peasant life. By the late 1950s, the Poor Peasants' Associations had ceased to function as mass organizations.[53] If they existed at all, it was merely as conduits for government propaganda and agencies for implementing policies established at higher levels. And that propaganda came to appear more and more absurd and those policies more and more capricious.

The Communist government's officials were capable of exerting even more painful control over the peasantry than the landlords had been. With the establishment of the communes, peasants saw cadres located in a distant headquarters issue ridiculous orders (under overwhelming pressure from higher levels of government) that would lead to terribly destructive consequences, without any consultation with the "masses."

---

49 Kane, *Famine in China*, 116–18.
50 The example is from Fei Xiaotung's interviews around 1980 with men of K'ai-hsien-kung about why they had been divorced. Fei Hsiao-t'ung, *Chinese village close up*, 251.
51 William Lavely provides demographic evidence to show that the education of most children in Nan-ch'uan, in Szechwan province, was halted during the three years of famine. W. R. Lavely, "The rural Chinese fertility transition: a report from Shifang Xian, Sichuan," *Population Studies*, 38 (1984), 370–71.
52 Chan, Madsen, and Unger, *Chen Village*, 25.   53 Vogel, *Canton under communism*, 315.

These same officials, moreover, had taken away peasants' belongings and forced them to eat in mess halls.

During the commune movement, peasants often expressed their feelings of powerlessness by complaining about the mess halls. They commonly complained about the quality of food, and expressed suspicions that the cooks and local officials kept extra portions of food for themselves. They protested about having to go to mess halls at set times and to eat food that did not necessarily suit their tastes. Cooking and eating had always in the past been carried out in the family unit. Indeed, one definition of an integral household had been a family unit that shared a kitchen. To have the preparation of food alienated from one's family, to be forced to eat somebody else's cooking at times and under circumstances set by somebody else, was perhaps the essence of powerlessness in peasant mentality.

As the failure of the GLF became more and more apparent, and as famine began to sweep through the countryside, a major theme in peasants' grumblings was a hatred of "commandism." Stories of local officials being afraid of going out alone after dark for fear of attack became part of the lore of the times.[54] Yet peasants' complaints about their fate rarely turned into active resistance to the system of authority responsible for their situation. In villages become "very quiet," the resistance was passive, manifesting itself in a profound lethargy and in a preoccupation with personal survival rather than public welfare. Part of this was doubtless the result of physical weakness caused by hunger. But part was the result of spiritual hopelessness derived from political impotence. Government policies had taught them once again to be fatalistic.

The GLF had been based on an extraordinarily optimistic view of human nature – the belief that China's people, when presented with the proper opportunities and indoctrinated with the proper political ideology, would be willing to work extraordinarily hard for the public good. Gross mismanagement of the GLF had undermined whatever basis there had been for that hope. Even as the grain supply began to improve by 1962, few farmers were willing to work hard, especially if hard work would bring their families no better rewards than lazier neighbors received. Few peasants were willing to put public concerns over private. Peasants working in public fields surreptitiously kept for themselves the produce they had collected.[55]

54 Ibid., 255.
55 Problems arising from low peasant morale are described with candor in a set of documents from Lien-chiang county in Fukien province captured by Kuomintang intelligence agents and published on Taiwan. See C. S. Chen, ed., *Rural people's communes in Lien-chiang*.

Retrenchment

To alleviate the economic disaster attendant on the GLF, the government needed, among other things, to raise peasant morale. Thus, as famine was widespread in the country, the government was announcing plans for a new rural political and economic order that would in effect give back to individual peasant households much of the control over their lives that had been lost in the radical phases of the collectivization movement. This new order was laid out in the revised draft "Work Regulations for Rural People's Communes" issued in September 1962 (popularly known as the "Sixty Articles").

The end product of a series of agricultural reforms that had begun as early as 1960, the new regulations retained the commune system in name while fundamentally transforming it in practice. Communes were, first of all, reduced in size, on the average to about a third of their original area and population, now often approximating traditional marketing areas in size. Even more important, commune headquarters no longer had the authority to manage day-to-day farming. They were responsible rather for overall coordination of agricultural plans formulated at lower levels and for managing certain economic enterprises and social services – such as middle schools, hospitals, small factories and repair shops – that could not be run efficiently at the village level. Below the commune level of administration were "production brigades," units of perhaps two hundred families encompassing one large village or several smaller ones, which corresponded to the old higher-stage APCs. These production brigades were responsible for directing basic-level militia units, assuring local public security, carrying out grassroots propaganda, running local primary schools, constructing modest-sized irrigation systems, and coordinating some of the economic planning of local farmers. But the control of this unit over the daily economic lives of ordinary peasants was limited. Responsibility for the daily management of farm work and the distribution of collectively produced wealth was decentralized to the level of the production team, a group of about twenty families (100 people), usually neighbors and often kinfolk, which corresponded in size and mode of organization to the old lower-stage APCs.[56]

The production teams were the primary units for the collective owner-

---

56 For thorough accounts of how communes, brigades, and production teams were organized and managed, see Ahn, "Political economy"; John C. Pelzel, "Economic management of a production brigade in post-Leap China," in W. E. Willmott, ed., *Economic organization in Chinese society*; and A. Doak Barnett, with a contribution from Ezra Vogel, *Cadres, bureaucracy, and political power in Communist China*, 313–424.

ship of farmland, draft animals, and large farm tools. No longer did peasants have to follow the orders of distant strangers about what crops to grow and where and how to grow them. Through its leaders (elected from slates prepared under the careful supervision of the local CCP organization),[57] each team would decide, within the framework of government regulations, how to utilize its farmland and how to deploy its laborers. No longer would industrious peasants have to share the wealth that their work had produced with strangers from outside of the zone of familiarity that constituted a production team. The net profit from each team's collective production would be divided up among its members, so that well-endowed and well-managed teams could distribute more to their members than their less fortunate neighbors. And no longer would highly skilled, hardworking individuals have to see less skilled and less energetic neighbors get just as large a share of the production team's profits as the good workers did. Each production team's profits were now divided up by means of a work-point system that rewarded team members according to how much work they had done.

The government promised that the Sixty Articles would provide the framework for agricultural organization for the next thirty years. They did, in fact, provide such a framework for the next decade and a half. It was a flexible framework. By manipulating the regulations specifying precisely how work was to be managed and labor remunerated by the production team leadership within the new framework, government officials could allow Chinese agriculture to look more like private or more like semisocialist collective farming.

To stimulate productivity in the early 1960s, the government instituted rules in such a way as to make peasants feel almost as if they were back in the presocialist era of private farming.[58] Production teams assigned responsibility for most farming tasks to small groups, in many places consisting of only two or three neighboring households. These groups were free to organize their work in any way they wanted, as long as they delivered a specified quota of grain for sale to the state each year. Working for the collective meant in practice carrying out a rudimentary form of mutual aid. In some places, production teams decentralized farming re-

---

57 See the description of an election in Chan, Madsen, and Unger, *Chen Village*, 66–71. Interviews with a variety of people from China suggest, however, that actual election procedures differed from place to place.

58 The Kwangtung province production brigade described by Pelzel in "Economic management of a production brigade in post-Leap China" is one in which responsibility for most production tasks was decentralized down to "a consortium that usually consisted of two friendly and cooperative households. Ideally, one of the two households would have a deficiency and the other a surplus of labor."

sponsibility all the way to the level of the individual household. In such instances, production teams assigned each of their member households a portion of land, and each household then negotiated a contract with its production team specifying that it would deliver a certain quota of grain each year for sale at the low price set by the state. The household could organize its work any way it wanted, keeping in mind only its responsibility to meet its agreed-upon quota. Anything it produced over this quota was its to keep, or to sell at a free market price.

Even this was not quite a return to free enterprise, however, because there was no free market for the basic commodities that peasants had to produce. In accordance with government orders that they "take grain as the basis," peasants were not free to grow whatever they chose, but were forced to plant most of their fields to grain. And they could not sell this grain on an open market, but had to deliver fixed quotas of it to the state at an artificially set low price.

But at least there was no longer a need to argue with unsympathetic, unrelated production team members about how many work points one was worth; and no longer a need to be told what to do every day by a production team leader. Control over work was in the hands of small, relatively private groups rather than large public organizations. This alone seemed to have had a salutary effect on peasant initiative and morale.

The sphere of the private was further expanded by the revival of limited free markets. Rural markets, which had been eliminated in the "socialist upsurge" of 1956, were now revived. The new regulations allowed each household to have a private plot of land (the exact size depended on the number of people in the household, but the total area allotted to these plots was limited to no more than 5 to 7 percent of a community's land) to grow vegetables on for consumption at home or sale at the newly revived markets. Peasants could also spend a limited amount of time on "sideline production" – handicraft manufacture, or beekeeping, or poultry raising, for example – which could also be sold on the market. A skilled, energetic, well-organized household could produce as much as 30 percent of its income from such private enterprise.

Even as these measures raised peasant morale, however, they also fostered inequalities and discouraged concern for the public welfare. Although all households in a given production team had access to approximately the same amount of material resources, households differed in their ability to farm. Thus, under the new decentralized production system, some households could meet their assigned quotas and have quite a bit left over for their own use, whereas other households – victims of sickness or poor planning or plain laziness – might have little to live on after meeting their quotas. Such successes and failures tended to perpetuate themselves, so that production teams – traditional neighborhoods or hamlets – once again began to be divided into rich and poor. The concern for tending to one's private plots, caring for one's own pigs, pursuing and marketing one's own sidelines, all pulled peasants' attention away from caring for the overall common good of the collective.[59]

That, at least, is the way the Maoists in the central government's leadership saw it. Concerned over the revival of such "spontaneous capitalist tendencies" in the countryside, the central government began by 1964 to move its system for managing and remunerating work in a more socialist direction. It moved more of the responsibility for managing production into the hands of team leaders. It took away the land assigned to individual households or to small groups of households and merged it into collectively tilled fields. Work points then had to play a bigger role in remuneration; and systems for calculating work points now became an increasingly important way either to stimulate individual peasant initiative, at the price of increasing inequalities within production teams, or to further the equality and solidarity of the collective.

Even these movements toward socialism, however, could never, under the framework of the Sixty Articles, lead to radical egalitarianism and highly rationalized labor management. The basic units of collective ownership, the production teams, were kept to a size that allowed them to correspond to the traditional social ecology of rural life, to localized kinship networks and to clusters of neighbors. Thus, there continued to be considerable inequality within the countryside, not necessarily so much within production teams as among them. A team in a productive agricultural area that was well endowed with strong, healthy workers and with good leadership could be much better off even than teams in nearby areas. One index of its well-being was the value of its work points. Because each work point entitled one to a share in the net profit of a production team, a team that was very profitable would pay more per work point than one that was not. In the most productive of the five side-by-side production teams that made up "Ch'en Village Production Brigade" in Kwangtung province, for example, ten work points (in 1971) were worth 1.10 yuan, whereas in the least productive teams (teams handicapped by poor leadership and weak labor power) they were worth only about .70. Ch'en Village, in turn, was much poorer than the neighboring villages in its people's commune. Yet the average standard of living in its commune

59 See Chan, Madsen, and Unger, *Chen Village*, 50–54, for a description of inequalities prevailing in one village during this period. Chen, *Rural people's communes in Lien-chiang* presents the views of county-level officials about this phenomenon.

was considerably higher than that of communes in impoverished provinces in other parts of China.[60]

Although production brigades, the next level of administration up
from a production team, could invest small amounts of the resources and
mobilize some of the labor power of their constituent production teams
for schools, small-scale industries, pumping stations, and the like, the
progress toward getting peasants to associate in work projects at the brigade level with people outside their production teams was slow. Progress
toward mobilizing peasants to work on common projects at the commune level was even slower in the 1960s and 1970s. Only rarely were
ordinary peasants called to work at the commune level. The division of
labor for most rural work was bounded by the confines of the small production team.

Indeed, during the 1960s and 1970s, the period when the Sixty Articles
were in effect, social life in the countryside became more cellular than it
had been for generations. During most periods of Chinese history, villages were open to the outside social world, integrated, albeit loosely, by
myriad ties into local marketing networks. As indicated earlier, they married their daughters into other villages and acquired wives from them.
They traded with other villagers at periodic markets located in nearby
towns. Sometimes they left their home villages to migrate to the cities or
to other regions where there might be better farmland. But now many of
these avenues of interchange were closed off.

By 1958, government regulations were in place restricting movement
out of one's production team without special permission. This did not
immediately freeze the rural population in place, because millions of
peasants (mostly single males hired as contract labor) were brought to the
cities to work on the grandiose construction projects being launched in
the GLF. But as the economy collapsed in the wake of the GLF, the government sent these laborers back to their rural communities – together
with other urbanites for whom there was no work in the cities. In 1961
and 1962, a total of 20 million people were sent from the cities to the
countryside. Most of these presumably did not want to go, and most rural
communities, just recovering from the worst year of the famine and still
suffering agonizing food shortages, presumably did not want to take
them in. The government's main response was to tighten the instru-

---

60 Chan, Madsen, and Unger, *Chen Village*, 247n. Compare this with the report of Liang Heng that
around 1968 ten work points in a poor region of Hunan provinice were worth only 14 cents.
Liang Heng and Judith Shapiro, *Son of the revolution*, 172–73. For a comprehensive account of
factors affecting work point values, see: William L. Parish and Martin King Whyte, *Village and
family life in contemporary China*, 47–72.

ments of coercion – to enforce strictly the regulations forbidding people
to move where they wanted. Thereafter, throughout the 1960s and 1970s,
almost all population movement was from the cities to the countryside. It
was virtually impossible for peasants to leave their villages for cities, and
increasingly difficult for peasants to move freely within the countryside.

Local free markets – important social institutions for bringing villagers
into contact with members of other communities in their regions – were
at first permitted in the early 1960s, but by the mid-1960s, in the name of
making progress toward socialism, they were largely suppressed. Wives
were still usually brought in from outside villages, but even this intimate
pattern of social exchange was in some places diminished as the government denounced as feudal superstition traditional taboos against marrying people from one's own village. Since the founding of the People's
Republic of China, the government had made major efforts to to saturate
Chinese society with progaganda in order to give its citizens a consciousness of belonging to a national society, but an unintended consequence of its rural policy in the 1960s and 1970s was to offset the effects of
its propaganda by encouraging local communities to turn in upon themselves.[61]

Another consequence of the government's efforts in the mid-1960s to
make at least the internal organization of rural production teams more
socialist was the eruption of local squabbles that sapped peasant morale
and undermined productivity. Often enough, these disputes centered
around the issue of work points.

There was a complicated variety of work-point systems, developed
during the mutual aid and collectivization movements of the 1950s.[62] The
systems mainly divided into two types, time-rate and task-rate systems. In

61 Parish and Whyte, ibid., 302–8.
62 Ibid., 59–71. Another issue concerning the distribution of a production teams's income was the
distribution of grain rations. As Parish and Whyte discuss it: "The distribution of grain is
technically separate from the assignment of work points. Work-point assignments affect a household's credits. Grain distribution affects a household's debits.... There are three ways in which
grain is commonly distributed. First, grain may be distributed on a per capita basis, with set
amounts being given according to the age and sex of each individual. Because these amounts
remain constant regardless of work performed during the year, grain distributed in this manner is
called 'basic grain.' This system provides a cushion of security. Second, grain may be distributed
according to the amount of work performed by household members during the year, or, more
precisely according to the work points they earn. When grain is distributed on this basis (called
work-point grain), one must work to eat. Third, a small amount (typically 10 percent) may be
given to induce people to turn over manure from their family pig to the team. This is manure or
fertilizer grain," (pp. 65–66). The greater the percentage of grain that is distributed as "basic
grain," the greater the degree of egalitarianism in consumption within a team – and the lesser the
incentive for strong workers to work hard, if the only motivation for such work is economic
self-interest. As the pressures to make villages more "socialist" increased in the late 1960s, the
proportions of basic grain to work-point grain increased.

time-rate systems, the members of each production team, through collective discussions, assigned a rating to each able-bodied worker once or
twice a year. Generally, healthy men between about 25 and 45 received
the highest ratings, usually set between nine and ten points for a day's
labor; women would get seven or eight points; and children, perhaps six.
To calculate the number of work points a team member had earned, one
would simply multiply his or her work-point rating by the number of
days worked. In task-rate systems, various jobs would be assigned a set
number of points, say fifty points for plowing a particular field. A farmer
would be given that many points upon finishing the job. Task rates encouraged individual effort and benefited strong and ambitious workers.
The faster one finished one's individual tasks, the more work points one
could earn relative to other team members. But by the same token, task
rates often discouraged cooperation among team members. They encouraged a one-sided attention to the quantity of work one did to the
detriment of concern for quality, and they fostered a narrow focus on
one's own individual task, while neglecting how that task should be coordinated with the work of other people. Thus, for example, women
transplanting rice shoots under a task-rate system (transplanting was considered women's work) were sometimes in such a rush to plant as many
rows as possible that they planted shoots in too shallow a fashion, causing
the roots to come loose when the paddies were flooded.

Time rates, on the other hand, encouraged attention to the overall
quality of a collective effort, since one's work-point rating depended
partly on one's overall capacity for teamwork. Time rates also to some
extent benefited the weak at the expense of the strong, because the
differentials between a first- and a second-rate male laborer, for instance,
were often relatively small, perhaps the difference between nine and ten
work points a day (which, in turn, might be worth the equivalent of 5 or
10 cents in Chinese money per day). Time rates, then, were more "socialist" than task rates, and – although most production teams used a mixture of both task rates and time rates – the balance tended to shift toward
time rates when the government wanted to increase the level of socialist
organization in the countryside.

More socialist yet was a work-point system called the "Ta-chai work-
point system," after a model production brigade in Shansi province.
From the early 1960s to the late 1970s, the government incessantly ex-
horted peasants, "In agriculture, learn from Ta-chai!" Although the truth
of the matter is obscure, Ta-chai was supposed to have been distinguished
for its self-reliance, its collective solidarity, its equality, and (the putative
cause of all of this) its high level of political awareness. Ta-chai had

evolved a work-point system that, like the time-rate system, gave each worker a rating, the range of which among men and among women workers was rather narrow. But the Ta-chai ratings were supposed to be based not only on laboring ability but also on political attitudes, and were to be set at meetings of one's peers after one had finished a period of work rather than before, as the time rates had usually been. The Ta-chai system thus involved a production team's members in extremely close scrutiny of one another, and demanded that they evaluate one another on the basis of some very intangible criteria. The Ta-chai system was promoted widely during periods of radical agricultural policy in the late 1960s. But in most places where it was introduced, the result was squabbling and acrimony. Peasants often used – or suspected one another of using – personal animosities to recommend low work-point ratings to their peers under the pretext of "political" criteria. Sometimes, work-point appraisal meetings lasted all through the night, and even then produced inconclusive results. Requiring a higher level of "socialist consciousness" than most communities could muster, the Ta-chai system usually had to be abandoned, at least in its pure form, soon after government policies forced it onto production teams.[63]

From the vantage point of the 1990s, the lesson of such failures seems clear, even though it apparently did not seem clear to the Maoists in the CCP leadership in the 1960s. The more peasant households were free to decide for themselves how to deploy their labor, the less they had to cooperate on production with numerous others; and the more they were allowed to reap the benefits of their own initiative, the more productive they would become. Although the Maoists recognized that this had in fact been the case during the early 1960s, they argued that peasant communities could become more egalitarian and more united, while continuing to be more productive, if the beliefs of the peasantry could change. This was to be the rationale for a massive new campaign in the mid-1960s to create a "new socialist person" by instilling in the hearts of peasants the values of a socialist society.

CREATING A "NEW SOCIALIST PERSON," 1963–1976

Struggles over leadership

This effort came in the form of a movement to upgrade the moral quality of local rural leadership. The movement was called the "Socialist Edu-

63 See Chan, Madsen, and Unger, *Chen Village*, 91–93; and Parish and Whyte, *Village and family life in contemporary China*, 63–71.

cation Campaign" and it was launched by Mao Tes-tung's plea at the CCP's Tenth Plenum of the Central Committee in September 1962 that the Party must never forget class struggle. The Chairman was worried that, if unchecked, the patterns of dominance characteristic of the old ruling classes could reassert themselves in the countryside, through the behavior of the regime's own, its local government and Party officials.[64]

From the beginnings of the Communist movement, the CCP had laid enormous stress on training and disciplining local leadership. Although major campaigns such as land reform were launched in villages by work teams of outside cadres, one of the first jobs of a work team was always to look for local activists who would become "backbone elements" for the coming campaign.[65] Those activists who proved themselves loyal and effective in the ensuing struggles would be recruited into the CCP. Each major campaign – land reform, mutual aid, collectivization, the Great Leap Forward – brought with it a substantial increase in new Party members. The CCP has always, however, been a highly exclusive group, and the increases never represented large percentages of the population. After land reform, less than 1 percent of the rural population belonged to the Party. By 1960, the proportion had risen to about 2 percent; and it was somewhat more than 3 percent in the 1980s.[66] To control the political and economic affairs of local communities, grassroots Party cadres must rely on the help of many local officials who are not Party members. And to be effective, local Party cadres depend on the general respect and loyalty of the people in their own community.

There were differences in the social composition of CCP members and other local leaders recruited during different stages of the history of the People's Republic. During land reform, work teams looked for tough, bold young men (and perhaps a few women) of poor peasant background to be spearheads in the struggles against the old elites. It was such people who were recruited into the CCP and became the guiding force behind local peasants' associations. But if they wanted institutions like the peasants' associations to command the respect of the rural population, the CCP had also to at least co-opt if not formally recruit older, more re-

64 See Baum, *Prelude to revolution*, 11–59; Madsen, *Morality and power in a Chinese village*, 67–101; and Chan, Madsen, and Unger, *Chen Village*, 37–73.
65 For a concise analysis of the relationship between "activists" and party leadership, see Richard H. Solomon, "On activism and activists: Maoist conceptions of motivation and political role linking state to society," *CQ*, 39 (July–September 1969), 76–114.
66 See Vogel, *Canton under communism*, 371–72, for statistics on CCP membership in rural areas up to 1960. I have not been able to find precise figures for rural Party membership after that. Reports to the Twelfth National Party Congress in 1982 stated that overall Party membership stood at 39 million, out of a total population of slightly more than 1 billion.

spected figures, more experienced in the art of making compromises and in cementing "good feeling" relations with exchanges of small favors. Such leaders would often come from middle-peasant social backgrounds. Usually relatively skilled in farming, such middle-peasant leaders were often especially important in guiding production.[67]

As the goals of the CCP changed, as the policy of "getting rich and building up a household" gave way to policies stressing mutual aid and then collectivization, the mix of local leaders set in place in the wake of earlier campaigns might become an obstacle to realizing the new policies. Thus, since the movement to establish APCs was threatening to many middle peasants, cadres from this background could not be relied on to carry out CCP policy. Nor, for that matter, could many cadres who had come from poor peasant backgrounds, because they had used their positions during land reform to prosper and thus to become "new middle peasants." So the CCP had to ease them aside if it were to carry out its programs.

It did this often by launching "rectification campaigns," in which the cadres were placed under investigation, cases of cadre misconduct were ferreted out, and the cadres were forced to undergo criticism and self-criticism, sometimes in the form of harrowing mass denunciation sessions. If suitably chastened, the cadres would be generally more willing to follow the proper CCP line, at least for the time being. At the same time, ambitious young local activists who had taken the lead in exposing the alleged misconduct were recruited as new members of the Party.[68]

There were major rectifications of rural cadres during land reform, especially to punish young local cadres who, failing to exercise proper moral discipline in their work, had appropriated some of the fruits of struggle for themselves or had taken bribes for protecting well-off peasants. In 1955, on the eve of the big push toward collectivization, a campaign against "hidden counterrevolutionaries" branded as counterrevolutionaries, among many others, some rural cadres who had assisted peasants in leaving APCs. As collectivization got under way, rural cadres were pushed to engage in criticism and self-criticism for being too sympathetic to middle peasants. As the GLF got going, cadres were criticized for being too cautious, too wedded to traditional ways. After the GLF, they were castigated for being too authoritarian, for pushing community mess halls too far, and for collectivizing too much private property –

67 Shue, *Peasant China in transition*, 95–96.
68 For vivid descriptions of such campaigns, see Hinton, *Fanshen*, 319–400. For a chronicle of the various campaigns affecting rural cadres in Kwangtung province during the 1950s, see Vogel, *Canton under communism*, esp. 109, 133, and 153.

errors for which their higher-level superiors were generally more responsible than they.

Besides being vulnerable to formal criticism launched from above, local cadres were constantly subject to informal complaints from below. "People treated you," said one local cadre to William Hinton, "like the father-in-law who carries his daughter-in-law across the creek. He puts forth a great deal of effort but gets nothing but curses in return. Why? Because he is suspected of wanting to take the daughter-in-law in his arms, of wanting to embrace her. The daughter-in-law considers the old man to be fresh, and the son thinks his pop is taking liberties with his bride!"[69]

Why would anyone want to be a cadre if the job entailed such insecurity and such vulnerability to criticism? Officially, the proper motivation was supposed to be a desire to serve the people, and at least some local cadres seemed, during the early parts of their careers anyway, to be idealistically committed to furthering the welfare of their communities. But for an ambitious poor peasant, at any rate, becoming a cadre was one of the only avenues toward increased power and prestige open in the society, and under such circumstances the potential gains may have outweighed the perceived risks.

In any case, the problem of local cadre quality became a key issue for the CCP after 1962. What was at stake, according to the "Former Ten Points," the key document launching the Socialist Education Campaign in May 1963, was nothing less than the question of "who will win in the struggle between socialism and capitalism ... between Marxism-Leninism and revisionism?"[70] Inflated though it was, the rhetoric was not totally inaccurate. Good local leadership was crucial to the success of collective agriculture. Collective labor was supposed to be better than private labor because it was more productive and thus more beneficial to those participating in it. But if one's local cadres were dishonestly siphoning off some of the collective's goods for their own use, or if they were unfairly favoring kinfolk or special friends with desirable work assignments and good work-point ratings, then peasant morale would fall and with it would decline the productivity of collective agriculture.

Thus, as the first phase in the Socialist Education Campaign, the CCP

---

69 Hinton, *Shenfan*, 157.
70 Quoted in Baum, *Prelude to revolution*, 24. For translations of this and other documents related to the Socialist Education Campaign, see Richard Baum and Frederick C. Teiwes, *Ssu-ch'ing: the Socialist Education Movement of 1962–1966*. For a comprehensive study of the characteristics of local leadership during this period, see Michel Oksenberg, "Local leaders in rural China, 1962–65: individual attributes, bureaucratic positions, and political recruitment," in A. Doak Barnett, ed., *Chinese Communist politics in action*, 155–215.

launched a "Four Cleanups Campaign" to cleanse rural cadres of economic, political, ideological, and managerial errors. The main problem to be cleaned up, though, was economic. Cadres were accused of embezzling collective funds and misusing public property. They were mainly accused of taking bribes, and of eating expensive meals and going on expensive trips at the collective's expense. They had fallen into these errors, it was said, because despite their coming from poor peasant origins, their consciousness was infected with ideology of the old capitalist and landlord classes.[71]

To many villagers, the Four Cleanups Campaign looked like the land reform campaign. Fanning out from keypoint communities, work teams of outside cadres came into villages; spent several months living in the village and "sinking roots"; sought out disgruntled poor peasants and recruited activists from their ranks; prepared accusations against the leading cadres in the local production teams and brigades, and, finally, mobilized the local peasants to attack those cadres who had been found guilty in angry "struggle sessions" and "denunciation sessions."[72]

If regulations against corruption were to be construed strictly, most local cadres had indeed been guilty of some wrongdoing. Local cadres got a share of their collective's profit like everybody else, and they got little more in the way of work points than any other good worker. They – and many of their fellow villagers – often felt it was acceptable to compensate themselves informally for their troubles, perhaps by enjoying some especially good meals in connection with their official meetings, perhaps by receiving some "gifts" from villagers petitioning for special favors. They also felt impelled often to give special consideration to their relatives and friends. Many villagers would not have condemned this behavior as long as it was not carried to extremes. But now outside work teams were calling in the strongest possible terms for sanctions against such irregular conduct. Cadres accused of such wrongdoing (work teams usually had a quota of local cadres to attack and forced confessions out of them in round-the-clock interrogation sessions) were stripped of their jobs and forced to pay back to the masses what they supposedly had improperly taken. As land reform had destroyed the old village elites, so did the Four Cleanups appear, upon its completion, to have destroyed the new local elites.

One disturbing aspect of the Four Cleanups Campaign was its revitalization of the idea of class struggle. The corrupt cadres had gone

71 See Baum, *Prelude to revolution*, 11–41; Chan, Madsen, and Unger, *Chen Village*, 37–40; Madsen, *Morality and power in a Chinese village*, 68–72.
72 Chan, Madsen, and Unger, *Chen Village*, 41–64.

wrong, it was suggested, because their thinking was that of the old classes. In a sense they really were members of the old classes, and thus could be struggled against vehemently. But most of the cadres were, in fact, of poor peasant origin. If one's personal conduct (or, for that matter, one's inner consciousness) was now the deciding factor that made one a member of the good or bad classes rather than one's objective sociological origin, the way was now open for extraordinarily arbitrary decisions about who was a class friend and who a class enemy. In the Four Clean-ups Campaign was rehearsed the logic of arbitary class struggle that would later characterize the Cultural Revolution.[73]

Indeed, the whole language of class analysis, which had been used by the CCP in land reform and was again becoming a major theme in the political rhetoric of the mid-1960s, was out of touch with the evolving realities of rural life. People who bore the label "landlord" or "rich peasant" were now no richer than anyone else, and because of the way they were systematically discriminated against they were often, in fact, poorer. Many poor peasants, on the other hand, had become relatively well-to-do. Which ones had prospered depended on a host of complex factors that were not touched upon in the official rhetoric about class exploitation. Once agriculture had been collectivized, economic success depended on such factors as how strong one was and how physically fit one's family members were (which in turn, of course, was related to what stage of the life cycle one was in); how good one's relations with kin and neighbors were (which would depend on how one fitted into the lineage networks that cut across village life); how favorably the government looked upon one's past political affiliations; or how disciplined, hard-working, and ambitious one was.[74] The confluence of factors like these created new interest groups and sometimes generated new antagonisms within villages, antagonisms that were incomprehensible in terms of the language of class analysis.

What the rhetoric of social class usually referred to at the village level was more akin to a new caste system. Everyone bore a class label, either conferred on one during land reform or inherited through one's father's line if one had been too young to receive a classification of one's own in the early 1950s. Although this classification bore only an indirect relation to one's present economic situation, it was a powerful determinant of one's political and social status. If one were a "poor" or "lower-middle peasant," one was eligible to be considered for cadre positions and for

73 Madsen, *Morality and power in a Chinese village*, 72–80. See also the analysis of Shue, *Peasant China in transition*, 339–41.
74 Chan, Madsen, and Unger, *Chen Village*, 52–53.

all kinds of favorable government treatment. If one were a "middle peasant," one might be eligible for a minor cadre position if one were extremely capable and extremely reliable, but one would always be somewhat vulnerable to political assault. If one were one of the "four bad types" – a landlord, rich peasant, counterrevolutionary, or "bad element" – one was permanently stigmatized. One had no right to attend production team or brigade meetings (although one would be assigned to clean up the meeting hall after the meeting was over), one could not vote in production team or brigade elections, any complaint one made about one's fate could be interpreted as a counterrevolutionary act and make one liable for severe punishment – and no poor or lower-middle peasant would marry one, except under the most desperate circumstances.

By the 1960s, these class labels had become fixed. They were completely ascribed, and no mobility out of them was possible. Though certainly miserable for the roughly 6 percent of the population who belonged to the four bad types, it was a situation of some security to the majority, who were classed as poor and lower-middle peasants. Their favorable class labels gave the latter a bedrock of political capital that could not normally be lost, unless one committed a major counterrevolutionary crime. But in the rhetoric of the Four Cleanups Campaign, it now became possible for poor and lower-middle peasants, and cadres at that, to lose their favorable class status because of some relatively minor misdeeds. Class labels became deadly weapons in local political warfare.[75]

The political warfare launched by the Four Cleanups Campaign was not as deadly as land reform had been to the old village elites. Although some local cadres had their careers destroyed and there were reports that at least a few had committed suicide, the destruction of the new elites did not turn out to be as final as the destruction of the landlords. Most of the local cadres, except those who had committed the most extreme infractions, had the accusations against them revised and were given their old jobs back. They were usually chastened enough, however, to refrain at least temporarily from particularistic relations and from private appropriation of public funds. And they had to share some of their local power with new, younger cadres, recruited by the work teams from among the ranks of activists in the campaign.

The Four Cleanups phase of the Socialist Education Campaign was followed by a more positive phase, in which villagers were supposed to learn to appreciate the values of socialism and to put those values more fully

---

75 See Richard Curt Kraus, *Class conflict in Chinese socialism*, esp. 39–114; and Madsen, *Morality and power in a Chinese village*, 75–80.

into practice. It was around this time – 1965 and 1966 – that the cult of Mao was introduced to villages. Peasants attended Mao study sessions in which they memorized passages from Mao's writings (such as the article entitled "Serve the people"), learned to sing revolutionary anthems, listened to older peasants emotionally testify as to how much better the glorious present was compared to the bitter past, and discussed among themselves the value of selflessly serving the people. These ideological revival sessions were often linked with introduction of such "socialist" reforms as the Ta-chai work-point system.[76]

The new emphasis on "absolute selflessness, without any thought of self" was perhaps temporarily made a little more palatable by the material improvements in peasants' lives in the mid-1960s. The economy in general had improved since the disastrous years just after the GLF. Some funds were becoming available for improved seed and fertilizers. Electricity was brought to many places in the countryside in the mid-1960s. Rural health clinics, staffed by local paramedics, were widely organized. The material quality of life was gradually improving. Perhaps many peasants were willing to give credit for this improvement to Chairman Mao, who, thanks to the efforts of an immense propaganda apparatus, appeared to them as almost a godlike figure. With the onset of the Cultural Revolution, however, that faith was severely tested.

The Cultural Revolution

The impact of the Cultural Revolution on villages was mainly indirect. The vast social movements that convulsed China during the Cultural Revolution were centered in the cities. Red Guard and Revolutionary Rebel factions were composed mostly of students and urban workers. But the unrest of the cities inevitably spilled over into the countryside. Most affected were those villages most closely connected with cities. Red Guards and Revolutionary Rebels traveled into suburban villages and sometimes into even remoter areas to spread their rebellious messages. Urban youth who had been "sent down" to the countryside in the early 1960s caught the revolutionary fever and organized Red Guard factions in their villages. City people seeking to escape the turmoil of the Cultural Revolution fled to visit their relatives in the countryside.[77]

Under the impetus, often, of outside agitators, some young villagers

---

76 Madsen, ibid., 130–50; Chan, Madsen, and Unger, *Chen Village*, 74–102.
77 Chan, Madsen, and Unger, ibid., 103–40; Hinton, *Shenfan*, 451–553; Liang and Shapiro, *Son of the revolution*, 161–88; Richard Baum, "The Cultural Revolution in the countryside: anatomy of a limited rebellion," in Thomas W. Robinson, ed., *The Cultural Revolution in China*, pp. 347–476.

formed their own Red Guard organizations, but these generally seemed to be rather tame and pale reflections of their urban exemplars. Some of these Red Guard organizations carried out "power seizures" at the production brigade level, taking over the official seals of office used by such officials and proclaiming themselves to be in charge now of local affairs. Though temporarily disruptive and annoying to many local peasants, such events did not profoundly alter the political situations of their localities. Villagers had little reason to respect or cooperate with the kinds of youngsters who did such things. More established local cadres often continued to run local events, at least informally. Villages, however, felt the consequences of the power seizures that took place in 1967 at higher levels, the level of the province, the county, and sometimes the commune headquarters. When these units were taken over by alliances of (mainly urban) Red Guards and Revolutionary Rebels, stable political links between villages and the outside world were cut, an unsettling and potentially disruptive experience for local communities. The potential for local unrest unleashed by the breakdown of state authority was not usually realized, however, because peasants were getting busy with harvesting and planting when much of it occurred, and because the military moved in to reestablish law and order in time to prevent major disruption. The most important effect of this brush with anarchy was not political but psychological and ultimately cultural. If nothing else, the Cultural Revolution reinforced for peasants the traditional idea that the outside world was a dangerous place and that strangers, especially representatives of the central government, were usually to be feared and avoided rather than trusted. Thus, the Cultural Revolution undid whatever progress had been made by the Socialist Education Campaign toward creating in the countryside a new socialist person with a new public-spirited morality. Villagers were left to fall back on older sources of meaning and morality, rooted in traditional religion and ritual.

Religion and ritual

Traditionally, peasants' ideas and feelings about the meaning of life and the fundamental dictates of morality had been textured, explained, and justified through an elaborate religious system. At the heart of this vision of the sacred had been a pantheon of gods, ghosts, and ancestors. In the peasant imagination, gods took on the form of larger-than-life government officials, arrayed in bureaucratic ranks under the Lord of Heaven. Ghosts were wraithful commoners, the dangerous spirits of deceased strangers. Good spirits were those of one's own deceased ancestors.

Regularly throughout the year and at crucial occasions of their lives, peasants had celebrated the meaning of life in rituals expressive of various facets of this world view.[78]

Major feasts like the lunar New Year, the Ch'ing Ming Festival, the Mid-Autumn Festival, and the Winter Solstice focused on worshiping a family's deceased ancestors and in the process celebrated the present solidarity of one's family. The religious dimensions of births, weddings, and deaths symbolized the integrity and centrality of the family, its links with the past and its hopes for the future. Festivals like the Hungry Ghost Festival aimed at placating the dangerous ghosts that roamed throughout the countryside. In addition, superstitious peasants practiced a variety of rituals day to day to protect themselves from the hostile spirits of strangers. Finally, every community had its earth god, its own local patron in the hierarchy of heavenly officials, whose birthday had to be celebrated; and religiously prudent villagers would want to appease their local god's superiors, the nearby city god, and the higher-echelon gods who periodically made the rounds of localities.

After the founding of the People's Republic, the old religious practices had not disappeared, in spite of the atheistic ideology of the ruling Communists. Official policy toward religion had been one of reluctant tolerance. Although religion is false, only its most politically dangerous or socially harmful aspects should be directly suppressed; the remaining religious practices will naturally wither away as the misery of economic exploitation is eliminated with socialist transformation.[79] At the rural level, this meant in practice that the property and other resources belonging to large lineage halls should be confiscated. Set up to worship the common ancestors who provided the basis for the unity of large groups of families, lineage halls, with their accompanying endowments, provided a moral and economic basis for political resistance to central authority and thus could not be tolerated; nor could temples to the local earth gods, which provided a focus for community solidarity against the outside world; nor could full-time religious practicioners such as shamans, fortune-tellers, and magical healers, because they operated independently of a political economy being brought under control by the government. But domestic worship of one's household's own ancestors could be permitted, along with the traditional rituals of passage punctuating the life cycle, as

---

78 The most systematic analysis of these dimensions of Chinese popular religion is based on anthropological fieldwork done in Taiwan: Arthur P. Wolf, "Gods, ghosts, and ancestors," in Arthur P. Wolf, ed., *Religion and ritual in Chinese society*. See also C. K. Yang, *Religion in Chinese society*.

79 Changing policies toward religion are documented in Donald E. MacInnis, comp., *Religious policy and practice in Communist China*.

long as these were kept modest in scale and did not disrupt agricultural production. A modicum of private rituals aimed at warding off dangerous ghosts and bringing good luck could also be officially sneered at but ignored in practice, as long as they remained essentially private.

One part of the Cultural Revolution, however, that affected most peasants directly was the campaign against the "four olds": old culture, old beliefs, old customs, and old habits. In effect this was an attack on traditional religious practices. Red Guards, mostly from the cities, demanded that all traditional ritual objects be destroyed. They forced peasant households to bring out and destroy their most precious sacred objects, the tablets engraved with the names of the ancestors that stood atop an altar in the front of the house. They confiscated and burned old books containing religious teaching. They destroyed images of the gods and symbols of good luck. In at least one place, they even broke the molds that housewives had used to imprint rice cakes with traditional good-luck symbols. Under the pressure of the antireligious zealotry unleashed by the Cultural Revolution, many peasants shied away from engaging in the traditional rituals surrounding births, marriages, and deaths.[80]

The Cultural Revolution created new gods and ghosts to replace the old ones. Mao, "the Reddest Sun That Shines in Our Hearts," became a sacred personage. His picture and slogans from his writings were stenciled everywhere on village walls. Copies of the little red book filled with his quotations – and in families that could afford them, copies of all four volumes of his collected works – graced the family altars where the ancestor tablets once stood. In some places villagers even began meetings by holding hands and performing "Loyalty Dances," which resembled a Virginia reel danced to the tune of "Sailing the Seas Depends on the Helmsman, Making Revolution Depends on Mao Tse-tung's Thought." If Mao took the place of the gods, class enemies took the place of the ghosts. Persons attacked, not only during the Cultural Revolution but also during earlier campaigns, were often called in official literature "cows, ghosts, snakes, and monsters," a traditional epithet composed of synonyms for dangerous supernatural strangers. New government holidays, like New Year's Day (in the Western calendar) and National Day on 1 October, were supposed to rival the old festivals in significance.[81]

One of the tragedies of the Cultural Revolution, however, was that the new symbols of the sacred that it proposed were so unbelievable. In the

80 Chan, Madsen, and Unger, *Chen Village*, 118.
81 Madsen, *Morality and power in a Chinese village*, 130–50; Chan, Madsen, and Unger, *Chen Village*, 169–74; Parish and Whyte, *Village and family life in contemporary China*, 287–97.

name of Mao, uncontrolled mobs committed atrocities. Having received access to modern mass communications, most villages could become aware of the anarchy that afflicted China's major cities. If those events were too far away to have a deep emotional and moral impact, campaigns like the Cleansing of the Class Ranks, launched in 1968 to punish disrupters of law and order during the anarchic phases of the Cultural Revolution, came all too close.

The Cleansing of the Class Ranks did extend into some rural areas, commanding peasants to search out certain quotas of fellow villagers (about 3 percent) who had been responsible for the most destructive parts of the Cultural Revolution. Some villages that had relatively few troublemakers during the Cultural Revolution had to invent them. In line with a further twist in the Maoist theory of social classes, members of the good classes would not usually commit counterrevolutionary acts. Therefore, those workers and poor peasants who wreaked havoc in the Cultural Revolution were probably not truly members of the good classes, but were infected with the hidden taint of bad class blood. And if the overt troublemakers could bear the secret taint of bad class origins, that hidden impurity might infect even those who apparently had not done anything obviously wrong. In the region around "Ch'en Village" in Kwangtung province, at least, this was the logic used to justify carrying out witch hunts against unpopular villagers, like gossipy old women, who villagers claimed had been improperly classified during land reform or who had had close relatives who had been improperly classified. All of this, done in the name of Chairman Mao in the heat of the anxieties generated by the Cultural Revolution, produced such flagrant miscarriages of justice that many peasants became thoroughly disillusioned by claims that Mao was the fountainhead of a glorious new revolutionary morality.[82]

Other campaigns followed in the early 1970s, such as the "One Hit Three Antis" Campaign of 1971 and the "Criticize Lin Piao, Criticize Confucius" campaign of 1973. Such campaigns, all done in the name of Mao, fostered the impression of a government undertaking totally unreasonable initiatives in the countryside. The Criticize Lin Piao Campaign exposed the population to the disillusioning spectacle of the fall from grace of the man who they were told during the Cultural Revolution had been Mao's closest comrade-in-arms. With the image of Mao becoming so tarnished, what was there left to believe in?

Many peasants, perhaps, found solace through a retreat into their families. Whatever basis there had been for a commitment to the public good,

---

82 Madsen, *Morality and power in a Chinese village*, 195–98.

whatever moral foundation had been built up for rural socialism, had been deeply eroded by the Cultural Revolution – a great irony because the avowed purpose of the Cultural Revolution was to create a new socialist morality. As fear of being punished for worshiping ancestors or for celebrating weddings and funerals in the traditional way subsided, many of the old family rituals came quietly back to life. Families had to be discreet, however, about visibly practicing such "feudal superstitions," and they often had to improvise ritual items, substituting mosquito-repellent coils for genuine incense sticks, for instance. Traditional public rituals were gone, perhaps for good. There was no worship of common ancestors of a lineage, no organized worship of local earth gods or city gods. Besides being officially forbidden, these would have required the expenditure of public funds that, since land reform, had become unavailable. But modern public rituals – celebrations of Chairman Mao, of the nation, or of the People's Liberation Army (PLA) – apparently evoked little enthusiasm and bore little meaning beyond the chance to get a few hours off from work. In spite of, or perhaps because of, the CCP's twenty years of propaganda, peasants lived in a family-centered, essentially private moral world, ill suited to the kind of collective discipline demanded by socialism.[83]

Beleaguered villages

Besides bombarding villages with propaganda in its attempt to tighten the moral and social links between villages and the national polity, the Maoist government had also sent them millions of young people from the cities. As already mentioned, by the early 1960s, the government virtually ended migration of peasants to the cities. Practically the only opportunity for mobility outside of the village was to join the PLA. Then one would be able to travel around the country and one might have the opportunity to learn a skill like truck driving, which could make one employable in county towns or even cities. The PLA, however, chose only a few of the strongest and most politically active village youths.

The eventual result of the barrier thus erected between city and countryside had been the formation of two separate, but decidedly unequal, social worlds. Patterns of work, community, and cultural life differed sharply between city and countryside. City people tended to see the countryside as a primitive, strange, and dangerous place and its people as decidedly inferior to urbanites. Peasants tended to accept their life as inferior to that of city people.

---

83 Parish and Whyte, *Village and family life in contemporary China*, 266–72, 287–97.

To bridge the gap between city and countryside, and to alleviate the demographic problems caused by overcrowding in the cities, the government began to send teenagers "up to the mountains and down to the countryside" in the early 1960s. At first, the program was voluntary. Idealistic middle school students were urged to devote themselves to the glorious work of building up the countryside. Even when conceived in these idealistic terms, however, the rationale for going to the countryside assumed that this was an act of sacrifice and by implication that country life was inferior to city life. Between 1962 and 1968, about 1.2 million urban youths had "gone down" to villages under this program. After 1968, the program was vastly increased. Between 1968 and 1978 around 12 million urban youths, approximately 11 percent of the total urban population, were sent down. Now, however, the program no longer even had a semblance of being voluntary.[84]

Even when relatively small numbers of relatively well-motivated young people had come into villages, their presence had often been disruptive. Often appalled by the dirt and poor hygiene of village life, inept at farm work, yet convinced of their own cultural superiority, many city youth quickly lost their idealism and wanted to go home, "to civilization," as a former sent-down youth interviewed by B. Michael Frolic put it.[85] To villagers, the city youth, unable to do enough farm work to support themselves, were "empty rice bowls," a drain on the local economy. Even when trying to serve the poor and lower-middle peasants, the urban youth often antagonized them with their patronizing attitudes. Sometimes, peasants saw urban youth as people to be taken advantage of. Former sent-down youth recount many anecdotes of peasants siphoning off for local village use money provided by the state for the care of urban youth. And there were enough cases of sexual abuse of young urban women by peasants to fuel ugly stereotypes about peasant immorality.[86]

Sometimes during the early years of the youth-to-the-countryside program, genuine progress had been made in developing mutual respect and understanding between city people and peasants; and urban youth helped promote literacy in the villages and to develop local technical expertise in health care and the use of new kinds of machinery. But few of these benefits were realized from the huge waves of youth sent down after

---

84 The most comprehensive study of the youth-to-the-countryside movement is Thomas P. Bernstein, *Up to the mountains and down to the villages: the transfer of youth from urban to rural China*. See also Peter J. Seybolt, ed., *The rustication of urban youth in China: a social experiment*; Chan, Madsen, and Unger, *Chen Village*, 8–11, 103–11, 231–35; and Madsen, *Morality and power in a Chinese village*, 105–29.
85 B. Michael Frolic, *Mao's people: sixteen portraits of life in revolutionary China*, 48.
86 Ibid., 51–53.

1968. Many of the first arrivals in the villages were former unruly Red Guards who perceived their exile to the countryside as a punishment for daring to rebel in 1966 and 1967. Having no motivation to integrate themselves with the lives of peasants, they drained away village resources, complained about their fate, fomented unrest, sometimes stole grain and vegetables from their village hosts, and spent much of their time thinking up ways to get out of their villages.[87] By the early 1970s government policy was decreeing that only one child per family could stay in the cities after middle school; practically all the rest had to go to the countryside. The influx of poorly motivated city people was often more than villages could comfortably absorb.

Thus, instead of narrowing the gap between city and countryside, the youth-to-the-countryside program may on balance have worsened it. Villagers may have perceived their communities as dumping grounds for the excess urban population, and urban youth may have seen themselves as having been dumped, "thrown into the garbage heap of history," as one such youth put it.[88] The hostility between city and countryside may have increased. To many villagers, the outside world – the world of cities and of government – must have seemed to be the source of few benefits and many problems.

This perception was enhanced by floods of unrealistic policies relating to agriculture that came down in the first half of the 1970s. Radicals in the central government began, for instance, to issue broad commands about what kinds of crops should be planted in various regions that were simply out of touch with economic realities. Peasants in South China, for instance, were commanded to plant cotton and wheat (on the rationale that these northern Chinese crops might be jeopardized in the event of a Soviet attack), even though such crops could not be grown effectively in the semitropical South China climate.[89] Throughout much of the 1960s, no matter what its other problems, the government's approach toward agriculture usually had at least been helpful toward increasing production. Now many peasants once again had to cope with increasingly rigid government commands that contradicted the realities with which they were most familiar – the conditions of successful farming.

They also had to cope with increasing grain exactions. Under a variety

87 Many of the articles from the official Chinese press translated in Seybolt, *The rustication of urban youth in China*, reflect concern on the part of officials about low morale among urban youth. For vivid examples of this loss of morale, see Liang and Shapiro, *Son of the revolution*, 189–92; Chan, Madsen, and Unger, *Chen Village*, 226–35; and Frolic, *Mao's people*, 42–57.
88 Madsen, *Morality and power in a Chinese village*, 129.
89 Chan, Madsen, and Unger, *Chen Village*, 236–43; stories about similar blunders appeared regularly in the Chinese press in 1978.

of pretexts, the government was demanding that larger quotas of grain be sold at the artificially low price set by the state, which would leave less for the peasants' own consumption. Peasant morale sank, and agricultural productivity gradually declined throughout the 1970s.

These alarming tendencies were partially offset by the success of small-scale industrialization at the rural level. By the early 1970s, the slogan that peasants should "take grain as the basis" had been modified to "grain as the basis and overall undertaking." At both the commune level and the production brigade level of rural organization, local cadres, encouraged by the government, were establishing more small factories for making and repairing agricultural tools, for manufacturing fertilizer, processing grain, and so forth. These industries provided welcome new services at the local level, rendering communities more self-sufficient. Profits from the industries also increased the amount of economic leverage communes and especially production brigades could exert on the relatively autonomous production teams. The new enterprises provided a new, "modern" kind of work experience for peasants, steady indoor work with machine tools, rather than seasonally fluctuating outside work with one's hands. Jobs in the new industries were attractive, and they whetted the appetite for more.[90]

These undeniably positive developments, however, sometimes had the effect of increasing the estrangement of the peasantry from the state. Localities had improved themselves largely by pulling themselves up by their own bootstraps. They were now more economically self-sufficient than ever. As far as improving the quality of their lives was concerned, they did not seem to have much need of the government, which in fact seemed to take away more than it gave.

The younger generation of peasants seemed particularly affected by this sense of estrangement. The sight of the modest new economic developments, the messages conveyed by the mass media, the knowledge provided by at least a primary school education, and the tales told by sent-down urban youth of the pleasures of city life – all served to raise expectations faster than they could be satisfied. "Our parents," said one Kwangtung peasant, "only wanted to be able to fill all our bellies. We young people want more out of life than just that."[91] But in the stagnant rural economy of the mid-1970s, more was not forthcoming.

90 See ibid., 213–23; Dwight Perkins, ed., *Rural small-scale industry in the People's Republic of China*; and Marianne Bastid, "Levels of economic decision-making" in Stuart R. Schram, ed., *Authority, participation and cultural change in China*, 159–97.
91 Chan, Madsen, and Unger, *Chen Village*, 252n.

UNDOING THE NEW, 1977 AND BEYOND

Decollectivization

As the 1970s were drawing to a close, the situation of peasant farmers changed suddenly and dramatically. Once Teng Hsiao-p'ing had consolidated his hold on the political coalition that succeeded Mao Tse-tung and his deposed supporters, his regime began to issue orders decollectivizing agriculture.

The new agricultural system, put into effect with considerable regional variation over a two-year period after December 1979, was not a full-fledged decollectivization. Peasants could not formally own land, in the sense of being able to buy or sell it or rent it out. But in most parts of the country, production responsibility was "decentralized to the household." In at least a few places, the land was divided up according to peasants' pre-1949 title deeds, a procedure that was officially criticized, however.[92] Under this popular "responsibility system," each household received responsibility for tilling, in whatever way it saw fit, a portion of what had once been collectively farmed land. After selling to the state a quota of grain and other produce (the state usually specified what crops had to be grown on the land), the household could dispose of its product in whatever way it wished. It was a situation of de facto tenancy, with the state now acting as the landlord.

The new system also allowed large increases in the size of peasants' private plots. Now up to 25 percent of the arable land could be used for such plots, on which peasants could grow anything they wanted for sale in the free market. Together with this came a great expansion in the scope of sideline production. Rural markets, which had been largely suppressed during the Cultural Revolution decade, now were permitted to come back with a vigor they had not enjoyed since the early 1950s. Peasants living near cities were allowed to set up "agricultural supplementary goods markets" inside the cities, something that had been forbidden since 1958. Production teams were still supposed to be the units that owned draft animals and large farm implements, and production brigades the units that owned heavy machinery, such as tractors, and small factories, workshops, and health clinics; but in some places even these kinds of public property were leased out to individuals to be operated for a profit.[93]

---

92 Jürgen Domes, "New policies in the communes: notes on rural societal structures in China, 1976–1981," *JAS*, 41.2 (February 1982), 264.
93 Chan, Madsen, and Unger, *Chen Village*, 272–73.

Condemned as antithetical to socialism for more than two decades, the individual pursuit of profit was now celebrated. "To get rich," a popular slogan went, "is glorious." This was one government slogan that most peasants embraced with alacrity. The countryside witnessed an extraordinary burst of entrepreneurial activity, and with this outpouring of individual initiative came extraordinary increases in agricultural production. More consumer goods were made available than ever before and newly prosperous peasants filled their households with new furniture, bicycles, radios, and even television sets. Although they were living in a system that was still socialist in name, peasants must have felt freer economically than at any time since their government had embarked on the socialist road.

With this economic freedom, however, returned many of the problems that socialism had partially alleviated. Disparities between rich and poor expanded. By the early 1980s there was talk of "new rich peasants," some of whom had incomes of as much as 10,000 yuan a year, as much as prosperous landlords of the prerevolutionary society. Unlike the old landed elites, however, these new rich peasants mainly made their money not from land rents but through commercial activities. Perhaps the quickest way to get rich was to obtain a monopoly over the local provision of an important service such as transport. Virtual monopolies in services such as trucking could sometimes be obtained through special relationships with cadres in charge of issuing licenses for them. Establishing such "good feeling" relationships with local cadres was often accomplished through bribery. Sometimes local cadres themselves were ones who set up the profitable new enterprises. With economic development, therefore, came increased temptations of corruption for local officials.[94]

The benefits of economic freedom, moreover, brought with them increased insecurities for the old, the weak, the poor, and the unlucky. With the new opportunities to get rich came new opportunities to become poor. If, because of sickness, poor planning, natural disaster, or just plain bad luck, a household could not coax a large enough yield out of its allotted land to give itself adequate income after transmission of its quotas to the state, there were fewer mechanisms available than before to help it out. Also left uncertain under the new system was how public works projects such as the development and maintenance of irrigation systems were to be managed in a world of independent small entrepreneurs.[95]

In the old society, help for the poor, the weak, and the elderly came, if it came at all, from the networks of familial relationships that textured

94 For examples, see ibid., 276–79.   95 Domes, "New policies in the communes," 264–65.

Chinese life.[96] Support, too, for communitywide public works projects was often organized along the lines of extended kinship relationships. In the new free enterprise system, traditional relations of kinship, friendship, and good human feeling would probably have to fill in for the social welfare arrangements provided under the commune system. Yet, just as family relationships were becoming more important for the long-range welfare of peasants than had been the ease for a generation, the government forcefully moved ahead with policies that could fundamentally weaken the ability of the peasant family to provide for that welfare.

Marriage and family

To understand the significance of these new policies, we should review the effects on family life of previous government policies since the founding of the People's Republic. One of the first acts of the new government was the promulgation, in 1950, of a sweeping new family law that abolished "the arbitrary and compulsory feudal marriage system, which is based on the superiority of man over women and which ignores the childrens' interests."[97] But because this law was not vigorously enforced in the countryside, it did not deeply affect the basic structure of rural family life. Peasants married and had children and took care of their children as they had done before the Communists came to power.

Based on "free choice of partners ... and on protection of lawful interests of women and children," the new marriage law had as its major premise the principle that marriage was a matter of the creation of a new family through the free choice of two equal individuals rather than an arrangement entered into by two existing families in which they would dispose of their children in a manner benefiting the family as a whole. But although under the new marriage law, men and women were to marry as a result of their own free decisions, marriages continued to be contracted under the strong guidance of parents.

To be sure, children gradually gained more of a say in who their spouse would be than they had had in the early twentieth century. Before 1949 it was usual for parents to arrange the marriages of their children in such a way that the bride and groom would not meet until the day of their wedding. Within a few decades after the founding of the People's Republic,

---

96 For a careful study of arrangements for the care of the elderly, see Deborah Davis-Friedmann, *Long lives: Chinese elderly and the communist revolution.*
97 Promulgated by the Central People's Government on 1 May 1950, the Marriage Law is translated in Yang, *The Chinese family in the communist revolution*, 221–26.

however, parental control over marriage arrangements had weakened significantly. Now, even when their parents had taken the initiative in arranging their marriage, the arrangement was usually made after consulting the children who would be married. With increasing frequency, young men and women, having gotten to know one another through going to school together or working in the same production unit, would themselves take the first steps toward getting married, although subsequent steps would be taken under the strong guidance of their parents. Still, these changes did not radically alter the fact that marriage was primarily an arrangement between families rather than individuals.[98]

The new marriage law was also based on "equal rights for both sexes," unlike traditional customs that made women clearly subordinate to men. In the rural areas of the People's Republic of China, however, women remained decidedly inferior to men. Marriages remained patrilocal, with women "marrying into" the families of their husbands (which usually meant marrying into a different village) and being obliged to contribute to the welfare of their in-laws. Sons, therefore, continued to be much favored over daughters – the birth of a son was called a "big happiness" while that of a daughter was a "small happiness," because after a daughter was raised, her services would be lost to another family. Within the family, wives remained clearly subordinate to their husbands and, indeed, to their husbands' parents. Ultimate decision-making power remained in the hands of a woman's husband or perhaps even of her husband's father, although, as in traditional times, women often eventually managed to gain considerable informal power in a household.

Although the three decades after 1949 did indeed bring some improvements in the lives of rural women, these improvements did not spring from, or give rise to, a fundamental transformation in the traditional patriarchal family system. Women gained some status when they were pressed into working in the fields after socialist transformation. Now the work points they earned were an essential part of a household's income. As women became worth more economically, there was an increase in the bride prices paid by a groom's family to the family of their future daughter-in-law. Within the family there seems to have been some softening of the authoritarian rule of the male family head. Yet when women went to work in the collective fields, they invariably were paid fewer work points than men, their income was not allocated to them personally but went to their entire household, and they were expected to take care of all of the housework in addition to doing farm work. Moreover, the vast

98   See Parish and Whyte, *Village and family life in contemporary China*, 155–99.

majority of rural cadres were men. Commonly, the only woman cadre at the production brigade level was one specifically in charge of women's work. Although a husband would now likely be punished if he beat his wife badly enough to cause severe injury, it was still not uncommon for husbands to beat their wives. A husband's sexual infidelity was considered far less serious than a wife's.[99]

At the foundation of this patriarchal system's durability was the vital role it played in providing for the welfare of its members, especially for its sick and elderly. As a husband and a wife became too old to support themselves, their sons and daughters-in-law would take care of them. In turn, elderly parents would take care of their sons' children when the children's parents were at work. The old ideal of an extended household in which married sons and their families would live together under the authority of an elderly patriarch thus survived. As in the past, it was an ideal that could be realized only partially by most families. The most common pattern was for an elderly couple to live together with one of their married sons, usually the eldest, and for the rest of one's married sons to live in separate households in close proximity to their parents' house.[100] But there are some indications that in the improved economic climate of today, there are more families living out the traditional ideal of the extended household than before 1949.[101]

Under the socialist agricultural system, those elderly without any children were supposed to be protected by the "Five Guarantees": guaranteed food, clothing, housing, medical care, and burial expenses. Each production team was supposed to put aside a portion of its annual income to pay for these services to its needy elderly. This system of social welfare, however, was based on the assumption that only a few elderly would need it, because most would be taken care of by their children. And despite government regulations that they be well taken care of, many of those rural elderly without any married sons to take care of them lived in pitiably poor conditions.[102]

With the decollectivization of agriculture at the end of the 1970s, the situation of peasants dependent on the Five Guarantees became even more precarious. Regulations implementing the new system specified that the livelihood of old and infirm people, as well as widowers, widows,

99 See ibid. 200–21; Judith Stacey, *Patriarchy and socialist revolution in China*; Kay Ann Johnson, *Women, the family, and peasant revolution in China*; and Margery Wolf, *Revolution postponed: women in contemporary China.*

100 Davis-Friedmann, *Long lives*, 34–46.

101 Fei Hsiao-tung, "On changes in the Chinese family structure," trans. in *Chinese Sociology and Anthropology*, 16. 1–2 (Fall–Winter, 1983–84), 32–45.

102 Davis-Friedmann, *Long lives*, 85–95.

and orphans, should be guaranteed. But because brigades and production teams had lost much of their authority over peasant households, who could guarantee that such programs for social welfare would in the long run be adequately funded?

It was quite reasonable in this context for peasants to be extremely concerned about maintaining the integrity of the traditional patriarchal family. Yet just as a new era of economic and political freedom seemed to be blossoming in the countryside, the government began to disrupt this integrity by means of a vigorous effort to limit each family to only one child.

Birth control campaigns were nothing new in the countryside. By the mid-1960s the government had begun extensive efforts to limit family sizes in rural areas. (Birth control programs had begun in the cities in the mid-1950s but had been interrupted by the GLF dogma that the larger the population the better.) There were some indications that many peasants, especially those of the younger generation, favored limiting births. Better health conditions had lowered the infant mortality rate. The requirement that women do field work had increased the burden of caring for large numbers of children. With opportunities for mobility out of the village restricted, and with the supply of land available for collective production relatively fixed, having many children could bring economic burdens on families. But any predisposition to limit family size was balanced out by the importance of having sons. Most families preferred to have two sons, to be well assured of at least one survivor to live with them, work together with them, and take care of them in old age. But it was essential to have at least one son.[103]

In the early 1970s, as the political and technical means for promoting birth control became well developed – as national and provincial commissions for promoting birth control gained the authority to put pressure directly on grassroots (mostly male) cadres, as cadres became able to impose material sanctions on families who had more than three children, as more efficient methods of birth control were developed, and as a better network for distributing birth control materials through local health clinics became available – the rural birthrate dropped significantly. The official slogan about family size was "One is good, two is enough, three is many, and four is excessive." Whether out of obedience to the government or (more likely) their own economic self-interest, most families were at least partially complying with this slogan, having no more than three children, and in many cases only two, especially if the two were

---

103 Parish and Whyte, *Village and family life in contemporary China*, 138–54.

sons. Still, few peasants, or even local cadres, would object if a couple with three or four daughters but no sons kept on having children until they had a boy.

By the late 1970s, however, as the potential problems posed for China's modernization by its huge population were acknowledged, the central government suddenly embarked on its drastic policy of one child per family. In many areas, the full resources of the state were brought to bear against those who failed to comply with the new policy. There were, in fact, reports of women as much as eight months pregnant being forced to have abortions. There are also indications that the incidence of female infanticide began to increase sharply as mothers and fathers grew fearful of the dire consequences of facing their old age without a married son nearby to take care of them. Although the draconian policy on family size remained in effect through the mid-1980s, there were indications that in many rural areas it was being pursued in a more flexible manner.[104]

The reforms of the Teng Hsiao-p'ing regime greatly expanded the scope of economic and political freedom in the countryside. Besides allowing more play to local market forces, the regime relaxed many of the harshest political constraints of the Maoist era. Most landlords and rich peasants had their "hats removed"; that is, they had the political stigma of their class status eliminated and were allowed to participate as full-fledged citizens in local life.[105] The era of violent political rectifications, carried out in the name of increasingly arbitrary conceptions of class struggle, was over, at least for the foreseeable future. The youth-to-the-countryside program was ended, removing a significant burden from the shoulders of rural and urban people alike. Yet in what was arguably the most important aspect of peasant life, the nature of its family life, the power of politics was felt more strongly than ever.

CONCLUSIONS

The ironies occasioned by a coercive family planning program being carried out alongside a liberalization in the rural economy illustrate how difficult it is to assess how the peasantry may have evaluated the complex historical changes we have described. Most changes that must have seemed good to many peasants were intertwined with changes that must

---

104 The allegations of late abortions and of infanticide have been made by Steven W. Mosher in *Broken earth*, 224–61. See, however, the suggestions of Norma Diamond, "Rural collectivization and decollectivization in China – a review article," *JAS*, 44.4 (August 1985), 785–92, that the locality where Mosher observed these extreme practices was unrepresentative.

105 According to the *Beijing Review*, 21 January 1980, more than 99 percent of landlords and rich peasants had had their "hats" removed; and whereas once they had numbered over 4 million, there were now only 50,000 "incorrigibles" left.

have seemed bad. Changes welcomed by the younger generation might not have been approved of by the older generation. And even changes that benefited a majority of the peasantry often were harmful to a substantial minority.

Take for example the ambiguities inherent in the economic history of villages. As of 1978, according to the Chinese government's own statistics, per capita grain production had hardly increased since the mid-1950s.[106] But even if the amount of food available on the average to villagers had not increased greatly, economic development had generally brought substantial material benefits to many communities: better roads, some electricity and mass communications, new health clinics and improved hygiene. For all of the eventual economic problems it might bring to the nation as a whole, the rising rural population was a sign of material well-being. And as a result of the three decades of history recounted here, these material benefits were more equally shared within villages than they had been before the revolution.

Most villagers who had been poor peasants at the time of land reform would therefore have reason to be grateful for the economic transformation of their communities. But if they were old enough to have been present at the time of land reform, they would be old enough to remember the massive famine of the early 1960s, when so many people suffered and even died as a result of their government's blundering attempts to create a radical form of socialism. They might consider, too, how many more hours of work they had to do in the service of their collectives since the socialist transformation of agriculture, how women had to leave the home to do farm labor, and how agricultural slack seasons had to be devoted to projects demanded by their collectives – and they might wonder how much more they had received for their extra work and how much had been taken away to the cities by the government and how much wasted in misguided agricultural programs.

On balance, though, older people may have more to be grateful for than the younger generation. One cost of the Chinese Communists' strategy for economic development was the restriction of mobility between countryside and city. Rooted in their local communities, most members of the older generation do not care much about being unable to move to the cities. But younger peasants may be frustrated, especially as they come to know a little more about the outside world through newspapers and

---

106 Graphs on page 2 of the *Chinese statistical yearbook, 1984*, indicate that grain production increased by about 50 percent from 1956 to 1978 (there was, of course, a steep decline during the Great Leap years followed by a steady recovery in the 1960s and 1970s), while China's total population increased by about the same percentage.

the radio, and now, increasingly, television. A poll conducted in an agricultural middle school in 1979 showed that only 6 percent of the students wanted to spend their life as farmers; and a poll conducted in an urban primary school showed that only one-half of 1 percent of the students wanted to be farmers.[107] But that is what more than 90 percent of school-age peasants will probably have to be. With their increasing opportunities for education, young people also may be even more aware than their elders of the inequalities that exist among rural communities and among regions, and those from poorer areas may wonder why such inequalities have to exist.

From the point of view of most peasants, however, the ratio of good to bad in the political realm has been even more ambiguous than the balance between costs and benefits in the economic realm. Peasants do not have to be afraid, as they were all too often in the 1930s and 1940s, of being threatened, abused, and exploited by local despots, or of being robbed by bandits, or of being killed by invading armies. The Communist government has brought them more order and stability, at least, than they had then. During land reform, the CCP organized poor and hired peasants into mass movements to strike down some of the most exploitative people on the rural scene. Although the power of mass associations of peasants was steadily stripped away, the CCP continued to organize poor and lower-middle peasants, at least to discuss how local affairs were being managed. Although the new system was by no means democratic, poor and lower-middle peasants participated more formally and more systematically in making decisions about the management of their local communities than ever before in history.[108]

Moreover, the basic-level cadres who governed production teams and production brigades almost all came from the same villages or hamlets that they governed, and were subject to all sorts of informal social controls from their neighbors and kinsfolk, even as they were scrutinized by higher-level authorities for signs of corruption. For all its imperfections, villagers may have had a more accountable and in general a more honest and well-disciplined local leadership than before the revolution. It was a system that perhaps gave villagers more of a sense of collective control over the routines of their day-to-day lives than they had known before.

107 Chen Yuefang [Ch'en Yueh-fang], Zhang Baichuan [Chang Pai-ch'uan], and Yu Duankang [Yu Tuan-k'ang], "A survey of primary school student aspirations and learning interests," trans. in *Chinese Sociology and Anthropology*, 16. 1–2 (Fall–Winter, 1983–84), 145–58; and Lan Chengdong [Lan Ch'eng-tung] and Zhang Zhangru [Chang Chung-ju], "Aspirations and inclinations of this year's senior high school graduates: a survey of three high schools in Shanghai," trans. in the same issue of *Chinese Sociology and Anthropology*, 159–69.
108 Such is the argument of Parish and Whyte, *Village and family life in contemporary China*, 327–8.

But whatever sympathies local cadres may have had toward the members of their communities, they were still chosen only after careful scrutiny by higher-level authorities in the CCP and were still subject to the immense power of the bureaucratically organized Party and state, a government whose constantly changing policies must often have seemed dangerous and capricious to many peasants. Traditionally, peasants had learned to avoid politics, letting local elites mediate disputes and keep order while keeping government officials at arm's length. But now the politics of the Chinese state could no longer be kept at arm's length. In the 1950s, the government's economic policies caused a massive famine; in the 1960s and 1970s, its political campaigns ruined careers and sometimes destroyed innocent lives in the name of unrealistic notions of class struggle.

Although the state inundated villages with propaganda attempting to justify its policies, to give peasants a sense of participating in a political cause that transcended the confines of their local community – and, at its most ambitious, fundamentally to transform peasant consciousness into a new, "socialist" mode of thinking – the peasant mentality for the most part retained a skepticism about government policies and remained closely focused on village and family life. To be sure, some peasants, such as local Party cadres and demobilized PLA soldiers, had more systematic exposure to Marxist-Leninist-Maoist ideology than others, and presumably this sometimes resulted in a modicum of appreciation for their place in the national polity. The younger generation, most of whom have by now completed at least six years of primary school, probably has a better intellectual grasp of the basic tenets of the government's ideology than their elders. But even such people remain overwhelmingly concerned with village life for the simple reason that under the present political economic system they have almost no prospect of leaving their villages and thus no way of participating directly in wider public affairs.

The central government remains, then, a distant, mysterious, yet powerful entity. During some periods of the three decades of history recounted here, the government seemed, at least to poor and lower-middle peasants, to be a basically benevolent entity, pregnant with an almost sacred moral promise. In the mid-1960s, many peasants revered, even worshiped, Mao as a godlike figure, in much the same way that they may have looked upon their emperors in former eras. But the destructive policies of the Cultural Revolution and its aftermath seem to have demythologized the central government. By the mid-1970s, it appears to have become in the minds of many peasants nothing but a dangerous, alien, meddlesome force. Whereas in the late 1950s the government could by its intervention in village life generate at least a short burst of high enthusiasm for its adventuristic GLF policies, in the late 1970s it generated enthusiasm mainly by withdrawing its grip on the local economy.

Peasants' evaluations of the changes in their modes of social life may have entailed less of a tension between positive and negative judgments than their evaluations of political and economic life, because, after all, the patterns of their social life did not change as drastically as their political economy. Contrary to the expectations of some Western social scientists in the 1950s, the socialist transformation of the Chinese countryside did not fundamentally change the structure of the peasant family or unravel the traditional fabric of community life. The Communists' attempts at socialist transformation were most successful precisely when they built their new organizations for collective agriculture closely around the traditional social ecology of the countryside. When they did make attempts to unravel some of the basic patterns of traditional social life, especially when organizing the higher-level APCs and the people's communes, the result was economic and political chaos. So in the end, they settled for leaving such patterns largely intact.

The traditional family, therefore, remained the most important moral, emotional, and economic presence in a person's life. Kinship remained patrilineal, family residence remained patrilocal, and authority in the family remained patriarchal. Old people continued to live with one of their married sons. Sons still accepted their obligations to care for their parents in old age and, indeed, to defer at least in a general way to their authority. Large, extended family households, with several married sons and their families living with their parents in one compound and eating from a common kitchen, were in at least some places even more common than in the past; and because of restrictions on mobility out of villages, it was increasingly likely that an elderly couple would at least have several married sons living nearby in separate households but remaining closely involved with providing for the welfare of their parents and in cooperating economically with one another.

Formally organized corporate lineages drawing together hundreds of households descended from a common ancestor were a thing of the past, their common property and temples confiscated by the Communist government and their leadership suppressed. But such lineage organizations had been on the decline even before the Communists took power.[109] Yet

---

109 See Yang, *The Chinese family in the communist revolution*, 191–96.

even today, ties of distant kinship are one important reinforcing strand in the particularistic webs of "good feeling" that shape local alliances and give substance to local patterns of cooperation.

As the 1980s began, the most socially disruptive and unwelcome government attempt to alter social life was its policy that married couples be limited to only one child. It is still too early, however, to gauge the effect of this program. Most of the lasting changes that have occurred in the rural family have taken place somewhat gradually as a response not to direct government pressure but to changing opportunity structures in rural life. Marriages are not as frequently arranged by parents without consulting their children, partly because young people have more of an opportunity to meet potential spouses at school or work groups. Women have slightly more standing within households because their field labor is now a more important economic asset. Such changes have probably been welcomed by most of the younger generation; and they have not been drastic enough or swift enough to upset the old seriously. Some of the young may indeed wish for swifter changes in rural family life. Women, in particular, have seen the burdens of their status lifted but slightly. Although they might welcome a lightening of that burden, however, they do not seem to have developed modes of consciousness or forms of organization that would allow them systematically to push for an improvement of their status.

Thus, for better or worse, at least three of the "thick ropes" that Mao in the 1920s saw as holding the peasantry in bondage are still thick and still constraining. Old ties of political authority have been dismantled, but have been replaced by strong new ones. The bonds of family life remain tight. And women are still tied to the authority of their husbands. What of the fourth rope, the bond of traditional religion?

Western research on this subject is scanty. It seems, though, that much of the authority of the old gods, the sacred symbols of a bureaucratically arranged political order, has died. Large temples to gods (like those so common in rural Taiwan) are gone. There are no more elaborate and expensive public festivals in honor of such sacred beings. On the eve of the Cultural Revolution, the government tried to substitute the worship of Mao for the worship of the traditional gods. But the cult of Mao failed; and official political celebrations evoke little emotional resonance in the rural populace. The sanctified ancestors of rural people, however, are still a revered, felt presence. Ancestor tablets, destroyed or hidden away during the Cultural Revolution, are now reconstructed or brought out of hiding. Peasants still celebrate the main festivals honoring the ancestors and affirming the transcendent unity and destiny of their families. Although shamans and fortune-tellers have been suppressed, the government at the end of the 1970s was expressing concern that some of them were still practicing their "feudal superstitions."[110] At least some ghosts, those traditional symbols of the dangerous, the alien, and the irrational that such religious practitioners evoke, seem, though outlawed, to be still alive.

110 Richard Madsen, "Religion and feudal superstition," *Chingfeng*, 190–96, 217–18.

CHAPTER 10

URBAN LIFE IN
THE PEOPLE'S REPUBLIC

When the Chinese Communists swept to power in 1949, they rapidly went from being a movement controlling large tracts of the Chinese countryside to a central government having to digest and manage the complexities of China's urban centers. China's new leaders were not, of course, country bumpkins: Most had had considerable urban experience before they took to the hills in 1927. Still, the task of bending the cities to suit the programs of the new government appeared formidable. For cities had been not only the center of power of the Chinese Nationalists but also the focus for much of the foreign influence that had streamed into China over the previous century. Their cosmopolitan natures made it appear difficult to transform them to suit the populist ideals of China's new rulers. Indeed, some urban elites and foreigners complacently assumed that their positions would not be threatened, because the Chinese Communists could not possibly run power stations, manage foreign trade, and deal with all the other complexities of urban life without relying on them.

This complacency turned out to be misguided. The Chinese Communists attempted to transform urban institutions and social life in fundamental ways. The record of this effort of urban transformation is mixed. In the short run the accomplishments of the new government were impressive. Many seemingly insuperable obstacles and immutable behavior patterns were overcome. In the long run, though, the difficulties of managing Chinese urban life gave rise to new problems and crises that organizational skill and ideological zeal alone could not resolve. In the process much of the popular goodwill accumulated as a result of early accomplishments was dissipated, leaving a sense of crisis and frustrated expectations as urbanites looked back over the record of more than three decades.

Conveying the human impact of drastic social change is never an easy matter, and this is particularly the case in dealing with contemporary China. Human reactions are inherently a subjective realm, recollections of earlier events are blurred and distorted, and most of the available sources of information are biased and unrepresentative. Then there is simply the matter of the diversity of the urban landscape. The experience of people in Peking and Shanghai has been different from that in Canton or Chungking, and the experience of people in county and commune towns even more different. Intellectuals have perceived events differently from cadres, workers, students, and soldiers, and people with overseas ties, Christians, Moslems, Long March veterans, and housewives all have had experiences that distinguish them from other urbanites. Furthermore, given the dramatic lurches in policies and campaigns in post-1949 China, it turns out that cohort differences are dramatic as well – people who were in school or who started work in different periods or even separated by only a year or two have often had quite different life experiences. A general account such as this cannot hope to present all of this diversity accurately, but an attempt will be made to discuss general trends and impressions about Chinese urban life, with a focus on the larger cities and occasional efforts to note the diversity of reactions of urban groups. In its attempt to describe popular feelings, this chapter is specifically intended not to focus on the reactions of the highly educated and urban elites. Insofar as possible, its aim is to see events from the standpoint of the urban *"lao-pai-hsing"* – "old hundred surnames," or, in other words, ordinary urbanites such as workers, shop clerks, students, technicians, and others.[1]

The Chinese Communists were not content to manage Chinese cities as they were. Although there have been important fluctuations over time, certain general orientations and policies in regard to cities can be identified. Chinese cities were seen as imbued with a number of negative features: They were based on capitalist property relationships and market exchanges; they were noted for glaring inequalities, conspicuous consumption, poverty, begging, unemployment, and slum conditions; they were subject to runaway inflation; the children of well-off families had considerable advantages in education and other realms; foreign control and cultural influence were centered there; urban bureaucrats were unresponsive to popular needs and often arbitrary and corrupt as well; crime,

1 This chapter draws on a number of kinds of information about urban life. First come the impressions gained from several stints of interviewing people who have left China for Hong Kong, and particularly from the most recent project, which has produced a monograph, Martin King Whyte and William L. Parish, *Urban life in contemporary China*. Second come the personal accounts published by a variety of people, Chinese and foreigners, who have lived in urban areas during the three decades, which will be cited later where appropriate. These sources are supplemented by the Chinese press, short stories and plays, and the secondary literature on China. Several types of sources often agree in regard to many of the themes stressed in this chapter, but still it is recognized that many points are impressionistic and debatable. The author wishes to thank the Center for Asian and Pacific Studies at the University of Hawaii, which provided a faculty fellowship that enabled him to carry out the research for this chapter. Thanks also to Stephen Uhalley, Donald Klein, Wei Zhangling, and my fellow volume authors for revision suggestions, not all of which could be incorporated.

prostitution, drug addiction, and secret society graft were endemic; cities did not serve rural needs well; and materialism, cynicism, and alienation were widespread.

The Chinese Communist Party (CCP) was determined to change the character of China's cities in fundamental ways, and this involved much more than simply a shift from capitalism to socialism. China's new leaders wanted to remake cities into places characterized by traits opposite to those just listed – into stable, production-oriented, egalitarian, Spartan, highly organized, cohesive, and economically secure places with low levels of crime, corruption, unemployment, and other urban evils. They also wanted to reorient cities to serve rural needs so as to reduce the "gap between town and country." This effort implied, in part, trying to limit the rate of urbanization generally, and in particular trying to control the growth of the largest, primarily coastal, cities while fostering growth mostly in small and medium-sized cities in the interior.[2]

China's new leaders expected progress toward these goals to lead to a citizenry that was involved, supportive, optimistic, and willing to sacrifice to contribute to the general change effort. Although the evaluation of the prevailing nature of Chinese urban society was decidedly negative, it would be misleading to simply characterize the CCP as "anti-urban." The CCP elite recognized the dual nature of Chinese cities – as both the focal points of many social evils but also the absolutely indispensable loci of economic and technological progress in the future. To mix our metaphors, the problem they faced was thus how to avoid "killing the goose that laid the golden eggs" while still making it over into a socialist swan. As already noted, in spite of considerable initial successes, the task of transforming, utilizing, and controlling China's cities proved to be no easy matter.

THE EARLY YEARS, 1949–1956

The job of consolidating control over urban areas and gaining popular support was made easier than expected in part because of the disorderly

---

2 China differed from many colonial societies in not having much of its urban population concentrated in a "primal" port city oriented toward foreign trade, but instead a fairly even distribution of urban places from small to large. The treaty port era, however, had produced a disproportionate growth of these foreign-oriented cities, and particularly of Shanghai, and led to a desire by the CCP to redress the balance somewhat. See Clifton Pannell, "Recent growth in China's urban system," in Laurence J. C. Ma and Edward Hanten, eds., *Urban development in modern China*, 91–113. At the time of the 1953 census 13.2 percent of the Chinese population was classified as urban, and fewer than 8 percent of China's urbanites were living in her largest city, Shanghai. (Typical figures for low-income countries are between approximately 20 percent and 40 percent.) See Morris Ullman, "Cities of mainland China: 1953–1959," in Gerald Breese, ed., *The city in newly developing countries*, 81–103.

conditions that prevailed during the last years of Nationalist rule. The story is by now a familiar one – of official corruption, incompetence, and brutality, and of runaway inflation, crime, and other disorders removing whatever portion of "the mandate of heaven" the Nationalists retained from the Anti-Japanese War period. By the time the CCP swept into the cities from mid-1948 onward, the urban mood was not uniform, but still a general eagerness for change and improvement existed. Many of the most ardent supporters of the Kuomintang (KMT) and those who had the most to lose and had the resources to do so left for Taiwan or for Hong Kong or points overseas. Some other urbanites of more humble means fled to the hills for a time, out of fear of their new rulers – a fear reinforced by rumors of the CCP's communizing wives, destroying the family, forcing Moslems to eat pork, and committing other barbarities. On the other hand some urbanites, particularly among students and radical intellectuals, anxiously awaited the chance to greet the arrival of the People's Liberation Army (PLA). Most urbanites, however, avoided both extremes, and awaited the change of regime with resignation and a wait-and-see attitude. Many felt that their new rulers could not be any worse than the Nationalists, but they nevertheless worried about how the change would affect them and their loved ones. A common response when the PLA troops started to arrive was to lock doors, shutter windows, and bury family heirlooms, assuming that some looting would be unavoidable. Many urban dwellers anxiously peeked out at the occupying troops from behind their shuttered windows and only felt safe to venture out after a day or so of cautious observation of the changed scene.

The initial reaction of Chinese urbanites after the brief interlude of fear was almost uniformly one of pleasant surprise. The PLA had clearly trained its troops well in how to make a positive impression, and particular caution seems to have been shown in taking over the largest cities. City dwellers accustomed to the arrogant and undisciplined behavior of the defeated Nationalist troops found that the PLA soldiers presented a very different image. Accounts from this period are filled with anecdotes conveying incredulity and gratitude at seeing soldiers politely asking urbanites for directions, helping civilians with chores, refusing or paying for food and other items offered them, and pitching in to perform manual-labor tasks. Even one bitter anti-Communist American priest who was imprisoned and then expelled after twenty-three years in China stated that these were "by far the finest and best disciplined troops I have seen in China."[3] The reactions of urbanites were not uniformly respectful toward the PLA, however, for almost immediately "yokel stories" about

3 Mark Tennien, *No secret is safe*, 64.

the behavior of rural recruits began to circulate. The favorite was the tale
of a soldier who thought a Western-style toilet was a device for washing
rice and promptly flushed away his ration. Indeed, the contrast between
peasant soldiers and their urban environment was so striking that one
journalist in China's most cosmopolitan city used the image of "Martians
in Shanghai."[4] The effect of such stories and humor was probably to help
humanize the occupying troops as well-intentioned, even if unsophisti-
cated, fellows.

Other elements in the CCP's urban takeover helped to smooth the transition. Particularly important was the policy of initial leniency promoted
under the "New Democracy" slogan. Although the Nationalists had
spread rumors of the streets running with the blood of victims of the new
government, the CCP hastened to reassure the populace that only selected
groups, particularly those closely associated with the KMT elite, would
become targets of coercion, and that the rest of the population would all
have valuable places in the new society. Initially these promises seemed to
be honored, again particularly in the largest cities, with honors and status
showered on many prominent non-communists and forgiveness shown
even toward some known KMT informers and other hostile elements.
Later on, of course, this leniency would evaporate, but by then control
over urban areas had been consolidated.

Perhaps no impression of the change in regimes was stronger than the
sense of a bewildering variety of new experiences to which people were
exposed. Almost immediately university students, intellectuals, and workers in key enterprises began participating in a whole range of novel activities. There were frequent meetings, political study, manual labor stints,
and campaign mobilizations – the hallmark features of the new regime.
People had to familiarize themselves with the ideas of what to them were
obscure philosophers – not only Marx and Engels, but also Kant and
Hegel. They were organized to discuss the theory of evolution and to
accept the idea that men were descended from apes (not a novel idea to
students and intellectuals, but decidedly so to many other urbanites). A
whole new set of phrases and political jargon had to be mastered, and an
enthusiasm for keeping diaries to record one's thoughts was fostered
among students. Young people in particular participated in demonstrations and marches, learned and performed the *yang-ko* harvest dance
then in official vogue, and even for a period engaged in an enthusiasm for
organized announcing of current events and news from rooftops.

4 The phrase is used by Robert Guillain in Otto van der Sprenkel, Robert Guillain, and Michael
Lindsay, *New China: three views*, 84.

Many kinds of activities awaited those willing to be mobilized. Recruits were organized in 1949 into "southbound work teams" that would accompany the PLA into other cities and help establish control there. Students and others were organized to clean urban drains, renovate slum areas, repair river embankments, and in other ways participate in the effort to improve the urban environment. Subsequently, large numbers of college students, intellectuals, and others went to selected villages for a few weeks to observe how land reform was progressing under the guidance of teams of cadres who had been mobilized earlier. Teams of urbanites also fanned out through urban areas to combat inflation by pressuring people to buy bonds and keeping an eye out for speculators. Similarly, drama troupes were organized to put on skits about the evils of the old marriage customs and to help propagate the new 1950 marriage law. Others joined the effort to teach literacy to their illiterate neighbors. The involvement of China in the Korean War in late 1950 brought with it a whole new range of similar activities – selling bonds, writing "pen pal" letters to soldiers at the front, and organizing drama troupes to tour factories and mines performing patriotic skits. Even Buddhist monks and nuns were mobilized to join in the patriotic demonstrations of the period, much to the amusement of those who noticed their ineptness at marching.

Reactions to this hectic range of new activities varied. Some were skeptical of the value of many of these projects and noted, for example, that students in these years spent too much time outside of their classrooms to learn much. And some of the new activities occasioned considerable conflict between friends and within families. For example, some parents were quite anxious and even angry to learn that their children (particularly their daughters) wanted to join the southbound work teams or the PLA. Others were upset when their offspring used the new marriage policies to reject a marital prospect chosen by their parents.

Not all of the changes were popular. For example, the authorities decided, for reasons that were never clearly explained, that all dogs had to be eliminated from urban areas, and sent out people who grabbed many pets on the street and killed them, causing anguish to the families that had owned them.[5] A revolutionary opera dealing with popular suffering like *The white-haired girl* found a tremendous audience response wherever it was performed, but some efforts in these years to present reformed versions of traditional operas aroused popular hostility. Derk Bodde noted an instance in Peking during the first year in which the audience viewing

---

5 Various explanations of the dog-killing episode were offered, including sanitation problems, dogs as carriers of disease, and the waste of food that ended up in the mouths of dogs instead of humans. A revival of dog raising in later years led to a new campaign to kill dogs in Peking in 1983.

a traditional play "cleansed of its feudal elements" shouted angrily and refused to leave the theater, pelting with melon seeds an official spokesman sent out to pacify them.[6] Many urbanites simply found it difficult, at least at first, to adapt to the new styles of behavior demanded of them – active involvement in, rather than avoidance of, politics; bluntly expressed criticisms of others, rather than conflicts hidden behind the appearance of harmony; and so forth.

On the other hand, many urbanites found these new activities exhilarating and rewarding. This was particularly the case for students, younger cadres, and some poorly educated urbanites. William Sewell describes the mood produced by what would appear to be a mundane and even menial task – urban drain cleaning: "The day was one not to be forgotten: The joy of united effort, the sense of accomplishment, the excitement of noise and colour."[7] Sewell also describes the gratification felt by workers and service personnel in the college in which he was teaching in Szechwan when they were included in political and administrative discussions and decision making along with faculty members and college administrators. He noted that a mah-jong–playing, nagging mother-in-law and the college gateman were transformed into enthusiastic participants in the new political activities, and he observed, "One of the unexpected facts of the new way of life was that it brought joy into colourless lives."[8]

The positive impression made by the new government was due not simply to involving people in many new activities, but also to many other factors. Particularly important was the impression that the new government was much more efficient and effective in getting things done. Problems long assumed to be endemic to Chinese society were quickly brought under control or eliminated – opium addiction, begging, prostitution, pocket-picking, secret society extortion, and so forth. The tactics used in dealing with such phenomena tended to follow a set pattern. First a period of leniency was declared during which those involved were pressured to register with the authorities and begin to repent the errors of their ways. When through a period of political study and mutual accusations the authorities felt that they had acquired enough information on those involved, a sudden shift was made toward proscription of the activity in question. Beggars and prostitutes were rounded up and assigned to "honest labor" or sent back to their villages, and anyone caught en-

6 Derk Bodde, *Peking diary: a year of revolution*, 235.
7 William Sewell, *I stayed in China*, 100.
8 Ibid., 107. A decidedly less enthusiastic picture of the effect of the change of regime on student life is given in Maria Yen, *The umbrella garden: a picture of student life in Red China*. But even Yen's account (dealing with Peking University) makes it clear that the majority of students were responding enthusiastically to the new demands placed on them.

gaging in such activities after the ban was liable to arrest and incarceration, with some leading recalcitrants executed to intimidate others. Within a year or two such tactics had produced dramatic changes.

The signs of government efficacy were visible in many other ways. Although skeptics had doubted the ability of the new government to manage complex cities, they soon found that electric power, coal, food, and other essentials were supplied more consistently than in the past. Inflation proved more difficult to combat, but by 1951 it had been brought under control, in spite of China's involvement in the Korean War. In the large cities some of the worst slum areas were renovated, new apartment blocks for workers began to be built, and in general an atmosphere of effective urban administration arose. Campaigns against "squeeze" (petty bribery) began, and rules requiring receipts and vigorous inspection systems rapidly changed the accustomed ways of transacting business. Perhaps an understandable amount of exaggeration is contained in the comment of an English observer on the immediate impact of the changeover in Shanghai: "On 24 May you could bribe everyone in Shanghai. On 26 May you could bribe no one – for perhaps the first time in a hundred years."[9] The enforcement of standard-price policies in stores and a new ban against tipping were similarly effective. Even the manner of pedicab drivers, described by observers as the last of the Chinese "rugged individualists," was altered – from trampling over each other in the competition for customers and haggling over fares to taking turns and adapting to the new standardized fare system. One common reaction to such changes is visible in the statement of a Chinese faculty member at Yenching University in 1951: "At last we have a government such as I have yearned for for years, a government that does not simply talk but gets things done."[10] An English missionary professor was similarly impressed, observing, "The increase in the general efficiency of life in Peking was ... almost unbelievable to a person versed in the ways of old China."[11]

This growing respect for the new government was heightened not just by its efficiency but also by the style of the new leaders, who were generally seen as more hardworking, less corrupt, and perhaps more accessible than their predecessors. Accounts from these early years mention surprise at seeing cadres working diligently at their desks rather than dozing, and also at their working late into the night, as well as engaging in the hectic round of new activities prescribed by the government – political study, group singing, and so forth. Many members of the population were

9 David Middleditch, quoted in Noel Barber, *The fall of Shanghai*, 159.
10 Quoted in Ralph Lapwood and Nancy Lapwood, *Through the Chinese revolution*, 69.
11 Ibid., 124.

impressed by the fact that old cadres remained on a supply system during the early years, rather than receiving a salary, so that they did not appear to be gaining materially from their service. An English observer described being struck at meeting an official from the Tientsin Public Security Bureau in the Peking train station and learning later that he had waited all afternoon for a train that was not sold out and finally ended up taking standing room back to Tientsin. The observer (Otto van der Sprenkel) remarked, "Such refusal on the part of an official to trade on his rank, and procure a seat by the simple method of having a few other passengers thrown off the train ... is the best propaganda in the world for showing the ordinary people what their new leaders and servants are like."[12]

Even the top leaders took pains to portray themselves as living Spartan lives and as being accessible to the public, although in fact many of their activities were not publicly visible. But through inspections tours of villages and factories, brief manual labor stints, and frequent meetings with "representatives of the masses" they helped to convey the desired impression. Many young cadres who served in the capital in the 1950s were impressed at seeing high state officials dancing, swimming, and engaging in other leisure activities in a relaxed fashion alongside junior personnel. Ralph Lapwood sums up the generally positive impression received of the cadres (*kan-pu*): "In the uncalculating service of the kanpu lies the secret of the success of the People's Government in enlisting for effective action ... the Chinese people in their hundreds of millions."[13]

Such views contain a degree of exaggeration produced by the contrast with the behavior of officials before 1949, and in reality ambition and self-interest were not alien to the new cadres. Accounts we have from inside the new bureaucracy in these years paint a somewhat different picture. One cadre who came to Wuhan with one of the southbound work teams describes his colleagues as waging "guerrilla warfare" over office space and furnishings, and others describe bureaucratic infighting and complaints over status as being endemic to state offices in these years.[14] Additionally, the existence of the supply system did not mean that cadres were all living on equal subsistence provisions. The supply system was graded, with three levels of dining privileges, access to limousines according to rank, and so forth, so that status competition was by no means absent. Still, the series of cadre rectification campaigns staged in the early years persuaded at least large parts of the urban public that the new

12 Van der Sprenkel et al., *New China: three views*, 8.
13 Lapwood, *Through the Chinese revolution*, 61.
14 Liu Shaw-tong, *Out of Red China*, 109; see also Esther Cheo Ying, *Black country girl in Red China*.

government was determined to deal strictly with cadre corruption and discipline problems as soon as they arose.[15] The overall impression of the new leadership was positive.

The appeal to nationalistic sentiments was also used to considerable effect during the early years. Formal extraterritoriality had ended in 1943, but in 1949 foreign ownership and influence were still considerable in China's major cities. Within a few years Western influence was dramatically reduced and only partially replaced by Soviet influence. Initially, foreigners in at least the largest cities benefited from the overall policy of leniency, and the complexity of the urban situation and concern for diplomatic recognition urged caution. But right from the start changes began to be made – street signs and official notices that had been in English now had to be in Chinese; the same change occurred in the trade names printed on manufactured products, and court hearings and other official functions were all conducted in Chinese. Foreigners were told that they could continue to live and work in China as long as they did not violate the laws and policies of the new government. How true this assurance might have proved to be we will never know, for the onset of the Korean War in 1950 changed the atmosphere considerably. Many foreigners were pressured to leave or were arrested and subsequently expelled, and a paranoia about espionage made the lives of those remaining uncomfortable. Some foreigners who wanted to leave had bureaucratic obstacles put in their way and were given to understand that being made to wait was part of an effort of China's new rulers to demonstrate that they were now complete masters on their own soil.

After 1950 pressure mounted across the board to reduce Western and particularly American influence. Hollywood movies were criticized and later banned, with Soviet movies as well as Chinese productions eventually taking their place. Western clothing and styles of dress were criticized, as were slit skirts and other "bourgeois" Chinese styles of apparel, and a more uniform wearing of what then was known variously as a Sun Yat-sen, liberation, or Lenin suit, and later became known abroad as the Mao jacket, began to be adopted. Within a short period people packed away or sold their high heels, furs, U.S. Army surplus jackets, and other out-of-favor items (some of which were snapped up by the new waves of Soviet visitors), and cosmetics began to disappear from female faces. In some instances individuals were directly criticized for their "bourgeois" dress, but in many others they simply anticipated the mood of the new society and fell into step on their own. In political study meetings and

15 An assessment of these early campaigns is offered in Frederick C. Teiwes, *Elite discipline in China: coercive and persuasive approaches to rectification, 1950–1953.*

published self-criticisms Western-influenced Chinese confessed to having felt that "the American moon is brighter than the Chinese moon" and pledged to correct such mistaken views.

The measures taken against foreign influence were not all simply symbolic. Many Western-owned businesses were forced out or taken over, hospitals, schools and other organizations financed or run by foreigners were nationalized, and in general Chinese assumed the leadership roles in organizations of all kinds. In 1950 the government began its "Three Self" Campaign designed to get Christian churches to cut their foreign ties and accept the government's leadership if they wanted to survive. In some cases extreme tactics were used to incite hostility against foreigners. In many different cities Catholic nuns had run foundling homes for abandoned infants and orphans. After 1950 such homes were charged with having willfully neglected and even murdered and dismembered Chinese babies. Newspapers printed lurid pictures of the disinterred bones of supposed victims, and nuns were hauled off for struggle sessions before angry mobs in sports stadiums.[16]

In general Western control and influence in China were dramatically reduced by such measures. One Indian observer commented that by 1952 British influence in China had been reduced to about what it had been before the Opium War 110 years earlier, with a base in Hong Kong, a few consuls, but no ambassador residing in Peking.[17] Reactions to the anti-Western assault of these years differed. Many Chinese Christians and others long associated with foreigners were severely threatened, and some were even incarcerated or executed. But it appears that most urbanites, and particularly ordinary workers and former peasants who had not benefited much from the foreign presence, felt pride in these changes. They saw their government for the first time in more than a century able to stand up to foreigners and end their special privileges in China. The Korean War helped to heighten such sentiments, with most urbanites swept up in the patriotic zeal of the period and proud of their country's showing against the more modernized UN forces. The political unity achieved by the CCP, initial progress in economic reconstruction, and the successful assault on foreign power and privileges all promoted a sense of national pride that the government did its best to amplify and reinforce.

These years were also, of course, the ones of "leaning to one side" by following the Soviet model, but the Soviet presence does not seem to have significantly compromised the new mood of national pride. Some

16 The account of one such incident, in Canton in 1951, is presented in Tennien, *No secret is safe*, 26ff. Resistance among Catholics to the enforced rupture of ties to the Vatican continued in Shanghai and some other locales until about 1960.
17 Frank Moraes, *Report on Mao's China*, 170.

Chinese were suspicious of Soviet motives and of such actions as the removal of industrial facilities from Manchuria after 1945. They felt that copying the Soviet Union in such detail – right down to substituting the Soviet-style five-point grading system in schools for the hundred-point system followed earlier – was ill-advised. But the government argued that Soviet advice and advisers were being invited to China rather than being imposed by force, and that it was only proper to learn from the Soviet "elder brother," since in their Marxist view "the Soviet present is China's future."

Public reactions varied to the thousands of Soviet advisers who began to flood into Peking's Friendship Hotel and similar establishments in other cities. Here age seems to have made an important difference. Those who were students at the time recall being inspired by the heroes and heroines in Soviet war novels translated during this period, and some adopted Russian nicknames and wrote to pen pals in the Soviet Union. Many cried when they heard the news of Stalin's death. Even many mature Chinese developed close relationships with individual Soviet advisers and were impressed by some of the early measures adopted by the Soviet government to create a good impression, such as not allowing visiting Soviet advisers to ride in rickshaws. But among many older Chinese these new Soviet visitors were looked upon with suspicion or even disgust. In spite of the public relations measures adopted, Chinese quickly noticed that many of the visitors seemed quite "bourgeois" in their style of dress and in their behavior, with their wives, in particular, showing a strong preference for tourism, shopping, and idle chatter.[18] Some of the Soviet advisers were perceived as arrogant and demanding, feeling it was natural for the Chinese to accept all of their advice and do things in the Soviet manner. In general, then, many of the actual representatives sent by the Soviet elder brother did not match the characters in the heroic novels very well.

In spite of such negative impressions of what one Chinese termed these Soviet "proletarian princes," the USSR was not seen as the threat to China's sovereignty that the West had once been. So Soviet ties did not detract in major ways from the new government's ability to make skillful use of patriotic feelings. One Chinese journalist from Hong Kong, who was imprisoned for several years after 1952 and then prevented from leaving China until 1957, nevertheless had the following reaction to viewing the 1 October parade in 1956: "I must admit that I was even choked with unspeakable feelings – never before had I felt so proud to be Chinese."[19]

18 A vivid picture of this sort of behavior is given in Mikhail Klochko, *Soviet scientist in Red China.*
19 Eric Chou, *A man must choose*, 223. The phrase "proletarian princes" also comes from ibid., 234.

Perhaps no influence on support of the new government was more important, however, than perceptions of chances for economic security and improvement. The CCP came to power when conditions were very insecure, of course. Because of inflation a cup of coffee cost more than 3 million yuan in Shanghai (and these were the supposedly "inflation-proof" new "gold yuan") and in a month a janitor in Szechwan earned only as much as it cost to send three airmail letters to Europe.[20] Part of the change came from bringing the ruinous inflation under control, but not all of it. Perhaps even more important was the way the new regime opened up mobility opportunities. The need to replace departed personnel, staff the burgeoning bureaucracy, and supply skills for the coming industrialization drive led to a wide range of personnel recruitment efforts – short-term training courses, "revolutionary universities," cadre schools, and so forth. Regular schools were also rapidly expanded, and as they were nationalized tuitions were reduced sharply, so that in large cities universal primary school enrollment was approached. Thus, many young and ambitious people saw doors opening up for them as a result of the change of regimes. Even peasants were drawn into the quest for mobility. The authorities tried repeatedly during the 1950s to disperse rural migrants back to their native villages, but up until nearly the end of the decade these efforts were not very successful, and many peasants managed to get a foothold in the city during this period and become urban workers.[21]

The new job opportunities were accompanied by a gradual standardization of regulations affecting wages, working conditions, and fringe benefits for those working in public enterprises (and even in large private ones). Initially the government vacillated on the issue of wage increases, first encouraging demands against capitalist owners, then pressuring workers to content themselves with less in order to keep their firms in business. But the improvements made in the food-supply and -distribution system and efforts to keep prices down impressed urbanites. Even with stable wages they were able to buy higher-quality grains (rice and wheat rather than corn or barley) and such items as fish much more regularly than in the late 1940s. With the general wage increases introduced in

---

20 The coffee price is noted in Barber, *The fall of Shanghai*, 134; the janitor's salary, in Sewell, *I stayed in China*, 38.

21 One estimate states that 20 million or more peasants migrated to the cities in the period 1949–57. See Etsuzo Onoye, "Regional distribution of urban population in China," *The developing economies*, 8.1 (1970), 92–122. Recent Chinese figures claim a net in-migration in these years of 18.5 million. See Chang Tse-hou and Ch'en Yü-kuang, "The relationship between population structure and economic development," *Chung-kuo she-hui k'o-hsueh*, no. 4 (1981), cited in Leo Orleans, "China's urban population: concepts, conglomerations, and concerns," in U.S. Congress, Joint Economic Committee, *China under the four modernizations*, 1.279.

1956, confidence in an improving standard of living increased.[22] In addition, a system of fringe benefits was implemented, including medical insurance, disability pay, paid maternity leave, pensions, and so forth, which provided a degree of security generally unknown to most employed people earlier (although initially many sectors of the labor force were not fully covered by such benefits). In general, an optimism about improved living conditions and mobility opportunities prevailed during this period.

The improved economic conditions and widening availability of fringe benefits paradoxically contributed to a trend that CCP policy was expressly designed to avoid: an increasingly privileged position of urbanites relative to the peasants who had brought the revolution to victory. In the cities, the state took the responsibility for providing the "welfare package" of benefits that socialism was seen as promising, but in the countryside the burden of providing any such benefits fell on collective units and the peasants themselves, rather than on the state. As a result, much less improvement occurred. In general, after 1949 the gap between Chinese town and countryside in incomes, access to consumer goods, cultural amenities, and simply secure jobs and welfare benefits widened, making urbanites increasingly aware, and peasants increasingly envious of, the advantages of urban life. Only in housing could it perhaps be argued that rural dwellers had the advantage, as by the late 1970s the typical housing space of peasants had expanded to close to three times that available to the average urbanite.[23] But even in this realm most urbanites could rent their housing for minimal cost – often 5 percent of their incomes or less – whereas peasants had to finance home construction and upkeep out of their own pockets.

Of course, there was downward mobility as well, with former urban elites losing many of their advantages and in some cases their lives. However, several factors kept such downward mobility from negating the impression of improved opportunities in the public mind. For one thing, those who lost out appeared to be fewer in number than those who gained, and some of their advantages had long been resented. But in many cases their fall was also softened somewhat – capitalists received

---

22 One Western effort to check the official claim that the urban standard of living had improved even in comparison with the 1930s concludes that there was a real improvement. See Bruce Reynolds, "Changes in the standard of living of Shanghai industrial workers, 1930–1973," in Christopher Howe, ed., *Shanghai: revolution and development in an Asian metropolis.*

23 In 1982 a figure of 10 square meters of living space per capita for peasants was published. (See *Beijing Review*, 20 [1982], 8.) A few years earlier, in 1978, the urban living space per capita was claimed to have been only 3.6 square meters. See Zhou Jin, "Housing China's 900 million people," *Beijing Review*, 48 (1979), 18.

interest payments on the official assessments of their capital after socialist transformation in 1956 (as well as good salaries, in many cases), some well-paid personages had "retained wage" levels set for them that were higher than the new standardized wage ranks, and the curtailing of income from house rents, royalties, and other nonwage sources was gradual rather than abrupt.

Perhaps more important, the offspring of capitalists and intellectuals still benefited disproportionately from the new opportunities made available in the 1950s. In spite of the official stance in favor of workers and peasants, the new government's need for highly skilled personnel was so great that urban students – who in these years tended to come from well-off families – were encouraged to pursue their studies and accept good positions in the new order. As long as they were willing to follow the new policies and make ritualized criticisms of the "bourgeois" values of their parents (and as long as their parents stayed out of serious political trouble), they could anticipate rewarding career prospects awaiting them. During the 1950s social relations within schools were not permeated by concern for class background labels, as they came to be later on. Students tended to form friendships with others who had similar grades or personal interests, rather than to base such ties on class background or political factors, and in general there was no perception of tight competition for a few desirable opportunities. For a period in the 1950s there were, in fact, more college places available each year than there were graduates of upper-middle schooling who could fill them.[24] Well into the 1960s, offspring of what were in theory the "bad classes" (capitalists, merchants, etc.) were still able to do better on average than the children from working-class families.[25]

In general, then, there was much about these early years that made urbanites three decades later look back on them nostalgically. Order had been restored, foreign privileges had been ended, economic conditions were improving, the government seemed efficient and concerned, and even the danger of crime seemed to have been sharply reduced. People who were in school in those years, in particular, remember them as rewarding and exciting – as filled with studying hard to make China strong, taking up hobbies, going on school hikes, reading heroic Soviet and Chinese novels, joining propaganda teams that traveled to villages and factories, and taking pride in the joy their achievements in school

24 According to Robert Taylor, *Education and university enrolment policies in China, 1949–1971*, 32, from 1953 to 1956 there were 15 percent more university places than upper middle school graduates.
25 Evidence on the continuing advantages of "bourgeois" children up to the Cultural Revolution is presented in Whyte and Parish, *Urban life in contemporary China*, ch. 3.

brought to their parents. It was an optimistic period in which many things seemed possible for China as a nation and for the lives of her urban residents, especially the young.

It would be misleading, however, to conclude that the initial doubts and skepticism of urbanites turned into unrestrained popular enthusiasm for the new government. From the first there were aspects of the new order that at least many urbanites saw as ominous. For one thing the new government implemented a much higher degree of regimentation and control over the population than its predecessor had, with much more penetration into the intimate details of urban lives and more pressure to change behavior and relationships. This degree of regimentation extended itself gradually and differentially after the period of initial leniency. Press control and censorship took effect within days after the changeover, but American movies continued to be shown until 1951. College students were almost immediately organized for political study, labor, and public marches, but they were still able to choose their own roommates and the courses they wished to study. By the 1951-52 school year, they began to have roommates assigned and course assignments had become mandatory, and a year or so later the centralized system of university assignment and subsequent job placement had taken effect. Workers in state-run textile mills began to be organized in officially sponsored trade unions in the initial weeks, but those in small workshops or operating as individual craftsmen and peddlers were only loosely supervised and organized until the mid-1950s. In urban neighborhoods life did not change dramatically at first, but by 1954 the standardized structure of residents' committees had begun to have an impact on everyone's activities.[26]

Although the changes in some sectors were gradual, by the mid-1950s an organizational system had begun to emerge that made it possible to control and mobilize the citizenry much more effectively than before. The building blocks of pre-1949 cities – guilds, native-place associations, clans, secret societies, neighborhood temple associations, and so forth – had either been eliminated or transformed. In their place a new urban infrastructure had been built that was firmly under Party control. In each urban neighborhood, residents' committees were organized under the leadership of ward government offices and police stations. These committees both organized useful service activities, such as lane cleanup efforts, bicycle repair stands, and first-aid stations, and also exerted control over the lives of local residents – organizing them for political indoctrination meetings, checking for unregistered individuals or deviant activity, or-

---

26 A vivid account of the gradual change at this level is presented in Shirley Wood, *A street in China.*

ganizing nighttime security patrols, and in later years pressuring families
to send their children to the countryside and to limit their fertility. The
other major pillar of the new organizational system became the work
units (*tan-wei*), which took it as their task to organize the lives of their
employees both on and off the job. Large work units not only provided
housing, medical clinics, and other resources for their employees but also
organized political study, supervised leisure activities, gave approval for
marriages and divorces, supervised released convicts, and engaged in other
social control activities similar to those of the residents' committees.

In addition to work units and neighborhoods, many urbanites also
came under the supervision of a wide range of new "mass associations"
that supervised professional and leisure-time activities – the Communist
Youth League, the Women's Federation, trade unions, businessmen's
associations, the Writer's Union, independent Christian churches, and so
forth. More and more of the vital resources needed for life were allocated
through these new bureaucratic systems rather than being distributed by
the market or by individual or voluntary association efforts. For example,
the 1st Five-Year Plan set in motion a process by which jobs would be
bureaucratically assigned, essentially for life, and the labor market began
to disappear. This period also set in motion the transition to a form of
urban life in which strict rationing (supervised by work units and residents' committees) controlled access to basic food and consumer items,
most housing was taken over by work units or city agencies, the private
practice of medicine was eliminated, and urbanites were increasingly dependent on authorities in the new bureaucratic structures controlled by
the CCP. As in bureaucratic systems elsewhere, the result was that individual preferences often lost out, for example, when spouses would find
themselves assigned to work in different cities and would have to put up
with living apart and seeing each other only on brief annual vacation
visits.

The transformations in the urban organizational system had a number
of important consequences. For one thing the sights and sounds of
Chinese cities began to change. The standardization and bureaucratization of commerce gradually eliminated the myriad trades and traders that
had always provided color to streets and back alleys – roving peddlers,
pot menders, letter writers, seal carvers, trinket sellers, and so forth. With
the state taking over the responsibility for providing for the needs of
urbanites, it was no longer necessary to beckon customers with colorful
signs and distinctive whistles or cries.

The status hierarchy was also transformed in important ways. Among
the elite, capitalists, merchants, and intellectuals lost status; and farther

down in the pecking order, groups such as service workers, peddlers, and ritual specialists also suffered declines. The new status hierarchy was dominated by high-ranking cadres (*kao-chi kan-pu*) and military officers, with high-ranking intellectuals and technical specialists next in line but firmly under the control of these bureaucratic elites. Workers, technicians, and others connected to industrial production gained in prestige, while a variety of new pariah groups (class enemies, bad class origin elements, controlled elements) were consigned to the bottom of the heap. Income and educational credentials became less important in where you stood in this new urban hierarchy, while bureaucratic rank and political credentials, such as Party membership, became increasingly important. But perhaps almost as important as this vertical pecking order was the differentiation among work units and administrative "systems" (*hsi-t'ung*). Some large and powerful bureaucracies, such as the military and the railways, could provide their members with a wide range of benefits and privileges, while smaller and less resourceful units, such as primary schools or neighborhood factories, were much less able to fill the needs of their personnel. One's status in the new urban structure therefore depended on one's work unit as well as on one's rank.

By 1956 China's unruly cities had come increasingly under the control of a new bureaucratic system, confounding the skeptics. Observers acquainted with urban life before 1949 were struck by the way even long-standing but relatively trivial forms of behavior, such as jaywalking and spitting on the street, seemed to be giving way under the new controls. One keen observer in Peking observed presciently in 1955, "This regime is probably the first in history which could officially adopt birth control as a compulsory measure, and make sure that its orders will be universally obeyed."[27]

This tight-knit organizational system helps to explain why what was in theory most major change in this period – the transition of the urban economy to socialist forms in 1955–56 – was in certain ways anticlimactic. Increasing state control over raw materials, markets, credit, and other resources; intimidation of capitalists and critics of socialism in the Five Antis Campaign of 1951–52 and the 1955 campaign against hidden counterrevolutionaries; and organizational pressure applied by trade unions and the Party-supervised Federation of Industry and Commerce – all

27 An unnamed observer quoted in Robert Guillain, *600 million Chinese*, 295. The observer goes on to describe how the residents' committee could fix birth quotas, give advice, and "keep an eye on married couples," and how the Agricultural Producers' Cooperatives (predecessors of people's communes) could distribute contraceptives in the villages and add the task of planning reproduction to that of planning agricultural production. All of these predictions came true in the 1970s.

produced a situation in which urban capitalists and merchants had little autonomy or room for maneuver left by 1955. When the campaign for socialist transformation was accelerated in the latter part of that year, it proceeded with little visible resistance, and much more rapidly than originally planned. In an extreme case, the whole campaign for socialist transformation was declared completed in Peking in January 1956 after only ten days.

The socialist transformation campaign, however, also revealed serious drawbacks of the potent organizational system the CCP had constructed. For one thing, it was easier to mobilize the population for change than to make the resulting new organizations work efficiently. The speedup of socialist transformation resulted in many cases in "paper successes," with factories and shops declared socialist even before full inventories of their capital and goods had been taken and before new systems of bookkeeping, trained managerial and accounting personnel, and other things needed to make socialist enterprises work were in place. So months of subsequent work were required to dispel the confusion before the reality began to approach the campaign slogans.

The impressive mobilizational skills of the Party also made it possible to introduce changes that were useless or even harmful. For example, during the "small leap" production campaign that followed socialist transformation in 1956, the enthusiasm for homegrown solutions to China's problems led to such innovations as a "double-wheeled, double-bladed plow" and a birth control technique that required women to swallow large numbers of live tadpoles. Neither was a notable success. Although these particular innovations were quickly repudiated, the capacity of the system to override popular misgivings and press forward with new technology and organizational forms would be demonstrated on a much larger and more disastrous scale in the bigger leap that followed in 1958.

The authorities argued that the much more highly organized form of life they had introduced was needed to deal with China's many problems, and much of the population could appreciate this argument. Still, the result was to subject urbanites to increasingly tight control by very demanding authorities who were not subject to popular influence. People found that many cherished customs and patterns of behavior had to be altered to avoid running afoul of the new authorities. Gambling, attending Christian church services, reading Western novels, hiring a spirit medium, worshiping one's ancestors, and many other activities became surrounded by uncertainties – did they violate the new rules or not? The Chinese penchant for humor came up against the humorlessness of the authorities when it came to their own aims and programs, and individuals who had been ganged up on in group criticism sessions for a wisecrack or political joke soon learned to keep their humor in check. Now it was not just the few informers one had to be careful to avoid saying the wrong thing to, as before 1949, but most people outside of a few close friends and family members. (This constricting of communications, however, appears to have been more marked among cadres, intellectuals, and students than among workers and others of lower status. Workers were both less suspected of harboring deviant views and more likely to be excused, because of their low level of education, if they did.)

It is true, of course, that down through the centuries Chinese have recognized the need to adapt to the whims of their new rulers, whether this involved renouncing Buddhism, wearing a queue, or adopting the symbols of the "New Life Movement" (the 1930s effort by the Nationalists to foster moral regeneration). What was different about the situation after 1949 was simply the scope of the changes required and the organizational penetration that backed up the new demands. An old professor confided to William Sewell at the time of the changeover that things would be all right because Chinese do not become martyrs. "We have learnt from the bamboos. They bend in the wind; and when the wind ceases to blow they go upright again."[28] Yet scarcely a year later this same professor, distraught at not being able to adjust to the new society, hanged himself.

The tightening of official control coincided with the end of the initial leniency period and the use of coercion against a wide range of target individuals and groups. In the campaign to suppress counterrevolutionaries, the Three and Five Antis campaigns, the thought reform campaign, the campaign against Hu Feng sympathizers, and the effort to dig out hidden counterrevolutionaries, large numbers of people were subjected to political struggles, arrested, and executed. Officials and sympathizers of the Nationalists, secret society and religious cult leaders, capitalists, labor gang bosses, foreign and native priests, corrupt cadres, disaffected intellectuals, black marketeers, and simply those who made the mistake of publicly criticizing the new government found themselves in serious trouble. The large number of arrests filled the jails, makeshift jails had to be used to accommodate the overflow, and many of the targets were executed or disappeared, never to be heard from again.[29] Each major cam-

---

28 Sewell, *I stayed in China*, 53-54.

29 Wildly differing estimates have been presented on the number of people executed in China in the period 1949-52 nationally. (Separate estimates of urban executions are not available, and the land reform campaign in the countryside bulks large in these estimates.) They vary from "a few tens of thousands" (Lapwood, *Through the Chinese revolution*, 146) through 800,000 (up until 1953, from an unpublished version of Mao Tse-tung's 1957 speech "On the correct handling of

paign of this period also set off waves of suicides of those who had become, or feared they would become, a target. In spite of reassurances from officials of the new government that criticisms were welcomed and that coercion would be used only against a handful of class enemies, it soon became clear to all that one had to be extraordinarily careful not to earn the animus of the new authorities, and that if one did get into trouble, the penalties could be severe.

How did this tight regimentation and widespread coercion balance off in the minds of urbanites against the accomplishments of the new government? Again reactions obviously differed, and some groups were clearly antagonized or intimidated by the new order. But most urbanites were not particularly threatened by these developments, and many even warmly approved them. We have already noted that many accepted the need for tighter organization. Was not regimentation an acceptable price to pay for safe streets, stable currency, and a unified and strong country? Then, too, the government was fairly successful in convincing urbanites that most of the coercion was being applied selectively against those who truly deserved it. Many felt it was a good thing to cleanse society of evil people. The skill with which the authorities presented lurid tales of the wicked deeds of Japanese collaborators, Nationalist informers, secret society bosses, and even Catholic nuns generated public hostility and played upon resentments that already existed.

Still, many urbanites who were not members of special target groups did have disturbing experiences during these early years. For some it was a parent hauled off temporarily to jail on a trumped-up charge; for others it was a favorite teacher who became a target in the 1955 campaign against hidden counterrevolutionaries and subsequently disappeared; for still others it was an old friend driven to suicide by the new political pressures.[30] Such personal experiences caused agonizing internal reexamination of the nature of the new society that left nagging doubts underneath the general optimism and commitment. But even in such cases there were convenient rationalizations available to ease troubled minds. After all, Mao had long ago noted that "a revolution is not a dinner party," and in the general turmoil some mistakes were bound to be made. For many

contradictions among the people," as cited in *NYT*, 13 June 1957, p. 8), 2 million (Maurice Meisner, *Mao's China: a history of the People's Republic*, 81); 5 million (Jacques Guillermaz, *The Chinese Communist Party in power, 1949–1976*, 24), and on up to 15 million or so (Tennien, *No secret is safe*, 195; Richard L. Walker, "The human cost of communism in China," report to the Subcommittee on Internal Security of the U.S. Senate Judiciary Committee, 16).

30 Shirley Wood noted (in *A street in China*, 107–8) that "in Shanghai nearly everyone could boast of being at least distantly related to someone who had got a comeuppance to one degree or another since Liberation, and the government suppression of 'counter-revolutionaries'... had thrown certain sections of the population into consternation."

the suitable explanation was the one long familiar to dictatorial regimes – "if Mao only knew." Official policies and leadership could be seen as wise and benevolent, but the manifestly poorly trained and inadequately disciplined basic-level cadres who carried out the policies tended to make lots of mistakes and fall into "deviations" and abuses. Urbanites could hope that the reexamination stages that followed most major campaigns would correct whatever injustices had been done. Therefore, in spite of the fact that coercive measures were applied on a sweeping scale during these years, many urbanites still saw the period as relatively optimistic and even benign. They felt that much of the coercion was acceptable and even laudable, and that abuses were not systemic but were due to problems of implementation. So the considerable personal misery produced by official coercion during these years did not significantly undercut the public involvement and optimism generated by the new order.

THE MIDDLE YEARS, 1957–1965

The tempo of life in the early years varied. The years through 1952 were ones of novelty and disruption, with campaigns to remake society disturbing orderly work and study routines. From 1953 through 1956, with the ending of the Korean War and the launching of the 1st Five-Year Plan, the emphasis shifted much more toward mobilizing commitments to study and work productively to help build up the country economically, and "extracurricular" activities were cut to a minimum. In 1957 and then in the ensuing Great Leap Forward the tempo began to change back toward campaign mobilizations once again, and China was plunged into first a political and then an economic crisis. Still the spirit of optimism and commitment that had been built up during the early years carried over to a considerable extent and enabled the government to weather these storms fairly successfully.

In 1957 a number of events contributed to public uneasiness. First, the Chinese became aware of the upheavals that had occurred in Eastern Europe in 1956, and some learned that Khrushchev had made a secret speech denouncing Stalin's crimes in that same year. They were at least dimly aware that these events were causing anxiety among China's leaders, and that they produced some uncertainty about the future of socialism. However, most people remained ignorant of the initial signs of Sino-Soviet conflict and remained convinced that the two countries would stay on the best of terms.

The Hundred Flowers Campaign and the Anti-Rightist Campaign that followed it hit closer to home. The liberalizations of 1956–57 and the call for open criticism of the CCP that followed met with mixed responses. The harsh penalties inflicted against critics of the government in earlier campaigns urged caution, and at the same time many people were, on balance, quite satisfied with the society around them and with their own lives. When, after several rounds of nudging and reassuring potential critics, the Hundred Flowers criticisms finally did erupt in the spring of 1957, they were wide-ranging, emotional, and mainly produced by an important but narrow segment of urban society – intellectuals, students, members of "democratic parties," and professional people. These were people who, while in theory close allies of the CCP's under its united front policies, had actually seen their prestige and autonomy sharply eroded. Their criticisms were diverse, but they primarily centered on the issue of professional and intellectual autonomy versus party control. As these criticisms unfolded in wall posters and in the national press, the majority of urbanites not actively involved looked on in some bewilderment. Many found it hard to comprehend the idea that the CCP would permit and even encourage such blunt criticism and were also somewhat shocked by the angry tone of some of the attacks. When in June 1957 the government struck back by launching the Anti-Rightist Campaign, the claim that the "masses" were demanding that the critics be silenced was not totally false. Many of the nonintellectuals in urban areas (and even a share of intellectuals) did feel that the criticism was going too far and was threatening the improvements and social cohesion the revolution had brought about.

While the Party's counterattack was supported by many, others still had their doubts. For students in universities and in some middle schools the Anti-Rightist Campaign represented an ominous change of pace. During previous years they had been exposed to criticism meetings involving fellow students and were aware of struggle and coercion used against various target groups, but many were now for the first time mobilized for a more or less life-and-death struggle against their own classmates. From a focus on study and organized recreation only infrequently disrupted by politics (the campaign against hidden counterrevolutionaries of 1955 had been conducted during the summer vacation, and mainly involved teachers), they now found their lives totally focused on political struggles. The pressure to inform on classmates was heavy, and many students were troubled that there appeared to be "target quotas" that made it necessary to brand a certain number of classmates as "rightists" even if they had committed no serious errors.

The aftermath was also unpleasant. Many of those labeled as rightists were taken away to forced labor – not only from schools but also from other organizations where the campaign was focused.[31] Some of those considered less serious rightists were not sent off to labor reeducation camps but were allowed to remain in their schools or work organizations or were transferred to less sensitive ones. But these people became pariahs. One émigré describes the prevailing situation: 'They still went to their offices, but nobody spoke to them or sat with them at the same table nor did 'rightists' talk among themselves. Former acquaintances turned their heads in the other direction when they saw a 'rightist' in the street, and visits, telephone calls, and letters were not to be expected."[32] In this atmosphere even people who had recognized the need to defend Chinese socialism against its critics sometimes had second thoughts.

The year 1957 also saw the launching of the *hsia-fang* campaign that resulted in many cadres being transferred downward to jobs in smaller towns or in the countryside. At least portions of the large numbers of people transferred downward in this campaign were given to understand that the shift was to be temporary, and that this was the beginning of a general policy of requiring all bureaucratic personnel periodically to "cleanse" themselves through manual labor and menial service. Many of the lesser rightists were, of course, also sent to the countryside under the banner of this campaign. Still, to urban personnel who had seen their lives and careers improving, the notion that mobility could run in the other direction, even if one had not committed any political errors, was clearly threatening.

However, many other events of 1957 helped to sustain the earlier optimism. This was the year of the launching of the Soviet Sputnik and of the completion of the Yangtze River bridge at Wuhan, and many newly built factories were also coming on line. Price increases for pork and ration shortages of cotton were used by Hundred Flowers critics to argue that the economy was not improving, but the government released a barrage of statistics designed to prove the opposite. Most urbanites accepted the government view. Their lives were getting better, new schools were opening, more and more novels and translated works were being published, and in general China still seemed on the move.

The continued optimism can be seen in the public response to the

---

31 An Indian employed in Foreign Languages Press in this period claims that thirty out of five hundred employees in that organization were declared rightists, and that four or five even earned the more serious label of counterrevolutionary. See Om Prakash Mantri, *Five years in Mao's China*, 31. At Peking University some 500 students and 100 faculty members were declared rightists. This constituted more than 7 percent of the university community. See Yue Daiyun and Carolyn Wakeman, *To the storm: the odyssey of a revolutionary Chinese woman*, 102–3.
32 Mu Fu-sheng, *The wilting of the hundred flowers: the Chinese intelligentsia under Mao*, 173. See also Morris Wills, *Turncoat: an American's 12 years in Communist China*, 100.

Great Leap Forward launched the following year. The prospect of accelerating the pace of economic improvement, overtaking Britain, and catapulting into communist abundance in fifteen years or so excited the imagination of many, particularly among the young. At this time were launched a wide variety of new or more intense activities that played on these feelings. In the spring of 1958 urbanites waged a battle against the "four pests" – flies, mosquitos, rats, and sparrows – with teams of enthusiastic participants competing to turn in the largest number of dead flies and perching on fences and roofs with pots and other noisemakers to keep sparrows from alighting so that they would eventually fall exhausted to their death.[33] In both urban and rural areas the famous "backyard steel furnaces" were run by students, office workers, and others. Using special instruction pamphlets prepared by the authorities and crude tools and raw materials (including scavenged pots and pans and fence posts), urbanites who had never even seen steel produced built crude brick furnaces and began to turn out imperfect ingots. In Peking many sectors of the population turned out to participate in breakneck round-the-clock construction of the Great Hall of the People, which was completed in an astonishing ten months. And tens of thousands were mobilized to haul earth by hand to construct the Ming Tombs water reservoir, outside the capital. Chou En-lai and other top leaders impressed participants by coming to take part in these mass labor stints, at least briefly. Similar if less grandiose projects were carried out in other cities, along with reforestation, factory construction, and other mass labor efforts.

This was also a period of a major new influx of rural residents into the cities. With the controls on urban migration temporarily relaxed in view of the rapid expansion anticipated in the urban economy and some active recruitment of manpower in rural areas by ambitious urban enterprises, the effects of the previous efforts to hold down city size were undone. An estimated 20 million peasants became new urbanites in 1958–59, particularly in the rapidly expanding new industrial cities in the interior, causing congestion and severe strain on urban resources.[34]

The events of the early Great Leap Forward were similar to those of the early 1950s in breaking down organizational barriers and bringing people into intense, if brief, contact with people from other work units

33 Campaigns had been conducted on more or less an annual basis against flies and some other pests since 1949, but the effort in 1958 was the largest and most ambitious. Subsequently, of course, it was determined that exterminating so many sparrows was harmful because the insects they had controlled began to run rampant. So bedbugs replaced sparrows on the list. One well-known Chinese doctor has told many foreigners that the most striking difference between pre-1949 cities and post-1949 ones is the elimination of flies. See William Kessen, ed., *Childhood in China*, 189.
34 See Onoye, "Regional distribution of urban population in China," 93–127.

and walks of life. They also had the effect of mobilizing and involving sectors of the population that had remained largely "on the sidelines" in earlier periods. This was particularly the case in regard to housewives, who were mobilized to come out of their homes and set up sewing groups, processing workshops, and other economically productive activities. To facilitate their involvement in work an active effort was made to open up nursery schools, mess halls, laundries, and other facilities that would lighten the burdens of housework. Subsequently, efforts were launched to create an entirely new organizational form, the urban commune, to correspond to the rural communes then being established, but the result had curiously little impact on public consciousness. To most urbanites the urban commune seems to have meant simply the added work organizations and service facilities run by neighborhoods, rather than the coherently organized residential and production complex envisioned by China's leaders. (And these work organizations and service facilities were all that remained when the effort to create urban communes was abandoned after 1960.)

The Great Leap Forward also brought with it new demands for change in popular habits and customs that also harked back to the early 1950s. In general more Spartan behavior was recommended, with "bourgeois" and traditional patterns of behavior falling under criticism. The populace became aware that the authorities frowned on those who engaged in ancestor worship, celebrated weddings in a lavish fashion, and continued to observe Chinese holidays in the traditional manner. At this time a major effort was launched to get urbanites to accept cremation, and to make it difficult for them to arrange for a traditional burial. (Many coffin shops and cemeteries were closed; but even so, until the Cultural Revolution, determined urbanites could arrange to acquire a coffin and have the deceased transported out to the countryside for burial.) A concerted effort was also made to eliminate the last vestiges of private enterprise and to crack down on roving street peddlers. It was also at this time that a then relatively little-known ideologist named Chang Ch'un-ch'iao argued that bureaucracy and inequality were getting out of hand and that China should return to the supply system used to reward officials before the revolution.[35]

For much of the urban population, though, and particularly for manual workers, what the Great Leap Forward signified most was simply a dizzying pace of work. During the earlier period the various emulation and socialist competition techniques developed in the Soviet Union were

35 Chang's article appeared in *JMJP*, 13 October 1958.

copied, and China produced its own Stakhanovites. But now these devices were pressed much more vigorously in the effort to break through
the obstacles to economic development. Workers were mobilized to
pledge to fulfill higher and higher work targets, and in periodic high tides
of production they were mobilized to stay at their posts for two or more
days at a stretch, producing at a breakneck pace. Machines intended to
run at one pace were speeded up to three, four, or more times that pace,
straining both machines and their operators to the breaking point. Even
nonmanual workers were affected. Writers, journalists, and others
pledged to produce designated numbers of written works that surpassed
their previous output. Groups of students worked without rest to develop their own textbooks suited to the new age. Many individuals slept
at thier posts and returned to their families only for a brief reunion once a
week. Students describe this as a period of constantly changing demands
and unexpected shifts in activities – a suddenly announced rural labor
stint would be succeeded by a call to devote one's energies to academic
study, which would in turn be disrupted by mobilization of students to
take part in marches and demonstrations, or involvement in an effort
to cleanse thoughts by "giving one's heart to the Party." Throughout
society the hectic campaign activities pervaded everyday life.

Immediate reactions to this societywide speedup were mixed. Many,
particularly among the young, found the atmosphere exhilarating and the
prospect of attaining the material abundance that loomed just over the
horizon gratifying. One former student conveys his reaction: "I was
caught up for the first time in this bewildering way of life. There seemed
no escape, but it was not wholly unpleasant. It was full of the unexpected."[36] Even those who found the physical effort involved very taxing
often reacted positively. An American who worked on the Ming Tombs
project reveals his thoughts: "By the end of the week we were filthy;
there was no place to take a bath. I was getting tired and sore and a bit fed
up. But there was a good atmosphere about it – of a big community
effort. And it did acquaint Chinese intellectuals with what it really means
to have to do that sort of work."[37] Among some segments of the population, however – particularly among older and more experienced manual
workers and technical experts – attitudes were often less positive. Such
people were much more skeptical of the wisdom of the speedups and
innovations and could foresee the quality problems, industrial accidents,
and disgruntled workers that this approach to economic development

36 Tung Chi-ping and Humphrey Evans, *The thought revolution*, 43. See also Sansan, as told to Bette
    Lord, *Eighth moon*, 57.
37 Wills, *Turncoat*, 103.

would foster. Still, on balance, most urbanites were initially willing to give the Great Leap Forward the benefit of the doubt and hope for the best.

The result was, of course, not the hoped-for abundance but the "three bitter years" of economic depression from 1959 through 1961. Food supplies began to drop dramatically by 1959, mess hall portions and rations had to be cut, and a period of nationwide hunger set in. Work units not only eliminated the speedups but were forced to cut down on work demands and other activities and to allow extra rest. In view of the low energy-levels of personnel, calisthenics, militia drills, and other activities were eliminated. In the resulting crisis many urban organizations experimented with food substitutes – for example, a special liquid prepared using algae that would provide some nutrition even if it would not meet the customary standards of the Chinese palate. Still, people lost weight and were constantly tired and hungry, and the rates of illness and sick leave from work shot up. One young Chinese recalls the situation in Changsha: "Many of the old people and almost all the children I knew had the 'water swelling disease,' dropsy. Our bodies puffed up and wouldn't recede, and we walked listlessly to school and arrived exhausted. When acquaintances met, they squeezed each other's legs to see how swollen they were, and examined each other's skins to see if they were yellow."[38] The quest for food became an obsession, and one person mentions having to get up at 3:00 A.M. in Tientsin in this period to claim a place in line in order to have any hope of buying the vegetables being brought into the city.[39] Still, conditions were much more severe in the countryside, and it was there that most of the excess deaths from this period occurred. In this case urban privilege turned out to be a life-and-death matter, as was explained to our young man from Changsha by his father: "You're lucky.... You live in a big capital city, and the Party and Chairman Mao are giving you food from the storage bins. The peasants have to find a way out for themselves."[40]

Perceptions varied about whether this suffering was equitably shared within the urban population. It was clear to some that high-ranking cadres and others continued to enjoy a variety of advantages – they received more and better food in their separate "small kitchen" dining facilities,

38 Liang Heng and Judith Shapiro, Son of the revolution, 17.
39 Sansan, Eighth moon, 75–76. The author would put her basket in line and then go home and sleep until about six, at which point she would return and start waiting in the line. The fact that an unattended basket could reserve one's place in line testifies to the high degree of social order that still prevailed at this time. Others describe even more extreme behavior under the stress of this period, such as students in Peking eating the spring buds off trees to still their hunger. See Sven Lindqvist, China in crisis.
40 Liang and Shapiro, Son of the revolution, 17.

they were able to attend luxurious banquets when foreign visitors were entertained, and so forth. One observer claimed that "the cooks and the big officials are the only people in China who stayed fat even during the hard times."[41] So a certain amount of popular grumbling arose. But many Chinese were impressed by the extent to which intellectuals and others of high status had to suffer along with the rest. They were further reassured when, in a minor campaign near the end of the "three bitter years," leading cadres in some organizations publicly confessed before their subordinates that they had used their positions to get extra food for themselves and their families. Many were convinced that at least the hunger had been more widely shared than it would have been before 1949, and that the CCP was concerned about punishing those who used rank to remain well fed.

There were consequences of the failure of the Great Leap Forward other than hunger. The economy was forced into retrenchment, with cutbacks in targets, some plant closings, and layoffs of personnel. A wage freeze was put into effect that would remain in place, with minor exceptions, until 1977. Some employees in state enterprises, seeing economic prospects there dim substantially, actually quit their jobs and began to work in collective enterprises where the principle of distributed profits seemed to promise higher earnings. The authorities were also forced to rescind the ban on private enterprise activities and allow peddlers, sidewalk seamstresses, and snack vendors to reemerge. Urban migration restrictions became extremely severe, and an estimated 20 million newly recruited urban workers were forced to return to the countryside.[42] The difficult economic conditions prevailing also fed a rise in crime and black marketeering, as well as in begging and other phenomena that had seemed under control a few years earlier.

General reactions to the failure of the Great Leap Forward again varied. Naturally, those who had accumulated grievances against the new order or were simply skeptical saw this crisis as further evidence of flaws in the system that allowed misguided policies to continue unchecked. One Soviet observer from this period offers a comment that resonates with views put forth by the post-Mao leadership:

One can compare the manner in which Mao governs China to the way in which a drunken bus driver would conduct his crowded bus along a precipitous and curving mountain road. The number of passengers who realize the danger grows

---

41 Wills, *Turncoat*, 94. See also Emmanuel John Hevi, *An African student in China*, 79ff.
42 This figure is cited in Tseng Ch'i-hsien, "The problem of employment in the economic development of China," unpublished paper cited in Orleans, "China's urban population: concepts, conglomerations, and concerns," 279.

with each passing moment, but no one dares to push the driver out of the way and take over for himself the responsibility of guiding the vehicle to safety.[43]

Within the Chinese leadership, of course, some recognition of this problem did arise, but it resulted at the time only in veiled criticism of Mao in the media. (P'eng Te-huai's more direct attempt to at least force the driver to his senses had resulted in P'eng being purged in 1959.) The public was given an explanation at the time that was quite different. In this official view the Great Leap Forward had been basically good, but a combination of disastrous weather, the treacherous withdrawal of Soviet advisers and plans in 1960, and overzealous actions of low-level cadres caused the resulting debacle.

It is difficult to judge with certainty, but it appears that at the time many if not most urbanites accepted this official view in large measure. The abrupt withdrawal of Russian advisers could quite easily be portrayed as treachery by the Soviet Union, the weather had been severe in many places, and it was easy to find examples of misguided and arrogant behavior by low-level cadres. At the same time, most urbanites remained largely unaware of the critiques of Mao that were then emerging within the CCP leadership. They knew, of course, that P'eng Te-huai had been replaced by Lin Piao as defense minister in 1959, but among at least low-level cadres and intellectuals the details of P'eng's criticism of the Great Leap policies were not widely known, and rumors about his disloyalty to Mao and sympathy toward the Soviet Union muddied the issue. And when Teng T'o, Wu Han, and other high-level Party intellectuals began to publish their veiled critiques of Mao in the early 1960s most urbanites remained unaware that Mao was the target (if they read them at all).

But perhaps most important, urbanites by and large simply wanted to believe the official explanations, however implausible. The idea that the strenuous efforts they had expended erecting buildings and constructing reservoirs had all been part of a gigantic official blunder was too painful to contemplate. So was the notion that Mao might be not only fallible but capable of leading China into chaos. At a deeper level most urbanites remained grateful for the improvements in their lives that had taken place during the 1950s and did not want to believe that the same leadership that enabled China to "stand up" could be responsible for the "three bitter years." Thus, for many urbanites, the Great Leap crisis sorely tried, but did not break, the confidence they had developed in the new order.[44]

43 Klochko, *Soviet scientist in Red China*, 211–12.
44 Sven Linqvist used the phrase "eclipse of the sun" to capture the mood during the three bitter years, a phrase by which he conveys the widespread feeling that the sun (i.e., better times) would come out again and people could hope and plan for the future. See his *China in crisis*, 35, 116.

It should also be noted that the break with the Soviet Union that the Great Leap crisis brought out into the open was not the cause of as much anxiety and concern as the rejection of the West after 1949. In part this was because the period of relying on the Soviet Union had been briefer than the earlier periods of contact with the West. But it also involved the fact that the rejection was not so total this time. Even though the alliance was broken, many of the ideas and institutions that had been borrowed remained in place. The thousands of Chinese sent to the Soviet Union for training did find some portions of their expertise less in demand than before (Russian rapidly fell out of favor in foreign-language study in China), but they did not have to denounce their former lives and activities the way many intellectuals educated in the West had had to do earlier. Their careers were therefore not seriously jeopardized. Furthermore, when the break occurred, it was easy to play on elements in Chinese popular perceptions that had always been present to some degree: feelings that Soviet advisers had been arrogant and bourgeois, that Khrushchev's crude and boorish ways contrasted negatively with Mao's sophistication, and that Soviet aid had never been as generous or devoid of strings as the USSR had portrayed it. So when the shift was made to an anti-Soviet posture, there was little sign of public opposition or resentment. To some this change meant that China had at last freed itself from its one final vestige of subordination to foreign powers.

After 1962 the economy was visibly improving and urban conditions seemed to be returning to something like their pre–Great Leap state. Market supplies increased, as did employment, and in 1963 a partial wage adjustment – mainly for those at the low end of the wage scale – was carried out. Problems of crime, speculation, and black marketeering seemed to be receding once again, and urbanites felt that the level of public safety was improving. Events occurred in which Chinese could take pride – for example, China's success in the border war with India in 1962, the recognition of China by France in 1964, and the explosion of China's first nuclear device in that same year. Although life continued to be a struggle – most of the women mobilized to work during the Leap continued to do so not only out of socialist duty but also out of recognition of financial necessity – but prospects for the future seemed to be looking brighter.

The government showed great concern in these years for repairing the damage to morale done by the three bitter years. This effort took the form of political study and propaganda that eventually was focused in the Socialist Education Campaign. In the countryside this movement in some places generated the most intense conflict since land reform, but in the cities it was a more benign effort to reinforce faith in socialism. The activities pursued were diverse – studying model figures such as Lei Feng, collecting family and factory histories that would demonstrate the great improvements brought about by Communist rule, hearing tales of past suffering from old workers and peasants, copying the political work systems used in the People's Liberation Army, and so forth.[45] Much of this activity was designed to drive home the idea that the suffering of the three bitter years would have been worse and less equitably shared if China had not turned socialist, an argument that many urbanites were still inclined to accept. A secondary theme was to grow in importance after 1962: Class enemies were still lurking about trying to undermine social-ism, and they had to be suppressed. People were still fairly vague about who such enemies might be in the urban context, but they were generally persuaded by all of the "speak bitterness" activities that the old landlords and KMT elements had been despicable people.

Underneath the atmosphere of restoration and improvement, however, were some more ominous trends. The most important was simply the matter of demography. During the optimistic 1950s a baby boom had occurred and schools had expanded rapidly, and in addition many peasant families had been able to stream in from the countryside (not all of whom were subsequently evicted). By the early 1960s larger and larger numbers of graduates were turned out by urban middle schools, but the retrench-ment in the economy and in higher education meant that there were not places to accommodate them all. Whereas we noted that for a time in the 1950s there were more college places than upper middle school graduates, by 1965 only about 45 percent of all general upper middle school grad-uates could be enrolled in college.[46]

The consequences of this changing demographic situation were many. Competition to get into the universities became more intense. In the school system of the time this meant that competition to get into the highest-quality, keypoint primary and middle schools became ferocious, since students in such schools had much better chances than others of gaining university acceptance. The relative decline in chances to go to college produced an increasingly competitive atmosphere within schools, and the uncertainties surrounding this competition were increased by shifting government policies in education. From one year to the next the

45 Lei Feng was an ordinary soldier who died in an accident. At his death he left a diary that recounted the good deeds he performed for other soldiers and his devotion to Chairman Mao. Recurrently after 1963 his exemplary behavior was held up as a model for students and others to copy, and he became the ultimate official hero. It appears that at least parts of Lei Feng's diary were manufactured after his death. See Wills, *Turncoat*, 127ff.
46 Figures cited in Stanley Rosen, "Obstacles to educational reform in China," *Modern China*, 8.1 (January 1982), 11.

stress to be placed on school grades, examination marks, political behavior, and class background labels shifted, thus altering the rules governing which students were most likely to succeed in the competition. But in general, those who had based their strategy on academic performance found that their chances of gaining university entrance were shrinking as political criteria were given added stress. Relations among students were affected, with class background and other political factors now becoming primary influences on friendship formation and school cliques. The educational policies of the time also in effect created a three-tier system of schools, with keypoint schools, ordinary state-run schools, and then people-run schools all enrolling portions of urban students. The atmosphere in the second and particularly the third rungs of this system was different and generally much less competitive. Students in such schools had but a slim chance of gaining college entrance and, at best, hoped for urban jobs, and in such schools student motivation and discipline were noticeably lower.[47]

Thus, in the years before the Cultural Revolution getting ahead in the educational system was an increasingly uncertain business in which many ambitious and talented young people had their hopes frustrated. For many with older siblings who had moved easily up through to the university and then into rewarding jobs only a few years earlier, their own uncertain prospects were particularly galling. A young woman who failed to get into a keypoint upper middle school conveys her anguish at the time in these terms: "At fourteen my life was fixed. I was to be an elementary-school teacher in three years and earn thirty-two yuan per month for the rest of my days. I would not have to wonder and plan for my future ever again."[48]

For the majority of urban youths who had few realistic hopes of gaining college entrance the issue became instead jobs, and here as well the situation had become more uncertain and competitive. The system of unified job placement developed in the 1950s had been premised on the idea that the economy would continue to expand vigorously to provide jobs for new entrants into the labor force, but that expectation had been thwarted by the collapse of the Great Leap Forward. Strict controls prevented state enterprises from taking on new personnel without permission, and not enough new jobs were created each year to accommodate the school-leavers. (The relatively "young" nature of the urban labor

47 For accounts of schooling in this period see Susan Shirk, *Competitive comrades: career incentives and student strategies in China*; Jonathan Unger, *Education under Mao: class and competition in Canton schools, 1960–1980*; Rosen, "Obstacles to educational reform."
48 Sansan, *Eighth moon*, 71.

force, swollen by newly employed people in the 1950s, meant that retirements freed only small numbers of places each year.) Even with peasants now strictly prohibited from streaming into the cities there were not enough jobs to go around. Some school leavers were assigned to jobs, but others were supposed to return to their homes and await possible future job assignments. These young people fell under urban residents' committee supervision, and often they engaged in occasional temporary work in construction or transportation, with stretches of unemployment interspersed, although a few might be lucky enough eventually to be assigned to a permanent job. These unallocated young people became known as "social youths," and they were recognized as a growing problem in these years. Neighborhood authorities tried to organize them for political study and other "wholesome" activities, and they mounted periodic drives to get them to volunteer to resettle in the countryside, but as their numbers multiplied it became increasingly difficult to deal with them. So in contrast to the optimism of the 1950s, urban youth and their parents in the 1960s saw the scene as one in which tight competition under shifting rules made planning their lives increasingly difficult.

For those already at work the situation was less worrisome, but still the atmosphere had changed from what had prevailed earlier. Whereas before the Great Leap there had been a feeling that new opportunities were opening up and that those who studied and applied themselves might be able to upgrade their jobs, shift to more interesting work, or simply anticipate wage increases every few years, in the 1960s the situation had changed. Most people continued working at the same job and at the same wage level year after year and worried about their ability to feed a growing family, even in the absence of inflation. People were fairly secure in their jobs and in the fringe benefits associated with them, but still they often felt that the chances of being transferred downward had become larger than the prospects for being promoted upward. With the economy just coming out of its retrenchment phase, they recognized that their fate lay for the foreseeable future in that of their work unit, and that individual efforts and contributions would not produce a major change in their situation. Indeed, with the continued specter of political campaigns and the renewed emphasis on class struggle they still had to worry about whether a careless statement or action would place them in serious jeopardy.

This atmosphere produced neither heroic efforts nor dedicated pursuit of expertise. In the increasingly rigid organizational cells that work units represented, the tendency instead was to strive for security in one's niche. Being careful to make the right impression in meetings, cultivating supportive relationships with superiors, and in general trying to avoid offending anyone became the orders of the day. In this structure those who did feel mistreated or abused could not readily raise complaints or go elsewhere, and instead they nursed their grievances privately until such time as these might be acted upon. That time arrived in 1966.

THE CULTURAL REVOLUTION DECADE, 1966–1976

Very few urbanites were aware of the clues that a major upheaval was in the offing in the early 1960s. Later on, events such as the satirical articles written by leading Party intellectuals and the changing directives that governed the Socialist Education Campaign were portrayed as efforts by others to attack Mao's authority, but at the time urbanites, if they were aware of such matters at all, tended to see them as simply part of the normal flux of Chinese politics. Even when the attacks on Wu Han, Teng T'o, and others escalated in early 1966, most people saw little reason for concern. Often in the past campaigns had started in the cultural sphere and then had moved into other areas, but urbanites had been through many such campaigns and had no reason to suspect that this new one might be out of the ordinary, or that instincts previously learned would not stand them in good stead in the days ahead. Only in the summer of 1966, with the purge of Peking's Mayor P'eng Chen, the mass rallies of Red Guards in Peking, and other unprecedented events, did people begin to realize they were in for something new. Then urbanites began watching new developments intently with both fascination and dread.

The course of events of the Cultural Revolution is well known from other sources and will not be repeated here.[49] Our aim is to comment on its impact on people's lives and feelings, and this is no easy task, since the Cultural Revolution had such a complex and varying impact. Whether or not the campaign succeeded in, as the slogan said, "touching men's souls," it is clear that in a brief span of time a variety of new and intense experiences became part of the consciousness of urbanites – Red Guards traveling all over the country, revelations about abuses of power and shabby behavior by powerful leaders, the paralysis of the CCP, searches of private homes for objects and symbols not in keeping with Maoist purity, the parading and humiliating of once-proud officials before angry mobs, the condemnation of many policies and cultural products of the previous seventeen years, the plunging of Red Guards into power seizures and factional warfare, the outbreak in many cities of pitched fighting involving

---

49 See, for example, Hong Yung Lee, *The politics of the Chinese Cultural Revolution*, and Chs. 2 and 4 in this volume.

the use of machine guns, mortars, and even tanks, the intervention of the army into civilian society, and unprecedented disruption of ordinary lives. As in previous periods, how people reacted to these intense experiences differed considerably.

For many urban young people this was an exhilarating time, at least initially. Instead of being locked into a tight competition to try and secure future opportunities in the urban job hierarchy, they found themselves called to act on a larger and more important stage as the vanguards in a new revolution. Although most were uncertain and even frightened at first and somewhat dubious about the "crimes" committed by their own teachers and Party leaders, many soon found the rewards of activism exciting. No longer required to study long hours and submit to school disciplinary rules, they played out their new role by traveling around the country, parading in front of national leaders, viewing places they had always wanted to see, and engaging in intense exchanges of ideas and experiences with other young people. They were able to take control in their own schools, draft new rules, require teachers and administrators to submit to humiliation, raid confidential files, and publish uncensored newssheets. They were able to march into neighborhoods and homes at will, carrying out searches for "four old" objects and engaging in other "communist wind" activities – giving streets and organizations new, more revolutionary names, requiring Mao's portrait and sayings to be posted everywhere, defacing ancient temples, and so forth. Some young people even changed their own given names from things like "Plum Blossom" to "Defend the East" or "Demands Revolution." Red Guards were able to march into factories, offices, and other organizations and freely proselytize for their revolution and in some cases even take part in local "power seizures." Perhaps most important, they were able to feel that Mao had particularly selected them to play the leading role in his effort to create a purer form of socialism. From being highly controlled political neophytes they were suddenly catapulted into positions of freedom and power, and the obstacles to their securing a valuable place in Chinese society seemed to have fallen away. In this heady atmosphere it is little wonder that it proved difficult to restrain young energies once they had been unleashed.

As these events unfolded they affected young people differentially, however. Already in 1966 factional cleavages began to emerge, and these led to violent confrontations in 1967 and 1968, and remaining hostility for many years afterward. In general, youths with good class backgrounds who had held student leadership roles tended to form more conservative factions, while young people with "middling" class backgrounds (e.g., petty bourgeois, professional, etc.) flowed into the more radical factions. The latter saw the Cultural Revolution as both a way to prove their revolutionary mettle and also to get back at those who had been lording it over them in the student hierarchy. In a curious sense this conflict involved the same social cleavage as in the Hundred Flowers Campaign in 1957, although this time the rhetoric and results were quite different. Young people from bad class backgrounds for the most part stayed on the sidelines, as they saw little chance of proving themselves or avoiding trouble by participating.[50] Over time, as factional violence escalated, the urban landscape became increasingly hazardous. Work units and residential lanes often put up gates and posted guards to protect themselves against the violence outside, and a simple trip to the market involved danger that one might be caught in factional crossfire and felled by a stray bullet. In this sort of environment more and more young people responded to their own fears and their parents' pleading and withdrew to the sidelines, leaving the field to a hard core of committed activists on both sides.

Within work organizations to a certain extent the same dynamics occurred, with conservative factions composed mostly of "good status" individuals, radical factions composed of those of intermediate political labels, and a minority of people of "bad status" who tried to stay out of the way. In work units other lines of cleavage tended to enter into the matter as well, though, with young versus old, temporary versus permanent employees, and mental versus manual workers all complicating the conflict.[51] In work units the conflict was slower to develop than in schools, as adults were more concerned about disruption of production and of their own lives. But within work units there were also more likely to be real and long-standing grievances, and the Cultural Revolution now allowed these grievances to be expressed, so that in some cases the resulting conflict was more intense and more difficult to resolve than in the schools. (In work organizations the need to keep work going at least intermittently also gave rise to awkward situations in which factional enemies tried to cooperate on the job, avoided each other at lunch, and attacked each other viciously after hours.) Even though some adults had initially been enthusiastic about the idea that the Cultural Revolution would counteract bureaucracy and entrenched privileges, the initial atmo-

---

50 See Anita Chan, Stanley Rosen, and Jonathan Unger, "Students and class warfare: the social roots of the Red Guard conflict in Guangzhou," *CQ*, 83 (September 1980), 397–446. Lee, *The politics of the Chinese Cultural Revolution*; and David Raddock, *Political behavior of adolescents in China*.

51 See, for example, Marc Blecher and Gordon White, *Micropolitics in contemporary China: a technical unit during and after the Cultural Revolution*.

sphere of heroic and enthusiastic struggle dissipated more rapidly than among the young, and many adults withdrew into their homes and families and brooded about the disorder they saw raging around them and what it portended for China.

The political consequences of the Cultural Revolution were complex. Initially the movement brought with it unprecedented freedom. Even though the flow of events was guided from above, it was not firmly under control, and with the CCP immobilized and new, relatively autonomous rebel groups as political actors the political scene changed. Gone, temporarily, were strictly organized political study groups enforcing consent for the current line. Instead, individuals could read the official and Red Guard press on their own, participate or not, investigate lives and dossiers, and engage in other enlightening activities. From these sorts of experiences they learned about the concealed privileges of elites, official corruption, vindictive feuds, and other abuses. As they traveled around they could learn of the experience of others in a fairly spontaneous atmosphere and be impressed with the fact that peasants, temporary workers, and many others had lives that were far different from the picture portrayed in official propaganda. Heated debates with factional opponents and midnight discussions with friends prompted people to think deeply about their society. A fairly common reaction was for urbanites to feel that they had been naive and gullible before the Cultural Revolution, but that now their "eyes had been opened." It is one of the paradoxes of the Cultural Revolution that what appeared to be the ultimate mobilization of blind faith actually left in its wake independent opinions and profound skepticism.

The Cultural Revolution also changed the whole emotional tone of political life. Before this time large parts of the population could feel trusted and secure even if they recognized the sharpness of official controls and the harshness of the treatment received by class enemies. As a result of the Cultural Revolution and subsequent campaigns (e.g., the cleaning of class ranks and the One Hit Three Antis campaigns, efforts to purge still further "hidden class enemies" in 1968–69 and 1970–71), this mood of relative security and trust was increasingly replaced by feelings of arbitrariness and anxiety. Partly, the scope of the struggle simply became broader, with many who had assumed they were immune from political danger suddenly finding themselves under attack. For many cadres and intellectuals, for instance, the experience of being confined to a "cowshed" (a makeshift work unit jail), seeing a father struggled against at a mass meeting, or being forced to move out of a spacious apartment and into a cramped hovel brought home for the first time what it was like to be a political victim. As the scope of struggles broadened even ordinary manual workers and shop clerks had rising anxiety about political victimization.[52]

Not only did the scope of political victimization increase, but the rules seemed to be more and more arbitrary and unpredictable. Patrons within one's organization with whom one had cultivated relations of trust over the years suddenly fell from grace, leaving people below without protection. The radicalization of politics meant that previous rules and procedures by which people had guided their lives were no longer valid, and people felt adrift in unpredictable political seas. Security in this situation might come from pleasing the new leaders who emerged, but given the political conflicts in Peking, which might produce still further changes, this was a risky strategy. Some tried to guess right and actively join the tide of the post-Cultural Revolution campaigns, but others tried to plead illness or "drop out" in other ways or simply to accept stoically whatever political fate came their way.

The increased political awareness and victimization of these years combined with other factors, such as the demise of Lin Piao, to promote a growing suspicion of authority figures. How much the behavior of leading personnel had really changed in comparison with that a decade or two earlier is uncertain, but much of the public clearly perceived a deterioration. The images of leaders as hardworking and public-spirited gave way to an increasing feeling that elites were more concerned about protecting their own power than about benefiting society. They were perceived as not only able but eager to use their power and "back door" methods to benefit themselves, their allies, and their families. New leaders seemed just as concerned with establishing their status and privileges as had those they replaced, and when old cadres were rehabilitated they seemed preoccupied with regaining lost perquisites and biding their time until they could seek revenge against those who had tormented them. So the Cultural Revolution heightened sensitivity to the problem of bureaucratic arrogance but did not succeed (or was even counterproductive) in the effort to combat this problem. And just as it could be argued in the 1950s that exemplary behavior by cadres was a major element in promoting respect for the new political system, the more

---

52 Some Chinese sources have spoken of as many as 100 million people having become in one way or another victims of the Cultural Revolution. Our own research indicates that in urban areas in this decade the number of people with political problems expanded considerably beyond the figure of 5 percent for targets often used in campaigns. See Whyte and Parish, *Urban life in contemporary China*, ch. 9.

jaundiced 1970s views of cadre behavior indicated growing disillusionment with China's political institutions.

The disorder in the political realm was matched by deteriorating economic conditions. To be sure, some people benefited – some temporary workers were converted into permanent employees in 1971, victors in factional struggles earned promotions, and members of the army catapulted into urban authority positions and in some cases were able to bring rural dependents into the city to live with them. Some nurses were promoted to work as doctors, and medical orderlies to work as nurses, even as doctors were required to empty bedpans and wash windows. But to the average urbanite prospects seemed to be worsening during the decade. The chances of being demoted or transferred downward as a result of political errors were seen as increasing. Bonuses and other incentive payments were converted into egalitarian wage supplements or abolished altogether, thus penalizing the most productive personnel. The freeze on wage increases remained in effect, except for another minor adjustment for those at the bottom of the scale that was carried out in 1971–72, so that the period of trying to meet family needs on the same wages stretched in many cases to fifteen years or longer.

Some social groups saw clear declines in their situations. People with Overseas Chinese ties lost many of their special privileges in housing, consumer goods, and other realms, and sometimes were even intimidated into refusing to accept remittances. Often, people with political problems or bad class backgrounds were forced to move into more cramped housing or had their pay docked, and a considerable number lost their urban registrations and had to relocate in entire family units back to their native villages (which in many cases were villages they had never lived in).[53] As the 1970s wore on some of these groups regained some of their lost ground, but others lost out in turn. For example, the army began to be eased out of its civilian leadership role, and official policies required rural recruits to return to their native villages after demobilization instead of being given an urban job assignment.

On top of the declining prospects many urbanites felt, there was a perceived deterioration in market supplies and living standards in these years. Some items, such as radios and wristwatches, were becoming more easily available, but they did not compensate for the feeling that food items were becoming scarcer, rations tighter, and shopping an increas-

[53] Chinese sources claim that as many as 13 million urbanites were sent into rural exile in this manner during the period 1966–76. See Kam Wing Chan and Xueqiang Xu, "Urban population growth and urbanization in China since 1949: reconstructing a baseline," *CQ*, 104 (December 1985), 606.

ingly time-consuming and frustrating business. One American woman
married to a Chinese gives the following picture:

Bit by bit, during the long years of revolutionary turmoil, the available raw
materials had become increasingly scanty. More and more of the time our meals
consisted of rice and a vegetable, stir-fried in a minimum of peanut oil.... The
situation was not one of famine; rice was still available, but a balanced diet was
nearly impossible to achieve.... Everyone, including myself, thought about food
more or less consciously all the time.... Planning how to use the meat-ration
tickets to best advantage would be the main topic of family conversation for
hours.[54]

An Australian student who lived in Peking from 1975 to 1977 mentions
the four key phrases heard when shopping: "there is none," "sold out,"
"tomorrow," and "it doesn't matter."[55] Housing was also a severe problem, since the housing boom of the early 1950s had not been maintained,
and even with strict controls on migration from the countryside, the
housing stock had become dilapidated, people had to make do with less
space, and those requesting new housing often had to wait years.[56]

One result of the Cultural Revolution was the promotion of somewhat
greater equality of distribution within cities. Inequalities in both incomes
and in access to consumer goods were truncated a bit.[57] However, the
social effects of this change were not so healthy as China's egalitarian
reformers had hoped. Equalizing distribution is always easiest when there
is a growing "pie" and everyone is getting more, while those at the bottom are gaining disproportionately. Then those at the bottom will be
happy and those at the top not too upset — precisely the sort of strategy
used to ease the transition to socialism in 1955–56. But in the Cultural
Revolution decade things worked differently. To urbanites it appeared
that the total "pie" was shrinking, and that equality was being promoted
mainly by chipping away at the advantages enjoyed by various privileged
groups, thus bringing them down closer to the level of other urbanites.
Thus, the groups that suffered were understandably upset, while those at

54 Ruth Earnshaw Lo and Katherine Kinderman, *In the eye of the typhoon: an American woman in China
during the Cultural Revolution*, 209, 283–84.
55 Beverley Hooper, *Inside Peking: a personal report*, 78 Hooper terms these the "4 Ms," as in Chinese
each term begins with an *M* sound.
56 A survey in 1978 in China's 192 largest cities found housing space per capita had declined 20
percent since 1949 – from 4.5 square meters to 3.6 square meters per person. See Zhou, "Housing
China's 900 million people," 8. Other sources use 1952 as the date to which the 4.5 square meter
figure pertained. See Chou Shu-lien and Lin Sen-mu, "T'an-t'an chu-chai wen-t'i" (Chatting on
the housing problem), *JMJP*, 5 August 1980, 5.
57 Details on the effectiveness of this equalizing effort are presented in Whyte and Parish, *Urban life
in contemporary China*, chs. 3–4.

the bottom saw little improvement in their lives. As a strategy for producing equality, this was bound to generate widespread dissatisfaction.

The increase in equality was also less beneficial than it might have been because to many urbanites it was increasingly clear that the distribution system was not as equitable as in the past.[58] Not only did those who worked harder or contributed more not find this reflected in their wage packet or in access to consumer goods – perhaps more important, people perceived that those who had connections could "beat the system" and gain access to consumer durables, medical care, housing, and other scarce resources that others could not obtain. In the tight conditions of the time everyone was forced to try to cultivate such connections to meet their needs, but some were more successful than others in "going by the back door." It was clear to all that those in positions of authority were able to play this game better than ordinary citizens, and anger mounted against the perceived advantages of Chinese elites.

Young people faced the most severe problems during these years. In the early stages of the Cultural Revolution they had been on top of the world, but by 1968 few of them had managed to escape a dramatic fall from grace. Most were bundled off to the countryside or border regions to settle down and become agriculturalists, and in the ensuing decade 17 million urban youths shared this fate. Although presented as a glorious crusade and maintained as a way of dealing with the employment problems presented by an excess of urban "intellectual youth," this proved to be a socially costly campaign. Many urban young people found the rigors of rural life more than they could take and soon began to drift illegally back to the cities for long periods. Since they had no urban registrations and could not legally be employed or receive rations, they had to live off family and friends or by illegal activities. By the early 1970s these returned youths were the main contributors to an urban crime wave. The fact that these young people had no niche in the urban system and in many cases had been embittered by their Cultural Revolution experiences made them unusually bold juvenile delinquents – much harder to control than registered urbanites or even peasants streaming in from the countryside. The many problems that resulted forced the authorities to modify the program in a number of ways even before Mao's death – by providing more funds to assist young people

58 The distinction between equality and equity should be kept in mind. Equality refers to the absolute differences in distribution, but equity refers to whether people receive what they deserve, in terms of the prevailing normative standards. Thus, a more equal distribution may or may not be perceived as more equitable.

in getting established and, particularly, by shifting from permanent rustication to a rotation system, with youth eligible for reassignment to urban jobs after a few years in the countryside.

Others besides former Red Guards were affected by the altered prospects of these years. The outlook for their younger brothers and sisters coming up through the school system was not much more secure. With the Cultural Revolution reforms of the educational system, they knew they could not go directly from middle school to the university, and that most would be sent to the countryside after graduation. Given the deemphasis on grades, and with automatic promotion and the lack of a tie-in between academic performance and future assignment, urban students felt they had little reason to study hard or behave themselves. No matter how they behaved, it would not make much difference in their futures. As a result, truancy and delinquent behavior by those still in school also increased. Parents were anxious about how their childern were behaving, but they were at a loss as to how to make their offspring follow the rules. Some youths and their parents hit on strategies they hoped would help – for example, cultivating special abilities in sports or music that might make them appeal to particular urban work units. But for many the task of planning for the future seemed almost hopeless. Some young people began to consult fortune-tellers or seek other mystical answers to the uncertainties surrounding their lives. In this general anxiety the perception that elites were able to get their children assigned to urban jobs, or "rescued" from the countryside to join the army or attend the university, added to the resentments felt against those in power.

The Cultural Revolution produced a drastic disruption of urban social order; but as already noted, the termination of the campaign upheavals in 1969 did not restore the degree of order that had existed in earlier years. Black marketeering, illegal peddling, and speculation proliferated. Pickpockets began to plague buses and streetcars, and laundry left out to dry or bicycles left unattended were increasingly likely to disappear. People walking alone at night were more fearful than in the past, and lurid cases of robbery, rape, and murder added to the popular fright. Perhaps most alarming, criminal gangs or "black societies" began to emerge in large cities and engage in behavior familiar in other parts of the world – defending turf, manufacturing homemade weapons, and fighting battles with rival gangs. Urban families were increasingly afraid of being in areas where such gangs were active, and they were even more worried that their children would fall under gang influence. In comparative terms the level of crime was still probably considerably less than in many other societies, yet Chinese urbanites sensed that the high degree of safety and public discipline that they had been so grateful for in the 1950s no longer existed.

Many other kinds of urban orderliness were also perceived as declining. Littering was seen as more common than in the past, as was spitting on the street. Shop personnel and waiters were perceived as increasingly surly, in spite of the extensive propaganda given to Mao's slogan "Serve the people." People were felt to be less likely than in the past to get up to give their seat on the bus to an old person, and buses and trains were not running on schedule as much as in the past. Even flies, rats, and other urban pests, which had been controlled relatively well a decade or so earlier, appeared to be making a comeback. Perhaps some of these perceptions are inaccurate and reflect a certain amount of nostalgia, but they do illustrate the increasing perception that the urban system was no longer working.

The Cultural Revolution also represented a massive effort to enforce conformity with the officially prescribed and narrowly defined version of proletarian culture. This effort penetrated every corner of the lives of urbanites. The Red Guard assaults set the process in motion, but the policies of succeeding years helped to keep the pressure on. The regime was hardly a bastion of liberalism to begin with, but now many forms of expression, customs, and cultural objects that had been permitted during the earlier years became taboo.[59]

During the Red Guard assaults on the "four olds" in 1966, many families found their jewelry, ancestral shrines, Bibles, old-style clothing, perfume, old books, and family heirlooms confiscated. Even some of those whose homes were not searched were seized by fear and destroyed or hid their own door-gods, foreign books, classical paintings, and other questionable items. At this time even the keeping of goldfish, birds, and other pets was proscribed as "bourgeois" in many locales. Families were required to post Mao's picture prominently in their homes and use Mao's sayings as decorations. In some organizations people performed "loyalty dances" to Mao each morning and answered the phone by saying, "Long live Chairman Mao."[60] In the early period of the Cultural Revolution people were in danger of being stopped on the street and having their hair cut or their clothing torn if they were not wearing the proper pro-

59 One vivid list of a hundred Red Guard proscriptions is translated in *Chinese Sociology and Anthropology* (Spring-Summer 1970), 215–27. (From a September 1966 Peking Red Guard document.)
60 Claudie Broyelle, Jacques Broyelle, and Evelyne Tschirhart, *China: a second Look*, 204. It might be noted that in 1952, Ralph Lapwood remarked approvingly (see *Through the Chinese revolution*, 81) that whereas under the Nationalists school children had to bow to Sun Yat-sen's portrait in the morning, no such worshiplike rituals had been adopted by the new government in regard to Mao Tse-tung.

letarian style. In a few work units showers and even laundry and other
service facilities were dismantled as representing too much catering to
"bourgeois" personal needs.

Bookstores and libraries scurried to take newly proscribed books off of
the shelves, and the repertoires of film companies and opera troupes were
similarly drastically affected. Some temples were defaced, the few remaining Christian churches were shut down, and those who wished to engage
in religious worship of any kind had to do so furtively, in the secrecy of
their own homes. Many kinds of recreational activities, such as dances,
camping outings, and hobby clubs also fell under suspicion for being
bourgeois and were cut back sharply. There were also attempts to take
much of the remaining life out of traditional festivals by encouraging
people to work right through them and by prohibiting the moon cakes,
incense, dragon boat races, and other ritual markers around which such
festivals turned. Cremation also began to be much more universally
required in the larger cities, with burials common only in smaller cities
and towns. Other ritual events were also affected – lavish wedding feasts,
pictures in Western-style wedding garments, and traditional mourning
rites were all taboo in these years. Maids, martial arts specialists, magi-
cians, and others found their occupations called into question as irrelevant to Chinese socialism. Owners of private homes in large cities had to
turn over their deeds and then begin paying rent on their premises. The
small-scale, licensed peddling and private handicraft activities that had
been allowed to operate in previous years were banned once again, and
even collective enterprises operated under more severe restrictions, unable to distribute their profits to employees. Even fertility began to be
strictly regulated in the 1970s, with births and contraceptive use monitored to try to prevent any urban family from having more than two
children, a limit that would be reduced to one child in 1979. (Actually,
energetic birth control efforts began to be pushed in urban areas in 1962,
in the wake of the failure of the Great Leap Forward, but both the demands made and the degree of organization of the effort escalated after
1970.)

Although some of these strictures began to be loosened a little even
before 1976, the effect of the Cultural Revolution on popular culture was
to disrupt previous customs and require conformity to a more limited
range of approved forms of behavior. The population had had ample previous experience in adapting to changing official demands, but the severity of the new controls nevertheless was agonizing for many, who saw
family heirlooms destroyed, were no longer able to worship as they
wished, and could not hold the sorts of wedding or funeral observances

they felt were proper. Another effect was to impoverish the cultural and recreational life of the populace. Instead of being involved in the organization and pursuit of a variety of activities, people found themselves required to participate in a narrow range of activities over and over again, the most dramatic case being the repetitiously performed model revolutionary operas.

In some cases the shortage of approved activities meant that nothing much was organized. Whereas in the past work units often celebrated national holidays with special food distributions, sports competitions, dances, and other recreational activities, in the 1970s some simply subjected employees to speeches on such occasions and then allowed them to go home. Students also found they had fewer and less varied extracurricular and vacation activities organized than used to be the case. A curious effect of the change in recreational activities was that urbanites were able more and more to retreat into the company of their families and close friends during their spare time, rather than being maximally involved in collective affairs as the radicals desired.

The effects of all of these changes on family life were complex. In the initial stages of the Cultural Revolution there were clearly some strains. Young people got involved in Red Guard activities that worried or even terrified their parents. In a few cases these activities brought young people into direct conflict with their parents – through participating in a "four olds" search of their own homes or denouncing or breaking ties with their parents. Sometimes differing factional sympathies or political troubles also created strain between spouses or even precipitated divorces. Later on, the inability to help children avoid rural rustication or assist them in planning their lives added to parental anguish, and families worried about how their offspring would survive their years in the countryside. Many adults were also forcibly separated from their spouses and children and required to undergo "remolding" in a penal institution or a May 7 cadre school.

Still, on balance, the forces in this period probably strengthened family ties and loyalties rather than weakened them, in spite of all the rhetoric about supreme loyalty to Mao Tse-tung. For one thing, families tended to share the fate of an individual member in trouble, producing in many cases a shared sense of resentment and solidarity in the face of discrimination. We have also noted that the poverty of recreational life during this time helped reinforce family ties. The importance of connections and "going by the back door" also tended to encourage people to rely on kin rather than conform to the bureaucratic rules. Perhaps most important, the severe disruptions and privations produced a need for allies and pro-

tection; but because the shifting political winds made many previous
allies unavailable or unreliable, people were impelled to rely even more
than in the past on their families and close friends in coping with the
many uncertainties of life. So families were in many cases driven inward
and found new strength and solidarity in this period. Even with the
resulting joint family efforts, however, many felt that important family
goals could not be met. The desire to become more prosperous, to keep
family members together, to see offspring married and started on rewarding careers, and to see family events celebrated in appropriate ways –
these very basic family goals were constantly frustrated in the Cultural
Revolution decade.

It should be noted that by this time one very important kind of kinship
tie had been dramatically undermined – that between urbanites and their
rural kin. In meeting the pressures of urban life one's own family would
certainly be relied upon, and close kin living elsewhere in the city or even
in other cities could often be of help. Many urbanites could tell tales of
kin in another city sending a "care package" of goods more plentiful
there, arranging for special surgery through their personal ties in that
city, or providing other kinds of assistance. But a number of factors over
the years – the migration restrictions, urban prohibitions of burials and
ancestor worship, tight work schedules, and simply diverging income
trends and patterns of life – made urban and rural areas in China increasingly into two separate worlds, as already noted.[61] The ties to one's
native place and a rural lineage, formerly prominent features of traditional Chinese cities, were much less in evidence three decades after the
revolution. To give one concrete example, an observer in Shanghai in
1952 had noted that "as the Lunar New Year drew near ... nearly the
entire older generation would pour out of the country, shouldering the
fatted calf, to visit their descendants in town."[62] These visits – which
according to the observer often lasted two months and often involved
substantial exchanges of food, gifts, and favors between rural and urban
kin – were decidedly rare by the 1970s.

By the time of Mao's death, in 1976, many of the important sources of
support for the government had been eroded, and a variety of grievances
were accumulating beneath the surface. The strict political controls of
the period generally kept such discontent hidden, but occasionally local
circumstances allowed disturbances to break out, and a number of strikes,

61 Detailed evidence on the divergence is provided in Martin King Whyte, "Town and country in
    contemporary China," *Comparative Urban Research*, 10 (1983), 9–20. For further details on the
    castelike barriers imposed between peasants and urbanites since 1949, see Sulamith Heins Potter,
    "The position of peasants in modern China's social order," *Modern China*, 9 (1983), 465–99.
62 Wood, *A street in China*, 149.

protests by veterans' groups, and similar events did occur. The sense
of problems seething beneath the surface, the death within months of
Chou En-lai and Chu Te as well as Mao, and the devastating earthquake
at T'ang-shan in 1976 – all added to popular anxieties about the future.

POST-MAO CHINA, 1977 AND BEYOND

In the wake of Mao's death and the arrest of his radical supporters, the
"Gang of Four," one month later, China's leaders had to operate in a
sense of crisis that had multiple dimensions: poor work motivation,
weakened Party authority, resentment against elite privileges, frustration
over poor supplies, rising juvenile delinquency, and other pressing problems. The reforms subsequently introduced took a variety of forms and
were meant to deal with various aspects of this crisis: revelations and
denunciations of the suffering caused by the Cultural Revolution, the curtailing of the program of sending urban youth to the countryside, introduction of elements of a legal code, a new openness to Western trade and
contacts, a loosening of controls over communications and culture and
over private enterprise activities, efforts to restore the pre–Cultural
Revolution educational system and revive a predictable opportunity
structure, a new emphasis on respect for intellectuals, and an effort to
downplay the importance of class struggle. In general an atmosphere of
agonizing reexamination of China's shortcomings replaced the revolutionary smugness of the Cultural Revolution decade.

In the economic realm the improvements in supplies of both food
items and manufactured goods after Mao's death helped reduce popular
grumbling. Wage increases carried out several times after 1977 terminated
the long wage freeze, and members of the labor force were once again
able to increase their pay via bonuses and piece-rate premiums. A new
push to build more urban housing helped provide some families with
long-overdue relief from cramped living conditions. In general, all of
these changes were welcomed, although they did not fully satisfy the
backlog of expectations that had been built up.

In terms of mobility and status enhancement, large numbers of people
who had been stigmatized or demoted were rehabilitated and promoted,
and many skilled people were transferred to jobs more appropriate to
their talents. Groups such as Overseas Chinese and intellectuals had their
former privileges restored, and some individuals even received windfalls
in the form of several years of back pay or rent payments (actually, such
compensation began before 1977). The pace of transfer of rusticated
youths back to urban jobs picked up, and the pressure on newly gradu-

ating urban youth to go to the countryside was effectively eliminated. With the restoration of exam competition, keypoint schools, and direct entry from middle schools to universities, urban youth could once again see a set of primarily academic hurdles that had to be cleared in order to obtain a high-prestige job. Expression of individual preferences and career aspirations was no longer taboo, and even the prospect of going abroad for advanced study was once again available to the select few. The previous efforts to ban private enterprise entirely and to restrict collective enterprises were repudiated, and large numbers of privately run restaurants and service facilities and collective firms began to spring up and to absorb the majority of the young people being employed for the first time. These changes and the reopening of the peasant "free markets" within the cities helped restore some color to the drab urban landscape.

A number of factors made urbanites less satisfied with these changes than the authorities would have liked. For one thing, several price increases instituted after 1979 for meat, vegetables, and other basic food items, and difficulties in maintaining firm control over prices, gave rise to a new surge of inflation that led many urbanites to wonder how much their increased pay was really gaining them. And although those rehabilitated and restored to former positions certainly appreciated the improvement, their primary feeling was often one of vindication. In such cases their gratitude was tempered by a grudge. At the same time the slowness and bureaucratic wrangling over these changes led to much anxiety and anger.

The basic problem was that virtually all people felt that improvement in their lot was long overdue but that, in implementing changes, some people were selected for raises or privileges and others were not, giving rise to much envy and resentment. In work units countless hours were spent after 1977 in meetings called to decide who should get raises and bonuses, and in some cases employees not selected broke down in tears before colleagues or superiors with tales of how difficult their lives would be if they were not included. Those who were left out in the process were understandably angry and sometimes showed their feelings in novel ways, such as the boiler-room operators in a steel factory who shut down the heat to demonstrate that they did make a vital contribution to production.[63] Thus, considerable numbers of urbanites began to feel that they had not benefited enough from these changes. In the prevailing atmosphere of skepticism the view that bureaucrats and upper intellectuals were

63 See Agence France Presse report, Peking, 4 February 1979, in FBIS *Daily Report: China*, 6 February 1979, E1.

benefiting more than ordinary urbanites was also widely believed. Subsequent efforts by the authorities to argue that enterprises had to become more efficient in part by "breaking the iron rice bowl" and laying off or firing poor-quality or troublesome workers have been particularly threatening in this context.

For young people who did not yet have the security of a job the situation remained particularly anxious. Efforts to phase out the rustication campaign did at least relieve them of the fear of being sent into rural exile. But large segments of earlier cohorts still remained stuck in the countryside and angry about their fate, and when the "democracy movement" of 1978–79 made it possible, some of these youths streamed back into the city and mounted demonstrations. Even youths able to obtain urban jobs found themselves mostly employed in the collective or newly revived private sectors, and many of these jobs had low pay, little prestige, and few fringe benefits, not to mention poor advancement prospects. So even youths who returned from the countryside in many cases felt their gratitude tinged with disappointment at not being able to use their talents and achieve their aspirations. Since being stuck in a low-prestige job could affect one for life – not only in terms of income but also with regard to access to housing, attracting a spouse, and other matters – some young people chose to refuse the job assigned to them and accepted unemployment in the hope of eventually passing the university entrance examination or getting assigned a better job.

The newly reformed school system reoriented most urban students to aim toward college enrollment and subsequent work as an expert as the highest calling in the China of the "four modernizations."[64] But the changing demographic situation made this an even more heartbreaking competition than in the past. Instead of the more than 40 percent of upper middle school graduates who could anticipate college entry in 1965 (and 100 percent in 1953–56), by the end of the 1970s less than 4 percent of them could anticipate such success.[65] So while the post-Mao changes restored a clear opportunity structure, they also gave rise to hopes and expectations that could not possibly be met. After 1979 the authorities began efforts to cope with the resulting problems, such as converting some general middle schools to vocational and technical training schools and encouraging parents to retire early and pass their jobs on to a son

64 For example, a visitor to China observed a musical performance in which the leading lady described in song whom she would bestow her red flower on: "For years we have praised the workers and peasants and ignored the scientists. I am saving my flower for the boy studying to be a scientist. He will lead the modernization of China." W. E. Garrett, "China's beauty spot," *National Geographic*, 156 (1979), 548–49.
65 The last figure is cited in Rosen, "Obstacles to educational reform," 11.

or daughter. Nevertheless, the problem of coping with the large number of disappointed urban school graduates (now called "waiting for
work youth" rather than "intellectual youth" or "social youth") remained
serious.

The more dismal prospects urbanites perceived in the 1970s also help
explain the unusual success of the official birth-control program, with
birthrates in some cities under ten per thousand during this period. In the
official accounts this success is often attributed to the birth-control campaign itself, which after being disrupted by the Cultural Revolution
disorders, became increasingly strict after 1970, with only two children
allowed, rewards and penalties to force compliance, birth quotas passed
out, and contraceptive usage and sometimes even menstrual periods
monitored in work units and neighborhoods. But such official claims
ignore the fact that urban birthrates generally had been dropping since
the early 1960s, and had already reached unusually low levels by 1971, just
as the vigorous birth control efforts were getting under way.[66] It would
appear that the uncertain prospects for the future of one's children,
combined with the general shortages of housing and consumer goods and
the heavy burdens of raising children with nearly universal female employment, made bearing two children or just one child acceptable to many
urbanites even before the government began to require them to have no
more than this.[67]

In any complex economy there are problems in the lack of perfect fit
between the material goods and opportunities available and the aspirations of the population. But in China the consequences of the disparity
were particularly worrisome to the authorities. For one thing, the long
years of pent-up demands acted to make aspirations rise faster than they
could possibly be satisfied, weakening or nullifying the popular gratitude
that improvements could be expected to produce. Additionally, the combination of new opportunity to express personal ambitions and the modest improvements in the ability to raise and share grievances meant that
urbanites became aware of how widely their own sense of deprivation
was shared by others. The nature of socialism makes such feelings politi-

66 For example, see the figures for Shanghai presented in Judith Banister, "Mortality, fertility, and
    contraceptive use in Shanghai," *CQ*, 70 (June 1977), 268. For the national picture, consult Ansley
    J. Coale, *Rapid population change in China, 1952–1982*, 5.
67 According to a Chinese time budget study in two cities, for instance, Chinese couples spend con-
    siderably more time per day on housework than do couples in other socialist or capitalist societies.
    Moreover, the time spent on domestic chores goes up with each extra child – from 3.4 hours each
    workday for childless women to 4.3 hours per day for women with one child and 4.7 hours per
    day for women with two children. See Wang Ya-lin and Li Chin-jung, "Ch'eng-shih chih-kung
    chia-wu lao-tung yen-chiu" (Research on the housework of urban workers and employees),
    Chung-kuo she-hui k'o-hsueh, no. 1 (1982), 177–90.

cally important because in such a system the state is supposed to regulate and provide resources to advance popular welfare, so that when people feel deprived they are likely to blame the state and not fate, their own personal inadequacy, or other "external" factors.

Frustrated aspirations do not by themselves, recent research tells us, produce revolts or revolutions, but still the frustrations and resentment of elite privileges that were fostered complicated the task of ensuring a hard-working, compliant population. Authorities in China today would probably agree with an observation R. H. Tawney made in 1932: "Political forces in China resemble Chinese rivers. The pressure on the dykes is enormous, but unseen; it is only when they burst that the strain is realized."[68]

Similar comments can be made about post-Mao changes in the political realm. The government tried to turn a new page so that individuals would once again feel relatively safe from political victimization, trust the equity and efficacy of their political institutions, and respect the authority of the Party and the state. But here as well the changes introduced were in certain ways counterproductive. The combination of revelations about the repression and abuses of power of the Cultural Revolution decade and increased freedom to speak openly and critically about the government led some to feel that China's political system was corrupt and to know that others shared this view. A wave of cynicism about Chinese politics spread that legal codes, Party rectification, and new rules and procedures could not totally check. Throughout urban China in the late 1970s and into the 1980s, and particularly in the largest cities, there were signs of a widespread authority crisis – of minimal sales of political tracts, student objections to required political courses, and of public opinion polls among young people that revealed skepticism about socialism and intense resentment of the "special privileges" of the elite. Michael Lindsay had observed as early as 1950 that there were two opposing tendencies at war within Chinese politics, "on the one hand, rational thought, good administration, and respect for the common man; on the other unreasoning faith in dogma, bureaucracy, and contempt for the individual.... The development of China is likely to take completely different paths according to which tendency predominates."[69] By the late 1970s many urbanites had concluded with regret that the second tendency had won out.

After 1979, one reaction of the authorities to these problems was to crack down again on dissent – by arresting prominent dissidents, by

68 Quoted in Gilbert Rozman, ed., *The modernization of China*, 310.
69 From van der Sprenkel et al., *New China: three views*, 130.

eliminating the "four freedoms" from the constitution, and by organizing criticism of writers who had strayed too far from orthodox lines. To some urbanites such actions only proved that the authorities were primarily interested in maintaining control rather than in allowing a full examination of the problems of Chinese society. In this respect the changes since 1957 made public support for the official crackdown much weaker than it had been in the Anti-Rightist Campaign. Still, the vigor with which segments of the urban population voiced critical views, despite the long history of such critics' being squashed, seems to indicate that the population felt more secure from political victimization than in the past.

The government tried to stimulate enthusiasm for political participation by forming workers' representative congresses, holding direct elections using secret ballots for local and county-level people's congress delegates, and through other devices. But the skepticism that developed in the late 1970s led many urbanites to doubt that such organs would have much autonomous power or that the Party would tolerate the election of outspoken critics to such posts. Given the events of recent years, many urbanites reverted to a traditional view of politics – that it is an unpredictable and dangerous realm that should be avoided if at all possible. The result was an important change in the political atmosphere. Fewer urbanites than in the past were eager to seek admission to the Party. And whereas in the 1950s and early 1960s individuals competed to display their activism, and those considered politically "backward" were in danger of being stigmatized, by the end of the 1970s it was often the activists who felt isolated and looked down upon. Official policies helped create this situation by lauding the contributions of experts and threatening poorly educated political cadres with demotion, but in the process they created a new and very important group with a grievance – the thousands of individuals who had made names for themselves primarily through their political activism and as a consequence felt their status threatened. Efforts to revive at least partly the stress on political work and the virtues of "redness" in the early 1980s were perhaps designed to placate the feelings of this group.

The legacy of crime and juvenile delinquency spawned by the Cultrual Revolution carried over into the post-Mao period, producing continued popular anxieties. Indeed, the phasing out of the rustication program and the return to the cities of many disgruntled and underemployed youths may have aggravated the crime problem. With media policy changed to allow coverage of major crime cases, and with widespread publicity surrounding the introduction of the new criminal code after 1979, public consciousness of the crime danger perhaps increased more than the actual crime rate. Nostalgia for the good old days, when one could walk alone in safety late at night and when public morality was seen as very high, remained strong in the post-Mao period.

Trends in cultural life and popular customs after 1976 were generally perceived in much more unambiguously positive terms by much of the public. The stultifying controls over literature and the arts in the preceding decade and the draconian effort to enforce conformity with a rigid socialist puritanism produced a cultural life that was unsatisfying and forced urbanites to abandon cherished customs and behavior. When the rules were relaxed modestly after 1976 the effects were dramatic and obvious. New literary and artistic creations flooded out, which although not daring in international terms, clearly broke the rigid conventions that had prevailed. Feelings of love, characters who were not all good or bad, sad endings – these and other elements promoted variety in Chinese literature. Bookstores, movie theaters, and stages were filled with more varied fare – revivals of banned works as well as new creations. Western works began to be allowed in on a scale that had had no parallel in the preceding thirty years. Foreign books were translated, foreign films and television shows were displayed, and foreign radio stations could be listened to legally once again (although Taiwan radio and Hong Kong television still fell beyond the pale). To the urban public, the switch from *The red detachment of women* to *The man from Atlantis* (an American television serial) was quite startling.

Efforts were also made to revive the neglected cultural and recreational life of units – school extracurricular activities, work unit social gatherings, and so forth. Religious activities also began to be tolerated once again, as were modest observances of traditional festivals, pet raising, and a long list of other customs that had previously been taboo. In areas like family ritual some urbanites eagerly took advantage of the modest liberalizations by spending lavishly and reviving old ritual forms in celebrating weddings and funerals. In general, then, there was a perceptible "coming alive" in social life and customs, with the public released from the rigid standards of the previous period. And predictably enough, this shift almost immediately gave rise to official concern that things were going too far, and to efforts to discourage wedding feasts, Western fashion fads, and other symbols of the post-Mao period. What's more, the liberalizing trend did not extend to every realm. As previously noted, it was in this period that traditional fertility desires were being most severely restricted, with strict rewards and penalties implemented to reinforce the new one-child-per-family policy.

Also broadly welcomed were changes in interpersonal relations. In part this involved the lessening of the paranoia and caution that the political tensions of the previous period had spawned. But the post-Mao policies also allowed many families to "retrieve" their offspring from the country-side and enabled a substantial number of cadres forced by job assignments to live apart from their spouses to arrange to be reunited and work in the same place. Large numbers of stigmatized people were also rehabilitated and were able to begin repairing the kinship and friendship ties their troubles had disrupted; there was even a minor wave of remarriages of couples who had been forced to divorce under political pressure. In a number of ways, then, urbanites were able to feel that their interpersonal relationships were beginning to be restored to something approaching normalcy. Of course, the restoration of contacts and ties had in some cases the effect of fostering the communication of grievances and tales of suffering that made the implications of this change for governmental authority decidedly mixed.

The role of cities in China's development also began to be reevaluated in the post-Mao years. The long-standing policy of controlling urban growth, and especially the growth of the largest cities, had been partially successful. Although no consistent set of urban population statistics had been released, it was apparent that cities had grown more rapidly than the total population under Communist rule, from constituting something on the order of 13 percent of the total population in 1953 to 18.4 percent in 1964 and 20.6 percent in 1982.[70] Still, in view of the privileged nature of urban areas, the growth of cities would almost certainly have been faster had it not been for the strict efforts over the years to restrict migration from the countryside and deport "excess" urbanites to China's rural areas. Although some cities, such as Peking and Wuhan, grew rapidly, China's largest city, Shanghai, was prevented from growing, so its "primacy" – its share of the total urban population – actually declined from about 8 percent in 1953 to about 4 percent in 1982.[71]

It became increasingly clear, however, that this control of urban growth had entailed considerable cost. In part this involved the anger and

70 This comparison is only approximate because definitions of what is urban have changed over time, and city boundaries have shifted too (although these figures refer to city areas proper, and not their surrounding rural counties). Figures here are from Ullman, "Cities of mainland China: 1953–1959," 81–103; and *Beijing Review*, 45 (1982), 21.

71 Actually, Shanghai's metropolitan population fluctuated over time – from 4.4 million in 1949 to 6.2 million in 1953, 7.2 million in 1958, 5.7 million in 1971, and 6.3 million in 1982. See Banister, "Mortality, fertility, and contraceptive use in Shanghai," 259–60; Ullman, "Cities of mainland China: 1953–1959," 81–103; and *Chung-kuo ti-san-tz'u jen-k'ou p'u-ch'a ti chu-yao shu-tzu* (Main figures from China's third population census), 14–15. It is now clear, however, that these urban statistics are somewhat misleading because they ignore the large number of rural residents who went into the cities in the 1960s and 1970s to work as "temporary workers." In the 1980s this large number of unregistered people residing in cities, often for long periods, began to be officially discussed as a potential problem.

heartbreak of the millions deported from their urban homes over the years and the disruptions in the lives of even those who were eventually able to return. But the official policy also failed in its goal of promoting rural-urban integration. By the late 1970s urbanites were more different from rural residents in living standards and patterns of life than before 1949, and peasants who were kept from taking advantage of urban opportunities often bridled at the privileged position of their urban counterparts.[72] Perhaps just as important, the post-Mao leaders perceived that China's cities were not playing as dynamic a role in spurring growth and innovation as they should. Although these leaders did not dismantle the barriers against permanent migration by peasants into the cities, they did take steps to stimulate growth and creativity in urban enterprises, lauded the leading role of large cities, and placed many small and medium-sized cities in direct command of their surrounding rural areas. Such measures indicated a growing realization that while the previous policies may have prevented the sort of urban sprawl and overurbanization common elsewhere in the Third World, perhaps by the same token they had stunted the dynamism of the entire economy and thus harmed rural as well as urban areas. What role cities should play in China's future development remained a topic of heated debate.

CONCLUSIONS

By the 1980s it had become clear that the effort to create a highly organized, egalitarian, Spartan, and productive urban community had gone awry, and that as a consequence urbanites were far from the involved and committed population that the authorities desired. Success in creating a new urban form in the 1950s had given way more than two decades later to agonizing reappraisals of what had gone wrong and efforts to find new answers (or revive old answers) to urban dilemmas.

The mood of the urban population as China entered the 1980s was not uniform, however. The dramatic shifts in events and policies over the years produced life experiences that differed sharply across the generations and were reflected in varying reactions to the post-Mao urban scene. A detailed analysis of these cohort differences cannot be offered here, but some rather rough generalizations can be attempted.[73]

72 It should be noted, though, that the major increase in procurement prices in 1979 and liberalizations in rural organization and policies initiated then did reverse the long-term trend, at least temporarily, and led to peasant incomes and consumption expenditures growing faster in the period 1979–84 than those of urbanites.
73 A more refined effort to look at age distinctions among youths is presented in Thomas B. Gold, "China's youth: problems and programs," *Issues & Studies*, 18.8 (1982), 39–62. The present discussion is influenced by Gold's article.

For those over 60, and particularly for those who had retired from the
work force, there was a general feeling that their day in the sun was over.
Some had been able to lead rich and rewarding lives, others saw most of
their talents wasted in the new society, and some had been through bitter
ordeals. But by the 1980s promises about the four modernizations and the
future had limited appeal, and, as with the aged in many societies, they
concentrated on deriving simple pleasures from family and friends and
enjoying their final years. Although few now could enjoy the carefree
final years that were traditionally aspired to – most, for example, had to
help out with child-care and household chores so that the younger generation could concentrate on their jobs – still the security and pleasures
enjoyed were substantial. Most urban aged had pensions, enjoyed free
medical care, and lived with a grown offspring who would care for them
until their deaths. And most continued to enjoy the sociability of ties with
neighbors and former workmates that the restrictions on residential and
occupational mobility had helped to reinforce. So although there are
many exceptions, on balance the urban aged tended to be more satisfied
than those in younger cohorts. An account of how people in this age
bracket reacted to the news of the death of Mao echoes this verdict:

The older people could compare the present with the past, with its illnesses and
famines, its crowds of beggars, its lack of work. Despite the shortages, the corruption, and the political troubles, most of the older people felt that Chairman
Mao's Socialism had brought them a better life. It didn't matter that for many the
improvement could be measured in pennies; they were deeply grateful, and wept
as if they had lost one of their own parents.[74]

Those in their forties and fifties at the start of the 1980s were the ones
most affected by what might be called the "Camelot syndrome." They
were the ones who matured and began work soon after 1949 and who
were most caught up in the optimism of that period. They saw the new
government then as perhaps ruthless and demanding, but nevertheless as
the vehicle that could create a better society and more rewarding lives for
all. They gave the authorities their energies and subordinated their personal goals to those of the state, and now many felt disillusioned. The
society they saw around them was less appealing than the one they had
worked to create, and they agonized over what had gone wrong. Many in
this generation felt anger and disappointment in substantial measure, but
at the same time most were not totally alienated from the system. Rather,
the experiences of their younger years left them with a wistful nostalgia
for what was and what might have been. Thus, although skeptical of re-

74 Liang and Shapiro, *Son of the revolution*, 263.

cent trends and official pronouncements, many in this age group wanted to believe that things could be set right again.[75]

The cohorts who were in their thirties in the early 1980s had a somewhat different outlook, and this was particularly true for the former Red Guards. They, too, grew up in an atmosphere of optimism and enthusiasm, although they experienced stiffer competition than their elder brothers and sisters. Because of this early optimism and commitment, the reality of their lives since 1966 was the most crushing – factional violence, rural exile, educational and marital disappointments, and for many at best eventual return to a low-status urban job. These were the ones who felt most cheated and were the most cynical and boldly critical of the system in which they lived. Even some of those in this age group who managed better fates – university admission or a secure state job – remained alienated. Perhaps the words of the famous 1974 Li I-che wall poster express their sentiments most vividly: "We are youths who harbor no fear of tigers, but this does not mean that we fail to understand the savagery and cruelty of tigers. It can be said that we have been mauled by tigers, but not having been chewed to death or swallowed, we are lucky survivors with scars left on our faces, no longer handsome young men."[76]

Younger cohorts who finished school in the 1970s and early 1980s presented a still different picture. Their experiences in the disrupted educational system and recurrent campaigns did not inculcate in them the same optimism and commitment that the older cohorts shared. Rather, the shifting standards and unpredictability of those years promoted in many an orientation to intimidate competitors and get one's own way by hook or by crook. Because the initial hopes of this group were never so high, their sense of disappointment and anger was less than in the older cohorts. But at the same time political slogans had little appeal, and many in this age range were preoccupied with consumer goods acquisition and unconventional life-styles to a degree that shocked members of older cohorts. Many of these youths were more "turned off" to politics than inclined to protest.[77]

In regard to the youngest urbanites – those still in school in the 1980s – the government was striving to set things aright by reestablishing predict-

---

75 John Hersey describes being surprised at the "loyal yearning for a bright future for China" rather than bitterness that many of the older intellectuals he met in China displayed. See "A reporter at large: homecoming," part 3, *The New Yorker*, 24 May 1982, 61. A personal account that reflects this sort of sentiment is Yue and Wakeman, *To the storm*.

76 Quoted in Yih-tang Lin, comp., *What they say: a collection of current Chinese underground publications*, xvii.

77 Hersey ("A reporter at large," 65) characterizes this cohort as "bland, undirected, cynical, and callow."

able rules, tightening discipline and moral indoctrination, and providing more rewarding opportunities to aim for. How successful such efforts would be, and how well the authorities would be able to provide adult lives that would meet the expectations of this group, remained to be seen.

In reevaluating what went wrong during the three decades after the revolution, one common analysis is to blame the radicals, and Mao Tse-tung in particular, for launching the Cultural Revolution (and earlier misguided campaigns) that disrupted lives and destroyed hopes. It should be clear from our retracing of urban moods over the years that this sort of analysis is too simple. The factors that promote or undermine popular enthusiasm for the political system are more complex than such a view would recognize.

After 1949 the authorities to a considerable extent operated on the assumption that a tight-knit organizational system and intense ideological commitment would lead to success in tackling urban problems. Such an assumption ignores the way popular values and aspirations shape responses to political authority. Chinese urbanites were not in 1949 "poor and blank" objects ready to absorb the will of the leadership. Rather, they held to certain time-honored values and desires that colored their views of the new system. These included the desire for national strength and political order, as well as for economic security, equity, and opportunity; concern about control over crime, prostitution, and other social evils; an eagerness for political security and trust; a desire for varied and satisfying cultural and recreational pursuits; and a thirst for circumstances in which family obligations could be met and cohesive interpersonal ties could be maintained. The relatively high levels of optimism and commitment achieved during the 1950s can be attributed in large part to the widespread perception that such desires were being realized much more fully after 1949 than before, and largely as a result of the actions and programs of the new government. The erosion of good feelings that occurred subsequently can similarly be linked to growing feelings that such desires were no longer being realized, and that official actions were substantially to blame.

The changing mood was not simply the product of radical policies and misguided campaigns, however. Some of the factors that contributed to the change, such as the growing demographic problem and the aging of the bureaucratic structure, were long-run processes set in motion by events of the optimistic 1950s. Other problematic policies – the wage freeze, for instance, or the migration restrictions – were not simply the product of radical campaign impulses. Furthermore, some events in the radical phases that have been denounced by China's post-Mao leaders enjoyed a measure of real popularity at the time – the crackdown on the rightists in 1957, for instance, and the early Great Leap mobilizations and the Cultural Revolution attacks on bureaucratic privilege.

Moreover, it would be misleading to imply that the popular support for the government that existed in the 1950s had been eroded entirely by the 1980s. In spite of harsh ordeals and insecurity experienced by many urbanites over the years, powerful sources of support for the government remained. In part there was simply the traditional inclination to show due respect for China's rulers, which provided the authorities with a measure of "benefit of the doubt." In addition, it must be noted that there were still millions of urbanites – particularly among the cadres and manual workers – who felt that, in spite of intervening difficulties, their lives were much better and more secure because of the revolution, and who remained hopeful that the political system that produced those improvements could deal with China's new problems. Urbanites who utilized free medical care, purchased a new television set, saw the neighbors organize to combat dirt and flies, or arranged for a son or daughter to succeed them in their job could still reflect on the benefits socialism had brought them.

Finally, one major source of support for the authorities had not eroded in the same way as the others – pride in national strength and autonomy. In many respects China was stronger and more of a force in the world in the 1980s than it had been in the 1950s, and most urban Chinese, heirs to a century-long concern over national humiliation and betrayal, felt a sense of intense pride at every sign of China's strength, whether it was an effective speech by its United Nations delegate, a respectful pilgrimage to Peking by a foreign head of state, or a Chinese victory in an international volleyball tournament. (The other side of the coin is a widely shared sense of shame, and potential for social unrest, when people feel that China is doing poorly or is being insulted by foreign powers.)

In some respects, it should be noted, the radical phases in Chinese politics had contributed more to this sense of national pride than the intervening moderate periods. In the Cultural Revolution decade, for instance, China engaged in what was popularly perceived as a relatively successful conflict with the Soviet Union, ended its diplomatic isolation and took its place in the United Nations, launched an earth satellite, and saw a wide variety of visitors ranging from Richard Nixon to Third World revolutionaries come to inspect the new China. In the ensuing post-Mao period China's continued backwardness relative to other East Asian developing societies was made more apparent, China lost its Cambodian client state and fought what was perceived as a relatively unsuccessful border war with Vietnam, and the nation was engulfed by a new wave of visitors, who came not to seek revolutionary wisdom but to gain concessions and advantages such as had not been permitted since the revolution.[78] If an intense patriotism remained the linchpin of popular support for the government, the program of opening China up to the world threatened to undermine the effort to restore public support for the authorities.

The post-Mao leaders faced, then, the sort of problem that Humpty Dumpty represented for all the king's horses and all the king's men. They wanted to be able to re-create the sense of optimism and public support that had prevailed during the 1950s. But since the mood of that time depended in part on conditions that could never be fully re-created – a scarcity of educated personnel, the need to create and staff a new bureaucratic structure, recent memories of the Anti-Japanese and civil wars, and so forth – restoring previous policies would not do the trick. Neither would tighter organizational discipline and new doses of ideological exhortation put things right. Only by finding ways to satisfy the basic values and demands of the urban population to an increasing extent would it be possible to overcome the sense of crisis that prevailed more than three decades after the revolution. The effort to do so will challenge the skills of China's elite in the 1990s and beyond.

78 These new foreign advantages involve not only things such as being able to invest directly in China and bring in large numbers of foreign personnel, but even such measures as converting workers' rest homes in the famous seaside resort of Peitaiho back into hotels for foreigners. Some popular opposition to the new openness can be seen in the press debate after 1978 over whether the nineteenth-century Chinese westernizers were good or bad, charges that crime was being fostered by foreign influences, and, more dramatically, in occasional incidents in which a Chinese assaults or spits on a foreign visitor. See, for example, Garrett, "China's beauty spot," 552. In the mid-1980s riots occurred in Peking and in other cities in reaction to such things as a loss to a Hong Kong team in a soccer match and the flooding of Chinese markets with Japanese goods that were seen as substandard.

CHAPTER 11

LITERATURE UNDER COMMUNISM

THE INSTITUTION OF A SOCIALIST LITERATURE, 1949–1956

The organization of literary production

The first national Congress of Literature and Art Workers assembled 650 delegates in Peking from 2 July through 19 July 1949, some three months before the formal establishment of the People's Republic itself.[1] Mao Tse-tung, Chou En-lai, and other national figures emphasized by their presence the importance the leadership would attach to the development of a new socialist culture and the establishment of the necessary organs for its direction. The umbrella organization under which all cultural activities were to be coordinated was later (1953) to be christened the All-China Federation of Literary and Art Circles. Beneath this umbrella have come into existence, through four decades and with a pronounced hiatus at the time of the Cultural Revolution (roughly the ten years 1966–76), ten unions, covering fiction and poetry (the Writers Union), drama (the Dramatists Union, the largest of all because it incorporates performers as well as writers), cinema, music, dance, fine arts, performing literature, folk literature, children's literature, and circus (this last the newest, established at its fourth congress, in November 1979).

Although the federation has been responsible for the important stock-takings during the four national congresses (1949, 1953, 1960, 1979), the central role in the ongoing work of the direction and development of the new literature has been played by the Writers Union. This organ, which traces its origins back at least to the patriotic associations formed from 1937 onward by Lao She, Kuo Mo-jo, and other eminent men of letters, provides a forum for writers, holding frequent discussion meetings in all parts of the country. While questions of literary and artistic theory and policy are discussed in the *Literary Gazette* (*Wen-i pao*), published by the

---

1 *Liu-shih-nien wen-i ta-shih-chi, 1919–79* (Major cultural events of sixty years, 1919–79), prepared in draft form for the fourth Congress of Literature and Art Workers, gives authoritative information on organizational matters.

federation itself, the Writers Union operates leading journals such as *People's Literature* (*Jen-min wen-hsueh*) for creative writings deemed to be of national significance. Committees of the Writers Union handle editorial policies, relations with writers and academies of other countries, and the assistance of promising young writers in terms of assignment to work units for collection of material, provision of travel facilities, and so forth.

The position of chairman of the federation went in 1949 to the poet and dramatist Kuo Mo-jo (1892–1978), who held the office until his death. He was succeeded by his first vice-chairman, the novelist Mao Tun (1896–1981), who on his death was in turn succeeded by the critic Chou Yang (b. 1908), second vice-chairman in the early years.

In a major report to the first congress,[2] Chou Yang described the achievements of writers in the Communist-governed sectors of the nation as a "great beginning," which he dated firmly from Mao Tse-tung's "Talks at the Yenan forum of writers and artists" of May 1942. Chou reiterated Mao's major theses: the assignment to literature and the arts of the functions of weapons in the struggle against class enemies and tools in the socialist reconstruction of the nation; the need to furnish the worker, peasant, and soldier masses with "what the Chinese people love to see and hear"; and the obligation of the writer or artist, in order to meet this need, to abolish the gap between his own consciousness and that of the people by "making himself one with the masses." The necessary standpoint of the artist must be that of the proletariat and broad masses, and his attitude toward the masses must be to praise their toil and struggle and to educate them. Artistic criteria were necessary conditions and were important, but precedence must go always to political criteria in art and literature as in all other aspects of the national life.

In line with these directives, a new literature had grown up in the liberated areas of North China, on which Chou Yang now reported in statistical terms: Of 177 new works, 101 dealt with war themes, 41 with peasant life, and only 16 with themes from industrial life (which must now take precedence).

The creators of these works, in Chou Yang's presentation, had succeeded in escaping the constrictions of the world of the "May Fourth" intelligentsia, first and foremost by pioneering the use of the language of the masses: Chao Shu-li (1906–70) was the shining example of success in this regard. But individual achievement mattered less than the entrance of folk cultural forms into the artistic consciousness: *yang-ko* plays (new musical dramas, the arias based on the melodies of "rice-planting songs")

2 Chou Yang, "Hsin ti jen-min ti wen-i" (The people's new literature and art), *Chung-hua ch'üan-kuo wen-hsueh i-shu kung-tso-che tai-piao ta-hui chi-nien wen-chi* (Documents commemorating China's national congress of literature and art workers), 69–99.

and ballads were forms preferred by folk artists who at New Year in the villages, or in army units or factories, were spontaneously developing new modes of expression.

With judicious praise for what had already been accomplished came admonition for the future. The very popularity of such forms as the traditional drama posed the threat of persistence of unwholesome values and customs. Drama reform must be undertaken forthwith. Writers must invent new ways to extol the emergent new man or woman of socialism so that negative characters in literature would no longer exceed the positive in interest and appeal. Although efforts must be made to improve both standards of creative writing and standards of criticism – "We must not forget the villages" – the fundamental task remained the provision of a mass literature and art for people viewed as traditionally starved of culture. To this end, the 1949 first congress directed the establishment, within months, of no fewer than forty branch organizations of writers and artists, in major cities across the nation.

One of the prominent themes of the first congress was the welcome into the fold of the People's Republic extended to writers who had not hitherto been part of the Yenan Communist establishment but had spent the war years in Shanghai or Chungking. Time was to show that few of these men and women found the new directives congenial to creative work. Mao Tun, minister of culture as well as head of the Writers Union, withdrew from the creation of new fiction, although he fulfilled a valuable function by reverting to his role as practical critic, assessing each new crop of stories for technical achievement and counseling on matters of character portrayal and the development of style. Pa Chin (b. 1904) wrote no new major work of fiction after 1949, and his stories of the Korean War contained so much hyperbole that they read almost as parodies of the desired heroic mode. Shen Ts'ung-wen (b. 1903) presented a paradox. No one in the past had written more movingly of peasant life. But he seemed to feel himself cut off from the villages of the new era and unable to accept the requirement to glorify the socialist transformation. Eventually a new role was found for him, as researcher into the history of Chinese textiles and costumes; his comprehensive report on these researches was handsomely published in the late 1970s. Not until 1981 were critics to reaffirm the value of Shen's fiction of four or five decades earlier.

Poetry

A number of established poets who had spent the war and postwar years in the Kuomintang-controlled areas of China made attempts, following the establishment of the People's Republic, to bring their work into accord with the new spirit of the age. The most eminent was Kuo Mo-jo, who published several new volumes in the 1950s. He reverted to the mode of fervent apostrophe that had characterized his poems of thirty years previously to celebrate a range of achievements and aspirations of the new regime that had so honored him: reservoirs, bridges, the Bandung Conference success of Chou En-lai, and the defiance of Britain at the time of the Suez crisis. The transparency and oversimplification of these effusions became more and more obvious, climaxing in his collection, *The blooming of the hundred flowers* (*Pai-hua ch'i fang*), 1958, at the time of the Great Leap Forward (when Mao's Hundred Flowers liberalization had already been nullified by the Anti-Rightist Campaign). Thereafter Kuo Mo-jo wrote very little beyond classical-style poems in genial exchanges with Mao and other leaders. Feng Chih (b. 1905) is best known for the metaphysical subtleties of his *Sonnets* of 1941. The mode of these quiet meditations so little matched the stridency of the new age that he sought new means of expression via folk legends, which came to him in his land reform work, or via short lyrics of everyday life. Occasionally a strong new metaphor is born, as in his identification of mining drills, the heart of the burgeoning new industrial economy, with the hearts of the people on the surface above:

> Day and night, day and night,
>   the mountain creek purls,
> Day and night, day and night,
>   on the rail the coal trains shuttle,
> At a hundred and fifty metres below ground
> Day and night dins the electric drills' sound.
> By the creek happily the market noises flow,
> Women laugh and talk, and children sing everywhere,
> But inaudible to people are the electric drills below,
> Like the people's own heartbeats that they cannot hear.[3]

No poet of the 1940s made more bitter denunciations of the unjust society than Tsang K'o-chia (b. 1905).[4] Although he too now did his share of extolling, his poems of the 1950s continue to hark back to the darkness of the past, as in "Some people" (*Yu ti jen*), in which he compares the great satirist Lu Hsun with those "who to survive cannot let others live." Yuan Shui-p'ai (1919–82), whose *Hill ballads of Ma Fan-t'o* were a scourge to the Nationalists in the civil war period, also

---

3 Feng Chih, "Coal-mining district," from *Poems of a decade* (*Shih-nien shih-ch'ao*), quoted in S. H. Chen, "Metaphor and the conscious in Chinese poetry," in Cyril Birch, ed., *Chinese communist literature*, 52.

4 See, for example, his "Zero degree of life" (1947), with its child corpses frozen in Shanghai gutters, in K. Y. Hsu, ed., *Twentieth century Chinese poetry: an anthology*, 289.

continued his satirical verse, but his aim now tended to veer toward over-seas targets, the capitalists and imperialists inimical to the infant republic.

Accomplished poets like Pien Chih-lin (b. 1910) and Ho Ch'i-fang (1912–77) turned, in the main, to literary scholarship and criticism and produced little new verse after 1949. Ho had the prestige of an ex–liberated area writer and occupied high positions in the hierarchy. In 1954 he published a series of articles that reiterated the need to continue the efforts of the 1930s to develop modern forms of regulated verse. Poets whose choice had lain between free verse and folk-ballad forms were en-couraged by these articles to experiment with "liberated quatrains" and other stanzaic forms, usually rhymed.

In contrast with these men, Ai Ch'ing (b. 1910) became active anew in the 1950s, visiting and hymning the Soviet Union, lamenting Hiroshima, comparing Vienna to

> A young wife stricken with rheumatism,
> Sweet face and paralyzed limbs,[5]

and reporting at length on the incipient revolutionary fervor of the Latin American countries he toured. Ai Ch'ing had been the leading figure among leftist poets before liberation, and was criticized, with Ting Ling and others, at the time of the Yenan talks of 1942. His work of that period could appear at first sight rather prosy, with its free verse form, avoidance of hyperbole and apostrophe, and hospitality to narrative elements and detailed description. But the strong, spare diction was perfectly suited to the harshness of his message, which centered on the contrast between the richness of the Chinese land and the suffering of the people who worked it. In the poems of the early 1950s he obediently experimented with more tightly structured stanza forms based on folk song rhythms, but the fighting spirit of the poet of protest is no less evident in the choice of sub-ject. His 1957 collection *On the headland (Hai-chia shang)* contains more than one poem whose central metaphor is of the poet himself as a jealous guardian of his independence, his right to speak out. His mind is "mother of pearl," slowly forming the pearls of his symbols; his person is a reef that staunchly resists the battering waves. In an allegorical prose poem of the Hundred Flowers period, the poet appears as a yellow bird, pecked at by the magpie critics about whom the sparrows flutter, but going on undaunted with his song. Another of Ai Ch'ing's poems of this time (1956) was viciously criticized for its apparent sympathy with the tragic figure of the last Ming emperor, whose suicide (on the tree on Coal Hill)

---

5 Quoted in Chang Chung et al., *Tang-tai wen-hsueh kai-kuan* (Survey of contemporary literature), 39.

is the subject. Ai Ch'ing's insistent independence of spirit, his intransigence in the face of earlier attacks, and his association with the "Ting Ling faction" combined to make him a foremost target of the Anti-Rightist Campaign of 1957. Two years later he was shipped to the wilds of Sinkiang. He did not return from this exile until 1975, and the loss of his voice for two decades has been the most grievous the new poetry has suffered.

Among the fifty-three titles reprinted in the *People's literary series* (*Chung-kuo jen-min wen-i ts'ung-shu*) in 1949 were two long narrative poems that between them represented the new verse of the 1940s and exerted strong influence on the work of later poets. The first was "The carter's story" (*Kan-ch'e chuan*), by T'ien Chien (b. 1916), whose poetic development had led him from the regular metrical patterning practiced by the Crescent Moon school to a pounding staccato line fashioned after the Soviet poet Mayakovsky. This is the line he uses in "The carter's story," some twelve thousand words long, which tells of the liberation of the carter's daughter from the clutches of a vicious landlord. In the following passage, the carter is forced to deliver his daughter to the landlord in settlement of his debt. Straightforward modern speech forms are the basis of the language, but they are organized on principles of symmetrical balance and reduplication familiar to classical song styles, and the powerful rhythmic climax is provided by a proverb:

> Who could guess, who could guess,
> poor man's cart
> filled with tears
> loaded with hate
> as if it were wrapped in fog
> drenched with driving rain.
> Though Lan-ni climbed on the cart
> she cried
> the cart cried
> the girl and the cart
> jolting on
> through the sound of weeping.
> It was so hard to go
> hard, so hard to go
> hard, so hard to go.
> Sorrow to go
> sorrow not to go.
> Truly, a hatred born in a day
> takes a thousand years to die! (pp. 29–30)

A representative passage from T'ien Chien almost twenty years later will show his movement away from the idiosyncratic "drumbeat rhythm" toward a more stereotyped diction. "Big iron man" (*T'ieh-ta-jen*), of 1964, teaches the need for continued vigilance against revisionists and saboteurs who, in the poem's terms, will pose as fox fairies to lure the defender of the commune from his post:

> Cunning fox, stop your dreaming,
> stop hoping for me to lay down my rifle.
> You are a fox, and nothing more, and
> you want to drag me into the mud pond.
> I have shed blood for the Revolution,
> I have been wounded defending my country,
> I have planted trees for the commune
> and now these trees are grown and covered with blooms.
> The moon should look only at red hearts
> as big trees should be timbers for the commune.
> Don't think you can come here to tempt me,
> I want to taste no honey on the tip of a sword.[6]

The rhythms here are more reminiscent of Li Chi (1922–80), the son of a poor peasant family in Honan who came to critical attention with his narrative poem "Wang Kuei and Li Hsiang-hsiang," the second of the ballads included in the literary series. The poem consists of some four hundred rhymed couplets with lines of seven syllables or slightly longer. The critic Chou Erh-fu[7] described the publication of this poem as "without a doubt an epoch-making event in the history of Chinese poetry. The author Li Chi is not a literary worker, nor a poet, but a man actually working among the masses, who at the same time has a love of literature.... Here is a poem born from the very midst of the people; its thought is completely the thought of the people, its feeling, its life, its language are entirely of the people, it is an authentic voice from the inmost core of the people."

"Wang Kuei and Li Hsiang-hsiang" uses a ballad form current in northern Shensi and known as *shun-t'ien-yu* (or *hsin-t'ien-yu*). Often the first line of each couplet is a metaphor, and the second a statement, thus:

> Flower of the lily blossoming red
> Hsiang-hsiang grew into a lovely girl

and its parallel, a few lines later,

> Thickets of willow clustering green
> Wang Kuei was a fine young lad. (pp. 11–12)

Images as well as metrical form come from the popular romantic tradition:

---

6 *Shih-k'an* (Poetry journal), 7 (1964), 4–7, trans. in K. Y. Hsu, ed., *Literature of the People's Republic of China*, 708–12.
7 Chou Erh-fu, *Hsin-ti ch'i-tien* (A new start), 120.

Watching from her window a wild goose fly south
Hsiang-hsiang's suffering is more than can be told:
People say the wild goose can carry a message
Take these words from me to the one I love:
"When you went away, the trees were just in bud;
Now the leaves have all gone, but still you don't return." (p. 49)

The romantic appeal of the triumph of young lovers sufficed to offset the frequent crudities and weaknesses of the verse, and "Wang Kuei and Li Hsiang-hsiang" became a popular successor to the traditional sentimental ballads of the type of "Liang Shan-po and Chu Ying-t'ai."

Li Chi has continued to write ballads, extolling the workers of the Yü-men oil fields and, in 1958, telling in "The story of Yang Kao" the life of a poor shepherd boy who learns the art of balladry from a blind singer who is also an underground Party worker. Much of his story concerns his heroic exploits in the fighting against the Japanese and the Nationalists, but no less significant to his development as a revolutionary hero is his participation in the land reform movement and, in the final sections, his entrance into the romance of the oil fields at Yü-men. Energy, whether surging from the underground reservoirs of oil or springing from the narrative line of his verse, is Li Chi's hallmark; his weaknesses come from his urgent desire to be understood at once by the simplest mind, which leads him into an enfeebling reiterative chattiness. Still, he is perhaps the most widely read poet in China, and he has recently exerted a strong influence for the popularization of diction as an editor of *Poetry journal* (*Shih-k'an*) and *People's literature*.

Shao Yen-hsiang (b. 1933), as a young radio journalist in the early fifties, typified the drive of the years of the 1st Five-Year Plan to glorify the industrial worker in song and story. In "Far journey" (*Tao yuan-fang ch'ü*) the speakers are young city dwellers leaving for distant construction projects:

On the railroad we are headed for
No sign yet of any tracks,
Where the mine I'm headed for will be drilled
Nothing yet but desert land ...
But what isn't there will surely come to be,
our splendid dreams cannot fail.[8]

Sun Yu-t'ien (b. 1936), the poet of the Huainan mines, also contributed to the movement to bring the figure of the industrial worker into Chinese verse, as did Li Hsueh-ao (b. 1933) with his volume *Printer's songs* (*Yin-shua kung-jen chih ko*), of 1956.

8 Shao Yen-hsiang, *Tao yuan-fang ch'ü* (Far journey), 65.

The peasant in fiction

The most highly praised and widely imitated of the writers on peasant life in these early years was Chao Shu-li (1906–70). In 1943 Chao published a story, "Blackie gets married" (*Hsiao Erh-hei chieh-hun*), which with the straightforward simplicity of a diagram celebrated the success of peasant lovers in overcoming the opposition of their reactionary parents, colorful representatives of bucolic superstition named, respectively, Auntie Three the Witch and Chu-ko Liang the Second. Chao had learned the craft of storytelling from village practitioners in his home in the hill country of Shansi, and his story offers instant appeal with its skillful use of familiar turns of phrase and methods of introducing characters, creating suspense, and explaining plot developments guaranteed to rivet the rustic attention. The extraordinary success of the story must be credited in part, however, to a conscious effort to promote this local journalist as a model of the new writer, no citified bourgeois intellectual but a genuine product of a peasant background (which indeed he was), whose rise to literary fame was undoubtedly the result of his work as a Party publicist and of his adherence to the injunctions of Mao Tse-tung in the Yenan "Talks" of the previous year.

Chao Shu-li soon followed up on "Blackie" with "The ballads of Li Yu-ts'ai" (*Li Yu-ts'ai pan-hua*), a long story that is certainly his best-loved work. The concreteness and economy of Chao's method may be seen in the opening vignette of "Li Yu-ts'ai," which defines the entire sociology of his chosen milieu:

There was a curious feature of this place Yen-chia-shan. At the western end of the village the houses were two-storied brick buildings. In the middle part they were only of one storey, and in the eastern part, by the village ash-tree, was a row of twenty or thirty cave-dwellings in the soil. The terrain of the village was level enough, but if you looked at the line made by the roofs of the houses, you would find a distinct slope running down from west to east. All the people who lived in the west part had the surname Yen. In the middle an assortment of surnames was mixed in with the Yen families; but all were natives of the region. Only the east end was in a special case. Half of the people here were pioneers from other parts of the country; the rest were local families of mixed surnames whose living had gone downhill. There were no more than three households with the surname Yen, and these had only moved into this part of the village after going broke and selling their property. (p. 1)

It is not surprising that the local tyrant has the surname Yen. He is pilloried by the village balladeer Li Yu-ts'ai, whose rhymes educate the villagers and voice their wrongs to the new Party authorities:

Our head is Yen Heng-yuan,
His hand blots out the sun,
Since headmen were invented
Ten years the only one.

Every year an election,
But when the voting's done,
Names proposed and rejected,
Still it's Yen Heng-yuan.

Why don't we make a big board,
Carve his name thereon,
Every year at election time
Just mark it with your thumb;

Save us the trouble of writing
Year by year the same one,
We could use it then a hundred years
Before it was finally done. (p. 3)

Chao Shu-li's first full-length novel, *Changes in Li Village* (*Li-chia-chuang ti pien-ch'ien*), appeared in 1946. The story is of the reversal in fortunes of landlord bosses (typified by Li Ju-chen) and oppressed peasants (Chang T'ieh-suo and his fellows) in a north Shansi village over the preceding two decades. The humor is much reduced in this dramatic, at times grim narrative: eyes are gouged out, hands cut off, the temple runs with blood in the fiercest phase of suppression of the Communist forces, and the people's ultimate revenge takes the form of tearing Li Ju-chen limb from limb (though this act is censured by the leading cadres when they learn of it). Ingenious trickery by the reactionaries and the growing confidence of the peasant progressives as fast-paced action proves their power, plus the vigorous colloquial language Chao uses at all times, kept *Changes* a best-seller until the early 1950s, when it was superseded by more sophisticated tales of the "turnabout" from Ting Ling and Chou Li-po.

In 1955, in response to calls from the leadership for the development of cooperatives, Chao Shu-li again rose to the occasion with a work that is his most ambitious, though not necessarily his best (for this we should look either at "The ballads of Li Yu-ts'ai" or among his shorter stories, "Registration" (*Teng-chi*), "The heirloom" (*Ch'uan-chia-pao*), or other tales of changes in the lives of peasants, especially peasant women). *Three mile bend (San-li-wan)* is the story of the completion of an irrigation project by the new-fangled agricultural production cooperative in a remote northern village. Practical lessons in adaptation to the new ways are given as the villagers with their cadre leaders overcome resistance from a self-serving headman and independent-minded middle peasants. Some of the humor of Chao's earliest works is recaptured, especially in the good-natured courtships of the young people, but in general the author's canvas is too broad, and *Three mile bend* lacks cohesion. The great pity is that Chao never completed *Magic spring caves* (*Ling-ch'üan-tung*), the first part of which he published in 1959. This story of the resistance of Shansi villagers to Japanese and marauding ex-Kuomintang troops in the years around 1940–41 represents a return to Chao's earliest and happiest style, a deliberate evocation of the heroic world of the old military romances, and a mining of the riches of the culture of the countryside, its elements of magic and superstition treated with amused affection rather than savagely pilloried.

Chao Shu-li in the 1960s was to produce only a small number of undistinguished short stories before his denunciation (for excessive concentration on dubious "middle characters") at the height of the Cultural Revolution, during one of whose mindless upheavals he was attacked and killed.

Ting Ling (b. 1907) wrote the outstanding work of "land reform" fiction in *The sun shines over the Sangkan River* (*T'ai-yang chao tsai Sang-kan ho-shang*), which was published in 1948 and awarded a Stalin Prize in 1951. A rough formula for such fiction had evolved through a considerable corpus of stories in the late 1940s, as the movement spread with the advances of the Communist armies across the northern part of the country. The stories would describe the initial rousing of the peasants to identify the landlord as their oppressor; the landlord's search for allies among prosperous villagers and their more gullible hangers-on; his stratagems to hoodwink the inexperienced cadres in charge; and at last, the emergence of progressives among the villagers, who with the aid of more experienced cadres from outside succeed in exposing the landlord and thwarting his reactionary designs.

Ting Ling could draw on years of training as a writer, from the romantic confessions of her early stories through the realist exposures of shortcomings in the Yenan scene that had gotten her into trouble in the early 1940s. In *Sangkan River* she blends romantic with realist in a manner (although this was never acknowledged) that could serve as a model for the next generation. The apple-laden orchards that will be the people's ultimate prize glisten with morning dew in idyllic description, yet the village urchins are bare-bottomed and smelly enough to dispel any doubts of idealization. In short chapters she traces the complex interactions between the obdurate landlord Ch'ien Wen-kui, his niece Hei-ni, whom he shrewdly uses as bait, and her lover, Ch'eng Jen, formerly hired hand, now slowly growing in assuredness as chairman of the peasants' association. Ku Yung is a middle peasant reluctant to be "communized," but finally persuaded that his hard-won dignity as a farmer will be respected. Negative characters who are interesting, yet not so much as to outshine the progressives, include a cynical, unscrupulous schoolteacher whose skillful rumor mongering is one of the landlord's major resources, and a pompous cadre, Wen Ts'ai, who demonstrates the absurd inapplicability of his book-learned socialist theory to the situation he is faced with on the ground.

A second Stalin Prize–winning land reform novel, also published in 1948, was *The hurricane* (*Pao-feng tsou-yü*), by the veteran Communist Chou Li-po (1908–79). The title is an allusion to an image used by Mao Tsetung for the wrath of the aroused peasants sweeping across the land; the model for Chou's book is Sholokhov's *Virgin soil upturned*, which Chou himself translated into Chinese. But Chou had not yet fully found himself as a creative writer, and although *Hurricane* exhibits a wealth of naturalistic detail of peasant life, testifying to conscientious fieldwork, its characters lack the depth and subtlety of Ting Ling's. Much more satisfactory is his later (1955) work *Great changes in a mountain village* (*Shan-hsiang chüpien*), describing the struggles required to establish an agricultural cooperative in a Hunan hill town in the middle fifties. The attention Chou pays to the holdouts and to the marriage relationships of his characters brought him under critical fire, but it is precisely these elements of human interest that lend conviction to this long novel, one of the half-dozen most successful works of the new writing.

War fiction

The Great War of 1914-18 virtually put an end to the glorification of the warrior in modern Western literature. Chinese Communist fiction, in contrast, has shown no trace of war weariness. Throughout the war of resistance to Japan, the civil war, and the Korean War, writers unflaggingly celebrated the valor and sagacity of the People's Liberation Army and its leaders, castigated the enemy, and extolled the love and trust between army and masses, close as members of one family.

New son and daughter heroes (*Hsin erh-nü ying-hsiung chuan*) is a novel by K'ung Chueh and Yuan Ching, husband-and-wife team who had already published short stories of peasant and army life (under the title of *Sufferers* (*Shou-k'u-jen*), 1947). Their collaboration did not survive their divorce in the early 1950s.

The original *Son and daughter heroes*, by the nineteenth-century Manchu author Wen-k'ang, attempts to show young people engaging in heroic acts through the motivation of filial piety; K'ung and Yuan's "new" heroes, Ta-shui and his sweetheart, Hsiao-mei, with their comrades, are motivated not by the old morality but by the new, the loyalty to country and to Party. They are at the center of a chronicle of the eight-year war against Japan, as it affected the dwellers on the shores of Poyang Lake in Hopei province. The book is carefully structured to demonstrate the growing scope of the Communist resistance, from small-scale collection of arms abandoned by the fleeing Kuomintang to attacks on lake steamers, the capture of forts, and at last all-out campaigns againt walled towns and cities. The widening scale of the action is accompanied by growth of understanding of the new revolutionary morality, so that skillfully paced narrative appeal enhances rather than overshadows the didactic function.

The attempt by K'ung and Yuan to repeat their success with a novel about the Korean War, *Together in life and death* (*Sheng-ssu-yuan*), was unsuccessful.

The second major work to popularize the resistance role of the Party was *Heroes of Lü-liang* (*Lü-liang ying-hsiung chuan*), also the product of collaboration. Ma Feng (b. 1922) developed as a writer with the army based at Yenan, and reached his peak of creativity with a prolific output of short stories in the 1950s. "I knew three years ago" (*San-nien tsao chih-tao*) and "Uncle Chao the stockman" (*Ssu-yang-yuan Chao ta-shu*) are among the best known of his stories, which present lively figures of peasants learning the ropes of cooperation.

Ma Feng's collaborator, Hsi Jung, was born one year later and has followed a similar though somewhat less celebrated career. *Heroes of Lü-liang* won instant popularity by reproducing the form, and often the specific idiom, of the old picaresque novels of derring-do. Many of its hundred chapters comprise self-contained episodes, unified only by their setting in the hills of Shansi province and by the centering of the action on the militiamen of a single village. The authors' re-creation of the racy, picturesque vernacular style of *Shui-hu-chuan* and comparable works must be counted a remarkably successful response to Mao Tse-tung's call (in the Yenan "Talks") for "what the Chinese people love to see and hear."

In the forties and early fifties, war furnished the bulk of material for both short story and novel. Liu Pai-yü (b. 1916) at that time was already writing the kind of fictionalized reportage he has continued to the present. Most recently he has written about the North China oil fields, but through most of his work his heroes' antagonists have been armed men – Japanese, Nationalists, or the Americans in Korea – rather than Mother Nature, as is only fitting for the army's chief cultural worker. Perhaps because of his absorption in army life, his prolific output consists mostly of sketches of comic-book heroes caring nothing for the enemy's bullets and bombs. His best-known work is the short novel *Flames ahead* (*Huo-kuang tsai ch'ien*), of 1952, depicting the hotly contested crossing of the Yangtze in the civil war. Soon after this he was reporting on the Korean War, but pride of place on this topic should go to Yang Shuo (1913–68) for his novel *A thousand miles of lovely land* (*San-ch'ien-li chiang-shan*). This is again a fairly short novel, which centers on the indomitable Wu T'ien-pao, railway engine driver for the People's Volunteers.

The technical problem facing these writers was to encompass the leap in scale from the exciting but isolated incidents of guerrilla fighting to the major campaigns of all-out warfare. Liu Ch'ing (1916–78), in his *Wall of bronze* (*T'ung-ch'iang t'ieh-pi*), of 1951, attempts to solve the problem by establishing a grain depot, rather than an individual hero, at the center of his action. But on the whole the attempt fails; there is much confusion in the narrative until the young cadre Shih Te-fu is captured by the Nationalists. From this point on the grain depot recedes into the background, and the author settles down into a fluent adventure of resistance and escape. Yang Shuo in *A thousand miles of lovely land* succeeds in projecting the train, bearing ammunition to the forward troops, as a powerful image of defiance of the bombs of an unseen airborne enemy. But perhaps because of the need to perpetuate the myth of a "volunteer" force, there is little attempt to represent the larger picture of the war in its strategic implications.

It is in this regard that *Defend Yenan* (*Pao-wei Yen-an*), of 1954, by Tu P'eng-ch'eng (b. 1921), sets a new standard, and remains outstanding among war novels. The exploits of his central protagonist, Chou Ta-yung, who is depicted as standing "like an iron statue but with blazing eyes," are set against the huge backdrop of the Nationalist campaign in 1947 to capture the seat of Communist authority. Leading Party strategists appear in person, most notably the feisty P'eng Te-huai. The political education of the hero is closely keyed to his growing recognition of the genuine strategic brilliance of the high command. When the defensive forces are temporarily withdrawn from Yenan, in a daring feint to lure the main force of the Nationalists beyond the reach of their supply lines, Chou Ta-yung's impetuosity leads him near to despair; only gradually is he brought to recognize that individual acts of heroism must be reinforced by the grand design of strategy, of stringing out the enemy until his weaknesses appear and he can be attacked: in contrast with the sporadic harassment of the Japanese occupation forces, the Communists were faced now with an enemy who could commit a hundred thousand troops at a time to a single battle. Chou Ta-yung's personal victories over wounds and weariness and powerfully armed enemy forces, which threaten again and again to overwhelm his small company, are firmly set in the massive framework of the Red Army's irresistible swing from defensive to offensive and final, total triumph.

P'eng Te-huai was disgraced in 1959 in consequence of his outspoken opposition to Mao's Great Leap Forward. It was a disastrous development for Tu P'eng-ch'eng and his epic novel, which was taken out of print and in 1963 ordered to be destroyed. Tu continued to write stories on themes drawn from commune development and socialist construction, but he has not again attempted a work of such major scope as *Defend Yenan*.

The worker in fiction

The Yenan talks of 1942 had established the masses of workers, peasants and soldiers as prime subjects and beneficiaries of the new literature. Of the three, the industrial worker was slowest to appear in the new works. Aside from Pa Chin's novel of mining, *Snow* (*Hsueh*), written largely in imitation of Zola's *Germinal*, and a few stories by Chang T'ien-i (b. 1906) and others, there was little in the way of precedent. Such models as could be found were from Soviet literature, Gladkov's *Cement*, for example; Upton Sinclair also was known in China in the 1930s.

The first major work in the genre of industrial fiction in China was *Prime moving force* (*Yuan-tung-li*) by Ts'ao Ming (b. 1913), the wife of the leading Cantonese novelist Ou-yang Shan (b. 1908). She based the story on her own political work in the hydroelectric and steel plants of the Northeast during their postwar rehabilitation. Although she places a veteran worker, Old Sun, in the midst of most of the action, she has a certain success in establishing the power station itself as a sort of collective central figure of the book. She devotes a number of lyrical passages to the plant as it is transformed from battered wreck, victim of Japanese and Kuomintang withdrawal, stranded in the frozen Manchurian winter landscape, to humming vitality after restoration (in Chapter 9, the plant forms part of a pastoral backdrop as the women pick flowers by the lake).

From the start Old Sun displays attributes of the hero, selflessly braving an ice-covered pond to salvage precious oil. He is tough, optimistic, resourceful. In a lively episode he shows diplomatic skills, even guile, when he cajoles local peasants into returning sheets of iron roofing they have looted. Wang Yung-ming, the dedicated cadre who is appointed director of the plant, achieves his own political education in application of the mass line by learning to trust this veteran worker in preference to the enthusiastic but officious union chairman or the Japan-educated technical specialists. The tensions with these men, in the terms used later by

Mao Tse-tung, are nonantagonistic contradictions, internal to the group of progressive workers themselves. The principal drama of the action, however, arises from antagonistic contradictions with Kuomintang-leaning saboteurs. These conflicts mark *Prime moving force* as belonging to the early, rehabilitation stage of industrial fiction.

Ts'ao Ming in earlier years had written short stories of peasant life. She followed up *Prime moving force* with *The locomotive (Huo-ch'e-t'ou)*, of 1950, whose central image is of Marxism as the locomotive force of history, conveyed through the growth in political consciousness of workers and cadres alike in a locomotive works; and with a long novel, *Riding the waves (Ch'eng-feng p'o-lang)*, of 1959, eulogizing the Great Leap Forward in steel production. These later works, however, were considerably less influential than *Prime moving force*, which had numerous imitators. Ko Yang's *Story of Wang Chin-chung* (1954) repeats the theme of growth in political understanding through the trials of the production process itself, though the eponymous hero, the subject of this fictional autobiography, is of the next generation after Old Sun. Lei Chia's *Spring comes to the Yalu River (Ch'un-t'ien lai-tao-le Ya-lü-chiang)*, of 1954, explores a situation parallel to that of *Prime moving force*, but with a paper mill substituted for the hydroelectric plant. Again, the workers must break down bureaucratic barriers between themselves and the Party cadres, as well as combat both intractable machines and human (class) enemies. This is the first volume of a lengthy trilogy, *Potential (Ch'ien-li)*. Lei Chia (b. 1915) has also written numerous short lives of labor heroes.

With the promulgation of the 1st Five-Year Plan (1953–57) pride of place was given to heavy industry and, within this area, to steel production. Wang Chin-chung was a fictionalized worker from the "steel capital," Anshan in the Northeast, but a construction worker rather than that elite figure the foundryman himself. The latter appears as hero in the next major work of industrial fiction to follow *Prime moving force*, Ai Wu's novel *Steeled and tempered (Pai-lien ch'eng-kang)*, of 1957. Ai Wu (b. 1904) was a prolific writer of pronounced left-wing sympathies in the years before 1949, and *Steeled and tempered* displays his technical skill, especially in passages in which detailed exposition of the problems and processes involved prepare the reader for the high drama of blast furnace operation. No image could more successfully capture the glamour of the steelworker, aristocrat of industry, than that of the protagonist, Ch'in Te-kui, emerging from the very mouth of the furnace at the beginning of the novel to throw off his flaming asbestos glove with a single sweep of his arm. In the jargon of the time, which opposed "red" and "expert," Ch'in is no more expert than his former mentor and jealous competitor, Yuan T'ing-fa. But he is more "red," motivated by ideological commitment to the cause of national advancement rather than by personal pride or material incentive. His true achievement is less the smashing of records in steel production than the "tempering" of his comrades, as under the guidance of the responsible cadres he works to resolve the major conflict. This is the conflict between the speeding up of production on the one hand and the welfare of both plant and workers on the other. These competing claims anchor the action in a satisfyingly real set of problems, and overshadow the melodramatic sabotage attempt that weakens the novel's ending.

Also in 1958 appeared *In days of peace* (*Tsai ho-p'ing ti jih-tzu-li*) by Tu P'eng-ch'eng, the author of the major war novel *Defend Yenan*. *In days of peace* is a much slighter work, which qualifies as "industrial fiction" in that its background is the construction of the Paochi–Chengtu railroad in Szechuan, but which in fact is a kind of continuation of Tu's war writing. The lead characters are war heroes, whose contrasting modes of adaptation to the demands of peace and reconstruction provide the book's theme. Yen Hsing succeeds in subjecting himself, born leader that he is, to the will of the masses. Liang Chien, death-defying in war, remains too much the individualist to adjust to the long haul of peacetime. He vacillates and is overwhelmed by pessimism, whereas Yen Hsing draws strength from adversity. Having no recourse to the romance of technology, Tu P'eng-ch'eng takes advantage (as in his war stories) of the outdoor setting to battle the forces of nature. The romantic fervor of his writing recalls Romain Rolland in such a passage as the following (a human chain of workers is rescuing huge sacks of cement from a flooding river):

Yen Hsing felt that:
    The violent wind lashing the workers seemed to arouse in them an inexhaustible strength!
    The foam from the river slapping the workers seemed to give them an even more ardent spirit!
    The flashes of lightning seemed to light their path![9]

The new theater

In the early 1950s, theaters were refurbished or newly erected in many cities, schools of acting founded, and dramatic works of the classical tradition edited and reprinted. Chou En-lai, an aficionado of the classical theater, gave powerful support. The first festival of regional drama was

9 *Tsai ho-p'ing ti jih-tzu li*, 93, quoted in Michael Gotz, "Images of the worker in contemporary Chinese fiction, 1949–64," 96.

held in Peking in 1952 with more than twenty different traditional forms of theater represented; the variety was increased in the second festival held in 1957. Hand in hand with support went censorship: Obscene dialogue and gestures were banned, and so were whole plays of the Peking Opera and other traditions if the contents were judged to be excessively superstitious or otherwise "feudal."

Rewriting, however, was more frequent than outright banning. An interesting example of a play salvaged by this means is *The white snake* (*Pai-she-chuan*), which the leading dramatist T'ien Han (1899–1968) treated to a major overhaul. The traditional versions are by no means free of ambiguities, but in general the White Snake, despite the bewitching beauty of the human form she has adopted, is clearly labeled as evil and ends up thoroughly suppressed by the power of the Buddha as exercised through the abbot Fa-hai. T'ien Han's version reverses the roles, discomfits Fa-hai and his superstitious nonsense and sends White Snake off into the sunset at the close of the play, the epitome of the liberated woman. The superb duos between White Snake and her maid Blue Snake, converted from fatal charm to mere celebration of feminine grace, inevitably lose something of their dramatic impact, but the play is saved, the show can and does go on. The 1956 revival of the Soochow *K'un-ch'ü* drama *Fifteen strings of cash* (*Shih-wu-kuan*), in an abridged and tightened version, was also hailed as an excellent product of the policy of "weeding through the old to let the new emerge."

Two plays of the early 1950s dealt with problems of contemporary society by the use of the spoken drama form developed in China from the 1920s. *Facing the new situation* (*Tsai hsin shih-wu ti mien-ch'ien*), of 1951, by Tu Yin (b. 1919) and others, explores the tensions between an army veteran who now finds himself as cadre in charge of a steel mill in Shenyang, and the technologists on whose cooperation he must depend to restore the mill to operation. *The test* (*K'ao-yen*), of 1953, is a similar but more complex play by Hsia Yen (b. 1900), who was a leading organizer of left-wing dramatists in the 1930s, wrote several wartime plays, and has made a major contribution to the development of the Chinese film. Hsia Yen's "industrial" play *The test*, written against the background of the Three Antis Campaign, in particular shows sympathy for the Western-trained engineer in his struggle against bureaucratic management, and functions as a plea for restraint and understanding in bringing the intellectuals into the service of the state.

On a closely related theme, Ts'ao Yü (b. 1910) in 1954 wrote *Bright skies* (*Ming-lang ti t'ien*) to depict the process whereby the faculty of a Peking medical school, a U.S. foundation, are able gradually to overcome their subservience to the American scientific culture. Another established playwright, Sung Chih-ti (1914–56), contributed to the spoken drama of the middle fifties by treating the Korean War, in *To protect peace* (*Pao-wei ho-p'ing*), and the socialist transformation of agriculture, in *Spring shoots* (*Ch'un-miao*), of 1956.

Ch'en Pai-ch'en (b. 1908) also belongs to the senior generation of Chinese playwrights. In the late 1950s he wrote plays satirizing the "paper tiger" of the United States, but it was almost two decades before his next major work appeared, *Song of the great wind* (*Ta feng ko*), written in 1977 after the deaths of Chou En-lai and Mao Tse-tung.

In 1954 Hsia Yen was appointed vice-minister of culture, and four years later he wrote and produced a major film, *The Lin family store* (*Lin-chia p'u-tzu*), based on the middle-length story written in 1932 by Mao Tun.

The generation gap provided the theme for two plays of 1963, *The young generation* (*Nien-ch'ing ti i-tai*), by Ch'en Yun and others, and *Don't ever forget* (*Ch'ien-wan pu-yao wang-chi*), by Ts'ung Shen (b. 1928). It was a particularly insidious problem of the time, the fear that the revolutionary spirit had somehow drained out of the young, who, insufficiently aware of the sacrifices made on their behalf, are in danger of bourgeois self-seeking in the new society they take for granted. An especially thorny problem is their reluctance to go to the countryside. In both plays, the revisionist-minded young protagonists fall inevitably into serious blunders and are brought to realize their faults.

Few novels of the 1930s were read with more enjoyment than those of Lao She (1899–1966), especially the satirical *City of cats* (*Mao-ch'eng chi*), of 1933, and his masterpiece, *Rickshaw boy* (*Lo-t'o hsiang-tzu*), of 1937, the harrowing story of a country boy's doomed struggle to survive in the corrupt and oppressive world of the Peking streets. During the Sino-Japanese War, Lao She as a leader of the patriotic organizations of writers in Nationalist-held China fostered the use of ballads and dramatic sketches as instrument of propaganda, and after 1949 he wrote no new fiction, unless we may view the unfinished but delightful autobiographical sketch *Beneath the red banner* (*Cheng-hung ch'i-hsia*) as an embryonic novel. Written in the early 1960s, this remained unpublished until the late 1970s. Lao She did, however, enjoy an extraordinarily successful new career as a dramatist. Of more than twenty plays, *Dragon beard ditch* (*Lung hsu kou*) was one of the earliest stage successes after the establishment of the People's Republic, but *Teahouse* (*Ch'a-kuan*), of 1957, although it had only a lukewarm first reception, is now recognized as his best play. It was revived with great éclat, and given a European tour, in 1979. Lao She's intimate knowledge of the Peking scene, especially the life of the urban poor, fills both plays with vigor and wit. "Dragon beard ditch" is the name of a noisome sewer whose festering from government neglect is no more than symbolic of the fates of the poor who live on its banks. This does not prevent the municipal authorities from levying a "sanitation tax" on their miserable hides. But this is the old, corrupt government. With the establishment of the Communist regime, the ditch is drained and covered, the inhabitants put to productive work, and a new life blossoms in the reinvigorated heart of the city. A similar contrast between old and new informs a later play by Lao She, *Family portrait (Ch'üan-chia-fu)*, in which the people's police spare no effort in securing the reunion of members of a family scattered in consequence of various abuses of the old society.

Teahouse traces precisely the decline of this "old society" by vividly evoking three stages in the lives of habitués of a Peking teahouse: 1898 (Act 1), the sunset years of the Manchu dynasty; 1916 (Act 2), when Peking lies at the mercy of the warlords; and 1946 (Act 3), when the Nationalists prove helpless to repair the ravages of war. As the teahouse set changes with the times one feature becomes gradually more conspicuous: a set of posters warning, "Do not discuss national affairs." If cynics in the audience, at the end of the third and final act, were to visualize an act 4 that would be set during the People's Republic and would feature still bigger posters, this could not be laid to Lao She's account. When the Cultural Revolution came, however, Lao She was savagely attacked as a bourgeois writer of unregenerate convictions, and he is widely believed to have died as the result of a beating by Red Guard hooligans.[10]

FROM THE "HUNDRED FLOWERS" TO THE SOCIALIST EDUCATION CAMPAIGN, 1956–1965

Critical realism in fiction

Liu Pin-yen (b. 1925) and Wang Meng (b. 1934) have been closely associated in the minds of readers. Both came to sudden prominence with writings startlingly critical of bureaucratism during the Hundred Flowers period from mid-1956 to mid-1957. Both were subsequently labeled rightists and published nothing for twenty years. And both, after the overthrow of the Gang of Four, seem to have picked up again very much where they left off in their writing careers. Liu, essentially the journalist,

10 Paul Bady, "Death and the novel – on Lao She's 'suicide,'" *Renditions*, 10 (Autumn 1978), 5–14.

still projects the rawer indignation. Wang showed a good deal of subtlety even in his first story, written when he was 22, and he is now regarded as the most accomplished practitioner of the short story in China.

Liu's work belongs to the genre of reportage, *pao-kao wen-hsueh*, which may be either revelatory or (more usually) adulatory, permits the use of factual material, and imposes little in the way of formal requirements, although it is expected that there will be a great deal of "verbatim" dialogue. His first piece, "At the bridge construction site" (*Tsai ch'iao-liang kung-ti shang*), made all the more of a stir because for April 1956 it achieved an unprecedented degree of outspokenness. Both the construction chief and the chief engineer at the bridge site, despite longtime Party membership and distinguished war records, are complacent, conservative, and concerned first and foremost with saving their own skins in the face of any misadventure. Some details of their behavior are well observed: There is a suggestion box on their wall, but the lock has rusted shut. An enthusiastic young engineer is transferred away from the site, and when the reporter-narrator revisits the construction chief, his old acquaintance, after an absence of months, nothing in his mode of conduct has improved in the slightest.

"Exclusive–confidential" (*Pen-pao nei-pu hsiao-hsi*) is a longer piece of reportage, published in two parts, June–October 1956.[11] Its accusations are more serious in that they involve distortion and suppression of the truth by editors who whether arrogant or apathetic are primarily self-seeking bureaucrats. An embryonic story line pursues the question, which remains unresolved, of whether the young woman reporter who is the principal center of vision will be admitted to Party membership. For this to happen it seems only too likely that she will have to forswear her practice of making unflattering reports on the actual state of affairs in the local mine and other places: "So this was his idea! To join the Party, one should give up defending its interests! To join the Party, one had to suppress one's own ideas!" (p. 21).

Wang Meng's *Young newcomer in the Organization Department* (*Tsu-chih-pu hsin-lai ti ch'ing-nien-jen*), of September 1956,[12] although it portrays the same world of bureaucratic lethargy as Liu Pin-yen's reportages, is a much more carefully worked piece of writing. Though not immediately recognizable, there is a subtle, inconclusive love story as a leading thread. This in itself is revolutionary for the time: Chou Yang had denied the possibility of love as a significant theme:

11 *Jen-min wen-hsueh*, 6 (1956), 6–21, and 10 (1956), 48–59.
12 Ibid., 9 (1956), 29–43.

Under new conditions in the villages, the bases of feudalism have already been smashed, the life of the people is filled with the content of struggle. Love has retired to a position in life of no importance; the new *yang-ko* works have themes a thousand times more important, a thousand times more significant than love.[13]

The critic Huang Ch'iu-yun at this same time of the Hundred Flowers classified the types of love as conceived by contemporary writers:

... the "no sooner meet than discuss industrial inventions" type of love, the "bashful, one smile and they're gone" type of love, the "I've a question to put to you: do you love me or not" type of love, the "postpone the wedding for the sake of production" type of love, the "thrice passed his home and never entered" type of love [the last in reference to a hero of ancient myth who neglected his wife for the welfare of humanity].[14]

But Lin Chen, the young ex-schoolteacher whose entrance into the work of Party recruitment in a factory provides the story line of "Young newcomer," finds in the disillusioned senior cadre, the grass widow Chao Hui-wen, his only source of encouragement and support. The drawing together of these two young people is delicately suggested and stands as an oasis of humanity in a world where Party officials pick their teeth in a manner reminiscent of Chang T'ien-i's petty bullies of the 1930s, where the head of the organization section admits his staleness – "The occupational disease of a cook is loss of appetite – the same applies to a Party official" (p. 40) – and where a recruitment officer reveals his bored cynicism in his first conversation with Lin:

"How many people did you develop [i.e., recruit into the party] in the first quarter of 1956?"
"One and a half."
"What does your half mean?"
"We sent one name in but the area committee have been a couple of months or more over admitting him." (p. 31)

Altogether, Wang Meng's story paints an unusually convincing picture of the involvement of cadres in a factory dispute, when all – cadres, workers, manager, foremen – walk the knife edge between one form of deviation and another.

Other influential stories of the years 1957–58 were denounced as deviationist, revisionist or even bourgeois because they were written too evidently as a kind of cadre literature, for the benefit of fellow intellectuals rather than the worker, peasant, and soldier public. They include "Beautiful" (*Mei-li*), by Feng Ts'un, and "The visitor" (*Lai-fang-che*), by Fang

13 Chou Yang, *Piao-hsien hsin ti ch'ün-chung ti shih-tai* (Expressing the new age of the masses), 67.
14 Huang Ch'iu-yun, "T'an ai-ch'ing" (On love), *Jen-min wen-hsueh*, 7 (1956), 59–61.

Chi (b. 1919). What is "beautiful" in Feng Ts'un's story is the mind of today's youth, in its devotion to work and self-sacrifice. But the story is in fact a study of frustration, of a young woman cadre who is so hopelessly overworked that she must give up all hope of courtship. Fang Chi's "visitor" is a far more pathetic figure, an intellectual broken by his love for a ballad singer. There are resonances of the well-known T'ang romance "The story of Li Wa," but where the protagonist in that story receives help from the courtesan who ruined him toward success in the examinations and an official career, Fang Chi's young student attempts suicide, turns for salvation to the Party, is heard out by an ostensibly unsympathetic cadre-narrator, and ends by leaving for reform through labor. Not only do both stories center on the personal tragedies of lovers, but they sketch in backgrounds of cold bureaucratic hostility, and (in Fang Chi's story) even of the persistence into the new society of an unsavory underworld of pimps and madames.

The most eloquent defense of the kind of writing represented by Wang Meng's "Young newcomer" appeared in the same month as that story, September 1956, in an article by Ch'in Chao-yang (b. 1916), writing under the pseudonym Ho Chih.[15] This was one of a small number of manifestos that were flown as banners into the mid-1960s by writers seeking a greater degree of autonomy, and cited equally frequently by censorious Party apologists. The young writer Liu Shao-t'ang (b. 1926) echoed Ch'in Chao-yang's arguments and was severely attacked; Ch'in himself had a stronger power base, being at the time an editor of the leading national literary journal, *People's Literature*. Both men paid lip service to Mao Tse-tung's directives to writers as laid down at Yenan in 1942. Liu Shao-t'ang reiterated Mao's basic principles as follows:

> Literature and art must serve the workers, peasants and soldiers; political criteria come first and artistic criteria second in literary criticism; and writers should deeply involve themselves with life and remould their thinking. These are fundamental and permanent guides for literature of the past, the present and the future. They cannot be revised or rescinded.[16]

But Mao's instructions had been misinterpreted, and Ch'in Chao-yang identified one of the greatest stumbling blocks to correct understanding as being the 1934 Soviet definition of "socialist realism:"

---

15 Ho Chih, "Hsien-shih chu-i – kuang-k'uo ti tao-lu" (Realism – the broad highway), *Jen-min wen-hsueh*, 9 (1956), 1–13.

16 Liu Shao-t'ang, "Wo tui tang-ch'ien wen-i wen-t'i ti i-hsieh ch'ien-chien" (Some thoughts on literary problems today), *Wen-i hsueh-hsi*, 5 (1957), 7–10, trans. in Hua-ling Nieh, ed., *Literature of the Hundred Flowers*, 1. 63–71.

Socialist realism demands of the artist a true, historically concrete portrayal of reality in its revolutionary development, in which truthfulness and historical concreteness must be combined with the task of ideological reform and the education of the working people in the spirit of socialism.[17]

As Liu Shao-t'ang commented:

If the realities of life are not considered real, and writing itself is supposed to involve the "revolutionary development" of reality, writers are forced to embellish life and ignore its true features. According to the principle of "reality in its revolutionary development," writers should not write of problems in a socialist society or depict the more negative aspects of the society, for these are temporary matters which can be resolved. Then, is there any meaning to "reality" as it pertains to realism?

Mechanical application of this Soviet theory – and, by implication, of Mao's directives that owed much to Ch'ü Ch'iu-pai (1899–1935) and his interpretation of the Soviet model – had led to dogmatism and the production of an artificial, monotonous literature in recent years. In place of "socialist realism," Ch'in Chao-yang called for a "realism of the socialist era." His description of this mode repeated basic principles from the theoretical writings of Hu Feng (b. 1904), who only a year previously had been the victim of the most bitter campaign yet launched: Its result had been the arrest of Hu as a counterrevolutionary and his elimination from the literary scene (his rehabilitation came only in 1981). Many of Hu Feng's formulations reappeared now in Ch'in Chao-yang's call for a realism that would be more honest, more critical, and more humane. Greater honesty would reduce the hyperbole of the descriptions of an unreal socialist paradise. A more critical spirit would permit the reflection and analysis in literary works of actual problems of the new society. Under the heading of "humane" there would be room for subjective expression, for the emotions, for aspects of reality not confined to the reflection of class struggle.

Certain models from the literature of the past reappear with great frequency in the theoretical writings of Hu Feng and those who, like Ch'in Chao-yang, in the Hundred Flowers period tried to expand the permissible scope of writing beyond the narrow bounds of orthodoxy. Gorky and Lu Hsun are the most commonly cited, Sholokhov only slightly less so, but discussion centered also on two of Hu Feng's old heroes, Balzac and Tolstoy. That a Catholic royalist and a mystical anarchist should both have written works that were cornerstones of nineteenth-century realism was a powerful argument for the dissociation of the artist from specific

17 See the discussion by D. W. Fokkema in *Literary doctrine in China and Soviet influence, 1956–60*, 116.

political activity. This was the crux of the theoretical and critical discussions of the time: the question of the artist's autonomy, his need for time to write, his horror of thought reform, his resistance to dictation. Something of the pettiness of the restrictions to which a writer could be subjected may be gathered from an anecdote told by Yao Hsueh-yin (b. 1910):

I once wrote a novella in which there appeared, as a minor character, a worker who was politically backward. He was prone to feelings of jealousy and factionalism. If he saw a cogwheel being put in a wrong place, he would simply fold his hands and do nothing. As a result, the machine was kept from operating properly. Certain editors at the publishing house thought that this was unseemly behavior for a worker, and insisted he be changed into a spy. I did not agree, and as a result the manuscript did not go to press.[18]

The Chinese public should perhaps be grateful to these "certain editors," for this rejection may have contributed to Yao Hsueh-yin's decision to dedicate himself to a theme remote from contemporary life, a massive, multivolume historical novel on the subject of Li Tzu-ch'eng, peasant leader of the rebellion that brought down the Ming dynasty. *Li Tzu-ch'eng* began publication in 1963, and successive volumes produced in the last few years remain very popular.

Revolutionary romanticism: poetry of the Great Leap Forward

Some of the most vociferous counterattacks against the pleas for liberalization came from Li Hsi-fan (b. 1927) and Yao Wen-yuan (b. 1930). Li had come to prominence in 1952 with his denunciation of Yü P'ing-po (b. 1899) for his "bourgeois" interpretation of the eighteenth-century classic *Dream of the red chamber*, a diatribe on which was built the regime's first major campaign for thought control of the intellectuals. Yao Wen-yuan was later, in 1965, to emerge as a chief instigator of the Cultural Revolution with his identification of the play *Hai Jui dismissed from office* (*Hai Jui pa-kuan*) by Wu Han (1909–69) as an unacceptable satire on Mao himself; later still, Yao was anathematized as a member of the hated Gang of Four. The major restatement of the orthodox line was left to Chou Yang, who in March 1958 published a definitive summary.[19]

Chou Yang's new formulation, attributed to Mao Tse-tung and

18 Yao Hsueh-yin, "Ta-k'ai ch'uang-hu shuo liang-hua" (Open the window to have a direct talk), *Wen-i pao*, 7 (1957), 10–11, trans. in Nieh, *Hundred Flowers*, 1. 81–96.
19 Chou Yang, "Wen-i chan-hsien ti i-ch'ang ta pien-lun" (A great debate on the literary front), *Wen-i pao*, 5 (1958), 2–14.

welcomed at once by Kuo Mo-jo, was a call for "the union of revolutionary realism with revolutionary romanticism." The optimistic, forward-
looking thrust of socialist realism, under this formula, was to become
mandatory. It was the perfect literary slogan for the Great Leap Forward
just beginning, just as the Great Leap itself was the perfect means for
distracting those writers who had not been declared rightists and effectively silenced as Liu Pin-yen and Wang Meng had been.

The general slogan of the Great Leap Forward was "more, faster, better, and more economically" as the guideline for all aspects of production.
Hsia Yen adapted this for his colleagues, calling for "large numbers of
plays, quickly and well written and economical to stage."[20] Writers in all
genres responded to such watchwords by announcing quotas: Pa Chin
undertook to write one long novel and three of medium length in
addition to translations in the course of one year. T'ien Han declared he
would write ten plays and ten film scenarios. None of these plans was
fulfilled. Mao Tun set ten thousand words as the optimum limit for the
short story and called for semifictional "reports" of five thousand to six
thousand words.[21] The "short short story," *hsiao hsiao-shuo*, came into
favor as a quotafiller.

It was in poetry, in the multimillion-poem movement, that literary production most immediately met the challenge of the Great Leap Forward.

The rhymed quatrain with lines of five or seven syllables has held an
honored place in Chinese poetry since the eighth century. At the time of
the Great Leap Forward in 1958, it proved the ideal instrument for a
quick jolt of incentive toward ever greater feats of production:

> Peanut shells, long and full,
> Scores of feet from side to side:
> Load them up with five hundred men
> And on the eastern sea we'll ride.[22]

Exaggeration at this level becomes comic, but still can be impressive
when the image is striking enough:

> Round and full the haystack climbs,
> The topmost comrade has reached the sky,
> Mops his sweat with a strip of cloud,
> Borrows the sun to light his pipe.[23]

20 Hsia Yen, "To, k'uai, hao, sheng, liang chung ch'iu chih" (Move faster, better, more economically
    and seek quality in quantity), Ibid., 6 (1958), 26.
21 Mao Tun, "T'an tsui-chin ti tuan-p'ien hsiao-shuo" (On recent short stories), *Jen-min wen-hsueh*, 6
    (1958), 4–8.
22 Quoted in Chao Ts'ung, "1958 nien ti Chung-kung wen-i" (Chinese communist literature and art,
    1958), *Tsu-kuo chou-k'an* (China weekly), 26.9–10 (June 1959), 43–46.
23 Kuo Mo-jo and Chou Yang, comps., *Hung-ch'i ko-yao* (Songs of the red flag), 218.

Not only bumper harvests (whether reaped or wished for) but also electrification, oil wells and steel plants, conservancy measures, and every aspect of production are extolled in these "new folksongs," which Mao Tse-tung asked for and the population at large hastened to create. The cream was dignified by selection into *Songs of the red flag*, to which Kuo Mo-jo and Chou Yang attached their names, but "multimillion-poem movement" was perhaps no exaggeration in itself for the extraordinary outpouring of the time. It was an attempt to hurl the nation into the Communist millennium, when every man and woman would be a poet. Festivals were held and prizes given, and model workers festooned their lathes with the verse tributes of their comrades. In Shanghai alone, it was claimed, two hundred thousand workers had participated in literary activity, producing more than 5 million items.

Through images of red flowers and red sun, of the "foolish old man who moved the mountain," of landscape redesigned by communal effort, the poems built up a crescendo of romanticism. Poet and laboring man merged into one gigantic figure, a towering Everyman:

> In Heaven there is no Jade Emperor,
> No Dragon King in the sea.
> I am the Jade Emperor,
> I am the Dragon King.
> Hey there, three sacred mountains and five holy peaks,
> Make way!
> Here I come.[24]

It was a new peak of romanticism, defined in Kuo Mo-jo's own gloss on the formula as "the reality of socialism together with the ideal of communism."[25] What was in front of one's eyes was less significant than the vision that frenzied words could conjure up.

The hyperbole of the Great Leap time was certainly not limited to the new, young (often anonymous) popular poets. In the disciplined imagination of a scholarly poet like Pien Chih-lin (b. 1910), the diggers of the Ming Tombs reservoir outside Peking appear as giants:

> "What's that you're doing,
> Shovel after shovel?"
> "A quarter million irrigated acres
> Are welling up in my palm!"[26]

24 Kuo and Chou, *Hung-ch'i ko-yao*, 172.
25 Kuo Mo-jo, "Chiu mu-ch'ien ch'uang-tso chung ti chi-ko wen-t'i" (Some current problems in creative writing), *Jen-min wen-hsueh*, 1 (1959), 4–9.
26 Pien Chih-lin, "Tung-t'u wen-ta" (Dialogue of the earth movers), *Shih-k'an*, 3 (1958), 10, trans. Lloyd Haft, in Hsu, *Literature of the People's Republic of China*, 380.

This kind of contribution to the "new folksong" gave Pien some room to maneuver at this tense time, so that with Ho Ch'i-fang and others he could protest the views of those who would enshrine such simplistic ditties as the only permissible new poetry. Neither Pien nor Ho has been a very prolific poet; but Ho's impeccable political position as a liberated area poet of the 1940s gave weight to the arguments he advanced in the 1950s in favor of the development of strict metrical forms in addition to free verse and loose narrative forms.

A phenomenon of the early 1950s was the involvement of a number of emergent young poets in the campaigns in the western regions, from the mountains of Yunnan and Tibet to the grasslands and deserts of Sinkiang and Inner Mongolia. The excitement of their personal discovery of these vast territories resulted in highly romanticized lyrics of celebration. Kung Liu (b. 1927) was born in Kiangsi, and commented on the contrast of stern North with languid South when he moved to Peking in 1956:

> The green south sends gifts to the north:
> The gifts are wet rice, saplings, and my songs,
> And in all the bustle
> I have lost my reed flute.
> But the north has given me a *so-na* horn
> And tells me, "This is your weapon!"[27]

Kung Liu rose to fame via the lead he took in transcribing and editing a Chinese version of "Ashima," an oral epic of the Sani tribesmen of Yunnan. Ashima is a Sani maiden whose heroic struggle to follow her lover leads to her death at the hands of vicious overlords but serves as immortal inspiration to her people to seek liberation (led at last, of course, by the Chinese Communist Party); the story was made into a popular movie.

Liang Shang-ch'üan (b. 1931) was born in Szechwan, which is his home today, but in the mid-1950s, after army service, he extolled the end of fighting in Inner Mongolia – very much from a Chinese point of view:

> Cattle and sheep, like jewels
> Glittering in the sun;
> Mongolian tents, like buds,
> Each one ready to burst into bloom.
> No smoke of war rises now on the beacon tower.
> A rainbow floats in the eyes, a smile in the heart.[28]

27 Quoted in Chang, *Tang-tai wen-hsueh kai-kuan*, 63.
28 Liang Shang-ch'üan, "Ch'ang-ch'eng nei-wai" (The great wall, within and beyond), *Shan-ch'üan chi*, 76–78, trans. in Hsu, *Literature of the People's Republic of China*, 181.

Kao P'ing (b. 1932) has a long narrative poem of a Tibetan girl, lost in snow when her landlord sends her, to get rid of her, on an impossible search for a strayed flock. Her story is told in first person up to the point of her death, and is impressive as one gradually becomes aware of the background of her unhappy fate. The pithy dialogue follows the model of T'ien Chien's "Carter's story," ten years earlier.

As the ethnic minorities began to produce their own writers capable of composition in Chinese, like the Tibetan poet Rabchai Tsazang (b. 1935) and the Mongolian short story writer Malchinhu (b. 1930), the temptation to borrow their local color diminished (although the playwright Ts'ao Yü fell heavily into the trap with *Wang Chao-chün*, written in 1978 in response to official request).

The Great Leap was simply an extension of romantic optimism for these young poets, and in 1959 Liang Shang-ch'üan was writing of commune orchards with the personification of nature common to Great Leap verse:

> Orchards race rivers into the distance.
> On both banks they stand, like guards of honour.
> They greet the boats, waving them on toward the mountain,
> Offering the passengers heavy loads of fruit.[29]

Liang's images are more finely worked than most, and he has an eye for significant contrast. To the revolutionary, the pagoda is a symbol of the repressive power of superstition, pressing down as it does on some saintly relic (or, in the case of the famous Thunder peak pagoda at Hangchow, on an imprisoned sprite). Liang describes, in his poem "Black pagoda," such a structure as the dominant feature of the skyline of a small town. But the town now boasts a power station:

> Gazing, from a distance I see
> Another Black Pagoda rising high against the old.
> Nearer at hand I recognize the power-station chimney,
> Ceaselessly emitting its ink-swirls of smoke,
> Painting, in the darkness, lights like stars on the earth,
> Painting, in the daylight, a black peony on the sky.[30]

One of the most ambitious poems to emerge from the Great Leap Forward was the "White cloud O-po symphony" (*Pai-yun O-po chiao-hsiang shih*) which Juan Chang-ching composed and revised over a period of five

29 Liang Shang-ch'üan, "Ts'ai-se ti ho-liu" (River of many colors), *Shih-k'an*, 6 (1961), 16–17, trans. in Hsu, *Literature of the PRC*, 549.
30 Liang Shang-ch'üan, *K'ai hua ti kuo-t'u* (Flowering homeland), 67.

years, 1958–63. Juan was born in Kwangtung in 1914, but he came to fame with a long narrative poem relating the "turnabout" of three down-trodden peasant women of the Northwest. This was "Waters of the Chang river" (*Chang-ho shui*), which in the early 1950s was regarded as a worthy successor to Li Chi's "Wang Kuei and Li Hsiang-hsiang." "White cloud" was too farfetched to repeat the early success. Its theme, the overcoming of the superstitious conservatism that goads Mongolian herdsmen to resist industrialization, is too heavy for the overromanticized narrative thread. Worse, the pastoral prettiness of the opening, the fierce heroism of the ancestor who gave his blood in exchange for precious water, the old herdsman's determination to protect the sacred springs – all these build up the reader's own resistance to the tapping of the water for mining purposes, and we are far from convinced that, in the end, the grassland will "leap forward in the era of steel" – the poet-propagandist fails to convince us that he has come anywhere near the minds of his herdsman protagonists.

Heroes and middle characters in fiction

One of the favorite patterns in the short fiction of the Great Leap period is the illustration of the process whereby the individualistic peasant or worker is brought to shed his doubts of the value of collective enterprise for rapid increase in production. The writer or cadre narrator, revisiting a village or work site, is startled to find that a model revolutionary worker is none other than the unregenerate holdout of two or three years earlier, and learns his story via a series of flashbacks. An example that stands out from the mass of such stories by virtue of its appealing humor is the story "I knew that three years ago" (*San-nien tsao chih-tao*) by Ma Feng. "I knew that three years ago" is the catch phrase of the smart-aleck peasant Chao, whose idea of contributing to his co-op's hog production drive is to way-lay a prize pig en route to service the sows of the neighboring village. When the neighbors' ensuing litters are so puny as to make his mach-inations obvious, Chao's pride in his "achievement" suffers a sad blow and he is brought to see the error of his ways. He ends the story in model fashion, restraining his fellows from rigging sluices to divert the neighbors' water for their own use.

Another kind of comparison pits bad old days against heroic present, and improves on the occasion to demonstrate the irresistible commitment of the model worker in the socialist era. The worker-author Fei Li-wen (b. 1929) in his story "Shipyard search" (*Ch'uan-ch'ang chui-tsung*) has two model workers reminisce over the maltreatment they suffered in their broken-down preliberation shipyard. Now, so great is his urge to get back to his riveting even after a hectic night shift, one of them has been locked in the senior workers' lounge by the Party branch secretary, only to escape, through a window, back to the surpassing of his quota. The idealized behavior patterns being held up for emulation in stories of this kind may carry little conviction, but what may be more important is the shipyard setting itself, which projects the glamour of modernized large-scale industry, the huge steamer hulls looming out of the darkness, lighted suddenly by riveters' torches high in the air above.

The widespread use of the vocabulary of war reflects the urgent mood of the Great Leap. The humblest laborer becomes a "warrior" in a production "brigade," and "elite" workers form "crash squads" who "declare war on heaven" in their struggles against natural forces. Actual warfare continued to provide a staple of heroic fiction at this time, whether in celebration of the Red Armies themselves or the militant workers and students of the revolutionary past. *Stormy petrel* (*Hai-yen*), by Ko Ch'in, portrays a young female revolutionary at the time of the white terror in Shanghai, 1926–27. It takes the form of a film scenario but is not without passages of lyrical fervor:

A burst of gunfire, compact as driving rain, comes from the workers on either side of the railway. This sacred and noble sound of gunfire shakes in its pride the hearts of men and shakes the darkness of heaven and earth. The beloved ones have risen to their feet and are courageously advancing through the storm.[31]

The shortage of satisfactory villains in the new society induced novelists to return not only to war themes but to the years of the Party's underground struggles before 1949. Two major novels treat this material with very different results. The first, *Song of youth* (*Ch'ing-ch'un chih ko*), both as a novel and movie has had enormous appeal to young people. It was written in 1958 by Yang Mo (b. 1914), a writer who projects a great deal of romantic aspiration into her heroine, Lin Tao-ching. From student theorist this girl matures into a dedicated underground worker during the early 1930s, her life and actions dominated by growing contempt for her lover (an admirer of the liberal intellectual Hu Shih) and ardent devotion to first one and then a second Party agitator. The style and atmosphere of *Song of youth* are heavily reminiscent of leftist writings of the May Fourth period (Hu Yeh-p'in, for example), and even the imprisonment and torture of the heroine (the culminating state of her psychological growth) are highly romanticized.

---

31 Ko Ch'in, "Hai-yen" (Stormy petrel), *Jen-min wen-hsueh*, 3 (1958), 31–50. For quotation, see p. 44.

The second major work to treat the theme of the Communist underground is *Red crag* (*Hung yen*), of 1961, by Lo Kuang-pin (1924–67) and Yang I-yen (b. 1925). The contrast with *Song of youth* is marked. Yang Mo's work was criticized, in a major debate soon after its publication, for the bourgeois stance of its idealized protagonist and specifically for the distance of her thinking, language, her whole conception of revolutionary action, from the life of the masses. In a pathetic effort to respond to this criticism, Yang Mo added a new section to a revised edition, in which her heroine Lin Tao-ching anachronistically is "sent down" – she goes to work as tutor in a landlord's house. This theoretical fusion with peasant life in the end does little to reduce our sense that both the author and her protagonist are viewing the student movement, the underground work of the Party, and the entire course of revolution through the rosy spectacles of the May Fourth intellectual.

Red crag, on the other hand, comes close to the ideal prescription for a work of socialist realism. It has virtually documentary status. Lo Kuang-pin and Yang I-yen were responsible for no other works of fiction. They began their work with a 1959 memoir, *Immortality in blazing fire* (*Tsai lieh-huo chung yung-sheng*), of the experiences of political prisoners, underground workers like themselves, in a concentration camp outside Chungking operated by the Sino-American Cooperation Organization. The time is the most intense late stages of the civil war, when the Nationalists are preparing a last-ditch defense of their former wartime capital. Lo and Yang are reputed to have worked for ten years on the conversion of their memoirs into fiction, and to have written 3 million words before finalizing the text of *Red crag* at some four hundred thousand. The complex narrative combines the resistance of the prisoners to deprivation, interrogation, temptation, and torture, with their persistent and ultimately successful efforts to maintain contact with outside forces, both Party underground and Red Army operations in the area. Rather than a single protagonist *Red crag* furnishes a gallery of portraits of disciplined revolutionaries both male and female, of waverers and turncoats, and of guileful but despairing functionaries of the Nationalist secret service. The great length and grim subject matter of the book are validated by a whole series of strongly written climactic scenes: Hsu Yun-feng's heartbreaking work on an escape hole, from solitary confinement and before his own martyrdom; Sister Chiang confronted with the display of her husband's severed head, and her calm preparations for her own execution; the revelation that Hua Tzu-liang has spent three years feigning madness in order to safeguard his role as intermediary.

Red crag is an impressive monument to the many dedicated Communists who died in the underground struggles of two decades. It has had more readers, probably, than any other work of Communist literature, and is even more widely known as film and stage play. The quality of incident and characterization place it squarely in the traditional line of the Chinese prose epic.

Of all the many works of fiction that have been attempts to project the new social ethic of the Chinese Communists, none has carried more conviction than Liu Ch'ing's *The builders (Ch'uang-yeh shih)*, of 1959. This was the first of four projected volumes, but the first part of a second volume was not published until 1977, one year before Liu Ch'ing's death. Liu Ch'ing's credentials were impeccable. He was born in 1916 in Shensi, joined the Party at the age of twenty, and moved to Yenan in 1938. He published short stories, then in 1947 wrote his first full-length novel, *Planting grain (Chung-ku chi)*, whose background is the development of mutual aid teams in the Shensi countryside during the Anti-Japanese War. Liu Ch'ing's participation in the civil war underlies his second novel, *Wall of bronze*. The central figure of this novel, Shih Te-fu, sets a new standard for the portrayal of the guerrilla hero who emerges from the peasant community and never loses either his dedication to his fellow peasants or the closest contact with them despite the rigors of capture by the Nationalists and the heroic adventures of full-scale warfare.

This heroic model is further developed in *The builders*. This is in essence the story of Liang Sheng-pao, a young peasant whose emergence as a leader is the natural consequence of his growing understanding of socialist cooperation and of his vision of the benefits it can bring to the Shensi village. The attractiveness of Liang Sheng-pao is the key to the success of the book. Hero he may be, but an understated hero. He is introduced only slowly into the action, and obliquely, through the highly critical intermediary, his father, Liang the Third, whose rugged individualism is affronted by Sheng-pao's everlasting readiness to put the common effort before the prosperity of his own family. Liang the Third is himself a notable figure, long unregenerate but at last converted to the new ways of self-sacrifice for the community, and rewarded at last with a new dignity as father of the cooperative's chairman. This "middle character" was frequently cited in the great debate of the mid-1960s as having occupied too much of Liu Ch'ing's attention, but the critics who called for more exclusive emphasis on the positive hero failed to appreciate the valuable function of this crusty old father as foil to the "new socialist man," his son Sheng-pao.

Slow in appearing, and then in an unremarkable light, demonstrating his frugality on an errand for the cooperative, Liang Sheng-pao ends the novel absent on another mission, and separated from his sweetheart who suspects that the two of them are too strong-willed ever to form a successful marriage.

A central episode in *The builders* is the story of the expedition Liang Sheng-pao organizes to cut bamboo in the mountains for the making of brooms. It is the slack season in the fields, and the cooperative needs funds; but much more important to Sheng-pao is the chance to prove the value of an organized communal effort. As the men he leads willingly band together to build a shelter, he wins through to a new level of faith in his vision:

The men's warm mutual affection, their good cheer, stirred the young leader deeply. They were giving him a new understanding. He used to think it would take years to change the selfish individualistic peasant mentality, with long meetings every winter, running far into the night. But now he had caught a glimmering of something. Could it be that the main way to change this mentality was through collective labor? That you shouldn't wait for their mentality to change before organizing them, but rather you should organize them in order to bring the change about? (p. 403)

Liu Ch'ing's concern throughout *The builders* is the essential ordinariness of Liang Sheng-pao, the believable hero who learns more from the experience of daily living than from the texts of speeches. Precisely because we can relate to the novel's central figure, the reader is the more prepared to accept Liu Ch'ing's own vision of a rosy future, expressed in rhapsodies to the bucolic beauties of the North China Plain.

The "middle character," stationed between hero and villain on the spectrum, is (to the outside observer) more recognizably a human being than either, and his presence in a literary work usually increases its degree of believability. He has no malicious intent to block the forward movement of humanity or undermine the revolution – he is not a villain – but falls short of the hero by placing his own interests or comfort first, by being, in other words, *l'homme moyen sensuel*, familiar in life and literature for centuries. In the view of the ideologues, this man had virtually disappeared from China, to be replaced by what Chou Yang called the "people of the new age":

Those writers with bourgeois prejudice have always held that the advanced characters ... whom we describe are untrue to life and that only colourless "petty individuals" or low, negative characters are "true." Their argument is that every man has some faults and defects, that there is a struggle between darkness and light in the depth of every heart; this is what they mean by the "complexity of the inner mind." We are against over-simplifying the minds of characters. The inner life of the people of the new age is of the richest and healthiest. They know what attitude to take with regard to labor, friendship, love and family life. Of course, they must have worries, inner conflicts, and shortcomings of one kind or another, or make this or that mistake; but they always endeavour to use communist ideas and morality as the highest criteria for all their actions.[32]

Mao Tun advanced a similar position:

The important thing in selecting a subject is its social significance and ability to reflect the spirit of the age. In characterization, reject the revisionist principle of describing men as they are; shortcomings in a character must be shown as transitory phenomena subject to correction, or if incorrigible, peculiar to class enemies doomed to failure. The dark side of society is depicted to show the reader the inevitability of the elimination of reaction and the resolution of contradiction.[33]

Therefore when Shao Ch'üan-lin (1906–71), Ch'in Chao-yang, and others, following a seminar held in Dairen in August 1962, advocated greater attention to the middle character in the interests of increased truth to life, they were accused of backsliding, even of counterrevolutionary activity in attempting to divert attention from the heroes dedicated to Chou Yang's "communist ideas and morality" who now, it was claimed, constituted the overwhelming mass of the population. The opposition engendered by the proponents of the middle character filled consecutive issues of the *Literary Gazette* for late 1964, and gained increasing momentum until the outbreak of the Cultural Revolution itself made all such debate for the moment irrelevant.

Ch'en Teng-k'o (b. 1918) is a writer of peasant origin who cut his teeth on stories of the Japanese and civil wars. His novel *Thunderstorm (Feng-lei)* of 1964 is one of the boldest and most violence-filled accounts of the imposition of cooperative institutions on a backward village (in this case, in Ch'en's native province of Anhwei) in the mid-1950s. The overcoming of peasant opposition to collaborative effort is the theme also of *Song of the pioneers (K'en-huang ch'ü)*, 1959–63, by Pai Wei (b. 1911): the wasteland against which the Party-led peasants struggle in this novel is the residue of disastrous flooding of the Yellow River in Honan province, where the author had worked in 1950–54.

Sun Li (b. 1913) won popularity in the late 1950s and early 1960s with his stories of rural life, depicting the contrasting attitudes toward cooperation of the older and younger generations somewhat in the manner of Chao Shu-li.

---

32 Chou Yang, "Wo kuo she-hui chu-i wen-hsueh i-shu ti tao-lu" (The path of our socialist literature and art), *Wen-i pao*, 13–14 (1960), 15–37.
33 Mao Tun, "Fan-ying she-hui chu-i yueh-chin ti shih-tai, t'ui-tung she-hui chu-i ti yueh-chin" (Reflect the age of the socialist leap forward, promote the socialist leap forward), *Jen-min wen-hsueh*, 8 (1960), 8–36.

The reflection in literary works of life in the factory or mine was begun by professional writers Ts'ao Ming, Ai Wu, and others, but by the late 1950s a group of young writers on industrial themes had emerged from among the workers themselves. T'ang K'o-hsin (b. 1928), as befits a man of Wusih, writes (mostly short stories) about textile workers. While the textile mill may lack the potential for high drama offered by the blast furnace or the coal mine, the relatively small, intimate scale of work (at least for the more old-fashioned spinner or weaver) makes for constant interaction among the workers, who in T'ang's stories are forever joking, trading insults, but in the end stimulating each other to improved attitudes and increased production. "Sha Kuei-ying," of 1962, is a middle-length story of the evolution of a model worker, a young woman power-loom operator. Her personal name is that of the woman warrior Mu Kuei-ying, familiar to all lovers of storytelling and traditional theater. Sha Kuei-ying's selfless dedication to the common welfare wins over a backsliding individualist comrade with whom she trades looms, willingly undertaking to work with an inferior machine (which she then proceeds to repair). Her superior political consciousness puts to shame a would-be lover, the male chauvinist Shao Shun-pao, whom, however, she imbues with a new readiness to take responsibility and accept criticism.

Hu Wan-Ch'un (b. 1929) has been closely associated with T'ang K'o-hsin, like him restricting his work largely to short stories (although he has also written plays and movie scripts), and remaining active in Shanghai through the years of the Cultural Revolution. Hu's background was the machine shop and steel mill, where most of his stories are set. He is a superior stylist, using everyday settings and symbols with effective economy. Some of his best stories concern the aging worker, like Shun-fa in the story "Twilight years" (*Wan-nien*), of 1962, whose feelings of uselessness in retirement are countered by realization of the social advances to which his work has contributed. While Hu's hotheaded young apprentices have physical strength and revolutionary zeal, his veteran workers are given an impressive dignity with their sense of responsibility as masters of the new society. Thus the ending of the story "What instructor Pu-kao thought" (*Pu-kao shih-fu so hsiang-tao ti*), of 1958, brings only satisfaction to the master steelmaker whose speed record has just been surpassed by his pupil:

The day dawned. The red sun threw off thousands of golden rays. From the rolling shop drifted the humming of machines mingled with the beats of drums and gongs. A new record had been set by Yang Hsiao-niu's shift. Everyone was in high spirits. Life was striding ahead.[34]

34 Hu Wan-ch'un, *Man of a special cut*, 96, quoted in Gotz, "Images of the worker," 265.

The song of Ou-yang Hai (Ou-yang Hai chih ko), of 1965, by Chin Ching-mai (b. 1930), may be read now as an ominous precursor of Cultural Revolution fanaticism. The real-life heroism of the young soldier who gave his life to avert a train crash is attributed to his harsh childhood in the old society and the redeeming inspiration of Mao Thought, but what is disturbing is the morbid insistence on sacrifice as the only truly acceptable course for a good Communist. The work vividly illustrates the weakness of the "three-in-one" creative formula, according to which the leadership supplies the thought content, the masses provide life experience, and the author contributes writing skills.

Poetry of the 1960s

In 1960, in a major policy statement, Chou Yang described the advances made in fostering the "national forms" Mao had called for in the Yenan "Talks":

Guided by the policy of letting a hundred flowers blossom and developing the new from the old, we have taken over and renovated our excellent heritage of literature and art to make it a part of our advanced socialist culture, and at the same time we are investing our new literature and art with different forms and styles with more dazzling national characteristics.[35]

Mao Tse-tung himself may serve as exemplar of the poet who under all the pressure to compose in the language of the masses nevertheless clings to a completely traditional classical diction. Mao could do this, of course, simply by claiming that his poetry was not meant seriously as a contribution to the new literature. It was merely his hobby, and must not be imitated as a model. But this is tongue-in-cheek: Mao was, in fact, a powerful poet, and by imbedding new themes and images in scrupulously conventional forms he has shown other poets a path they have not been slow to follow.

Mao's best poems, such as "Changsha" (1925) and "Snow" (*Hsueh*) (1936), were written before the People's Republic was established, although they appeared in public view for the first time on New Year's Day of 1957.[36] But we may demonstrate his achievement with "Swimming," his celebration of his own much publicized swim across the Yangtze River in 1956:

> I drank the waters of Changsha,
> Now enjoy fish of Wuchang;
> Ruled a bar across river's miles,

---

35 Chou Yang, "Tao-lu," 15.   36 *JMJP*, 1 January 1957.

> Stretched sight horizon-long,
> Preferring beat of wind and wave
> To aimless stroll in idle court.
> These hours to me belong.
> The master's words at stream-side:
> "Thus ever does it run."
>
> Wind-sway of masts
> Repose of Tortoise and Snake
> And a great plan begun:
> North and south across nature's moat
> Bridged by a soaring span.
> West, we erect new cliffs of stone
> To block the rains of Witch's Gorge:
> Calm lake from sheer walls sprung.
> If still the goddess flourish,
> What changes since she was young![37]

"Swimming" fulfills with the greatest exactness the requirements of meter and rhyme imposed by the classical lyric pattern *Shui-tiao ko-t'ou* It alludes to a third-century folk ditty concerning the establishment of a new capital and to a historic epithet for the Yangtze, "nature's moat." Tortoise and Snake are the names of hills on either bank of the Yangtze at Wuhan; the "goddess" appeared to a royal lover in an ode of the third century B.C., and the "Master" is Confucius, whose conviction of time's changelessness Mao's whole poem refutes. With masterful irony Mao superimposes on these ancient allusions the achievements of today, the new reservoir at Witch's Gorge and the new Wuhan bridge. Out of it all comes the symbol of his own personal achievement: His own strong arms and legs have carried him across history and geography to unify the country and bear it into the modern age.

Of other national leaders who, like Mao, indulged in the composition of classical-style verse, the most serious was probably Ch'en I (1901–72), the war hero who eventually served as foreign minister. He was a popular figure: A witty comedy, *Mayor Ch'en I*, by Sha Yeh-hsin, pleased audiences in 1979 with its portrayal of his resourcefulness during his years as mayor of Shanghai.[38] In the same year a selection of one hundred and fifty of his poems was published. Though his command of technicalities of traditional-style verse is not as sure as Mao's, and his heroic vision is less cosmic in scale, his poems are certainly livelier than Chu Te's or Tung Pi-wu's.

---

37 Mao Tse-tung, "Yu-yung" (Swimming), in *Mao Chu-hsi shih-tz'u san-shih-ch'i shou* (Thirty-seven poems by Chairman Mao).
38 The controversy surrounding Sha Yeh-hsin as coauthor of the play *If I were genuine*, earlier in 1979, will be discussed later in this chapter.

Kuo Mo-jo reverted to classical modes for his exchanges with Mao in the 1960s. But there was an attractiveness about the power of the concise classical quatrain that proved irresistible to many writers, even to one like Hsiao Chün (b. 1908) better known for his modern realist prose. Hsiao Chün fell foul of the Party leadership in the early days and was removed from the literary scene even during the Yenan period. But through all the years of disgrace and exile he maintained his independence of spirit, which he expresses through the symbol of the tiger in the following quatrain:

> One roar, this hill to that,
>   and all the beasts take fright!
> Limitless space, lone prowler,
>   moon's uncertain light.
> Though hunger, frost cut bone-deep,
>   and hero heart grow old,
> For me no docile tail
>   to wag in others' sight![39]

Mao's fusion of old and new is clearly apparent in the work of Ko Pi-chou (b. 1916), whose emergence as a poet dates from the 1950s. In 1962 he published four "New songs of Pei-mang mountain." Pei-mang is the site of ancient royal tombs near Loyang, and a familiar classical locus of mournful reflection. But these songs are anything but mournful. The third ends as follows:

> In our new town of Loyang
> Where is the old city to be found?
> Among nimbuses of many hues the I River dances like a phoenix,
> In the white clouds the river Lo arches like a dragon;
> See the immense ocean of green trees,
> And jungles of smoking chimneys row after row.
> Factories stand like gunboats in battle array.
> O fighting ships one by one,
> A voyage of ten thousand *li* you have begun.[40]

The outlook of the early-1960s lyricists is altogether less rosy than that of their predecessors of a decade earlier. The revolution, clearly, has not abolished class privilege. The poet may sing of the joys of the new society, but he must be mindful also of the forces that had to be vanquished and that still may threaten again. Lu Ch'i (b. 1931) presents an

---

39 Hsiao Chün presented a calligraphic scroll of this poem to the writer during his visit to Berkeley in August 1981.
40 Ko Pi-chou, "Pei-mang-shan hsin-hsing ssu-shou" *JMJP*, 24 March 1962, trans. in S. H. Chen, "Metaphor and the conscious," 44.

effective ledger of revolutionary credit and debit in "The abacus clicks," one poem in a sequence ("poems-in-series," *tsu-shih*, were very popular at this time) entitled "Return to Willow village" (*Ch'ung-fan yang-liu ts'un*), of 1964. The clicking the poet hears is not made by crowding livestock or by the loading of the commune's plentiful harvest, but by the abacus, relic of the old days of miserly calculation, and of the campaigns to "square accounts" with the landlords. But the abacus too has "turned about," and now reckons not rents but work points.[41]

Yen Chen (b. 1930) won praise for his first poem, "Chang's hands" (*Lao Chang ti shou*), which vividly realizes the "turnabout" of a landless peasant by concentrating attention on his hands as they work the soil for the landlord, then hold out the beggar's bowl, take up a gun in the revolution, dig a new channel for the Huai River, and at last return to "banging the door-knocker of the good earth" in Chang's own fields.

Yen Chen's collection *Southern ballads* (*Chiang-nan ch'ü*), of 1961, presents pretty lyrics of country life, idealized in a way that recalls the lush vocabulary of the old dramatic romances. But by the mid-1960s Yen's smiling fields, it was clear, had known their winters also:

> Pine forests of the snowy plateau: I sing your praise
> For the depth and strength of your green,
> Wax-plum blossom deep in the hills: I sing your praise
> For the spirit of your blooming, and your lasting fragrance.
> Praise for the branch, which under the snow still puts out fresh green,
> Praise for the root, which down in the mud still nurtures fragrance,
> While under the ice the stream still chuckles by day and by night,
> While up in the sky spring thunder brews in the clouds of sunset.
> Who says the winter is a world of snowstorm?
> No, the snowstorm's but one of winter's aspects.[42]

In this poem, "Song of winter" (*Tung chih ko*), Yen Chen has passed through the "three bad years" of 1959–61, and celebrates the endurance of his people with the image of the wax plum that blooms in January, rather than the blood-red peony that ten years earlier was all but mandatory.

Kuo Hsiao-ch'uan (1919–76) began to write poetry in Yenan in the 1940s and by the 1960s was a leading practitioner, experimenting with a wide variety of forms and subjects. His moving, meditative "drumbeat" lyric "Gazing at the starry sky" (*Wang hsing k'ung*), of 1959, was attacked as excessively individualistic, but his themes are more often public, as in the "new rhymeprose" (*hsin tz'u-fu*) "Carved on the northern wasteland" (*K'o tsai pei-ta-huang ti t'u-ti shang*), of 1963:

---

41 See translation by Hsu in *Literature of the People's Republic of China*, 728.
42 Quoted in Chang, *Tang-tai wen-hsueh kai-kuan*, 74.

This land slumbers on, as in an immense dream.
No voice of man to be heard, only howling wolves, bears, and tigers;
This land, always covered in tall grass.
For days on end, no man casts any shadow on it, only the sky, and the water, and
the red sun large as a cartwheel ...
No tractors, no motor caravans, no pack horses,
But here is the land, tens of thousands of acres, turning over in the warm spring
breeze.
No houses, no inns, no hamlets sending up wafts of smoke of evening cooking.
But here are several state farms, taking root among a forest of tents...[43]

The seventeen quatrains of this poem, with their long symmetrically balanced lines alternately rhymed, effectively shoulder their burden of dedication to the stern, long-neglected, but now rewarding homeland.

Kuo Hsiao-ch'uan is a prolific poet of intense commitment. For him as for many of his contemporaries the sea provides a fecund metaphor of the revolutionary strength of the masses, but his apostrophe to it in "To the ocean" (*Chih ta-hai*) has the overtones of a kind of verbal rape:

> Like a stormy petrel
> I want to draw the milk from your bosom
> And suckle with it the vast sky, broader than your sea,
> Like the red clouds of dawn
> I want to bathe in your embrace
> Then with my own blood dye your waves crimson,
> Like the spring thunder
> I'll learn from you how to roar
> Then fly far and wide driving back winter from the earth,
> And like the drenching rain
> I'll turn your warm vapours into liquid drops,
> Shower them across the land, make the crops grow
> Make the sea surge for joy...[44]

Kuo is best known for his sequences "To young citizens" (*Chih ch'ing-nien kung-min*), of 1955; "Trilogy: the general" (*Chiang-chün san-pu ch'ü*), from the late 1950s; and "Sugarcane forest – green gauze tents" (*Kan-che-lin – ch'ing-sha-chang*) in which he ranges with his customary breathless freedom comparing landscapes north and south in their socialistic transformation.

Like Kuo Hsiao-ch'uan, Ho Ching-chih (b. 1924) displays the influence of the Soviet poet Mayakovsky, and he has continued to write "ladder-style verse" (very short lines used in reiterative patterns) to the present time, though in his earlier work he made much use also of the *hsin-t'ien-yu* couplet that Li Chi borrowed from folk ballads for use in "Wang Kuei

43 Kuo Hsiao-ch'uan, *Kan-che lin* (Sugarcane forest), 3–7, trans. in Hsu, *Literature of the People's Republic of China*, 685.
44 Quoted in Chang, *Tang-tai wen-hsueh kai-kuan*, 82.

and Li Hsiang-hsiang." Ho's poems are even more overtly political than Kuo Hsiao-ch'uan's. He has written on the popular theme of "Return to Yenan" (*Hui Yen-an*), of 1956, and his "Song of Lei Feng" of 1963 stood out among the great mass of works of all genres promoting this self-sacrificing model soldier as a prime lesson of the Socialist Education Campaign.

Both Kuo Hsiao-ch'uan and Ho Ching-chih, perhaps because of the impeccable enthusiasm they maintained throughout their work, succeeded in continuing to write during the lean years of the Cultural Revolution.

Li Ying (b. 1926) through thirty years of army life has celebrated his comrades and his travels in some twenty collections of verse. Before he became a soldier he studied at Peking University, but his debt to the classical tradition of the Chinese lyric seems to come out in the trained poet's eye that sees fresh images, rather than in any indulgence in allusion or secondhand diction. In a poem on a hallowed theme of T'ang times, "Night song at the frontier" (*Pien-sai yeh-ko*), Li Ying may be hoping to invoke the illustrious Li Po:

> Border night, calm and still,
> Mountains too high, moon too small,
> The moon sleeps on the mountain's shoulder
> As the mountain on the shoulder of the warrior.[45]

Although like others Li Ying has felt compelled to issue some overtly patriotic, anti-imperialist poems, his themes are more commonly the every-day life of the soldier, his joy in the sunrise (like "golden pheasant fea-thers" over the Gobi) or the crashing sea below his coastal fort. He can start from a small symbol, a lookout lantern or a date palm or a windbreak of bamboos, and conjure up the spirit of a landscape; he can also fall vic-tim to the sentimentalism that lies ever in wait for the determined roman-tic, as when he extols the cook who steps lighter than the deer and rises earlier than the eagles. But again, this poem on the cook is redeemed by the bold image of the closing lines, wherein the cook appears bearing buckets of water for his breakfast chores – one bucket full of red sun; the other, of blue hills.

Wen Chieh (1923–71) was another poet who wrote of the frontier, in *Turfan lovesongs* (*T'u-lu-fan ch'ing-ko*), of 1954, and later poems into the 1960s. The beauties of the Chinese land were sung impressively at this time also by Yen Ch'en (b. 1914), who in the post-Mao era was to become one of the most influential sponsors of new poetry as chief editor of the national journal *Poetry* (*Shih-k'an*).

The historical play as a vehicle for protest

Chinese theatergoers tell a favorite anecdote to illustrate the popularity of the traditional operatic forms and the resistance to the new spoken drama (*hua-chü*). The creator of one of these newfangled pieces, late for his own opening night, found a group of his friends still idling in the foyer though the performance had begun. Remonstrating with them, he was told, "Oh, they haven't started yet, they're just standing around on the stage talking" – obviously, something that lacked music, song, and balletic movement could not be considered theater.

It was the conviction that operatic forms were the quintessence of Chinese theater that led to the development of the "revolutionary modern operas" as the prime expression (and almost the sole product) of the Cultural Revolution. The true progenitor of these works was *The white-haired girl (Pai-mao-nü)*.

The use of quickly composed, easily staged propaganda sketches, to encourage peasant audiences to confront landlords or resist the Japanese invaders, had been a feature of the cultural life of Communist areas since the 1930s. *The white-haired girl* was the most ambitious work to develop out of this tradition, a full-length play based on an actual happening in Hopei province in the early 1940s. Ho Ching-chih took the lead in the creating of the finished version of the play, which was billed as a cooperative work by members of the Lu Hsun Academy and was one of the most popular stage offerings in the early years of the People's Republic.

The story is of a girl, abducted by a villainous landlord, who runs away and hides for months in a cave, subsisting on roots and berries. These privations result in the growth of white hair all over her body, so that she is feared as a demon by superstitious villagers who chance upon her at dusk. The landlord uses this "demon" for his own unscrupulous ends, until the day of liberation by the Eighth Route Army. With the army returns the girl's sweetheart of former days, who, setting out undaunted to exorcise the demon, rediscovers his lost love. The moral comes through triumphantly in the girl's closing lines: "The old society turned human beings into demons; the new society turns demons into human beings." An opera version of *The white-haired girl* won a Stalin Prize in 1951, but during the Cultural Revolution the story was turned into a model ballet for stage and screen rather than a "model opera" as such.

T'ien Han's drama *Kuan Han-ching* (1958) has been at the same time one of the most impressive new plays staged in the People's Republic and one of the most outspoken appeals for autonomy for the artist. T'ien Han had been a prolific dramatist for more than thirty years and was head of the

Dramatists Union. His choice of subject was brilliant: Kuan Han-ch'ing was a leading playwright of the thirteenth century, the classical age of Yuan drama, currently being feted as a folk artist with performances and publications of plays and intense scholarly study of his art. Although little is known for certain about Kuan's life, he seems to have practiced medicine and acted on stage at times; more importantly, more than one of his plays revolves around the defense of an oppressed woman against the abuses of a rich and powerful bully.

T'ien Han's play about Kuan, though essentially a spoken drama highly realistic in presentation, is composed of rapidly shifting scenes like a traditional opera, offers a great deal of historical color and incorporates extracts from the operatic performance of Kuan's masterpiece, *The injustice to Tou O*. Some of the lines of this play are the most inflammatory in all of Chinese drama: The magistrate's court is pictured as an overturned bowl into which no light of truth can penetrate, the officials turn deaf ears to the laments of the populace, and in the climactic scene of the young widow's execution heavenly portents reveal her innocence. T'ien Han draws special attention to these lines, and builds the central conflict of his own play around the intolerance for such outspokenness on the part of the Mongol overlords of the day. Kuan Han-ch'ing is ordered to revise his script to make it less offensive for performance before a chief minister. Kuan refuses and his cast supports his courageous resistance. Threats and punishment fail to bring about the changing of Kuan's text, and the play ends with his departure for exile. The denouement prefigures the fate T'ien Han brought upon himself with this play and a second one, *Hsieh Yao-huan*: He died during imprisonment at the height of the Cultural Revolution.

Hsieh Yao-huan, published in February 1961, was T'ien Han's adaptation for Peking Opera of a folk-dance opera entitled *The woman governor* (*Nü-hsun-an*). It is set in the reign of the Empress Wu of the T'ang dynasty, depicted as a ruler misled by her own seclusion and excessive trust in ambitious, tyrannous ministers. Hsieh is her envoy to resolve incipient rebellion in the countryside, which these men and their local subordinates have stirred up by their oppressive actions. Destroyed by the machinations of self-seeking officials, Hsieh with her dying breath warns the empress against their destructive power.

For its evident reference to the impending failure of Mao's leadership, *Hsieh Yao-huan* was eventually criticized as one of the "three most poisonous weeds" among contemporary plays. The other two were *Li Hui-niang*, a ghost drama set in the Sung period, by Meng Ch'ao, and *Hai Jui dismissed from office* (*Hai Jui pa-kuan*), published one month before *Hsieh*

Yao-huan. The most controversial of all of these plays, *Hai Jui dismissed from office* was the work of the distinguished historian Wu Han (1909–69). He had published little since 1949, and had been disturbed by the excesses of the Great Leap Forward. He found in the historical figure of Hai Jui an opportunity to "make the past serve the present" by establishing a model of resistance to the abuse of power. Hai Jui was a scholar-official of the sixteenth century, outstanding among a number of brave censors, local officials, and other servants of the Ming throne who spoke out and often sacrificed their lives in opposition to tyranny. Hai Jui's memorial of protest to the emperor, for which he was at first condemned to death, had already featured in a new historical drama by the Shanghai actor-dramatist Chou Hsin-fang. Wu Han's treatment of Hai Jui follows the lines of a traditonal courtroom drama (*kung-an chü*), in which Hai as a newly appointed governor uncovers crimes of abduction and expropriation committed by the son of a retired grand secretary. Hai Jui takes the side of the peasant victims and resists the grand secretary's bribes and threats. Machinations by local landlords and their allies at court lead to Hai Jui's dismissal from office, but in a dramatic finale to the play he refuses to hand over his seal of office to his successor until the sound of a cannon tells him that his officers have executed the criminal according to his orders.

In form *Hai Jui dismissed from office* is a standard Peking opera, in nine scenes, with some pleasantly old-fashioned touches such as the thoroughly Confucian exhortation to virtue by Hai Jui's aged mother. It created no great stir at the time of its appearance, less for example than such similar pleas for resistance to falsehood and tyranny as T'ien Han's *Kuan Han-ch'ing*. Its eventual fate as ignition coil for the entire Cultural Revolution was bestowed upon it by the critic Yao Wen-yuan, who began a process of interpretation of the play late in 1965. As a *pièce à clef*, the play is read as a vindication of Marshal P'eng Te-huai, whose opposition to the Great Leap Forward led to his demotion and eventual purge. Hai Jui is P'eng, the restoration of lands to the peasants is a proposal to dismantle the people's communes, and behind all (though hardly mentioned in the play) is the deluded emperor, Mao Tse-tung himself.

CULTURAL REVOLUTION IN CHINA,
NEW WRITERS IN TAIWAN, 1966–1976

The revolutionary model operas

In a speech made at a major festival of Peking Opera on contemporary themes held in Peking in June and July 1964, Chiang Ch'ing, former actress who as Mao Tse-tung's wife was devoting herself to a theatrical renaissance, condemned the traditional opera as offering nothing but "emperors and princes, generals and ministers, beauties and geniuses, plus ox-headed demons and snake spirits."[46] This feudalistic bourgeois rubbish must be swept from the stage to make room for works that would treat contemporary themes, but with all the resources of music and dance that could be culled from the tradition itself and from the recently popular Western opera and ballet in addition. From the early 1960s on, five pieces took shape that were declared to be "blueprint works," *yang-pan-hsi*. *On the docks* (*Hai-kang*) is the only one of the five with a strictly contemporary and nonmartial topic, the struggle against a dockside saboteur. *Red lantern* (*Hung teng chi*) and *Sha-chia-pang* were the most popular of the five, both set during the Anti-Japanese War, the former celebrating the heroism of a railway worker and the latter that of a teashop proprietress as they aid the army in resistance. The remaining model operas (of the original group – a handful more followed in the early 1970s) were *Taking Tiger Mountain by strategy* (*Chih-ch'ü Wei-hu-shan*), in which a People's Liberation Army company takes a bandit's lair in 1946, and *Raid on the White Tiger Regiment* (*Ch'i-hsi Pai-hu-t'uan*), a Korean War story. In line with the theory of continuous revolution, a concept of continuous creation led to constant revision of the model operas. From early to late versions there is a sharpening of antagonisms so that shades of gray disappear from hero and villain portrayals alike, and no vestige of bourgeois behavior is left to the heroic types. The central part in the action of *Sha-chia-pang* is played by the teashop proprietress and underground party worker A-ch'ing-sao, but in performance of the work more and more stress falls on the PLA men under their leader, Kuo, whose dazzling white uniform dominates the eye as he leaps and postures about the stage.

Despite the simplistic renderings of the good-and-evil struggles and the objections of the purists to Tchaikovskian orchestration and elaborate sets and lighting effects, the model plays offered splendid dramatic moments and were genuinely popular before reiterated performance dulled their impact. The part of A-ch'ing-sao is a prime role for a mature actress. Fending off suspicions that she is in fact in league with the Reds, she claims to treat all patrons of her teahouse on an equal basis, including the Nationalist officer Tiao. "When the customer leaves, the tea grows cold," she sings, and fits action to words by pouring out at that precise moment the slops from the bowl the discomfited Tiao is holding. Her finest moment comes in the long, climactic seventh scene. Puppet soldiers drag off

46 Chiang Ch'ing, "On the revolution in Peking Opera," *Chinese Literature*, 8 (1967), 118–24.

an old village woman to be shot as a Communist spy. The Nationalist officers, who have been trying every means to break down A-ch'ing-sao's false front of unconcern, gaze expectantly at her – surely now she will reveal her Communist affiliation. A moment of silence, then she springs to her feet. "Commander!" she begins. They wait. With superb lightness and casualness she says, "I must be on my way." The balloon of the villain's expectation is pricked, and before long they let themselves be manipulated into sparing the old woman's life in the hope that they can use her as bait to catch other Communists in this enigmatic village society.

Chang Yung-mei (b. 1925) was one of the few authors able to continue work through the Cultural Revolution: His long poem "Battle at Hsisha" (*Hsi-sha chih chan*) appeared in 1974 to the enthusiastic approval of Chiang Ch'ing. Chang had had long experience with the incorporation of revolutionary fervor into poetic writings about army life. Since the early 1950s he had written of the romance of soldiering ("Rifle slung, I ride the world over" [*Ch'i-ma kua-ch'iang tsou t'ien-hsia*] was one of his popular ditties), of comradely devotion and the "fish in water" relationship of troops with civilian population, and of militant resistance in Korea and Vietnam.

The novels of Hao Jan

In the early 1970s it sometimes seemed, at least to outside observers, that aside from revisions of revolutionary operas the only things being written in China were stories by Hao Jan. And indeed, so prolific was this writer that the suspicion grew that "Hao Jan" was simply a pseudonym being shared by a group of adherents of the Cultural Revolution. In fact, the pseudonym belongs to Liang Chin-kuang (b. 1932), whose stories of peasant life are in direct line of descent from such mainstream writers as Chao Shu-li and Liu Ch'ing.

Hao Jan can make a story out of the salvaging of a sick horse ("A skinny chestnut horse" [*I-p'i shou hung-ma*]) or the repairing of a wheelbarrow ("The wheels are flying" [*Ch'e-lun fei-chuan*]). For the first of these he uses a formula that he did not invent but has developed and made characteristically his own: The narrator, a cadre or reporter, revisits a village and finds a new phenomenon of progress, in this case a glossy, handsome draft horse. To his astonishment he discovers this is the miserable nag he saw on his last visit. A flashback tells the story of the dedicated effort of the young commune member who refused to let this precious communal asset go to waste. Not only has the horse been saved, of course, but more important, the protagonist and his mates have learned an effective lesson in self-reliance. A similar theme informs the second story, whose method of narration, however, has been described as "incremental repetition," a building up of tiny incidents for cumulative effect that is familiar from the lyrical tradition of Chinese fiction. Individual episodes in this history of wheelbarrow repair may seem almost absurdly trivial, the dialogue such as one might overhear between teenagers in a schoolyard. But in the end a convincing relationship has developed between two attractive young people and their farming environment. An image Hao Jan has used for the reading of his stories describes a child with sugarcane – the longer you chew, the tastier it gets.

Since his first stories appeared in 1956, Hao Jan has published over a hundred, in many collections. But he is best known for two multivolume novels: *Bright sunny skies* (*Yen-yang t'ien*), in three volumes, of 1964–66, and *The golden highway* (*Chin-kuang ta-tao*), in two volumes, of 1972–74 (like *The builders*, with which indeed it shares many features, this work was originally projected in four volumes, but has not been completed). The two novels tell the complicated history of collectivization in the countryside, but in reverse chronological order: *Bright sunny skies* is restricted to a month or so in the summer of 1957, the time of the wheat harvest, when progressive poor peasants must struggle to thwart the machinations of their middle or rich peasant neighbors seeking to enrich themselves at the communal expense. Hao Jan's method here is panoramic, juxtaposing the experiences of a vast range of vivid and distinct characters of both sexes and all ages. *Golden highway* ends in time just about where *Bright sunny skies* begins, being concerned in the main with the sometimes pathetic, but finally heroic, efforts of poor peasants in the early 1950s to overcome the aftermath of war, famine, and landlord depredations, to break out of poverty by organized collective endeavor. The time-scale of *Golden highway* is more extended (as with Liu Ch'ing's *The builders*, there is a prerevolutionary prologue), and Hao Jan focuses more exclusively on a group of representative types, positive and negative, and the processes of their respective vindication or overthrow. The work is very much a product of the Cultural Revolution, dedicated to "line struggle" and structured according to the "three saliences." The "golden highway" is, of course, the socialist line, of cooperation for mutual benefit and self-sacrifice in the public interest. It is represented by Kao Ta-ch'üan and his friends among the poorest of the peasants, and resisted by ex-landlords, rich peasants, and misguided hangers-on of these men, whose capitalist-individualist line fails to lead even to their own self-enrichment. "Three saliences" (*san t'u-ch'u*) is the shorthand of the time for the formula for artistic creation favored by the Cultural Revolution leadership: Among all characters, emphasize the positive; among the positive, emphasize the main heroic characters; and among the main characters, emphasize the primary central character.

Like Liang Sheng-pao in *The builders*, Kao Ta-ch'üan receives guidance from Party secretaries and other cadres, and from his painstaking readings in the works of Chairman Mao. As a typical product of the ideologically intense years of the Cultural Revolution, however, *Golden highway* sets the words of the Great Helmsman in bold print. Kao Ta-ch'üan himself is altogether more of a type (*tien-hsing*) than Liang Sheng-pao, physically stronger, morally more self-negating, the fires of revolutionary fervor burning with a fiercer flame. He conspicuously stands out (*t'u-ch'u*) from his fellows, who may be more aggressive but less thoughtful, or more cautious but less determined: In a word, Kao Ta-ch'üan is perfect. Perfect, and therefore less than human. Already in *Bright sunny skies* Hao Jan had shown a tendency toward excess, as when the Party branch secretary Hsiao Ch'ang-chun "for the sake of socialism" – that is, to avoid the loss of a precious day of harvesting – calls off the search for his infant son, abducted by the ex-landlord in an attempt at sabotage. With *Golden highway* there is a further intensification of the heroic image, which can lead at times to removal from reality. Kao Ta-ch'üan is reduced from a believable hero to a mere Paul Bunyan projection of folk fantasy when he single-handedly rights an overturned cart, throws his knee out in the process, but has a friend wrench the joint back into the socket and stumps undaunted on his way down the mountain track.

With *Sons and daughters of Hsi-sha* (*Hsi-sha erh-nü*), of 1974, a novella of the fisher folk of Hainan island and their wartime exploits, Hao Jan reached a level of abstract lyrical romanticism that proved unacceptable to the critics, who understood it as adulation of Chiang Ch'ing, and with the fall of the Gang of Four, Hao Jan lost his own position as the most widely published fiction writer in China.

It is hard to imagine that he will not make a comeback. For sheer fluency of storytelling he has had no equal. Character, pinpointed by the selection of appealing detail of stance or feature or diction; incident, rescued from the trivial by recognition of its potential for parable; symbol, the ax that clears away intransigence or the rope that finds strength in the joining of strands: All these components of a lively tale seem to flow from Hao Jan in an effortless stream. His chief artistic (as distinct from political) fault in *Sons and daughters of Hsi-sha* was his failure to recognize that the subject was beyond his knowledge. Peasant life on the North China Plain is something he knows intimately, has lived and felt deeply, and can interpret as he wishes.

New fiction in Taiwan

By an irony of history, precisely the years during which literary creation was most rigidly fettered on the mainland were a time of the most vigorous new activity in Taiwan. Writers publishing there (whether resident or not: Eileen Chang, Pai Hsien-yung, and some others have resided in the United States for many years), untrammeled by the prescriptions of ideology, have drawn sustenance from worldwide currents of thought as well as from their individual interpretations of the native heritage. Their number includes poets and writers of fiction, the distinction of whose work is unsurpassed among living writers of Chinese. Some began in 1980 to be published on the mainland, and a future development of the greatest interest will be the effect on mainland writers of their discovery of the technical advances and unflinching social commitment of the Taiwan writers.

Chang Ai-ling (Eileen Chang, b. 1921) began her career in Japanese-occupied Shanghai with a brilliant series of short stories under the general title of *Romances* (*Ch'uan-ch'i*). After leaving the mainland for Hong Kong in 1952, she wrote two novels, *Rice-sprout song* (*Yang-ko*), of 1954, and *Love in Redland* (*Ch'ih-ti chih lien*), also of 1954, which were decades ahead of their time in expressing bitter disillusionment with the "new" morality of Communism. Powerful as they are, however, neither work matches the achievement of a novelette she wrote in 1943 that has continued to haunt her own imagination as well as that of her readers.

This is *The golden cangue* (*Chin so chi*), a story of corruption and decadence in a gentry family closely modeled on the home of her own unhappy childhood in Tientsin and Shanghai. Ch'i-ch'iao, the girl whose youth and vigor are sacrificed in her presentation as wife to a wealthy cripple, grows old and bitter in a claustrophobic household heavy with the smell of opium, and avenges the frustrations of her own life on her own children. Despite its severe economy, the story is rich with sensuous imagery and sharply observed behavior.

Eileen Chang has never enjoyed robust health and has lived a secluded life since moving to the United States in 1955. In 1967 she published *The rouge of the north*, which is a revision and expansion, in her own English, of the basic pattern of events of *The golden cangue*; the following year her Chinese version, again with some modifications of the story, was published in Taipei under the title *Yuan-nü* (The embittered woman).

The intensity of evil, as it is perpetuated by unjust social systems and compounded by warped psychologies, is Eileen Chang's burden in these retellings and elaborations of the *Golden cangue* theme. It has not been so effectively depicted in Chinese fiction since the eighteenth-century *Dream of the red chamber*, and it is this masterpiece of the traditional literature that has been her primary literary inspiration.

Fiction of real distinction was slow to develop in Taiwan after 1949. One man who might have contributed was Yang K'uei, who had written stories notable for their social realism during the Japanese occupation, but he was imprisoned for some twelve years after criticizing the Kuomintang in 1949. He recommended publishing in the mid-1970s and, as a native-born Taiwanese writer, came to be regarded as something of a symbol of the "native soil" movement. *The whirlwind* (*Hsuan-feng*), of 1957, by Chiang Kuei (b. 1907), and *Fool in the reeds* (*Ti-ts'un chuan*), by Ch'en Chi-ying (b. 1908), drew much attention at the time for their vivid narration of the decades of upheaval that culminated in the Communist victory.

Chu Hsi-ning (b. 1926) is a major talent who has been publishing since the 1950s and continues to write both short stories and novels. He is a devout Christian and has spent many years in army service, and his stories are remarkable for their presentation of moral dilemmas through strongly drawn lines of plot. In one of his best-known pieces, "Molten iron" (*T'ieh-chiang*), of 1961, a heroic clan head kills himself in grotesque fashion by drinking molten iron on a dare, but his self-sacrifice is shown by the structure of the story to symbolize at once an assertion of heroic values and a protest against the encroachment of the modern age. For another story, "Daybreak" (*P'o-hsiao shih-fen*), of 1963, Chu Hsi-ning draws on a late medieval tale, but shifts the significance by the use of an introspective narrator in place of the storyteller of traditional times. Still, there is a strong element of the traditional love of the well-told tale in Chu Hsi-ning. He shares this with another born storyteller close in age and in the atmosphere his stories often evoke, Ssu-ma Chung-yuan (b. 1929).

Pai Hsien-yung was born in 1937, the son of General Pai Ch'ung-hsi, one of the Kuomintang's most powerful military leaders: It is no accident that some of his most moving stories ("The dirge of Liang-fu," for example) portray the pathos of the aging military man, his bent back stiffening to the salute as he recalls gallant exploits of decades earlier. With Wang Wen-hsing (b. 1939), Pai in 1960 founded the influential journal *Modern Literature* (*Hsien-tai wen-hsueh*). The writers who published here achieved levels of sophistication new to Chinese fiction. Pai's particular contribution, with which we can compare only the work of Chang Ai-ling, has been his fusion of modernistic techniques of introspection, time structuring, and the use of narrators of widely varying kinds, with a superb command of the elite Chinese culture in its material and intellectual delicacies of taste. Pai's early story "Yü-ch'ing-sao" powerfully exhibits elements that permeate his work: the subtle limitations on the narrator's perception (in this case, reminiscence of boyhood); depth of feeling for the under-ling, the aging servant; and the sudden descent into appalling violence of overwhelming sexual passion. Pai's most celebrated work is the collec-tion *Taipei characters (T'ai-pei jen)*, of 1971. "The eternal 'Snow Beauty'" (*Yung-yuan ti Yin Hsueh-yen*), in this collection, was the first story from Taiwan to be reprinted in the People's Republic, in the journal *Contempor-ary (Tang-tai)* in 1980, and one can easily see why: "Snow Beauty," with her meticulously maintained, ageless allure, and the hideous tycoon Wu, with his rotting eyelashes, between them represent the corrupt quintes-sence of bourgeois Shanghai fattening anew on the newly rich of Taipei.

Aside from a small number of short stories, Wang Wen-hsing has writ-ten only two novels, but each has become something of a cause célèbre. *Family changes (Chia-pien)*, of 1972–73, is innovative in form and aggres-sively idiosyncratic in diction, but in the end a profoundly moving work. Its 157 numbered sections, some consisting of only a few lines, present an impressionistic account of Fan Yeh's childhood and youth. Dominant is the shift from adoration to contempt for his father. Interspersed let-tered sections gradually inform us that the father has been driven off by Fan Yeh's cruelty to him, and that Fan Yeh is unsuccessfully prosecuting a search for him motivated by a complicated mixture of curiosity and re-morse. The novel has been read as unacceptably iconoclastic, but readers in many cases have reacted as strongly against the written style as the moral implications. Somewhat in the manner of James Joyce, who is obviously at the back of Wang Wen-hsing's mind much of the time, the diction is highly self-conscious, playing with words and inventing neo-logisms, experimenting with phonetic script and outrageous syntax. This process is taken farther in Wang's newer novel *The man with his back to the sea (Pei hai ti jen)*, of 1981. This story opens with a long paragraph of obscenities (perhaps to dismiss from the start the unwanted reader of overconventional propriety) and goes on to reveal, in the musings of a "failure," a world even more nihilistic yet morally anxious than that of *Family changes*.

Ch'en Ying-chen (b. 1936) is a native Taiwanese writer whose influence has been out of all proportion to the modest volume of his output of short stories and essays. In part this is due to the uncompromising ideal-ism of his stand for free intellectual inquiry, which has endured a seven-year imprisonment (1968–75) and further harassment since that time. Christianity in Ch'en's family background and the use of Christ images in his fiction enhance the aura of the martyr to truth in a world of clashing despotisms. He studied English in college but for long was not permitted to travel outside Taiwan.

He writes lean, spare stories, sometimes satirical but more commonly suffused with a profound compassion, in many of which an unfortunate or an outcast confronts failure, bitter suffering, or death and attempts to wring out some kind of understanding of the truths of existence. The situations into which Ch'en plunges his protagonists are contrived with little cunning but may border on melodrama. Unexplained deaths occur, endings bring little resolution. Symbols develop great force but operate sometimes on a level of some abstraction, incompletely fused with the action. Yet few stories written in Chinese in this century have achieved the power of Ch'en Ying-chen's best work. "A race of generals" (*Chiang-chün tsu*) bestows an unearthly beauty on two wandering musicians, an aging mainlander and a runaway prostitute young enough to be his daughter. "Roses in June" (*Liu-yueh li ti mei-kuei-hua*), of 1967, portrays another doomed love, between a black GI and the barmaid who shares his leave from Vietnam: The identifications in this story, of killer with victim and of girlfriend with mother with innocent Vietnamese child, set up deep resonances of pity and horror.

The intensity of his stand against political hypocrisy, joined with the thematic representation in his work of the deepest social issues of contemporary Taiwan, have placed Ch'en Ying-chen at the forefront of the "native soil" (*hsiang-t'u*) movement in literature, which in the 1970s began to vie with the "modernist" movement in the evolution of serious Chinese writing. Ch'en Ying-chen has been a leading theorist of the "native soil" movement.

Three of the best-known female writers publishing in Taiwan reside in the United States. Nieh Hua-ling (b. 1926) and Yü Li-hua (b. 1931) have both been productive over a number of years, and their women characters have been especially memorable. Frustration is a common theme in their work, whether of the desires of young girls or the ambitions of women past their youth. Yü Li-hua has been described as a spokeswoman for the "rootless generation"; one of Nieh Hua-ling's most daringly innovative novels is *Mulberry green and peach red* (*Sang-ch'ing yü t'ao-hung*), of 1976, in which the anguish of a Chinese woman whose identity threatens to be riven apart by the turmoil of national events is interwoven with the sufferings of the ill-fated Donner party in the snows of the nineteenth-century migration to California.

Ch'en Jo-hsi (b. 1938) had begun to make a name for herself as a writer of short stories before she returned to the mainland with her husband in 1967. Her dreams of service to the motherland turned to bitter disillusionment in the seven years begun by the Cultural Revolution, and on leaving the country she wrote stories, most notably "The execution of Mayor Yin" (*Yin hsien-chang*), of 1976, which for the first time depicted the oppressive life of the period in convincing detail for the outside world.

The "native soil" movement that gained momentum through the 1970s has given rise to a considerable body of work, especially of fiction, of impressive originality and power. "Native soil" writers, as the term implies, are Taiwan-born and spurn the themes of exile, nostalgia, and wandering in favor of the vivid evocation of life in the villages and small towns of Taiwan. The work of Ch'en Ying-chen has already been referred to in this connection. Huang Ch'un-ming (b. 1939), Wang Chen-ho (b. 1940), and Wang T'o have all been extraordinarily successful in articulating the sufferings, the courage, and often, too, the black or absurd comedy they have found at the bottom of the social scale, among the illiterates, the aging, the deaf, and the defeated. Huang Ch'un-ming's satires carry the force of parable, as in "Little widows" (*Hsiao kua-fu*), of 1975, in which a slick entrepreneur has the brainwave of opening a bar stocked with girls who will pass themselves off as young widows, and dress in traditional style and behave with classical decorum to titillate the jaded appetites of patrons. It is a perfect emblem of the prostitution of the indigenous culture of China to the modern commercial age. Wang Chen-ho's best-known story is the superb fable of cuckoldry "An oxcart for dowry" (*Chia-chuang i niu-ch'e*), of 1966, in which the pathetic deaf carter Wan-fa swaps his singularly ugly wife for a cart from a man one rung above him on the economic ladder, the repulsive Chien, whose armpits are inhabited by ringworms. The vivid realism of Wang's stories is often enhanced by his use of dialect, so extreme as to require the provision of footnotes in explanation. Wang T'o is more aggressively ideological in his writings than either Huang Ch'un-ming or Wang Chen-ho, and in the aftermath of demonstrations in Kaohsiung in December 1979 was arrested along with Yang Ch'ing-ch'u and others. The fiction of Yang Ch'ing-ch'u (b. 1940) bears a resemblance to Huang Ch'un-ming's fables of poor devils caught in the web of prostitution, corruption, and crime, but is marked by a more Zolaesque degree of sexual and physical violence.

Of all the overseas writers, perhaps none continues to be more obsessed with the problem of Chinese identity than Chang Hsi-kuo, born in Chungking in 1944. Chang is a highly trained mathematician and engineer who not only writes fiction but is distinguished by his readiness to make formal experiments and his eclectic command of modern written styles. He has written stories, essays, and novels, of which *The chess champion* (*Ch'i-wang*), of 1975, is the best known. His characteristic subjects are intellectuals caught up in political dilemmas, torn between claims of friendship and patriotism, desperately struggling with what it means to be Chinese in the second half of the twentieth century.

New poetry in Taiwan

One of the most widely read poets publishing in Taiwan, although he is currently resident in Hong Kong, is Yu Kuang-chung (b. 1928). His founding of the Blue Stars school in 1954 was one of the first stimuli to the new poetry movements among mainland writers who reached Taiwan in the years following 1948–49. The school was characterized by aestheticism and the kind of romantic moods familiar to classical Chinese verse and translated into the modern idiom by Hsu Chih-mo and the Crescent Moon poets of the post–May Fourth period, but Yu himself has moved through major phases of development since his early days. He is prolific, constantly experimenting, but exerting always great technical control over the sensual richness of his images. His 1964 collection *Associations of the lotus* (*Lien ti lien-hsiang*) securely established his popularity, especially with young people, as the poet of romantic love, but six years later the poems in *In time of cold war* (*Tsai leng-chan ti nien-tai*) demonstrated his preoccupation with China's fate among the nations and asserted his faith in subjective lyricism against the destructiveness of the modern industrial world and its wars. The title poem of the *Lotus* collection sounds several of his most typical notes and has the formal rigor of most of his work:

> Still so credulous am I, now young no more
> > So credulous of
> Beauty. I wish to kneel to the lotus pond.
>
> Now long have died the ecstasies of love.
> > Ah, love and love –
> That last of toys, and first of annoys.
>
> Now Narcissus dies thirsty in Greece:
> > On Byron's tomb
> Crows are quarreling over a dead cicada.
>
> War stops not at Hemingway's death.
> > Still men are fond
> Of writing their diaries in the light of Mars.
>
> A fashionable cancer is Nihilism.
> > When evening comes,
> Many a soul takes leave of its flesh.

Yet mine divorces me not. Here it stays
   With every lotus,
Watchful over its cosmos and mystery.

All at once very near and far is the East.
   With Buddha in you,
The lotus flowers form a divine seat.

Lo! Graceful are the flowers, cool the leaves!
   You can visualize
Beauty within them, and Deity above,

And me beside, and me between, I'm the dragon-fly.
   Dust is in the wind,
And powder. They need wiping, my weeping eyes.[47]

Chi Hsien (b. 1913) began writing poetry on the mainland in the 1930s under the influence of the Chinese Symbolists, Tai Wang-shu and others. He became the leading theorist and practitioner of "modernist" poetry, officially announcing the formation of the modernist school in 1956. In contradistinction to the Blue Stars, Chi Hsien and his fellows stressed exotic, often aggressively "difficult" imagery, declaring their preference for the "horizontal transplant" (from the West) over the "vertical inheritance" (from the classical tradition) and demanding the divorce of poetry from song and the abandonment of rhyme and strict meter. Chi Hsien's use of startling metaphors for shock effect may be seen as foreshadowing the surrealist poems of Ya Hsien (b. 1932) and Lo Fu (b. 1928). Ya Hsien's best-known poem is "Abyss" (*Shen-yuan*), of 1957, a long summation of the modern malaise that reads at times like a Chinese *Waste land*. Ya Hsien indulges at times a taste for the satiric, as in descriptions of cities (Rome, Chicago) he has not necessarily visited.

Although Cheng Ch'ou-yü (b. 1933) was associated with the modernists and is certainly difficult at times, his verses are entraordinarily serene and have a strongly classical flavor to them. He has not been prolific, but his love poems with their almost hallucinogenic quality are widely known and admired. An older poet, Chou Meng-tieh (b. 1920), shows less sign of Western influence than any of the poets mentioned so far, but like Cheng Ch'ou-yü draws on sources of inspiration in the native tradition. In his case the specific line of descent is Buddhist. He treats of transcendental themes, of mystical states, of the modes of perception known to the Zen school.

Yeh Wei-lien (Yip Wai-lim, b. 1937) and Yang Mu (Wang Ching-hsien, b. 1940; published for some years under the pseudonym Yeh Shan)

---

47 Yu Kuang-chung's own translation, in Ch'i Pang-yuan et al., eds. and comps., *An anthology of contemporary Chinese literature: Taiwan, 1949–1974*, 103–4.

both reside in the United States but continue to be productive poets. Yeh Wei-lien's verse is erudite, intellectual in the manner of T. S. Eliot, whom he has translated, or Ezra Pound, on whom he has conducted research. "Fugue" (*Fu-ko*), of 1960, is a densely elliptical study of the exile's loneliness and nostalgia, strong in feeling and in musical value despite its highly wrought diction. Taiwan is Yang Mu's native province, a fact reflected in the landscapes of his poems and in his fondness for allusion to Taiwanese legend and folklore. His poetic drama, *Wu Feng*, is on the subject of a hero of Taiwanese history.

The excesses of the modernists in the direction of esoteric Western allusions and purely private references provoked a reaction in the early 1970s in the form of increased concern for direct address of a wider public and for themes less involuted and more public. The "native soil" movement of 1977–78 was a natural culmination of these tendencies. One of its spokesmen in the realm of verse was Wu Sheng (b. 1941), whose village home and family provide his verse with a yardstick for the measurement of modern alienations. Already in 1974 he is writing, in his fresh, easy diction, of his mother, in the following lines from "The earth" (*Ni-t'u*):

> Day after day, from sunrise to sunset
> Mother who is blind to fatigue says –
> The fresh breeze is the best electric fan
> The rice field is the best scenery
> Water and bird songs are the sweetest music.
>
> Undisturbed by the taunts of
> The civilization of distant cities, my mother
> On this our family's land
> Waters her dreams with a lifetime of sweat.[48]

THE POST-MAO ERA

"Scar literature," exposure, and the new romantics

The death of Mao and the overthrow of the Gang of Four opened the floodgates to literary creation in all genres. Writers in their forties and fifties led the way but were soon followed by younger men and women. Once again the short story was the favored form, filling the pages of the many new journals both national and local. A long-starved readership joined in avid discussion as one new story, play, or film after another created headlines.

---

48 Trans. in Julia Lin, *Modern Chinese poetry.*

Three areas of concern rapidly took shape. First came the recognition that the topsy-turvy moral world of the Cultural Revolution and its aftermath had left traces, deep and perhaps ineradicable, on the minds of all Chinese and especially of the young. The result was "scar literature," or "literature of the wounded," which derived its label from the short story "Scar" (*Shang-hen*), of August 1978, by a young man in his twenties, Lu Hsin-hua. It is a sad story of a zealous young woman who fails to achieve reconciliation with her dying mother, a cadre unjustly disgraced during the Gang era.

As the immediate heat of indignation against the Gang and their followers began to wane, writers undertook more searching examinations of the entire course of events since the late 1950s and of a persistent range of wholly contemporary abuses and injustices. With the destruction of the myth of infallible leadership, these could now be reflected in a "literature of exposure." A period of exceptional openness began in mid-1979 and continued into the following year as writers hastened to portray corrupt bureaucrats, hypocrites, and bullies, to accuse and to satirize in ways absent from the Chinese literary scene since the 1940s.

The third great theme of post-Mao writing was the private values of personal life. The proper place of love in socialist life, the damage done by love's denial – these above all are matters that occupy fictional confessions, romances veering between melodrama and fantasy, and an impressive number of quietly thoughtful stories, poems, and plays.

The first manifestation, and actual manifesto, of "scar literature" was the story "The class teacher" (*Pan chu-jen*) by Liu Hsin-wu (b. 1924), published in November 1977. The high school teacher, first-person narrator and favorite persona used by Liu in several later stories as well, tells a tale that is undramatic in itself but that economically establishes contrasting types of young people. One is a remnant delinquent of the Gang period, whose rehabilitation the teacher undertakes in the face of his colleagues' skepticism. But the delinquent is not the problem: The problem is the blinkered mind, less receptive if anything than that of the young scapegrace himself, of the Youth League secretary, who is overly zealous and naively ready to denounce as obscene works of literature she has never even read. In positive contrast is a third student, whose home environment has guarded her sanity through the years of turmoil by continuing to give shelf space to the works of Tolstoy and Goethe, Mao Tun and Lo Kuang-pin.

Liu Hsin-wu has been an eloquent spokesman for the emerging young writers. In his speech before the fourth Congress of Literature and Art Workers in November 1979 he commented movingly on the reading out of one hundred names of writers who lost their lives, many by violence, during the decade 1966–76:

Years ago, when the five martyrs from the League of Left-wing Writers were killed, it was said that they were Communists, plotters of revolution. In other words, they were killed for being leftists. Although they were cruelly sacrificed, I do not think that their souls suffered the least agony. Now what sort of charges were leveled against the sacrificial victims we now mourn? "Counter-revolutionary revisionists," "bourgeois reactionary authorities," "old rightists," "rightists who slipped through the net," "sinister gang," ... in short, they were all turned into rightist forces and then killed. The souls of these martyrs from the fields of literature and art who never lived to see the Gang of Four smashed certainly suffered all the agonizing torment imaginable! As we listened to their names being read and lowered our heads in silent mourning, we could not help asking questions like: Why, in a socialist nation led by the Communist Party, does committing oneself to serving the people by promoting a rich, strong literary and artistic enterprise require making mental preparations to lay down one's life? No wonder so many of my friends and relatives said to me with the best of intentions after the meeting: "Don't consider yourself fortunate to be mounting the podium. The world of literature and art is a mine field. Look at how many people were killed in the Cultural Revolution alone! Now you have stepped into that circle. Are you prepared to be blown up?"[49]

Liu Hsin-wu has advanced rapidly in technical control of the short story form. In June 1979 he published "I love every green leaf" (*Wo ai mei-i-p'ien lü-yeh*), a story that successfully melds metaphor, dramatic incident, and complex time structure into a portrait that stays in the reader's mind, of a brilliant but victimized eccentric. A central image in the story is the photograph of a woman that the protagonist keeps in his desk – his relationship with her is never explicitly stated. He undergoes agony when the photograph is discovered by a snooping colleague and publicly displayed. The woman later visits him – evidently he is shielding her from political attack. Liu transforms the image of the hidden photograph into the striking metaphor of a "private plot" for the intellectual. The peasant is allowed a private plot for cultivation for his own use. Should not the intellectual, too, be permitted his private plot, an autonomous corner of his mind, a spiritual retreat? It is a concept of explosive potential in the Chinese context.

Intellectuals feature as protagonists of many works of the "literature of the wounded," replacing the obligatory worker, peasant, and soldier heroes of the preceding decade. Middle characters, with their flaws and vacillations, reappear for the first time since the mid-1960s, and good

---

49 Liu Hsin-wu, "Hsiang mu-ch'in shuo-shuo hsin-li hua" (Telling mother what's on my mind), *Shang-hai wen-hsueh*, 12 (1979), 80–85, tr. Helena Kolenda, in Howard Goldblatt, ed., *Chinese literature for the 1980s*, 137–38.

people suffer tragic fates again. Outcomes are still generally optimistic; however, there are still more or less formulaic expressions of faith in the glorious future of the revolution, and the level of engagement with actuality does not yet reach that of the works that were so soon to follow, and which would be characterized as a "literature of exposure" or even (by hostile critics) as a "literature of despair." The story "Three professors" (*San-ko chiao-shou*) by Ts'ao Kuan-lung (b. 1945) still deals with "wounds" inflicted by the Cultural Revolution, but its tone is dark enough to warrant its classification under the "exposure" label. This tale, which is of an intricacy worthy almost of Borges, pillories the abuse of talent. One of the three professors has had a student commit suicide while in detention. The boy's completed dissertation is impounded in a room locked with a new-style lock. The professor's mathematical genius enables him to crack the formula of the lock, and he sits, rapt in reading and correcting the dissertation, until "they" come to arrest him in turn. One of the remarkable features of the story (as also of the work of some other young writers) is the imaginative use of scientific terminology: The professor's brain as it races is compared to the fluorescent screen of an oscilloscope, and the intricate wire shapes he uses to pick the lock are carefully detailed.

An example of the expansion of scope beyond the disastrous decade of 1966–76 is "The good-luck bun" (*K'an-k'an shui chia yu fu*), by Liu Ch'ing-pang (b. 1951), a straightforward exposure of rural famine in the "three bad years" of 1959–61. The peasants' desperate search for food, when even the cooking pot has been sacrificed to the backyard steel furnace, is counterpointed by the incompetence and callousness of the cadres.

The two "revisionist" writers of the Hundred Flowers period who have drawn the greatest attention since the fall of the Gang of Four are Liu Pin-yen and Wang Meng. Liu Pin-yen's "reportage" "People or monsters" (*Jen-yao chih chien*), of 1979, is regarded as the outstanding example of exposure of the corruptions prevalent during the Gang period, but Liu's dedicated courage is evident in his insistence that the abuses he describes still persist. Liu's prime "monster" is Wang Shou-hsin, a female cadre who during the Gang period, by blackmail, backbiting, flirtation, or bribery as the case might demand, fights her way up to become manager and Party secretary of a coal company in the Northeast. From this base she builds a private empire of money and political power. Liu's indictment is not limited to the years following 1966: He describes the earlier "three bad years" in an image of the people eating tree bark while the children of cadres toss meat-filled dumplings to dogs in the street. Nor is his target one woman alone, for he makes thumbnail sketches of a whole range of sycophantic conspirators. In his latest works Liu Pin-yen shows no more concern than formerly for delicacy of language or economy of structure, and his tone has grown if anything more strident, resulting in the cancellation of his Party membership in 1986.

Wang Meng emerged as one of the most prolific and influential figures on the literary scene, and his appointment as minister of culture for some years did much to ingratiate Teng Hsiao-p'ing's regime with men and women of letters. Wang Meng's major concerns have continued to be the morality of officialdom, the preservation of integrity through an official career, the individual intellectual's struggle to retain or regain faith in the revolution after the cataclysms of the Cultural Revolution and the Gang period. Willingness to experiment with technical innovation puts his writing at the forefront of current Chinese fiction. Already in his notorious 1956 piece "Young newcomer in the Organization Department," there was considerable ironic distance between author and protagonist: Although Wang Meng was only 22 at that time, he was obviously a great deal less starry-eyed than his "young newcomer." Wang Meng's departures from the naively autobiographical give special power to recent stories like "The Bolshevik salute" (*Pu-li*), in which a local official traces the development of his own attitude to the Party from early fervor, through suffering as a rightist and labour reformer, to recent readmission to membership; in "The eye of night" (*Yeh ti yen*) an intellectual returns to the city after a twenty-year absence to be confronted with the problem of "backdoor" corruption. The central figure of "Anxious wisp of heart" (*Yu-yu ts'un-ts'ao hsin*) is especially cleverly crafted, a barber whose attempts to "serve the party" meet with the same frustrations at the hands of arrogant or wrongheaded cadres as, one must assume, the author's own have encountered. The three Wang Meng stories just described were all published in 1979.

Wang Meng weathered controversy and survived charges of negativism by ingeniously contriving upbeat endings to his stories, although these are sometimes seen as mere tacked-on "tails of brightness" (*kuang-ming wei-pa*).

In the move toward a more genuine, as against a specifically "socialist" realism, Chiang Tzu-lung is playing an interesting role. He is very much a mainstream rather than a revisionist writer, whose first stories appeared in 1976, well before the "rightists" of the Liu Pin-yen or Wang Meng stamp were admitted back into print. Chiang is that Maoist ideal, the worker-writer, and his heroes resolutely overcome obstacles to production. These obstacles may be posed by bourgeois-minded technicians, complacent cadres, or leftist extremists, depending on the prevailing ideological climate. But Chiang Tzu-lung, acceptable as he may be to the leadership, has secured some room for his own brand of outspokenness. His story "Base" (*Chi-ch'u*), of 1979, describes the refusal of one top cadre after another to take responsibility or even to recognize that a concrete base for heavy machinery is defective, crumbling, and completely unusable. One honest old foreman urges his steelworkers to dismantle the base so it can be rebuilt, but the workers, idle for months because of lack of supplies, are interested only in working on holidays for overtime pay. At last a young woman activist succeeds in galvanizing the workers into action, but not before she has expressed some of her own agonizing doubts concerning the failure to catch up with capitalist nations in productivity and technology.

The writer Ju Chih-chüan (b. 1925) in 1958 wrote one of her best-received stories, "Lilies" (*Pai-ho-hua*), a heavily sentimental account of the death of a civil war soldier that nevertheless was remarkable for the suppressed sexuality of its first-person narrator, a young woman cadre. One of Ju Chih-chüan's contributions to the "literature of exposure" is "A story out of sequence" (*Chien-chi ts'o-le ti ku-shih*), of 1979, which criticizes the excesses of the Great Leap Forward and the coverups that followed.

The new proliferation of regional literary journals engendered varying degrees of daring: Those of Anhwei and Kwangtung tended to countenance the greatest outspokenness. Stories published in 1979–80 with the intention of bringing home to the public the wrongs that had been committed presented details that could never have seen print in earlier years. The underground or "unofficial" journals, which flourished during the "Peking spring" of 1979, also carried protests and warnings from such writers as the poet Huang Hsiang. During the years before 1976 Huang was reported to have hidden his manuscripts in plastic bags around which he molded candles, melting them to retrieve his writings when the political climate made publication a possibility.[50] Among stories that evaded censorship by publication in these short-lived journals were some that came to attract widespread attention. "A tragedy of the year 2000" (*K'o-neng fa-hsien tsai 2,000 nien ti pei-chü*), by Su Ming, is a political fantasy that predicts a repeat of the disasters of the Cultural Revolution one generation hence. "In the ruins" (*Tsai fei-hsu shang*), though powerful in its evocation of the wasteland bequeathed by the recent past, still draws hope in its conclusion from the musings of the protagonist, an aging professor, on the long perspective of history.

Other leading works of "exposure literature" include Ts'ung Wei-hsi's

50 Roger Garside, *Coming alive!: China after Mao.*

"The red magnolia under the wall" (*Ta-ch'iang hsia ti hung yü-lan*), which opens with the arrival of a new prisoner at the labor camp complete with armed guards: the magnolia stains red with innocent blood. Liu Chen's "Girl who seemed to understand" (*T'a hao-hsiang ming-pai le i-tien-tien*) exposes village poverty leading to famine in the early sixties, and Chu Lin's novel *Road of life* (*Sheng-huo ti lu*) reports the persistence of begging in the countryside in 1975. Kao Hsiao-sheng's stories at this time, although they have wit and warmth, convey a sense of the bleakness of village life, in the persistent but apparently doomed efforts of his protagonists to improve their meager livelihood: "Li Shun-ta builds a house" (*Li Shun-ta tsao wu*) and "Ch'en Huan-sheng goes to town" (*Ch'en Huan-sheng shang ch'eng*) are among his most popular stories.

Some stories use a framework through which the reader is invited to identify his own awakening to brutal realities with that of a senior cadre, who gradually becomes cognizant of sufferings he himself has caused by past actions: "History be my judge" (*Li-shih a, ni shen-p'an wo pa*) by Ch'ien Yü-hsiang is an example. Other stories juxtapose generations, portraying aging cadres or intellectuals in their realization that they have failed young followers: Ch'en Ts'un's "Two generations" (*Liang-tai jen*) and Chin Ho's "Reunion" (*Ch'ung-feng*) explore this theme from different angles.

The memorial essay for the man of letters has a long history in China. For some years it appeared that the only permissible subject was Lu Hsun, but in 1979 a number of moving tributes appeared to writers who had suffered persecution in the dark decade. Shao Ch'üan-lin and his wife were commemorated by their daughter: Shao, as chief proponent of the need to portray "middle characters" in fiction, had been a prime target of the doctrinaire critics in the mid-1960s. The most admired of many pieces of this kind was the reminiscence of his late wife by Pa Chin.

The preoccupation with romantic love was but one symptom of the reemergence of personal concerns in fiction, in stories patterned around the evaluation of an individual life-history. The novella "When a person reaches middle age" (*Jen tao chung-nien*), of 1980, by Chen Jung (b. 1935), deepened the introspective mood of its time by presenting the reminiscences of a female eye surgeon who now herself lies in a hospital bed following a heart attack and nervous collapse. Highly charged prose conveys the romance of medicine; there is a dramatic eye operation among the souvenirs; but more fundamental to the mood projected is the sense of strain, overwork, bureaucratic frustrations and lack of reward. The protagonists of Chen Jung's story, older intellectuals, are seen as carrying the brunt of society's burdens while receiving the least recognition and attention. A colleague's plan to emigrate draws more sympathy than criticism, and indeed the emigrant's letter from the airport totally undercuts the upbeat ending (the healing of an old peasant).

"Love must not be forgotten" (*Ai shih pu-neng wang-chi ti*), of 1980, by the female writer Chang Chieh (b. 1938), was welcomed as a courageous affirmation of romantic love and, by the same token, attacked as morally lax. The story consists of a girl's sad recollection of her mother, married to a mediocre husband but in love with a senior cadre. He has placed himself out of reach by marrying, to protect her, the widow of a revolutionary martyr, and the romance has remained unconsummated.

Two novels aroused considerable controversy for what was seen as excessive dedication to personal or emotional gratification under the guise of "humanism" (*jen-hsing*). *The second handshake* (*Ti-erh tz'u wo-shou*) was the work of a young writer named Chang Yang. It circulated in manuscript in the late 1960s but was not published until 1979, after its author's release from imprisonment for what was judged an anti-Party work. A harmless fantasy of the love lives of an "eternal triangle" of distinguished and progressive scientists, *Second handshake* spoke to the new liberalization, to modernization, and to the demand for an old-fashioned "good read" in the genre of romance.

Tai Hou-ying's novel *Man, ah man!* (*Jen a, jen*), published late in 1981, is more up-to-date in its fictional techniques, although the "innovations" of interior monologue, dream sequences, and the profuse use of symbols and metaphors are mild indeed in comparison with fiction from Taiwan, Japan, or the Western world. Much of the book revolves around the struggle to publish a manuscript on the explosive topic of "Marxism and humanism," the credo of the long-suppressed intellectual Ho Ching-fu, who is the lover of Sun Yueh, the author's alter ego. This woman's reflections and reminiscences of the past two decades convey a strong disillusionment with the concept of class struggle as a key to the future, and contribute to the argument and plea for a return to more humane values.

New poets of protest

Of all the poems written in recent years using classical modes, one of the most impressive is anonymous, a simple quatrain in traditional five-syllable form that was posted on the martyrs' memorial in T'ien An Men Square at the beginning of April 1976, in commemoration of Chou En-lai, whose funeral had taken place three months earlier. A dignified and appropriate poem of mourning, it served notice at the same time that

Chou's enemies (notably the notorious Gang and their adherents) might have their own reaction to his death:

> I mourn, but in my ears demons shriek,
> I weep, but wolves and jackals grin.
> Though tears commemorate the hero
> My eyes flash and my sword is drawn.

Although most of the poems in the *Gate of Heavenly Peace collection* (*T'ien-An-Men shih-wen chi*)[51] used simple modern diction and the popular folk quatrain form, others like the one just quoted gained their effectiveness from their traditional styling, and have reinforced the lesson taught by Mao's own poems, that the classical forms of verse are far from obsolete in the new society.

New poets played a part in the literature of exposure. Yeh Wen-fu's poem "General, you can't do this!" (*Chiang-chün, pu-neng che-yang tso*), as the title suggests, castigates the abuse of power for personal ends. Han Han, Lei Shu-yen and the female poet Shu T'ing have all written poems of a new depth of personal feeling; and established poets like Ai Ch'ing and Pai Hua emerged, sometimes from years of silence, to issue stern warnings against any return to tyrannous oppression:

> How can the truth become private property?
> No! Truth is the shared wealth of the people,
> Like the sun
> It can be no one's monopoly![52]

One of the more extreme formal reversions is to the Whitmanesque prose-poem style, with its unrhymed, complex, but rhythmic line. Pi Shuo-wang uses this line in "Just because" (*Chih yin*), his dirge for the female cadre Chang Chih-hsin, whose cruel execution in 1975 was one of the most spectacular crimes of the Gang of Four henchmen (before she was led in front of the firing squad, a hole was drilled in her throat to prevent her crying out; it was said that one of her guards fainted from the horror).

Pei Tao (Chao Chen-k'ai, b. 1949) and Ku Ch'eng (b. 1958) are leading young poets of the early 1980s and were prominent targets in the controversy over "obscurity" (*meng-lung*, "mistiness," which can suggest a pleasing suggestive delicacy to the cultivated poetic eye and ear, or an unnecessary and suspect degree of difficulty to critics bludgeoned by decades

51 The collection was edited by a group of teachers using the collective pseudonym T'ung Huai-chou, indicating "together cherish Chou (Enlai)," and was published in 1978.
52 Pai Hua, "The sunlight is no one's monopoly" (*Yang-kuang, shui yeh pu-neng lung-tuan*).

of dedicatedly popularized diction). Inevitably, a poem like Pei Tao's "Snowline" (*Hsueh-hsien*) recalls the Symbolists of nineteenth-century France or 1930s China:

> forget what I've said
> forget the bird shot down from the sky
> forget the reef
> let them sink once more into the deep
> forget even the sun
> only a lamp left full of dust and ashes
> is shining
> in that eternal position
>
> after a series of avalanches
> the cliffs above the snowline
> seal everything in silence
> from gentle grassy shores
> below the snowline
> trickles a stream.[53]

The question of how directly these young poets could have received the influences of their predecessors remains moot.

Female poets of the years since 1976 include Shu T'ing, whose poem "Parting gift" (*Tseng pieh*) recalls the sonnets of Feng Chih in its calm, meditative, but sonorous flow and its dedication to re-creating a precious past moment; and Mei Shao-ching, whose "Question" (*Wen*) is posed to those who endured the twenty years of silence "like oysters / shrunk within hard shells of their own making" or "like silkworms, scalded" for the filament they create. A stern sense of what is needed for survival in present-day Chinese society is conveyed by a poet named Lei Wen writing in December 1979:

> The water-chestnut
> Having no soil of its own
> Uses its
> Prickly fruit
> To protect its
> Bitter life.[54]

One man at least who originally made his name as a poet has turned to a new form of expression. Hsu Ch'ih (b. 1916) has developed an interesting form of poetic prose in the genre of reportage. "The Goldbach conjecture" (*Ko-ti-pa-ho ts'ai-hsiang*), of 1978, and other pieces describe the

---

53 Trans. in Bonnie S. McDougall, *Notes from the city of the sun: poems by Bei Dao*, 73.
54 Lei Wen, "Hsiao-shih i-shu" (A handful of poems), *Shih-k'an*, 12 (1979), 56, trans. in W. J. F. Jenner, "1979: a new start for literature in China?" *CQ* 86 (June 1981), 274.

lives and triumphs of a mathematician, a geologist, and others, and while making an impressive contribution to the romanticization of science at the same time exert a plea on behalf of the occasionally eccentric individual who creates scientific knowledge.

The new spoken drama

It is possible that the very excesses of the Cultural Revolution in forcing revolutionary model operas down the audience's throat have produced a reaction in favor of spoken drama. The swing may be seen as an aspect of genuine modernization, or the fact may simply be that a new generation of playwrights and playgoers feels more comfortable with this more contemporary idiom. For whatever reason, where the controversial plays of the early 1960s wore the guise of historical drama, in the late 1970s the spoken drama dominated a new outburst of stage activity.

Only a brief interval divided the fall of the Gang of Four from the appearance of stage plays that pilloried their abuses of power. *When the maple leaves turn red* (*Feng-yeh hung le ti shih-hou*) offered a burlesque of the attempts of Gang followers to sabotage the work of a research institute, whose members while mourning the death of Mao still dedicate themselves to renewed scientific effort in his memory. More sentimental, but more popular, was *Loyal hearts* (*Tan-hsin p'u*), of 1977, by Su Shu-yang. A dramatic highlight of this play is the onstage reception of a telephone call from the sickbed of the beloved leader Chou En-lai. The pro-Chou, anti-Gang demonstrations at T'ien An Men Square in April 1976 are the subject matter of *In the silence* (*Yü wu-sheng ch'u*) by Tsung Fu-hsien, of 1978. Chou was represented onstage (a meticulously exact physical likeness) in *Storm over the fatherland* (*Shen-chou feng-lei*), of 1979, by Chao Huan and Chin Ching-mai. Chu Te was another hero of this popular melodrama, the villain roles going to the Gang members themselves.

This outpouring of indignation against the Gang was followed in 1979–80 by the more searching investigation of persistent abuses, in a number of new plays, of which *Authority and law* (*Ch'üan yü fa*) by Hsing I-hsun was one of the most impressive. Set in May 1978, the play exposes a former victim of Gang machinations who is now reinstated in power. This man has successfully covered up crimes originally committed twenty years earlier, including the misuse of famine funds that led to many deaths. Realistically presented characters engage the audience's sympathy as they bemoan the near impossibility, under the system they and their elders have created, of ever getting at the truth.

Save her (*Chiu-chiu t'a*) by Chao Kuo-ch'ing, treats the newly recognized problem of rampant juvenile delinquency. Seduced by a cadre's son, the female protagonist becomes a gun-toting member of a hoodlum gang and bears an illegitimate child before her honest former boyfriend is brought staunchly to accept her back in the finale.

The title of the 1979 play *If I were genuine* (*Chia-ju wo shih chen-ti*)[55] carried the satiric ring of the plot itself: If the young protagonist had really been the son of a high-ranking cadre instead of merely an impostor, he could have held on to the privileges showered on him by the sycophantic underlings of the perennial Chinese bureaucracy. The play cuts much closer to the bone than its model, Gogol's *Inspector general*. It was given only a handful of performances, mostly before restricted audiences in Shanghai and Peking, before being shut down late in the year. More innocuous, though still highly effective in its satire of self-seeking cadres, was Su Shu-yang's *Neighbors* (*Tso-lin yu-she*), of 1980. The play manifests its indebtedness to Lao She and his *Teahouse* by celebrating the national days of the years 1976–78 as they impinge on a residential compound in Peking.

Wang Ching's *In society's archives* (*Tsai she-hui ti tang-an-li*) is a screenplay that tells of criminal acts – rape and murder – covered up by the army to protect high-ranking officers. *A girl thief* (*Nü-tsei*) by Li K'o-wei is another among many films portraying young people, children of persecuted parents or victims of seduction, who have fallen afoul of society. Along with *If I were genuine*, these films were discussed at a major forum in Peking in February 1980, at which Hu Yao-pang delivered the keynote address. Writers, it was accepted, should not ignore the persistence of difficult social problems. They should, however, recognize the contributory role of remnant vices from the old society, and be concerned to stress the positive forces of the new, which can bring about rehabilitation. Above all, writers should consider the effects of their work.

Among a host of new domestic dramas, many treating the long-suppressed subject of romantic love, *She* (*T'a*), of 1980, by T'ien Fen and Ch'ien Man-lan, stands out as an honest treatment of the pursuit of love and marriage by mature adults. *She* reaffirms the right to happiness of a young widow, the mother-in-law to whom she has hitherto devoted herself, and the man who seeks the widow's love despite opposition from his own family. In its insistence on private problems and their solution, a play of this kind is a far cry from the propagandistic call for sacrifice that dominated the stage for so many years.

---

55 By Sha Yeh-hsin et al.; also known as *The cheat* (*P'ien-tsu*).

POSTSCRIPT

"The corner love forsook" (*Pei ai-ch'ing i-wang ti chiao-lo*) is the title of a 1980 story by Chang Hsien. Its wording could be taken as symbolic of a view of China's past three decades, a view being expressed by writers, in their forties or younger, who have come to dominate the Chinese literary scene since 1976. From Yü Lo-chin's "Winter fairytale" (*I-ko tung-t'ien ti t'ung-hua*), of 1979, to Chang Hsin-hsin's "Dreams of our generation" (*Wo-men che-ko nien-chi ti meng*), of 1982, there has been an outpouring of works, often autobiographical in nature or in mode, reaffirming the value of the individual, the woman especially, her need for consideration and her need for love.

During these three decades literature under communism has stocked the cultural desert of the Chinese countryside with nourishment of a kind. It has provided heroes, role models, lessons in practical socialism. The small number of works generally acknowledged as successful – *Red crag, The builders*, a few poems and plays – continue to be reprinted and reaffirmed. At the same time, the attempts of writers to advance their techniques in the direction of modernism, and to confront in their art the genuine problems of life in the new society, continue to meet with discouragement. The attack in 1981 on Pai Hua's film *Bitter love* (*K'u-lien*) was the first major condemnation of a creative work since the end of the Mao era. Chou Yang has reemerged as a determining voice in the setting of literary policy.[56] Though Hu Ch'iao-mu late in 1981 denied the immutable relevance of Mao's literary principles to present-day conditions, he reaffirmed the Party's insistence that writers continue to support Marxism, socialism, the dictatorship of the proletariat and the Party's own leadership.[57]

The satirist Alexander Zinoviev has one of his characters say the following about the Soviet Union:

Soviet history really (and not merely apparently) is a history of congresses, meetings, plans, obligations, overfulfillments, conquests of new fields, new departures, demonstrations, decorations, applause, folk-dances, farewell ceremonies, arrival ceremonies, and so on; in brief, everything which can be read in official Soviet newspapers, journals, novels, or which can be seen on Soviet television, and so on. There are certain things which happen in the Soviet Union which do

---

56 Chou Yang, "Chi wang k'ai lai, fan-jung she-hui chu-i hsin shih-ch'i ti wen-i" (Inherit the past and usher in the future prosperity of the literature and art of the new socialist age), *Wen-i pao*, 11–12 (1979), 8–26.

57 Hu Ch'iao-mu, "Tang-ch'ien ssu-hsiang chan-hsien ti jo-kan wen-t'i' (Some current problems on the thought front), *HC*, 23 (1981), 2–22.

not appear in the media of mass information, education, persuasion, and entertainment. But all this represents in this context an immaterial non-historic background to real Soviet history. Everything which, to an outside observer who has
not passed through the school of the Soviet way of life, may seem a falsehood,
demagogy, formalism, a bureaucratic comedy, propaganda, and so on, in fact
represents the flesh and blood of this way of life, in fact this life itself. And everything which may seem to be bitter truth, the actual state of things, commonsense
considerations and so on is, in fact nothing but the insignificant outer skin of the
real process.[58]

Since the end of the Mao era, the outer skin of "bitter truth ... and so
on" has revealed itself more and more in Chinese literary works. Writers
both new and established continue to press against the frontiers of theme
and technique. The process of ever tightening restriction has been
slowed, although it is not yet clear that it has been reversed. Literature
under communism has survived the imposition of all but intolerable
burdens. It has reflected much of the vision of the makers of the new
society, and may now have begun to cope with some greater part of the
reality, in its slow advance into the world of modernism.

58 Alexander Zinoviev, *The radiant future*, quoted in Clive James, "Laughter in the dark," *New York
Review of Books*, 19 March 1981, 20.

PART V

THE SEPARATED PROVINCE

CHAPTER 12

TAIWAN UNDER NATIONALIST RULE, 1949–1982

When the Nationalist General Ch'en I received the Japanese surrender in Taipei on 25 October 1945 and took over as governor of Taiwan province, he assumed control of an area with a history very different from that of other parts of China. Settled relatively late, mainly by Chinese from Fukien province during and after the sixteenth century, Taiwan became a Japanese colony in 1895.[1] The changes in material conditions and attitudes of the people of Taiwan during the fifty years of Japanese rule affected in important ways the subsequent development of Taiwan under the Nationalists.

An early and central objective of the Japanese was the establishment of law and order among a sometimes rebellious people. First through military operations and later through the creation of an extensive police apparatus, the Japanese introduced an administrative and legal system that fostered an orderly and peaceful society. Strict, and at times harsh and arbitrary, the Japanese rulers created an environment conducive to economic development and modernization that stood in sharp contrast to the civil war, warlordism, banditry, and military invasion by Japanese forces that plagued the Chinese mainland during the first half of the twentieth century.

Economic development in Taiwan was carried out along lines aimed primarily at benefiting the Japanese Empire rather than the people of Taiwan, but the process conferred on the Taiwanese a steadily rising standard of living. By 1945 the people of Taiwan enjoyed a style of life considerably more advanced than that of the average citizen on the mainland. For example, in the early 1930s Taiwan had 2,857 miles of railways as

---

1 The bulk of the people of Taiwan are descended from immigrants from southern Fukien and speak the Amoy dialect. A smaller number, whose ancestors came from Kwangtung, speak Hakka. These two groups are usually referred to collectively as "Taiwanese." The "mainlanders" on Taiwan consist of those Chinese who emigrated from the mainland after 1945. They speak a variety of dialects, but their common means of communication is the national language (*kuo yü* in Chinese), based on the dialect spoken in North China. As of 1982 the total population of Taiwan was 18 million, some 2 million of whom were "mainlanders" or their children. The total also includes some 200,000 aboriginal tribespeople, living mainly in the mountains, whose ancestors inhabited Taiwan before the Chinese came. They are related to the Malays and speak a variety of languages.

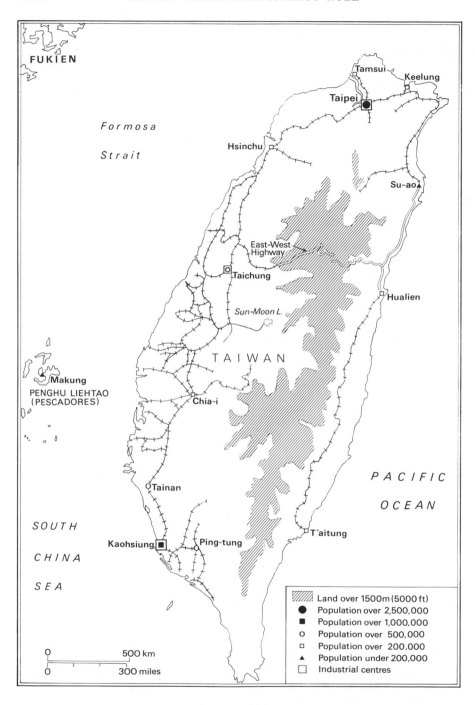

MAP 12. Taiwan

compared to only 9,400 for all of continental China, and power plants in Taiwan generated nearly as much electric power as all the power plants in China.[2] The Japanese vastly improved public health conditions, expanded primary education, built harbors and highways, and began the creation of an industrial base. They modernized public finance by means of land surveys that clearly established land ownership, ended large-scale evasion of the land tax, and provided a basis that later helped the Nationalist government to carry out land reform. Through the expansion of irrigation, the introduction of new farming techniques, and the organization of agricultural associations they greatly increased agricultural production.

The Taiwanese, while appreciating the material gains they had made under Japanese rule, resented their treatment by the Japanese as second-class citizens. All the higher positions in government in Taiwan, as well as the senior managerial, technical, and administrative jobs, were in the hands of Japanese. Few Taiwanese were able to get more than a primary school education.[3] A long struggle by Taiwanese activists to obtain representative government in Taiwan and Taiwanese representation in the Japanese Diet had produced only meager results by the time the war in the Pacific broke out in 1941. Some Japanese liberals sympathized with the Taiwanese desire for political representation, but the mainstream of the Japanese ruling group believed that only when the Taiwanese had been fully assimilated as Japanese in language, culture, and devotion to the emperor could they be accorded equal political rights. Extreme Japanese nationalists rejected the very idea that these colonial subjects could ever be assimilated and become true Japanese.

At the war's end in 1945 the Taiwanese enthusiastically welcomed the expulsion of the Japanese and the reattachment of Taiwan to China, believing that they would fall heir to confiscated Japanese properties and take over the jobs formerly held by Japanese. They were grievously disappointed to find Taiwan taken over by a new group of overlords – Chinese, to be sure, but speaking a different dialect and often looking down on and discriminating against the local people. Taiwanese resentment was to explode in violence in 1947 and tension between mainlanders and Taiwanese became a lasting political problem for the Nationalists.

Three main themes have dominated the history of Taiwan under the Nationalists since the government of the Republic of China retreated there in 1949: the struggle for the survival of Taiwan as a separate politi-

---

2 George H. Kerr, *Formosa: licensed revolution and the Home Rule movement, 1895–1945*, 185.
3 Ibid., 177.

cal entity in the world community, the drive for economic development, and the adjustments in domestic politics under the pressures of changing circumstances. For twenty years the U.S. guarantee of the security of Taiwan, extended at the outbreak of the Korean War in June 1950, provided a reliable shield behind which the modernization of the island could confidently proceed. But after President Nixon's opening to the People's Republic of China (PRC) in 1971 and the Republic of China's loss of its seat in the United Nations, the constancy of the U.S. commitment came increasingly under question by the people of Taiwan. American concessions to Peking on the Taiwan issue in 1972, 1979, and 1982 in order to maintain fruitful relations with the billion people of China were deemed essential to the United States for broad geopolitical reasons; but they created uneasiness in Taiwan, despite U.S. efforts to reassure the people there. Peking's promises of political autonomy if Taiwan "returned to the motherland" were unconvincing to the government and people of Taiwan, who saw their interests best served by a continued struggle to maintain a separate status.

Taiwan's economic development has been widely recognized as one of the outstanding success stories of the past thirty years. It grew out of an unusual combination of circumstances: the relatively developed infrastructure left by the Japanese; the influx of thousands of experienced and well-educated technicians, businessmen, and government administrators from China; large amounts of U.S. economic aid for the first fifteen years; political stability; and the willingness of the top national leaders to accept the advice of the technocrats. Taiwan entered the 1980s approaching the status of a developed nation, with one of the highest per capita standards of living in Asia, and with the fruits of economic development widely shared among the population.

Taiwan has been free of armed rebellion and military coups and, since the 1947 Taiwanese uprising, has only rarely suffered from politically inspired riots and other disorders common to many developing countries. The threat from Peking, the rising living standard, and the widely accepted legitimacy of rule by the two top leaders – Chiang Kai-shek, followed by his son, Chiang Ching-kuo – combined to favor political stability. Critics condemned the political system as rigid and repressive, stressing the monopoly of power by Chinese from the mainland through a single party, the Kuomintang (KMT), the ban on opposition parties, the maintenance of martial law, the arrests of political opponents, and controls over the media. Nevertheless, the political scene has changed substantially over the years. Tens of thousands of Taiwanese have been admitted to the KMT, and Taiwanese have risen to high positions in the Party and government.

Independent politicians have run in local and provincial elections and sometimes have defeated KMT candidates in important contests. Since 1969, elections have been held to add increasing numbers of new members to the national elective bodies. Although some sensitive topics remain taboo, the scope of permitted political debate in the media has broadened in recent years. Economic and social modernization has produced a general recognition both within the government and among the political opposition that the pace of political change will inevitably quicken.

When Chiang Kai-shek resumed the presidency of the government of the Republic of China in Taipei on 1 March 1950, the outlook was grim. Nationalist defenses on the Chinese mainland had crumbled more rapidly than even Mao Tse-tung had anticipated. The loss of Shantung province in September 1948, facilitated by the defection of the Nationalist commander of Tsinan, was quickly followed by the encirclement and defeat of the elite Nationalist forces in Manchuria (the Northeast). Communist troops promptly laid siege to Peking and Tientsin, while others massed for the climactic Huaihai battle north of Nanking involving a total of a million men on the two sides. The loss of the key city of Hsu-chou in December 1948 broke the back of the defenses and the entire Yangtze River line lay open to attack. Nanking fell in April 1949, Shanghai and Hankow in May, and Canton in October. In little more than a year almost the entire Chinese mainland had come under Communist control. The Nationalist government fled from Nanking first to Canton, then to Chungking, then to Chengtu, and finally, in December 1949, to Taipei.

Military reverses destroyed confidence in Nationalist currency. Paper money depreciated in value until by the summer of 1948 the value of the notes had dropped to little more than the actual cost of printing them. The new "gold yuan" replacement currency issued in August 1948 met a similar fate, but only after thousands of trusting citizens had turned in their holdings of gold, silver, and foreign currencies as required by law in exchange for the soon to be worthless money.

Military defeat and economic collapse gave rise to growing demands in high Kuomintang circles for the retirement of Chiang Kai-shek and peace negotiations with the Communists. In January 1949 Chiang retired to his native place, Fenghua in Chekiang province, formally turning the government over to Li Tsung-jen, who became acting president. Chiang did not, however, resign the presidency or give up his position as head of the Kuomintang. From retirement he continued to intervene in national affairs and began to prepare for a last-ditch stand in Taiwan. Shortly before his retirement he appointed his trusted colleague, 52-year-old General Ch'en Ch'eng, as governor of Taiwan and commander of the Taiwan garrison, and his son, 40-year-old Chiang Ching-kuo, as director of the Taiwan headquarters of the KMT. In February 1949, without informing the acting president, he ordered the governor of the Central Bank of China to transfer the government's gold reserves secretly to Taiwan. He himself went to Taiwan in May 1949 and established a residence there, where he stayed between trips to the Philippines, South Korea, and the China mainland, which he left for the last time in December 1949, flying out of Chengtu to Taipei just before the Communists took the city.

When Chiang Kai-shek resumed the presidency (Acting President Li Tsung-jen having fled to the United States and declined to go to Taiwan) the Chinese Communist leaders were already planning the invasion of Hainan island in the South China Sea and the Choushan Islands, seventy-five miles southeast of Shanghai, which were taken in April and May 1950, respectively. The "liberation" of Taiwan had been declared the principal task for 1950 and Su Yu, deputy commander of the Third Field Army, had been put in charge of the operation. For Chiang the only bright spot in the military picture had been the defeat with heavy losses of the Communist force that had assaulted Quemoy, a small island just off Amoy harbor, in October 1949.

Chiang could expect little help from the United States. Madame Chiang Kai-shek had returned from there in January 1950 after a year-long unsuccessful quest for $3 billion in aid and the appointment of a high-ranking U.S. military officer to direct strategic and supply planning. The U.S. government was concerned at the strategic consequences of the conquest of Taiwan by the PRC, but was unwilling to divert thinly stretched forces from more important commitments elsewhere to prevent it. After an agonizing debate within and outside the U.S. government, in which influential Republican senators and the Joint Chiefs of Staff pressed for military aid to Taiwan, President Harry S. Truman, in the light of the sorry performance of the Nationalist government on the mainland, decided against it. The Department of State issued a confidential policy memorandum to information officers abroad in December 1949 informing them that the fall of Taiwan was expected and instructing them how to handle the event so as to minimize damage to U.S. interests. In January 1950 President Truman announced that

the United States has no desire to obtain special rights or privileges or to establish military bases in Formosa at this time. Nor does it have any intention of utilizing its armed forces to interfere in the present situation. The United States Government will not pursue a course which will lead to involvement in the civil conflict in China. Similarly, the United States Government will not provide military aid or advice to Formosa.[4]

Compelled to face the threat of Chinese Communist invasion without hope of U.S. military intervention or aid, Chiang Kai-shek vigorously set about strengthening his last redoubt. The first essentials were to reorganize the motley 800,000 troops withdrawn from the mainland and to eliminate Communist infiltration. In December 1949 he had appointed Wu Kuo-chen (K. C. Wu), the American-educated former mayor of Shanghai, in place of Ch'en Ch'eng as governor of Taiwan, in part to relieve Ch'en to concentrate on military reorganization. Ch'en dismissed tens of thousands of overage and ineffectual officers and reduced the number of troop units by two-thirds. Ch'en was made premier and General Sun Li-jen, an American-educated officer who had commanded the American-trained New First Army in Burma and Manchuria and had later headed a training command in Taiwan, was appointed commander in chief of the newly streamlined army.

Chiang was convinced that an important cause of the debacle on the mainland was the absence of a mechanism for the political control and indoctrination of the armed forces. To perform this function he established a General Political Warfare Department with Chiang Ching-kuo at its head, which placed political officers in each military unit. Security agencies, also under Chiang Ching-kuo's supervision, arrested hundreds of persons charged with being Communist agents, including the deputy chief of the general staff and his wife. The ferreting out of spies and the improved organization and command of the armed forces significantly strengthened Taiwan's defenses, but could not remedy a woeful lack of weapons, ammunition, and supplies.[5]

CONSOLIDATING THE BASE, 1949–1959

The American intervention

While the Nationalists gathered their strength to meet the Communist onslaught fortune intervened in the form of the reversal of President

4 *Department of State Bulletin*, 16 January 1950, 79.

5 For assessments of conditions on Taiwan in the late 1940s and early 1950s, see Joseph W. Ballantine, *Formosa: a problem for the United States foreign policy*; Fred W. Riggs, *Formosa under Chinese Nationalist rule*; Hollington K. Tong, *Chiang Kai-shek*; A. Doak Barnett, *China on the eve of communist takeover*, ch. 20, "Island refuge"; Albert Ravenholt, "Formosa today," *Foreign Affairs*, 30.4 (July 1952), 612–24; Mark Mancall, ed., *Formosa today*, derived from a special issue of the *China Quarterly*, 15 (July–September 1963).

Truman's hands-off policy toward Taiwan. The president and his advisers viewed the Soviet-backed invasion of South Korea in June 1950 as an attempt to expand the area dominated by the Soviet Union, which might be followed by other probes for weak spots in the circle of containment maintained by the United States and its allies. In these circumstances it would be imprudent, the president thought, to permit Taiwan to come under the control of the communist bloc. Moreover, the bipartisan support he needed for U.S. military intervention in Korea would be weakened if he continued to reject the demands of Republican senators to help the Nationalists defend their island against the Chinese Communists. Consequently, he declared:

The occupation of Formosa by Communist forces would be a direct threat to the security of the Pacific area and to United States forces performing their lawful and necessary functions in that area. Accordingly, I have ordered the Seventh Fleet to prevent any attack on Formosa. As a corollary of this action, I am calling upon the Chinese Government on Formosa to cease all air and sea operations against the mainland. The Seventh Fleet will see that this is done. The determination of the future status of Formosa must await the restoration of security in the Pacific, a peace settlement with Japan, or consideration by the United Nations.[6]

The Chinese Communist armed forces, almost totally lacking in naval and air power, were in no position to defy the Seventh Fleet. They discontinued preparations for the invasion of Taiwan, began strengthening their coastal defenses, and shifted the main focus of their military concerns to the Korean border. A great sense of relief and revived hope for the future swept Taiwan at the extension of U.S. military protection to the island. Nationalist morale was bolstered further by the prompt institution of a military aid program and increased economic aid.

The Korean War was a turning point in American attitudes toward Taiwan and the People's Republic of China. The hope that a Chinese form of "Titoism" would develop on the China mainland withered as evidence of close Sino-Soviet cooperation mounted. The PRC put meat on the bones of the Sino-Soviet alliance signed in February 1950 when it sent Chinese "volunteers" pouring across the Yalu River in November to strike a devastating blow at overextended U.S. and South Korean forces. The Soviets began methodically equipping the Chinese Communist armed forces with large numbers of modern automatic rifles, artillery, planes, tanks, and naval craft. They also instituted a large-scale economic aid program designed to expand and modernize China's heavy industry.

---

6 *Department of State Bulletin*, 3 July 1950, 5.

In the early 1950s the Sino-Soviet bloc seemed to Americans to be firmly established, growing in strength, and posing a threat to all the noncommunist nations on its periphery. The bloody fighting in Korea between Chinese Communist and American troops created deeply felt hostility among the people of the two countries toward each other. In the PRC it was fanned by a virulent anti-American propaganda campaign; and in the United States, by the fear of communism whipped up by the reckless charges of Senator Joseph R. McCarthy.

The intensification of the global Cold War, which had exploded into a hot war in Korea, changed the attitudes of the U.S. government and the American people toward Taiwan. Instead of being resigned to the PRC's occupation of the island, the U.S. government now came to see it as a vital link in a rapidly evolving security system in the western Pacific. Strategically located between U.S. allies to the north – Japan and South Korea – and U.S. allies to the south – the Philippines, Thailand, Australia, and New Zealand – Taiwan could play an important role in containing the spread of communism in East Asia. In General Douglas MacArthur's memorable phrase, following his visit to Taiwan in the summer of 1950, the island was "an unsinkable aircraft carrier." In order to bring Taiwan formally into the U.S.-sponsored security system and to provide a stable framework for long-term economic and military aid programs on the island, the United States signed a mutual security treaty with the Republic of China (ROC) in December 1954.

Entering into a formal defense alliance with the Republic of China created a problem for the United States because its objectives differed from those of its partner. Chiang Kai-shek's goal was to counterattack the mainland, overthrow the Chinese Communist regime, and restore Nationalist rule. His troops occupied a number of islands close to the mainland coast, as a political symbol of the Nationalists' determination to return. But the United States was unwilling to underwrite any such venture; its concern was limited to the defense of Taiwan and the nearby Penghu islands. Therefore, the application of the treaty was carefully limited to the defense of Taiwan and the Penghus and in an accompanying exchange of notes the ROC agreed that except for "action of an emergency character which is clearly an exercise of the inherent right of self-defense," it would launch its forces from Taiwan, Penghu, or the offshore islands only in "joint agreement" with the United States.[7]

Occupation of the offshore islands by the Nationalists posed a dilemma for the United States. Loss of one of the larger islands would be a serious

---

[7] Hungdah Chiu, ed., *China and the question of Taiwan*, 250–53.

blow to its ally, yet the United States government did not wish to be committed to the defense of these relatively vulnerable positions. In September 1954, before the signing of the security treaty, the PRC heavily bombarded Quemoy, the largest of the offshore islands. In early January 1955 its amphibious forces captured one of the Ta Chen Islands, off Chekiang province. Because these islands were beyond the range of air support from Taiwan, the Nationalists withdrew the remainder of their forces there with the help of the Seventh Fleet. In order to discourage the PRC from attacking other offshore islands, President Dwight Eisenhower got Congress to pass the "Formosa Resolution" in late January 1955, which authorized the president to employ U.S. forces to defend Taiwan and Penghu against armed attack and "such related positions and territories of that area now in friendly hands" as he might find necessary to assure the defense of Taiwan and Penghu.[8]

For the next three years no serious conflict occurred in the Taiwan Strait. Responding to a proposal by Premier Chou En-lai, the United States agreed to open ambassadorial-level talks with the PRC in August 1955. The ROC strongly opposed the talks, fearing a deal might be made behind its back, but the United States had its own interests to consider, especially obtaining the release of American citizens imprisoned in the PRC. Most of the jailed Americans were released as a result of an agreement reached in the talks, but no agreement was reached on PRC proposals for a foreign ministers' conference, removal of the U.S. embargo on trade with China, and the exchange of journalists. The PRC rejected a U.S. proposal for the renunciation of the use of force in the Taiwan area, and the talks were suspended in December 1957.

In August 1958 Mao Tse-tung decided to test the will of the United States to assist the ROC in defending the offshore islands. He may have been encouraged to launch this probe by the orbiting of the Soviet Sputnik and other trends in world affairs that caused him to declare on a visit to Moscow in 1957 that "the East wind is prevailing over the West wind." On 23 August, PRC artillery opened a massive bombardment of Quemoy, which initially cut off the supply lines to the defenders. President Eisenhower and Secretary of State John Foster Dulles were determined to prevent the capture of the island by the PRC, even at the cost of using nuclear weapons. The Seventh Fleet assembled in force, assumed responsibility for the air defense of Taiwan, and began to convoy ROC supply ships up to the three-mile limit off Quemoy. Within a month the blockade was broken. At the ambassadorial talks, resumed in Warsaw

8 Ibid., 257.

soon after the bombardment began, no agreement was reached on U.S. proposals for a cease-fire, but the bombardment eventually slackened, finally taking the form of a token bombardment on odd days of the month only, in order to underline the PRC's rejection of a cease-fire and its ability to impede or permit at will the resupply of Quemoy.[9]

The 1958 offshore island crisis had both positive and negative effects on the U.S.-ROC alliance. It demonstrated U.S. determination not to permit Quemoy to be captured. U.S. and Nationalist forces cooperated successfully to force the PRC to give up its effort to interdict the island's supply lines. In the course of the fighting, the Nationalists acquired improved weapons for their armed forces, notably eight-inch howitzers for Quemoy and Sidewinder missiles for their air force. On the other hand, the crisis imposed severe strains on the alliance because of differences over military operations and opposition to U.S. policy within the United States and among its allies elsewhere in the world. According to Secretary of State Dulles, the Eisenhower administration had been forced to strain its relations with the Congress and its allies almost to the breaking point in the struggle to save Quemoy. Chiang Kai-shek bitterly opposed U.S. efforts to bring about a cease-fire between the offshore islands and the mainland, for a cease-fire would undercut the symbolic value of the islands as stepping-stones to his cherished goal of mainland recovery. Dulles eventually persuaded Chiang to reduce his forces on the offshore islands by 15,000 men in exchange for an increase in firepower there, and to issue a declaration that the ROC's principal means of recovering the mainland would be through Sun Yat-sen's Three People's Principles and not the use of force.

The PRC had second thoughts about the wisdom of trying to cut Taiwan off from the offshore islands. During the Warsaw talks the United States had pressed strongly for a special regime for the islands, and world opinion, expressed at the United Nations and elsewhere, favored withdrawal of Taiwan's forces from the islands in order to reduce the risk of conflict in the area. But Peking had a stake in Chiang Kai-shek's commitment to "one China" and was alarmed at the growth of international support for the concept of an independent Taiwan. Consequently, when Defense Minister P'eng Te-huai announced the shift to odd-day shelling, he broadcast to "his compatriots in Taiwan" that he wanted them to be able to ship enough supplies to the offshore islands to entrench themselves for a long time to come. Foreign Minister Ch'en I informed foreign

---

9 For a detailed analysis of the offshore islands confrontations of 1954–55 and 1958, see J. H. Kalicki, *The pattern of Sino-American crises.*

diplomats in Peking in December 1958 that the PRC's policy was either to
liberate Taiwan and the offshore islands all at once or to preserve the
present situation.

The security aspects of the American intervention in support of the
Nationalist government on Taiwan were reinforced by U.S. diplomatic
support for the presence of the Republic of China in the United Nations,
where it was a charter member and one of the five permanent members of
the Security Council. In the early 1950s U.S. influence on United Nations
members was strong. In January 1950 it organized the defeat of a Soviet
resolution in the Security Council that called for the expulsion of the
ROC, at which the Soviet representative walked out vowing not to return
so long as the ROC representative remained. The absence of the Soviet
representative when the Korean War broke out made it possible to pass
two Security Council resolutions condemning the North Korean invasion
and appealing to UN members to aid South Korea. Further efforts by the
Soviet representative, after his return to the Security Council in July
1950, to have the Council replace the ROC with the PRC failed. In 1951,
following the PRC's armed intervention in Korea, the United States was
able to obtain the passage of a General Assembly resolution condemning
the PRC as an aggressor for attacking United Nations forces in Korea.
During the remainder of the 1950s Washington mobilized support annually in the UN General Assembly for a resolution "not to consider" any
change in China's representation in the UN.

The PRC's intervention in Korea seriously impeded its efforts to win
a seat in the UN and gain international recognition. In the United States a
Committee of One Million was organized in 1954, including many members of Congress, which rallied public opinion in support of the ROC and
against the PRC. Every year the U.S. Congress passed a resolution opposing the seating of the PRC in the United Nations. By January 1950,
twenty-six countries, mostly Soviet-bloc and neutralist states, had recognized the PRC, but during the succeeding five years no additional state
did so, even though the PRC clearly possessed the attributes normally
required for its recognition as the legitimate government of China. Many
governments would have been willing to maintain diplomatic relations
with both the PRC and the ROC, but neither of the two would tolerate
dual recognition. Forced to choose, many governments hesitated to abandon the ROC and establish relations with the PRC, because they did not
wish to offend the United States, because their leaders were strongly anti-
communist, or because they wanted to follow the lead of the United
Nations. The ROC itself vigorously sought support, particularly among
the emerging African nations, by inviting national leaders on red carpet
visits to Taiwan.

By the end of the 1950s the outlook for the ROC on Taiwan was immeasurably brighter than it had been a decade before. It was no longer just a beleaguered refugee government, bereft of international support and facing a probable early demise. It had a formal defense treaty with the United States and large ongoing U.S. military and economic aid programs. With U.S. help it had retained its position in the United Nations and had diplomatic relations with more countries than the PRC did. Although heavily dependent on the United States, Taiwan was not merely a passive object of U.S. foreign policy; taking advantage of the Cold War climate of the 1950s it had acquired substantial influence through domestic politics in the United States. It had hired American public relations firms to publicize its cause. The "China Lobby," a loose coalition of staunchly anticommunist publishers, businessmen, and U.S. senators and representatives, continually stressed the importance of supporting anti-communist Taiwan as a vital component in the global struggle against the Sino-Soviet bloc. Taiwan had also acquired a constituency within the Washington bureaucracy that had a stake in the growing military and economic aid programs on Taiwan.

For many Americans, trends in East Asia bolstered the rationale for strengthening Taiwan and keeping it part of the "free world." The French defeat at Dienbienphu and the division of Indochina in 1954 constituted another advance by the Sino-Soviet bloc and a threat to the rest of Southeast Asia. The United States did not establish a military base in Taiwan comparable to those in Okinawa, Japan, and the Philippines, but it stationed a Matador missile unit there, capable of striking targets on the China mainland, and spent $25 million on improvements to Kung Kuan airfield in central Taiwan so that it could serve as an emergency recovery base for B-52 bombers of the Strategic Air Command. In 1959 the emerging doctrinal and policy dispute between Moscow and Peking seemed to most Americans but a tiny crack in the solid edifice of Sino-Soviet cooperation, and few foresaw the gaping rift that was soon to develop.[10]

Defense modernization

No longer faced with the need to prepare urgently against impending attack, the military authorities in Taiwan set in motion with American help a long-term program of military modernization. The first and most needed reform was to replace the traditional system of unit loyalty to the

10 The expanding U.S. relationship with the Republic of China in the 1950s and 1960s is discussed in Ralph N. Clough, *Island China*; Foster Rhea Dulles, *American foreign policy toward Communist China, 1949–1969*; Chiu, *China and the question of Taiwan*; Hungdah Chiu, ed., *China and the Taiwan issue*; and Karl Lott Rankin, *China assignment*.

commander rather than to the service with a modern recruitment and personnel management system. Newly established military academies for each of the services began training young officers. The institution of universal two- or three-year military service provided a self-replenishing source of young conscripts, making possible the retirement of aging, ill, or crippled soldiers from the mainland. A Vocational Assistance Commission for Retired Servicemen, initially financed with U.S. aid funds, helped the retirees find jobs. A centralized modern finance system ended the customary practice of commanding officers pocketing part of the pay intended for the troops. An expanding force of reserves was created composed of young men who had completed their military service and were recalled annually for refresher training. In order to increase professionalism, to reduce the tendency for high-ranking officers to aspire to political influence, and to provide openings for competent younger officers, the chief of staff and the commanders of the services were changed every two to three years. A combined service force handled finances and procurement for all the services and managed the arsenals.

A U.S. Military Assistance Advisory Group (MAAG) administered the military aid program and gave advice and training to the ROC armed forces. The first unit, commanded by a major general, had grown to 2,000 persons by 1960, one of the largest of such U.S. military advisory groups in the world. It supervised the reequipment of the armed forces in Taiwan with modern automatic rifles, trucks, communications equipment, artillery, tanks, planes, radar, destroyers, and other naval craft. Thousands of military personnel were sent to the United States for training. By the end of the 1950s the ragtag defeated forces rescued from the mainland had been transformed into a modern armed force 600,000 strong. Although inferior in quantitative terms to its adversary across the strait, it was capable of giving a good account of itself, as demonstrated in the 1958 offshore islands crisis when the ROC's F-86s achieved a kill ratio of 8:1 against the PRC's MiG-15s.

Political consolidation

The defeat of the Nationalists on the China mainland was as much political as military.[11] The Communists surpassed them in organizational skills and propaganda techniques, especially in the countryside. When Chiang Kai-shek withdrew his battered government to Taiwan, he knew he must

---

11 Political developments in the 1950s and 1960s are analyzed in Clough, *Island China*; Chiu, *China and the question of Taiwan* and *China and the Taiwan issue*; Douglas H. Mendel, *The politics of Formosan nationalism*; Peng Ming-min, *A taste of freedom*; and Paul T. K. Sih, ed., *Taiwan in modern times*.

give high priority to creating a more effective government and Party, reviving morale, and drastically reducing corruption and factional squabbling.[12] His prestige was tarnished, but through trusted subordinates he still maintained control of the principal instruments of power: the national treasury, the security services, and the best units among the armed forces. His task was eased by the failure of Vice-President Li Tsung-jen and other political adversaries to come to Taiwan. Some who stayed away were warlords or senior army commanders who had defected to the Communists. Others, including his relatives T. V. Soong and H. H. Kung, were wealthy men who sought in the United States, Hong Kong, or Europe a safer refuge than Taiwan. Senior political figures who came to Taiwan were cut off from their local political bases and sources of income, leaving most of them heavily dependent on the government and Party for their positions and livelihood.

In many ways conditions in Taiwan favored a fresh start by the Nationalists. The area was small and had been well provided by the Japanese with railways, highways and electric power. Agriculture was highly developed, and the economy had made a rapid recovery from the damage caused by World War II. The level of literacy was much higher than on the China mainland. Society in Taiwan was orderly and well organized; it did not suffer from the bandits, warlord armies, and periodic famines that had afflicted large parts of the mainland. No significant Communist underground existed in Taiwan, and protection of the island from Communist infiltration was much easier than it would have been in any mainland province. The arrival between 1946 and 1950 of 2 million refugees burdened the economy, but among them were thousands of trained and experienced technicians and senior bureaucrats to fill the vacuum left by repatriated Japanese, who had reserved all the higher positions on the island for themselves.

The Nationalists brought the structure of their government unchanged from the mainland. Based on the Three People's Principles enunciated by the founder of the Republic of China, Sun Yat-sen, which were an amalgam of traditional Chinese and Western political concepts, it was established in accordance with a constitution adopted at Nanking in 1946. The government consisted of a National Assembly to elect the president and vice-president and amend the constitution, a Legislative Yuan to pass the laws, an Executive Yuan to carry out the laws, a Judicial Yuan to interpret the constitution and serve as a court of last resort, a Control

12 Chiang set his goal as building Taiwan into a model province to be a solid foundation for reconstructing a recovered mainland. See Tong, *Chiang Kai-shek*, 490; also Brian Crozier, *The man who lost China*, 353.

Yuan to supervise officials, and an Examination Yuan to conduct civil service examinations. Members of the National Assembly, the Legislative Yuan, and the Control Yuan were elected in 1947 and 1948 from all the provinces of China. A substantial number of the members of these elective bodies did not go to Taiwan, but emergency measures adopted for "the period of Communist rebellion" extended the terms of those who did go and enabled these bodies to continue to function with reduced numbers.

Chiang Kai-shek served both as president of the nation and as the head of the ruling party, the Kuomintang, which had been established by Sun Yat-sen in 1919 as the successor to earlier revolutionary parties. His position in the party had been strengthened by the failure of other powerful party figures to come to Taiwan. In 1950 he gained approval of the party's highest executive body for a sweeping party reform that purged the membership of wavering and disloyal members in preparation for the 1952 party congress, which elected a new central committee and standing committee. Two minor parties, the Young China Party and the Democratic Socialist Party, moved to Taiwan along with the KMT, but they were small parties with little influence. No new parties were permitted; the political system in Taiwan was essentially a one-party system. Thus, the reform of the KMT was an essential prelude to making a new political start in Taiwan.

The most serious threat to political stability when Chiang Kai-shek resumed the presidency, aside from the Communist menace, was tension between the 2 million refugees from the mainland and the 6 million native Taiwanese. Although the Taiwanese spoke Chinese dialects and retained Chinese cultural practices brought over by their ancestors from the mainland, fifty years under the Japanese had given them a sense of identity that distinguished them from the recently arrived mainlanders. They had learned to speak Japanese, some had studied in Japan, and all had been influenced to some extent by the music, magazines, motion pictures, and other elements of Japanese popular culture that had flowed in from Japan. The Taiwanese had hoped to be given a greater role in administering their island than the Japanese had permitted. They were dismayed to see the positions vacated by the Japanese occupied by mainlanders, many of whom were more interested in making personal fortunes out of confiscated Japanese properties than in establishing a just and efficient provincial government.

On 28 February 1947, growing Taiwanese resentment erupted in riots in which a number of mainlanders were killed or injured. Taiwanese quickly organized throughout the island, demanding reforms from the

Nationalist governor, General Ch'en I.[13] Ch'en temporized until military reinforcements arrived from Shanghai, then carried out a brutal suppression of the Taiwanese, killing thousands, including those who had demonstrated political leadership during the uprising. The KMT Central Executive Committee censured Ch'en and he was removed from office, but the "2/28 affair" had created lasting bitterness among Taiwanese toward their mainlander overlords. Some fled to Hong Kong, where they established a Taiwan independence movement. The movement soon split into a procommunist wing that moved to Peking and advocated the "liberation" of Taiwan and its integration into the PRC and an anticommunist wing that moved to Tokyo and advocated an independent Taiwan.

Mainlanders and Taiwanese were divided by a more fundamental difference than the animosity created by the avarice of mainlander carpetbaggers and the bloodshed in the "2/28 affair." The long-term goal of Chiang Kai-shek and his colleagues was the recovery of the mainland from the Communists; the development of Taiwan was secondary to that objective. The Taiwanese, on the other hand, were primarily concerned with the security and prosperity of Taiwan. They had little interest in mainland recovery, except perhaps as a means of getting most of the mainlanders to go back home. From the mainlander viewpoint, the Nationalist government, originally elected on the mainland, was to be the vehicle for the recovery. Therefore, it had to hold its seat in the United Nations as the legitimate government of China and had to be representative of all the people of China, not just the people on Taiwan. The provincial and local governments could be largely composed of Taiwanese, but to do the same at the national level would undercut the mainland recovery rationale. The Taiwanese, conscious of being the bulk of Taiwan's population, resented being reduced to a minor role in the national government, where the most important decisions concerning their lives were being made.

13 No accurate figures are available for those killed in the days and months following the "2/28 incident." The most detailed account by a foreign observer is in George Kerr, *Formosa betrayed*, ch. 14, "The March massacre," 291–310. Kerr was American vice-consul in Taipei. He estimates mainlander deaths at from 30 to more than 100 and deaths of Taiwanese at possibly as many as "the 20,000 figure often given by Formosan writers." He says, however, that each group exaggerated its losses. In a later book (*Formosa: licensed revolution*, xvi) he states more conservatively that "at least ten thousand Formosans were killed or imprisoned and thousands were forced to seek safety overseas." Other estimates of those killed are: Victor H. Li, "several thousand" ("Taiwan and America's China policy: an introduction," in Victor H. Li, ed., *The future of Taiwan* 2); John Slimming, "seven thousand" (*Green plums and a bamboo horse*, 133); Douglas Mendel, "from 10,000 to 20,000" (*The politics of Formosan nationalism*, 37, quoting Kerr); and Lim T'ianbeng, "20,000" ("The Black March of 1947," in *The Formosan Taiwandang* [Spring 1969], 33. His reference is Kerr).

During the late 1940s and early 1950s the Nationalist government adopted a number of economic, political, and social measures that moderated the strains between mainlanders and Taiwanese. None was taken exclusively for that purpose, but over a period of years they collectively helped to achieve that result.

The most important and effective single measure probably was the land reform, carried out under the slogan "land to the tiller." Land reform made a vital contribution to Taiwan's notable economic development, but it was adopted initially as much for political as for economic reasons. Nationalist leaders were well aware of how effectively the Communists had exploited the grievances of the poor peasants against the landlords on the mainland. As Ch'en Ch'eng wrote after he had presided over the carrying out of land reform in Taiwan:

To allow the tenant farmers and farm hands ... to groan under the exploitation of the landlords was not merely a land and economic problem, but a social and political matter. If this problem had not been solved in good time, it would have adversely affected the stability and very existence of the nation.[14]

At the time of land reform 50 percent of Taiwan's population was engaged in agriculture, and almost all of these farmers were Taiwanese. Land reform significantly improved the livelihood of those buying the land they tilled, who greatly outnumbered the landlords forced to sell their land to the government for resale to tenants. The result was to assure stability and growing prosperity in the countryside. The success of the Nationalists in carrying out land reform in Taiwan when they had failed in attempts to do so on the mainland can be attributed to several factors: the lack of political ties between landlords and the officials pushing through the land reform, the absence of civil war and Communist infiltration in the Taiwan countryside, and the existence of accurate land records developed during the Japanese colonial period.

Land reform set the stage for the rapid economic development discussed below, which benefited both mainlanders and Taiwanese. Although the mainlanders reserved for themselves senior positions in the government, the KMT, the government corporations, and the military, the ownership of land, both rural and urban, was overwhelmingly in the hands of Taiwanese. They benefited from rising land prices and from the flourishing enterprises in the private sector which also were owned by Taiwanese. Thus, economic gains to some extent offset Taiwanese resentment at being excluded from political power.

Measures to increase political participation at the local and provincial

14 Chen Cheng, *Land reform in Taiwan*, 21.

levels also helped to mitigate Taiwanese resentment. For example, farmers' associations had been established under the Japanese at township, county, and provincial levels. They performed a variety of services for farm families, including rural credit and savings deposits, marketing of agricultural products, extension services, health services, settlement of disputes, and sale of daily necessities. Under the Japanese the directors of farmers' associations at the various levels were appointed by Japanese officials. Under the Nationalists, regulations were modified to limit voting membership in the associations to families deriving more than half their income from farming and to provide for election of directors by the membership. Thus, the Nationalist government assisted large numbers of Taiwanese farm families not only to acquire the land they tilled, but also to have greater influence in the organizations that most affected their daily lives.

The Nationalists also greatly expanded the elective process at the provincial and local levels. The Japanese had permitted no islandwide elective body. Local administrative officials were appointed, as was half of the membership of the local assemblies. Chiang Kai-shek approved a system of popular election of county and city councils, magistrates, and mayors, beginning in 1950. A provincial assembly was elected in 1951 by the county and city councils, but after 1959 it, too, was popularly elected. All citizens over age 20 were given the right to vote in local and provincial elections.

Provincial and local elections opened an important avenue to Taiwanese engagement in political activity. Since the formation of new parties was prohibited, large numbers of Taiwanese joined the KMT, which had to run Taiwanese candidates in local elections in order to win the votes of the predominantly Taiwanese electorate. Local office conferred prestige and in some cases control of patronage on ambitious Taiwanese. Competent performance in a local elective office sometimes served as a stepping-stone for appointment to a position in the provincial government and even the national government. Although they could not form their own party, candidates could run as nonparty independents against the approved KMT candidates and were sometimes elected. The KMT candidates had the substantial advantage of party funds and the party apparatus to help them campaign, but some independents, despite numerous restrictions on campaigning, found they could appeal successfully to a Taiwanese protest vote against the mainlander-dominated KMT. Experience gained in provincial and local elections was to prove valuable later to the KMT, to the nonparty politicians, and to the voters when it became necessary to hold elections to fill vacancies in elective bodies at the national level.

Other important measures that helped gradually diminish the tension between mainlanders and Taiwanese were the use of the national language (*kuo yü*, usually called Mandarin in English) throughout the school system and the introduction of an equitable examination system for admission to high school or college and for appointment to civil service positions. The Nationalists had adopted measures to generalize the use of the national language on the mainland, but the Japanese invasion and the civil war had prevented their thorough implementation. In compact Taiwan the job was easier; schools at all levels were taught in the national language from 1946 on. By the end of the 1950s most of those in the rising generation had acquired a useful knowledge of the language, and the barrier to effective spoken communication between Taiwanese and mainlanders was eroding.

Parents, whether mainlander or Taiwanese, considered it highly important to the future of the family to give their children the best education they could afford. Entry into high school and college was governed by standardized examinations, and the grades received determined whether an applicant was admitted to a prestigious institution or a mediocre one. Administration of the examinations was scrupulously fair. Whether a child was admitted to a school or (in college) a course of his or her choice depended on examination scores, not on the position of the parent. The same was true of the civil service examinations. Consequently, although mainlander children had some advantage in the early years because their schooling had prepared them better for the examinations, this advantage disappeared as soon as all those taking examinations were products of the post-1945 school system in Taiwan. Taiwanese felt discriminated against in terms of political power, but their equality of access to education and civil service jobs prevented more serious social divisions from developing. Mixing in the schools and government offices also tended to break down barriers and improve communication.

The introduction of democratic procedures in local politics did not fundamentally alter the authoritarian nature of the Nationalist government, although it served as a safety valve by providing scope for many Taiwanese to pursue political aspirations. The central government remained under the firm control of Chiang Kai-shek, who was reelected to the presidency in 1954 and again in 1960. He appointed the top military and civilian officials and consolidated his power by shrewdly balancing one group against another. Martial law had been declared in 1949 to permit secret trials in military courts of persons accused of subversive activity. Although security measures were eased somewhat after American intervention removed fear of an imminent Communist attack, security agencies continued active. Governor K. C. Wu found the atmosphere in Taiwan so oppressive that he resigned in 1953 and went to the United States, whence he sent open letters to the National Assembly and Chiang Kai-shek denouncing Taiwan's lack of democracy and security excesses. The commander in chief of the armed forces, General Sun Li-jen, was removed from his post in 1955 and placed under house arrest on charges of responsibility for demands presented to Chiang Kai-shek at a military review by disaffected officers.

Economic stabilization

When Chiang Kai-shek resumed the presidency in 1950, Taiwan's economy was in a shaky condition as a result of a succession of shocks.[15] Under the Japanese, Taiwan had been an export-oriented economy, in 1937 exporting 44 percent of its production, mainly processed foods, almost entirely to Japan. At the end of World War II agricultural production in Taiwan, affected by the disruption of shipping lanes to Japan, had dropped to one-half the 1939 level. Three-fourths of Taiwan's industry, two-thirds of its power plants, and one-half of its transport network had been put out of operation by American bombers. Cut off from its traditional market by order of the U.S. occupation authorities in Japan, Taiwan shifted its principal economic relations to the China mainland, but trade with that war-ravaged region by 1948 amounted to only one-quarter of Taiwan's prewar external trade volume. With the fall of Shanghai in 1949, Taiwan's mainland market was cut off and it was again forced to find new markets for its exports. In 1949 the Taiwan authorities established a new currency, severed from the expiring Nationalist currency on the mainland, with 100 percent reserves in gold and foreign exchange and pegged to the U.S. dollar. Inflation continued to soar, however, as the Bank of Taiwan pumped out paper currency to meet the extraordinary military expenses. Moreover, infected by mainland inflation, Taiwan's prices rose an average of 100 percent annually from 1946 on, surging to 500 percent in 1949–50.

Despite the monetary crisis and the severe damage suffered by Taiwan's economy during the 1940s, the island possessed a sound base from

15 The most comprehensive and up-to-date analysis of economic development in Taiwan from the 1950s through the mid-1970s is Walter Galenson, ed., *Economic growth and structural change in Taiwan: the postwar experience of the Republic of China.* Also useful are Neil H. Jacoby, *U.S. aid to Taiwan: a study of foreign aid, self-help and development*; T. H. Shen, ed., *Agriculture's place in the strategy of development: the Taiwan experience*; K. T. Li, *The experience of dynamic economic growth on Taiwan*; Jan S. Prybyla, *The societal objective of wealth, growth, stability and equity in Taiwan*; and Shirley W. Y. Kuo, *The Taiwan economy in transition.*

which to recover and forge ahead in the 1950s. Most important were its human resources. Public health conditions were good and the population well educated, by Asian standards. Farmers were skillful and productive, and a small but well-trained force of industrial workers existed. During the 1930s, in recognition of Taiwan's strategic importance, the Japanese had expanded industry beyond food processing for the Japanese market, establishing textile, bicycle, cement, chemical, pulp and paper, fertilizer, petroleum refining, aluminum, and steel plants. Managers, engineers, and technicians arrived in large numbers among the refugees from the China mainland to take the places of some thirty thousand departed Japanese. Power plants, railways, and highways were in place and capable, once war damage had been repaired, of supporting the revival of agriculture and industry.

By 1950 favorable trends were already apparent in industry and agriculture. Industry reached its prewar production peak in 1951 and agriculture in 1952. The reassuring effect of the U.S. decision to protect Taiwan, combined with restrictive monetary measures by the authorities and the arrival of large amounts of U.S. aid commodities, beginning in 1951, made possible the control of inflation. By 1953 the rise in the consumer price index had been brought down to 19 percent and from 1954 through 1960 averaged under 9 percent annually.

The land reform, begun in 1949 with the limitation of land rents to 37.5 percent of the principal crop instead of the 50 percent commonly collected, made an important contribution to agricultural production and industrialization and set the stage for Taiwan's rapid economic growth in the 1960s and 1970s. In the second phase of land reform the government sold to farm families a large amount of public land acquired from Japanese owners. In the third phase, completed in 1953, landlords were required to sell to the government for resale to tenants all land exceeding three hectares of rice paddy or six hectares of dry land. Landlords were compensated partly in ten-year bonds denominated in terms of rice or sweet potatoes, and partly in stock in four government corporations confiscated from the Japanese. The tenants paid the government for the land in ten equal annual installments.

Land reform greatly diminished the power of the landlord class in the countryside and turned Taiwan's agriculture into a system of owner-tillers cultivating small plots of land, most of them under two hectares. It increased the income of the farmers and the productivity of agriculture in general as the new owners worked harder and invested more. It also reduced the wealth of the landlords, because the government purchased their excess land at less than market value and the interest paid on their bonds was well below the market rate. It transferred to private ownership four large corporations by turning landlords into stockholders.

The carrying out of the land reform and the further development of agriculture in Taiwan were greatly facilitated by the work of a unique institution, the Chinese-American Joint Commission on Rural Reconstruction (JCRR). Established in 1948 and supported by U.S. aid funds, it was headed by three Chinese and two American commissioners. For many years the chairman was Chiang Monlin, a distinguished educator who had served as chancellor of Peking University and minister of education. Shen Tsung-han, one of the Chinese commissioners, received his Ph.D. degree from Cornell University, as did Lee Teng-hui, an agricultural economist with the commission, who later became mayor of Taipei and governor of Taiwan and was to succeed Chiang Ching-kuo as president of the Republic of China in 1988. Since it was outside the normal Chinese government structure and could pay higher salaries, it was able to recruit exceptionally able agricultural specialists. The commission performed a dual function, serving in the place of a ministry of agriculture in the Chinese government and as the agricultural arm of the U.S. aid mission. It was responsible for directing into agriculture approximately one-third of U.S. economic aid to Taiwan, which generated almost 60 percent of net domestic capital formation in agriculture during the entire period that Taiwan received U.S. economic aid (1951–65). The JCRR carried on a wide range of rural development activities, including crop and livestock improvement, water resource development, soil conservation, agricultural organization and extension, agricultural financing, rural health improvement, and agricultural research. It was a pioneer in promoting integrated rural development in a developing country.[16]

Under the combined stimulus of the land reform and the agricultural development programs instituted by the JCRR, agricultural production increased at an average annual rate of 4 percent from 1952 through 1959, exceeding the high population growth rate of 3.6 percent annually during this period. Livestock production increased 73 percent. Nearly one-fourth of the U.S. economic aid flowing in at the rate of $90 million per year was in the form of surplus agricultural commodities. Thus, Taiwan had ample food supplies to sustain a rapidly growing population, improve the quality of nutrition, and maintain unchanged the level of agricultural exports, which constituted the bulk of its exports during this period.

16 A recent book-length study of the JCRR is Joseph A. Yager's *Transforming agriculture in Taiwan: the experience of the Joint Commission on Rural Reconstruction.*

Agriculture also served as an important source of government revenues, through land taxes payable in rice, compulsory purchases of rice at
below market prices, and a rice-fertilizer barter program. Chemical fertilizer was a government monopoly. The exchange of fertilizer for rice at
a high fixed rate in terms of rice gave the government a substantial
income as well as a supply of rice that it allocated as rations to military
and civilian government employees and sold on the open market from
time to time to maintain price stability. Government control of this basic
foodstuff enabled the authorities to ensure an adequate supply for government employees and to prevent the wide swings in rice prices and hoarding by merchants that had contributed to public demoralization on the
mainland.

Taiwan's early emphasis on agriculture made possible a balanced
growth of both industry and agriculture unusual among developing
countries. Although agriculture was "squeezed" to provide the bulk of
the capital needed for industrial growth, the terms of trade were not
nearly so unfavorable to the agricultural sector as customary elsewhere.
Land reform increased the income of individual farm families enough
to provide a substantial market for the nondurable consumer goods
produced by industry. People who had been landlords in the past,
because they were now no longer permitted to invest in farmland as they
had traditionally done, began to invest in industry.

Other early economic decisions by the Taiwan authorities contributed
to the pattern of balanced growth that developed during the 1950s. At the
beginning of the decade government-owned corporations acquired from
the Japanese (mainly in chemicals, fertilizer, and petroleum) accounted for
56 percent of industrial production. Instead of expanding the government
sector, the leaders decided to maintain these industries at roughly the
existing level, invest government funds in the expansion of infrastructure,
and create a climate conducive to the growth of import-substituting consumer goods industries operated by private entrepreneurs. The government thus began to put money into the expansion of the rural road
network, improvement of the railways (already second in density only to
Japan in Asia), and increases in the production of electric power in order
to keep ahead of rising demand.

Measures designed to encourage the growth of import-substituting
industries resulted in a gradual shift of industrial production away from
food processing for export to textiles, rubber and leather goods, bicycles,
wood products, and other consumer items produced for the domestic
market. Because the manufacture of these goods required small amounts
of capital and a relatively low level of technical skill, it could be un-

dertaken by the largely inexperienced Taiwanese entrepreneurs. They built small plants on the fringes of the large cities or small towns where they had easy access to labor off the farms. The decentralization of industry kept the influx of rural population into the large cities relatively low during the 1950s. The well-developed bus and train service caused many new industrial workers to choose to commute to work from the farm rather than move into the cities. The maxim of "developing agriculture by means of industry; fostering industry by virtue of agriculture" was being followed.

Industrial production increased during the 1950s at 10 percent a year. By the end of the decade, however, the scope for further expanding import-substituting industries had been exhausted. The import of consumer goods as a proportion of the total domestic supply of such goods had dropped to 5 percent, and excess production capacity was appearing in some areas. The government had to decide whether to shift its emphasis to the production of previously imported consumer durables and capital goods or to the export of nondurable consumer goods already being produced in Taiwan. After some hesitation, it chose the latter route. Even before the decision was made, the export of manufactured goods from Taiwan had increased significantly. In 1952 92 percent of all exports had consisted of agricultural or processed agricultural products and only 8 percent were manufactured. By 1959 exported manufactured goods had climbed to 24 percent of total exports. A series of changes in foreign exchange, monetary, and fiscal policies taken in the late 1950s and early 1960s opened the door to a more rapid expansion in the export of manufactures. Taiwan was to shift from an industry producing largely from domestic raw materials for the domestic market to one relying on imported raw materials to be processed for export by a labor-intensive industry.[17]

Taiwan in 1960 differed from other developing countries in several important respects. Its agriculture did not consist of a large-scale, modern sector coexisting with a mass of backward peasants, but almost entirely of smallholders, mostly literate and relatively efficient. Its industry had not gone in for government-owned prestige heavy-industry projects, but had concentrated on providing the infrastructure and business climate to encourage labor-intensive production of consumer goods by private entrepreneurs. Growth was well balanced between the rural and urban sectors and income was fairly evenly distributed among the population.

17 See K. T. Li's paper "Public policy and economic development," written in 1969 and published in Li, *The experience of dynamic economic growth on Taiwan*, 30–73.

Chiang Kai-shek and his colleagues, including a remarkable group of Western-educated technocrats headed by K. Y. Yin, C. K. Yen, K. T. Li, and Chiang Monlin, had built the foundation for the extraordinary economic growth that was to take place in the 1960s and 1970s.

In 1960, however, no one foresaw the approaching economic takeoff. Memory of the Quemoy conflict was still fresh. Military expenditures were consuming 11 percent of national income. Food shortages in mainland China, combined with the failure of the utopian Great Leap Forward and the sudden withdrawal of Soviet experts, raised hopes in Taipei that Communism in China might indeed be, in the words of Secretary of State Dulles, "a passing and not a perpetual phase." Chiang Kai-shek and many other senior KMT leaders continued to view the development of Taiwan as preparation for the day when the inevitable popular rising against Communist tyranny would provide the opportunity to recover the mainland.

ECONOMIC TAKEOFF, 1960–1970

International position

In 1961 more than a decade had passed since Chou En-lai had demanded the ROC's seat in the United Nations for the PRC. An increasing number of UN members opposed setting aside the China question each year by a procedural motion "not to consider" any change in China's representation. Consequently, the United States and its allies agreed to debate and vote on the question, but they succeeded in keeping the ROC in the UN and excluding the PRC for the rest of the decade by mobilizing majority support each year for a resolution providing that the question of China's representation could be resolved only by a two-thirds majority. Further decline in support for the ROC was checked temporarily by the international ill-will provoked by the Cultural Revolution in China. The decline soon resumed. In 1970 for the first time a simple majority of UN members voted to expel the ROC and admit the PRC, although the resolution failed to pass for lack of a two-thirds majority.

Throughout the 1960s, in addition to the struggle to retain its seat in the United Nations, the ROC was engaged in a contest with the PRC for recognition by individual countries. It invited a stream of dignitaries from all over the world to observe progress in Taiwan. It also instituted in 1961 a program of technical missions to developing countries, mainly in agriculture. By 1970 it had 702 technicians in twenty-three African countries on short-term or long-term assignments. It had 111 others in eleven Asian and Latin American countries. In addition it had trained in Taiwan thousands of technicians from developing countries. The ROC's imaginative diplomacy helped to retain diplomatic relations with a sizable number of countries, but the PRC, holding the trump card of control over mainland China, was slowly gaining. France switched recognition in 1964 and Canada and Italy in 1970. By that year fifty-three countries had recognized the PRC, while sixty-eight still recognized the ROC.

The preservation of the ROC's international position throughout the 1960s owed much to U.S. policy. The United States had the power to veto the PRC's admission to the United Nations, and it expended large amounts of political capital every year to persuade allied and friendly countries to support the ROC's position. But the decisions by close allies such as France, Canada, and Italy to oppose the United States on this issue showed that U.S. influence was waning. Moreover, the attitude of Americans toward the China issue was gradually changing. By the late 1960s few could deny that the Sino-Soviet rift was genuine, serious, and likely to last a long time. Polemics between the two grew more strident, the Soviets stationed powerful forces along the China border, and in 1969 the hostility between Moscow and Peking erupted in military clashes at Chen-pao Tao (Damansky Island). The bipolar world of the 1950s had disappeared and in the emerging multipolar system the advantages of developing links with the Soviet Union's giant adversary appeared compelling to increasing numbers of Americans.

The Vietnam War and the Cultural Revolution in China delayed serious official consideration of a shift in policy on the China question. Taiwan, although not the site of a permanent U.S. military base, proved to be a useful auxiliary position from which to conduct the war in Vietnam. The United States stationed a wing of C-130 transport aircraft and a KC-135 tanker squadron at Ch'ing Ch'üan Kang (formerly Kung Kuan) airfield, the runway of which had been extended in the 1950s at U.S. expense for contingency use. Two units of fighter aircraft from the U.S. 13th Air Force in the Philippines were stationed in Taiwan also. The U.S. overhauled fighter aircraft, tanks, and personnel carriers in Taiwan, which provided the best facilities in the western Pacific for these purposes outside of Japan. By the late 1960s U.S. military personnel stationed in Taiwan, exclusive of dependents, numbered close to ten thousand. Thus, the practical value of Taiwan to the war effort, the preoccupation of the U.S. government with conducting an increasingly unpopular war, and the chaos of a China in the throes of the Cultural Revolution combined to cause reconsideration of the China issue to be deferred.

Meanwhile, the network of substantive relations between the United

States and Taiwan was proliferating. Military aid continued throughout the 1960s, reaching a total by mid-1969 of over $3 billion. The F-86 fighter aircraft, of Korean War vintage, were replaced by F-100, F-104, and F-5 aircraft. The ROC acquired C-119 transports and received authorization to coproduce military helicopters with Bell Helicopter Company. Nike-Hercules and Hawk missiles strengthened Taiwan's anti-aircraft capability while additional destroyers and LSTs improved its ability to resupply the offshore islands. More tanks and howitzers arrived. Taiwan was also developing an armaments industry that by the end of the 1960s was producing M-14 rifles, machine guns, artillery shells, mortars, and other types of military equipment. Thousands of military men from Taiwan received training in the United States.

The United States phased out economic aid in 1965, having provided $1.4 billion since 1951. Taiwan was now able to stand on its own economically, and U.S. officials pointed to it proudly as the first developing nation to "graduate" from a U.S. economic aid program. American businessmen found Taiwan a congenial place to invest; by the end of 1968, twenty-three American firms employed more than 22,000 Chinese employees in plants in Taiwan. Two American banks had established branches there. American missionaries, denied access to the China mainland, settled by the hundreds in Taiwan. Universities in the United States developed various exchange relationships with universities in Taiwan, and every year the former received several thousand graduate students from the island.

Economic growth

The decade of the 1960s in Taiwan was notable for the spurt in overall economic growth that sent the rate of increase in per capita income from 2.7 percent annually in the 1950s to 5.8 percent in the 1960s. The surge in the export of manufactured goods, the primary cause of the high growth rate, brought about basic structural changes in the economy. Agricultural production dropped from 33 percent of net demestic product in 1960 to 18 percent in 1970, while industrial production climbed from 25 percent to 35 percent. The public sector share of industrial production dropped from 48 percent in 1960 to 28 percent in 1970, the private sector share increasing from 52 percent to 72 percent over that period. Foreign trade soared from $461 million in 1960 to $3 billion in 1970 and the proportion of industrial products in that trade leaped from 32 percent in 1960 to 79 percent in 1970.

No single factor accounts for Taiwan's success in achieving exceptionally high economic growth based on a rapid increase in the export of labor-intensive manufactures using imported raw materials. It resulted from a combination of political stability, continuation of the emphasis on the rural sector begun in the 1950s, and the adoption of new foreign exchange, monetary, and fiscal measures designed to encourage exports.

Agriculture continued to perform well, although production increased at a somewhat slower rate than in the 1950s. At a 3.6 percent annual increase it still remained well ahead of population growth, for that rate declined from 3.5 percent in 1960 to 2.4 percent in 1970, owing to the effects of industrialization and an official policy adopted in the early 1960s of encouraging family planning. Because nearly all arable land in Taiwan was already under cultivation, the increase in agricultural production had to come from increased yield per hectare. This was made possible through improved crop varieties, increased labor, and, most important, the increased use of chemical fertilizers. The share of rice in the agricultural product dropped sharply as farmers stepped up output of the more profitable fruits, vegetables, and livestock and the public demanded a more varied diet as their income increased.

Industrial production grew at 20 percent annually during the 1960s, twice the rate achieved during the previous decade. The products that became the cutting edge of Taiwan's export drive during this period were textiles, wood, and leather and paper products. During the second half of the decade electronic components increased in importance. Foreign manufacturers began to build plants in Taiwan to take advantage of its inexpensive, easily trained labor to produce parts for their finished products assembled elsewhere. This process was furthered by Taiwan's establishment of export processing zones in which materials could be imported free of duty, processed by Taiwanese labor, and exported with a minimum of red tape.

Taiwan's rapid industrial growth was made possible by a continuing ample supply of inexpensive labor, increasing income in both rural and urban sectors, which provided a growing domestic market to complement the drive into the export market, and a boom in the savings ratio to GNP from 5 percent to 10 percent in the 1950s to close to 30 percent by 1970. The ready supply of labor and the rise in rural income, at a somewhat slower rate than the rise in urban income, were both closely related to the relative dispersion of industry in Taiwan. A study of labor distribution in Taiwan between 1956 and 1966 shows that employment in manufacturing in Taiwan's sixteen largest cities and towns containing 32 percent of the population actually declined relatively, while manufacturing employment in rural areas *increased* from 47 percent to 52 percent of the total.[18] With such a dispersal of industry it is not surprising that by 1972 more than half of farm family income came from nonagricultural sources. The rise in savings, which largely took the form of an enormous increase in bank deposits and provided the investment funds to support rapid industrialization, probably can be explained by a combination of increased confidence, rising income, and the Chinese propensity to put something away for the future. The outcome of the offshore islands crisis of 1958 had demonstrated that Taiwan was safe from military attack by the PRC. Government measures had brought inflation down to only 2–3 percent annually during the 1960s. Banks were paying high interest rates on savings deposits, the economy was humming, unemployment was low, and people were more optimistic about their personal future than in the 1950s.

The phasing out of U.S. economic aid in 1965, although viewed with uneasiness at the time by government officials, had no deleterious effect on the growth of Taiwan's economy. By the time the pipeline had run dry in 1968, private foreign investment had increased so that it exceeded the annual $90 million that had come in through U.S. aid. By 1970 Taiwan had accumulated foreign exchange reserves of $627 million, equivalent to more than five months of imports, and had no difficulty in qualifying for loans from foreign banks at commercial rates.

Political stability

During the 1960s no structural change occurred in the political system on Taiwan. Chiang Kai-shek, reelected president in 1960 and again in 1966 and reelected *tsung-ts'ai* (director-general) of the KMT in 1969, frequently reiterated the ROC's claim to be the legitimate government of all China, as well as its determination to recover the lost mainland. The remaining members of the National Assembly, Legislative Yuan, and Control Yuan elected on the mainland in 1947 and 1948 continued to perform their constitutional functions. Political stability provided the necessary foundation for Taiwan's rapid economic growth, which, by affording the mass of the population opportunities to improve their living standard, helped maintain political stability.

Although the structure of the political system remained unchanged, a subtle but unmistakable change occurred in the emphasis of government policy. The influence of those who saw Taiwan principally as a base for

---

18 Gustav Ranis, "Industrial development," in Galenson, *Economic growth*, 224, quoting Samuel P. S. Ho, "The rural non-farm sector in Taiwan," in *World Bank studies in employment and rural development*, vol. 32.

mainland recovery declined, while the influence of those whose main concern was the development of Taiwan itself increased. Hope for return to
the mainland rose briefly in 1961–62 when the PRC was suffering from
severe economic difficulties. Chiang Kai-shek readied his forces to take
advantage of possible rebellion on the mainland, and the PRC countered
by moving reinforcements into Fukien province. President John F.
Kennedy informed the PRC, both publicly and through the Warsaw
channel, that the United States opposed the use of force in the region and
would not back offensive action by the ROC. Thereafter. with the exception of an occasional very small-scale raid on the mainland, the ROC's
military preparations were directed exclusively to the defense of Taiwan
and the offshore islands. The technocrats, concerned with the economic
development of Taiwan, gained increasing support from Chiang Kai-shek
for their plans and policies.

The fading of the hope for mainland recovery did not affect the determination of the mainlander ruling group to retain control of the levers of
power. The top positions in the KMT, the security services, the military,
and the financial and economic ministries remained in their hands. They
applied martial law selectively to eliminate threats to the government
coming either from the Communists or from partisans of the Taiwan
independence movement. The mainlander editor of the political journal
Free China Fortnightly, Lei Chen, who attempted to organize an opposition political party composed of both mainlanders and Taiwanese, was
sentenced to ten years in jail in 1960 for failing to report a former Communist on his staff. The leadership would brook no organized opposition
to the KMT.

The ruling party, with a membership aproaching one million by the
end of the decade, played an important role in maintaining political
stability. It had primary responsibility for establishing and controlling
the limits of public debate, through media it owned and operated and
through monitoring the privately owned media, suspending organs that
transgressed established bounds. It ran candidates in local and provincial
elections, securing the election of between 78 percent and 92 percent of its
candidates in elections conducted between 1964 and 1968. It provided a
link between government and people through the China Youth Corps
(successor to the San-min chu-i Youth Corps) and through party connections with farmers' associations, labor unions, fishermen's associations,
cooperatives, and women's organizations. Party officials on college campuses closely monitored student opinions and activities.

Tension between mainlanders and Taiwanese eased as the 2/28 incident
of 1947 receded into the past, but Taiwanese resentment at the main-

lander monopoly of power did not disappear. In 1965 the former chairman of the Political Science Department at Taiwan National University, Professor P'eng Ming-min, secretly had a manifesto printed calling on Taiwanese to rise up and overthrow "Chiang's dictatorial regime," for which he and two associates were sentenced to eight years in prison. His sentence was later commuted and he escaped from Taiwan. The Taiwan independence movement, operating mainly in Japan and the United States, continued to agitate for an independent Taiwan, but the movement remained small and faction-ridden and had little influence within Taiwan itself. In 1965 Thomas Liao (Liao Wen-i), who eleven years before had been named president of the "Provisional Government of the Republic of Formosa" by a group of Taiwanese exiles in Tokyo, deserted the movement and returned to Taiwan followed by others.

The failure of anti-KMT movements based abroad to gain much influence in Taiwan can be ascribed in part to the effectiveness of the security agencies on the island, although the extent of surveillance of Taiwanese in itself engendered resentment. An equally important reason may have been the benefits accruing from the economic growth that provided job and business opportunities and rising incomes to a large number of Taiwanese. Taiwanese businessmen, in particular, were developing relations with mainlanders in the bureaucracy, and both groups had an interest in continued political stability. In addition, Taiwanese politicians were finding greater scope for political participation. Even though denied the right to organize an opposition party, they were becoming more skillful in running as independents against KMT candidates. Kao Yü-shu (Henry Kao), a Taiwanese engineer educated in Japan, in 1964 outwitted the KMT and gained election for the second time as mayor of Taipei. In that same year independents won elections to the mayoralties in Keelung and Tainan, making non-KMT politicians mayors in three of Taiwan's five largest cities. In order to relieve the KMT from having to contest the Taipei mayoralty in future elections, Chiang Kai-shek in 1967 made the city a "special municipality" under the Executive Yuan, but shrewdly blunted Taiwanese displeasure with this move by making Kao the first appointed mayor. In 1969 Taiwanese politicians had their first opportunity to run for national office. It had become evident to everyone that the membership in the national elective bodies was shrinking at an accelerating pace as the members elected on the mainland died. Consequently, fifteen new members were elected to the National Assembly, eleven to the Legislative Yuan, and two to the Control Yuan. Thus, during the 1960s the Taiwanese were increasingly finding ways to gain more influence within the mainlander-dominated society, by success in business, by challenging the KMT on the hustings, and by advancement within the KMT itself.

Throughout the decade Chiang remained the unchallenged leader. Head of the party since 1938, president of the republic since 1948, and commander in chief of the armed forces, he retained in his hands the power to make all senior civil and military appointments and was the final authority for all important decisions. He ruled in a traditional Confucian style: paternalistic, apart from the people, feeling an obligation to look after them and expecting from them in return loyalty to his person. Austere in his personal life, he enforced austerity among his subordinates. Chiang was already in his seventies at the beginning of the decade and speculation concerning his successor focused on the vice-president, Ch'en Ch'eng, and the president's son, Chiang Ching-kuo, who at that time headed up all security and intelligence activities in Taiwan. Each had a substantial group of supporters in top KMT circles. Chiang Kai-shek did not indicate where his preference lay; on the contrary, his style of rule was to keep power in his own hands and not allow anyone else to build too strong a power base of his own. Ch'en Ch'eng's death in 1965 at the age of 68 removed Chiang Ching-kuo's only serious rival. He became vice-minister of defense in 1964 and minister in 1965, and after Ch'en's death it was widely assumed that he was being groomed as Chiang Kai-shek's successor.

Social change

The economic and political developments of the 1960s were accompanied by significant changes in education, urbanization, and the composition of the labor force. Level of education had long been associated with income and social status among the Chinese, and they traditionally sought the best education for their children, particularly sons. In Taiwan as early as 1950 a substantial number of girls also received education. In that year girls constituted more than one-third of the students in primary schools and one-fourth of those in secondary schools. At the college level, however, they constituted only about 11 percent of the student body. By 1960 the proportion of girls among primary school students had increased to nearly one-half, in secondary schools to 34 percent, and in higher education to 23 percent. As incomes rose during the 1960s, parents avidly sought more education for their children. The proportion of the population with primary education declined slightly by 1970, as a result of the decline in the population growth rate, but the proportions both of those with secondary education and of those with higher education doubled.

Illiteracy dropped from 27.1 percent of the population 6 years or older to 14.7 percent. The proportion of girls among secondary school students reached 44 percent and in higher educational institutions 36 percent. Enrollment increases at the secondary level resulted in part from the extension of free public education from six to nine years in 1968.

University graduates flocked in large numbers to the United States for graduate study, averaging 2,000 to 3,000 per year. Many of them became permanent residents of the United States, as there were numerous jobs available in the 1960s for holders of advanced degrees, especially in science and engineering. Only about 5 percent of those leaving for graduate study during this period returned. This "brain drain" had both good and bad effects. It deprived Taiwan of the services of talented persons in whose education the government had made a substantial investment. On the other hand, Taiwan could not have absorbed such a large number of highly educated people in the kinds of positions for which they were qualified. A surplus of highly educated, underemployed, and dissatisfied young people could have created political problems. The lure of graduate study in the United States kept many of Taiwan's best and brightest university students concentrating on their studies rather than, as in some other developing countries, turning their energies to political agitation. Moreover, the growing pool of well-trained Chinese in the United States with family ties in Taiwan could be drawn upon later as Taiwan's industry and scientific research became more sophisticated.

In common with many other developing countries, Taiwan was becoming more urbanized as industry and commerce expanded. The population of the large cities increased by 87 percent during the 1960s and that of the towns by 73 percent, whereas the population of the island as a whole was increasing by only 35 percent. The impact of urbanization on the society has not been thoroughly studied, but certain conclusions can be drawn from the data available.[19] The migration from rural to urban areas did not, as in many other places, result from population pressure on the land, for rural population growth had been more than offset by increases in agricultural yield. It seems to have resulted more from the availability of industrial and commercial jobs in the cities and the attractions of city life than a flight from grinding poverty. Urbanization reflected drastic changes in the composition of the labor force. The number employed in agriculture, fisheries, and forestry increased only 16 percent during the 1960s, while workers in the commerce, manufacturing, and ser-

19 See Emily Martin Ahern and Hill Gates, eds., *The anthropology of Taiwanese society*; and James C. Hsiung et al., eds., *The Taiwan experience, 1950–1980*.

vice sectors increased by 43, 82, and 115 percent, respectively. Rural-urban migration had a less disruptive effect on family life and traditional values than elsewhere, for the cleavage between urban and rural society was less sharp. The island was small, bus and train transportation was good, and it was relatively easy for migrants to the city to keep in touch with their home village. Many migrants, after a period in the city, returned to the village. One study concluded that for every four migrants who entered Taiwan's largest cities, three left.[20] The information gap between city dwellers and rural people was bridged by radios, owned by one in ten of the population, and daily newspapers that circulated throughout the island. Newspaper circulation and the publication of books and magazines soared during the decade.

NEW CHALLENGES, 1971–1978

During the 1970s Taiwan's ability to survive in a hostile environment was tested more severely than at any time since the late 1940s. It suffered heavy blows to its international position and to its economy. It also had to manage the transition from the rule of Chiang Kai-shek to that of a new political leader. Its ability to surmount these challenges and continue to advance and prosper testified to the soundness of the political and economic systems established in previous decades by Taiwan's governing elite.

Diplomatic setbacks

The decade began inauspiciously for Taiwan with the startling announcement from Washington in July 1971 that President Richard M. Nixon intended to visit Peking. He and his national security adviser, Henry Kissinger, had concluded that opening relations with the PRC would facilitate the settlement of the unpopular war in Vietnam and would give the United States greater leverage in seeking détente with the Soviet Union. They judged correctly that American public opinion on the China issue had changed and would support the move. The U.S. Congress, for the first time in twenty years, failed to adopt its customary resolution opposing entry of the PRC into the United Nations. President Nixon withdrew U.S. opposition to the admission of the PRC and, although his representatives worked to preserve a seat for Taiwan also, showed that he placed a low priority on that objective by sending Henry Kissinger to

20 Alden Speare, Jr. "Urbanization and migration in Taiwan," in Hsiung et al., *The Taiwan experience*, 281.

Peking at the height of the UN debate on the question. The members of the United Nations in October 1971 voted to admit the PRC and to expel Taiwan, because Peking had insisted that it would not join if Taiwan remained a member.

Once Taiwan had been ousted from the UN, most of the nations that still maintained diplomatic relations with it severed those relations and recognized the PRC as the sole legitimate government of China. One of the first to do so, in September 1972, was Japan, whose leaders were profoundly shocked by President Nixon's decision to change U.S. China policy without prior consultation with them. By 1977 only twenty-three countries still maintained diplomatic relations with Taipei. Taiwan's loss of its UN seat also greatly facilitated the PRC's campaign to have it expelled from other international organizations. Within a few years Taiwan had lost its membership in nearly all intergovernmental bodies and was steadily losing ground in the struggle to maintain its place in international nongovernmental organizations. The PRC was determined not only to prevent the government in Taiwan from claiming to represent China, but also to deny Taiwan international acceptance as a separate political entity. "One China, one Taiwan" was just as repugnant to Peking's leaders as "two Chinas."

Denied diplomatic relations with most countries, Taiwan was compelled to resort to unorthodox methods of maintaining international intercourse. Foreign trade was vital to its survival, for exports constituted half of its GNP. Japan was Taiwan's most important trading partner except for the United States, taking 12 percent of its exports and supplying 42 percent of its imports in 1972. Both Tokyo and Taipei wanted to maintain close substantive relations for political as well as economic reasons. As Foreign Minister Masayoshi Ohira said to his fellow members of the Liberal Democratic Party after diplomatic relations with Taipei had been ended: "There are strong and deep ties between Japan and Taiwan. Consequently, even if diplomatic relations are severed, administrative relations must be respected and treasured. So long as they do not touch upon the very roots of the maintenance of Japan-China relations, we intend to devote utmost efforts for the maintenance of administrative relations between Japan and Taiwan."[21]

Within three months after the severance of diplomatic relations Japan and Taiwan agreed on an unofficial arrangement to take their place.[22] The

---

21 *Asahi*, 1 October 1972.
22 David Nelson Rowe, *Informal diplomatic relations: the case of Japan and the Republic of China, 1972–74*, provides a detailed account of the unorthodox substitute for formal diplomatic relations created between Japan and Taiwan. See also Clough, *Island China*, ch. 7.

Japanese established an Interchange Association with an office in Taipei headed by a former Japanese ambassador, while Taiwan set up an East Asia Relations Association with offices in Tokyo, Yokohama, Osaka, and Fukuoka headed by a member of the Central Committee of the KMT. Both associations were staffed principally by active or retired foreign service personnel, assigned in a private capacity. Although these offices did not receive the full range of privileges and immunities accorded foreign diplomats, they enjoyed sufficiently special treatment to permit them to perform most of the functions normally carried out by diplomatic missions. Trade between Japan and Taiwan continued without interruption; imports from Japan quadrupled in value between 1972 and 1979, while exports increased sixfold. Japanese investments in Taiwan paused for a year, then resumed their upward trend.

The only serious disruption in substantive relations between Japan and Taiwan was the suspension of flights by their national airlines for more than a year in 1974–75. Taipei ordered the flights halted because of a slighting reference to the flag of the Republic of China made by Foreign Minister Ohira in connection with an announcement of the establishment of aviation relations with the PRC. Foreign airlines quickly picked up the traffic formerly carried by Japan Air Lines and China Airlines, so there was no interruption in air travel. Lengthy negotiations between the Interchange Association and the East Asia Relations Association and a mollifying statement in the Diet by Ohira's successor, Foreign Minister Kiichi Miyazawa, eventually brought about resumption of flights by China Airlines and a subsidiary of Japan Air Lines, Japan Asia Airways.

In order to promote trade throughout the world, Taiwan created a China External Trade Development Council (CETDC), a private organization supported by compulsory donations from exporters. Its offices abroad operated under various names, depending on the political posture of the country. In places where the use of the word "China" might cause problems, the office was referred to as representing the Far East Trade Services, Inc. Lacking consular officers in most countries, Taiwan devised various ways of providing visas to foreigners wanting to visit Taiwan. In West Germany, for example, travelers were able to obtain from the Taiwan Travel Service "letters of recommendation" that could be exchanged for entry visas upon arrival in Taiwan. The East Asia Relations Association in Tokyo provided visas bearing a stamp reading, "Chinese Embassy, Seoul, Korea." In Malaysia and Thailand visas were issued by China Airlines. The absence of diplomatic relations with many countries made it more difficult for Taiwan to work out problems requiring governmental action and imposed inconvenience and delay on the conduct of international relations, but did not significantly impair the substantive relationships that enabled Taiwan to continue to prosper as a separate political entity in the world community.

Of course, during most of the decade Taiwan continued to enjoy diplomatic relations with its most important supporter and trading partner, the United States, which accounted for 22–27 percent of Taiwan's imports during the 1970s and 34–42 percent of its exports. In the carefully drafted joint communiqué issued in Shanghai in February 1972 the United States agreed to "concrete consultations to further the normalization of relations" with the PRC, but made no commitment as to when or under what conditions normalization might be achieved. It stated that it did not challenge the position held by Chinese on both sides of the Taiwan Strait that there was but one China and that Taiwan was a part of it. Reaffirming an interest in the peaceful settlement of the Taiwan question by the Chinese themselves, the United States declared that it would reduce its military forces and installations in Taiwan as tension in the area diminished, with the ultimate objective of their total withdrawal. The communiqué symbolized an agreement between Washington and Peking to set aside the Taiwan issue for the time being in order to develop various kinds of relations with each other. The establishment of liaison offices in the two capitals in 1973 provided a mechanism for doing this. The communiqué and the exchange of liaison offices dismayed the government and people of Taiwan, who saw in them bad omens for the future, but they did not prevent the United States from strengthening its economic links with Taiwan at the same time as it developed relations with the PRC.

Soon after President Nixon's visit to China, the president of the U.S. Export-Import Bank arrived in Taiwan to offer long-term credits for public and private projects there. By 1975 the bank's loans and guarantees in Taiwan approached $2 billion, the bank's largest exposure in any country except Brazil. In 1973 the United States established a trade center in Taipei. American private investment continued to flow to Taiwan; American companies represented in the American Chamber of Commerce in Taipei increased from 60 to 200 between 1972 and 1975. Imports from the United States multiplied six times in value between 1971 and 1978, while exports increased over five times. Total two-way trade between the United States and Taiwan in 1978 reached $7.4 billion, compared with $1.1 billion between the United States and the PRC.

While economic ties between the United States and Taiwan were growing, the military relationship was changing. As promised in the Shanghai Communiqué, the United States gradually withdrew its military personnel from the island, cutting back from 10,000 in 1972 to 750 by late 1978.

In 1974 the U.S. Congress quietly repealed the Formosa Resolution of 1955. Taiwan continued to acquire military equipment from the United States, but was now buying it on credit or for cash rather than receiving it in the form of grants. The United States also continued to help Taiwan to improve its own arms industry, notably through approving an agreement with the Northrop Corporation for the coproduction in Taiwan of F-5 E fighter aircraft, beginning in 1974.

The flow of graduate students to the United States continued in the 1970s, although the number returning to Taiwan increased, particularly at the end of the decade when job opportunities for highly educated specialists increased in Taiwan and the recession in the United States reduced job opportunities there. Many parents sent children to study in the United States, not only for education and financial betterment, but also because a son or daughter who had acquired the right of permanent residence in the United States or American citizenship provided an escape hatch for their families in Taiwan should the island's security come under serious threat. The "green card" issued to those who had acquired the right of permanent residence in the United States became a prized possession.

Economic stress

The 1970s were notable for the first serious economic recession encountered by Taiwan after two decades of rapid economic growth. A boom in the first three years of the decade during which GNP grew at an average annual rate of 13 percent was halted abruptly by the sudden rise in oil prices, which struck Taiwan particularly hard because of its total dependence on imported oil. GNP growth dropped to 1.1 percent in 1974, and industrial production actually declined by 4.5 percent, the first decline in twenty years. The consumer price index shot up 47 percent. Taiwan proved exceptionally resilient, however, in coping with the crisis. The "ten big projects" discussed later in this section had been initiated at the beginning of the decade. Though opposed by some economists at the time for pumping too much government money into an overheated economy, they proved useful in counteracting the effects of the decline in private sector industrial production. The prompt adoption of draconian measures in early 1975 brought inflation for that year down to 5 percent. Large numbers of young women, laid off from their jobs in the textile industry, which was hard hit by a shrinking international market, returned to their farm homes. Families provided a substitute for nonexistent unemployment insurance. The economy gradually recovered during

1975, growing by a modest 4.5 percent, then rebounded in the later years of the decade, achieving a real annual growth averaging 12 percent from 1976 through 1979.

The rate of increase in agricultural production slowed during the 1970s, to an average annual rate of 2.3 percent. Rice production remained constant, the increases coming mainly in vegetables, fruit, and livestock. In an effort to sustain farm income, which had been declining relative to urban income, the government reversed its farm policy. In 1973 it abolished the rice-fertilizer barter system, thereby reducing the price of fertilizer and sharply increasing its use. It dropped compulsory purchases of rice at below market prices and began subsidizing rice farmers by buying at above market prices. Thus, instead of squeezing the farmer to produce capital for industry, as in the past, the government, like those of most industrialized countries, introduced agricultural subsidies. As they have elsewhere, these subsidies produced large rice surpluses and constituted a significant burden on the treasury, but were regarded as necessary to reduce the gap between urban and rural income and to prevent political dissatisfaction on the farms. By 1970 the number of workers engaged in agriculture had peaked. A growing labor shortage in the countryside spurred mechanization, and the number of power tillers, tractors, combines, rice dryers, and power sprayers in use increased fairly rapidly. Mechanization was retarded, however, by the small size of farms, averaging only about one hectare, making it difficult for individual farmers to afford the investment in mechanization. The government promoted various forms of cooperation among farmers to facilitate mechanization, but with only moderate success. Thus, at the end of the decade the government faced difficult decisions among a variety of competing objectives: retaining the family farm as the norm, substituting machines for increasingly scarce and costly agricultural labor, avoiding excessive rice surpluses and a heavy burden on the treasury, minimizing the gap between rural and urban incomes, and keeping Taiwan self-sufficient in basic foods.

The rate of increase in industrial production also slowed during the 1970s, but achieved a remarkable 15 percent average annual growth rate despite the drop in 1974 and the relatively small increase in 1975. Industrial production increased more rapidly than during the 1950s, but at a slower rate than in the boom years of the 1960s. The rapid increase in the share of industrial production in the private sector as compared with the public sector came to an end in the 1970s, the ratio stabilizing at approximately 81 percent for the private sector and 19 percent for the public sector. This change reflected the need for heavier government investments in infrastructure and in industrial projects too large to be financed by private entrepreneurs. The government-financed "ten big projects" included the construction of a new port at Taichung and the expansion of one at Suao, the construction of a north-south freeway and a new international airport, and railway electrification, as well as the construction of an integrated steel mill, a large shipyard, and new petrochemical plants.

Taiwan's two-way trade soared from $3.9 billion in 1971 to $31 billion in 1979. The proportion of industrial products in this trade continued to climb, from 81 percent in 1971 to 91 percent in 1979. Taiwan remained dependent on foreign trade for its survival and the government recognized the need to upgrade steadily the quality and sophistication of its exports in order to compete with countries with cheaper labor, such as the Philippines, Indonesia, and the PRC. During the 1970s Taiwan began to shift out of labor-intensive industry to capital-intensive and technology-intensive manufacturing. Locally manufactured machinery and equipment was increasingly substituted for items formerly imported and the export of capital goods to Southeast Asia and other developing countries began. The leadership sought through a larger investment in education and training, and probably more government intervention than in the past, to accomplish the transition from the predominantly family-owned small businesses to large-scale modern corporations capable of competing internationally in sophisticated products.

Political transition

Chiang Kai-shek was reelected president in 1972 at the age of 85 for another six-year term, but his health was failing and he had largely withdrawn from active participation in government. By this time the grooming of Chiang Ching-kuo as his successor was far advanced. After serving four years as vice-premier, he became premier in 1972. As premier he became in effect the top decision maker in the government, although he faithfully performed his filial duty of consulting with his father on important questions. When Chiang Kai-shek died in 1975, C. K. Yen, the vice-president, succeeded to the presidency, as provided by the constitution, but Chiang Ching-kuo became the real leader, for Yen was a technocrat with no political base. Chiang Ching-kuo was elected chairman of the KMT soon after his father's death and in 1978 was elected president of the ROC.

The authoritarian character of the political system did not change immediately under Chiang Ching-kuo, but his emphasis and style of governance differed substantially from that of his father. He sought to establish clearer lines of responsibility within the bureaucracy; factions and personal ties with the leader declined in importance. His practice of traveling about the island constantly in sport shirt and slacks to hear directly the views of soldiers, farmers, workers, and fishermen contrasted with Chiang Kai-shek's Confucian aloofness. He launched a well-publicized drive against corruption that led to the conviction of highly placed individuals. He continued his interest in youth activities developed during his twenty-one years as director of the China Youth Corps and appointed young men to high posts. Most important, he took a number of actions to improve the position of Taiwanese, appointing Taiwanese to the posts of vice-premier, governor, and other senior positions. He took a particular interest in promoting agricultural reforms aimed at improving the livelihood of the farmers, nearly all of whom were Taiwanese. Relations between mainlanders and Taiwanese had mellowed in the twenty-five years since the 2/28 incident, and the shock of President Nixon's change in policy toward the PRC highlighted the importance of cooperating with each other in facing the heightened threat from the mainland.

Martial law continued in effect during the 1970s and other forms of political control remained firmly in place, but Chiang Ching-kuo, influenced by some of the more liberal-minded among the senior leadership, permitted some broadening of political activity and debate. During 1971–72 lively political discussion among intellectuals at Taiwan National University appeared in the public print, touching on sensitive subjects such as the extent of academic freedom, the role of the security police, and the distribution of income. The government and party, responding gingerly but effectively, brought the debate back within the limits they considered proper. A new monthly, the *Taiwan Political Review*, which had audaciously quoted an anti-KMT intellectual abroad as saying that the choice for the people of Taiwan was either overthrowing the KMT and establishing an independent state or negotiating reunification with the PRC, was closed down in 1975 after only five issues, and the following year its editor was sentenced to ten years in prison for sedition. Some subjects remained taboo.[23]

A number of factors combined to produce pressures for political change during the 1970s. The decease at an accelerating rate of members of the national elective bodies who had been chosen on the mainland highlighted more insistently the need to rethink as a basic national policy that these organs must be representative of all China. Elections were held in 1972 and 1973 to add a small number of new members to the National

---

23 For an account of political trends in the early 1970s, see Mab Huang, *Intellectual ferment for political forms in Taiwan, 1971–1973.*

Assembly, Control Yuan, and Legislative Yuan, but these were palliatives, merely permitting postponement of the difficult task of devising a long-term solution. Local political activity became more vigorous, as Taiwanese politicians sought, within the limits permitted them, to gain greater influence within the system. They found new ways of appealing to the large numbers of migrants to the cities, no longer bound by their traditional local political loyalties and obligations. Rising levels of education increased popular interest in the voting process and affluent Taiwanese businessmen found it in their interest to contribute larger sums to the campaigns of particular candidates. In the provincial and local elections of 1977 nonparty candidates for the first time developed methods of cooperating on an island-wide basis. Some publicly warned the KMT against trying to manipulate election returns, and in Chungli, where a KMT official was suspected of tampering with ballots, a mob rioted, setting fire to police and fire department vehicles. The government showed great caution in containing the riot. Nonparty candidates won one-fifth of the seats, more than they had in the 1973 election, but not more than they had in some earlier elections. Tainan and Taichung, the third and fourth largest cities, both elected nonparty mayors. Nonparty politicians were much heartened by the election, which they perceived as a small but significant step toward a more democratic system.

Cultural and intellectual life

The Chinese culture transplanted from mainland China to Taiwan has undergone a vast transformation since the arrival of the Nationalist government. New shoots, imported from the West and grafted onto native Chinese stock, have produced myriad hybrids. New technology and mass education have given rise to a popular culture that is disseminated almost instantly throughout the island and is linked more and more closely to world cultural trends. Traditional Chinese cultural pursuits, despite official efforts to encourage them, attract a declining band of aficionados.

In their efforts to influence cultural trends, the KMT and the government have been buffeted by cross-currents. To support their struggle for survival against the Chinese Communist Party, the authorities wanted to enlist culture and the intellectuals in the service of anticommunism. For example, as early as 1950 the government established literature awards to encourage writers to produce "a positive literature in the defense of humanity and freedom against totalitarianism and Communism."[24] Much

---

24 Ch'i Pang-yuan et al., eds., *An anthology of contemporary Chinese literature: Taiwan, 1949–1974*, 2.1.

writing, especially in the 1950s, was colored by the need to paint the Communist mainland in the blackest colors and to avoid themes considered subversive to the government in Taiwan. The works of the leading Chinese writers of the 1930s, nearly all of them leftists who remained on the mainland, were banned in Taiwan.

Taiwan's leaders portrayed Taiwan as a repository for traditional Chinese culture, which the Chinese Communists by their inculcation of a foreign ideology were trying to destroy. The brutal attacks on the intellectuals in the Anti-Rightist Campaign and the Cultural Revolution and the wholesale destruction of books and art objects by Red Guards in the campaign against the "four olds" gave substance to the Nationalist charges. Nationalist leaders considered the emphasis on traditional Chinese culture vital, not only to draw as sharp a line as possible between themselves and the Chinese Communists and to increase Taiwan's attraction for the Overseas Chinese, but also to emphasize their commitment to "one China."

In order to strengthen the Taiwanese sense of belonging to the stream of Chinese culture, the government prohibited the importation of Japanese publications and motion pictures and banned the playing of Japanese songs on local radio stations. It introduced into the schools courses on Chinese history and civilization, stressing the inculcation of traditional Chinese values, such as respect for parents and for authority. During the 1960s it built the Palace Museum, an elegant showplace for the large collection of priceless Chinese art objects brought from the mainland. It sponsored innumerable exhibits of traditional Chinese painting and calligraphy by artists in Taiwan and performances of Chinese classical music. The military services supported four separate Peking Opera troupes, which performed not only for the armed services in Taiwan and on the offshore islands, but also for the public.[25]

Academic life was led by surviving members of the May Fourth generation. Lo Chia-lun headed the historiographical office that began compiling the official history of the 1911 Revolution and the Chinese Republic. Fu Ssu-nien, also a student leader at Peita in 1919, became president of Taiwan National University. The Academia Sinica Institute of History and Philology, which he had headed on the mainland, moved to new quarters for it and other institutes at Nan-kang, a Taipei suburb. Publication of documents from the foreign office (Tsung-li ya-men) archives on imperialist wars and Chinese domestic movements contributed to historical research worldwide.

25 See Irmgard Johnson, "The reform of Peking Opera in Taiwan," *CQ*, 57 (January–March 1974), 140–45.

Some of the mainland universities were reincarnated in Taiwan. Peking's Tsing-hua University and Shanghai's Chiao-t'ung University were reestablished in Hsinchu, where they provided scientific and engineering support to the Hsinchu Science-based Industrial Park. Chengchih University and National Central University, originally in Nanking, were relocated in Taipei and Chungli, respectively. Alumni of Soochow University established a new Soochow University in Taipei, and the Catholic Church, which had supported Fu Jen University in Peking, opened a Fu Jen University in Taipei. The United Board for Christian Higher Education in Asia established Tunghai University in Taichung. The former Tai-hoku Imperial University in Taipei became Taiwan National University, the island's most prestigious educational institution. These are only a few of the 105 schools of higher education that by 1987 had 443,000 students.

As time passed, the effort to weld the intellectuals of Taiwan into a uniform anticommunist phalanx as defenders of traditional Chinese culture came increasingly into conflict with ideas sweeping in from the West, particularly from the United States. In the official view, Taiwan was both a repository of Chinese tradition and a bastion of the free world. In order to retain the U.S. support deemed vital to Taiwan's survival, the authorities could not permit too great a gap to develop between the official rhetoric concerning freedom in Taiwan and the extent of freedom actually accorded the intellectuals. This basic political requirement, combined with the rapid modernization of Taiwan's society, widened the scope for intellectuals, particularly those from the younger generation who grew up in Taiwan, to experiment with Western themes and artistic forms in literature, music, drama, art, and dance.

The most remarkable feature of Taiwan's cultural transformation has been the spread of popular culture, a blend of the old and new, made possible by modern technology. The transistor radio emerged early and multiplied rapidly in numbers, enabling news broadcasts, Chinese opera, and popular music to be heard by millions throughout the island. Later, stereo systems playing records or tapes, often pirated and cheap, became popular. By 1980 many Taipei taxi drivers had installed tape decks so that they could listen to their own favorite music. Cassettes featuring Taiwan's leading singers of popular songs were eagerly sought by young people in the cities of mainland China.

Government-owned and private studios produced increasing numbers of motion picture films for use on the island and for distribution in Hong Kong and in Overseas Chinese communities in Southeast Asia and elsewhere. By the late 1970s Taiwan's studios were turning out 150 to 200 films a year, mainly historical dramas, *kung fu* films, romances, and comedies. In terms of quality, Taiwan's films did not rank with those produced by the best Japanese directors, but they reached a large audience. By the early 1980s TV had become the most effective means of reaching the public. The number of sets on the island exceeded 3 million in 1979, or nearly one set for every five persons.[26] Influenced by American television, but also incorporating modified elements of traditional Chinese culture, TV programming was devoted mainly to news and entertainment. Programs included variety shows, Taiwan opera, modern soap operas, historical plays, and some educational and public service features. The three networks, which by 1979 broadcast almost entirely in color, supported themselves by advertising.

The number of daily newspapers published in Taiwan has not varied much, remaining at about thirty for the past three decades. The circulation of the most popular newspapers has, however, risen dramatically with the rise in literacy and affluence, especially since 1965. The installation of modern high-speed presses and facsimile printers to speed up transmission of reports from various parts of the island have enabled the production of newspapers to meet the demand. Total circulation of the big four – the privately owned *China Times, United Daily News*, and *Taiwan Times*, and the KMT-owned *Central Daily News* – approached 3 million by 1980. The total circulation of all newspapers was between 4 million and 5 million, or approximately one copy for every four persons on the island.[27] The leading newspapers subscribe to the principal international news services, as well as Taiwan's Central News Agency's worldwide service, and publish a substantial amount of news from abroad. The *China Times* and the *United Daily News* contain literary supplements that provide important outlets for writers in Taiwan. The *United Daily News* produces an American edition, published in the United States for the Chinese community there.

Other aspects of cultural life range from the traditional Taiwanese *pai pai* celebrations – banquets in honor of local gods accompanied by opera and puppet shows in villages throughout Taiwan – to experimentation by avant-garde artists and writers with abstract art and with forms of writing used by symbolist and existentialist writers in the West. A vogue has developed for reviving and modernizing Chinese folk dances. A dynamic young dance company, the Cloud Gate Dance Ensemble, which combines Chinese and modern dance techniques in interesting ways, has performed in the United States and Europe.

---

26 *Statistical yearbook of the Republic of China, 1980*, 595.
27 Cho-yun Hsu, "Cultural values and cultural continuity," in Hsiung et al., *The Taiwan experience, 1950–1980*, 24.

Dramatic changes have occurred in Chinese fiction produced in Taiwan since the establishment of the Nationalist government there.[28] During the 1950s novels and short stories were politically inspired anticommunist works or escapist literature by mainlander writers drenched with nostalgia for the past life on the China mainland. T. A. Hsia commented at the end of that decade: "I do not know of a single novel published in Taiwan in the last ten years that deals, seriously or humorously, with the life of peasants, workers, or the petty-bourgeois class of teachers and government clerks to which the writers themselves, with few exceptions, belong."[29]

In 1960, however, a group of talented young Taiwan university students established the journal *Modern Literature* in which to publish their own writings and introduce in translation modern Western writers such as Kafka, D. H. Lawrence, Virginia Woolf, Joyce, Sartre, Fitzgerald, Faulkner, and Steinbeck. Cut off for political reasons from the mainstream of modern Chinese literature of the 1930s, which drew on Western literary techniques, these young writers had to begin anew the task of adapting modern Western ideas to the writing of Chinese fiction. The best of that work, such as Pai Hsien-yung's *Taipei people*, achieved a high level of artistic excellence. His writing and that of his colleagues Wang Wen-hsing, Ch'en Jo-hsi, and Ou-yang Tzu broke away from the stereotypes of the 1950s and made Taiwan's literary arena more lively and interesting. These writers have been criticized, however, for being more concerned with form than with content and for lacking the insight into the cultural and historical roots of the problems faced by individuals in present-day Taiwan.[30]

During the 1970s a new voice in Chinese fiction in Taiwan emerged: the Taiwan-born writer concerned with the lives of the poor and socially deprived, especially in the villages. These practitioners of the so-called *hsiang-t'u wen-hsueh*, or regional literature, such as Ch'en Ying-chen, Wang T'o, Wang Chen-ho, Yang Ch'ing-ch'u, and Huang Ch'un-ming, sprinkled their writing with Taiwanese colloquialisms and wrote about the distress of the "little people" from rural Taiwan caught up in the rapid social change produced by modernization. Some became political activists and were jailed for their activities. Ch'en Ying-chen served a seven-year sentence for "subversive activities," and Wang T'o and Yang Ch'ing-ch'u were sentenced to twelve years in 1980 for involvement in the December 1979 Kaohsiung riot.

---

28 See Jeannette L. Faurot, ed., *Chinese fiction from Taiwan: critical perspectives*.
29 C. T. Hsia, *A history of modern Chinese fiction 1917–1957*, appendix by T. A. Hsia, 511.
30 Leo Ou-fan Lee, "Modernism and romanticism in Taiwanese literature," in Faurot, *Chinese fiction from Taiwan*, 6–30.

In Taiwan, as elsewhere, writers of popular fiction far outsell both the "modernists" seeking innovative ways to use Western literary techniques in their writing and the "nativists" concerned with the impact of modernization on those on the bottom rung of the social ladder. The outstanding example is Ch'iung Yao, a writer who has produced twenty novels, most of them later made into motion pictures. She has developed a mass audience for her love romances with happy endings; her first novel, published in 1963, has been through thirty printings.[31]

The three cultural trends in Taiwan – a struggle to preserve aspects of traditional Chinese culture, efforts by intellectuals to produce original and innovative works of art and literature, and the emergence of a modernized mass culture – all can be discerned in mainland China also, but with significant differences. Children no longer chant the Confucian classics or spend long hours practicing calligraphy with the writing brush in either China or Taiwan. Few officials can compose poetry or paint. Classical art and literature have been largely relegated to the museums in both places. The mainland, however, has the great advantage over Taiwan of possessing renowned historic monuments, such as the Great Wall and the Forbidden City. Mainland archaeologists have continued to discover treasures from the past, including the spectacular tomb of Ch'in Shih-huang-ti at Sian. Traditional popular arts, suppressed during the Cultural Revolution – Chinese opera, acrobats, puppeteers and itinerant sword-swallowers – enjoyed a remarkable revival in the late 1970s, much to the delight of an entertainment-starved populace. Thus, the Peking government's emphasis on preserving China's cultural relics, its academies for traning young people in acrobatics, folk dancing, and Chinese opera, and a general loosening of restraints on traditional popular entertainment undermined Taiwan's claim to be the sole preserver of Chinese tradition.

In Taiwan traditional popular culture has been in retreat before the onrushing tide of modern, Western-influenced popular culture. Increasingly, Taiwan's popular culture has become internationalized and commercialized. On the mainland the demand for translations of Western books, the extraordinary popularity of the foreign films and TV programs shown in China, and the interest shown by young people in music from Taiwan and the West testified to the popular desire, at least in the coastal cities, for access to the world culture that had swept across Taiwan.

Those committed to serious literature and art enjoyed greater freedom to practice their skills in Taiwan than on the mainland. The compulsion in the communist system to make art "serve the people" in ways defined by the current leadership hobbled creativity. In Taiwan, on the other hand, while the KMT placed limits on the freedom to write on sensitive subjects, it did not try to force writers into a mold. Party officials may not have understood or approved of abstract art, but painters and sculptors were free to experiment. Over the years the creativity of Taiwan's artists and writers grew in liveliness and sophistication.

By 1980 some Taiwan fiction writers had seen their works published on the mainland. At the same time, the works of the great mainland authors of the 1920s and 1930s, such as Lu Hsun and Lao She, while still officially banned, were readily available to those who knew where to look in pirated editions of books published in Hong Kong. Thus, in the early 1980s cross-fertilization was beginning.

PRC overtures

After President Nixon's visit to China in 1972 and the issuance of the Shanghai Communiqué, the PRC redoubled its efforts to convince the government and people of Taiwan that "liberation" was inevitable. PRC spokesmen warned that the United States could not be relied on and called on the Taiwan authorities to begin negotiations for unification with the mainland. In contrast with the past, when such appeals were directed almost exclusively to mainlanders on Taiwan, Peking began to pay attention to the Taiwanese. It was evident to PRC leaders that mainlander dominance of the government in Taiwan would eventually come to an end and the Taiwanese majority would take over. When that time came, it was essential, they felt, that the leadership in Taiwan continue to hold to the one-China position.

Chou En-lai himself met with several groups of Overseas Chinese, including people of Taiwanese origin, in the early 1970s. He assured them that the incorporation of Taiwan into the PRC would not lower living standards on the island and that the transformation of the social and political system there would be gradual. He invited people from Taiwan to visit the mainland and see for themselves conditions there. He emphasized the great importance of the role of Taiwanese in "liberating" Taiwan. In such meetings both Chou and Teng Hsiao-p'ing stressed the need to work patiently over a long period of time to bring about unification, but they did not exclude the possibility of resort to force if peaceful methods failed. In their efforts to appeal to Taiwanese, PRC authorities noticeably softened their attitude toward the Taiwan independence movement, viewing its leaders as wrongheaded but capable of redemption.

While paying attention to the Taiwanese, the PRC did not neglect the mainlanders. It assured them that past sins, however serious, would be forgiven if they now worked for the unification of Taiwan with the motherland. It invited them to visit the mainland, openly or secretly. It freed several hundred senior Nationalist officials who had been in prison for twenty-five years or longer, as well as a substantial number of agents captured in the 1960s, allowing them to go to Hong Kong or Taiwan if they wished. But PRC appeals made no greater impact on Taiwan than they had in earlier years. "Our stance is that we will never establish any type of contact with the Communists," Premier Chiang Ching-kuo told the Legislative Yuan in 1976.[32] Few in Taiwan, either mainlander or Taiwanese, saw any personal advantage to be gained from Taiwan's coming under Peking's control. On the contrary, they feared that the standard of living in Taiwan would be brought down to the mainland level and they would be subjected to the same kind of oppressive controls imposed on mainland Chinese. Eyewitness accounts of conditions on the mainland relayed to them by the large numbers of Overseas Chinese visiting the PRC from the United States and Japan had little to appeal to them in comparison with the relatively comfortable life they enjoyed in Taiwan.

TAIWAN AFTER NORMALIZATION

During 1977 and 1978 the U.S. ambassador in Taipei warned Taiwan's leaders that the U.S. government was working toward the establishment of formal diplomatic relations with Peking. Nevertheless, the government and people of Taiwan were shocked when, on 15 December 1978, President Jimmy Carter announced the normalization of relations with the PRC with only a few hours' advance notice to Chiang Ching-kuo. The United States agreed to recognize the PRC as the sole legal government of China, to establish diplomatic relations with it on 1 January 1979, simultaneously breaking diplomatic relations with the ROC, to terminate the mutual defense treaty with the ROC by one year from that date, and to withdraw all remaining military personnel from Taiwan within four months. The joint communiqué agreed between Washington and Peking declared that the United States would maintain cultural, commercial, and other unofficial relations with the people of Taiwan. The United States also acknowledged "the Chinese position that there is but one China and Taiwan is part of China." In separate statements the U.S. government

---

32 *Daily Report: China*, 20, September 1976, B1.

stated that it continued to have an interest in the peaceful resolution of the Taiwan issue, which it expected to be settled peacefully by the Chinese themselves. The Chinese government declared that the method by which Taiwan would be reunited with the motherland was entirely China's internal affair. At a press conference in connection with the normalization announcement, Chinese Communist Party Chairman Hua Kuo-feng revealed that the two governments differed on the issue of arms sales to Taiwan. During the negotiations the United States had said that it would continue to supply limited amounts of defensive arms to Taiwan, to which the PRC did not agree.

Government officials in Taiwan immediately denounced the normalization agreement in bitter terms. When Deputy Secretary of State Warren Christopher arrived in Taiwan in late December to discuss postnormalization relations between Washington and Taipei, his delegation was met by an angry crowd shouting epithets and breaking through the police cordon to beat on the delegations' automobiles with sticks. Christopher rejected Chiang Ching-kuo's demand that some form of government-to-government relations be established between Washington and Taipei after the severing of diplomatic relations, as the U.S. government was committed to maintaining unofficial relations only.

Members of the U.S. Congress, displeased by what they regarded as insufficient advance consultation with them by the executive branch and dissatisfied with the draft legislation it had prepared to govern future relations with Taiwan, made extensive revisions in the draft and passed it as the Taiwan Relations Act in late March 1979.[33] The act conformed to the principle accepted by the Carter administration in its negotiations with Peking, that future relations with Taiwan be unofficial, and it provided for the establishment of a private agency, the American Institute in Taiwan, with offices in Washington and Taipei, to handle those relations. The act also provided the legal basis for continuing to treat Taiwan as a legal entity under U.S. law and for the continuation in force of existing treaties and agreements until changed. Provision was made for American

33 For the text of the act and an analysis of it, see Chiu, *China and the Taiwan issue*; for other analyses, see A. Doak Barnett, *U.S. arms sales: the China-Taiwan tangle*; Robert L. Downen, *Of grave concern: U.S.-Taiwan relations on the threshold of the 1980s*; William Kintner and John F. Copper, *A matter of two Chinas: the China-Taiwan issue in U.S. foreign policy*; Edwin K. Snyder, A. James Gregor, and Maria Hsia Chang, *The Taiwan Relations Act and the defense of the Republic of China*. See also *Implementation of the Taiwan Relations Act: the first year*, a staff report to the Committee on Foreign Relations of the U.S. Senate, June 1980; *Taiwan: one year after United States–China normalization*, a workshop sponsored by the Committee on Foreign Relations, U.S. Senate and Congressional Research Service, Library of Congress, June 1980; and *Oversight of the Taiwan Relations Act*, hearing before the Subcommittee on East Asian and Pacific Affairs of the Committee on Foreign Relations, U.S. Senate, 14 May 1980.

officials to be temporarily separated from their official positions to serve in the American Institute in Taiwan in a private capacity.

For the principal congressional architects of the act, however, its key provisions were those aimed at assuring Taiwan's security after the termination of the mutual defense treaty. The act made clear that the establishment of diplomatic relations with the PRC rested on the expectation that the future of Taiwan would be determined by peaceful means and that any effort to determine it by other than peaceful means would be of grave concern to the United States. It stated the U.S. intention to provide Taiwan with defensive weapons and to maintain the U.S. capacity to resist any resort to force or to other forms of coercion that would jeopardize the security, or the social or economic system, of the people of Taiwan.

The authorities in Taiwan, while still much worried about the implications of the drastic change in U.S. policy for the future of the island, welcomed the Taiwan Relations Act and began to accommodate to the new situation. They set up a Coordination Council for North American Affairs as their unofficial counterpart of the American Institute in Taiwan to carry out the functions formerly performed by the embassy and consular offices in the United States. The PRC vigorously protested the Taiwan Relations Act as violating the terms of the normalization agreement and constituting interference in Chinese domestic affairs. Having made their position clear for the record, however, they did not immediately pursue the issue and went ahead with the establishment of extensive relations with the United States during 1979 and 1980.

In the latter part of 1980 PRC leaders became increasingly concerned about relations between the United States and Taiwan. They were disturbed by the Carter administration's decision to permit American aircraft companies to discuss with Taiwan the possible purchase of an advanced fighter aircraft and the signing of an agreement between the American Institute in Taiwan and the Coordination Council for North American Affairs on privileges and immunities, approximating those enjoyed by diplomatic missions. President Ronald Reagan's pro-Taiwan statements during the election campaign of 1980, including a statement of intention to "upgrade" relations with Taiwan, further alarmed Peking. In official statements and published commentaries the PRC began to remind Washington that it had never agreed to continued arms sales to Taiwan. Chinese leaders underlined their opposition to foreign arms supply to Taiwan by downgrading relations with the Netherlands to the chargé level in March 1981 because the Dutch had sold two submarines to Taipei. By the fall of 1981 they were warning Washington that relations between the two countries would deteriorate unless the United States set a date by which its weapons sales to Taiwan would end.

Long-drawn-out negotiations finally produced a carefully crafted joint communiqué issued on 17 August 1982 in which the United States, in the light of the conciliatory policy toward Taiwan followed by the PRC since 1 January 1979 and a reaffirmation in the communiqué that peaceful reunification of Taiwan was its "fundamental policy," stated that it did not intend to carry out a long-term policy of arms sales to Taiwan, that its arms sales would not exceed in quantity or quality the levels of recent years, and that it would reduce gradually its sales of arms to Taiwan,[34] leading over a period of time to the final resolution of the issue. Taiwanese officials sharply criticized the communiqué for contradicting the letter and spirit of the Taiwan Relations Act. They expressed regret that the United States had refused to sell them an advanced fighter aircraft, although they were somewhat mollified by the U.S. decision to extend the coproduction agreement to provide an additional sixty F-5 E fighters. Meanwhile, the *People's Daily*, while welcoming the agreement, declared in an editorial that "the clouds hanging over Sino-U.S. relations have not been completely cleared away." It expressed the hope that "the U.S. government will truly live up to its promises by honestly but not perfunctorily reducing its arms sales to Taiwan," so that the problem could "be resolved thoroughly and at an early date."[35]

Peking-Taipei interaction

In agreeing to phase down arms sales to Taiwan, the United States had relied heavily on proposals for peaceful reunification of Taiwan with the mainland made by the PRC. Simultaneously with the establishment of diplomatic relations with the United States, Peking announced an end to the bombardment of the offshore islands with shells loaded with propaganda leaflets, which had been carried out on odd days of the month since the early 1960s. Mainland TV carried an unprecedented nonpolitical documentary on Taiwan, showing its scenic beauty and bustling streets, and the PRC media began to refer to Taiwan's leaders as "the Taiwan authorities" instead of "the Chiang clique." The National People's Congress appealed to Taiwan to authorize trade with the mainland, personal visits, and the opening of shipping and postal services. The message said that China would respect the status quo in Taiwan and would adopt reasonable policies in settling the question of reunification so as not to

34 The text of the joint communiqué is in *NYT*, 18 August 1982.
35 *Washington Post*, 18 August 1982.

cause the people of Taiwan any losses. Vice-Premier Teng Hsiao-p'ing went further, assuring a visiting delegation of U.S. senators that after reunification Taiwan would be fully autonomous, retaining its existing social and economic system and its armed forces. Teng told the senators that the PRC would use force against Taiwan only if the authorities there refused indefinitely to negotiate or if the Soviet Union interfered.

In September 1981 Yeh Chien-ying, chairman of the Standing Committee of the National People's Congress, made a comprehensive nine-point proposal on reunification, offering Taiwan a "high degree of autonomy" as a special administrative region with its own armed forces. He said that the central government would not interfere with local affairs in Taiwan and that its socioeconomic system and economic and cultural relations with foreign countries would remain unchanged. There would be no encroachment on proprietary rights, the right of inheritance of private property or foreign investments, Yeh promised. Yeh also offered economic assistance to Taiwan and posts of leadership in national political bodies on the mainland for Taiwanese officials. He called on representatives of the KMT to meet with Chinese Communist Party officials for an exhaustive exchange of views on reunification.[36]

The Taiwanese authorities flatly rejected Yeh's proposals, as they had previous overtures from Peking, reiterating their policy of having no negotiations and no contacts with the PRC. They characterized the proposals as propaganda aimed primarily at the United States and intended to persuade Washington that Taiwan had no need for American arms. They pointed out the inconsistency between Yeh's offer to permit Taiwan to retain its own armed forces and the PRC's efforts to bar Taiwan from obtaining new weapons for those forces from the United States or elsewhere. Any genuine PRC proposal to negotiate would be made secretly, they asserted, not in the public media. The basic fear in Taiwan, widely felt within the government and among the public, was that if the Taiwanese authorities ever began to negotiate the terms by which the island would become a subordinate region within the PRC, they would be on a slippery slope leading to eventual control by Peking and the imposition of the communist system in Taiwan. They lacked confidence in the promises made by PRC leaders, for even if the aging Teng Hsiao-p'ing should be sincere, there was no assurance that his successors would carry out his commitments. Peking's refusal to exclude the use of force against Taiwan added to their apprehension.

Despite the impasse with regard to negotiations, various forms of

36 For the text of Yeh's statement, see *Beijing Review*, 24.40 (5 October 1981).

unofficial contact between the people of Taiwan and the Chinese on the mainland steadily increased between 1979 and 1982. Two-way trade, which had been negligible before 1978, grew to some $500 million by 1981, conducted mostly by way of Hong Kong. A compromise reached in the International Olympic Committee and later extended to other international sports federations, accepting the mainland organization as the "Chinese Olympic Committee" and its Taiwan counterpart as the "Chinese Taipei Olympic Committee," enabled teams from both to compete in international sports events. Scientists from Taiwan and the mainland met with increasing frequency at international conferences. Scholars and students from both places studying in American universities and elsewhere came to know each other. Although direct correspondence between Taiwan and the mainland was forbidden by the government in Taiwan, the exchange of letters between relatives via friends or relatives in Hong Kong, the United States, or Japan became increasingly common. A small number of persons in Taiwan even visited their relatives on the mainland without being arrested, although it was technically illegal for them to do so. Through these various forms of interchange people were coming to have a more realistic view of conditions on either side of the Taiwan Strait.

Political strains and economic recession

Taiwan had scheduled elections for the Legislative Yuan and National Assembly to take place in December 1978. Opposition politicians, showing new aggressiveness and confidence after the successes scored by nonparty candidates in the 1977 local elections, coordinated their islandwide activities more closely than before and proclaimed more boldly demands for an end to martial law, the release of political prisoners, and an increase in the number of elected officials. The unexpected announcement of U.S. normalization of relations with Peking a few days before the elections were to have taken place caused the government to postpone them. In the tense atmosphere immediately following U.S. severance of diplomatic relations, the government jailed a Taiwanese opposition politician and his son for alleged association with a communist agent and suspended a nonparty county magistrate, in part for having attended a demonstration protesting the former's imprisonment.

The trend toward more open debate of sensitive issues was checked by the temporary ascendancy of conservative KMT elements who demanded unity at a time of national crisis, but soon resumed. In February 1979 the government, influenced by more liberal-minded KMT leaders, lifted a

one-year ban on the registration of new periodicals. New political journals quickly appeared, ranging in views from the stridently anticommunist *Chi Feng* to the strongly anti-KMT *Mei Li Tao* (Formosa
Magazine). In the middle ground were journals backed by moderate
KMT members and middle-of-the-road opposition politicians. A lively
political debate soon developed, unprecedented in its public treatment of
sensitive topics. Political commentators put forward concrete proposals
for far-reaching political and judicial reform, demanded the right to form
opposition parties, and harshly criticized the KMT.

A number of prominent Taiwanese opposition politicians, headed by
Legislative Yuan member Huang Hsin-chieh, associated themselves with
Mei Li Tao, which styled itself "The Magazine of Taiwan's Democratic
Movement." The principal objective of the *Mei Li Tao* group was a new
government elected by the people of Taiwan and, by implication, an
independent state of Taiwan, although this goal could not be publicly
proclaimed. The group quickly established ten branch offices around the
island, each headed by a prominent local Taiwanese opposition politician,
and began to hold anti-KMT receptions and rallies. The group became, in
effect, a shadow political party, united in its opposition to the KMT but
loosely organized and lacking in discipline. It became the prime target of
the hard-line *Chi Feng*, which virulently denounced it as procommunist.
As its rallies became larger and noisier, it was criticized not only by
Taiwanese politicians within the KMT but also by moderate Taiwanese
opposition politicians, who felt it was unwisely provoking a showdown
with the KMT.

The showdown came on 10 December 1979. A demonstration organized in Kaohsiung by the *Mei Li Tao* group ended in a riot. Fourteen of
the leaders of the group were arrested. Eight, including Legislative Yuan
member Huang Hsin-chieh, were convicted of sedition and sentenced to
prison terms ranging from twelve years to life.[37] The government thus
eliminated at one stroke the principal leaders of the radical wing of the
Taiwanese opposition. In retrospect it is evident that the *Mei Li Tao*
group overestimated their public support and underestimated the determination and capability of the government not to permit any political
group to stir up popular passions against the KMT with an appeal to
"Taiwan for the Taiwanese." Although the majority of Taiwanese
favored greater influence for Taiwanese in the national government,
many disapproved of the methods used by the *Mei Li Tao* group. A con-

37 John Kaplan, *The court-martial of the Kaohsiung defendants.*

sensus among Taiwanese and mainlanders alike strongly favored gradual political reform by orderly means over mass confrontation with the ruling party that could jeopardize the political stability, public order, and economic growth from which nearly all had benefited.

The Kaohsiung incident and the convictions that followed ushered in a period of tighter controls on political debate. The Legislative Yuan passed a new election law designed to preserve the predominant position of the KMT and prevent public disorders during election campaigns, but still permit opposition candidates to run with some prospect of success. Under the new law the Legislative Yuan and National Assembly elections of 1980 (those originally scheduled for December 1978 and postponed) and the provincial and local elections of 1981 proceeded smoothly, although larger amounts of money were spent by candidates in the latter elections than ever before and vote buying was widely criticized in the media.

Taiwan suffered from the world recession beginning in 1979, but the severing of diplomatic relations by the United States had no perceptible adverse effect on its economy. Taiwan's gross national product (GNP) increased by 8 percent in 1979 and 6.8 percent in 1980. New foreign investment hit a record high of $329 million in 1979 and surged to $466 million in 1980. Taiwan had no difficulty in securing foreign loans. It borrowed more than $1.2 billion from American, European, and Japanese banks during 1980, but its long-term foreign debt totalled only $5 billion and its debt-service ratio was in the neighborhood of 6 percent, extraordinarily low for a developing country. Foreign banks were eager to open branches in Taiwan and the government had to place a limit on the number admitted each year in order to hold down competition. Eight foreign banks opened branches in Taipei in 1980, five of them European, making a total of twenty-three foreign banks with branches in Taiwan as of early 1981.

Two-way trade with more than a hundred countries exceeded $39 billion in 1980. Economic decision makers emphasized trade with Western Europe, partly in order to diversify Taiwan's trading pattern, but also to raise its visibility among Europeans and build political support for the long run. Trade with Western Europe increased faster than overall trade, and in 1980 the EEC countries became Taiwan's second largest market, surpassing Japan. In a departure from its stringent anticommunist posture of the past, the government in 1979 removed the ban on direct trade with five Eastern European countries and permitted indirect trade with the rest.

Looking back and looking ahead

Taiwan's history since 1949 has two main strands: externally, the struggle for survival in the face of a massive threat; and internally, the modernization of an agrarian society.

Survival was made possible by the hundred-mile-wide moat that separated the island from the mainland and the support and protection extended by the United States. The water barrier made successful invasion by PRC forces impossible, so long as the U.S. Seventh Fleet was committed to preventing it. An island was also much easier to protect against infiltration and subversion than was a mainland province. Even after the termination of the United States–Republic of China security treaty at the end of 1979, the Taiwan Strait, defended by Taiwan's 500,000 U.S.-equipped armed forces, was a formidable obstacle. The United States continued to be Taiwan's main source of new weapons and military spare parts after the termination of the security treaty. U.S. support was not only vital to Taiwan's defense, but also for many years maintained the status of the Republic of China in the international community and provided the economic aid that contributed importantly to Taiwan's economic takeoff. It provided the people of the island with a breathing space that they used well, so that by the 1970s, when the United States began to cut back its support out of deference to its newly established relations with the PRC, they were much more self-confident and self-reliant.

Taiwan not only survived, it prospered. Per capita GNP soared from around U.S. $200 in the early 1950s to U.S. $1,800 in 1982. It is far advanced in the transformation from an agrarian to an industrial society. Along with South Korea, Singapore, and Hong Kong it became known as one of the "four tigers" of the western Pacific, outstanding among developing countries for their rapid economic growth, based heavily on foreign trade. The example of these countries, together with that of Japan, may have been partly responsible for China's decision under Teng Hsiao-p'ing to expand its foreign trade and use material incentives to spur agricultural and industrial production. Taiwan's exceptional economic growth was brought about, however, by a number of factors discussed earlier in this chapter, not all of which could be replicated by the PRC: the relatively developed base left by the Japanese; the influx of large numbers of experienced administrators and technicians from the mainland; the large amount of U.S. economic aid in the early years; the land reform; the stress on education; the decision to switch to export-led industrial growth in the early 1960s, just as a period of unprecedentedly rapid expansion of world trade was getting under way; the encouragement given to private enterprise; conservative but flexible monetary and fiscal policies; and the willingness of the top leaders to rely on the advice of able technocrats.

Economic progress was made possible by a stable political environment. Political stability, in turn, depended in considerable degree on economic progress – the two were reciprocally supportive. People who saw their standard of living rising year by year and who were optimistic that their children could look forward to a still better life could not easily be stirred by revolutionary rhetoric to support confrontational politics or the use of violence to force political change. The great majority felt more comfortable with the government's emphasis on law and order and its commitment to gradual, incremental change. Other factors that made for a political stability unusual among developing countries were the accepted legitimacy of the top leaders, the firm but only moderately repressive rule of the KMT, and the threat from the communist system on the mainland, which was widely seen as far more repressive. Moreover, the early institution of local elections, the admission of large numbers of Taiwanese to the KMT, and the appointment of Taiwanese to increasingly senior positions in the government and party helped to moderate differences between the mainlander leadership and the bulk of the people.

During the late 1980s, despite a slowing in the growth of world trade, Taiwan was successful in expanding its exports and in continuing its rapid economic growth. By the end of 1987, per capita GNP had grown to $5,000 and foreign exchange reserves had surged to an astonishing $76 billion, a level exceeded only by West Germany and Japan. Friction over trade issues developed between the United States and Taiwan because of the large deficit in U.S. trade with Taiwan. Under U.S. pressure, Taiwan reluctantly reduced trade barriers and allowed the appreciation of its currency against the U.S. dollar. Taiwan faced several serious economic problems, particularly the need to shift out of labor-intensive manufactures to more sophisticated products rapidly enough to keep ahead of its competitors. It also needed to modernize its banking system in order to stimulate domestic investment. Its problems – an excess of exports, savings, and foreign exchange reserves – were the opposite of those confronted by most developing countries, and the prospects for Taiwan's skilled economic managers to make the necessary adjustments were good.

Responding to pressures from the increasingly affluent middle class and a well-educated younger generation, Chiang Ching-kuo in 1986 announced his intention to end martial law, lift the ban on new political parties, and permit the establishment of new newspapers. Most of the opposition leaders jailed as a result of the 1979 Kaohsiung riot were released and some became leading figures in a new opposition political party, the Democratic Progressive Party. Restrictions on political debate were greatly eased and politics became more lively. Street demonstrations on a variety of issues became commonplace. By the early 1990s nearly all members of the Legislative Yuan, the National Assembly, and the Control Yuan elected on the mainland in 1947 and 1948 will have died or retired and will have been replaced by younger politicians elected by the people of Taiwan. The KMT probably will retain its position as the dominant party, but it will face increased competition from the Democratic Progressive Party and other new parties.

The process of democratization, which is unlikely to be reversed, will increasingly bring Taiwanese into top positions in the KMT and the government, as symbolized by Taiwanese native Lee Teng-hui's assumption of the positions of president and acting chairman of the KMT immediately after Chiang Ching-kuo's death in January 1988. The "Taiwanization" of the leadership raises the question of whether the new leaders will drop the "one China" position and declare Taiwan an independent state. The PRC's threat to prevent secession by military force is a powerful deterrent to such action. More likely is a continuation of Taiwan's ambiguous status as a de facto independent political entity and a further increase in trade and other forms of interaction between Taiwan and the mainland, a trend that gained momentum after Chiang Ching-kuo's decision in 1987 to allow visits to relatives on the mainland.

If tension between Taiwan and the PRC declines further and a stable state of peaceful coexistence develops, the risk of military action against Taiwan will also decline and the diminishing flow of weapons from the United States, as provided for in the U.S.-PRC joint communiqué of August 1982, will not adversely affect Taiwan's security. Should this trend be reversed for any reason, the United States, as well as the two Chinese parties, would face difficult decisions.

EPILOGUE: THE ONUS OF UNITY

In the preface to Volume 14, we said that a rounded perspective on the Communist enterprise in China might be possible only after a century. An epilogue appended to the final volume of a history of China covering two thousand years is a hazardous venture. Yet to take our narrative so close to the present and not offer some contemporary reflections seems craven, even if the result will only provide harmless amusement for future historians.

In our introduction to these final two volumes, entitled "The Reunification of China," we pointed out that "*a billion or so Europeans in Europe and the Americas live divided into some fifty separate and sovereign states, while more than a billion Chinese live in only one state.*"[1] We rejected geography and ethnic diversity as sufficient explanations for the failure of Europeans to revive the Roman empire, as compared with the success of the Chinese in restoring theirs. We argued, rather, that the disorder of the Warring States period (403–221 B.C.) led Chinese political philosophers such as Confucius to enshrine peace and order as central ideals, thus transforming unity into an overriding political goal. Once achieved, unity was preserved by the invention of bureaucratic government.[2] The bureaucracy's function was facilitated by the unifying symbol of the emperor and legitimized by a universal ideology of which it was the guardian.

Placed in that long historical trajectory, the Chinese Communists can be seen as another unifying "dynasty," equipped with "imperial" chairman, bureaucracy, and ideology. Yet their achievement, so startling to contemporaries, pales by comparison with that of the Ch'in (221–206 B.C.), who imposed the first true empire upon the chaos of the Warring States, and the Sui (A.D. 589–617), who reestablished the Ch'in-Han system after three centuries of disunity, thereby transforming it from a vanished ideal into the norm of political organization for another thirteen hundred years. The feat of Mao and his colleagues in setting up their

---

1 John K. Fairbank, "The reunification of China," *CHOC*, 14.14; emphasis in original.
2 Ibid., 19–20.

regime after fewer than forty years of disorder resembles more the relatively speedy takeovers by the Han, T'ang, Ming, and Ch'ing.

Whatever the extent of their achievement, the Communists' commitment to unity had the support of all patriotic Chinese. The Nationalists would obviously have preferred a China united under their own banner, but no one questioned that age-old ideal, especially after the fragmentation of the warlord era from 1916 to 1928. Indeed, if unity was "the legitimator of dynasties," as we put it, then the CCP's success in uniting mainland China, which Chiang Kai-shek had never achieved, conferred upon it the traditional "mandate of heaven."

Implicit in most histories of China is acceptance of and indeed admiration for the unifying imperative of Chinese politics.[3] Yet looked at from today's perspective, after forty years of Communist rule, negative consequences of that historic Chinese achievement are beginning to emerge.

As we pointed out, governing the vast Chinese population as a unit is a "gargantuan task." Traditionally, the emperors had claimed absolute rights over the lives and ideas of their citizens. In practice, the steel frame of the imperial civil service was able to maintain only general and superficial oversight of law and order and the economy, and, especially after the population explosion in the eighteenth century, was heavily dependent on local gentry for detailed supervision of society. While the gentry subscribed to the bureaucracy's desire for stability and to its Confucian ideology, the imperial pattern of rule permitted great diversity of custom and belief, as well as freedom of economic activity, among the population at large. That equilibrium between center and locality, state and society was destabilized by the Communists.

During its decades in the wilderness, the CCP had been honed under Mao into a superb instrument for control and mobilization: "Fortunately for the CCP, the modern development of transport and communications, of firepower and police networks, had given the new government of the People's Republic various means to control the Chinese state and, for a time, the society."[4] CCP cadres penetrated the remotest villages.

The superior organizational and technical resources of the CCP were not all that differentiated it from the traditional mandarinate. Even more significant was its Promethean urge to change nature. This alteration of ethos from the traditional acceptance of the natural order compares with the innovative breakthroughs of the Ch'in and Sui. The mandarinate had been committed to a steady-state agrarian society; now the CCP was bent on transforming China into a modern industrialized nation, and at a rapid rate.

3 Ibid., 21.

As a result of its advantages and in line with its aims, by 1957 a

strong centralized state had been established after decades of disunity, China's national pride and international prestige had grown significantly as a result of fighting the world's greatest power to a stalemate in Korea, the country had taken major steps on the road to industrialization and achieved an impressive rate of economic growth, the living standards of its people had made noticeable if modest progress, and the nation's social system had been transformed according to Marxist precepts in relatively smooth fashion.[5]

Abroad, especially in non-communist Asia, the CCP's achievements were regarded with awe.

But the tools of success were also weapons of destruction, when the aims were pursued with arrogant fervor. The CCP could train downtrodden peasants into victorious soldiers and transform smallholders into collective farmers, but it could also mobilize them for the disastrous Great Leap Forward in which millions perished.[6] Only in a state as united and controlled as China could so terrible a calamity have taken place nationwide.

If the GLF underlined the negative aspect of the combination of transformative goals and mobilizational skills, the Cultural Revolution exposed the disastrous consequences of the newfound ability to inculcate a national ideology directly from the center. Imperial Confucianism had inevitably been adulterated by the time it filtered down to the grass roots, but pure Mao Tse-tung Thought could be transmitted directly throughout the land by radio, television, and the circulation of millions of "little red books."

The Cultural Revolution also magnified another aspect of the traditional political culture: the power of the imperial symbol. The emperor had been dependent mainly on sober mandarins and gentry to inspire and maintain respect for him, and they had their own national and local agendas, whereas the cult of the "imperial" Chairman could be nurtured by direct contact between Mao and fervent Red Guards and opportunistic acolytes, and spread abroad by them and by incessant media propaganda. In the name of Mao and his Thought, numberless atrocities could be committed and the country could be brought to the brink of anarchy.

By Mao's death in 1976, the disastrous consequences of combining the traditional stress on unity and the traditional political instruments for preserving it – emperor, bureaucracy, and ideology – with modern propaganda and organization, plus the modern goal of transforming society,

---

5 Frederick C. Teiwes, "Establishment and consolidation of the new regime," *CHOC*, 14.51.
6 See Nicholas Lardy, "The Chinese economy under stress, 1958–1965," *CHOC*, 14.360–97; Roderick MacFarquhar, *The origins of the Cultural Revolution, 2: the Great Leap Forward 1958–1960.*

was clear for all to see. The mixture was so powerful that China had been brought successively to the brink of economic ruin and political anarchy.

Teng Hsiao-p'ing's actions after his assumption of paramount power at the Third Plenum of the Eleventh Central Committee in December 1978 suggested that he had learned at least some of these lessons. He did not abandon the notion of unity, for its restoration had been too central a goal of the Communist revolution; nor did he abandon the hope of transforming society, another central revolutionary goal. But he did alter the role of the traditional political instruments and moderate the use of the modern techniques that had rendered them so devastating. He tried to diminish the critical role of the "imperial" symbol by personally eschewing the formal leading roles in Party and state and, unlike Mao, genuinely sought to assign increasing power to his chosen successors. He diminished the role of ideology and he also encouraged the unleashing of society from the bonds of bureaucratic rule, a process initiated by Mao's assault on the CCP during the Cultural Revolution.

Mao had long railed against bureaucrats, particularly when he felt they were trying to tie his hands. He became convinced that the CCP, once in power, had served to suppress the people rather than to unleash them. Teng appeared to share Mao's view, though mainly about the deadening effect of Party control on the economy. He cut back the role of the Party by unshackling the peasantry from collectivism and encouraging private enterprise in the urban areas. He undermined the role of ideology, already on the retreat as a result of the hyperbole of the Cultural Revolution, by extolling practice as the sole criterion of truth. The media ceased to be primarily an instrument of ideological indoctrination.

But there was one profound difference between Mao and Teng: Whereas Mao appeared to revel in upheaval or *luan*, Teng abhorred it, especially after he had witnessed the national chaos and personal tragedies resulting from the Cultural Revolution. Like China's traditional political philosophers he sought peace and order, and saw national unity as their necessary prerequisite.

Yet Teng's reform program had undermined the symbols and instruments that had ensured order and unity, and had not substituted new ones. As an increasingly diverse society began to flex its muscles and make new demands on the state from the mid-1980s on, the state had only one instrument for ensuring order and unity, the PLA.

The suppression of the prodemocracy movement in T'ien An Men Square by tanks in mid-1989 exposed the political vacuum at the heart of Teng Hsiao-p'ing's reform program. It laid bare the continuing fundamental problem for Chinese politicians attempting to lead their country into the modern world: how to maintain the unity of a billion persons while allowing them sufficient political, economic, and social freedom to make their country prosper.

The Communists, like the Confucians before them, have feared factionalism and suppressed provincialism. This has been their onus of unity. In this light, the European inability to preserve or restore Roman unity was not failure but actually the key to Europe's pluralistic future. In his analysis of the impact of the fall of the western Roman empire, Gibbon pointed to the benefits of what would have been for Chinese a traumatic experience:

Europe is now divided into twelve powerful, though unequal kingdoms, three respectable commonwealths, and a variety of smaller, though independent states: the chances of royal and ministerial talent are multiplied, at least, with the number of its rulers.... The abuses of tyranny are restrained by the mutual influence of fear and shame; republics have acquired order and stability; monarchies have imbibed the principles of freedom, or, at least, of moderation; and some sense of honour and justice is introduced into the most defective constitutions by the general manners of the times. In peace, the progress of knowledge and industry is accelerated by the emulation of so many active rivals; in war, the European forces are exercised by temperate and undecisive contests.[7]

Gibbon went on to argue that modern freedom was secured by the emergence of this new European polity comprising a concert of smaller, independent states hammered out of the fragments of the old empire. The rivalry associated with the balance of power was greatly preferable to the stifling, deadening uniformity of empire. After the experience of twentieth-century slaughter and holocaust, one winces at Gibbon's eighteenth-century insouciance about "temperate and undecisive" war. But his confident assertion that the failure to reestablish the Roman empire was beneficial for Europeans because it liquidated a stifling uniformity and encouraged a productive international emulation is relevant today, and particularly for China.

In this age of nationalism and especially of China's cultural nationalism, no Chinese statesman can contemplate dissolving a 2,000-year-old state. But Peking politicians inevitably must acknowledge the necessity of institutional innovation in politics as well as in the economy. As many Chinese and foreign observers have told them, one cannot move far toward a free market for goods without permitting a free market for ideas, nor sponsor economic initiatives without creating channels of political expression and participation.

7 Edward Gibbon, *The decline and fall of the Roman Empire*, 2.95.

On this frontier of development, history may offer suggestions. The success stories of Taiwan and Singapore suggest that in a trading community, a strong but supportive Chinese bureaucracy can maintain political control and simultaneously allow and indeed encourage industry and commerce. In Hong Kong, Chinese entrepreneurs have proved that they can develop dynamically even under an alien bureaucracy that is content simply to stand by and let trade expand.

In the PRC, five Special Economic Zones and the fourteen ports open for foreign trade testify to the ingenuity of mainland economic reformers. What political equivalents can be imagined? How can the world's most populous state with the longest political continuity re-create its polity? The American example of federalism was contemplated by some in the 1920s. As of 1990, the modification of party dictatorship was under way in Taiwan, Eastern Europe, and even the Soviet Union.

Of course, the mandarins running the three "little dragons" have only relatively tiny populations to worry about compared with that of the mainland, and they preside over a public mainly devoted to urban life and commerce instead of still mired in the remote villages of a largely agrarian subcontinent. But that only underlines the urgency for the CCP to find forms of political, economic, and social disaggregation if China's modernization is not to founder. The dead hand of the central bureaucracy must not be allowed to stifle the talents of the people.

Both Mao and Teng have understood this in their different ways. In July 1957, Mao called on his colleagues "to create a political climate in which there is both centralism and democracy, discipline and freedom, unity of purpose and personal ease of mind and liveliness"[8] as the basis for developing China. At the historic Third Plenum in December 1978, Teng repeated that call, and put it in a more concrete context:

At present, we must lay particular stress on democracy, because for quite a long time democratic centralism was not genuinely practised: centralism was divorced from democracy and there was too little democracy. Even today, only a few advanced people dare to speak up.... If this doesn't change, how can we persuade everyone to emancipate his mind and use his head? And how can we bring about the four modernizations?[9]

Teng had a vision of the contrast between China and Europe and the constraints imposed upon him and his colleagues by the gargantuan size and the still agrarian-centered economy of their country:

8 Quoted in MacFarquhar, *The origins of the Cultural Revolution, 1: contradictions among the people 1956–1957*, 287.
9 *Selected works of Deng Xiaoping (1975–1982)*, 155, 156.

There are many provinces, municipalities and autonomous regions in China, and some of our medium-sized provinces are as big as a large European country. They must be given greater powers of decision in economic planning, finance and foreign trade – always within the framework of a nationwide unity of views, policies, planning, guidance and action.[10]

Here, of course, is the rub. "Unity of views, policies, planning, guidance and action" is to be desired no doubt, but for a polity of more than a billion people it is plainly impossible and in fact undesirable if thought is to develop. A "unity of views" enforced by state and Party police is an empty facade without efficacy. Here the idea of unity can only be self-defeating.

The narrative in the bulk of this volume ends in the early 1980s to permit a measure of historical perspective. Those were years of hope, with a genuine sense of a new beginning under Teng's leadership. The Chinese people were beginning to demonstrate their willingness and capacity to exploit new freedoms in order to improve their lot.

But the argument within the Chinese leadership over unity and diversity persisted. Throughout the 1980s, Teng threw his weight behind economic diversity, opening up China to outside intellectual influences in order to encourage it. But he became increasingly dissatisfied with their corrosive impact upon political unity. Briefly in 1983–84, more toughly in 1986–87, and then with armed force in the summer of 1989, he acted to reimpose central political control over the burgeoning forces of society set in motion by his own reforms.

Neither Mao nor Teng was able to square the Chinese circle, preserving unity while simultaneously permitting freedoms. The tragedies of the campaigns against counterrevolutionaries, the Anti-Rightist Campaign, the Great Leap Forward, the Cultural Revolution, and the T'ien An Men Square massacre are sufficient proof of that. In the last analysis, unity, and the disciplined order of which it is the basis, have always seemed more important, and freedom, and the loss of control that it spawns, too dangerous to China's leaders.

But the onus of unity assumed by China's leaders is increasingly an incubus for the Chinese people. If there is one historic lesson to be drawn from the four decades of the People's Republic, it is that there has to be fundamental change in the political system which over the centuries welded the Chinese people together. If not, the pressures of an increasingly self-confident developing society will finally grow so powerful that the system will burst asunder. In the 1990s and beyond, unity will be preserved only by diversity.

10 Ibid., 157.

APPENDIXES:
MEETINGS AND LEADERS

TABLE 32
High-level formal[a] Party meetings, 1966–1982

11th plenum, 8th CC, Peking	1–12 Aug. 1966
12th plenum, 8th CC, Peking	13–31 Oct. 1968
CCP Ninth National Congress, Peking	1–24 Apr. 1969
1st plenum, 9th CC, Peking[b]	28 Apr. 1969
2nd plenum, 9th CC, Lushan	23 Aug.–6 Sep. 1970
CCP Tenth National Congress, Peking	24–28 Aug. 1973
1st plenum, 10th CC, Peking[b c]	30 Aug. 1973
2nd plenum, 10th CC, Peking	8–10 Jan. 1975
3rd plenum, 10th CC, Peking	16–21 July 1977
CCP Eleventh National Congress, Peking	12–18 Aug. 1977
1st plenum, 11th CC, Peking[b]	19 Aug. 1977
2nd plenum, 11th CC, Peking	18–23 Feb. 1978
3rd plenum, 11th CC, Peking	18–22 Dec. 1978
4th plenum, 11th CC, Peking	25–28 Sep. 1979
5th plenum, 11th CC, Peking	23–29 Feb. 1980
6th plenum, 11th CC, Peking	27–29 June 1981
7th plenum, 11th CC, Peking	6 Aug. 1982
CCP Twelfth National Congress, Peking	1–11 Sep. 1982
1st plenum, 12th CC, Peking[b]	12–13 Sep. 1982

[a] "Formal" is used to distinguish these meetings from other important high-level meetings, such as Politburo or central work conferences, that often preceded CC plenums. For a more detailed listing and discussion of both formal and informal central meetings, see Lieberthal and Dickson, *A research guide to central Party and government meetings in China, 1949–1986.*
[b] 1st plenums are usually held immediately after National Congresses for the purpose of formally voting in the new Politburo and other central organs, such as the Secretariat.
[c] This source gives 31 August, but most others give 30 August.
Source: *Chung-kuo kung-ch'an-tang li-tz'u chung-yao hui-i chi, hsia* (Collection of various important conferences of the CCP, 2). Chung-kung chung-yang tang-hsiao tang-shih chiao-yen-shih tzu-liao tsu, ed.

TABLE 33
Party leadership, 1965–1969[a]

Eve of GPCR 1965	11th plenum, 8th CC 1–12 Aug. 1966	Ninth Congress, 1–24 Apr. 1969
	Politburo	
	Standing Committee	
Mao Tse-tung[b]	Mao Tse-tung[b]	Mao Tse-tung[b]
Liu Shao-ch'i[c]	Lin Piao[c]	Lin Piao[c,f]
Chou En-lai[c]	Chou En-lai	Chou En-lai
Chu Te[c]	T'ao Chu	Ch'en Po-ta
Ch'en Yun[c]	Ch'en Po-ta	K'ang Sheng
Lin Piao[c]	Teng Hsiao-p'ing	
Teng Hsiao-p'ing[d]	K'ang Sheng	
	Liu Shao-ch'i	
	Chu Te	
	Li Fu-ch'un	
	Ch'en Yun	
	Full members[e]	
Tung Pi-wu	Tung Pi-wu	Yeh Ch'ün[f]
P'eng Chen	Ch'en I	Yeh Chien-ying
Ch'en I	Liu Po-ch'eng	Liu Po-ch'eng
Li Fu-ch'un	Ho Lung	Chiang Ch'ing
P'eng Te-huai	Li Hsien-nien	Chu Te
Liu Po-ch'eng	Li Ching-ch'üan	Hsu Shih-yu
Ho Lung	T'an Chen-lin	Ch'en Hsi-lien
Li Hsien-nien	Hsu Hiang-ch'ien	Li Hsien-nien
Li Ching-ch'üan	Nieh Jung-chen	Li Tso-p'eng[f]
T'an Chen-lin	Yeh Chien-ying	Wu Fa-Hsien[f]
		Chang Ch'un-ch'iao
		Ch'iu Hui-tso[f]
		Yao Wen-yuan
		Huang Yung-sheng[f]
		Tung Pi-wu
		Hsieh Fu-chih
	Alternate members[e]	
Ulanfu	Ulanfu	Chi Teng-k'uei
Chang Wen-t'ien	Po I-po	Li Hsueh-feng
Lu Ting-i	Li Hsueh-feng	Li Te-sheng
Ch'en Po-ta	Sung Jen-ch'iung	Wang Tung-hsing
K'ang Sheng	Hsieh Fu-chih	
Po I-po		

[a] The precise date on which a leader lost his post during the early period of the GPCR is not always easy to establish.
[b] CC Chairman
[c] CC Vice-chairman
[d] General Secretary
[e] Mao and Lin Piao apart, full and alternate members of the post–Ninth Congress Politburo were listed by the number of strokes in the characters of their names and are so listed here, except for the Standing Committee, whose ranking is easy to pinpoint.
[f] Lin Piao and Yeh Ch'ün died in a plane crash on 13 September 1971 while fleeing the country; Li, Wu, Ch'iu, and Huang were arrested 24 September 1971.

TABLE 34
Party leadership, 1973–1982

Tenth Congress 24–28 Aug. 1973	Eleventh Congress 12–18 Aug. 1977	Twelfth Congress 1–11 Sep. 1982
	Politburo *Standing Committee*	
Mao Tse-tung[a]	Hua Kuo-feng[al]	Hu Yao-pang[b]
Chou En-lai[c]	Yeh Chien-ying[c]	Yeh Chien-ying
Wang Hung-wen[cd]	Teng Hsiao-p'ing[c]	Teng Hsiao-p'ing
K'ang Sheng[c]	Li Hsien-nien[c]	Chao Tzu-yang
Yeh Chien-ying[c]	Wang Tung-hsing[ck]	Li Hsien-nien
Li Te-sheng[cf]	Ch'en Yun[bc]	Ch'en Yun
Chu Te[c]		
Chang Ch'un-ch'iao[cd]		
Tung Pi-wu[c]		
Teng Hsiao-p'ing[fc]		
	Full members[e]	
Wei Kuo-ch'ing	Wei Kuo-ch'ing	Wan Li
Liu Po-ch'eng	Ulanfu	Hsi Chung-hsun
Chiang Ch'ing[d]	Fang I	Wang Chen
Hsu Shih-yu	Liu Po-ch'eng	Wei Kuo-ch'ing
Hua Kuo-feng	Hsu Shih-yu	Ulanhu[n]
Chi Teng-k'uei	Chi Teng-k'uei[k]	Fang I
Wu Te	Su Chen-hua	Teng Ying-ch'ao
Wang Tung-hsing	Li Te-sheng	Li Te-sheng
Ch'en Yung-kuei	Wu Te[k]	Yang Shang-k'un
Ch'en Hsi-lien	Yü Ch'iu-li	Yang Te-chih
Li Hsien-nien	Chang T'ing-fa	Yü Ch'iu-li
Yao Wen-yuan[d]	Ch'en Yung-kuei	Sung Jen-ch'ing
	Ch'en Hsi-lien[k]	Chang T'ing-fa
	Keng Piao	Hu Ch'iao-mu
	Nieh Jung-chen	Nieh Jung-chen
	Ni Chih-fu	Ni Chih-fu
	Hsu Hsiang-ch'ien	Hsu Hsiang-ch'ien
	P'eng Ch'ung	P'eng Chen
	Teng Ying-ch'ao[b]	Liao Ch'eng-chih
	Hu Yao-pang[bjl]	
	Wang Chen[b]	
	P'eng Chen[i]	
	Alternate members[g]	
Wu Kuei-hsien	Ch'en Mu-hua	Yao I-lin
Su Chen-hua	Chao Tzu-yang[ijm]	Ch'in Chi-wei
Ni Chih-fu	Saifudin	Ch'en Mu-hua
Saifudin		

[a] CC Chairman. Mao Tse-tung died on 9 September 1976. Hua Kuo-feng became chairman on 7 October 1976, but was replaced by Hu Yao-pang at the 6th plenum (27–29 June 1981) of the 11th CC.

[b] General Secretary; this congress abolished the chairmanship and the General Secretary formally became Party leader.

[c] CC Vice-chairman.

[d] The Gang of Four was arrested on 6 October 1976.

[e] These members were listed in stroke order.

f Teng Hsiao-p'ing was reappointed to the Politburo in December 1973, and to the Standing Committee as a vice-chairman at the 10th CC's 2nd plenum (8–10 January 1975), on the latter occasion apparently in place of Li Te-sheng, who reverted to full Politburo member.
g Full members and alternate members were listed in stroke order except at the Twelfth Congress when alternates were listed in order of votes received.
h Appointed at 11th CC's 3rd plenum (18–22 December 1980).
i Appointed full member at 11th CC's 4th plenum (25–28 September 1978).
j Appointed member of Standing Committee at 11th CC's 5th plenum (23–29 February 1980).
k Dismissed at 11th CC's 5th plenum.
l Hu Yao-pang replaced Hua Kuo-feng as chairman at 11th CC's 6th plenum (27–29 June 1981). Hua was reduced to vice-chairman.
m Appointed a vice-chairman at the 11th CC's 6th plenum.
n Romanization was changed between Congresses.
Sources: Wang Chien-ying, *Chang-kuo kung-ch'an-tang tsu-chih shih tzu-liao hui-pien* (A collection of materials on the organizational history of the CCP). Peking: Hung-ch'i, 1983; Hao Meng-pi and Tuan Hao-jan, eds., *Chung-kuo kung-ch'an-tang liu-shih-nien, xia.*

TABLE 35

State leaders, 1965–1983[a]

1965	1975	1978	1983
		Head of state[b]	
Liu Shao-ch'i			Li Hsien-nien
		Vice heads of state[b]	
Soong Ching-ling			Ulanhu
Tung Pi-wu			
		Chairman, NPC[b]	
Chu Te	Chu Te	Yeh Chien-ying	P'eng Chen
		Premier	
Chou Eu-lai	Chou En-lai[c]	Hua Kuo-feng[d]	Chao Tzu-yang
		Vice-premiers	
Lin Piao	Teng Hsiao-p'ing	Teng Hsiao-p'ing[b]	Wan Li
Ch'en Yun	Chang Ch'un-ch'iao[g]	Li Hsien-nien[b]	Yao I-lin
Teng Hsiao-p'ing	Li Hsien-nien	Hsu Hsiang-ch'ien[b]	Li P'eng
Ho Lung	Ch'en Hsi-lien	Chi Teng-k'uei[i]	T'ien Chi-yun
Ch'en I	Chi Teng-k'uei	Yü Ch'iu-li	
K'o Ch'ing-shih[e]	Hua Kuo-feng[e]	Ch'en Hsi-lien[i]	
Ulanfu	Ch'en Yung-kuei	Keng Piao	
Li Fu-ch'un	Wu Kuei-hsien	Ch'en Yung-kuei[b]	
Li Hsien-nien[f]	Wang Chen	Fang I	
T'an Chen-lin	Yü Ch'iu-li	Wang Chen[b]	
Nieh Jung-chen	Ku Mu	Ku Mu	
Po I-po	Sun Chien	K'ang Shih-en	
Lu Ting-i		Ch'en Mu-hua	
Lo Jui-ch'ing		Wang Jen-chung[jb]	
T'ao Chu		Ch'en Yun[jb]	
Hsieh Fu-chih		Po I-po[j]	
		Yao I-lin[j]	
		Chi P'eng-fei	
		Chao Tzu-yang[jd]	
		Wan Li	
		Yang Ching-jen[j]	
		Chang Ai-p'ing[j]	
		Huang Hua[j]	

[a] These appointments were made at the end of the first sessions of the 3rd (21 December–4 January 1964–65), 4th (13–17 January 1975), 5th (26 February–5 March 1978), and 6th (6–21 June 1983) National People's Congresses respectively. Dismissals and additional appointments made between these sessions are annotated.

[b] The posts of head of state and vice head of state were abolished in both new state constitutions promulgated at the first sessions of the 4th and 5th NPCs, in line with the views expressed by Mao Tse-tung in 1970. The chairman of the NPC acted as head of state.

[c] Chou En-lai died on 8 January 1976 and Hua Kuo-feng became acting premier on 3 February. On 8 April, *JMJP* published the decision that he would no longer be "acting" but would now be premier in his own right.

[d] Hua Kuo-feng was replaced by Chao Tzu-yang as premier at the third session (30 August–10 September 1980) of the 5th NPC.

e Died in 1965.

f Li Hsien-nien was the only vice-premier appointed in 1965 to serve throughout the GPCR; the precise dates of formal dismissal of the others are difficult to establish.

g Arrested on 6 October 1976.

h Resigned in September 1980.

i Dismissed in April 1980.

j Wang Jen-chung was appointed in December 1978; Ch'en Yun, Po I-po, and Yao I-lin in July 1979, Chi P'eng-fei in September 1979, Chao Tzu-yang and Wan Li in April 1980; and Yang Ching-jen, Chang Ai-p'ing, and Huang Hua in September 1980.

Sources: Successive editions of *Chung-hua jen-min kung-ho-kuo ti X chie ch'üan-kuo jen-min tai-piao ta-hui ti X tz'u hui-i wen-chien* (Documents of the X session of the X NPC of the PRC); Hao and Tuan, *Chung-kuo kung-ch'an-tang liu-shih-nien.*

BIBLIOGRAPHICAL ESSAYS

1. MAO TSE-TUNG'S THOUGHT FROM 1949 TO 1976

This essay continues the bibliographical essay on Mao's thought to 1949 published in Volume 14 of *The Cambridge History of China* in 1987. The study of Mao Tse-tung's thought for the period after 1949 has long been impeded by the fact that many writings of crucial importance were not available at all, and those issued in China had often been so extensively revised as to constitute an unreliable guide as to what he originally said. Although large numbers of previously unpublished documents were put into circulation in the early years of the Cultural Revolution, there is, even today, no comprehensive edition of the Chinese texts of Mao's post-1949 writings comparable to the twenty-volume compilation for the earlier period produced in Japan. (For details regarding this edition of the pre-1949 works, supervised by Takeuchi Minoru, see the bibliographic essay on Mao Tse-tung Thought to 1949 in Volume 13, and the entry below in the Bibliography under *Mao Tse-tung chi*.)

Volume V of the official *Selected works*, covering the period 1949–1957, which appeared in 1977 in Chinese (and also in English translation) is very selective indeed, and has now been withdrawn from sale because the editorial work is considered to have been marred by leftist errors. In the course of the 1980s, the organ under the Central Committee entrusted with this work, the *Chung-yang wen-hsien yen-chiu shih* (known in English as the Department for Research on Party Literature), published several thematic volumes, including collections of letters and journalistic writings, but it was only in 1987 that the first volume of what promised to be a very full chronological series was issued for restricted circulation. (See *Chien-kuo i-lai Mao Tse-tung wen-kao* [Draft writings by Mao Tse-tung since the establishment of the regime], vol. 1, September 1949–December 1950.) The fact that this first volume, of 784 pages, includes materials for only one and a quarter years suffices to underscore both the scope of the collection and how long it is likely to take to complete the work down to 1976.

Meanwhile, scholars in Germany, the United States, and Japan began, not long after Mao's death, to collect materials with a view to producing editions of his works respectively in German, English, and Chinese. The first group, led by Helmut Martin, successfully completed work on its edition within a few years. (See *Mao Zedong, Texte*.) Their efficiency was, however, ill-rewarded, for at about the time when the last volume came off the press, a flood of new material emerged. This came both from the official Chinese activities already mentioned, and from the much wider circulation abroad of "Red Guard" compilations of the Cultural Revolution period, as a result of the new open climate. The German edition, while useful (especially as it contains many of the Chinese texts as appendixes), is therefore already out of date and unsatisfactory.

At the opposite extreme, the Japanese scholars, led by Takeuchi Minoru and Nakamura Kimiyoshi, have decided to give up the attempt to continue their earlier series of Chinese texts for the period after October 1949, on the grounds that all the key manuscript and documentary sources are under the control of the authorities of the Chinese Communist Party and it is hopeless to try to compete with them. (The situation is, of course, quite different from that for the earlier years, covered by the *Mao Tse-tung chi*, when many of Mao's writings were published at the time he produced them, and can thus be found in libraries.)

The American group, led by Ying-mao Kau, is doing its best to steer a course between these two extremes. Only a first volume, covering the period to 1955, has thus far appeared. (See *The writings of Mao Zedong 1949–1976*, edited by Michael Y. M. Kau and John K. Leung, vol. 1, *September 1949–December 1955*.) An effort is being made to translate all new Chinese-language materials and to include them in the series, either in their chronological place or in a concluding supplementary volume.

For the time being, therefore, there is no complete and convenient source either in Chinese or in any foreign language, and little prospect of having one available soon. Those interested in Mao Tse-tung Thought are thus obliged to rely, for the most part, on selections made by various scholars or agencies, from their own perspectives.

A substantial quantity of useful, but not very good, translations of some of the Red Guard materials was published by the JPRS in 1974 in two volumes entitled *Miscellany of Mao Tse-tung Thought*. An important recent publication, drawing on more than twenty newly available unofficial collections, is *The secret speeches of Chairman Mao* (1989), edited by Roderick MacFarquhar, Timothy Cheek, and Eugene Wu. A volume of Mao's talks and letters from 1956 to 1971 was published in English in 1974 as *Mao Tse-tung unrehearsed* (U.S. title: *Chairman Mao talks to the people*), edited by Stuart R. Schram. See also Jerome Ch'en, *Mao papers* (1970), and Mao Tse-tung, *A critique of Soviet economics* (1977), translated by Moss Roberts.

Among Western interpretations of Mao's thought, John Bryan Starr, *Continuing the revolution: the political thought of Mao* (1979), is a comprehensive overview that suffers from a tendency to treat everything Mao wrote from the 1920s to the 1970s as a single corpus, and to analyze it in such a way that the whole of Mao's life and thought appears to find its culmination in the Cultural Revolution. Frederic E. Wakeman, in his *History and will* (1973), also links Mao Tse-tung's ideas of the May Fourth period with those of his later years, but in less simplistic and uncritical fashion. Among the older works, Arthut Cohen, *The communism of Mao Tse-tung* (1971 [1964]), stresses the Stalinist roots of Mao's thought. James Hsiung, *Ideology and practice* (1970), emphasizes rather its links with the Chinese tradition. Although his view of *ssu-hsiang* or thought as a characteristically Chinese mode of intellectual activity different from the systematic doctrines common in the West can be questioned, his study is assuredly one of the most stimulating on the topic as a whole. See also Stuart R. Schram, ed., *The political thought of Mao Tse-tung* (rev. ed., 1969). A series of useful, if somewhat premature, appreciations of various aspects of Mao's contribution are to be found in Dick Wilson, ed., *Mao Tse-tung in the scales of history* (1977).

Among recent books on Mao's ideas after 1949, two collections of essays are perhaps most notable. The first of these to appear was Maurice Meisner's *Marxism, Maoism, and utopianism* (1982). Taking the view that although the social goals proclaimed by Mao were "Marxist-inspired," the means with which he sought to achieve them were not, Meisner holds that his thought and action during the Great Leap Forward, and especially during the Cultural Revolution, had a profoundly positive historical impact. Not many Chinese would today share this position, but Meisner argues it with much talent. More balanced, judicious, and incisive is the analysis of Tang Tsou in his *Cultural Revolution and post-Mao reforms* (1988), of which more than half deals with theory and policy during Mao's later years.

Much of the most interesting and original work on Mao's thought is today going on in China itself, where standards both of textual accuracy and of scholarly independence have greatly improved. The official interpretation of Mao Tse-tung's historical role contained in the Central Committee Resolution of 27 June 1981 (*Resolution on CPC history [1949–1981]*) deals, of course, at some length with his thought. For several years thereafter, it was not easy for Chinese scholars to depart from the frame-

work thus laid down, but increasingly these constraints are being challenged or interpreted very flexibly. This flexibility is less evident in the
articles appearing in the journal *Mao Tse-tung ssu-hsiang yen-chiu* (Research
on Mao Tse-tung Thought), published in Chengtu under the influence of
the last surviving active member of Mao's own philosophical study group
in Yenan (Yang Ch'ao). Less orthodox interpretations appear in articles
published, for example, in *Ma-k'o-ssu-chu-i yen-chiu* (Research on Marxism), edited by Su Shao-chih. Yang Ch'ao's *Wei-wu pien-cheng-fa ti jo-kan
li-lun wen-t'i* (Some theoretical problems of materialist dialectics) (1980),
originally titled *Lun Mao Chu-hsi che-hsueh t'i-hsi* (On Chairman Mao's
philosophical system) (1978), might almost have been published in Mao's
lifetime. A work such as *Wan-nien Mao Tse-tung: kuan-yü li-lun yü shih-
chien ti yen-chiu* (Mao Tse-tung in his later years: research on the relation
between theory and practice) (1989), edited by Hsiao Yen-chung, with a
preface by Li Jui, most decidedly would not have appeared when Mao
was alive. Very interesting analyses are also published, for internal circulation, in the organ of the Department for Research on Party Literature,
Wen-hsien ho yen-chiu (Documents and research), and in other *nei-pu* journals. Indeed, many of the essays in the volume just mentioned on Mao's
later years come from such sources.

2. THE CHINESE STATE IN CRISIS

Like virtually every other urban institution, the official Chinese press was
seriously disrupted by the turmoil of the Cultural Revolution. Few new
books appeared; virtually all specialized journals ceased operations; and
even *Hung-ch'i* (Red flag), the Party's theoretical magazine, suspended
publication for several months. The national media that did continue
to function – principally the New China News Agency, *Jen-min jih-pao*
(People's daily), *Chieh-fang-chün pao* (Liberation Army news), and *Peking
Review* – assumed a highly polemical and bombastic tone. A relatively
large portion of this meager fare was translated by the U.S. Consulate
General in Hong Kong, and published in their three periodicals: *Survey
of the China Mainland Press, Selections from China Mainland Magazines*, and
Current Background. In addition, both the American and British governments continued monitoring and translating national and provincial radio
broadcasts, and placed the results in the Foreign Broadcast Information
Service *Daily Report* and *Summary of World Broadcasts*.
   China's central authorities attempted to maintain order during the Cultural Revolution by issuing a series of central directives and by circulating
major speeches by national leaders. Most such speeches and directives

were distributed through internal channels, but many of them were published by Red Guard organizations and later compiled by foreign research institutions. Useful compendiums include *CCP documents of the Great Proletarian Cultural Revolution, 1966–1967*; "Collection of documents concerning the Great Proletarian Cultural Revolution"; and "Speeches and statements alleged to have been made by Chinese communist leaders in July through October, 1966." The most important statements by Mao Tse-tung during this period can be found in Jerome Ch'en, ed., *Mao papers: anthology and bibliography; Miscellany of Mao Tse-tung Thought (1949–1968)*; and Stuart R. Schram, ed., *Chairman Mao talks to the people: talks and letters 1956–1971*. They are catalogued and indexed in John Bryan Starr and Nancy Anne Dyer, *Post-liberation works of Mao Zedong: a bibliography and index*. Michael Y. M. Kau, ed., *The Lin Piao affair: power politics and military coup*, contains a comparable collection of statements by Lin Piao.

The dearth of official publications was counterbalanced by a plethora of unofficial newspapers and magazines published by Red Guard organizations of varying political orientations. These publications contained inflammatory denunciations of central and provincial leaders, critical commentaries on major policies since 1949, chronologies of the Cultural Revolution, and highly emotional accounts of factional struggle within various units and institutions. Some Red Guard publications also contain what purport to be self-criticisms by the principal victims of the Cultural Revolution. The accuracy of the Red Guard media is, of course, highly suspect; but they remain an invaluable research tool if used with care.

Because few Red Guard publications have apparently been preserved inside China itself, interested scholars must rely on collections maintained outside the PRC. Eight batches of Red Guard materials were collected by the Center for Chinese Research Materials in Washington and distributed by microfilm and photocopies to interested libraries. Many of these publications, in turn, were translated in *Selections from China Mainland Magazines* and *Current Background*. The best bibliographic guide to these Red Guard materials is Hong Yung Lee, *Research guide to Red Guard publications, 1966–1969*. In addition, both the Union Research Institute and the University of Michigan have published catalogues of their own Red Guard holdings: *Catalogue of Red Guard publications held by URI*; and Raymond N. Tang and Wei-yi Ma, *Source materials on Red Guards and the Great Proletarian Cultural Revolution*.

Since the death of Mao Tse-tung, the purge of the Gang of Four, and the demotion of Hua Kuo-feng, there has been a second wave of Chinese publications on the Cultural Revolution, as part of a broad effort to assess the origins and outcomes of the movement. Among these new materials are the documentation from the trial of the Gang of Four and the supporters of Lin Piao, in *A great trial in Chinese history – the trial of the Lin Biao and Jiang Qing counter-revolutionary cliques, Nov. 1980–Jan. 1981*. Equally important is the description and evaluation of the Cultural Revolution contained in the official *Resolution on certain questions in the history of our Party since the founding of the People's Republic of China*.

The drafting and promulgation of the historical resolution provided an occasion for publication of additional detailed materials on the Cultural Revolution. See, for example, Ch'üan-kuo tang-shih tzu-liao cheng-chi kung-tso hui-yi ho chi-nien Chung-kuo kung-ch'an-tang liu-shih chou-nien hsueh-shu t'ao-lun-hui mi-shu-ch'u (Secretariat of the National Work Conference on Collecting Party Historical Materials and the Academic Conference in Commemoration of the Sixtieth Anniversary of the Chinese Communist Party), eds., *Tang-shih hui-yi pao-kao-chi* (Collected reports from the Conference on Party History); Chung-kung tang-shih yen-chiu-hui (Research Society on the History of the Chinese Communist Party), ed., *Hsueh-hsi li-shih chueh-i chuan-chi* (Special publication on studying the resolution on history); and Sun Tun-fan et al., eds., *Chung-kuo kung-ch'an-tang li-shih chiang-i* (Teaching materials on the history of the Chinese Communist Party).

A number of memoirs and biographies published since 1976 contain interesting information about particular episodes in the Cultural Revolution. An article by Ch'en Tsai-tao, "Wu-han 'ch'i-erh-ling shih-chien' shih-mo" ("The beginning and end of the 'July 20th incident' in Wuhan"), recounts his involvement in the Wuhan Incident of July 1967. The memoirs of Nieh Jung-chen, one of China's most senior military commanders, published in 1983–84, also reveal much about his involvement during the Cultural Revolution. An account by Teng Hsiao-p'ing's daughter Mao Mao, "In the days spent in Kiangsi," tells of her father's confinement and internal exile between 1967 and 1973. A generally laudatory account of Chou En-lai is Percy Jucheng Fang and Lucy Guinong J. Fang, *Zhou Enlai: a profile*. A much more critical study of K'ang Sheng is Chung K'an, *K'ang Sheng p'ing-chuan* (A critical biography of K'ang Sheng).

The "scar literature" of the late 1970s and early 1980s offers considerable insight into the ways in which Chinese intellectuals view the Cultural Revolution. Collections of stories revealing how individual lives were affected by the movement include Chen Jo-hsi, *The execution of Mayor Yin and other stories from the Great Proletarian Cultural Revolution*; Perry Link, ed., *Stubborn weeds: popular and controversial Chinese literature after the Cultural Revolution*; Perry Link, ed., *Roses and thorns: the second blooming of the Hundred Flowers in Chinese fiction, 1979–80*; and Helen F. Siu and Zelda Stern, eds., *Mao's harvest: voices from China's new generation*.

The protest literature of the so-called Peking Spring movement, as well as other analytical essays written more recently, also offers clues as to how contemporary Chinese intellectuals interpret and assess the origins, evolution, and consequences of the Cultural Revolution. One of the most impassioned condemnations of the movement, going far beyond the official interpretation, is Wang Xizhe, "Mao Zedong and the Cultural Revolution." An interesting collection of essays by younger intellectuals appears in the Spring 1986 issue of *Chih-shih-fen-tzu* (The Chinese intellectual), published in New York.

Outside China, the Cultural Revolution has been the subject of a wide range of secondary literature, much of which is cited in James C. F. Wang, *The Cultural Revolution in China: an annotated bibliography*. The earliest works were produced by Western journalists and government officials, many of them based in Hong Kong. Much of their work, although written without the benefit of hindsight and perspective, represents the China-watching profession at its best. Of particular value are two Hong Kong newsletters: *China News Analysis*, edited (and largely written) by Father L. Ladany; and *China News Summary*, published by the British government. Full-length and relatively comprehensive contemporary accounts include Robert S. Elegant, *Mao's great revolution*; Stanley Karnow, *Mao and China: from revolution to revolution*; and Edward E. Rice, *Mao's way*. Also valuable is the series of articles, published in *CQ*, by Philip Bridgham, an analyst in the U.S. government: "Mao's Cultural Revolution: origin and development"; "Mao's Cultural Revolution: the struggle to seize power"; and "Mao's Cultural Revolution: the struggle to consolidate power."

All major political histories of the People's Republic contain some discussion of the Cultural Revolution. The best are Parris H. Chang, *Power and policy in China*, 2nd ed.; Jürgen Domes, *The internal politics of China, 1949–1972*; Jacques Guillermaz, *The Chinese Communist Party in power, 1949–1976*; and Maurice Meisner, *Mao's China: a history of the People's Republic*. Interestingly, there have been few full-length scholarly studies devoted to the Cultural Revolution. The exceptions are Jean Daubier, *A history of the Chinese Cultural Revolution*, written from a somewhat Maoist perspective; and Hong Yung Lee, *The politics of the Chinese Cultural Revolution: a case study*, a more objective treatment. Byung-joon Ahn, *Chinese politics and the Cultural Revolution: dynamics of policy processes*, although principally concerned with the early 1960s, does contain a detailed account of the earliest months of the Cultural Revolution.

A full understanding of the Cultural Revolution can be obtained only by examining the way in which the movement unfolded in particular places and institutions. A partial list of case studies of the Cultural Revolution in major cities and provinces includes Victor Falkenheim, "The Cultural Revolution in Kwangsi, Yunnan, and Fukien"; Gardel Feurtado, "The formation of provincial revolutionary committees, 1966–1968: Heilungkiang and Hopei"; Neale Hunter, *Shanghai journal: an eyewitness account of the Cultural Revolution*; Paul Hyer and William Heaton, "The Cultural Revolution in Inner Mongolia"; Victor Nee, "Revolution and bureaucracy: Shanghai in the Cultural Revolution"; *The Cultural Revolution in the provinces*; and Andrew G. Walder, *Chang Ch'un-ch'iao and Shanghai's January Revolution*.

Comparable analyses of Cultural Revolutionary activities, in particular basic-level units, include Marc J. Blecher and Gordon White, *Micropolitics in contemporary China: a technical unit during and after the Cultural Revolution*; William Hinton, *Hundred day war: the Cultural Revolution at Tsinghua University*; David Milton and Nancy Dall Milton, *The wind will not subside: years in revolutionary China, 1964–1969*; and Victor Nee, *The Cultural Revolution at Peking University*.

Yet another way of studying the Cultural Revolution is to examine the individuals who were actively engaged in it. Intriguingly, although a chapter on the Cultural Revolution usually ends most biographies of Mao, little has been written that focuses specifically on Mao's role in the movement. More is available on other leaders. On Chou En-lai, see Thomas W. Robinson, "Chou En-lai and the Cultural Revolution" in Robinson, ed., *The Cultural Revolution in China;* on Liu Shao-ch'i, see Lowell Dittmer, *Liu Shao-ch'i and the Chinese Cultural Revolution: the politics of mass criticism.* The Cultural Revolution figures prominently in two biographies of Chiang Ch'ing: Roxane Witke, *Comrade Chiang Ch'ing*; and Ross Terrill, *The white-boned demon: a biography of Madame Mao Zedong.* Furthermore, the memoirs of several former Red Guards have now been published: Gordon A. Bennett and Ronald N. Montaperto, *Red Guard: the political biography of Dai Hsiao-ai*; Gao Yuan, *Born red: a chronicle of the Cultural Revolution*; Liang Heng and Judith Shapiro, *Son of the revolution*; and Ken Ling, *The revenge of heaven: journal of a young Chinese.*

Three of the social groups most centrally involved in the Cultural Revolution were the state and Party cadres, who were the target of the movement; the Red Guards, who served as its shock troops; and the People's

Liberation Army, which was its principal immediate beneficiary. The attempts of the nation's officials to survive the onslaught of the Red Guards are analyzed in Parris H. Chang, "Provincial Party leaders' strategies for survival during the Cultural Revolution"; and Richard Baum, "Elite behavior under conditions of stress: the lesson of the 'Tang-ch'üan p'ai' in the Cultural Revolution." The effect of the Cultural Revolution on the composition of the government and Party elites is discussed in Richard K. Diao, "The impact of the Cultural Revolution on China's economic elite"; Donald W. Klein, "The State Council and the Cultural Revolution"; Charles Neuhauser, "The impact of the Cultural Revolution on the CCP machine"; and Frederick C. Teiwes, *Provincial leadership in China: the Cultural Revolution and its aftermath.* On the changes in the Central Committee and Politburo made at the Ninth Party Congress, see Donald W. Klein and Lois B. Hager, "The Ninth Central Committee"; and Robert A. Scalapino, "The transition in Chinese Party leadership: a comparison of the Eighth and Ninth Central Committees."

On the Red Guard movement, and the radical intellectuals who sought to lead it, the following works are of interest: Anita Chan, "Images of China's social structure: the changing perspectives of Canton students"; Parris H. Chang, *Radicals and radical ideology in China's Cultural Revolution*; Klaus Mehnert, *Peking and the New Left: at home and abroad*; Stanley Rosen, *Red Guard factionalism and the Cultural Revolution in Guangzhou (Canton)*; and Martin Singer, *Educated youth and the Cultural Revolution.* The dispatch of former Red Guards to rural areas after their movement was disbanded in 1968 is treated in Thomas P. Bernstein, *Up to the mountains and down to the villages: the transfer of youth from urban to rural China.*

The role of the People's Liberation Army in the Cultural Revolution is surveyed in Chien Yu-shen, *China's fading revolution: army dissent and military divisions, 1967–68*; Jürgen Domes, "The Cultural Revolution and the army"; Jürgen Domes, "The role of the military in the formation of revolutionary committees, 1967–68"; Harvey W. Nelsen, "Military forces in the Cultural Revolution"; and Harvey W. Nelsen, "Military bureaucracy in the Cultural Revolution."

Other social groups affected by the Cultural Revolution have received somewhat less extensive treatment. On peasants, see Richard Baum, "The Cultural Revolution in the countryside: anatomy of a limited rebellion." On intellectuals, see Merle Goldman, *China's intellectuals: advise and dissent*; and Anne F. Thurston, "Victims of China's Cultural Revolution: the invisible wounds."

Finally, there is a large body of interpretative literature on the Cultural Revolution, which surveys its origins, assesses its outcomes, and places it in a broader theoretical, comparative, or historical context. Generally speaking, works written before the death of Mao and the purge of the Gang of Four were more sympathetic toward the Cultural Revolution, whereas those produced since that time are more critical. A useful sampler is contained in Richard Baum with Louise B. Bennett, eds., *China in ferment: perspectives on the Cultural Revolution*. Other interpretive essays worthy of note are Byung-joon Ahn, "The Cultural Revolution and China's search for political order"; John Israel, "Continuities and discontinuities in the ideology of the Great Proletarian Cultural Revolution"; Robert Jay Lifton, *Revolutionary immortality: Mao Tse-tung and the Chinese Cultural Revolution*; Maurice Meisner, "Leninism and Maoism: some populist perspectives on Marxism-Leninism in China"; Stuart R. Schram, "The Cultural Revolution in historical perspective"; Richard Solomon, *Mao's revolution and the Chinese political culture*; and Tang Tsou, "The Cultural Revolution and the Chinese political system." Three articles in John Lewis's *Party leadership and revolutionary power in China* are also valuable: Leonard Schapiro and John Wilson Lewis, "The roles of the monolithic Party under the totalitarian leader"; Benjamin I. Schwartz, "The reign of virtue: some broad perspectives on leader and Party in the Cultural Revolution"; and Stuart R. Schram, "The Party in Chinese Communist ideology."

3. CHINA CONFRONTS THE SOVIET UNION

Little primary material is available from the Chinese Foreign Ministry or the Chinese Communist Party, the two institutions where Peking's foreign policy was made during the period, other than standard (and often propagandistic) official pronouncements. Aside from Red Guard materials, the scholar must therefore rely principally on speeches, official newspaper accounts, government press releases, propaganda tracts, and above all on radio broadcast intercepts – all of which must be used with great care and according to the unperfected technique of interlinear analysis – and secondly on non-Chinese sources, mostly English- and Russian-language primary and secondary sources in the case of this chapter. Even the opening up of Chinese sources during the post–Cultural Revolution years did not produce much in memoirs, solidly based Chinese analyses, or *neipu* materials. That may change for the better in the future.

Work on Chinese foreign policy requires using all available sources and taking an additive approach, that is, building up inductively from a base in Chinese documents but incorporating data from external sources. One must seek logical congruence among many and diverse sources. Often, most of the sources are non-Chinese – in the case of this chapter, Russian.

Given that most of what is going to be available for a considerable period will already be at hand quite soon after events occur, a careful sifting and condensation may produce satisfactory and sometimes definitive results.

The Red Guard material is now under solid library control. See the *Red Guard publications* (twenty-three volumes and eight supplements) of the Center for Chinese Research Materials. The major American university research libraries with strong Chinese collections (Berkeley, Chicago, Columbia, Harvard, Michigan, and Hoover at Stanford) all have their own indexes, as docs the Library of Congress.

Beyond that, one must have recourse to the standard official Chinese publications, such as *Jen-min jih-pao* (People's daily), *Chieh-fang-chün pao* (Liberation Army news), *Peking (Beijing) review*, *Shih-chieh chih-shih* (World knowledge), and *Hung-ch'i* (Red flag). The most important source by far, however, is the American government translation series *Daily report: China*, published by the Foreign Broadcast Information Service. (The British publication *Survey of world broadcasts: Far East* does not, in general, massively overlap the *Daily Report*. The two must be used in conjunction.) Without the *Daily Report*, no work on primary sources for Chinese foreign policy is possible without enormous inconvenience and many gaps. It should be supplemented by the other American government translation series, *Translations on the People's Republic of China* (with various subtitles according to subject matter), published by the Joint Publications Research Service, and the *Survey of the China Mainland Press*, and the associated minor series, published, until 30 September 1977, by the American Consulate General, Hong Kong. Soviet sources have the same limitations as official Chinese sources. These include: *Pravda*, *Izvestia*, and TASS. Indispensable for control of Russian sources are the Foreign Broadcast Information Service *Daily report: Soviet Union* and the *Current Digest of the Soviet Press* (weekly).

A few collections of Chinese documents include the major pronouncements on foreign policy and Sino-Soviet relations. These include Harold Hinton, ed., *The People's Republic of China, 1949–1979*, 5 volumes (supplemented by *The People's Republic of China, 1979–1984*, 2 volumes); John Gittings, *Survey of the Sino-Soviet dispute*; and James T. Myers, ed., *Chinese politics: documents and analysis*, 2 volumes. Unfortunately, the authoritative *Modern Chinese society: an analytical bibliography* (G. William Skinner, general editor) does not include entries on Chinese foreign policy.

A few Chinese-language studies, memoirs, and collections relevant to foreign policy were beginning to appear by the 1980s. These included: Kao Kao and Yen Chia-ch'i, *"Wen-hua ta-ko-ming" shih-nien shih, 1966–1976* (A history of the ten years of the "Great Cultural Revolution," 1966–1976);

Cheng Te-jung et al., eds., *Hsin Chung-kuo chi-shih, 1949–1984* (Records of the new China); *Chung-kuo kung-ch'an-tang li-shih chiang-i* (Teaching materials for a brief history of the Chinese Communist Party); *Tang-tai Chung-kuo wai-chiao* (Diplomacy of contemporary China): Hao Meng-pi and Tuan Hao-jan, eds., *Chung-kuo kung-ch'an-tang liu-shih-nien* (Sixty years of the Chinese Communist Party).

Certain English-language journals are quite useful for studying Chinese foreign policy, particularly the indispensable *China Quarterly*, which has a "Quarterly chronicle and documentation" that surveys Chinese foreign relations by country and subject. Also worthy of consultation are: *Issues & Studies* (Taipei), *Asian Survey, Problems of Communism, Far Eastern Economic Review, Current Scene* (Hong Kong, 1961–72), *Contemporary China* (1974–1979), *The China Mainland Review* (Hong Kong, 1965–1967), *Pacific Affairs*, and *China News Summary*. Quite useful also is the Korean journal *Chong-Sa Yan-gu* (Sino-Soviet relations), which has a portion of its contents in English. Two Taiwan journals that often contain information unavailable elsewhere, but that must be used with caution, are *Inside Mainland China* and *Chung-kung yen-chiu* (English title, *Studies on Chinese communism*). The most important Russian journal is *Problemy Dal'nego Vostoka* (Problems of the Far East), which is principally devoted to China. Other Russian-language journals of relevance include *Mirovaia ekonomika i mezhdunarodnye otnosheniia* (World economy and international relations), *Kommunist*, and *Mezhdunarodnaia zhizn'* (International affairs). Reference should also be made to the internal annual *Gosudarstvo i obshchestvo v Kitaie* (State and society in China), the product of annual conferences at the China Branch of the Institute of Oriental Studies in Moscow, which occasionally contains insights into Soviet policies toward China.

Bibliographies of Chinese foreign policy are hardly numerous. Recourse must be had to the Library of Congress computer printout service for particular topics, but care must be taken not to cast too wide or too narrow a search in terms of key words. Thomas W. Robinson has an unpublished *Bibliography of Chinese foreign relations, 1949–1975* with 3,637 entries, which is cross-indexed by subject and author. See also Jessica S. Brown et al., *Sino-Soviet conflict: a historical bibliography*. For more recent works in English, recourse must be had to *Foreign Affairs* and its *Recent books on international relations* for books, *ABC Pol Sci* for articles, and *Doctoral dissertations on China*. The *Journal of Asian Studies* does list material on Chinese foreign policy in its annual bibliography but varies considerably in comprehensiveness from year to year. On the Soviet side, the *Slavic Review* publishes an annual bibliography but with the same limitations. Russian-language material is, fortunately, well indexed, first in V. P.

Zhuravleva's annual *Bibliographiia Kitaia*, which supplements on an annual basis (but which so far has not been published as a single volume) the earlier classic of the same name by P. E. Skachkov, and beyond that in the review pages of *Problemy Dal'nego Vostoka*, the annual *Kitaiskaia Narodnaia Respublika, Narody Azii i Afriki*, and the standard Russian annual indexes of books, articles, and the important newspapers. (*Pravda* and *Izvestia* are, incidentally, indexed in English by the *Current Digest of the Soviet Press*.)

English-language books on Sino-Soviet relations are quite numerous. Most are essentially policy analyses. Only those based on original sources or whose analytic quality is superior are noted here. Unfortunately, space does not permit more than a sampling of a large field, and only for the period covered in this chapter.

Oton Ambroz, *Realignment of world power: the Russo-Chinese schism under the impact of Mao Tse-tung's last revolution*; An Tai-sung, *The Sino-Soviet territorial dispute*; A. Doak Barnett, *China and the major powers in East Asia*; Robert Boardman, *Britain and the People's Republic of China 1949–1974*; O. B. Borisov and B. T. Koloskov, *Sino-Soviet relations, 1945–1973*; O. Edmund Clubb, *China and Russia: The "Great Game"*; Dennis J. Doolin, *Territorial claims in the Sino-Soviet conflict: documents and analysis*; Herbert J. Ellison, ed., *The Sino-Soviet conflict: a global perspective;* David Floyd, *Mao against Khrushchev: A short history of the Sino-Soviet conflict*; Raymond L. Garthoff, ed., *Sino-Soviet military relations*; Harry Gelman, *The Soviet Far East buildup and Soviet risk-taking against China*; George Ginsburgs and Carl F. Pinkele, *Sino-Soviet territorial dispute, 1949–64*; John Gittings, *Survey of the Sino-Soviet dispute: a commentary and extracts from the recent polemics, 1963–67*; John Gittings, *The world and China, 1922–1972*; Thomas M. Gottlieb, *Chinese foreign policy factionalism and the origins of the strategic triangle*; William E. Griffith, *Sino-Soviet relations, 1964–1965*; Willliam E. Griffith, *The Sino-Soviet rift*; Melvin Gurrov and Byong-Moo Hwang, *China under threat: the politics of strategy and diplomacy*; Morton H. Halperin, ed., *Sino-Soviet relations and arms control*; Harold Hinton, *The bear at the gate: Chinese policy making under Soviet pressure*; Harold Hinton, *Three and a half powers: the new power balance in Asia*; G. F. Hudson, Richard Lowenthal, and Roderick MacFarquhar, *The Sino-Soviet dispute*; C. G. Jacobsen, *Sino-Soviet relations since Mao: the Chairman's legacy*; Geoffrey Jukes, *The Soviet Union in Asia*; Keesing's Research Report, *The Sino-Soviet dispute*; Mikhail A. Klochko, *Soviet scientist in Red China*; Kenneth G. Lieberthal, *Sino-Soviet conflict in the 1970s: its evolution and implications for the strategic triangle*; Alfred D. Low, *The Sino-Soviet dispute: an analysis of the polemics*; Klaus Mehnert, *Peking and Moscow*; Jonathan D. Pollack, *The lessons of coalition politics: Sino-American security relations; The Sino-Soviet conflict in the 1980s: its dynamics and policy implications*; and *The Sino-Soviet rivalry and Chinese security debate*; Thomas W. Robinson, *The border negotiations and the future of Sino-Soviet-American relations* and *The Sino-Soviet border dispute: Background, development, and the March 1969 clashes*; Harrison E. Salisbury, *War between Russia and China*; Gretchen Ann Sandles, "Soviet images of the People's Republic of China, 1949–1979"; Harry Schwartz, *Tsars, mandarins, and commissars: a history of Chinese-Russian relations*; Bhabani Sen Gupta, *Soviet-Asian relations in the 1970s and beyond: an interperceptional study*; Richard H. Solomon and Masataka Kosaka, eds., *The Soviet Far East military buildup; nuclear dilemmas and Asian security*; Robert G. Sutter, *Chinese foreign policy after the Cultural Revolution, 1966–1977*; Rodger Swearingen, *The Soviet Union and postwar Japan*; Donald S. Zagoria, *The Sino-Soviet conflict, 1956–1961*; Kenneth G. Weiss, *Power grows out of the barrel of a gunboat; the U.S. in Sino-Soviet crises*; Allen S. Whiting, *The Chinese calculus of deterrence: India and Indochina*; Richard Wich, *Sino-Soviet crisis politics: a study of political change and communication*; Michael B. Yahuda, *China's role in world affairs*; Donald S. Zagoria, ed., *Soviet policy in East Asia; The Sino-Soviet conflict, 1956–1961*; and *Vietnam triangle: Moscow/Peking/Hanoi*.

Although Russian-language books on the subject are often propagandistic, several excellent analyses have been published. Moreover, Soviet materials on other aspects of China seemingly unconnected with Chinese foreign policy actually may contain insightful material on the latter, as it is a Russian propensity to speak only indirectly about one's actual interest. The following list thus is on-subject if not always so evidenced by title.

O. B. Borisov, *Vnutrenniaia i vneshniaia politika Kitaia v 70-e gody* (Internal and external policies of China in the seventies); O. B. Borisov and B. T. Koloskov, *Sovetsko-Kitaiskie otnosheniia 1945–1970: kratkii ocherk* (Soviet-Chinese relations 1945–1970: a brief sketch); Fedor Burlatsky, *Mao Tse-tung: an ideological and psychological portrait*; L. P. Deliusin, *The sociopolitical essence of Maoism*; K. A. Egorov, *Gosudarstvennyi apparat KNR, 1967–1981* (The governmental apparatus of the PRC, 1967–1981); V. G. Gel'bras, *Kitai: krizis prodolzhaetsia* (China: the crisis continues); B. N. Gorbachev, *Sotsial'no-politicheskaia rol'kitaiskoi armii (1958–1969)* (The social and political role of the Chinese army [1958–1969]); L. M. Gudoshnikov, *Politicheskii mekhanizm Kitaiskoi Narodnoi Respubliki* (Political mechanisms of the People's Republic of China); *Kitai: obshchestvo i gosudarstvo* (China: society and the state); *Kitai: poiski putei sotsial'nogo razvitiia* (China: the search for the path of socialist development); *Kitai: traditsii i sovremennost'* (China: traditions and the present); *Kitai i sosedi*

(China and its neighbors); *Kitaiskaia Narodnaia Respublika 1973 (−1979)* (The People's Republic of China 1973 [−1979]); L. S. Kiuzazhian, *Ideologicheskie kampanii v KNR 1949–1966* (Ideological campaigns in the PRC 1949–1966); M. I. Makarov et al., *Vneshniaia politika KNR* (Foreign policy of the PRC); Raisa Mirovitskaya and Yuri Semyonov, *The Soviet Union and China: a brief history of relations*; G. N. Mos'ko, *Armiia Kitaia: orudie avantiuristicheskoi politiki Maoistov* (The Chinese army: instrument of the adventuristic policies of the Maoists); *Opasnyi kurs* (Dangerous course); *Problemy i protivorechiia v razvitii rabochego klassa KNR* (Problems and contradictions in the development of the working class of the PRC); *Problemy sovetskogo kitaevedeniia* (Topics in Soviet Sinology); A. M. Rumiantsev, *Istoki i evoliutsiia "Idei Mao Tsze-duna"* (Sources and evolution of "Mao Tse-tung Thought"); *Sotsial'no-ekonomicheskii stroi i ekonomicheskaia politika KNR* (Social-economic structure and economic policies of the PRC); *Sovremennyi Kitai v zarubeznykh issledovaniiakh* (Contemporary China in foreign research); S. L. Tikhvinskii, *Istoriia Kitaia i sovremennost'* (The history of China and the present); O. Vladimirov and V. Ryazantsev, *Mao Tse-tung: a political portrait*; and B. Zanegin, A. Mironov, and Ia. Mikhailov, *K sobitiiam v Kitae* (On developments in China).

4. THE SUCCESSION TO MAO AND THE END OF MAOISM

Before the Cultural Revolution, the Western student of Chinese politics had a simple task as far as sources were concerned. There were a few central newspapers and magazines, a few public speeches, and a few refugees in Hong Kong to consult. Some copies of provincial newspapers were smuggled out to Hong Kong, and provincial radio broadcasts were monitored along with Radio Peking. These simple tools of the trade still involved much reading and even more interpretation, but it was an easily manageable data base.

During the Cultural Revolution, such sources were supplemented by a flood of new and different material, much of it released by Red Guards who ransacked the offices of deposed officials. The most important type of new data was the collections of hitherto unpublished Mao speeches, many of them confusingly given the same title, most commonly *Mao Tse-tung ssu-hsiang wan sui!* (Long live Mao Tse-tung Thought!), translations of which appeared in various forms, notably in Stuart Schram's *Mao Tse-tung unrehearsed; talks and letters, 1956–71* (American edition entitled *Chairman Mao talks to the people*), Jerome Ch'en's *Mao* and his *Mao papers: anthology and bibliography*, in the two volumes published by the JPRS entitled *Miscellany of Mao Tse-tung Thought*, and in issues of *Chinese Law and Government* (1.4,

9.3, 9.4, 10.2, 10.4, 11.4). These collections had evidently been put to-gether by different units, and many new versions continued to emerge from China even after the Cultural Revolution, resulting in a new set of translations in Roderick MacFarquhar, Timothy Cheek, and Eugene Wu, eds., *The secret speeches of Chairman Mao*. A comprehensive collection of all Mao's post-1949 works is being prepared by Michael Y. M. Kau and John K. Leung under the title *The writings of Mao Zedong, 1949–1976*, of which the first volume has appeared. Most of the material in these collec-tions, however, related to the pre–Cultural Revolution period; post-1966 speeches were confined for obvious reasons to the period up to the rusti-cation of the Red Guards in the summer of 1968.

The other voluminous type of material produced by the Red Guards was their newspapers, which gave often tendentious accounts of current and pre–Cultural Revolution CCP affairs, but which were mined to good effect by Hong Yung Lee in *The politics of the Chinese Cultural Revolution*. Again, these materials related only to the period up to the summer of 1968. After that, the flow of materials ebbed, although internal CCP documents about the Lin Piao affair became available. In addition, the increasing presence of Westerners in China in the 1970s resulted in some eyewitness reports like Roger Garside's *Coming alive!: China after Mao*, which, despite its title, also covers the events from January 1976.

Only after the end of the Cultural Revolution did a significant amount of new material relevant to the 1969–76 period become available. It took a number of forms. There are some general accounts, produced in spite of an official ban on research into the subject. The most solid and compre-hensive (and certainly most recent) is that by Wang Nien-i, *1949–1989-nien-ti Chung-kuo: ta-tung-luan-ti nien-tai* (China from 1949–1989: a decade of great upheaval), whose author, a professor at the National Defense University, clearly has access to sources not generally available. A very creditable earlier work by the political scientists Kao Kao and Yen Chia-ch'i (the former director of the Political Science Institute of the Chinese Academy of Social Sciences), *"Wen-hua ta-ko-ming" shih-nien shih, 1966–1976* (A history of the ten years of the "Great Cultural Revolution," 1966–1976) was banned on the eve of publication and appeared first in a Hong Kong edition, but the original Tientsin edition is widely available in the West. The authors felt constrained to rely only on publicly available material, and were criticized for the number of errors that crept in; a second edition taking account of the criticisms is apparently under preparation. A flawed English translation of the first edition has been published in Taiwan. Among general Western works, Jürgen

Domes's *Internal politics of China, 1949–1972* and *The government and politics of the PRC: a time of transition* combine broad description and close analysis of specific episodes. Laszlo Ladany, *The Communist Party of China and Marxism, 1921–1985: a self-portrait,* presents a summation based on many years of China-watching by the longtime editor of the Hong Kong newsletter *China News Analysis.*

There are also Chinese collections of essays on different aspects, events or experiences of the Cultural Revolution. Chou Ming, *Li-shih tsai che-li ch'en-ssu: 1966–1976 nien chi-shih* (History is reflected here: a record of the years 1966–1976) is in six volumes: The first deals with the fate or activities of senior leaders during the decade and includes some articles by surviving relatives, notably the children of Liu Shao-ch'i; the second volume concerns itself with major episodes, such as the attack on Wu Han in 1965, the February "counter-current" in 1967, and the Lin Piao affair in 1971; the third volume deals again with the fates of individuals, such as somewhat less senior leaders and intellectuals, again with articles by close relatives, such as T'ao Chu's wife. Chin Ch'un-ming's *"Wen-hua ta-ko-ming" lun-hsi* (An analysis of the "Great Cultural Revolution") is a collection of essays by a senior Party historian on major episodes of the decade and includes interesting information relevant to the period covered in this chapter. *Shih-nien-hou-ti p'ing-shuo – "Wen-hua ta-ko-ming" shih lun-chi* (Appraisals and explanations after one decade – a collection of essays on the history of the "Great Cultural Revolution"), edited by T'an Tsung-chi and Cheng Ch'ien, is a similar type of volume.

More general histories of the Chinese Communist movement are now available from virtually every provincial publishing house. Most are repetitious, but it is worth scanning a number on any issue of interest to see if a fact has surfaced in one that is not in any of the others. For instance, the 1981 edition of the Kwangtung Jen-min ch'u-pan-she's *Chung-kuo kung-ch'an-tang chien-shih chiang-i* (Teaching materials for a brief history of the Chinese Communist Party) appears to have been the first such work to reveal (*hsia,* 353) that, in between the work conference and the CC plenum at Lushan in 1959, there had been a meeting of the Politburo Standing Committee at which P'eng Te-huai had been criticized. Of all the works in this category examined by the present author, easily the most comprehensive, usually combining precise dates for meetings with lists of participants, is Hao Meng-pi and Tuan Hao-jan, eds., *Chung-kuo kung-ch'an-tang liu-shih-nien* (Sixty years of the Chinese Communist Party), of which the second volume covers the post-1949 period. Also extremely useful is a work by the late Hu Hua, a doyen among Party historians,

Chung-kuo she-hui-chu-i ko-ming ho chien-she shih chiang-i (Teaching materials on the history of China's socialist revolution and construction). The *Resolution on CPC history (1949–81)* is the document published by the CC on the occasion of the CCP's sixtieth anniversary as its assessment of the Cultural Revolution and the years preceding. The explanatory commentary on it is: Chung-kung chung-yang wen-hsien yen-chiu-shih, 《*Kuan-yü chien-kuo-i-lai tang-ti jo-kan li-shih wen-t'i ti chueh-i*》 *chu-shih-pen (hsiu-ting)* (Revised annotated edition of the resolution on certain historical problems of the Party since the founding of the People's Republic). Both are essential reading to ascertain the official analysis of key events. As in the case of the Hu Hua book, this latter volume was available in the West in a *nei-pu* (internal) edition before it was openly published; the differences in the two editions appear to be for the most part insignificant enough for the open edition to be acceptable for research purposes.

Another valuable type of work is the chronological volume, which is not just a simple repetition of dates but contains helpful summaries of major meetings and events. Important examples include: Teaching and Research Office for CCP History of the [PLA] Political Academy, ed., *Chung-kuo kung-ch'an-tang liu-shih-nien ta-shih chien-chieh* (A summary of the principal events in the 60 years of the Chinese Communist Party); *Chung-kung tang-shih ta-shih nien-piao* (A chronological table of major events in the history of the Chinese Communist Party); *Chung-kuo kung-ch'an-tang li-tz'u chung-yao hui-i-chi* (Collection of various important conferences of the CCP; in two volumes); Fang wei-chung, ed., *Chung-hua jen-min kung-ho-kuo ching-chi ta-shih-chi (1949–1980)* (A record of the major economic events of the PRC [1949–1980]), which is of interest to a far wider circle than just economists.

Yet another type of work is that devoted to the individual episode, including Party congresses and People's Congress sessions that are covered in official publications like *Tenth National Congress of the Communist Party of China (Documents)*. The documents on the Lin Piao affair were never officially published, but a Western compilation and translation is to be found in Michael Y. M. Kau, ed., *The Lin Piao affair: power politics and military coup*. One Chinese analysis is Yü Nan, "Chou tsung-li ch'u-chih '9.13' Lin Piao p'an-t'ao shih-chien ti i-hsieh ch'ing-k'uang" (Some of the circumstances regarding Premier Chou's management of the 13 September incident when Lin Piao committed treachery and fled). A Western account by a Dutch journalist is Jaap van Ginneken, *The rise and fall of Lin Piao*. More recently, a version of this episode based on the account of Lin Piao's daughter appeared in a series of articles "Sheng-huo tsai li-shih yin-ying chung-ti Lin Tou-tou" (Lin Tou-tou who lives in the shadow of history) in the *Hua-ch'iao jih-pao* (14–23 June 1988). It has also been discussed by T'an Tsung-chi in "Lin Piao fan-ko-ming chi-t'uan ti chueh-ch'i chi-ch'i fu-mieh" (The sudden rise of the Lin Piao counterrevolutionary clique and its destruction) in *Chiao-hsueh ts'an-k'ao, hsia* (Reference for teaching and study, vol. 2). The way in which Lin Piao's crime was transformed from an example of leftism to one of rightism is described by Wang Jo-shui in another series of articles in the *Hua-ch'iao jih-pao* entitled "Ts'ung p'i 'tso' tao-hsiang fan-yu ti i-tz'u ko-jen ching-li" (The experience of one individual of the reversal from criticizing "leftism" to opposing rightism).

The activities of the Gang of Four's Liang Hsiao writing group are described by the wife of one of the group in Yue Daiyun and Carolyn Wakeman, *To the storm*, which is in addition a fascinating account of the whole sweep of the post-1949 period from the perspective of a committed Party member who fell foul of the Party line. The poems put up in memory of Chou En-lai in the period preceding the T'ien An Men incident in April 1976 are collected in *Ko-ming shih ch'ao* (A transcript of revolutionary poems), and *T'ien An Men shih-wen chi* (Collection of T'ien An Men poems), and an English edition, Xiao Lan, *The Tiananmen poems*. The official transcript of the trial of the Gang of Four is available in Tsui-kao jen-min fa-yuan yen-chiu-shih, *Chung-hua jen-min kung-ho-kuo tsui-kao jen-min fa-yuan t'e-pieh fa-t'ing shen-p'an Lin Piao, Chiang Ch'ing fan-ko-ming chi-t'uan an chu-fan chi-shih* (A record of the trial by the Special Tribunal of the PRC's Supreme People's Court of the principal criminals of the Lin Piao and Chiang Ch'ing counter-revolutionary cliques). The Chinese have also published shorter Chinese and English editions: *Li-shih ti shen-p'an* (A historic trial); *A great trial in Chinese history*. David Bonavia's *Verdict in Peking: the trial of the Gang of Four* contains translated extracts with commentary. As its title indicates, John Gardner's *Chinese politics and the succession to Mao* discusses many of these episodes. Merle Goldman in *China's intellectuals: advise and dissent* deals with the struggles in the intellectual sphere in great detail. David Zweig, *Agrarian radicalism in China, 1968–1981*, covers the struggle of the Gang of Four to chart a leftist path in an important policy arena. It is among the first monographs to benefit from lengthy field research in rural China.

The above-mentioned Hu Hua was also the chief editor of the mammoth series of books *Chung-kung tang-shih jen-wu-chuan* (Biographies of personalities in the history of the Chinese Communist Party) (Sian: Shensi Jen-min), of which more than thirty volumes had appeared by the time of his death. This is an invaluable compendium. Each volume contains a dozen or more biographies of dead party leaders, usually a mix of early martyrs and those who survived as leaders of the PRC at the outbreak of the Cultural Revolution.

Since the first of these volumes was published in 1980, however, booklength lives, collections of memorial essays on individual leaders, and their selected works have appeared, many of which contain more detail than the briefer essays in the Hu Hua series. Although some are clearly "fiction," containing records of conversations it is doubtful were ever recorded, all are worth consulting. For the period covered in this chapter, the most important so far are: *Chou En-lai shu-hsin hsuan-chi* (Chou En-lai's selected letters); *Chou En-lai hsuan-chi, hsia* (The selected works of Chou En-lai, vol. 2); *Chou tsung-li sheng-p'ing ta-shih-chi* (Major events in the life of Premier Chou); *Pu-chin-ti ssu-nien* (Inexhaustible memories), also on Chou; *Selected works of Deng Xiaoping (1975–1982)*; Chang Yun-sheng, *Mao-chia-wan chi-shih: Lin Piao mi-shu hui-i-lu* (An on-the-spot report on Mao-chia-wan: the memoirs of Lin Piao's secretary); Nan Chih, *Yeh Ch'ün yeh-shih* (An unofficial history of Yeh Ch'ün); Chu Chung-li (the widow of a former senior official, Wang Chia-hsiang), *Nü-huang meng: Chiang Ch'ing wai-chuan* (Empress dream: an unofficial biography of Chiang Ch'ing); Yeh Yung-lieh, *Chang Ch'un-ch'iao fu-ch'en shih* (The history of Chang Ch'un-ch'iao's rise and fall); Chung K'an, *K'ang Sheng p'ing-chuan* (A critical biography of K'ang Sheng); Lin Ch'ing-shan, *K'ang Sheng wai-chuan* (An unofficial biography of K'ang Sheng); Hsueh Yeh-sheng, ed., *Yeh Chien-ying kuang-hui-ti i-sheng* (Yeh Chien-ying's glorious life); *Ying-ssu lu: huai-nien Yeh Chien-ying* (A record of contemplation: remembering Yeh Chien-ying); *Nieh Jung-chen hui-i-lu, hsia* (The memoirs of Nieh Jung-chen, vol. 3). Articles on individuals often appear first in the regular press before being collected in book form; the two digests *Hsin-hua yueh-pan* (New China monthly) and *Hsin-hua wen-chai* (New China digest) feature regular sections reproducing a few of these articles.

Western lives of Chinese leaders are far fewer. They include: Lucian Pye, *Mao Tse-tung: the man in the leader* (a psychological analysis); Dick Wilson, ed., *Mao Tse-tung in the scales of history*, a series of essays by leading scholars published shortly after the Chairman's death; Ross Terrill, *Mao*; the same author's *The white-boned demon* (on Chiang Ch'ing); Roxane Witke, *Comrade Chiang Ch'ing*, which is based largely on the personal account given by its subject to the author in a series of interviews; Roger Faligot and Remi Kauffer, *Kang Sheng et les services secrets chinois (1927–1987)*; Ting Wang, *Wang Hung-wen, Chang Ch'un-ch'iao p'ing-chuan* (Biographies of Wang Hung-wen and Chang Ch'un-ch'iao), and the same author's *Chairman Hua: leader of the Chinese Communists*.

It is obviously not enough to rely only on Chinese (and Western) books. Chinese journals and other publications on Party history, many of them *nei-pu*, have to be consulted when copies become available: *Tang-shih yen-chiu* (Research on Party history) (1980–87), once *nei-pu*, now openly published and with the new name *Chung-kung tang-shih yen-chiu* (Research into the history of the CCP) (1988–); *Tang-ti wen-hsien* (Party documents); *Tang-shih t'ung-hsun* (Party history newsletter); *Wen-hsien ho yen-chiu* (Documents and research); *Tang-shih yen-chiu tzu-liao* (Research materials on Party history); *Nei-pu wen-kao* (Internal manuscripts); *Tang-shih tzu-liao cheng-chi t'ung-hsun* (Newsletter on the collection of materials on Party history). Articles from such journals and collections occasionally surface elsewhere, most notably in the three-volume collection edited by Chu Ch'eng-chia, *Chung-kung tang-shih yen-chiu lun-wen hsuan* (Selection of research papers on the history of the CCP). Access to these more arcane sources should not, however, blind one to the fact that important articles often appear in the regular press.

So much material now appears in so many PRC sources, that a group of younger Western scholars have got together to publish the *CCP Research Newsletter* (Fall 1988–) under the editorship of Timothy Cheek in order to inform the field about the most important new items. This journal is required reading for anyone seeking to keep abreast of the floodtide of new items of interest. It is to be hoped that when the Chinese authorities notice this journal and realize that *nei-pu* became an almost irrelevant classification in the era of *k'ai-fang*, a more realistic view as to what material really needs to be kept secret will emerge.

Among more generalist Western journals, *The China Quarterly* and *The Australian Journal of Chinese Affairs* are most likely to carry articles dealing with the Cultural Revolution; the *CQ*'s "Quarterly Chronicle and Documentation" section is a useful reference. *Issues & Studies* (Taipei) has often been the first to publish translations of important Communist documents.

The politics of the post-Cultural Revolution period have been less closely analyzed by Chinese publications, principally because China's leader for most of the years since 1976, Teng Hsiao-p'ing, has been alive and in charge. On the other hand, the nature of the contemporary material has been quite different from any previous period in the history of the PRC. It is far more voluminous: there has been an explosion of publications, both books and serials. Official publications have been far more honest and less propagandistic, and they can be measured against openly expressed divergent opinions. Moreover, so porous did the Chinese political process become, that detailed accounts of top-level discussion and debate appeared very quickly in Hong Kong Chinese publications like *Cheng-ming* (Contention) and *Chiu-shih nien-tai* (The nineties).

Again, chronologies focusing on the post-Mao era are important, notably: Li Sheng-p'ing and Chang Ming-shu, *1976–1986: Shih-nien cheng-chih ta-shih-chi* (A record of the great political events of the ten years 1976–1986); Huang Chien-ch'iu, Sun Ta-li, Wei Hsin-sheng, Chang Chan-pin, Wang Hung-mo, eds., *Hsin shih-ch'i chuan-t'i chi-shih* (Oct. 1976–Oct. *1986*) (Important events and special problems of the new period); Li Yung-ch'un, Shih Yuan-ch'un, and Kuo Hsiu-chih, eds., *Shih-i chieh san chung ch'üan-hui i-lai cheng-chih t'i-chih kai-ko ta-shih-chi* (A record of the major events of the reform of the political system since the Third Plenum of the 11th Central Committee). An invaluable Western version of the chronological volume is Kenneth Lieberthal and Bruce J. Dickson, *A research guide to central Party and government meetings in China, 1949–1986.*

A major documentary collection, in addition to the *Selected works of Deng Xiaoping (1975–1982)*, already cited, is *Shih-i chieh san chung ch'üan-hui i-lai chung-yao wen-hsien hsuan-tu* (Selected readings of important documents since the third plenum of the 11th Central Committee) which is in two volumes. A Western documentary collection approaching the period from a different angle is John P. Burns and Stanley Rosen, eds., *Policy conflicts in post-Mao China: a documentary survey, with analysis*; *Central documents and Politburo politics in China*, by Kenneth Lieberthal, with James Tong and Sai-cheung Yeung, explains how such documents get produced and distributed.

Western accounts of Teng Hsiao-p'ing's reform program are numerous, ranging from general works through monographs to journalists' analyses. Among the best general works are: A. Doak Barnett and Ralph N. Clough, eds., *Modernizing China: post-Mao reform and development*; Harry Harding, *China's second revolution: reform after Mao*; David M. Lampton, ed., *Policy implementation in post-Mao China*; Elizabeth J. Perry and Christine Wong, eds., *The political economy of reform in post-Mao China*; Tsou Tang, *The Cultural Revolution and post-Mao reforms*. A useful background series is the *China briefing* annual volume produced by the China Council of the Asia Society. Monographs include: David S. G. Goodman, *Beijing street voices: the poetry and politics of China's democracy movement*; Ellis Joffe, *The Chinese army after Mao*; Kenneth Lieberthal and Michel Oksenberg, *Policy making in China: leaders, structures, and processes*, which analyzes the energy industry before, during, and after the Cultural Revolution; Jean C. Oi, *State and peasant in contemporary China: the political economy of village government*, which covers from the mid-1950s to the late 1980s, and like the Zweig volume is informed by rural research during the later years of the period.

Many of the Western newspaper correspondents based in China during the Cultural Revolution or, in the case of American journalists, just after, had training on China or learned fast. Among the best of the early books of reportage were: Richard Bernstein, *From the center of the earth: the search for the truth about China*; David Bonavia, *The Chinese: a portrait*; Fox Butterfield, *China: alive in the bitter sea*; John Fraser, *The Chinese: portrait of a people*; Jay and Linda Mathews, *One billion: a China chronicle*; Philip Short, *The dragon and the bear: inside China and Russia today*. Steven W. Mosher's controversial *Broken earth: the rural Chinese* and *Journey to the forbidden China* are reports by a doctoral student in anthropology who was among the first American scholars to spend time in the Chinese countryside after the normalization of Sino-American relations in January 1979. Simon Leys is a scholar-essayist who laces his mordant commentaries on the PRC with exposés of any humbug that can be found in Western works on China; his main books are *Chinese shadows*; *The Chairman's new clothes: Mao and the Cultural Revolution*; *Broken images: essays on Chinese culture and politics*.

5. THE OPENING TO AMERICA

Despite an extensive secondary literature, Chinese foreign policy between the Ninth and Twelfth CCP National Congresses remains understudied. The principal inhibiting factor is informational: The available materials do not permit a full rendering of Chinese decision making during this period. The Chinese remain extraordinarily sensitive about the inner workings of their foreign policy process. These inhibitions have eased somewhat in recent years, enabling enhanced access to officials and research institutes concerned with external affairs. But the available historical materials shed little light on deliberations over foreign policy or on the relationship between domestic and international politics, especially in periods of intense leadership conflict.

However, as a consequence of increased official encouragement of archival work, Chinese researchers have compiled a more comprehensive record of the history of Chinese foreign relations, including the 1970s. These efforts culminated with the publication of *Tang-tai Chung-kuo wai-chiao* (Diplomacy of contemporary China), which provides an authoritative recapitulation of the events of this period, even if it reveals little about the workings of the political process. In addition, some memoirs and reminiscences of senior officials offer revealing insights into China's foreign policy reassessment of the late 1960s and early 1970s, though not in great detail. These include *Nieh Jung-chen hui-i lu* (Memoirs of Nieh Jung-chen); Tieh Tzu-wei, "Ch'en I tsai 'Wen-hua ta-ko-ming' chung" (Ch'en I during the "Great Cultural Revolution"), in *Kun-lun*; and Yeh

Chien-ying Biographical Writing Group, *Yeh Chien-ying chuan-leuh* (A brief biography of Yeh Chien-ying). Edgar Snow's discussions with senior Chinese officials before Henry Kissinger's secret visit are an additional valuable source; they are published in their fullest form in Snow, *The long revolution*.

Scholars have also benefited immeasurably from the writings of U.S. officials involved in Sino-American relations during the 1970s. These sources include Zbigniew Brzezinski, *Power and principle*; Henry Kissinger, *White House years*, and *Years of upheaval*; Richard Nixon, *RN – the memoirs of Richard Nixon*; Michel Oksenberg, "A decade of Sino-American relations," in *Foreign Affairs*; Richard H. Solomon, *Chinese political negotiating behavior*; and Cyrus Vance, *Hard choices*.

The basic primary sources for Chinese foreign policy after the Cultural Revolution remain the major CCP media, especially editorials and commentary in *Jen-min jih-pao* (People's daily) and *Hung-ch'i* (Red flag). *Beijing Review* also serves as a useful source for major foreign policy pronouncements. During the late 1970s and early 1980s, China resumed publication of important foreign affairs periodicals that had been interrupted since 1966. These include *Shih-chieh chih-shih* (World knowledge) and *Kuo-chi wen-t'i yen-chiu* (Journal of international studies), both publications of the Ministry of Foreign Affairs. For monitoring foreign policy developments, the Foreign Broadcast Information Service *Daily Report: China*, issued by the U.S. Government, and *Summary of World Broadcasts: Far East*, issued by the British Broadcasting Corporation, constitute essential sources. Several periodic publication series of the Joint Publications Research Service, issued by the U.S. Government, also contain important primary source documentation.

In addition, Teng Hsiao-p'ing's speeches (including several major commentaries of Chinese foreign policy) are compiled in *Teng Hsiao-p'ing wen-hsuan 1975–1982* (Selected works of Teng Hsiao-p'ing 1975–1982). These sources have also been supplemented by internal leadership documents and speeches disseminated in Taiwan or in the West. Although the authenticity of these materials is sometimes subject to dispute, many have provided important insights at times of major policy conflict. Two collections that incorporate these documents include King C. Chen, ed., *China and the three worlds – a foreign policy reader*; and Michael Y. M. Kau, ed., *The Lin Piao affair: power politics and military coup*. An additional primary source, though its value is disputed by some scholars, concerns allegorical literature that appears to reflect internal debate on sensitive foreign policy questions. For alternative interpretations that draw on such sources, consult Kenneth G. Lieberthal, "The foreign policy debate as seen through allegorical articles, 1973–76," in *CQ*; and Harry Harding, "The domestic politics of China's global posture, 1973–78," in Thomas Fingar et al., eds., *China's quest for independence: policy evolution in the 1970s.*

Despite the limitations on information, scholars have produced some important interpretative volumes, as well as monographs on more discrete issues and periods. Among the interpretive volumes, see in particular, Joseph Camilleri, *Chinese foreign policy: the Maoist era and its aftermath*; Golam W. Choudhury, *China in world affairs: the foreign policy of the PRC since 1970*; Harry Harding, ed., *China's foreign relations in the 1980s*; Samuel Kim, ed., *China and the world: Chinese foreign policy in the post-Mao era;* Richard H. Solomon, ed., *The China factor: Sino-American relations and the global scene*; and Michael Yahuda, *Towards the end of isolationism: China's foreign policy after Mao.*

Among the factors contributing to the Sino-American accommodation, greatest weight has been accorded Peking's shifting security calculations following the militarization of the Sino-Soviet conflict. On this topic, see John W. Garver, *China's decision for rapprochement with the United States, 1968–1971*; Harry Gelman, *The Soviet Far East buildup and Soviet risk-taking against China*; Thomas M. Gottlieb, *Chinese foreign policy factionalism and the origins of the strategic triangle*; Melvin Gurtov and Byong-Moo Hwang, *China under threat: the politics of strategy and diplomacy*; Gene T. Hsiao and Michael Witunski, eds., *Sino-American normalization and its policy implications*; and Richard Wich, *Sino-Soviet crisis politics: a study of political change and communication.*

The shifting geostrategic context of Sino-American and Sino-Soviet relations during the 1970s and early 1980s has also been explored in various monographs and edited volumes, including Herbert J. Ellison, ed., *The Sino-Soviet conflict: a global perspective*; Banning N. Garrett and Bonnie S. Glaser, *War and peace: the views from Moscow and Beijing*; Kenneth G. Lieberthal, *Sino-Soviet conflict in the 1970s: its evolution and implications for the strategic triangle*; Jonathan D. Pollack, *The Sino-Soviet rivalry and Chinese security debate*, and *The lessons of coalition politics: Sino-American security relations*; Gerald Segal, *Sino-Soviet relations after Mao*; Douglas T. Stuart and William T. Tow, eds., *China, the Soviet Union, and the West: strategic and political dimensions in the 1980s*; Chi Su, "Soviet image of and policy toward China, 1969–1979"; Robert G. Sutter, *Chinese foreign policy: developments after Mao*; and Allen S. Whiting, *Siberian development and East Asia: threat or promise?*

Compared to Sino-American and Sino-Soviet politics, Sino-Japanese relations remain extraordinarily understudied. However, see Robert E. Bedeski, *The fragile entente: the 1978 Japan-China peace treaty in a global con-*

text; Chae-jin Lee, *Japan faces China: political and economic relations in the postwar era*, and *China and Japan: new economic diplomacy*; and Robert Taylor, *The Sino-Japanese axis: a new force in Asia?* For several important articles, see Shinkichi Etō, "Japan and China – a new stage?" in *Problems of Communism*, and "Recent developments in Sino-Japanese relations," in *Asian Survey*; and Ryosei Kokubun, "The politics of foreign economic policy-making in China: the case of plant cancellations with Japan," in *CQ*.

The literature on China's relations with Southeast Asia (especially the deterioration of relations with Vietnam) is extensive and detailed. For an especially evocative account, see Nayan Chanda, *Brother enemy: the war after the war*. See also Chang Pao-min, *Beijing, Hanoi, and the Overseas Chinese*, and *Kampuchea between China and Vietnam;* William J. Duiker, *China and Vietnam: the roots of conflict*; Eugene K. Lawson, *The Sino-Vietnamese conflict*; and Robert S. Ross, *The Indochina tangle: China's Vietnam policy, 1975–1979*.

The implications of China's emergence in international organizations during the 1970s are exhaustively studied in Samuel S. Kim, *China, the United Nations, and world order*. For reviews of the economic dimensions of Chinese foreign policy in the 1970s, see A. Doak Barnett, *China's economy in global perspective*; and Allen S. Whiting, *Chinese domestic politics and foreign policy in the 1970s*.

6. CHINA'S ECONOMIC POLICY AND PERFORMANCE

Research and publications dealing with China's economic reforms of the 1980s is ongoing just as the reforms themselves are ongoing. Work on economic policy and performance during the Cultural Revolution period (1966–76) is also in its infancy. There were, to be sure, many articles and books written about the Chinese economy in the 1960s and 1970s, but those dealing with the contemporary period were forced to rely on very limited data of questionable reliability. In fact, much of the Western literature on China's economy in this period was devoted to reconstructing production estimates for agriculture, industry, gross national product, and various other subsectors. Despite these limitations, valuable work was accomplished, and the reader interested in the English-language works of lasting value written in the 1960s and 1970s should look at the bibliography in the survey article by Dwight H. Perkins, "Research on the economy of the People's Republic of China: a survey of the field," in *JAS*.

Beginning in 1979 the Chinese government began once again to publish official statistical series after a nearly twenty-year hiatus when all economic data had been treated as state secrets. What began as a trickle of statistics in 1979 became an ever widening flood in the 1980s. The single most useful source, published in both English and Chinese, is the State Statistical Bureau's *Statistical yearbook of China*, published annually beginning in 1981 and covering more and more data, not only for the 1980s but for the earlier periods as well. The 1,029 pages in the 1989 *Statistical yearbook* contrasts with the 200-plus, much smaller pages of the State Statistical Bureau's *Wei-ta ti shih-nien* (Ten great years), the principal statistical source of the 1950s. And there are now dozens of specialized statistical handbooks for different sectors (for example, the *Chung-kuo nung-yeh nien-chien* [Agricultural yearbook of China]), for many of the individual provinces (for example, the Kwangtung Statistical Office's *Kwangtung-sheng t'ung-chi nien-chien* [Kwangtung province statistical yearbook]), and many specialized studies including the State Statistical Bureau's *Chung-kuo ku-ting tzu-ch'an t'ou-tzu t'ung-chi tzu-liao, 1950–1985* (Statistical materials on fixed capital investment in China, 1950–1985).

In addition to these statistical sources, there is a growing literature in English based on fieldwork in China, some of it carried out in collaborative projects between the Chinese Academy of Social Sciences and the World Bank. Two of the important products of this latter collaborative effort are Gene Tidrick and Chen Jiyuan, eds., *China's industrial reform*, and William Byrd and Lin Qingsong, eds., *China's rural industry: structure, development, and reform*.

Among the various efforts to look at the 1960s and 1970s in the light of the newly available information and data, the most work has been done on the rural sector. Studies of both the pre- and post-reform period based on fieldwork in China are found in William L. Parish, ed., *Chinese rural development: the great transformation*. Broad-based economic analysis of agricultural development for the entire period since 1949 that is based in part on the new data can be found in Nicholas Lardy, *Agriculture in China's modern economic development*, and Dwight Perkins and Shahid Yusuf, *Rural development in China*. Much less work has been done on industrial development strategies in the 1960s and 1970s based on information available only since the 1980s. A notable exception is Barry Naughton, "The third front: defence industrialization in the Chinese interior," in *CQ*.

Several general collections of essays concentrate on issues of economic reform and economic performance in China in the 1980s. These include the U.S. Congress Joint Economic Committee's two-volume work, *China's economy looks toward the year 2000*, and Elizabeth J. Perry and Christine Wong, eds., *The political economy of reform in post-Mao China*. Many of the collections of essays now coming out are joint efforts of Chinese and foreign economists. One of the most useful of these is Bruce L. Reynolds, ed., *Chinese economic reform*, a special issue of the *Journal of Comparative Economics*. The World Bank also puts out a general volume on the Chinese economy approximately every four years. A general analysis of China's reform efforts together with an extensive bibliography is Dwight H. Perkins's "Reforming China's Economic System," in the *Journal of Economic Literature*.

One difference between the 1980s and the previous two decades is the growing number of economic analyses by Chinese authors. These publications appear in literally dozens of economic journals, most of which did not even exist before 1979. Others appear as articles in newspapers. The *World Economic Herald* published in Shanghai was particularly energetic in bringing debates over controversial economic reform issues to a wider audience. Most such articles, however, are available only in the Chinese language, although there have been a number of efforts to translate some of these articles into English in order to reach an international audience. One particularly noteworthy English translation is of the Chinese Economic System Reform Research Institute's *Reform in China: challenges and choices* (ed. with an introduction by Bruce L. Reynolds), published by M. E. Sharpe, which also puts out a regular journal of translations of economic works under the title *Chinese Economic Studies*.

Finally, there is a literature on China's economy written mainly with a business audience in mind but containing articles on current economic issues of general interest. Notable in this category is *The China Business Review,* a publication of the U.S.–China Business Council, and the *China Newsletter* of the Japan External Trade Organization (JETRO). A useful collection of essays emphasizing trade issues is Eugene K. Lawson, ed., *U.S.-China Trade: problems and prospects*.

7. EDUCATION

This essay continues the discussion presented for Chapters 4 and 9 of *CHOC* 14. Sources and research methodologies described there are necessary background for the further comments and data offered here. In general, official Chinese newspapers and journals remained the primary source, but certain changes should be noted. The Union Research Institute's clipping file service in Hong Kong became much less useful after the Chinese government began to restrict the circulation of newspapers outside the country beginning in the late 1950s. The URI service nevertheless continued through the early 1970s. The entire collection of files going back to 1950 was moved to the Baptist College library in Hong Kong, when the Institute itself finally closed in 1983. Meanwhile, the profusion of unofficial Red Guard publications chronicled the events of 1966–68, and provided a critical retrospective on earlier years. Once the Red Guards "returned to school to make revolution," however, their independent publishing activities ceased. Local official newspapers continued to be published throughout the entire Cultural Revolution decade (1966–76), with only brief interruptions, which varied with the locality during the most chaotic years, 1967–69.

Nevertheless, the circulation of these publications outside the country remained tightly restricted. Thus between 1969 and 1976, foreigners' access to the Chinese media was essentially confined to the "two newspapers and one journal" (*liang pao i k'an*). These were the national publications controlled by the Maoist central administration, with sole authority to serve as the publicity organs for the new order it aimed to build in the wake of the Red Guard mass mobilization phase. These three publications – *Jen-min jih-pao* (People's daily), *Chieh-fang-chün pao* (Liberation Army news), and *Hung-ch'i* (Red flag); plus *Kuang-ming jih-pao* (Enlightenment daily), which followed their lead; and later the journal *Hsueh-hsi yü p'i-p'an* (Study and criticism) – remained the chief documentary sources for the "revolution in education" experiments as well as everything else that occurred between 1968 and 1976. Also, occasional issues of a few local study journals were spirited out of China, such as *Chiao-yü ko-ming* (Education revolution) published by Kwangtung Normal College, and *Chiao-yü shih-chien* (Education practice) from the Shanghai Normal University.

Such was the research environment within which the oral history or interview method became popular in the late 1960s and early 1970s. At the time, when there was also an upsurge of interest in China both scholarly and otherwise, interviews with former residents of China were virtually the only alternative to the tightly controlled media. These were conducted mainly in Hong Kong by American graduate students and professors during those years when the Universities Service Centre, established in 1963, became their main field research base once removed from China itself. As mentioned in the Volume 14 bibliographical essay, the books on education that relied most heavily on interview data were those by Stanley Rosen, Susan Shirk, and Jonathan Unger. All three began as Ph.D. dissertation research at the Universities Service Centre.

The proliferation of official publications after 1976, and the relaxation of their sale outside China, have served to remedy somewhat the paucity of documentary sources for the preceding decade. The most noteworthy addition to date is a major acquisition of provincial newspapers made in 1987 by the Universities Service Centre in Hong Kong. The Centre has since closed as an independent institution, but its library, now housed at Hong Kong's Chinese University, retains the most complete and readily accessible collection of national and provincial newspapers available anywhere. Virtually every province is represented in consecutive issues from 1949 to the present. This collection provides a unique source for the Cultural Revolution decade and supersedes the old URI materials for the earlier years as well, since the newspaper clipping files (according to the published index) were based on a far from complete selection of local publications. In addition, the collection supersedes those available in China itself, not only because of accessibility but also because libraries there do not maintain so extensive an array of publications under one roof.

Specialized official and semiofficial publications on education, youth, and science also proliferated in the post-1976 era. By the mid-1980s, a selection of the main newspapers that concentrated on these subjects included: *Kuang-ming jih-pao*; *Chung-kuo chiao-yü pao* (China education news); *Chiao-yü wen-chai* (Education extracts); *Chiao-shih pao* ('Teachers' news); *Chung-kuo ch'ing-nien pao* (China youth news); *Chung-kuo shao-nien pao* (China children's news); *K'o-chi jih-pao* (Science and technology news); *K'o-hsueh wen-hua pao* (Scientific culture news); and *Liang yung jen-ts'ai pao* (Dual-purpose personnel news, specializing in military education news). The *Jen-min ta-hsueh* (People's University) newspaper clipping reprint series included several relevant categories and provided a useful though not comprehensive collection of articles on education-related subjects.

The major journals included: *Jen-min chiao-yü* (People's education); *Chiao-yü yen-chiu* (Education research); *Chiao-hsueh yü yen-chiu* (Teaching and research); *Kao chiao chan-hsien* (Higher education battlefront), changed in the mid-1980s to *Chung-kuo kao-teng chiao-yü* (Chinese higher education); *Kao-teng chiao-yü yen-chiu* (Higher education research); *Chiao-yü li-lun yu shih-chien* (Education theory and practice); *Chiao-yü yü chih-yeh* (Education and occupation); and *Chiao-hsueh t'ung-hsun* (Teaching bulletin). Many of these specialized newspapers and periodicals were replicated in provincial and local versions. Most common were those concerning education. Most provinces and Peking and Shanghai published their own magazines as, for example, *Shang-hai chiao-yü*, *Shan-hsi chiao-yü*, *Fu-chien chiao-yü*. In format, these provincial education magazines were all similar; they were written for teachers and concentrated on teaching news.

Another source was the journals that most major universities and colleges published. These contained a wide range of scholarly articles; most pertinent for the education field itself were the journals of the teacher training universities, for example: *Pei-ching shih-fan ta-hsueh hsueh-pao* (Peking Normal University journal); *Hua-tung shih-fan ta-hsueh hsueh-pao* (East China Normal University journal); *Hua-nan shih-fan ta-huseh hsueh-pao* (South China Normal University journal); *Hua-chung shih-fan ta-hsueh hsueh-pao* (Central China Normal University journal); and *Tung-pei shih-ta hsueh-pao* (Northeast Normal University journal).

Ironically, the output of the various translation services has moved inversely with the growth in number of Chinese publications. The reduction in translated materials occurred both generally and for education-related subjects in particular. The main U.S. government translations (the press survey, magazine extracts, *Current Background*, and supplements) were all collapsed in 1977 into the Foreign Broadcast Information Service (FBIS) – *Daily Report: China* series. This provides a brief compilation of major news items each day. The reason for the decision to consolidate, according to members of the U.S. Consulate in Hong Kong who helped to make it in 1976, was that the "two newspapers and one journal" formula then dominating the official Chinese media had made so extensive a translation service superfluous. But that decision must go down as yet another in a list of several historic failures on the part of U.S. government China analysts to anticipate the direction of things to come. As soon as the consolidation was implemented, the publication explosion in China commenced. In 1979, therefore, the need to cover the increased volume of materials led to a reorganization of the old U.S. Joint Publications Research Service (JPRS) into a more streamlined series of specialty publications. Between 1979 and 1987, items on education and youth were translated in *China report: political, sociological and military affairs* under the joint JPRS/FBIS logo. In the mid-1980s, the various JPRS series were further focused. As of 1987, relevant items could be found translated in three JPRS series: *China Area Report (CAR)*, *China/Red Flag (CRF)*, and *China/State Council Bulletin (CSB)*. Translations of scientific and technical articles appeared in a separate series. Unfortunately, however, interest in education topics as reflected in these various translations series peaked during 1977–79, when the Maoist experiments were being overturned. Once the education system was restored to its pre–Cultural Revolution form, the subject fell rapidly in the priority ratings. As a result, it became impossible from about 1980 to gain even a superficial overview of developments in the education field by relying on English translations alone. The one bright spot for those who do not read Chinese is *Chinese Education: a journal of translations*, formerly published by the International Arts and Sciences Press (IASP) and since 1977 by M. E. Sharpe. This journal provides a good but limited topical compilation of articles four times annually.

Probably more than other areas of regional specialization, the China field remains peculiarly sensitive to changing political fashions and public moods, including both those in China and those in the world outside. In particular, the changes that have overtaken foreign research and reporting about contemporary China reflect the political events that have occurred there, and with no less ironic consequences than they have produced for the Chinese themselves. Thus, even though our access to China both physically and via its publications has improved dramatically since 1976, the information now available to the interested English-language audience has not expanded accordingly. For better or worse, however, the supply of information in this case probably reflects the demand because the interested reading public itself has shrunk. The intensity of concern that China generated, first as enemy and later as newfound friend, continued in one form or another for three decades. But by 1980, the earlier orientation had become obsolete and the novelty of the latest phase was beginning to wear off. The China that had emerged through its newly reopened door after 1976 was, by its own admission, a poor and backward society seeking aid and acceptance from the Western international community. China as just another friendly and familiar Third World country was very different, in terms of the curiosity it aroused, from the China that had invited sympathetic observers to view its revolutionary experiments in the early 1970s.

Drawing inspiration as it does in this field from the larger arena of public interest, scholarly research also suffered a deflation of energy. The Cold War conflicts of the post-1945 era had generated the earlier motivation: first, to show that China was Asian Communist enemy number one and, then, to prove that it was not. By 1980, both missions had passed into history and no comparable new ones were emerging. These and other currents were combining to produce a level of intellectual inertia that was probably unprecedented in the China field since the late 1940s. Suddenly gone were the days when the discovery of some new document could produce a flurry of excitement and scholars vied with each other in the search for interviewees who could help to explain how this or that policy was being implemented in any given city or village. Nor was it simply a matter of jaded appetites, too many available "internal" documents, and an unlimited supply of potential informants. Topics remained unresearched and unexplored, even while the resources for doing so were greater than ever before.

The study of Chinese education remained in the forefront of all these political and generational trends. Thought reform of the intellectuals was the dominant theme of 1950s research. Then a range of questions related to educational sociology and development emerged quickly into the limelight at the start of the Cultural Revolution. They retained a high profile thereafter as Mao's "education revolution" struck responsive cords among an international audience eager to learn what, if any, wider application the Chinese experiments might have and the lessons that might be learned from them. Once the post-Mao administration in China disassociated itself categorically from those experiments, however, the effect was to discredit the earlier sympathetic reporters as naive apologists for a revolutionary movement gone awry. Thereafter, the subject receded to a more modest place on the priority list of scholarly and public concerns. Whether Mao's successors have succeeded in permanently removing education from the arena of public policy debates within China itself remains to be seen. But for the time being, events have combined to dampen quite effectively wider foreign interest in this sector of the Chinese experience. Everybody, of course, knows that Chinese dynasties and governments have from time immemorial sought legitimacy by exaggerating their own accomplishments and denigrating those of their predecessors. But the mood was such by the end of the 1980s, and the lack of curiosity was so pervasive, that few troubled to verify the new administration's claims either about itself or about its Maoist predecessor with respect to education-related subjects and many others as well. In effect, the new opportunities to combine documentary and field research that the improved access to Chinese sources offered were being left largely unexploited for a range of issue areas.

Finally, besides those already mentioned, there was one additional important reason for the state of research on Chinese education specifically. This concerned the "liberation" of the Chinese intellectual community, or large numbers thereof, from their suspect status as actual or potential enemies of the revolution. They had also emerged further as friends and colleagues speaking authoritatively about Chinese education within the international academic community. But in the process of that interaction, it became increasingly difficult for the foreign observer to differentiate the various roles being filled by their Chinese counterparts, that is, either as participants within the Chinese political arena or as scholarly researchers whose views and writings on the Cultural Revolution and more specialized education topics meshed perfectly with the orientations of the post-Mao government. Viewing education within the context of Chinese tradition, one might interpret the intellectual-bureaucratic establishment as once again helping to rewrite history for a new political administration. Viewing education within the more immediate context of post-1949 events, one might also interpret the exonerated intellectual community as victim of the revolution and by extension as a firm ally of the new postrevolutionary order, in terms both of commitments and of self-interest. Perhaps several more years must pass to distance everyone farther from the upheavals of 1949–79, before Chinese academics and their foreign counterparts will regain the perspective and motivation necessary to produce a new generation of scholarship in this area.

8. CREATIVITY AND POLITICS

Sources about intellectual life during the Cultural Revolution – in particular, about the fate of literature and the arts – can be divided into the following categories: (1) Chinese sources published in China, (2) Chinese sources published outside China, (3) sources in English published in China, and (4) sources in English and other languages published outside China.

1. The first category consists largely of the official and unofficial newspapers, as well as books of fiction, poetry, essays, opera texts, and criticism. *People's daily* and *Red flag* carried the major official documents revealing cultural change; Red Guard newspapers based themselves largely on rumors, and they cannot be considered reliable except for providing an excellent impression of the "revolutionary atmosphere." The number of Chinese learned and literary journals was sharply reduced during the Cultural Revolution; they reappeared gradually during the 1970s.

2. Chinese sources published in Taiwan and Hong Kong grew more valuable as the Cultural Revolution proceeded. Initially they tended to be rather partisan in "the struggle between the two lines." In June 1967, for instance, Tzu-lien ch'u-pan-she in Hong Kong published a red booklet with sayings by Liu Shao-ch'i (*Liu chu-hsi yü-lu*) as an antidote to the *Quotations from Chairman Mao Tse-tung.* A serious and reliable study, however, is Chao Ts'ung, *Chung-kuo ta-lu ti hsi-chü kai-ko* (The reform of drama in mainland China), a publication of the Chinese University Press.

3. English sources published in China have the advantage of giving official translations of the major documents and reports. A well-known specimen of the early period of the Cultural Revolution is *Important documents on the Great Proletarian Cultural Revolution in China. Chinese Literature*, which continued publication throughout the Cultural Revolution except for a brief period in 1967, is of particular importance for our topic. The rehabilitations of writers and artists after the death of Mao Tse-tung

were published not only in the Chinese press, but usually also in English in *Chinese Literature.*

4. Apart from the publications in English by the Union Research Institute in Hong Kong or the journal *Issues & Studies* printed in Taiwan – which only incidentally refer to literature, the arts, and intellectual life – a great number of books and articles appeared in Europe and America. A distinction should be made between eyewitness reports and academic analyses.

Some of the eyewitness reports were written by Europeans and published rather promptly, others were written by Chinese and published mainly in the 1980s. An early report by Alexei Zhelokhovtsev, a Russian sinologist, was published in *Novyi Mir* in 1968; a German version appeared under the title *Chinesische Kulturrevolution aus der Nähe.* In German the name of the author is spelled A. N. Schelochowzew. As usual in Soviet publications of this period, the tone of the book is unfriendly and polemical, but the description of the early stage of the Cultural Revolution is precise and quite reliable. The polemical tone predominates also in the collective volume *Sud'by kul'tury KNR 1949–1974* (The fate of culture in the People's Republic of China 1949–1974), edited by V. A. Krivtsov, S. D. Markova, and V.F. Sorokin. Both Zhelokhovtsev and Markova have published more on literature under the Cultural Revolution. An eyewitness account by a diplomat from the Netherlands focusing on ideological and intellectual matters is D. W. Fokkema, *Report from Peking.* A French diplomat, Jean Esmein, wrote *La Révolution culturelle chinoise.* A valuable eyewitness account that describes the vicissitudes of a young Chinese who became a Red Guard at the age of 12 is Liang Heng and Judith Shapiro, *Son of the revolution.* Yue Daiyun, now a professor of Chinese literature at Peking University, told her story of suppression and survival to Carolyn Wakeman, which resulted in the book *To the storm: the odyssey of a revolutionary Chinese woman.*

Among the academic analyses Merle Goldman's *China's intellectuals: advise and dissent* stands out as a comprehensive and reliable summary of political and intellectual history between 1960 and 1980. This book was preceded by a great number of publications, such as Richard H. Solomon, *Mao's revolution and the Chinese political culture* and Thomas W. Robinson, ed., *The Cultural Revolution in China.* A unique source is Roxane Witke, *Comrade Chiang Ch'ing,* partly based on interviews granted by Chiang Ch'ing to the American author.

Analyses dealing with literature and the arts are less numerous. Joe C. Huang, *Heroes and villains in communist China: the contemporary Chinese novel as a reflection of life* includes the early stage of the Cultural Revolution.

Kai-yu Hsu combines analysis and interviews in *The Chinese literary scene*. After the death of Mao Tse-tung, and in particular when the phenomenon of "scar literature" had been discovered by Western sinologists, several publications devoted to the new literature appeared, of which only a selection can be mentioned here: David S. G. Goodman, *Beijing street voices: the poetry and politics of China's democracy movement*; Howard Goldblatt, ed., *Chinese literature for the 1980s: the Fourth Congress of Writers and Artists*; Wolfgang Kubin and Rudolf G. Wagner, ed., *Essays in modern Chinese literature and literary criticism: papers of the Berlin Conference 1978*; Rudolf G. Wagner, ed., *Literatur und Politik in der Volksrepublik China*; Jeffrey C. Kinkley, ed., *After Mao: Chinese literature and society, 1978–1981*; Michael S. Duke, *Blooming and contending: Chinese literature in the post-Mao era*.

9. THE COUNTRYSIDE UNDER COMMUNISM

Before 1949, some of the best rural sociology and anthropology in the world was done in China, some of it by Westerners such as Sidney Gamble and Morton Fried, but much of it by such brilliant Chinese social scientists as Fei Hsiao-t'ung, Lin Yueh-hwa, and C. K. Yang. Books produced by such scholars – notably, Sidney Gamble, *Ting Hsien: a North China rural community*, Morton Fried, *The fabric of Chinese society*, Fei Hsiao-t'ung, *Peasant life in China*, Lin Yueh-hwa, *The golden wing* – provide a superb basis for understanding the texture of Chinese village life in the decades preceding the victory of the Communists.

But soon after the founding of the People's Republic of China the new government suppressed academic sociology and anthropology, which according to it were carriers of bourgeois ideology. Besides doing tragic damage to the careers of superb scholars like Fei Hsiao-t'ung, the suppression of academic social science also greatly harmed the cause of international understanding. Solid information on the experience of China's vast peasant population was simply unavailable to foreigners.

Throughout China there were published a rich variety of local histories, often describing in fresh, fascinating detail the experience of a particular village, commune, or county. These documents, however, were usually published in extremely limited editions and were not available outside of China. In the Chinese-language documents that could be purchased from outside China or that were available in foreign libraries, such major events as land reform, collectivization, the Great Leap Forward, the Socialist Education Campaign, and the Cultural Revolution in the countryside were mainly described in highly stereotyped terms, so colored by the current political line that they gave little direct reliable information about what ordinary peasants actually felt about the events. During the 1960s and 1970s, for example, a vast number of newspaper articles and books were written extolling Ta-chai, the production brigade in Shansi province that was supposedly a model of economic productivity and revolutionary spirit. A good representative of this literature in English is *Ta-chai: standard-bearer in China's agriculture*. But in the late 1970s, after the defeat of the Maoists by the allies of Teng Hsiao-p'ing, the official press claimed that Ta-chai's success was illusory, and denounced its supposedly heroic leader, Ch'en Yung-kuei, as a fraud.

A hint of the wealth of frank information that may be available in documents normally restricted from foreigners can be had from a perusal of the "Lien-chiang documents," local reports on post–Great Leap Forward problems in Fukien province that were obtained by Taiwan intelligence agents. These documents are translated in C. S. Chen, ed., *Rural people's communes in Lien-chiang*.

Newspapers, books, and periodicals published in China and available in the West during the 1950s, 1960s, and most of the 1970s did, however, afford plenty of clues about what was going on in China's villages, and from the mid-1950s to the mid-1970s, China scholars in the West devoted enormous amounts of effort sifting through and interpreting those clues. The most successful accounts of rural life produced by this method include the sections on villages in Franz Schurmann, *Ideology and organization in Communist China*; Ezra Vogel, *Canton under Communism: programs and politics in a provincial capital, 1949–1968*; Richard Baum, *Prelude to revolution*; and Vivienne Shue, *Peasant China in transition: the dynamics of development toward socialism, 1949–1956*. C. K. Yang, *The Chinese family in the communist revolution* and *A Chinese village in early communist transition* combine a sensitive analysis of ethnography conducted in a Kwangtung village on the eve of the Communist takeover with a careful analysis of documents on village life published during the 1950s.

From the mid-1960s to the mid-1970s, these efforts to puzzle out clues contained in official Chinese publications were increasingly supplemented by interviews with émigrés from China to Hong Kong. One problem with using this methodology to understand the processes of rural life, however, was that most of the émigrés from China were from the cities rather than the countryside. When Western scholars wrote about rural life, therefore, their information was at best secondhand; memories of rural life recounted by city people, usually from the Kwangtung area, who had spent some time in the countryside (often as a result of being sent down to rural areas against their will). John C. Pelzel, "Economic management of a production brigade in post-Leap China" (published in

W. E. Willmott, ed., *Economic organization in Chinese society*), was one of the best of such works based primarily on interviews conducted in the mid- to late 1960s. By the early 1970s, enough émigrés had come to Hong Kong who had lived long periods of time in the countryside, and enough sophistication had been obtained in methods for locating and interviewing them, that some extremely informative accounts of rural life could be produced. William L. Parish and Martin King Whyte, *Village and family life in contemporary China* used a combination of quantitative and qualitative sociological analysis to paint a subtle picture of social continuity and change in the rural areas of Kwangtung province. Anita Chan, Richard Madsen, and Jonathan Unger, *Chen Village: the recent history of a peasant community in Mao's China* and Richard Madsen, *Morality and power in a Chinese village* utilized accounts of émigrés from a single Kwangtung village to build an integrated account of social history in that community from the 1950s to 1980.

Complementing these attempts by professional social scientists to understand China from the outside were a series of books by foreigners who, because of special personal or political connections, were able to visit Chinese villages and produce eyewitness accounts of what life was like there. These accounts often lack social scientific analysis and are strongly colored by the political commitments of their authors to the Chinese revolution. The best of them, however, provide vivid, detailed, honest descriptions of village life, even when these descriptions do not support the hopes of their authors about socialism. The finest works of this genre are William Hinton's *Fanshen* and *Shenfan* – epic eyewitness stories of the vicissitudes of "Long Bow" village in Shansi province. Other books of this genre are Jack Chen, *A year in Upper Felicity*; Isabel and David Crook, *Revolution in a Chinese village: Ten Mile Inn* and *Ten Mile Inn: mass movement in a Chinese village*; and Jan Myrdal's transcriptions of interviews with peasants in Liu Lin: *Report from a Chinese village*, Jan Myrdal and Gun Kessle, *China: the revolution continued*, and Jan Myrdal, *Return to a Chinese village*.

By 1978, China began cautiously to allow professional social scientists to conduct research in villages. The first product of such access was Steven Mosher, *Broken earth: the rural Chinese*, a work based on a year of research in a Kwangtung village, but engulfed in controversy because of Chinese allegations that the author used unethical research methods. David Zweig's *Agrarian radicalism in China, 1968–1981* was based on fieldwork near Nanking. Edward Friedman, Paul G. Pickowicz, and Mark Selden, *Chinese village, socialist state*, is based on research conducted over a period of eight years in Hopei province, near the area where Sidney

Gamble did the fieldwork for his *Ting Hsien*; and *Agents and victims in South China: accomplices in rural revolution* by Helen Siu is based on research in Kwangtung.

Of even greater long-range importance for a systematic understanding of rural life in the People's Republic is the slow but steady reemergence in the 1980s of sociology as a legitimate enterprise in Chinese academic life. Fei Hsiao-t'ung has begun to restudy the rural village of Kai-hsien-kung, which was the basis for his 1939 classic *Peasant life in China*. A steady stream of articles is beginning to appear in journals like *She-hui* (Society) based on this renewed work by Fei and other Chinese rural sociologists. Some of the results of Fei's new work is available in English translation in Fei Xiaotong, *Chinese village close-up*.

Sociologists and other scholars of rural China can benefit from a huge outpouring of statistical data about China's demography and rural economy. Until the early 1980s, accurate, detailed population and economic statistics were simply not available. Before that, what compilations of statistics were published belonged to a genre that might be characterized as "social science fiction." An example was the State Statistical Bureau's account of the first decade of the PRC, *Ten great years: statistics of the economic and cultural achievements of the People's Republic of China* (translation published by Western Washington State College, Program in East Asian Studies, 1974). As with science fiction, real facts might be found embedded in an imaginative account. Digging the useful facts out, however, required considerable effort.

With China's policies of reform and opening to the West in the 1980s, came a professionalization of the gathering of statistics and open publication of many statistical compilations. A nationwide population census was carried out in 1982, using the most modern techniques. The census yielded a wealth of data useful to scholars studying rural demographic trends. Data from the census were published in English translation in *The 1982 population census of China* and *New China's population*. Yearly "Almanacs of China's population" are published by the Population Research Center of the Chinese Academy of Social Sciences.

In 1981, an *Almanac of China's economy, with economic statistics for 1949–1980* was published under the editorship of Hsueh Mu-ch'iao by the Economic Research Centre of the State Council of the PRC and by the State Statistical Bureau. Every year thereafter, a *Statistical yearbook of China* has been published by the China Statistical Information and Consultancy Service Center. A Chinese economic yearbook (*Chung-kuo ching-chi nien-chien*) has been published since 1981, and a Chinese agricultural yearbook (*Chung-kuo nung-yeh nien-chien*) has been published since 1980. Most provinces also now publish their own economic almanacs, copies of which are available in major research center libraries in the West.

10. URBAN LIFE IN THE PEOPLE'S REPUBLIC

General works in Chinese on urban social organization and patterns of life since 1949 are scarce. However, two major Chinese urban planning journals, *Chien-chu hsueh-pao* (Architectural journal) and *Ch'eng-shih chien-she* (Urban construction), contain informative articles on urban policy and on the transformation of particular urban areas. A variety of works on official urban policies and programs also exist. See, for example, Lai Chih-yen, ed., *Chieh-kuan ch'eng-shih ti kung-tso ching-yen* (Experience in the takeover work in cities); Liu Shao-ch'i et al., *Hsin-min-chu chu-yi ch'eng-shih cheng-ts'e* (New democratic urban policies); Lu Hung, *Lun ch'eng-hsiang ho-tso* (On urban–rural cooperation); *Lun ch'eng-hsiang kuan-hsi* (On the urban–rural relationship); *Tsu-kuo hsin-hsing ch'eng-shih* (The motherland's new type cities); and Wu-han shih ch'eng-shih kuei-hua she-chi yuan (Wuhan City Urban Planning and Design Academy), *Ch'eng-shih kuei-hua ts'an-k'ao t'u-li* (Reference key to urban planning). A few accounts of the transformations of particular cities are also available. See, for example, Lao She, *Wo je-ai hsin Pei-ching* (I love new Peking), and *Chao-chia-pang ti pien-ch'ien* (The transformation of Chao-chia-pang) – a Shanghai slum. Since 1979 several new sociological journals have begun to publish informative empirical studies of urban social life. See, in particular, *She-hui k'o-hsueh chan-hsien* (Social science front), *She-hui* (Society), and *Chung-kuo she-hui k'o-hsueh* (Chinese social science). There is also an English-language journal published in China, *Social Sciences in China*, and a Western journal of translations, *Chinese Sociology and Anthropology*, which from time to time have articles of interest on urban social patterns.

In Western scholarship there are a number of useful studies of Chinese urban organization and social life before 1949 that provide an essential background for the understanding of the post-1949 changes. Particularly important are G. William Skinner, ed., *The city in late imperial China*; Mark Elvin and G. William Skinner, eds., *The Chinese city between two worlds*; William Rowe, *Hankow: commerce and society in a Chinese city, 1796–1889* and *Hankow: conflict and community in a Chinese city, 1796–1895*; Sidney Gamble, *Peking: a social survey*; George Kates, *The years that were fat*; Olga Lang, *Chinese family and society*; Edward Lee, *Modern Canton*; Morton Fried, *The fabric of Chinese society*; H. Y. Lowe, *The adventures of Wu*; Rhoads Murphey, *Shanghai: key to modern China*; and Ida Pruitt, *A daughter of Han* and *Old Madam Yin*.

Several scholars have focused on post-1949 changes in particular cities.

See, in particular, Ezra Vogel, *Canton under communism*; Lynn T. White III, *Careers in Shanghai*; and Kenneth Lieberthal, *Revolution and tradition in Tientsin, 1949–1952*. See also the informative conference volume edited by Christopher Howe, *Shanghai: revolution and development in an Asian metropolis*. The best work on the organizational changes made in Chinese cities generally after 1949 is still Franz Schurmann, *Ideology and organization in communist China* (ch. 6). A useful conference volume on urban organization and trends up to the Cultural Revolution is John Lewis, ed., *The city in communist China*. *Urban life in contemporary China*, by Martin King Whyte and William L. Parish, presents a sociological overview of how Chinese cities are organized and of their distinctive patterns of social life, with a focus on the 1970s. In *The Chinese hospital*, Gail Henderson and Myron S. Cohen present an ethnographic portrait and analysis of patterns of social life in a Wuhan hospital.

Several monographs and collections deal with urban population trends and urban geography and urban planning before and after 1949. See Gilbert Rozman, *Urban networks in Ch'ing China and Tokugawa Japan*; C. K. Leung and Norton Ginsburg, eds., *China: urbanization and national development*; Morris Ullman, *Cities of mainland China, 1953 and 1958*; Rhoads Murphey, *The fading of the Maoist vision*; Laurence Ma and Edward Hanten, eds., *Urban development in modern China*; Edwin Winckler and Janet Cady, eds., *Urban planning in China*; and Richard Kirkby, *Urbanization in China: town and country in a developing economy, 1949—2000 AD*. (See also G. William Skinner, *The city in late imperial China*.) Laurence Ma also provides a useful bibliography with a similar focus: *Cities and city planning in the PRC: an annotated bibliography*. See also the discussion of the confusion in the official Chinese statistics on urban population trends in Leo Orleans, "China's urban population: concepts, conglomerations, and concerns," in U.S. Congress, Joint Economic Committee, *China under the four modernizations*, vol. 1, and in Kirkby, *Urbanization in China*.

Several of the works just cited are concerned with the effort to limit urban population growth, and this effort is also the focus of several specialized monographs, such as H. Yuan Tien, *China's population struggle*; Thomas Bernstein, *Up to the mountains and down to the villages*; and Judith Banister, "Mortality, fertility, and contraceptive use in Shanghai." Problems of providing urban employment are dealt with in Charles Hoffmann, *The Chinese worker*; Christopher Howe, *Employment and economic growth in urban China, 1949–1957*; Christopher Howe, *Wage patterns and wage policy in modern China, 1919–1972*; and Thomas Rawski, *Economic growth and employment in China*. Problems of urban social control are addressed by several articles in John Lewis, ed., *The city in Communist*

China; in Amy Wilson, Sidney Greenblatt, and Richard Wilson, eds., *Deviance and social control in Chinese society*; and in Jerome Alan Cohen, *The criminal process in the People's Republic of China, 1949–1963* (particularly ch. 2).

A variety of first-person accounts by Chinese and foreigners who were former residents of various Chinese cities give vivid pictures of what their lives were like in particular periods. Particularly informative are Derk Bodde, *Peking diary, a year of revolution*; Emmanuel John Hevi, *An African student in China*; Beverley Hooper, *Inside Peking*; Mikhail Klochko, *Soviet scientist in Red China*; Ralph and Nancy Lapwood, *Through the Chinese revolution*; Liang Heng and Judith Shapiro, *Son of the revolution*; Sven Lindqvist, *China in crisis*; Ruth Earnshaw Lo and Katherine Kinderman, *In the eye of the Typhoon*; Robert Loh, *Escape from Red China*; Peter Lum, *Peking, 1950– 1953*; Sansan, *Eighth Moon*; William Sewell, *I stayed in China*; Tung Chi-ping and Humphrey Evans, *The thought revolution*; Shirley Wood, *A street in China*; Esther Cheo Ying, *Black country girl in Red China*; Maria Yen, *The umbrella garden*; and Yue Daiyun and Carolyn Wakeman, *To the storm*. Similar vividness is conveyed in some of the portraits in M. Bernard Frolic, *Mao's people*, and in the fictionalized tales in Chen Jo-hsi, *The execution of Mayor Yin*. Also useful for comments on the atmosphere in Chinese cities at particular times are various journalistic accounts, such as Richard Bernstein, *From the center of the earth*; Fox Butterfield, *China: alive in the bitter sea*; James Cameron, *Mandarin red*; John Fraser, *The Chinese*; Robert Guilllain, *600 million Chinese*; Frank Moraes, *Report on Mao's China*; Frederick Nossal, *Dateline Peking*; Ruth Sidel, *Families of Fengsheng*; William Stevenson, *The yellow wind*; and Ross Terrill, *Flowers on an iron tree*. China's capital is also well represented in picture books and guidebooks. See, for example, Hu Chia, *Peking today and yesterday*; Nigel Cameron and Brian Brake, *Peking: a tale of three cities*; Felix Greene, *Peking*; Ando Hikotarō, *Peking*; and Odile Cail, *Peking*.

11. LITERATURE UNDER COMMUNISM

Primary sources for the study of contemporary Chinese literature consist of texts published in book form (novels, plays, collections of short stories, essays, theoretical writings, and poems) and literary journals. In recent years the People's Literature Press (Jen-min wen-hsueh ch'u-pan-she) of Peking and other publishers have issued annual collections of prize-winning or other selected new literary works. Periodicals have proliferated in the post-Mao period. Among older established journals, resuming publication after suspension during the Cultural Revolution, *Jen-min wen-hsueh* (People's literature) for creative writing; *Wen-i pao* (Literary gazette) for theory; and *Wen-hsueh p'ing-lun* (Literary review) for practical criticism all tend to represent establishment opinion. More adventurous in their publication of new writing are *Shou-huo* (Harvest); *Shih-yueh* (October); *Tang-tai* (Contemporary); and especially provincial journals such as *Kuang-chou wen-i* and *Tso-p'in* (Canton), *Ho-pei wen-i*, *Ch'ang-chiang wen-i* (Hupei), *Ya-lu chiang* (Liaoning), *An-hui wen-hsueh*, and *Shang-hai wen-hsueh*. Journals specializing in drama include *Chü-pen* (Plays), *Hsi-chü pao* (Theater news), and *Shang-hai hsi-chü* (Shanghai theater). For cinema there is *Chung-kuo tien-ying* (Chinese film). Leading periodicals for new poetry are *Shih-k'an* (Poetry journal), *Hsing-hsing* (Stars), and *Shih t'an-so* (Poetry exploration). *Wen-i hsueh-hsi* (Literary studies), *Wen-i yen-chiu* (Literary research), and *Tu-shu* (Reading) carry important critical articles. The Shanghai Library publishes a monthly index to periodicals, including literary journals, *Ch'üan-kuo pao-k'an so-yin*. *Wen-hsueh pao* (Literary gazette) is a Shanghai weekly newsletter. Some mainland underground publications have been reprinted in Taiwan in the series *Ta-lu ti-hsia k'an-wu hui-pien*, issued by Institute for the Study of Chinese Communist Problems, Taipei, from 1980 on.

Hong Kong journals which pay close attention to Chinese literary developments include *Chiu-shih nien-tai* (The nineties), *Tung-hsiang* (Directions), and *Ming-pao yueh-k'an*. In the United States, the *Modern Chinese Literature Newsletter* is published by Center for Chinese Studies, University of Illinois. Articles on contemporary literature have appeared from time to time in *Journal of Asian Studies*, *CLEAR*, *Contemporary China,* and *The China Quarterly* (London). For new writing in Taiwan, the leading journals are *Ch'un wen-hsueh* (Pure literature), *Chung-wai wen-hsueh* (Chinese and foreign literature), *Hsien-tai wen-hsueh* (Contemporary literature), *T'ai-wan wen-i* (Taiwanese literature) and *Yu-shih wen-i* (Young lion literature and art).

Many English translations from contemporary mainland writing have been published by the Foreign Languages Press, Peking, and new translations appear monthly in their journal *Chinese Literature*. Indices to this journal covering the years to 1976 have been published separately by Hans J. Hinrup and Donald Gibbs. The late Kai-yu Hsu edited two important anthologies: *Literature of the People's Republic of China*, and *Twentieth century Chinese poetry*. Nieh Hua-ling's two-volume *Literature of the Hundred Flowers* is a useful compilation of creative, critical, and theoretical texts from the crucial years 1956–57, and Howard Goldblatt has edited documents from the Fourth Congress of Writers and Artists in *Chinese literature for the 1980s*. Post-Mao creative works in translation appear in *Contemporary Chinese literature*, ed. Michael S. Duke; *The new realism*, ed. Lee Yee; *Roses and thorns* and *Stubborn weeds*, ed. Perry Link; *Trees on the mountain*, ed. Stephen C. Soong and John Minford; and *Mao's harvest,* ed. Helen F. Siu and Zelda Stern. Ch'i Pang-yuan has a two-volume anthology of Taiwan writing in all genres, *Anthology of contemporary Chinese literature, Taiwan: 1949–74,* published in both Chinese and English versions.

Tsai Mei-hsi, *Contemporary Chinese novels and short stories, 1949–74: an annotated bibliography* is useful for fiction. Much bibliographical material is also contained in *Liu-shih nien wen-i ta-shih-chi, 1919–79* (Major cultural events of sixty years), prepared by the Institute of Literary and Artistic Research, Ministry of Culture, for the fourth congress in late 1979. Chen Ruoxi, "Democracy wall and the unofficial journals" gives details of *samizdat* literature from the years 1978–79. Two helpful biographical dictionaries are *Chung-kuo tang-tai tso-chia hsiao chuan* and the Hong Kong publication *Chung-kuo wen-hsueh-chia tz'u-tien.*

Two major new histories of contemporary literature, compiled by teams of scholars from several universities, have appeared under the title *Chung-kuo tang-tai wen-hsueh shih,* from Fukien People's Press (1980 onward) and Kirin People's Press respectively. A two-volume "draft history," *Chung-kuo tang-tai wen-hsueh shih ch'u-kao,* was published by People's Literature Press, Peking, in 1981. Lin Man-shu et al., *Chung-kuo tang-tai wen-hsueh shih-kao* ends its account with the year 1965. Some major mainland writers are treated unsympathetically in C. T. Hsia, *A history of modern Chinese fiction.* The late chapters of Colin Mackerras, *The Chinese theatre in modern times,* contain valuable information on the period since 1949, and an older but more detailed study is Chao Ts'ung, *Chung-kuo ta-lu ti hsi-chü kai-ko* (The reform of drama in mainland China). Post-1949 cinema is the subject of Jay Leyda, *Dianying.* Julia Lin has done a study of mainland poets, *Contemporary Chinese poetry.*

Valuable volumes of critical studies are Chang Chung et al, *Tang-tai wen-hsueh kai-kuan* (Survey of contemporary literature), the 1980 collection *Chung-kuo tang-tai wen-hsueh tso-p'in hsuan chiang* (Lectures on selected contemporary Chinese literary works), and, for the new writers of the post-Mao period, the special issue no. 10, *Tang-tai tso-chia p'ing-lun* (Review of contemporary writers) of *Wen-hsueh p'ing-lun ts'ung-k'an* (Literary review series). C. T. Hsia (Hsia Chih-ch'ing) makes a penetrating study of contemporary Taiwan writers in *Hsin wen-hsueh ti ch'uan-t'ung* (The tradition of the new literature). Taiwan fiction is also covered by Ho Hsin, *Chung-kuo hsien-tai hsiao-shuo ti chu-ch'ao* (Major trends in modern Chinese fiction), and in two important volumes of critical essays, Yeh Wei-lien, ed., *Chung-kuo hsien-tai tso-chia lun* (Contemporary Chinese writers) and Wei T'ien-ts'ung, ed., *Hsiang-t'u wen-hsueh t'ao-lun chi* (Collected essays on "native soil" literature).

Research conferences have resulted in symposia of critical studies.

Early years are treated in Cyril Birch, ed., *Chinese communist literature*. More recent volumes include Wolfgang Kubin and Rudolf G. Wagner, eds., *Essays in modern Chinese literature and literary criticism: papers of the Berlin Conference 1978*; Bonnie McDougall, ed., *Popular Chinese literature and the performing arts in the People's Republic of China, 1949–1979*, from a conference held at Harvard in 1979; and Jeffrey C. Kinkley, ed., *After Mao: Chinese literature and society, 1978–81*, from a 1982 conference at St. John's University. A conference on Taiwan fiction held at the University of Texas in 1979 is reported in Jeannette L. Faurot, ed., *Chinese fiction from Taiwan: critical perspectives*.

Aspects of mainland literature since 1949 have been studied in a number of monographs. Jaroslav Průšek, *Die Literatur des befreiten China und ihre Volkstraditionen* (The literature of liberated China and its folk traditions) is valuable for the use of folk forms in the early years. D. W. Fokkema, *Literary doctrine in China and Soviet influence, 1956–60*, and Merle Goldman, *Literary dissent in communist China* both cover important debates of the 1950s. Joe C. Huang's *Heroes and villains in communist China* analyzes major works of mainstream fiction, and Michael Gotz has done an unpublished dissertation on "Images of the worker in contemporary Chinese fiction, 1949–64." Recent writing is analyzed in Michael S. Duke, *Blooming and contending: Chinese literature in the post-Mao era*. The most sophisticated study of a single writer is Yi-tse Mei Feuerwerker, *Ding Ling's fiction*. The ideologue (and member of the Gang of Four) Yao Wen-yuan is the subject of a monograph by Lars Ragvald, *Yao Wen-yuan as a literary critic and theorist*.

12. TAIWAN UNDER NATIONALIST RULE, 1949–1982

Taiwan's ten years as a Chinese province after 1885 are appraised in *CHOC* 11.258–66, which gives details of the tax reform and Westernization projects in Taiwan under the vigorous modernizing Governor Liu Ming-ch'uan (1885–91). The authors, Professors K. C. Liu and R. J. Smith, cite studies by William M. Speidel, Kuo T'ing-i, Leonard H. D. Gordon, and others. Secondary sources in English on Taiwan's history before 1949 are: James W. Davidson, *The island of Formosa: historical view from 1430 to 1900*; W. G. Goddard, *Formosa: a study in Chinese history*; George W. Barclay, *Colonial development and population in Taiwan*; and George H. Kerr, *Formosa: licensed revolution and the Home Rule movement, 1895–1945*. Paul K. T. Sih, ed., *Taiwan in modern times*, contains chapters on Taiwan's pre-1949 history. Chiao-min Hsieh's *Taiwan-Ilha Formosa: a geography in perspective* (1964) is the standard geography, though now out of date.

The history of Taiwan since 1945 has of course been profoundly influenced by the preceding half century of Japanese rule after 1895. The fact that *The Cambridge History of China* does not deal with Taiwan under Japanese colonialism is both understandable and regrettable. No *CHOC* volume has traced the experience of Chinese living within the Japanese empire of the early twentieth century. This subject is still comparatively underresearched, although Japanese studies of the empire have proliferated in recent decades; many sources have been used and issues discussed. Out of this work historians of China should find many opportunities for further study.

One leader in surveying the 1895–1945 era has been Ramon Myers, whose articles on Taiwan as an imperial colony of Japan and Taiwan's agrarian economy under Japanese rule have been followed by a comprehensive symposium volume, *The Japanese colonial empire, 1895–1945*, edited by Ramon H. Myers and Mark R. Peattie with fourteen contributors, which originated from a 1979 conference. This volume is focused mainly on Japanese motives, management, economic dynamics, and historiography concerning both Korea and Taiwan, but several chapters offer data and cite publications on specific aspects of Taiwan's history. See especially chapter 5 ("Police and community control systems in the empire") by Ching-chih Chen; chapter 6 ("The attempt to integrate the empire: legal perspectives") by Edward I-te Chen; chapter 9 ("Colonialism and development: Korea, Taiwan, and Kwantung"), by Samuel Pao-San Ho; chapter 10 ("Capital formation in Taiwan and Korea"), by Toshiyuki Mizoguchi and Yuzo Yamamoto; and chapter 11 ("Agricultural development in the empire"), by Ramon H. Myers and Yamada Saburō. One pioneer monograph is Patricia Tsurumi, *Japanese colonial education in Taiwan 1895–1945*.

For a Japanese bibliography of 636 items on Taiwan published 1945–79, see the journal *Taiwan kingendaishi kenkyū* (Historical studies of Taiwan in modern times), no. 3 (1980). For publications in English, see *Taiwan: a comprehensive bibliography of English-language publications*, comp. by J. Bruce Jacobs, Jean Hagger, and Anne Sedgley, introduction by J. Bruce Jacobs.

Scholarly writing on developments on Taiwan since 1949 has been sparser than that on the People's Republic of China, even though research materials from Taiwan on most topics are richer and more readily available. Few European or Japanese scholars have taken much interest in Taiwan; the field has been dominated by Americans. Moreover, the writing by Americans has focused overwhelmingly on the problem posed for U.S. China policy by relations with Taiwan.

The topic that has attracted most attention in writings on Taiwan, aside from U.S.-Taiwanese relations, has been Taiwan's economic development. Taiwan's success in this area has caused it to be viewed as a model and studied for the possible application to other developing countries of economic policies adopted there. A recent example is the well-informed study by Joseph A. Yager, *Transforming agriculture in Taiwan: the experience of the Joint Commission on Rural Reconstruction.* Anthropologists and sociologists, denied access to the China mainland from 1950 to 1979, have published a number of books and articles based on fieldwork in Taiwan. During the 1970s the poetry and fiction produced in Taiwan began receiving increasing attention from scholars of comparative literature. Relatively little basic research has been done on the sensitive areas of Taiwan's military establishment or its political evolution. Another neglected subject is the conduct of Taiwan's foreign relations since the Republic of China lost its UN seat as well as its diplomatic relations with most countries.

Important primary sources for research on Taiwan are the many publications of organs of the national and provincial governments. Among the most useful are the annual *China yearbook* (Government Information Office), the *Statistical yearbook* (Directorate-General of Budget, Accounting and Statistics), and the *Taiwan statistical data book* (Council on Economic Planning and Development). Published data on the Kuomintang is available from the party headquarters in Taipei. Newspapers include particularly the *Chung-yang jih-pao* (Central daily news), published by the KMT, and the privately-owned *Chung-kuo shih-pao* (China times) and *Lien-ho pao* (United daily news). The latter two publish Chinese-language editions in the United States as well. Political journals such as the *Shih-pao chou-k'an* (Sunday times weekly), *Pa-shih nien-tai* (The eighties), *Shen keng* (Plow deeply), and *Huang-ho* (Yellow River) contain analyses of current politics and views of the United States and the PRC. Because writers had to avoid sensitive subjects such as the succession to Chiang Ching-kuo or policies toward Peking, published political analyses had to be supplemented by interviews with knowledgeable people in Taiwan. Numerous periodicals on economics, literature, and other specialized topics are available.

Primary sources for U.S. policy toward Taiwan include the China volumes of the *Foreign Relations of the United States* series, now available through 1957, the *China white paper* (1949), reissued by Stanford University in two volumes in 1968, and the monthly *U.S. State Department Bulletin.* Periodic hearings in the Congress on China policy contain valuable material, particularly those held by the Senate Foreign Relations Committee and the House Foreign Affairs Committee. Useful memoirs include: Harry S. Truman, *Year of decisions* (1955) and *Years of trial and hope*

(1956); Dean Acheson, *Present at the creation* (1969); Dwight Eisenhower, *Mandate for change, 1953–1956* (1963), and *Waging peace 1956–61* (1965); Arthur M. Schlesinger, Jr., *A thousand days* (1965); Theodore Sorensen, *Kennedy* (1965); and Roger Hilsman, *To move a nation* (1968). *The New York Times* and *The Washington Post* are indispensable sources. Convenient summaries of U.S. policy toward China and Taiwan are contained in *China and U.S. Far East policy, 1945–1967* (1967), and *China and U.S. foreign policy* (1973) published by the Congressional Quarterly, Inc., Washington, D.C.

Articles on Taiwan appear frequently in the weekly *Far Eastern Economic Review* and *Asian Wall Street Journal*, published in Hong Kong. A summary of developments in Taiwan during the previous year appears in the *Far Eastern Economic Review*'s *Yearbook* and in an annual survey article in the January or February issue of *Asian Survey*. *The China Quarterly* and the *Journal of Asian Studies* occasionally carry articles on Taiwan.

The *Jen-min jih-pao* (People's daily) is the primary source for the PRC's policy toward Taiwan and its views of U.S. Taiwan policy. The most important editorials and government statements appear in English in the *Beijing Review*. The *Daily Report: China*, issued by the Foreign Broadcast Information Service (FBIS), Washington, D.C., is the most important single source in English, containing translations of Chinese broadcasts. Chinese journals, such as *Shih-chieh chih-shih* (World knowledge) and *Kuo-chi wen-t'i yen-chiu* (Journal of international studies) contain articles on Taiwan and U.S. policy toward Taiwan, as do the Peking-owned newspapers *Ta-kung pao* and *Wen-hui pao* in Hong Kong.

Few books treat comprehensively Taiwan's economic, military, political, and foreign relations history. The most complete is Ralph N. Clough, *Island China* (1978). Hungdah Chiu, ed., *China and the question of Taiwan* (1973) and *China and the Taiwan issue* (1979) contain chapters on Taiwan's early history and its economic and political development, as well as useful collections of documents. All three of these books give principal emphasis to U.S.-Taiwanese relations. James Hsiung, et al., eds., *The Taiwan experience, 1950–1980* (1981) contains excerpts from many books and articles on a variety of subjects, including cultural values, education, social conditions, law and justice, and defense capabilities. Yung-hwan Jo, ed., *Taiwan's future?* (1974), looks at Taiwan from a variety of perspectives, while Victor H. Li, ed., *The future of Taiwan* (1980) contains a debate among Chinese in the United States with widely varying viewpoints on the future relationship of Taiwan with the PRC.

Books on U.S.-Taiwanese relations in the context of U.S. China policy, in addition to those mentioned above, include Foster Rhea Dulles,

American foreign policy toward Communist China, 1949–1969; Ross Y. Koen, *The China lobby in American politics*; William J. Barnds, ed., *China and America: the search for a new relationship*; A. Doak Barnett, *China policy*, *The FX decision*, and *U.S. arms sales: the China-Taiwan tangle*; Ralph N. Clough, Robert B. Oxnam and William Watts, *The United States and China: American perceptions and future alternatives*; Jerome Cohen, Edward Friedman, Harold Hinton, and Allen S. Whiting, *Taiwan and American policy*; Richard Moorsteen and Morton Abramowitz, *Remaking China policy*; former ambassador to the Republic of China Karl L. Rankin, *China assignment*; Tang Tsou, *Embroilment over Quemoy: Mao, Chiang and Dulles*; Ramon H. Myers, ed., *Two Chinese states: U.S. foreign policy and interests*; Edwin K. Snyder, A. James Gregor, and Maria Hsia Chang, *The Taiwan Relations Act and the defense of the Republic of China*; Robert L. Downen, *Of grave concern: U.S. Taiwan relations on the threshold of the 1980s*; William Kintner and John F. Copper, *A matter of two Chinas: the China-Taiwan issue in U.S. foreign policy*. J. H. Kalicki, *The pattern of Sino-American crises*, analyzes in detail the confrontations over the offshore islands in 1954–55 and 1958.

For analysis of Taiwan's economic development, see Neil H. Jacoby, *U.S. aid to Taiwan: a study of foreign aid, self-help, and development*; Chen Cheng, *Land reform in Taiwan*; Walter Galenson, ed., *Economic growth and structural change in Taiwan: the postwar experience of the Republic of China*; John C. H. Fei, Gustav Ranis, and Shirley W. Y. Kuo, *Growth with equity: the Taiwan case*; Martin M. C. Yang, *Socio-economic results of land reform in Taiwan*; Anthony Y. C. Koo, *The role of land reform in economic development*; T. H. Shen, ed., *Agriculture's place in the strategy of development: the Taiwan experience*; A. James Gregor, with Maria Hsia Chang and Andrew B. Zimmerman, *Ideology and development: Sun Yat-sen and the economic history of Taiwan*; Jan S. Prybyla, *The societal objective of wealth, growth, stability and equity in Taiwan*; K. T. Li, *The experience of dynamic economic growth on Taiwan*; and Shirley W. Y. Kuo, *The Taiwan economy in transition*. Also of interest is Lawrence J. Lau, ed., *Models of development: a comparative study of economic growth in South Korea and Taiwan*.

The principal works on political developments in Taiwan are: George H. Kerr, *Formosa betrayed*; Peng Ming-min, *A taste of freedom*; Douglas Mendel, *The politics of Formosan nationalism*; Mab Huang, *Intellectual ferment for political reforms in Taiwan, 1971–1973*; Arthur J. Lerman, *Taiwan's politics: the provincial assemblyman's world*; J. Bruce Jacobs, *Local politics in a rural Chinese cultural setting: a field study of Mazu Township, Taiwan*. The two books edited by Hungdah Chiu and the one by Paul K. T. Sih cited above also have chapters on political development in Taiwan. A recent study is by John F. Copper with George P. Chen, *Taiwan's elections: political development and democratization in the Republic of China* (1984). See also the special issue on Taiwan since 1949 of *The China Quarterly* 99 (September 1984), 462–568.

Sociological and anthropological studies include: Emily Martin Ahern and Hill Gates, eds., *The anthropology of Taiwanese society*: Myron L. Cohen, *House united, house divided: the Chinese family in Taiwan*; Bernard Gallin, *Hsin Hsing, Taiwan: a Chinese village in change*; Wolfgang L. Grichting, *The value system in Taiwan 1970: a preliminary report*; Burton Pasternak, *Kinship and community in two Chinese villages*; Richard W. Wilson, *Learning to be Chinese: the political socialization of children in Taiwan*; Richard W. Wilson, Amy A. Wilson, and Sidney L. Greenblatt, eds., *Value change in Chinese society*; Norma Diamond, *K'un Shen: a Taiwan village*; and, most recently, Thomas B. Gold, *State and society in the Taiwan miracle*.

For biographies of Chiang Kai-shek, see Hollington K. Tong, *Chiang Kai-shek*; and Brian Crozier, *The man who lost China*.

For military capability, see Stuart E. Johnson with Joseph A. Yager, *The military equation in northeast Asia*, and William H. Overholt, "Nuclear proliferation in Eastern Asia."

David Nelson Rowe, *Informal diplomatic relations: the case of Japan and the Republic of China, 1972–74* is the only monograph on Taiwan's international relations since its exclusion from the United Nations. Hungdah Chiu, with Shao-chuan Leng, ed., *China: seventy years after the 1911 Hsin-Hai Revolution* contains a chapter on Taiwan's international relations from 1949 to 1981.

The principal collections of literature from Taiwan are: Ch'i Pang-yuan et al., eds., *An anthology of contemporary Chinese literature: Taiwan, 1949–1974, vol. 1: Poems and essays; vol. 2: Short stories*; Vivian Ling Hsu, ed., *Born of the same roots: stories of modern Chinese women*, Hwang [or Huang] Chun-ming (trans. Howard Goldblatt), *The drowning of an old cat and other stories*; Joseph S. M. Lau and Timothy A. Ross, eds., *Chinese stories from Taiwan, 1960–1970*. Jeannette L. Faurot, ed., *Chinese fiction from Taiwan: critical perspectives*, contains critical evaluations of the principal writers and trends in fiction on Taiwan. See also the discussion of new fiction and poetry in Taiwan in Chapter 11 of the present volume, by Cyril Birch.

BIBLIOGRAPHY

A built-in ambiguity haunts any bibliography of Chinese writings: entries that are immediately intelligible to the reader of English, like *Central Daily News* or *Liberation Daily*, are not directly clued to the Chinese characters in which the originals are written (*Chung-yang jih-pao, Chieh-fang jih-pao*). Yet, on the other hand, an entry like *Chin-tai shih yen-chiu-so*, though more accurate in the esoteric script of romanization, may be translated variously as Modern History Institute or Institute of Modern History. In this situation we have put romanized accuracy ahead of English-translated intelligibility, but with occasional cross-references.

Another problem in that large compilations of documents are usually edited by committees, departments, or other institutional organs, so that listing such works by compiler or editor would confront the reader with many words but little information. In such cases we prefer to list by title. Compilers and editors are then cited in the body of the entry.

Footnote notation systems, like romanization systems, may appeal only to certain people. Yet they are necessary and have to be arbitrary. The sole test is their accuracy and economy. Numbers of issues within volumes of periodicals we unite with a period. (If pages are within a volume only, they are united with its number by a period: e.g., Mao, *SW*, 5.27.) For journals that use the year as the volume number, the year is treated as a volume number; the citation therefore appears as, say, 1981.4, 17–21.

Materials such as speeches, reports, and articles of and about the Chinese leadership are normally cited with reference to their place of origin in the press or published collections, but a certain number of such materials are listed independently in the bibliography.

A great part of Chinese publications are put out by the People's Publishing House, Jen-min ch'u-pan-she, which we abbreviate to Jen-min. We have similarly abbreviated the names of most other publishing houses by omitting ch'u-pan-she.

Acheson, Dean. *Present at the creation: my years in the State Department.* New York: Norton, 1987 [1969].
Adie, W. A. C. "Chou En-lai on safari." *CQ*, 18 (April–June 1964), 174–94.
Adie, W. A. C. "China and the war in Vietnam." *Mizan*, 8.6 (November–December 1966), 233–41.

Agence France Presse. Press service. Paris.

Ahern, Emily Martin, and Gates, Hill, eds. *The anthropology of Taiwanese society*. Stanford, Calif.: Stanford University Press, 1981.

Ahn, Byung-joon. *Chinese politics and the Cultural Revolution: dynamics of policy processes*. Seattle: University of Washington Press, 1976.

Ahn, Byung-joon. "The Cultural Revolution and China's search for political order." *CQ*, 58 (April–June 1974), 249–85.

Ahn, Byung-joon. "The political economy of the People's Commune in China: changes and continuities." *JAS*, 34.3 (May 1975), 631–58.

Ai Ch'ing 艾青. "Liao-chieh tso-chia, tsun-chung tso-chia" 瞭解作家,尊重作家 (Understand writers, respect writers). *CFJP*, 11 March 1942.

Albinski, Henry S. "Chinese and Soviet policies in the Vietnam crisis." *Australian Quarterly*, 40.1 (March 1968), 65–74.

Ambroz, Oton. *Realignment of world power: the Russo-Chinese schism under the impact of Mao Tse-tung's last revolution*. 2 vols. New York: Speller, 1972.

American Association for the Advancement of Science. *See* Gould, Sidney H.

American Political Science Review. Quarterly. Washington, D.C.: American Political Science Association, 1906– .

An-hui wen-hsueh 安徽文學 (Anhwei literature). Monthly. Hofei: 1979– .

An Tai-sung. *The Sino-Soviet territorial dispute*. Philadelphia: Westminster Press, 1973.

An Tai-sung. "The Sino-Soviet dispute and Vietnam." *Orbis*, 9.2 (Summer 1965), 426–36.

Ando Hikotar 安藤彦太郎. *Peking*. Tokyo: Kodansha International, 1986.

Ashbrook, Arthur G., Jr. "China: economic modernization and long-term performance," in U.S. Congress [97th], Joint Economic Committee, *China under the Four Modernizations*, 1.99–118.

Asia Quarterly: journal from Europe. Quarterly. Bruxelles: Centre d'étude du Sud-Est asiatique et de l'Extrême-Orient, Institut de Sociologie, Université libre de Bruxelles, 1970– . Supersedes *Revue du Sud-Est asiatique et de l'Extrême Orient*.

Asian Survey: a monthly review of contemporary Asian affairs. Monthly. Berkeley: Institute of East Asian Studies, University of California Press, 1961– .

Asian Wall Street Journal. Weekly. [Hong Kong]: Dow Jones, April 30, 1979– .

Aspaturian, Vernon D. "The USSR, the USA and China in the seventies." *Survey*, 19.2 (87) (Spring 1973), 103–22.

Atlas. See *World Press Review*.

Atlas World Press Review. See *World Press Review*.

Australian Journal of Chinese Affairs, The, Semi-annual. Canberra: Contemporary China Centre, Australian National University, 1979– .

Australian Quarterly. Quarterly. Sydney: Australian Institute of Political Science, 1929– .

Aviation Week & Space Technology. Weekly. New York: McGraw-Hill, 1916– .

Badgley, John H. "Burma and China: policy of a small neighbor," in A. M. Halpern, ed., *Policies toward China*, 303–28.

Bady, Paul. "Death and the novel: on Lao She's 'suicide.'" *Renditions*, 10 (Autumn 1978), 5–14.

Balassa, Bela, and Williamson, John. *Adjusting to success: balance of payments policies in the East Asian NICs*. Washington, D.C.: Institute for International Economics, 1987.

Ballantine, Joseph W[illiam]. *Formosa: a problem for United States foreign policy*. Washington, D.C.: The Brookings Institution, 1952.

Banister, Judith. "Mortality, fertility, and contraceptive use in Shanghai." *CQ*, 70 (June 1977), 254–95.

Barber, Noel. *The fall of Shanghai*. New York: Coward, McCann & Geoghegan, 1979.

Barclay, George W. *Colonial development and population in Taiwan*. Port Washington, N.Y.: Kennikat Press, 1972; Princeton, N.J.: Princeton University Press, 1954.

Barnds, William J., ed. *The two Koreas in East Asian affairs*. New York: New York University Press, 1976.

Barnds, William J., ed. *China and America: the search for a new relationship*. New York: New York University Press, 1977.

Barnes, A. C. *See* Kuo Mo-jo.

Barnett, A. Doak. *China on the eve of Communist takeover*. New York: Praeger, 1963.

Barnett, A. Doak. *China policy: old problems and new challenges*. Washington, D.C.: The Brookings Institution, 1977.

Barnett, A. Doak. *China and the major powers in East Asia*. Washington, D.C.: The Brookings Institution, 1977.

Barnett, A. Doak. *The FX decision: "another crucial moment" in U.S.-China-Taiwan relations*. Washington, D.C.: The Brookings Institution, 1981.

Barnett, A. Doak. *China's economy in global perspective*. Washington, D.C.: The Brookings Institution, 1981.

Barnett, A. Doak. *U.S. arms sales: the China-Taiwan tangle*. Washington, D.C.: The Brookings Institution, 1982.

Barnett, A. Doak. *The making of foreign policy in China – structure and process*. Boulder, Colo.: Westview Press, 1985.

Barnett, A. Doak, ed. *Chinese Communist politics in action*. Seattle: University of Washington Press, 1969.

Barnett, A. Doak, and Clough, Ralph N., eds. *Modernizing China: post-Mao reform and development*. Boulder, Colo.: Westview Press, 1986.

Barnett, A. Doak, with Ezra Vogel. *Cadres, bureaucracy, and political power in Communist China*. New York: Columbia University Press, 1967.

Bastid, Marianne. "Levels of economic decision-making," in Stuart R. Schram, ed., *Authority, participation and cultural change in China*, 159–97.

Bastid, Marianne. "Economic necessity and political ideals in educational reform during the Cultural Revolution." *CQ*, 42 (April–June 1970), 16–45.

Baum, Richard. *Prelude to revolution: Mao, the Party, and the peasant question, 1962–66.* New York: Columbia University Press, 1975.

Baum, Richard, ed., *China's four modernizations: the new technological revolution.* Boulder, Colo.: Westview Press, 1980.

Baum, Richard. "The Cultural Revolution in the countryside: anatomy of a limited rebellion," in Thomas W. Robinson, ed., *The Cultural Revolution in China*, 367–476.

Baum, Richard. "Elite behavior under conditions of stress: the lesson of the 'T'ang-ch'üan p'ai' in the Cultural Revolution," in Robert A. Scalapino, ed., *Elites in the People's Republic of China*, 540–74.

Baum, Richard. "China: year of the mangoes." *Asian Survey*, 9.1 (January 1969), 1–17.

Baum, Richard, ed., with Louise B. Bennett, *China in ferment: perspectives on the Cultural Revolution.* Englewood Cliffs, N.J.: Prentice-Hall, 1971.

Baum, Richard, and Teiwes, Frederick C. *Ssu-ch'ing: the Socialist Education Movement of 1962–1966.* Berkeley: Center for Chinese Studies, University of California, 1968.

BBC. *See* British Broadcasting Corporation.

Bedeski, Robert E. *The fragile entente: the 1978 Japan-China peace treaty in a global context.* Boulder, Colo.: Westview Press, 1983.

Bei Dao. *See* McDougall, Bonnie S.

Beijing Review. See *Peking Review.*

Bell, Carol. "Korea and the balance of power." *Political Quarterly*, 25.1 (January–March and April–June, 1976).

Bennett, Gordon A. *China's Eighth, Ninth, and Tenth Congresses, Constitutions, and Central Committees: an institutional overview and comparison.* Occasional Paper, no. 1. Austin: Center for Asian Studies, University of Texas, 1978.

Bennett, Gordon A., and Montaperto, Ronald N. *Red Guard: the political biography of Dai Hsiao-ai.* New York: Anchor Books, 1972; Garden City, N.Y.: Doubleday, 1971.

Berninghausen, John, and Huters, Ted, eds. *Revolutionary literature in China: an anthology.* White Plains, N.Y.: M. E. Sharpe, 1976. Originally published as two special issues of *Bulletin of Concerned Asian Scholars*, 8.1 and 8.2 (January–March and April–June, 1976).

Bernstein, Richard. *From the center of the earth: the search for the truth about China.* Boston: Little, Brown, 1982.

Bernstein, Thomas P. *Up to the mountains and down to the villages: the transfer of youth from urban to rural China.* New Haven, Conn.: Yale University Press, 1977.

Binder, Leonard, et al., contribs. *Crises and sequences in political development.* Studies in political Development, no. 7. Princeton, N.J.: Princeton University Press, 1971.

Birch, Cyril, ed. *Chinese communist literature*. New York: Praeger, 1962. Published as special issue of *CQ*, 13 (January–March 1963).

Birch, Cyril. "Fiction of the Yenan period." *CQ*, 4 (October–December 1960), 1–11.

Blecher, Marc J., and White, Gordon. *Micropolitics in contemporary China: a technical unit during and after the Cultural Revolution*. White Plains, N.Y.: M. E. Sharpe, 1979.

Boardman, Robert. *Britain and the People's Republic of China 1949–1974*. New York: Macmillan, 1976.

Bodde, Derk. *Peking diary: a year of revolution*. Greenwich, Conn.: Fawcett Publications, 1967; New York: Henry Schuman, 1950.

Bonavia, David. *The Chinese: a portrait*. Harmondsworth: Penguin, 1982; London: Allen Lane, 1981.

Bonavia, David. *Verdict in Peking: the trial of the Gang of Four*. New York: Putnam; London: Burnett Books, 1984.

Borisov, O. B. *Vnutrenniaia i vneshniaia politika Kitaia v 70-e gody* (Internal and external policies of China in the seventies). Moscow: Politizdat, 1982.

Borisov, O. B., and Koloskov, B. T. *Sovetsko-Kitaiskie otnosheniia 1945–1970: kratkii ocherk* (Soviet-Chinese relations 1945–1970: a brief sketch). Moscow: Mysl', 1972.

Borisov, O. B. [Rakhmanin, Oleg B.], and Koloskov, B. T. [Kulik, S]. Ed. with an introductory essay by Vladimir Petrov. *Soviet-Chinese relations, 1945–1970*. Bloomington: Indiana University Press, 1975.

Borisov, O. B., and Koloskov, B. T. *Sino-Soviet relations 1945–1973: a brief history*. Trans. from the Russian by Yuri Shirokov. Moscow: Progress, 1975.

BR. Beijing Review.

Bradsher, Henry. "The Sovietization of Mongolia." *Foreign Affairs*, 5.3 (July 1972), 545–53.

Breese, Gerald, ed. *The city in newly developing countries: readings on urbanism and urbanization*. Englewood Cliffs, N.J.: Prentice-Hall, 1969.

Bridgham, Philip. "Mao's Cultural Revolution: origin and development." *CQ*, 29 (January–March 1967), 1–35.

Bridgham, Philip. "Mao's Cultural Revolution: the struggle to seize power." *CQ*, 34 (April–June 1968), 6–37.

Bridgham, Philip. "Mao's Cultural Revolution: the struggle to consolidate power." *CQ*, 41 (January–March 1970), 1–25.

Bridgham, Philip. "The fall of Lin Piao." *CQ*, 55 (July–September 1973), 427–29.

British Broadcasting Corporation. *Summary of world broadcasts. Part 3. The Far East*. Caversham Park, Reading: British Broadcasting Corporation, 1966– . Cited as *SWB*.

Brown, Jessica, et al. *Sino-Soviet conflict: a historical bibliography*. ABC Clio Research Guides: 13. Santa Barbara, Calif.: ABC-Clio Information Services, 1985.

Broyelle, Claudie; Broyelle, Jacques; and Tschirhart, Evelyne. *China: a second look*. Trans. by Sarah Matthews. Brighton: Harvester Press; Atlantic Highlands N. J.: Humanities Press, 1980.

Brzezinski, Zbigniew. *Power and principle*. New York: Farrar, Straus, Giroux, 1983.

Bulletin of Concerned Asian Scholars. Quarterly. Boulder, Colo.: 1969– . Continues *CCAS Newsletter*.

Bulletin of the State Council of the People's Republic of China. See *Chung-hua jen-min kung-ho-kuo kuo-wu-yuan kung-pao*.

Bullock, Mary Brown. *An American transplant: the Rockefeller Foundation and Peking Union Medical College*. Berkeley: University of California Press, 1980.

Burki, Shahid Javed. *A study of Chinese communes, 1965*. Cambridge, Mass.: East Asian Research Center, Harvard University, 1969.

Burlatsky, Fedor. *Mao Tse-tung: an ideological and psychological portrait*. Moscow: Progress, 1980.

Burns, John P., and Rosen, Stanley, eds. *Policy conflicts in post-Mao China: a documentary survey with analysis*. Armonk, N.Y.: M. E. Sharpe, 1986.

Burton, Barry. "The Cultural Revolution's ultraleft conspiracy: the 'May 16 Group.'" *Asian Survey*, 11.11 (November 1971), 1029–53.

Butterfield, Fox. *China: alive in the bitter sea*. New York: Bantam Books, 1983; New York: Times Books, 1982.

Byrd, William, et al. *Recent Chinese economic reforms: studies of two industrial enterprises*. World Bank Staff Working Papers, no. 652. Washington, D.C.: World Bank, 1984.

Byrd, William, and Lin Qingsong, eds. *China's rural industry: structure, development, and reform*. New York: Oxford University Press, for the World Bank, 1990.

Byrd, William, and Tidrick, Gene. "Factor allocation in Chinese industry." [Paper prepared for conference on Chinese enterprise management, Peking, August 1985.]

Cail, Odile. *Peking*. New York: McKay, 1972. [Fodor's *Peking*, Eugene Fodor, ed.]

Cambridge History of China, The (CHOC). Vol. 1. *The Ch'in and Han empires, 221 B.C. – A.D. 220*, ed. Denis Twitchett and Michael Loewe (1986). Vol. 3. *Sui and T'ang China, 589–906, Part 1*, ed. Denis Twitchett (1979). Vol. 7. *The Ming Dynasty, 1368–1644, Part 1*, ed. Frederick W. Mote and Denis Twitchett (1988). Vol. 10. *Late Ch'ing 1800–1911, Part 1*, ed. John K. Fairbank (1978). Vol. 11. *Late Ch'ing 1800–1911, Part 2*, ed. John K. Fairbank and Kwang-Ching Liu (1980). Vol. 12. *Republican China 1912–1949, Part 1*, ed. John K. Fairbank (1983). Vol. 13. *Republican China 1912–1949, Part 2*, ed. John K. Fairbank and Albert Feuerwerker (1986). Vol. 14. *The People's Republic, Part 1: the emergence of revolutionary China*, ed. Roderick MacFarquhar and John K. Fairbank (1987). Cambridge: Cambridge University Press.

Cameron, James. *Mandarin red: a journey behind the "Bamboo Curtain."* London: Michael Joseph, 1955.

Cameron, Nigel, and Brake, Brian. *Peking: a tale of three cities.* Foreword by L. Carrington Goodrich. New York: Harper & Row, 1965.

Camilleri, Joseph. *Chinese foreign policy: the Maoist era and its aftermath.* Seattle: University of Washington Press, 1980.

CAR. China Area Report. See JPRS, *China Area Report (CAR).*

Carrère d'Encausse, Helène, and Schram, Stuart R., comps. *Marxism and Asia: an introduction with readings.* London: Allen Lane, Penguin Press, 1969.

Catalogue of Red Guard publications held by URI. See Union Research Institute.

CB. See U.S. Consulate General. Hong Kong. *Current Background.*

CCP. Chinese Communist Party. Chung-kuo kung-ch'an-tang.

CCP CC Documentary Research Office. Chung-kung chung-yang wen-hsien yen-chiu-shih.

CCP CC Party History Research Office. Chung-kung chung-yang tang-shih yen-chiu-shih.

CCP documents of the Great Proletarian Cultural Revolution, 1966–1967. See Union Research Institute.

CCP Research Newsletter. 3/yr. Colorado Springs, Colo.: Chinese Communism Research Group, 1988– .

CDSP. The Current Digest of the Soviet Press.

Central China Normal University Journal. See Hua-chung shih-fan ta-hsueh hsueh-pao.

Central Intelligence Agency. *See* United States, Central Intelligence Agency.

CFJP. Chieh-fang jih-pao.

Chan, Anita. *Children of Mao: a study of politically active Chinese youths.* London: Macmillan; Seattle: University of Washington Press, 1985, with subtitle *Personality development and political activism in the Red Guard generation.*

Chan, Anita. "Images of China's social structure: the changing perspectives of Canton students." *World Politics,* 34.3 (April 1982), 295–323.

Chan, Anita; Madsen, Richard; and Unger, Jonathan. *Chen Village: the recent history of a peasant community in Mao's China.* Berkeley: University of California Press, 1984.

Chan, Anita; Rosen, Stanley; and Unger, Jonathan, eds. *On socialist democracy and the Chinese legal system: the Li Yizhe debates.* Armonk, N.Y.: M. E. Sharpe, 1985.

Chan, Anita; Rosen, Stanley; and Unger, Jonathan. "Students and class warfare: the social roots of the Red Guard conflict in Guangzhou." *CQ,* 83 (September 1980), 397–446.

Chan Kam Wing and Xu Xueqiang. "Urban population growth and urbanization in China since 1949: reconstructing a baseline." *CQ,* 104 (December 1985), 583–613.

Chanda, Nayan. *Brother enemy: the war after the war.* New York: Harcourt Brace Jovanovich, 1986.

Chang Ch'un-ch'iao 張春橋. "P'o-ch'u tzu-ch'an-chieh-chi ti fa-ch'uan ssu-hsiang" 破除資產階級的法權思想 (Eliminate the ideology of bourgeois right). *JMJP,* 13 October 1958.

Chang Ch'un-ch'iao. "On exercising all-round dictatorship over the bourgeoisie," in Raymond Lotta, ed., *And Mao makes 5*, 209–20.

Chang Chung 張鍾 et al. *Tang-tai wen-hsueh kai-kuan* 當代文學概觀 (Survey of contemporary literature). Peking: Peking University Press, 1980.

Chang Chung-li 張中禮. *The Chinese gentry: studies on their role in nineteenth-century Chinese society*. Intro. by Franz Michael. Seattle: University of Washington Press, 1955.

Chang Ming-yang 張明養. "An analysis of Lin Piao and the 'Gang of Four's' ultraleft foreign policy line." *Fu-tan hsueh-pao* 復旦學報 (Fudan journal), 2 (March 1980), in JPRS 76141 *China Report*, 103 (30 July 1980), 40–51.

Chang Pao-min. *Beijing, Hanoi, and the Overseas Chinese*. Berkeley: Institute of East Asian Studies, University of California, 1982.

Chang Pao-min. *Kampuchea between China and Vietnam*. Singapore: Singapore University Press, 1985.

Chang, Parris H. *Radicals and radical ideology in China's Cultural Revolution*. New York: Research Institute on Communist Affairs, School of International Affairs, Columbia University, 1973.

Chang, Parris H. *Power and policy in China*. University Park: Pennsylvania State University Press, 1975; revised and enlarged ed., 1978.

Chang, Parris H. "Provincial Party leaders' strategies for survival during the Cultural Revolution," in Robert A. Scalapino, ed., *Elites in the People's Republic of China*, 501–39.

Chang Tse-hou 張澤厚 and Ch'en Yü-kuang 陳玉光. "The relationship between population structure and economic development." *Chung-kuo she-hui k'o-hsueh*, 4 (1981), 29–46.

[Chang Wen-t'ien]. *Chang Wen-t'ien hsuan-chi* 張聞天選集 (Selected works of Chang Wen-t'ien). Peking: Jen-min, 1985.

Chang Wen-t'ien 張聞天. "Lu-shan hui-i shang ti fa-yen" 廬山會議上的發言 (Intervention at Lu-shan), in *Chang Wen-t'ien hsuan-chi*, 480–506.

Chang Yü-feng 張玉鳳. "Anecdotes of Mao Zedong and Zhou Enlai in their later years." *Kuang-ming jih-pao*, 26 December 1988 – 6 January 1989, trans. in FBIS *Daily Report: China*, 27 January 1989, 16–19 and 31 January 1989, 30–37.

Chang Yun-sheng 張雲生. *Mao-chia-wan chi-shih: Lin Piao mi-shu hui-i-lu* 毛家灣紀實: 林彪秘書回憶錄 (An on-the-spot report on Mao-chia-wan: the memoirs of Lin Piao's secretary). Peking: Ch'un-ch'iu, 1988.

Ch'ang-chiang wen-i 長江文藝 (Yangtze literature and art). Monthly. Wuhan: 1978– .

Chao-chia-pang ti pien-ch'ien 肇家濱的變遷 (The transformation of Chao-chia-pang). Editorial Group. Shanghai: Shanghai Jen-min, 1976.

Chao Shu-li 趙樹理. *Li Yu-ts'ai pan-hua* 李有才板話 (The ballads of Li Yu-ts'ai). Peking: Chung-kuo jen-min wen-i ts'ung-shu, 1949.

Chao Ts'ung 趙聰. *Chung-kuo ta-lu ti hsi-chü kai-ko* 中國大陸的戲劇改革 (The reform of drama in mainland China). Hong Kong: Chinese University Press, 1969.

Chao Ts'ung. "1958 nien-ti Chung-kung wen-i" 1958年的中共文藝 (Chinese communist literature and art, 1958). *Tsu-kuo chou-k'an*, 26.9–10 (June 1959), 43–46.

Chao Tzu-yang [Zhao Ziyang] 趙紫陽. "Advance along the road of socialism with Chinese characteristics – report delivered at the 13th National Congress of the Communist Party of China on October 25, 1987." *Beijing Review*, 30.45 (9–15 November 1987), I–XXVII.

Che-hsueh yen-chiu 哲學研究 (Philosophical research). Peking: 1956–   .

Cheek, Timothy. *See* MacFarquhar, Roderick.

Chen, C. S., ed. *Rural people's communes in Lien-chiang: documents concerning communes in Lien-chiang county, Fukien province, 1962–1963*. Trans. Charles Price Ridley. Stanford, Calif.: Hoover Institution Press, 1969.

Chen Cheng [Ch'en Ch'eng] 陳誠. *Land reform in Taiwan*. Taipei: China Publishing Co., 1961.

Chen, Ching-chih. "Police and community control systems in the empire," in Ramon H. Myers and Mark R. Peattie, eds., *The Japanese colonial empire*, 213–39.

Chen, Edward I-te 陳以德. "The attempt to integrate the empire: legal perspectives," in Ramon H. Myers and Mark R. Peattie, eds., *The Japanese colonial empire*, 270–74.

Chen, Jack. *A year in Upper Felicity: life in a Chinese village during the Cultural Revolution*. New York: Macmillan; London: Collier Macmillan, 1973.

Chen Jo-hsi. *See also* Chen Ruoxi.

Chen Jo-hsi. *The execution of Mayor Yin and other stories from the Great Proletarian Cultural Revolution*. Trans. Nancy Ing and Howard Goldblatt. Bloomington: Indiana University Press, 1978.

Chen, King C. 陳慶, ed. *China and the three worlds – a foreign policy reader*. White Plains, N.Y.: M. E. Sharpe, 1974.

Chen, King C. *China's war with Vietnam, 1979: issues, decisions, and implications*. Stanford, Calif.: Hoover Institution Press, 1987.

Chen, King C. "Hanoi vs. Peking: policies and relations – a survey." *Asian Survey*, 12.9 (September 1972), 807–17.

Chen Ruoxi. "Democracy Wall and the unofficial journals." *Studies in Chinese terminology*, no. 20. Berkeley, Calif.: Center for Chinese Studies, Institute of East Asian Studies, University of California, 1982.

Chen, S. H. 陳世驤. "Metaphor and the conscious in Chinese poetry," in Cyril Birch, ed., *Chinese communist literature*, 39–59.

Chen, Theodore Hsi-en 陳錫恩. *The Maoist educational revolution*. New York: Praeger, 1974.

Chen, Theodore Hsi-en. *Chinese education since 1949: academic and revolutionary models*. New York: Pergamon Press, 1981.

Chen Yun. *See* Ch'en Yun.

Ch'en, Jerome. *Mao Tse-tung and the Chinese revolution*. London: Oxford University Press, 1965.

Ch'en, Jerome, ed. *Mao*. Englewood Cliffs, N.J.: Prentice-Hall, 1969.

Ch'en, Jerome, ed. *Mao papers: anthology and bibliography*. London and New York: Oxford University Press, 1970.

Ch'en Pei-ou 陳北鷗. *Jen-min hsueh-hsi tz'u-tien* 人民學習辭典 (People's study dictionary). 2nd ed., Shanghai: Kuang-i shu-chü, 1953.

Ch'en Tsai-tao 陳再道. "Wu-han 'ch'i-erh-ling shih-chien' shih-mo" 武漢"七·二零事件"始末 (The beginning and end of the "July 20th incident" in Wuhan). *Ko-ming-shih tzu-liao*, 2 (September 1981), 7–45.

Ch'en Yue-fang; Chang Pai-chuan; and Yu Tuan-k'ang. "A survey of primary school student aspirations and learning interests." Trans. in *Chinese Sociology and Anthropology*, 16.1–2 (Fall–Winter 1983–84), 145–58.

[Ch'en Yun] *Ch'en Yun wen-hsuan (1956–1985)* 陳雲文選 (Selected works of Ch'en Yun). Peking: Jen-min, 1986.

Chen Yun [Ch'en Yun]. Speech, in *Eighth National Congress of the Communist Party of China*, 2.157–76.

Chen Yun [Ch'en Yun]. "Planning and the market." *Beijing Review*, 29.29 (21 July 1986), 14–15.

Chenery, Hollis, and Syrquin, Moises, with the assistance of Hazel Elkington. *Patterns of development, 1950–1970*. London: Oxford University Press, for the World Bank, 1975.

Cheng, J. Chester, ed., with the collaboration of Ch'ing-lien Han et al. *The politics of the Chinese Red Army: a translation of the Bulletin of Activities of the People's Liberation Army*. Stanford, Calif.: Hoover Institution Press, 1966.

Cheng-ming 爭鳴 (Contention). Monthly. Hong Kong: 1977–   .

Cheng, Nien 鄭念. *Life and death in Shanghai*. New York: Grove Press, 1987; London: Grafton Books, 1986.

Cheng Te-jung 新中國紀事 et al., eds. Hsin Chung-kuo chi-shih, 1949–89. (Records of the new China). Changchun: Tung-pei shih-fan ta-hsueh, 1986.

Ch'eng-shih chien-she 城市建設 (Urban construction). Bimonthly. Peking: 1980–   .

Cheo Ying, Esther. *Black country girl in red China*. London: Hutchinson, 1980.

Chi Hsin 齊辛. *The case of the Gang of Four*. Hong Kong: Cosmos Books, 1977.

Ch'i Pang-yuan 齊邦媛 et al., eds. and comps. *An anthology of contemporary Chinese literature, Taiwan: 1949–1974*. 2 vols. Taipei: National Institute for Compilation and Translation, 1975.

Ch'i Pang-yuan et al., eds. *Chung-kuo hsien-tai wen-hsueh hsuan-chi* 中國現代文學選集 (Anthology of contemporary Chinese literature). 2 vols. Taipei: Shu-p'ing shu-mu, 1976.

Ch'i Pang-yuan et al., eds. *An anthology of contemporary Chinese literature: Taiwan, 1949–1974*. Vol. 1: *Poems and essays*. Vol. 2: *Short stories*. Seattle: University of Washington Press, 1977.

Ch'i-shih nien-tai 七十年代 (The seventies). Monthly. Hong Kong: 1970–1983. From 1984, title changed to *Chiu-shih nien-tai* 九十年代 (The nineties).

Chiang Ch'ing 江青. "On the revolution in Peking opera: speech made in July

1964 at a forum of theatrical workers participating in the Festival of Peking Operas on Contemporary Themes." *Chinese Literature*, 8 (August 1967), 118–24.

Chiang Yi-shan 江一山. "Military affairs of communist China, 1968." *Tsu-kuo*, 59 (February 1969), 20–36.

Chiao-hsueh ts'an-k'ao: ch'üan-kuo tang-hsiao hsi-t'ung Chung-kung tang-shih hsueh-shu t'ao-lun-hui, shang, hsia 教學參攷：全國黨校系統中共黨史學術討論會, 上、下 (Reference for teaching and study: national Party school system's academic conference on CCP history, vols. 1 and 2). Anhwei: December 1980. Cited as *Chiao-hsueh ts'an-k'ao, hsia*.

Chiao-hsueh t'ung-hsun 教學通訊 (Teaching bulletin). Various sources and editions.

Chiao-hsueh yü yen-chiu 教學與研究 (Teaching and research). Monthly. Peking: 1953– .

Chiao-shih pao 教師報 (Teachers' news). Formerly *Shan-hsi chiao-yü pao* 陝西教育報 (Shensi education news). Weekly. Sian: 1984– .

Chiao-yü ko-ming 教育革命 (Education revolution). Monthly. Canton: Kwangtung Normal College, 1972–76.

Chiao-yü li-lun yü shih-chien 教育理論與實踐 (Education theory and practice). Bimonthly. Taiyuan: 1981– .

Chiao-yü shih-chien 教育實踐 (Education practice). Monthly. Shanghai: 1975–76.

Chiao-yü wen-chai 教育文摘 (Education extracts). Fortnightly. Peking: 1984– .

Chiao-yü yen-chiu 教育研究 (Education research). Monthly. Peking: 1979– .

Chiao-yü yü chih-yeh 教育與職業 (Education and occupation). Bimonthly. Peking: 1917–1949; 1985– .

Ch'iao Huan-t'ien [Qiao Huantian] 喬還田. "A discussion of Li Hung-chang's Westernization activities." *JMJP*, 30 March 1981, in FBIS *Daily Report: China*, 3 April 1981, K8–12.

Ch'iao Huan-t'ien. "The diplomatic activities of the Westernization proponents should not be cut off from the Westernization movement." *JMJP*, 7 May 1981, in FBIS *Daily Report: China*, 15 May 1981, K4–7.

Chieh-fang-chün pao 解放軍報 (Liberation Army news). 1956– .

Chieh-fang jih-pao 解放日報 (Liberation daily). Yenan. 1941–46. Shanghai. 1949– . Cited as *CFJP*.

Chien-chu hsueh-pao 建築學報 (Architectural journal). Monthly. Peking: 1954– .

Chien-kuo i-lai ... See Mao Tse-tung.

Chien Yu-shen. *China's fading revolution: army dissent and military divisions, 1967–68*. Hong Kong: Centre of Contemporary Chinese Studies, 1969.

Ch'ien-ko wan-ch'ü hsien-kei tang 千歌萬曲獻給黨 (A myriad of songs and poems devoted to the Party). Shanghai: Jen-min, 1971.

Chih-shih-fen-tzu 知識分子 (The Chinese intellectual). New York: 1984–1988, 1989– .

Chin Chih-pai 靳志柏. "P'i-K'ung yü lu-hsien tou-cheng" 批孔與路綫鬥爭 (Criticism of Confucius and two-line struggle). *HC*, 7 (1974), 23–34. Trans. in *PR*, 32 (1974), 6–10, 12, and 33 (1974), 8–12.

Chin Ching-mai 金敬邁. *Ou-yang Hai chih ko* 歐陽海之歌 (The song of Ouyang Hai). Peking: Chieh-fang-chün wen-i-she, 1965.

Chin Ch'un-ming 金春明. "*Wen-hua ta-ko-ming*" *lun-hsi* "文化大革命"論析 (An analysis of the "Great Cultural Revolution"). Shanghai: Jen-min, 1985.

Chin Ch'un-ming, " 'Wen-hua ta-ko-ming' ti shih-nien" "文化大革命"的十年 (The decade of the "Great Cultural Revolution"), in Chung-kung tang-shih yen-chiu-hui, ed., *Hsueh-hsi li-shih chueh-i chuan-chi*, 144–69.

Chin, Steve S. K. *The thought of Mao Tse-tung: form and content*. Hong Kong: Centre of Chinese Studies, University of Hong Kong, 1979. [Preface to Chinese edition dated 1976.]

China (CAR). *See* JPRS.

China briefing. Annual. New York: China Council of the Asia Society, 1980– .

China Business Review, The. Bimonthly, Washington, D.C.: National Council on U.S.-China Trade [name changed to U.S.-China Business Council], 1974– .

China Children's News. See *Chung-kuo shao-nien pao*.

China Daily. Peking: 1981– . [Printed and distributed in Peking, Hong Kong, New York, et al.]

China Education News. See *Chung-kuo chiao-yü pao*.

China Mainland Review, The. Quarterly. Hong Kong: Institute of Modern Asian Studies, University of Hong Kong, 1965–1967.

China News Analysis. Fortnightly. Hong Kong: 1953–82; 1984– . [1953–82 published by Fr. Ladany.]

China News Summary. Hong Kong: British Regional Information Office.

China Newsletter. Bimonthly: Tokyo: Japan External Trade Organization (JETRO), 1975– .

China Quarterly, The. Quarterly. London: Congress for Cultural Freedom (Paris), 1960–68; Contemporary China Institute, School of Oriental and African Studies, 1968– .

China/Red Flag (CRF). See JPRS.

China Report. Quarterly since 1986 (formerly bimonthly). (Centre for the Study of Developing Societies, India). Newbury Park, Calif.: Sage, 1964– .

China: socialist economic development. *See* World Bank.

China/State Council Bulletin (CSB). Cited as *CSB*. *See* JPRS.

China Statistical Information and Consultancy Service Center. *Statistical yearbook of China*. Annual.

China Topics. Hong Kong: British Regional Information Office, 1964– ; [London: n.p., "Y.B" [T.B.], 1961–Irregular.]

China white paper. See U.S. Department of State.

China Yearbook. Annual. 1957–79. Compiled by the China Yearbook Editorial Board. Taipei: China Publishing Company. Continues *China Handbook* 1937–45. New York: Macmillan. Continued by *Republic of China* 1983– .

China Youth News. See *Chung-kuo ch'ing-nien pao*.

Chinese Agricultural Yearbook. See *Chung-kuo nung-yeh nien-chien* ...

Chinese Agricultural Yearbook Compilation Commission. See *Chung-kuo nung-yeh nien-chien.*

Chinese Communist Affairs: a quarterly review. Quarterly. Taipei: Institute of Political Research, 1964–69.

Chinese Communist internal politics and foreign policy: reviews on. Reference materials concerning education. Taipei: Institute of International Relations, 1974.

Chinese Economic Studies, Armonk, N.Y.: M. E. Sharpe Quarterly, 1967– .

Chinese Economic System Reform Research Institute. *See* Reynolds, Bruce, ed.

Chinese economic yearbook. See *Chung-kuo ching-chi nien-chien.*

Chinese Education: a journal of translations. Quarterly. Armonk, N.Y.: M. E. Sharpe, 1968– . [Before 1977 published by IASP.]

Chinese Higher Education. See *Chung-kuo kao-teng chiao-yü.*

Chinese Law and Government: a journal of translations. Quarterly. Armonk, N.Y.: M. E. Sharpe, Cited as *CLG.* 1968– .

Chinese Literature. Monthly. Peking: FLP, 1951– .

Chinese Sociology and Anthropology: a journal of translations. Quarterly. Armonk, N.Y.: M. E. Sharpe, 1968– .

Chinese statistical yearbook. See *Chung-kuo t'ung-chi nien-chien.* Cited as *TCNC.*

Chinese Studies in History: a journal of translations. Quarterly. Armonk, N.Y.: M. E. Sharpe, 1967– . [Formerly *Chinese studies in history and philosophy.*]

Ching-chi kuan-li 經濟管理 (Economic management). Monthly. Peking: 1979– .

"Ching-chung ch'iao-hsiang liao" 警鐘敲響了 (An alarm has been sounded). Observer. *JMJP,* 15 January 1980, 6.

Chinnery, John. "Lu Xun and contemporary Chinese literature." *CQ,* 91 (September 1982), 411–23.

Chiu, Hungdah 丘宏達, ed. *China and the question of Taiwan: documents and analysis.* New York: Praeger, 1973.

Chiu, Hungdah, ed. *China and the Taiwan issue.* New York: Praeger, 1979.

Chiu, Hungdah, ed., with Leng, Shao-chuan 冷紹佺. *China: seventy years after the 1911 Hsin-Hai Revolution.* Charlottesville: University Press of Virginia, 1984.

Chiu-shih nien-tai. See *Ch'i-shih nien-tai.*

Ch'iu Chih-cho 裘之倬. "Teng Hsiao-p'ing tsai 1969–1972" 鄧小平在1969–1972 (Teng Hsiao-p'ing in 1969–1972). *Hsin-hua wen-chai,* 4 (April 1988), 133–55.

CHOC. Cambridge history of China, The.

Chou En-lai hsuan-chi, hsia 周恩來選集,下 (The selected works of Chou En-lai, 2). Peking: Jen-min, 1984.

Chou En-lai shu-hsin hsuan-chi 周恩來書信選集 (Chou En-lai's selected letters). Peking: Chung-yang wen-hsien, 1988.

Chou En-lai. See *Chou tsung-li …*

[Chou En-lai]. "Chinese government and people strongly condemn Soviet revisionist clique's armed occupation of Czechoslovakia." *PR,* supplement to 34 (23 August 1968), III–IV.

Chou En-lai. "Report to the Tenth National Congress of the Communist Party of China" (delivered 24 August 1973). *PR*, 35 and 36 (7 September 1973), 17–25.

Chou En-lai. "Internal report to the Party on the international situation," in King C. Chen, ed., *China and the three worlds*, 137–38.

Chou Erh-fu 周而復. *Hsin-ti ch'i-tien* 新的起點 (A new start). Peking: Ch'ün-i, 1949.

Chou, Eric. *A man must choose*. New York: Knopf, 1963.

Chou Ming 周明, ed. *Li-shih tsai che-li ch'en-ssu: 1966–1976 nien chi-shih* 歷史在這裏沉思:1966–1976年記實 (History is reflected here: a record of the years 1966–1976). vols. 1–3: Peking: Hua-hsia, 1986; vols. 4–6: T'ai-yuan: Pei-yueh, 1989.

Chou Shu-lien 周叔蓮, and Lin Shen-mu 林森木. "T'an-t'an chu-chai wen-t'i" 談談住宅問題 (Chatting on the housing problem). *JMJP*, 5 August 1980, 5.

Chou tsung-li sheng-p'ing ta-shih-chi 周總理生平大事記 (Major events in the life of Premier Chou). Chengtu: Szechwan jen-min, 1986.

Chou Yang 周揚. *Piao-hsien hsin-ti ch'ün-chung ti shih-tai* 表現新的羣眾的時代 (Expressing the new age of the masses). Peking: Hsin-hua shu-tien, 1949.

Chou Yang. *The path of socialist literature and art in China*. Peking: FLP, 1960.

Chou Yang. "Hsin ti jen-min ti wen-i" 新的人民的文藝 (The people's new literature and art), in *Chung-hua ch'üan-kuo wen-hsueh i-shu kung-tso-che tai-piao ta-hui chi-nien wen-chi*, 69–99.

Chou Yang. "Wen-i chan-hsien ti i-ch'ang ta pien-lun" 文藝戰綫的一場大辯論 (A great debate on the literary front). *Wen-i pao*, 5 (1958), 2–14.

Chou Yang. "Wo kuo she-hui chu-i wen-hsueh i-shu ti tao-lu" 我國社會主義文學藝術的道路. *Wen-i pao*, 13–14 (1960), 15–37. Trans. as Chou Yang, *The path of socialist literature…*

Chou Yang "The fighting task confronting workers in philosophy and the social sciences." (Speech at the fourth enlarged session of the Committee of the Department of Philosophy and Social Science of the Chinese Academy of Sciences held 26 October 1963). *PR*, 1 (3 January 1964), 10–27.

Chou Yang. "Chi wang k'ai lai, fan-jung she-hui chu-i hsin shih-ch'i ti wen-i" 繼往開來,繁榮社會主義新時期的文藝 (Inherit the past and usher in the future prosperity of the literature and art of the new socialist age). *Wen-i pao*, 11–12 (1979), 8–26.

Chou Yang. "Yeh t'an-t'an tang ho wen-i ti kuan-hsi" 也談談黨和文藝的關係 (Speaking again of the relation between the Party and literature and the arts). *HC*, 11 (1979), 26–29.

[Chou Yang] [Zhou Yang]. "Zhou Yang on reality in literature and other questions." [Interview with Zhou Yang.] *Chinese Literature*, 1980.1 (January), 92–96.

Chou Yang. "Kuan-yü Ma-k'o-ssu-chu-i ti chi-ko li-lun wen-t'i ti t'an-t'ao" 關於馬克思主義的幾個理論問題的探討 (An exploration of some theoretical questions of Marxism). *JMJP*, 16 March 1983.

Choudhury, G[olam] W. *China in world affairs: the foreign policy of the PRC since 1970*. Boulder, Colo.: Westview Press, 1982.

Christman, Henry M. *See* Lenin, Vladimir Il'ich.

Chu Ch'eng-chia 朱成甲, ed. *Chung-kung tang-shih yen-chiu lun-wen hsuan, hsia* 中共黨史研究論文選(下) (Selection of research papers on the history of the CCP, vol. 3). Changsha: Hunan jen-min, 1984.

Chu Chung-li 朱仲麗.ʹ *Nü-huang meng: Chiang Ch'ing wai-chuan* 女皇夢:江青外傳 (Empress dream: an unofficial biography of Chiang Ch'ing). Peking: Tung-fang, 1988.

Chu-shih-pen. See *Kuan-yü chien-kuo-i-lai.* . . .

Chü-pen 劇本 (Plays). Monthly. Peking: 1952–   .

Ch'ü Po 曲波. *Lin hai hsueh yuan* 林海雪原 (Tracks in the snowy forest). Peking: Tso-chia, 1957.

Ch'üan-kuo Mao Tse-tung che-hsüeh ssu-hsiang t'ao-lun hui lun-wen hsuan 全國毛澤東哲學思想討論會論文選 (Selected essays from the national conference to discuss Mao Tse-tung's philosophical thought). Nanning: Kwangsi jen-min, 1982.

Ch'üan-kuo pao-k'an so-yin 全國報刊索引 (Index to newspapers and periodicals published in China). Monthly. Shanghai: Shanghai Municipal Library, 1973–   .

Ch'üan-kuo tang-shih tzu-liao ... See *Tang-shih hui-yi pao-kao-chi.*

Ch'un wen-hsueh 純文學 (Pure literature). Monthly. Taipei: 1967–   .

Chung, Chin O. *P'yongyang between Peking and Moscow: North Korea's involvement in the Sino-Soviet dispute, 1958–1975.* University: University of Alabama Press, 1978.

Chung-hua ch'üan-kuo wen-hsueh i-shu kung-tso-che tai-piao ta-hui chi-nien wen-chi 中華全國文學藝術工作者代表大會紀念文集 (Documents commemorating China's national congress of literature and art workers). Peking: Hsin-hua shu-tien, 1950.

Chung-hua jen-min kung-ho-kuo chiao-yü ta-shih-chi, 1949–1982 中華人民共和國教育大事記,1949–1982 (Education chronology of the People's Republic of China, 1949–1982). Peking: Chiao-yüʺk'o-hsueh, 1983.

Chung-hua jen-min kung-ho-kuo ching-chi ho she-hui fa-chan ti-ch'i ko wu-nien chi-hua, 1986–1990 中華人民共和國經濟和社會發展第七個五年計劃, 1986–1990 (The 7th Five-Year Plan for the economic and social development of the People's Republic of China, 1986–1990). Peking: Jen-min, 1986.

Chung-hua jen-min kung-ho-kuo kuo-wu-yuan kung-pao 中華人民共和國國務院公報 (Bulletin of the State Council of the People's Republic of China). Peking: State Council.

Chung-hua jen-min kung-ho-kuo ti-wu-chieh ch'üan-kuo jen-min tai-piao ta-hui ti-san-tz'u hui-i wen-chien 中華人民共和國第五屆全國人民代表大會第三次會議文件 (Documents of the third session of the 5th NPC of the PRC). Peking: Jen-min, 1980.

Chung-So Yongu 中蘇研究 (Sino-Soviet Affairs). Quarterly. Seoul: Institute for Sino-Soviet Studies, Hanyang University, 1980–   .

Chung-hua jen-min kung-ho-kuo tsui-kao jen-min fa-yuan t'e-pieh fa-t'ing shen-p'an Lin Piao, Chiang Ch'ing fan-ko-ming chi-t'uan an chu-fan chi-shih 中華人民共和國最高人民法院特別法庭審判林彪、江青反革命集團案主犯紀實 (A record of the trial by the Special Tribunal of the PRC's Supreme People's Court of the principal criminals of the Lin Piao and Chiang Ch'ing counterrevolutionary cliques). Tsui-kao jen-min fa-yuan yen-chiu-shih 最高人民法院研究室 (Research Office, Supreme People's Court), ed. Peking: Fa-lü, 1982.

Chung K'an 仲侃. *K'ang Sheng p'ing-chuan* 康生評傳 (A critical biography of K'ang Sheng). Peking: Hung-ch'i, 1982.

Chung-kung chung-yang tang-hsiao nien-chien, 1984 中共中央黨校年鑒, 1984 (CCP Central Party School Yearbook, 1984). Peking: Chung-kung chung-yang tang-hsiao, 1985.

Chung-kung shih-yi-chieh san-chung ch'üan-hui yi-lai chung-yang shou-yao chiang-hua chi wen-chien hsuan-pien 中共十一屆三中全會以來中央首要講話及文件選編 (Compilation of major central speeches and documents since the Third Plenum of the Eleventh Central Committee). 2 vols. Taipei: Chung-kung yen-chiu tsa-chih-she, 1983.

Chung-kung tang-shih ta-shih nien-piao 中共黨史大事年報 (A chronological table of major events in the history of the Chinese Communist Party). Chung-kung chung-yang tang-shih yen-chiu-shih, ed. Peking: Jen-min, 1987.

Chung-kung tang-shih yen-chiu 中共黨史研究 (Research into the history of the CCP). Bimonthly. Peking: Chung-kung chung-yang tang-hsiap, 1988– . Replaced *Tang-shih yen-chiu.*

Chung-kung tang-shih yen-chiu-hui 中共黨史研究會 (Research Society on the History of the Chinese Communist Party), ed. *Hsueh-hsi li-shih chueh-i chuan-chi* 學習歷史決議專集 (Special publication on studying the resolution on history). Peking: Chung-kung chung-yang tang-hsiao, 1982.

Chung-kung yen-chiu 中共研究 (Studies on Chinese communism). Monthly. Taipei: 1967– . Cited as *CKYC.*

Chung-kuo chiao-yü nien-chien, 1949–1981 中國教育年鑒, 1949–1981 (China education yearbook, 1949–1981). Peking: Chung-kuo ta-pai-k'o ch'üan-shu, 1984.

Chung-kuo chiao-yü pao 中國教育報 (China education news). 3/yr. Peking: 1983– .

Chung-kuo ching-chi nien-chien 中國經濟年鑒 (Almanac of China's economy). Annual. Hong Kong: Hsien-tai wen-hua ch'i-yeh kung-szu, 1981– .

Chung-kuo ching-chi nien-chien (Almanac of China's economy). Peking: Chung-kuo ching-chi nien-chien yu-hsien kung-szu, 1983– .

Chung-kuo ch'ing-nien 中國青年 (China youth). Monthly. Peking: 1949–1966, 1978– .

Chung-kuo ch'ing-nien pao 中國青年報 (China youth news). Peking: 1951– .

Chung-kuo jen-k'ou nien-chien 中國人口年鑒 (Chinese population yearbook). Annual. Population Research Center of the Chinese Academy of Social Sciences, 1985– .

Chung-kuo jen-min chieh-fang-chün chiang-shuai ming-lu 中國人民解放軍將帥名錄 (The names and records of marshals and generals of the Chinese People's Liberation Army). Hsing-huo liao-yuan pien-chi-pu 星火燎原編輯部 (A single spark can start a prairie fire editorial department). Peking: Chieh-fang-chün, vol. 1, 1986; vol. 2, 1987; vol. 3, 1987.

Chung-kuo kao-teng chiao-yü. 中國高等教育 (Chinese higher education). Formerly *Kao-chiao chan-hsien* 高教戰綫 (Higher education battlefront). Monthly. Peking: 1965– .

Chung-kuo kung-ch'an-tang. Chinese Communist Party.

Chung-kuo kung-ch'an-tang chien-shih chiang-i 中國共產黨簡史講義 (Teaching materials for a brief history of the Chinese Communist Party). 2 vols. Canton: Kwang-tung jen-min, 1981.

Chung-kuo kung-ch'an-tang li-shih chiang-i (Teaching materials on the history of the Chinese Communist Party). Wuhan: Jen-min, 1984.

Chung-kuo kung-ch'an-tang li-tz'u chung-yao hui-i-chi 中國共產黨歷次重要會議集 (Collection of various important conferences of the CCP). Chung-kung chung-yang tang-hsiao tang-shih chiao-yen-shih tzu-liao tsu, ed. Shanghai: Jen-min, vol. 1, 1982; vol. 2, 1983.

Chung-kuo kung-ch'an-tang liu-shih-nien ta-shih chien-chieh 中國共產黨六十年大事簡介 (A summary of the principal events in the 60 years of the Chinese Communist Party). Cheng-chih hsueh-yuan Chung-kung-tang shih chiao-yen-shih, 政治學院 中共黨史教研室. Cited as Teaching and Research Office for CCP History of the [PLA] Political Academy, *Chung-kuo kung-ch'an-tang....* Peking: Kuo-fang ta-hsueh, 1985.

Chung-kuo kung-ch'an-tang ti-chiu tz'u ch'üan-kuo tai-piao ta hui (hua-ts'e) 中國共產黨第 九次全國代表大會(畫冊) (Ninth Congress of the Chinese Communist Party [pictorial volume]). Hong Kong: San-lien shu-tien, 1969.

Chung-kuo nung-yeh nien-chien 中國農業年鑑 (Chinese agricultural yearbook, 1980). Chinese Agricultural Yearbook Compilation Commission. Peking: Agricultural Publishing House, 1980– .

Chung-kuo pai-k'o nien-chien 中國百科年鑑 (China encyclopedic yearbook). Annual. Peking and Shanghai: Chung-kuo ta-pai-k'o ch'üan-shu, 1980– .

Chung-kuo shao-nien pao 中國少年報 (China children's news). Weekly. Peking: 1951– .

Chung-kuo she-hui k'o-hsueh 中國社會科學 (Chinese social science). Bimonthly. Peking: 1980– .

Chung-kuo shih-pao 中國時報 (China times). Taiwan.

Chung-kuo tang-tai tso-chia hsiao chuan 中國當代作家小傳 (Brief biographies of contemporary Chinese writers). Paris: Centre de Publication Asie Orientale, 1967.

Chung-kuo tang-tai wen-hsueh shih 中國當代文學史 (History of contemporary Chinese literature). Comp. by Shantung and nineteen other universities. Foochow: Fukien jen-min, 1980.

Chung-kuo tang-tai wen-hsueh shih ch'u-kao 中國當代文學史初稿 (First draft history of contemporary Chinese literature). 2 vols. Ministry of Education editorial committee advised by Ch'en Huang-mei. 陳荒煤 Peking: Jen-min wen-hsueh, 1981.

Chung-kuo tang-tai wen-hsueh tso-p'in hsuan-chiang 中國當代文學作品選講 (Lectures on selected contemporary Chinese literary works). Comp. by sixteen institutions of higher education. Nanning: Kwangsi jen-min wen-hsueh, 1980.

Chung-kuo ti-san-tz'u jen-k'ou p'u-ch'a ti chu-yao shu-tzu 中國第三次人口普查的主要數字 (Main figures from China's third population census). Peking: Chung-Kuo t'eng-chi, 1982.

Chung-kuo tien-ying 中國電影 (Chinese film). Quarterly. Peking: 1958– .

Chung-kuo tui-wai mao-i nien-chien, 1984 中國對外貿易年鑑, 1984 (China's foreign trade yearbook, 1984). Peking: Chung-kuo tui-wai ching-chi mao-i, 1984.

Chung-kuo t'ung-chi nien-chien, 1981 中國統計年鑑, 1981 (Statistical yearbook of China, 1981). Chung-hua jen-min kung-ho-kuo kuo-chia t'ung-chi chü 中華人民共和國國家統計局, ed. Peking: Chung-kuo t'ung-chi nien-chien, 1982. Cited as *TCNC*.

Chung-kuo t'ung-chi nien-chien 中國統計年鑑 (Statistical yearbook of China, 1981). Hong Kong: Ching-chi tao-pao she, 1981– . Cited as *TCNC*.

Chung-kuo t'ung-chi nien-chien 中國統計年鑑 (Statistical yearbook of China, 1983). Chung-hua jen-min kung-ho-kuo kuo-chia t'ung-chi chü, ed. Peking: Chung-kuo t'ung-chi nien-chien, 1983. Cited as *TCNC*.

Chung-kuo wen-hsueh-chia tz'u-tien: hsien-tai 中國文學家辭典:現代 (Biographical dictionary of Chinese writers: modern). Hong Kong: Wen-hua tzu-liao kung-ying she, 1979; part two, 1980.

Chung-wai wen-hsueh 中外文學 (Chinese and foreign literature). Monthly. Taipei: 1972– .

Chung-yang jih-pao 中央日報 (Central daily news). Taipei: 1947– .

Chung-yang wen-hsien yen-chiu-shih. Department for Research on Party Literature.

"Circular of [the] Central Committee of [the] CCP [on the Cultural Revolution]." (16 May 1966). *PR*, 21 (19 May 1967), 6–9.

CKYC. Chung-kung yen-chiu.

Clark, Paul. "The film industry in the 1970s," in Bonnie S. McDougall, ed., *Popular Chinese literature and performing arts in the People's Republic of China, 1949–1979*, 177–96.

Clark, Paul. "Film-making in China: from the Cultural Revolution to 1981." *CQ*, 94 (June 1983), 304–22.

CLEAR [Chinese literature, essays, articles, reviews]. Madison, Wis.: Coda Press, 1979– .

Cleverley, John. *The schooling of China: tradition and modernity in Chinese education.* London: George Allen & Unwin, 1985.

CLG. Chinese Law and Government.

Clough, Ralph N. *Island China.* Cambridge, Mass.: Harvard University Press, 1978.

Clough, Ralph N., et al. *The United States, China, and arms control.* Washington, D.C.: The Brookings Institution, 1975.

Clough, Ralph N.; Oxnam, Robert B.; and Watts, William. *The United States and China: American perceptions and future alternatives.* Washington, D.C.: Potomac Associates, 1977.

Clubb, O. Edmund. *China and Russia: the "Great Game."* New York and London: Columbia University Press, 1971.

Coale, Ansley J. *Rapid population change in China, 1952–1982.* Washington, D.C.: National Academy Press, 1984.

Cohen, Arthur A. *The communism of Mao Tse-tung*. Chicago: University of Chicago Press, 1971 [1964].

Cohen, Arthur A. "How original is 'Maoism'?" *Problems of Communism*, 10.6 (November–December 1961), 34–42.

Cohen, Jerome Alan. *The criminal process in the People's Republic of China, 1949–1963: an introduction*. Cambridge, Mass.: Harvard University Press, 1968.

Cohen, Jerome Alan; Friedman, Edward; Hinton, Harold; and Whiting, Allen S. *Taiwan and American policy: the dilemma in U.S.-China relations*. New York: Praeger, 1971.

Cohen, Myron L. *House united, house divided: the Chinese family in Taiwan*. New York: Columbia University Press, 1976.

"Collection of documents concerning the Great Proletarian Cultural Revolution." *CB*, 852 (6 May 1968).

Commentator. "Ts'ung Yueh-nan tang-chü fan-hua k'an Su-lien ti chan-lueh i-t'u" 從越南當局反華看蘇聯的戰略意圖 (Soviet strategic intention as viewed from the Vietnamese authorities anti-Chinese activities). *HC*, 8 (1 August 1978), 101–4.

Commentator. "Tang-ch'ien chan-cheng wei-hsien yü pao-wei shih-chieh ho-p'ing" 當前戰爭危險與保衛世界和平 (The current danger of war and the defense of world peace). *HC*, 11 (2 November 1979), 53–58.

Commentator. "Fan-mien chiao-yuan tsai kei ta-chia shang hsin-k'o: p'ing Su-lien ch'in-lueh ho chan-ling A-fu-k'an" 反面教員在給大家上新課:評蘇聯侵略和占領阿富汗 (The teacher who teaches by negative example is giving everyone a lesson: commentary on the Soviet invasion and occupation of Afghanistan). *HC*, 2 (16 January 1980), 46–48.

"Communiqué of the Eleventh Plenary Session of the Eighth Central Committee of the Communist Party of China (adopted on August 12, 1966)." *PR*, 34 (19 August 1966), 4–8.

"Communiqué of the Third Plenary Session of the 11th Central Committee of the Communist Party of China" (adopted on 22 December 1978). *PR*, 52 (29 December 1978), 6–16.

Communist Affairs: documents and analyses. Quarterly. Guilford, Surrey: Butterworth Scientific, 1982– .

Comparative Urban Research. New York: 1972–85. Continued by *Comparative Urban and Community Research*.

Compton, Boyd, trans. and intro. *Mao's China: party reform documents, 1942–44*. Seattle: University of Washington Press, 1966 [1952]; Westport, Conn.: Greenwood Press, 1982 [c. 1952].

Congressional Quarterly, Inc. *China and U.S. foreign policy*. Ed. William B. Dickinson, Jr. Washington, D.C.: 1973 [2nd ed.].

Congressional Quarterly Service. *China and U.S. Far East policy, 1945–1967*. Washington, D.C.: 1967 [rev.].

"The Constitution of the People's Republic of China." *PR*, 4 (24 January 1975), 12–17.

Contemporary China. Vol. 1. *1955*. Hong Kong: Hong Kong University Press, 1956. Vol. 2. *1956–1957*, 1958. Vol. 3. *1958–1959*, 1960. Vol. 4. *1959–1960*, 1961. Vol. 5. *1961–1962*, 1963. Vol. 6. *1962–1964*, 1968.

Contemporary China. See Sorich, Richard.

Contemporary China. Ed. Edwin Winckler. Boulder, Colo.: Westview Press, October 1976–Winter 1979.

Copper, John F., with George P. Chen, *Taiwan's elections: political development and democratization in the Republic of China*. Occasional Papers in Contemporary Asian Studies. Baltimore: University of Maryland School of Law, 1984.

Corbett, Charles Hodge. *Lingnan University*. New York: Trustees of Lingnan University, 1963.

Cordier, Andrew W., ed. *Columbia essays in international affairs: the dean's papers, 1965*. New York: Columbia University Press, 1966.

Council for Economic Planning and Development. *Taiwan statistical data book, 1986*. Taipei: Council for Economic Planning and Development, 1986.

CQ. The China Quarterly.

CRF. See JPRS. *China/Red Flag (CRF)*.

Crook, Frederick W. "The reform of the commune system and the rise of the township-collective-household system," in U.S. Congress, Joint Economic Committee, *China's economy looks toward the year 2000*, 1.354–75.

Crook, Isabel, and Crook, David. *Revolution in a Chinese village: Ten Mile Inn*. London: Routledge & Kegan Paul, 1959.

Crook, Isabel, and Crook, David. *Ten Mile Inn: mass movement in a Chinese village*. New York: Pantheon, 1979.

Crozier, Brian, with the collaboration of Eric Chou. *The man who lost China: the first full biography of Chiang Kai-shek*. New York: Scribner, 1976.

CSB. See JPRS. *China/State Council Bulletin (CSB)*.

CSCPRC. Committee on Scholarly Communication with the People's Republic of China.

CSM. Christian Science Monitor.

CSYB. Chinese statistical yearbook.

Cultural Revolution. See *Important documents on the Great Proletarian Cultural Revolution in China*.

Cultural Revolution in the provinces, The. Cambridge, Mass.: East Asian Research Center, Harvard University, 1971.

Current Background. See U.S. Consulate General.

Current Digest of the Soviet Press, The. Weekly. Columbus, Ohio: 1949– . Cited as CDSP.

Current History. 9/year (monthly except June, July, August). Philadelphia: Current History, Inc., 1914– .

Current scene: developments in mainland China. Irregular. Hong Kong: The Green Pagoda Press, 1961–1972. Supersedes mimeographed publication by the same title, 1959–1961. After December 1972 "no longer available for American distribution."

Daily Report: China. See FBIS.

Daily Report: Far East. See FBIS.

Daily Report: People's Republic of China. See FBIS.

Daily Report: Soviet Union. See FBIS.

Daily Report: USSR. See FBIS.

Daily Telegraph. London.

Dake, Antonie C. A. *In the spirit of the Red Banteng: Indonesian communists between Moscow and Peking 1959–1965.* The Hague: Mouton, 1973.

Dallin, Alexander, with Jonathan Harris, and Grey Hodnett, eds. *Diversity in international communism: a documentary record, 1961–1963.* New York: Columbia University Press, 1963.

Daubier, Jean. *A history of the Chinese Cultural Revolution.* Trans. Richard Seaver. Preface by Han Suyin. New York: Vintage Books, 1974.

Davidson, James W. *The island of Formosa: historical view from 1430 to 1900.* London: Privately published, 1903.

Davis-Friedmann, Deborah. *Long lives: Chinese elderly and the communist revolution.* Cambridge. Mass.: Harvard University Press, 1983.

Decision of the Central Committee of the Chinese Communist Party concerning the Great Proletarian Cultural Revolution. Peking: FLP, 1966.

"Decision of the Central Committee of the Communist Party of China on reform of the economic structure," 20 October 1984. *Beijing Review,* 27.44 (29 October 1984), I–XVI.

Deliusin, L. P. *The socio-political essence of Maoism.* Moscow: Novosti, 1976.

Deng Xiaoping. *See also* Teng Hsiao-p'ing.

Deng Xiaoping. *Selected works of Deng Xiaoping (1975–1982).* Peking: FLP, 1984.

Deshpande, G. P. "China and Vietnam." *International Studies,* 12.4 (October–December 1973), 568–81.

Developing Economies, The. Quarterly. Tokyo: Institute of Developing Economies – Ajia Keizai Kenkyūshō, 1962– .

Diamond, Norma. *K'un Shen: a Taiwan village.* New York: Holt, Rinehart & Winston, 1969.

Diamond, Norma. "Rural collectivization and decolléctivization in China: a review article." *JAS,* 44.4 (August 1985), 785–92.

Diao, Richard K. "The impact of the Cultural Revolution on China's economic elite." *CQ,* 42 (April–June 1970), 65–87.

Dickinson, William B. *See* Congressional Quarterly, Inc.

Die Welt. Daily. Hamburg: 1946– .

Dittmer, Lowell. *Liu Shao-ch'i and the Chinese Cultural Revolution: the politics of mass criticism.* Berkeley: University of California Press, 1974.

Dittmer, Lowell. *China's continuous revolution: the post-liberation epoch, 1949–1981.* Berkeley: University of California Press, 1987.

Dittmer, Lowell. "Bases of power in Chinese politics: a theory and an analysis of the fall of the 'Gang of Four.'" *World Politics,* 31.1 (October 1978), 26–60.

Dittmer, Lowell, and Chen Ruoxi. *Ethics and rhetoric of the Chinese Cultural Revo-*

lution. Studies in Chinese Terminology, no. 19. Berkeley: Center for Chinese Studies, Institute of East Asian Studies, University of California, 1981.

Djilas, Milovan. *The new class: an analysis of the Communist system.* New York: Praeger, 1957.

"Document of the Ministry of Foreign Affairs of the People's Republic of China" (9 October 1969). *PR*, 41 (10 October 1969), 8–15.

Documents of the Chinese Communist Party Central Committee, September 1956–April 1969. See Union Research Institute.

Documents of the Thirteenth National Congress of the Communist Party of China (1987). Peking: FLP, 1987.

Domes, Jürgen. *The internal politics of China, 1949–1972.* Trans. Rudiger Machetzki. New York: Praeger; London: C. Hurst, 1973.

Domes, Jürgen. *The government and politics of the PRC: a time of transition.* Boulder, Colo.: Westview Press, 1985.

Domes, Jürgen. "The Cultural Revolution and the army." *Asian Survey*, 8.5 (May 1968), 349–63.

Domes, Jürgen. "The role of the military in the formation of revolutionary committees, 1967–68." *CQ*, 44 (October–December 1970), 112–45.

Domes, Jürgen. "New policies in the communes: notes on rural societal structures in China, 1976–1981." *JAS*, 41.2 (February 1982), 253–67.

Dommen, Arthur J. "The attempted coup in Indonesia." *CQ*, 25 (January–March 1966), 144–70.

Doolin, Dennis J. *Territorial claims in the Sino-Soviet conflict: documents and analysis.* Stanford, Calif.: Hoover Institution, 1965.

Dore, Ronald. *The diploma disease: education, qualification and development.* London: George Allen & Unwin, 1976.

Dorrell, William F. "Power, policy, and ideology in the making of the Chinese Cultural Revolution," in Thomas W. Robinson, ed., *The Cultural Revolution in China*, 21–112.

"Down with the new tsars!" Editorial in *JMJP*, 4 March 1969, in *SCMP*, 4373 (11 March 1969), 17–19.

Downen, Robert L. *Of grave concern: U.S.-Taiwan relations on the threshold of the 1980s.* Washington, D.C.: Center for Strategic and International Studies, Georgetown University, 1981.

Downen, Robert L. *To bridge the Taiwan Strait: the complexities of China's reunification.* Washington, D.C.: The Council for Social and Economic Studies, 1984.

Dual Purpose Personnel News. See Liang yung jen-ts'ai pao.

Duiker, William J. *China and Vietnam: the roots of conflict.* Berkeley: Institute of East Asian Studies, University of California, 1986.

Duke, Michael S. *Blooming and contending: Chinese literature in the post-Mao era.* Bloomington: Indiana University Press, 1985.

Duke, Michael S., ed. *Contemporary Chinese literature: an anthology of post-Mao fiction and poetry.* Ed. and intro. by Michael S. Duke for the *Bulletin of Concerned Asian Scholars.* Armonk, N.Y.: M. E. Sharpe, 1985.

Duke, Michael S. "The second blooming of the hundred flowers, Chinese literature in the post-Mao era," in Mason Y. H. Wang, ed., *Perspectives in contemporary Chinese literature*, 1–48.

Dulles, Foster Rhea. *American policy toward Communist China, 1949–1969*. Foreword by John K. Fairbank. New York: Thomas Y. Crowell, 1972.

East China Normal University Journal. See *Hua-tung shih-fan ta-hsueh hsueh-pao*.

Eastman, Lloyd E. *The abortive revolution: China under Nationalist rule, 1927–1937*. Cambridge, Mass.: Harvard University Press, 1974.

ECMM. See U.S. Consulate General. Hong Kong. *Extracts from China Mainland Magazines*.

Economic Planning Board. *Handbook of Korean economy, 1980*. Seoul: Economic Planning Board, 1980.

Economic Planning Board. *Major statistics of Korean economy, 1986*. Seoul: Economic Planning Board, 1986.

Economist, The. Weekly. London: Economist Newspaper Ltd., 1843– .

Education and Occupation. See *Chiao-yü yü chih-yeh*.

Education Extracts. See *Chiao-yü wen-chai*.

Education Practice. See *Chiao-yü shih-chien*.

Education Research. See *Chiao-yü yen-chiu*.

Education Revolution. See *Chiao-yü ko-ming*.

Education Theory and Practice. See *Chiao-yü li-lun yü shih-chien*.

Edwards, R. Randle; Henkin, Louis; and Nathan, Andrew J. *Human rights in contemporary China*. New York: Columbia University Press, 1986.

Egorov, K. A. *Gosudarstvennyi apparat KNR, 1967–1981* (The governmental apparatus of the PRC, 1967–1981). Moscow: Nauka, 1982.

Eighth National Congress of the Communist Party of China. Peking: FLP, 1956.

Eighth National Congress of the Communist Party of China. Vol. 1: *Documents*. Vol. 2: *Speeches*. Peking: FLP, 1981.

Eisenhower, Dwight. *Mandate for change, 1953–1956: the White House years*. Garden City, N.Y.: Doubleday, 1963.

Eisenhower, Dwight. *Waging peace 1956–1961: the White House years*. Garden City, N.Y.: Doubleday, 1965.

Elegant, Robert S. *Mao's great revolution*. New York: World, 1971.

Eleventh National Congress of the Communist Party of China (documents). Peking: FLP, 1977.

Elkin, Jerrold F., and Fredericks, Brian. "Sino-Indian border talks: the view from New Delhi." *Asian Survey*, 23.10 (October 1983), 1128–39.

Elliott, David W. P., ed. *The third Indochina conflict*. Boulder, Colo.: Westview Press, 1981.

Ellison, Herbert J., ed. *The Sino-Soviet conflict: a global perspective*. Seattle: University of Washington Press, 1982.

Elvin, Mark, and Skinner, G. William, eds. *The Chinese city between two worlds*. Stanford Calif.: Stanford University Press, 1974.

Enlightenment Daily. See *Kuang-ming jih-pao*.

Erisman, Alva Lewis. "Potential costs of and benefits from diverting river flow for irrigation in the North China plain." University of Maryland, Ph.D. dissertation, 1967.

Esherick, Joseph W. "On the 'restoration of capitalism': Mao and Marxist theory." *Modern China*, 5.1 (January 1979), 41–77.

Esmein, Jean. *La Révolution culturelle chinoise*. Paris: Seuil, 1970.

Eto, Shinkichi 衛藤瀋吉. "Japan and China – a new stage?" *Problems of Communism*, 16.6 (November–December 1972), 1–17.

Eto, Shinkichi. "Recent developments in Sino-Japanese relations." *Asian Survey*, 20.7 (July 1980), 726–743.

Evans, Humphrey. *See* Loh, Robert.

Extracts from China Mainland Magazines. See U.S. Consulate General.

Fairbank, John K., ed. *The missionary enterprise in China and America*. Cambridge, Mass.: Harvard University Press, 1974.

Faligot, Roger, and Kauffer, Remi. *Kang Sheng et les services secrets chinois (1927–1987)*. Paris: Robert Laffont, 1987.

Falkenheim, Victor. "The Cultural Revolution in Kwangsi, Yunnan, and Fukien." *Asian Survey*, 9.8 (August 1969), 580–97.

Fan Shuo. "The tempestuous October – a chronicle of the complete collapse of the 'Gang of Four.'" *Yang-ch'eng wan pao*, 10 February 1989, trans. in FBIS *Daily Report: China*, 14 February 1989, 16–22.

Fang, Percy Jucheng 方鉅成, and Fang, Lucy Guinong J. 姜桂儂. *Zhou Enlai: a profile*. Peking: FLP, 1986.

Fang Wei-chung 房維中, ed. *Chung-hua jen-min kung-ho-kuo ching-chi ta-shih-chi (1949–1980)* 中華人民共和國經濟大事記 (1949–1980) (A record of the major economic events of the PRC [1949–1980]). Peking: Chung-kuo she-hui k'o hsueh, 1984.

Far Eastern Economic Review. Weekly. Hong Kong: Far Eastern Economic Review Ltd., 1946–   . Cited as *FEER*.

Far Eastern Economic Review. *Yearbook*. Annual. Hong Kong: Far Eastern Economic Review, Ltd., 1962–1972. Continues in part: *Far Eastern Economic Review … Yearbook and Asian textile survey*. Continued by *Asia Yearbook*, 1973–   .

Faurot, Jeannette L., ed. *Chinese fiction from Taiwan: critical perspectives*. Bloomington: Indiana University Press, 1980. [Symposium on Taiwan fiction, 1979, University of Texas at Austin.]

FBIS. *Foreign Broadcast Information Service*.

FEER. *Far Eastern Economic Review*.

Fei Hsiao-t'ung 費孝通. *Peasant life in China: a field study of country life in the Yangtze valley*. Preface by Bronislaw Malinowski. New York: E. P. Dutton, 1939; London: Routledge & Kegan Paul, 1932.

Fei Hsiao-t'ung. "On changes in the Chinese family structure." *Chinese Sociology and Anthropology*, 16.1–2 (Fall–Winter 1983–84), 32–45.

Fei Xiaotong [Fei Hsiao-t'ung]. *Chinese village close up*. Beijing: New World Press, 1983.

Fei, John C. H.; Ranis, Gustav; and Kuo, Shirley W. Y. *Growth with equity: the Taiwan case.* New York: Oxford University Press, for the World Bank, 1980.

Feng Chih 馮至. *Shih-nien shih-ch'ao* 十年詩鈔 (Poems of a decade). Peking: Jen-min wen-hsueh, 1959.

Feuerwerker Yi-tsi Mei 梅儀慈. *Ding Ling's fiction: ideology and narrative in modern Chinese literature.* Cambridge, Mass.: Harvard University Press, 1982.

Feurtado, Gardel. "The formation of provincial revolutionary committees, 1966–1968: Heilungkiang and Hopei." *Asian Survey*, 12.12 (December 1972), 1014–31.

Field, Robert Michael; Lardy, Nicholas; and Emerson, John Philip. *A reconstruction of the gross value of industrial output by provinces in the People's Republic of China: 1949–73.* Washington, D.C.: U.S. Department of Commerce, 1975.

Field, Robert Michael; McGlynn, Kathleen M.; and Abnett, William B. "Political conflict and industrial growth in China: 1965–1977," in U.S. Congress, Joint Economic Committee, *The Chinese economy post-Mao*, 1.239–83.

Fifth session of the Fifth National People's Congress (main documents). Peking: FLP, 1983.

The Financial Times. Daily. London: 1888– .

Fingar, Thomas, et al., eds. *China's quest for independence: policy evolution in the 1970s.* Boulder, Colo.: Westview Press, 1980.

Fitzpatrick, Sheila, ed. *Cultural Revolution in Russia, 1928–1931.* Bloomington: Indiana University Press, 1984 [1978].

Floyd, David. *Mao against Khrushchev: a short history of the Sino-Soviet conflict.* New York: Praeger, 1964.

FLP. Foreign Languages Press.

Fokkema, D[ouwe] W. *Literary doctrine in China and Soviet influence, 1956–1960.* Foreword by S. H. Chen. The Hague: Mouton, 1965.

Fokkema, D. W. *Report from Peking: observations of a Western diplomat on the Cultural Revolution.* London: C. Hurst; Montreal: McGill-Queen's University Press, 1972. [Originally published in Dutch as *Standplaats Peking.*]

Fokkema, Douwe W. "Chinese criticism of humanism: campaign against the intellectuals, 1964–66." *CQ*, 26 (April–June 1966), 68–81.

Fokkema, D. W. "Chinese literature under the Cultural Revolution." *Literature East and West*, 13 (1969), 335–58.

Fokkema, D. W. "The Maoist myth and its exemplification in the new Peking Opera." *Asia Quarterly*, 2 (1972), 341–61.

Fokkema, D. W., and [Kunne–] Ibsch, Elrud. *Theories of literature in the twentieth century: structuralism, Marxism, aesthetics of reception, semiotics.* London: C. Hurst, 1986 [1979, 1977]; New York: St. Martin's Press, 1986.

Foreign Affairs. 5/year. New York: Council on Foreign Relations, 1922– .

Foreign Broadcast Information Service. Washington, D.C.: U.S. Department of Commerce, 1941– . Cited as FBIS. The *Daily Report* of this agency has appeared in sections designated for specific regions but the names of these regions have been changed from time to time in a manner that makes it difficult to construct a precise genealogy. These designations have been used at various times: Asia and Pacific, China, Communist China, East Asia, Eastern Europe, Far East, People's Republic of China, USSR, USSR and Eastern Europe. FBIS is discussed in *CHOC* 14.557 et passim.

Foreign Languages Press 外文出版社. Cited as FLP.

Foreign Relations of the United States, 1866– . Washington, D.C.: U.S. Government Printing Office. Cited as *FRUS*.

Formosan Taiwandang, The. Irregular. New York: Formosan Readers Association.

Franke, Wolfgang. *The reform and abolition of the traditional Chinese examination system*. Cambridge, Mass.: East Asian Research Center, Harvard University, 1972.

Fraser, John. *The Chinese: portrait of a people*. London; Fontana/Collins, 1982; New York: Summit Books, 1980.

Fraser, Stewart E., ed. *Education and communism in China: an anthology of commentary and documents*. Hong Kong: International Studies Group, 1969.

Free China Journal. Weekly. Taipei: Kwang Hwa Publishing Co., 1964– . (From 1964 to 1983 was *Free China Weekly*.)

Free China Weekly. See *Free China Journal*.

Freedman, Maurice. *Lineage organization in southeastern China*. London: Athlone Press, 1958.

Fried, Morton H. *Fabric of Chinese society: a study of the social life of a Chinese county seat*. New York: Octagon Books, 1969; New York: Praeger, 1953.

Friedman, Edward; Pickowicz, Paul G.; and Selden, Mark. *Chinese village, socialist state*. New Haven, Conn.: Yale University Press, 1991.

Frolic, B. Michael. *Mao's people: sixteen portraits of life in revolutionary China*. Cambridge, Mass.: Harvard University Press, 1980.

FRUS. *Foreign Relations of the United States*.

Fu-yin pao-k'an tzu-liao 復印報刊資料 (Reference materials reprinted from newspapers and periodicals). Monthly. Peking: Chung-kuo jen-min ta-hsueh.

Furuya, Keiji, ed. *Chiang Kai-shek, his life and times*. New York: St. John's University, 1981. [Abridged English edition/Chunming Chang?]

Galenson, Walter, ed. *Economic growth and structural change in Taiwan: the postwar experience of the Republic of China*. Ithaca, N.Y.: Cornell University Press, 1979.

Gallin, Bernard. *Hsin Hsing, Taiwan: a Chinese village in change*. Berkeley: University of California Press, 1966.

Gamble, Sidney D., assisted by John Stewart Burgess. *Peking: a social survey*. Foreword by G. Sherwood Eddy and Robert A. Woods. New York: George H. Doran, 1921.

Gamble, Sidney D. *Ting Hsien: a North China rural community*. Foreword by Y. C. James Yen. Stanford, Calif.: Stanford University Press, 1968; New York: Institute of Pacific Relations, 1954.

Gao Yuan 高原. *Born red: a chronicle of the Cultural Revolution*. Stanford, Calif.: Stanford University Press, 1987.

Gardner, John. *Chinese politics and the succession to Mao*. London: Macmillan, 1982.

Gardner, John. "Educated youth and urban-rural inequalities, 1958–66," in John Wilson Lewis, ed., *The city in communist China*, 235–86.

Garrett, Banning N., and Glaser, Bonnie S. *War and peace: the views from Moscow and Beijing*. Berkeley: Institute of International Studies, University of California, 1984.

Garrett, W. E. "China's beauty spot." *National Geographic*, 156 (1979), 536–63.

Garside, Roger. *Coming alive!: China after Mao*. New York: McGraw-Hill; London: Andre Deutsch, 1981.

Garthoff, Raymond L., ed. *Sino-Soviet military relations*. New York: Praeger, 1966.

Garver, John W. *China's decision for rapprochement with the United States, 1968–1971*. Boulder, Colo.: Westview Press, 1982.

Gelb, Leslie H., with Richard K. Betts. *The irony of Vietnam: the system worked*. Washington, D.C.: The Brookings Institution, 1979.

Gelber, Harry. "Nuclear weapons and Chinese policy." London: IISS Adelphi Paper, no. 99, 1973.

Gel'bras, V. G. *Kitai: krizis prodolzhaetsia* (China: the crisis continues). Moscow: Izdatel'stvo "Mezhdunarodnye Otnosheniia," 1973.

Gelman, Harry. *The Soviet Far East buildup and Soviet risk-taking against China*. Santa Monica, Calif: The RAND Corporation, R-2943, August 1982.

Gernet, Jacques. "Introduction," in Stuart Schram, ed., *Foundations and limits of state power in China*, xv–xxvii.

Gibbs, Donald A. *Subject and author index to "Chinese literature" monthly (1951–1976)*. New Haven, Conn.: Far Eastern Publications, Yale University, 1978.

Ginsburg, Norton. *See* Leung, C. K.

Ginsburgs, George, and Pinkele, Carl F. *The Sino-Soviet territorial dispute, 1949–64*. New York: Praeger, 1976.

Gittings, John. *The role of the Chinese army*. London and New York: Oxford University Press, 1967.

Gittings, John. *Survey of the Sino-Soviet dispute: a commentary and extracts from the recent polemics 1963–1967*. London: Oxford University Press, 1968.

Gittings, John. *The world and China, 1922–1972*. New York: Harper & Row, 1975.

Gittings, John. "Army-Party relations in the light of the Cultural Revolution," in John Wilson Lewis, ed., *Party leadership and revolutionary power in China*, 373–403.

Gittings, John. "The 'Learn from the army' campaign." *CQ*, 18 (April–June 1964), 153–59.

Gittings, John. "The Chinese army's role in the Cultural Revolution." *Pacific Affairs*, 39.3–4 (Fall–Winter 1966–67), 269–89.

Goddard, W. G. *Formosa: a study in Chinese history*. London: Macmillan, 1966.

Gold, Thomas B. *State and society in the Taiwan miracle*. Armonk, N.Y.: M. E. Sharpe, 1986.

Gold, Thomas B. "China's youth: problems and programs." *Issues & Studies*, 18.8 (August 1982), 39–62.

Goldblatt, Howard, ed. *Chinese literature for the 1980s: the Fourth Congress of Writers and Artists.* Armonk, N.Y.: M. E. Sharpe, 1982.

Goldblatt, Howard. *See* Hwang Chun-ming.

Goldman, Merle. *Literary dissent in Communist China.* New York: Atheneum, 1971; Cambridge, Mass.: Harvard University Press, 1967.

Goldman, Merle, *China's intellectuals: advise and dissent.* Cambridge, Mass.: Harvard University Press, 1981.

Goodman, David S. G. *Beijing street voices: the poetry and politics of China's democracy movement.* London and Boston: Marion Boyars, 1981.

Goodman, David S. G. *Centre and province in the People's Republic of China: Sichuan and Guizhou, 1955–1965.* Cambridge and New York: Cambridge University Press, 1986

Goodman, David S. G., ed. *Groups and politics in the People's Republic of China.* Armonk, N.Y.: M. E. Sharpe, 1984.

Gorbachev, B. N. *Sotsial'no-politicheskaia rol'Kitaiskoi armii (1958–1969)* (The social and political role of the Chinese army [1958–1969]). Moscow: Nauka, 1980.

Gosudarstvo i obshchestvo v Kitaie. (State and society in China). Annual. Moscow: Institute of Oriental Studies (China branch).

Gottlieb, Thomas M. *Chinese foreign policy factionalism and the origins of the strategic triangle.* Santa Monica, Calif.: The RAND Corporation, R-1902-NA, November 1977.

Gotz, Michael. "Images of the worker in contemporary Chinese fiction, 1949–64." University of California at Berkeley, Ph.D. dissertation, 1977.

Gould, Sidney H., ed. *Sciences in communist China.* Washington, D.C.: American Association for the Advancement of Science, 1961. [A symposium presented at the New York Meeting of the American Association for the Advancement of Science, 26–27 December 1960.]

Graham, Angus. *The book of Lieh-tzu.* London: John Murray, 1960.

Graham, Angus. *Chuang-tzu. The seven inner chapters and other writings from the book "Chuang-tzu."* London: Allen & Unwin, 1981.

Gray, Jack, and Cavendish, Patrick. *Chinese communism in crisis: Maoism and the Cultural Revolution.* New York: Praeger, 1968.

"The Great Proletarian Cultural Revolution: a record of major events – September 1965 to December 1966." JPRS, 42,349 *Translations on Communist China: Political and Sociological Information* (25 August 1967).

A great revolution on the cultural front. Peking: FLP, 1965.

A great trial in Chinese history: the trial of the Lin Biao and Jiang Qing counter-revolutionary cliques, Nov. 1980–Jan. 1981. Peking: New World Press, 1981.

Greene, Felix. *Peking.* London: Cape, 1978.

Gregor, A. James, with Maria Hsia Chang and Andrew B. Zimmerman.*Ideology and development: Sun Yat-sen and the economic history of Taiwan.* Berkeley: Center for Chinese Studies, Institute of East Asian Studies, University of California, 1981.

Grichting, Wolfgang L. *The value system in Taiwan 1970: a preliminary report.* Taipei: n.p., 1971.

Griffith, William E. *The Sino-Soviet rift.* Cambridge, Mass.: MIT Press; London: Allen & Unwin, 1964.

Griffith, William E. *Sino-Soviet relations, 1964–1965.* Cambridge, Mass.: MIT Press, 1967.

Griffith, William E., ed. *The world and the great power triangles.* Cambridge, Mass.: MIT Press, 1975.

Griffith, William E. "Sino-Soviet relations, 1964–65." *CQ,* 25 (January–March 1966), 66–76.

Gudoshnikov, L. M. *Politicheskii mekhanizm Kitaiskoi Narodnoi Respubliki* (Political mechanisms of the People's Republic of China). Moscow: Nauka, 1974.

Guillain, Robert. *600 million Chinese.* Trans. from the French by Mervyn Savill. New York: Criterion Books, 1957. [Published in England as *The blue ants.* London: Secker & Warburg, 1957.]

Guillain, Robert. *When China wakes.* New York: Walker, 1966.

Guillermaz, Jacques. *The Chinese Communist Party in power, 1949–1976.* Trans. Anne Destenay. Boulder, Colo.: Westview Press, 1976.

Gurtov, Melvin. *China and Southeast Asia, the politics of survival: a study of foreign policy interaction.* Baltimore: Johns Hopkins University Press, 1975; Lexington, Mass.: [Heath] Lexington Books, 1971.

Gurtov, Melvin. "The foreign ministry and foreign affairs in the Chinese Cultural Revolution," in Thomas W. Robinson, ed., *The Cultural Revolution in China,* 313–66.

Gurtov, Melvin, and Hwang, Byong-Moo. *China under threat: the politics of strategy and diplomacy.* Baltimore: Johns Hopkins University Press, 1980.

Halperin, Morton H., ed. *Sino-Soviet relations and arms control.* Cambridge, Mass.: MIT Press, 1967.

Halpern, A. M., ed. *Policies toward China: views from six continents.* New York: McGraw-Hill, 1965.

Han Suyin 韓素音. *My house has two doors.* London: Jonathan Cape; New York: Putnam, 1980.

Hao Jan 浩然. *Yen-yang t'ien* 艷陽天 (Bright days). 3 vols. Peking: Jen-min wen-hsueh, 1964–66.

Hao Jan. *Chin-kuang ta-tao* 金光大道 (A golden road). 2 vols. Peking: Jen-min wen-hsueh, 1972–74.

Hao Jan. "Bright clouds." *Chinese Literature,* 4 (April 1972), 13–28.

Hao Meng-pi 郝夢筆 and Tuan Hao-jan 段浩然, eds. *Chung-kuo kung-ch'an-tang liu-shih-nien, hsia* 中國共產黨六十年(下) (Sixty years of the Chinese Communist Party, part 2). Peking: Chieh-fang-chün, 1984.

Harding, Harry. *Organizing China: the problem of bureaucracy, 1949–1976.* Stanford Calif.: Stanford University Press, 1981.

Harding, Harry, ed. *China's foreign relations in the 1980s.* New Haven, Conn. Yale University Press, 1984.

Harding, Harry. *China's second revolution: reform after Mao.* Washington, D.C.: The Brookings Institution, 1987.

Harding, Harry. "The domestic politics of China's global posture, 1973–78," in Thomas Fingar et al., eds., *China's quest for independence,* 93–146.

Harding, Harry. "Reappraising the Cultural Revolution." *The Wilson Quarterly,* 4.4 (Autumn 1980), 132–41.

Harding, Harry. "From China, with disdain: new trends in the study of China." *Asian Survey,* 22.10 (October 1982), 934–58.

Harding, Harry, and Gurtov, Melvin. *The purge of Lo Jui-ch'ing: the politics of Chinese strategic planning.* Santa Monica, Calif.: The RAND Corporation, R-548-PR, February 1971.

Hartford, Kathleen. "Socialist agriculture is dead; long live socialist agriculture!: organizational transformations in rural China," in Elizabeth J. Perry and Christine Wong, eds., *The political economy of reform in post-Mao China,* 31–61.

Hawkins, John N. *Mao Tse-tung and education: his thoughts and teachings.* Hamden, Conn.: Linnet Books/Shoestring Press, 1974.

Hawkins, John N. *Education and social change in the People's Republic of China.* New York: Praeger, 1983.

Hayhoe, Ruth, ed. *Contemporary Chinese education.* London: Croom Helm, 1984.

Hayhoe, Ruth, and Bastid, Marianne, eds. *China's education and the industrialized world: studies in cultural transfer.* Armonk, N.Y.: M. E. Sharpe, 1987.

HC. Hung-ch'i.

Heaton, William. "Maoist revolutionary strategy and modern colonization: the Cultural Revolution in Hong Kong." *Asian Survey,* 10.9 (September 1970), 840–857.

Hellmann, Donald C., ed. *China and Japan: a new balance of power.* Lexington, Mass.: [Heath] Lexington Books, 1976.

Henderson, Gail, and Cohen, Myron S. *The Chinese hospital.* New Haven, Conn.: Yale University Press, 1984.

Hersey, John. "A reporter at large: homecoming, part 3." *The New Yorker,* 24 May 1982, 44–66.

Hersh, Seymour. *The price of power: Kissinger in the Nixon White House.* New York: Summit Books, 1983.

Hevi, Emmanuel John. *An African student in China.* New York: Praeger, 1963 [1962].

HHPYK. Hsin-hua pan-yueh k'an.

HHYP. Hsin-hua yueh-pao.

Higher Education Battlefront. See *Chung-kuo kao-teng chiao-yü.*

Higher Education Research. See *Kao-teng chiao-yü yen-chiu.*

Hilsman, Roger. *To move a nation: the politics of foreign policy in the administration of John F. Kennedy.* New York: Dell, 1968.

Hindley, Donald. "Political power and the October 1965 coup in Indonesia." *JAS,* 27 (1969), 237–49.

Hinrup, Hans J. *An index to "Chinese literature," 1951–1976.* London: Curzon Press, 1978.

Hinton, Harold. *The bear at the gate: Chinese policy making under Soviet pressure.* Washington, D.C.: American Enterprise Institute, 1971.

Hinton, Harold. *Three and a half powers: the new power balance in Asia.* Bloomington: Indiana University Press, 1975.

Hinton, Harold C., ed. *The People's Republic of China, 1949–1979: a documentary survey.* 5 vols. Wilmington, Del.: Scholarly Resources, 1980.

Hinton, Harold C., ed., *The People's Republic of China, 1979–1984: a documentary survey.* 2 vols. Wilmington, Del.: Scholarly Resources, 1986.

Hinton, Harold C. "China and Vietnam," in Tang Tsou, ed., *China in crisis,* 2. 201–36.

Hinton, William. *Fanshen: a documentary of revolution in a Chinese village.* New York: Vintage Books, 1967; New York: Monthly Review Press, 1966.

Hinton, William. *Hundred day war: the Cultural Revolution at Tsinghua University.* New York: Monthly Review Press, 1972.

Hinton, William. *Shenfan: the continuing revolution in a Chinese village.* New York: Random House, 1983.

The historical experience of the dictatorship of the proletariat. Peking: FLP, 1959.

History of the Communist Party of the Soviet Union (Bolshevik). Short course. Moscow: Foreign Languages Publishing House; New York: International Publishers, 1939.

History Writing Group of the CCP Kwangtung Provincial Committee. "The ghost of Empress Lü and Chiang Ch'ing's empress dream." *Chinese Studies in History,* 12.1 (Fall 1978), 37–54.

Ho, Samuel Pao-San. "Colonialism and development: Korea, Taiwan, and Kwantung," in Ramon H. Myers and Mark R. Peattie, eds., *The Japanese colonial empire,* 347–98.

Ho Chih 何直 [Ch'in Chao-yang 秦兆陽]. "Hsien-shih chu-i – kuang-k'uo ti tao-lu" 現實主義－廣闊的道路 (Realism – the broad highway). *Jen-min wen-hsueh,* 9 (1956), 1–13.

Ho Hsin 何欣. *Chung-kuo hsien-tai hsiao-shuo ti chu-ch'ao* 中國現代小説的主潮 (Major trends in modern Chinese fiction). Taipei: Yuan-ching, 1979.

Ho-pei wen-i 河北文藝 (Hopei literature and art). Monthly. Shih-chia-chuang: 1949– . Title changed to *Ho-pei wen-hsueh* 河北文學 (Hopei literature) after 1987.

Ho Ping-ti 何炳棣 and Tsou, Tang 鄒讜, eds. *China in crisis: China's heritage and the communist political system.* Vol. 1, in two books. Foreword by Charles U. Daly. Chicago: University of Chicago Press, 1968.

Hoffmann, Charles. *The Chinese worker.* Albany, N.Y.: State University of New York Press, 1975 [1974].

Holden, Reuben. *Yale in China: the mainland, 1901–1951.* New Haven, Conn.: Yale in China Association, 1964.

Holmes, Robert A. "Burma's foreign policy toward China since 1962." *Pacific Affairs*, 45.2 (Summer 1972), 240–54.

Holsti, K[al] J. [Kalevi Jaakko], et al. *Why nations realign: foreign policy restructuring in the postwar world*. London and Boston: Allen & Unwin, 1982.

Hooper, Beverley. *Inside Peking: a personal report*. Foreword by Stephen Fitz-Gerald. London: Macdonald & Jane's, 1979.

Howe, Christopher. *Employment and economic growth in urban China, 1949–1957*. Cambridge: Cambridge University Press, 1971.

Howe, Christopher. *Wage patterns and wage policy in modern China, 1919–1972*. Cambridge: Cambridge University Press, 1973.

Howe, Christopher, ed. *Shanghai: revolution and development in an Asian metropolis*. New York: Cambridge University Press, 1981.

Hsi-chü pao 戲劇報 (Theater news). Monthly. Peking: 1950–   . Formerly *Jen-min hsi-chü* 人民戲劇 (People's theater).

Hsia, C. T. *A history of modern Chinese fiction 1917–1957*. With an appendix on Taiwan by Tsi-an Hsia. New Haven, Conn.: Yale University Press, 1971 [1961].

Hsia, C. T. "The continuing obsession with China: three contemporary writers." *Review of National Literatures*, 6.1 (1975), 76–99.

Hsia Chih-ch'ing 夏志清 [C. T. Hsia]. *Hsin wen-hsueh ti ch'uan-t'ung* 新文學的傳統 (The tradition of the new literature). Taipei: Shih-pao wen-hua kung-ssu, 1979.

Hsia Yen 夏衍. "To, k'uai, hao, sheng, liang chung ch'iu chih" 多、快、好、省、量中求質 (More, faster, better, more economically, seeking quality in quantity). *Wen-i pao*, 6 (1958), 26.

Hsiang, Nai-kuang. "The relations between Hanoi and Peiping." *Chinese Communist Affairs*, 1.4 (December 1964), 9–21.

Hsiao, Gene T. 蕭錚, and Witunski, Michael, eds. *Sino-American normalization and its policy implications*. New York: Praeger, 1974.

Hsiao Yen-chung 蕭延中, ed. *Wan-nien Mao Tse-tung: kuan-yü li-lun yü shih-chien ti yen-chiu* 晚年毛澤東.關於理論與實踐的研究 (Mao Tse-tung in his later years: research on the relation between theory and practice). Preface by Li Jui. Peking: Ch'un-ch'iu, 1989.

Hsieh, Chiao-min 謝覺民. *Taiwan-Ilha Formosa, a geography in perspective*. Washington, D.C.: Butterworth, 1964.

Hsien-tai wen-hsueh 現代文學 (Modern literature). Bimonthly. Taipei: 1960–73, 1977–   .

Hsin-hua pan-yueh k'an 新華半月刊 (New China semi-monthly). Peking: 1956–61. Formerly *Hsin-hua yueh pao* 新華月報 (New China monthly). Peking: 1949–55. In 1962, again became known as *Hsin-hua yueh-pao*, the name it retains at present.

Hsin-hua t'ung-hsun-she 新華通訊社 (New China News Agency).

Hsin Hua-wen. *Tachai, standard-bearer in China's agriculture*. Peking: FLP, 1972.

Hsin-hua wen-chai 新華文摘 (New China digest). Monthly. Peking: 1981–   .

Formerly (1979–81) *Hsin-hua yueh-pao wen-chai-pan* 新華月報文摘版 (New China monthly digest).

Hsing-hsing 星星 (Stars). Monthly. Chengtu: 1957–60, 1979– .

Hsiung, James Chieh 熊玠. *Ideology and practice: the evolution of Chinese communism.* New York: Praeger, 1970.

Hsiung, James C[hieh]., et al., eds. *The Taiwan experience, 1950–1980: contemporary Republic of China.* New York: Praeger, 1981.

Hsu, Cho-yun 許綽雲, ed. "Cultural values and cultural continuity," Section 1 in James C. Hsiung et al., eds., *The Taiwan experience, 1950–1980,* 19–61.

Hsu, Kai-yu 許芥煜, ed. and trans. *Twentieth century Chinese poetry: an anthology.* Garden City, N.Y.: Doubleday, 1964.

Hsu, Kai-yu. *The Chinese literary scene: a writer's visit to the People's Republic.* New York: Vintage Books, 1975.

Hsu, Kai-yu, ed., with Ting Wang, co-editor, and special assistance of Howard Goldblatt, Donald Gibbs, and George Cheng. *Literature of the People's Republic of China.* Bloomington: Indiana University Press, 1980.

Hsu, Vivian Ling, ed. *Born of the same roots: stories of modern Chinese women.* Bloomington: Indiana University Press, 1981.

Hsueh-hsi tzu-liao 學習資料 (Materials for Study).

Hsueh-hsi wen-hsuan 學習文選 (Documents for study). 1967.

Hsueh-hsi yü p'i-p'an 學習與批判 (Study and criticism). Monthly. Shanghai: 1973–76.

[Hsueh Mu-ch'iao] Xue Muqiao 薛暮橋, ed. *Almanac of China's economy, 1981, with economic statistics for 1949–1980.* Economic Research Centre of the State Council of the People's Republic of China and the State Statistical Bureau, comps. Hong Kong: Modern Cultural Co., 1982.

Hsueh Yeh-sheng 薛冶生, ed. *Yeh Chien-ying kuang-hui-ti i-sheng* 葉劍英光輝的一生 (Yeh Chien-ying's glorious life). Peking: Chieh-fang-chün, 1987.

Hu Chia. *Peking today and yesterday.* Peking: FLP, 1956.

Hu Ch'iao-mu 胡喬木. "Tang-ch'ien ssu-hsiang chan-hsien ti jo-kan wen-t'i" 當前思想戰綫的若干問題 (Some current problems on the thought front). *HC,* 23 (1981), 2–22.

Hu Hua 胡華. *Chung-kuo she-hui-chu-i ko-ming ho chien-she shih chiang-i* 中國社會主義革命和建設史講義 (Teaching materials on the history of China's socialist revolution and construction). Peking: Chung-kuo jen-min ta-hsueh, 1985.

Hu Hua, ed. *Chung-kung tang-shih jen-wu-chuan* 中共黨史人物傳 (Biographies of personalities in the history of the Chinese Communist Party). Sian: Shensi Jen-min. More than 40 volumes.

Hu Hui-ch'iang 胡惠強. "Ta lien kang-t'ieh yun-tung chien-k'uang" 大煉鋼鐵運動簡況 (A brief account of the campaign to make steel in a big way). *Tang-shih yen-chiu tzu-liao,* 4 (1983), 762–65.

Hu Shi Ming and Seifman, Eli, eds. *Toward a new world outlook: a documentay history of education in the People's Republic of China, 1949–1976.* New York: AMS Press, 1976.

Hu Wan-ch'un 胡萬春. *Man of a special cut.* Peking: FLP, 1963.

Hu Yao-pang 胡耀邦. "Li-lun kung-tso wu-hsu-hui yin-yen" 理論工作務虛會引言 (Introduction to theoretical work conference). In *Chung-kung shih-i-chieh san-chung ch'üan-hui i-lai chung-yang shou-yao chiang-hua chi wen-chien hsuan-pien*, 2. 48–63.

Hua-ch'iao jih-pao 華僑日報 (China daily news). New York: 1940–89.

Hua-chung shih-fan ta-hsueh hsueh-pao 華中師範大學學報 (Central China Normal University journal). Bimonthly. Wuhan: 1955– .

Hua Fang. "Lin Piao's abortive counter-revolutionary coup d'état." *PR*, 23.51 (22 December 1980), 19–28.

Hua Kuo-feng 華國鋒. "Political report to the 11th National Congress of the Communist Party of China (12 August 1977)." *PR*, 20.35 (26 August 1977), 23–57.

Hua Kuo-feng. "Report on the work of the government" at the First Session of the Fifth National People's Congress, 26 February 1978. *PR*, 21.10 (10 March 1978).

Hua Kuo-feng. "Unite and strive to build a modern, powerful socialist country! – Report on the work of the government delivered at the First Session of the Fifth National People's Congress on 26 February 1978." *PR*, 21.10 (10 March 1978), 7–40.

Hua-nan shih-fan ta-hsueh hsueh-pao 華南師範大學學報 (South China Normal University Journal). Quarterly. Canton: 1956– .

Hua-tung shih-fan ta-hsueh hsueh-pao 華東師範大學學報 (East China Normal University journal). Bimonthly. Shanghai: 1955– .

Huai-nien Chou En-lai (懷念周恩來) (Longing for Chou En-lai). Peking: Jen-min, 1986.

Huang Chien-ch'iu 黃見秋; Sun Ta-li 孫大力; Wei Hsin-sheng 魏新生; Chang Chan-pin 張占斌; and Wang Hung-mo 王洪模. eds. *Hsin shih-ch'i chuan-t'i chi-shih (1976.10–1986.10)* 新時期專題紀事 (1976.10–1986.10) (Important events and special problems of the new period). Peking: Chung-kung tang-shih tzu-liao, 1988.

Huang Ch'iu-yun 黃秋耘. "T'an ai-ch'ing" 談愛情 (On love). *Jen-min wen-hsueh*, 7 (1965), 59–61.

Huang Ho 黃河 (Yellow River). Monthly. Taipei: 1979– .

Huang, Joe C. 黃冑. *Heroes and villains in communist China: the contemporary Chinese novel as a reflection of life*. London: C. Hurst; New York: Pica Press, 1973.

Huang, Mab. *Intellectual ferment for political reforms in Taiwan, 1971–1973*. Ann Arbor: Center for Chinese Studies, University of Michigan, 1976.

Hudson, G. F.; Lowenthal, Richard; and MacFarquhar, Roderick. *The Sino-Soviet dispute*. New York: Praeger, 1961.

Hughes, John. "China and Indonesia: the romance that failed." *Current Scene*, 19 (4 November 1969), 1–15.

Hung-ch'i 紅旗 (Red flag). Peking: 1958–88. Cited as *HC*.

Hung-wei pao 紅衛報 (Red Guard news). Peking: Foreign Languages Institute, 1966–67.

Hunter, Neale. *Shanghai journal: an eyewitness account of the Cultural Revolution.* Boston: Beacon Press, 1971; New York: Praeger, 1969.

Hwang, Chun-ming [Huang Ch'un-ming]. *The drowning of an old cat, and other stories.* Trans. Howard Goldblatt. Bloomington: Indiana University Press, 1980.

Hyer, Paul, and Heaton, William. "The Cultural Revolution in Inner Mongolia." *CQ,* 36 (October–December 1968), 114–28.

I-chiu-ch'i-pa nien ch'üan-kuo yu-hsiu tuan-p'ien hsiao-shuo p'ing-hsuan tso-p'in-chi 一九七八年全國優秀短篇小説評選作品集 (Critical selection of the best short stories of the whole nation published in 1978). Peking: Jen-min wen-hsueh, 1980.

IASP. International Arts and Sciences Press.

Important documents on the Great Proletarian Cultural Revolution in China. Peking: FLP, 1970.

Index Foreign Broadcast Information Service Daily Report: China. Monthly plus annual cum. (New Canaan, Conn.: NewsBank, Inc., 1975–). From 1975 to 1982, the index was published quarterly, but with Volume 9 in 1983, the publication became a monthly, with an annual cumulative index as well. Beginning in October 1977, FBIS began to compile an index to the *Daily Report* as well as the JPRS translations. With the fifteenth number in this series covering April to June 1981 (published 28 August 1981), the series acquired the designation "For Official Use Only" and was no longer available to libraries.

Inside China Mainland. Monthly. Taipei: Institute of Current Chian Studies, 1979– .

International Affairs/Mezhdunarodnaya zhizn'. Monthly. Moscow: Vsesoyuznoe Obshchestvo "Znani", 1955– . Editions in English, French, and Russian.

International Herald Tribune. Daily. Paris.

International Journal. Quarterly. Toronto: Canadian Institute of International Affairs, 1946– .

International Studies. Quarterly. Newbury Park, Calif.: Sage Publications. (School of International Studies, Jawaharlal Nehru University) 1961– . Formerly *International Studies Newsletter.*

Iowa Review. Iowa City: School of Letters and the Graduate College of the University of Iowa, 1970– .

Israel, John. *Student nationalism in China, 1927–1937.* Stanford, Calif.: Stanford University Press, 1966.

Israel, John. "Continuities and discontinuities in the ideology of the Great Proletarian Cultural Revolution," in Chalmers A. Johnson, ed., *Ideology and politics in contemporary China,* 3–46.

Issues & Studies. Monthly. Taipei: Institute of International Relations, 1964– .

Izvestia. Daily. Moscow: Presidium of Supreme Soviet of the USSR, 1917– .

Jacobs, J. Bruce. *Local politics in a rural Chinese cultural setting: a field study of Mazu Township, Taiwan.* Canberra: Contemporary China Centre, Research School of Pacific Studies, Australian National University, 1980.

Jacobs, J. Bruce; Hagger, Jean; and Sedgley, Anne, comps. *Taiwan: a comprehen-*

sive bibliography of English-language publications. Introduction by J. Bruce Jacobs. Bundoor, Victoria: Borchardt Library, La Trobe University; New York: East Asian Institute, Columbia University, 1984.

Jacobsen, C. G. [Carl G.]. *Sino-Soviet relations since Mao: the Chairman's legacy.* New York: Praeger, 1981.

Jacobson, Harold K., and Oksenberg, Michel. "China and the keystone international economic organizations." Unpublished manuscript, 1987.

Jacoby, Neil H. *U.S. aid to Taiwan: a study of foreign aid, self-help and development.* New York: Praeger, 1966.

Jacques, Tania. "'Shärqiy Türkstan' or 'Sinkiang'?" *Radio Liberty Research*, RL 98/75 (7 March 1975), 1–4.

James, Clive. "Laughter in the dark." *New York Review of Books*, 19 March 1981, 19–20.

JAS. Journal of Asian Studies.

Jen Ku-p'ing 任谷平. "The Munich tragedy and contemporary appeasement." *JMJP*, 26 November 1977; *PR*, 20.50 (9 December 1977), 6–11.

Jen-min chiao yü 人民教育 (People's education). Monthly. Peking: 1950– .

Jen-min ch'u-pan-she. People's Publishing House. Cited as Jen-min.

Jen-min jih-pao Editorial Department. "Chairman Mao's theory of the differentiation of the three worlds is a major contribution to Marxism-Leninism." *PR*, 20.45 (4 November 1977), 10–41.

Jen-min jih-pao 人民日報 (People's daily). Peking: 1949– . Cited as *JMJP*.

Jen-min jih-pao so-yin (Index to People's daily). Peking: 1951– .

Jen-min shou-ts'e 人民手冊 (People's handbook). Peking: 1950–53, 1956–65, 1979.

Jen-min ta hsien-chang hsueh-hsi shou-ts'e 人民大憲章學習手冊 (Handbook for the study of the great people's constitution). Shanghai: Chan-wang chou-k'an, November 1949.

Jen-min ta hsien-chang hsueh-hsi tzu-liao 人民大憲章學習資料 (Materials for the study of the great people's constitution). Tientsin: Lien-ho t'u-shu, 1949.

Jen-min wen-hsueh 人民文學 (People's literature). Peking: 1949–66, 1976– .

Jenner, W. J. F. "1979: a new start for literature in China?" *CQ*, 86 (June 1981), 274–303.

JMJP. Jen-min jih-pao.

Jo, Yung-Hwan, ed. *Taiwan's future:* Tempe: Center for Asian Studies, Arizona State University, 1974.

Joffe, Ellis, *Party and army: professionalism and political control in the Chinese officer corps, 1949–1964.* Cambridge, Mass.: East Asian Research Center, Harvard University, 1965.

Joffe, Ellis. *The Chinese army after Mao.* Cambridge, Mass.: Harvard University Press, 1987.

Joffe, Ellis. "The Chinese army under Lin Piao: prelude to political intervention," in John M. H. Lindbeck, ed., *China: management of a revolutionary society*, 343–74.

Johnson, Cecil. *Communist China and Latin America, 1959–1967.* New York: Columbia University Press, 1970.

Johnson, Chalmers A., ed. *Ideology and politics in contemporary China*. Seattle: University of Washington Press, 1973.

Johnson, Irmgard. "The reform of Peking Opera in Taiwan." *CQ*, 57 (January–March 1974), 140–45.

Johnson, Kay Ann. *Women, the family, and peasant revolution in China*. Chicago: University of Chicago Press, 1983.

Johnson, Stuart E., with Joseph A. Yager. *The military equation in northeast Asia*. Washington, D.C.: The Brookings Institution, 1979.

Joint Economic Committee. *See* United States Congress.

Joint Publications Research Service (JPRS). Washington, D.C.: U.S. Government. Various series. See Peter Berton and Eugene Wu, *Contemporary China: A Research Guide*. Standford, Calif.: Standford University Press, 1967, 409–30, and M. Oksenberg summary in *CHOC*, 14.557–58. Includes regional, worldwide and topical translations and reports. Published periodically. The following items are cited in footnotes:

    Joint Publications Research Service. *Miscellany of Mao Tse-tung Thought*. See Mao Tse-tung, *Miscellany*...

    Joint Publications Research Service. *Translations on international communist developments*.

    Joint Publications Research Service, *Bibliography-index to U.S. JPRS research translations*. See Kyriak, Theodore.

    Joint Publications Research Service. *China Area Report (CAR)*. 1987– .

    Joint Publications Research Service. *China report: Red Flag*. Monthly. Continues *Translations from Red Flag*.

    Joint Publications Research Service. *China/State Council Bulletin (CSB)*. 1987– . Cited as *CSB*.

    Joint Publications Research Service. *China report: political, sociological and military affairs*. 1979–87.

    Joint Publications Research Service. *Translations on Communist China: political and sociological information*. 1962–68.

Jones, Hywell G. *An introduction to modern theories of economic growth*. New York: McGraw-Hill, 1976.

Joseph, William A. *The critique of ultra-leftism in China, 1958–1981*. Stanford, Calif.: Stanford University Press, 1984.

Journal of Asian Studies. Quarterly (irregular). Ann Arbor: Association for Asian Studies, University of Michigan, 1941– . Cited as *JAS*.

Journal of Comparative Economics. San Diego, Calif.: Academic Press, 1977– .

Journal of Economic Literature. Quarterly. Nashville, Tenn.: American Economic Association, 1963– .

JPRS. *See* Joint Publications Research Service.

Jukes, Geoffrey. *The Soviet Union in Asia*. Sydney: Angus & Robertson; Berkeley: University of California Press, 1973.

Kai-ko: wo-men mien-lin ti t'iao-chan yü hsuan-tzu 改革:我們面臨的挑戰與選擇 (Reform: we face challenge and alternative). General Survey Group of the Chinese Institute for Economic Systems Reform. Peking: Chung-kuo ching-chi, 1986.

Kalicki, J. H. *The pattern of Sino-American crises*. Cambridge: Cambridge University Press, 1975.

Kan yu ko yin tung ti ai 敢有歌唫動地哀 (Dare a song to move the earth to grieve). Hong Kong: Ch'i-shih nien-tai, 1974.

Kane, Penny. *Famine in China, 1959–61: demographic and social implications*. New York: St. Martin's Press, 1988.

Kao chiao chan-hsien. See *Chung-kuo kao-teng chiao-yü*.

Kao Kao 高皋 and Yen Chia-ch'i 嚴家其. *"Wen-hua ta-ko-ming"shih-nien shih, 1966–1976* "文化大革命"十年史, 1966–1976 (A history of the ten years of the "Great Cultural Revolution," 1966–1976). Tientsin: Jen-min, 1986.

Kao-teng chiao-yü yen-chiu 高等教育研究 (Higher education research). Quarterly. Wuhan: 1980– .

Kao Wen-hsi. "China's cement industry," in *Chung-kuo ching-chi nien-chien, 1982*, Part V.

Kao Yü-pao 高玉寶. "How I became a writer." *Chinese Literature*, 6 (June 1972), 111–18.

Kaplan, John. *The court-martial of the Kaohsiung defendants*. Berkeley: Institute of East Asian Studies, University of California, 1981.

Karnow, Stanley. *Mao and China: from revolution to revolution*. New York: Viking Press, 1972.

Karnow, Stanley. *Vietnam, a history*. New York: Penguin Books; New York: Viking Press, 1983.

Kates, George N. *The years that were fat: the last of old China*. Cambridge, Mass.: MIT Press, 1976 [1952]. Intro. by John K. Fairbank.

Kau, Michael Y. M. [Ying-mao] 高英茂, ed. *The Lin Piao affair: power politics and military coup*. White Plains, N.Y.: IASP, 1975.

Kau, Michael Y. M., and Leung, John K., eds. *The writings of Mao Zedong 1949–1976*. Vol. 1. *September 1949–December 1955*. Armonk, N.Y.: M. E. Sharpe, 1986.

Kau, Ying-mao. "The case against Lin Piao." *CLG*, 5.3–4 (Fall–Winter 1972–73), 3–30.

Keesing's Research Report. *The Sino-Soviet dispute*. Bristol: Keesing's, 1970; New York: Scribner, 1969.

Kerr, Clark, et al. *Observations on the relations between education and work in the People's Republic of China: report of a study group*. Berkeley, Calif.: The Carnegie Council on Policy Studies in Higher Education, 1978.

Kerr, George H. *Formosa betrayed*. Boston: Houghton Mifflin, 1965.

Kerr, George H. *Formosa: licensed revolution and the Home Rule movement, 1895–1945*. Honolulu: University Press of Hawaii, 1974.

Kessen, William, ed. *Childhood in China*. New Haven, Conn: Yale University Press, 1975.

Kessler, Lawrence D. *K'ang-hsi and the consolidation of Ch'ing rule, 1661–1684*. Chicago: University of Chicago Press, 1976.

Kim, Ilpyong J. "Chinese Communist relations with North Korea: continuity and change." *JAS*, 13.4 (December 1970), 59–78.

Kim, Roy U. T. "Sino–North Korean relations." *Asian Survey*, 8 (August 1968), 17–25.

Kim, Samuel S. *China, the United Nations, and world order*. Princeton, N.J.: Princeton University Press, 1979.

Kim, Samuel S., ed. *China and the world: Chinese foreign policy in the post-Mao era*. Boulder, Colo.: Westview Press, 1984.

Kim, Samuel S. "Chinese world policy in transition." *World Policy Journal*, 1.3 (Spring 1984), 603–33.

Kinkley, Jeffrey C., ed. *After Mao: Chinese literature and society, 1978–1981*. Cambridge, Mass.: Council on East Asian Studies, Harvard University, 1985.

Kintner, William R., and Copper, John F. *A matter of two Chinas: the China-Taiwan issue in U.S. foreign policy*. Philadelphia: Foreign Policy Research Institute, 1979.

Kirkby, Richard. *Urbanization in China: town and country in a developing economy, 1949–2000 A.D.* New York: Columbia University Press, 1985.

Kissinger, Henry. *White House years*. Boston: Little, Brown, 1979.

Kissinger, Henry. *Years of upheaval*. Boston: Little, Brown, 1982.

Kitai: obshchestvo i gosudarstvo (China: society and the state). Moscow: Nauka, 1973.

Kitai: poiski putei sotsial'nogo razvitiia (China: the search for the path of socialist development). Moscow: Nauka, 1979.

Kitai: traditsii i sovremennost' (China: traditions and the present). Moscow: Nauka, 1976.

Kitai i sosedi (China and its neighbors). Moscow: Nauka, 1982.

Kitaiskaia Narodnaia Respublika 1973 (–1979). (The People's Republic of China 1973 [–1979]. Annual. Moscow: Nauka, 1975–81.

Kiuzazhian, L. S. *Ideologicheskie kampanii v KNR 1949–1966* (Ideological campaigns in the PRC 1949–1966). Moscow: Nauka, 1970.

Klein, Donald W. "The State Council and the Cultural Revolution," in John W. Lewis, ed., *Party leadership and revolutionary power in China*, 351–72.

Klein, Donald W. "Peking's diplomats in Africa." *Current Scene*, 2.36 (1 July 1964), 1–9.

Klein, Donald W., and Clark, Anne B. *Biographic dictionary of Chinese communism, 1921–1965*. 2 vols. Cambridge, Mass.: Harvard University Press, 1971.

Klein, Donald W., and Hager, Lois B. "The Ninth Central Committee." *CQ*, 45 (January–March 1971), 37–56.

Klenner, Makiko. *Literaturkritik und politische Kritik in China: die Auseinandersetzungen um die Literaturpolitik Zhou Yangs*. Bochum: Studienverlag Brockmeyer, 1979.

Klochko, Mikhail A. *Soviet scientist in Red China*. Trans. Andrew MacAndrew. New York: Praeger, 1964.

KMJP. Kuang-ming jih-pao.

Knight, Nick. *Mao Zedong's "On contradiction": an annotated translation of the pre-liberation text*. Griffith Asian Papers Series. Nathan, Queensland: Griffith University, 1981.

Knight, Nick. "Mao Zedong's *On contradiction* and *On practice*: pre-liberation texts." *CQ*, 84 (December 1980), 641–68.

Ko Ch'in 葛琴. "Hai-yen" 海鷰 (Stormy petrel). *Jen-min wen-hsueh*, 3 (1958), 31–50.

Ko-ming shih ch'ao 革命詩鈔 (A transcript of revolutionary poems). 2 vols. Peking: Ti-erh wai-kuo-yü'hsueh-yuan, 1977.

Ko-ming-shih tzu-liao 革命史資料 (Reference materials of revolutionary history). Quarterly. Shanghai: 1979– . Formerly *Tang-shih tzu-liao* 黨史資料 (Reference materials of Party history).

Ko Pi-chou 戈壁舟. *Pei-mang-shan hsin-hsing ssu-shou* 北邙山新行四首 (Four new songs of Pei-mang Mountain). *JMJP*, 24 March 1962.

K'o-chi jih-pao 科技日報 (Science and technology news). 3/week. Peking: 1986– .

K'o-hsueh wen-hua pao 科學文化報 (Scientific culture news). 3/week. Canton: 1984– .

Koen, Ross Y. *The China lobby in American politics*. Ed. with an introduction by Richard C. Kagan. New York: Octagon Books, 1974; New York: Macmillan, 1960.

Kokubun, Ryosei. "The politics of foreign economic policy-making in China: the case of plant cancellations with Japan." *CQ*, 105 (March 1986), 19–44.

Kommunist. 18/yr. Moscow: Pravda Tsentral'nogo Komiteta KPSS, 1924– . [Until 1952 published as *Bolshevik*.]

Komsomolskaya Pravda. 300/yr. Moscow: Central Committee of the YCL, 1925– .

Koo, Anthony Y. C. *The role of land reform in economic development: a case study of Taiwan*. New York: Praeger, 1968.

Krasnaia Zvezda (Red star). Daily. Moscow: 1924– . [Central organ of the Ministry of Defense of the USSR.]

Kraus, Richard Curt. *Class conflict in Chinese socialism*. New York: Columbia University Press, 1981.

Krivtsov, V[ladimir] A[leksaevich]; Markova, S. D.; and Sorokin, V. F., eds. *Sud'by kul'tury KNR 1949–1974* (The fate of culture in the People's Republic of China 1949–1974). Moscow: Nauka, 1978.

《*Kuan-yü chien-kuo-i-lai tang-ti jo-kan li-shih wen-t'i ti chueh-i*》*chu-shih-pen* (*hsiu-ting*). 《關於建國以來黨的若干歷史問題決議》註釋本(修訂) (Revised annotated edition of the resolution on certain questions in the history of our party since the founding of the People's Republic). Peking: Jen-min, 1985.

"Kuan-yü kuo-min-tang tsao-yao wu-mieh ti teng-tsai so-wei 'Wu Hao ch'i-shih' wen-t'i ti wen-chien" 關於國民黨造謠誣衊地登載所謂"伍豪啟事"問題的文件 (Document on the problems of the Kuomintang maliciously concocting and publishing the so-called 'Wu Hao notice'). *Tang-shih yen-chiu*, 1 (1980), 8.

"Kuan-yü'wo-kuo ti tui-wai ching-chi kuan-hsi wen-t'i" 關於我國的對外經濟關係問題 (On the question of our country's external economic relations). Editorial Department. *HC*, 8 (16 April 1982), 2–10.

Kuang-chou wen-i 廣州文藝 (Canton literature and art). Monthly. Canton: 1973– .

Formerly *Kung-nung-ping wen-i* 工農兵文藝 (Worker-peasant-soldier literature and art).

Kuang-ming jih-pao 光明日報. (Enlightenment daily). Peking: 1949– .

Kubin, Wolfgang, and Wagner, Rudolf G., eds. *Essays in modern Chinese literature and literary criticism: papers of the Berlin Conference, 1978*. Bochum: Germany: N. Brockmeyer, 1982.

Kuhn, Philip A. *Rebellion and its enemies in late imperial China: militarization and social structure, 1796–1864*. Cambridge, Mass.: Harvard University Press, 1970; paperback ed. with new preface, 1980.

Kun, Joseph C. "North Korea: between Moscow and Peking." *CQ*, 31 (July–September 1967), 48–58.

Kung Yü-chih 龔育之. "Fa-chan k'o-hsueh pi-yu chih lu – chieh-shao Mao Tse-tung t'ung-chih wei ch'uan-tai 'Ts'ung i-ch'uan hsueh t'an pai-chia cheng-ming' i wen hsieh ti hsin ho an-yü" 發展科學必由之路－介紹毛澤東同志為傳代 "從遺傳學談百家爭鳴"－文寫的信和案語 (The way which the development of science must follow – presenting Comrade Mao Tse-tung's letter and annotation relating to the republication of "Let a hundred schools of thought contend viewed from the perspective of genetics"). *Kuang-ming jih-pao*, 28 December 1983.

Kung Yü-chih. "Mao Tse-tung yü tzu-jan k'o-hsueh" 毛澤東與自然科學 (Mao Tse-tung and the natural sciences), in Kung Yü-chih et al., eds., *Mao Tse-tung ti tu-shu sheng-huo*, 83–114.

Kung Yü-chih. "'Shih-chien lun' san t'i" "實踐論"三題 (Three points regarding "On practice"), in *Lun Mao Tse-tung che-hsueh ssu-hsiang*, 66–86.

Kung Yü-chih, P'ang Hsien-chih 逢先知, and Shih Chung-ch'üan 石仲泉. *Mao Tse-tung ti tu-shu sheng-huo* 毛澤東的讀書生活 (Mao Tse-tung's reading activities). Peking: San-lien shu-tien, 1986.

Kun-lun 崑崙 (Kunlun literary bimonthly). Bimonthly. Peking: 1982– .

Kuo-chi wen-t'i yen-chiu 國際問題研究 (Journal of international studies). Quarterly. Peking: 1959– .

Kuo Hsiao-ch'uan 郭小川. *Kan-che-lin* 甘蔗林 (Sugarcane forest). Peking: Tso-chia, 1963.

Kuo Mo-jo 郭沫若. *Li Po yü Tu Fu* 李白與杜甫 (Li T'ai-po and Tu Fu). Peking: Jen-min wen-hsueh, 1971.

Kuo Mo-jo. *Mo-jo shi-tz'u hsuan* 沫若詩詞選 (Selected poems of [Kuo] Mo-jo). Peking: Jen-min wen-hsueh, 1977.

Kuo Mo-jo. "Chiu mu-ch'ien ch'uang-tso chung ti chi-ko wen-t'i" 就目前創作中的幾個問題 (Some current problems in creative writing). *Jen-min wen-hsueh*, 1 (1959), 4–9.

Kuo Mo-jo. "Three poems." *Chinese Literature*, 1 (1972), 50–52.

Kuo Mo-jo. "On seeing 'The monkey subdues the demon.'" *Chinese Literature*, 4 (1976), 44.

Kuo Mo-jo. "Kuo Mo-jo's poem." *Chinese Literature*, 4 (1976), 50.

Kuo Mo-jo and Chou Yang, comps. *Hung-ch'i ko-yao* 紅旗歌謠 (Songs of the red flag). Peking: Hung-ch'i tsa-chih she, 1959. Trans. A. C. Barnes. *Songs of the red flag*. Peking: FLP, 1961.

Kuo, Shirley W. Y. *The Taiwan economy in transition*. Boulder, Colo.: Westview Press, 1983.

Kwangtung-sheng t'ung-chi nien-chien 廣東省統計年鑑 (Kwangtung province statistical yearbook). Kwangtung Statistical Office, 1985– .

Kwong, Julia. *Chinese education in transition: prelude to the Cultural Revolution*. Montreal: McGill–Queen's University Press, 1979.

Kwong, Julia. *Cultural Revolution in China's schools, May 1966 – April 1969*. Stanford, Calif.: Hoover Institution Press, 1988.

Kyodo. News service.

Kyoto Daigaku Jimbun Kagaku Kenkyusho 京都大學人文科學研究所. *Mō Takutō chosaku nenpyō* 毛澤東著作年表 (Chronological table of Mao Tse-tung's works). Vol. 2. *Goi sakuin* (Glossary and index). Kyoto: Kyoto Daigaku Jimbun Kagaku Kenkyūsho, 1980.

Kyriak, Theodore, ed. *Bibliography-index to U.S. JPRS research translations*, vols. 1–8. Annapolis, Md.: Research and Microfilm Publications, 1962– .

Ladany, Laszlo. *The Communist Party of China and Marxism, 1921–1985: a self-portrait*. Stanford, Calif.: Hoover Institution Press. 1988.

Lai Chih-yen 賴志衍, ed. *Chieh-kuan ch'eng-shih ti kung-tso ching-yen* 接管城市的工作經驗 (Experience in the takeover work in cities). Peking: Jen-min, 1949.

Lampton, David M. *Policy implementation in post-Mao China*. Berkeley: University of California Press, 1987 [1985].

Lan Ch'eng-tung 藍成東 and Chang Chung-ju 張鍾汝. "Aspirations and inclinations of this year's senior high school graduates: a survey of three high schools in Shanghai." Trans. *Chinese Sociology and Anthropology*, 16.1–2 (Fall–Winter 1983–84), 159–69.

Lang, Olga. *Chinese family and society*. New Haven, Conn.: Yale University Press; London: G. Cumberlege, Oxford University Press, 1946. Published under the auspices of the International Secretariat, Institute of Pacific Relations and the Institute of Social Research.

Lao She 老舍. *Wo je-ai hsin Pei-ching* 我熱愛新北京 (I love new Peking). Peking: Peking ch'u-pan-she, 1979.

Lapwood, Ralph, and Lapwood, Nancy. *Through the Chinese revolution*. London: Spalding & Levy, 1954.

Lardy, Nicholas R. *Economic growth and distribution in China*. Cambridge: Cambridge University Press, 1978.

Lardy, Nicholas R. *Agriculture in China's modern economic development*. Cambridge: Cambridge University Press, 1983.

Lardy, Nicholas. "Prices, markets and the Chinese peasant." Center Discussion Paper, no. 428. New Haven, Conn.: Yale Economic Growth Center, December 1982.

Lardy, Nicholas. "Agricultural prices in China." World Bank Staff Working Paper, no. 606. Washington, D.C.: The World Bank, 1983.

Lardy, Nicholas R. "The Chinese economy under stress, 1958–1965." *CHOC*, 14.360–97.

Lardy, Nicholas R., and Lieberthal, Kenneth, eds. *Chen Yun's strategy for China's development: a non-Maoist alternative.* Trans. Ma Fong and Du Anxia; introduction by the editors. Armonk, N.Y.: M. E. Sharpe, 1983.

Larkin, Bruce D. *China and Africa, 1949–1970: the foreign policy of the People's Republic of China.* Berkeley: University of California Press, 1971.

Lasater, Martin L. *The Taiwan issue in Sino-American strategic relations.* Boulder, Colo.: Westview Press, 1984.

Lasater, Martin L. *Taiwan: facing mounting threats.* Washington, D.C.: Heritage Foundation, 1984 [rev. 1987].

Latham, Richard J. "The implications of rural reforms for grass-roots cadres," in Elizabeth J. Perry and Christine Wong, eds., *The political economy of reform in post-Mao China,* 157–73.

Lau, D. C. *Mencius.* Harmondsworth: Penguin Books, 1970.

Lau, Joseph S. M. "The concepts of time and reality in modern Chinese fiction." *Tamkang Review,* 4.1 (1973), 25–40.

Lau, Joseph S. M. "'How much truth can a blade of grass carry?': Ch'en Ying-chen and the emergence of native Taiwan writers." *JAS,* 32.4 (1973), 623–38.

Lau, Joseph S. M. "'Crowded hours' revisited: the evocation of the past in *Taipei jen.*" *JAS,* 35.1 (1975), 31–47.

Lau, Joseph S. M., and Ross, Timothy A., eds. *Chinese stories from Taiwan, 1960–1970.* Foreword by C. T. Hsia. New York: Columbia University Press, 1976.

Lau, Lawrence J., ed. *Models of development: a comparative study of economic growth in South Korea and Taiwan.* San Francisco: Institute for Contemporary Studies Press, 1986.

Lavely, W. R. "The rural Chinese fertility transition: a report from Shifang Xian, Sichuan." *Population Studies,* 38 (1984), 365–84.

Lawson, Eugene K. *The Sino-Vietnamese conflict.* New York: Praeger, 1984.

Lawson, Eugene K., ed. *U.S.-China trade: problems and prospects.* New York: Praeger, 1988.

Le Monde. Daily. Paris: 19 December 1944–   .

Lee, Chae-jin. *Japan faces China: political and economic relations in the postwar era.* Baltimore: Johns Hopkins University Press, 1976.

Lee, Chae-jin. *China and Japan: new economic diplomacy.* Stanford, Calif.: Hoover Institution Press, 1984.

Lee, Edward Bing-Shuey [Li Ping-jui]. *Modern Canton.* Shanghai: Mercury Press, 1936.

Lee, Hong Yung. *The politics of the Chinese Cultural Revolution: a case study.* Berkeley: University of California Press, 1978.

Lee, Hong Yung. *Research guide to Red Guard publications, 1966–1969.* Armonk, N.Y.: M. E. Sharpe, 1991.

Lee, Leo Ou-fan 李歐凡. "Modernism and romanticism in Taiwanese literature," in Jeannette L. Faurot, ed., *Chinese fiction from Taiwan*, 6–30.

Lee, Leo Ou-fan. "Dissent literature from the Cultural Revolution." *CLEAR* [*Chinese Literature: essays, articles, reviews*], 1 (January 1979), 59–79.

Lee Yee 李怡, ed. *The new realism: writings from China after the Cultural Revolution*. New York: Hippocrene Books, 1983.

Legge, James, trans. *The Chinese classics*. 5 vols. Reprinted Hong Kong: Hong Kong University Press, 1960 [1866].

Lei Wen 雷雯. "Hsiao-shih i-shu" 小詩一束 (A handful of poems). *Shih-k'an*, 12 (1979), 56.

Leifer, Michael. *Cambodia: the search for security*. New York: Praeger, 1967.

Leifer, Michael. "Cambodia and China: neutralism, 'neutrality,' and national security, " in A. M. Halpern, ed., *Policies toward China: views from six continents*, 329–47.

Lenin, Vladimir I. "The state and revolution," in Henry M. Christman, ed., *Essential works of Lenin*. New York: Bantam Books, 1966, 271–364.

Lerman, Arthur J. *Taiwan's politics: the provincial assemblyman's world*. Washington, D.C.: University Press of America, 1978.

"Letter of the Central Committee of the Party of Labour of Albania and the Council of Ministers of the P. S. R. of Albania to the Central Committee of the Communist Party of China and the State Council of the People's Republic of China on July 29, 1978." *Zeri i Popullit*, 30 July 1978, in FBIS *Daily Report: Eastern Europe*, 1 August 1978, B1–24.

Leung, C. K., and Ginsburg, Norton, eds. *China: urbanization and national development*. Chicago: Department of Geography, University of Chicago, 1980.

Lewis, John Wilson, ed. *Party leadership and revolutionary power in China*. Cambridge: Cambridge University Press, 1970.

Lewis, John Wilson, ed. *The city in Communist China*. Stanford, Calif.: Stanford University Press, 1971.

Lewis, John Wilson. "China and Vietnam," in University of Chicago Center for Policy Studies, *China briefing*, 53–56.

Leyda, Jay. *Dianying: an account of films and the film audience in China*. Cambridge, Mass.: MIT Press, 1972.

Leys, Simon. *The Chairman's new clothes: Mao and the Cultural Revolution*. London: Allison & Busby, 1977.

Leys, Simon. *Chinese shadows*. Harmondsworth: Penguin Books, 1978.

Leys, Simon. *Broken images: essays on Chinese culture and politics*. London: Allison & Busby, 1979.

Li Chi 李季. *Wang Kuei yü Li Hsiang-hsiang* 王貴與李香香 (Wang Kuei and Li Hsiang-hsiang). Peking: Chung-kuo jen-min wen-i ts'ung-shu, 1949.

Li Hsi-fan 李希凡. "Intellectuals of a bygone age." *Chinese Literature*, 12 (December 1972), 24–32.

Li Hung-k'uan. "Ode to the constitution," in David S. G. Goodman, *Beijing street voices: the poetry and politics of China's democracy movement*, 70.

Li Jui 李銳. *Lun San-hsia kung-ch'eng* 論三峽工程 (On the Three Gorges project). Changsha: Hunan k'o-hsueh chi-shu, 1985.

Li Jui. "Ch'ung tu Chang Wen-t'ien ti 'Lu-shan ti fa-yen'" 重讀張聞天的"廬山的發言"(On rereading Chang Wen-t'ien's intervention at Lu-shan). *Tu-shu*, 8 (1985), 28–38.

Li, K. T. [Kuo-ting] 李國鼎. *The experience of dynamic economic growth on Taiwan.* Taipei: Mei Ya Publications, 1976.

Li Sheng-p'ing 李盛平 and Chang Ming-shu 張明澍, eds. *1976–1986: Shih-nien cheng-chih ta-shih-chi* 1976–1986: 十年政治大事記 (A record of the great political events of the ten years 1976–1986). Peking: Kuang-ming jih-pao, 1988.

Li-shih-ti shen-p'an 歷史的審判 (A historic trial). Peking: Ch'ün-chung, 1981.

Li-shih yen-chiu 歷史研究 (Historical research). Bimonthly. Peking: 1954–　.

Li, Victor H. *De-recognizing Taiwan: the legal problems.* Washington, D.C.: Carnegie Endowment for International Peace, 1977.

Li, Victor H., ed. *The future of Taiwan: a difference of opinion: a dialogue* [among Trong R. Chai et al.] White Plains, N.Y.: M. E. Sharpe, 1980.

Li Ying 李瑛. *Tsao-lin ts'un-chi* 棗林村集 (Jujube village collection). Peking: Jen-min, 1972.

Li Ying. "Hsiao" 笑 (Laughter), in Li Ying, *Tsao-lin ts'un-chi*, 71–73. Trans. in *Chinese Literature*, 8 (August 1972), 33–35.

Li Yung-ch'un 李永春, Shih Yuan-ch'in 史遠芹, and Kuo Hsiu-chih 郭秀芝, eds. *Shih-i chieh san chung ch'üan-hui i-lai cheng-chih t'i-chih kai-ko ta-shih-chi* 十一屆三中全會以來政治體製改革大事紀 (A record of the major events of the reform of the political system since the Third Plenum of the 11th Central Committee). Peking: Ch'un-ch'iu, 1987.

Liang Heng 梁恆 and Shapiro, Judith. *Son of the revolution.* New York: Vintage, 1984; New York: Knopf, 1983.

Liang Hsiao 梁效. "Yen-chiu Ju-Fa tou-cheng ti li-shih ching-yen" 研究儒法鬥爭的歷史經驗 (Study the historical experience of the struggle between the Confucian and Legalist schools). *HC*, 10 (1974), 56–70.

Liang Shang-ch'üan 梁上泉. *K'ai hua ti kuo-t'u* 開花的國土 (Flowering homeland). Peking: Chung-kuo ch'ing-nien, 1957.

Liang Shang-ch'üan. *Shan-ch'üan chi* 山泉集 (Mountain spring poems). Peking: Tso-chia, 1963.

Liang yung jen-ts'ai pao 兩用人材報 (Dual purpose personnel news). Weekly. Chengtu: 1984–　.

Liao Kai-lung 廖蓋隆. *Ch'üan-mien chien-she she-hui-chu-i ti tao-lu* 全面建設社會主義的道路 (The road to building socialism in an all-round way). *Yun-nan she-hui k'o-hsueh*, 2 (March 1982), 1–8, and Peking: Chung-kung chung-yang tang-hsiao, 1983.

Liao Kai-lung. *Tang-shih t'an-so* 黨史探索 (Explorations in Party history). Peking: Chung-kung chung-yang tang-hsiao, 1983.

Liao Kai-lung. "Kuan-yü hsueh-hsi 'chueh-i' chung t'i-ch'u ti i-hsieh wen-t'i ti chieh-ta" 關於學習《決議》中提出的一些問題的解答 (Answers and explanations regarding some questions which have been posed in connection with the study of the "Resolution [of 27 June 1981]"). *Yun-nan she-hui k'o-hsueh*, 2 (March 1982), 101–10.

Liao Kai-lung. "Kuan-yü Mao Tse-tung kung-kuo p'ing-chia ho she-hui-chu-i kao-tu min-chu – tui Shih-la-mu chiao-shou lun Mao Tse-tung ti chi p'ien wen-chang ti p'ing-shu" 關於毛澤東功過評价和社會主義高度民主－對施拉姆教授論毛澤東的幾篇文章的評述 (Regarding the evaluation of Mao Tse-tung's merits and faults, and high-level socialist democracy – a commentary and evaluation on several articles by Professor Schram on Mao Tse-tung), in Liao Kai-lung, *Ch'üan-mien...*, 319–37.

Liao Kai-lung. "Li-shih ti ching-yen ho wo-men ti fa-chan tao-lu" 歷史的經驗和我們的發展道路 (The experience of history and the path of our development). *CKYC*, 9 (September 1981), 101–77.

Liao Kai-lung. "She-hui-chu-i she-hui chung ti chieh-chi tou-cheng ho jen-min nei-pu mao-tun wen-t'i" 社會主義社會中的階級鬥爭和人民內部矛盾問題 (The problem of class struggle and of contradictions among the people in socialist society), in Liao Kai-lung, *Ch'üan-mien...*, 229–83.

Liao Kuang-sheng. *Antiforeignism and modernization in China, 1860–1980: linkage between domestic politics and foreign policy.* Foreword by Allen S. Whiting. Hong Kong: Chinese University Press; New York: St. Martin's Press, 1984.

Liberation Army News. See Chieh-fang-chün pao.

Lieberthal, Kenneth. *A research guide to central Party and government meetings in China 1949–1975.* Foreword by Michel Oksenberg. Michigan Papers in Chinese Studies, Special Number. White Plains, N.Y.: International Arts and Sciences Press, 1976.

Lieberthal, Kenneth G. *Sino-Soviet conflict in the 1970s: its evolution and implications for the strategic triangle.* Santa Monica, Calif.: The RAND Corporation, R-2342-NA, July 1978.

Lieberthal, Kenneth G. *Revolution and tradition in Tientsin, 1949–1952.* Stanford, Calif.: Stanford University Press, 1980.

Lieberthal, Kenneth G. "The foreign policy debate as seen through allegorical articles, 1973–76." *CQ*, 71 (September 1977), 528–54.

Lieberthal, Kenneth. "The Great Leap Forward and the split in the Yenan leadership." *CHOC*, 14. 293–395.

Lieberthal, Kenneth, and Dickson, Bruce J. *A research guide to central Party and government meetings in China 1949–1986.* Armonk, N.Y.: M. E. Sharpe, rev. and expanded ed., 1989.

Lieberthal, Kenneth, and Oksenberg, Michel. *Policy making in China: leaders, structures, and processes.* Princeton, N.J.: Princeton University Press, 1988.

Lieberthal, Kenneth, with the assistance of James Tong and Sai-cheung Yeung. *Central documents and Politburo politics in China.* Ann Arbor: Center for Chinese Studies, University of Michigan, 1978.

Lien-ho pao 聯合報 (United daily news). Taipei: 1951– .

Lifton, Robert Jay. *Revolutionary immortality: Mao Tse-tung and the Chinese Cultural Revolution.* New York: Random House, 1968.

Lim T'ianbeng. "The Black March of 1947." *The Formosan Taiwandang* (Spring 1969).

Lin Ch'ing-shan 林青山. *K'ang Sheng wai-chuan* 康生外傳 (An unofficial biography of K'ang Sheng). Peking: Chung-kuo ch'ing-nien, 1988.

Lin, Julia. *Modern Chinese poetry: an introduction.* Seattle: University of Washington Press, 1972.

Lin Man-shu 林曼叔 et al. *Chung-kuo tang-tai wen-hsueh shih-kao* 中國當代文學史稿 (Draft history of contemporary Chinese literature). Paris: Pa-li ti-ch'i ta-hsueh tung-ya ch'u-pan chung-hsin 巴黎第七大學東亞出版中心 (University of Paris VII, East Asian Publication Center), 1978.

Lin Piao 林彪. "Long live the victory of People's War!" *PR*, 8.36 (3 September 1965), 9–30. Also Peking: FLP, 1965.

Lin Piao. "Report to the Ninth National Congress of the Communist Party of China." *PR*, 12.18 (30 April 1969), 16–35.

Lin Piao. "Address to Politburo" (18 May 1966). *CLG*, 2.4 (Winter 1969–70), 42–62.

"Lin Piao's speech at the Military Academy." *Issues & Studies* (Taipei), 8.6 (March 1972), 75–79.

Lin Tou-tou 林豆豆. "Vice-chairman Lin Piao on writing." *Huo-chü t'ung-hsun* (Torch bulletin [Canton]), 1 (July 1968). Quoted from *SCMM*, 630 (1968), 1–7.

Lin, Yih-tang, comp. *What they say: a collection of current Chinese underground publications.* Taipei: Institute of Current China Studies, n. d. [1980?].

Lin Yueh-hwa [Yao-hua]. *The golden wing: a sociological study of Chinese familism.* London: Kegan Paul, Trench, Trubner, 1948. Issued under the auspices of the International Secretariat, Institute of Pacific Relations.

Lindbeck, John M. H. *Understanding China: a report to the Ford Foundation.* New York: Praeger, 1971.

Lindbeck, John M. H., ed. *China: management of a revolutionary society.* Seattle: University of Washington Press, 1971.

Lindqvist, Sven. *China in crisis.* Trans. Sylvia Clayton. New York: Crowell, 1963.

Ling, Ken. *The revenge of heaven: journal of a young Chinese.* Trans. Miriam London, and Lee Ta-ling. New York: Putnam, 1972.

Ling, Ken. *Red Guard: from schoolboy to "Little General" in Mao's China.* New York: Putnam, 1972.

Link, Perry, ed., *Stubborn weeds: popular and controversial Chinese literature after the Cultural Revolution.* Bloomington: Indiana University Press, 1983.

Link, Perry, ed. *Roses and thorns: the second blooming of the Hundred Flowers in Chinese fiction, 1979–80.* Berkeley: University of California Press, 1984.

Literature East and West. Quarterly. New York: Modern Language Association of America, 1953– .

Literaturnaya Gazeta. Weekly. Moscow: Soyuz Pisatelei SSSR, 1929– .

Liu Ch'ing 柳青. *The builders.* Peking: FLP, 1964.

Liu Hsin-wu 劉心武. "Pan-chu-jen" 班主任 (The class teacher). *Jen-min wen-hsueh*, 11 (November 1977), 16–29. Trans. in *Chinese Literature*, 1 (January 1979), 15–36.

Liu Hsin-wu. "Hsiang mu-ch'in shuo-shuo hsin-li hua" 向母親說説心裏話 (Telling mother what's on my mind). *Shang-hai wen-hsueh*, 12 (1979), 80–85.

Liu Hsin-wu. "Telling mother what's on my mind." Trans. Helena Kolenda, in Howard Goldblatt, ed. *Chinese literature for the 1980s …*, 137–38.

Liu, James J. Y. *The Chinese knight-errant.* Chicago: University of Chicago Press; London: Routledge & Kegan Paul, 1967.

Liu, Kwang-ching, and Smith, Richard J. "The military challenge: The north-west and the coast." *CHOC*, 11.202–73.

Liu Pin-yen 劉賓雁. "Pen-pao nei-pu hsiao-hsi" 本報內部消息 (Exclusive – confidential). *Jen-min wen-hsueh*, 6 (1956), 6–21 and 10 (1956), 48–59.

[Liu Shao-ch'i] 劉少奇. *Collected works of Liu Shao-ch'i, 1945–1957.* Hong Kong: Union Research Institute, 1969. *Collected works of Liu Shao-ch'i, 1958–1967.* Hong Kong: Union Research Institute, 1968.

Liu Shao-ch'i. "Report on the question of agrarian reform" delivered at the Committee of the Chinese People's Political Consultative Conference, 14 June 1950, in *Collected works of Liu Shao-ch'i*, 2.215–233.

Liu Shao-ch'i et al. *Hsin-min-chu chu-yi ch'eng-shih cheng-ts'e* 新民主主義城市政策 (New democratic urban policies). Hong Kong: Hsin-min-chu, 1949.

[Liu Shao-ch'i]. *Liu chu-hsi yü-lu* (Sayings by Chairman Liu) Hong Kong: Tzu-lien, 1967.

[Liu Shao-ch'i]. *Liu Shao-ch'i hsuan-chi* 劉少奇選集 (Selected works of Liu Shao-ch'i). Peking: Jen-min, vol. 1, 1981; vol. 2, 1985.

Liu Shao-t'ang 劉紹棠. "Wo tui tang-ch'ien wen-i wen-t'i ti i-hsieh ch'ien-chien" 我對當前文藝問題的一些淺見 (Some thoughts on literary problems today). *Wen-i hsueh-hsi*, 5 (1957), 7–10.

Liu Shaw-tong. *Out of Red China.* Trans. Jack Chia and Henry Walter; introduction by Dr. Hu Shih. New York: Duell, Sloan & Pearce; Boston: Little, Brown, 1953.

Liu-shih-nien wen-i ta-shih-chi, 1919–79 六十年文藝大事記 1919–79 (Major cultural events of sixty years, 1919–79). Peking: Institute of Literary and Artistic Research, Ministry of Culture, October 1979.

Liu Shu-mao 劉緒茂. "An introduction to the several types of production responsibility systems currently in use in our rural areas." *Ching-chi kuan-li*, 9 (15 September 1981), 12–14.

Lo Jui-ch'ing 羅瑞卿. "Commemorate the victory over German fascism! Carry the struggle against U.S. imperialism through to the end!" *HC*, 5 (1965), in *PR*, 8. 20 (14 May 1965), 7–15.

Lo Jui-ch'ing. "The people defeated Japanese fascism and they can certainly defeat U.S. imperialism too." *NCNA*, 4 September 1965, in *CB*, 770 (14 September 1965), 1–12.

Lo, Ruth Earnshaw, and Kinderman, Katherine S. *In the eye of the typhoon: an American woman in China during the Cultural Revolution.* Introduction by John K. Fairbank. New York: Harcourt Brace Jovanovich, 1980.

Löfstedt, Jan-Ingvar. *Chinese educational policy: changes and contradictions, 1949–79.*

Stockholm: Almqvist & Wiksell International; Atlantic Highlands, N.J.: Humanities Press, 1980.

Loh, Robert, as told to Humphrey Evans. *Escape from Red China*. New York: Coward-McCann, 1962.

Look. Biweekly. Des Moines, Iowa: Cowles Pub, 1937–71.

Lord, Bette [Bao], [Sansan, as told to]. *Eighth moon: the true story of a young girl's life in Communist China*. New York: Harper & Row, 1964.

Los Angeles Times. Daily. Los Angeles Times Mirror Co.: 4 December 1881– .

Lotta, Raymond, ed. *And Mao makes 5: Mao Tse-tung's last great battle*. Chicago: Banner Press, 1978.

Lovelace, Daniel D. *China and "People's War" in Thailand, 1964–1969*. Berkeley: Center for Chinese Studies; University of California, 1971.

Low, Alfred D. *The Sino-Soviet dispute: an analysis of the polemics*. Rutherford, N.J.: Fairleigh Dickinson University Press, 1976.

Lowe, H. Y. *The adventures of Wu: the life cycle of a Peking man*. Introduction by Derk Bodde. Princeton, N.J.: Princeton University Press, 1983.

Lowenthal, Richard. *World communism: the disintegration of a secular faith*. New York: Oxford University Press, 1964.

Lu Hsin-hua 盧新華. "Shang-hen" 傷痕 (The scar), in *I-chiu-ch'i-pa nien ch'üan-kuo yu-hsiu tuan-p'ien hsiao-shuo p'ing-hsuan tso-p'in-chi*, 244–58.

Lu Hung 盧燕. *Lun ch'eng-hsiang ho-tso* 論城鄉合作 (On urban–rural cooperation). Peking: San-lien shu-tien, 1949.

Lu Ting-i 陸定一. "Speech at the opening ceremony of the Festival of Peking Opera on Contemporary Themes," in *A great revolution on the cultural front*, 78–86.

Lum, Peter. *Peking: 1950–1953*. London: Robert Hale, 1958.

Lun Mao Tse-tung che-hsueh ssu-hsiang 論毛澤東哲學思想 (On Mao Tse-tung's philosophical thought). Peking: Jen-min, 1983.

Lutz, Jessie Gregory. *China and the Christian colleges, 1850–1950*. Ithaca, N.Y.: Cornell University Press, 1971.

Ma, Laurence J. C. *Cities and city planning in the People's Republic of China: an annotated bibliography*. Washington, D.C.: Office of Policy Development and Research, U.S. Department of Housing and Urban Development, 1980.

Ma, Laurence J. C., and Hanten, Edward W., eds. *Urban development in modern China*. Boulder, Colo.: Westview Press, 1981.

MacFarquhar, Roderick. *The origins of the Cultural Revolution, 1: contradictions among the people 1956–1957*. London: Oxford University Press; New York: Columbia University Press, 1974.

MacFarquhar, Roderick. *The origins of the Cultural Revolution, 2: the Great Leap Forward 1958–1960*. London: Oxford University Press; New York: Columbia University Press, 1983.

MacFarquhar, Roderick; Cheek, Timothy; and Wu, Eugene, eds. *The secret speeches of Chairman Mao: from the Hundred Flowers to the Great Leap Forward*. Cambridge, Mass.: Council on East Asian Studies, Harvard University, 1989.

MacFarquhar, Roderick. "Passing the baton in Beijing." *The New York Review of Books*, 35.2 (18 February 1988), 21–22.

MacInnis, Donald E., comp. *Religious policy and practice in communist China: a documentary history*. New York: Macmillan, 1972.

Mackerras, Colin. *The Chinese theatre in modern times, from 1840 to the present day*. Amherst: University of Massachusetts Press, 1975.

Mackerras, Colin. "Chinese opera after the Cultural Revolution (1970–72)." *CQ*, 55 (July–September 1973), 478–510.

Madsen, Richard. *Morality and power in a Chinese village*. Berkeley: University of California Press, 1984.

Madsen, Richard. "Religion and feudal superstition." *Chingfeng* (Hong Kong), 1980, 190–218.

Major, John S., ed. *China briefing, 1985*. Boulder, Colo.: Westview Press, 1987 [1986].

Makarov, M. I., et al. *Vneshniaia politika KNR* (Foreign policy of the PRC). Moscow: Izdatel'stvo Mezdunarodnye Otnosheniia, 1971.

Mancall, Mark, ed. *Formosa today*. Derived from a special issue of *CQ*, 15 (July–September 1963). New York: Praeger, 1963.

Manchester Guardian. Daily. Manchester: 1 May 1821–22 August 1959. Continued by *Guardian*, 24 August 1959– .

Mantri, Om Prakash. *Five years in Mao's China*. New Delhi: Perspective Publications, 1964.

Mao Chu-hsi chiao-yü yü-lu 毛主席教育語錄 (Quotations from Chairman Mao on education). Peking: Peking tien-chi hsueh-hsiao Tung-fang-hung kung-she 北京電機學校東方紅公社 (East is Red Commune of the Peking Electrical School), July 1967.

Mao Chu-hsi kuan-yü kuo-nei min-tsu wen-t'i ti lun-shu hsuan-pien 毛主席關於國內民族問題的論述選篇 (Selections from Chairman Mao's expositions regarding problems of nationalities within the country). Peking: Kuo-chia min-tsu shih-wu wei-yuan-hui ti-san ssu 國家民族事務委員會第三司 (Third Department of the State Commission on Minority Affairs), October 1978.

Mao Chu-hsi tui P'eng, Huang, Chang, Chou fan-tang chi-t'uan ti p'i-p'an 毛主席對彭、黃、張、周反黨集團的批判 (Chairman Mao's criticism and repudiation of the P'eng, Huang, Chang, Chou anti-Party clique). Peking: n.p., 1967.

Mao Chu-hsi wen-hsuan 毛主席文選 (Selected writings by Chairman Mao). n.p., n.d.

Mao Mao 毛毛. "In the days spent in Kiangsi." *JMJP*, 22 August 1984, in FBIS *Daily Report: China*, 23 August 1984, K1–K6.

Mao, *MTHC*. See Mao Tse-tung. *Hsuan-chi*.

Mao Tse-tung. See also *Mao Chu-hsi*....

Mao Tse-tung. *Hsuan-chi* 選集 (Selected works). Peking: Jen-min, vols. 1–4, 1960; vol. 5, 1977. Cited as *MTHC*.

Mao, *SW*. *See* Mao Tse-tung, *Selected works of Mao Tse-tung*.

Mao Tse-tung. *Selected works of Mao Tse-tung* [English trans.]. Peking: FLP, vols. 1–3, 1965; vol. 4, 1961; vol. 5, 1977. Cited as Mao, *SW*.

Mao Tse-tung. *Selected readings*. Peking: FLP, 1967. Trans. of an earlier, and substantially different, version of *Mao Tse-tung chu-tso hsuan-tu*.

Mao Tse-tung. *Miscellany of Mao Tse-tung Thought (1949–1968)*. 2 vols. Arlington, Va.: Joint Publications Research Service, Nos. 61269–1 and –2, 20 February 1974. [Trans. of materials from *Mao Tse-tung ssu-hsiang wan-sui*.]

Mao Tse-tung. *Pien-cheng wei-wu-lun: chiang-shou t'i-kang* 辯證唯物論:講授提綱 (Dialectical materialism: lecture notes). Dairen: Ta-chung shu-tien, n.d. [c. 1946].

Mao Tse-tung ssu-hsiang wan-sui! 毛澤東思想萬歲! (Long live Mao Tse-tung Thought!). Peking: n.p., 1967. Cited as *Wan-sui* (1967).

Mao Tse-tung ssu-hsiang wan-sui. Peking: n.p., 1967. Supplement. Cited as *Wan-sui* (Supplement).

Mao Tse-tung ssu-hsiang wan-sui! Peking: n.p., 1969. Cited as *Wan-sui* (1969).

Mao Tse-tung che-hsueh ssu-hsiang (chai-lu) 毛澤東哲學思想(摘錄) (Mao Tse-tung's philosophical thought [extracts]). Compiled by the Department of Philosophy of Peking University. Peking: 1960.

Mao Tse-tung t'ung-chih lun Ma-k'o-ssu-chu-i che-hsueh (chai-lu) 毛澤東同志論馬克思主義哲學(摘錄) (Comrade Mao Tse-tung on Marxist philosophy [extracts]). Urumchi: Sinkiang: ch'ing-nien, 1960. Compiled by the Office for Teaching and Research in Philosophy of the Party School under the Chinese Communist Party Committee, Sinkiang Uighur Autonomous Region.

Mao Tse-tung chu-tso, yen-lun, wen-tien mu-lu 毛澤東著作、言論、文電目錄 (A bibliography of Mao Tse-tung's writings, speeches, and telegrams). Peking: Chung-kuo jen-min chieh-fang-chün cheng-chih hsueh-yuan hsun-lien pu t'u-shu tzu-liao kuan, February 1961.

Mao Tse-tung. *Selected letters*. See *Mao tse-tung shu-hsin hsuan-chi*.

Mao Tse-tung. *Quotations from Chairman Mao Tse-tung*. Peking: Jen-min, 1966.

Mao Tse-tung. *A critique of Soviet economics*. Trans by Moss Roberts. New York: Monthly Review Press, 1977. [A translation of Mao Tse-tung, "Tu 'cheng-chih ching-chi-hsueh …'"].

Mao Tse-tung shu-hsin hsuan-chi 毛澤東書信選集 (Selected letters of Mao Tse-tung). Peking: Jen-min, 1983.

[Mao Tse-tung]. *Chien-kuo i-lai Mao Tse-tung wen-kao* 建國以來毛澤東文稿 (Draft writings by Mao Tse-tung since the establishment of the regime). Vol. 1: *September 1949–December 1950*. Vol. 2: 1951. vol. 3: 1952. vol. 4: 1953–54. Peking: Chung-yang wen-hsien, 1987–90.

Mao Tse-tung. *Mao Chu-hsi shih-tz'u san-shih-ch'i shou* 毛主席詩詞三十七首 (Thirty-seven poems by Chairman Mao). Peking: Wen-wu, 1963.

Mao Tse-tung chu-tso hsuan-tu 毛澤東著作選讀 (Selected readings from Mao Tse-tung's writings). 2 vols. Peking: Jen-min, 1986.

Mao Tse-tung che-hsueh p'i-chu-chi 毛澤東哲學批註集 (Mao Tse-tung's collected annotations on philosophy). Peking: Chung-yang wen-hsien, 1988.

Mao Tse-tung. "Mao-tun lun" 矛盾論 (On contradiction). *MTHC*, 1.278–326.

Mao Tse-tung. "Ch'ing-nien yun-tung ti fang-hsiang" 青年運動的方向 (The orientation of the youth movement). [Speech on the 20th anniversary of the May 4th Movement]. *MTHC*, 2.549–57.

Mao Tse-tung. "Chung-kuo ko-ming yü Chung-kuo kung-ch'an-tang" 中國革命與中國共產黨 (The Chinese revolution and the Chinese Communist Party). *MTHC*, 2.615–50.

Mao Tse-tung. "Hsin min-chu chu-i lun" 新民主主義論 (On new democracy). *MTHC*, 2.655–704.

Mao Tse-tung. "Lun jen-min min-chu chuan-cheng: chi-nien Chung-kuo kung-ch'an-tang erh-shih-pa chou-nien" 論人民民主專政:紀念中國共產黨二十八週年 (On the People's Democratic Dictatorship: in commemoration of the 28th anniversary of the Chinese Communist Party). *MTHC*, 4.1473–86.

Mao Tse-tung. "Tsai sheng, shih, tzu-chih-ch'ü tang-wei shu-chi hui-i shang ti chiang-hua" 在省、市、自治區黨委書記會議上的講話 (Talk at the meeting of provincial, municipal, and autonomous area Party secretaries) [27 January 1957]. *MTHC*, 5.368.

Mao Tse-tung. "Kuan-yü cheng-ch'üeh ch'u-li jen-min nei-pu mao-tun ti wen-t'i" 關於正確處理人民內部矛盾的問題 (On the correct handling of contradictions among the people). [Talk of 27 February 1957]. *MTHC*, 5.392.

Mao Tse-tung. "Tso ko-ming ti ts'u-chin-p'ai" 作革命的促進派 (Be promoters of progress) [Speech at the Third Plenum 9 October 1957]. *MTHC*, 5.497.

Mao Tse-tung. "I-ch'ieh fan-tung-p'ai to shih chih lao-hu" 一切反動派都是紙老虎 (All reactionaries are paper tigers). [Speech of 18 November 1957 in Moscow]. *MTHC*, 5.531.

Mao Tse-tung. "Lun shih ta kuan-hsi" 論十大關係 (On the ten great relationships). *MTHC*, 5.267–88. Trans. in Stuart R. Schram, ed., *Mao Tse-tung unrehearsed*.

Mao Tse-tung. "Report on an investigation of the peasant movement in Hunan." [March 1927]. Mao, *SW*, 1.23–59. (Pages vary in different editions.)

Mao Tse-tung. "Talks at the Yenan forum on literature and art." Mao, *SW*, 3. 69–98.

Mao Tse-tung. "Tu 'cheng-chih ching-chi-hsueh chiao-k'o shu'" 讀《政治經濟學教科書》 (Reading notes on the [Soviet] textbook of political economy). *Wan-sui* (1967), 167–247. The best English version is Mao Tse-tung, *A critique of Soviet economics*, q.v.

Mao Tse-tung. "Tsai Hangchow hui-i shang ti chiang-hua" 在杭州會議上的講話 (Talk at the Hangchow meeting) [December 1965]. *Wan-sui* (1969).

Mao Tse-tung. "Tsai Ch'eng-tu hui-i shang ti chiang-hua" 在成都會議上的講話 (Talks at the Chengtu conference) [March 1958]. *Wan-sui* (1969), 159–80.

Mao Tse-tung. "Tsai Hankow hui-i shang ti chiang-hua" 在漢口會議上的講話 (Talk at the Hankow meeting) [April 1957]. *Wan-sui* (1969), 180.

Mao Tse-tung. "Tsai k'uo-ta ti chung-yang kung-tso hui-i shang ti chiang-hua" 在擴大的中央工作會議上的講話 (Speech at the enlarged Central Work Conference) [30 January 1962]. *Wan-sui* (1969), 399–423.

Mao Tse-tung. "San-ko fu tsung-li hui-pao shih ti ch'a-hua" 三個副總理滙報時的插

話 (Interjections at a report meeting with three vice-premiers) [May 1964]. *Wan-sui* (1969), 494.

Mao Tse-tung. "Ch'un-chieh t'an-hua chi-yao" 春節談話紀要 (Summary of talk at the Spring Festival) [13 February 1964]. *Wan-sui* (1969), 455–65.

Mao Tse-tung. "Chao-chien shou-tu hung-tai-hui fu-tse jen ti t'an-hua" 召見首都紅 代會負責人的談話 (Talk with responsible Red Guard leaders from the capital). *Wan-sui* (1969), 687–716.

Mao Tse-tung. "Kei Lin Piao, Ho Lung, Nieh Jung-chen, Hsiao Hua chu t'ung-chih ti hsin" 給林彪、賀龍、聶榮臻、蕭華諸同志的信 (Letter to Comrades Lin Piao, Ho Lung, Nieh Jung-chen, and Hsiao Hua) [December 1963]. [Mao], *Tzu-liao Hsuan-pien*. Reproduced by Center for Chinese Research Materials, 287.

Mao Tse-tung. "Kei yin-yueh kung-tso-che t'an-hua" 給音樂工作者談話 (Talk to music workers). Trans. in Stuart R. Schram, ed. *Mao Tse-tung unrehearsed*, 84–90.

Mao Tse-tung. "Tsai Chung-kuo kung-ch'an-tang ti-chiu-chieh chung-yang wei-yuan-hui ti-i-tz'u ch'üan-t'i hui-i shang ti chiang-hua" 在中國共產黨第九屆中 央委員會第一次全體會議上的講話 (Talk at the First Plenum of the Ninth Central Committee of the Chinese Communist Party) [28 April 1969]. *CKYC*, 4.3 (March 1970), 120–26.

Mao Tse-tung. "Reply to Comrade Kuo Mo-jo" (17 November 1961). *Chinese Literature*, 4 (1976), 43.

Mao Tse-tung. "Reply to Comrade Kuo Mo-jo" (9 January 1963). *Chinese Literature*, 4 (1976), 48–49.

"Mao Tse-tung's private letter to Chiang Ch'ing (July 8, 1966)." *CLG*, 6.2 (Summer 1973), 96–100.

Mao Tse-tung. "Tsai Pei-tai-ho hui-i shang ti chiang-hua" 在北戴河會議上的講話 (Talk at the Pei-tai-ho conference) [August 1958]. *Hsueh-hsi tzu-liao*.

Mao Tse-tung. "Speech at the Lushan Conference," 23 July 1959, in Stuart R. Schram, ed., *Chairman Mao talks to the people*, 131–46.

Mao Tse-tung. "Fan-tui pen-pen chu-i" 反對本本主義 (Oppose bookism). In Mao, *Selected readings*, 48–58.

Mao Tse-tung. "Tsai pa-chieh shih-chung ch'üan-hui shang ti chiang-hua" 在八屆 十中全會上的講話 (Address at the Tenth Plenum of the Eighth Central Committee) [24 September 1962]. *Wan-sui* (1969), 430–36.

Mao Tse-tung ssu-hsiang yen-chiu 毛澤東思想研究 (Research on Mao Tse-tung Thought). Quarterly. Ch'eng-tu: 1983– .

Mao Tun 茅盾. "T'an tsui-chin ti tuan-p'ien hsiao-shuo" 談最近的短篇小説 (On recent short stories). *Jen-min wen-hsueh*, 6 (1958), 4–8.

Mao Tun. "Fan-ying she-hui chu-i yueh-chin ti shih-tai, t'ui-tung she-hui chu-i ti yueh-chin" 反映社會主義躍進的時代, 推動社會主義的躍進 (Reflect the age of the socialist leap forward, promote the socialist leap forward). *Jen-min wen-hsueh*, 8 (1960), 8–36.

Mao Zedong's "On contradiction." See Knight, Nick.

Martin, Helmut, ed. *Mao Zedong. Texte.* 6 vols. in 7. Munich: Carl Hanser Verlag, 1979–82.

Marx, Karl. "Critique of the Gotha Programme," in Karl Marx and Friedrich Engels, *Selected works.* London: Laurence & Wishart, 1970, 311–31.

Materials Group of the Party History Teaching and Research Office of the CCP Central Party School. See *Chung-kuo kung-chan tang li-t'zu chung-yao hui-i-chi.*

Mathews, Jay, and Mathews, Linda. *One billion: a China chronicle.* New York: Ballantine Books, 1983.

Matthews, Mervyn. *Education in the Soviet Union: policies and institutions since Stalin.* London: George Allen & Unwin, 1982.

Maxwell, Neville. "The Chinese account of the 1969 fighting at Chenpao." *CQ,* 56 (October–December, 1973), 730–39.

Maxwell, Neville. "A note on the Amur/Ussuri sector of the Sino-Soviet boundaries." *Modern China,* 1.1 (January 1975), 116–26.

McDougall, Bonnie S. *Mao Zedong's Talks at the Yan'an conference on literature and art": a translation of the 1943 text with commentary.* Ann Arbor: Center for Chinese Studies, University of Michigan, 1980.

McDougall, Bonnie S., ed. *Popular Chinese literature and performing arts in the People's Republic of China, 1949–1979.* Berkeley: University of California Press, 1984.

McDougall, Bonnie S., ed. and trans. *Notes from the city of the sun: poems by Bei Dao.* Ithaca, N.Y.: China-Japan Program, Cornell University, rev. ed. 1984 [1983].

McDougall, Bonnie S. "Poems, poets and *Poetry* 1976: an exercise in the typology of modern Chinese literature." *Contemporary China,* 2.4 (Winter 1978), 76–124.

Mehnert, Klaus. *Peking and Moscow.* Trans. Leila Vennewitz. New York: Putnam, 1963.

Mehnert, Klaus. *Peking and the New Left: at home and abroad.* Berkeley: Center for Chinese Studies, University of California, 1969.

Meisner, Maurice. *Mao's China: a history of the People's Republic.* New York: Free Press, 1977.

Meisner, Maurice. *Marxism, Maoism, and utopianism: eight essays.* Madison: University of Wisconsin Press, 1982.

Meisner, Maurice. "Leninism and Maoism: some populist perspectives on Marxism-Leninism in China." *CQ,* 45 (January–March 1971), 2–36.

Melanson, Richard A., ed. *Neither cold war nor détente?: Soviet-American relations in the 1980s.* Charlottesville: University Press of Virginia, 1982.

Mendel, Douglas H. *The politics of Formosan nationalism.* Berkeley: University of California Press, 1970.

Mezhdunarodnaia zhizn' (International affairs). Monthly. Moscow: "Znanie," 1955–   .

Miksche, F. O. "USSR: Rot-China – An der Ostgrenze Russlands Wacht die Dritte Weltmacht." *Wehr und Wirtschaft* (October 1974), 424–428.

The Military Balance. Annual. London: International Institute for Strategic Studies, 1959– . Various titles.

Miller, H. Lyman. "China's administrative revolution." *Current History,* 82.485 (September 1983), 270–74.

Milton, David, and Milton, Nancy Dall. *The wind will not subside: years in revolutionary China, 1964–1969.* New York: Pantheon, 1976.

Ming-pao yueh-k'an 明報月刊 (Ming Pao monthly). Monthly. Hong Kong: 1966– .

Mirovaia ekonomika i mezhdunarodnye otnosheniia (World economy and international relations). Monthly. Moscow: Institut mirovoi ekonomiki i mezhdunarodnykh otnoshenii, 1957– .

Mirovitskaya, Raisa, and Semyonov, Yuri. *The Soviet Union and China: a brief history of relations.* Moscow: Novosti, 1981.

Miscellany of Mao Tse-tung Thought. See Mao Tse-tung.

Mitchell, Ronald G. "Chinese defense spending in transition," in U.S. Congress, Joint Economic Committee, *China under the four modernizations,* 1. 605–10.

Mizan. Bimonthly (irregular). London: Central Asian Research Centre, 1959–71. Incorporating *Central Asian Review.*

Mizoguchi Toshiyuki 溝口敏行 and Yamamoto Yūzō 山本有三. "Capital formation in Taiwan and Korea," in Ramon H. Myers and Mark R. Peattie, eds., *The Japanese colonial empire,* 399–419.

Modern China: an international quarterly of history and social science. Quarterly. Newbury Park, Calif.: Sage, 1975– .

Modern Chinese Literature Newsletter. Semi-annual. Various publishers, 1975–78.

Montaperto, Ronald N., and Henderson, Jay, eds. *China's schools in flux: report.* White Plains, N.Y.: M. E. Sharpe, 1979.

Moorsteen, Richard, and Abramowitz, Morton. *Remaking China policy: U.S.-China relations and governmental decisionmaking.* Cambridge, Mass.: Harvard University Press, 1971.

Moraes, Frank. *Report on Mao's China.* New York: Macmillan, 1954.

"More on the historical experience of the dictatorship of the proletariat." *JMJP,* 29 December 1956, 21–64. Trans. in *The historical experience . . .*

Mosher, Steven W. *Broken earth: the rural Chinese.* New York: Free Press; London: Collier Macmillan, 1983.

Mosher, Steven W. *Journey to the forbidden China.* New York: Free Press; London: Collier Macmillan, 1985.

Mos'ko, G. N. *Armiia Kitaia: orudie avantiuristicheskoi politiki Maoistov* (The Chinese army: instrument of the adventuristic policies of the Maoists). Moscow: Voennoe izdatel'stvo Ministerstva Oborony SSSR, 1980.

Mozingo, David P. *Chinese policy toward Indonesia, 1949–1967.* Ithaca, N.Y.: Cornell University Press, 1976.

MTHC. See Mao Tse-tung. *Hsuan-chi* (Selected works of Mao Tse-tung).

Mu Fu-sheng [pseud.]. *The wilting of the hundred flowers: the Chinese intelligentsia under Mao.* New York: Praeger, 1963 [1962].

Munro, Donald J. "Egalitarian ideal and educational fact in communist China," in John M. H. Lindbeck, ed., *China: management of a revolutionary society*, 256–301.

Murphey, Rhoads. *Shanghai: key to modern China*. Cambridge, Mass.: Harvard University Press, 1953.

Murphey, Rhoads. *The fading of the Maoist vision: city and country in China's development*. New York: Methuen, 1980.

Myers, James T.; Domes, Jürgen; and Groeling, Erik von, eds. *Chinese politics: documents and analysis*. Vol. 1. *Cultural Revolution to 1969*. Vol. 2. *Ninth Party Congress (1969) to the death of Mao (1976)*. Columbia: University of South Carolina Press, 1986, 1989.

Myers, Ramon H., ed. *Two Chinese states: U.S. foreign policy and interests*. Introduction by Robert A. Scalapino. Stanford, Calif.: Hoover Institution Press, 1978.

Myers, Ramon H., and Peattie, Mark R., eds. *The Japanese colonial empire, 1895–1945*. Princeton, N. J.: Princeton University Press, 1984.

Myers, Ramon H. "Taiwan's agrarian economy under Japanese rule." *Journal of the Institute of Chinese Studies of the Chinese University of Hong Kong*, 7.2 (December 1974), 451–74.

Myers, Ramon H., and Yamada, Saburō. "Agricultural development in the empire," in Ramon H. Myers and Mark R. Peattie, eds., *The Japanese colonial empire*, 420–452.

Myrdal, Jan. *Report from a Chinese village*. Trans. Maurice Michael. New York: Pantheon, 1965.

Myrdal, Jan. *Return to a Chinese village*. Trans. Alan Bernstein. Foreword by Harrision E. Salisbury. New York: Pantheon, 1984.

Myrdal, Jan, and Kessle, Gun. *China: the revolution continued*. Trans. Paul Britten Austin. New York: Pantheon, 1970.

Nan Chih 南枝. *Yeh Ch'ün yeh-shih* 葉群野史 (An unofficial history of Yeh Ch'ün). 3rd ed. Hong Kong: Mirror Post Cultural Enterprises, 1988.

Narody Azii i Afriki (The peoples of Asia and Africa). Bimonthly. Moscow: Nauka, 1955–   . Continues *Problemy vostokovedeniia*.

National Foreign Assessment Center. *See* United States.

National Geographic Magazine. Monthly. Washington, D.C.: National Geographic Society, 1888–   .

Naughton, Barry. "Finance and planning reforms in industry," in U.S. Congress, Joint Economic Committee, *China's economy looks toward the year 2000*, 1.604–629.

Naughton, Barry. "The third front: defence industrialization in the Chinese interior." *CQ*, 115 (September 1988), 351–86.

NCNA. New China News Agency.

Nee, Victor, with Don Layman. *The Cultural Revolution at Peking University*. New York: Monthly Review Press, 1969.

Nee, Victor. "Revolution and bureaucracy: Shanghai in the Cultural Revolution," in Victor Nee and James Peck, eds., *China's uninterrupted revolution: from 1840 to the present*, 322–414.

Nee, Victor, and Peck, James, eds. *China's uninterrupted revolution: from 1840 to the present*. New York: Pantheon, 1975.

Nei-pu wen-kao 內部文告 (Internal manuscripts). Nos. 7, 13 (1981), No. 10 (1987). Peking: Hung-ch'i tsa-chih-she "nei-pu wen-kao" pien-chi pu 紅旗雜誌社《內部文告》編輯部.

Nelsen, Harvey W. *The Chinese military system: an organizational study of the Chinese People's Liberation Army*. 2nd ed., rev. and updated. Boulder, Colo.: Westview Press, 1981 [1977].

Nelsen, Harvey W. "Military forces in the Cultural Revolution." *CQ*, 51 (July–September 1972), 444–74.

Nelsen, Harvey W. "Military bureaucracy in the Cultural Revolution." *Asian Survey*, 14.4 (April 1974), 372–95.

Neuhauser, Charles. *Third World politics: China and the Afro-Asian People's Solidarity Organization, 1957–1967*. Cambridge, Mass.: East Asian Research Center, Harvard University, 1968.

Neuhauser, Charles. "The impact of the Cultural Revolution on the CCP machine." *Asian Survey*, 8.6 (June 1968), 465–88.

New China Monthly. See *Hsin-hua yueh-pao*.

New China News Agency. (*Hsin-hua-she*). Cited as NCNA. See *Hsin-hua t'ung-hsun-she*.

New China News Agency. *Daily News Release*. Hong Kong: 1948– .

New China Semi-monthly. See *Hsin-hua pan-yueh-k'an*.

New China's population. China Financial and Economic Publishing House. English trans. New York: Macmillan, 1988.

New Republic: a journal of opinion. 48/yr. Washington, D.C.: 1914– .

New Times. A Soviet weekly of world affairs. Moscow: Trud, 1943– .

New York Review of Books, The. 21/yr. New York: NYRB, 1963– .

New York Times, The. Daily. New York: 13 September 1857– .

New Yorker, The. Weekly. New York: The New Yorker Magazine, 1925– .

News from Chinese provincial radio stations. See United Kingdom Regional Information Office for Southeast Asia.

Nickum, James E. *Hydraulic engineering and water resources in the People's Republic of China*. Stanford, Calif.: U.S.-China Relations Program, Stanford University, 1977. [Report of the U.S. Water Resources delegation, August–September 1974.]

Nieh, Hua-ling 聶華苓, ed. *Literature of the Hundred Flowers*. 2 vols. New York: Columbia University Press, 1981.

Nieh Jung-chen. "Several questions concerning Lin Biao," *Hsin-hua jih-pao*, 18 and 19 October 1984, in FBIS, *Daily Report: China* 5 November 1984, K18–21.

Nieh Jung-chen hui-i lu 聶榮臻回憶錄 (Memoirs of Nieh Jung-chen). 3 vols. Peking: Chieh-fang-chün, 1983, 1984.

1982 population census of China (major figures), The. Hong Kong: Economic Information Agency, 1982.

Ning Lao T'ai-t'ai. *See* Pruitt, Ida.

Nixon, Richard M. *RN: the memoirs of Richard Nixon*. New York: Grosset & Dunlap, 1978.

Northeast Normal University Journal. See *Tung-pei shih-ta hsueh-pao*.

Nossal, Frederick. *Dateline Peking*. London: Macdonald, 1962.

"Nothing is hard in this world if you dare to scale the heights." *JMJP*, *HC*, *Chieh-fang-chün pao* (Liberation Army news) joint editorial, 1 January 1976. Trans. in "Quarterly chronicle and documentation." *CQ*, 66 (June 1976), 411–16.

Oi, Jean C. *State and peasant in contemporary China: the political economy of village government*. Berkeley: University of California Press, 1989.

Ojha, Ishwer C. *The changing pattern of China's attitude toward a negotiated settlement in Vietnam, 1964–1971*. Edwardsville: Southern Illinois University Press, 1973.

Oksenberg, Michel. "Local leaders in rural China, 1962–65: individual attributes, bureaucratic positions, and political recruitment," in A. Doak Barnett, ed., *Chinese communist politics in action*, 155–215.

Oksenberg, Michel, and Yeung Sai-cheung. "Hua Kuo-feng's pre–Cultural Revolution Hunan years, 1949–1966: the making of a political generalist." *CQ*, 69 (March 1977), 3–53.

Oksenberg, Michel. "A decade of Sino-American relations." *Foreign Affairs*, 61.1 (Fall 1982), 175–95.

"On the historical experience of the dictatorship of the proletariat." Editorial Department, *JMJP*, 5 April 1956. Trans. in *The historical experience . . .*

Onoye, Etsuzō. "Regional distribution of urban population in China." *The Developing Economies*, 8.1 (March 1970), 93–127.

Opasnyi kurs (Dangerous course). Moscow: Politizdat, 1969–81.

Orbis: a journal of world affairs. Quarterly. Philadelphia: Foreign Policy Research Institute, 1956– .

Orleans, Leo A., ed., with the assistance of Caroline Davidson. *Science in contemporary China*. Stanford, Calif.: Stanford University Press, 1980.

Orleans, Leo A. "China's urban population: concepts, conglomerations, and concerns," in U.S. Congress, Joint Economic Committee, *China under the four modernizations*, 1.268–302.

Overholt, William H. "Nuclear proliferation in Eastern Asia," in William Overholt, ed., *Asia's nuclear future*. Boulder, Colo.: Westview Press, 1977, 133–59.

Pa-shih nien-tai 八十年代 (The eighties). Monthly. Taipei: 1979– .

Pacific Affairs: an international review of Asia and the Pacific. Quarterly. Vancouver, B.C.: 1926– . Vols. 1–33 published by the Institute of Pacific Relations. Vols. 34– published by the University of British Columbia, Vancouver.

Pai-chia cheng-ming – fa-chan k'o-hsueh ti pi-yu chih lu. 1956 nien 8 yueh Ch'ing-tao i-ch'uan hsueh tso-t'an hui chi-shu. 百家爭鳴－發展科學的必由之路. 一九五六年八月青島遺傳學座談會記述 (Let a hundred schools contend – the way which the development of science must follow. The record of the August 1956 Tsingtao Conference on Genetics). Peking: Commercial Press, 1985.

Pai Hsien-yung 白先勇. "The wandering Chinese: the theme of exile in Chinese fiction." *Iowa Review*, 7.2–3 (Spring–Summer 1976), 205–12.

Pan Ku 班固. *The history of the former Han Dynasty*. Trans. Homer H. Dubs. 3 vols. Baltimore: Waverly Press, 1955 [1944, 1938].

Pannell, Clifton. "Recent growth in China's urban system," in Laurence J. C. Ma and Edward Hanten, eds., *Urban development in modern China*, 91–113.

Parish, William L., ed. *Chinese rural development: the great transformation*. Armonk, N.Y.: M. E. Sharpe, 1985.

Parish, William L. "Factions in Chinese military politics." *CQ*, 56 (October–December 1973), 667–99.

Parish, William L., and Whyte, Martin King. *Village and family life in contemporary China*. Chicago: University of Chicago Press, 1978.

Pascoe, B. Lynn. "China's relations with Burma, 1949–1964," in Andrew W. Cordier, ed., *Columbia essays in international affairs: the dean's papers, 1965*, 175–204.

Pasternak, Burton. *Kinship and community in two Chinese villages*. Stanford, Calif.: Stanford University Press, 1972.

Payne, Robert. *Chiang Kai-shek*. New York: Weybright & Talley, 1969.

Peck, James. *See* Nee, Victor.

Pei-ching jih-pao 北京日報 (Peking daily). 1954– . (Ceased publication for a time during Cultural Revolution.)

Pei-ching kung-jen 北京工人 (The Peking worker). Monthly. Peking: 1984– .

Pei-ching shih-fan ta-hsueh hsueh-pao 北京師大學學報 (Peking Normal University journal). Bimonthly. Peking: 1956– .

Peking Daily. See *Pei-ching jih-pao*.

Peking Normal University Journal. See *Pei-ching shih-fan ta-hsueh hsueh-pao*.

Peking Review. Weekly. Peking: 1958– . (From January 1979, *Beijing Review*.)

Pelzel, John C. "Economic management of a production brigade in post-Leap China," in W. E. Willmott, ed., *Economic organization in Chinese society*, 387–414.

Peng Dehuai [P'eng Te-huai] 彭德懷. *Memoirs of a Chinese marshal: the autobiographical notes of Peng Dehuai (1898–1974)*. Trans. Zheng Longpu; English text edited by Sara Grimes. Peking: FLP, 1984.

Peng Ming-min 彭明敏. *A taste of freedom: memoirs of a Formosan independence leader*. New York: Holt, Rinehart & Winston, 1972.

[P'eng Te-huai]. *The case of P'eng Te-huai, 1959–1968*. Hong Kong: Union Research Institute, 1968.

P'eng Te-huai. "Letter of opinion," in *The case of P'eng Te-huai, 1959–1968*, 7–13.

P'eng Te-huai tzu-shu 彭德懷自述 (P'eng Te-huai's own account). Peking: Jen-min, 1981. Trans. as *Memoirs of a Chinese marshal*. Peking: FLP, 1984.

People's Daily. See *Jen-min jih-pao*.

People's Education. See *Jen-min chiao-yü*.

People's Publishing House. Jen-min ch'u-pan-she. Cited as Jen-min.

Pepper, Suzanne. *China's universities: post-Mao enrollment policies and their impact on the structure of secondary education: a research report.* Ann Arbor: Center for Chinese Studies, University of Michigan, 1984.

Pepper, Suzanne. "An interview on changes in Chinese education after the 'Gang of Four.'" *CQ*, 72 (December 1977), 815–24.

Pepper, Suzanne. "Education and revolution: the 'Chinese model' revised." *Asian Survey*, 18.9 (September 1978), 847–890.

Pepper, Suzanne. "Chinese education after Mao." *CQ*, 81 (March 1980), 1–65.

Pepper, Suzanne. "China's universities: new experiments in socialist democracy and administrative reform – a research report." *Modern China*, 8:2 (April 1982), 147–204.

Perkins, Dwight H. *Agricultural development in China, 1368–1968.* Chicago: Aldine, 1969.

Perkins, Dwight, ed. *Rural small-scale industry in the People's Republic of China.* Berkeley: University of California Press, 1977. [Report of the American Rural Small-Scale Industry Delegation.]

Perkins, Dwight H. "Research on the economy of the People's Republic of China: a survey of the field." *JAS*, 42.2 (February 1983), 345–72.

Perkins, Dwight H. "Reforming China's economic system." *Journal of Economic Literature*, 26 (June 1988), 601–45.

Perkins, Dwight, and Yusuf, Shahid. *Rural development in China.* Baltimore: Johns Hopkins University Press, for the World Bank, 1984.

Perry, Elizabeth J. "Social ferment: grumbling amidst growth," in John S. Major, ed., *China briefing, 1985,* 39–52.

Perry, Elizabeth J., and Wong, Christine, eds. *The political economy of reform in post-Mao China.* Cambridge, Mass.: Council on East Asian Studies, Harvard University, 1985.

Pien Chih-lin 卞之琳. "Tung t'u wen-ta" 動土問答 (Dialogue of the earth movers). *Shih-k'an*, 3 (1958), 10.

Polemic on the general line of the international communist movement, The. Peking: FLP, 1965.

Political Quarterly. Quarterly. Oxford: Basil Blackwell, 1930– .

Pollack, Jonathan D. *The Sino-Soviet conflict in the 1980s: its dynamics and policy implications.* Santa Monica, Calif.: The RAND Corporation, 1981.

Pollack, Jonathan D. *The Sino-Soviet rivalry and Chinese security debate.* Santa Monica, Calif.: The RAND Corporation, R-2907-AF, October 1982.

Pollack, Jonathan D. *The lessons of coalition politics: Sino-American security relations.* Santa Monica, Calif.: The RAND Corporation, R-3133-AF, February 1984.

Pollard, D. E. "The short story in the Cultural Revolution." *CQ*, 73 (March 1978), 99–121.

Pollard, D. E. "The controversy over modernism 1979–84." *CQ*, 104 (December 1985), 641–57.

Potter, Sulamith Heins. "The position of peasants in modern China's social order." *Modern China*, 9.4 (October 1983), 465–99.

Powell, Ralph L. "Commissars in the economy: the 'Learn from the PLA' movement in China." *Asian Survey*, 5.3 (March 1965), 125–38.

PR. Peking Review.

Pratt, Lawrence. *North Vietnam and Sino-Soviet tension*. Toronto: Baxter, 1967.

Pravda. Daily. Moscow: CPSUCC, 1912– .

PRC State Statistical Bureau. Chung-hua jen-min kung-ho-kuo kuo-chia t'ung-chi chü. See *Chung-kuo t'ung-chi nien-chien.*

Price, Jane L. *Cadres, commanders and commissars: the training of the Chinese Communist leadership, 1920–1945*. Boulder, Colo.: Westview Press, 1976.

Price, Ronald F. *Education in communist China*. London: Routledge & Kegan Paul, 1970; 2nd ed. published under the title *Education in modern China*. London and Boston: Routledge & Kegan Paul, 1979.

Price, Ronald F. *Marx and education in Russia and China*. London: Croom Helm; Totowa, N.J.: Rowman & Littlefield, 1977.

Problems of communism. Bimonthly. United States Information Agency. Washington, D.C.: U.S. Government Printing Office, 1952– .

Problemy Dal'nego Vostoka (Problems of the Far East). Quarterly through 1986; bimonthly 1987– . Institute of the Far East, USSR Academy of Sciences. Trans. as *Far Eastern Affairs*. Moscow: Progress, 1972– .

Problemy i protivorechiia v razvitii rabochego klassa KNR (Problems and contradictions in the development of the working class of the PRC). Moscow: Institute of the International Workers' Movement, Academy of Sciences, 1978.

Problemy sovetskogo kitaevedeniia (Topics in Soviet Sinology). Moscow: Institute of the Far East, 1973.

Pruitt, Ida. *A daughter of Han: the autobiography of a Chinese working woman [by] Ida Pruitt, from the story told her by Ning Lao T'ai-t'ai*. Stanford, Calif.: Stanford University Press, 1967; New Haven, Conn.: Yale University Press; London: H. Milford, Oxford University Press, 1945.

Pruitt, Ida. *Old Madam Yin: a memoir of Peking life, 1926–1938*. Stanford, Calif.: Stanford University Press, 1979.

Průšek, Jaroslav. *Die Literatur des befreiten China und ihre Volkstraditionen*. (The literature of liberated China and its folk traditions). Prague: Artia, 1955.

Prybyla, Jan S. *The societal objective of wealth, growth, stability and equity in Taiwan*. Occasional Paper in Contemporary Asian Studies, no. 4. Baltimore: University of Maryland School of Law, 1978.

Pu-chin-ti ssu-nien 不盡的思念 (Inexhaustible memories). Peking: Chung-yang wen-hsien, 1987.

Pusey, James R. *Wu Han: attacking the present through the past*. Cambridge, Mass.: East Asian Research Center, Harvard University, 1969.

Pye, Lucian W. *Mao Tse-tung: the man in the leader*. New York: Basic Books, 1976.

Pye, Lucian. *The dynamics of Chinese politics*. Cambridge, Mass.: Oelgeschlager, Gunn & Hain, 1981.

Pye, Lucian W., with Mary W. Pye. *Asian power and politics: the cultural dimensions of authority*. Cambridge, Mass.: Harvard University Press, 1985.

"Quarterly chronicle and documentation." *CQ*, in each issue.

Ra'anan, Uri. "Peking's foreign policy 'debate,' 1965–1966," in Tang Tsou, ed., *China in crisis*, 2.23–71.

Raddock, David. *Political behavior of adolescents in China*. Tucson: University of Arizona Press, 1977.

Radio Liberty Dispatch. Weekly. Various titles. From 1989 became *Report on the USSR*. New York: Radio Liberty Committee.

Radio Liberty Research Bulletins on the Soviet Union. Weekly. Munich: RFERL, Inc., 1956– . Formerly *Radio Liberty Research Bulletins*.

Ragvald, Lars. *Yao Wen-yuan as a literary critic and theorist*. Stockholm: Department of Oriental Languages, University of Stockholm, 1978.

Ranis, Gustav. "Industrial development," in Walter Galenson, ed., *Economic growth and structural change in Taiwan*, 206–62.

Rankin, Karl Lott. *China assignment*. Seattle: University of Washington Press, 1964.

Ravenholt, Albert. "Formosa today." *Foreign Affairs*, 30.4 (July 1952), 612–24.

Rawski, Thomas G. *Economic growth and employment in China*. New York: Oxford University Press, for the World Bank, 1979.

Red Flag. See *Hung-ch'i*.

Renditions: a Chinese-English translation magazine. Semi-annual. Hong Kong: Research Centre for Translations, Chinese University of Hong Kong, 1973– .

"Report on the investigation of the counterrevolutionary crimes of the Lin Piao anti-Party clique." From *Chung-fa*, No. 34 (1973), in Michael Y. M. Kau, ed., *The Lin Piao affair*, 110–17.

Research Office of the Supreme People's Court. See *Chung-hua jen-min kung-ho-kuo* …

Resolution on certain questions in the history of our Party since the founding of the People's Republic of China [27 June 1981]. NCNA, 30 June 1981; FBIS *Daily Report: China*, 1 July 1981, K1–38; published as *Resolution on CPC History* (1949–1981). Peking: FLP, 1981.

Review of National Literatures. Annual. Whitestone, N.Y.: Council on National Literatures, Griffon House Publications, 1970– .

Reynolds, Bruce L. "Changes in the standard of living of Shanghai industrial workers, 1930–1973," in Christopher Howe, ed., *Shanghai: revolution and development in an Asian metropolis*, 222–239.

Reynolds, Bruce L, ed. and intro. *Reform in China: challenges and choices*. Chinese Economic System Reform Research Institute, Peking. Armonk, N.Y.: M. E. Sharpe, 1987.

Reynolds, Bruce L., ed. *Chinese economic reform*. A special issue of the *Journal of Comparative Economics*, 11.3 (September 1987). Boston, Mass.: Academic Press, 1988.

Rice, Edward Earl. *Mao's way*. Berkeley: University of California Press, 1972.

Riggs, Fred W. *Formosa under Chinese Nationalist rule*. New York: Octagon Books, 1972; New York: Institute for Pacific Relations, 1952.

Riollot, Jean. "Soviet reaction to the Paracel Islands dispute." *Radio Liberty Dispatch* (11 February 1974), 1–3.

Riskin, Carl. "Small industry and the Chinese model of development." *CQ*, 46 (April–June 1971), 245–73.

Robinson, Thomas W. *The Sino-Soviet border dispute: background, development, and the March 1969 clashes.* Santa Monica, Calif.: The RAND Corporation, RM-6171-PR, 1970; *American Political Science Review*, 66.4 (December 1972), 1175–1202.

Robinson, Thomas W., ed. *The Cultural Revolution in China.* Berkeley: University of California Press, 1971.

Robinson, Thomas W. *The border negotiations and the future of Sino-Soviet-American relations.* Santa Monica, Calif.: The RAND Corporation, P-4661, 1971.

Robinson, Thomas W. "A politico-military biography of Lin Piao, part II, 1950–1971." Draft manuscript, August 1971.

Robinson, Thomas W. "Explaining Chinese foreign policy: contributing elements and levels of analysis." Unpublished manuscript, 1978.

Robinson, Thomas W. "Chou En-lai and the Cultural Revolution," in Thomas W. Robinson, ed., *The Cultural Revolution in China*, 165–312.

Robinson, Thomas W. "The Wuhan Incident: local strife and provincial rebellion during the Cultural Revolution." *CQ*, 47 (July–September 1971), 413–38.

Robinson, Thomas W. "China in 1972: socio-economic progress amidst political uncertainty." *Asian Survey*, 13.1 (January 1973), 1–18.

Robinson, Thomas W. "China in 1973: renewed leftism threatens the 'New Course.'" *Asian Survey*, 14.1 (January 1974), 1–21.

Robinson, Thomas W. "American policy in the strategic triangle," in Richard A. Melanson, ed., *Neither cold war nor détente?*, 112–33.

Robinson, Thomas W. "Political and strategic aspects of Chinese foreign policy," in Donald C. Hellmann, ed., *China and Japan: a new balance of power*, 197–268.

Robinson, Thomas W. "Detente and the Sino-Soviet-U.S. triangle," in Della W. Sheldon, ed., *Dimensions of detente*, 50–83.

Robinson, Thomas W. "Restructuring Chinese foreign policy, 1959–1976: three episodes," in K [al] J. Holsti, et al., *Why nations realign: foreign policy restructuring in the postwar world*, 134–71.

Robinson, Thomas W., and Mozingo, David P. "Lin Piao on People's War: China takes a second look at Vietnam." Santa Monica, Calif.: The RAND Corporation, Rm-4814-PR, November 1965.

Roll, C. R. "The distribution of rural income in China: a comparison of the 1930s and the 1950s." Harvard University, Ph.D. dissertation, 1974.

Rosen, Stanley. *The role of sent-down youth in the Chinese Cultural Revolution: the case of Guangzhou.* Berkeley: Center for Chinese Studies, University of California, 1981.

Rosen, Stanley. *Red Guard factionalism and the Cultural Revolution in Guangzhou (Canton).* Boulder, Colo.: Westview Press, 1982.

Rosen, Stanley. "Obstacles to educational reform in China." *Modern China*, 8.1 (January 1982), 3–40.

Ross, Robert S. *The Indochina tangle: China's Vietnam policy, 1975–1979.* New York: Columbia University Press, 1988.

Rowe, David Nelson. *Informal diplomatic relations: the case of Japan and the Republic of China, 1972–74.* Hamden, Conn.: Shoestring Press, 1975.

Rowe, William. *Hankow: conflict and community in a Chinese city, 1796–1895.* Stanford, Calif.: Stanford University Press, 1984.

Rowe, William. "Urban society in late imperial China: Hankow 1796–1889." Columbia University, Ph.D. dissertation, 1980. Published as *Hankow: commerce and society in a Chinese city, 1796–1889.* Stanford, Calif.: Stanford University Press, 1989.

Rozman, Gilbert. *Urban networks in Ch'ing China and Tokugawa Japan.* Princeton, N.J.: Princeton University Press, 1974 [1973].

Rozman, Gilbert. *The Chinese debate about Soviet socialism, 1978–85.* Princeton, N.J.: Princeton University Press, 1987.

Rozman, Gilbert, ed. *The modernization of China.* New York: Free Press, 1981.

Rumiantsev, A. *Istoki i evoliutsiia Idei Mao Tsze-duna"* (Sources and evolution of "Mao Tse-tung Thought"). Moscow: Nauka, 1972.

Rupen, Robert A., and Farrell, Robert, eds. *Vietnam and the Sino-Soviet dispute.* New York: Praeger, 1967.

Salisbury, Harrison E. *War between Russia and China.* New York: Norton, 1969.

Salisbury, Harrison E. "Marco Polo would recognize Mao's Sinkiang." *New York Times Magazine*, 23 November 1969.

Sandles, Gretchen Ann. "Soviet images of the People's Republic of China, 1949–1979." University of Michigan, Ph.D. dissertation, 1981.

Sansan. *See* Lord, Bette [Bao].

Sardesar, D. R. "China and peace in Vietnam." *China Report*, 5.3 (May–June 1969), 13–18.

Scalapino, Robert A. *On the trail of Chou En-lai in Africa.* Santa Monica, Calif.: The RAND Corporation, Rm-4061-PR, April 1964.

Scalapino, Robert A., ed. *Elites in the People's Republic of China.* Seattle: University of Washington Press, 1972.

Scalapino, Robert A. "Africa and Peking's united front." *Current Scene*, 3.26 (1 September 1965), 1–11.

Scalapino, Robert A. "The transition in Chinese party leadership: a comparison of the Eighth and Ninth Central Committees," in Robert A. Scalapino, ed., *Elites in the People's Republic of China*, 67–148.

Schapiro, Leonard, and Lewis, John Wilson. "The roles of the monolithic party under the totalitarian leader," in John Wilson Lewis, ed., *Party leadership and revolutionary power in China*, 114–45.

Schelochowzew, A. N. *See* Zhelokhovtsev, A.

Schlesinger, Arthur M., Jr. *A thousand days: John F. Kennedy in the White House.* Boston: Houghton Mifflin, 1965.

Schram, Stuart [R.]. *Documents sur la théorie de la révolution permanente" en Chine*. Paris: Mouton, 1963.

Schram, Stuart [R.]. *Mao Tse-tung*. Rev. ed. Harmondsworth: Penguin Books, 1967.

Schram, Stuart R. *The political thought of Mao Tse-tung*. Rev. ed. New York: Praeger, 1969.

Schram, Stuart R. *Authority, participation and cultural change in China*. Cambridge: Cambridge University Press, 1973.

Schram, Stuart [R.]. *Mao Zedong: a preliminary reassessment*. Hong Kong: The Chinese University Press, 1983.

Schram, Stuart [R.]. *Ideology and policy in China since the Third Plenum, 1978–1984*. London: School of Oriental and African Studies, 1984.

Schram, Stuart R., ed. *Chairman Mao talks to the people. See* Schram, Stuart R., ed., *Mao Tse-tung unrehearsed*.

Schram, Stuart R., ed. *Mao Tse-tung unrehearsed: talks and letters, 1956–71*. Harmondsworth: Penguin Books, 1974. Published in the United States as *Chairman Mao talks to the people: talks and letters 1956–1971*. New York: Pantheon, 1974.

Schram, Stuart [R.], ed. *The scope of state power in China*. London: School of Oriental and African Studies, and Hong Kong: The Chinese University Press, 1985.

Schram, Stuart [R.], ed. *Foundations and limits of state power in China*. London: School of Oriental and African Studies, and Hong Kong: The Chinese University Press, 1987.

Schram, Stuart R. "The Cultural Revolution in historical perspective," in Stuart R. Schram, ed., *Authority, participation and cultural change in China*, 1–108.

Schram, Stuart R. "The party in Chinese communist ideology," in John Wilson Lewis, ed., *Party leadership and revolutionary power in China*, 170–202.

Schram, Stuart [R.]. "Decentralization in a unitary state: theory and practice 1940–1984," in Stuart Schram, ed., *The scope of state power in China*, 81–125.

Schram, Stuart [R.]. "Mao Tse-tung's thought to 1949." *CHOC*, 13.789–870.

Schram, Stuart [R.]. "Party leader or true ruler? Foundations and significance of Mao Zedong's personal power," in Stuart R. Schram, ed., *Foundations and limits of state power in China*, 203–56.

Schram, Stuart [R.]. "The Marxist," in Dick Wilson, ed., *Mao Tse-tung in the scales of history*, 35–69.

Schram, Stuart [R.]. "Mao Tse-tung and the theory of the permanent revolution, 1958–1969." *CQ*, 46 (April–June 1971), 221–44.

Schram, Stuart R. "From the 'Great Union of the Popular Masses' to the 'Great Alliance.'" *CQ*, 49 (January–March 1972), 88–105.

Schram, Stuart [R.]. "Chairman Hua edits Mao's literary heritage: 'On the ten great relationships.'" *CQ*, 69 (March 1977), 126–35.

Schram, Stuart [R.]. "New texts by Mao Zedong, 1921–1966." *Communist Affairs*, 2.2 (April 1983), 143–165.

Schram, Stuart [R.]. "'Economics in command?' Ideology and policy since the Third Plenum, 1978–1984." *CQ*, 99 (September 1984), 417–61.

Schram, Stuart [R.]. "The limits of cataclysmic change: reflections on the place of the 'Great Proletarian Cultural Revolution' in the political development of the People's Republic of China." *CQ*, 108 (December 1986), 613–24.

Schram, Stuart [R.]. "China after the Thirteenth Congress." *CQ*, 114 (June 1988), 177–97.

Schurmann, Franz. *Ideology and organization in Communist China*. Berkeley: University of California Press, 1968 [1966].

Schwartz, Benjamin I. *Chinese communism and the rise of Mao*. Cambridge, Mass.: Harvard University Press, 1964 [1951].

Schwartz, Benjamin I. "The reign of virtue: some broad perspectives on leader and party in the Cultural Revolution," in John Wilson Lewis, ed., *Party leadership and revolutionary power in China*, 149–69.

Schwartz, Benjamin I. "The primacy of the political order in East Asian societies," in Stuart Schram, ed., *Foundations and limits of state power in China*, 1–10.

Schwartz, Harry. *Tsars, mandarins, and commissars: a history of Chinese-Russian relations*. Philadelphia: Lippincott, 1964; Rev. ed. Garden City, N.Y.: Doubleday, 1973.

Science and technology in the People's Republic of China. Paris: Organization for Economic Co-operation and Development, 1977.

Science and Technology News. See *K'o-chi jih-pao*.

Scientific Culture News. See *K'o-hsueh wen-hua pao*.

SCMM. *See* U.S. Consulate General (Hong Kong). *Selections from China Mainland Magazines*.

SCMP. See U.S. Consulate General (Hong Kong). *Survey from China Mainland Press*.

Segal, Gerald. *Sino-Soviet relations after Mao*. London: International Institute for Strategic Studies, Adelphi Paper, no. 202, Autumn 1985.

Selected works of Deng Xiaoping [*Teng Hsiao-p'ing*] (*1975–1982*). Peking: FLP, 1984.

Sen Gupta, Bhabani [Sena Canakya]. *The fulcrum of Asia: relations among China, India, Pakistan and the USSR*. New York: Pegasus, 1970.

Sen Gupta, Bhabani. *Soviet-Asian relations in the 1970s and beyond: an interperceptional study*. New York: Praeger, 1976.

Sewell, William. *I stayed in China*. New York: A. S. Barnes, 1966.

Seybolt, Peter J., ed. *Revolutionary education in China: documents and commentary*. White Plains, N.Y.: International Arts and Sciences Press, 1973.

Seybolt, Peter J., ed. *The rustication of urban youth in China: a social experiment*. Introduction by Thomas P. Bernstein. White Plains, N.Y.: M. E. Sharpe, 1977 [1976, 1975].

Shambaugh, David L. "China's America watchers: images of the United States, 1972–1986. " University of Michigan, Ph.D. dissertation, 1989.

Shang-hai hsi-chü 上海戲劇 (Shanghai theater). Bimonthly. Shanghai: 1956– .

Shang-hai wen-hsueh 上海文學 (Shanghai literature). Monthly. Shanghai: 1953– . Formerly *Wen-i yueh-k'an* 文藝月刊 (Literature and art monthly).

Shao Hua-tse 邵華澤. "Kuan-yü 'wen-hua ta ko-ming' ti chi-ko wen-t'i" 關於"文化大革命"的幾個問題 (On several questions concerning the "Great Cultural Revolution"), in *Tang-shih hui-i pao-kao-chi*, 337–92.

Shao Yen-hsiang 邵燕祥. *Tao yuan-fang ch'ü* 到遠方去 (Far journey). Peking: Tso-chia, 1956.

Shaw, Brian. "China and North Vietnam: two revolutionary paths." *Current Scene*, 9.11 (November 1971), 1–12.

She-hui 社會 (Society). Bimonthly. Shanghai: 1981– .

She-hui k'o-hsueh chan-hsien 社會科學戰綫 (Social science front). Quarterly. Ch'ang-ch'un: 1978– .

Sheldon, Della W., ed. *Dimensions of detente*. New York: Praeger, 1978.

Shen keng 深耕 (Plow deeply). Taiwan.

Shen, T. H., ed. *Agriculture's place in the strategy of development: the Taiwan experience*. Taipei: Joint Commission on Rural Reconstruction, 1974.

"Sheng-huo tsai li-shih yin-ying chung-ti Lin Tou-tou" 生活在歷史陰影中的林荳荳 (Lin Tou-tou who lives in the shadow of history). New York: *Hua-ch'iao jih-pao*, 14–23 June 1988.

Shih-chieh chih-shih 世界知識 (World knowledge). Monthly. Peking: 1934– .

Shih-chieh ching-chi tao-pao 世界經濟導報 (World Economic Herald). Weekly. Shanghai: 1980–1989.

Shih Chung-ch'üan 石仲泉. "Tu Su-lien 'Cheng-chih ching-chi hsueh chiao-k'o shu' ti t'an-hua" 讀蘇聯《政治經濟學教科書》的談話 (Talks on reading the Soviet textbook of political economy), in Kung Yü-chih et al., *Mao Tse-tung ti tu-shu sheng-huo*, 148–78.

Shih Chung-ch'üan. "Ma-k'o-ssu so-shuo-ti 'tzu-ch'an-chieh-chi ch'üan-li' ho Mao Tse-tung t'ung-chih tui t'a ti wu-chieh" 馬克思所説的"資產階級權利"和毛澤東同志對它的誤解 (The "bourgeois right" referred to by Marx, and Comrade Mao Tse-tung's misunderstanding of it). *Wen-hsien ho yen-chiu*, 1983, 405–17.

Shih Chung-ch'üan. "Review of *Mao Tse-tung che-hsueh p'i-chu-chi*." *Che-hsueh yen-chiu*, 10 (1987), 3–9, 40.

Shih-i chieh san chung ch'üan-hui i-lai chung-yao wen-hsien hsuan-tu 十一屆三中全會以來重要文獻選讀 (Selected readings of important documents since the Third Plenum of the 11th Central Committee). 2 vols. Peking: Jen-min, 1987.

Shih-k'an 詩刊 (Poetry journal). Monthly. Peking: 1957– .

Shih-pao chou-k'an 時報週刊 (Sunday times weekly). Taipei: 1977– .

Shih t'an-so 詩探索 (Poetry exploration). Quarterly. Peking: 1980– .

Shih-yueh 十月 (October). Bimonthly. Peking: 1978– .

Shirk, Susan L. *Competitive comrades: career incentives and student strategies in China*. Berkeley: University of California Press, 1982.

Short, Philip. *The dragon and the bear: inside China and Russia today*. London: Abacus, 1982.

Shou-huo 收穫 (Harvest). Bimonthly. Shanghai: 1957–60, 1964–   .

Shue, Vivienne. *Peasant China in transition: the dynamics of development toward socialism, 1949–1956*. Berkeley: University of California Press, 1980.

Sicular, Terry. "Rural marketing and exchange in the wake of recent reforms," in Elizabeth J. Perry and Christine Wong, eds., *The political economy of reform in post-Mao China*, 83–109.

Sidel, Ruth. *Families of Fengsheng: urban life in China*. Baltimore: Penguin Books, 1974.

Sigurdson, John. *Rural industrialization in China*. Cambridge, Mass.: Council on East Asian Studies, Harvard University, 1977.

Sih, Paul K. T. 薛光前, ed. *Taiwan in modern times*. New York: St. John's University Press, 1973.

Simon, Sheldon W. *The broken triangle: Peking, Djakarta and the PKI*. Baltimore: Johns Hopkins University Press, 1969.

Singer, Martin. *Educated youth and the Cultural Revolution*. Ann Arbor: Center for Chinese Studies, University of Michigan, 1971.

Siu, Helen F. *Agents and victims in South China: accomplices in rural revolution*. New Haven, Conn.: Yale University Press, 1989.

Siu, Helen F., and Stern, Zelda, eds. *Mao's harvest: voices from China's new generation*. New York: Oxford University Press, 1983.

Sixth Five-Year Plan of the People's Republic of China for Economic and Social Development (1981–1985). Peking: FLP, 1984.

Skachkov, Petr Emel'ianovich. *Bibliografiia Kitaia*. Moscow: Izdatel'stvo vostochnoi literaturi, Institut narodov Azii, Akademiia nauk SSSR, 1960.

Skinner, G. William, ed. *The city in late imperial China*. Stanford, Calif.: Stanford University Press, 1977.

Skinner, G. William, et al., eds. *Modern Chinese society: an analytical bibliography*. Vol. 1: G. W. Skinner, ed. *Publications in Western languages, 1644–1972*. Vol. 2: G. W. Skinner and W. Hsieh, eds., *Publications in Chinese, 1644–1969*. Vol. 3: G. W. Skinner and S. Tomita, eds., *Publications in Japanese, 1644–1971*. Stanford, Calif.: Stanford University Press, 1973.

Skinner, G. William. "Marketing and social structure in rural China." *JAS*, Part I, 24.1 (November 1964), 3–43; Part II, 24.2 (February 1965), 195–228; Part III, 24.3 (May 1965), 363–99.

Slavic Review. Quarterly. Stanford, Calif.: American Association for the Advancement of Slavic Studies, 1941–   . [Formerly *The American Slavic and East European Review*.]

Slimming, John. *Green plums and a bamboo horse: a picture of Formosa*. London: John Murray, 1964.

Smith, Roger M. *Cambodia's foreign policy*. Ithaca, N.Y.: Cornell University Press, 1965.

Snow, Edgar. *Red star over China*. New York: Bantam, 1978; 1st rev. and enlarged ed. New York: Grove Press, 1968; New York: Random House, 1938; London: Godancz, 1937.

Snow, Edgar. *The long revolution*. New York: Vintage Books; London: Hutchinson, 1973.

Snow, Edgar. "Interview with Mao." *New Republic*, 152 (27 February 1965), 17–23.

Snow, Lois Wheeler. *China on stage: an American actress in the People's Republic*. New York: Random House, 1972.

Snyder, Edwin K.; Gregor, A. James; and Chang, Maria Hsia. *The Taiwan Relations Act and the defense of the Republic of China*. Berkeley: Institute of International Studies, University of California, 1980.

Social Sciences in China: a quarterly journal in English. Quarterly. Peking: Chinese Academy of Social Sciences, 1980– .

Socialist upsurge in China's countryside. Peking: FLP, 1957; and General Office of the Central Committee of the Communist Party of China, ed. Peking: FLP, 1978.

Soeya, Yoshihide. "Japan's postwar economic diplomacy with China: three decades of non-governmental experiences." University of Michigan, Ph.D. dissertation, 1987.

Solomon, Richard H. *Mao's revolution and the Chinese political culture*. Berkeley: University of California Press, 1971.

Solomon, Richard H., ed. *The China factor: Sino-American relations and the global scene*. Englewood Cliffs, N.J.: Prentice-Hall, 1981.

Solomon, Richard H. *Chinese political negotiating behavior: a briefing analysis*. Santa Monica, Calif.: The RAND Corporation, R-3295, December 1985.

Solomon, Richard H. "On activism and activists: Maoist conceptions of motivation and political role linking state to society." *CQ*, 39 (July–September 1969), 76–114.

Solomon, Richard H., and Kosaka Masataka, eds. *The Soviet Far East military buildup: nuclear dilemmas and Asian security*. Dover, Mass.: Auburn House, 1986.

Soo Chin-yee (Sansan). *Eighth moon. See* Lord, Bette [Bao].

Soong, Stephen C., and Minford, John, eds. *Trees on the mountain: an anthology of new Chinese writing*. Hong Kong: Chinese University Press, 1984.

Sorenson, Theodore C. *Kennedy*. New York: Harper & Row, 1965.

Sorich, Richard, ed. *Contemporary China: a bibliography of reports on China published by the United States Joint Publications Research Service*. Prepared for the Joint Committee on Contemporary China of the American Council of Learned Societies and the Social Sciences Research Council. New York: n.p., 1961.

Sotsial'no-ekonomicheskii stroi i ekonomicheskaia politika KNR (Social-economic structure and economic policies of the PRC). Moscow: Nauka, 1978.

South China Normal University Journal. See Hua-nan shih-fan ta-hsueh hsueh-pao.

Soviet Analyst. Semi-monthly. Richmond, Surrey: n.p. [Ed. Iain Elliot], 1972– .

Sovremennyi Kitai v zarubezhnykh issledovaniiakh (Contemporary China in foreign research). Moscow: Nauka, 1979.

Speare, Alden, Jr. "Urbanization and migration in Taiwan," in James C. Hsiung et al., eds., *The Taiwan experience, 1950–1980*, 271–281.

Special Commentator. "Su-lien cheng-pa shih-chieh ti chün-shih chan-lueh" 蘇聯

稱霸世界的軍事戰略 (The military strategy of the Soviet Union for world domination). *JMJP*, 11 January 1980, 7.

"Speeches and statements alleged to have been made by Chinese communist leaders in July through October, 1966." *CB*, 819 (10 March 1967), 1–84.

Spence, Jonathan. *To change China: Western advisers in China, 1620–1960.* Harmondsworth: Penguin Books, 1980.

Spence, Jonathan. *The Gate of Heavenly Peace: the Chinese and their revolution, 1895–1980.* Harmondsworth: Penguin Books, 1982.

Spitz, Allan A., ed. *Contemporary China.* Pullman: Washington State University Press, 1967.

Stacey, Judith. *Patriarchy and socialist revolution in China.* Berkeley: University of California Press, 1983.

Stalin, Joseph. *Economic problems of socialism in the USSR.* Peking: FLP, 1972.

Stalin, Joseph. *Marxism and problems of linguistics.* Peking: FLP, 1972.

Starr, John Bryan. *Continuing the revolution: the political thought of Mao.* Princeton, N.J.: Princeton University Press, 1979.

Starr, John Bryan. "Revolution in retrospect: the Paris Commune through Chinese eyes." *CQ*, 49 (January–March 1972), 106–25.

Starr, John Bryan, and Dyer, Nancy Anne, comps. *Post-Liberation works of Mao Zedong: a bibliography and index.* Berkeley: Center for Chinese Studies, University of California, 1976.

State Council of the People's Republic of China, Bulletin of. See *Chung-hua jen-min kung-ho-kuo kuo-wu-yuan kung-pao.*

State Statistical Bureau. *Ten great years: statistics of the economic and cultural achievements of the People's Republic of China.* Introduction by Feng-hwa Mah. Bellingham: Western Washington State College, 1974. Information compiled by the State Statistical Bureau. Originally published 1960.

State Statistical Bureau. *Statistical yearbook of China.* Annual. 1981–   . Compiled by the State Statistical Bureau, People's Republic of China. English edition. Hong Kong: Economic Information Agency, 1982–   .

State Statistical Bureau. *Chung-kuo t'ung-chi chai-yao, 1987* 中國統計摘要 (Chinese statistical summary, 1987). Peking: Chung-kuo t'ung-chi, 1987.

State Statistical Bureau. *Chung-kuo ku-ting tzu-ch'an t'ou-tzu t'ung-chi tzu-liao, 1950–1985* 中國固定資產投資統計資料 (Statistical materials on fixed capital investment in China). Peking: Chung-Kuo t'ung-chi, 1987.

State Statistical Bureau. *Wei-ta ti shih-nien* 偉大的十年 (Ten great years). Peking: 1960; English edition. Peking: FLP, 1960.

"State Statistical Bureau report on the results of the 1981 National Economic Plan." *Chung-kuo ching-chi nien-chien, 1982,* 8.79, 82–83.

"Statement of the government of the People's Republic of China." *PR*, 41 (10 October 1969), 3–4.

"Statement of the government of the People's Republic of China," 24 May 1969. NCNA, 24 May 1969.

Statistical yearbook of China. See State Statistical Bureau.

Statistical yearbook of the Republic of China. Annual. Taiwan: Directorate-General of Budget, Accounting and Statistics, Executive Yuan, 1975– .

Stavis, Benedict. *The politics of agricultural mechanization in China*. Ithaca, N.Y.: Cornell University Press, 1978.

Stevenson, William. *The yellow wind, an excursion in and around Red China with a traveller in the yellow wind*. London: Cassell; Boston: Houghton Mifflin, 1959.

Stolper, Thomas E. *China, Taiwan and the offshore islands, together with an implication for Outer Mongolia and Sino-Soviet relations*. Armonk, N.Y.: M. E. Sharpe, 1985.

Strategic Survey. Annual. London: International Institute for Strategic Studies, 1967– .

Strategic Survey 1966. London: International Institute for Strategic Studies, 1966.

"Strive to create the brilliant images of proletarian heroes: appreciations in creating the heroic images of Yang Tzu-jung and others," by the Taking Tiger Mountain by Strategy Group of the Peking Opera Troupe of Shanghai. *Chinese Literature*, 1 (January 1970), 58–75.

Strong, Anna Louise. "Three interviews with Chairman Mao Zedong." *CQ*, 103 (September 1985), 489–509.

Stuart, Douglas T., and Tow, William T., eds. *China, the Soviet Union, and the West: strategic and political dimensions in the 1980s*. Boulder, Colo.: Westview Press, 1982.

Study and Criticism. See *Hsueh-hsi yü p'i-p'an*.

Su Chi. "Soviet image of and policy toward China, 1969–1979." Columbia University, Ph.D. dissertation, 1983.

Su Shao-chih 蘇紹智. *Tentative views on the class situation and class struggle in China at the present stage*. Peking: Institute of Marxism-Leninism–Mao Zedong Thought, Chinese Academy of Social Sciences, 1981.

Su Shao-chih, ed. *Ma-k'o-ssu-chu-i yen-chiu* 馬克思主義研究 (Research on Marxism). Peking: Institute of Marxism-Leninism–Mao Zedong Thought, Chinese Academy of Social Sciences, 1984.

"Summary of Chairman Mao's talks to responsible local comrades during his tour of inspection (mid-August to September 12, 1971)." *CLG*, 5.3–4 (Fall–Winter 1972–73), 31–42.

Summary of the Forum on the Work in Literature and Art in the Armed Forces with which Comrade Lin Piao entrusted Comrade Chiang Ch'ing. Peking: FLP, 1968.

"Summary of the Forum on the Work in Literature and Art in the Armed Forces with which Comrade Lin Piao entrusted Comrade Chiang Ch'ing," in *Important documents on the Great Proletarian Cultural Revolution in China*, 201–38.

Summary of World Broadcasts. Daily and weekly reports. Caversham Park, Reading: British Broadcasting Corporation, Monitoring Service, 1963– . Cited as *SWB*.

Sun Tun-fan 孫敦番, et al., eds. *Chung-kuo kung-ch'an-tang li-shih chiang-i* 中國共產黨歷史講義 (Teaching materials on the history of the Chinese Communist Party). 2 vols. Tsinan: Shan-tung jen-min, 1983.

Sung Chien 宋健. "Jen-K'ou yü chiao-yü" 人口與教育 (Population and education).

Tzu-jan pien-cheng-fa t'ung-hsun 自然辯證法通訊 (Journal of the dialectics of nature), 3 (June 1980). Trans. in JPRS. 77745 *China report: Political, sociological, and military affairs*, 178, 3 April 1981, 43–47.

Sung-ko hsien-kei Mao Chu-hsi 頌歌獻給毛主席 (Odes to Chairman Mao). Shanghai: Shanghai jen-min, 1970.

Survey. 1957, 1962–1989. London and Paris: various publishers. Formerly *Soviet survey* (1956–57 and 1958–61) and *Soviet culture* (1956). Bimonthly 1961–62; quarterly 1963 82; irregular, 1983, 1989.

Survey: a journal of East and West studies. London: Institute for Defence and Strategic Studies, 1959– .

Sutter, Robert G. *Chinese foreign policy after the Cultural Revolution, 1966–1977*. Boulder, Colo.: Westview Press, 1978.

Sutter, Robert G. *Chinese foreign policy: developments after Mao*. New York: Praeger, 1985.

Suttmeier, Richard P. *Science, technology and China's drive for modernization*. Stanford, Calif.: Hoover Institution Press, 1980.

SWB. Summary of World Broadcasts.

Swearingen, Rodger. *The Soviet Union and postwar Japan*. Stanford, Calif.: Hoover Institution Press, 1978.

Swetz, Frank. *Mathematics education in China: its growth and development*. Cambridge, Mass.: MIT Press, 1974.

Ta-kung pao 大公報 ("L'Impartial"). Hong Kong.

Ta-lu ti-hsia k'an-wu hui-pien 大陸地下刊物滙編 (Collection of the mainland underground publications). Taipei: Institute for the Study of Chinese Communist Problems, 1980– .

Tachai. See Hsin Hua-wen.

T'ai-wan wen-i 臺灣文藝 (Taiwanese literature and art). Bimonthly. Taipei: 1953– .

"Taiwan briefing." Special section on Taiwan. *CQ*, 99 (September 1984), 462–568.

Taiwan statistical data book. Taipei: Council for Economic Planning and Development, Executive Yuan, 1971– .

Taiwan kingendaishi kenkyū (Historical studies of Taiwan in modern times), 3 (1980).

Takeuchi Minoru 竹內實, ed. *Mao Tse-tung chi* 毛澤東集 (Collected writings of Mao Tse-tung). 10 vols. Tokyo: Hokuboshe, 1970–72; 2nd ed., Tokyo: Sososha, 1983.

Takeuchi Minoru, ed. *Mao Tse-tung chi pu chüan* 毛澤東集補卷 (Supplements to the collected writings of Mao Tse-tung). 10 vols. Tokyo: Sososha, 1983–86.

Tamkang Review. Semi-annual 1970–77: Quarterly 1978– . Taipei: Graduate Institute of Western Languages and Literature, Tamkang College of Arts and Sciences, 1970– .

T'an Tsung-chi 譚宗級. "Lin Piao fan-ko-ming chi-t'uan ti chueh-ch'i chi-ch'i fu-mieh" 林彪反革命集團的堀起及其覆滅 (The sudden rise of the Lin Piao counter-revolutionary clique and its destruction), in *Chiao-hsueh ts'an-k'ao, hsia*, 38–57.

T'an Tsung-chi and Cheng Ch'ien 鄭謙, eds. *Shih-nien-hou-ti p'ing-shuo – "Wen-hua ta-ko-ming" shih lun-chi.* 十年後的評說－"文化大革命"史論集 (Appraisals and explanations after one decade: a collection of essays on the history of the "Great Cultural Revolution"). Peking: Chung-kung tang-shih tzu-liao, 1987.

Tang, Raymond N., 湯迺文 and Ma, Wei-yi 馬惟一. *Source materials on Red Guards and the Great Proletarian Cultural Revolution.* Ann Arbor: Asian Library, University Library, University of Michigan, 1969.

Tang-shih hui-yi pao-kao-chi 黨史會議報告集 (Collected reports from the Conference on Party History). Ch'üan-kuo tang-shih tzu-liao cheng-chi kung-tso hui-yi ho chi-nien Chung-kuo kung-ch'an-tang liu-shih chou-nien hsueh-shu t'ao-lun-hui mi-shu-ch'u 全國黨史資料徵集工作會議和紀念中國共產黨六十週年學術討論會秘書處 Secretariat of the National Work Conference on Collecting Party Historical Materials and the Academic Conference in Commemoration of the Sixtieth Anniversary of the Chinese Communist Party), eds. Peking: Chung-kung chung-yang tang-hsiao, 1982.

Tang-shih t'ung-hsun 黨史通訊 (Party history newsletter). Bimonthly 1980–84; monthly 1984–88. Biweekly 1989– . Title changed to *Chung-Kung tang-shih t'ung hsun.* Peking.

Tang-shih tzu-liao cheng-chi t'ung-hsun 黨史資料徵集通訊 (Newsletter on the collection of materials on Party history). Peking: Chung-kung tang-shih tzu-liao, 1984– .

Tang-shih yen-chiu 黨史研究 (Research on Party history). Peking: Chung-kung chung-yang tang-hsiao, 1980– . Also see *Chung-kung tang-shih yen-chiu.*

Tang-shih yen-chiu tzu-liao 黨史研究資料 (Research materials on Party history). Chengtu: Szechwan jen-min (for the Museum on the History of the Chinese Revolution), 1980– .

Tang-tai 當代 (Contemporary). Bimonthly. Peking: 1979– .

Tang-tai Chung-kuo wai-chiao 當代中國外交 (Diplomacy of contemporary China). Peking: Chung-kuo she-hui k'o-hsueh, 1987.

Tang-ti wen-hsien 黨的文獻 (Party documents). Bimonthly. Peking: 1988– .

T'ao K'ai 陶凱. "K'ai-shih ch'üan-mien chien-she she-hui-chu-i ti shih-nien" 開始全面建設社會主義的十年 (The ten years which saw the beginning of the all-round construction of socialism), in Chung-kung tang-shih yen-chiu-hui, ed., *Hsueh-hsi li-shih chueh-i chuan-chi.*

TASS News Agency.

Tatu, Michael. *The great power triangle: Washington, Moscow, Peking.* Paris: Atlantic Institute, 1970.

Taylor, Robert. *Education and university enrolment policies in China, 1949–1971.* Canberra: Australian National University Press, 1973.

Taylor, Robert. *China's intellectual dilemma: politics and university enrolment, 1949–1978.* Vancouver: University of British Columbia Press, 1981.

Taylor, Robert. *The Sino-Japanese axis: a new force in Asia?* New York: St. Martin's Press, 1985.

Teachers' News. See *Chiao-shih pao.*

Teaching and Research. See *Chiao-hsueh yü yen-chiu.*

Teaching and Research Office on CCP History of the [PLA] Political Academy. *See* Chung-kuo kung-chan-tang liu-shih-nien ta-shih chien-chieh.

Teaching Bulletin. See Chiao-hsueh tung-hsun.

Teiwes, Frederick C. *Provincial leadership in China: the Cultural Revolution and its aftermath.* Ithaca, N.Y.: China–Japan Program, Cornell University, 1974.

Teiwes, Frederick C. *Elite discipline in China: coercive and persuasive approaches to rectification, 1950–1953.* Canberra: Contemporary China Centre, Research School of Pacific Studies, Australian National University, 1978.

Teiwes, Frederick C. *Politics and purges in China: rectification and the decline of Party norms, 1950–1965.* White Plains, N.Y.: M. E. Sharpe, 1979.

Teiwes, Frederick C. *Leadership, legitimacy and conflict in China: from a charismatic Mao to the politics of succession.* Armonk, N.Y.: M. E. Sharpe, 1984.

Ten great years. See State Statistical Bureau.

Teng Hsiao-p'ing 鄧小平. *Teng-Hsiao-p'ing wen-hsuan 1975–1982.* 《鄧小平文選》 (Selected works of Teng Hsiao-p'ing). Peking: Jen-min, 1983.

Teng Hsiao-p'ing. *Selected works of Deng Xiaoping (1975–1982).* Peking: FLP, 1984.

Teng Hsiao-p'ing. *Fundamental issues in present-day China.* Peking: FLP, 1987.

Teng Hsiao-p'ing. "Memorial speech for Chou En-lai," in "Quarterly Chronicle and Documentation." *CQ*, 66 (June 1976), 420–24.

Teng Hsiao-p'ing. "Answers to the Italian journalist Oriana Fallaci," in *Selected works of Deng Xiaoping [Teng Hsiao-p'ing] (1975–1982),* 326–34.

Teng Hsiao-p'ing. "Uphold the four cardinal principles," in Teng Hsiao-p'ing, *Selected works,* 166–91.

Teng Hsiao-p'ing. "On the reform of the system of Party and state leadership," in Teng Hsiao-p'ing, *Selected works,* 302–25.

Teng Hsiao-p'ing. "Conversation of 26 April 1987 with Lubomir Strougal," in Teng Hsiao-p'ing, *Fundamental issues in present-day China,* 174–79.

Teng Li-ch'ün 鄧力羣. "Hsueh-hsi 'Kuan-yü chien-kuo-i-lai tang-ti jo-kan li-shih wen-t'i ti chueh-i' ti wen-t'i ho hui-ta" 學習《關於建國以來黨的若干歷史問題的決議》的問題和回答 (Questions and answers in studying the "Resolution on certain historical questions since the founding of the state"), in *Tang-shih hui-i pao-kao-chi,* 74–174.

Teng Li-ch'ün. "Comments of 11-12 August 1981 on the Resolution of 27 June 1981," in *Tang-shih hui-i pao-kao-chi.*

Tennien, Mark. *No secret is safe.* New York: Farrar, Straus, & Young, 1952.

The Tenth National Congress of the Communist Party of China (documents). Peking: FLP, 1973.

Terrill, Ross. *Flowers on an iron tree: five cities of China.* Boston: Little, Brown, 1975.

Terrill, Ross. *Mao: a biography.* New York: Harper Colophon Books, 1981.

Terrill, Ross. *The white-boned demon: a biography of Madame Mao Zedong.* New York: William Morrow, 1984.

Thomson, James C., Jr. *While China faced west: American reformers in Nationalist China, 1928–1937.* Cambridge, Mass.: Harvard University Press, 1969.

Thurston, Anne F. *Enemies of the people: the ordeal of the intellectuals in China's Great Cultural Revolution*. New York: Knopf, 1987.

Thurston, Anne. "Victims of China's Cultural Revolution: the invisible wounds." *Pacific Affairs*, Part I, 57.4 (Winter 1984–85), 599–620; and Part II, 58.1 (Spring 1985), 5–27.

Tidrick, Gene, and Chen Jiyuan, eds. *China's industrial reform*. London: Oxford University Press, 1987.

Tieh Tzu-wei 鐵竹偉. "Ch'en I tsai 'wen-hua ta-ko-ming' chung" 陳毅在"文化大革命"中 (Ch'en I during the Great Cultural Revolution). *Kun-lun*, 5 (September 1985), 121–43.

Tien, H. Yuan 田心源. *China's population struggle: demographic decisions of the People's Republic, 1949–1969*. Columbus: Ohio State University Press, 1973.

T'ien An Men shih-wen chi 天安門詩文集 (Collection of T'ien An Men poems). Peking: Peking ch'u-pan-she, 1979.

T'ien Chien 田間. *Kan ch'e chuan* 趕車傳 (The carter's story). Peking: Chung-kuo jen-min wen-i ts'ung-shu, 1949.

T'ien Chien. "T'ieh-ta-jen" 鐵大人 (Big iron man). *Shih-k'an*, 7 (1964), 4–7.

Tikhvinskii, S. L. *Istoriia Kitaia i sovremennost'* (The history of China and the present). Moscow: Nauka, 1976.

Times [London]. Daily. London: 1785– .

Ting Wang 丁望. *Chairman Hua: leader of the Chinese Communists*. Montreal: McGill–Queen's University Press, 1980.

Ting Wang. *Wang Hung-wen, Chang Ch'un-ch'iao p'ing-chuan* 王洪文、張春橋評傳 (Biographies of Wang Hung-wen and Chang Ch'un-ch'iao). Hong Kong: *Ming-pao yueh-k'an*, 1977.

Ting Wei-chih 丁偉志 and Shih Chung-ch'üan 石仲泉. "Ch'ün-chung lu-hsien shih wo-men tang ti li-shih ching-yen ti tsung-chieh" 群眾路綫是我們黨的歷史經驗的總結 (The mass line is the summation of the historical experience of our Party). *Wen-hsien ho yen-chiu*, 1983, 420–28.

Tong, Hollington K. 董顯光. *Chiang Kai-shek*. Taipei: China Publishing Co., 1953.

Townsend, James R. *The revolutionization of Chinese youth: a study of* Chung-kuo Ch'ing-nien. Berkeley: Center for Chinese Studies, University of California, 1967.

Trager, Frank N. "Sino-Burmese relations: the end of the Pauk Phaw era." *Orbis*, 11.4 (Winter 1968), 1034–54.

Treadgold, Donald W., ed. *Soviet and Chinese communism: similarities and differences*. Seattle: University of Washington Press, 1967.

Tretiak, Daniel. "The Sino-Japanese Treaty of 1978: the Senkaku incident prelude." *Asian Survey*, 18.12 (December 1978), 1235–49.

Truman, Harry S. *Memoirs*. Vol. 1: *Year of decisions*. Vol. 2: *Years of trial and hope*. Garden City, N.Y.: Doubleday, 1955–56.

The truth about Vietnam-China relations over the last 30 years. Hanoi: Ministry of Foreign Affairs, 4 October 1979. In FBIS *Daily Report: Asia and Pacific*, supplement, 19 October 1979.

Tsai Mei-hsi. *Contemporary Chinese novels and short stories, 1949–74: an annotated bibliography*. Cambridge, Mass.: Harvard University Press, 1979.

Tsedenbal, Yu[mjagin]. "K Sotsialisticheskomu Obshchestvennomu Stroiu Minuya Kapitalizm" (Toward a socialist social order, by-passing capitalism). *Problemy Dal'nego Vostoka*, 4 (1974), 6–29.

Tso-chuan. Legge's translation. *The Ch'un Tseu with The Tso Chuen*, in *The Chinese Classics*, V.

Tso-p'in 作品 (Literary works). Monthly. Canton: 1954– .

Tsou, Tang 鄒讜. *Embroilment over Quemoy: Mao, Chiang and Dulles*. Salt Lake City: University of Utah Press, 1959.

Tsou, Tang, ed. *China in crisis*. Vol. 2: *China's policies in Asia and America's alternatives*. Foreword by Charles U. Daly. Chicago: University of Chicago Press, 1968.

Tsou, Tang. *The Cultural Revolution and post-Mao reforms: a historical perspective*. Chicago: University of Chicago Press, 1986.

Tsou, Tang. "The Cultural Revolution and the Chinese political system." *CQ*, 38 (April–June 1969), 63–91.

Tsou, Tang. "Marxism, the Leninist party, the masses and the citizens in the rebuilding of the Chinese state," in Stuart R. Schram, ed., *Foundations and limits of state power in China*, 257–89.

Tsu-kuo 祖國 (The fatherland [China monthly?]). Monthly. Taipei: 1964– .

Tsu-kuo chou-k'an 祖國週刊 (China weekly). Weekly. Taipei: 1953– .

Tsu-kuo hsin-hsing ch'eng-shih 祖國新形城市 (The motherland's new type cities). Shanghai People's Press Editorial Group. Shanghai: Shanghai Jen-min, 1974.

Tsurumi, Patricia. *Japanese colonial education in Taiwan 1895–1945*. Cambridge, Mass.: Harvard University Press, 1977.

Tu P'eng-ch'eng 杜鵬程. *Tsai ho-p'ing ti jih-tzu li* 在和平的日子裏 (In days of peace). Sian: Tung-feng wen-i, 1958.

Tu-shu 讀書 (Reading). Monthly. Peking: 1979– .

"T'uan-chieh jen-min chan-sheng ti-jen ti ch'iang-ta wu-chi: hsueh-hsi 'Lun cheng-t'se'" 團結人民戰勝敵人的強大武器:學習"論政策" (A powerful weapon to unite the people and defeat the enemy: a study of "On policy"). Writing Group of the CCP Hopei Provincial Committee. *HC*, 9 (2 August 1971), 10–17.

Tung, Chi-ping, and Evans, Humphrey. *The thought revolution*. London: Leslie Frewin, 1967; New York: Coward-McCann, 1966.

Tung-hsiang 動向 (The trend). Monthly. Hong Kong: 1978– .

Tung-pei shih-ta hsueh-pao 東北師大學報 (Northeast Normal University Journal). Bimonthly. Changchun: 1955– . Formerly *Chi-lin shih-ta hsueh-pao* 吉林師大學報.

T'ung Huai-chou 童懷周 [pseud.], ed. *T'ien-an-men shih-wen chi* 天安門詩文集 (Poems from the Gate of Heavenly Peace). Peking: Jen-min wen-hsueh, 1978.

Turkmenskaya Iskra. Daily. Ashkhabad: Turkmenistan CPCC, Supreme Soviet, and Council of Ministers of Turkmen SSR.

Twelfth National Congress of the CPC (September 1982). Peking: FLP, 1982.

Tzu-liao hsuan-pien 資料選編 (Selected materials). Peking: n.p., January 1967.

Ullman, Morris. *Cities of mainland China: 1953 and 1958*. [Washington, D.C.]: Foreign Manpower Research Office, Bureau of the Census, U.S. Department of Commerce, 1961.

Ullman, Morris B. "Cities of mainland China: 1953–1959," in Gerald Breese, ed., *The city in newly developing countries*, 81–103.

Unger, Jonathan. *Education under Mao: class and competition in Canton schools, 1960– 1980*. New York: Columbia University Press, 1982.

Union Research Institute [URI]. *CCP documents of the Great Proletarian Cultural Revolution, 1966–1967*. Hong Kong: Union Research Institute, 1968.

Union Research Institute [URI]. *Catalogue of Red Guard publications held by URI*. Hong Kong: Union Research Institute, 1970.

Union Research Institute [URI]. *Documents of the Chinese Communist Party Central Committee, September 1956–April 1969*. Hong Kong: Union Research Institute, 1971.

Union Research Service. Hong Kong: Union Research Institute, 1955– .

United Kingdom Regional Information Office for Southeast Asia. Hong Kong Branch. *News from Chinese provincial radio stations*. Hong Kong. 1960s. Irregular.

United Nations. Economic and Social Commission for Asia and the Pacific. *Statistical yearbook for Asia and the Pacific*. Annual. Bangkok: Economic and Social Commission for Asia and the Pacific, 1973– . Continues *Statistical yearbook for Asia and the Far East*.

United States. Central Intelligence Agency. *People's Republic of China: international trade handbook*. Washington, D.C.: Central Intelligence Agency, December 1972.

United States. [Central Intelligence Agency]. National Foreign Assessment Center. *China: the steel industry in the 1970s and 1980s*. Washington, D.C.: Central Intelligence Agency, May 1979.

United States. Central Intelligence Agency. National Foreign Assessment Center. *Chinese defense spending, 1965–79*. Washington, D.C.: Central Intelligence Agency, July 1980.

United States Congress [92nd]. Joint Economic Committee. *People's Republic of China: an economic assessment*. Washington, D.C.: U.S. Government Printing Office, 1972.

United States Congress [95th]. Joint Economic Committee. *The Chinese economy post-Mao*. Vol. 1: *Policy and performance*. Washington, D.C.: U.S. Government Printing Office, 1978.

United States Congress [97th]. Joint Economic Committee. *China under the four modernizations*. 2 vols. Washington, D.C.: U.S. Government Printing Office, 1982.

United States Congress [99th]. Joint Economic Committee. *China's economy looks toward the year 2000*. Vol. 1: *The four modernizations*. Vol. 2: *Economic openness in modernizing China*. Washington, D.C.: U.S. Government Printing Office, 1986.

U.S. Consulate General. Hong Kong. *Current Background*. Weekly (approx.). 1950–77. Cited as *CB*.

U.S. Consulate General. Hong Kong. *Extracts from China Mainland Magazines*. 1955–60. Cited as *ECMM*. Title changed to *Selections from China Mainland Magazines*, 1960–77.

U.S. Consulate General. Hong Kong. *Selections from China Mainland Magazines*. 1960–77. Cited as *SCMM*. Formerly *Extracts from China Mainland Magazines*.

U.S. Consulate General. Hong Kong. *Survey of China Mainland Press*. Daily (approx.). 1950–77. Cited as *SCMP*.

U.S. Consulate General. Hong Kong. *Survey of China Mainland Press, Supplement*. 1960–73.

U.S. Department of State. *State Department Bulletin*. Monthly. Washington, D.C.: 1922– .

U.S. Department of State. *United States relations with China, with special reference to the period 1944–1949*. Washington, D.C.: 1949. Reissued with intro. and index by Lyman Van Slyke as *China white paper*. 2 vols. Stanford, Calif.: Stanford University Press, 1967.

United States Government. Joint Publications Research Service. *See* Joint Publications Research Service.

United States. National Foreign Assessment Center. *See* United States. Central Intelligence Agency.

University of Chicago Center for Policy Studies. *China briefing*. Chicago: Center for Policy Studies, University of Chicago, 1968.

Urban, George, ed. and intro. *The miracles of Chairman Mao: a compendium of devotional literature, 1966–1970*. London: Tom Stacey, 1971.

URI. Union Research Institute. Hong Kong.

Usack, A. H., and Batsavage, R. E. "The international trade of the People's Republic of China," in United States Congress [92nd], Joint Economic Committee, *People's Republic of China: an economic assessment*, 335–70.

Van der Kroef, Justus M. "The Sino-Indonesian partnership." *Orbis*, 8.2 (Summer 1964), 332–56.

Van der Kroef, Justus M. "Chinese subversion in Burma." *Indian Communist*, 3 (March–June 1970), 6–13.

van der Sprenkel, Otto; Guillain, Robert; and Lindsay, Michael. *New China: three views*. London: Turnstile Press, 1950.

van Ginneken, Jaap. *The rise and fall of Lin Piao*. Harmondsworth: Penguin Books, 1976.

Van Ness, Peter. *Revolution and Chinese foreign policy: Peking's support for wars of national liberation*. Berkeley: University of California Press, 1970.

Van Slyke, Lyman. See U.S. Department of State.

Vance, Cyrus. *Hard choices*. New York: Simon & Schuster, 1983.

Varg, Paul A. *Missionaries, Chinese and diplomats: the American Protestant missionary movement in China, 1890–1952.* Princeton, N.J.: Princeton University Press, 1958.

Vertzberger, Yaacov Y. I. *China's southwestern strategy: encirclement and counterencirclement.* New York: Praeger, 1985.

Vladimirov, O., and Ryazantsev, V. *Mao Tse-tung: a political portrait.* Moscow: Progress, 1976.

Vogel, Ezra F. *Canton under communism: programs and politics in a provincial capital, 1949–1968.* New York: Harper & Row, 1980; Cambridge, Mass.: Harvard University Press, 1969.

Wagner, Rudolf G. *Literatur und Politik in der Volksrepublik China.* Frankfurt: Suhrkamp, 1983.

Wakeman, Frederic. *History and will: philosophical persepectives of Mao Tse-tung's thought.* Berkeley: University of California Press, 1973.

Walder, Andrew G. *Chang Ch'un-ch'iao and Shanghai's January Revolution.* Ann Arbor: Center for Chinese Studies, University of Michigan, 1978.

Walder, Andrew G. "The informal dimension of enterprise financial reforms," in United States Congress, Joint Economic Committee, *China's economy looks toward the year 2000,* 1.630–645.

Walker, Kenneth R. *Food grain procurement and consumption in China.* New York: Cambridge University Press, 1984.

Walker, Richard L. "The human cost of communism in China." Report to the Subcommittee on Internal Security of the U.S. Senate Judiciary Committee. Washington, D.C.: U.S. Government Printing Office, 1971.

Wan-sui (1967) (1969). See *Mao Tse-tung ssu-hsiang wan-sui.*

Wang, James C. F. *The Cultural Revolution in China: an annotated bibliography.* New York and London: Garland, 1976.

Wang Jo-shui 王若水. "Ts'ung p'i 'tso' tao-hsiang fan-yu ti i-tz'u ko-jen ching-li" 從批"左"倒向反右的一次個人經歷 (The experience of one individual of the reversal from criticizing "leftism" to opposing rightism). *Hua-ch'iao jih-pao,* 12–21 March 1989.

Wang Ling-shu 王靈書. "Ji Dengkui [Chi Teng-k'uei] on Mao Zedong." *Liao-wang* 瞭望 (Outlook) overseas edition, 6–13 February, 1989, trans. in FBIS *Daily Report: China,* 14 February 1989, 22–26.

Wang, Mason Y. H., ed. *Perspectives in contemporary Chinese literature.* University Center, Mich.: Green River Press, 1983.

Wang Meng 王蒙. "Tsu-chih-pu hsin lai ti ch'ing-nien-jen" 組織部新來的青年人 (The young newcomer to the organization department). *Jen-min wen-hsueh,* 9 (1956), 29–43.

Wang Nien-i 王年一. *1949–1989 nien-ti Chung-kuo: ta-tung-luan-ti nien-tai* 1949–1989 年的中國:大動亂的年代 (China from 1949–1989: a decade of great upheaval). Honan: Honan jen-min, 1988.

Wang Nien-i. "Mao Tse-tung t'ung-chih fa-tung 'wen-hua ta-ko-ming' shih tui hsing-shih ti ku-chi" 毛澤東同志發動文化大革命時對形勢的估計 (Comrade Mao Tse-tung's estimate of the situation at the time when he launched the "Great Cultural Revolution"), in *Tang-shih yen-chiu tzu-liao*, 4 (1983), 766–74.

Wang Nien-i. " 'Wen-hua ta-ko-ming' ts'o-wu fa-chan mai-lo" '文化大革命' 錯誤發展的脈絡 (Analysis of the development of the errors of the "Great Cultural Revolution"). *Tang-shih t'ung-hsun*, October 1986.

Wang Xizhe 王希哲. "Mao Zedong and the Cultural Revolution," in Anita Chan, Stanley Rosen, and Jonathan Unger, eds., *On socialist democracy and the Chinese legal system: the Li Yizhe debates*, 177–260.

Wang Ya-lin 王雅林 and Li Chin-jung 李金榮. "Ch'eng-shih chih-kung chia-wu lao-tung yen-chiu" 城市職工家務勞動研究 (Research on the housework of urban workers and employees). *Chung-kuo she-hui k'o-hsueh*, 1 (1982), 177–90.

Washington Post, The. Daily. Washington, D.C.: The Washington Post Co., 1877– .

Watson, Andrew. *Mao Zedong and the political economy of the border region*. Cambridge: Cambridge University Press, 1980.

Watts, William. *See* Clough, Ralph N.

Wehr und Wirtschaft. See *Wehrtechnik ...*

Wehrtechnik, vereinigt mit Wehr und Wirtschaft. Monthly. Monatsschrift für wirtschaftliche Fragen der Verteidigung, Luftfahrt und Industrie. Bonn–Duisdorf: Wehr und Wissen Verlagsgesselschaft gmbH, 1969– .

"Wei shih-mo yao cheng-feng?" 為什麼要整風? (Why do we want to rectify?). Editorial. *JMJP*, 2 May 1957.

Wei T'ien-ts'ung 尉天聰, ed. *Hsiang-t'u wen-hsueh t'ao-lun chi* 鄉土文學討論集 (Collected essays on "native soil" literature). Taipei: Hsia-ch'ao tsa-chih she, 1978.

Weiss, Kenneth G. *Power grows out of the barrel of a gunboat: the U.S. in Sino-Soviet crises*. Alexandria, Va.: Center for Naval Analyses, December 1982.

Wen Chi-tse 溫濟澤. "Mao Tse-tung t'ung-chih tsai Yenan shih-ch'i shih tsen-yang chiao-tao wo-men hsueh che-hsueh ti? " 毛澤東同志在延安時期是怎樣教導我們學哲學的? (How did Comrade Mao Tse-tung teach us to study philosophy during the Yenan period?), in *Ch'üan-kuo Mao Tse-tung che-hsueh ssu-hsiang t'ao-lun hui lun-wen hsuan*, 68–82.

Wen-hsien ho yen-chiu 文獻和研究 (Documents and research). Peking: Chung-yang wen-hsien yen-chiu-shih, 1983– .

Wen-hsueh pao 文學報 (Literary gazette). Weekly. Shanghai: 1981– .

Wen-hsueh p'ing-lun 文學評論 (Literary review). Bimonthly. Peking: 1957– . Formerly *Wen-hsueh yen-chiu* 文學研究 (Literary research).

Wen-hsueh p'ing-lun ts'ung-k'an, 10: tang-tai tso-chia p'ing-lun chuan-hao 文學評論叢刊, 10: 當代作家評論專號 (Literary review series, 10: special issue, critiques of contemporary writers). Peking: Chung-kuo she-hui k'o-hsueh, 1981.

Wen-hui pao 文滙報 (Wenhui daily). Shanghai: 1938– .

Wen-i hsueh-hsi 文藝學習 (Literary studies). Monthly. Peking: 1954– .

Wen-i pao 文藝報 (Literary gazette). Weekly. Peking: 1949– .

Wen-i yen-chiu 文藝研究 (Research on literature and art). Monthly. Peking: 1979–.

West, Philip. *Yenching University and Sino-Western relations, 1916–1952.* Cambridge, Mass.: Harvard University Press, 1976.

White, D. Gordon. "The politics of *Hsia-hsiang* youth." *CQ*, 59 (July–September 1974), 491–517.

White, Gordon. *The politics of class and class origin: the case of the Cultural Revolution.* Canberra: The Australian National University, 1976.

White, Gordon. *Party and professionals: the political role of teachers in contemporary China.* Armonk, N.Y.: M. E. Sharpe, 1981.

White, Lynn T., III. *Careers in Shanghai: the social guidance of personal energies in a developing Chinese city, 1949–1966.* Berkeley: University of California Press, 1978.

Whiting, Allen S. *The Chinese calculus of deterrence: India and Indochina.* Ann Arbor: University of Michigan Press, 1975.

Whiting, Allen S. *Chinese domestic politics and foreign policy in the 1970s.* Ann Arbor: University of Michigan Press, 1979.

Whiting, Allen S. *Siberian development and East Asia: threat or promise?* Stanford, Calif.: Stanford University Press, 1981.

Whiting, Allen S. *China eyes Japan.* Berkeley: University of California Press, 1989.

Whiting, Allen S. "How we almost went to war with China." *Look*, 33 (29 April 1969), 76.

Whiting, Allen S. "The use of force in foreign policy by the People's Republic of China." *The Annals of the American Academy of Political and Social Science*, 402 (July 1972), 55–66.

Whiting, Allen S. "Sino-American detente." *CQ*, 82 (June 1980), 334–41.

Whitson, William W., with Huang Chen-hsia. *The Chinese high command: a history of communist military politics, 1927–71.* New York: Praeger, 1973.

Whyte, Martin King. *Small groups and political rituals in China.* Berkeley: University of California Press, 1974.

Whyte, Martin King. "Town and country in contemporary China." *Comparative Urban Research*, 10.1 (1983), 9–20.

Whyte, Martin King, and Parish, William L. *Urban life in contemporary China.* Chicago: University of Chicago Press, 1984.

Wich, Richard. *Sino-Soviet crisis politics: a study of political change and communication.* Cambridge, Mass.: Council on East Asian Studies, Harvard University, 1980.

Willmott, W. E., ed. *Economic organization in Chinese society.* Stanford, Calif.: Stanford University Press, 1972.

Wills, Morris. *Turncoat: an American's 12 years in Communist China.* Englewood Cliffs, N.J.: Prentice-Hall, 1968. [The story of Morris R. Wills as told to J. Robert Moskin.]

Wilson, Amy Auerbacher; Greenblatt, Sidney Leonard; and Wilson, Richard Whittingham, eds. *Deviance and social control in Chinese society.* New York: Praeger, 1977.

Wilson, Dick, ed. *Mao Tse-tung in the scales of history: a preliminary assessment*. New York: Cambridge University Press, 1977.

Wilson Quarterly. 5/yr. Washington, D.C.: Woodrow Wilson International Center for Scholars, 1976– .

Wilson, Richard W. *Learning to be Chinese: the political socialization of children in Taiwan*. Cambridge, Mass.: MIT Press, 1970.

Wilson, Richard W.; Wilson, Amy A.; and Greenblatt, Sidney L., eds. *Value change in Chinese society*. New York: Praeger, 1979.

Winckler, Edwin A., and Cady, Janet A., eds. *Urban planning in China: report of the U.S. urban planners delegation to the People's Republic of China*. New York: National Committee on U.S.-China Relations, 1980.

Witke, Roxane. *Comrade Chiang Ch'ing*. Boston: Little, Brown, 1977.

Wolf, Arthur P., ed. *Religion and ritual in Chinese society*. Stanford, Calif.: Stanford University Press, 1974.

Wolf, Arthur P. "Gods, ghosts, and ancestors," in Arthur P. Wolf, ed., *Religion and ritual in Chinese society*, 131–82.

Wolf, Margery. *The house of Lim: a study of a Chinese farm family*. New York: Appleton-Century-Crofts, 1968.

Wolf, Margery. *Revolution postponed: women in contemporary China*. Stanford, Calif.: Stanford University Press, 1985.

Wolff, Lester L., and Simon, David L., eds. *Legislative history of the Taiwan Relations Act: an analytic compilation with documents on subsequent developments*. Jamaica, N.Y.: American Association for Chinese Studies, United States, 1982.

Wong, Christine Pui Wah. "Rural industrialization in the People's Republic of China: lessons from the Cultural Revolution decade," in United States Congress, Joint Economic Committee, *China under the four modernizations*, 1. 394–418.

Wood, Shirley. *A street in China*. London: Michael Joseph, 1959.

Woodside, Alexander. "Peking and Hanoi: anatomy of a revolutionary partnership." *International Journal*, 24.1 (Winter 1968–69), 65–85.

World Bank. *See* Chenery, Hollis.

World Bank. Papers prepared for the Chinese Academy of Social Sciences–World Bank Conference on Township Village and Private Enterprise, Peking, November 1987.

World Bank. *China: socialist economic development*. Annex G: *Education Sector*. World Bank Document (1 June 1981). Washington, D.C.: World Bank, 1981.

World Bank. *China: socialist economic development*. Vol. 1: *The economy, statistical system, and basic data*. Vol. 2: *The economic sectors: agriculture, industry, energy and transport and external trade and finance*. Vol. 3: *The social sectors: population, health, nutrition and education*. Washington, D.C.: World Bank, 1983.

World Economic Herald. See *Shih-chieh ching-chi tao-pao*.

World Policy Journal. Quarterly. New York: World Policy Institute, 1983– .

World Politics: a quarterly journal of international relations. Quarterly. Princeton, N.J.: Center of International Studies, Princeton University Press, 1948– .

World Press Review. Monthly. New York: Stanley Foundation, 1961– . Formerly *Atlas* (1961–72); *Atlas World Press Review* (1972–80).

Wu Chiang 吳江. "Pu-tuan ko-ming lun-che pi-hsu shih ch'e-ti ti pien-chang wei-wu lun-che" 不斷革命論者必須是徹底的辯證唯物論者 (A partisan of the theory of the permanent revolution must be a thoroughgoing dialectical materialist). *Che-hsueh yen-chiu*, 8 (1958), 25–28.

Wu, Eugene. *See* MacFarquhar, Roderick.

Wu Han 吳晗. *Hai Jui pa kuan* 海瑞罷官. (Hai Jui dismissed from office). Peking: Ch'u-pan-she, 1961.

Wu Han. "Shen-hua-chü shih pu-shih hsüan-ch'uan mi-hsin?" 神話劇是不是宣傳迷信? (Do plays of fairy tales spread superstition?). *Chung-kuo ch'ing-nien*, 15 (1961), 9–11.

Wu-han shih ch'eng-shih kuei-hua she-chi yuan 武漢市城市槼劃設計院 (Wuhan City Urban Planning and Design Academy). *Ch'eng-shih kuei-hua ts'an-k'ao t'u-li* 城市槼劃參攷圖例 (Reference key to urban planning). Wu-han: China Construction Industry Press, 1977.

Wylie, Raymond F. *The emergence of Maoism: Mao Tse-tung, Ch'en Po-ta and the search for Chinese theory, 1935–1945*. Stanford, Calif.: Stanford University Press, 1980.

Xiao Lan [Hsiao Lan] 蕭蘭, ed. *The Tiananmen poems*. Peking: FLP, 1979.

Xu Liangying 許良英 and Fan Dainian 范岱年. *Science and socialist construction in China*. Armonk, N.Y.: M. E. Sharpe, 1982.

Ya-lu chiang 鴨綠江 (Yalu River). Monthly. Shenyang: 1950– . Formerly *Tung-pei wen-i* 東北文藝 (Northeast literature and art).

Yager, Joseph A. *Transforming agriculture in Taiwan: the experience of the Joint Commission on Rural Reconstruction*. Ithaca, N.Y.: Cornell University Press, 1988.

Yahuda, Michael B. *China's role in world affairs*. New York: St. Martin's Press, 1978.

Yahuda, Michael. *Towards the end of isolationism: China's foreign policy after Mao*. New York: St. Martin's Press, 1983.

Yahuda, Michael. "Kremlinology and the Chinese strategic debate, 1965–66." *CQ*, 49 (January–March 1972), 32–75.

Yalem, R[onald] J. "Tripolarity and world politics." *Yearbook of world affairs, 1974*, 28.23–42.

Yang, C. K. [Ch'ing-k'un] 楊慶堃. *The Chinese family in the communist revolution*. Cambridge, Mass.: MIT Press, 1959.

Yang, C. K. *A Chinese village in early communist transition*. Cambridge, Mass.: MIT Press, 1959.

Yang, C. K. *Religion in Chinese society*. Berkeley: University of California Press, 1961.

Yang Ch'ao 楊超. *Lun Mao Chu-hsi che-hsueh t'i-hsi* 論毛主席哲學體係 (On Chairman Mao's philosophical system). 2 vols. Hsi-yang ti-ch'ü yin-shua-so, 1978.

Yang Ch'ao. *Wei-wu pien-cheng-fa ti jo-kan li-lun wen-t'i* 唯物辯證法的若干理論問題

(Some theoretical problems of materialist dialectics). Chengtu: Szechwan jen-min, 1980. [Rev. ed. of *Lun Mao Chu-hsi che-hsueh t'i-hsi.*]

Yang-ch'eng wan pao 羊城晚報 (Yang-ch'eng evening news). Daily. Canton: 1957–1966, 1980– .

Yang Kuo-yü 楊國宇 et al., eds., *Liu Teng ta-chün cheng-chan chi* 劉鄧大軍征戰記 (A record of the great military campaigns of Liu [Po-ch'eng] and Teng [Hsiao-p'ing]). 3 vols, Kunming: Yun-nan jen-min, 1984.

Yang, Martin M. C. 楊懋春. *Socio-economic results of land reform in Taiwan*. Honolulu: East-West Center Press, 1970.

Yang Tung-liang 楊東梁. "A brief analysis of the debate on coastal defense versus land border defense." *KMJP*, 10 February 1981 in FBIS *Daily Report: China*, 5 March 1981, L3-L7.

Yao Hsueh-yin 姚雪 . "Ta-k'ai ch'uang-hu shuo liang-hua" 打開窗戶說亮話 (Open the window to have a direct talk). *Wen-i pao*, 7 (1957), 10–11.

Yao Meng-hsien. "Chinese communists and the Vietnam War." *Issues & Studies*, 1.9 (June 1965), 1–13.

Yao Ming-le 姚明樂. *The conspiracy and death of Lin Biao*. Trans. with introduction by Stanley Karnow. New York: Knopf, 1983. Published in Britain as *The conspiracy and murder of Mao's heir*. London: Collins, 1983.

Yao Wen-yuan 姚文元. *On the social basis of the Lin Piao anti-Party clique*. Peking: FLP, 1975. Also in Raymond Lotta, ed., *And Mao makes 5*, 196–208.

Yao Wen-yuan. "She-hui-chu-i hsien-shih-chu-i wen-hsueh shih wu-ch'an chieh-chi ko-ming shih-tai ti hsin wen-hsueh" 社會主義現實主義文學是無產階級革命時代的新文學 (Socialist realist literature is the new literature of the age of proletarian revolution). *Jen-min wen-hsueh*, 9 (1957), 99–112.

Yao Wen-yuan. "On the new historical play *Hai Jui dismissed from office*." *Wen-hui pao*, Shanghai, 10 November 1965. Reprinted in *CFJP*, 10 November 1965; *CB*, 783 (21 March 1966), 1–18.

Yearbook of world affairs. Annual. London Institute of World Affairs. London: Stevens & Sons, 1947–1984.

Yeh Chien-ying. *See* "Ying-ssu lu" pien-chi hsiao-tsu.

Yeh Chien-ying Biographical Writing Group of the Military Science Academy. *Yeh Chien-ying chuan-lueh* 葉劍英傳略 (A brief biography of Yeh Chien-ying). Peking: Chün-shih k'o-hsueh yuan, 1987. *See also* Hsueh Yeh-sheng.

Yeh Wei-lien 葉維廉, ed. *Chung-kuo hsien-tai tso-chia lun* 中國現代作家論 (Contemporary Chinese writers). Taipei: Lien-ching, 1976.

Yeh Yung-lieh 葉永烈. *Chang Ch'un-ch'iao fu-ch'en shih* 張春橋浮沉史 (The history of Chang Ch'un-ch'iao's rise and fall). Changchun: Shih-tai wen-i, 1988.

Yen Ching-t'ang 閻景堂. "Chung-yang chün-wei yen-ko kai-k'uang" 中央軍委沿革概況 (Survey of the evolution of the Central Military Commission), in Chu Ch'eng-chia, ed., *Chung-kung tang-shih yen-chiu lun-wen hsuan, hsia*, 567–87.

Yen Fang-ming 閻放鳴 and Wang Ya-p'ing 王亞平. "Ch'i-shih nien-tai ch'u-ch'i wo-kuo ching-chi chien-she ti mao-chin chi ch'i t'iao-cheng" 七十年代初期我國經濟建設的冒進及其調整 (The blind advance in our national economic construction in the early 1970s and its correction). *Tang-shih yen-chiu*, 5 (1985), 55–60.

Yen, Maria. *The umbrella garden: a picture of student life in red China.* New York: Macmillan, 1954.

Yen Yuan-shu 顏元叔. *T'an min-tsu wen-hsueh* 談民族文學 (On national literature). Taipei: Hsueh-sheng, 1973.

Ying, Esther Cheo. *See* Cheo Ying, Esther.

"Ying-ssu lu" pien-chi hsiao-tsu "縈思錄"編輯小組. *Ying-ssu lu: huai-nien Yeh Chien-ying* 縈思錄:懷念葉劍英 (A record of contemplation: remembering Yeh Chien-ying). Peking: Jen-min, 1987. Cited as *Ying-ssu lu.*

Yu, George T. "Sino-African relations: a survey." *Asian Survey*, 5.7 (July 1965), 321–32.

Yu Shiao-ling. "Voice of protest: political poetry in the post-Mao era." *CQ*, 96 (December 1983), 703–20.

Yu-shih wen-i 幼獅文藝 (Young lion literature and art). Monthly. Taipei.

Yü Ch'iu-li 余秋里. "Report on the 1979 draft national economic plan." *JMJP*, 29 June 1979, 1, 3.

Yü Kuang-chung 于光中. *Lien ti lien-hsiang* 蓮的聯想 (Associations of the lotus). Taipei: Wen-hsing shu-tien, 1964.

Yü Nan 于南. "Chou tsung-li ch'u-chih '9.13' Lin Piao p'an-t'ao shih-chien ti i-hsieh ch'ing-k'uang" 周總理處置"九·一三"林彪叛逃事件的一些情況 (Some of the circumstances regarding Premier Chou's management of the 13 September incident when Lin Piao committed treachery and fled). *Tang-shih yen-chiu*, 3 (1981), 59.

Yuan Ssu. "Bankruptcy of Empress Lü's dream." *Chinese Studies in History*, 12.2 (Winter 1978–79), 66–73.

Yue Daiyun 樂黛雲, and Wakeman, Carolyn. *To the storm: the odyssey of a revolutionary Chinese woman.* Berkeley: University of California Press, 1985.

Yun-nan she-hui k'o-hsueh 雲南社會科學 (Yunnan social sciences). Bimonthly. Kunming: 1981– .

Zagoria, Donald S. *The Sino-Soviet conflict 1956–1961.* New York: Atheneum, 1964; Princeton, N.J.: Princeton University Press, 1962; London: Oxford University Press, 1962.

Zagoria, Donald S. *Vietnam triangle: Moscow/Peking/ Hanoi.* New York: Western Publishing, Pegasus, 1967.

Zagoria, Donald S., ed. *Soviet policy in East Asia.* New Haven, Conn.: Yale University Press, 1982.

Zagoria, Donald S. "Moscow, Peking, Washington, and the War in Vietnam," in Allan A. Spitz, ed., *Contemporary China*, 14–20.

Zagoria, Donald S., and Kim, Young Kun. "North Korea and the major powers," in William J. Barnds, ed., *The two Koreas in East Asian affairs*, 19–59.

Zagoria, Donald. "The strategic debate in Peking," in Tang Tsou, ed., *China in crisis*, 2.237–268.

Zagoria, Donald S., and Ra'anan, Uri. "On Kremlinology: a reply to Michael Yahuda." *CQ*, 50 (April–June 1972), 343–50.

Zanegin, B.; Mironov, A.; and Mikhailov, Ia. *K sobitiiam v Kitae* (On developments in China). Moscow: Politizdat, 1967.

Zhelokhovtsev, Aleksei Nikolaevich. [Schelochowzew, A. N.] *Chinesishe Kultur-revolution aus der Nähe*. Stuttgart: Deutsche Verlags-Anstalt, 1969.

Zhelokhovtsev, A. *"Kul'turnaya revolitusiya" s blizkogo rasstoyaniya (zapiski ochevidtsa)*. Moscow: Politizdat, 1973. Originally published as a three-part article in *Novyi Mir*, 44.1, 2, 3 (January, February, March 1968). Published in English as *The "Cultural Revolution": a close-up (An eyewitness account)*. Moscow: Progress, 1975.

Zhou Enlai. *See* Chou En-lai.

Zhou Jin. "Housing China's 900 million people." *Beijing Review*, 48 (1979), 17–27.

Zinoviev, Alexander [Aleksandr]. *The radiant future*. Trans. Gordon Clough. London: Bodley Head, 1981; New York: Random House, 1980.

Zweig, David. *Agrarian radicalism in China, 1968–1981*. Cambridge, Mass.: Harvard University Press, 1989.

Zweig, David. "Opposition to change in rural China: the system of responsibility and people's communes." *Asian Survey*, 23.7 (July 1983), 879–900.

Zweig, David. "Strategies of policy implementation: policy 'winds' and brigade accounting in rural China, 1966–1978." *World Politics*, 37.2 (January 1985), 267–93.

GLOSSARY-INDEX